Australian
Baby Guide

Goose Books Pty Ltd
25 William Street
Richmond 3121 Victoria
Tel: (03) 9427 0499
email: info@goosebooks.com.au
website: www.australianbabyguide.com.au

Other titles published:
Dog Poo on the Pram Wheels
Dog Poo on the Tricycle Wheels
Mummy Doesn't Do It Like That
Grandpa Gave Us Chocolate at Bedtime

National Library of Australia
cataloguing-in-publication entry:

Attiwill, Penny, 1962-

Australian baby guide:
all the information a parent needs from pregnancy to 3 years.

ISBN: 9780977539451 (pbk.)

Includes index.

Infants – Care – Australia – Handbooks, manuals, etc
Toddlers – Care – Australia – Handbooks, manuals, etc
Child rearing – Australia – Handbooks, manuals, etc

649.1220994

Cover image: Lifeworks Photography
Distributed by Pan Macmillan 1300 135 113
Design by Parkhouse 03 9427 7866
Printed in China

THANK YOU to all the industry professionals for your editorial input; to the many businesses for your support; to my freelance contributors for your continued enthusiasm; to the Vox Pop participants for your contributions that will give other new parents an insight into how it is or might be; and to the hundreds of mums and dads that responded to my request for feedback on what you want to see in a guide for Australian parents.
THANKS also to the people with whom I work so closely on a day-to-day basis: Nikki, Matt, Rich, Sean, Aaron, Jackie & Nathan.

Thank you all for your assistance in bringing the *Australian Baby Guide* to life.

Australian
Childhood Foundation
Protecting Children

The *Australian Baby Guide* proudly supports the work of the Australian Childhood Foundation
(see pages 614 & 615) by donating $1.00 from every book sold.

Welcome to the *Australian Baby Guide*.

With a new title and a new format this book has been ten years in the making. In 1999, almost two years after the birth of my eldest child, I published the first edition of *The Nappy Bag Book*. It was a Melbourne-specific resource for parents and just over 100 pages. Demand for a similar book in other states took hold and before I knew it we were publishing five separate editions each year. In 2005 we amalgamated it into a single national resource, and the book quickly gained an enviable reputation as the most comprehensive resource for parents available. With that came strong endorsement by midwives, obstetricians and childbirth educators in leading maternity hospitals nationally.

In early 2008 I decided it was time for an updated look. I wanted a new title that would truly reflect the book's content and a complete overhaul of internal pages, so I emailed a few hundred parents that had recently bought the book direct from our website and asked for constructive criticism. As a result our new book, the *Australian Baby Guide*, has a self-explanatory and strong title, a modern design, a better structure of content, more articles from peak authorities on a broad range of topics, a new Vox Pop section and the not-so-popular bits have been ditched!

On any one day parenting can encompass the full spectrum of emotions. I remember holding Tilly soon after she was born and having a good old cry (one of many) because of the overpowering love I had for her and because I had never before felt so mind-numbingly tired.

My aim with this book is to make your life easier as a parent of a young child by providing you with trusted practical information, by giving you a reassuring glimpse into the lives of other parents and by giving you the heads up on what's out there and available to you.

If only this book had been around when I had my first child, perhaps there would have been fewer tears and the realisation that good parenting can come in many guises, so long as you're happy and your kids are happy.

Cheers for now and I would love to hear what you think,

pen@goosebooks.com.au
www.australianbabyguide.com.au

Contents

NAPPIES, BATHTIME & SKINCARE   238

MILK & FOOD   172

Contents

Contents

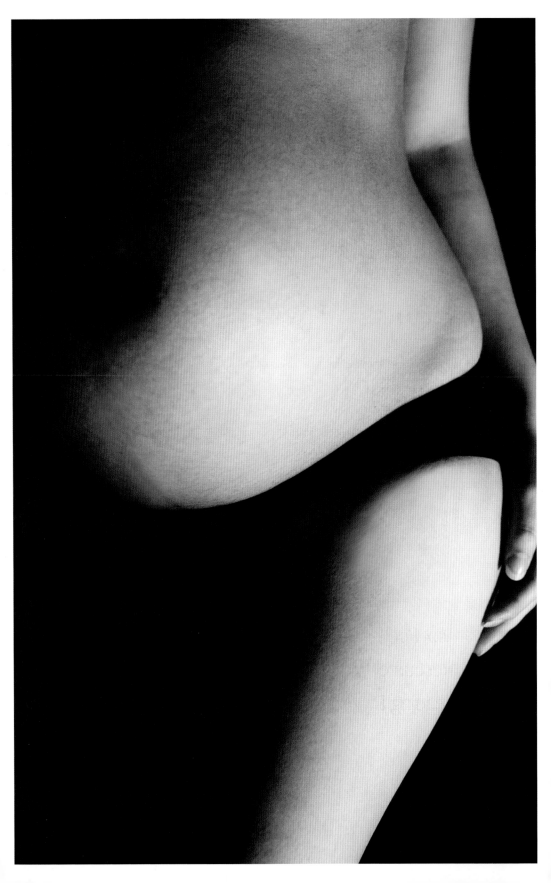

Pregnancy:
the first
nine months

Photograph by Iris Creations Photography, Melbourne & Geelong.

A weekly guide to your pregnancy

This pregnancy guide, compiled by Sandra Robinson and Catherine Price from birth.com.au, summarises the 9-month miracle unfolding for you and your baby. Each pregnancy and baby is unique, with normal pregnancies taking 37 to 42 weeks, meaning the measurements and development stages can vary depending on a woman's cycle, when conception occurred and the rate at which her baby grows.

FIRST TRIMESTER – CONCEPTION TO 12 WEEKS

Conception to 4 weeks

Your baby develops from a ball of cells into an embryo, measuring 1.5mm (0.06 inch) by 4 weeks of pregnancy (2 weeks after conception). Their spinal cord and brain (neural tube) begins forming and by 21 days after conception this is complete.

You may have tender, swollen breasts and sensitive nipples. Your period is due or late! A pregnancy urine test may still show negative, so re-test in a few days if a period doesn't eventuate. Blood pregnancy tests show positive results 8 to 12 days after conception.

Consider:

- Taking folic acid to help your baby's neural tube develop and grow healthy new body cells.
- Eating a well-balanced diet and changing lifestyle habits such as caffeine, cigarettes, alcohol or recreational drugs. Check with your caregiver about medications, over-the-counter treatments and natural therapies.

5 weeks

Your baby is curled up, measuring 2–4mm (0.08 to 0.16 inch) from the crown of their head to the base of their back (crown to rump length or CRL). Their heart begins beating with their blood stream flowing separately from their mother's. Their umbilical cord has two arteries and one vein. Small hands and feet start budding from their upper and lower body.

You may feel bloated and experience pulling, tugging or mild cramping sensations, and perhaps lower backache as the uterus grows. Breasts feel fuller and you may be tired or extremely fatigued. Some women crave certain foods. Emotions can feel like a roller-coaster ride.

Consider going to bed early, having weekend naps and resting when possible. Use heat packs for mild aches and pains.

6 weeks

Your baby measures 5mm (0.2 inch) from crown to rump. Their facial features start building around a wide mouth with their lower jaw forming before their upper jaw. Their head is comparatively large and their brain is forming, with eyes developing on each side of their head. Arms and legs lengthen with hands and feet resembling ridged paddles, later forming fingers and toes. Their oesophagus, stomach, kidneys and bowel are developing with two small buds growing into lungs. Their heart now has four chambers and beats between 90 and 200 per minute!

You may need to pass more urine, due to increased kidney blood flow and pressure on your bladder from the growing uterus. About 30% of pregnant women experience light bleeding in the early weeks (pink, brown or bright red) which may be of concern. For around half these women, their pregnancy continues and they have a healthy baby. If bleeding persists or is heavy with cramping, speak with your caregiver.

Consider choosing your maternity caregiver and place of birth. Options include a hospital antenatal clinic, team midwifery, birth centres, shared care with your local GP, an obstetrician or your own midwife. Be aware that some caregivers and hospitals book out quickly.

7 weeks

Your baby is just over 1cm long (0.4 inch) and each eye has an optic cup, retina and lens. Their nasal pits, inner ears and tongue are developing and their upper jaw and palate come together, fusing as one. Their pancreas, appendix and reproductive organs start forming and their body has a fine transparent skin layer, with fingers and thumbs becoming more defined.

You may have morning sickness or "all day and all night sickness" and notice an increase in saliva, with a heightened sense of smell. Tiredness can feel never-ending, even after long hours of sleep.

Consider:

- Eating small, regular meals, snacking on dried fruits, biscuits or toast before getting out of bed and separating food and drinks at meal times to help with morning sickness. Try vitamin B6 or ginger. Peppermint, anise, fennel seed or chamomile teas may help. Some women use homeopathy, acupressure points or seasickness bands.
- Taking time out from busy work and social schedules to help with stress levels, try a massage or holiday (if possible), bathe at the end of the day.
- Partaking in physical activity, which releases endorphins, helps with wellbeing. Spend time with your partner, family or friends.

8 weeks

Your baby measures 1.5cm (0.6 inch) and their head is more rounded with defined cheeks, mouth, lips, chin and nasal passages. Tiny blood vessels network under their fine skin and their eyelids develop but remain closed until 24 weeks of pregnancy. Internal and external ears develop, but they cannot hear until 19 to 24 weeks. Immature taste buds grow on their tongue and their arms and legs lengthen, extending forwards and across their body.

You may experience nose bleeds or bleeding gums. Hormonal changes and emotions can fluctuate, with mood swings shifting quickly. These feelings are very normal but may catch you by surprise!

Consider:

- Having a dental check-up if you are due for one.
- Optional early genetic testing to screen for abnormalities or disorders. These are performed before 12 to 14 weeks. Discuss options with your local doctor or genetic counsellor at the maternity hospital.
- Avoiding or limiting fish with high mercury levels such as shark (flake), swordfish barramundi, gemfish or ling.

9 weeks

Your baby is 2.5cm (1 inch) in length. Their fingers and toes have formed and nail beds begin growing. Their heart has valves and blood is produced by their liver. Their bone marrow takes over blood

A weekly guide
to your pregnancy

production once bones mature. Lungs are growing bronchi and spreading through their chest. Their anus and ovaries or testes have developed but both sexes look similar until external sex organs fully form.

Your baby's elbows, knees, wrists and ankles develop and muscles form between skin and bones. Their neck is stronger and they can lift and turn their head. Their hands can reach out to touch their face and some may suck their thumb!

You may experience headaches due to hormonal changes and increased blood volume, or if prone to migraines these may improve. Dizziness and feeling light-headed is common as blood vessels naturally relax. Your libido may either rise or decline. Making love throughout pregnancy is perfectly safe, providing there are no health complications.

Consider:

- Taking care with hair dyes. Some women opt for foils or a cap to avoid skin contact with hair dyes.
- Avoiding chemical hair-removal methods and some types of laser. Speak with your caregiver or beautician.
- Avoiding tanning creams and lotions. Most caregivers err on the side of caution, not recommending artificial tanning during pregnancy.

10 weeks

Your baby measures 3.5cm (1.4 inches) and weighs about 5 grams (0.18 ounces). Their brain and nervous system matures and their legs are now longer than their arms. Growing muscles work together with nerves to facilitate their first movements and their jaw can now open. Small ribs can be seen through their chest and their digestive system is developing rapidly.

You may notice you are passing more wind and perhaps experiencing wind pain and constipation. Emotions can begin to feel more balanced, accepting the reality of the pregnancy. It may be hard to keep the pregnancy a secret.

Consider:

- Drinking 8 glasses of water a day, including fruit juice, prunes, fibre, bran, fruit and vegetables to help with constipation. Reduce refined foods or try some liquorice. Gentle physical activity can help stimulate the bowel.
- Investigating maternity and paternity leave entitlements, if working.
- When to announce your pregnancy to family, friends and work colleagues.
- Discussing occupational health and safety issues in your workplace.

11 weeks

Your baby is 5cm long (2 inches) and weighs about 8 grams (0.28 ounces). All their major organs are now in place and their kidneys secrete fluid into their bladder, passing this into the amniotic fluid. Sucking and swallowing begins and mature taste buds allow tasting of the amniotic fluid surrounding them. The cycle of swallowing and urinating sterile amniotic fluid continues until birth. Your baby also breathes amniotic fluid to help strengthen their lungs and diaphragm. They now have about 20 baby teeth inside their gums.

Your uterus grows out of the pelvic bones and increased blood flow makes your skin feel warmer. It is common to wonder about your baby, what they may look like and if they are growing normally.

Consider writing down questions for your first pregnancy visit. First visits involve providing information about your health, medical and pregnancy history and perhaps taking blood for some routine tests (if not already done).

12 weeks

Your baby measures 7.6cm (3.04 inches) and weighs around 30 grams (1 ounce). They have eyebrows and fine whiskers of hair on their face. Their placenta is fully functional, supplying oxygen and nutrients and removing carbon dioxide and waste materials. Their bowel expands and contracts, filling with a tar-like substance that becomes their first bowel motion after the birth, called meconium. They can now make creeping and climbing movements but you are unlikely to feel them just yet, although a few women describe fluttering sensations at this early stage.

You may feel healthier and stronger as tiredness and morning sickness start subsiding, although for some this may take a little longer. Your skin may glow and eyes and hair shine, as your waistline thickens making clothes feel tighter. Your appetite may return if this has been affected and emotions may feel more balanced with a sense of calmness.

Consider continuing a well-balanced diet, making sure you have sufficient calcium and starting or resuming mild to moderate physical activity.

SECOND TRIMESTER – 13 TO 28 WEEKS

13 weeks

Your baby is 9cm (3.6 inches) from head to toe and weighs approximately 45 grams (1.56 ounces). Their gag and swallow reflexes develop and nasal passages form. Amniotic fluid passes through their nose and mouth triggering their sense of smell for life after birth.

Your stomach may start bulging and a growth spurt soon causes your belly to pop! You may feel emotionally more comfortable about the pregnancy.

Consider various childbirth classes in your area.

14 weeks

Your baby measures 12cm and weighs around 85 grams (3 ounces). Their heart beat can be heard using an electronic Doppler and their placenta is bigger than they are.

You may experience a metallic taste and have weird food cravings. Physical and emotional changes can impact on how you feel about your body and sexuality. Some women have a renewed interest in love-making as energy levels increase, with perhaps less concerns about miscarriage.

Consider regular pelvic floor exercises.

15 weeks

Your baby measures 15cm (6 inches) and weighs 120 grams (4.2 ounces), with their head being one third of their body size. Vocal chords form and they make various facial expressions. Their hands and feet explore your uterus. If you press on your belly they respond with small startle reflexes.

You may feel aches, pains and strange sensations as your body grows, ranging from stretching, burning, mild cramping, tugging, pulling or stitch pains. Fears and tears may quickly surface and dreams can be vivid, strange and scary.

Consider writing down questions for future pregnancy visits.

A weekly guide to your pregnancy

16 weeks
Your baby is 17cm from head to toe and weighs approximately 200 grams (7 ounces). They are now bigger than their placenta and amniotic fluid increases. Their umbilical cord is covered by a thick, gristle-like substance called Wharton's Jelly.

You may notice colostrum leaking from your nipples (although not for all women). The top of your uterus is about halfway between your pubic bone and belly button.

Consider how you would like to feed your baby, breast or formula.

17 weeks
Your baby measures 19cm and weighs about 280 grams (9.8 ounces). Their fine transparent skin is purple-red in colour from the many blood vessels flowing underneath. They change positions frequently and touch their own body. If having twins or triplets, they reach out to locate each other.

You may feel warmer and prefer to sleep with only a sheet, even in winter. Forgetfulness and feeling vague are common. Don't worry you are not alone!

Consider writing lists to help with forgetfulness.

18 weeks
Your baby measures 20cm (7.9 inches) and weighs approximately 310 grams (11 ounces). A fine layer of hair (lanugo) covers their skin, which sheds before birth.

You may sense your baby move with faint fluttering sensations (like butterflies) or small 'popping' bubbles or mild scratching feelings. Movements become stronger with more definite kicks over coming weeks.

Consider an ultrasound to look at body structures such as their heart, lungs, kidneys, brain and spine. Determining their sex is not 100% accurate!

19 weeks
Your baby is 22cm long and weighs about 340 grams (12 ounces). Their inner ear bones and nerve endings develop so they can hear your heartbeat, breathing and voice, although their ears are not structurally complete until 24 weeks.

You may experience sharp groin pains from the growing uterus. Walking, sudden movement, coughing, sneezing or exercise can trigger pains. Sore hips are also common with loosening ligaments.

Consider:
- Gentle yoga, heat packs, massage and resting for aches and pains.
- Sleeping with pillows between your legs for hip pain.

20 weeks
Your baby is 23cm (9 inches) long and weighs approximately 420 grams (14.8 ounces). Their nails have formed and fingerprints are visible.

You may feel your baby move for the first time, or later if the placenta is positioned at the front of your belly reducing sensations. The top of your uterus is felt near your belly button when lying down. It is normal for different women to look bigger or smaller at similar stages of pregnancy.

Consider shopping for maternity clothes and comfortable footwear.

21 weeks

Your baby is 25cm long and weighs about 500 grams (1 pound). A thick, white, greasy cream called vernix protects their skin and their eyelids remain fused shut. Their retinas are fully developed and they have eyelashes and eyebrows with hair pigments showing hair colour.

You may feel irregular sensations called Braxton Hicks contractions. These tone the uterus and massage your baby and may be felt as mild cramping, a hardness or tightness or you may not notice them at all. Many women experience them during love-making, which is normal.

Consider practising deep breathing during Braxton Hicks contractions if they are uncomfortable.

22 weeks

Your baby is 26cm long and weighs about 550 grams (1.2 pounds). Their brain and spinal cord matures with nerve cells making vigorous connections. They recognise warmth, light and sound, and may jump to loud, sudden noises. Their placenta processes a litre of blood per hour, increasing to 12 litres by 40 weeks.

You may experience fluid retention in the legs, feet and hands, usually at the end of the day, being worse in hot weather or if standing for long periods. If swelling is noticeable first thing in the morning, advise your caregiver. Sometimes nausea and vomiting returns unexpectedly, particularly if feeling stressed.

Consider baby items - essentials and nice-to-haves, perhaps borrowing or lay-buying items now.

23 weeks

Your baby is 28cm long and weighs about 600 grams (1lb 5oz). Their head moves from side to side and they may have hiccups. A fine layer of fat forms between muscles and skin, covering blood vessels, and they now have sweat glands.

Your legs may feel jittery and perhaps ache, called restless legs, which can interfere with sleep. Sitting for long periods may also be difficult.

Consider:
- Using cell salts or magnesium phosphate for restless legs.
- Removing your belly ring or replacing it with a flexible PTEF bar as your belly grows.

24 weeks

Your baby is 30cm long and weighs around 700 grams (1lb 8oz). Their lungs produce surfactant, which helps with breathing after birth. Other people may feel your baby kicking when placing their hand on your belly.

You may experience shortness of breath even when resting, or your heart race in your chest (palpitations). Exercising, feeling anxious, excited or stressed can trigger palpitations or they may happen for no apparent reason, usually subsiding after a few minutes.

Consider not lying flat on your back if it makes you feel dizzy, breathless or nauseous.

25 weeks

Your baby measures 33cm (13.2 inches) and weighs about 800 grams (1lb 12oz). Their heart rate is 110 to 170 beats per minute. Their eyes can open and their vision is perfectly focused to around 30cm away. Your baby will be able to see your face when held, once born. Movements are regular and they respond if you press on their protruding feet, bottom or hands.

A weekly guide to your pregnancy

You may have sore or tender spots on your belly from your baby continually pressing on the same area. Your caregiver can feel the position of your baby's head and body.

Consider further routine tests such as a glucose tolerance test for gestational diabetes, a blood count for anaemia and perhaps a vaginal swab for Group B strep.

26 weeks
Your baby is 35cm long and weighs around 950 grams (2lb). They recognise your voice and respond to different types of music.

You may experience upper or lower backache or sciatica (felt as a shooting nerve pain down the buttock and back of one leg).

Consider massage, acupuncture, chiropractic or osteopathy for back pain and sciatica.

27 weeks
Your baby is 37cm long and weighs about 1,100 grams (2lb 7oz). Their immune system develops and antibodies pass to them from you. They can distinguish light from dark and track movement.

You may feel rib pain as your uterus grows. Leg cramps may occur at night making you jolt awake, contributing to tiredness.

Consider pain management methods for labour such as breathing, hot (cold) packs, showers, the bath, massage, movement and positions, music, hypnosis, a TENS machine, visualisation, acupressure, natural remedies or medical gas, pethidine or an epidural.

28 weeks
Your baby measures 38cm (15 inches) and weighs around 1.2kg (2lbs 10oz). Their bone marrow matures, producing their own blood supply, taking over from their liver and spleen. Their liver begins to store iron.

You may start feeling heavy and tired as your pregnancy progresses into the third trimester.

Consider resting more and taking iron supplements if levels are low.

THIRD TRIMESTER – 29 WEEKS TO BIRTH
29 weeks
Your baby measures 40cm from head to toe and weighs about 1,350 grams (3lb). A layer of fat called brown adipose tissue starts forming to help regulate body warmth after birth. Unlike older babies and children, newborns have a limited ability to shiver, sweat or move to maintain their body temperature.

You may hear strange clicking or popping sounds coming from your uterus. While this is not common and strange when heard, it is not an indication of a problem. There are no known reasons for these sounds – simply a mystery of pregnancy?

Consider:
- Birth plans
- Choices and options if planning a Caesarean or VBAC (Vaginal Birth After Caesarean).
- Preparing siblings for the new baby's arrival.
- Cord blood donation at birth.

30 weeks

Your baby is around 42cm long (16.5 inches) and weighs approximately 1.5kg (3lb 5oz). Their brain increases in size and complexity, the pupils of their eyes respond to light and they see dim shapes. Unborn babies have sleep and wake cycles, often being more active when their mother is resting.

You may notice feeling larger, heavier and tireder as your baby grows. Some women experience fluid retention in their hands, legs and feet (called oedema), even when their blood pressure is normal.

Consider:

- Changes in your baby's movements to being stretches, pushes and rolls as they take up more space.
- The type of nappies you will use - cloth, disposable or a combination of both.
- What to pack for the hospital or birth centre or preparations for a homebirth.

31 weeks

Your baby is around 43cm long and weighs about 1.7kg (3lb 12 oz), and is starting to look a little chubby now! Fine hair disappears from their face, but remains on their body. They sleep about 90% of the time, in between short bursts of movement when awake.

You may experience heartburn (indigestion or reflux) in the chest and throat after eating.

Consider:

- Eating small, regular meals and avoiding foods or fluids that trigger heartburn.
- Having extra support people organised for the labour.
- Taking raspberry leaf tea, tablets or tincture for uterine toning.

32 weeks

Your baby measures 44cm in length and weighs approximately 1.9kg (4lb 3oz). Their lungs are maturing and their sucking and swallowing action starts to co-ordinate.

You may experience constipation and haemorrhoids which can be painful, itchy and may bleed.

Consider:

- Slowing down and resting when possible.
- Drinking plenty of fluids and increasing fruit and fibre in your diet.
- Organising a tour of your birth place.

33 weeks

Your baby is about 45cm long and weighs about 2,100 grams (4 lbs 10oz) and is now fully developed physically with a firm grasp reflex. They can taste sweet and sour, detecting subtle changes in amniotic fluid flavour, depending on what their mother eats. This is thought to act as a flavour bridge to their mother's breast milk.

You may notice varicose veins in your legs and/or genital area, caused by blood pooling. These can feel uncomfortable but do not cause a problem during birth. They improve in the weeks after birth.

Consider:

- Moving with gentle exercise, elevating your feet, resting and wearing support stockings.
- Pelvic floor exercises.
- Using perineal massage to prepare for birth.

A weekly guide to your pregnancy

34 weeks

Your baby is about 46cm long (18 inches) and weighs about 2,350 grams (5lb 3oz). From here on in, unborn babies gain weight, grow a little longer and mature their lungs, sucking reflex and immune system.

You may need to urinate more frequently. Some women experience numbness or pins and needles in their hands called carpal tunnel syndrome, caused by fluid accumulating in the wrists. Your thoughts may drift to the labour and birth with feelings surfacing about your impending baby's birthday.

Consider your baby's position at check-ups with your caregiver. They should start lying head-down by this stage.

35 weeks

Your baby measures 47cm from head to toe (18.5 inches) and weighs around 2.6kg (5lb 12oz) and now looks quite plump! Their head may move lower into your pelvis, possibly bringing discomfort or cramping sensations.

You may experience pain at the front of your pelvis called symphysis pubis, caused by the pubic joint loosening. Pain is felt low, in the middle or at the front, and can range from an annoying twinge or ache to a sharp, shooting pain or a clicking sensation.

Consider:

- Taking care with posture and lifting.
- Possibly stopping work soon if not already at home.
- Re-testing iron levels, if previously low.

36 weeks

Your baby is around 48cm long and weighs approximately 2,850 grams (6lb 5oz) and is now in normal proportions. At 36 to 37 weeks their lungs fully mature but this can be delayed to 38 to 40 weeks for babies of diabetic mothers.

You may not sleep well during the final weeks, waking frequently because of discomfort and needing urinate.

Consider:

- Resting and napping when you can.
- Seeing your caregiver weekly throughout the last month.
- Asking about routine procedures for the birth and vitamin K for your newborn.

37 weeks

Your baby measures about 48.5cm long (19 inches) and weighs about 3.1kg (6lb 13oz). Babies born after 37 weeks are regarded as being on time (not premature). Term babies have small pads of breast tissue under their nipples (both boys and girls) and fingernails reaching the tips of their fingers, often looking manicured! Their overall growth slows now and amniotic fluid starts slightly decreasing.

You may notice an increase in mucus coming away as your baby's head engages. This may be mistaken for the waters breaking. If unsure, contact your caregiver. During the last weeks the mucus plug (or show) can come away, which does not necessarily mean labour is imminent.

Consider:

◗ Knowing the physical and emotional signs of labour starting.

◗ Discussing the role of your support people and what will happen with older siblings.

◗ What to prepare for a planned caesarean.

38 weeks

Your baby is about 49cm long and weighs around 3,200 grams (just over 7lb) – this can vary widely! The fine hair disappears from their body but their skin is still covered with thick, creamy vernix. The placenta covers one third of the uterus and processes around 12 litres of blood per hour. For boys, their testes descend into their scrotum.

You may feel fed up and ready to have your baby, or you may not want the pregnancy to end! Some women experience pre-labour signs such as period pain, a mucus show, loose bowel motions, nausea or vomiting, backache, the waters breaking or mild to moderate contractions. During pre-labour the cervix softens and ripens, thins out and starts to open or dilate slightly from 1 to 3 centimetres.

Consider:

◗ Having your hospital/birth centre bag packed.

39 weeks

Your baby will be born soon (if not already!). The greasy vernix cream all but disappears, leaving remnants in their armpits and groin. Newborns naturally slow or stop their practice breathing patterns 24 to 48 hours before labour commences. The amniotic fluid in their lungs absorbs into their blood stream during labour, with small remaining amounts absorbed within 24 hours after birth.

You may be enjoying the last week of pregnancy, perhaps being pampered or catching up with friends. Some women feel so uncomfortable they just want their baby to be born!

Consider:

◗ Remembering your baby may not be ready for another week or more yet.

◗ Cooking and freezing meals for the early weeks of parenting. Stocking up on kitchen and household items to reduce shopping needs after the birth.

40 weeks

Your baby is ready but only 5% of babies are born on their due date, most naturally arriving within the week afterwards. The average Australian birth weight is 3,300 grams, ranging from 2,800–4,500 grams (6lb 3oz to 9lb 15oz). An average length is 50cm (20 inches), ranging from 46–56 cms (18 to 22 inches). Their head circumference may be 33cm to 37cm.

You may be feeling a range of emotions if your baby hasn't arrived yet. Bear in mind the normal length of pregnancy is anytime from 37 to 42 weeks.

Consider:

◗ Induction options and choices, normally offered 7 to 10 days past the due date.

◗ Local community support services once your baby is home.

◗ Postnatal support and mothers' groups.

Written by Sandra Robinson (childbirth educator) & Catherine Price (midwife): authors of *BIRTH* & directors of www.birth.com.au.

Prenatal tests
& what to expect

Pregnant women undergo a variety of tests at different stages before their baby is born. Many tests are considered routine, but a few are optional choices. Women with medical conditions such as diabetes, high blood pressure, epilepsy, thyroid or metabolic disorders often require additional tests, and women with multiple pregnancies or babies with suspected health issues may also require more testing than normal.

Routine tests during the first 20 weeks

Blood group and antibodies is a three-in-one blood test that identifies your blood group (A, B, AB or O), Rhesus factor (positive or negative e.g. A positive) and screens for blood antibodies. The results should ideally be negative or nil.

Full blood count (FBC) measures haemoglobin, related to anaemia. The normal pregnancy range is 10.5 to 15.0 gm% (or 105 to 150g/L). Platelets are also measured (cells that clot the blood to control bleeding), with normal ranges being 140,000 to 450,000 per uL. A serum ferritin measures iron stores, the normal being 20 to 150 ng/ml.

Rubella screens for immunity to German measles. Most adults have good immunity due to experiencing the virus as a child or being previously vaccinated. A rubella titre above 10 to 20 IU/ml is regarded as being immune to rubella.

Syphilis tests are called VDRL/RPR and TPHA. Results are 'non-reactive' if no infection is present and 'reactive' if present.

Hepatitis B and C and HIV/AIDS screenings have now become fairly standard, although they are not compulsory and some women do decline them.

Thalassaemia testing is now fairly routine. It is an inherited condition affecting haemoglobin production (cells that carry oxygen in the blood). If a woman has thalassaemia, her unborn baby could be at risk of anaemia to varying degrees. The father of the baby should also be tested to help determine how severely the baby may be affected.

Ultrasounds may be performed during the first 12 weeks to confirm or date the pregnancy or to help with genetic testing. An ultrasound may also be used to identify twins or investigate unexplained bleeding.

Routine ultrasounds are often performed at 18 to 20 weeks to screen for physical abnormalities in unborn babies and check the position of the placenta. When estimating the stage of pregnancy (or baby's due date) ultrasounds done between 8 and 12 weeks are generally within 3 to 5 days of accuracy, from 12 to 22 weeks are plus or minus 10 days of the due date, and if performed after 22 weeks can be 2 to 3 weeks out.

A sterile urine test is often done to screen for a possible infection.

Prenatal tests
& what to expect

A pap test may be done if one has not been performed in the past 2 years. Some caregivers also do a routine breast check for lumps.

Optional genetic tests

Genetic tests are optional and aim to detect specific inherited disorders. They range from non-invasive nuchal translucency ultrasounds with blood tests, to more invasive procedures that obtain cells from inside the uterus. Ultrasounds done at around 18 weeks can detect obvious physical abnormalities, such as kidney, spine or heart defects, but can't reveal the actual genetic make-up of a baby such as Down's syndrome.

Nuchal translucency (NT) ultrasound is now the most common screening test. It measures a normal fluid-filled sac at the back of the unborn baby's neck which is present after 10 weeks + 3 days of pregnancy and before 13 weeks + 6 days. It aims to identify babies at possible risk of having a genetic disorder.

NT scans can only estimate the risk as being either high or low, they are not 100% accurate. Therefore some women with a normal healthy baby are given a 'high risk' result and others can be given a 'low risk' result, yet their baby may have a genetic disorder. Accurate results are more likely if the ultrasonographer is experienced at performing NT scans and if a blood test is also performed, increasing the accuracy from 75% to 85%. If the result comes back as 'high risk', counselling and an amniocentesis test are generally offered.

Amniocentesis involves the caregiver taking a sample of amniotic fluid with a fine needle through the woman's belly to obtain cells naturally shed from the baby floating in the fluid. It is usually performed between 15 and 18 weeks. The cells are grown in a laboratory to map the baby's genes or chromosomes, which then definitely proves or disproves a specific genetic disorder exists.

Chorionic villus sampling (CVS) can be performed between 10 and 12 weeks of pregnancy, taking a small sample of cells from the placenta via the woman's vagina to map the baby's genes and providing a definite diagnosis.

Both amniocentesis and CVS procedures carry a small risk of miscarriage. Ultrasound is used to guide the caregiver during the test to obtain the required sample. Preliminary results can sometimes be obtained after 48 to 72 hours, but final results usually take around 2 weeks.

Routine tests from 20 to 40 weeks

Glucose tolerance blood test (GTT) is taken after the woman has a special sweet drink. It detects diabetes caused by pregnancy (gestational diabetes). Normal ranges are 3.5 to 6.5 mmol/L but can be up to 8.0 mmol/L and still be normal. Blood sugar levels frequently above 8 mmol/L may cause health complications for the baby. A GTT is often performed around 26 to 30 weeks but may be recommended earlier for women considered at risk of developing diabetes.

Group B Streptococcus (GBS) uses a vaginal swab or urine test at around 28 weeks to screen for this bacterium. GBS is regarded as a normal body organism (not an infection) and does not generally cause a problem unless it grows and multiplies, particularly if the waters break before labour starts.

Anti-D. Women with a Rhesus negative blood type (eg. O negative), have further antibody blood tests at 28 and 34 weeks of pregnancy and may be given Anti-D immunoglobulin injections. Ask your caregiver for details.

Ultrasounds are not usually performed after 20 weeks unless there are health concerns for the unborn baby. These may include not growing as expected or unexplained bleeding. If the routine 19 week ultrasound showed the placenta was low, another ultrasound is usually done at around 34 weeks to check it has moved up with the growing uterus. Ultrasounds may also be done to check the baby's well-being if the pregnancy is overdue, or establish the baby's position (e.g. breech or head-down), if your caregiver is unsure.

Routine pregnancy visit procedures and tests

Blood pressure is usually performed at every visit, with normal pregnancy levels ranging from 90/50 to 135/80, the average being 110/70. Health concerns can be an issue if your blood pressure rises significantly higher than what is normal for you, especially after 28 weeks.

Feeling/measuring your belly is done after 12 weeks to monitor your baby's growth. When lying down, caregivers may also use a tape measure starting from the pubic bone to the top of the uterus (or fundus). After 34 weeks the position of your baby also becomes important.

Listening to your baby's heart beat is exciting and reassuring. By 8 to 10 weeks the rate is around 170 to 200 beats per minute (only measurable with ultrasound). By about 20 weeks the rate drops to around 110 to 170 beats. Caregivers can detect an unborn baby's heart rate with an electronic Doppler after 12 to 14 weeks.

Urine tests may be used to detect protein (related to high blood pressure). Glucose in the urine during pregnancy is common for healthy women and does not necessarily mean diabetes. Some caregivers request a urine sample at every visit although this is now less common.

Weighing at every visit is not usually done these days, although some caregivers still do this.

Written by Sandra Robinson (childbirth educator) & Catherine Price (midwife): authors of *BIRTH* & directors of www.birth.com.au.

The importance of folic acid in your diet

Taking folic acid before pregnancy and for the first three months of pregnancy can reduce your chances of having a baby with spina bifida or problems with the development of the brain (called neural tube defects). Spina bifida is where the spinal cord, and the bones, muscle and skin that cover it, do not form normally. The abnormal development occurs when the spinal cord and brain are forming during the sixth week of pregnancy (4 weeks after conception). This is often before a woman knows that she is pregnant.

Why take folic acid?

Research has shown that the chance of having a baby with spina bifida is much less if a woman increases her intake of folic acid for at least one month before she gets pregnant and for the first three months of her pregnancy.

- Every woman who could become pregnant should be sure she gets enough folate and this is best done by taking folic acid tablets.
- The risk is much lower, but taking extra folic acid does not totally eliminate the risk.
- Taking folic acid before pregnancy may also lower the risk of some other heart, kidney and limb abnormalities. The evidence for this is not as strong as for spina bifida, and more research is being done.
- There is no evidence that other vitamins or minerals will protect your baby against spina bifida.

What is folate or folic acid?

- Folic acid is a water-soluble B-group vitamin that is needed for healthy growth and development. The vitamin is known as 'folate' when it is found naturally in food, and 'folic acid' when it is added to foods or when it is in tablets. Folic acid is turned into folate in the body.
- It can be found naturally in most plant foods, especially green vegetables, wholegrain breads and cereals, peas and dried beans.
- Extra folic acid is also added to some foods, such as some breakfast cereals, some breads and fruit juices. If folic acid is added, this will be marked on the labelling.

How can you increase your folic acid?

- The easiest and most effective way is by taking a daily folic acid tablet. A healthy diet is important, but it is very difficult to get enough folate from foods to prevent spina bifida.
- Folic acid tablets are quite safe to take. The tablets recommended are 0.5 milligrams (which is 500 micrograms). One tablet each day is enough. (Note: tablets in other countries may contain a different amount of folic acid.)
- Folic acid tablets are available from chemist shops (without a prescription), health food shops and some supermarkets.
- Some multivitamins contain folic acid, but often at a lower dose, so it is best to take the separate tablets.

Who should take folic acid tablets?

- Folic acid works best if it is taken for at least one month before starting a pregnancy.
- As many pregnancies are unplanned, it is recommended that all women of child bearing age who could become pregnant, take a folic acid tablet (0.5 milligrams) every day.
- If you have a family history of spina bifida, or take medication for epilepsy, you may need a higher dose of folic acid. Ask your doctor about this.
- Extra folate is not as effective if you start to take it after you know you are pregnant, but it is worth taking it if you suspect you may be pregnant (for example if you have missed a period).
- The risk of having a baby with spina bifida if extra folic acid was not taken is still small.

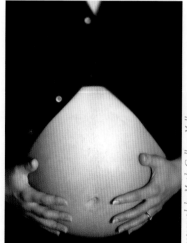

Photograph by Maple Gallery, Melbourne.

What is spina bifida?

Spina bifida is a serious abnormality of the spinal cord and the bones, muscles and skin covering it. 'Spina' means spine, and 'bifida' means divided or split.

- Babies with spina bifida usually have an obvious abnormality on their back when they are born. Some will die soon after birth and most need a lot of treatment.
- Spina bifida can cause permanently weak legs, no feeling in the legs and problems walking. Many people with spina bifida will need to use a wheelchair.
- There can also be problems with bladder and bowel control.
- Other neural tube defects affect the development of the brain as well as the spinal cord.
- There is no cure for spina bifida.

What is the risk of spina bifida?

- Any woman could have a baby with spina bifida or other neural tube defects.
- About 1 in 1,000 babies in South Australia is born with spina bifida and another 1 in 1,000 babies has another type of neural tube defect.
- The risk is higher if another family member has had spina bifida. You can have tests to check for neural tube defects during pregnancy.
- Taking folate for at least 1 month before getting pregnant and during the first 3 months has been shown to reduce the risk by up to 70%.

Finding out whether an unborn baby has spina bifida

- Most women in Australia have an ultrasound examination during early to mid pregnancy. Most babies with spina bifida will be diagnosed by that ultrasound.
- Blood tests which find most neural tube defects may also be done.

What to eat & what not to eat

Nutrition is crucial during pregnancy to maintain optimal health for both the mother and the child. Dieting is not recommended during pregnancy as a decrease in weight could potentially cause problems to the health of both mother and baby.

Are you eating for two?

Many people believe that during pregnancy the mother is eating for two. While the mother needs to increase her nutrients, the amount of food does not necessarily need to be increased. It is the quality and nutritious value of food that is important.

Healthy foods

During pregnancy it is important that a variety of healthy foods are included as part of your daily eating pattern. Eating balanced amounts of the following foods will be beneficial to both mother and baby:

- Lots of fruit and vegetables, which provide an array of vitamins and minerals and help to increase folate. Ensuring plenty of folate is in your diet can assist in preventing neural tube birth defects such as spina bifida. Green leafy vegetables are excellent sources of folate and dietary fibre. Other good sources include oranges, sweet potatoes, peas, corn, avocado and tomatoes. During pregnancy try to include at least 5 servings of well-washed vegetables and 2 serves of fruit each day.
- Moderate amounts of lean meats provide extra protein and are a great source of iron. During pregnancy protein requirements increase slightly, to allow the baby to grow and develop, as well as allowing the mother's own breast tissue to develop. Pregnant and breastfeeding women should eat at least two servings of lean meat, poultry, seafood, eggs, nuts and seeds or legumes per day. If there is a family history of allergic disease, peanut and peanut products should be avoided.
- Moderate amounts of dairy. Pregnant women should eat at least three servings of calcium-rich foods such as milk, cheese and yoghurt every day to ensure an adequate intake of calcium. This ensures that there is enough calcium in the mother's body for both herself and her baby, so calcium is not drawn from the mother's bones. Choosing pasteurised milks ensures bacterial effects are minimised.
- Breads and cereals. Pregnant mothers need to consume more dietary energy to cope with the growing changes of their body. This is not required in the first three months of pregnancy, but is necessary in the last six months as the baby is growing rapidly. A variety of bread and cereal foods should be included in the diet. Wholemeal & wholegrain varieties are preferred, or alternatively choose breakfast cereals that are fortified with iron. Pregnant women should eat four to six servings daily of breads and cereals. This will help to provide adequate carbohydrate and dietary fibre.
- Nuts and seeds. They can provide extra energy, protein, healthy fats, iron and other vitamins and minerals.
- Legumes, for example lentils, chick peas and baked beans. These are a great source of both carbohydrate and protein, and are a good source of folate. They can be mixed in with meat and vegetable dishes, e.g. casseroles and stir fries, or salads.
- Some fats and oils in the form of plant oils, butter, avocado, margarine and fish (fresh or canned) – for vitamins A, D, E and K and essential fatty acids.

Foods to choose carefully

Fish is nutritious for mother and baby and is an important part of a healthy diet as it is high in omega-3 oils and a good source of protein. "The Australian Dietary Guidelines advise eating one or two fish meals per week for good health. The good news is that FSANZ has found it is safe for all population groups to eat 2–3 serves per week of most types of fish. There are only a few types of fish which FSANZ recommends limiting in the diet – these are billfish (swordfish/broadbill and marlin), shark/flake, orange roughy and catfish." These should be avoided during pregnancy because of high levels of mercury.

Foods that may be harmful

There are some foods that should be avoided as they can contain listeria and lead to bacterial contamination. This can be harmful to both the mother and unborn child.

Risk of listeria is managed by ensuring hygienic preparation, storage and handling of food and by avoiding high risk foods.

It is recommended that pregnant women avoid consuming the following foods, especially if it is unsure if hygienic practices have been followed:

◉ **Cold meats**	Unpackaged ready-to-eat from delicatessen counters, sandwich bars, etc. Packaged, sliced ready-to-eat
◉ **Cold cooked chicken**	Purchased (whole, portions, or diced) ready-to-eat
◉ **Pate**	Refrigerated pate or meat spreads
◉ **Salads** (fruit & vegetables)	Pre-prepared or pre-packaged salads e.g. from salad bars, smorgasbords, etc.
◉ **Chilled seafood**	Raw (e.g. oysters, sashimi or sushi) Smoked ready-to-eat Ready-to-eat peeled prawns (cooked) e.g. in prawn cocktails, sandwich fillings, and prawn salads
◉ **Cheese**	Soft, semi-soft and surface ripened cheeses (pre-packaged and delicatessen) e.g. brie, camembert, ricotta, feta and blue
◉ **Ice cream**	Soft serve
◉ **Other dairy products**	Unpasteurised dairy products (e.g. raw goats' milk)

Food preparation and safety

The way foods are prepared can influence their safety and risk of bacterial contamination. Therefore:

◉ Vegetable, fruits and any food that has had contact with soil should be washed thoroughly.

◉ Only freshly prepared foods should be consumed, no pre-packaged foods.

◉ Always keep cooked and raw foods separate, and store fresh food in the refrigerator.

Enjoying a wide variety of nutritious foods is one of the best ways that women can help to ensure good health for both themselves and their baby during pregnancy.

Information provided by Nutrition Australia, www.nutritionaustralia.org. Written by Marianne Glennon.

Why testing for pre-eclampsia is so important

Women should always report worrying signs or symptoms to their doctor during pregnancy. Often there may turn out to be no cause for alarm, but it is a simple matter to have a blood pressure measurement, a urine check, a blood test or other investigations/examinations to be sure that pre-eclampsia is not the cause of the symptoms or signs of concern. Unfortunately, pre-eclampsia does not provide a woman with early warning symptoms or signs, so never miss an ante-natal appointment.

Pre-eclampsia is the most common serious medical disorder of human pregnancy. It can affect both the mother and her unborn baby. It usually arises during the second half of pregnancy, and can even occur some days after delivery. In the mother, it can cause several problems of which she may be unaware – high blood pressure (hypertension), leakage of protein into the urine (proteinuria), thinning of the blood (coagulopathy) and liver dysfunction.

Occasionally, pre-eclampsia can lead to convulsions (fits), a serious complication known as eclampsia. Also, when a pregnancy is complicated by PE, the baby may grow more slowly than normal in the womb or suffer a potentially harmful oxygen deficiency.

Pre-eclampsia can affect as many as 10% of pregnancies, which makes it one of the most common pregnancy complications. It occurs more often in first pregnancies. Occasionally, women who have suffered it once find that it recurs in one or more subsequent pregnancies, and rarely a woman who has not experienced it in earlier pregnancies may develop it in a subsequent pregnancy.

The precise cause of pre-eclampsia is unknown. However, genetic factors are probably involved, given women whose mothers and/or sisters have suffered pre-eclampsia are at increased risk of the disease themselves. There is good evidence that the placenta is centrally involved in the development of pre-eclampsia.

During pregnancy the placenta requires a large blood supply from the mother to sustain the growing baby. It seems that in pre-eclampsia the placenta does not receive sufficient maternal blood for its requirements. When this occurs, damage to the mother's blood vessels follows, the result of which is increasing blood pressure. Kidney function is also disturbed and blood proteins leak from the mother's circulation through the kidney into the urine.

As pre-eclampsia worsens, other organs are affected, including the mother's liver, lungs, brain, heart and blood clotting system. Dangerous complications such as eclampsia (convulsions), cerebral haemorrhage (stroke), pulmonary oedema (fluid in the lungs from heart failure), kidney failure, liver damage and thinning of the blood (disseminated intravascularcoagulation) can occur in serious cases. However, these complications are fortunately rare.

A combination of rising blood pressure and protein in the urine can suggest pre-eclampsia may be developing. As yet, there is no precise diagnostic test for pre-eclampsia. However, if a previously healthy pregnant woman develops high blood pressure and proteinuria in the latter half of her pregnancy, then the diagnosis is almost always pre-eclampsia.

Some swelling (oedema) is common in normal pregnancy, but excessive swelling which also involves the face can occur in pre-eclampsia.

In severe pre-eclampsia, other symptoms can appear, including severe headaches, visual disturbances (such as flashing lights), vomiting and pain in the upper abdomen. While such symptoms may have other less dangerous causes, they should never be ignored during pregnancy.

The relative deficiency in the blood supply from the mother to the placenta limits the baby's supply of nutrients and oxygen, which may lead to reduced growth of the baby (intrauterine growth restriction) and even oxygen deprivation. The timing of delivery in cases of pre-eclampsia which arise early in the second half of pregnancy can be particularly difficult, because a very premature fetus may be severely affected by pre-eclampsia, but on the other hand, cannot be certain of survival outside the womb either.

Once a woman with pre-eclampsia has developed persistent hypertension and significant proteinuria, the disease is considered to be severe and hospitalisation is required for careful monitoring of maternal and fetal welfare, stabilisation of various complications of pre-eclampsia and preparation for delivery. Even though some features of pre-eclampsia can be temporarily improved by treatments, the disease itself is progressive (sometimes slowly, but sometimes rapidly) until delivery. Blood pressure lowering drugs may often be necessary to reduce the risks of complications such as heart failure and stroke. Anticonvulsant drugs such as magnesium may also be required to prevent or treat eclamptic fits.

Because of the progressive nature of pre-eclampsia, once admitted, women are not usually discharged until after delivery.

The best way to minimise the harm that pre-eclampsia may cause in a pregnancy is to regularly attend for antenatal check-ups, so that the chance of detecting pre-eclampsia in its earliest stages is optimised. If a woman is at particular risk of pre-eclampsia, then it would be wise for her to attend a specialist obstetrician or maternity hospital with skill and experience in the management of pre-eclampsia and its complications. Such women especially should consult with their doctors early in pregnancy, or even before pregnancy, to plan their antenatal care.

All women should ensure that their blood pressure is checked regularly during pregnancy and that their urine is examined for the presence of protein.

While small amounts of protein in urine specimens may be normal during pregnancy, amounts greater than a 'trace' should not be ignored and should lead to further investigations to determine the cause of the proteinuria. Besides pre-eclampsia, attention may be drawn by this simple ante-natal test to other pregnancy problems such as urinary tract infections.

Information provided by Australian Action on Pre-eclampsia Inc. (AAPEC), www.aapec.org.au.

Dressing to support your body

Having a baby is an exciting time, but accommodating your bump and changing figure can be daunting. Luckily the days of kangaroo pouches are gone, so you can dress comfortably and stylishly when pregnant. Many women wait until near the end of their pregnancy before buying maternity-specific clothing, thinking they will be able to 'get by' with what they already have. Investing in quality maternity wear that fits properly and looks fabulous will do much for your confidence at a time when you may feel unsure of your changing body. Labels that cater specifically for the pregnant shape have spent time developing and refining styles and systems that grow with your expanding bump.

Well designed maternity clothing can be worn right through your pregnancy and after as your body goes back to its natural size. As more and more women are working and socialising through their pregnancies it is important that they have a functional wardrobe that they feel great in.

"It's really important to carry your pre-pregnancy style preferences through to your maternity wardrobe," says fashion designer Charlotte Devereux. "If you feel your best in smart pants and a shirt don't suddenly start wearing track pants and your partner's jeans just because you're pregnant. The same goes with colour – it looks amazing on the pregnant figure and so many women feel they have to stick with black."

It's a good idea to build your pregnancy wardrobe around a few key pieces that you can adapt for different situations. A really fabulous cut of maternity jean can look fantastic dressed up with a gorgeous floaty top for a night out, teamed with a jacket and shirt for a smart casual look or thrown on with a t-shirt for maximum comfort.

Many of the current fashion trends are really flattering when adapted to maternity designs; empire-waist dresses and tops; trapeze dresses; shifts; leggings and slim cut pants. Just like a non-pregnant silhouette it is important to go for volume up top or on the bottom – not both. Slim cut jeans and tailored pants are effective at balancing looser top garments. For a laidback look, match an oversized top or short shift dress with leggings. Leggings which are especially designed for pregnancy will be comfortable and also help support your bump.

The increased media interest in celebrity pregnancies has put figure-flaunting style on the map. You should celebrate your bump and new found curves with some really gorgeous outfits – the time of the tent has gone. Most maternity labels do beautiful dresses in the latest season's colours and fabrics. Celebrities are great at accessorising and you can be too. Buy a fabulous new oversized handbag – it can double as a nappy bag later.

Get some gorgeous slouchy new boots – your feet will expand and you will be more comfortable in shoes with give. Bring some variety to your outfits by wrapping a gorgeous scarf around your neck.

Just like in pre-pregnancy show off the body parts you really love and make sure you wear garments that hug your bump. Long-line tee shirts and tank tops look great teamed with shorts or skirts in soft, stretchy fabrics. A deep v-neck is flattering and you can always throw on a scarf in cooler months. Your body temperature increases when pregnant so easy-to-remove layers will be your best friend.

Keep a soft and luxurious wrap with you for whenever the temperature drops.

It is important to get the right underwear for your changing shape. Breasts swell during pregnancy and the best maternity bras will provide support without rigid underwire that can begin to dig and squeeze. They will also have more hooks for changing the band size than a normal bra, and adjustable and detachable straps that make them ideal for breastfeeding. A v-neck that crosses over at the front and gathers over your bump can also double as an excellent breastfeeding top after you give birth.

Dressing to support your body during pregnancy can be confusing and this is when shopping at a maternity-specific store is so beneficial. The sales assistants know their stuff and will be able to advise you on what to expect and how to accommodate your changing shape. The best stores will usually have a removable bump that you can try on with the clothes, letting you see how the garments will look and fit as you get further along.

Celebrate your pregnancy, dress to flaunt it and flatter it, not hide it. A few key pieces can make all the difference to your comfort and style over this special time. Remember, when you bring home the bags after your shopping, it's probably the one time your partner will truly understand that it was because you really did have nothing to wear!

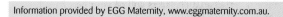

Information provided by EGG Maternity, www.eggmaternity.com.au.

Vox Pop

We asked a number of women and men around Australia to send in their advice, tips and personal experiences on a range of topics so that you have an insight into how others cope being a new parent. We hope you find their comments interesting, informative and reassuring. Vox Pop biographies: page 652

Jess Tamblyn
Mum of one, SA

Having a couple of drinks and devouring a cheese platter with friends was my favourite way to spend a sunny Sunday afternoon, so I was shattered to learn that not only could I not indulge in the wine but I also had to give up my favourite cheeses – I was devastated! But overall I had a great pregnancy and enjoyed being pregnant. I did find it interesting though how all of a sudden everyone thought it was okay to comment on your size. In one day I would have someone tell me I was looking rather big and was most likely further along in my pregnancy than I thought and then someone else would tell me I looked small and hinted there might be a problem – and these were complete strangers! Everyone becomes a pregnancy expert. I especially loved the childless male pregnancy experts – somehow they just knew everything!

Kaz Cooke
Mum of one, Melbourne

Motherhood is hilarious, messy, revolutionary, tedious, full of wonder, exciting, drudgery, liberating, enslaving, fascinating, worrying, fun, selfish, responsible, infuriating, cuddly, ever-changing, relentlessly repetitive, full-time shiftwork, full of love, educational, exhausting. Parenthood requires patience, help, and as many wipe-down surfaces as possible.

Katherine Twigg
Mum of one, VIC

My advice for anyone who is pregnant is to enjoy every minute, it is such an amazing experience. Make the most of every kick you feel and every time you see your baby on the ultrasound … I smile even now when I think back to those times.

I liked to give my belly cuddles and talk to my baby all the time. I said good morning to him every morning and he always responded with a kick or some kind of movement. I think that it is important that they get used to your voice as when they are born it must be so scary for them, but at least they have that comfort and familiarity when they hear your voice!

If you are having problems sleeping, invest in a pregnancy pillow that you can cuddle and wrap your legs around (particularly if you usually like sleeping on your belly); it made all the difference to me for a good night's sleep, particularly towards the end of my pregnancy.

Louise Cruz
Mum of three, NSW

When I discovered I was pregnant with my first child I was only 20 and had been married 3 months. After the initial shock wore off, I was really excited and made the decision to be fully informed on everything that was likely take place over the next 8 months or so. I set off to buy some books and attended antenatal classes at the hospital, although found these focussed mainly on the labour and birth side of things. It was good though to be armed with all the medical terminology for the various procedures that may arise in the course of the birth, and to be told what my options might be for pain relief during labour.

As a first-time mum I would highly recommend making the time to do some reading and research or even just talk to other mums so that the whole process of pregnancy and labour doesn't feel so daunting. I think the fear many first-time mums experience in the lead up to the birth is due to the unknown.

With that said, all the research and reading can't tell you what your labour will be like or exactly what to expect, and it is important to remember that everyone's experience is different!

Tony Wilson
Dad of one, Melbourne

Given the ratio of women to men who read baby books, there is only one answer to the question "How did you feel about your partner's changing body shape when pregnant?" Beautiful! The rounded belly, the physical reminder for both of us of what was about to happen, 'the glow' that either really happens, or is actually a rosy-cheeked flush that comes from having your head upside down in a toilet for three months. The baby bump is undoubtedly the best part of the body transformation, or at least equal with the who-needs-a-plastic-surgeon breast augmentation. The week thirty-five and beyond ankle bloat is perhaps overrated, although I did get plenty of laughs pushing my finger into Tam's foot, and then marvelling at the fact that the divot would stay there for ages. We took to calling Tamsin's ankles 'cankles' — no sign of where the calf ended and the ankle began!

Cindy Fraser
Mum of three, Melbourne

I seemed to sail through my first pregnancy without any worries. Then when I found out I was having twins with my second pregnancy I went into complete shock! A standard initial appointment (which I assured my husband he needn't bother coming to) revealed that we were expecting twins … well I cried for three days! I was told I was considered high risk because I was carrying twins and at each subsequent appointment I was made aware of the dangers associated with twin pregnancies. My obstetrician was also adamant that I would be having these babies early (as often happens with twin births) so we found ourselves counting the weeks aiming to make it that little bit further along. None of the concerns eventuated and I carried the twins to a healthy full term.

Linda Bull
Mum of two, Melbourne

For me motherhood has involved a massive shift in lifestyle, all for the better. Before I had my kids I never understood the meaning of the word 'tired'. I used to be out a lot, sleep late, be on tour for five or six months at a time, come home for two weeks and go back out again. I always used to think that I was tired from the workload and the travel but on reflection it all seems like leisure in comparison to being a mum. On balance, the fatigue is outweighed by the joy and love that all mothers feel, and if I had the choice of going back to the hedonistic lifestyle I had before, I still wouldn't do it. I prefer being a mother to a tour animal.

Lucy Mulvany
Mum of three, SA

No matter how many times someone tells you how much your life will change once you have a baby, no matter how much you intellectually understand that of course your life will change, I don't think you truly emotionally understand this until you finally bring your baby home for the first time.

I waited a very long time to get pregnant the first time. I was, in theory, totally 'ready' for a baby, totally ready to share my life with a new baby. Financially and materially we were ready. And I thought I understood what being a parent meant. I totally understood that small babies involve sleepless nights, a lot of poo and a lot of spew. I was ready to embrace all that.

So many friends and family members kept saying to me "Oh, you won't believe how much your life will change". At the time I found this bizarre: of course I understood that my life would change! When I gave birth to my eldest daughter Olivia, it was truly the happiest day in my life. She was quite perfect in every way and I fell head over heels in

Vox Pop

We asked a number of women and men around Australia to send in their advice, tips and personal experiences on a range of topics so that you have an insight into how others cope being a new parent. We hope you find their comments interesting, informative and reassuring. Vox Pop biographies: page 652

love with her. But a week later, when I took her home for the first time from hospital, it hit me. I was *totally* responsible for a tiny life. My life was no longer my own … Olivia would now control my every waking (and an awful lot of my sleeping) moments! This wasn't like a job that I could knock off from. This was a real and dramatic shift in my world. It was the little things: I could no longer nip to the shops without taking a nappy bag, a stroller and a baby. This previously-easy task used to take all of five minutes; now it took at least an hour.

I no longer was revered as a successful career woman. I was the stay-at-home mummy with bags under her eyes and milk stains on her shoulders. My husband and I could no longer enjoy lazy Sundays with toast and coffee in front of video clips … babies have no concept of sleeping in, ever. A hot date with my husband? Even if I had a babysitter lined up, I would stall at the last minute, as I couldn't stand to leave my daughter just in case she needed me. Fancy a curry or some chocolate? Nope, I realised I couldn't even eat what I wanted to anymore as it seemed to affect my breastmilk.

All of a sudden I was no longer me. I was a mother, which, for all its amazing treasured moments, robbed me of some spontaneity, stole a little freedom, and diminished my selfishness totally. I was no longer playing at an individual level; I was now playing a team sport. And while I wouldn't change a thing, the shock of the change of tactics was unbelievable.

Tracey Thompson
Mum of one, Brisbane

I found pregnancy a wonderful experience. Knowing that I was growing a little miracle inside my body was wonderful! Yes, your body does change shape and you may get some stretch marks – embrace it. You are creating a beautiful new life! My advice for you while pregnant is to make sure you spend lots of quality time with your partner, friends and family. Go out to dinner, go to the movies, or whatever you usually do for

entertainment as once the little one comes it won't happen as often! I wish I had been given that little piece of advice, as I was a little naive about how life-changing a baby is. Don't get me wrong … I still spend heaps of time with my friends, family and partner and have lots of fun, but you just can't do things at the last minute and as often as you used to.

Michelle Eicholtz
Mum of one, VIC

The first thing I would like to say to expectant mums and dads is don't just read up about what is happening to your body now. I know it's fascinating but I really wish that I had found out a little bit more of what it was going to be like when I had the baby at home. I think that I did ask my friends and family, but there must be some sort of secrecy going on because it was nothing like I expected it to be. My first nine months were great – I was an older mum at 40 so I guess I had a lot more to worry about, and I was also overweight which was against everything they recommended.

I worked up until my 34th week with no problems at all. At week 38 I went for my check up and they found out I had pre-eclampsia and so I was admitted straight away; I was so glad that I had packed those bags a couple of days beforehand! I guess that getting everything ready before the baby comes is important – I kept putting it off because I still couldn't believe it was real. I kept thinking it was a dream that I was pregnant or that if I bought a lot I would jinx myself and then something would happen with the baby. But the best advise would be to go mad and buy everything! Make sure you have everything you think you might need later like nappies, wipes, bath soap, nail clippers, a thermometer and get that carseat fitted – don't keep putting it off – test out that new pram and stock up on household items like soap powder, dishwashing liquid, tissues, toilet paper. Anything you can think of that you buy often, buy it! My baby is now 16 weeks old and I am just about to run out of washing powder so maybe I went a bit overboard!

Sarah Murdoch
Mum of two, Sydney

I absolutely loved being pregnant … even when I had morning sickness. We tried so long to get pregnant the first time so I just could never get used to what a miracle it is. It's funny, I thought that maybe the second time around it wouldn't feel as exciting but it was just as amazing to feel the baby kicking and to see the baby with ultrasound. I always thought being pregnant would feel so alien but instead it always felt incredibly natural. The second pregnancy was much more tiring having a toddler in tow. Especially as mine is so heavy! I was walking around with him sitting on my tummy!

Wow … it is so many things. Who knew you could feel this much love? Who knew you could be this busy! It is just more amazing than I could have ever imagined. I absolutely love being a mum. I really love every minute of it. Even the tantrums. Okay, maybe they aren't the best thing ever! But quite seriously having children makes everything else I have achieved in my life pale in comparison.

Amanda Jephtha
Mum of one, Sydney

With what seems to be an infinite amount of baby products to choose from, how will you know what to buy or, more importantly, what not to buy? Plan early. The 18 to 24 week mark is the optimum time to shop for your baby. You still have a small belly, you should be feeling more energetic in your second trimester, and it also allows for plenty of time for delays in deliveries.

Take the time to find out what's available, and don't buy the first thing you see, no matter how tempting. Don't be pressured into buying because of a special offer or price. Most stores will discount, particularly when buying several big-ticket items.

Don't be afraid to ask someone pushing the same model of pram you are thinking of buying what

they think. Most people will stop and give you the full low-down, including demonstrations. This is a great way to seek objective advice.

Nicole Hambling
Mum of one, VIC

It was one of the best birthday presents I could have asked for. The home pregnancy test was positive and the doctor confirmed it. However our joy was short lived when I had what they call a spontaneous miscarriage a couple of weeks later. About 4 months later I started to suspect I might be pregnant again, however this time I was a little reluctant to have my suspicions confirmed. I didn't want to get my hopes up again. I happened to go to the doctor for a cough I couldn't shake and mentioned that I thought I might pregnant. My suspicions were confirmed.

It was all too good to be true. Within a week I started to spot and given past history I was a little worried. Two weeks worth of blood tests testing hormone levels and a couple of ultrasounds and we were in the clear, however I had difficulty shaking the feeling that something might go wrong.

I had an easy pregnancy, no real morning sickness, but I just couldn't get excited about it. I was worried something would go wrong.

I didn't, nor would I let anyone else for that matter, buy anything for the baby until after Christmas. I remember my mother worrying that the baby would be born with nowhere to sleep and no clothes to wear. But I was still worried that something might go wrong.

Christmas came and went and by now my little action man was starting to move around (I was convinced I was having a boy.) I was still going to uni part time and working full time. Finishing work was hard because it meant that I was at home alone with my thoughts. I was only home for two weeks when Amy Grace was born. Boy did I get it all wrong! There are times now when I just wish I could have relaxed a little more and really enjoyed being pregnant.

Vox Pop

We asked a number of women and men around Australia to send in their advice, tips and personal experiences on a range of topics so that you have an insight into how others cope being a new parent. We hope you find their comments interesting, informative and reassuring. Vox Pop biographies: page 652

Martine Pekarsky
Mum of two, Melbourne

We struggled for so long to get pregnant that now I wish we had sought professional help sooner. We spent 12 months on fertility drugs which didn't resolve the issue. In the end we were injecting needles into my tummy every evening and going for two internal ultrasounds a week for three months but finally we were pregnant and there were 'two heartbeats'. We were so excited and tried not to get our hopes up too much as it had been such an emotional rollercoaster ride that we couldn't bear the thought of anything going wrong. All in all I had a pretty standard twin pregnancy but I loved being pregnant and really didn't care about how uncomfortable it all was. I had to stop driving at 20 weeks as my tummy was hitting the steering wheel so that made things interesting!

Everything had been going well, then at 28 weeks I went in for a standard ultrasound and the operator kept popping in and out of the room and it seemed to be taking an awfully long time. I had to get back to work so I was ready to just sneak out the door when she came in and said "your doctor's on the phone". How lovely of him to call I thought, but he began telling me that I was 5cm dilated and had to go to the closest hospital with a neonatal unit immediately. No going home to pack my bags and no going back to work until after the babies were born … it was time. Luckily my husband was with me; we were both terrified. We were so unprepared with no baby clothes, no carseat, no nappies – all these things I was going to sort out when I finished up at work of course.

Fortunately for us the babies didn't arrive that day nor the next – in fact they stayed in another 7 weeks and were delivered by c-section on their original due date. Staying in the same hospital bed for weeks and weeks on end was quite an experience but I did make some incredible friends with my roommates in the antenatal wards, two of whom were having twins themselves and were able to share stories in those early days when we all had newborns.

Anastasia Jones
Mum of two, Melbourne

The year my daughter was conceived and born we moved to a new city and I started a new job so I was stressed in the first trimester of the pregnancy and very, very moody but I just put this down to everything that was going on around us – new jobs, new apartment, new city.

For me, my biggest source of information during the pregnancy, and in the weeks after, was an old friend and ex-colleague who was also pregnant with her second child (her son is three weeks older than my daughter) and I don't think she thought I would take her up on the offer to "call me at any time of the day or night".

I often called her for advice, to have a whine or just to have a conversation with someone other than my husband. Her mantra, which I live by to this day, is "whatever works"!

Bianca McCulloch
Mum of two, Melbourne

My first pregnancy was so different from my second in so many ways. With my first I had a beautiful little boy and although he was diagnosed with minor kidney problems at my 20-week scan I had a pretty good pregnancy – no morning sickness at all and a pretty breezy first 8 months.

Things got a bit harder towards the end as I really bad pelvic pain and simple things like turning over in bed were painful but that was really all that was negative about my first pregnancy.

This time around I'm having a girl and I have had extremely bad morning sickness and abdominal pain caused by stretching stomach muscles. When I first started feeling the pain I panicked a bit as I hadn't had this problem in my first pregnancy and so I didn't know what was wrong. I thought that I might have been having a miscarriage but luckily all is fine with the baby.

The ultrasound showed that my little girl is completely healthy. It just goes to show that every pregnancy is different and you just can't compare your pregnancy with anyone else's.

Christine Walsh
Mum of two, Broome

My first pregnancy went quite smoothly and I had no problems working full-time up to 38 weeks. (I had my year 1-2 class trained to come and see me at my desk as I was too big to kneel down at their desks to do marking!) I ate healthy foods especially in the first four months of pregnancy switching to grainy bread, taking folic tablets etcetera.

I never actually threw up while pregnant though during the first few months I did feel nauseous in the early evenings and went off a few foods like tea and chocolate. I walked a few times during the week and also did my exercise DVD – all in all I gained approximately 13kg.

My second pregnancy was similar at the beginning in that I felt nauseous in the evenings and lost my appetite for chocolate and tea. At 28 weeks I was diagnosed with gestational diabetes – I had to watch my diet, reduce carbs and cut out sugary foods and do a blood test every evening. I was quite upset by this as the stereotype of being pregnant and eating whatever you wanted to eat was out the window. However for the sake of my baby's health I tried to be good about the food I ate.

Only on a handful of occasions did my blood levels go over what they should have been. I gained 18kg in this pregnancy and was only working 2 days a week towards the end of my pregnancy but did struggle and finished work at 36 weeks.

Not sure if I struggled because I had a toddler at home and couldn't rest as often as I would have liked or because of the extra weight I gained.

Andrea Tulloch
Mum of one, NSW

Being an older first time mum in my late thirties, I found that everyone I knew (and even many that I didn't including strangers on the street) suddenly became experts on pregnancy. I had found it difficult to fall pregnant but was very glad and excited when we had a positive result. My older brother and his partner suggested that we withhold telling everyone until it became evident and in retrospect they had the right idea. We were so excited that we told everyone the news just after the twelve week scan. I was suddenly overwhelmed with opinions. Generally they were imparted with the best of intentions, however they were mainly horror stories of what can go wrong not only during the pregnancy but also what can happen during the birth. I tried to stop people telling me horror pregnancy stories – it was just too much information. I had to block negative thoughts and focus on positive things. In the end we had a very good pregnancy with few complications.

Anna Ngo
Mum of one, Perth

My first inkling of being pregnant came from just feeling somehow different. My husband claims to have suspected it all along and convinced me to take a pregnancy test. But it actually took two tests to confirm the good news and needless to say we were both ecstatic.

As the pregnancy was planned I had already familiarised myself with the wave of changes about to take place. But I soon found out that reading about them is one thing, experiencing them is quite another. Early on I felt most of the classic symptoms such as nausea, vomiting, heartburn and fatigue. Certain foods which I normally ate were suddenly less palatable (due to a heightened sense of smell). In the later stages I experienced spontaneous cramping

Vox Pop

We asked a number of women, men and industry professionals around Australia to send in their advice, tips and personal experiences on a wide range of topics so that you have an insight into how others cope being a new parent. We hope you find their comments interesting, informative and reassuring.

in my legs and feet, shortness of breath, more heartburn and rollercoaster emotions (albeit mostly excitement and anxiousness). Oddly, however, I never once had any strange food cravings.

By about the 7th and 8th month my stomach was very, very large and I was frequently approached by friends and strangers and asked whether or not I was carrying twins. This was just one big baby girl for her small mother to carry! However sleeping did become quite a challenge in the latter months. During this stage I also began to feel regular kicks and bumps (which always kept me reassured that all was in order).

Surprisingly I kept very active and busy right up until labour. Somehow I was expecting that the last month would be so physically demanding that I would be housebound. But luckily for me this wasn't the case, and on Boxing Day after an 18-hour labour, baby Mikaela entered the world and changed our lives forever.

Bernadette Vella
Mum of two, Brisbane

My first pregnancy was a textbook pregnancy. I was on top of the world. I had pretty bad morning sickness (actually all day and all night) until week 20 but other than that it was a trouble-free pregnancy. I grew enormous putting on a third of my normal weight and when my due date came around I was very eager for my bub to come. I decided to be induced and had a reasonably trouble-free birth and my son Tiernan was born weighing a healthy 3.27 kg. He is now 4 years old.

My second pregnancy however was a different story. At 14 weeks I was diagnosed with cancer and told I had to terminate in order to start chemotherapy and survive. I decided to go ahead with treatment but also to keep my baby. The morning sickness blended together with the nausea from the chemotherapy and I was quite unwell throughout the pregnancy. I was closely monitored and at 33 weeks my darling daughter Arielle was born by caesarean.. She was born healthy but only

weighed 1.5kg. She spent 4 weeks in hospital before coming home weighing just 2kg. She is now nearly 2 and has had no health complications.

Kerri Harding
Mum of one, VIC

I was 30 when my son was born. Previously when I had thought about starting a family, there was always some small element of doubt in my mind, some trivial reason as to why it wasn't the right time. For some reason though things changed for me when I celebrated my 30th birthday. It was like a switch had suddenly been turned on inside me. For the first time I felt a real urge to start a family.

It was a huge shock when I discovered that I was pregnant after only our first month of trying. I had expected it to take a lot longer. I was absolutely ecstatic for the first couple of weeks but then reality started to sink in.

I was amazed at how much the thought of being pregnant occupied my mind. I was suffering from morning sickness and questioning whether I was really ready to be a parent, to make a life-long commitment to a person I didn't even know yet. I had never had much to do with babies before and was wondering how on earth I would deal with a newborn.

I had never been (and still am not) the type of person who goes weak at the knees at the sight of someone else's baby. I was worried that I would feel the same way towards my own baby. I was also starting to feel overwhelmed by everything that all the books said that we would need in readiness for a new baby.

Every time I made up my mind that I was going to go and purchase something, the number of different brands that I had to choose from would make my head spin and I would inevitably come out of the shop empty handed and even more confused than when I went in. I hated feeling like I wasn't in control of everything.

From all accounts, a lot of women go into 'nesting mode' as their pregnancy progresses but I was out of control! I felt as though everything had to be perfect for when the baby came home. I was cleaning, washing, dusting and vacuuming for the pure sake of it. Hindsight is a wonderful thing and when I look back now I realise I made a lot of unnecessary work and stress for myself. Nobody (certainly not the baby) would even notice a lot of things I was obsessing over at the time.

It pays to take a reality check and ask yourself if something is really that important in the grand scheme of things.

I was very fortunate in that I had a very good pregnancy, all plain sailing. I just wish that I had taken more time to sit back, relax and savour the experience rather than get caught up in a lot of the small details that seemed so important at the time.

The conception, growth and development of a baby really is a small miracle in progress and not one that we should take for granted. Enjoy the experience!

Leanne Cummins
Mum of two, NSW

Pregnancy can take its toll on you physically and mentally not only in the early weeks, but right throughout the 40–42 weeks. To feel at your best you need to get a good night's sleep, eat a healthy diet and get some exercise.

Rest is not always easy as your belly grows and it becomes uncomfortable to sleep on your back, or to roll from one side to the other without waking up fully. It can help to snooze (if you can) through the day. Rest doesn't always mean 'sleeping' though, so try to stop what you are doing, sit and practice a short relaxation for 5 minutes. Or just stop and make time to breathe.

Even though you may not feel like going for a walk, a swim or a yoga class, try to motivate yourself to get there and do it – you will feel a whole lot better. Exercise stimulates hormones that make us feel great, and also helps to move extra blood supply around to eliminate waste products from you and your baby.

A healthy diet is sometimes easier said than done, especially if you are feeling sick. If you cannot take in essential nutrients due to nausea, try taking a supplement. There are also some foods that should be avoided in pregnancy particularly those that may contain listeria.

De-stress and don't worry! You will hear many stories and be given many pieces of advice over the next few years. Some of the main things women seem to worry about are weight gain and sleeping on their backs. Just know that the weight will come off later and sleeping on your back does not affect baby, only you. Talk to your midwife about everything as there is no such thing as a silly question.

Learn to sift through the information now, and keep only those snippets that you might want to try later. Everybody thinks they know better than you because they've done it their way… but you know yourself better so trust your gut instincts.

Michelle Winduss
Mum of one, Sydney

My pregnancy was pretty smooth sailing. I experienced quite a lot of fatigue (like most pregnant women) and more often than not, restless legs. During my pregnancy my biggest fear was the actual birth. I was worried about where I would be when my contractions started or my waters broke, how much pain I would be in … all the normal things that expectant mothers go through.

Even though these concerns were on my mind, I made an effort to enjoy my pregnancy and I always enjoyed finding out about my baby's progress at each stage. Even though I concentrated on my pregnancy and giving birth, nothing prepared me for what it would be like looking after a newborn for the first time.

The sleepless nights were really hard and not knowing what to do when your baby is crying can be heartbreaking. I really wish that during the nine months of pregnancy I had done some more reading on what life would be like when the baby was actually born.

Resources

These Resources pages list products and services relevant to "Pregnancy: the first nine months".
To make your life easier as a parent, editorial listings have been grouped into sub categories.
Businesses then appear alphabetically under a national or a state-based subhead depending on reach.

SUB-CATEGORIES

ADVISORY & SUPPORT SERVICES: PREGNANCY

NATIONAL

Australian Action on Pre-eclampsia (AAPEC)
Tel: (03) 9330 0441
email: info@aapec.org.au
website: www.aapec.org.au

Australian Action on Pre-eclampsia (AAPEC) is a national organisation offering support and information on pre-eclampsia and HELLP Syndrome to members of the general public and health professionals. Their aim is to raise awareness of pre-eclampsia and inform all women of the signs and symptoms of this potentially dangerous pregnancy condition. An annual membership fee of $20 entitles members to receive their quarterly newsletter including current research into pre-eclampsia, fundraising activities and member stories.

Australian Multiple Birth Association (AMBA)
Tel: 1300 886 499
email: secretary@amba.org.au
website: www.amba.org.au

AMBA is a voluntary community organisation of families with twins, triplets, quadruplets and more. A national network of associated groups provides activities and services that encourage the exchange of information, education and mutual support. AMBA is committed to increasing awareness of the special needs of multiple birth families, and to improve the resources available to them. AMBA is a non-profit, non-political and non-sectarian organisation co-operating with organisations having related interests.

VICTORIA

Caroline Chisholm Society
41 Park Street
Moonee Ponds VIC 3039
Tel: 1800 134 863 or (03) 9370 3933
email: info@carolinechisholmsociety.com.au
website: www.carolinechisholmsociety.com.au

The Caroline Chisholm Society provides counselling (pregnancy, grief – pregnancy loss and post abortion – individual and family counselling, parent/child relationships counselling and financial counselling), a 7-day-a-week counselling line, free pregnancy testing, support groups (postnatal depression support groups and constructive parenting programs), in-home family support program, material aid and accommodation service.

Fertile Ground Health Group

Suite 3, Level 6, 372–376 Albert Street
East Melbourne VIC 3002
Tel: (03) 9419 9988
email: reception@fertileground.com.au
website: www.fertileground.com.au

Fertile Ground Health Group specialise in preconception care for men and women, infertility, IVF support, health in pregnancy, birth preparation and labour support, postnatal and baby health, as well as general health. They also treat menstrual issues throughout the lifecycle, including menarche and menopause. Specialist services include naturopathy, acupuncture, osteopathy, massage, kinesiology and counselling. There is a range of supplementary services to help you stay on track including massage, home and hospital visiting services, midwife/lactation support services and infant massage instruction.

Parent Infant Research Institute

Austin Health 330 Waterdale Road
Heidelberg Heights VIC 3081
Tel: (03) 9496 4496
email: Jennifer.ericksen@austin.org.au
website: www.piri.org.au

The Infant Clinic is a not-for-profit clinic staffed by specialist psychologists who provide a comprehensive service to families in the ante and postnatal period. Cutting edge research, teaching and treatment programs are available to address the needs of parents facing the challenges of parenthood, especially prematurity, relationship changes, anxiety, depression and understanding and managing babies and toddlers. The Infant Clinic also has antenatal programs to assist in the transition to parenthood.

The Royal Women's Hospital

132 Grattan Street
Carlton VIC 3053
Tel: (03) 8345 2127
email: angela.steele@thewomens.org.au
website: www.ypp.org.au

The Young Women's Health Program offers antenatal and postnatal support and outreach services for women aged 19 years and under who are pregnant and parenting. Service hours are 9.00am to 5.00pm Monday to Friday.

NEW SOUTH WALES

Childbirth Education Association of Australia (NSW)

PO Box 240
Sutherland NSW 2232
Tel: (02) 8539 7188
email: info@cea-nsw.com.au
website: www.cea-nsw.com.au

The Childbirth Education Association of Australia (NSW) has been preparing women and their partners and families for childbirth and early parenting since 1961. Services offered by CEA include prenatal classes throughout Sydney metro as well as video and book borrowing libraries. CEA has also produced a number of videos and publications on pregnancy and childbirth. Visit the CEA's website or phone the number above.

Planning for Babe

PO Box 3313
St Pauls NSW 2031
Tel: 0411 126 325
email: amanda@planningforbabe.com.au
website: www.planningforbabe.com.au

Planning for Babe offers professional, time-poor, pregnant women the latest must-have – their own exclusive baby planner. Through private consultations and extensive research, Planning for Babe matches the perfect baby products to your individual lifestyle – just like a wedding planner to a wedding. From organising all the essentials, to arranging private product viewings, to having a label create a custom gown for you, this fully tailored service covers all bases for the discerning pregnant woman.

QUEENSLAND

Women's Health Queensland Wide

165 Gregory Terrace
Spring Hill QLD 4000
Tel: (07) 3839 9962
Health Information Line (07) 3839 9988
Toll Free outside Brisbane 1800 017 676
TTY (07) 3831 5508
email: admin@womhealth.org.au
website: www.womhealth.org.au

Women's Health Queensland Wide is a non-profit health promotion service providing information and education services to women and health workers throughout the state. Services include a Health Information Line staffed by registered nurses and midwives, library services, fact sheets and quarterly publication, as well as a website and health education programs. Women can contact the service for information on a wide range of topics including pregnancy, childbirth, breastfeeding, early childhood and postnatal depression.

YHES House

11 Hicks Street
Southport QLD 4215
Tel: (07) 5531 1577
email: yypcoord@yhes.org.au
website: www.yhes.org.au

The Youth Health and Education Service (YHES House) Young Parents Support Program aims to improve the health and wellbeing of young parents aged 12 to 25 years, and their children, during the prenatal and early childhood periods. By offering a Childbirth Education Support Group and a New Parents Group, YHES House provides information, socialisation and ongoing support to empower young people to make informed decisions about their own and their child's health and wellbeing.

Resources

PREGNANCY: THE FIRST NINE MONTHS

Baby clubs ➡ Books, DVDs & CDs

BABY CLUBS

NATIONAL

Australian Pacific Paper Products

Tel: 1800 224 332 toll free
website: www.babyloveclub.com.au

Join the BabyLove club free. Great hints and tips and information on baby care, ask BabyLove's registered Maternal and Child Health Nurse questions, chat to other mums, and save money on great offers. Start your own online baby diary and album to share with family and friends around the world. A fun and engaging site for mums and dads. Don't forget that each member has a chance to win great prizes on a regular basis.

Huggies Mum To Be Club

Tel: 1800 028 334
email: via website
website: www.huggies.com.au

The Huggies Mum To Be Club is all about pregnancy and getting ready for the most important job you will ever undertake – parenthood. Membership to the Huggies Club is free and you will receive regular email newsletters with lots of information, special offers and feature articles relevant to your stage of pregnancy and beyond. You will also have access to exclusive Club member competitions and special discount offers, access to a help panel where you can speak to a midwife whenever you like and access to the Huggies Forum where you can chat to other pregnant women about anything you like. Join the Huggies Mum to Be Club at www.huggies.com.au.

BOOKS, DVDs & CDs:
PREGNANCY & GENERAL PARENTING

NATIONAL

Active Birth – Wonderful Birth Services

PO Box 3039
Kew VIC 3101
website: www.wonderfulbirth.com

Guided Relaxation and Inspiration for Joyful Pregnancy, Birth and Beyond is a double CD produced by Lina Clerke, an experienced childbirth educator, midwife and mother. It offers valuable prenatal relaxation skills and positive preparation for birth and early parenting. The CD also includes a guided postnatal/general relaxation, and lovely music to help your baby to settle. For further details and to order visit www.wonderfulbirth.com.

Australian Childhood Foundation

Tel: (03) 9874 3922
email: info@childhood.org.au
website: www.childhood.org.au

The *Every Child is Important* booklet for parents is a free parenting resource that provides positive strategies for parents to enhance their relationship with their children as well as including ways for responding to children's behaviour. This relevant, positively focused booklet is a part of the award-winning Every Child is Important program and is a must-have for all mums and dads. The booklet is also available as a free-talking book translated into 12 different languages.

Babywise Bliss

Tel: 0411 156 265
email: info@babywisebliss.com.au
website: www.babywisebliss.com.au

Following the best-selling *Baby Wise* book, Babywise Bliss present the long awaited support DVD. In this contemporary, one-hour long presentation they take you through the basics of life with a newborn to 6-month-old baby. You will find practical advice and solutions to some of parenting's most commonly asked questions. Topics covered include Babies and Sleep, When Babies Cry, Tired Signs, Dad's Role in Parenting and many more.

Being Dad DVDs

website: www.beyondhomeentertainment.com.au or www.beingdad.com.au

The DVD *Being Dad* provides inspiration and information for dads to be. A sneak peek into pregnancy from a guy's point of view. *Pregnancy & Birth* uncovers the mysteries of pregnancy and birth. A ground breaking, hilarious and emotional documentary film. *Being Dad 2* offers inspiration and information for new dads. A sneak peek into parenthood from a guy's perspective. This DVD follows six first-time dads and their families as they cope with the whirlwind experience of bringing the baby home all the way through to raising two year olds. Featuring interviews with a world class psychologist, paediatrician, financial planners, sleep expert and safety expert and includes the dad group's advice on travelling with your baby, kids wisdom, immunisation, circumcision, overcoming difficult times and the difference between boys and girls. Visit www.beyondhomeentertainment.com.au or www.beingdad.com.au for more information.

Belly

email: sass.e.nicholson@gmail.com
website: www.bellyjournal.blogspot.com

Belly is a pregnancy journal which features a beautiful collection of poetry, prose and art themed around pregnancy, birth and early motherhood and provides plenty of space for personal contributions.

Birthing Sense Birth Education DVDs

Tel: 0411 255 535
email: leanne@birthingsense.com
website: www.birthingsense.com

Compliment or substitute your prenatal class with three DVDs. Australian midwife and antenatal educator Leanne Cummins has interviewed over 26 experts and parents to bring your childbirth education class to your own home. Fifty segments over three DVDs help you make sense of your pregnancy, birth and new baby. Order your birth class online at www.birthingsense.com.

Birthnet Pty Ltd

Tel: (02) 9662 6019
email: management@birth.com.au
website: www.birth.com.au

Birth.com.au and *BIRTH* the book are invaluable resources for women and partners on their journey to parenthood. Written and supported by a midwife and a childbirth educator with over 30 years collective experience, they provide everything you need to know about fertility, conception, pregnancy, birth and early parenting. Birthnet's online birthtalks® community is a great way to network with other parents and parents-to-be.

Calm Baby Confident Mum

Tel: (02) 4272 5077
email: simone@boswellbunch.com
website: www.calmbabyconfidentmum.com

Calm Baby Confident Mum: A Commonsense Guide to Managing Your Baby is a practical book for new mums which covers feeding your baby, settling your baby and playing with your baby. A flexible routine is encouraged, so that both baby and mum can stay calm and confident that their days will flow smoothly, and that they will enjoy each other's company. Chapters cover significant ages of baby during the first year, as well as breastfeeding, crying and settling, sleeping and playtime. Twins, premmies and special needs babies, dads and second babies are also discussed.

Choice

Tel: 1800 069 552
email: ausconsumer@choice.com.au
website: www.choice.com.au/baby

Leave the guesswork behind with the essential buying guide for parents. Now in its twelfth edition, *The CHOICE Guide to Baby Products* is packed with independent and practical information based on CHOICE research and tests. Information covered includes test results on baby carriers, strollers, cots and highchairs. There is also general buying advice on bath time, bedtime and changing accessories, feeding, toys, walkers plus safety advice and handy "What to look for" checklists.

Dadstheword Pty Ltd

Tel: 1300 306 802
email: rosvroom@bigpond.net.au
website: www.dadstheword.com

Discover the secrets to your baby and quickly become a great dad – this DVD shows you all you need to know. It will save you hours of distress and quickly skyrocket you to enjoying those first days home with your baby. Endorsed by Australian College of Midwives and Steve Biddulph. Information on the DVD is suitable for all new mums and dads.

Dr. Janet Hall – Author

Tel: (03) 9419 3010
email: info@drjanethall.com.au
website: www.drjanethall.com.au

Dr. Janet Hall is the author of several books to assist parents including: *How You Can Be Boss of the Bladder*, *Boss of Bedtime, Easy Toilet Training, Fear Free Children, Fight Free Families* and her latest book, *Super-Parent Survival Guide*. Dr. Hall has a user friendly way of delivering information and talks in easy to understand terms to help you get maximum benefit in applying her suggested ideas to achieve success.

Full Belly

Tel: (08) 8278 4342
email: info@parentwellbeing.com
website: www.parentwellbeing.com

In pregnancy there are obvious physical changes but the emotional changes are no less powerful. As your body changes so does your perspective on the world and what's important. There are wonders at the baby you are growing, and worries about birth and beyond. Jodie Benveniste, bestselling author of *Little Bundle: Comfort and inspiration for new parents*, has a new book titled *Full Belly* which will help you enjoy the wonders and calm the worries.

Gentle Birth, Gentle Mothering

email: info@sarahjbuckley.com
website: www.sarahjbuckley.com

Gentle Birth, Gentle Mothering is the internationally-acclaimed bible for 21st century parents and parents-to-be. Dr Sarah J Buckley, GP and mother of four, gives essential medical information as well as her gentle mothering wisdom on ultrasound, ecstatic birth, epidurals, caesarean risks, cord blood banking, breastfeeding, attachment, sound sleeping and more. New edition out March 2009 in bookstores and online at www.sarahjbuckley.com.

Growing Families Australia

Tel: (08) 8322 3770
email: enquiries@gfi.org.au
website: www.gfi.org.au

Growing Families Australia provides books and courses that provide clear strategies for parenting that have been successful and effective worldwide. Their resources give a clear pathway to influencing and raising emotionally balanced, intellectually assertive and morally sensible children. They give parents practical 'tools' to help them in the important role of parenting and the confidence to follow through and therefore enjoy their children.

Resources

PREGNANCY: THE FIRST NINE MONTHS

Books, DVDs & CDs

Home Fitness Delivered

Tel: (03) 9412 3594
email: info@homefitnessdelivered.com.au
website: www.homefitnessdelivered.com.au

Home Fitness Delivered is Australia's largest online retailer of fitness and lifestyle entertainment products, including a comprehensive list of pregnancy related books, CDs and DVDs. Homefitnessdelivered.com.au caters for mums at every stage of their pregnancy, with pre and postnatal yoga DVDs right through to the Baby Einstein range featuring products such as Baby Vivaldi, Music Box Orchestra and more. Home Fitness Delivered provide terrific customer service and fast, reliable delivery.

It's Time to Sleep Pty Ltd

Tel: 1300 137 110
email: info@itstimetosleep.com
website: www.itstimetosleep.com

It's Time to Sleep is an educational DVD and book that teaches parents how to get babies and toddlers to sleep independently. It was produced with Rhonda Abrahams who created and runs the Baby Sleep and Settling Centre in the Sunshine Hospital. The DVD covers all aspects of baby sleep and settling that Rhonda uses in the centre, educating parents on why babies have trouble sleeping and demonstrating techniques used to teach babies and toddlers to sleep independently. Phone 1300 137 110.

Julia Sundin, Physiotherapist

Tel: (02) 9417 6467
website: www.jujusundin.com

Julia Sundin's new CD titled *"Hypno Active" Visualisation for Childbirth* will help you master the stress, anxiety, fear and pain in labour through imagery, mantras, key words and suggestion. There are two sessions – one for pregnancy stress management and one for labour pain management. A cut out cribb sheet for partners is included. Visit www.jujusundin.com for more information and price.

Julia Sundin, Physiotherapist

Tel: (02) 9417 6467
website: www.jujusundin.com

Julia Sundin's *Baby Visualisation* CD provides an invitation to use guided imagery to enter life inside the womb, to deepen the process of natural bonding, to peer into the world of your baby and come closer to the living, breathing child you have created together. $25.00 plus p&h. Available from www.jujusundin.com.

Julia Sundin, Physiotherapist

Tel: (02) 9417 6467
website: www.jujusundin.com

Julia Sundin's *Pelvic Floor Exercise Program* CD is a bit like having your own 'pelvic floor personal trainer' in your own home with over 30 varied pelvic floor toning and strengthening exercises alternating with education about the pelvic floor during pregnancy, childbirth and the post partum period. $42.00 plus p&h – available from www.jujusundin.com.

Julia Sundin, Physiotherapist

Tel: (02) 9417 6467
website: www.jujusundin.com

JuJu Sundin's *Birth Skills with Sarah Murdoch* ($40.00 + p&p) details the proven tools and techniques required for helping the birthing couple deal with labour pain, pushing out the baby, crowning, posterior, backache birth, motivation and much more. Sarah Murdoch writes about her experiences of being in JuJu's classes and applying the techniques with her husband during labour.

Kindred Magazine

Tel: (02) 6684 4353
website: www.kindredmagazine.com.au

Kindred magazine supports the important movement towards sustainable living and natural parenting. Featuring articles from leading thinkers and visionaries on the frontlines of social change, *Kindred* covers topics such as optimal development, gentle discipline, social ecology, the environment, education reform, relationships and much more. *Kindred* is more than a magazine, it is an engaging and active global community, a platform and a networking hub from which springs many diverse and progressive initiatives. Phone or visit the website for further information.

Mum to Mum Pty Ltd

website: www.beyondhomeentertainment.com.au or www.mumtomumdvd.com.au

Mum to Mum has created five DVDs which will help you prepare for, and then look after, your baby. DVD 1 is titled *Preparing to Bring Home Your Baby* and it shows you everything you'll need to buy and where it all goes before you actually bring home your baby. It takes you through how to buy according to the SIDS guidelines, safety proofing your house, preparing your pet for the new addition to the family and there is lots of talk with mums to prepare you for life ahead. DVD 2 is titled *Caring for Your Baby (in the first 3 months)* and it takes you through all you need to know for the daily care of your new baby. It covers loads of information including settling techniques, development milestones, establishing basic routines, how to bath and change your baby and feeding options. DVD 3, *Caring for Your Baby 3 to 6 months*, addresses issues such as "how many feeds does my baby now need?", establishing a good sleeping routine, what to do with an unsettled baby, how to be prepared for getting out and about with your baby and how to identify basic illnesses.

DVD 4, *Caring for your Baby 6 to 12 months* covers nutritional advice, CPR, pets and play time and DVD 5, *Caring for your toddler 1 to 2 years*, includes helpful info on allergies, quality childcare and milestones in development. Visit the websites www.beyondhomeentertainment.com.au or www.mumtomumdvd.com.au for more information.

Pan Macmillan Australia Pty Ltd
Tel: (02) 9285 9100
email: pansyd@macmillan.com.au
website: www.panmacmillan.com.au

Pan Macmillan is one of Australia's leading publishers of young adult, children's, first concept and parenting books and has a strong focus on Australian authors. Their authors include John Marsden, Andy Griffiths, Mem Fox, Robin Barker and Tim Winton. Their range of parenting books includes Peter Mayle's classics *What's Happening To Me?* and *Where Did I Come From?*, Robin Barker's bestselling *Baby Love*, *The Mighty Toddler* and *Baby & Toddler Meals*, Mem Fox's *Reading Magic*, Tizzie Hall's *Save Our Sleep* and the *Save Our Sleep Diaries* and many more. Pan Macmillan titles are available from all good booksellers.

Parenting SA
Tel: (08) 8303 1660
website: www.parenting.sa.gov.au

Parent Easy Guides, produced by Parenting SA, provide information on more than 90 different parenting topics, from birth through to adolescence. Developed from research in conjunction with appropriate experts, the Parent Easy Guides are used widely throughout Australia. Parenting SA is an initiative of the Children, Youth and Women's Health Service (CYWHS) which forms part of the State Government department, SA Health. Parenting SA supports parents to build their knowledge, skills and confidence.

Parenting With Ease
Tel: (08) 9408 1372
website: www.parentingwithease.com.au

Parenting With Ease offers real solutions to real problems including sleep issues, the daily battle of wills with your toddler and feeling a greater sense of calm and ease in your role as a parent. Parenting With Ease helps parents to enter the world of a child and understand how to integrate with it through the manuals *The 12 Ingredients to Miracle Parenting* and *The Baby Ease Sleep Solution* and the CD *Harmonious Mother Harmonious Baby*.

Penguin Group (Australia)
Tel: (03) 9811 2400
website: www.penguin.com.au

Up the Duff, Kaz Cooke's week-by-week guide to pregnancy, covers everything from body changes to the birth experience to coping with a newborn baby. The big new 2009 edition has bonus sections on preparing for pregnancy, fertility treatments, the latest screenings and tests, medical intervention, and post-baby sex, all written in the down-to-earth, funny and medically informed way that has made *Up the Duff* the Australian bible for pregnant women and their partners.

Penguin Group (Australia)
Tel: (03) 9811 2400
website: www.penguin.com.au

Kidwrangling, the regularly updated sequel to *Up the Duff*, has everything a parent needs to know about caring for babies, toddlers and preschoolers, including sleeping, crying, bosoms and bottles, food, teeth, common illnesses, immunisation schedules, mental and physical development, teaching kids how to behave, parties, toys, travel, being at home, paid work, and much more. This is a sane, witty and reassuring guide backed by Australian research and expert advice.

Physiotherapy Pilates Proactive
Tel: (08) 8271 3144
email: parkside@pilatesproactive.com.au
website: www.pilatesproactive.com.au

Recorded by highly-qualified pilates expert and physiotherapist, Rachel Combe, the *Pilates Proactive*™ *Pregnancy & Post Natal* CD includes three separate pilates exercise programs – first trimester; second and third trimester; and postnatal which each run for 30 minutes. The CD also includes a comprehensive instruction booklet which accompanies the exercises. The routines will improve posture, alleviate pain and tone the body during pregnancy and post-natally. These exercises are designed to be done at home in conjunction with regular Pilates Mat Class attendance as initial supervision is essential for safe, proficient technique. CDs may be purchased online at www.pilatesproactive.com.au.

Pinky McKay
Tel: (03) 9801 1997
website: www.pinkymckay.com.au

Internationally Certified Lactation Consultant and Infant Massage Instructor, Pinky McKay offers a natural, intuitive approach to solving baby and toddler sleep problems. In *Sleeping Like a Baby*, as well as offering the latest research about infant sleep, Pinky offers practical tips to gently settle babies and toddlers without resorting to 'cry it out' regimes; how to create a safe sleeping environment; read your baby's body language so that learning to sleep becomes a stress-free process for parent and child and what and how to feed infants to encourage sleep.

Preggi Bellies
Tel: 1300 727 171
email: info@preggibellies.com.au
website: www.preggibellies.com

Developed by physiotherapists, Preggi Bellies is a complete motivational workout incorporating correct exercise on a MediBall for pregnant women and women who have had or are planning to have children. Due to demand, the Preggi Bellies program is also available on DVD. Visit www.preggibellies.com.au for full details

Resources

PREGNANCY: THE FIRST NINE MONTHS

Books, DVDs & CDs

➔ Education classes & workshops

about the program, timetables, a complete list of stockists or to purchase the DVD online. Alternatively you can phone 1300 72 71 71 for more information.

Sound Impressions Pty Ltd

Tel: (03) 9867 8338
email: info@soundimpressions.com.au
website: www.musicfordreaming.com

The *Music for Dreaming Collection for Mother and Baby*, a two-CD pack, consists of *Music for Dreaming for baby* and *Music for Dreaming II for mother*. It has been created to be in harmony with you and your baby's natural biological rhythm by replicating the resting heartbeat and human pulse. The pure sound of this music is created by traditional instruments rather than synthesised sounds to protect your baby's delicate ears as well as the sensitive nervous system of both mother and baby. Two hours of continuous calming music performed by an ensemble from the internationally acclaimed Melbourne Symphony Orchestra. Scientifically researched and designed to deeply relax mother and assist baby to feed effectively and be gently soothed to sleep. Trusted and used for more than a decade by leading maternity and children's hospitals, nursing mothers and childcare centres Australia wide.

Terrific Toddlers

Tel: (02) 9623 4810
email: mel@terrifictoddlers.com.au
website: www.terrifictoddlers.com.au

The refreshing message of the book *Terrific Toddlers* is that as a parent, you can make a difference in your toddler's behaviour. In this straightforward and practical book, Mel Hayde is profoundly positive – encouraging mums to proactively guide and train their children. *Terrific Toddlers* offers practical and positive suggestions for turning your day with a toddler from chaos into calm.

The Fatherhood Project

Tel: (02) 6684 2309
email: info@fatherhood.com.au
website: www.fatherhood.net.au

The *Fatherhood* CD and DVD is a great gift to give to a new dad. It is a beautiful collection of songs about being a father or having a father by Australia's finest contemporary songwriters including John Butler, Xavier Rudd and Paul Kelly. It's a powerful gift for new dads or for your own father. Available from the website www.fatherhood.net.au or www.natureschild.com.au.

The Healing Mind Pty Ltd

Tel: (03) 5442 6757
email: info@thehealingmind.com.au
website: www.thehealingmind.com.au

These are innovative CDs that use the power of your mind to allow you to relax and let go through guided visualisations. *Relaxed Mother ... Calm Baby* will assist in an easier, calmer pregnancy and birth; *Relaxation CDs for Adults & Children* – great for getting kids off to sleep in a fun, relaxed way; *Our Special Place* CDs – working through grief and loss associated with the loss of a loved one; *Dr Tom* assists children with dental anxieties. All CDs are available through www.sleeptalk.com.au and www.ourspecialplace.com.au.

Tweddle Child & Family Health Service

Tel: (03) 9689 1577
email: tweddle@tweddle.org.au
website: www.tweddle.org.au

Tweddle staff have produced a range of books and videos to assist parents. *Sleep Right Sleep Tight* is a book with answers for sleep deprived parents. It is a practical guide to solving sleep problems in babies and young children. *Eat Right Don't Fight* contains absolutely everything you need to know from early feeding to managing fussy eaters. *Breastfeeding, A Beginner's Guide* is a DVD that covers many aspects of breastfeeding in the early days and weeks. First time mothers and their babies demonstrate a range of techniques. In *Sleep Right Sleep Tight*, the video and DVD parents demonstrate settling and sleep techniques with their babies and toddlers, and talk about their experience of using the techniques.

Yoga Babes

Tel: (02) 9944 0255
email: yogababes@optusnet.com.au
website: www.yogababes.com.au

Yoga for Pregnancy and Birth is a 70-minute DVD including two 20-minute yoga routines, baby bonding, relaxation and a section on using yoga and massage for childbirth. Pre and postnatal yoga relaxations CDs for every mum-to-be and new mums feature music by Ian Cameron Smith and each run for 65 minutes with three guided meditations. $29.95 for the DVD, $25 for each CD or $70 for all three (including $5 p&h).

Yoga Babes

Tel: (02) 9944 0255
email: yogababes@optusnet.com.au
website: www.yogababes.com.au

Mother Me is an easy-to-read book offering practical solutions and advice for those navigating the rocky path of motherhood. Mother-of-three and yoga teacher Katie Brown 'gave birth' to the idea for the book after the arrival of her first child, Lucas. Katie also spoke to hundreds of other mums and scores of experts in her research and their experiences and wisdom help to make this essential reading for new mums. The book is based on seven building blocks physical, emotional, relationship, parenting, work and finance, friends and family and keeping the balance. *Mother Me* is available at all major bookstores; published by Pan Macmillan and rrp$32.95. For more information visit www.yogababes.com.au.

EDUCATION CLASSES & WORKSHOPS: PREGNANCY

VICTORIA

Eastside Midwives
Tel: 0425 770 316
email: enquiries@eastsidemidwives.com
website: www.eastsidemidwives.com

Eastside Midwives is a group of three registered midwives who provide care throughout your pregnancy, birth and postnatal period for both you and your baby. They can provide hospital support, homebirth support, breastfeeding support as well as early parenting support. All care is provided in the comfort of your own home. Eastside Midwives also run antenatal classes; visit the website for further details.

Renee Kam
Tel: 0412 094 961
email: reneekam@iprimus.com.au

Renee Kam is a physiotherapist (with experience in women's health), an antenatal educator and a mum. She is passionate about educating expectant parents about breastfeeding and infant sleep prior to the arrival of their babies to ensure good habits are set in motion from the outset. The class runs for approximately three hours from her house in East Bentleigh on a Saturday or Sunday. Email Renee for more information.

The Northern Hospital: Childbirth Programs
185 Cooper Street
Epping VIC 3076
Tel: (03) 8405 8220
website: www.nh.org.au

Childbirth education and parenting classes offered by The Northern Hospital include: the 'Early Bird Class' (early pregnancy related issues and information); Evening Series (runs over 6 weeks); Sunday Workshop (an alternative to a 6-week class); Father Class (a specifically designed class to meet the needs of fathers and provides an opportunity to meet new dads with their babies); a Multiple Birth Class (specially designed for the needs of twin/triplet families) and the Breastfeeding Ante-Natal Class (this session is offered to all pregnant women who want more indepth breastfeeding information). Phone the number above for further information.

Waverley Private Hospital
347–352 Blackburn Road
Mount Waverley VIC 3149
Tel: (03) 9802 0522
website: www.waverleyprivate.com.au

Waverley Private Hospital has a long and proud tradition in delivering a family-focused yet innovative approach to maternity services. Right from the start, they provide relevant education and information programs so your choices are the best possible to guide you in the planning and development of your pregnancy and assist you in the care of your newborn. The maternity unit boasts a collaborative team of experienced obstetricians, medical staff, nurses and lactation consultants, comfortable and well-appointed rooms, an onsite Level II Special Care nursery, 3 modern and fully-equipped birthing suites, 5 state-of-the-art operating theatres and 24-hour anaesthetic roster, as well as the option to participate in the innovative Parenting Program at the five-star Novotel Hotel.

NEW SOUTH WALES

Beer + Bubs
Tel: (02) 9440 9099
email: cheers@beerandbubs.com.au
website: www.beerandbubs.com.au

Beer + Bubs is all about learning how to be the best childbirth support person you can be at this two-and-a-half-hour workshop at the pub. Learn what to say and what not to say, great ideas for pain relief, how to be an advocate for the birthing mother, practical tips on what to do at each stage of labour and much more. Cost is $50 per person which includes dinner.

Birth Right Pty Ltd
Suite 5, 670 Darling Street
Rozelle NSW 2039
Tel: 0419 606 171
email: susan@birthright.com.au
website: www.birthright.com.au

Birth Right provides a range of services for pregnancy, including Active Birth classes, HypnoBirthing, calmbirth, pregnancy belly dancing, doula service, birth de-brief and early parenting classes. Birth Right is the only doula training school run by a midwife with over 30 years experience. Susan Ross is the founder and director of Birth Right; she is a midwife, childbirth educator, doula trainer, HypnoBirthing practitioner, mother and author of the book *Birth Right*. Susan is passionate about helping women understand their choices.

Essential Birth Consulting
Home visits around Sydney
Tel: 0400 418 448
email: melissam@idx.com.au

Do you leave your check-ups with unanswered questions? Are you having your first baby or planning to do things differently this time? Essential Birth Consulting can help you experience your birth your way. They provide home birth services; assistance to choose a hospital, doctor or birth centre to complement your needs; personalised, one-on-one childbirth education; assistance through the maze of options for birth; and birth debriefing. All the research is done for you, saving you valuable time.

Resources

PREGNANCY: THE FIRST NINE MONTHS

Education classes & workshops
➡ Exercise classes, yoga & massage

Julia Sundin, Physiotherapist
PO Box 139
Roseville NSW 2069
Tel: (02) 9417 6467
website: www.jujusundin.com

JuJu Sundin's Pain Mastery Class for Labour course is an inspiring and motivating series including safe pregnancy exercise, posture, backcare, pelvic floor awareness and lots of practice of strategic management of labour pain. These classes mainly focus on birth skills. For bookings phone (02) 9417 6467 or visit the website for more information.

Mater Hospital
Rocklands Road
North Sydney NSW 2060
Tel: (02) 9900 7300
email: maternity@matersydney.com.au
website: www.matersydney.com.au

The maternity department at the Mater Hospital provides women and their families with supportive, high quality care before, during and after the birth of their baby. They offer an integrated, collaborative team of obstetricians, paediatricians, midwives, maternity social workers and lactation experts to guide in the planning and development of your pregnancy. In recognition of your right to choose and to ensure mothers and partners are adequately prepared, the hospital provides education and information programs so that your choices are the best possible. Mater Hospital has 6 delivery suites, 38 postnatal beds and 10 Level II Special Care Nursery beds. Phone the number above or visit the website for further information.

Pregnancy, Birth & Beyond
27 Hart Street
Dundas Valley NSW 2117
Tel: (02) 9873 1750
email: jane@pregnancy.com.au
website: www.pregnancy.com.au

Pregnancy, Birth & Beyond provides quality prenatal courses to help you and your partner prepare for the birth of your baby. All courses are comprehensive, personal and tailor made. The programs are based on informed choice so as to help you understand your options and achieve the birth experience you desire. Information on breastfeeding and early parenting included. The programs are facilitated by Jane Palmer, accredited independent midwife, childbirth educator and mother. Phone the number above or visit the website for further information.

Transition Into Parenthood
9 Withybrook Place
Sylvania NSW 2224
Tel: (02) 9544 6441
email: julie@julieclarke.com.au
website: www.julieclarke.com.au

Transition Into Parenthood offers comprehensive and great value birth and parenting-preparation courses in Sydney. Choose from either a six-session course Monday or Tuesday nights, or a two-day Saturday condensed, or a one-day super condensed Sunday course, designed for couples who are busy or have had a baby before and need to refresh. The popular new Australian calmbirth® courses day, evening or weekends are also offered by Julie. Discount applies when two courses booked. Dates and details are listed on Julie's website www.julieclarke.com.au.

QUEENSLAND

birth@mackay
Tel: 0437 695 819
email: birthatmackay@bigpond.com
website: www.birthatmackay.com.au

Birth@mackay is a unique midwifery service giving women more choices in pregnancy, birth and early parenting care. birth@mackay provides individually tailored ante-natal, breastfeeding and parenting classes. The midwives are available for consultation and support during pregnancy and birth. Postnatal home visiting is also available including breastfeeding support.

WESTERN AUSTRALIA

Bentley Health Service - Maternity
35–39 Mill Street
Bentley WA 6102
Tel: (08) 9334 3666

Bentley Health Service provides a range of services to support women during pregnancy and birth. There is a midwife/GP Clinic, ante-natal education, parenting classes and postnatal fitness classes. Early discharge with home visiting midwifery service and lactation consultant for breastfeeding problems are available.

St John of God Hospital Murdoch
100 Murdoch Drive
Murdoch WA 6150
Tel: (08) 9366 1111

A comprehensive range of classes are provided by midwives at St John of God Hospital Murdoch to meet all your needs whether you are pregnant or planning a pregnancy. "Focus on Lifestyle" is a free evening class for couples contemplating pregnancy, or who are in the early stages of pregnancy. Parent Education classes include the topics of birth, breastfeeding and parenting. Day and evening classes are available. Bookings are necessary and fees apply. St John of God Hospital Murdoch has been providing obstetric care for more than 13 years, developing an outstanding reputation as one of the finest maternity services in Perth.

SOUTH AUSTRALIA

Flinders Medical Centre (FMC)
Flinders Drive
Bedford Park SA 5042
Tel: (08) 8204 4680
website: www.flinders.sa.gov.au

Flinders Medical Centre (FMC) offers women, their partners and support people a variety of childbirth education classes run by midwives and physiotherapists. These classes provide the opportunity to learn and discuss aspects of pregnancy, birth and parenting. They also provide a chance to interact with others sharing a similar experience. There is no charge to attend any of the childbirth education programs. As classes fill quickly, bookings should be made by the 20th to 22nd week of pregnancy. Classes commence at about the 30th week of pregnancy. Phone the number above or visit the website for further information.

EXERCISE CLASSES, YOGA & MASSAGE: PREGNANCY

NATIONAL

Preggi Bellies
Tel: 1300 727 171
email: info@preggibellies.com.au
website: www.preggibellies.com

Developed by physiotherapists, Preggi Bellies is a complete motivational workout incorporating correct exercise on a MediBall for pregnant women and women who have had or are planning to have children. Classes are available throughout Melbourne, Sydney, Brisbane and Auckland. Due to demand, the Preggi Bellies program is also available on DVD. Visit www.preggibellies.com.au for full details about the program, timetables, a complete list of stockists or to purchase the DVD online. Alternatively you can phone 1300 72 71 71 for more information.

VICTORIA

Aquamums Pty Ltd
58 Mathoura Road
Toorak VIC 3142
Tel: (03) 9826 6346
email: mandy@aquamums.com.au
website: www.aquamums.com.au

Aquamums runs aquaerobics for pre and postnatal women. Classes consist of 45 minutes of fitness work, stretching and toning under the instruction of qualified physiotherapists. This non-jarring workout is also excellent for those women with back or pelvic joint pain associated with pregnancy. Classes can be claimed on private insurance 'extras'. Aquamums classes are located in Armadale, the city, Ashburton, Kew, Berwick, Cheltenham and St Kilda. Daytime and evening sessions available. Phone the number above or visit the website for further information.

Fitwise Physiotherapy
4th Floor, 372 Albert Street
East Melbourne VIC 3002
Tel: (03) 9486 0512
email: fitwise@fitwise.com.au
website: www.fitwise.com.au

Growing a baby is hard work and hard on your body. This complimentary Early Pregnancy Seminar provides vital tips on keeping happy and healthy, including advice about appropriate exercise, back care and pelvic floor care. You can also book your first free class with the Fitwise Physiotherapy exercise and pilates program.

Madelaine Akras
26 Merton Street
Box Hill VIC 3128
Tel: 1800 003 902 or (03) 9849 0096 or 0418 351 979
website: www.hypnobirthingvictoria.com.au

Pregnancy massage offers a safe and comfortable treatment to simply relax and support you throughout your pregnancy and birth. Pregnancy massage and/or naturopathic supports may help to alleviate a range of ailments from back and neck aches, cramps, swollen ankles, sciatica to depression, anxiety and stress. These treatments can be used individually or together to also assist with the induction of labour as well as being beneficial to promote the healing process after birth.

Marcelle Oppermann
Tooronga Road
Malvern East VIC 3145
Tel: 0432 856 532
email: massagetherapy@marcelleoppermann.com
website: www.marcelleoppermann.com

Marcelle Oppermann offers relaxation, sports, pregnancy and postnatal massage and infant massage classes. Enjoy a deeply nurturing and relaxing massage that helps soothe away the aches and pains so commonly experienced during pregnancy. Postnatally, massage will help your body back into homeostasis, alleviating fatique and stress. Phone for more information.

Marie Cardamone
Tel: 0409 178 782
email: marie_cardamone@hotmail.com

Marie offers pregnancy massage therapy to ease the discomfort, aches and pain you experience as your body changes throughout pregnancy. Massage can also help increase your confidence and control by preparing your body for labour, and after birth it can help restore your body to pre-pregnancy condition. Phone or email for more information.

Marietje Stuckey
26 Merton Street
Box Hill VIC 3128
Tel: 1800 003 902 or (03) 9849 0096 or 0418 351 979
email: makras@optusnet.com.au
website: www.hypnobirthingvictoria.com.au

Resources

PREGNANCY: THE FIRST NINE MONTHS

Exercise classes, yoga & massage

Marietje Stuckey offers women antenatal and postnatal massage as well as induction massage which can be given at 39–40 weeks. With ante-natal massage time is spent by connecting the mother and baby, the mother visualising the baby in the womb at different stages during pregnancy as well as learning breathing techniques. Simple exercises can also be given at this time. Partners and birth support can learn techniques that can be useful during pregnancy and labour. Marietje is available to attend the birth.

Moksha Yoga

493 Centre Road
Bentleigh VIC 3204
Tel: (03) 9766 4880 or 0415 631 058
email: info@mokshayoga.com.au
website: www.mokshayoga.com.au

Moksha Yoga offers a wide range of yoga classes including pre and postnatal yoga and mother and baby yoga. Moksha Yoga believes consistent practice is the key which subsequently provides a deeper sense of personal awareness, enhances recuperative abilities, supports you through your pregnancy labour and beyond and promotes healing at every level of being.

Qi Rhythm Pregnancy Massage

Tel: 0417 035 497
email: melaniemyres@ozemail.com.au
website: www.qirhythm.com.au

Qi Rhythm practitioners offer pre and postnatal massage in the convenience and comfort of your own home as well as visits to women in hospital. They use a supportive pregnancy table enabling you to lay on your belly – a true luxury! Qi Rhythm believes a mother's wellbeing is fundamental to the caring and nurturing of a newborn. Massage therapies provide emotional relief and physical improvement for muscular pain and imbalance, helping mother's relax and cope with the heavy demands of motherhood. Gift vouchers are available.

Yoga Concepts

Level 1/458 Bridge Road
Richmond VIC 3121
Tel: (03) 9429 8697 or 0412 183 379
email: info@yogaconcepts.com.au
website: www.yogaconcepts.com.au

Yoga Concepts Wellness Centre in Richmond offers dynamic programs to assist with your daily life. With a family focus they have highly skilled and accredited teachers offering pre and postnatal yoga, mother and baby yoga, baby massage, prenatal massage, general relaxation massage, kids yoga, kids creative movement, pilates and parenting seminars along with general yoga, pilates and meditation classes and workshops. Phone the Centre on (03) 9429 8697 or visit www.yogaconcepts.com.au for further information.

Yoga Moves

2 William Street
Balaclava VIC 3183
Tel: (03) 9527 5198
email: info@yogamoves.org
website: www.yogamoves.org

Yoga Moves classes are conducted in a warm, supported environment. The focus is on creating an individualised approach to yoga poses, breathing and meditation. Prenatal yoga postures are designed to meet individual needs. Discover the benefits of a yoga practice to keep the body strong, supple and toned for carrying your baby and the birthing process.

Yoga Sweet Yoga

Tel: (03) 9761 0631
email: yogasweetyoga@alphalink.com.au

Yoga Sweet Yoga offers classes to nurture yourself and your growing baby. 'Pregnancy Yoga' will help you connect deeply with your baby, strengthen your body and mind in preparation for birth and release tension to enjoy a blissful pregnancy. 'Mother and Baby Yoga' classes strengthen your body after birth, while playing, stretching and relaxing with your baby. Your teacher, Cathy, is a mother of three children, a qualified yoga and meditation teacher, doula and HypnoChildbirth practitioner. She is able to support your journey into motherhood with calmness and clarity. Phone the number above or email for further information.

NEW SOUTH WALES

Essential Yoga

2/80 Bellingara Road
Miranda NSW 2228
Tel: (02) 9522 4363
email: essentialyoga@bigpond.com
website: www.essentialyoga.com.au

Pregnancy is a time of growth and change for every woman's body and emotions. Prenatal yoga classes guide you to a more comfortable pregnancy and easier birth through exercise and relaxation. Postures will improve your fitness and wellbeing, aid circulation, improve muscular control, strengthen back and abdominal muscles, and speed recovery after birth. Yoga will keep you in touch with the changes in your body and provide a positive environment for the growing child. Phone the number above or visit the website for further information.

Hypnobirth

Tel: 0414 949 546
email: info@hypnobirth.com.au
website: www.yogabhoga.com.au

A regular yoga practice during pregnancy is a wonderful

way to maintain wellbeing during this unique and transient time. Classes are designed to be gentle, nurturing and safe as you move through a transformational phase of body and mind in preparation to become a mother. The physical benefits of yoga can transform your experience of pregnancy from a time of weakness, discomfort and indisposition to one in which you feel healthy and strong. Increased stamina and strength prepare you for labour and birth together with breathing, relaxation and meditation techniques to calm, relax and empower you. A regular practice of relaxation and inner reflection can provide the path to a deeper connection with your unborn baby and your own inherent feminine wisdom. For further information visit www.yogabhoga.com.au or phone 0414 949 546 and speak with Helen Scard, Diploma of Health & Yoga, Meditation Teacher, Certified HypnoBirthing Childbirth Educator, Reiki Master Teacher.

QUEENSLAND

Brisbane Active Birth and Yoga
Tel: (07) 3379 1896
email: janec@kayemob.com
website: www.activebirthyoga.org

Jane Campbell-Kaye offers Active Birth Pregnancy Yoga classes for women from 12 weeks right up until birth. Classes are weekly and contain some childbirth education interwoven with yoga, which strengthens the body, calms the mind and develops the ability to relax. Jane trained with Janet Balaskas in London and has 25 years teaching experience. For details see the website www.activebirthyoga.org. Brisbane area only.

Merendi Health & Wellness
4/255 Leitchs Road
Brendale QLD 4500
Tel: 1300 881 536
email: info@merendi.com.au
website: www.merendi.com.au

Merendi Health & Wellness has a multidisciplinary allied and alternative health team consisting of exercise physiologists, dieticians, massage therapists, Bowen therapists, yoga and pilates instructors offering health and wellbeing programs aimed specifically for women during pregnancy and after giving birth. They combine education, hands-on workshops, individual consultations and exercise programs to teach you how to manage the many symptoms associated with pregnancy, losing post-baby bulge and to enhance your quality of life.

WESTERN AUSTRALIA

A Labour of Love
PO Box 526
South Fremantle WA 6162
Tel: 0418 336 362
email: info@alabouroflove.com.au
website: www.alabouroflove.com.au

Gabrielle Targett, BA Phys Ed and registered fitness leader (18 years), runs pregnancy-specific deep water running classes and hydrotherapy classes at the Fremantle Leisure Centre all year round. This class has been running for 14 years now with many women coming back for second and third pregnancies. Pregnancy massage is also available on a specially designed table with a belly hole which means you can lay flat on your front with no strain to your pregnant body. Gabrielle offers one hour and one-and-a-half hour massages. A massage voucher makes a perfect gift for a pregnant woman.

belly flower
Margaret River
Tel: 0417 186 673
email: info@bellyflower.com.au
website: www.bellyflower.com.au

belly flower offers yoga classes to women in the south west of Western Australia: Margaret River, Busselton and surrounding areas. Programs include pregnancy yoga, relaxation for birth classes, childbirth education workshops, midwifery consults, labour and birth support, mother and baby yoga, infant massage and breastfeeding consultations. A yoga book 'Yoga for Belly, Birth & Baby' is also available.

Eve Naturopathy & Massage
West Leederville
Tel: 0409 102 238
email: eve4health@yahoo.com.au

Kate Krasenstein has been a massage therapist for 11 years and a naturopath and aromatherapist for 9. Specialising in pre and postnatal massage since 2004, she has extensive training in this field. Kate has worked with hundreds of women throughout their pregnancies providing emotional support and physical nurturing. As a naturopath she provides pre-conception, pregnancy and postnatal care. She is the state representative for Infant Massage Australia and teaches the art of baby massage in individual or group class settings.

Monkey Bars Play & Learn Centre
Unit 1/2 Batman Road
Canning Vale WA 6155
Tel: (08) 6254 2555
email: info@monkeybars.com.au
website: www.monkeybars.com.au

As well as running fun activity programs for children aged 0 to 5 years, Monkey Bars Play & Learn Centre hosts sessions for new mums including Mums & Bubs Yoga and for expectant mums there are antenatal yoga classes. An after-school program offers a variety of fitness and yoga classes for school-aged children. Phone for more details.

SOUTH AUSTRALIA

Active Birth Centre @ Coast Yoga
1 Rose Street
Glenelg SA 5045
Tel: (08) 8295 2298
email: enquiries@coastyoga.com.au
website: www.coastyoga.com.au

Resources

PREGNANCY: THE FIRST NINE MONTHS

Exercise classes, yoga & massage
➡ Maternity clothing labels

Practical skills for pregnancy and childbirth classes offer yoga-based techniques to deal with pain and the challenges of birth, breathing techniques, encouraging the mind to think positively, and to assist you in discovering your own resources to birth your baby as naturally as possible. Active Birth Centre @ Coast Yoga also holds birthing workshops for couples as well as mothers and babies yoga classes.

Physiotherapy Pilates Proactive
86 Glen Osmond Road
Parkside SA 4807
Tel: (08) 8271 3144
website: www.pilatesproactive.com.au

Physiotherapy Pilates Proactive specialises in women's health and pilates. With locations in Stirling, Parkside and Littlehampton, they offer over 15 Pilates Mat classes that are suitable for pregnancy. All the physiotherapists have a passion for pre/postnatal care and are highly experienced in the treatment of pregnancy-related conditions. Physiotherapy Pilates Proactive aims to pamper clients from the moment they join PPP – all are given a complimentary Chi Ball for home-use, sample bags full of high quality organic products and information handouts. Pregnancy-safe aromatherapy oils burn during class with relaxing classical music and dimmed soft lighting.

Roz Donnellan-Fernandez:
Community Midwifery Services
Tel: (08) 8278 1429
email: elduende@chariot.net.au

Roz is a community midwife who has practised midwifery continuity of care for the past 13 years. She attends women during pregnancy, labour and birth and the postnatal period to 6 weeks following childbirth in homes, hospitals and birthing centres. She is also a qualified lactation consultant, facilitates preparation for parenthood groups with a local yoga centre and is involved in the education of midwives. Roz implemented and was Joint Co-ordinator of the inaugural Midwifery Group Practice service at (WCH) from 2004 to 2008, a public model of midwife-led care.

TASMANIA

Special Delivery
Level 1, 42 Brisbane Street
Launceston TAS 7250
Tel: 0408 538 875
email: sarah@specialdelivery.net.au
website: www.specialdelivery.net.au

Prepare your body and mind for a healthy pregnancy and birth with Special Delivery. Explore your birthing possibilities and meet the challenges of pregnancy and birth with confidence, strength and grace. As a certified doula and yoga instructor, Sarah offers practical physical and emotional support and care to birthing couples through pregnancy, birth and the post birth period. You can experience a joyous and empowering birth. Special Delivery services include: birth doula, postnatal doula, yoga in pregnancy for women and couples, mummy and baby yoga, one-on-one yoga tuition and aromatherapy products for pregnancy, birth, mum and baby. Phone the number above or visit the website for further information.

FAMILY PLANNING

NATIONAL

Australian Council of Natural Family Planning
Tel: (02) 9639 7381
email: acnfp@ozemail.com.au
website: www.acnfp.com.au

The Australian Council of Natural Family Planning has centres throughout Australia teaching natural fertility. Phone or visit the website for more information.

Care Pharmaceuticals Pty Ltd
Tel: 1800 788 870
email: info@carepharmaceuticals.com.au
website: www.maybebaby.com.au

MAYBE BABY™ helps you pinpoint the days when you are most likely to conceive. The size of a lipstick, MAYBE BABY™ is the clean accurate and non-invasive way to keep a close eye on your ovulation cycle. Simply place your saliva on the mini-microscope, let it dry, then check it in the viewfinder. Plus you can reuse the same MAYBE BABY™ day after day, cycle after cycle, until you get your good news. Visit the website for further information.

Centacare Natural Fertility Services
Tel: 1800 114 010
email: cfcs@centacarebrisbane.net.au
website: www.centacarebrisbane.net.au

Centacare Natural Fertility Services offers instruction in natural fertility control postpartum. The highly effective Lactational Amenorrhoea Method (LAM) is safe, completely natural and ideal for breastfeeding mothers, with less than 2% chance of pregnancy if used correctly. LAM is taught by experienced NFS teachers accredited with the Australian Council of Natural Family Planning. Other services include natural fertility control following completion of breastfeeding, support to achieve pregnancy and education and counselling services.

NFM Kits Pty Ltd
Tel: (03) 5474 3213
email: info@nfmcontraception.com
website: www.nfmcontraception.com

The Natural Fertility Management Contraception Kit shows you how to observe and interpret your body's signs of fertility so you can avoid unplanned conceptions. The NFM methods are easy to use, have no side effects and offer you the freedom to have unprotected intercourse for most of your cycle, or even before your cycle returns after childbirth. Studies show a success rate of between 97% and 99.8% when these methods are used correctly. Phone the number above or visit the website for further information.

VICTORIA

Mercy Hospital for Women
163 Studley Road
Heidelberg VIC 3084
Tel: (03) 8458 4082
email: mhwfbc@mercy.com.au

The Natural Family Planning Clinic at the Mercy Hospital is targeted at all women trying to achieve and avoid pregnancy without the use of chemicals and devices. But in particular the clinic offers new parents the opportunity to learn how to use natural methods of family planning during breastfeeding. Phone the number listed above or email for further information.

QUEENSLAND

Children by Choice
Tel: (07) 3357 5377
email: info@childrenbychoice.org.au
website: www.childrenbychoice.org.au

Children by Choice provide counselling, information and referral services to women experiencing unplanned pregnancy. They offer non-judgemental support on all options with an unplanned pregnancy – abortion, adoption and parenting. All women and their partners can access Australia-wide pregnancy options information from this comprehensive website at www.childrenbychoice.org.au. Children by Choice also provide a confidential face-to-face and Queensland-wide telephone counselling and information service. Children by Choice services are provided by professionally trained counsellors. Phone the number listed above or visit their website for further information.

Family Planning Queensland (FPQ)
100 Alfred Street
Fortitude Valley QLD 4006
Tel: (07) 3250 0240
email: enquiries@fpq.com.au
website: www.fpq.com.au

FPQ can assist with women's sexual health checks and contraception advice. FPQ is a leading provider of sexual and reproductive health services throughout Queensland with centres in Cairns, Townsville, Bundaberg, Rockhampton, Toowoomba, Sunshine Coast and Gold Coast, Brisbane and Ipswich. For more information visit www.fpq.com.au or phone the number listed above.

MATERNITY CLOTHING LABELS

NATIONAL

Barefoot Maternity & Nursing Wear
Tel: (02) 4959 9050
email: sales@barefootmaternity.com.au
website: www.barefootmaternity.com.au

Barefoot Maternity are makers of stylish, comfortable and affordable maternity and nursing wear. The Barefoot range is designed and manufactured in Australia and includes garments for corporate, casual, evening and nursing. New in store for the down-to-earth girl are Barefoot Organics, soft and silky garments in organic cotton. Shop online at www.barefootmaternity.com.au.

Belly Basics
Tel: 1800 004 009
email: bellybasics@krites.com
website: www.bellybasicsaustralia.com

Belly Basics®, the brand that brought you the style and comfort of 'The Pregnancy Survival Kit', now makes your choices even easier. Phone 1800 004 009 for a copy of their catalogue or visit their website www.bellybasicsaustralia.com. You will find a range of clothes that take away your worries of everyday wear, work wear, evening wear and swimwear. All with the comfort, style and wearability that you associate with Belly Basics®.

EGG Maternity
Tel: (07) 3846 6268
website: www.eggmaternity.com.au

Celebrate your pregnancy with EGG, one of the finest maternity lifestyle brands in Australia. The seven ranges in the EGG collection mean you can find the perfect garment for your budget and lifestyle. This includes all the necessities with EGG Basics, Charlotte Devereux designer range, timeless cuts of EGG Classic and the vibrant, value range Chic by EGG. Visit www.eggmaternity.com.au for more information.

Fertile Mind
Tel: 1800 757 777
website: www.fertilemind.com.au

The Belly Belt kit contains all you need to turn your regular jeans, skirts, pants and shorts into maternity wear. The Belly Bra is clinically proven to significantly reduce the severity of back pain commonly experienced during pregnancy. The BellyBra lifts weight off the pelvis and supports the abdomen and lower back. The 6waydress can be worn more than six ways to flatter every shape. Jersey fabric and in-built boob tube support the bust. Maternity tights offer microfibre for stretch and comfort and a wide cotton gusset for breathability. The super stretchy, seamless and gently supportive Bando extends tops and helps keep up regular jeans, skirts and trousers.

Resources

PREGNANCY: THE FIRST NINE MONTHS

Maternity clothing labels

➔ Memorabilia: pregnancy

Fragile

Tel: (02) 9362 0085

email: info@fragile.com.au

website: www.fragile.com.au

Established in 1995, Fragile has over the years become somewhat of an Australian icon — the place to visit when shopping for all things beautiful. Fragile offers an exquisite range of maternity wear, designed in-house, for the new mum-to-be, as well as a collection of beautiful, local and imported clothing for the newborn to 6 years. Visit www.fragile.com.au or phone the number above for more information.

JK Kids Gear

8 stores in Australia plus an online shop

Tel: 1800 155 255 for your nearest store

website: www.jkonline.com.au

JK Maternity offers street-smart pregnancy designs that dress the mum-to-be with confidence and style. The range features everyday maternity wear that offers great value for money on casual yet contemporary styling. This is innovative clothing that has the edge in urban simplicity and style. To view the entire range visit JK's new website at www.jkonline.com.au.

New Beginnings

Tel: (02) 9316 9810

email: sales@havenhall.com.au

website: www.newbeginnings.com.au

New Beginnings has you covered from pregnancy to breastfeeding with a wide range of maternity/feeding bras (with ugrow technology), sleeping bras, pregnancy briefs, disposable undies, back support products as well as maternity pads. The range is practical, comfortable, healthy and of the best quality. Purchases can be made direct at www.newbeginnings.com.au (stockists can also be viewed online). Phone or visit the website for further details.

Nursingwear

Tel: 0410 290 849

email: info@nursingwear.com.au

website: www.nursingwear.com.au

Made especially for pregnant and breastfeeding mums, the Kyrawear sleep bra offers enough support to keep breast shields in place, yet is un-restrictive enough for a comfortable night's rest. It is lovely and soft and has no hooks or clips. Available in black or white. Phone the number above or visit the website for further information.

Pumpkin Patch

Tel: 1800 123 430

email: info@pumpkinpatch.com.au

website: www.pumpkinpatch.com.au

Patch Maternity will make you glow with the most gorgeous collections yet. Once again the Patch designers have combined cosy comfort with the latest design-driven style. All occasions are covered: from easy-wear casual pieces for everyday, through to work outfitting and fashion-forward looks for those fun nights out. See in store or online at www.pumpkinpatch.com.au.

Ramalama

Tel: 1300 729 834

email: hello@ramalama.com.au

website: www.ramalama.com.au

Ramalama offers a truly organic range of maternity essentials to take you through pregnancy and beyond. Classic tees, bamboo tanks and their amazing wrap dress will take you effortlessly from day to night. All made from a unique organically grown and dyed cotton or from gorgeous silk-like bamboo fibres for their minimal impact on you and the earth. With elegant styling and delicate detailing to flatter your belly, all pieces can also be worn post pregnancy. Phone the number above or visit the website for further information.

SunRos Pty Ltd

Tel: (02) 9997 7625

info@labellyband.com.au

www.labellyband.com.au

La Belly maternity band is a high quality maternity accessory you can use throughout your pregnancy and beyond. Ultrasoft and easy to wear, La Belly Band is a seamless knit band that you can wear at your waistline. It will cover undone buttons or just conceal elastic waistbands. Enjoy your favourite pre-pregnancy and pregnancy clothes longer in a fashionable way. La Belly Band: 93 % cotton, Oeko-tex certified and available in trendy prints and colours. Phone the number listed above or visit the website for further information.

Top Secret Maternity

Tel: (03) 9704 8677

email: sales@topsecretmaternity.com.au

website: www.topsecretmaternity.com.au

Top Secret Maternity is maternity fashion with a built-in nursing bra. For the discerning new mums who want to breastfeed in style, Top Secret Maternity offers a comprehensive range of fashion nursingwear for all occasions which can also be worn throughout the pregnancy. They have a range of garments which make breastfeeding as discreet as it can possibly get, thanks to the exclusive, patented "Privacy Layer" – it's supportive, discreet, versatile and stylish. View the collection and order online at www.topsecretmaternity.com.au or phone (03) 9704 8677 for your nearest stockist.

Triumph International

Tel: 1800 777 208
email: queries.brisbane@triumph.com
website: www.triumph.com

Triumph understands how motherhood brings changes to your body and can help answer your questions regarding maternity bras. Triumph offers a wide range of maternity bras, as well as everyday and fashion bras, for all women, regardless of size, shape or lifestyle. Triumph lingerie is available at leading department and specialty lingerie retailers, and now also has its own stores in Queensland at Wynnum West, Stones Corner, and in Western Australia at Joondalup, Centro Galleria, Garden City. Call in for a personalised consultation with a Triumph bras tylist to ensure you're wearing the correct size. For a maternity brochure or more information freecall 1800 777 208 or visit www.triumph.com/au.

Yim Maternity

Tel: 0412 409 088
email: info@yim.com.au
website: www.yim.com.au

YIM Maternity Jeans are a normal stretch jean fitted for a pregnant woman and are designed to wear throughout your pregnancy (the entire 40 weeks) and then until you can fit back into your old jeans. With adjustable elastic inside the waistband, these pull-on, low cut jeans grow and shrink as your body does. Phone the number above or visit the website for further information.

MEMORABILIA: PREGNANCY

NATIONAL

A Pregnancy Keepsake

Tel: 0404 017 326 or 0419 870 495
email: josie@minnelli.com.au

A Pregnancy Keepsake is a beautifully presented journal ideal for personal use or as a gift for the expectant mother. It is designed to be used as a diary to record ones experiences while pregnant. It begins at week 4 through to week 42 and includes a monthly update where details such as weight can be recorded. Photos of the expectant mother can be included. Available at all major bookstores (rrp$29.95) or order via email for the special price of $14.95 plus postage and handling. Phone for more details.

Aide-Memoire Pregnant Belly Casting

Tel: (08) 8358 4555
email: itsybitsy1@bigpond.com
website: www.itsybitsystudios.com

You can now remember your pregnancy in a beautiful 3D life casting and be able to share your beautiful pregnant form with your unborn child when they grow older. You may make an appointment to have your cast professionally created in their studio or may order a DIY Kit via internet/phone. If selecting the DIY option you will need an assistant – ask your partner and this will be a unique bonding experience for them, the baby

and you. These kits are also popular at baby showers. Their professional artist can design your cast, alternatively decorate it yourself, even waiting until your child is able to help you. They use only top quality materials and state-of-the-art techniques in both products and service. Phone the number listed above or visit the website for more information.

Belly Art

Tel: 0411 405 834
email: info@bellyart.com.au
website: www.bellyart.com.au

Belly Art specialises in creating professional belly casts for pregnant women to cherish as 'priceless' works of art. Belly Art also produce 3D sculptures of baby's hand and feet mounted or box framed in a multitude of colour options from traditional to modern. The range includes safe, easy-to-use DIY Casting kits and Inkless Print kits, personalised gifts, life sculptures and gift certificates. Visit their website www.bellyart.com.au and online store for full and illustrated details of their extensive product range.

Belly Babies

Tel: (02) 9365 5451 or 0417 060 964
email: casts@bellybabies.com.au
website: www.bellybabies.com.au

Belly Babies specialise in creating plaster casts of your pregnant belly. These capture unique 3D images and are lasting mementoes of your pregnancy. Belly Babies offer home or studio visits and do-it-yourself kits. Belly Babies products are ideal presents and an exciting, fun way to involve family and friends in a miraculous time in your life. Visit their website to view their artwork or phone for more information.

Birthing Bellies

Tel: 0411 039 239
email: enquiries@birthingbellies.com.au
website: www.birthingbellies.com.au

Birthing Bellies specialise in professional belly casting and beautifully presented Pregnant Belly Casting Kits. A belly cast is a plaster casting of your belly made during the final months of pregnancy. It preserves, in great detail, the shape of your belly, including your belly button and is one of the most beautiful ways to remember those intimate months you shared with your baby. The kits come complete with instructions, materials and decorative ideas. Birthing Bellies products are 100% safe and are a perfect gift idea. Birthing Bellies can offer home and studio visits in NSW only. Phone the number above or visit the website for further information.

Itsy Bitsy Baby Hand & Feet Sculptures

Tel: (08) 8358 4555
email: itsybitsy1@bigpond.com
website: www.itsybitsystudios.com

Itsy Bitsy offer a DIY Pregnant Belly Casting Kit. Available nationally by phone or via their website at www.itsybitsystudios.com.

Resources

PREGNANCY: THE FIRST NINE MONTHS

Memorabilia: pregnancy

Milestone Press

Tel: 0401 671 707
email: sales@milestonepress.com.au
website: www.milestonepress.com.au

Milestone Press publishes *A Book About Me* for memories of pregnancy through to age five. Designed in Australia, the book's loose-leaf format allows you to remove the pages that don't suit your family. No more blank space or empty pages. There is also a ziplock plastic pocket to store items that are too special to glue such as clippings and photos. *A Book About Me* is the perfect way to record important milestones and funny moments in a book that will look just as stylish when they have their own children. Phone or visit the website for more information.

Mother's Helper

Tel: 0429 950 227
email: samantha@mothershelpers.com.au
website: www.mothershelpers.com.au

Mother's Helper Diary Second Edition is now complete with a pregnancy journal – everything you will need from pregnancy to birth and parenting. There are sections for: recording your pregnancy, birth plan, hospital bag and labour and birth; baby's birth details, emergency contacts and notes; a practical guide for baby's first eight months; medication, Illness and allergy. The activity and feeding companion is the best way to make sense of those early, sleep deprived days with your baby. The simple layout prompts you to jot down baby's feeds, sleeps, nappies and routines – all those things that will fly out of your mind in the first few weeks after birth. *Mother's Helper*: everything you will need to know about you and your baby in one convenient place. Phone or visit the website for more information.

Serenity Belly Masking

Tel: 0414 864 994
email: paula@serenitybellymasking.com.au
website: www.serenitybellymasking.com

A pregnant Belly Mask or Belly Cast can be created personally for you by Serenity Belly Masking (if you live in Queensland) or with the Do-It-Yourself Kit (available nationally) for that pregnancy keepsake. This unique three-dimensional cast of your belly, during pregnancy, is something to cherish forever. The mask can be decorated, themed and displayed in your baby's room or anywhere in your home. Visit the website for further information.

VICTORIA

Iris Creations Photography

Point Cook (servicing Melbourne & Geelong)
Tel: 0413 036 634
email: gemma@iriscreationsphotography.com
website: www.iriscreationsphotography.com

Gemma Higgins-Sears is one of Melbourne's most sought after photographers for maternity, newborn and baby portraiture. Iris Creations Photography is dedicated to capturing the special moments in life that matter the most and creating art. Sessions are performed in the comfort of your own home or at the studio. Offering affordable packages (including christenings and namings) tailored to suit you. Phone the number listed above or visit the website for more information.

Kristen Cook

Tel: 0411 447 011
email: kristen@kristencook.com.au
website: www.kristencook.com.au

Kristen Cook is a boutique lifestyle photographer based in Melbourne specialising in pregnancy, newborns, babies, toddlers, children and families. Kristen works exclusively on location, either at your home or at your chosen venue so that your child will be comfortable, engaged and most importantly have fun! To view Kristen's work and find out more information about how she can capture those tickles, giggles and love for your family, visit Kristen's website at www.kristencook.com.au.

Leanne Temme Photography

38 Windella Avenue
East Kew VIC 3102
Tel: (03) 9859 5345
email: leanne@leannetemme.com.au
website: www.leannetemme.com.au

Celebrate your curves with a sensitive, artistic pregnancy portrait by Leanne Temme to treasure this special time. Taken in a relaxed, private all female studio, Leanne's experience as a mother and magazine photographer will guarantee your results are beautiful. Birth announcements and thank-you cards are available featuring your baby. A special offer with pregnancy bookings is a free baby photo session. Phone the number above or email to make an appointment.

Lifeworks Photography

28 Stafford Street
Northcote VIC 3070
Tel: (03) 9482 2006
email: info@lifeworksphotography.com.au
website: www.lifeworksphotography.com.au

Lifeworks Photography all female team specialise in portraits of pregnancy, newborn, children of all ages and families. Over the last 17 years they have gained an enviable reputation for a high standard of ethics and superb quality photography along with exceptional personal service. With the release of their 'true expressions' photographic techniques of watchmegrow, jigsaw, angelart, lifeart, they can offer photographically designed portraiture that goes beyond the ordinary. Allow the team at Lifeworks to create images that not only capture your family's essence, but design photographic pieces of art that are naturally and personally expressive. Phone (03) 9482 2006 or view their beautiful images on their website.

Maple Gallery
11 Cavalry Circuit
Maribyrnong VIC 3032
Tel: (03) 9317 9413 or 0413 480 781
website: www.maplegallery.com.au

Maple Gallery offers natural and creative portrait photography specialising in pregnant bellies, newborn babies, cheeky children and families. Maple Gallery will capture your unique story with beautifully designed wall portraits with your choice of traditional frames, metallic art mounts or artistic canvas. Join them for a fun and relaxed day in their studio or on location in the gardens or beach as they create truly personal portraits that exhibit the real you. For further information phone Maple Gallery on the number above or visit www.maplegallery.com.au.

Vicki Bell Photography
Tel: 0412 875 584
email: vicki@vickibell.com.au
website: www.vickibell.com.au

Capturing the classical beauty and shape of each woman on their incredible journey to motherhood is truly an experience. Vicki Bells' pregnancy photography celebrates the female form. Her images are created to be simple, sophisticated and sensual. Most often partners and other family members are included in the session and Vicki creates a relaxed and tranquil atmosphere to capture all the emotion and tenderness a family shares at this time. To view samples of her photographs visit www.vickibell.com.au.

NEW SOUTH WALES

AMcSeveny Creations
Tel: 0409 396 513
email: info@amcsevenycreations.com.au
website: www.amcsevenycreations.com.au

A belly cast is a precious memento recording forever the miracle of your pregnancy and makes a fabulous addition to any nursery. AMcSeveny Creations belly casts are created using lace and casting plaster to capture your unique feminine impression, and adorned with an original artwork. Included in your baby shower, the creation of your belly cast can be shared with those nearest and dearest to you. To book your casting session or to purchase a gift voucher visit their website.

Corinne Dany Photography & Design
Suite 1, 10 Boolwey Street
Bowral NSW 2576
Tel: (02) 4862 4088 or 0415 490 626
email: petrola@hinet.net.au
website: www.corinnedany.com

From her convenient studio in downtown Bowral or on location in the gorgeous Southern Highlands, Sydney and The Blue Mountains, Corinne Dany captures mothers-to-be, newborns and families with a relaxed and creative approach. Visit her website to see a slideshow of her work and look out for her fabulous range of products including the very special, individually-designed coffee table books, canvas prints and birth announcement cards.

Forever Bliss Photography
Tel: 0400 829 449
email: chantelle@foreverblissphotography.com.au
website: www.foreverblissphotography.com.au

forever bliss photography
creative custom portraiture

Award-winning photographer Chantelle Bliss is a leading pregnancy, maternity, newborn, baby, child and family photographer in Sydney, New South Wales. Chantelle is available for sessions in the greater Sydney area and for commercial and advertising assignments. Member of the AIPP – Australian Institute of Professional Photographers.

LK Photography
Newcastle to Gosford
Tel: 0413 144 603 or (02) 4973 4456
email: laura@lkphotography.com.au
website: www.lkphotography.com.au

With 14 years experience, LK Photography services Newcastle to Gosford, 7 days a week, at your home or location of your choice. Their photography for pregnancy, babies and children and birthday parties is modern, fun, natural and beautifully delivered in a professional, non-obtrusive, friendly and customer-focussed environment. Sitting fee includes high resolution DVD of unlimited portraits, index sheets, consultation and viewing appointments. See their website, phone or email for price list with sample portraits.

Newlife Photography
Tel: (02) 9660 7143
email: galia@newlifephotography.com
website: www.newlifephotography.com.au

Newlife Photography specialises exclusively in photographing babies from pregnancy to 12 weeks old. Newlife Photography has a gentle approach and special ability to capture the beauty that is newborn babies: precious, ethereal, full of love and trust, peace, innocence, personality, quirkiness and joy. The style

Resources

PREGNANCY: THE FIRST NINE MONTHS

Memorabilia: pregnancy ➡ Pregnancy retreats

manages to stay contemporary, fresh and always innovative. Blessed to be able to work with newborn babies everyday, they strive to provide their clients with exceptional keepsakes of such a memorable time. Phone or visit the website for more information.

QUEENSLAND

Ashford Studio

116 Varsity Parade
Varsity Lakes QLD 4227
Tel: (07) 5562 2295
email: info@ashfordstudio.com.au
website: www.ashfordstudio.com.au

More women today are baring their pregnant bellies for the camera to capture their blossoming beauty. Kathryn Ashford, principal photographer at Ashford Studio, specialises in pregnancy and newborn photography and loves to create emotional images that touch the heart. For more information or to make an appointment phone Kathy on (07) 5562 2295 or visit the Ashford Studio website at www.ashfordstudio.com.au.

Catherine Lowe Photography

Tel: (07) 5528 2060 or 0402 023 241
email: cathlowe@iinet.net.au
website: www.celebrationsstudios.com.au

Celebrations Studios offers competitive prices, award-winning imagery and an outstanding commitment to their clients. Specialising in maternity, babies and family, they also photograph family events. Phone or visit the website for more information.

WESTERN AUSTRALIA

Kin Photography

U5/258 Newcastle Street
Northbridge WA 6003
Tel: 0419 957 060 or 0412 501 194
email: enquiries@kinphotography.com.au
website: www.kinphotography.com.au

Whether it is photos to celebrate your pregnancy, the arrival of your new baby, or a portrait session to capture the essence of your family, Kin Photography aims to provide you with photos that you will be proud to have in your home, and to make your photo shoot an enjoyable experience. Photo sessions can be done at home or on location and gift certificates are available. Phone or visit the website for more information.

SOUTH AUSTRALIA

Appleseed Photography

All areas in Adelaide
Tel: 0414 805 423
email: info@appleseedphotography.com.au
website: www.appleseedphotography.com.au

Kirsty from Appleseed Photography specialises in creative pregnancy and newborn portraiture as well as babies and toddlers in Adelaide. Working on location with natural light and a relaxed and unhurried approach, Kirsty ensures your children are comfortable and familiar with herself and their surrounding environment. Appleseed Photography is recognised for providing excellent personalised service, exclusive online viewing and ordering and exquisite hand made products. A mother herself, Kirsty's passion is to help other parents preserve precious memories by creating high quality fine art to cherish for a lifetime. Visit the website for further information.

PARENTING EXPOS

NATIONAL

Pregnancy Babies & Children's Expo

Tel: (08) 8341 5940
email: info@pbcexpo.com.au
website: www.pbcexpo.com.au

If you are a parent or planning to be then you should visit this Expo which caters to all those planning or who have a young family. All the needs of mums, dads and their children are represented under the one roof with stalls, exhibits and experts on hand to offer knowledgeable advice on parenting requirements. There is also great entertainment for the kids. Dates for the 2009 expos are: Adelaide 13th to 15th March; Sydney 15th to 17th May; Brisbane 19th to 21st June; Perth 14th to 16th August and Melbourne 16th to 18th October. Visit www.pbcexpo.com.au for further information.

PHYSIOTHERAPISTS

NATIONAL

Australian Physiotherapy Association

Tel: (03) 9092 0888
email: national.office@physiotherapy.asn.au
website: www.physiotherapy.asn.au

Physiotherapists around Australia offer excellent antenatal and postnatal support. Physiotherapy can help you stay healthier, fitter and stronger before and after the birth. Physiotherapists can also help you to look after your back, improve recovery of bladder control, use a baby sling and protect the head shape of your baby. To find a local physiotherapist, contact the Australian Physiotherapy Association office in your state or go to 'Find a Physio' on the APA's website at http://physiotherapy.asn.au.

VICTORIA

Fitwise Physiotherapy
4th Floor, 372 Albert Street
East Melbourne VIC 3002
Tel: (03) 9486 0512
email: fitwise@fitwise.com.au
website: www.fitwise.com.au

Back pain, incontinence and pelvic girdle pain are not normal features of pregnancy and the postnatal period. Fitwise Physiotherapy offers a highly qualified and experienced team to provide excellent evidence based treatments, exercise and pilates programs.

Health 4 Women (H4W)
Suite 327/55 Flemington Road
North Melbourne VIC 3051
Tel: (03) 9329 0999
website: www.health4women.com.au

Back pain, pelvic joint pain and incontinence are not acceptable complications of pregnancy. The H4W Practice is located across the road from the new Women's Hospital and Frances Perry House. Inpatient and outpatient physiotherapy services include individual consultations prenatally, postnatally and for older women. There is also now a small pilates studio offering one-on-one or small group classes.

QUEENSLAND

Narangba Physiotherapy & Sports Injury Clinic
Shop 4, Narangba Station Plaza, 20 Main Street
Narangba QLD 4504
Tel: (07) 3886 9470
email: narangbaphysio1@aapt.net.au

Narangba Physiotherapy & Sports Injury Clinic offers prenatal and postnatal physiotherapy treatment including exercise programs, pilates classes and massage for new mums and mums-to-be. They now also offer paediatric physiotherapy services. Phone or email for more information.

Yummy Mummy Physio
Locations at Grange and Bulimba
Tel: (07) 3352 3666
email: info@yummymummyphysio.com.au
website: www.yummymummyphysio.com.au

Yummy Mummy Physio is a specialised and professional physio practice designed to enhance your experience of pregnancy and motherhood. Services include physiotherapy for the treatment of back and neck pain, pubic symphysis and SIJ pain, sciatic and buttock pain, abdominal weakness and separation and pelvic floor weakness. They also offer pregnancy massage, baby massage workshops, pregnancy and post-natal exercise classes, boot camp, actve labour classes and more. Phone or visit their website for further information.

PREGNANCY PILLOWS

NATIONAL

Bubbaliscious
Tel: 0410 637 306
email: cleo@bubbaliscious.com.au
website: www.bubbaliscious.com.au

Bubbaliscious is an Australian-owned business providing specialty products for mums and babies. It is the home of the Body Wrap Pillow, a patented maternity sleeping aid. The Body Wrap is a full body contact pillow that wraps the body providing both back and stomach support during pregnancy and eliminates the need for several pillows, enabling a good night's sleep. For more information visit www.bubbaliscious.com.au. Available nationally.

Clever Babies (Kushies)
Tel: 1800 114 443
email: info@cleverbabies.com.au
website: www.cleverbabies.com.au

Kushies® Pregnancy Pillow Plus is a multi-purpose pillow, angled for stomach support and promotes a proper sleeping position for the expectant mother. The Pregnancy Pillow Plus is angled shaped which is also ideal for propping up baby and it can be used as a foot rest to elevate swollen ankles or as a lower back support. It also has a removable cover that makes machine washing and drying easy. Log onto www.cleverbabies.com.au or phone 1800 114 443 for a free mail order catalogue for the full range of Kushies®.

Inspired Living
Tel: (03) 9826 5870
email: info@inspiredlivingaus.com
website: www.inspiredlivingaus.com

Inspired Living designs and manufactures a range of innovative lifestyle accessories. Their product range includes a maternity pillow designed to assist sleeping during pregnancy and to assist with breastfeeding. As recommended by medical practitioners it is best to sleep on your side during pregnancy for optimum comfort, support and for the health of your baby. The Inspired Living pillow was designed by a mother-to-be and has been trialled by many pregnant women with positive results. Available at selected retail outlets. Visit their website, email or phone for more information.

PREGNANCY RETREATS

NATIONAL

Byron Pregnancy Retreat
Tel: (02) 6684 4429
email: anna@celebrationofbirth.com
website: www.celebrationofbirth.com

The 'Celebration of Birth' weekend is a fun, nurturing, creative experience for pregnant women and their

Resources

PREGNANCY: THE FIRST NINE MONTHS
Pregnancy scans ➔ Stores online

partners to look forward to the birth with confidence and joy. Enjoy yoga and meditation, holistic birth preparation, blessingway celebration and more as you connect with your inner wisdom for harmonious birth, in a relaxing environment. Facilitated by professional childbirth educator Anna Watts. Weekends are held throughout the year in the beautiful Byron Bay hinterland. They also offer personalised pregnancy packages and individual pregnancy sessions at a time to suit you. Phone (02) 6684 4429 or visit www.celebrationofbirth.com for further information.

PREGNANCY SCANS

VICTORIA

Early Image
Tel: (03) 9529 7433
email: info@earlyimage.com.au
website: www.earlyimage.com.au
From 25 weeks onwards Early Image's 4D Superscan allows you to watch live action of your baby smiling, opening its eyes, yawning and sucking its thumb in colour. What's more, you can bring your family and friends along for the show. You will be amazed once you see your beautiful baby in ultravision. Early Image are also experts in gender determination and confirmation from 17 weeks onwards and no referral is necessary.

STORES ONLINE: PREGNANCY

NATIONAL

Belly Babes
email: info@bellybabesmaternity.com.au
website: www.bellybabesmaternity.com.au
Belly Babes are proud to say that their staff are all mothers, have a great eye for fashion and believe that pregnancy is no barrier to looking and feeling fantastic about your changing body. They cater for mums-to-be, the fuller figured women and the little ones too. Enjoy looking at a selection of their beautiful garments and products online. Visit www.bellybabesmaternity.com.au.

Bellycan Maternity Wear
email: amy@bellycanmaternity.com.au
website: www.bellycanmaternity.com.au
Bellycan Maternity Wear stocks suitable corporate, evening, formal, lingerie, sleepwear, swimwear, smart and casual wear. Labels include HOTmilk Lingerie,

Ripe, Soon Melbourne, Ilant Swimwear, Rosa Morena Sleepwear, Dress 4 Two, Mango Jam, Barefoot, Szabo Fashion, Top Secret, Yim, Egg, OiOi Sophisticated Baby Bags, The Zaky, Reminder Bracelets, Dunstan Baby Language DVDs, pregnancy books, baby shower games and associated products. Gift vouchers and mail order available. Visit the website for further information.

Cedar Leaf
email: info@cedarleaf.com.au
website: www.cedarleaf.com.au

Cedar Leaf is one of Australia's leading online luxury maternity boutiques. Specialists in combining labels like Mishka'n'Milka and Blossom Mother & Child from the UK with the likes of M Missoni, BY Malene Birger and Billion Dollar Babes, you are offered a diffusion of maternity and non-maternity labels to wear during your pregnancy and many years beyond. With an express postage fee of $15 to anywhere in Australia and beautiful complimentary gift packaging on every order, you will be truly hooked on the Cedar Leaf experience.

Down to Earth Baby
email: info@downtoearthbaby.com
website: www.downtoearthbaby.com
Down to Earth Baby is a one-stop organic and eco-friendly mother and baby shop. With natural products for pregnancy through to baby including fabulous skincare and aromatherapy products, organic herbal teas, as well as organic and eczema-friendly clothing. They also offer support packs and organic gifts for each stage of pregnancy, labour, postnatal recovery, breastfeeding and baby plus non-toxic toys and baby bottles. Great babycare products include cloth and disposable nappies for environmentally-conscious families.

Gayle Petrie Designs
Tel: 1300 768 608
website: www.gaylepetriedesigns.com.au
Gayle Petrie Designs offers a comprehensive selection of maternity wear online. Labels include Gayle Petrie, Szabo, Belly Basics, Ripe, Pea in a Pod, Soon Maternity, Maternity Plus, Mishkanmilka, Anita Lingerie, Lovable Lingerie, OiOi Baby Bags, Ilant Swimwear, GlamourMom, Bonds and Angel Maternity Wear just to name a few. Stock constantly arriving and updated daily and next-day delivery on most occasions. Payment with Mastercard, Visa, Amex, Diners and Paypal available.

GlowMama Maternity
Tel: (07) 3861 0010
email: shop@glowmama.com.au
website: www.glowmama.com.au
The GlowMama online boutique offers stylish and fashionable clothing for pregnant women. GlowMama aims to provide you with outstanding customer service with helpful assistance on sizing and maternity style tips. Visit www.glowmama.com.au for further details.

Just 4 Mums Maternitywear

Tel: (03) 9704 9994
email: info@just4mums.com.au
website: www.just4mums.com.au

Just 4 Mums Maternitywear online stocks all the major brands including casual, work, swim, gym, plus sizes, lingerie, hosiery, breastfeeding wear, jeans, formal evening wear and they also offer an evening wear hire service to help you save money. Spoil yourself and look great throughout your pregnancy with some great pieces that make you feel good about your new pregnancy figure. Phone the number above or visit the website for more information.

Kids Exclusive

Tel: 0405 152 549
email: sales@kidsexclusive.com.au
website: www.kidsexclusive.com.au

Kids Exclusive sell a selection of long and short-sleeved maternity tees by Preggers & Proud as well as high quality European kids' shoes and clothing. Phone or visit the website for further information.

Lili Aurora

Tel: (02) 8509 5533
email: info@liliaurora.com.au
website: www.liliaurora.com.au

Lili Aurora is an e-boutique stocking the best from maternity designers worldwide. Lili Aurora seeks out pieces that will become wardrobe favourites during pregnancy and beyond – they are constantly searching for innovative designers that offer comfort together with that eye-catching special something. They are also passionate about providing a website to revive the spirit – a cyber-retreat for all mums and mums-to-be. Phone or visit the website for more information.

Maternity Revolution

Tel: (07) 3205 1818
email: lisa@maternityrevolution.com.au
website: www.maternityrevolution.com.au

Maternity Revolution is an impressive online store offering bargains from $15. Subscribe to their newsletter to receive regular discounts – orders are usually processed same day and you are welcome to chat to their friendly staff if you have questions. The range includes maternity clothes, sleepwear, bras, feeding garments, support belts, nappy bags, books, premmie baby wear and much more. Visit their website for the full range. For those without a credit card Maternity Revolution accepts direct deposit and money orders.

Mums 'n Bubs Maternity Wear

Tel: (08) 8945 6867
email: info@mumsnbubsmaternity.com
website: www.mumsnbubsmaternity.com

Mums 'n Bubs Maternity Wear stock maternity wear, baby nappy bags, baby gifts, premature baby wear, children's wear, breastfeeding tops as well as baby and toddler hats. Visit the online store at www.mumsnbubsmaternity.com.

Nature's Child

Tel: 1300 555 632
email: orders@natureschild.com.au
website: www.natureschild.com.au

 Nature's Child sell organic cotton breast pads, breast tops and bras, meditation CDs, prenatal yoga DVD, belly oils, belly casting and more. See their Fathers 2B section and enjoy the free pages of information helping you to research the best nappy options and parenting styles. Lots of beautiful baby goods too. Nature's Child is Australia's largest organic baby store since 2000. Ask to see their product range at Babies Galore or view their website for full details.

Parents' Essentials

Tel: 1800 782 022
email: customerservice@parentsessentials.com.au
website: www.parentsessentials.com.au

Parents' Essentials makes parents' lives easier by providing innovative product solutions. They offer a collection of packs including The Maternity Hospital Pack: all your essential products for your hospital stay; the Bath Time Pack that contains the innovative Tummy Tub as the baby bath; and a Toilet Training Pack to get your toilet training journey off to a smooth start. A Parents' Essentials Pack makes a practical baby shower gift, gift for a newborn or as a solution to one of many childhood milestones. Phone or visit the website for more information.

pop maternity

Tel: 0429 693 984
email: info@popmaternity.com.au
website: www.popmaternity.com.au

Pop Maternity is the exclusive Australian distributor of the beautiful Eve Alexander Maternity range of nursing bras and lingerie as well as the designer behind the invisible comfort of the Perfect Fit Maternity Undies. Visit www.popmaternity.com.au for more information as well as great gift ideas. Wholesale enquiries welcome.

Queen Bee Maternity & Nursing Wear

Tel: 1300 773 449
email: sales@queenbee.com.au
website: www.queenbee.com.au

Queen Bee is a great place to shop for fabulous maternity clothing, designer maternity jeans and stylish breastfeeding clothes. Shop securely online 24 hours a day at www.queenbee.com.au. Fast shipping Australia wide.

ready set mama

Tel: 0412 627 749
email: nicole@readysetmama.com.au
website: www.readysetmama.com.au

ready set mama stocks the gorgeous WOMAMA range of maternity and breastfeeding wear from New Zealand. See the range on their website or phone the number above for more details.

Resources

PREGNANCY: THE FIRST NINE MONTHS

Stores online ➜ Stores retail

Sparrows Nest Maternity

Tel: (08) 8177 0911
email: sparrowsnestmaternity@bigpond.com
website: www.sparrowsnestmaternity.com

Sparrows Nest Maternity is an online maternity superstore. They offer maternity and breastfeeding wear in sizes 6 to 24 XXXL as well as gift baskets and vouchers. Family owned and offering personal service. Online purchases welcome.

Stork Maternity Wear & Accessories

Tel: (02) 6023 4800
email: sales@storkmaternity.com.au
website: www.storkmaternity.com.au

Stork Maternity offers an extensive range of maternity wear for all occasions including maternity bras up to a J cup and a great range of breastfeeding tops from all the leading maternity labels. Experienced friendly staff will help you capture the beautiful woman inside the loving mother. Stork Maternity also has a great range of nappy bags and baby accessories.

Sweet Lilly Maternity

Tel: 0410 590 889
email: info@sweetlillymaternity.com.au
website: www.sweetlillymaternity.com.au

Sweet Lilly Maternity is home to a great collection of fun, fabulous, edgy maternity and breastfeeding clothes. If you are a pregnant Web Queen, then this is your place for up to the minute runway maternity fashion that has been imported from around the world and now available for you to purchase. Sweet Lilly Maternity has hot maternity jeans from Mama Black New York, practical and stylish breastfeeding clothes at realistic prices and dreamy maternity evening wear and dresses that have been constantly featured throughout Australian and international press. Over 50 labels in the range – visit www.sweetlillymaternity.com.au for more information.

STORES RETAIL: PREGNANCY

VICTORIA

Belly Babes

85 Cunninghame Street
Sale VIC 3850
Tel: (03) 5144 4600
Also located at:
Shop 2, 108 Franklin Street
Traralgon VIC 3844
Tel: (03) 5176 0610

email: info@bellybabesmaternity.com.au
website: www.bellybabesmaternity.com.au

Belly Babes has become one of Gippsland's favourite maternity, baby and children's fashion stores. They have created a relaxed and comfortable atmosphere where their experienced staff can take you through the extensive range of clothing and offer expert advice or just leave you to browse. Belly Babes cater for women of all shapes and sizes, from the beginning of pregnancy right through to the breastfeeding stage. They are continually expanding the clothing lines at Belly Babes in order to meet the fashion needs of mums-to-be for all occasions. Drop in and say hi or call for any assistance, they are happy to post Australia wide.

Fragile

285-287 Coventry Street
South Melbourne VIC 3202
Tel: (03) 9686 4111
email: info@fragile.com.au
website: www.fragile.com.au

Established in 1995, Fragile has over the years become somewhat of an Australian icon — the place to visit when shopping for all things beautiful. Fragile offers an exquisite range of maternity wear, designed in-house, for the new mum-to-be, as well as a collection of beautiful, local and imported clothing for the newborn to 6 years.

Glow Maternity & Newborn

197 Main Street
Mornington VIC 3931
Tel: (03) 5973 5655
email: sales@glowmaternitywear.com.au
website: www.glowmaternitywear.com.au

Glow Maternity & Newborn stocks fashionable and affordable maternity wear and evening wear hire is now available. They also have a great range of baby clothes and gifts from prem to size 4.

Just 4 Mums Maternitywear

Shop 4, Fountain Gate Super Centre (next to Spotlight)
Narre Warren VIC 3805
Tel: (03) 9704 9994
email: info@just4mums.com.au
website: www.just4mums.com.au

Just 4 Mums Maternitywear is conveniently located in BabyCo at Narre Warren and also sells online. Stocking all the major brands the range includes casual, work, swim, gym, plus sizes, lingerie, hosiery, breastfeeding wear, jeans, formal evening wear and they also offer an evening wear hire service to help you save money. Spoil yourself and look great throughout your pregnancy with some great pieces that make you feel good about your new pregnancy figure.

Little Wonders Baby Shop

1–36 Station Street
Cranbourne VIC 3977
Tel: (03) 5995 3464
email: sales@littlewonders.com.au
website: www.littlewonders.com.au

Little Wonders Baby Shop offers a range of pre-loved items such as children's clothes for newborns through to size 10, maternity clothes and a range of items and accessories to make your pregnancy more comfortable. Located in Cranbourne with an outlet in Baranduda, this shop is run by mothers with young children. Open 10.30am to 3.00pm Tuesday to Friday or by appointment.

Maternal Instinct
235 Moorabool Street
Geelong VIC 3220
Tel: (03) 5229 2293
email: mmaterna@bigpond.net.au
website: www.maternalinstinct.com.au

Maternal Instinct stocks one of the widest ranges of maternity labels in Victoria from high end fashion to budget conscious. Phone or visit the website for further details.

Motherhood Maternity Warehouse
487 North Road
Ormond VIC 3204
Tel: (03) 9578 0589
email: sales@motherhoodmaternitywear.com.au
website: www.motherhoodmaternitywear.com.au

Since 1974 Motherhood Maternity Warehouse has offered generations of expectant mums a huge range of maternity items at truly great prices. Specialising in everyday basics and smart casual, the range now also includes nursing tops, accessories and swimwear. All the latest looks from the top maternity brands at affordable prices with helpful advice and offering something for every mother to be. Free parking next to Ormond Station. Open Tuesdays to Saturdays 10.00am to 5.00pm.

Mumma Mia Maternity Lifestyle
365 Glenhuntly Road
Elsternwick VIC 3185
Tel: (03) 9528 1375
website: www.mummamia.com.au

Mumma Mia Maternity Lifestyle offers a great shopping experience for parents-to-be. They stock everything you need from maternity wear through to clothing for children size 3. They specialise in funky maternity wear in sizes small to extra large and kids' wear in sizes 0000 to 3. There is also a playroom, a feeding and change area and the shop is pram-friendly. Open Monday to friday 9.30am to 5.30pm and Saturday 9.30am to 4.00pm.

Ostara Maternity & Lifestyle
393 Bay Street
Brighton VIC 3186
Tel: (03) 9596 9248
website: www.ostaramaternity.com.au

Ostara offers a great range of maternity and fashion labels suitable for pregnancy and beyond including Soon, Yim, Metalicus, Mishka & Milka, Bumpology, Szabo, Precious Cargo, Two of Us, Bliss, Il Tutto and Oi Oi. Ostara offers a true fashion edge to ensure you will look and feel fabulous! They are also maternity jeans specialists.

Out'N Front
149 Glenferrie Road
Malvern VIC 3144
Tel: (03) 9509 4397
email: bmichaels@outnfront.com.au
website: www.outnfront.com.au

Out'N Front has an inherent understanding of women. They fully understand your need to feel in control during during your nine months of pregnancy. Nothing could be easier. With styles boasting exquisite appeal and designed for all circumstances (work, sport, lingerie, sleepwear and hosiery), their garments are of good quality, fashionable and comfortable at prices you can afford.

Swimwear Galore
430 Brunswick Street
Fitzroy VIC 3065
Tel: (03) 9417 2222
Also located at:
310 St. Kilda Road
St. Kilda VIC 3182
Tel: (03) 9534 6222
1297 Nepean Highway
Cheltenham VIC 3192
Tel: (03) 9585 5622
131 Ocean Beach Road
Sorrento VIC 3943
Tel: (03) 5984 0322
138 Malop Street
Geelong VIC 3220
Tel: (03) 9529 9100
email: enquiries@swimweargalore.com.au
website: www.swimweargalore.com.au

Swimwear Galore is the largest retail swimwear shop in Australia. They cater for the whole family including a large range of maternity and mastectomy swimwear. The maternity styles include one piece as well as the new singlet two-piece style, sizes 8–18. Open Monday to Friday 9.30am to 5.30pm, Saturday 9.00am to 5.00pm, extended hours during summer.

NEW SOUTH WALES

BJ's Maternity Boutique
Shop 38 Wills Road
North Woolooware NSW 2230
Tel: (02) 9523 6855
email: shop-jayne@bjs.com.au
website: www.bjsmaternity.com.au

BJ's Maternity Boutique offers a massive range of the latest styles in maternity clothing with swim, party, work, evening and breastfeeding wear, many below recommended retail price. Sizes 6–24 are available on selected items and a huge selection of reduced price stock is also available. Labels include Belly Basics, Pea in a Pod, Szabo, Ripe, Dress4Two, New Beginnings and Ninth Moon. BJ's is open Wednesday to Saturday (during January open Saturdays only) or by appointment.

Resources

PREGNANCY: THE FIRST NINE MONTHS

Stores retail

Fragile

76a Paddington Street
Paddington NSW 2021
Tel: (02) 9362 0085
Also located at:
Shop 5003, Level 5
Westfield Shopping Centre
Bondi Junction NSW 2022
Tel: (02) 9389 3522
email: info@fragile.com.au
website: www.fragile.com.au

Established in 1995, Fragile has over the years become somewhat of an Australian icon — the place to visit when shopping for all things beautiful. Fragile offers an exquisite range of maternity wear, designed in-house, for the new mum-to-be, as well as a collection of beautiful, local and imported clothing for the newborn to 6 years.

Just Maternity

Shop 22, Ground floor Piccadilly Centre
210 Pitt Street
Sydney NSW 2000
Tel: (02) 9266 0132
Also located at:
Piccadilly Arcade
210 Pitt Street
Sydney NSW 2000
Tel: (02) 9266 0132
Shop 4, 39 Tramore Place
Killarney Heights NSW 2087
Tel: (02) 9452 3066
website: www.justmaternity.com.au

Just Maternity has all the top maternity labels including Ripe, Pea in a Pod and Szabo. There are over 5,000 garments to choose from including off-season stock for travellers which are carried all year round. Friendly, helpful service will help you look your best.

Mums the Word Maternity Wear

Shop 5, Masonic Centre, Showground Road
(corner of Old Northern Road)
Castle Hill NSW 2154
Tel: (02) 9894 0900

Mums the Word Maternity Wear has a fabulous range of maternity clothing to suit all shapes and changing sizes. For casual, formal, sporty and business wear, Mums the Word Maternity Wear can provide all you need during your pregnancy – fashionable, stylish, practical and affordable. Phone or visit the website for more information.

Stork Maternity Wear & Accessories

465B Dean Street
Albury NSW 2640
Tel: (02) 6023 4800
email: sales@storkmaternity.com.au
website: www.storkmaternity.com.au

Stork Maternity offers an extensive range of maternity wear for all occasions including maternity bras up to a J cup and a great range of breastfeeding tops from all the leading maternity labels. Experienced friendly staff will help you capture the beautiful woman inside the loving mother. Stork Maternity also has a great range of nappy bags and baby accessories.

AUSTRALIAN CAPITAL TERRITORY

Motherly Instincts

Shop 17, Homeworld Centre
Greenway (Tuggeranong Centre) ACT 2900
Tel: (02) 6293 4452
email: beck@motherlyinstincts.com.au
website: www.motherlyinstincts.com.au

Be pregnant and proud in comfort and style with the fantastic range, service and price at Motherly Instincts. They have everything you need for a happy and healthy pregnancy. Open 7 days.

QUEENSLAND

GlowMama Maternity

3 Days Road
Grange QLD 4051
Tel: (07) 3861 0010
email: shop@glowmama.com.au
website: www.glowmama.com.au

The GlowMama boutique in Grange, Brisbane, has been designed to be more than just a maternity wear shop. The relaxed and comfortable atmosphere and the genuine enthusiasm for stylish and fashionable clothing has helped establish this beautiful boutique into a haven for pregnant women. GlowMama aims to provide you with outstanding customer service and will be happy to take you through the extensive collection of clothing, suggest outfit options or just leave you to browse. If you choose to shop online you will find that the same level of attention is provided, with helpful assistance on sizing and maternity style tips.

Maternity Revolution

1/124 South Pine Road
Brendale QLD 4500
Tel: (07) 3205 1818
email: lisa@maternityrevolution.com.au
website: www.maternityrevolution.com.au

Maternity Revolution is one of Brisbane's largest maternity wear stores with a mind boggling range, great prices and bargains from $15. They also stock feeding bras, breastfeeding garments, nappy bags, books, creams, support belts and stockings, sleepwear, premmie baby wear and more. Visit the superstore (open 7 days) with kids play area, toilets and off-street parking or shop online. Sizes range from 6 to 26.

Maternity Super Store
4/50 Kremzow Road
Brendale QLD 4500
Tel: (07) 3205 3837
email: maternitysuperstore@hotmail.com
website: www.maternitysuperstore.com.au

Maternity Super Store stocks items all under $50 (excludes formal gowns). They stock over 6,000 items in sizes 6 to 28 ranging from casual through to corporate, swim wear, breastfeeding garments, belly bands and maternity body pillows. There is a children's play area, TV, bathroom and parking out the front. Open Monday to Friday 9.00am to 5.00pm and Saturday 9.00am to 3.00pm.

NORTHERN TERRITORY

Bellycan Maternity Wear
Oasis Shopping Centre, 15 Temple Terrace
Palmerston NT 0830
Tel: (08) 8932 7650
email: amy@bellycanmaternity.com.au
website: www.bellycanmaternity.com.au

Bellycan Maternity Wear stocks suitable corporate, evening, formal, lingerie, sleepwear, swimwear, smart and casual wear. Labels include HOTmilk Lingerie, Ripe, Soon Melbourne, Ilant Swimwear, Rosa Morena Sleepwear, Dress 4 Two, Mango Jam, Barefoot, Szabo Fashion, Top Secret, Yim, Egg, OiOi Sophisticated Baby Bags, The Zaky, Reminder Bracelets, Dunstan Baby Language DVDs, pregnancy books, baby shower games and associated products. Gift vouchers and mail order available.

Mums 'n Bubs Maternity Wear
Shop 16B Hibiscus Shopping Town
Leanyer Darwin NT 0812
Tel: (08) 8945 6867
email: info@mumsnbubsmaternity.com
website: www.mumsnbubsmaternity.com

Mums 'n Bubs Maternity Wear stock maternity wear, baby nappy bags, baby gifts, premature baby wear, children's wear, breastfeeding tops as well as baby and toddler hats. Visit the store at the address above or online at www.mumsnbubsmaternity.com.

WESTERN AUSTRALIA

Aura Woman
16 Forrest Street
Subiaco WA 6008
Tel: (08) 9388 1992
Also located at:
Shop 7, 30–32 Ardross Street
Applecross WA 6153
email: aura01@westnet.com.au
website: www.aurawoman.com.au

Aura Woman is the stylish alternative for modern women who can stay true to their sense of style with versatile, cutting edge designs. You will find clothes to complement your existing wardrobe, with garments that can be worn before, during and after pregnancy. Aura

Woman offers an exciting new concept for mothers-to-be who have decided against buying a pregnancy wardrobe and just "making do". WA designed and made, the collections cater for size 4 to 20 and provides a unique flexibility in your wardrobe. Visit www.aurawoman.com.au to see the full range.

BabyBelly
Shop 4b Bunbury City Plaza
123 Spencer Street
Bunbury WA 6230
Tel: (08) 9792 5550
email: babybelly@westnet.com.au

BabyBelly specialises in maternity clothing stocking labels such as Ripe, Bloom, Barefoot, BellyButton, Cosmic, Fertile Mind, Bellybasics Yim, Boho Mama and Ilant swimwear. They also stock a variety of Berlei and Hotmilk maternity bras and a range of baby clothing plus gr8x nappy bags, baby gifts, nursing pillows and accessories. The maternity clothing range consists of casual, corporate, evening, leisure and underwear; sizes range from 6 to plus sizes. Open Monday, Tuesday, Wednesday and Friday 9:30am to 5:00pm, Thursday 9:30am to 6:00pm and Saturday 9:30am to 1:30pm.

Bates Street Babies
36 Bates Street
Merredin WA 6415
Tel: (08) 9041 2200
email: batesstreetbabies@bigpond.com.au
website: www.batesstreetbabies.com.au

Bates St Babies is the only dedicated baby and maternity shop in wheatbelt WA. They stock lots of gorgeous bits and pieces for baby and little kids as well as maternity and breastfeeding clothes. They also have a lovely feeding lounge and baby change area and a great play zone for the kids to have fun while mum and dad shop. So whatever you need – cots, prams, change tables, linen, clothes, books, cards, creams, potties, bookends, motifs – visit this beautiful shop.

SOUTH AUSTRALIA

Bug-a-lugs Baby Store
31 Light Crescent
Mt Barker SA 5251
Tel: (08) 8398 3521
email: info@bugalugsbaby.com.au
website: www.bugalugsbaby.com.au

Bug-a-lugs Baby Store stocks a gorgeous range of maternity clothes including brands such as Ripe, Ninth Moon, Belly Basics, plus bras to size 20G from Hot Milk, Bravado, Lovable, Goddess and Bonds. Bug-a-lugs also has a great children's clothing range as well as a huge range of nursery furniture and equipment.

Sparrows Nest Maternity
1289 South Road
St Marys SA 5042
Tel: (08) 8177 0911
email: sparrowsnestmaternity@bigpond.com
website: www.sparrowsnestmaternity.com

Resources

PREGNANCY: THE FIRST NINE MONTHS

Stores retail
➔ Websites: pregnancy & general parenting

Sparrows Nest Maternity is a maternity superstore. They offer maternity and breastfeeding wear in sizes 6-24 xxxl. The store also has gift baskets and vouchers. Family owned and offering personal service. Open 7 days (next to Babyco) and online purchases welcome. Phone or visit the website for more information.

TASMANIA

The Growing Years
175 Elphin Road
Newstead TAS 7250
Tel: (03) 6334 7200

The Growing Years stock a good range of maternity wear. Open Monday to Friday 9.00am to 5.00pm and Saturday by appointment. Phone for further details.

WEBSITES: PREGNANCY & GENERAL PARENTING

NATIONAL

Australian Childhood Foundation
Tel: 1800 176 453
email: info@childhood.org.au
website: www.kidscount.com.au

www.kidscount.com.au is a website for parents all about childhood. It has information to help you raise happy and confident children.

Babypoo Pty Ltd
email: info@babypoo.com.au
website: www.babypoo.com.au

www.babypoo.com.au features free street-smart video parenting tips from real parents. The site also includes an online shop specialising in Australian-made parenting DVDs revealing all the secrets from the experts. Visit the website for more information.

BellyBelly.com.au
Tel: (03) 9836 7734
email: info@bellybelly.com.au
website: www.bellybelly.com.au

Prepare for pregnancy, birth and baby online at BellyBelly. Feel reassured, educated and informed with the best support and information available at your fingertips. BellyBelly is a friendly and respected online parenting social network where everything is explained in black and white without the jargon, so you can make your own informed decisions on all things conception, pregnancy, birth and baby. No fluff. Real stuff.

Birthnet Pty Ltd
Tel: (02) 9662 6019
email: management@birth.com.au
website: www.birth.com.au

Birth.com.au and *BIRTH* the book are invaluable resources for women and partners on their journey to parenthood. Written and supported by a midwife and a childbirth educator with over 30 years collective experience, they provide everything you need to know about fertility, conception, pregnancy, birth and early parenting. Birthnet's online birthtalks® community is a great way to network with other parents and parents-to-be.

Blackmores
Tel: 1800 803 760 tollfree Advisory Service
website: www.preconception.com.au

The decision to try for a baby is an exciting step and once made, a healthy, timely conception is a key concern. Blackmores has developed a website www.preconception.com.au, a one-stop shop providing key information when trying to conceive. The steps women can take to improve their chance of conceiving are outlined in detail looking at "cleaning up and removing hurdles" by avoiding toxins like tobacco and alcohol and shedding excess weight, "getting healthy" physically, mentally and emotionally, scheduling a pre-conception check up with a healthcare practitioner and "knowing your cycle" to help determine the most fertile time.

Earlybirds
Tel: 1800 666 550
email: info@earlybirds.com.au
website: www.earlybirds.com.au

Earlybirds' website is a useful source for parents and carers of premature babies. Earlybirds Network page provides access to information and links to national and local premature support groups together with latest copies of newsletters from Austprem and Premmie Press. Earlybirds proudly supports Austprem and the National Premmie Foundation.

KidsLife Foundation
Tel: (03) 9276 7743
email: kidslife@asg.com.au
website: www.kidslife.com.au

KidsLife, a community initiative of the Australian Scholarships Group (ASG), aims to help parents understand their children's development and support them in forming effective parenting strategies that work for their family. To achieve this KidsLife offers free access to parenting information via its website, and free subscription to its e-newsletter and unique parent briefings series. KidsLife aims to encourage parents to explore their parenting choices and discover positive ways that enable them, their children and family to grow and develop.

Mum Zone
email: admin@mumzone.com.au
website: www.mumzone.com.au

Mum Zone is a parenting website designed especially for busy Australian mums by busy Australian mums. Mum Zone is a one-stop, interactive site full of useful and practical resources, ideas and tips to make life as a mum that bit easier and fun. It will also save you precious time so you have more to spend with your child. Mum Zone provides useful resources as well as allowing you to share your experiences, tips and ideas with others.

Mum's Grapevine
Tel: 0422 932 033
email: sales@mumsgrapevine.com.au
website: www.mumsgrapevine.com.au

Mum's Grapevine is the site for mums and mums-to-be to find out about the best deals, discounts, special offers, sales and new products for all things relating to mums, babies and kids. You will save on maternity wear and accessories, baby and children's clothes, toys, manchester, nursery items and more. Simply register online to receive the free weekly e-newsletter giving you the inside scoop on all the best offers. Register online and it's free to join.

Natural Family Publishing
Tel: 0407 739 862
email: susan@naturalparenting.com.au
website: www.naturalparenting.com.au

www.naturalparenting.com.au is a comprehensive online resource offering well researched articles on pregnancy, birth, babies and parenting. Access to all content is free of charge and includes many controversial topics and information not easily found elsewhere. The site also offers a popular forum where members can enjoy the support and company of a like-minded parenting community.

Natural Parenting Tips
Tel: (08) 9206 1275
email: kiera@naturalparentingtips.com
website: www.naturalparentingtips.com

Natural Parenting Tips is your resource for gentle discipline ideas, recipes, resources, and creative play ideas for infants and toddlers. Updated daily with new articles and resources check out www.naturalparentingtips.com.

Parent Wellbeing
Tel: (08) 8278 4342
email: info@parentwellbeing.com
website: www.parentwellbeing.com

All parents want the best for their children and want to raise happy, healthy, successful children. But how can parents help their children embrace and succeed in life? Jodie Benveniste believes it begins with their own wellbeing – happy, healthy parents raise happy, healthy children. Parent Wellbeing is an online resource that helps parents increase their wellbeing so parents and children benefit.

Pinky McKay
Tel: (03) 9801 1997
website: www.pinkymckay.com.au

Pinky offers gentle solutions to sleep and settling, breastfeeding education and support and infant massage classes. Her website, My Child, offers a wealth of information and support for gentle parenting options, including articles, a forum, comprehensive links to pregnancy, birth, health and nurturing sites, as well as details of Pinky's services,which include Preparation For Breastfeeding sessions for pregnant parents. You can order Pinky's books and DVDs via her website.

Preschool Entertainment
Tel: (02) 4977 1079
website: www.preschoolentertainment.com

Preschool Entertainment is a free site for parents of children aged six months to six years and explores the educational and entertainment value of products aimed at this age group. There is also a free ezine, regular give-aways, discussion board, interviews, news and more.

Raising Children Network
email: info@raisingchildren.net.au
website: www.raisingchildren.net.au

www.raisingchildren.net.au is Australia's first national quality-assured parenting website, covering all the basics about raising children 0 to 8 years. Features include: 50 film clips including a breastfeeding demonstration, parents tips on sleep and settling, and safety and CPR information; interactive maps showing local services and community resources; baby karaoke featuring favourite children's songs; Parenting in Pictures (visual guides for essential parenting skills); and access to the Raising Children DVD. Supported by Australian Government and quality-assured by experts.

Real Mums
Tel: 0414 548 103
email: admin@realmums.com.au
website: www.realmums.com.au

www.realmums.com.au is a new and unique website that explores what it means to be a real mum in Australia today. The site embraces the fact that women are not 'just mums' but are individuals in their own right. The 'real mums' behind the site are fun, funny and just a little bit naughty.

Smart-Mums
Tel: 0417 892 155
email: shelley@smart-mums.com.au
website: www.smart-mums.com.au

www.smart-mums.com.au is a quick, easy-to-use website for busy Australian mums, grandparents and carers. It provides parenting and lifestyle articles, quick links to informative and relevant websites, a fantastic shopping directory, healthy recipes as well as great competitions. Everything is in the one location – whether you need to help the children with their homework, send a gift, organise the family holiday or cook a quick nutritious meal – save time and do it online.

Resources

PREGNANCY: THE FIRST NINE MONTHS

Websites: pregnancy & general parenting
➦ Women's health & wellbeing

Think Twins
Tel: (03) 8802 9446
email: info@thinktwins.com.au
website: www.thinktwins.com.au

Think Twins is Australia's biggest online store for families with twins, triplets and more. Whether it's finding a birthday gift or accessing a terrific range of articles and resources including a huge range of twin-specific books for parents and children, Think Twins will make life as a parent of twins a little easier. Phone the number above or visit the website for more information.

www.happychild.com.au
Tel: (02) 9889 0999
email: publisher@happychild.com.au
website: www.happychild.com.au

This Australian website keeps you informed about the latest parenting advice and best parenting books. www.happychild.com.au is a quality website with no membership fees, a free newsletter guaranteeing you don't miss new information, and friendly online forums to connect you with other parents. Interactive features such as forums, polls, blogs and book reviews allow you to use the website to suit your family's needs. Specialising in the social and emotional development of children, www.happychild.com.au helps parents raise happy, successful kids.

www.ninemonths.com.au
Tel: (03) 9569 3938
email: services@ninemonths.com.au
website: www.ninemonths.com.au

Ninemonths.com.au is an online Australian guide to pregnancy, birth and life. Special features include a comprehensive resource centre, weekly baby email, parents forum and database of 30,000 baby names.

Young Mums Online
Tel: 0431 173 053
email: admin@youngmumsonline.com
website: www.youngmumsonline.com

Young Mums Online is an online community dedicated to young parents around Australia. YMO is designed to be a non-judgemental environment where new or young mothers won't feel silly asking questions and/or giving advice. Visit the website for further details.

WOMEN'S HEALTH & WELLBEING: PREGNANCY

NATIONAL

Ahava Dead Sea Skincare
Tel: 0402 033 382
email: info@deadsea.com.au
website: www.deadsea.com.au

Ahava Dead Sea mineral products are now available online. These affordable professional products have ingredients from the Dead Sea to help skin conditions like eczema, dermatitis and dry skin, as well as ranges for normal skin, ageing skin, sensitive skin and men. There are face, body and home spa products available for delivery anywhere in Australia. You can fill out the online skin analysis form for professional advice and samples. www.deadsea.com.au are the only authorised online seller of Ahava Dead Sea mineral products. Phone or visit the website for more information.

Aromababy Natural Skincare
Tel: (03) 9464 0888
email: info@aromababy.com
website: www.aromababy.com

New from Aromababy the organic Essentials for pregnancy, labour and postnatal use. Choose from a selection of exquisite organic massage/bath oil blends formulated using a base of pesticide-free pure, cold pressed sweet almond oil. Each product contains added natural gm free vitamin E and nourishing oils such as organic rosehip, calendula and evening primrose. This range includes the luscious Stretched to the Limit (also available in a rich cream) body oil, ideal to help skin maintain its elasticity pre/post baby, On the Run to help relieve tired, aching legs and Pure Love to uplift and energise during labour and postnatally. Visit www.aromababy.com for stockists or to order online.

Aspen Pharmacare Pty Ltd
Tel: (02) 8436 8300
email: sales@aspenpharmacare.com.au
website: www.aspenpharmacare.com.au

Heartburn and indigestion can be a real problem during pregnancy. Thankfully there is an effective antacid remedy called Andrews* TUMS* which can do much to relieve these symptoms. Andrews* TUMS* contains calcium carbonate so it works fast to alleviate heartburn and indigestion. And it provides important calcium for normal growth and development of the skeleton. It's aluminium and magnesium free and comes in great tasting chewable tablets.
Always read the label. Use only as directed. If symptoms persist see your doctor.

Bayer Consumer Healthcare
Tel: (02) 9391 6000

Elevit* is based on the only pregnancy supplement proven in a clinical trial to reduce the risk of neural tube defects, such as spina bifida, by 92%[1]. Just one tablet of

Elevit contains more folic acid, 800ug, and iron, 60mg, in combination than any other pregnancy supplement. Elevit should be taken at least one month before falling pregnant, throughout your pregnancy and while breastfeeding. Elevit is only available in pharmacy. For more information visit www.elevit.com.au.

Always read the label. Use only as directed.

The Australian formulation of Elevit is the same as that used in the Czeizel study except that it does not contain vitamin A. [1] Czeizel A.E. Paed Drugs 2000; 2(6): 437-49.

Bellamy's Organic

Tel: 1800 010 460
email: sales@bellamysorganic.com.au
website: www.bellamysorganic.com.au

Bellamy's Organic produce a range of organic snackfoods which are particularly good for mums-to-be. They use only 100% Australian grown organic ingredients, free from any synthetic fertilisers, pesticides or GMOs. Bellamy's Organic product range is gently processed without the addition of processing aids, additives or preservatives. Great foods to nurture both mum and baby.

Belli Skin Care Australia

PO Box 2044
Clovelly NSW 2031
Tel: 1300 884 916
email: sales@hotmama.com.au
website: www.belliskincare.com.au

Experience total pampering for your body and mind with Belli Pregnancy. Indulge and soothe your skin with luxurious formulations created specifically for pregnant mothers. Belli Pregnancy is the only line in the world that teratology screens each ingredient to help you guard against chemicals. Every product is allergy tested and free of artificial dyes and parabens. Visit www.belliskincare.com.au for more information.

Blackmores

Tel: 1800 803 760 tollfree Advisory Service
website: www.blackmores.com.au

Because pregnancy and breastfeeding bring specific nutritional needs, Blackmores makes a Pregnancy & Breast-Feeding Gold Formula to help both you and your baby through this special period of your life. Just two capsules a day provide 250 µg of iodine, a nutrient essential for the development of your baby's brain, hearing and eyesight, plus 16 other essential nutrients including folic acid, iron, calcium, vitamin D3, and omega-3 fatty acids. For free advice from Blackmores naturopaths phone 1800 803 760 or visit their website at www.blackmores.com.au/pregnancy.

Always read the label. Use only as directed.

CHC 36211-10/06

Blackmores

Tel: 1800 803 760 tollfree Advisory Service
website: www.blackmores.com.au

Blackmores CONCEIVE WELL™ GOLD has been specially formulated to prepare the body for conception.

Blackmores CONCEIVE WELL™ GOLD supplies nutrients associated with healthy ovulation and normal conception, helps protect the female reproductive system from free radical damage, and supplies nutrients needed for hormone production. For free advice from Blackmores naturopaths phone 1800 803 760 or visit their website at www.blackmores.com.au/pregnancy.

Always read the label. Use only as directed.

CHC 36964-07/07

Floradix

Tel: (02) 9499 7023
email: sales@cornell.com.au

FLORADIX is an easily absorbed form of iron balanced with a range of B Vitamins (B1, B2, B6 and B12) and Vitamin C, as well as other herbal extracts to fortify the body. Taken twice daily, FLORADIX can assist in the health of the whole family. FLORADIX is well tolerated and helps maintain vitality, energy, stamina, fitness and general good health. FLORADIX can provide iron at times when the requirement is particularly high, eg. during pregnancy and when breastfeeding (lactation). FLORADIX is a source of iron and can assist in maintaining normal blood and is excellent during convalescence and helpful for athletes to replenish iron stores in blood and muscle.

Always read the label. Use only as directed.

House of Camylle

Tel: 0416 806 655
email: sales@houseofcamylle.com.au
website: www.houseofcamylle.com.au

Relaxation is important for you and your baby. House of Camylle sells a complete range of relaxation products online – quality products to cater for all your personal relaxation needs and a range of unique gift ideas.

Kimberly-Clark Australia – Poise

Tel: 1800 028 334
website: www.poise.com.au

Pregnancy and childbirth may cause pelvic floor muscles to become weak. For pregnant women, doing pelvic floor exercises helps the body to cope with the increasing weight of the baby. If your pelvic floor muscles are healthy, fit and strong prior to giving birth, chances are your muscles will recover back to normal after giving birth. Visit www.poise.com.au for hints and tips on how to identify and exercise your pelvic floor muscles and for information on how to best manage slight bladder loss.

Made By Mums

Tel: 0411 018 245 or (03) 9827 4770
email: info@madebymums.com.au
website: www.madebymums.com.au

Made by Mums' organic teas for pregnancy, postnatal and lactation are specially blended for your needs during the various stages of pregnancy and childrearing. Caffeine free, organic certified and great tasting. Available in resealable foil packs for freshness. Phone or visit the website for more information.

Resources

PREGNANCY: THE FIRST NINE MONTHS
Women's health & wellbeing

National Prescribing Service
Tel: 1300 888 763
email: info@nps.org.au
website: www.nps.org.au

NPS Medicines Line is a national telephone service providing Australians with confidential, independent information about prescription medicines, over-the-counter medicines and herbal and natural remedies. Medicines Line pharmacists can advise how medicines work; how to take medicines; doses; side effects; interactions with other medicines; medicines during pregnancy and breastfeeding; medicines for children and storage. Medicines Line is available from 9.00am to 6.00pm EST Monday to Friday for the cost of a local call (calls from mobiles may cost more).

Pelvic Floor Exercise
Tel: 1300 763 940
email: info@pelvicfloorexercise.com.au
website: www.pelvicfloorexercise.com.au

Pelvic Floor Exercise is Australia's specialist pelvic floor shop, packed with quality products for strengthening the pelvic floor muscles. This online shop offers books, DVDs and CDs, gymballs, and other exercise aids perfect for use during pregnancy. For postnatal use, you'll find feedback exercisers, vaginal cones and electrical stimulation devices recommended by health professionals, yet easy to use at home. Phone for a brochure or visit their website for everything you need to know about strengthening your pelvic floor, plus up-to-date research and links.

Perfect Potion
Tel: 1800 988 999
email: customerservice@perfectpotion.com.au
website: www.perfectpotion.com.au

Perfect Potion provides you with certified natural and certified organic products including a large range of pure, natural and safe skincare and bodycare products for mums during pregnancy and for newborn babies. The Beautiful Baby range is made with the purest essential oils and gentle plant extracts to caress, soothe and pamper your baby's every need. Using Perfect Potion's aromatherapy products during the birthing process is a wonderful way to create a calming atmosphere that comforts and nurtures new mothers, helping to ease pain, maintain focus and sustain motivation.

Philips AVENT
Tel: 1300 364 474
email: inquiry@avent.com.au
website: www.avent.com.au

The Philips Avent Future Mother Skincare range is specifically designed for mothers-to-be. Made with a combination of marine extracts, minerals, vitamins, amino acids and plant extracts, the Avent products were developed to nurture the future mother during pregnancy and beyond. Future Mother skincare consists of four products: an indulgent body cream, a leg and foot reviver, a relaxing bath and shower essence and a lightly absorbed oil to combat the effects of dry skin and stretchmarks. Available individually or as a pack in travel sizes from leading pharmacies and specialist baby outlets.

Poisons Information Centre
Tel: 13 11 26
Victorian Poisons Information Centre:
www.austin.org.au/poisons
NSW Poisons Information Centre:
www.chw.edu.au/parents/factsheets/safpoisj.htm
QLD Poisons Information Centre:
www.health.qld.gov.au/PoisonsInformationCentre/
WA Poisons Information Centre:
www.scgh.health.wa.gov.au/departments/wapic/index.html

Poisons Information Centre provides telephone advice to callers needing information about first aid for poisoning, bites, stings, mistakes with medicines and poisoning prevention. The service is available 24-hours a day, seven days a week. If you or someone in your care has been poisoned, ring the Poisons Information Centre to find out what to do next. The advice is up-to-date unlike many books and charts and you may avoid an unnecessary trip to the doctor or hospital.

Pure Spa®
Tel: (03) 9464 0888
email: info@purespa.com.au
website: www.purespa.com.au

Pure Spa® offers pure and natural, organic-rich products formulated by a leading Melbourne natural therapist. Up to 99% certified organic ingredients have been combined to provide the purest solution to all your and your baby's skincare needs. Used in select hospitals, naturally Pure Spa® is free from mineral oil, cocoamphodiacetate, parabens and sulphate. Eczema-friendly and suitable for sensitive skin, Pure Spa offers a specialist product that won't cost the earth. Go ahead and pamper yourself. Available online at www.purespa.com.au or from select baby boutiques, pharmacies and online stores.

The Kinder Kompany Pty Ltd
Tel: 1300 661 060
email: info@kinderkot.com.au
website: www.kinderkot.com.au

In the event of a car collision an adult is thrown forward with a force of 3 to 5 tons. When pregnant the car's hip belt which lies across the stomach can hurt the unborn baby, or even cause miscarriage. BeSafe Pregnant is a simple belt system which is used together with the car's seatbelt. It keeps the hip belt low across the hips and prevents it from sliding up on the tummy thereby protecting the unborn baby. It is recommended to use the BeSafe Pregnant from the second month of pregnancy. BeSafe Pregnant is available through selected retailers and online. For your nearest retailer visit www.kinderkot.com.au/besafe/.

VICTORIA

PANDA
810 Nicholson Street
North Fitzroy VIC 3068
Tel: Phone support: 1300 726 306; Admin (03) 9481 3377
email: info@panda.org.au
website: www.panda.org.au

PANDA is a statewide, not-for-profit organisation for women and families affected by postnatal and antenatal depression in Victoria. PANDA acknowledges that social, biological and psychological factors play a role in postnatal and antenatal depression. PANDA works to: support and inform women and their families who are affected by postnatal and antenatal mood disorders; and educate health care professionals and the wider community about postnatal and antenatal mood disorders. PANDA runs a support, information and referral helpline which is staffed by specially trained volunteers and staff, many of whom have experienced postnatal or antenatal depression.

BellyBelly Pregnancy Centre
Level 1, 89 Canterbury Road
Canterbury VIC 3126
Tel: (03) 9836 7734
website: www.bellybelly.com.au/pregnancy-centre

At the BellyBelly Pregnancy Centre you're in safe hands during conception, pregnancy and into parenthood. The centre offers a range of services including natural health therapies, informative and empowering workshops and education, as well as products and services available for sale. Therapists – including osteopaths, massage therapists, acupuncturists, a counsellor, naturopaths and others – are passionate and experienced about pre-conception and pre and postnatal care. Books, DVDs and other products are carefully selected to ensure you get great information and products helping you to have a safe, informed and educated journey.

Women's Health Information Centre (WHIC)
Corner Flemngton Road & Grattan Street
Carlton VIC 3053
Tel: (03) 8345 3045, 1800 442 007 country callers
email: whic@thewomens.org.au
website: www.thewomens.org.au

The Women's Health Information Centre is a free confidential statewide health service offering information, individualised support and referral options on a wide range of women's health issues. The experienced women's health nurses and midwives are available by telephone, email or visit the centre for one-on-one support.

QUEENSLAND

Mater Health & Wellness Clinic
550 Stanley Street
South Brisbane QLD 4101
Tel: (07) 3010 5744
website: www.wellnessclinic.mater.org.au

The Mater Health & Wellness Clinic provides access to a team of leading allied health specialists who work together with clients, parents, their children and the greater medical community to provide individual treatment programs to ensure optimal health and wellness. Specialised services include nutrition counselling, physiotherapy, speech pathology, occupational therapy, psychology, counselling and massage. A range of services are offered for children as well as adults, including a focus on women's health and maternity services. Visit their website for individual service and clinician details.

Women's Health Queensland Wide
165 Gregory Terrace
Spring Hill QLD 4000
Tel: (07) 3839 9962
Health Information Line (07) 3839 9988
Toll Free outside Brisbane 1800 017 676
TTY (07) 3831 5508
email: admin@womhealth.org.au
website: www.womhealth.org.au

Women's Health Queensland Wide is a non-profit health promotion service providing information and education services to women and health workers throughout the state. Services include a Health Information Line staffed by registered nurses and midwives, library services, fact sheets and quarterly publication, as well as a website and health education programs. Women can contact the service for information on a wide range of topics including pregnancy, childbirth, breastfeeding, early childhood and postnatal depression. Phone or visit the website for more information.

EGG Maternity

Summer or winter, spring or autumn, no matter what your style or budget – conservative through to high fashion, simple to extravagant – EGG designs and produces 7 quality, stylish apparel and accessory ranges for women to wear during their nine months of pregnancy and beyond.

EGG Classic features the best selling, timeless pregnancy shapes updated each season to reflect the trends – perfect for the working mother-to-be.

Chic by EGG is a diffusion value line featuring fun, accessible items in contemporary styles and colours.

EGG Organic is a capsule wardrobe of 100% pure organic cotton pieces for expectant mums who want to look fabulous and care for the environment.

Charlotte Devereux for EGG is all about Goddess Luxe. Sumptuous light silks and gorgeous fine knits are perfect for special occasions or any time a woman wants to feel like a goddess.

EGGShell is an infant range of essential pieces in soft organic cotton.

EGG Basics is available year round and has the full range of wardrobe staples on which to build your pregnancy wardrobe – jeans, tee's, dresses, pants, exercise wear, swimwear, nightwear, underwear, breastfeeding bras and tops, tummy supports, hosiery and more.

EGG for all Seasons is all about taking you from summer to winter and back – trans-seasonal garments you can layer up or mix and match to maximise your pregnancy wardrobe.

New for 2009 is EGG Essential Care bath and beauty range. Personal care products that harness the aromatherapy and cosmetic benefits of lavender, tangerine and organic rosehip oil, all proven to be beneficial during pregnancy.

Up the Duff

The one, the only brilliant Aussie bible on being 'up the duff'. Kaz gives you the up-to-date lowdown on pregnancy, birth and coping when you get home. No bossy boots rules. Just lots of cartoons and the soundest, sanest, wittiest advice you'll ever get. Everything you need to know about the scary parts, the funny parts and your private parts.

Week by week: what's happening to you and the baby – Hermoine the Modern Girl's funny and useful pregnancy diary.

Also: how to prepare for pregnancy and trying to conceive, including IVF, and all the latest info on new medical advances and tests: what they're like and why you have them; finding your birth team; giving birth and the debate on "natural vs medical" approaches, and the rest: crying eating, weeing and working; blokes, bosoms, busybodies and bunny rugs; nausea and other 'side effects'; choosing an obstetrician and a midwife; the best services and books on everything; stretchmarks; maternity and baby clothes; childbirth classes, travel, safety, baby names and how to be rude to complete strangers; what to expect in hospital; breastfeeding, post-baby body image and sex life, and what it's like with a newborn baby.

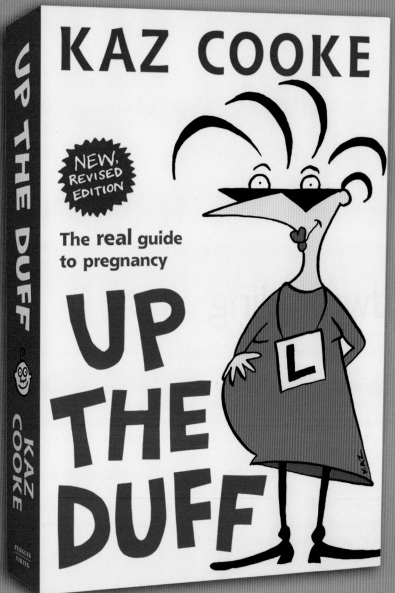

Kidwrangling

Now you have a baby, what on earth are you going to do with it? Kaz Cooke delivers all the up-to-date, reliable info, with advice from the experts, including real mums and dads.

Kidwrangling is funny, reassuring and practical, with no judgemental guruspeak about the right way to do things – just a range of great solutions for you to choose from.

Babies: getting through the first weeks • bosoms • bottles • sleeping • crying • coping • new mum & newborn health • bonding • the blues • mum's post-baby body • equipment • first food • teething • dummies

Toddlers and Preschoolers: using the loo • family food • teaching kids how to behave • child care • dealing with common illnesses • exercise • getting ready for school

Plus: emotional and physical development 0 to 5 • immunisation • safety • what dads need to know • birthday parties & presents • being at home • paid work • travel • best-ever lists of where to go for extra help • games, toys & activities & much more.

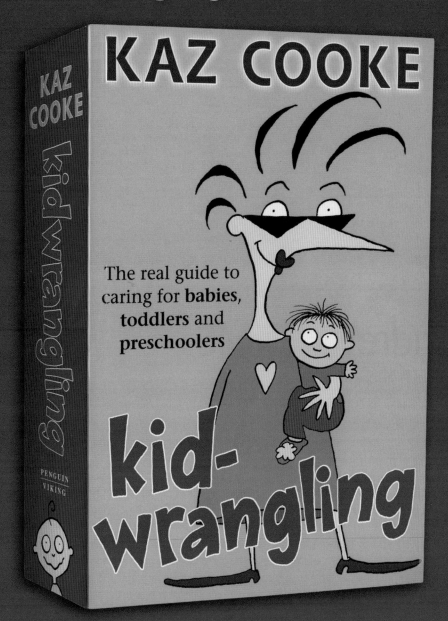

Andrews TUMS

Heartburn, indigestion, upset stomachs and discomfort after eating may occur when your stomach produces too much acid. Symptoms of heartburn and indigestion can be very distressing and debilitating for sufferers, especially for women who are pregnant and unable to use most heartburn remedies. It is sometimes during pregnancy that gastro-oesophageal reflux and heartburn is experienced for the first time.

Thankfully, there is an effective antacid remedy called Andrews* TUMS* which can do much to relieve these symptoms. Andrews TUMS Antacid tablets provide fast relief of heartburn and indigestion, by effectively neutralizing the stomach acid that causes these symptoms.

Andrews TUMS can also be used as a daily source of extra calcium as it contains calcium carbonate. It works by treating symptoms with something your body needs anyway – calcium – which is important to protect bones and can help in the prevention of osteoporosis in later life.

Aluminium and magnesium free, it is suitable to use in pregnancy from the fourth month onwards. Andrews TUMS is available in convenient, great tasting chewable orange tablets, available in supermarkets and pharmacies.

Always read the label. Use only as directed. If symptoms persist see your healthcare professional.

*Trademark of GlaxoSmithKline group of companies
ASMI/15763-10/08

TUMS* FOR MUMS

Fast[1] heartburn relief, with all the goodness of calcium for mums to be.

If heartburn and indigestion affect your life as a mum to be[2] then 'TUMS* for MUMS' is the antacid for you. Each calcium-rich chewable tablet is an excellent antacid for both pregnant mums and women in general. What's more, it contains no aluminium or magnesium, so TUMS* is gentle on the stomach and just right for mums to be.

TUMS* FOR MUMS

Robin Barker

Robin Barker has over thirty years' experience in the early childhood world. Her expert advice, wisdom, humour and sheer commonsense will keep you sane and smiling throughout the wonderful years with your child. Robin's books *Baby Love* and *The Mighty Toddler*, continue to be seen as essential reading for any parent and have been updated to provide the most current information on raising your child.

Baby Love is the only book you'll need to guide you through your baby's first year. Australia's bestselling babycare book is loved by thousands of new parents every year. With expert advice for the first twelve months of every baby's life and full of Robin Barker's wisdom and humour, this classic guide has been fully revised, including new material on nutrition, food allergy and intolerance, and updates on safe sleeping, breastfeeding, 'reflux' and immunisation.

Practical and essential, *The Mighty Toddler* includes key milestones for each age group; a complete ABC of toddler behaviour and responses; a guide to day-to-day toddler care; explanations about toddler health, medical conditions and illnesses; and Robin's down-to-earth advice on how to keep your life on track! Recently revised to include up-to-date information about immunisation, food allergies and intolerances, and 'sleep', *The Mighty Toddler* is the most comprehensive guide available to Australian parents.

Together these books have continued to provide mothers across the world with practical and reassuring advice on raising their children. They are an absolute must for any new parent. Robin's advice has helped generations of parents and the revised and updated editions of this book prove that Robin is still regarded as the most widely read and trusted authority on helping parents and children grow to be the best they can be.

ROBIN BARKER

BABY LOVE AND **THE MIGHTY TODDLER**
ARE THE ONLY BOOKS YOU'LL NEED TO GUIDE
YOU THROUGH YOUR BABY'S FIRST FEW YEARS

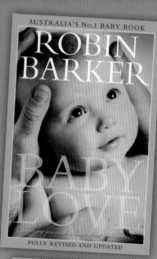

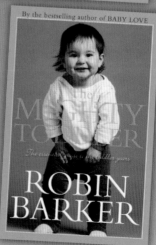

AVAILABLE NOW WHERE ALL GREAT BOOKS ARE SOLD

Beyond Baby

Beyond Baby is a new DVD label specialising in parenting DVDs, proudly Australian and made by real mums and dads. They were created by mums and dads who were frustrated by the lack of visual aids available in parenting and they are the perfect survival guide for any first-time parent and make ideal gifts for parents to be.

Titles available:

Certified Infant Massage Instructor, Internationally Certified Lactation Consultant (IBCLC), mother of five and respected baby care author, Pinky McKay will show you how to calm and connect with your baby as you follow her simple step-by-step instructions. *Pinky McKay's Baby Massage* covers the complete baby massage, mini massage, safety issues and much more.

Being Dad DVD provides inspiration and information for dads-to-be. A sneak peek into pregnancy from a guy's point of view, *Pregnancy & Birth* DVD uncovers the mysteries of pregnancy and birth – this is a ground-breaking, hilarious and emotional documentary film. *Being Dad 2* DVD provides inspiration and information for new dads; it's a sneak peek into parenthood from a guy's perspective. This DVD follows six first-time dads and their families as they cope with the whirlwind experience of bringing the baby home all the way through to raising two year olds.

Mum to Mum has created five DVDs which will help you prepare for, and then look after, your baby. DVD 1 – *Preparing to Bring Home Your Baby*; DVD 2 – *Caring for Your Baby (in the first 3 months)*; DVD 3 – *Caring for Your Baby 3 to 6 months*; DVD 4 – *Caring for your Baby 6 to 12 months*; and DVD 5 – *Caring for your toddler 1 to 2 years*.

For more information on Beyond Baby's range of ultimate baby survival guides on DVD please visit our website www.beyondhomeentertainment.com.au.

BEYOND BABY

Your Ultimate Baby Survival Guides on DVD

Mum To Mum Vol 1 – 5

The complete visual guide by real mums for real mums.

This series of "How To Guides" covers every stage of caring for your new baby that will empower first time parents. The DVD's feature interviews with mums and experts in all fields including nutrition, psychology and pets. Great handy tips also included.

Collect all 5 volumes!
For stockists visit **www.mumtomumdvd.com.au**

Being Dad 1 & 2

Ever wondered what men are REALLY thinking about pregnancy?

Being Dad is a collection of two DVD's that covers the pregnancy through to bringing the baby home. This hilarious and insightful DVD follows six Aussie Dads and their families as they cope with the whirlwind experience.

Features include interviews with a world class psychologist, paediatrician, financial planners, sleep expert, safety expert and a dads groups' advice on a range of topics.

For stockists visit **www.beingdad.com.au**

Pinky McKay's Baby Massage

Pinky McKay, mother of five and author of Sleeping Like a Baby, Toddler Tactics and 100 Ways to Calm the Crying, has released her very first DVD, Pinky McKay's Baby Massage.

Baby Massage is proven to help your baby be smarter, happier and to sleep better. Certified Infant Massage Instructor, Internationally Certified Lactation Consultant, Pinky McKay will show you how to calm and connect with your baby as you follow her step by step instructions. This DVD covers the complete baby massage, mini massage, safety issues and much more.

For more information visit **www.pinkymckay.com.au**

DK Books

DK's comprehensive range of pregnancy and parenting titles have been helping to guide parents around the world for more than 30 years. From conception and birth, through to the teenage years, DK offers a range of books with practical and proven advice from names you can trust – including Su Laurent, Lesley Regan and Miriam Stoppard, whose bestselling *Conception, Pregnancy and Birth* has helped more than a million women through the first stages of motherhood.

For more information about the DK range of parenting titles visit www.dk.com.au/parenting.

Everything you'll ever need to know about
pregnancy, birth and childcare

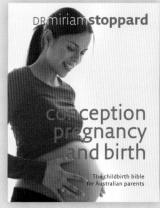

Dr Miriam Stoppard's helpful guidance provides all the information you'll need while you're expecting: from advice on antenatal care and the latest obstetric procedures to tips on nutrition and exercise

Expert advice and clear step-by-step photographs demonstrate the correct procedure for every childhood emergency

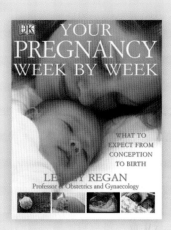
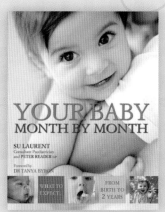

Full of practical information about what to expect and how to influence your baby and toddler's development every step of the way

look inside the books at **dk.com.au/parenting**

Floradix

FLORADIX is an easily absorbed form of iron balanced with a range of B Vitamins (B1, B2, B6 and B12) and Vitamin C, as well as other herbal extracts to fortify the body. Taken twice daily, FLORADIX can assist in the health of the whole family. FLORADIX is well tolerated and helps maintain vitality, energy, stamina, fitness and general good health. FLORADIX can provide iron at times when the requirement is particularly high, e.g. during pregnancy and when breastfeeding (lactation). FLORADIX is a source of iron and can assist in maintaining normal blood and is excellent during convalescence and helpful for athletes to replenish iron stores in blood and muscle.

Floradix is just one of the many natural products made by Salus, a family-run Bavarian company. Salus prides itself on cultivating and growing the very finest, purest herbs and fruits, gathering them from all over the world to create an outstanding range of supplements designed to promote good health and good living the natural way.

Salus has a global policy of environmental consciousness, and co-operates with countries worldwide to promote sustainable farming which benefits local people and contributes to a healthier, safer environment.

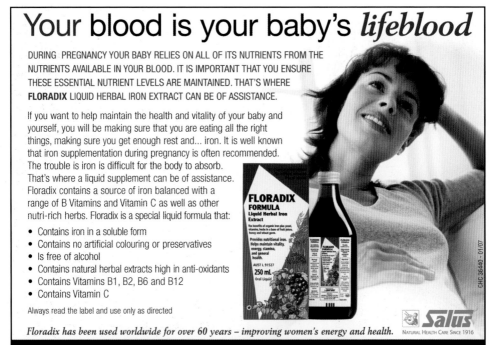

Bambini Pronto

Bambini Pronto has been recognised as the 'Best Online Small Business in Australia' and has been awarded the National Small Business Champion Award.

Bambini Pronto is an online store that produces a unique catalogue specializing in exclusive products for maternity, newborns and toddlers. Winning the National Award highlights Bambini Pronto's fast growing success that has made it a household name within Australian families.

Bambini Pronto thrives on superb customer service whilst sourcing innovative products from around the world before delivering them to Australian families in a fast and friendly way. "Our team all work towards this on a daily basis, so it's wonderful to receive this award in recognition of our hard work and careful product selection," said Julie DeSilva, Director.

Bambini Pronto have recently added a wish list capability to their site which allows people to create their own wish list and allow friends and family to access this when they are deciding what might be the perfect gift for baby showers, birthdays and Christmas.

Go online to request the beautiful FREE catalogue and bring the best to your family – fast!

WEB: www.bambinipronto.com.au PH: 1800 777 107

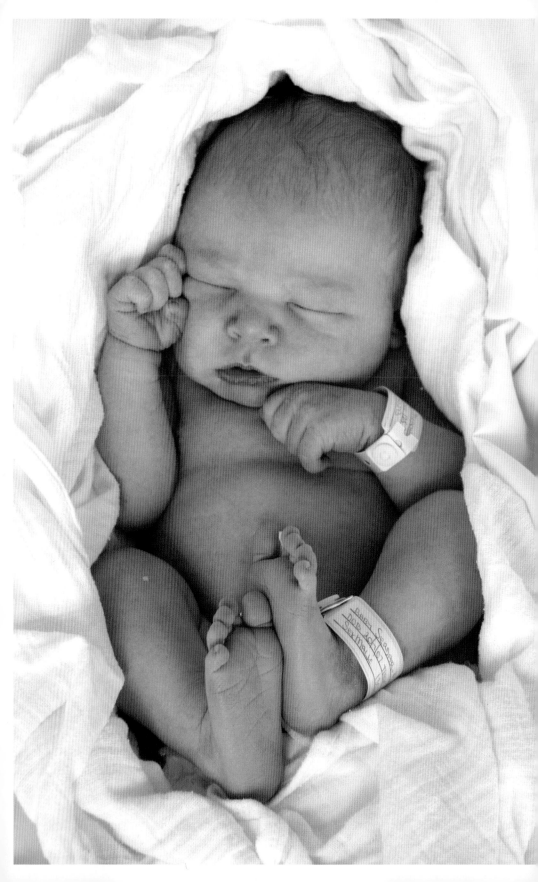

Childbirth & postnatal services

Photograph by Appleseed Photography, Adelaide.

Childbirth: an inspiring adventure

Just for a moment, think of all the things that you have learned in your life so far. You could identify many thousands of physical, psychological, emotional, intellectual and social skills, facts and behaviours that have helped you through life – but dealing with childbirth wasn't one of them. So here you are – the accomplished, intelligent, mature and capable individual that you have become, and yet with all those years and opportunities of learning, nothing and no-one has taught you about one of the greatest challenges (and adventures) you will ever face in your life: your own childbirth experience. Is it any wonder you are scared? Is it any wonder so many of you say "I want the baby, but I don't want the labour and I certainly don't want the pain!" Is it any wonder that so many are deciding upon epidurals and caesareans in the early weeks of pregnancy? So many women today don't even wish to give labour a try.

How is it possible to put into the too-hard-basket an activity that women have been doing for thousands of years? An activity that we as women are specifically designed to do? It's worth pondering over the fact that with human intellectual supremacy, increasingly civilised and sophisticated lifestyles and the drive for overall control and command, we seem to have lost our belief in our ability to actually endure the act of childbirth; perhaps more deeply embedded in our psyche is the fact that in modern life, pain has no place in our value system.

Medical choice and support is vital in our modern and civilised world. The health and safety of mother and baby is paramount and should never be compromised. But it is possible – with comprehensive preparation including knowledge of the birth process, realistic labour skills acquisition, insight into your partner's role and the development of courage and confidence – to actually look forward to labour with excitement, enthusiasm, curiosity and a spirit of adventure, whether or not you have chosen medical pain relief.

The first fact you need to understand is that the pain associated with contractions is normal and healthy. For most women it builds up slowly from mild period-like pain to a very intense sensation. It's a bit like your body ringing a bell (albeit a painful bell) each time labour work is to be done. Mostly, that 'contraction bell' lasts for only sixty seconds, and then there is a pain-free rest period in between. Remember, the pain is healthy pain (as opposed to sickness, disease or traumatic or injury pain) and so it is feasible that you can have a healthy response.

A drug-free birth is not possible for everyone, and it is not what everyone wants. But if you do want to give it a try, it is a matter of 'ordinary people', for a few hours, doing a few 'extraordinary' things. In one of my preparation sessions we actually practise labour management in the lift, the stairwell, the carpark, the mall and the street. Brilliant for breaking down those inhibitions!

Women today are strongly conditioned to be pleasant, polite, compassionate, and charming. Is it possible for you to let go of these things for just a few hours? Two of the most articulated fears that labouring women lament over are creating a disturbance to the woman in the next room in labour and upsetting and embarrassing their partner with their coping techniques. Should we criticise these two fears? Absolutely not. They are both quite normal. Social conditioning is both powerful and automatic, inbuilt and hard to stop … but you can suspend it for the few hours that you need when it will not be helpful.

Working towards a natural birth, or simply 'giving it a go' using a combination of both human resources and medical resources, involves decision, commitment, conviction and an openness to accept whatever plan B or plan C holds for you if things don't go exactly as planned. Get yourself fit with walking, yoga, pilates, swimming or any physical activity that appeals to you. Do some research to find the antenatal class that best suits your needs and read books that are relevant to birth in Australia.

Sometimes it is said that there is too much focus on the birth and not enough on being a parent. It is actually impossible to see beyond the birth until you have passed through the experience. It is fair to say that the childbirth experience is less than one day for most women, and yet parenting goes on for years. After the birth take each day as it comes, for it too is an adventure all of its own!

Photograph by Appleseed Photography, Adelaide.

A useful way to approach the first stage of labour

This is when the cervix is opening from 0 to 10 centimetres and is usually the longest part of labour:

- Mobilise your own in-built pain relieving chemistry to dull the sensations with your endorphin production. Everyone has the potential to do this simply by being active.
- Deal with the by-product of the painful contractions with your stress management techniques. You will learn these at antenatal classes.
- Influence the efficiency of contractions as they dilate the cervix, rotate the baby and help the baby descend, with your proactivity and use of gravity.
- Make a decision to 'step outside of the box' of your normal ego boundaries of comfortable behaviour. Have the courage and confidence to tread into territory you have not been to before. You cannot deal with labour pain with your normal day-to-day behaviour. You can deal with labour pain, however, with increasingly powerful labour behaviour that you will learn.

Written by Juju Sundin, physiotherapist & health educator, www.jujusundin.com.

Childbirth education

There is no doubt that we limit our thoughts about birth and parenting until we find ourselves pregnant. We are a society that thrives on self-confidence and empowerment and we need to know what we are doing, what is happening to us, and where to get help if we need it. Childbirth education today has changed and our options have evolved to meet the needs of a new generation.

Adults having babies today are comfortable with emails, blogs and podcasts and have an abundance of information at their fingertips. But how do we make sense of it all? How do we: develop our skills for birth and parenting; have the confidence to make informed decisions; develop a foundation of support for after our baby arrives; and do that while we maintain our busy lifestyles?

Childbirth education starts with your caregiver. Their job is to give you information and allay your fears throughout your childbirth journey. Who you choose can impact on this. It is important to develop a rapport with your caregiver and be comfortable asking them questions while letting them know what your wants and needs are. Your options for care during pregnancy are to see your GP, be referred to an obstetrician or see a midwife – either through a hospital or at home. Some people choose a combination of doctor/midwife care (known as 'shared care').

Traditionally, we have also attended hospital-based prenatal classes for more detailed information about birth and babies. We were often supported by other pregnant families over the 5-6 weeks of classes. Now classes can be over one or two days to fit in with our busy schedules. Support can be gained through internet forums or community support groups, such as the Australian Breastfeeding Association or Multiple Births Association.

Responses from prenatal class attendees can vary from being a 'great learning experience' to 'I didn't learn anything new at all'. Time restraints often impact on what you learn in a class. Research has shown that many attendees focus on birth during prenatal classes, hence birth information tends to dominate the program. It also shows that information relating to your new baby is not retained by many attendees as they believe they can learn it after their baby arrives.

It is important therefore to get your childbirth information from a variety of means to help to fill any gaps in your learning. Your prenatal class can form the basis for your questions with your caregiver. Other forms of media from reputable authors are becoming more widely available and you can revisit the information as required.

In addition to reading books and magazines, watching and listening to podcasts and DVDs are becoming more popular. We can even download short segments onto our mobile phones to watch over and over again! Look for endorsements from midwives' associations and current Australian support groups for up-to-date information.

It is now easier than ever before to access the information you need. At the click of your mouse you can be instilled with the skills and confidence to make informed decisions regarding your birth and new baby. Try to use a combination of media and birth classes for quality information, and ask your health care provider lots of questions to become empowered and to make the choices that will best suit you, your lifestyle, and your new baby.

Written by Leanne Cummins, midwife & childbirth educator, www.birthingsense.com.

TENS pain-relief

Today we are fortunate to have many tools, both medical and natural, available to assist with pain-relief during labour. However, most women recognise the advantages of trying to avoid or delay the use of drugs during their labour. It is important to investigate your options long before your due date so that when the big day arrives, you are making an informed choice about which medical and non-drug pain-relief options might be right for you.

What is TENS?

TENS stands for Transcutaneous Electrical Nerve Stimulation. TENS produces electrical signals to stimulate nerves via self-adhesive pads which are attached to your back, releasing endorphins. Similar to the way we rub our knee after we knock it into something, TENS confuses the pain signal to the brain, and effectively lessens the pain sensation. The endorphins released also help you cope with the pain.

Advantages

TENS is used extensively in the UK, and is fast gaining in popularity here in Australia. TENS is portable, non-invasive and easy to use. It doesn't affect your mobility during labour, and the research indicates that there are no negative side effects for mother or baby. The fact that it is controlled by the labouring mother helps enhance her feelings of control during childbirth. It can be used in conjunction with other pain-relief techniques, but must be removed before using the bath or shower.

How effective is TENS?

As with other pain-relief methods, the effectiveness varies from person to person. Some mothers find that TENS provides sufficient pain-relief for the entire labour, and others may need a little more help. At the end of the day, the important thing is that mother and baby are both happy and healthy.

The research findings

Many studies have been conducted into the use of TENS during labour. A study by Kaplan et al. in 1998 concluded that TENS was effective and non-invasive. It helped reduce the duration of the first stage of labour and the amount of analgesic drug administered.

There are a variety of TENS available, so it makes sense to use a TENS that is specifically designed for use in labour. Ease of use, fewer wires, and a built-in boost button all help make life easier. Consider too how convenient it will be to hold.

Availability

TENS are available to hire or buy, at a very reasonable price, particularly when you consider the cost of some pain-relief alternatives. Ensure you have it at least 2 weeks before your due date, so it is on hand when labour starts. You can try your hospital, your physiotherapist, or search on the internet, where you can hire online and have it delivered straight to your door.

Written by Nicole Ronay Sundin, www.birthpartner.com.au.

What are some early labour signs?

If you are late in your last trimester of pregnancy, you are probably eagerly awaiting a sign that labour has begun or is imminent. So what might you notice in early labour?

Spontaneous rupture of membranes (SROM)

Commonly known as the 'breaking of the waters', this happens when the amniotic sac (which surrounds the baby) ruptures, resulting in amniotic fluid trickling or gushing from your vagina. This happens as the first sign of labour in around 15-25% of labours, so it's not as common as the TV soap operas would have you believe. You may notice a smaller gush of waters or sometimes it may be an enormous flood. Some women also notice a 'popping' sensation as their waters break.

Amniotic fluid can leak for days and even after the waters have broken, the fluid will still be replenished. If you suspect you have broken your waters, pop a pad on (do not use tampons) and call your midwife or labour ward who will ask a few questions to help determine what has happened. Sometimes it may be a bladder leak – don't feel embarrassed if this is the case as it's quite common in the latter stages of pregnancy.

Some indicators that your waters have broken are: having no control over the flow; a panty liner is inadequate to absorb the fluid; the pad is wet more than once, and it doesn't smell like urine.

Contractions

Regular contractions are a good indicator that you are in labour. Early labour contractions usually feel like period pain or you may experience a lower backache at around 20 to 30 minute intervals. Sometimes these pains may radiate from back to front or vice versa. There is no need to start timing the contractions straight away – if they are mild contractions, ignore them. If you feel there has been progress with early contractions (e.g. getting stronger, longer and closer together), time 5 contractions and see how they are panning out, then time another 5 when you feel there has been further progress.

To time your contractions, count how many seconds there are between the start and the end of the contraction. You can also time how long it is between contractions by counting how many minutes there are between the start of one contraction and the start of the next contraction.

Approximately 3-5 minutes apart and roughly a minute long are good signs that you are in labour. Labour contractions can start off coming at irregular intervals but usually become more regular – this is why ignoring early contractions is helpful as it avoids unnecessary disappointment and anxiety when the contractions aren't progressing as you hoped. If you are in labour, the contractions will become stronger and last longer. It is possible to experience contractions without your cervix dilating.

You may still be in pre-labour and not established labour if:

❯ Your contractions are irregular.

❯ The contractions aren't getting increasingly stronger.

❯ A change in position, massage, walking, eating or drinking relieves or stops the contractions.

❯ The contractions are short or may last several minutes.

Labour contractions will:

❯ Not stop or slow down, regardless of frequency and your activity.

❯ Be in a fairly predictable pattern (e.g. every eight minutes, although some women will have regular contractions every 5-10 minutes throughout).

- Become increasingly closer together.
- Last longer.
- Become stronger (walking usually makes them stronger).
- Build up, have a peak, then reduce.

Mucus plug

As your cervix begins to dilate (open), the thick mucus plug which sealed off your cervix during pregnancy (to prevent infection reaching the baby) may come loose and partially or wholly discharge from your vagina. It may be watery or sticky and be jelly-like in appearance, and sometimes has a brown, pink or red tinge to it. The show may occur over several days and sometimes you can lose your show up to two weeks before labour starts. Most women who do notice their show will go into labour over the following few days.

Involuntary shivering

Even if you are not cold, you may experience shivering or trembling in early labour. The same thing can happen during or after birth, and can be frightening if you aren't sure why your body is doing it. It's simply your body's way of relieving tension and often lasts only a few minutes. Try doing something relaxing like taking a warm shower, having massage or breathing deeply. Holding your breath to the count of 5 several times consecutively can stop the shivers.

Lightening

When your baby has dropped and settled deeper into your pelvis, you might notice that you can breathe a little easier than before. This happens because it relieves some pressure on your diaphragm. However, as a pay-off, you may then feel more pressure on your bladder, which means more trips to the bathroom!

Diarrhoea

In the days prior to birth, production of prostaglandin will stimulate your bowels to open more frequently. As labour approaches, you may notice diarrhoea – the body is naturally emptying the bowels to make way for baby. A very common fear is that you will open your bowels in labour, however you may find this emptying of the bowel prior to going into labour prevents that. Sometimes there can be some passing of stools during labour. Some women don't even notice as midwives quickly attend to this, however keep in mind that the midwives are used to this and it is very normal. Anxiety in labour can slow or stall contractions, so if it is of great concern to you, have a chat with your midwife.

Increased Braxton Hicks contractions

These 'practice' contractions which you may have felt during pregnancy may occur more frequently and be more intense and painful. Some women may not feel any Braxton Hicks throughout pregnancy so don't feel alarmed if you haven't. This doesn't mean labour is any further away. Remember, to distinguish Braxton Hicks from labour contractions, if they are labour contractions and not Braxton Hicks, they need to be getting stronger, more regular, closer together and they do not stop.

Written by Kelly Winder, www.bellybelly.com.au.

Routine newborn screening tests

The newborn screening test (NBST) is a government-funded program involving maternity caregivers taking a small sample of blood from newborn babies, usually by pricking their heel. The baby's blood is tested for several rare disorders that usually relate to their body possibly lacking a specific enzyme necessary for metabolism. The NBST used to be known as the Guthrie test, named in the mid 1960s when it only detected phenylketonuria. However, since the late 1970s additional tests for other disorders have been included.

The NBST is routinely performed around 3 to 5 days of age. The aim is to detect specific disorders so that treatment can commence before an affected baby shows physical signs of illness and perhaps suffers health consequences due to a late diagnosis. Metabolic disorders can be treated by either altering the baby's diet (in most cases the baby is placed on a special formula, stopping breastfeeding if doing so), and/or giving medications, depending on the disorder the baby has.

There are four main metabolic disorders commonly tested for: cystic fibrosis, galactosaemia, phenylketonuria and hypothyroidism. However, laboratories in some Australian states have extended their testing in recent years to 30 or so other rare metabolic disorders relating to protein and fat metabolism, e.g. congenital adrenal hyperplasia and maple syrup urine disease. The incidence of these other rare disorders is about 1 in 6,000 babies (or 0.00017%).

The four main rare disorders:

Cystic fibrosis (CF) is a genetically inherited disorder that causes a baby's intestines and lungs to produce very thick, tenacious mucus as well as affecting the functioning of their pancreas. The mucus in the lungs is associated with inflammation and can make the baby susceptible to frequent chest infections, requiring antibiotics. The mucus in the intestines creates problems with the baby absorbing and digesting food, slows the passing of bowel motions and the baby's pancreas is unable to produce sufficient enzymes to adequately digest food.

Cystic fibrosis affects about 1 in 2,500 babies (0.0004%) in white Caucasian populations, but is less common in Asian and black African races. The disorder can be carried by healthy parents and passed to their baby if both parents carry the gene for CF. When both parents are healthy but carry the CF gene, they have a 25% chance of having a baby who has CF, a 50% chance of having a baby who is healthy but is a carrier of the CF gene (like themselves) and a 25% chance of having a baby who is neither a carrier nor a sufferer of CF.

It is possible for parents with a family history of CF to be tested to see if they carry the CF gene. This can give them an opportunity to seek genetic counselling prior to conceiving a baby or to consider genetic tests for their baby early in the pregnancy to detect CF. If CF is detected by the newborn screening test, the baby has a DNA test to detect the CF gene as well as their sweat tested at about 6 weeks of age. These further tests can confirm whether the baby actually has the disorder, or is only a carrier of the CF gene. The aim is to start treatment for the baby before 2 months of age.

In the past, babies born with CF were not expected to live beyond teenage years. Today, with more advanced treatments and possibly the early detection of the disorder with the newborn screening test, the outlook for babies with CF has improved and many live until 40-years or older.

Galactosaemia is a very rare metabolic disorder caused by the accumulation of galactose, a sugar present in milk, breast milk and most formulas (also known as lactose). It is for this reason that babies diagnosed with galactosaemia cannot breastfeed and need to be on a milk-free diet for life.

Babies with galactosaemia generally appear well during the first 48 hours after birth. However, in later days they can suffer from severe, prolonged jaundice and infections and may be ill with vomiting and diarrhoea to the point of the disorder becoming life-threatening, until they are diagnosed and started on special milk without lactose. The aim is to start treatment as soon as the disorder is detected and before the baby becomes ill.

It is possible for children with galactosaemia to have learning difficulties and in some cases require speech therapy. The baby may also have eye problems within a few months of life (called cataracts or a clouding of the eye lens). It is for this reason that babies with galactosaemia should have their eyes tested by an Ophthalmologist, a consultant health professional who checks sight and can prescribe glasses.

Galactosaemia affects about 1 in every 40,000 babies (0.000025%). The disorder can be carried by healthy parents and passed onto their baby, if both parents carry the gene for galactosaemia. When both parents are healthy but carriers of the gene, they have a 25% chance of having a baby who has galactosaemia, a 50% chance of having a baby who is a healthy carrier of the galactosaemia gene (like themselves) and a 25% chance of having a baby who is neither a carrier nor a sufferer of galactosaemia.

It is possible for parents with a family history of galactosaemia to be tested to see if they carry the gene. This can give them the opportunity to seek genetic counselling prior to conceiving a baby or to consider genetic tests for their baby early during the pregnancy to detect galactosaemia.

Babies with galactosaemia need to be on a milk-free diet for life. This includes any type of milk, cheese, yoghurt and ice cream. Lactose can also be present in many other foods such as cereals, baked beans, canned spaghetti, lentils and chickpeas. It is for this reason that parents of children with galactosaemia often rely on the guidance and advice of a qualified dietician.

Congenital hypothyroidism (CH) in babies results from either a small, absent or poorly functioning thyroid gland, which is located in the throat. Hypothyroidism in babies is referred to as congenital because the baby is born with the disorder, rather than developing it later in life. An old term for this disorder used to be cretinism.

The thyroid gland is responsible for the overall control of the body's metabolism. If it is not functioning properly, then a baby's brain development can be slow (possibly leading to mental handicap) and physical development may be delayed (such as dwarfism) if the baby is not treated early. Congenital hypothyroidism can sometimes be inherited from both parents (who carry the CH gene, but are themselves healthy), but for some babies the cause may be unknown.

The signs of congenital hypothyroidism may not be obvious at birth. However babies with CH can sometimes have severe, prolonged jaundice, a large tongue, a hoarse cry, be lethargic and sleep for long periods and occasionally have a hernia near their belly button (although hernias can also occur in healthy babies). Damage to the brain may be permanent if babies with CH are not treated early. They are also at increased risk of hearing impairment. It is for this reason babies with CH should have their hearing checked when they are older.

Congenital hypothyroidism affects about 1 in 3,500 babies (0.00033%) and has been included with the NBST since about 1977. The test looks for a hormone called thyroid-stimulating hormone (TSH) and T4, which are not usually elevated in an affected baby's system until they are at least 24 hours old.

Routine newborn screening tests

Phenylketonuria (PKU) is a rare inherited disorder where the baby has an absence, or low level of a liver enzyme called phenylalanine hydroxylase. This enzyme is needed by the body to break down part of the protein in the diet called phenylalanine, an amino acid - one of many amino acids that make up protein. Our bodies cannot use phenylalanine until it is broken down by the phenylalanine hydroxylase enzyme to a substance called tyrosine. A lack of the phenylalanine hydroxylase enzyme causes a build up of phenylalanine to toxic concentrations in the body that can cause permanent brain damage if not treated early.

There are no obvious physical signs of PKU. Brain impairment can be prevented or reduced if the baby is placed on a special phenylalanine-free formula within the first 20 days of life. Babies with PKU are unable to breastfeed.

PKU affects about 1 in 10,000 babies (0.0001%) and can be carried by healthy parents and passed onto their baby if both parents carry the gene for PKU. When both parents are healthy but carry the PKU gene they have a 25% chance of having a baby who has PKU, a 50% chance of having a baby who is a healthy carrier of the PKU gene (like themselves) and a 25% chance of having a baby who is neither a carrier nor a sufferer of PKU. It is possible for parents with a family history of PKU to be tested to see if they carry the PKU gene. This can give them an opportunity to seek genetic counselling prior to conceiving a baby or to consider genetic tests early in the pregnancy to see if their baby has PKU.

If a baby is born with PKU, the phenylalanine starts to accumulate within hours of the birth, reaching relatively high levels within a week or so. The newborn screening test aims to detect PKU early, so an affected baby can be placed on a special phenylalanine-free formula. The baby needs to have at least 48 hours of milk feeds (breast or bottle) to increase the accuracy of the test. It is for this reason that the newborn screening test is delayed 3 to 5 days after birth. If the test is done when the baby is less than 48 hours old, it is recommended the test be repeated a few days later.

Once PKU is detected the baby should have further blood tests to confirm the diagnosis. Sometimes a baby produces low levels of phenylalanine hydroxylase, which is capable of breaking down some of the phenylalanine to tyrosine. This condition is a form of PKU called hyperphenylalaninaemia but still requires some dietary modification. However, the health risks to the baby are not as severe.

Babies with PKU need to be on a special low-protein diet, usually for the rest of their lives. They also need to have regular blood tests to monitor their phenylalanine levels. It is important for parents of affected babies to have access to a qualified dietician to advise them about foods recommended for their child. The aim being to keep phenylalanine levels low, but high enough to provide a healthy, balanced diet that supports their child's growth and development.

How the test is done

The newborn screening test entails taking a few drops of the baby's blood, either by pricking their heel or taking blood from their vein. The blood is soaked onto a pre-printed, specially designed absorbent paper card (similar to blotting paper) for testing. The paper card has 3 or 4 marked circles about 1cm in diameter that the caregiver must fill-in with the blood for the testing required.

The newborn screening test is usually taken by the midwife in the hospital before going home, or by a visiting midwife for mothers and babies who go home early (within 48 hours) or after a home birth.

A step-by-step overview of how the test is performed can be found on www.birth.com.au.

Written by Sandra Robinson (childbirth educator) & Catherine Price (midwife): authors of *BIRTH* & directors of www.birth.com.au.

The Apgar score

The newborn Apgar scoring system was named after an American doctor, Virginia Apgar, and was first introduced in the 1960s. The Apgar score utilises five physical signs of a baby at birth, giving each a possible score of 0, 1 or 2, reaching a total assessment of up to 10 points. The midwife or doctor present at the baby's birth performs the Apgar score when the baby is one minute old and then repeats the score when the baby is five minutes old. However, if the baby takes longer to fully respond and breathe, the scoring may continue, repeated at seven minutes of age and possibly again at ten minutes if the baby is unwell.

The Apgar score was designed to standardise the way caregivers evaluated a baby's physical wellbeing at birth, helping to provide a general understanding of how well each baby makes the physical transition to independent life from their mother. These days there is much controversy about whether the Apgar score is a valid tool and opinions vary about its importance. Currently in Australia, a newborn's Apgar score is documented by maternity caregivers on the baby's medical records as well as government health department statistics and publications. It may also be used by researchers comparing groups of babies' health at birth for studies relating to this issue.

The table below shows the five physical signs used when giving each Apgar score with a description of the observations a caregiver makes for each level of scoring. The five minute Apgar score is regarded as more important than the 1 minute score because it is believed to be more reflective of the baby's overall health. A total Apgar score of 8 to 10 is regarded as good, 5 to 7 can indicate that the baby is mildly unwell, 3 to 4 reflects moderate to severe poor health and 0 to 2 is extremely poor health.

SIGNS	0	1 point	2 points
Colour	Blue, pale	Body pink, limbs blue	Completely pink
Breathing	Absent	Slow, irregular breaths - less than 40 per min	Strong cry, 40 breaths per minute or more
Heart beat	Absent	Less than 100 per minute	Over 100 per minute
Muscle tone	Limp, flaccid	Limbs have some movement	Actively moving
Response to touch	Absent	Some response	Active response

How is the Apgar score done?

The Apgar score is done visually by the caregiver and in many cases parents are unaware it is taking place. When a baby cries straight away and appears alert and vigorous, most caregivers automatically give a score of 9 or 10 at one minute, usually taking one point off for colour because the baby's hands and feet are often blue. The score given at five minutes is usually 10 if the baby is well and looks like they have fully adjusted to being in the outside world. Sometimes the caregiver physically checks the baby's heart rate is above 100 beats per minute by gently placing their hand on the baby's chest or their

The Apgar score

Photograph by Iris Creations Photography, Melbourne & Geelong.

umbilical cord to see how fast it is pulsating. It is automatically presumed that the baby's heart rate is over 100 if they are very responsive and/or crying.

A few caregivers routinely give a score of 9 at one minute and then 9 again at five minutes, because the baby's hands and feet are still looking blue. However, blue hands and feet are a normal physical feature for newborns which can persist or occur periodically for days or weeks after the birth. In reality this type of scoring is technically incorrect as the Apgar score is designed to reflect the baby's adjustment to life outside the womb. Nevertheless, a score of 9 at five minutes is generally accepted by most professionals and will often be recorded in this way. As a rule, scores of 8, 9 or 10 at one minute and 9 or 10 at five minutes are all considered a reflection of a well and healthy baby at birth, the only difference being the individual way a caregiver tends to score.

In the excitement of the birth (but more out of habit), the caregiver could allocate a score for your baby well before the first minute has been reached, resulting in a lower first Apgar score than they probably deserve. While this can be a source of concern for many parents, bear in mind that the Apgar score at five minutes is much more important and a better indicator of your baby's health than the one minute score. Many hospitals now have stop clocks in delivery rooms (usually on the resuscitation examination table for unwell babies) to try and guide the caregiver with their scoring, while they concentrate on caring for the baby.

Did you know? A widespread problem with the Apgar scoring system is the tendency for many caregivers to give the baby a score as soon as they leave the mother's body, instead of waiting for a minute to pass. If you think about standing for one minute's silence you can understand that this is quite a substantial time before the first score should be given.

What causes baby to respond slowly and be given a low Apgar score?

There are many physical reasons why a baby can be slow to respond soon after birth and therefore be given a lower Apgar score, usually at one minute of age. These can be any of the following, or a combination of these factors:

Fast birth. If the baby descends down the birth canal very rapidly either through a short pushing phase with a natural birth or by a caregiver using a ventouse suction cap or forceps, they may be born a little stunned, taking 2 to 3 minutes to breathe and respond.

Cord around the neck. Occasionally the umbilical cord can be around the baby's neck quite tightly, or on very rare occasions wrapped around their neck 2 or 3 times. This can momentarily constrict blood flow to the baby at birth and cause them to take a little longer to respond. Be aware that about 25% of babies are born with the cord around their neck or body loosely, most of the time it doesn't bother them and they have high Apgar scores.

Baby distressed. The baby may have been distressed during the labour or just before the birth. Possibly the baby's heart beat was dropping below the normal rate and/or the amniotic fluid was stained green with the baby having their first bowel movement, called meconium. These signs are not definite predictors that the baby will be slow to respond at birth, but they can increase the chances of this happening.

Narcotic pain-relief or a general anaesthetic. Narcotic drugs taken by the mother for pain-relief during labour, such as injections of pethidine, can suppress the baby's ability to take a breath at birth. This is especially the case if the drug was administered within 2 to 4 hours before the birth. If the baby is affected and not responding, the caregiver may give the baby an injection of a medication called naloxone or Narcan, which temporarily reverses the effects of the narcotic for about 4 hours. The injection may need to be repeated if the baby becomes very drowsy again.

A general anaesthetic (GA) for the mother during a caesarean birth (being made unconscious) can also affect her unborn baby, making them slower to respond at birth. This is because the anaesthetic is capable of moving quickly from the mother's blood stream through the placenta to her baby in the minutes before the birth.

Baby is unwell. A newborn baby may be unwell because they are very premature, have a genetic disorder or perhaps heart or lung problems. This may be evident soon after the birth, often requiring immediate medical attention. Their five minute Apgar score may be low as well, indicating longer term health issues for the baby.

Written by Sandra Robinson (childbirth educator) & Catherine Price (midwife): authors of *BIRTH* & directors of www.birth.com.au.

Newborn jaundice

Jaundice is a common yellowing of the baby's skin and eyes due to a build up of a substance called bilirubin in their body. Bilirubin is the by-product of the normal cell breakdown of a baby's surplus red blood cells during the first week after birth. Red blood cells are called haemoglobin and their main function is to carry oxygen. Excess haemoglobin is no longer needed by babies after birth because they start breathing their own oxygen, rather than sharing oxygen breathed in by their mother while they grow and develop in the womb.

When haemoglobin is broken down the bilirubin by-product needs to be processed (called conjugated) by the baby's liver before it can be excreted through their bowel motions. Health professionals often refer to unconjugated and conjugated bilirubin, especially when performing blood tests. Unconjugated bilirubin refers to the bilirubin that needs to be processed by the liver before it can be excreted by the baby's bowel. Conjugated bilirubin refers to the bilirubin that has already been processed by the baby's liver and is ready for excretion.

About 50% to 70% of babies process and excrete all the bilirubin in their system before it has a chance to accumulate. These babies show no signs of yellowing. However, 30% to 50% of babies temporarily accumulate varying levels of unconjugated bilirubin in their blood stream. This is because their liver doesn't keep up with the amount of bilirubin that needs to be broken down and processed for excretion, which is normal if it remains mild. The accumulation of unconjugated bilirubin gives the baby's skin and eyes a yellow discolouration, known as jaundice.

Most babies with jaundice have only a slight yellow discoloration that does not cause them any health problems. Their liver eventually processes all the accumulated bilirubin within a week or so, without it becoming very high. In some cases though, the levels of bilirubin accumulate to high levels, usually requiring some form of treatment, mainly phototherapy.

Very high levels of bilirubin in the baby's system (known as hyperbilirubinaemia) can cause a degree of brain damage if not treated. If brain damage occurs due to extremely high levels of bilirubin, this is known as kernicterus. Babies rarely develop kernicterus these days because treatments are now available, as well as the fact that caregivers closely monitor newborns to ensure treatments are used before levels reach this point.

There are three different types of jaundice:

Physiological jaundice is the most common type, where bilirubin temporarily accumulates to a moderate degree and in most cases does not require any treatment because the levels of bilirubin do not become very high.

Breast milk jaundice is a term given to a common type of mild jaundice that becomes persistent, or prolonged, for up to 6 to 12 weeks after birth. The baby appears slightly yellow, but is well and healthy. Breast milk jaundice does not require any treatment because the levels of bilirubin remain very low. *NOTE:* Breast milk jaundice is harmless and should not be a reason to stop breastfeeding. In the past, mothers were often asked to stop breastfeeding for 24 to 48 hours and place their baby on formula. The only advantage of doing this is that it may reassure the caregiver that it is indeed only breast milk jaundice. If you are advised to do this, and are not happy about it, you may wish to seek a second opinion.

Non-physiological jaundice is the most uncommon form of jaundice caused by the baby being ill or having a health disorder. Non-physiological jaundice can appear early (within 24 hours of birth) and may persist for more than 2 weeks after birth, possibly being quite severe and usually requiring treatment.

Signs of physiological jaundice

The pale yellow discolouration of jaundice usually starts to appear on the baby's face and neck, as well as the whites of their eyes, about 24 to 48 hours after birth. As the levels of bilirubin accumulate, the yellowing deepens and moves down the baby's body (over a day or two) to their chest, belly, and sometimes upper arms and legs, usually peaking at around 3 to 6 days of age. If the bilirubin levels become very high, the jaundice can be seen right down to the baby's hands and feet.

After a week or so, the bilirubin levels start to lower and the yellow discolouration disappears in reverse. That is, the baby's chest, neck, head and eyes are the last areas to lose their yellow appearance.

Most jaundice is mild to moderate, with the yellow discolouration being mainly confined to the baby's head, neck, chest and belly areas and possibly to their upper arms and thighs. The baby usually remains well and healthy and feeds normally. If the jaundice becomes severe (moving down to their feet and hands), the baby may show signs of being drowsy, lethargic and reluctant or disinterested in feeding. Most babies have treatment commenced before they reach this stage, if it is diagnosed.

Measuring jaundice levels

The easiest (and most common) method a caregiver will use to monitor a baby for jaundice levels is to observe their physical appearance and behaviour. This is usually done on a daily basis. If there is concern about the baby's bilirubin level becoming too high, the caregiver may suggest a blood test to accurately measure the baby's exact bilirubin level. Paediatric doctors have written guidelines stating what an acceptable level of bilirubin should be and at what level treatments are recommended.

Since the early 1980s, jaundice meters have been used by many caregivers to estimate bilirubin levels. This device is held on the baby's forehead by the caregiver who then presses a button to emit a brief beam of bright light onto the baby's skin. The reflection of light is interpreted by the machine as a measurement of the degree of yellowness in the skin, displaying a reading called a transcutaneous bilirubin index or TcBI. This measure is a guide only. It does not directly measure bilirubin levels and the results can be affected by the baby's skin colour, their birth weight, if they are premature and if phototherapy is already in use. However, jaundice meters have been shown to reduce unnecessary blood tests by about 20%, compared to the caregiver just using physical observation.

For further information on the different treatments used for jaundice visit www.birth.com.au.

Written by Sandra Robinson (childbirth educator) & Catherine Price (midwife): authors of *BIRTH* & directors of www.birth.com.au.

Weighing, measuring & bathing your baby

When a baby is born and excitement fills the room, there is often the urge to ring everyone and spread the good news. After "Congratulations!", the inevitable question comes – "How heavy is he or she?" – prompting many parents to ask for their baby to be weighed.

It is common practice to weigh a baby within 30 minutes or so of birth. However, you may request this to be delayed for an hour or longer, to enable more close bonding time with your baby and perhaps breastfeed them. Many parents cherish having some undisturbed time with their new baby before caregivers attend to the formalities, including weighing. Be aware that feeding your baby does not make much difference to their birth weight. Often they wee or poo during this time which usually makes up for any small gains!

Some birthplaces have preset routines as to when babies are weighed and perhaps bathed. There may also be pressure to move you and your baby to the postnatal ward if caregivers are busy, meaning that procedures are done within an hour of birth. Babies who are unwell and need medical attention are usually weighed swiftly on arrival to the intensive care nursery, in case medications or intravenous fluids are required as dosages are prescribed according to the baby's weight.

These days most birthplaces weigh and measure newborns in the birth room with the parents present, using portable equipment. When the birth is by caesarean the baby may be weighed outside the operating room or on the postnatal ward. If your baby needs to be taken to another room to be weighed your partner or support person can go with them, or you could ask that the weighing be delayed until you are ready (or feeling able) to go with your baby to see this done. Don't forget the camera!

Weighing is usually done on electronic scales with a cradle attached for the baby to lie in, which is lined with a disposable cloth or baby blanket for warmth and hygiene. The baby's weight is done as a bare weigh (no clothes) and in Australia is recorded metrically, for example 3,600 grams or 3.6kg. The scales may come with a conversion option to show pounds and ounces or your caregiver may have a conversion chart to show both metric and imperial measures.

The average weight of babies born at term (37 to 42 weeks) is about 3,300 grams or 7lb 4.5oz, but it is normal for a baby's weight to range from 2,800 grams to 4,500 grams (approx. 6lb to 10lb).

Head circumference is recorded in centimetres. It is normal for a newborn's head to have a degree of moulding after birth, making their head circumference slightly less, by up to 1cm or so. This original measurement is still recorded. However don't be concerned if your baby's head is larger on re-measuring a few days later. This is just the baby's head-shape becoming more rounded after birth. The average head circumference of a newborn is about 35 centimetres, but can range from 33 to 37 centimetres. This measure is not usually converted to inches.

Length is measured in centimetres from the crown of your baby's head to their heels. Your baby may be measured while lying on their side, with the caregiver trailing a measuring tape down their back and leg, or by placing your baby on a special measuring board. The caregiver could ask your partner or another carer to gently hold your baby's legs straight while the measure is being done, as newborns prefer to be in a fetal position and are generally not keen on straightening their legs.

The average length of babies born at term (37 to 42 weeks) is about 50cm or 20 inches, but can range from 46 to 56 centimetres (18 to 22 inches). Again, don't be too concerned if your baby has 'shrunk' or 'grown' dramatically between their measurement at birth and at subsequent measures at the health clinic a week or so later. This is usually more to do with the inaccuracy of measuring and the different carers' methods, rather than a physical problem with your baby.

Bathing your baby. For many years, giving a newborn baby a bath soon after birth has been a commonly accepted practice, probably originating from parents and caregivers seeing their baby as soiled and wanting them to look clean. In recent years bathing has also played a role in medical beliefs about controlling possible blood-born infections such as hepatitis B and C and HIV-AIDS.

While these factors have contributed to perpetuating routine bathing practices, other issues are now coming into play. Dermatologists (skin specialists) question the benefits of excessively bathing babies, especially with soaps, detergents and perfumed or medicated products, as they can irritate the baby's skin, drying it and making the baby more prone to rashes and skin infections.

The other issue is one of hospital-acquired infections. A baby is born with 'friendly' bacteria on their skin from contact with their mother and family. If this is washed away then foreign hostile bacteria from hospitals and caregivers may take over and cause infections of the baby's skin or umbilical cord. This is one of the many reasons (along with bonding and demand breastfeeding) behind encouraging babies to room in with the mothers in hospital, rather than being cared for in a large nursery with other babies.

With all this in mind, there is no real medical reason why a healthy baby needs to be bathed soon after birth, and many parents now wait a day or more before bathing their baby to allow the rich vernix cream often present on their skin to soak in, and reduce skin irritations and possible infections. If you prefer your baby's bath to be delayed, request this or include it in your birth plan.

Most babies are born looking fairly unsoiled, but if you think they need to be cleaned before grandma arrives, consider just wiping their face and scalp with a warm cloth, and/or their bottom, without having a full bath (known as a top and tail). If you do bath your baby, use just plain water. You may wish to use non-perfumed creams, oils or lotions such as sorbelene.

Ideally, bathing a baby soon after birth should be performed with the parents present in the birth room, but it may be done in another room with the father or support person to watch or hold the baby. If a baby's body temperature is below 36ºC, or they are born premature or very small, or they are unwell and need medical attention, then bathing will probably be delayed.

To read a step-by-step guide for bathing your baby, visit www.birth.com.au.

Written by Sandra Robinson (childbirth educator) & Catherine Price (midwife): authors of *BIRTH* & directors of www.birth.com.au.

All about babies: what makes them tick?

These days many parents have not had a lot of experience with babies until their first baby comes along. If you are one of these parents you will probably find you have many questions about this new person who has come into your life. It can be overwhelming and scary when you realise your baby is so dependent on you for everything, especially if you feel you don't know a lot about babies. Understanding what babies are like may help to make it easier to care for your baby.

What are babies like?

Every baby is different:

- Babies do some things 'automatically' without knowing they are doing them. These are called *reflexes*. For example, if something is put in their mouths they suck on it (sucking reflex), and if something is put in their hands they hold on tight (grasp reflex). If they are startled or upset they fling their arms out and throw their heads back (startle reflex).
- *Babies' heads* can sometimes be uneven in shape after the birth or because of the way they sleep. This is nothing to worry about and goes away as they grow.
- The '*soft spot*' (fontanelle) on top of a baby's head is there so the baby can more easily fit through the birth passage when he is being born. This spot will close over in the baby's first year or so. The skin over the soft spot is strong and you cannot hurt babies by gently washing or brushing their heads. Sometimes the fontanelle swells when the baby is crying and goes flat when the crying stops.
- *Cradle cap* is crusty scales on the head. You can rub it with olive oil or petroleum jelly to soften it one evening and wash it off the next day. Gently lift off the scales with a fine-toothed comb or fingernail. If it is really bad and does not improve see your doctor.
- Some babies have *sticky eyes* due to a blocked tear duct. Ask your doctor how to manage this. It is not serious.
- Some babies have *little white lumps* like tiny pearls in their mouth, especially on the gums. These are normal and go away when the baby grows.
- Babies are often born with *puffy genitals and breasts* (sometimes 'milk' even comes from the breasts). This is from the mother's hormones, is not a problem and it does not last long.
- Babies sometimes get a *lump* (hernia) *underneath their belly button* (umbilicus). It may swell if the baby is crying. This is a small gap in the 'tummy' muscle and will nearly always go away in time. It does not need treatment and does not cause health problems.
- Most babies have *spots on their faces* and often on parts of the body in the first few weeks. These can look like acne – red spots with white centres. They are not acne and they do not need any treatment. They seem to be a reaction to the skin being exposed to air rather than to fluid in the womb (uterus) before birth. Sometimes the spots come when the baby gets hot or has been lying on that side. If they go away within an hour or so they are probably this kind of spot.
- Lots of babies have *hiccups after feeds*. This is normal.
- Some babies *spill a little milk* after feeds. If they are growing well and happy this is nothing to worry about. If your baby is bringing up milk in big spurts much of the time you need to see your doctor. If your baby is not putting on weight or is miserable, talk to your doctor or child health nurse.

- Very young breastfed babies do several '*poos*' a day. Even if baby seems to be pushing hard, the poo is usually very soft. After a few weeks baby may only have a poo every few days and it will still be soft. All this is normal.
- Bottle fed babies might have firmer poos. If the poos seem very hard, try a teaspoon of brown sugar in a little boiled water before a feed (once or twice). Don't keep doing this after the poos are soft again.
- Babies usually start to get their *teeth* at about six months and usually have all their baby teeth by the time they are three years old. These teeth need to be looked after and brushed. Avoid giving bottles of juice or milk at bedtime. The sugars in these drinks stay in the mouth and can cause decay.
- Some babies don't have any teeth until they are one year old. Occasionally a baby is born with a tooth.

What your baby can do

Remember that every baby is different. While babies usually follow similar patterns with their development, your baby might do things faster or slower or differently from other babies and this is usually fine. If your baby is doing things much more slowly or not doing some things at all, it is a good idea to check with your doctor to make sure that all is going well. Here are some of the things your baby will probably be able to do:

- *By six or seven weeks* he can smile at you when you smile at him.
- *By two months* he can hold up his head when you are holding him upright and lift his head up if he is lying on his tummy.
- *By three months* he will enjoy hitting toys that make a noise and he can hold a rattle for a short time.
- *By four months* he may be able to roll from his front to his back, but it may be another couple of months, or more, before he can roll from his back to his front.
- *By seven months* he will be sitting up and might be starting to crawl.
- *By nine months* many babies can pull themselves up to stand. Some babies take longer. It takes another two or three months or so before he can stand without holding onto something and then a few more weeks before he can actually walk.
- *By twelve months* babies will 'talk' to you in their own language and may say one or two clear words – one of them will probably be "No!". Your baby will be able to hold something with his thumb and forefinger and play little games like 'wave goodbye' and 'pat-a-cake'.

What your baby can see, hear, taste and feel

Newborn babies may seem very helpless and vulnerable, and in many ways they are, but they can see, hear, taste, smell and feel. They can move their arms and legs (though they cannot control the movements) and they can suck! They communicate their feelings and needs (such as their need for comfort and feeds) by crying.

Seeing:

Your baby can see quite well at birth, especially things that are close:

- She will be able to see your face and will soon learn to recognise you.
- She will be able to see objects that are further away, but they will be blurry. Her distance vision will develop over the next few months.

All about babies:
what makes them tick?

- Babies can see the different colours, but as they do not understand colours they may like simple shapes, each in one colour.
- In the first few weeks, a baby's eyes often cross, or wander in different directions some of the time.
- By the age of 3 months the eyes should be lined up so that they both look at the same object.
- If a young baby's eyes are turned in or out most of the time, or if a baby over 3 months old has turned eyes, the baby needs to have his eyes checked.
- Some babies and young children have turned eyes some of the time (more often when they are tired or unwell). These babies should also have their eyes checked.
- Babies' eyes may change colour and you may not know what colour their eyes will be for several months.

Hearing:

- Your baby has been hearing since well before birth. He is familiar with your voice and the sounds of your household.
- You may notice that he tends to calm down if you make soft noises, and that he startles if there is a sudden loud noise.
- Babies seem to like high voices and animated faces (this might be why people often talk to babies in a higher voice).
- Your baby can hear voices, but he cannot understand any words yet. By talking to your baby from the time that he is born, you can help him start to understand that sounds make words and have meaning.
- Listen to your baby's noises and sounds and copy them. When you copy your baby it is like saying "I can hear you" and this is the start of teaching your baby to talk.

Smell and taste:

- Babies are born with senses of smell and taste. They are said to be able to recognise the smell and taste of their mother's milk, and they may refuse to drink if the milk tastes different.
- Babies can tell different tastes such as salty, sweet, sour and bitter.
- They certainly react to unpleasant tastes such as some medicines.
- They do not need salt or sugar on their foods when they start eating solids and they learn to like the tastes they are given.

Feeling:

- Babies are sensitive to touch from the time they are born and they can feel pain.
- Gentle, caring touch is very important so babies feel loved and cared for. Some parents enjoy learning how to give baby a massage.
- Nappy rash is very painful for babies, and they will be quite unsettled.

Moving:

- Most of a baby's movements are random and the baby is not able to control them at first. These are called reflexes.
- There are several reflexes, such as the startle reflex (the baby's arms stretch out and his back arches

and his head goes back), and the grasp reflex (he will grip something that is put onto the palm of his hand – such as your finger). These reflexes will decrease over the next few months as your baby gets more conscious control of his movements.

● When something touches his face he will turn towards it (the rooting reflex) and he will suck on it. Sucking is a reflex too; your baby will suck on things that are put into his mouth. Some babies will even be sucking their thumbs when they are newborns. Babies need to suck so that they can survive.

● Babies also have a 'tongue thrust' reflex. When something is placed into their mouth, they will, in the early months, tend to push it out using their tongue. This often happens when they are started on solids. It does not mean that they do not like the taste of the food; it is because they need to learn how to control their tongue.

● Most babies will start to smile by the time that they are around 6 weeks old, and they will be able to move their head a little.

THINGS TO KEEP IN MIND:

● Every baby is different, even in the same family.

● The best way to get to know what babies are like is to watch and learn from your own baby.

● Babies grow and learn faster than they will at any other stage of life, so what they do will be continually changing.

● Take time to enjoy the new things your baby is learning and doing.

● If you have questions, ask for information. Most other parents have exactly the same question.

● Ask for help if you have any worries about your baby. This shows you are interested in learning about your baby and that you care.

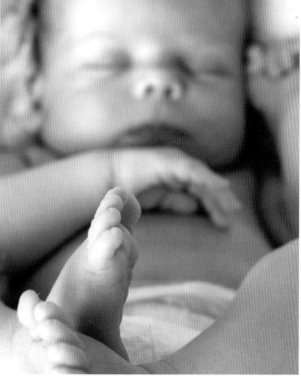

Photograph by Appleseed Photography, Adelaide.

Adapted from Parenting SA Parent Easy Guide #49 with permission. Copyright Government of South Australia, www.parenting.sa.gov.au.

Government assistance for parents

There are a number of payments that may be available through the Family Assistance Office to help families with the cost of raising children. Some are one-off payments while others provide ongoing support.

Baby Bonus

Baby Bonus is available to families to help with the costs of a new baby. Parents who adopt a child under the age of 16 years are also eligible to receive the payment. The payment is for each child, so a mother who gives birth to twins would receive two payments.

Baby Bonus is paid in 13 fortnightly instalments to families whose combined income is less than $75,000 in the first six months after the birth or adoption of a child. Baby Bonus is currently $5,000 and the rate is adjusted on 1 July each year.

You must lodge your claim with the Family Assistance Office within 52 weeks of the birth or, in the case of adoption, within 52 weeks of the child being entrusted into your care.

New mothers should get a claim form from the hospital when the child is born. For more information, go to www.centrelink.gov.au, call 13 6150 or visit any Family Assistance Office.

Family Tax Benefit Part A

Family Tax Benefit Part A is an annual tax benefit to help families with the cost of raising children. Guardians, including foster parents and grandparents, responsible for the day-to-day care of children/grandchildren are also eligible for this assistance. Family Tax Benefit Part A is paid for each child in a person's care.

Families can choose to receive this payment as fortnightly assistance through the Family Assistance Office or as a lump sum at the end of the financial year.

There is an income test for this payment but no assets test. The amount families receive depends on their actual annual family income as well as the number of dependent children and their ages. Parents can get an estimate of how much they may be entitled to by using the 'Centrelink/Family Assistance/Child Support estimator' in the Online Services section of the Centrelink website. Payment rates and income test limits for this payment are adjusted on 1 July each year.

For more information, go to www.centrelink.gov.au, call 13 6150 or visit any Family Assistance Office.

Family Tax Benefit Part B

Family Tax Benefit Part B gives extra assistance to families with one main income, including sole parents, where the youngest dependent child is under 16. It can also be paid for dependent children up to 18 years if age if they are a full time student and do not receive Youth Allowance or a similar payment. It also gives extra assistance to families who have a child under the age of five.

Family Tax Benefit Part B is paid per family. It is paid to families where the higher income earner in a couple, or a sole parent, has a taxable income of $150,000 or less. Eligible single parent families receive the maximum rate of Family Tax Benefit Part B. For members of a couple, the rate of payment is based on the income of the lower earner.

Parents can get an estimate of how much they may be entitled to by using the 'Centrelink/Family

Assistance/Child Support estimator' in the Online Services section of the Centrelink website. Payment rates and income test limits for this payment are adjusted on 1 July each year.

For more information, go to www.centrelink.gov.au, call 13 6150 or visit any Family Assistance Office.

Parenting Payment

This payment provides financial help for people who are the principal carers of children. Parenting Payment can only be paid to one person who cares for a child.

To qualify for Parenting Payment, a person must be the principal carer for at least one child under 8 (if the parent is single) or at least one child under 6 (if the parent is a member of a couple). Please Note: People receiving Parenting Payment before 1 July 2006 can remain on that payment until their youngest child turns 16, as long as they remain eligible.

The amount someone can get depends on their income and assets and whether they have a partner.

For more information, go to www.centrelink.gov.au, call 13 6150 or visit any Centrelink Customer Service Centre.

Maternity Immunisation Allowance

Maternity Immunisation Allowance is a payment for children who have been fully immunised or are exempt from immunisation. The payment is currently $243.30 and the rate is adjusted on 1 July each year. There is no income or assets test for this payment.

From 1 January 2009 Maternity Immunisation Allowance will be paid in two instalments– the first instalment will be made when the child is fully immunised and between 18 and 24 months and the second instalment is made when the child is fully immunised and between 4 years, 3 months and 5 years.

For more information, go to www.centrelink.gov.au, call 13 1650 or visit any Family Assistance Office.

Child Care Benefit

Child Care Benefit helps with the cost of child care. There are two types of payment – one for approved care and one for registered care.

Approved care is where the child care service have been approved to receive Child Care Benefit directly from the Family Assistance Office on behalf of families, so families pay less out of their own pocket. This includes most long day care, family day care, before and after school care, vacation care, in-home care, and some occasional care services offer approved care.

Child Care Benefit can be paid to the child care service who will pass this on as reduced fees, or families can choose to receive a lump sum at the end of the financial year.

Registered care is care provided by nannies, grandparents, relatives or friends and, in some circumstances, private pre-schools, kindergartens, occasional care centres and outside school hours care centres that are registered with the Family Assistance Office.

Government assistance for parents

This payment is paid by direct credit when people lodge a claim and their receipts with the Family Assistance Office.

There is an income test for approved care but not for registered care. The amount of Child Care Benefit someone can receive for approved care depends on their income, the number of children being cared for and if they are undertaking work, training or study.

Parents can get an estimate of how much they may be entitled to by using the 'Centrelink/Family Assistance/Child Support estimator' in the Online Services section of the Centrelink website.

Payment rates and income test limits for this payment are adjusted on 1 July each year.

Child Care Tax Rebate

In addition to Child Care Benefit, a person may be entitled to Child Care Tax Rebate if they use approved care. A person doesn't need to get Child Care Benefit to get the rebate.

From July 2008 and onwards, a person can claim 50 per cent of out-of-pocket expenses up to a maximum of $7,500 per child. The rebate is paid every three months, however a person can ask to receive it annually.

A person only needs to complete a claim form for Child Care Benefit and the Family Assistance Office will work out whether they are entitled to Child Care Benefit and Child Care Tax Rebate.

Jobs, Education and Training (JET) Child Care fee assistance

Families who receive certain payments from Centrelink, may be able to get Jobs, Education and Training (JET) Child Care fee assistance. This payment helps people with the cost of approved child care by paying some of the 'gap fee' while they are working, training or studying so you can enter or re-enter the workforce for a limited period of time.

The 'gap fee' is the difference between the amount someone is charged for child care and the amount they pay after Child Care Benefit (CCB).

For more information, go to www.centrelink.gov.au, call 13 1650 or visit any Centrelink Customer Service Centre.

OTHER SERVICES AVAILABLE

Personal/family counselling service

Centrelink social workers provide counselling and support to Centrelink customers with difficult personal or family issues. Social workers can also refer people to a range of other services to help them, such as housing assistance, counselling, health services, legal services, support groups and emergency financial assistance.

People can call 13 1794 to speak to a social worker over the phone or to arrange an appointment at a Centrelink Customer Service Centre.

Financial Information Service

Centrelink's Financial Information Service helps people understand their financial options so they can make more informed decisions. The service is free and confidential and is available for everyone – not just people who receive a payment from Centrelink.

Centrelink has a network of Financial Information Service Officers throughout Australia and people can make an appointment to talk about their situation. They also conduct seminars on financial options and concepts, like understanding financial planning and investments, understanding basic taxation requirements and social security provisions.

It's important people know Financial Information Service Officers are not financial planners. They don't sell advice or purchase investment products, and aren't able to make decisions on anyone's pension or financial choices.

People can arrange to talk to a Financial Information Service Officer over the phone or face to face. For more information, go to www.centrelink.gov.au, call 13 2300 or visit any Centrelink Customer Service Centre.

Centrepay

Centrepay is available to most customers who receive a payment from Centrelink. It is a free direct bill-paying service that helps people manage their household expenses.

This service allows people to have regular fortnightly amounts deducted from their payments, which are paid directly to the customer's nominated organisation or service provider. Customers can pay a range of bills, including rent, electricity, gas and water, telephone, household goods, child care, court fines, education fees, no interest loans, and medical services.

Customers can contact Centrelink or the service provider directly to check to see if the provider is registered with Centrepay. The minimum payment amount for Centrepay is $10 per fortnight, but customers should check with individual organisations or service providers as some may require a different minimum amount, e.g. Telstra have a $20 minimum payment.

Customers can change, suspend or cancel the deduction at any time by simply calling Centrelink or using Centrelink's online Self Service. For more information, customers should contact Centrelink on their normal payment number.

Information supplied by Centrelink, www.centrelink.gov.au.

Looking after your pelvic floor

Pregnancy and birth put tremendous demands on the pelvic floor. Women who have had children are more likely to suffer from urinary incontinence as they age, and the risk of pelvic floor disorders increases with the number of babies a woman gives birth to. Pelvic floor disorders that emerge in middle or later life often have their origin in the childbearing years.

What can you do to build a stronger pelvic floor?

Effective pelvic floor muscle exercise is essential in preventing and addressing pelvic floor-related problems including incontinence, prolapse, and reduced sexual satisfaction. So it's important to exercise those pelvic floor muscles both before birth and post-natally. There are two recommended pelvic floor exercises that should be done regularly.

- **Exercise 1:** Tighten the muscles around your back passage, vagina and front passage and lift up inside as if trying to stop passing wind and urine at the same time. It is very easy to bring other, irrelevant muscles into play, so try to isolate your pelvic floor as much as possible by not pulling in your tummy, not squeezing your legs together, not tightening your buttocks and not holding your breath. The effort should be coming from the pelvic floor. Try holding the squeeze as long and as hard as you can. Build up to a maximum of 10 seconds. Rest for 4 seconds and then repeat the contraction as many times as you can up to a maximum of 10 contractions. Try to do these exercises in a slow and controlled way with a rest of 4 seconds between each muscle contraction. Practise your maximum number of held contractions (up to 10) about six times each day.

- **Exercise 2:** The ability to work these muscles quickly helps them react to sudden stresses from coughing, laughing or exercise. Practise some quick contractions, drawing in the pelvic floor and holding for just one second before releasing the muscles. Do these steadily, aiming for a strong muscle-tightening with each contraction up to a maximum of 10 times. Try to do one set of slow contractions (exercise 1) followed by one set of quick contractions (exercise 2) six times each day. If you do pelvic floor exercises regularly, you will see optimum results within 3 to 6 months, but you should continue them for life to fully protect your pelvic floor.

What if you can't squeeze your pelvic floor muscles?

Many women just can't learn how to contract their pelvic floor muscles effectively from written instructions. If you are one of these women, there are many helpful resources, exercise aids and devices available. These aids can also be helpful if you having difficulty regaining control over your pelvic floor muscles after giving birth. This takes time, and persistence will often pay off. Alternatively, women's health physiotherapists specialise in helping women strengthen their pelvic floor muscles.

Pelvic floor weakness and stress incontinence symptoms often diminish naturally in the weeks after birth. But, remember that the exercises you do now will help you to avoid problems in future pregnancies and later in life. Incorporate your pelvic floor exercises into your own routines and maintain them for life for a strong, healthy pelvic floor.

Written by Linda McClelland, www.pelvicfloorexercise.com.au.

Vox Pop

We asked a number of women and men around Australia to send in their advice, tips and personal experiences on a range of topics so that you have an insight into how others cope being a new parent. We hope you find their comments interesting, informative and reassuring. Vox Pop biographies: page 652

Sarah Murdoch
Mum of two, Sydney

All my life I imagined childbirth to be just a terribly scary part of having a baby. I couldn't even imagine what the pain would be like and really didn't want to know … until I found Juju Sundin. My obstetrician recommended her childbirth classes and I thought I would give them a try.

I absolutely loved the classes and learned so much about my body, about labour, about my baby, and finally about the actual birth and the pain. More importantly I learned what the pain would be like and how to manage it.

Because of this my births were the most amazing, exciting and overwhelmingly mind-blowing adventures for my husband and me! We worked through my contractions together never losing sight of just how incredible it was. We both felt we brought our children into the world together, as a team. I can't imagine what it would be like to have not experienced that.

I feel really lucky. Having said that, I say to my friends who are pregnant that it really doesn't matter how babies come into the world so long as you are all healthy.

Andrew Weldon
Dad of one, Melbourne

The labour took 6 hours, 3 days, 5 minutes. It was urgent, scary, exhilarating, upsetting, humbling, violent, disgusting and absolutely beautiful. It was the greatest display of human achievement and endurance I have seen – in real life, on television, wherever. My partner awed me. My partner and child, working in combination, awed me. I felt a part of it, but separate. I clutched my partner's hand in the final stages and watched her strain, and knew it was her challenge, she was alone with it. I was supporting her, but at that moment, in

the final hours, it was theoretical. The midwives called me round to see my baby's head – rumpled purple scalp, blood. I was horrified and moved beyond words or action. I stood dumb.

The head further out – purple, blue. Only the overjoyed midwives to remind me that this was normal. I saw neither of us – me, my partner - in these fresh features, shown to the world for the first time but my heart filled with a protective love. My child. She slid out, finally. "A boy!" I gasped, but they were engorged labia not testicles and I'll feel foolish about this forever.

Later as my partner pushed to expel the placenta – a relative skip in the park, a parody of childbirth – I held the slippery little stranger, slimy skin sliding over ribcage.

My head empty of thought, only awe at my partner, my child, the body.

I think I cried.

Amanda Jephtha
Mum of one, Sydney

Don't wait until you're in the throes of labour to pack your hospital bag. Babies are considered full term at 37 weeks, so make sure you are packed and ready by then. The key is to write a detailed checklist and pin it to the bag.

Tick items as you pack, so if someone else needs to finish the packing for you, they will know exactly what's missing – and nothing will be left open to interpretation!

Your hospital stay will be split into two distinct periods – the delivery of your baby, and the recovery in the maternity ward. So why not pack two separate, smaller bags?

Rather than rifling through a beautifully packed large bag, everything will be on hand when you need something quick smart. Also, someone can take the delivery bag home once you've settled into the maternity ward meaning one less thing to carry home at the end of your stay.

Tip: don't forget to pack plenty of plastic bags for your laundry in the maternity ward bag.

Ros Pittard
Mum of two, VIC

I gave birth to my first baby in a private hospital with my own obstetrician. It was a very long and challenging 20 hour labour, but I felt safe in their hands. We had a long de-briefing with the mid-wife who spent the final seven hours of labour with us. My husband and I really appreciated that, as it was a wonderful but quite traumatic experience.

The first weeks post-birth were very difficult. I was madly in love with our baby, but struggled to know how to manage his unsettled behaviour. The midwives at our hospital provided phone support for the first few weeks at home.

Christine Walsh
Mum of two, Broome

My two birthing experiences were not all that pleasant, though when you put it all into perspective it really doesn't really matter as all in all it was less than 24 hours of my life. Plus if it wasn't for the fact I gave birth I wouldn't have my two healthy gorgeous children.

Two days before my daughter was born I thought I was in labour as I was experiencing cramping and had lost my mucous plug. False alarm, though I was really uncomfortable for the next few days.

The night I actually went into labour I still wasn't 100% convinced I was in labour so I crept out into the lounge room not wanting to wake up my husband who had to work early that morning. He finally woke up to my cries in pain as I was hunched over the fit ball.

We called the hospital and the midwife talked me through a contraction and said it was time to come in. By the time I reached the hospital I was 3cm dilated. I requested an epidural but because it was the middle of the night we had to wait nearly two hours for one. I had a hot shower and some gas to relieve the pain. I'm not entirely sure if the gas worked but it did give me (and my husband) something to concentrate on when a contraction came. The shower was such a lovely relief; I sure wasn't thinking about the environment and saving water that night!

Things were progressing fine once I had the epidural. The doctor came in and said we would have the baby by mid morning. Mid morning came and still no baby. They let the epidural wear off as it was time to push. I pushed for an hour and a half and there was not much progress.

The midwives then realised that my baby's head was transverse (lying on the side). I was told they would try and use forceps to deliver the baby and if that didn't work I would have to have a caesarean. At 2.35pm our daughter Savannah was born with the aid of forceps and a lot of pulling. It was the most amazing experience of my life with overwhelming feelings of wanting to protect and love this child.

The baby blues hit me hard as I couldn't get my head around the thought of how I would look after the baby and juggle all the housework. I think because no-one had told me that I would feel like this – I had no close friends that had had babies – I had no idea. And I, being the super organised person that I am, was really at loss.

So be prepared that you really do have no idea of how it will be for you until your baby is born and yes your hormones do throw you out of whack for a while. Though if these feelings do continue and you grow more anxious you may need to seek medical advice as a few of my friends have suffered from postnatal depression.

I think the most important thing to remember is that you want a healthy baby as the final outcome. If you keep an open mind about the whole birthing experience it will help you as unfortunately in life things don't always go to plan. There is no point getting too upset if things don't go exactly as you had planned as the safe arrival of your baby is really the ultimate aim.

Vox Pop

We asked a number of women and men around Australia to send in their advice, tips and personal experiences on a range of topics so that you have an insight into how others cope being a new parent. We hope you find their comments interesting, informative and reassuring. Vox Pop biographies: page 652

Lee Norman
Mum of one, Melbourne

When I first met with my obstetrician I was keen on a 'celebrity birth' scheduled caesarean – my obstetrician talked to me about my lifestyle and asked about the things that I would like to do within the weeks after the birth. He then slipped in that none of that would be possible if I had a caesar, so rather than telling me I couldn't have a scheduled caesarean he used reverse psychology to convince me that if I was going to have a caesar it was going to be as a last resort.

This was a common theme during our discussions; he never said I couldn't have or do something, he usually just worked out what else was important to me and let me know that would or wouldn't be possible.

I am pleased that we went with a natural birth as our baby was ill after she was born and taken from St Francis Xavier Cabrini Hospital (Melbourne) to the Mercy (Melbourne). As I had had a natural birth I was well enough to travel with her in the NETS ambulance to the Mercy and return to Cabrini at night. The other mums that I met who had had caesars weren't mobile for several days.

Jessica Hatherall
Mum of two, Sydney

I had two babies in the birth centre in the Royal Hospital for Women Randwick. I was extremely lucky and had both my children naturally. The birth centre and the midwives were fantastic and I can't recommend them enough. I wasn't sure if I would really be able to give birth without drugs but by going to the birth centre I knew if I changed my mind I could just walk down the hall to the delivery suite where an epidural would be waiting. I also had the comfort of knowing that if there was an emergency they could just push a button and lots of doctors would descend.

My top tips for childbirth would be as follows:
Lots of yoga while pregnant.
The TENs machine is a great distraction during labour.
An EPI-NO is also a good option for a first pregnancy to help prepare your pelvic floor muscles.
Lots of water during labour – the bath, the shower – great for pain relief.
Make sure your birth partner knows what kind of labour you want and is prepared to be a huge support to help you achieve it.

At the end of the day all that matters is that you and the baby are healthy. For the first few weeks post-birth I felt pretty good. I really enjoyed my 'babymoon'. I had the baby blues for about one night which I think is pretty typical. Physically I was a little bit sore for a few weeks but otherwise my physical recovery was really fast.

Tony Wilson
Dad of one, Melbourne

I remember being amazed at Tam's endurance, her ability to keep going despite how tired she was, and how long the ordeal had gone on for. When the head crowned I was definitely relieved, both for the fact that it would soon be over, and because Pam, our midwife, kept reassuring us that we were making textbook progress. I remember saying something naff, something like 'we're having a baby' to Tam, and thank god she wasn't comprehending much or she might have slapped me across the face and told me that SHE was having the effing baby! My voice did crack though, and it was all very emotional.

Tam was physically sick from 8 weeks pregnant to half an hour after the birth, so it was just such a relief to be finished, and for both Tam and Polly to be well. The midwife asked me to do the gender identification, to tell Tam whether it was a boy or a girl. I've never particularly trusted my eyesight, so I remember being a bit tentative. "A girl?" I said, but there was a question in my voice. I think Tam was hoping I'd be a bit more certain.

Tanya Byrnes
Mum of one, VIC

Once you're in labour the best instructions and advice come from your midwife. Listen and talk as much as you can to your midwife as they soon become your best friend. Even if you don't feel up to the task, try to eat and keep your fluid intake up. The hours which lay ahead for yourself and your partner are exhausting. Try to take naps as regularly as possible to keep up your strength. Talk to each other while in labour and during those last moments before you have your newborn child in your arms – you are both going through this together.

Alana White
Mum of one, SA

My labour experience is something I will never forget. I went into labour at 39 weeks and 5 days. It started off with what I thought were my waters breaking. I called up the Women's and Children's Hospital here in SA to see what I should do. I was advised to go into the women's assessment centre to be checked out. I was told that I was not yet dilated and to go back home. As soon as I returned home I started to have contractions that were about 15 minutes apart and so four hours later I returned to hospital. Once back at the hospital I was told I was now 3cm dilated and I was taken up to the birthing room where my waters broke and I started getting the worst period pains I had ever experienced. After 14 hours of nothing happening I was induced and told to start pushing – 40 minutes later Jaylan John Buhagiar was born, a perfectly healthy boy.

To cope through labour you need a very good support person. My partner, Jake, was amazing and without him it would have been a lot harder. After that you really need your friends and family as most women experience the baby blues just like I did. Your whole life changes so be ready for it!

Andrea Tulloch
Mum of one, NSW

Originally from Melbourne I was really concerned when we decided to start our family in the south western slopes area of NSW, but I have been extremely impressed by the rural health services in our area. Our farm is a 45minute drive down the Hume and Sturt Highways to the hospital where we were to deliver our baby. Also being a first time mum I was concerned about isolation and any follow up care once we got home. I can honestly say that I have been spoilt for care. We were fortunate enough to deliver at a private hospital that had rooms set up for couples from out of town so my husband was able to stay some nights with me. The midwives were great and very friendly with a wealth of information about babies.

I went by the one-step-at-a-time principal so I didn't overwhelm myself with details and consequences. The midwives were very patient with my bevy of questions once our little boy arrived. I have also been very impressed with the follow up care from the local midwife and health care nurse. She has been available at any time to answer questions by mobile phone, and in the early days when we were battling through weight gain issues she was able to come and offer support at our home on the farm and talk through any issues we had. I understand that everyone has a different experience of childbirth but we were very lucky for the support and care we received.

Anna Ngo
Mum of one, Perth

I had labour all worked out: from what to bring to hospital to what painkillers to choose to the entire birthing plan. I also watched and read a good deal of videos and books on the topic, and so formed my own expectations of how labour would start and how the delivery would go. But if there was one event that would not go according to plan,

Vox Pop

We asked a number of women and men around Australia to send in their advice, tips and personal experiences on a range of topics so that you have an insight into how others cope being a new parent. We hope you find their comments interesting, informative and reassuring. Vox Pop biographies: page 652

this would be the one. My daughter Mikaela was born late on Boxing Day. The night before I had very little sleep as I was feeling 'strange'. After a few hours of pacing around the house and reading, the strange feeling soon became intermittent sharp pains. I knew it wasn't Braxton Hicks contractions because they never really hurt. I was sure this was the genuine thing so I woke my husband and we nonchalantly made for the hospital (somehow I expected the drive to be a little more suspenseful!).

The midwife at the hospital was convinced it was just a false alarm and assured me that it would likely be days before I would go into real labour. But as a precaution she did her usual examinations and found that I was already a few centimetres dilated. Lucky me, because if this was a false alarm then what would the real thing feel like! But in the grand scheme of things it was still considered early days so we chose to wait it out at home for a few hours before returning again just before sunrise.

On my birth plan I noted that I would try and cope with the pain by using gas. But when I was offered an epidural I quickly accepted, and from there my birth plan went straight out the window. About 18 or so hours passed from the moment I experienced those sharp pains at home until the moment Mikaela was finally born.

In all that time my epidural was regularly dosed, my waters were manually broken, I slept, ate, I was given a shot to hasten the dilation, was very close to having a caesarean, pushed like I've never pushed before, and was helped along by forceps after being given a small incision down below. All in all, I did not expect any of those things to happen and yet they did!

It was supposed to be a very normal labour, of average length, painful but manageable, and the baby would arrive after a dozen or so pushes.

But now that I'm a bit wiser I realise that 'normal' is only a matter of perspective.

Ultimately it's about bringing a healthy baby into the world, and I know it's probably been said endlessly before, but when this happens it's worth everything you've been through and more.

Kaz Cooke
Mum of one, Melbourne

Apart from putting on 27 kilos my pregnancy wasn't too bad. By the end I rather resembled a befuddled heffalump who didn't know what she was in for. I'd been to all the classes and researched until my bosoms nearly fell off and in the end I had no labour at all, just an induction followed by a graph that was frowned at by many medical staff and then an incredibly fast emergency caesarean. It wasn't so much a journey as an exclamation mark.

Katherine Twigg
Mum of one, VIC

I got so much help from the midwives in the week I was in hospital and it really made the difference for when I came home.

The advice I would give in relation to childbirth is that although it is a good idea to have a birth plan, be prepared that this may change.

My son was born by caesarean section because after all day in labour I was only 6cm dilated and it really just wasn't progressing. My son was not struggling with labour, it was that my pelvis was just too small for him to fit through so I really had no alternative.

Luckily the only birth plan I had was to do whatever it took to ensure the safe arrival of my son and that's exactly what happened. Sometimes it doesn't quite go to plan so as long as you are aware of this you won't be disappointed.

The day I brought my baby home, I was overwhelmed. All the manuals for the sterilizer and breast pump came out in a hurry, so my recommendation to all new mums and dads is to really understand all the equipment you may have to use prior to your baby being born … it will save you a lot of stress!

Danielle Murrihy
Mum of two, Melbourne

I went into labour at 34.4 weeks; my waters broke and I called the hospital and they advised me to come in straight away. I assumed that they would keep me in for a few days, stop the leak and let my babies cook a little longer but no! I was on the table within half an hour having a spinal and getting prepped for an emergency caesarean. I was a mum to twins just one and a half hours later! I was a mess – it was not what I was expecting and it all happened too fast.

My mum talked her way into the theatre along with my partner. Thank goodness she was there as my partner fainted and took a nurse down with him! He missed the actual delivery but he was the first to cuddle the boys. My mum shoved a baby into my arms but I was crying and shaking and I was terrified I would drop him. The boys were whisked away to the Special Care Nursery and my partner went with them. I didn't get to see them again until the following afternoon. Our two little boys in the isolettes – they were so beautiful and so little. They stayed in SCN for 17 days and I was discharged at 6 days. The drive home with an empty back seat was devastating. But all in all it turned out to be a good situation. It meant I had time to recover from my c-section, I had time to get breastfeeding down pat and also to get things ready at home. Each morning my partner would drop me off at hospital while he did a couple of hours work, then he would pick me up in the afternoon. At home we would have dinner and then go back into the hospital for bathtime, a last feed and to put the boys to bed. The staff were just beautiful and night times were my favourite time. The wards and nursery were quiet and everything was so peaceful and relaxed and I was happy to leave them with the staff.

I was one very nervous mum when I was told that I could take my babies home. We drove up to the hospital knowing that this was the last time; we said our goodbyes and as soon as we got home there was no way those babies were ever leaving me again!

Jess Tamblyn
Mum of one, SA

I wanted an all natural birth with no chemical pain relief nor medical intervention. This all sounded great and quite easy until I was actually in labour! During the final stages I cried out for an epidural although the anaesthetist was unavailable straight away and by the time he arrived I was ready to push! Turns out I had coped just fine until right at the end and it wasn't until transition that the pain became unbearable but this only lasted a short time.

I was so glad I didn't have the epidural. My daughter's birth ended up being a wonderful experience just as I had planned and I was so proud of myself for achieving what many people thought I was crazy to attempt.

Kerri Harding
Mum of one, VIC

My husband and I attended childbirth education classes at our local St. John of God hospital where I was booked in to give birth to our child. In our experience, by far one of the more informative sessions was the discussion concerning labour and childbirth. I think it is normal for any expectant mum to be nervous and scared when thinking about these things, especially when you inevitably get told the horror story of somebody else's nightmare labour and birth by some well meaning soul who just wanted to be prepared for all possible scenarios ... yeah, thanks for that!

I remember walking away from this class and saying to my husband that the only thing I really didn't want to consider was a caesarean section. As far as everything else was concerned, I was determined to keep an open mind. You can plan for the labour and birth as much as you like but the reality is until you are there experiencing it, it is impossible to know how it feels, what will happen and how you will react. Labour and childbirth are

Vox Pop

We asked a number of women and men around Australia to send in their advice, tips and personal experiences on a range of topics so that you have an insight into how others cope being a new parent. We hope you find their comments interesting, informative and reassuring. Vox Pop biographies: page 652

an intensely personal experience that you can only prepare yourself so much for. My pregnancy was all smooth sailing right through until my final visit with the obstetrician when I was 9 days overdue. We decided that I would go into the hospital the following morning and that my labour would be induced. I was so excited I could hardly sleep. All going well, I would give birth to a healthy baby sometime the next day!

After having two lots of prostaglandin gel inserted at different intervals, having my waters broken and an intravenous oxytocin drip inserted, I was still only 3cm dilated at midnight and, worse still, no further dilated at 6.00am the next morning after enduring irregular contractions all night while my husband slept in a bean bag beside me!

It turned out that my baby was posterior and was going nowhere fast and that the best scenario was to have an emergency caesarean … just what I didn't want. To be honest though, at that point I was so tired (both physically and mentally) that the idea of a caesarean was actually quite appealing and the procedure was a lot less scary than I had imagined. At the end of it all I got to kiss and cuddle a healthy baby boy. What more could you want?

Kirstin Amos
Mum of one, QLD

Childbirth was not as I expected even though we had attended all the antenatal classes and been shown and told of what was to happen. When the time arrived I was a little shocked. My waters broke at home at about 11.00pm and I did as the hospital advised which was to go back to bed and try and relax and if the pain increased then to make my way to hospital. The nurses at the Wesley were so supportive and caring. I had my son Carter at 7.05pm Saturday night and once I held him in my arms and saw that little face with the bent nose, the pain and discomfort was all worthwhile. Once I returned home from hospital the follow-up care from a health nurse was a great help, especially since

I was having a little problem with breastfeeding. I also had my mum who was a great help in the fact that she allowed me to do simple things like have a shower and even a nap.

Leanne Cummins
Mum of two, NSW

In my experience as a midwife and doula, I have found that the people who cope 'best' with labour are those who have practiced relaxation. Not many couples understand that the contractions you get while in labour will subside. They usually progress to last 60–90 seconds at their peak, and then allow you rest time to recover. The closer you get to having your baby, the shorter the rest time.

Couples can use their own techniques of breathing or distraction to help get through the work of labour. In between the contractions, it is most important to let go and rest – flop over something and breathe in the oxygen for you and your baby.

Let that contraction go and allow the next one to come – breathe through the contraction as effectively as the last one, and let it go again (forget about it). Focus on the job at hand and your labour will progress much faster than someone who has 'lost it'.

Louise Cruz
Mum of three, NSW

Going into labour with my first child was both a relief that the pregnancy would finally be over (as I had suffered through a very hot summer with no air conditioning) and also a very scary proposition as I had no idea what would happen. I remember thinking that my worst scenario for the labour would be to have to have a caesarean. After about 4 hours of labour and trying the gas to ease the pain (which made me very nauseous) I opted to have an epidural. It gave me a rest from the pain for a few hours, but did wear off just in time for me to feel the delivery. My labour was timed to be 9.5

hours long. With my second child I think I was again weary of the possibility of a caesarean, but was determined to do all I could to avoid another epidural. I had a hot bath and walked around the room in the early stages. The gas again made me feel sick so I tried standing in the shower while my husband massaged my back. I had a shot of pethidine in the later stages of the labour and my son was delivered while I was still standing in the shower. He weighed 3.5kg and my labour was recorded at just 1 hour and 15 minutes.

Lucy Mulvany
Mum of three, SA

I gave birth to all three of my children in a private hospital without intervention. Sometimes it really is possible to have the birth you want, in the environment you want. Be armed with that knowledge, and the confidence that you are designed to give birth.

Martine Pekarsky
Mum of two, Melbourne

We had a pretty straightforward birth experience in the end, and I was quite comfortable with the idea of having a caesarean. The discomfort of the operation was far outweighed by the comfort of not having the twins inside me – they were born at 7lb and 6lb so quite a good size and I felt like I was walking on air! I was finally able to get up on a stool and sit down on a couch and do all those normal things.

Our hospital experience once the babies arrived was a disaster. My husband and I tried to brave it out by keeping the babies in our room with us instead of in the hospital nursery, so by the time we left we were exhausted and running on one hour of sleep in 3-hour sleep cycles. We were teary and emotional and by the time we worked out where we had gone wrong it was too late. Visitors were

discouraged and we felt as though we would never cope at home on our own. Due to a medical condition the nurses told me I probably would not be able to breastfeed, so we started learning about formula and sterilizing bottles which I was very disappointed about.

Fortunately as soon as the babies came home they slept and slept and slept and so we started to worry about that instead. I had the 'baby blues' which lasted 3 weeks until my husband went back to work. I kept crying but didn't know why, went off my food, and panicked when I heard them cry, then once the hormones were out of my system it was amazing. One morning I woke up and felt on top of the world and loved my new life!

Melanie Smoothy
Mum of one, NSW

Eager to be as prepared and informed as possible, my husband and I attended an antenatal class which was held at the hospital we'd selected for the impending birth of our son. The antenatal class covered a variety of topics including what to pack, pain relief options, techniques and positions for birth, breastfeeding, general care and what to expect post birth.

One topic you seem to repeatedly read or hear about during your pregnancy is a birth plan. Priding myself on my organisation and time management skills (courtesy of years of office administration and management), this concept sounded very appealing! After attending our antenatal class and studying the multitude of information we had on hand, we chose the birthing position and pain relief option (a quick and pain free birth please!).

Brayden's birth began with a false start on the Sunday – a trip to the hospital and a visit from our obstetrician confirming I was pre-labour (mild contractions without dilating). After being monitored for several hours, we were advised to return home until my labour progressed. We soldiered on until my waters broke early on the Tuesday evening when we made the trip back to the hospital.

Vox Pop

We asked a number of women and men around Australia to send in their advice, tips and personal experiences on a range of topics so that you have an insight into how others cope being a new parent. We hope you find their comments interesting, informative and reassuring. Vox Pop biographies: page 652

In the birthing suite of our hospital, our obstetrician confirmed that I was now in labour and was progressing well. I was convinced he was going to tell me I was at least 8cm dilated (mind you, I'm not sure if that was just wishful thinking or the effect of the gas). He informed me that I was in fact not that far and I had some time to go.

A few hours later, with the foetal monitor monitoring Brayden's progress during the labour, we were advised that he was in distress and that I was being rushed to theatre for an emergency caesarean section. Needless to say, neither my husband nor I remember ticking that box as part of our birth plan.

As much as I support the notion of having a birth plan, realistically it is just a concept that encourages you to look into all the options available and decide what is best for you. The important factor is to remember to be flexible with your birth plan; there are no certainties when it comes to labour. Furthermore, it's not the process of how your baby is delivered, but the end result that is the most important. After having the emergency caesarean I felt as though I had failed to do what came to women naturally. It took time, but eventually I realised the situation was beyond our control and the most important thing was in fact the end result – the safe arrival of our baby.

Anna Brandt
Mum of one, QLD

Two things I went through pregnancy remembering and was absolutely thankful that I kept them in mind the whole way through: Whatever happens happens! You can't plan or pre-empt anything that is going to happen during your pregnancy and if you set yourself a 'plan', then make sure you add to 'the plan' to be disappointed that it didn't go 'to plan'. Guaranteed!

You have the option to write your own 'birth plan' which the obstetrician and midwife will work with, but I didn't understand how I could tell the 'professionals' how to do their job. I'm no

professional, I didn't study this for five-plus years; I'm certainly not now going to start thinking I know what is best in this situation. I heard so many horror stories and the thing I noticed about the majority of them was that the couples all had preconceptions about what they wanted and how they wanted 'it' to be. My theory is plan to have no plan and trust your obstetrician/ midwife; they've been through this a thousand times.

The second point is that this is no time to be a hero! If I'm in pain and there's something that's going to help then I'm going to try it. I knew I would probably end up having an epidural however if something else less invasive was likely to work then I would have had that. One thing I hate women saying to me about my childbirth is "did you have an epidural? If so don't talk to me about childbirth." Women who have epidurals are no less of a woman than those who don't have an epidural. At the end of the day we all had to push (unless of course you had a caesarean and then that's a whole other ball game).

Tracey Thompson
Mum of one, Brisbane

As with all first time mums, I had so many questions floating around in my head coming up to my due date – how do I actually know for sure that I am in labour, when do I actually go to the hospital, what pain relief do I want to take, etcetera, etcetera. As I have now experienced childbirth my advice is to just go with how you're feeling at the time and trust your gut instinct. I stayed at home for about 5 hours in labour as I felt more comfortable in my own surroundings and felt I could deal with the pain a lot better. I went to hospital when the pain became regular and constant and was 8cm dilated on arrival. I am so glad I experienced most of my labour at home in my own comfortable surroundings. The most valuable piece of advice I received for the first week or two, post labour, was that it is okay to cry! Don't hold back and just let those tears flow. It's all a big change …

Michelle Winduss
Mum of one, Sydney

During my pregnancy I tried to prepare myself as much as I could by doing a lot of reading. I also heard from a lot of mothers what childbirth was like and what to 'expect'. I thought the normal things that most expectant mothers thought: how early do I pack my bags, will I be able to have a natural birth, what if my baby does not arrive on time.

I worked throughout my entire pregnancy – full time as an accountant. I decided to finish work approximately 4 to 5 weeks before my due date so that I could have some much-talked-about 'rest' before the baby arrived. Approximately nine hours after I finished work my waters broke. My husband and I rushed to Sydney South West Private Hospital and we were taken by the nurse to the delivery room. Once settled, I asked the nurse "so when can I go home?" The nurse gave me a puzzled look and said "you will not be going home any time soon. This baby will be here before lunch". Panic immediately set in. I thought to myself "this is not the way this was supposed to happen – what about my 4 week rest?" Sure enough at 12:07pm our son was born. He had some minor complications and needed to stay in the nursery at the hospital but after 13 days we were able to go home.

My advice to expecting mothers: be as prepared as you can but always expect the unexpected!

Rebecca Tragear Whiting
Mum of four, Melbourne

My first two babies were two weeks late and induced. I had pain relief and felt out of control as I slept between contractions and played no real role in the birth. I decided with number three it would be different! I began yoga once a week after my initial morning sickness wore off. The instructor gave me little tips on breathing after each session and reminded me to focus on my baby floating in the womb and its incredible journey into the world. I appointed the services of a fantastic obstetrician and booked into Masada Private Hospital. Everyone involved knew about my previous births and my goals for the next one. My third baby came 3 days late but I went into labour naturally and I focused on the baby and my breathing throughout the labour. I felt very in control and got completely in the zone and delivered after 6 hours with no pain relief. I felt empowered for days after and could not believe how different the experience had been. I was induced again for number four but still controlled my labour with the same techniques and delivered successfully after 7 hours. The midwives are fantastic so make sure you glean as much information and advice from these amazing professionals as you can.

Rowena Raats
Mum of three, Kalgoorlie

Childbirth can sometimes be the easiest part! I know this sounds crazy but I have had three quite easy births all without any complications. I know it's the part of pregnancy that many women focus on but for me the hardest part is getting through the first 2 to 6 weeks after the baby arrives!

With my body sore, hormones all over the place, milk coming in, lack of sleep and caring for this tiny bundle of joy things can easily get on top of you. The strange part is I struggle more with each subsequent child. I think sometimes we are expected to 'snap' back, cope with everything and be that supermum we see in magazines but the reality of it can be so different.

Great support (and I mean real support: someone that does the washing, cooks meals, takes kids to school and just listens) is so important. We live in a country town away from any family and I can't imagine how I would have coped without a support network. I think it's important that support is in place before the baby is born because a lot of times we need help a long time before we actually ask.

Resources

These Resources pages list products and services relevant to "Childbirth & postnatal services".
To make your life easier as a parent, editorial listings have been grouped into sub categories.
Businesses then appear alphabetically under a national or a state-based subhead depending on reach.

SUB-CATEGORIES

ADVISORY & SUPPORT SERVICES: CHILDBIRTH & POSTNATAL SERVICES

NATIONAL

Australian Multiple Birth Association (AMBA)
Tel: 1300 886 499
email: secretary@amba.org.au
website: www.amba.org.au
AMBA is a voluntary community organisation of families with twins, triplets, quadruplets and more. A national network of associated groups provides activities and services that encourage the exchange of information, education and mutual support. AMBA is committed to increasing awareness of the special needs of multiple birth families, and to improve the resources available to them. AMBA is a non-profit, non-political and non-sectarian organisation co-operating with organisations having related interests. Visit the website for more information.

Australian Physiotherapy Association
Tel: (03) 9092 0888
email: national.office@physiotherapy.asn.au
website: www.physiotherapy.asn.au
Physiotherapists around Australia offer excellent antenatal and postnatal support. Physiotherapy can help you stay healthier, fitter and stronger before and after the birth. Physiotherapists can also help you to look after your back, improve recovery of bladder control, use a baby sling and protect the head shape of your baby. To find a local physiotherapist, contact the Australian Physiotherapy Association office in your state or go to 'Find a Physio' on the APA's website at http://physiotherapy.asn.au.

beyondblue: the national depression initiative
email: Info line: 1300 22 4636
website: www.beyondblue.org.au

beyondblue

One of the key roles of beyondblue is to produce, and refer people to, accurate, up-to-date, easy-to-read information on depression, anxiety and related disorders. This includes information relating to: depression, anxiety disorders, postnatal depression, bipolar disorder, diagnosis, treatment, recovery, young people, men, family and friends and chronic physical illness. Phone their Information Line 1300 22 4636 or visit the website at www.beyondblue.org.au for more information.

Bonnie Babes Foundation Inc

Tel: (03) 9803 1800
email: enquiry@bbf.org.au
website: www.bbf.org.au

The Bonnie Babes Foundation is a non-profit volunteer based charity which is established for the health and wellbeing of families. Sadly one in every four pregnancies ends in a loss from miscarriage and stillbirth. Over 17,000 babies are born prematurely, many of them often struggling for life. The Bonnie Babes Foundation helps to save babies' lives and counsel families through this extreme hardship. All proceeds the Foundation raises are for vital medical research projects, and for the 24-hour, 7-day-per-week family counselling services. They also support families with seriously ill babies and infants with childhood diseases.

Child Abuse Prevention Service

Tel: 1800 688 009 or (02) 9716 8000
email: mail@childabuseprevention.com.au
website: www.childabuseprevention.com.au

For the past 30 years CAPS has offered support to parents and carers when the stress and pressures have become too great. CAPS offer 24-hour, 7 days a week confidential telephone support and referrals. For help please phone 1800 688 009 or (02) 9716 8000.

Cradle 2 Kindy Parenting Solutions

Tel: 1300 786 101
email: info@cradle2kindy.com.au
website: www.cradle2kindy.com.au

Cradle 2 Kindy Parenting Solutions provides an optimum start for any parent. This includes ongoing help, bi-monthly newsletters and age-appropriate e-letters. This service includes advice on setting up the nursery, newborn care, breast and bottle feeding, weaning, age-appropriate routines, sleep and settling, night waking, colic/reflux, behavioural and twin management all in the comfort of your home. Cradle 2 Kindy also provide phone and email consultation to those in rural areas. Their motto is "bringing confidence to parenting". Read more about their services on their website www.cradle2kindy.com.au.

goingtohospital.com

email: info@goingtohospital.com
website: www.goingtohospital.com

goingtohospital.com puts together everything you need for going to hospital and delivers it to your home or hospital within 48 hours – soft jersey casual pieces that look as good out of bed as in; pants that fit over your bump but still look good later; front-opening nightshirts and t/shirts. Great pieces that you will wear for months to come. They can also pack a bath bag and a shawl or slippers that you just haven't had time to shop for. Visit www.goingtohospital.com for further information.

L'il Aussie Prems

Tel: 0412 248 583
email: admin@lilaussieprems.com.au
website: www.lilaussieprems.com.au

L'il Aussie Prems is an Australian online support site for parents and families of premature babies. You will find links to Australian support groups, clothing stores, read amazing birth stories, blogs, premmie articles and view premature baby galleries. They have a great community forum featuring live chats, personal diaries, premmie buddies and more.

Labour TENS

Tel: (02) 9400 2709
email: heather@labourtens.com.au
website: www.labourtens.com.au

Labour TENS is an advanced maternity TENS machine providing pain relief from the first contraction through birth and beyond. This safe, highly effective TENS can be used alone for a drug-free birth or with any other pain relief method. The Labour TENS unit has been highly recommended by midwives and obstetricians since the 1960s. This TENS hire company provides a quality product and service specifically designed for pain relief in childbirth at minimal cost. Health fund rebates up to 100%.

Maternity Coalition Inc.

email: inquiries@maternitycoalition.org.au
website: www.maternitycoalition.org.au

Maternity Coalition is a national, non-profit umbrella organisation of groups and individuals committed to improving maternity care for all Australian women, encouraging and promoting informed choice for maternity care and birthing options. MC activities and initiatives include: a national network of branches and local groups in all states; consumer information on choices in childbirth; lobbying governments and health care providers; providing consumer representation on government and professional working groups; information, education, and support programs for all women and their families; Participating Organisations Midwives in Private Practice, Homebirth Australia Inc and Caesarean Awareness Network Australia. Email info@maternitycoalition.org.au for a brochure outlining their aims, activities, and benefits of membership.

Miracle Babies

Tel: 1300 PREMMIE (1300 773 664)
email: info@miraclebabies.com.au
website: www.miraclebabies.com.au

Miracle Babies supports families of babies who enter the world challenged by prematurity or sickness. Their mission is to help families during their journey through a Neonatal Intensive Care Unit (NICU), the transition to home and onwards. They provide support through hospital visits, newsletters, an online forum, playgroups and a 1300 phone number. Founding members have all experienced the birth of a premature or sick newborn. By sharing their strength and knowledge, they can help families celebrate their own miracle babies.

National Council of Single Mothers & their Children

Tel: (08) 8226 2505 or tollfree 1300 725 470
email: ncsmc@ncsmc.org.au
website: www.ncsmc.org.au

Resources

CHILDBIRTH & POSTNATAL SERVICES
Advisory & support services

The National Council of Single Mothers and their Children fights for the rights of single mothers and their children to the benefit of all single parent families. NCSMC offers practical help and support for single mothers and their children in every state and territory including lobby and advocacy work for Centrelink, family law, child support and domestic violence issues. NCSMC is a peak body representing the rights and voice of single mothers and their children nationally.

Parent Infant Research Institute
Tel: (03) 9496 4496
email: carol.newnham@austin.org.au

The birth of a premature baby affects both the baby and his/her parents in unexpected ways. *Premiepress* explains these differences along with the normal emotional, physical and social needs of babies. By understanding these needs as well as the baby's difficulties, parents are encouraged to help their baby's development.

Pelvic Floor Exercise
Tel: 1300 763 940
email: info@pelvicfloorexercise.com.au
website: www.pelvicfloorexercise.com.au

Pelvic Floor Exercise is Australia's specialist pelvic floor shop, packed with quality products to help you regain strength and control of your pelvic floor muscles after childbirth. They stock feedback exercisers, vaginal cones and electrical stimulation devices that are recommended by health professionals, yet easy to use in privacy at home, at times that suit you and your baby. Phone for a brochure or visit their website for everything you need to know about strengthening your pelvic floor, plus up-to-date research and links.

Positive Parenting Network of Australia
email: lois.haultain@parent.net.au
website: www.parent.net.au

The Positive Parenting Network is an alliance of professional educators who support and encourage parents in their challenging and important job. They help parents understand how to deal with misbehaving children in loving, positive ways and how they can bring peace to their families. Visit the website www.parent.net.au to find classes, workshops, resources and private consultations ('supernanny' visit or by phone) with experienced and certified educators. Sign up for a free email newsletter with helpful hints at www.parent.net.au. Educators are available in NSW, Victoria and Queensland.

prisms.com.au
Tel: 0438 007 059
email: info@prisms.com.au
website: www.prisms.com.au

prisms provides newly separated and single mothers with a comprehensive range of information, online resources and support. The website includes an online forum, resource centre, expert panel (with advice about child psychology, career, early childhood education, finance, real estate, health and fitness) and inspirational case studies of single mothers who have survived separation and divorce. prisms holds regular meetings for single mothers around Australia. Phone or visit the website for more information; the prisms website is updated daily.

SIDS and Kids
Tel: National Office (03) 9819 4595 or 1300 308 307
email: national@sidsandkids.org
website: www.sidsandkids.org

SIDS and Kids offers a range of support and counselling services to Australian families following the death of a baby or child during pregnancy, birth, infancy and childhood, regardless of the cause. Bereavement support is offered 24 hours a day, 7 days a week and is completely free of charge. If you or someone you know is in need of these services phone SIDS and Kids on 1300 308 307 or visit the website for more information.

Sleep Rescue & Home Support Services
Tel: (03) 9439 1367 or 0428 439 136
email: admin@sleeprescue.com
website: www.sleeprescue.com

If your baby is not sleeping there is help. The Sleep Rescue and Home Support Service provides practical support, education and advice to help parents develop skills to confidently manage the challenges of early parenthood. Staff provide guidance and continuity of support to assist families achieve their goals in their home environment. Families receive care and support for infant settling, feeding issues, sleep problems and routines. They offer day/night overstays, 24 hours and no waiting list. Phone or visit the website for more information.

Tresillian Family Care Centres
24-hour Parents Help Line: (02) 9787 0855 or 1800 637 357
website: www.tresillian.net

Messenger Mums is an exciting initiative between Tresillian Family Care Centres and ninemsn for parents having difficulties in the early years of their child's life. Tresillian's registered nurses are available online from Monday to Friday between 9.00am to 3.30pm to offer parenting advice and support via 'instant-messaging'. This is a free service. Visit http://health.ninemsn.com.au/messengermums/default.aspx.

VICTORIA

Being a Mother
Tel: (03) 9882 7958 or 0407 819 519
email: betty@beingamother.com
website: www.beingamother.com

Feel like you're the only one who struggles with being a mum? Tired of yelling or being frustrated? Want to know how to feel happier and less stressed? Being a Mother is a tailored workshop addressing these issues with techniques that are practical, easy to use and work immediately. East Hawthorn venue. Rebates and concession available. For more information phone Betty Chetcuti, Psychologist (BBSc (Hons.), MEdPysch, MAPS), wife and mother of three. Private appointments also available.

BellyBelly Pregnancy Centre
Level 1, 89 Canterbury Road
Canterbury VIC 3126
Tel: (03) 9836 7734
email: info@bellybelly.com.au
website: www.bellybelly.com.au/pregnancy-centre

At the BellyBelly Pregnancy Centre you're in safe hands during conception, pregnancy and into parenthood. The centre offers a range of services including natural health therapies, informative and empowering workshops and education, as well as products and services available for sale. Therapists – including osteopaths, massage therapists, acupuncturists, a counsellor, naturopaths and others – are passionate and experienced about pre-conception and pre and postnatal care. Books, DVDs and other products are carefully selected to ensure you get great information and products helping you to have a safe, informed and educated journey.

Centre for Child & Family Development
721A Riversdale Road
Camberwell VIC 3124
Tel: (03) 9830 0422
email: ccfdau@ozemail.com.au
website: www.childandfamily.com.au

The Under Fives Counselling Service provides skilled psychotherapy help for problems which may arise for new babies and new parents and for toddlers and young children with eating, sleeping, toilet training difficulties and general behavioural problems.

Fertile Ground Health Group
Suite 3, Level 6, 372–376 Albert Street
East Melbourne VIC 3002
Tel: (03) 9419 9988
email: reception@fertileground.com.au
website: www.fertileground.com.au

Fertile Ground Health Group specialise in preconception care for men and women, infertility, IVF support, health in pregnancy, birth preparation and labour support, postnatal and baby health, as well as general health. They also treat menstrual issues throughout the lifecycle, including menarche and menopause. Specialist services include naturopathy, acupuncture, osteopathy, massage, kinesiology and counselling. There is a range of supplementary services to help you stay on track including massage, home and hospital visiting services, midwife/lactation support services and infant massage instruction.

Health 4 Women (H4W)
Suite 327/55 Flemington Road
North Melbourne VIC 3051
Tel: (03) 9329 0999
website: www.health4women.com.au

The H4W Practice is located across the road from the new Women's Hospital and Frances Perry House. Inpatient and outpatient physiotherapy services include individual consultations pre-natally and postnatally to prepare for childbirth and to facilitate postnatal recovery. There is also now a small pilates studio offering one-on-one or small group classes.

Hospital to Home
Tel: (03) 9818 8807 or 0427 818 848
email: hospitaltohome@bigpond.com
website: www.hospitaltohome.com.au

Hospital to Home is a quality home nursing support service caring for mothers and families. Services include: home nursing (home visit by an experienced midwife providing breastfeeding support, settling techniques and parentcraft assistance); lactation consultants; maternal massage, aromatherapy facial, feet treat; infant massage tuition; luscious meals, gourmet biscuits and champagne; home assistance, house cleaning or home and family support; nappy service (Huggies and cloth); classic flowers and gift vouchers. All in the comfort of your home either as an Early Discharge Package or purchased singularly.

Immaculate Reception
10 Landen Avenue
North Balwyn VIC 3104
Tel: 0414 943 365
email: sarah@immaculatereception.com.au
website: www.immaculatereception.com.au

Immaculate Reception creates a fabulous experience for new parents. Specialising in fully preparing your home for mum and baby's arrival, they can give you the time to relax, recover and bond with your new baby. Services include New Arrivals packages, creating a pristine and baby-ready home; organising and setting up baby equipment; delicious dinners delivered and other home-style meals delivered to your door, post-natal doulas and referral to a professional team of post-natal specialists. Fabulous gift packages make the perfect surprise for any new mum.

Life's Little Treasures
Tel: 0437 254 360
email: contact_us@lifeslittletreasures.org.au
website: www.lifeslittletreasures.org.au

Life's Little Treasures is a charity run by volunteer parents who themselves have had a premature baby. They provide support and assistance to other families of

Resources

CHILDBIRTH & POSTNATAL SERVICES

Advisory & support services

premature babies throughout Victoria, either in hospital, neonatal intensive care units, special care nurseries or in the community when families get home. They provide this support and information to parents via a supportive parent network to match like parents together for support; morning teas/playgroups at various venues including hospitals and community settings; a quarterly newsletter and website to provide parents with updated and relevant information on premature baby issues; a Parent Information guide and parent packs providing relevant tips and information specific to these families. Social occasions are also organised throughout the year.

Madelaine Akras

26 Merton Street
Box Hill VIC 3128
Tel: 1800 003 902 or (03) 9849 0096 or 0418 351 979
email: makras@optusnet.com.au
website: www.hypnobirthingvictoria.com.au

The Journey into Motherhood Birthing Kit is designed to support you before, during and after your labour and birth. The Journey into Motherhood Birthing Kit consists of 8 homeopathic remedies, calendula tincture and flower essences which are safe for both mother and baby as well as an easy-to-follow instruction booklet detailing effective use of the remedies.

Maternal and Child Health Line

Tel: 13 22 29

The Maternal and Child Health Line is a state-wide, 24-hour telephone service. Callers can access information, advice and support regarding child health, nutrition, breastfeeding, maternal and family health. The service is available to Victorian families with children 0 to school age and complements the locally based service. Phone 13 22 29.

Mercy Health O'Connell Family Centre

6 Mont Albert Road
Canterbury VIC 3126
Tel: (03) 8416 7600
website: www.mercy.com.au

Mercy Health O'Connell Family Centre, a facility of Mercy Health, is a government-funded service providing family focused education and support to families experiencing parenting difficulties with children up to four years of age. Services include day-stay programs and a residential program and most costs are covered by Medicare. The Centre also conducts parent education workshops around various early parenting topics and issues in response to community request and need.

PANDA

810 Nicholson Street
North Fitzroy VIC 3068
Phone support: 1300 726 306; Admin (03) 9481 3377
email: info@panda.org.au
website: www.panda.org.au

PANDA is a statewide, not-for-profit organisation for women and families affected by postnatal and antenatal depression in Victoria. PANDA acknowledges that social, biological and psychological factors play a role in postnatal and antenatal depression. PANDA works to: support and inform women and their families who are affected by postnatal and antenatal mood disorders; and educate health care professionals and the wider community about postnatal and antenatal mood disorders. PANDA runs a support, information and referral helpline which is staffed by specially trained volunteers and staff, many of whom have experienced postnatal or antenatal depression.

Parent Infant Research Institute

Austin Health 330 Waterdale Road
Heidelberg Heights VIC 3081
Tel: (03) 9496 4496
email: Jennifer.ericksen@austin.org.au
website: www.piri.org.au

The Infant Clinic is a not-for-profit clinic staffed by specialist psychologists who provide a comprehensive service to families in the ante and postnatal period. Cutting edge research, teaching and treatment programs are available to address the needs of parents facing the challenges of parenthood, especially prematurity, relationship changes, anxiety, depression and understanding and managing babies and toddlers. The Infant Clinic also has antenatal programs to assist in the transition to parenthood.

Positive Parenting Services

Tel: 0408 102 552
email: katieshafar@yahoo.com.au
website: www.positiveparenting.com.au

Never underestimate the impact on a family of sleeplessness due to a wakeful baby or child/infant. Katie Shafar provides child sleep and behavioural management in your own home. Her work is to keep families together by decreasing family stresses, to encourage quiet times and talking, and to empower people to solve their own problems by giving them the knowledge and confidence to trust their own intuition and follow through. Phone Katie on the number above or visit her website www.positveparenting.com.au for more information.

ready set mama

PO Box 255
Ormond VIC 3204
Tel: 0412 627 749
email: nicole@readysetmama.com.au
website: www.readysetmama.com.au

ready set mama helps mums-to-be prepare for baby's arrival and their time in hospital by providing the essentials for both mother and baby when they pack their bags. Fabulous for busy expectant mums to help maximise precious rest time both before and after baby's arrival. Ideal, practical and beautifully presented – a wonderful gift idea from family, friends or work colleagues for the mum-to-be. ready set mama also stocks the gorgeous WOMAMA range of maternity and breastfeeding wear from New Zealand – see the range on the website or phone for more details.

SANDS (Vic)
Suite 208, 901 Whitehorse Road
Box Hill VIC 3128
Tel: (03) 9899 0217 (admin) or (03) 9899 0218 (support)
email: info@sandsvic.org.au
website: www.sandsvic.org.au

SANDS (Vic) is a state-wide self-help support organisation for parents who have experienced the death of a baby through miscarriage, stillbirth or shortly after birth. SANDS offers 24-hour phone support for bereaved parents, families and friends. It holds monthly support meetings and has a bi-monthly newsletter. SANDS has also produced the book *Your Baby has Died* and many other pamphlets and educates parents, professionals and the general community through seminars, workshops, media releases and literature.

The Featherweight Club
C/- Mercy Hospital for Women, 163 Studley Road
Heidelberg VIC 3084
Tel: 0412 976 224
email: fwc@featherweightclub.com
website: www.featherweightclub.com

The Featherweight Club is a voluntary organisation established to support families who have had an infant admitted to a Special Care Nursery, including the Neonatal Intensive Care Unit, due to prematurity or other complications. It seeks to raise awareness of these families' needs within the hospital environment and the broader community. Members have all had personal experiences of babies in a Special Care Nursery and they support families using the practical experiences of, and funds raised by, their volunteer members.

The Royal Women's Hospital
132 Grattan Street
Carlton VIC 3053
Tel: (03) 8345 2127
email: angela.steele@thewomens.org.au
website: www.ypp.org.au

The Young Women's Health Program offers antenatal and postnatal support and outreach services for women aged 19 years and under who are pregnant and parenting. Service hours are 9.00am to 5.00pm Monday to Friday.

Tweddle Child & Family Health Service
53 Adelaide Street
Footscray VIC 3011
Tel: (03) 9689 1577
email: tweddle@tweddle.org.au
website: www.tweddle.org.au

tweddle
child + family health service

Tweddle is an early parenting centre which provides support and education for families with children up to four years of age. Tweddle has day-stay and residential programs for parents who are experiencing sleeping, feeding and behaviour problems with their baby or young child. Tweddle's range of services and programs are tailored to suit an individual family's needs. Tweddle also has two new services: Tweddle@Home is a fee-based, home-visiting service with expert advice tailored to your individual needs in the privacy of your own home; Tweddle Psychology Service has recently commenced where clients can be referred by a health professional or contact them direct. Rebates may be available through Medicare and private insurance agencies.

NEW SOUTH WALES

babybliss
Tel: 0417 487 439
email: jo@babybliss.com.au
website: www.babybliss.com.au

Babybliss is a home visiting service, established by Jo Ryan, for parents of babies and toddlers. Jo's calm and relaxed approach to tackling early childhood issues like sleeping, feeding and establishing routines makes her a welcome inclusion for young families and empowers parents to feel confident in dealing with their children. Jo works with families in their own home or remotely, to their own standards and in a way that is suitable to each family's unique beliefs and practice. Her support and advice will ultimately assist in reducing the stress that is felt by all parents, creating a better experience of early parenthood and young family life.

Blissful Babies
PO Box 7263
Penrith South LPO NSW 2750
Tel: 0400 673 881
website: www.blissfulbabies.com.au

Blissful Babies has over 20 years experience and can assist families with setting up a nursery, providing support for newborns, establishing a flexible daily routine, assisting and coaching parents in Mothercraft skills, teaching feeding techniques, breastfeeding care and advice, reflux management, teaching settling techniques, relaxation bathing and baby massage, night waking and looking after pre-term and special needs infants. Blissful Babies has also worked extensively with neonates, postnatal depression and other medical conditions. Effective techniques for managing multiple births. A follow-up phone service is also offered.

Blue Mountains Homebirth Support Group
Tel: (02) 4757 2080 or 0410 428 307
email: nataliedash@optusnet.com.au

The Blue Mountains Homebirth Support Group is for women and families seeking information on homebirth in the Blue Mountains. Details of independent midwives, support groups, waterbirth, childbirth classes, doulas and birthing options are provided.

Resources

CHILDBIRTH & POSTNATAL SERVICES

Advisory & support services

Childbirth Education Association of Australia (NSW)

PO Box 240
Sutherland NSW 2232
Tel: (02) 8539 7188
email: info@cea-nsw.com.au
website: www.cea-nsw.com.au

The Childbirth Education Association of Australia (NSW) has been preparing women and their partners and families for childbirth and early parenting since 1961. Services offered by CEA include prenatal classes throughout Sydney metro as well as video and book borrowing libraries. CEA has also produced a number of videos and publications on pregnancy and childbirth.

Dial-A-Mum Inc

Tel: (02) 9477 6777
email: dial_a_mum@hotmail.com
website: www.dial-a-mum.org.au

Dial-A-Mum is a telephone support service that has been in operation since 1979 and is operated and funded by a group of trained, volunteer mothers. Callers come from all age groups, from all areas of Sydney and New South Wales and from all walks of life. Their issues are varied: conflict in relationships (spouse/partner, family, friends, neighbours and the workplace), domestic abuse, parenting, mental health, grief and isolation. Callers are adults and children who just want to talk to a mum.

Karitane

PO Box 241
Villawood NSW 2163
Careline (7 days/week): 1300 227 464 or
(02) 9794 2300, Karitane@Home: (02) 9399 7147
email: karitane.online@sswahs.nsw.gov.au
website: www.karitane.com.au

Karitane provides support, guidance and information to families with children 0 to 5 years who are experiencing parenting difficulties. Assistance is available through Careline (7 day per week State-wide Service: 1300 CARING 1300 227 464), Family Care Centres, Jade House (PND support), the Toddler Clinic, Residential Unit, volunteer home visiting, Karitane@Home (private home visiting for a fee for service) and Connecting Carers NSW (for foster and kinship carer support). A specialised team of Child and Family Health professionals are available for consultation on a wide range of issues such as feeding problems, sleep and settle routines, toddler behaviour management, parent anxiety, pre and post-natal depression and other issues.

stepbystep Parenting

Tel: 0458 536 137
email: stacy@stepbystepparenting.com.au
website: www.stepbystepparenting.com.au

The one-on-one services stepbystep Parenting provides to clients are developed and targeted to meet the individual needs of each family situation. Their home visits provide a comfortable and secure environment for both parent and child. Each team member has more than 20 years experience, specialising in midwifery, parentcraft and lactation consultancy. stepbystep staff have trained and worked at Tresillian and Karitane, as well as private and public hospitals in southern Sydney.

The Hills Parenting Centre

105 Showground Road
Castle Hill NSW 2154
Tel: (02) 9659 7760
website: www.hillsparentingcentre.com.au

The Hills Parenting Centre provides for families from birth to five years of age with a speciality in infant sleep programs. Services include pregnancy groups, help with the management of a newborn infants, setting up routines, avoiding problems. Their other area of expertise is in providing help throughout the toddler years with a focus on building healthy relationships and teaching parents how to understand and manage difficult toddler behaviour. This is the first private service of its kind in Australia.

Tresillian Family Care Centres

Head Office: McKenzie Street
Belmore NSW 2192
24-hour Parents Help Line: (02) 9787 0855 or
1800 637 357
Other locations:
25 Shirley Road
Wollstonecraft NSW 2065
Tel: (02) 9432 4000
2 Second Avenue
Willoughby NSW 2068
Tel: (02) 8962 8300
1b Barber Avenue
Kingswood NSW 2747
Tel: (02) 4734 2124
website: www.tresillian.net

Arriving home with a new baby can be daunting and often it's hard to know who to turn to for help. If you need assistance with any issue relating to the care of your baby contact the Tresillian 24-hour Parents Help Line on (02) 9787 0855 in Sydney or 1800 637 357(outside Sydney). Parents needing help from Tresillian are usually experiencing difficulties ranging from breastfeeding, settling the newborn, a baby who continues to wake several times a night, toddler behaviour, nightwaking and postnatal depression. Tresillian employs professional staff including Child and Family Health Nurses, Paediatricians, Psychologists, Psychiatrists and Social Workers who offer families practical advice. They also hold a range of Parent Education Seminars across Sydney.

AUSTRALIAN CAPITAL TERRITORY

ParentLine
Tel: (02) 6287 3833
website: www.parentlineact.org.au

ParentLine is open from 9.00am to 9.00pm, Monday to Friday for parents and other people concerned with issues of parenting. The service aims to enhance the development, health and emotional wellbeing of children by supporting parents and carers and connecting them with the network of services available to families in the ACT and surrounding areas. The assistance provided is confidential, immediate and anonymous. Professionally trained staff provide callers with counselling, guidance, information about parenting issues and programs offered by other agencies, and referral to other organisations. ParentLine also provides face-to-face counselling and ongoing telephone support through trained volunteers.

QUEENSLAND

Child Health Line
Tel: (07) 3862 2333 or 1800 177 279 (24 hours)
website: www.health.qld.gov.au/cchs

The Child Health Line is a 24-hour telephone information and support service for parents, carers and service providers with infants, children and young people aged 0–18 years.

Childbirth Education Association (Brisbane) Inc.
PO Box 206
Petrie QLD 4502
Tel: (07) 3285 8233
email: mail@ceabrisbane.asn.au
website: www.ceabrisbane.asn.au

Childbirth Education Association (Brisbane) is a non-profit community group which began in 1965 and provides quality independent childbirth education and support services. Services include prenatal active birth course; private one-on-one sessions for first births, subsequent births or vaginal births after caesarean; information on VBAC and positive caesarean birth; information on choosing a care provider and place of birth. The benefits of these courses include a small group environment; addressing individual needs and concerns; exploring all the options in birth; and developing strategies to implement informed choices. Phone or visit the website for more information.

Friends of the Birth Centre Assoc Qld
PO Box 93
Grange QLD 4051
Tel: (07) 3289 9789
email: info@fbc.org.au
website: www.fbc.org.au

Friends of the Birth Centre Assoc Qld is a non-profit association dedicated to midwifery and birth centre advocacy. Branches in Mackay, Townsville, Gold Coast, Darling Downs and Brisbane. If you believe your community could benefit from a birth centre then give them a ring. Expectant and young families in Brisbane are invited to monthly Tuesday playgroups. Make friends among facilitated discussion in a child-friendly environment. Details on website.

Healthcare Belmont Private Hospital
1220 Creek Road
Carina QLD 4152
Tel: (07) 3398 0238

The Brisbane Centre for Post Natal Disorders is an in-patient and day patient specialised unit for women experiencing emotional disturbances during the childbearing period. Mothers and their babies are supported by a multi-disciplinary team, a comprehensive therapy program and supportive environment with an opportunity to gain insight, develop more satisfactory ways of relating to others, build a sense of confidence and enhance enjoyment of parenting. For further information contact the unit on (07) 3398 0238.

My Helping Hand
Tel: 0405 222 153
email: lynne@myhelpinghand.com.au
website: www.myhelpinghand.com.au

My Helping Hand provides a personalised, in-home service to help you in the first few weeks at home with your baby. The service is tailored to suit your individual requirements and needs. My Helping Hand is beneficial to all mums and especially those who do not have any family close by. They are passionate about helping others and providing a professional and friendly service so let them take care of your housework while you have time with your baby.

The Home Midwifery Association (QLD) Inc.
PO Box 655
Spring Hill QLD 4004
Tel: (07) 3839 5883
email: info@homebirth.org.au
website: www.homebirth.org.au

The Homebirth Support Group is a group of mothers and midwives and their families working towards real choice in childbirth. They view birthing as a family event rather than a medical emergency, and celebrate babies' births rather than deliveries. They meet each second and fourth Monday of the month in Brisbane, each first and third Friday at the Sunshine Coast and the first Wednesday of the month at the Gold Coast. HMA publishes a quarterly magazine, Down to Birth, providing information on natural birth, nutrition, natural healing methods and pain relief. HMA have contact details of midwives who attend homebirths.

Women's Health Queensland Wide
165 Gregory Terrace
Spring Hill QLD 4000
Tel: (07) 3839 9962
Health Information Line (07) 3839 9988
Toll Free outside Brisbane 1800 017 676
TTY (07) 3831 5508
email: admin@womhealth.org.au
website: www.womhealth.org.au

Resources

CHILDBIRTH & POSTNATAL SERVICES

Advisory & support services
→ Birth announcements, cards & stationery

Women's Health Queensland Wide is a non-profit health promotion service providing information and education services to women and health workers throughout the state. Services include a Health Information Line staffed by registered nurses and midwives, library services, fact sheets and quarterly publication, as well as a website and health education programs. Women can contact the service for information on a wide range of topics including pregnancy, childbirth, breastfeeding, early childhood and postnatal depression.

YHES House
11 Hicks Street
Southport QLD 4215
Tel: (07) 5531 1577
email: yypcoord@yhes.org.au
website: www.yhes.org.au

The Youth Health and Education Service (YHES House) Young Parents Support Program aims to improve the health and wellbeing of young parents aged 12 to 25 years, and their children, during the prenatal and early childhood periods. By offering a Childbirth Education Support Group and a New Parents Group, YHES House provides information, socialisation and ongoing support to empower young people to make informed decisions about their own and their child's health and wellbeing. Phone or visit the website for more information.

WESTERN AUSTRALIA

Hush Postnatal Services
PO Box 479
Greenwood WA 6924
Tel: (08) 9448 5459
email: info@hushpostnatal.com.au
website: www.hushpostnatal.com.au

Hush provides a private postnatal support service in the comfort of your own home. Established by Paula Baildham and Zoe Islip, Hush is dedicated to the education and empowerment of new parents. As midwives/lactation consultants and parents, Paula and Zoe realise how daunting it can be taking your new baby home. Hush promotes knowledge, self-confidence and practical skills in all facets of newborn care. Individualised care may include breastfeeding, identification of tired signs, gentle settling techniques, bathing and baby massage and gift certificates. Private antenatal classes are also available. Visit their website for further details.

Ngala Inc.
9 George Street
Kensington WA 6151
Tel: (08) 9368 9368
website: www.ngala.com.au

Ngala is an early parenting centre with a passion for supporting and guiding families through the journey of early parenting via a range of opportunities to increase and enhance knowledge of parenting skills. They offer education courses, coffee mornings, consults, day stay and overnight stay and the Ngala Helpline. Helpline staff provide guidelines and reassurance for parents, and seek to encourage confidence. Parents can contact the Ngala Helpline between the hours of 8.00am and 8.00pm on (08) 9368 9368 (metro callers) or 1800 111 546 (country) 7 days a week.

SOUTH AUSTRALIA

24/7 Parent Helpline
Tel: 1300 364 100

The Parent Helpline is a 24/7 service providing information, support and referral to parents and young people from birth to 25 years. Parents can access information on a large range of topics including behaviour, feeding or sleeping difficulties, diet and toilet training, risk taking and managing the transition to adulthood. The information is provided by a multi-disciplinary team of registered nurses, community health workers, social workers and specially trained volunteers. The Helpline has a local call cost. The Parent Helpline is an initiative of the Children Youth and Women's Health Service, which forms part of the State Government Department SA Health.

CARES SA Inc.
(Caesarean Awareness Recovery Education Support)
Tel: (08) 8280 6667
email: cares.sa.org@gmail.com
website: www.cares-sa.org.au

CARES SA Inc. is a non-profit community support group for women and families dealing with any issues surrounding caesarean or vaginal birth after caesarean (VBAC). They are not anti-caesarean; they aim to provide balanced information to assist women planning a safe and empowered birth. They provide a caring and understanding environment for women and their partners to find emotional healing. Options for support are coffee meetings, email, website and by phone.

Women's and Children's Hospital
72 King William Road
North Adelaide SA 5006
Tel: (08) 8161 7592
website: www.wch.sa.gov.au

Midwifery Group Practice through the Women's and Children's Hospital (WCH) offers midwifery-led care during pregnancy, labour, birth and the postnatal period up to four weeks after childbirth. The WCH and community based care is provided by the Children, Youth and Women's Health Service, a division of SA Health.

BIRTH ANNOUNCEMENTS, CARDS & STATIONERY

NATIONAL

Alannah Rose – Exclusive Stationery Boutique

Tel: 0417 572 528

email: info@alannahrose.com.au

website: www.alannahrose.com.au

Introduce your little one to the world with a stylish personalised baby announcement, thank-you card or christening invitation from Alannah Rose. Simply select a design from their online boutique at www.alannahrose.com.au, supply a photo of your child and they will deliver your cards in a beautiful box ready for you to write on and send to the world. This professionally printed range includes stylish folding birth announcement cards, christening and party invitations as well as Christmas cards. Delivery is Australia wide.

Announcements & Invitations by Little Dance

Tel: (03) 9752 6602

email: enquiries@littledanceinvitations.com

website: www.littledanceinvitations.com

Announcements & Invitations by Little Dance specialise in beautiful photo invitations for birth announcements, Christenings, namings, baptisms, birthdays, Christmas and other special and fun occasions. They offer an original range of invitations from funny to stylish, classic designs as well as RSVP cards, place cards and bomboniere tags, also fantasy art and photo montages. Announcements & Invitations by Little Dance create gorgeous photo memory gifts. Phone or visit the website for more information.

cardamon seed

Tel: (03) 9383 3247

email: info@cardamonseed.com.au

website: www.cardamonseed.com.au

cardamon seed makes it easy for you to have birth announcement cards for your new baby using your own photos. Their designs are original and can be changed to suit your taste. Their website displays a range of card designs to choose from for birth announcements, thank you cards, christening invitations, Christmas cards, birthday and wedding invitations. All you need to do is send them a photo by email and then choose the design you like, the message and quantity. Within 24 hours they will email you a proof for your approval, before sending your cards to print. The cardamon seed service takes between 5 to 10 working days from the time you order through to receipt of your cards. The cards are available nationally and internationally. Visit their website or phone for further information.

Creative Cards

Tel: (03) 9873 4081

email: info@creativecards.com.au

website: www.creativecards.com.au

Creative Cards specialise in creating personalised, beautiful and unique photo cards using your photo and words. Their high quality yet affordable range includes, birth announcements, thank you cards, birthday invitations, Christmas cards and much more. Simply choose from the wide range of gorgeous designs, email a photo from your collection, write your own words or choose theirs and let them do the rest. Your personalised cards and free envelopes will be returned to you within 10 days. Available nationally.

Designed with Love

email: designedwithlove@bigpond.com

website: www.designedwithlove.com.au

Designed with Love offers beautiful, affordable stationery for all of your child's events – birth announcements, christening invitations, birthday invitations and much more. Each is personalised with your photos and many different colour combinations. Starting at only $1 each.

Designer Photo Cards

Tel: 0412 579 599

email: enquiry@designerphotocards.com.au

website: www.designerphotocards.com.au

Designer Photo Cards design customised cards for special occasions and they also offer standard designs as well. Designer Photo Cards can be created for just about anything – announcements, invitations, greetings and thank you cards. Once you've purchased a customised design it is yours to do what you like with. Some people like to use their design to make matching mugs, calendars, mouse-mats – the possibilities are endless. Phone or visit the website for more information.

InkPink Design

Tel: 0407 545 925

email: cards@inkpinkdesign.com.au

website: www.inkpinkdesign.com.au

Announce your new baby in style with a personalised photo greeting card that will grab the attention of your guests when they receive it and can be added to the family photo album after the event is over. InkPink Design can create invitation and announcement designs for all occasions: baby showers, baby birth announcements, christenings and naming days, birthdays and thank-you cards. Cards come with optional magnets on the back, envelopes and folding cards. Enlargement prints of photo collages and family keepsake designs are also available.

Inviting Invitations

Tel: (02) 9999 6597

email: enquiries@invitinginvitations.com.au

website: www.invitinginvitations.com.au

Inviting Invitations sells unique, personalised baby invitations and cards. The range includes baby shower invitations, birth announcement cards, christening invites, birthday party invitations and cards. You can also customise your own unique and personalised invitations and cards with your child's photo. Prices range from $2.95 including envelopes and delivery Australia wide within 7 days. Phone or visit the website for more information.

Resources

Leanne Temme Photography

38 Windella Avenue
East Kew VIC 3102
Tel: (03) 9859 5345
website: www.leannetemme.com.au

Leanne Temme, a photographer and mother, can create beautiful birth announcements and thank-you cards that feature your baby. Visit Leanne's website to see her photography portfolio or phone or email for more information.

Mini Ink

Tel: 0408 936 031
email: design@miniink.com.au
website: www.miniink.com.au

Mini Ink creates individually designed baby announcement, birthday and christening photo cards. These cards aim to make parents, family and friends smile, as well as convey a message of joy or an invitation to celebrate, using your own personal photos of your special little one. Each contemporary and stylish baby card is custom created and printed onto archive quality photo paper, then delivered to your door ready to make a big impression. Visit www.miniink.com.au for more information or phone the number above.

Nanny Pickle

Tel: (07) 3366 9006
email: nannypickle@nannypickle.com.au
website: www.nannypickle.com.au

Once upon a time, not so very long ago, there lived a sweet, savvy and slightly quirky nanny, known throughout the land as Nanny Pickle. From the wonderful world of Nanny Pickle comes her playful range of infant wear and accessories for babies and toddlers. Born out of whimsy and a daydream, Nanny Pickle creates beautiful collections of delightful infant wear, divine cards for baby and mama, sweet hand-made toys and delectable co-ordinated nursery accessories. Visit Nanny Pickle's divine website to explore the entire range.

Photocards

email: lexandscott@unwired.com.au
website: www.photocards.ueuo.com

Photocards custom design the perfect photo announcement, invitation or greeting card for birthday parties, farewells, thank-you cards, baby showers, birth announcements, christenings and baptisms, congratulations, anniversaries, graduations, change of address, Christmas cards, engagements, weddings, kitchen teas, hens nights and much more. Visit the website for further information or phone the number listed above.

Stationery Online

Tel: 1800 501 075
email: sales@stationeryonline.com
website: www.stationeryonline.com.au

Stationery Online offers beautiful pregnancy and birth announcements to share your proudest moments with family and friends. Add your own photo to their many designs. Available in traditional card or magnetic formats. They also offer wonderful Christening, naming day and party invitations and stationery. View and order online or phone. They deliver anywhere in Australia.

BOOKS, DVDs & CDs: CHILDBIRTH

NATIONAL

A Labour of Love

Tel: 0418 336 362
email: info@alabouroflove.com.au
website: www.alabouroflove.com.au

Gabrielle Targett's inspiration for writing *A Labour of Love – an Australian guide to natural childbirth* came from her own experiences and attending births as a professional (birth support person) doula over the last eleven years. Gabrielle is also a trained independent national childbirth educator, running empowered couples/women's childbirth educational workshops and courses. She has presented at many birth-related conferences in Western Australia and nationally. Her outstanding ability to speak publicly with honesty, humour and passion makes her a sought-after presenter and a person who has much to offer both other professionals and the pregnant women she educates all over Australia. Working currently as a certified hypnosis practitioner, Gabrielle offers CDs through her online shop to women who want to prepare for birth in a positive and empowered way.

birth

Tel: 0400 484 620
email: di@birtheducation.com.au
website: www.birtheducation.com.au

Dusty's Big Day Out DVD follows the labour and birth of baby Dusty. A very real birth film that shows how the mother deals with pain and how the people around her are involved. An excellent resource for parents, midwives, and birth educators. Produced by Di Diddle, birth attendant/educator. For copies phone 0400 484 620 or visit www.birtheducation.com.au.

Birthing Sense Birth Education DVDs

Tel: 0411 255 535
email: leanne@birthingsense.com
website: www.birthingsense.com

Compliment or substitute your prenatal class with three DVDs. Australian midwife and antenatal educator Leanne Cummins has interviewed over 26 experts and parents to bring your childbirth education class to your own home. Fifty segments over three DVDs help you make sense of your pregnancy, birth and new baby. Order your birth class online at www.birthingsense.com.

Birthnet Pty Ltd
Tel: (02) 9662 6019
email: management@birth.com.au
website: www.birth.com.au

Birth.com.au and *BIRTH* the book are invaluable resources for women and partners on their journey to parenthood. Written and supported by a midwife and a childbirth educator with over 30 years collective experience, they provide everything you need to know about fertility, conception, pregnancy, birth and early parenting. Birthnet's online birthtalks® community is a great way to network with other parents and parents-to-be.

Gentle Birth, Gentle Mothering
email: info@sarahjbuckley.com
website: www.sarahjbuckley.com

Want the best birth for you and your baby? Need more confidence and less fear? *Gentle Birth, Gentle Mothering* by Dr Sarah J Buckley, GP and mother of four, gives essential information on prenatal testing, pain relief and epidurals, caesarean versus natural birth, cord blood banking and more. Learn about the ecstatic hormones of labour, and how superbly designed your body is for a safe and satisfying birth. New edition out March 2009 in bookstores and online at www.sarahjbuckley.com.

Julia Sundin, Physiotherapist
Tel: (02) 9417 6467
website: www.jujusundin.com

Face to Face with Childbirth ($30 inc. p&p) includes body exercise, ways of developing confidence and courage, understanding the birth process, focussing on your partner's role, medical backup should you need it, and powerful ideas and input on mastering labour pain. Available through mail order or phone (02) 8539 7188. Visit www.jujusundin.com for more information.

Julia Sundin, Physiotherapist
Tel: (02) 9417 6467
website: www.jujusundin.com

Julia Sundin's new CD titled *"Hypno Active" Visualisation for Childbirth* will help you master the stress, anxiety, fear and pain in labour through imagery, mantras, key words and suggestion. There are two sessions – one for pregnancy stress management and one for labour pain management. A cut out cribb sheet for partners is included. Visit www.jujusundin.com for more information and price.

Julia Sundin, Physiotherapist
Tel: (02) 9417 6467
website: www.jujusundin.com

The *Father's Role in Birth* CD is for fathers/partners who want to know exactly what they will be doing on the day of the birth – from the moment they receive the phone call from you to say you are in labour, throughout labour at home, in the car and during your time in the delivery suite/birthcentre. $42.00 plus p&h. Available from www.jujusundin.com.

Julia Sundin, Physiotherapist
Tel: (02) 9417 6467
website: www.jujusundin.com

All You've Wanted to Know About Labour Pain CD is positive 'what, why, when, where, how' education about the pain of childbirth and will help you come to terms with the healthy, fascinating and extraordinary sensation that comes with contractions. It will also assist you to learn the tools to help you keep control on the day of the birth. $42.00 plus p&h. Available from www.jujusundin.com.

Julia Sundin, Physiotherapist
Tel: (02) 9417 6467
website: www.jujusundin.com

JuJu Sundin's *Birth Skills with Sarah Murdoch* ($40.00 + p&p) details the proven tools and techniques required for helping the birthing couple deal with labour pain, pushing out the baby, crowning, posterior, backache birth, motivation and much more. Sarah Murdoch writes about her experiences of being in JuJu's classes and applying the techniques with her husband during labour. Visit www.jujusundin.com or phone for further information.

Little Bundle
Tel: (08) 8278 4342
email: info@parentwellbeing.com
website: www.parentwellbeing.com

Exhausted from broken sleep? Confused by conflicting advice? Overwhelmed by your baby's constant needs? You are not alone. The book *Little Bundle* provides consolation and inspiration during the first year of your baby's life. Like a good friend, Jodie Benveniste does not tell you how to look after your baby, instead she helps you care for yourself. "Dip into Little Bundle for reassurance, comfort and companionship in the middle of the night." Robin Barker, author of *Baby Love*.

Nuhouse Press
Tel: 0409 808 852
email: email@nuhousepress.com
website: www.nuhousepress.com

The Baby Doctor is a book for children about IVF. *The Baby Doctor* uses IVF technology to make babies and he's helping the family in this story have their second IVF baby. Read it with the big brother or sister-to-be in your family to help explain why mummy is feeling tired and going to see the doctor a lot. Read it with your own miracle baby to help explain the special way they came into the world. $30 including postage from www.nuhousepress.com.

Resources

CHILDBIRTH & POSTNATAL SERVICES

Books, DVDs & CDs

➡ Education classes & workshops

Physiotherapy Pilates Proactive

Tel: (08) 8271 3144

email: parkside@pilatesproactive.com.au

website: www.pilatesproactive.com.au

Recorded by highly-qualified pilates expert and physiotherapist, Rachel Combe, the *Pilates Proactive™ Pregnancy & Post Natal* CD includes three separate pilates exercise programs – first trimester; second and third trimester; and postnatal which each run for 30 minutes. The CD also includes a comprehensive instruction booklet which accompanies the exercises. The routines will improve posture, alleviate pain and tone the body during pregnancy and post-natally. These exercises are designed to be done at home in conjunction with regular Pilates Mat Class attendance as initial supervision is essential for safe, proficient technique. CDs may be purchased online at www.pilatesproactive.com.au.

The Healing Mind Pty Ltd

Tel: (03) 5442 6757

email: info@thehealingmind.com.au

website: www.thehealingmind.com.au

This is an innovative CD that uses the power of your mind to allow you to relax and let go through guided visualisations. *Relaxed Mother ... Calm Baby* will assist in an easier, calmer pregnancy and birth. Available through www.sleeptalk.com.au and www.ourspecialplace.com.au.

Yoga Babes

Tel: (02) 9944 0255

email: yogababes@optusnet.com.au

website: www.yogababes.com.au

Yoga for Pregnancy and Birth is a 70-minute DVD including two 20-minute yoga routines, baby bonding, relaxation and a section on using yoga and massage for childbirth. Pre and postnatal yoga relaxations CDs for every mum-to-be and new mums feature music by Ian Cameron Smith and each run for 65 minutes with three guided meditations. $29.95 for the DVD, $25 for each CD or $70 for all three (including $5 p&h).

CORD BLOOD BANKS

NATIONAL

Biocell Pty Ltd

Tel: 1800 071 075 Free Call

email: info@biocell.com.au

website: www.biocell.com.au

Of all the decisions parents make for their children, choosing to store their cord blood stem cells may well prove to be the most important. Stem cells are currently useful in the treatment of a number of diseases and the amazing progress of stem cell research around the world has prompted a growing number of Australian families to consider cord blood banking. Contact Biocell, Australia's premier cord blood bank today, for information on how cord blood banking can benefit your family.

EDUCATION CLASSES & WORKSHOPS: CHILDBIRTH

VICTORIA

About Birth

Tel: 0411 660 884

email: lael@aboutbirth.com.au

website: www.aboutbirth.com.au

About Birth workshops offer calmbirth. Calmbirth is a unique education that focuses on equipping parents with the tools to achieve a calm, peaceful and empowering experience. By learning breathing, relaxation and how to overcome fears, couples that experience calmbirth rate their birth as an amazing, stress free, beautiful journey. About Birth workshops also explore all the ante-natal education that is needed to prepare you for the hospital system or birthing at home.

birth

North Fitzroy

Tel: 0400 484 620

email: di@birtheducation.com.au

website: www.birtheducation.com.au

birth is a series of dynamic childbirth education classes presented by well-known educator Di Diddle and guest speakers (including Rhea Dempsey). The series of four classes take the mystery out of labour, birth and life with a newborn and will help empower you for a positive birth experience and confident early parenting. Explore active birth positions, pain management, support techniques, breastfeeding and settling a newborn in a supportive and friendly environment. Attend at any time during your pregnancy, the earlier the better.

Birth Confidence

Tel: (03) 9484 2749

email: ingrid@birthconfidence.com.au

website: www.birthconfidence.com.au

Workshops run by Birth Confidence focus on teaching practical skills to partners and support people to assist women during labour and birth. Participants learn specific breathing techniques, active birth positions, massage skills and acupressure points as well as general tips and information. Facilitated by Annie Fogarty – yoga teacher, childbirth educator and doula – and Ingrid Holmes – massage therapist and doula – these workshops draw on their experience of attending births and of working with women with pre-natal yoga and massage.

Fitwise Physiotherapy
4th Floor, 372 Albert Street
East Melbourne VIC 3002
Tel: (03) 9486 0512
email: fitwise@fitwise.com.au
website: www.fitwise.com.au

 In Fitwise Physiotherapy's Birthwise classes, their focus is to empower you to explore ways to physically and mentally prepare for an active birth. Classes include massage, breathing, effective pushing techniques, coping mechanisms for pain, practising positions and scenarios to gain confidence for what's ahead.

Neighbourhood Childbirth Education
Community Drive
Greensborough VIC 3088
Tel: 0411 606 325
email: alleahy@optusnet.com.au

Neighbourhood Childbirth Education runs community-based and non-profit childbirth education sessions in a small informal group setting encouraging participation, discussion and the development of support and friendship. Discover a woman's inbuilt mechanisms to cope with pain in labour, breastfeeding and much more. Expect a self-motivated learning environment. Childbirth education and preparation – the pathway to informed choice.

The Northern Hospital: Childbirth Programs
185 Cooper Street
Epping VIC 3076
Tel: (03) 8405 8220
email: karen.macdonald2@nh.org.au
website: www.nh.org.au

Childbirth education and parenting classes offered by The Northern Hospital include: the 'Early Bird Class' (early pregnancy related issues and information); Evening Series (runs over 6 weeks); Sunday Workshop (an alternative to a 6-week class); Father Class (a specifically designed class to meet the needs of fathers and provides an opportunity to meet new dads with their babies); a Multiple Birth Class (specially designed for the needs of twin/triplet families) and the Breastfeeding Ante-Natal Class (this session is offered to all pregnant women who want more indepth breastfeeding information). Phone the number above for further information.

NEW SOUTH WALES

All About Birth
North Sydney & Northern Beaches
Tel: 0408 231 759
email: info@allaboutbirth.com.au
website: www.allaboutbirth.com.au

The focus of All About Birth is to provide positive information on labour, birth and beyond. Programs include calmbirth® course, or half day birth and half day early parenting programs. Private sessions are also available. The calmbirth® course is an enriching two-day course that teaches breathing, relaxation and visualisation skills, as well as life skills that are birth specific. All programs are facilitated by Louise Luscri, midwife and childbirth educator. Phone Louise or visit the website for more details. Health rebates are available.

Innate Birth
Blue Mountains
Tel: (02) 4757 2080 or 0410 428 307
email: nataliedash@optusnet.com.au

Innate Birth offers childbirth education workshops in the Blue Mountains and Western Sydney. Women/couples are provided with reassurance, information and techniques for natural active birth preparation. Birth support, sibling care and a photography/video service are available.

Julia Sundin, Physiotherapist
PO Box 139
Roseville NSW 2069
Tel: (02) 9417 6467
website: www.JuJuSundin.com

JuJu Sundin's Pain Mastery Class for Labour course is an inspiring and motivating series including safe pregnancy exercise, posture, backcare, pelvic floor awareness and lots of practice of strategic management of labour pain. These classes mainly focus on birth skills. For bookings phone (02) 9417 6467.

Naturalbirth.net.au
30 Lewis Street
Balgowlah Heights NSW 2093
Tel: (02) 9400 2709
email: info@naturalbirth.com.au
website: www.naturalbirth.com.au

If you re considering a natural birth then classes are essential to give you plenty of tools and choices for birth. These classes will give you confidence, help you feel more relaxed and in control of the birth process – they will inspire, educate and empower you to make the right choices for you and your baby. Services offered include natural birth education, hypnotherapy for childbirth, pre and post natal yoga and massage, natural remedies for pregnancy and birth.

Pregnancy, Birth & Beyond
27 Hart Street
Dundas Valley NSW 2117
Tel: (02) 9873 1750
email: jane@pregnancy.com.au
website: www.pregnancy.com.au

Pregnancy, Birth & Beyond provides quality prenatal courses to help you and your partner prepare for the birth of your baby. All courses are comprehensive, personal and tailor made. The programs are based on informed choice so as to help you understand your options and achieve the birth experience you desire. Information on breastfeeding and early parenting included. The programs are facilitated by Jane Palmer, accredited independent midwife, childbirth educator and mother.

Resources

CHILDBIRTH & POSTNATAL SERVICES

Education classes & workshops
➔ Independent practitioners

Royal North Shore & Ryde Hospital
Pacific Highway
St Leonards NSW 2065
Tel: (02) 9926 6855 Maternity enquiries
website: www.nsh.nsw.gov.au/rnsh/info/DWCH/
NEWBORNS.shtml

RNSH Childbirth & Early Parenting Education offers a wide range of prenatal preparation-for-birth and parenting classes and pre and postnatal exercise classes. Phone (02) 9926 7248 for further information on these classes.

Sydney Southwest Private Hospital
40 Bigge Street
Liverpool NSW 2170
Tel: (02) 9821 0333

The Sydney Southwest Private Hospital offers classes designed to help you adjust and feel at ease with the changes that parenthood brings. They are held in a friendly, informal atmosphere and encourage both parents to be involved in learning about pregnancy, childbirth and parenting skills. The classes are offered in two formats – a two-part, comprehensive class on consecutive Saturdays and weekly classes run one night per week for seven weeks. A fee is charged for these services. Fund rebates available.

Transition Into Parenthood
9 Withybrook Place
Sylvania NSW 2224
Tel: (02) 9544 6441
email: julie@julieclarke.com.au
website: www.julieclarke.com.au

Transition Into Parenthood offers comprehensive and great value birth and parenting-preparation courses in Sydney. Choose from either a six-session course Monday or Tuesday nights, or a two-day Saturday condensed, or a one-day super condensed Sunday course, designed for couples who are busy or have had a baby before and need to refresh. The popular new Australian calmbirth® courses day, evening or weekends are also offered by Julie. Discount applies when two courses booked. Dates and details are listed on Julie's website www.julieclarke.com.au.

QUEENSLAND

Kate Hooghuis registered calmbirth® practitioner
Central Coast
Tel: (02) 4340 5663
email: khooghuis@optusnet.com.au

Kate Hooghuis provides an inspirational childbirth education program designed to guide expectant parents on how to use techniques of deep relaxation, focused breathing and other natural inner resources to birth their baby calmly and joyfully. This course will greatly enhance your understanding and experience of childbirth.

WESTERN AUSTRALIA

St John of God Hospital, Subiaco
12 Salvado Road
Subiaco WA 6008
Tel: (08) 9382 6111
email: info@subiaco@sjog.org.au
website: www.sjog.org.au/subiaco

The St. John of God Hospital, Subiaco offers an extensive parent education program, inclusive of preparing for birth through to breastfeeding and transition to parenting. The Childbirth and Parenting Classes are conducted by experienced midwives in comprehensive evening and day courses that cover labour, relaxation and breathing awareness, birth, nursery needs and breastfeeding. Parenting skills are also introduced and a tour of the maternity unit is included in this program.

SOUTH AUSTRALIA

Active Birth Centre @ Coast Yoga
1 Rose Street
Glenelg SA 5045
Tel: (08) 8295 2298
email: enquiries@coastyoga.com.au
website: www.coastyoga.com.au

Practical skills for pregnancy and childbirth classes offer yoga-based techniques to deal with pain and the challenges of birth, breathing techniques, encouraging the mind to think positively, and to assist you in discovering your own resources to birth your baby as naturally as possible. Active Birth Centre @ Coast Yoga also holds birthing workshops for couples as well as mothers and babies yoga classes.

EXERCISE CLASSES, YOGA & MASSAGE: POSTNATAL

VICTORIA

My Trainer Corporation
Mobile service to all suburbs in Melbourne metro
Tel: (03) 9836 5599
email: advisors@mytrainer.com.au
website: www.mytrainer.com.au

A My Trainer mobile personal trainer can help you improve your fitness, lose weight, increase strength and re-charge your energy. Pre or post baby, their team of experienced personal trainers can help. They offer: mums with babies outdoor group training, one-on-one mobile personal training; kids fitness programs and weight-loss programs. Phone for more details.

Prams in the Park Personal Training
Several central locations
Tel: 0411 527 465
email: martine@pramsinthepark.com.au
website: www.pramsinthepark.com.au

Pram's in the Park is a specially designed, affordable workout for parents of babies and young children. Bring your children with you and enjoy an hour of strength training suitable for all fitness levels. Prams in the Park allows you to do something positive for yourself while caring for your children in a supportive, fun and flexible environment right in a beautiful park. In addition to a great workout you will also meet other parents in the area. Stay and have coffee afterwards. All equipment supplied. Pregnant women welcome.

NEW SOUTH WALES

Fitness 4 mums with bubs
Parramatta, Ingleburn and Camden
Tel: 0410 565 390
email: paulene@fitness4mumswithbubs.com.au
website: www.fitness4mumswithbubs.com.au

Fitness 4 mums with bubs is a specific exercise program to get new mums back into shape after pregnancy and childbirth. Benefits include: re-strengthen your pelvic floor muscles and abdominals, improve muscle tone and lose weight, increase back strength, socialise with other mums and increase well being. Classes are $15 and run for one hour in Parramatta, Ingleburn, Camden. For more information and availability on class times contact Paulene Smallwood on 0410 565 390. Personal training and nutrition plans are also available.

QUEENSLAND

Complete Performance Solutions
Carindale and Kangaroo Point, Brisbane
Tel: 0402 076 311 & (07) 3166 8183
email: info@completeperformancesolutions.com
website: www.completeperformancesolutions.com

Complete Performance Solutions can develop a personalised plan to get you back to your pre-pregnancy body the healthy way. Their professional dieticians and exercise physiologists will provide you with personalised advice and genuine support. They provide an in-person mobile service in Brisbane and a personalised phone/email program and support program throughout Australia. Gift vouchers available. Visit the website for further information: www.completeperformancesolutions.com.

WESTERN AUSTRALIA

Babes on the Run
Various locations
Tel: 0419 935 690
email: info@babesontherun.com.au
website: www.babesontherun.com.au

The Babes Pram-Fit program is specifically designed to meet the needs of mums: weight loss, strengthening and toning. Babes on the Run clients work in small groups with a Personal Trainer to receive effective, results driven exercise programs. Trainers provide ongoing support and education in a social atmosphere that makes training fun. Bring your baby, get outside and get gorgeous! Gift vouchers are available. Phone or visit the website for further information.

belly flower
Margaret River
Tel: 0417 186 673
email: info@bellyflower.com.au
website: www.bellyflower.com.au

belly flower offers yoga classes to women in the south west of Western Australia: Margaret River, Busselton and surrounding areas. Programs include pregnancy yoga, relaxation for birth classes, childbirth education workshops, midwifery consults, labour and birth support, mother and baby yoga, infant massage and breastfeeding consultations. A yoga book *Yoga for Belly, Birth & Baby* is also available.

SOUTH AUSTRALIA

Physiotherapy Pilates Proactive
86 Glen Osmond Road
Parkside SA 4807
Tel: (08) 8271 3144
email: parkside@pilatesproactive.com.au
website: www.pilatesproactive.com.au

Physiotherapy Pilates Proactive specialises in women's health and pilates. With locations in Stirling, Parkside and Littlehampton, they offer over 40 pilates mat classes that are suitable postnatally. All the physiotherapists have a passion for pre/postnatal care and are highly experienced in the treatment of pregnancy-related conditions as well as pelvic floor retraining. Their practices are baby-friendly and they encourage clients to attend the Mums & Bubs classes for pilates exercises and networking with other new mums. Physiotherapy Pilates Proactive also offers one-on-one personal pilates training packages to assist clients with their health goals.

INDEPENDENT CHILDBIRTH & EARLY PARENTING PRACTITIONERS

NATIONAL

Australian Society of Independent Midwives
Tel: (02) 9319 2090
email: midwife@ozemail.com.au
website: www.australiansocietyofindependentmidwives.com

The Australian Society of Independent Midwives is made up of midwives and midwifery advocates committed to supporting women's birth choices, sensitive midwifery practice, continuity of care and carer and the protection and promotion of breastfeeding. The Society produces a quarterly newsletter, Communique, and an annual Members Directory that connect members with colleagues, consumers and commerce. The mission of The Australian Society of Independent Midwives is to advance independent midwifery through

Resources

CHILDBIRTH & POSTNATAL SERVICES

Independent practitioners

creating greater public awareness of natural birth opportunities for women, promoting best midwifery practice through continuity of care, advising government and health authorities on the benefits of independent midwifery practice to women and society at large and collaborating with like-minded groups at a national and international level. For further information about midwives and natural birth choices in your state contact: Jan Robinson NSW (02) 9319 2090, Liz Wilkes QLD (07) 4638 0005, Robyn Thompson VIC (03) 9398 2020, Marijke Eastaugh SA (08) 8388 3146, Meryl Hammond NT (08) 8981 3865, Mary Murphy WA (08) 9440 1310, Margie Perkins ACT (02) 6241 6031 and Jean Vasic TAS (03) 6394 3305.

Birth Partner

Tel: 0402 405 889
email: nicole@birthpartner.com.au
website: www.birthpartner.com.au

Birth Partner can help make the birth of your baby easier. They hire and sell a variety of useful tools for your labour including TENS, birth balls, electric aromatherapy oil burners and more. Nicole is a doula and so she has seen what works. Birth Partner also has a select range of gorgeous gifts for baby, mum and dad. You can order online, or by phone, for quick delivery Australia-wide. Visit www.birthpartner.com.au for more information.

calmbirth Pty Ltd

Tel: (02) 4862 1156
email: pjackson@calmbirth.com.au
website: www.calmbirth.com.au

calmbirth® childbirth preparation programme assists couples to create a calm and joyful birth experience. The calmbirth® programme's aim is to dismantle fear, stress and anxiety experienced by many women during pregnancy and childbirth. The important factors addressed by calmbirth® are understanding, confidence and fearlessness. The knowledge and skills taught prepares the mother to remain relaxed and focused during her labour, to make informed choices, and to be in tune with the natural energy and rhythm of her baby's birth. (Available all states except Western Australia and Northern Territory.)

www.findadoula.com.au

Tel: (02) 9440 9099
email: doula@findadoula.com.au
website: www.findadoula.com.au

This website details trained, experienced doulas from all over Australia as well as doulas in training. A doula is a professional birth support person who is trained to give emotional and physical support to the birthing mother and her partner before, during and after childbirth. This website is free for all to use.

VICTORIA

About Birth

Tel: 0408 020 916
website: www.aboutbirth.com.au

Lael Stone and Jules Brooks are experienced birth attendants that work in supporting both the birthing woman and her partner. They are passionate about assisting couples to achieve the birth experience they desire – whether it be in a Birth Centre or private hospital, a home birth, water birth, Hypnobirth or vaginal birth after caesarean.

Active Birth – Wonderful Birth Services

PO Box 3039
Kew VIC 3101
email: lina@wonderfulbirth.com
website: www.wonderfulbirth.com

Lina Clerke offers an effective, positive approach to preparing for birth with dynamic weekend workshops, classes and private sessions guaranteed to inspire, empower and prepare you. Lina has over 20 years experience teaching about and attending births. She also offers pre and postnatal CDs, massage, counselling, debriefing and phone consultations. For more information visit www.wonderfulbirth.com.

Andrea Bilcliff

8 Raleigh Drive
Narre Warren South VIC 3805
Tel: (03) 9704 2386
email: midwife@netspace.net.au
website: www.homebirths.com.au

Andrea Bilcliff provides midwifery care throughout pregnancy, birth and in the postnatal period. She works in partnership with women providing individualised care based on their families unique needs and beliefs. Andrea supports the right of women to be able to choose how, where and with whom they give birth. She is also experienced in homebirths and waterbirths and has birth pools for hire.

BaBs – Birthing and Babies Support Inc

Tel: 0422 522 986
email: erikamunton@yahoo.com.au
website: www.birthingandbabies.info

BaBs offers local peer support groups for pregnant and parenting women and their families in their own communities. They work to support women to make informed choices, take action about pregnancy, birth and parenting, to feel empowered and confident in their choices to improve their health, parenting and life skills.

Dial a Doula

Tel: 0401 626 883
email: sunfel@foxall.com.au
website: www.womenofspirit.asn.au

Dial a Doula provides support during pregnancy, birth and postnatally. Prenatal support includes information to assist you in making informed choices in all aspects of childbirth; support in the home prior to the birth, building a rapport with you, your partner and family; and information about local resources and other support available. Support during labour includes presence at all times during labour and birth; support for your partner or chosen birth companions emotionally and physically; assistance in the care of your children who may be present; physical support such as massage, hot/cold compresses, and whatever else may be required. Postnatal support includes breastfeeding support; nurturing massage; emotional support; overnight support in the home; assistance in the home such as cooking, cleaning, shopping and childcare; and flexible arrangements and availability to suit your needs.

Eastside Midwives

Tel: 0425 770 316
email: enquiries@eastsidemidwives.com
website: www.eastsidemidwives.com

Eastside Midwives is a group of three registered midwives who provide care throughout your pregnancy, birth and postnatal period for both you and your baby. They can provide hospital support, homebirth support, breastfeeding support as well as early parenting support. All care is provided in the comfort of your own home. Eastside Midwives also run antenatal classes; visit the website for further details.

Echuca Moama Midwifery & Parenting Service

2/100 Haverfield Street
Echuca VIC 3564
Tel: (03) 5482 6283 or 0419 246 303
email: idacq223@mcmedia.com.au
website: www.echucabirthandbaby.com.au

Echuca Moama Midwifery & Parenting Service, operated by midwife Andrea Quanchi, offers women the choice of one-to-one midwifery care during pregnancy, labour, birth and beyond. This includes maternal and child health care to families including sleep and settling. Phone the number above for more details or visit the website.

Erika Munton Birth Works

Tel: (03) 9720 8058
email: erikamunton@yahoo.com.au
website: www.birthworks.info

Erika Munton is an experienced doula/birth attendant with over 10 years experience. Erika provides a caring and empowering service for people seeking additional support, information and guidance through the journey to parenthood with individual sessions, birth attendance and support groups. She will work with you to build trust in your natural mothering abilities; increase your awareness of the birth culture we live in; make informed choices; experience an empowering birth and feel resourced and ready for the ongoing journey of motherhood. Phone the number above for more details or visit the website.

Fourth Trimester

Tel: 1800 462 669
email: info@fourthtrimester.com.au
website: www.fourthtrimester.com.au

Fourth Trimester is an innovative service organisation committed to providing quality postnatal care and support to women and their families in the first weeks after birth. The one-hour, in-home postnatal consultation includes: support and advice with breastfeeding; mothercraft skills; infant care; settling techniques; emotional support; and wound care and management. Fees start at $65 per one hour postnatal visit.

Joy Johnston

25 Eley Road
Blackburn South VIC 3130
Tel: (03) 9808 9614
email: johnston@aitex.com.au
website: www.aitex.com.au/joy.htm

Joy Johnston is an independent midwife providing midwifery services for women and babies in the Melbourne area (and surrounds). A midwife since 1973 and practising independently since 1993, Joy attends many births in the home. The *Midwife's Journal* is the story of her practice, and can be accessed on her website, and you can find midwifery stories and critical comment on current issues at her online blog http://villagemidwife.blogspot.com/.

Leigh Greenaway-Lock

Tel: 0411 487 953

If you are feeling sleep deprived, disorganised and totally overwhelmed then call Leigh Greenaway-Lock, a Mothercraft Nurse with over 25 years experience. In a two-hour consultation Leigh can teach you and your baby routine and sleep strategies to let you feel back in control. She specialises in newborns to children 3 years of age in the areas of routines, feeding, solids and weaning.

Madelaine Akras

26 Merton Street
Box Hill VIC 3128
Tel: 1800 003 902 or (03) 9849 0096 or 0418 351 979
website: www.hypnobirthingvictoria.com.au

Madelaine is passionate about the birthing process and offers couples the ability to work as a team to achieve the birth they desire. calmbirth® provides couples with the appropriate tools to learn to relinquish their fears and trust in their body's natural instinct to take over. Madelaine has helped many couples during pregnancy, birth and postnally and believes calmbirth® provides a clearer and more fulfilling way for couples to approach and undergo their birthing experience.

Marietje Stuckey

26 Merton Street
Box Hill VIC 3128
Tel: 1800 003 902 or (03) 9849 0096 or 0418 351 979
email: makras@optusnet.com.au
website: www.hypnobirthingvictoria.com.au

Resources

HypnoBirthing®/calmbirth teaches couples, and their birth support, methods for a safe and more comfortable childbirth through guided imagery, visualisation, special breathing and deep relaxation techniques. HypnoBirthing®/calmbirth eliminates the fear and tension that cause long labour and pain, replacing it with confidence, calm and comfort. Marietje Stuckey is a HypnoBirthing®/calmbirth practitioner with a background in nursing. HypnoBirthing®/calmbirth assists a woman to have a natural childbirth as nature intended.

Marietje Stuckey

26 Merton Street
Box Hill VIC 3128
Tel: 1800 003 902 or (03) 9849 0096 or 0418 351 979
email: makras@optusnet.com.au
website: www.hypnobirthingvictoria.com.au

A Birth Attendant (BA) brings essential added support not only to the mother but also for the staff attending the birth, and especially for the partner during the birth experience. Having a BA present at the birth has shown to shorten labour, decrease the chances of a caesarean and lessens the level of anxiety. Support is given in a hospital or home. Marietje Stuckey is a registered nurse and NACE certified. Marietje offers support before, during and after childbirth.

Maternity CRAFT

PO Box 3155
Mentone East VIC 3194
Tel: 0418 590 814
email: meales@tpg.com.au

Maternity CRAFT offers educational activities for expectant women and health professionals. Their ante-natal service is designed for people who may either be unable or uninterested in attending hospital-based courses. Each ante-natal program is designed to meet your specific needs relating to pre-labour, labour, pain management, birthing options, breastfeeding, the postnatal period and newborn infants. All information is based on fact, current trends and research statistics, helping you to make informed decisions about your care and in turn enhance your birthing and new parenthood experience.

Midwives In Private Practice

Tel: (03) 9704 2386
email: mipps@maternitycoalition.org.au
website: www.maternitycoalition.org.au

Midwives in Private Practice (MIPP) are all members of Maternity Coalition, and are working with other groups and individuals to improve maternity services and outcomes for all women in Australia. Members work on a one-to-one basis to provide primary maternity services, giving personal expert professional care through pregnancy, birth and postnatally. They attend births in the home or accompany women to hospital for birth.

Midwives Naturally

9 Winding Way
Warrandyte North VIC 3113
Tel: (03) 9844 2523
email: jennieteskey@yahoo.com
website: www.midwivesnaturally.com.au

Midwives Naturally is a midwifery group practice offering continuity of care whether you choose to birth at home or in hospital. They have a special interest in waterbirth and vaginal birth after caesarean. Midwives Naturally also offers ante-natal and sibling preparation classes as well as birth pools for hire. Visit their website for further information.

Nurturing Women

Tel: 0402 109 519
email: lisa@nurturingwomen.com.au
website: www.nurturingwomen.com.au

Nurturing Women postnatal healing services are designed to support mothers in their recovery from pregnancy and childbirth and restore their natural state of inner balance. Complementary therapies such as therapeutic massage, bowen therapy and reiki are offered in the comfort of the mother's own home. Home visits are carefully planned providing all that is needed to create a peaceful and soothing atmosphere for the treatment. Enquire about Nurturing Women's exclusive first treatment offer. Health card concessions and gift packages available.

Sue Power calmbirth®

Tel: 0413 189 864
email: sue_june@hotmail.com

The calmbirth® philosophy is about believing that pregnancy, labour and birth are normal life events and birth a natural process to be experienced joyfully and calmly. Classes gives a greater understanding of birth, allay fear and anxiety, aiming to provide the necessary tools to achieve a calmer, more satisfying birth experience. Fear and anxiety create a physiological response that can negatively affect birth. Learning ways to relax and trust in the body, and what it is designed to do, can assist in achieving a more positive and rewarding birthing experience.

The InnerWoman

PO Box 1014
Healesville VIC 3777
Tel: (03) 5962 3304 or 0411 037 306
email: esther@innerwoman.com.au
website: www.innerwoman.com.au

Learn techniques that can help you tap into your own natural birthing instincts and hormones, greatly reducing fear and tension. HypnoBirthing is a natural approach for a safer, easier and more comfortable birth experience. It is every woman's right to birth her baby as gently and naturally as possible and have control over her own birthing. Regular evening or weekend classes are held at Healesville, Balwyn or in your own home. The professional doula (with or without HypnoBirthing classes) is the ultimate companion for the expecting, birthing and new mother and her family, who will do her utmost so you'll experience the best birth outcome possible.

TLC Doula Support

3/1288 Burwood Highway
Upper Ferntree Gully VIC 3156
Tel: 0419 517 636
email: info@tlcbirth.com.au
website: www.tlcbirth.com.au

TLC Birth provides calmbirth® classes by a registered practitioner as well as complete and comprehensive doula support before and during birth. They also offer practical and emotional support in the early postnatal period including breastfeeding assistance. Reasonable rates and packages available.

NEW SOUTH WALES

Australian Doula College

31 Brighton Street
Petersham NSW 2049
Tel: 1300 139 507
website: www.australiandoulacollege.com.au

The Australian Doula College is an integrated health care centre providing education, support and continuity of care for women during pregnancy, childbirth and beyond. Through a network of qualified and experienced doulas, educators and practitioners, they offer a variety of services, treatments and support. They look forward to empowering you on your amazing journey, however that journey unfolds for you.

Birth Right Pty Ltd

Suite 5, 670 Darling Street
Rozelle NSW 2039
Tel: 0419 606 171
website: www.birthright.com.au

Birth Right provides a range of services for pregnancy, including Active Birth classes, HypnoBirthing, calmbirth®, pregnancy belly dancing, doula service, birth de-brief and early parenting classes. Birth Right is the only doula training school run by a midwife with over 30 years experience. Susan Ross is the founder and director of Birth Right; she is a midwife, childbirth educator, doula trainer, HypnoBirthing practitioner, mother and author of the book *Birth Right*. Susan is passionate about helping women understand their choices.

Birth Without Fear

Berkeley Vale, Terrigal
Tel: 0402 127 940
email: lindajwinter@hotmail.com

calmbirth® classes are based on the belief that pregnancy and birth are normal life events. Some of the things you will learn include: how the body is designed to birth; skills to eliminate fear, tension and anxiety; simple deep relaxation techniques and breathing techniques. The end result is that you can feel good about your birth experience.

Blissful Birthing

Pottsville Beach
Tel: 0438 269 889
email: blissfulbirthing@internode.on.net
website: www.blissfulbirthing.com.au

Blissful Birthing offers doula support, birth preparation workshops and blessingway planning. Michelle services the far-north coast of NSW and the southern Gold Coast. She is a certified doula, childbirth educator and volunteer counsellor with the Australian Breastfeeding Association. She believes birth is the most amazing experience of your life and with support and knowledge you can become empowered to enjoy a truly blissful birth.

Brighid's Hands Birth Support Doulas

Tel: (02) 4782 5670 or (02) 4753 7863
email: info@brighidshands.com.au
website: www.brighidshands.com.au

Brighid's Hands offers a birth support service for women and couples who would like extra support throughout pregnancy and birth. They are passionate about supporting women to achieve the births they want, and about women having access to a range of information and experiences to support them into their new roles as mothers. They are committed to giving pregnant women confidence in their innate ability to birth their babies in an environment in which they feel nurtured and safe. Servicing the Blue Mountains and western Sydney.

calm Connexions

48 Wyndham Way
Eleebana NSW 2282
Tel: (02) 4946 7871
email: penny@calmconnexions.com.au
website: www.calmconnexions.com.au

calmbirth® offers a gentle yet effective way to prepare for the birth of a baby and embodies the phiosophy of helping couples help themselves. Using knowledge and simple techniques which enhance inner resources. Calmbirth® skills enable couples to birth their babies as calmly and joyfully as possible. Calmbirth® not only enhances the birth experience, but becomes valuable life skills as well; ones that foster communication, connection and joy. Phone Penny Williams for more information.

Caroline Foldes

Tel: 0423 358 851
email: caroline@sacred.net.au
website: www.sacred.net.au

Women and their families should be supported to birth how, where and when they wish. Adequate preparation

Resources

CHILDBIRTH & POSTNATAL SERVICES
Independent practitioners

and support ensures that you will be much closer to achieving your desired outcome. Caroline provides extensive guidance and preparation for parents-to-be so that they enter birth calmly, feeling positive. She has attended births at home, and in hospital labour wards and birth centres. Her photographs and book, Joyous Birth, are a testament to the beautiful memories of these births and the precious first days of postnatal bonding. Caroline can assist in the North Shore, eastern suburbs, northern beaches and inner west areas of Sydney.

Cindy Turner – Midwife
15 Dr George Mountain Road
Tanja NSW 2550
Tel: (02) 6494 0131
email: midwife@bordernet.com.au

Midwife Cindy Turner offers independent midwifery services including pregnancy, birth and early parenting care, both at home or in hospital. The area she covers ranges from Narooma to Eden on the far south coast.

Essential Birth Consulting
Home visits around Sydney
Tel: 0400 418 448
email: melissam@idx.com.au

Do you leave your check-ups with unanswered questions? Are you having your first baby or planning to do things differently this time? Essential Birth Consulting can help you experience your birth your way. They provide home birth services; assistance to choose a hospital, doctor or birth centre to complement your needs; personalised, one-on-one childbirth education; assistance through the maze of options for birth; and birth debriefing. All the research is done for you, saving you valuable time.

Heli Murray – Loving Birth
Byron Bay
Tel: (02) 6685 6523
email: helim@bigpond.com

Heli Murray at Loving Birth provides professional, loving support through pregnancy, birth and early post partum. Heli is a mother, certified doula, calmbirth® practitioner and HypnoBirthing® practitioner. Heli supports women in Ballina, Byron, Lismore and Tweed areas. She sees birth as a transformational life-experience and loves supporting new parents to discover their own innate knowledge and maximise enjoyment of this wondrous time. Heli also facilitates calmbirth® classes for couples and small groups. Phone the number above for more information.

Hypnobirth
Tel: 0414 949 546
email: info@hypnobirth.com.au
website: www.hypnobirth.com.au

The HypnoBirthing® childbirth method is as much a philosophy of birth as it is a technique for achieving a satisfying, relaxing, and stress-free method of birthing. Over five sessions of 2.5 hours each you will learn how to bring your mind and body into harmony with nature allowing you to receive your child gently into the world. When enrolling in a HypnoBirthing course you will receive a copy of Marie Mongan's book HypnoBirthing together with 2 relaxation CDs, course notes in a folder, healthy snacks and drinks. Helen Scard is a HypnoBirthing Certified Educator and holds a Diploma of Health & Yoga teaching pre-natal yoga classes, relaxation and meditation. She also co-facilitates with a colleague monthly gatherings at The Women's Circle.

Innate Birth
Blue Mountains
Tel: (02) 4757 2080 or 0410 428 307
email: nataliedash@optusnet.com.au

Innate Birth offers a birth support (doula) service for pregnant women/couples who would like extra support during pregnancy, labour, birth and postpartum. Natalie and Jo offer information, encouragement and physical and emotional assistance and are experienced in attending births at home, hospital and birth centres. Servicing Western Sydney, Macarthur, Hawkesbury and the Blue Mountains. Active Birth workshops regularly held in the Blue Mountains.

Kate Hale
North Shore and the inner west of Sydney
Tel: (02) 9416 4386

Kate Hale is a midwife, lactation consultant and mother of four children. Kate does private consultations in your own home from birth to toddler covering all feeding issues along with settling, baby management and routines.

Luv-Bub Baby Massage and Successful Parenting
PO Box 392
Balmain East NSW 2041
Tel: 0438 648 465
email: whisperer@luvbub.com.au
website: www.luvbub.com.au

Moira is a qualified midwife and neo-natal specialist with over 20 years experience and offers a range of specialist parenting and baby support services including: preterm and newborn support; sleep rescue and settling routines; lactation and nutrition consultations; baby massage courses; father's parenting sessions; return to work advice and support; and a babysitting and nanny service. Moira's range of caring services are personalised and are available for home visits or group sessions Sydney wide and nationally upon request. Phone the number above for more information.

Pregnancy, Birth & Beyond
27 Hart Street
Dundas Valley NSW 2117
Tel: (02) 9873 1750
email: jane@pregnancy.com.au
website: www.pregnancy.com.au

Jane Palmer works as an independent midwife in the
Sydney metropolitan area. Jane provides continuity of
care through pregnancy, birth and beyond, supporting
women and their families giving birth at home, in a birth
centre or a hospital. Additional services include
breastfeeding counselling, postnatal visits and parenting
support. To find out more visit Jane's website
www.pregnancy.com.au.

Wendy Jarratt
Tel: 0412 277 251
email: wendy.jarratt@gmail.com

Wendy provides doula services to women in the eastern
suburbs and inner west areas of Sydney.

AUSTRALIAN CAPITAL TERRITORY

Confident Birth & WellBeing
Tel: (02) 6294 0069
email: info@confidentbirth.com.au
website: www.confidentbirth.com.au

Make the birth of your baby a joyous event and your
life healthy and stress free. For calm constant care
before, during and after the birth of your baby, as well as
complementary therapies for the whole family, talk to
Vickie Hingston-Jones, an experienced professional
doula and natural therapist. Phone the number above for
more information.

The Birth Yurt
Tel: (02) 6288 7275
email: thebirthyurt@gmail.com
website: www.calmbirth.com.au

Rachel is a doula and calmbirth practitioner in Canberra
and is passionate about supporting women and couples
to use their own inner resources to birth with calm and
joy. She trusts a woman's body to birth the way that is
right for her believing that birth is a very normal and
also very simple process that, with proper nurturing and
support, can be most enjoyable and satisfying. Rachel is
there to provide information, practical skills, and
support and nurturing during pregnancy as well as
offering one-on-one support during labour. She also
offers private and group calmbirth classes and doula
support. Phone for an appointment or for more details.

QUEENSLAND

Birth Connection
Tel: 0406 412 354
email: pernillep@optusnet.com.au
website: www.birthconnection.com.au

A doula is a trained birth attendant who understands the
process of birth both physically and emotionally. She
supports and empowers the birthing woman and her
partner during pregnancy, labour, birth and early

parenting and provides that much needed continuity of
care. At Birth Connection you can get the full package:
childbirth education, doula service and post doula
service.

birth@mackay
Tel: 0437 695 819
email: birthatmackay@bigpond.com
website: www.birthatmackay.com.au

Birth@mackay is a unique midwifery service giving
women more choices in pregnancy, birth and early
parenting care. birth@mackay provides individually
tailored ante-natal, breastfeeding and parenting classes.
The midwives are available for consultation and support
during pregnancy and birth. Postnatal home visiting is
also available including breastfeeding support.

GentleBirth Pregnancy and Birth Education
Tel: (07) 4993 1213
email: info@gentlebirth.com.au
website: www.gentlebirth.com.au

Rachael Austin is an independent midwife providing
homebirth and home waterbirth in the central
Queensland district. Rachael will negotiate distance, up
to three hours approximately from Theodore.

Judy Chapman
PO Box 1524
Mareeba QLD 4880
Tel: (07) 4093 2748
email: judyc5201@yahoo.com.au

Judy Chapman is available for homebirth services in the
Mareeba area of far north Queensland.

Pre-Natal Centre
274 Toohey Road
Tarragindi QLD 4121
Tel: (07) 3392 7517
email: annmt@iprimus.com.au
website: www.prenatalcentre.com.au

Pre-Natal Centre provides information and knowledge
so you can make informed choices with your caregivers
during your pregnancy and birth. As a midwife of 40
years, Ann provides information for a variety of
situations having worked in private, public and
community services. Currently working as a Labour
Ward Midwife (and previously as a Lactation
Consultant) Ann covers vaginal births, c/sections and
VBACs in groups of 1 to 5 at a variety of times. Phone
her for further details.

WESTERN AUSTRALIA

A Labour of Love
PO Box 526
South Fremantle WA 6162
Tel: 0418 336 362
email: info@alabouroflove.com.au
website: www.alabouroflove.com.au

Gabrielle Targett is a childbirth educator, doula and
author of *A Labour of Love – an Australian guide to
natural childbirth*. Gabrielle's business, A Labour of

Resources

CHILDBIRTH & POSTNATAL SERVICES

Independent practitioners
➔ Maternity hospitals & birth centres

Love, offers empowered independent childbirth educational workshops, doula services (formally known as doulas down under network), birth support during pregnancy, hypnosis for birth preparation, support and guidance through labour and birth and postnatal support. Gabrielle has an online shop offering Hypnosis for Birth CDs, A Labour of Love book, Labour Heat Hug and Hypnosis and childbirth educational home study workbooks.

Australian Doulas
Tel: (08) 9305 2003
email: info@australiandoulas.com.au
website: www.australiandoulas.com.au

Australian Doulas is the place to find a doula in Western Australia. If you are looking for a doula they offer a huge choice covering mainly Perth, the Avon Valley and south-west areas. Visit their website to see profiles on all doulas.

BodyWise BirthWise
Tel: 0402 576 451
email: kristin@bodywisebirthwise.com.au
website: www.bodywisebirthwise.com.au

BodyWise BirthWise offers women (and their partners) holistic care from preconception to the postnatal period. The naturopathic services include women's hormonal health, natural fertility management, preconception, pregnancy and postnatal care. The prenatal services include active birth workshops, birth and parenting courses and birth support (doula). BodyWise BirthWise offers empowering and inspiring prenatal education for informed and confident birthing, respecting every woman's – and baby's – birthright.

Community Midwifery WA
1/40 Pearse Street
North Fremantle WA 6159
Tel: (08) 9430 6882
website: www.cmwa.net.au

Community Midwifery WA (CMWA) vision is for all women to birth safely in an environment of respect and love. CMWA co-ordinates the Community Midwifery Program (CMP) offering a midwife-led model of maternity care for low risk women. Women on the CMP are cared for by a known midwife throughout pregnancy, labour and the postnatal period and predominately have home births. CMWA also offers prenatal education and support, an extensive pregnancy and childbirth library, consultation and referral by qualified midwives, and pre and postnatal support groups.

Malavisi Midwifery
10 Duchess Street
Busselton WA 6280
Tel: (08) 9754 8281
email: petemalavisi@dodo.com.au
website: www.freewebs.com/homebirthingsouthwest/

Pete Malavisi of Malavisi Midwifery has been working as an independent midwife in the south west for over eight years. He is committed to continuity of carer for birthing services and is also an active member of Birth Choices, believing that every woman should have the choice to choose her primary carer and place of birth and that it should all be available via the public health system. Phone the number above or visit the website for more information.

Mary Murphy
336 Oxford Street
Leederville WA 6007
Tel: 0418 952 498
email: midwife1@iinet.net.au

Mary Murphy offers pre-pregnancy information as well as personalised pregnancy, birth and postnatal care. She has a pregnancy, birth and parenting resource library including books, videos and DVDs and offers the hire of birth pools. Phone the number above for more information.

Theresa Clifford
Tel: 0419 923 182
email: theresaclifford@optusnet.com.au

Theresa Clifford has been a midwife in private practice in WA for 29 years. She offers holistic women-centred care to all women including those experiencing twins, breach and VBAC. She also facilitates active birth workshops, homeopathics for childbirth and homeopathics for family health workshops several times a year. Theresa is based in South Fremantle. Phone the number above for more information.

SOUTH AUSTRALIA

Flinders Medical Centre (FMC)
Flinders Drive
Bedford Park SA 5042
Tel: (08) 8204 4680
website: www.flinders.sa.gov.au

The Flinders Maternity Outreach Service (formerly Domiciliary Midwife Service) offers women continued postnatal support by Flinders Medical Centre (FMC) midwives, in their own home, seven days a week. For the majority of women, support is only required for the first week, but occasionally it is required for several weeks. While this service is available to all women, it is particularly relevant to women who are discharged within the first 24 hours of birth. It is discussed with mothers prior to discharge. The service can help with: feeding problems; settling techniques; the baby's growth and weight gain; assessment of the baby's health; coping with an older sibling's reaction to the new baby and maternal care, both physical and emotional.

Roz Donnellan-Fernandez: Community Midwifery Services

Tel: (08) 8278 1429
email: elduende@chariot.net.au

Roz is a community midwife who has practised midwifery continuity of care for the past 13 years. She attends women during pregnancy, labour and birth and the postnatal period to 6 weeks following childbirth in homes, hospitals and birthing centres. She is also a qualified lactation consultant, facilitates preparation for parenthood groups with a local yoga centre and is involved in the education of midwives. Roz implemented and was Joint Co-ordinator of the inaugural Midwifery Group Practice service at (WCH) from 2004 to 2008, a public model of midwife-led care.

TASMANIA

Special Delivery

Level 1, 42 Brisbane Street
Launceston TAS 7250
Tel: 0408 538 875
email: sarah@specialdelivery.net.au
website: www.specialdelivery.net.au

Prepare your body and mind for a healthy pregnancy and birth with Special Delivery. Explore your birthing possibilities and meet the challenges of pregnancy and birth with confidence, strength and grace. As a certified doula and yoga instructor, Sarah offers practical physical and emotional support and care to birthing couples through pregnancy, birth and the post birth period. You can experience a joyous and empowering birth. Special Delivery services include: birth doula, postnatal doula, yoga in pregnancy for women and couples, mummy and baby yoga, one-on-one yoga tuition and aromatherapy products for pregnancy, birth, mum and baby.

MATERNITY HOSPITALS & BIRTH CENTRES

VICTORIA

Box Hill Hospital (Birralee)

Nelson Road
Box Hill VIC 3128
Tel: (03) 9895 3333
email: boxhill.hospital@boxhill.org.au
website: www.easternhealth.org.au

Birralee Maternity Service offers a range of models of care including midwife shared care and GP shared care. In addition to the antenatal clinics at Box Hill Hospital, Birralee now has an Antenatal Clinic based at Yarra Ranges Health in Lilydale. Birralee provides a variety of childbirth and parenting classes in English and Cantonese. Their professional and caring midwives will assist you in learning to care for your newborn both in hospital and at home. Birralee Maternity Service includes 24-hour medical cover, a Special Care Nursery for sick and premature babies, Home Midwife Visiting Service and a Lactation Support Unit if required. Tours of the facility are available Saturday and Sunday at 2.30pm.

Epworth Freemasons Hospital

2nd Floor, 320 Victoria Parade
East Melbourne VIC 3002
Tel: (03) 9418 8333
email: info@fmh.com.au
website: www.fmh.com.au

Epworth Freemasons Hospital is a private hospital offering modern, spacious facilities, experienced midwives, doctors and a fully-equipped Level 2 Special Care Nursery. There are nine delivery suites and a number of birth options are available. Partners and siblings are welcome to stay in rooms with queen-sized beds. They have 38 rooms at the Victoria Street Campus and also have 12 maternity rooms in the newly renovated Women's Health Unit at Clarendon Street. The hospital also has allocated rooms at The Park Hyatt Melbourne for suitable patients who may wish to spend the remainder of their hospital stay supported with midwife care.

Frances Perry House

Level 6 & 7, Corner Flemington Road and Grattan Street
Parkville VIC 3052
Tel: (03) 9344 5000
website: www.francesperryhouse.com.au

Frances Perry House is a private hospital (with a Level 2 Special Care Nursery) providing comprehensive maternity services, with the advantage of being co-located with the Royal Women's Hospital. Their facility boasts private rooms (many with double beds) which have panoramic views of the Melbourne skyline. Their experienced and supportive staff provide excellent educational programs throughout the pregnancy, birth and postnatal periods. In June 2008 Frances Perry House together with the Women's Hospital moved to a brand new hospital on the corner of Flemington Road and Grattan Street in Parkville. The new Frances Perry is located on the top two levels of the new Royal Women's Hospital. Frances Perry continues to offer a range of private hospital services including general surgery, gynaecology, breast reconstruction, plastic surgery and urogynaecology.

Frankston Hospital – Maternity Unit

Hastings Road
Frankston VIC 3199
Tel: (03) 9784 7777
website: www.phcn.vic.gov.au

Phone the number above for information on maternity facilities and services.

Health Scope – Knox Private Hospital

262 Mountain Highway
Wantirna VIC 3152
Tel: (03) 9210 7231

Risby Maternity Unit is a 12 bed unit with a Level 2 Nursery. Ten rooms are equipped with double beds and ensuite facilities and partners may stay overnight free of charge. Ante-natal classes and an early physioexercise class are offered at the hospital as are monthly pre-pregnancy information nights. Knox Private is serviced

Resources

CHILDBIRTH & POSTNATAL SERVICES

Maternity hospitals & birth centres

with a 24 hour accident and emergency department as well as an intensive care and coronary care unit and pathology is on site.

Masada Private Hospital

26 Balaclava Road
East St Kilda VIC 3182
Tel: (03) 9038 1370
email: maternity.msp@ramsayhealth.com.au
website: www.ramsayhealth.com.au

Masada knows that the birth of your baby is a special occasion and is committed to providing an environment which is flexible, personalised and supportive. The Masada Perinatal Services offer a full range of childbirth and parenting education as well as Mother Baby Unit parenting support. For more information contact the Masada Maternity Unit on the number above.

Mercy Hospital for Women

163 Studley Road
Heidelberg VIC 3084
Tel: (03) 8458 4082
email: mhwfbc@mercy.com.au

The birth centre at The Mercy Hospital for Women is a home-like place to have your baby when the pregnancy and birth are straight forward. It provides midwifery led care throughout pregnancy, birth and postnatal period. If a complication occurs the hospital provides specialist obstetric backup. They also offer care to women choosing to have a private obstetrician, as well as shared-care with your local doctor. The centre is fully equipped with a lounge, play area, kitchen and individual bedrooms for you and your family. A team of experienced midwives provide regular check-ups throughout your pregnancy as well as conducting pre-natal classes. They are flexible with times, offering classes and check-ups on some evenings and weekends. Couples are encouraged to stay together at the centre following the birth for one night. This is followed up with regular home visits from the domiciliary midwives.

Mercy Hospital for Women

163 Studley Road
Heidelberg VIC 3084
Tel: (03) 8458 4082
email: mhwfbc@mercy.com.au

Mercy Hospital for Women is a specialist women's hospital offering obstetrics, care of the premature baby, gynaecology, treatment of women's cancer, postnatal depression and reproductive medicine. As a public teaching hospital, the Mercy is recognised as a centre of

excellence and is accustomed to dealing with emergency and complicated cases. The hospital caters for women of all ages and backgrounds and treats public and private patients.

Mitcham Private Hospital

27 Doncaster East Road
Mitcham VIC 3132
Tel: (03) 9210 3222
website: www.mitchamprivate.com.au

Mitcham Private Hospital is located at the gateway of Melbourne's growing eastern corridor, and is well recognised in the local community for its range of acute surgical and medical services, and is known nationally for its maternity services as a WHO Baby Friendly Hospital. From the earliest stages of your pregnancy, Mitcham Private Hospital works with you to provide consistent care, information and advice, tailored to address the real issues that new parents are going to encounter. Refurbished private rooms at Mitcham Private Hospital offer comfort and luxury and are equipped with the latest medical technology. With the support of a 24 hour anaesthetic roster, and onsite Level II Special Care Nursery, the experienced team of obstetricians, nurses and midwives are dedicated to providing the most caring and comfortable childbirth experience possible for mother and child.

Monash Medical Centre – Clayton (Southern Health)

246 Clayton Road
Clayton VIC 3168
Tel: (03) 9594 2488
email: birth.centre@southernhealth.org.au

The midwives at the Birth Centre provide pregnancy and labour care supporting the natural birth process. You may have flexible appointment times, attend childbirth and parenting classes and enjoy postnatal care in a home-like environment where your family can stay too. The Birth Centre has also been providing water birth facilities for the past 16 years.

Northpark Private Hospital

Corner Greenhills & Plenty Roads
Bundoora VIC 3083
Tel: (03) 9467 6022
website: www.healthscope.com.au

Northpark Private Hospital Maternity Unit is located in the northern suburbs of Melbourne. The unit is spacious with a sunny outlook consisting of 16 beds, 5 birthing suites and a Level 2 nursery. They offer modern luxurious double bed accommodation in private rooms, and the nursing staff are dedicated to ensuring quality care in a supportive environment while at the same time building confidence and independence in families caring for newborn infants.

St Frances Xavier Cabrini Hospital – Maternity

183 Wattletree Road
Malvern VIC 3144
Tel: (03) 9508 1222

Phone the number above for information on maternity facilities and services.

St John of God Health Care
Gibb Street
Berwick VIC 3806
Tel: (03) 9709 1400

St John of God Health Care offers a family-centred maternity unit with assistance and education with feeding, antenatally and postnatally. They have a Level One nursery, postnatal depression service and lactation consultants on staff. Staff are approachable and friendly.

St Vincents and Mercy Private Hospital
59–61 Victoria Parade
Fitzroy VIC 3065
Tel: (03) 9411 7111
email: info@stvmph.org.au
website: www.stvincentsmercy.com.au

At the St Vincents Private Campus they have been delivering Melbourne's babies for over 60 years, and are one of Melbourne's finest midwifery units. The exceptional facilities include modern, well-equipped delivery suites, a two-level Special Care Nursery and all single private accommodation including some rooms with double beds. In addition, patients are treated to beautiful, fresh, innovative meals and have access to childbirth education, breastfeeding support and the guidance and support of caring midwives.

The Bays Hospital
Vale Street
Mornington VIC 3931
Tel: (03) 5975 2009

The Maternity Unit at The Bays provides family centred care through a committed team of passionate, professional midwives ensuring excellent support and care. Their deluxe birthing suites include an ensuite and deep bath, innovative pain management therapies and complimentary therapies including aromatherapy. They provide a complete birthing experience, ensuring your level of care and support extends far beyond your baby's birthday.

The Northern Hospital Epping
185 Cooper Street
Epping VIC 3076
Tel: (03) 8405 8000
website: www.nh.org.au

The Northern Hospital's Maternity & Women's Health Unit offers comfortable mainly single and two-bed rooms with ensuites, as well as spacious birthing rooms each with an ensuite and telephone. Their Special Care Nursery caters for babies requiring extra care after birth, including sick and premature babies transferred from other hospitals. Expectant parents are supported by a number of ante-natal services including midwives clinics, shared care with locals GPs and ante-natal education classes.

The Royal Women's Hospital
Corner of Grattan Street & Flemington Road
Parkville VIC 3052
Tel: (03) 8345 2000
website: www.thewomens.org.au

The Royal Women's Hospital is Australia's largest specialist hospital dedicated to improving the health of women and newborn babies. As a major teaching hospital, the Women's provides comprehensive services ranging from health promotion to clinical expertise and leadership in maternity services, gynaecology, cancer services and specialist care of newborn babies.

Waverley Private Hospital
347–352 Blackburn Road
Mount Waverley VIC 3149
Tel: (03) 9802 0522
website: www.waverleyprivate.com.au

Waverley Private Hospital has a long and proud tradition in delivering a family-focused yet innovative approach to maternity services. Right from the start, they provide relevant education and information programs so your choices are the best possible to guide you in the planning and development of your pregnancy and assist you in the care of your newborn. The maternity unit boasts a collaborative team of experienced obstetricians, medical staff, nurses and lactation consultants, comfortable and well-appointed rooms, an onsite Level II Special Care nursery, 3 modern and fully-equipped birthing suites, 5 state-of-the-art operating theatres and 24-hour anaesthetic roster, as well as the option to participate in the innovative Parenting Program at the five-star Novotel Hotel.

NEW SOUTH WALES

Auburn Hospital
Norval Street
Auburn NSW 2144
Tel: (02) 9563 9500

Auburn Maternity Service provides a range of services to support you before, during and after your baby's birth. The unit provides women-centred care with a focus on midwifery input. Ante-natal outpatient services include early pregnancy assessment clinic, midwives clinics or GP-shared care and ante-natal day stay. All six birthing rooms have ensuites and the maternity ward offers early discharge with midwifery at home program, 24-hour room-in and a special care nursery. Parent education is available in English, Arabic, Mandarin/Cantonese and Turkish.

Bankstown-Lidcombe Hospital - Maternity Unit
Eldridge Road
Bankstown NSW 2200
Tel: (02) 9722 8000

Phone the number above for information on maternity facilities and services.

Bowral & District Hospital
2 Mona Road
Bowral NSW 2576
Tel: (02) 4861 0224

In the Maternity Unit of Bowral Hospital located in the Southern Highlands of New South Wales, midwives, two specialist obstetricians, one staff specialist ostetrician, two paediatricians and GP obstetricians

Resources

CHILDBIRTH & POSTNATAL SERVICES
Maternity hospitals & birth centres

along with midwives provide various models of care for approximately 700 births yearly. Ante-natal care, 3 birthing rooms and 12 postnatal beds are available. Home visits are also available via a Midwifery Support Program for early discharge. The Maternity Unit is closely aligned with the Child & Family Health Nurses, enabling ongoing care provision for growing babies and their families.

Camden & Campbelltown Hospital
Therry Road
Campbelltown NSW 2560
Tel: (02) 4634 3000

Phone the number above for information on maternity facilities and services.

Hurstville Community Private Hospital
37 Gloucester Road
Hurstville NSW 2220
Tel: (02) 9579 7777
email: maternity@calvaryhurstville.com.au

Hurstville Community Private Hospital is increasing its capacity from 71 to 85 in-patients beds including a new Special Care Nursery, High Dependency Unit and 15 new adult beds. The hospitals specialities include colorectal, general, gynaecology, orthopaedics, urology surgery and obstetrics. More than 1,000 babies are born in five (5) delivery suites and the hospital has a Level 2 Special Care Nursery. The hospital is fully accredited by the Australian Council on Healthcare Standards and is now accredited with teaching hospital status by the University of New South Wales.

Kareena Private Hospital
86 Kareena Road
Caringbah NSW 2229
Tel: (02) 9717 0000
email: kareenaprivate@ramsayhealth.com.au
website: www.kareenaprivate.com.au

Kareena Private Hospital provides antenatal, labour and postnatal care. Rooms are either single or double and all feature an ensuite, television and phone. Mothercraft care and education is provided in a friendly caring environment. The hospital also has lactation consultants and mothercraft classes and a good range of videos and books to assist you in preparing for parenthood. They also provide comprehensive ante-natal classes.

Manly Hospital
Darley Road
Manly NSW 2095
Tel: (02) 9976 9624

Manly Maternity is a twenty-bed unit with a strong community focus that has approximately 980 births each year. There are three birthing rooms and spas and antenatal exercise classes are available. Manly Maternity also has a flourishing midwives clinic and provides both a medical obstetric clinic for high risk pregnancies and a maternal antenatal mental support program.

Mater Hospital
Rocklands Road
North Sydney NSW 2060
Tel: (02) 9900 7300
email: maternity@matersydney.com.au
website: www.matersydney.com.au

The maternity department at the Mater Hospital provides women and their families with supportive, high quality care before, during and after the birth of their baby. They offer an integrated, collaborative team of obstetricians, paediatricians, midwives, maternity social workers and lactation experts to guide in the planning and development of your pregnancy. In recognition of your right to choose and to ensure mothers and partners are adequately prepared, the hospital provides education and information programs so that your choices are the best possible. Mater Hospital has 6 delivery suites, 38 postnatal beds and 10 Level II Special Care Nursery beds.

Mona Vale Hospital – Maternity Service
Coronation Street
Mona Vale NSW 2103
Tel: (02) 9998 0333

The Mona Vale Hospital Maternity Service is designated as category Level 4. The staff ensures mother, baby and family are recognised as individuals, guaranteeing flexibility to enable maternity care to encompass customs, ideals and the needs of women. Natural childbirth, wellness and aftercare is promoted to assist the new family. There are parenting education programs, birthing unit, nursery, ward for prenatal, postnatal care, midwifery support program for home and maternity clinics. There are activities including aqua-aerobics and access to high risk care if required as part of the NSCCAHS Network. The Maternity Service endeavours to continually maintain and improve service value for women and the community.

Natural Birth Education & Research Centre
273 Lindendale Road
Lismore NSW 2480
Tel: (02) 6629 5312
email: info@naturalbirth.org.au
website: www.naturalbirth.org.au

The Natural Birth Education & Research Centre (NBERC) is a world leader in natural birth. NBERC offers safe, midwife-led pregnancy and birth care, 24-hour post-natal support, childbirth preparation classes and birth support (doula) training. Their beautifully appointed birthing and accommodation suites are situated on 18 quiet acres of rainforest and gardens. You can come and birth your baby in this wonderful, natural environment with midwives who care for the well being of you and your baby. The Natural Birth Education & Research Centre welcomes women from all over Australia.

Nepean Private Hospital
Barber Avenue
Kingswood NSW 2550
Tel: (02) 4732 7333

Nepean Private Hospital Women's Health Unit has been recently refurbished and provides quality obstetric care to women in the Nepean region. It is co-located with Nepean Public Hospital. Consisting of 28 single rooms with ensuites, 4 fully-equipped birthing rooms and "state of the art" Level 2 Special Care Nursery. The hospital has a dedicated team of doctors, midwives, lactation specialists, mothercraft and neonatal trained nurses to staff the unit providing education and support for new parents. Other services provided to the women and their families in the antenatal and postnatal period include: antenatal education classes, postnatal education, lactation support and postnatal clinic for on-going follow-up.

North Gosford Private Hospital
Burrabil Avenue
Gosford NSW 2250
Tel: (02) 4324 7111

Phone the number above for information on maternity facilities and services.

Prince of Wales Private Hospital
Barker Street
Randwick NSW 2031
Tel: (02) 9650 4693
email: powprivate.maternity@healthscope.com.au
website: www.powprivate.com.au

Prince of Wales Private Hospital is located in the heart of the eastern suburbs of Sydney and offers premium maternity services with a reputation for quality care. Prince of Wales Private Hospital delivers over 2,000 babies each year, and offers 6 fully equipped delivery suites, a full range of antenatal education, pre-admission consultations and a great team of experienced midwives. Prince of Wales Private Hospital also offers 24-hour midwife and medical cover, 24-hour theatre access and 24-hour on-call anaesthetist and neonatology services. The Level 2 Special Care Nursery facilities care for babies born from 32 weeks onwards and those that require extra clinical support. In 2008 Prince of Wales Private Hospital introduced the Little Luxuries Program at the Crowne Plaza Coogee Beach which offers eligible mothers the opportunity to experience their postnatal recovery in the luxurious surrounds of a beachfront hotel room. New parents bond with their baby in the comfort of deluxe accommodation offering ocean views; access to a specialised room service menu; and a large plasma screen TV with Foxtel channels, while midwifery staff from Prince of Wales Private Hospital are on site 24-hours to provide personalised parenting and breastfeeding support.

Royal Hospital for Women
Barker Street
Randwick NSW 2031
Tel: (02) 9382 6111
website: www.sesiahs.health.nsw.gov.au/rhw

For more than a century, the Royal Hospital for Women has provided specialist health care in partnership with women. The RHW was not only the first women's hospital in Australia, but also the country's first lying in hospital. As the state's only women's hospital and a tertiary referral hospital, they also provide highly specialised services including level three newborn intensive care, acute care services for women, reproductive medicine, telephone counselling services and the leading maternal fetal medicine.

Royal North Shore & Ryde Hospital
Pacific Highway
St Leonards NSW 2065
Tel: (02) 9926 6855 Maternity enquiries
website: www.nsh.nsw.gov.au/rnsh/info/DWCH/NEWBORNS.shtml

Royal North Shore Hospital has a long and distinguished history offering maternity care to the women in Northern Sydney since the early 1900s. The new Maternity Unit, opened in 2003, offers state-of-the-art facilities and a range of models of care, including the Midwifery Group Practice. As a tertiary referral hospital, specialised services include the Maternal Fetal Medicine Unit, Level 3 Newborn Care Centre, and acute care services.

St George Hospital
Gray Street
Kogarah NSW 2217
Tel: (02) 9350 1111

Phone the number above for information on maternity facilities and services.

St George Private Hospital
1 South Street
Kogarah NSW 2217
Tel: (02) 9598 5172
website: www.stgeorgeprivate.com.au

St George Private Hospital prides itself on providing the highest standard of clinical care. In February 2007 St George Private Maternity underwent extensive renovation to upgrade all delivery suites, the special care nursery and patient rooms. Obstetricians and paediatricians work in collaboration with all Maternity Unit staff to ensure all patients and new families receive the optimal standard of care. The Maternity Team are dedicated to ensuring your first few days as a parent are supported and focused on your individual needs throughout the process of your pregnancy, birth and postnatal period. Expert clinical care and services include: caring and experienced midwifery and nursing team, comprehensive education sessions, obstetricians on site 24 hours, Level 2 Special Care Nursery, in-patient breastfeeding and settling sessions and lactation services.

Resources

CHILDBIRTH & POSTNATAL SERVICES

Maternity hospitals & birth centres

Sydney Southwest Private Hospital

40 Bigge Street
Liverpool NSW 2170
Tel: (02) 9821 0333

The Sydney Southwest Private Hospital Maternity Unit provides all private accommodation with ensuites and four rooms have double beds. They have three modern birthing suites and a Level 2B nursery with state-of-the-art equipment. Their lactation consultants provide support to mums while establishing breastfeeding and the Unit also offers the services of a physiotherapist. A new Mood Disorder Unit has opened with qualified staff to help those with anxiety or PND.

Sydney Southwest Private Hospital

40 Bigge Street
Liverpool NSW 2170
Tel: (02) 9821 0333

The Sydney Southwest Private Hospital Birthing Unit has three modern birthing suites complete with spacious ensuites. Their highly trained midwives are on hand to assist and guide you and your partner through labour and the postnatal period. To help maintain a relaxed atmosphere they provide CD players and televisions in all rooms. They also offer aromatherapy on request. They have 24-hour, on-call anaesthetic and neo-natal cover to provide you and your baby with the best possible care. Phone the number above for more information.

The Hills Private Hospital

499 Windsor Road
Baulkham Hills NSW 2153
Tel: (02) 9639 3333

The attractive birthing facilities at this hospital comprise five tastefully furnished birthing suites allowing you to experience childbirth in home-like surroundings. The postnatal area comprises both private and twin share rooms all with ensuite, personal telephone and television. Some rooms also have double beds so partners can stay. They offer a high standard of care within a family environment.

AUSTRALIAN CAPITAL TERRITORY

Calvary Hospital

Corner Belconnen Way & Haydon Drive
Bruce ACT 2617
Tel: (02) 6201 6111
website: www.calvary.act.gov.au

The Maternity Unit at Calvary Public Hospital is situated on the 3rd level in the Marian Building. The Maternity ward offers single rooms and two or four-bed rooms all with ensuite facilities. There are six birthing rooms, five with ensuite facilities.

Calvary Hospital

Corner Belconnen Way & Haydon Drive
Bruce ACT 2617
Tel: (02) 6201 6359
website: www.calvary.act.gov.au

The Calvary Public Hospital offers a range of classes for women birthing at Calvary Maternity Unit. 'First Time Parents' is a series of 5 sessions of 2 hours duration beginning at approximately 28 weeks or there is a 'One Day Group' for first time parents held monthly on a Tuesday. Other classes include: Refresher Group; Elective Caesarean Section Sessions; Antenatal Breastfeeding Education; Postnatal Fitness Sessions, Multiple Births and Vaginal Birth after Caesarean Section sessions. Phone Childbirth Education for further information on (02) 6201 6359.

Calvary John James Hospital

173 Strickland Crescent
Deakin ACT 2600
Tel: (02) 6281 8100
email: wendy.prowse@calvary-act.com.au

Calvary John James Hospital is the largest private hospital in Canberra providing a caring and supportive environment throughout your pregnancy. They offer you the opportunity to discuss your individual birth plan with one of their highly skilled midwives as well as ante-natal and postnatal courses. The hospital provides private rooms with ensuites, postnatal baby massage classes and a special 'Romantic Couples' dinner on the night before discharge. Tours of the unit are available via appointment by phoning (02) 6281 8730.

Calvary Private Hospital

Conrer Haydon Drive & Belconnen Way
Bruce ACT 2617
Tel: (02) 6201 6586
email: wendy.prowse@calvary-act.com.au
website: www.calvary-act.com.au

Calvary Private Hospital has the only private maternity unit on the north side of Canberra. The hospital offers you the opportunity to discuss your individual birth plan with an experienced midwife as well as ante-natal and post-natal classes. You will be guaranteed a private room with ensuite and the majority of rooms have double beds with partners welcome to stay. You will also receive complimentary champagne and a baby t-shirt. The care, compassion and support provided at Calvary is renown.

Queanbeyan District Hospital & Health Service

Collett Street
Queanbeyan ACT 2620
Tel: (02) 6298 9211

Phone the number above for information on maternity facilities and services.

QUEENSLAND

Gold Coast Hospital
108 Nerang Street
Southport QLD 4215
Tel: (07) 5519 8211

The Gold Coast Maternity Service offers residents of the Gold Coast district a comprehensive choice of maternity care options. These include Birth Centre care, hospital/community-based medical and midwifery clinics, GP shared-care and private Obstetric care. In addition to the birthing suites, services include parenthood classes, in-patient ante/post-natal unit, a healthy hearing program, Special Care Nursery and midwifery postnatal home visiting. Referral to specialty services as required include Lactation Consultant, Physiotherapy, Dietitian, Social Work and Child Health Services.

Logan Hospital - 2D Maternity
Armstrong Road
Meadowbrook QLD 4131
Tel: (07) 3299 9565
website: www.health.qld.gov.au

If you live in the Logan city and Beaudessert Shire and surrounding areas, Logan Hospital is your community hospital offering many advantages as the first choice for your birth. Logan Hospital has the ability to handle 3,600 births each year. The Maternity Unit has 30 beds, nine birthing suites and a 16-cot Special Care Nursery – Level 2.

Mater Mothers' Hospital
Raymond Terrace
South Brisbane QLD 4101
Tel: (07) 3163 8664
website: www.mater.org.au

Opened in May 2008 the new Mater Mothers' Hospital has been designed to deliver real benefits to women and babies, along with providing a family-focussed environment in terms of care and support. The state-of-the-art facility offers women a choice of maternity care options including community-based shared care and midwifery clinics, midwifery group practice, early parenting education, and postnatal home care. For women and babies experiencing complications, the hospital provides specialist care in maternal fetal medicine, early pregnancy assessment and neonatology (for premature or sick newborn babies). Other special services include Queensland Cord Blood Bank; Breastfeeding Support Centre; allied health (physiotherapy, occupational therapy, nutrition and dietetics); natural fertility services; and tailored clinics for young women, women from non-English speaking backgrounds and women with substance use issues.

Mater Mothers' Private Hospital
Raymond Terrace
South Brisbane QLD 4101
Tel: (07) 3163 8622
website: www.mater.org.au

Collocated with Mater Mothers' Hospital, the new 90-bed Mater Mothers' Private Hospital offers the highest level of specialist private maternity and neonatal care. The pre-admission service, antenatal education (including Pre-pregnancy, Exercise in Pregnancy and Dads Only sessions) birth suite and postnatal care support your individual birthing and early parenting plans. The contemporary state-of-the-art facility is designed to provide privacy and comfort, with all rooms single-bed accommodation equipped with ensuites, telephones, televisions and mini-fridges. Other special services include the Queensland Cord Blood Bank; Breastfeeding Support Centre; allied health; natural fertility services; early parenting education; and advice and support from qualified lactation consultants.

Redland Hospital
Weippin Street
Cleveland QLD 4163
Tel: (07) 3488 3111

The Women and Birthing Service provides care to families within its Antenatal Service, Antenatal/Postnatal Inpatient Unit, Birthing Unit, Home Visiting Service and Special Care Baby Unit. The Women and Birthing Service provides care for pregnant women recognising individual needs and the concept of partnership and choice within the context of a multidisciplinary maternity team.

Royal Brisbane Women's Hospital - Maternity
Butterfield Street
Herston QLD 4029
Tel: (07) 3636 8111
website: www.health.qld.gov.au/rbwh

Phone the number above for information on maternity facilities and services.

St. Vincent's Hospital Maternity Unit
Scott Street
Toowoomba QLD 4350
Tel: (07) 4690 4000
website: www.stvincents.org.au

St. Vincent's Hospital Maternity Unit provides a range of services to support you before, during and after your baby's birth. Services offered include pre-admission service and parenting program. A highly skilled unit to provide you and your family with the very best of health care. The private rooms are beautifully appointed with ensuite, refreshment refrigerator, tea and coffee making facilities, TV and telephone. The birthing suites provide a relaxed atmosphere with private ensuites, balcony and sitting room. They are fully equipped to handle any emergency and are able to provide a range of options and choices to meet your needs. For babies who may require extra care and attention there is a fully-equipped special care nursery with the latest technology.

Sunshine Coast Private Hospital
Syd Lingard Drive
Buderim QLD 4556
Tel: (07) 5430 3150

The Sunshine Coast Private Hospital has a new 27-bed unit, all with private ensuites as well as TV, direct dial

Resources

CHILDBIRTH & POSTNATAL SERVICES
Maternity hospitals & birth centres

phones and some rooms have double beds and fridges. The special care nursery facilities are available along with ante-natal classes, pre-admission clinics and post-natal reunions. Sunshine Coast Private Hospital is a Baby Friendly Accredited hospital set in a very tranquil bush environment. Tours of the unit are available on the first Sunday of every month at 2.00pm or at other times by appointment.

The Wesley Hospital
451 Coronation Drive
Auchenflower QLD 4066
Tel: (07) 3232 7000
website: www.wesley.com.au

The Wesley Hospital has both private and shared accommodation. All rooms have external views, a television and telephone, and their four delivery suites are comfortable and spacious. Phone 3232 7000 to organise a tour of the hospital.

NORTHERN TERRITORY

Alice Springs Hospital
Gap Road
Alice Springs NT 0870
Tel: (08) 8951 7777

Alice Springs Hospital provides a full maternity service including midwife clinics and early discharge. A variety of birthing choices is supported by the Alice Springs Hospital Maternity Unit.

Darwin Private Hospital
Rocklands Drive
Tiwi NT 0810
Tel: (08) 8920 6011

Phone the number above for information on maternity facilities and services.

Gove District Hospital
Matthew Flinders Way
Nhulunbuy NT 0880
Tel: (08) 8987 0211

Phone the number above for information on maternity facilities and services.

Katherine Hospital
Gorge Road
Katherine NT 0850
Tel: (08) 8973 9211

Phone the number above for information on maternity facilities and services.

Royal Darwin Hospital
Rocklands Drive
Tiwi NT 0810
Tel: (08) 8922 8888

Phone the number above for information on maternity facilities and services.

Tennant Creek Hospital
Schmidt Street
Tennant Creek NT 0860
Tel: (08) 8962 4399

Phone the number above for information on maternity facilities and services.

WESTERN AUSTRALIA

Albany Regional Hospital
Warden Avenue
Albany WA 6330
Tel: (08) 9892 2222

Albany Hospital provides a supportive and professional service to women and their families of the Great Southern region. This includes a comprehensive obstetric service incorporating GP obstetricians, a team of highly skilled midwives with the support of an on-site obstetrician/gynaecologist. Antenatal education classes, home visiting service for early discharge clients 7 days a week and lactation consultant are available. Phone the number above for further information.

Attadale Private Hospital – Maternity
21 Hislop Road
Attadale WA 6156
Tel: (08) 9330 1000

Attadale Private Hospital is a 38-bed hospital located in the suburb of Attadale, centrally located within the City of Melville in Perth's southern suburbs. The hospital is located adjacent to lush parkland. Medical and surgical services are offered which include maternity, gynaecology, urology and medical rehabilitation. Attadale Private Hospital specialises in obstetrics. Phone the number above for more information.

Bentley Health Service – Maternity
35–39 Mill Street
Bentley WA 6102
Tel: (08) 9334 3666

Bentley Health Service provides a range of services to support women during pregnancy and birth. There is a midwife/GP Clinic, ante-natal education, parenting classes and postnatal fitness classes. Early discharge with home visiting midwifery service and lactation consultant for breastfeeding problems are available. Phone the number above for more information.

Galliers Private Wing, Armadale Hospital
3056 Albany Highway
Armadale WA 6112
Tel: (08) 9391 1050

Galliers Private Wing, Armadale Hospital, provides private care and accommodation with a difference.

Midwifery model of care, supportive doctors and a shared-care program with midwives and doctors. Appointments are available at weekends with midwives. The hospital provides individual personalised care from all team members. Partners and family are welcome to support you at this very special time. Phone to arrange an individual appointment to meet a happy team of dedicated midwives and tour this comfortable and relaxed unit.

Glengarry Private Hospital
53 Arnisdale Road
Duncraig WA 6023
Tel: (08) 9447 0111
website: www.ramsayhealth.com.au

Glengarry Private Hospital has been a leader in the provision of maternity services in Perth's northern suburbs for 31 years. This maternity service offers women and their families access to a comprehensive spectrum of modern maternity facilities. The Women's Health Unit has 28 beds which include a Level II neonatal nursery and four birthing suites. Lactation Consultancy is also available to assist with breastfeeding. On discharge a Midwifery Home Visiting Service is available so mums can return home early with the support of experienced domiciliary midwives. There is also a variety of parent education classes including pre-pregnancy classes that are scheduled regularly. At Glengarry a team of dedicated midwives, obstetricians, anaesthetists and paediatricians work together to provide families with a memorable childbirth experience. There is 24-hour access to the hospital's operating theatres for patients requiring an emergency or planned caesarean section. The hospital also has 24-hour anaesthetic cover. Glengarry Hospital delivers quality private health care and has a strong community reputation. Easy parking with excellent access to medical suites and services.

Joondalup Health Campus
Shenton Avenue
Joondalup WA 6027
Tel: (08) 9400 9400

Highly trained doctors and midwives staff the maternity unit at Joondalup Health Campus. This vast experience is backed up by well-equipped facilities including 24-hour onsite laboratory services, adult intensive care facilities and 24-hour anaesthetic, medical and surgical services in case of an emergency. Midwives have formulated a program of classes for prospective parents with the aim to share knowledge and, through discussion, assist in making your birth experience as pleasurable as possible. Joondalup Health Campus was Western Australia's first Baby Friendly Accredited Hospital. Aside from the main nursery the hospital has a Special Care Nursery for babies requiring a little extra support and observation. The following services are also provided: lactation consultant, social worker, pastoral care upon request and a physiotherapy department. For more information on the services they provide phone the number above.

Kalgoorlie Regional Hospital
Piccadilly Street
Kalgoorlie WA 6430
Tel: (08) 9080 5888

Phone the number above for information on maternity facilities and services.

King Edward Hospital – Family Birth Centre
374 Bagot Road
Subiaco WA 6008
Tel: (08) 9340 2222
website: www.wnhs.wa.gov.au

The Family Birth Centre is located at King Edward Memorial Hospital (KEMH) and caters for WA women with low-risk pregnancies who wish to have a family-centred, active birth. A team of midwives provide continuity of pregnancy and birth care in a relaxed and comfortable home-like setting. Women can access KEMH's services including medical care, the breastfeeding centre, physiotherapy and mental health support if required. Visit KEMH's website or phone for more information about services.

King Edward Memorial Hospital (KEMH)
374 Bagot Road
Subiaco WA 6008
Tel: (08) 9340 2222
website: www.wnhs.wa.gov.au

King Edward Memorial Hospital (KEMH) is WA's tertiary referral centre for complex pregnancies and high risk births. It offers world-class care and wide-ranging support services to WA women with complicated pregnancies and infants born prematurely. The KEMH Women and Newborn Health Library provides information to the public on women's and newborn health. Visit KEMH's website or phone for more information about services.

Mercy Hospital Mt Lawley
Thirlmere Road
Mount Lawley WA 6050
Tel: (08) 9370 9420
email: fbu@mercycare.com.au
website: www.mercycare.com.au/hospital.asp

The Mercy Family Birthing Unit offers intimate, home-style accommodation, caring personalised attention, along with state-of-the art clinical facilities. The rooms are beautifully appointed. All private rooms have double beds enabling parents to stay together for the duration of hospitalisation. Many rooms have extensive views of the Swan River. Their team is committed to preparing mothers, fathers and families for all aspects of childbirth, guiding you toward the safe arrival of your new baby, to taking your baby home and beyond.

Osborne Park Hospital (OPH)
Osborne Place
Stirling   WA 6021
Tel: (08) 9346 8000
website: www.oph.halth.gov.au

OPH provides care to women with low to moderate

Resources

CHILDBIRTH & POSTNATAL SERVICES

Maternity hospitals & birth centres

risk pregnancies throughout the antenatal, intrapartum and postnatal period by a team of midwives, doctors and allied health staff. Labour care is provided in luxuriously appointed birth suites with individual sitting rooms and ensuite bathrooms. Postnatal care is provided on the ward and at home (for women within the catchment area). The midwifery and obstetric staff form part of an experienced team dedicated to providing excellent care to all women. Support services consist of social workers, physiotherapists, dieticians, lactation consultants and psychiatrists.

Port Hedland Regional Hospital
Kingsmill Street
Port Hedland WA 6721
Tel: (08) 9158 1666

Phone the number above for information on maternity facilities and services.

Rockingham Kwinana Health Service
Elenora Drive
Rockingham WA 6168
Tel: (08) 9592 0600

The midwives at Rockingham Kwinana Health Service know that giving birth is a special time for parents and their families and take care to support each person as they go through this unique experience. Maternity services at Rockingham Kwinana Hospital will boast a brand new, state- of-the-art obstetric facility which includes a planned 24 bed unit with five birthing suites. A full range of services include preparation for birth classes, home-visiting midwifery service for parents requiring home support and lactation consultant. Parents interested in having their baby at RKHS are encouraged to contact the hospital and access the many support and education resources available to them.

South West Health Campus
Cnr Bussell Highway & Robinson Drive
Bunbury WA 6230
Tel: (08) 9722 1000

Phone the number above for information on maternity facilities and services.

St John of God Hospital Murdoch
100 Murdoch Drive
Murdoch WA 6150
Tel: (08) 9366 1111

St John of God Hospital Murdoch aims to provide the safest, most relaxed environment for you and your family. The Maternity Unit is a new, modern, technologically advanced and well-equipped facility, with 29 luxurious private and three spacious shared suites. Double and single bed suites are available. The Unit is supported by highly dedicated obstetricians, GP obstetricians, paediatricians and staffed by qualified, experienced midwives. The Birth Suite provides a private and safe environment where individual birthing needs can be accommodated. Five birthing suites are available each with bedroom décor, an ensuite, television, sitting area and tea and coffee making facilities. One birth suite has a bath. The Nursery and Special Care Nursery adjoin the ward. The breastfeeding room and breastfeeding clinic further enhance the exclusive experience of this facility. Murdoch Maternity at Home provides the opportunity for you to return home early with support and care from the Midwives of St Mary's Ward. Maternity Unit Tours are conducted by a midwife every Saturday and Sunday at 2.30pm so you can view the facilities.

St John of God Hospital, Subiaco
12 Salvado Road
Subiaco WA 6008
Tel: (08) 9382 6111
website: www.sjog.org.au/subiaco

The St. John of God Hospital, Subiaco maternity unit, has been operating for over 60 years and has an outstanding reputation. The unit is supported by Western Australia's leading obstetricians and caters for the full range of birthing needs. The delivery suite provides a safe and supportive birthing environment where the individual preferences of parents are acknowledged. In addition to the delivery suites offered, a family birthing suite is available which provides a home-like atmosphere. The delivery suite also includes a dedicated obstetric theatre to ensure there is no delay should an emergency arise. St. John of God Hospital, Subiaco also offers an extensive parent education program, inclusive of preparing for birth through to breastfeeding and transition to parenting.

Swan District Hospital
Eveline Road
Middle Swan WA 6056
Tel: (08) 9347 5244

Swan District Hospital is a 17-bed maternity facility with midwifery care and consultant obstetrician service available on site. Supported by consultant paediatricians and anaesthetists. The unit is also supported by extensive allied health facilities. The unit provides antenatal care, childbirth preparation classes, delivery facilities, postnatal ward, special care nursing and a home visiting midwifery service. Situated in the heart of the Swan Valley.

The Margaret River District Hospital
Farrelly Street
Margaret River WA 6285
Tel: (08) 9757 2000

Margaret River Hospital is a small district hospital that provides a personal interment service to low-risk pregnant women.

SOUTH AUSTRALIA

Ashford Hospital
55 Anzac Highway
Ashford SA 5035
Tel: (08) 8375 5222

Ashford Hospital is the largest private hospital providing obstetric services in South Australia. These up-to-date facilities include 6 delivery suites, 20 modern postnatal rooms all fitted with ensuite bathroom, DVD, sofa couch and a small refrigerator. The hospital is able to look after babies born from 32 weeks gestation in the level 2 nursery. The Baby Bliss program based at the Hilton Adelaide enables families to receive five star treatment in five star facilities. They also offer the full range of preparation for birth and parenting programs which are able to be adapted to suit your individual requirements.

Calvary North Adelaide Hospital
89 Strangways Terrace
North Adelaide SA 5006
Tel: (08) 8239 9100
email: maternity@calvarysa.com.au
website: www.calvarysa.com.au

The Maternity Unit offers personalised care and attention from visiting obstetricians, paediatricians and highly qualified midwives. The unit has a proud tradition of providing maternity services to the people of South Australia with over 66,000 babies born here. It's a well-equipped unit with highly qualified midwives and allied health professionals plus obstetrician, paediatrician and gynaecology consultants on site all supported by a 24-hour onsite medical officer. Staff care for you from preconception to the postnatal phase: Planning a Baby seminars; parent education classes; lactation consultants; a postnatal clinic and parent pampering packages. If special care is required there is a Level 2A Nursery for premature and highly dependant newborn babies as well as an Adult Critical Care unit for the care of mothers. For further information on the maternity services available at Calvary North Adelaide Hospital, to take a tour of the facilities or to make a booking phone the Maternity Unit Ward Clerk during office hours on 8239 9146 or email maternity@calvarysa.com.au.

Flinders Medical Centre (FMC)
Flinders Drive
Bedford Park SA 5042
Tel: (08) 8204 4680
website: www.flinders.sa.gov.au

Flinders Medical Centre (FMC) offers women the choice of giving birth in the traditional Labour & Delivery Suite or the Birth Centre. The Labour & Delivery Suite comprises ten pleasant birthing rooms, and two comfortable rooms that are used for high dependency medical care. The Birth Centre offers an alternative to traditional maternity care and is suitable for those who wish to have a natural approach to childbirth. The Birth Centre offers a comfortable homelike environment where women can give birth in a relaxed and friendly atmosphere supported by family and friends. Children are welcome provided they are in the care of an adult. Facilities include a double bed, a deep bath, en-suite bathroom and kitchen. Techniques such as massage, aromatherapy and water therapy are offered to reduce the need for pain-relieving drugs during labour. Women are encouraged to remain active and create a homely environment by bringing their favourite music, pillow, photos or flowers. Care is provided by Birth Centre midwives who assist women to make choices and actively participate in their care.

Flinders Private Hospital
1 Flinders Drive
Bedford Park SA 5042
Tel: (08) 8275 3333
email: ksax@acha.org.au
website: www.flindersprivate.com.au

Flinders Private Hospital Maternity Unit provides a luxurious and safe environment for you and your baby. It has well appointed birthing suites, private rooms, a spa bathroom and the nursery can accommodate babies from 34-weeks gestation. Neo-natal intensive care services are readily accessible if a higher level of care is needed.

Gawler Health Service
21 Hutchinson Road
Gawler East SA 5118
Tel: (08) 8521 2369
email: sonia.angus@health.sa.gov.au
website: www.ghs.sa.gov.au

Gawler Health Service offers a range of public health options within a rural community setting. It offers suitably appointed maternity facilities for you and your family's birthing experience within a professional and friendly environment. Their service promotes a continuum of care as they believe pregnancy, childbirth and the post-partum period is a special time in your life and they feel privileged to share the journey with you and your family. Gawler offers the option of midwifery care only, GP shared care or Obstetric Medical Consultant care. Gawler Health Service has 24-hour, on-call paediatricians, anaesthetists, obstetricians and theatre staff as well as boarder and private facilities.

North Eastern Community Hospital
580 Lower North East Road
Campbelltown SA 5074
Tel: (08) 8337 7200
website: www.northeasternhospital.com.au

North Eastern Community Hospital has 22 private maternity rooms each with its own ensuite, and 4 birthing rooms plus a Level 2, low dependency, accredited nursery. They offer ante-natal education plus specific ante-natal breastfeeding classes and also provide a comprehensive post-natal education and support system until Child & Youth Health can see their new mothers. Their staff includes qualified lactation consultants, neonatal nurses and midwives who provide a caring and efficient level of service to all clients and also on-site obstetricians.

Resources

CHILDBIRTH & POSTNATAL SERVICES

Maternity hospitals & birth centres
➔ Memorabilia: newborn, baby & childhood

Queen Elizabeth Hospital
28 Woodville Road
Woodville South SA 5011
Tel: (08) 8222 6000

Phone the number above for information on maternity facilities and services.

South Coast District Hospital
Bay Road
Victor Harbor SA 5211
Tel: (08) 8552 0500
website: www.encounterhealth.sa.gov.au

Phone the number above for information on maternity facilities and services.

The Whyalla Hospital & Health Services
Wood Terrace
Whyalla SA 5600
Tel: (08) 8648 8300
website: www.nfwrhs.sa.gov.au

Phone the number above for information on maternity facilities and services.

TASMANIA

Calvary Hospital Lenah Valley
49 Augusta Road
Lenah Valley TAS 7008
Tel: (03) 6278 5333
website: www.calvarytas.com.au

Phone the number above for information on maternity facilities and services.

Hobart Private Hospital
Argyle Street
Hobart TAS 7000
Tel: (03) 6214 3000 or Hotline 1800 033 480
website: www.healthscope.com.au

Celebrate the birth of your baby in the tasteful environment of Hobart Private Hospital's Maternity Unit, where the focus is on family-centred care and development of parenting knowledge and skills for the mother and the entire family. Ante-natal classes are offered at flexible times by the midwives who will be sharing your experience. You may choose to participate in the private Know Your Midwife (KYM) scheme – a new and unique program for privately insured women and women who are self-insured. The KYM model gives women the best of both obstetrician and midwife care. Women alternate visits between their obstetrician and the KYM midwives. This will allow them to form a

relationship with their private obstetrician as well as meeting and forming close ties with a small group of midwives, who are directly involved in care throughout the pregnancy, labour and after the birth. Patients suggest it is like being among friends. The Maternity Unit provides double beds in large suites, where women can birth their babies, and partners are encouraged to stay, to ease the transition into new parenting roles. The Unit acknowledges your celebration with a congratulatory gift of gourmet foods and champagne, baby products and a special teddy bear. Staff work closely with parents to ensure the best possible start in life for your baby and to provide ongoing care and support for the continued well being of your whole family.

Launceston Hospital - Queen Victoria Maternity
Charles Street
Launceston TAS 7250
Tel: (03) 6348 7111

Phone the number above for information on maternity facilities and services.

Mersey Community Hospital
Bass Highway
Latrobe TAS 7307
Tel: (03) 6426 5111

The Women's & Children's Health Unit is a 22-bed facility offering obstetric and midwifery services to women on the north west coast of Tasmania. Ante-natal women attending the Public Out Patient Clinic will attend either a Low Risk Midwife Clinic or a High Risk Doctors Clinic. Childbirth and parent craft classes are offered to all women attending this facility. Postnatal care is supported by experienced midwives and lactation consultants. Early discharge is an option and all women birthing at Mersey are offered visits form the Extended Care Midwife following discharge.

North West Private Hospital
Brickport Road
Burnie TAS 7320
Tel: (03) 6432 6000
website: www.northwestprivate.com.au

North West Private Hospital, Burnie, not only offers maternity services to women with private health insurance, the hospital holds the contract with DHHS to provide maternity services to the public sector. Services include antenatal classes, antenatal clinic, midwives clinic, Know Your Midwife Scheme and an Extended Midwifery Service for home visits after discharge. The maternity unit also has a Level II Special Care Nursery. Phone the number above for more information.

The Royal Hobart Hospital
48 Liverpool Street
Hobart TAS 7000
Tel: (03) 6222 8308

Phone the number above for information on maternity facilities and services.

MEMORABILIA: NEWBORN, BABY & CHILDHOOD

NATIONAL

Ageless-Bronzing Shoes & Dummies
Tel: (08) 8358 4555
email: itsybitsy1@bigpond.com
website: www.itsybitsystudios.com

Ageless-Bronzing Shoes & Dummies can preserve your priceless keepsakes in handcrafted everlasting metal, which is polished and lacquered to protect the metal's lustrous shine, eliminating any ongoing upkeep. They offer finishes in copper, antique copper, silver and gold and specialise in baby shoes, hospital id tags, tummy clips, first ballet shoes and football boots (even footballs. Upon request they will frame or mount your treasures on a beautiful rosewood base with personalised inscribed name plaque. Mail order service or if you live in South Australia you can visit their studio – phone first for an appointment. Gift vouchers available.

Always Gifts
Tel: 0412 223 118
email: enquiries@alwaysgifts.com.au
website: www.alwaysgifts.com.au

Always Gifts Candles include a stylish collection of personalised photo candles for your baby's special occasion such as births, naming days, baptisms and christenings. These Australian made pillar candles are personalised with your baby's name and photo on the front, and the back features a poem or prayer of your choice. For godparents or guests, the collection includes matching personalised taper candles which will serve as a meaningful keepsake as a remembrance of your baby's special day. Phone the number above for more information.

BellaBee Candle Designz
Tel: 0404 507 227
email: info@bellabeecandles.com.au
website: www.bellabeecandles.com.au

BellaBee takes pride in creating personalised keepsake candles for all occasions and specialising in christenings and baptisms. Phone the number above for more information.

Belly Art
Tel: 0411 405 834
email: info@bellyart.com.au
website: www.bellyart.com.au

Belly Art specialises in creating professional belly casts for pregnant women to cherish as 'priceless' works of art. Belly Art also produce 3D sculptures of baby's hand and feet mounted or box framed in a multitude of colour options from traditional to modern. The range includes safe, easy-to-use DIY Casting kits and Inkless Print kits, personalised gifts, life sculptures and gift certificates. Visit their website and online store for full and illustrated details of their extensive product range.

Birthing Bellies
Tel: 0411 039 239
email: enquiries@birthingbellies.com.au
website: www.birthingbellies.com.au

Capture the detail of every fingernail on your baby's tiny hand and every wrinkle on their foot with a sculpture that can be remembered in years to come. Birthing Bellies offers hands and feet sculptures in a range of colours including gold, bronze, silver, stone or off-white. Each set is presented with an inscribed gold plaque and mounted on hand crafted native hardwood or they can be beautifully framed with a photo. All materials used in the sculpting process are non-allergenic. Birthing Bellies offer home or studio visits in NSW only as well as the exclusive Baby Hand & Feet Sculpture Kit, allowing you to create professional sculptures of your baby's hands and feet. Birthing Bellies also specialise in baby hand and feet imprints, memorabilia bronzing, pregnant belly casting and Pregnant Belly Casting Kits.

Bubbalicious Blankies
Tel: 0427 762 774
email: mitch252@hotmail.com
website: www.bubbaliciousblankies.com.au

Bubbalicious Blankies produce top quality, personalised products for the special people in your life. They offer a huge selection of products including blankets, bunny rugs, towels, art smocks, reader bags, placemats, Santa sacks and stockings and much more. Visit their site to see the full range. Each item is embroidered individually.

Celebration Candles
Tel: (02) 9580 3010
email: info@celebrationcandles.com.au
website: www.celebrationcandles.com.au

Celebration Candles offer personalised hand painted candles for christenings, baptisms, naming days and for all special occasions. Beautiful candles are hand painted to your specifications with different designs available, making an ideal gift to celebrate the birth of a new baby. Delivery Australia wide.

Created By You
Tel: 0418 153 877
email: createdbyyou@ylt.net.au
website: www.createdbyyou.com.au

Now your favourite memories can be with you all the time with individual personalised products by Created By You. Your favourite photograph can be printed and displayed on your own canvas bag or cushion. The tote bag is made from canvas and is 37cm x 37cm – the perfect size for everyday use. The cushion is fully backed with canvas and comes complete with a full cushion inner. Ordering is as simple as sending an email. For further information or to request a sales leaflet and order form contact createdbyyou@ylt.net.au or visit www.createdbyyou.com.au.

Creative Memories
Tel: (03) 9561 6089 or 0414 299 923
Don't let photos of your baby's first smile end up in a

Resources

CHILDBIRTH & POSTNATAL SERVICES
Memorabilia: newborn, baby & childhood

box or worse, an album that destroys your precious photos. Creative Memories offers beginner classes and ongoing workshops to help you create safe and meaningful albums which tell your family's story. They also offer an exclusive collection of photo-safe albums and supplies. Private classes are also available in your home. Consultants available Australia-wide.

Etched In Memories
Tel: 0416 021 498
email: info@etchedinmemories.com.au
website: www.etchedinmemories.com.au

Etched In Memories is an online store specialising in photo engraving. You can send in your favourite photo and have it engraved onto a pendant as a beautiful personalised gift, keepsake or jewellery. Choose from the standard plated pendants or premium 9ct gold and sterling silver pendants. Etched In Memories also offer an engraving-only service, fundraising plus a 100% satisfaction guarantee, free regular postage and free gift wrapping.

IGC DOREL Pty Ltd
Tel: 1300 809 526
email: sales@igcdorel.com.au
website: www.pearhead.com

Pearhead products are designed to celebrate memories for generations to come. Crafted from only the finest materials, Pearhead frames, albums, keepsake boxes and scrapbooks help turn memories into timeless classics. Pearhead offers a stylish alternative in a variety of styles, sizes and colours. To view the latest range visit www.pearhead.com or phone IGC Dorel's Customer Service team on 1300 809 526 for your nearest stockist.

Impressionable Kids
Tel: 1300 885 868
email: contact@impressionablekids.com.au
website: www.impressionablekids.com.au

 Impressionable Kids specialise in framed baby hand and feet sculptures and are Australia's leader in framed children's memorabilia. Their product range includes 3D framed hand and feet sculptures, canvas prints, name frames, bronzing, custom framing, photo art and free-standing hand and feet sculptures. Impressions only take moments to take and are completely non-toxic to baby and can be framed with or without a photo. Visit www.impressionablekids.com.au for more information. Branches Australia wide. For franchise opportunities phone (02) 9543 1633.

Inky Feet
Franchises Australia wide
Tel: 1300 465 933 (1300 inky feet)
email: info@inkyfeet.com.au
website: www.inkyfeet.com.au

Inky Feet is an affordable, funky way of capturing a moment in time. Footprints and handprints of your newborn are taken at an Inky Feet home-based studio and personalised with birth details or a special message for family members. Coffee mugs, clocks and plates are just some of the pieces available. Franchises are also available nationally.

Katydid Decor Company
Tel: 1300 655 069
email: info@katydiddecor.com.au
website: www.katydiddecor.com.au

 The Katydid Décor Company can create a beautiful personalised ceramic keepsake for your child or gift for someone special. The range includes commemorative plates, cups or money boxes to mark a special occasion, nameplates for a child's bedroom door and new and exclusive to Katydid, a lovely range of free-standing ceramic letters. They are a perfect gift for any child and any occasion. Select a set of letters in your child's name or special word to reflect your feelings. Your chosen gift will be enjoyed now and treasured as a keepsake in the future.

Kazoku Kids
Tel: (08) 9470 2851
email: info@kazokukids.com.au
website: www.kazokukids.com.au

ImpPrints are paint swab products used to make keepsake hand or footprints of small children and babies. They are currently available in pink, blue, purple and now green. The range enables you to make your own keepsakes with a very quick and simple method or creating great gifts to hand on to relatives when that new family member arrives. The range consists of the swabs, cards, birth announcements, posters, grow charts and display photo mats. All feature acid free paper for Impprints to last a lifetime. To find out more visit www.kazokukids.com.au or phone (08) 9470 2851 for a free brochure or to find a store near you.

Keepsakes To Cherish
Tel: 0405 687 252
email: lisa@keepsakestocherish.com.au
website: www.keepsakestocherish.com.au

Create a gorgeous 3D-replica sculpture of your baby's hands and feet with these easy-to-use DIY baby hand and feet casting kits.

Little Tesoro
Tel: 0413 069 610
email: info@littletesoro.com.au
website: www.littletesoro.com.au

There's nothing quite like the memories we create with our children, especially during the early years. Little

Tesoro has created a way to capture those special moments with a contemporary hand and feet home sculpture kit. Created specifically for its ease of use and presented in a beautiful Corban and Blair designer box frame, the sculpture kit is available online and via retail stockists at rrp$68.95. So whether you're looking to express a unique creativity in your own surroundings or through your gift giving, there's nothing quite like Little Tesoro. For more information visit www.littletesoro.com.au.

Milestone Press
Tel: 0401 671 707
email: sales@milestonepress.com.au
website: www.milestonepress.com.au

Milestone Press publishes *A Book About Me* for memories of pregnancy through to age five. Designed in Australia, the book's loose-leaf format allows you to remove the pages that don't suit your family. No more blank space or empty pages. There is also a ziplock plastic pocket to store items that are too special to glue such as clippings and photos. *A Book About Me* is the perfect way to record important milestones and funny moments in a book that will look just as stylish when they have their own children.

My Reflections Photobooks
Tel: (08) 9529 3351
email: info@myreflections.com.au
website: www.myreflections.com.au

Have fun creating your own personalised photobook quickly and easily with My Reflections Photobooks. Use the free (easy to use) Photobook Designer software to drag your photos into the templates, add your text and order online or CD. They print and bind in three days. Visit www.myreflections.com.au for more information.

Our Baby Website
email: sales@ourbabywebsite.com.au
website: www.ourbabywebsite.com.au

A personal baby website is the perfect way to capture and share all those priceless moments and milestones online with your family and friends. With many beautiful designs to choose from, Our Baby Website have the look and feel of a custom-designed website but at an affordable price. Journal and share your personal stories and photos as well as notify family and friends of upcoming baby events and celebrations. Visit the website to read more about the free 14-day trial.

Piktorize
Tel: 0400 883 556
email: enquiries@piktorize.com.au
website: www.piktorize.com.au

Piktorize offers beautiful high-quality photo canvases, stunning professionally bound photo books, gorgeous photo engraved pendants and fun novelty photo gift items. They also have an extensive range of personalised gift ideas and all products come with a satisfaction guarantee.

ScrapFrames
Tel: (02) 9481 4263
website: www.scrapframes.com.au

Scrapbooking has become a very popular way to preserve precious memories and for many people the birth of a child sparks an interest in this creative and enjoyable hobby. ScrapFrames sell quality archival page frames that make great gifts for a new parent or grandparent, and are also perfect for displaying your own special pages for all to enjoy. ScrapFrames also offers a wide range of scrapbooking and stamping supplies at discounted prices and great customer service.

Smallprint
Tel: see website for nearest franchisee
email: sales@smallp.com.au
website: www.smallp.com.au

 Give a unique first impression with Smallprint and capture your child's fingerprint in silver. No moulds are used, so the finished piece has been actually touched by someone you love. No matter where you are, your child, grandchild, niece or godson is always with you – their little fingerprint captured in your necklace, cufflink or keyring. Each item comes beautifully packaged to create a perfect gift. Ideal for birthdays, christenings, Christmas, Mothers' Day or Fathers' Day.

Splosh
Tel: (07) 3208 4077
website: www.splosh.com.au

With the gorgeous range of baby keepsake boxes from Splosh, every little step can be remembered in style. Bring your baby memories alive and store them in style. Beautifully embossed with sparkling jewels and a unique baby poem, the Keepsake Box offers a personal touch with a special slot to store a photo of your child. Create the perfect gift for your baby and store special mementoes in the Splosh Baby Keepsake Box (rrp$49.95), in pink for girls, blue for boys and white for both.

Sticky Baby Company Pty Ltd
Tel: (02) 6652 2299
email: stickybabycompany@bigpond.com
website: www.stickybabycompany.com.au

 The *Sticky Baby Journal* is an easy solution to remembering those precious moments in your baby's life. This stylish and new journal has 410 stickers and 52 acid free weekly pages to record the moments you want to remember, without the need to fill in sections which may be irrelevant to your family. The stylish, modern D-ring design means you can add or delete pages as you wish. Visit their website for further information.

The Bronzing Studio
Tel: (02) 9899 9122
email: info@bronzingstudio.com.au
website: www.bronzingstudio.com.au

The Bronzing Studio specializes in bronzing baby shoes,

Resources

CHILDBIRTH & POSTNATAL SERVICES
Memorabilia: newborn, baby & childhood

dummies, hospital ID bands, umbilical cord clips, baby's first tooth or first lock of hair and much more. They transform sentimental items into meaningful and valuable memories with a rich coating of copper, silver or 24k gold. Bronzed baby items are a beautiful way to treasure the memory of your baby's special moments forever. Gift certificates available.

Trisha Lambi
Tel: (07) 3294 7285
website: www.trishalambi.com
Trisha Lambi is a visual artist specialising in portraiture from photographs. A portrait of your child makes a beautiful gift or you may commission an artwork for your own enjoyment. A portrait by Trisha Lambi will become a treasured keepsake of the family, even a family heirloom. Portraits are done in pencil/charcoal, sepia, pastel or oils and can be of an individual or group.

Twinkle Toes Baby Hand & Feet Sculptures
Tel: 1300 781 155
email: twinkletoesinternational@tpg.com.au
website: www.twinkletoes.com.au
Twinkle Toes Baby Hand & Feet Sculptures specialise in the quality framing of 3-dimensional sculptures of your child's hands and/or feet. Sculptures can be created in gold colour, mounted with an inscription and then beautifully framed. It is also a great gift for a new baby, a christening gift or as a beautiful memento for grandparents.

www.photomax.com.au
Tel: 1300 654 360
email: info@photomax.com.au
website: www.photomax.com.au
Order your photos, gifts, photo cards and photo books from home and get them delivered Australia wide. Photomax is a real photo lab with an easy-to-use online ordering process. They have a large range of photo gifts and photo cards including birth announcements, thank you, Christmas, season's greetings and many more.

VICTORIA

Amanda's Photography
Tel: (03) 9435 8339 or 0403 988 744
email: amanda@amandasphotography.com.au
website: www.amandasphotography.com.au
Amanda's Photography offers both lifestyle photography in your home or chosen location and affordable studio sessions at her home studio or beautiful, outside location. A mother of two, her understanding of babies and children really helps to illicit and recognise those magic, heart-melting moments. Amanda offers many digital negative packages to suit all budgets – starting from only $195. Visit www.amandasphotography.com.au for a complete price list of available services and products.

Casey Ann Photography
6 Oakland Avenue
Upwey VIC 3158
Tel: 0408 050 701
email: enquiry@caseyannphotography.com.au
Casey Ann Photography captures naturally beautiful images to immortalise your precious memories.

David Fowler Photography
1st Floor, 95 Victoria Street
Fitzroy VIC 3065
Tel: (03) 9417 7744
email: info@davidfowler.com.au
website: www.davidfowler.com.au
David is an award-winning AIPP Master Photographer specialising in capturing those gorgeous eyes and special smiles ... the character unique to each child that will be yours forever and cherished for generations to come. Celebrate life and experience the difference this passionate, relaxed professional will make, whether at your home, a park/beach adventure or the studio. Exciting presentation ideas are available and an appointment is recommended.

Iris Creations Photography
Point Cook (servicing Melbourne & Geelong)
Tel: 0413 036 634
email: gemma@iriscreationsphotography.com
website: www.iriscreationsphotography.com

Gemma Higgins-Sears is one of Melbourne's most sought after photographers for maternity, newborn and baby portraiture. Iris Creations Photography is dedicated to capturing the special moments in life that matter the most and creating art. Sessions are performed in the comfort of your own home or at the studio. Offering affordable packages (including christenings and namings) tailored to suit you.

Kristen Cook
Tel: 0411 447 011
email: kristen@kristencook.com.au
website: www.kristencook.com.au

Kristen Cook is a boutique lifestyle photographer based in Melbourne specialising in pregnancy, newborns, babies, toddlers, children and families. Kristen works exclusively on location, either at your home or at your chosen venue so that your child will be comfortable, engaged and most importantly have fun! To view Kristen's work and find out more information about how she can capture those tickles, giggles and love for your family, visit Kristen's website at www.kristencook.com.au.

Leanne Temme Photography

38 Windella Avenue
East Kew VIC 3102
Tel: (03) 9859 5345
email: leanne@leannetemme.com.au
website: www.leannetemme.com.au

Leanne Temme specialises in natural, sensitive, high quality photographs of newborns, babies and children. Drawing on her background photographing for baby magazines, Leanne's experience as a mother guarantees she captures the essence of your child. Choose from wall prints, albums, canvas, books, or birth announcement cards to treasure your memories. Sensitive mother and baby moments, proud father and sibling images and Christening portraits are a specialty. Your precious child will be treated with love, patience and care with personalised service and quality. Phone the number above for more information.

Lifeworks Photography

28 Stafford Street
Northcote VIC 3070
Tel: (03) 9482 2006
email: info@lifeworksphotography.com.au
website: www.lifeworksphotography.com.au

Lifeworks Photography all female team specialise in portraits of pregnancy, newborn, children of all ages and families. Over the last 17 years they have gained an enviable reputation for a high standard of ethics and superb quality photography along with exceptional personal service. With the release of their TRUE EXPRESSIONS photographic techniques of watchmegrow, jigsaw, angelart, lifeart, they can offer photographically designed portraiture that goes beyond the ordinary. Allow the team at Lifeworks to create images that not only capture your family's essence, but design photographic pieces of art that are naturally and personally expressive. Phone (03) 9482 2006 or view their beautiful images on their website www.lifeworksphotography.com.au.

Maple Gallery

11 Cavalry Circuit
Maribyrnong VIC 3032
Tel: (03) 9317 9413 or 0413 480 781
website: www.maplegallery.com.au

Maple Gallery offers natural and creative portrait photography specialising in pregnant bellies, newborn babies, cheeky children and families. Maple Gallery will capture your unique story with beautifully designed wall portraits with your choice of traditional frames, metallic art mounts or artistic canvas. Join them for a fun and relaxed day in their studio or on location in the gardens or beach as they create truly personal portraits that exhibit the real you. For further information phone Maple Gallery on the number above or visit www.maplegallery.com.au.

Vicki Bell Photography

Tel: 0412 875 584
email: vicki@vickibell.com.au
website: www.vickibell.com.au

Each day in the life of a baby welcomes new changes and no matter what stage your baby is at, Vicki Bell Photography creates delicate and timeless images that will be cherished for generations. Vicki photographs their dainty, cherub features, capturing their delicate gestures and tenderness so you will have professional images that will make you feel a sense of joy at every glimpse. To view samples of her work click onto www.vickibell.com.au.

NEW SOUTH WALES

Colour Me Mine

Shop 1, 29 Holtermann Street
Crows Nest NSW 2065
Tel: (02) 9436 2020
email: babies@colourmemine.com.au
website: www.colourmemine.com.au

Colour Me Mine is a paint-it-yourself ceramics studio in Crows Nest. You can paint ceramic gifts and keepsakes using your baby's and toddler's hand and feet. The professional staff will help you with design, paint selection and even imprint your baby's painted feet on your chosen ceramic items. They will also glaze and fire the pieces for your collection in 4 to 6 days time. Visit the website for prices and opening hours.

Corinne Dany Photography & Design

Suite 1, 10 Boolwey Street
Bowral NSW 2576
Tel: (02) 4862 4088 or 0415 490 626
email: petrola@hinet.net.au
website: www.corinnedany.com

From her convenient studio in downtown Bowral or on location in the gorgeous Southern Highlands, Sydney and The Blue Mountains, Corinne Dany captures mothers-to-be, newborns and families with a relaxed and creative approach. Visit her website to see a slideshow of her work and look out for her fabulous range of products including the very special, individually-designed coffee table books, canvas prints and birth announcement cards.

Forever Bliss Photography

Tel: 0400 829 449
email: chantelle@foreverblissphotography.com.au
website: www.foreverblissphotography.com.au

forever bliss photography
creative custom portraiture

Award-winning photographer Chantelle Bliss is a leading pregnancy, maternity, newborn, baby, child and family photographer in Sydney, New South Wales. Chantelle is available for sessions in the greater Sydney area and for commercial and advertising assignments. Member of the AIPP – Australian Institute of Professional Photographers. Phone the number above for more information.

Resources

LK Photography

Newcastle to Gosford
Tel: 0413 144 603 or (02) 4973 4456
email: laura@lkphotography.com.au
website: www.lkphotography.com.au

With 14 years experience, LK Photography services Newcastle to Gosford, 7 days a week, at your home or location of your choice. Their photography for pregnancy, babies and children and birthday parties is modern, fun, natural and beautifully delivered in a professional, non-obtrusive, friendly and customer-focussed environment. Sitting fee includes high resolution DVD of unlimited portraits, index sheets, consultation and viewing appointments. See their website, phone or email for price list with sample portraits.

Newlife Photography

Tel: (02) 9660 7143
email: galia@newlifephotography.com
website: www.newlifephotography.com.au

Newlife Photography specialises exclusively in photographing babies from pregnancy to 12 weeks old. Newlife Photography has a gentle approach and special ability to capture the beauty that is newborn babies: precious, ethereal, full of love and trust, peace, innocence, personality, quirkiness and joy. The style manages to stay contemporary, fresh and always innovative. Blessed to be able to work with newborn babies everyday, they strive to provide their clients with exceptional keepsakes of such a memorable time. Phone the number above for more information.

Vivid Imagination

Tel: (02) 6545 9354
email: sophie@vividimagination.com.au
website: www.vividimagination.com.au

Photography packages from Vivid Imagination cater for individuals and groups. With a great range of print and design choices available, make sure you capture those special moments in your child's life forever. Phone or email Sophie for further information.

QUEENSLAND

All Our Babies Photography

7 Stanley Terrace
Brighton QLD 4017
Tel: (07) 3869 4472
email: allourbabies@gmail.com
website: www.allourbabies.com.au

All Our Babies Photography capture simple and timeless images – a look, an expression, a smile. Phone the number above for more information or visit their website.

Ashford Studio

116 Varsity Parade
Varsity Lakes QLD 4227
Tel: (07) 5562 2295
email: info@ashfordstudio.com.au
website: www.ashfordstudio.com.au

More women today are baring their pregnant bellies for the camera to capture their blossoming beauty. Kathryn Ashford, principal photographer at Ashford Studio, specialises in pregnancy and newborn photography and loves to create emotional images that touch the heart. For more information or to make an appointment phone Kathy on (07) 5562 2295 or visit the Ashford Studio website.

Catherine Lowe Photography

Tel: (07) 5528 2060 or 0402 023 241
email: cathlowe@iinet.net.au
website: www.celebrationsstudios.com.au

Celebrations Studios offers competitive prices, award-winning imagery and an outstanding commitment to their clients. Specialising in maternity, babies and family, they also photograph family events. Phone the number above for more information.

Colour Me Mine

Tel: (07) 5545 0890
email: babies@colourmemine.com.au
website: www.colourmemine.com.au

Colour Me Mine is a paint-it-yourself ceramics studio in Eagle Heights. You can paint ceramic gifts and keepsakes using your baby's and toddler's hand and feet. The professional staff will help you with design, paint selection and even imprint your baby's painted feet on your chosen ceramic items. They will also glaze and fire the pieces for your collection in 4 to 6 days time. Visit the website for prices and opening hours or phone for further information.

WESTERN AUSTRALIA

Kin Photography

U5/258 Newcastle Street
Northbridge WA 6003
Tel: 0419 957 060 or 0412 501 194
email: enquiries@kinphotography.com.au
website: www.kinphotography.com.au

Whether it is photos to celebrate your pregnancy, the arrival of your new baby, or a portrait session to capture the essence of your family, Kin Photography aims to provide you with photos that you will be proud to have in your home, and to make your photo shoot an enjoyable experience. Photo sessions can be done at home or on location and gift certificates are available. Phone the number above for more information.

Playful Portraits

PO Box 258
Kingsway WA 6065
Tel: (08) 9388 3475 or 0411 454 735
email: playfulportraits@ii.net
website: www.playfulportraits.com.au

Playful Portraits is owned and operated by Perth-based mother Lynda Reed. Formerly located in the Subiaco Pavilion Markets Lynda can now come to you. She has a cheerful, friendly and professional approach to photography and aims to provide professional portraits at affordable prices. Specialising in exquisite children's and family portraiture in her portable studio or at the park or beach with the option to print in colour, black and white or sepia. Lynda has a range of props and costumes for themed portraits, and caters for simple and natural portraits to truly capture your child's personality. Your portrait session will be loads of fun while in the comfort of your home or outside in the sunshine. All ages are welcome – from newborn to grandparents – creating memories to be cherished forever.

SOUTH AUSTRALIA

Appleseed Photography

All areas in Adelaide
Tel: 0414 805 423
email: info@appleseedphotography.com.au
website: www.appleseedphotography.com.au

Kirsty from Appleseed Photography specialises in creative pregnancy and newborn portraiture as well as babies and toddlers in Adelaide. Working on location with natural light and a relaxed and unhurried approach, Kirsty ensures your children are comfortable and familiar with herself and their surrounding environment. Appleseed Photography is recognised for providing excellent personalised service, exclusive online viewing and ordering and exquisite hand made products. A mother herself, Kirsty's passion is to help other parents preserve precious memories by creating high quality fine art to cherish for a lifetime. Visit the website for further information.

Itsy Bitsy Baby Hand & Feet Sculptures

5 Ophir Crescent
Seacliff Park SA 5049
Tel: (08) 8358 4555
email: itsybitsy1@bigpond.com
website: www.itsybitsystudios.com

Itsy Bitsy Baby Hand & Feet Sculptures capture your baby's little hands and feet forever, in a gold or silver stone casting, mounted in custom-made frames with a personalised inscribed name plaque. Matching frames are also made for memorabilia such as photos, first shoes and birth certificates. Bronzing of shoes is available in copper, silver and gold. Available via phone or visit www.itsybitsystudios.com.

WEBSITES: CHILDBIRTH

NATIONAL

Active Birth – Wonderful Birth Services

email: lina@wonderfulbirth.com
website: www.wonderfulbirth.com

Be inspired, empowered and better prepared for your wonderful birth experience and beyond by visiting www.wonderfulbirth.com. The website of Lina Clerke, Australian childbirth educator, midwife and mother, offers wonderful stories, articles, links and services including relaxation CDs.

BellyBelly.com.au

Tel: (03) 9836 7734
website: www.bellybelly.com.au

Prepare for pregnancy, birth and baby online at BellyBelly. Feel reassured, educated and informed with the best support and information available at your fingertips. BellyBelly is a friendly and respected online parenting social network where everything is explained in black and white without the jargon, so you can make your own informed decisions on all things conception, pregnancy, birth and baby. No fluff. Real stuff.

Birthnet Pty Ltd

Tel: (02) 9662 6019
email: management@birth.com.au
website: www.birth.com.au

Birth.com.au and *BIRTH* the book are invaluable resources for women and partners on their journey to parenthood. Written and supported by a midwife and a childbirth educator with over 30 years collective experience, they provide everything you need to know about fertility, conception, pregnancy, birth and early parenting. Birthnet's online birthtalks® community is a great way to network with other parents and parents-to-be.

Earlybirds

Tel: 1800 666 550
email: info@earlybirds.com.au
website: www.earlybirds.com.au

Earlybirds' website is a useful source for parents and carers of premature babies. Earlybirds Network page provides access to information and links to national and local premature support groups together with latest copies of newsletters from Austprem and Premmie Press. Earlybirds proudly supports Austprem and the National Premmie Foundation.

www.ninemonths.com.au

Tel: (03) 9569 3938
website: www.ninemonths.com.au

Ninemonths.com.au is an online Australian guide to pregnancy, birth and life. Special features include a comprehensive resource centre, weekly baby email, parents forum and database of 30,000 baby names.

birth.com.au

Birth.com.au was conceived in 1999 and born on the internet late 2001. What started as an idea to provide childbirth classes online quickly mushroomed into a vast information library resource dealing with everything relating to preconception, fertility, pregnancy, labour, birth, Caesarean and parenting.

Co-authors and mothers Catherine Price (a midwife) and Sandra Robinson (a childbirth educator) have drawn from over 30 years experience working with women and their families. They provide sensitive, balanced, thoroughly researched and comprehensive information dealing with both medical care and natural therapies. This makes birth.com.au as relevant to women choosing their own doctor in a hospital, as women choosing to homebirth.

Birth.com.au hosts a vibrant, supportive community called birthtalks® and provides weekly pregnancy and parenting emails for women and their families. Parents can announce their baby's birth in birtharrivals® or shop and find local services in the birthpages® directory.

From the website came the book *BIRTH - Conceiving, Nurturing and Giving Birth to Your Baby*, published by Pan Macmillan in 2004. Now in its 4th reprint, with a foreword by Robyn Barker (author of *Baby Love*), BIRTH regularly receives rave reviews from parents and health professionals as being the best pregnancy and birth book available in Australia.

Birth.com.au is a much-loved site, bookmarked by thousands of Australian parents.

"I highly recommend Birth to all women and men on the road to parenthood and to anyone whose work is related to pregnancy, birth and the well-being of the families who come to them for help."
Robin Barker, author of *Baby Love & The Mighty Toddler*.

Milk & food

Photograph by Appleseed Photography, Adelaide.

Nutrition while feeding

While breastfeeding it is important to maintain a healthy lifestyle. You will be producing about 600ml of milk per day during the first few months and this will increase to around 1 litre per day by the time your baby is 4-6 months. If you are undernourished then you run the risk of depleting your nutritional reserves and this may affect the nutrient levels in your milk. You need to maintain good nutrition for both yourself and your baby.

Additional kilojoules are needed to help you keep up with the needs of your growing baby. The energy requirements of a non-pregnant woman are around 8,000kj/day. When breastfeeding you will need an extra 2,000kj/day to sustain your growing baby.

So now is the time to start eating into the body fat reserves that were laid down during pregnancy! Breast milk production utilises these fat stores and breastfeeding mums can lose about 1kg each month just by making breast milk. It may take up to a year to return to your pre-pregnancy weight but many women find the weight drops off quickly.

Limiting your energy intake, especially during the first few weeks of lactation, can affect your milk supply. Rapid weight loss can also release higher than normal levels of toxins from fat stores which can end up in the breast milk and may be harmful to your baby. It is not recommended that breastfeeding mothers follow a weight loss diet, just wait until you have finished breastfeeding and re-assess your weight then.

You should follow the same healthy lifestyle that you established during pregnancy. You need a lot of nutrients from your food so be sure that your diet contains foods with minimal processing such as whole grains and cereals, fruit and vegetables.

Your baby needs protein for both mental and physical growth, and so do you. Good sources of protein include lean meat, chicken or fish, soy products, nuts, legumes, eggs and dairy products.

You also need to eat good quality carbohydrates like wholegrain cereals and breads, brown rice, fruit and vegetables. Your intake does not affect the levels of carbohydrates in the breast milk, but carbohydrates prevent fatigue and contain fibre to maintain a healthy digestive system. If you are buying pre-packaged foods, look for 'Low GI' or foods with a low proportion of refined sugars.

Your baby's brain, eyes and nervous system require fatty acids. A source of good fats is essential in the first 3 years of your child's development. Good fats are unsaturated and omega-3, especially DHA, for brain and eye function, intelligence and behavioural growth. Fish is the preferred source of DHA, particularly salmon, tuna and sardines, but good fats (non-DHA) are also found in avocado and nuts.

Calcium is vital for strong teeth and bones as well as for nerve and muscle function. If there is not enough calcium in your diet then it will be leached right out of your bones. So eat low fat dairy, nuts and green leafy vegetables.

Iron helps many body systems develop including the immune system. It produces red blood cells which carries oxygen from the lungs. You will lose iron not only to breast milk but also during your period so it is essential that you maintain a high iron intake to avoid feeling tired. Iron found in meat is the most easily absorbed, but iron is also found in wholegrain cereals, legumes, green leafy vegetables and soy products.

Zinc is required in every cell and is essential for the production of white blood cells and a healthy immune system. For you it can prevent stretch marks, cracked nipples and assists post-birth healing. Zinc is found in lean meat, chicken and fish, as well as legumes, whole grains and egg yolks.

Be sure to drink plenty of fluids, in particular drink plenty of water to help with the production of breast milk and to keep your body hydrated.

Some babies will react to different substances in breast milk. Often women report that hot or spicy foods upset their babies, so just use trial and error, and of course common sense. Caffeine and alcohol pass from your blood into your milk so you should consider if you wish to consume these while you are breastfeeding. Nicotine and other drugs also pass from blood to breast milk so avoid smoking and taking medication. If you need some advice, speak to your doctor.

Maintaining a healthy lifestyle also helps you to sleep, enables you to better cope mentally, and can prevent fatigue and post-natal depression.

Breast milk will taste different depending on what you have eaten. When your baby begins on solids they are more willing to try different foods than bottle-fed babies who have only experienced one flavour.

Babies should not be fed cows' milk in the first year of their life and certainly not as a substitute for breast milk.

There are so many micro-nutrients in breast milk that can't be commercially replicated, such as antibodies to help baby resist infection, not to mention the countless other benefits to both mother and baby, so give it your best shot.

Written by Helen La Fontaine, BAppSc(FoodSc+Nutr), nutritional scientist & mother of two.

Daily routines

Babies are all very different.
These routines are a guide only.

4 to 6 months

Early morning **(5–7am)**	Milk feed on waking Sleep
Mid morning **(9–11am)**	Milk Play Sleep Play (optional)
Midday **(1–3pm)**	Milk Play Sleep Play (optional)
Evening **(5–7pm)**	Milk Bath Quiet time Sleep
9–11pm	Milk
2-3am (optional)	Milk

Some babies may be ready for the gradual introduction of solids
Sleep is according to tired signs
Milk = breast/bottle

6 to 8 months

Early morning (5–7am)	Milk feed on waking May return to sleep
Breakfast (7–9am)	Food Milk feed (optional) Play Sleep Play
Lunch (11.30am–1pm)	Food Milk feed Play Sleep
Mid afternoon	Water Play Short sleep (wake by approx. 4.30pm)
Dinner (5–6.30pm)	Food Bath Milk feed Quiet time Sleep

Optional evening milk feed prior to midnight
Baby is ready for the gradual introduction to solids
Sleep is according to tired signs
Milk = breast/bottle/cup

Daily routines

Babies are all very different.
These routines are a guide only.

8 to 10 months

Early morning **(6am)**	Milk feed on waking or after breakfast
Breakfast **(7–8.30am)**	Food Milk feed (if not given at 6am) Play Sleep
Mid morning **(if awake)**	Water/snack (optional)
Lunch **(11.30am–1pm)**	Food Milk feed Play Sleep
Mid afternoon **(if awake)**	Water (optional) Play Short sleep if needed (wake by approx. 4pm)
Dinner **(5–6.30pm)**	Food Bath Milk feed Quiet time
Sleep (6.30–7.30pm)	

Baby is ready to have solids up to 3 times a day
Sleep is according to tired signs
Milk = breast/bottle/cup

10 to 14 months

Early morning	Water on waking
Breakfast **(7–9am)**	Food Milk Play
Mid morning	Snack/water/diluted juice (optional)
Lunch **(11.30am–1pm)**	Food Milk Play Sleep
Mid afternoon	Snack Water/diluted juice
Dinner **(5–6.30pm)**	Food Bath Milk Quiet time Bed (7-7.30pm)

Continue with 2 day sleeps until your baby is approximately 14-18 months old
Sleep is according to tired signs
Milk = breast/bottle/cup

Daily routines

**Babies are all very different.
These routines are a guide only.**

14 to 18 months

Early morning	Water on waking (optional)
Breakfast (7–8.30am)	Food Milk Play
Mid morning	Snack/water (optional) Play
Lunch (11.30am–1pm)	Food Milk Play Sleep
Mid Afternoon	Snack Water
Dinner (5–6.30pm)	Food Bath Milk Quiet time
Bed (7-7.30pm)	

Sleep is according to tired signs
Milk = breast/bottle/cup

Information supplied by Tresillian, www.tresillian.net.

Breastfeeding your baby

The experience of breastfeeding is unique as no two mothers and babies are the same. Successful breastfeeding starts with correct positioning and attachment and may take up to 6-8 weeks to establish.

Positioning

Sit comfortably in an upright position. Allow your breast to fall naturally and lie baby on his/her side – chest to chest. Bring your baby to the breast, supporting his/her weight on your forearm and put your hand around his/her shoulder. Position your baby so that your nipple is in line with your baby's nose. This enables your baby's chin to tuck into your breast and his/her nose to be free when attached.

Attachment

Ensure your baby's mouth is open wide and the tongue is down before attaching. Bring your baby to the breast, NOT breast to baby. It is usual to experience some discomfort when you start the feed, however this should ease after a minute or two. If discomfort persists detach and start again.

Frequency

All babies will have different feeding and sleeping patterns. Some can feed more often at one time of the day and have less feeds and a longer sleep at another. It can be normal for a newborn to feed at intervals of two to five hours. Babies needs a minimum of 6 to 8 feeds in a 24 hour period.

The feeding process

Alternate breasts at each feed. Allow baby to suck on the first breast for as long as he/she wants (up to 30 minutes). Time spent feeding will vary with each baby, up to an hour can be quite normal. When your baby is feeding, a drawing rhythmical suck should be seen. Initially your baby may suck vigorously, then slow down to a pattern of a few sucks followed by a pause. This cycle may continue for the length of the feed. Your baby may pull off the breast or become very sleepy. This does not always mean the feed has finished. Your baby may need waking to continue feeding by changing his/her nappy and/or allowing a few minutes for your baby to burp (though they do not always need to burp). Offer your baby the second breast. Allow baby to suck for as long as he/she wants (up to 30 minutes). Don't be concerned if your baby doesn't want the second breast, but it is important to offer it.

Detachment

Slip your clean little finger between your baby's gums and detach from the nipple.

Principles

- Minimum of 6 breast feeds in 24 hours.
- Feed every two to five hours.
- Mother to sit in a comfortable position.
- Correct positioning and attachment.
- A baby needs adequate sleep to feed well.

Information supplied by Tresillian, www.tresillian.net.

How a lactation consultant can help

Lactation Consultants (LCs) offer specialist assistance and work with women and their baby/babies to benefit both before, during and through the weaning stage of breastfeeding. Both common and the more unusual breastfeeding concerns are seen to by these specialists. Apart from teaching the art of breastfeeding and assisting mothers to develop and improve their mothering skills, they also provide ongoing support for them.

Who are lactation consultants?
Many are employed as midwives, neonatal nurses, child/family health nurses, dietitians, medical officers, childbirth educators and breastfeeding counsellors working in public, private and community health facilities. There are many who also work in private practice. The highest international qualification for a lactation consultant is International Board Certified Lactation Consultant (IBCLC).

When should you call a lactation consultant?
If you:
- are pregnant and want help to prepare yourself to breastfeed.
- have concerns about your ability to feed
- are experiencing pain while breastfeeding
- have damaged nipples that are not improving
- are having difficulty with your baby waking for feeds
- find your baby/babies are not gaining weight well
- feel your milk supply is low
- think you have too much milk
- suspect that you have a blocked duct or mastitis
- notice that your baby shows signs of thrush or you have an infection of your nipples
- are concerned about medications/drugs and breastfeeding
- have a medical condition or surgical condition that may make breastfeeding challenging
- are returning to work and need advice on how to manage your breastfeeding
- need help with weaning.

If your baby:
- breastfeeds less than six times in 24 hours in the first 4-6 weeks
- is not wetting at least 6 nappies a day, especially in the first 6 weeks
- is frequently difficult to wake for feeds
- does not seem to be sleeping enough between feeds
- is not gaining weight
- shows signs of thrush
- seems unhappy at your breast or refuses to breastfeed
- has a medical or surgical problem that is impacting on the baby's ability to feed.

or you should also call a lactation consultant if you:

- ever have questions about any aspect of breastfeeding or simply wish to clarify things, including the science around breastmilk and breastfeeding.
- require information about breastfeeding equipment such as breast pumps and other supplies that are helpful to breastfeeding mothers and infants.

How do I find a lactation consultant?

A lactation consultant will have the credentials IBCLC after her name. To find a lactation consultant in your community talk to your childbirth educator, healthcare provider or maternity hospital.

Another way to find a lactation consultant is to contact the Australian Lactation Consultants' Association (ALCA) by emailing info@alca.asn.au or through the website www.alca.asn.au.

The Australian Breastfeeding Association may also be able to refer you to a lactation consultant.

Lactation Consultants give information and practical help to women and their families:

- who are preparing to breastfeed
- who are learning to breastfeed
- who want to breastfeed for longer
- at any stage in the breastfeeding process in order to prevent or solve difficulties and to make the experience as enjoyable as possible
- who wish to return to work and want to continue to feed their toddlers
- with the science and facts about breastfeeding.

Photograph by Appleseed Photography, Adelaide.

Information supplied by Gwen Moody IBCLC, on behalf of the Australian Lactation Consultants' Association, www.alca.asn.au.

Starting your baby on solid food

Starting your little one on solids can be an intimidating prospect. For first-time mums, the thought of baby having a solid piece of food in their mouth can be scary. Who hasn't heard the tale about a baby choking on a grape? And before you ask: yes, grapes are one of the highest risk foods for choking!

While starting on solids can certainly be challenging – especially when you have other little ones to feed and time is an issue – it is also a lot of fun. And as the weeks turn to months, what a relief when finally your little one is able to handle food and gobble down bits of food themselves!

So, I hear you ask, how can you overcome this hurdle safely? How can both you and your baby manage the transition from runny food to finger foods? Don't worry, try these tips below; they are aimed at helping you to make this move – even to enjoy it – and encourage you to set up healthy eating habits for your baby which will then take them into their toddler years and beyond.

When to start?
It is important that your baby is eating chunky food by nine months. Chunky food is important for your baby's dentition and it seems to have a preventative effect on the development of fussy eating habits a little later on. Try not to fall into the habit of providing soft foods for too long or you may find you have dug a rather large hole you can't get out of.

Finger foods commonly start around this time, although some babies start self-feeding earlier, and this is fine too. Remember, baby is your best guide. In fact, some babies refuse food unless they can feed it to themselves, the spoon becomes redundant and this new-found freedom is enjoyed with gusto!

Your baby may also start to show some clear preferences, and dislikes, for certain foods. Keep offering a good variety of foods, even if they have been rejected before. Just because baby said no today doesn't mean they won't want to have a nibble of it tomorrow. Rotating food so that you offer a variety of vegetables, fruit, breads, cereals, crackers, pastas etc. is a great way of spreading the selection of nutrients, making baby's diet interesting and varied.

Food and safe eating
Infants and young children don't have back teeth which we use to chew and grind food down to make smaller pieces. Combined with their still-developing eating methods, this puts them at risk of choking.

Most babies will gag quite often while eating; this is caused by food sitting at the back of the tongue and is simply a mechanical issue of moving food around the mouth. Nevertheless, despite there being no cause for alarm, most parents find it a little unsettling. It's worth noting that this is quite different from choking where the airways are blocked by a food or object.

Always supervise babies and children while eating. Too many toddlers and preschoolers think of eating as an inconvenience in a day that is otherwise filled with play. A common tendency is to take large mouthfuls of food and get it down as fast as possible. (Of course there are others who have a complete lack of interest, but that's a different story.)

The age groups most at risk from food-related choking: 90% occurs in infants and children under the age of five years; 65% in children under two.

Foods that are the most common offenders: sweets, nuts and grapes.

Getting fussy?

It is common for babies to appear to go off their food as they begin walking. This new-found independence and mastery of the world may get in the way of eating for a period of time, but most will emerge from this phase. Just stick with how you have been doing things. Picky eating tends to hit around 18 months.

Encouraging healthy eating in children

All babies are born with preferences for certain tastes (namely sweet and salty) but there are ways these preferences can be influenced (positively, in the perfect world). We know that early exposure to a variety of foods and food textures has a beneficial influence on eating patterns. Of course, other influences include role models, TV, culture and religion, books, peers, food rules, and even the family structure.

But by far the most influential factor on your little one's early preferences is you. Parents' attitudes towards food and meal-times – along with the actual foods they themselves consume – will help to shape their child's eating habits from a very early age. So while of course baby's own personality will influence what they eat, it is the combination of this inherent aspect with their environment that determines the outcome.

It's all starting to sound a little hard, but really, just keep in mind you ultimately have control over the environment (you as a role model, your values towards food and meals) and your child has control over what they choose to eat. Offer healthy foods, leave the junk for outside the home, and you will be doing great!

Tips for making food safer:

- Always sit down to eat in a calm manner.
- Supervise infants or young children while they eat.
- Avoid hard, round, small foods or chop them into irregular small pieces.
- Encourage children to take small to medium bites, to eat slowly and to chew their food well.
- Never force food into a child's mouth.
- Cut meat, poultry etc. into small non-spherical pieces and remove skin and excess fat.
- Grate, cook or mash small hard fruit and vegies.
- Cut hard fruit and vegetables into odd shapes (e.g. quarter grapes) or thin strips (e.g. apple or pear) and non-chokeable sized pieces (this may just enable air to pass if the food does get stuck in the throat).
- Avoid or be extra vigilant with nuts, seeds, popcorn, whole grapes and sweets.
- Also watch out for melted cheese that has solidified as it can also be a hazard.

Information supplied by Leanne Cooper © 2009, nutritionist & director of Sneakys www.sneakys.com.au.

Fabulous recipes for fussy eaters

Remember that food rejection is a normal behaviour for most young children. Meal-times should always be family-oriented and enjoyable, and don't forget that children learn from you so be a good example.

- Always encourage your child's choices: they are more likely to eat a food they themselves have chosen.
- Involve your little one in meal preparation, cooking, serving etcetera.
- Grow vegies or vegie bits (i.e. carrots and sprouts in containers on the bench).
- Another way of involving your child in their food selection is allowing them to gather food, i.e. growing/picking vegetables in your own garden or picking them at the supermarket.
- Be clever with food by hiding fruit and vegies where you can. For example, you can include pumpkin in scones, grate vegies into meals, puree fruit into smoothies or include fruit in their yoghurt.
- Try to involve others in your child's meal-time. For example, if your child attends family day-care, try asking the carer to give them a main meal at lunch.
- Try to be creative with food: make hedgehogs, faces, houses, and discuss the foods your child is selecting. It is a great way to make meal-times fun.
- Consider using iron-fortified cereals as they offer more absorbable iron than many foods and this will help with growth and immunity. Low iron can influence fussy eating habits. If you suspect this is the case seek professional advice.
- Be persistent and don't give up. Continue to put a variety of foods on your child's plate and don't make a fuss if it goes uneaten. Simply take the plate away (even if it means the dog is getting a little plump!). Even if the meal is rejected, your child is still being exposed to food that will form a part of their diet later on.
- Don't let children fill up on snacks too close to meal-time.
- Remember, excessive milk can affect iron uptake so don't rely too heavily on this drink.
- Ensure all meals – including snacks – include some form of protein (meat, dairy, egg, nuts, seeds, pulses, fish). Grind up nuts and seeds and add them to your child's breakfast each morning; add to smoothies and frittatas. With smoothies, don't forget to add natural yoghurt and opt for additions such as almonds, oats or rice that have around 100mg of calcium per 100ml.
- Freeze smoothies and make cool ice-blocks that are a meal in themselves.
- Add tiny amounts of treats to foods, for example, make cream-cheese crackers with a smidge of additive-free hundreds and thousands. Or pop a few on a banana and freeze!
- Limit distractions such as toys and TV.
- Offer your child's main meal when they are hungriest; this may mean dinner is at lunch time.
- Don't overfill plates; an empty plate is pleasing for everyone.
- Offer three main meals and three small snacks a day, one of which may be a healthy supper, to increase the spread of nutrients over the day.
- Remove the plate when they have finished and offer a healthy snack later if you feel they may still be hungry.

BREKKY BLAST OFF

Breakfast is your little one's first meal after some 8–12 hours of sleep (if you are lucky!). While your child obviously hasn't been burning up as much energy while asleep, they have still used a considerable amount regenerating the body and growing; indeed, some children literally seem taller in the morning than when they went to bed! Also, the body's metabolic rate is highest in the morning so your child's need for refuelling is at its greatest.

When they wake up, their little bodies' sugar levels are low, and need replenishing with something quick and healthy. There are few things worse than a hungry and cranky child.

Breakfast is the meal that will kick-start the brain and body, providing it with the fuel it needs.

Skipping breakfast commonly results in an energy slump mid-morning. With fuel for the brain in scarce supply, it's not hard to work out that even basic mental and physical tasks become taxing. This is most pronounced in children and in fact, many studies point to the influence of a good breakfast on a child's behaviour and overall eating habits. Children who skip breakfast tend to have more body fat and may struggle with learning.

Munchie muesli

Ingredients

4 cups of whole oats
½ cup of dried coconut
¼ cup of roughly chopped sunflower seeds
¼ cup of roughly chopped pumpkin seeds
2 tablespoons of linseeds
¾ cup of honey
1 cup of mixed dried fruit

Preparation

1.   Preheat your oven to 180°C.
2.   Line a large baking tray with grease-proof paper and leave ready for the ingredients.
3.   Combine the oats, seeds and coconut and mix well.
4.   Carefully melt the honey in a microwave or pan.
5.   Add the melted honey to the ingredients and combine well.
6.   Place the muesli mix in the baking tray and spread out evenly.
7.   Bake for 10 minutes and then mix.
8.   Return to the oven for another 10 minutes.
9.   Remove from the oven and allow to cool.
10. Add the dried fruit and mix.
11. Place in an air-tight container for about 10 days.

Option: Top with fresh fruit and yoghurt. Munchie muesli is also great as a quick snack..

Fabulous recipes for fussy eaters

Perfect porridge

Ingredients

⅓ cup of whole rolled oats (not the fast-cook kind)

¾ cup of your choice of milk or you can use water

¼ teaspoon of vanilla essence

a sprinkle of spice

extra milk of your choice for topping

1 tablespoon of natural yoghurt

½ banana chopped

Preparation

You can, of course, opt to use the microwave, but I have used the stove here.

1. Combine the oats, milk, vanilla and spice in a pot.
2. Bring to the boil, turn down to a moderate heat and stir until thickened.
3. Top with yoghurt and banana and a little extra milk.

Cookie-cutter brekky

Ingredients

1 or 2 slices of wholemeal or wholegrain bread

1 egg

A little butter

Preparation

1. Using a cookie-cutter, cut out a shape from the middle of the bread slice and carefully remove.
2. Butter both the leftover bread and the cut-out piece.
3. Melt a little butter in a frying pan (to help brown the bread).
4. Place the unbuttered side of the bread into the pan.
5. Break the egg into a small bowl or cup and pour into the hole left in bread slice (you could also beat the egg first if you choose to).
6. Fry egg until it is cooked through.
7. Flip the bread and fry until browned.

Serves one.

SNACKS AND PACKS

Children up to 10 years need to eat every four to six hours (maybe more) to ensure they have enough energy. Keep in mind, however, that grazing all day isn't ideal due to the continual exposure of the teeth to food. Your child should eat regularly and include two to three snacks a day. Snacks are vital to reduce hunger, maintain energy and provide nutrients. In fact, many children (particularly those in childcare) get around 50% of their nutrient requirements in meals and snacks prior to the evening meal.

Ensure that snacks are as nutritious as meals, avoid overly fatty foods and sweetened foods or drinks (e.g. fruit juices) that are energy dense and may displace other foods. Giving milk after a snack rather than before or with can be a good idea. It can also be helpful to have jars of healthy snacks in the fridge and cupboard that can be rotated, for example sun-ripened sultanas, dates, figs and apricots, choosing one fruit each day and rotating them. Another may be crackers which can vary from wholemeal, rice crackers, rye and even gluten-free, again rotating. You can do the same thing with breads, varying brown bread, rye bread, spelt bread, pumpernickel and so on. These foods can be stored and will keep for some time; they can then be combined with fresh fruit, yoghurt and other fresh foods. So, for example, a child may have snacks composed of strawberries, sun-dried figs, wholemeal pumpkin scones and natural yoghurt one day; then apple, sun-dried apricot halves, rye crackers and cheese the next, and so on. The following ideas are provided in order to assist you in meeting one of the most important dietary guidelines – VARIETY. Some are for home while others can be used for lunchboxes and bags.

Snack ideas

Personally, I like to offer both fruit and something more sustaining at every snack – for example: fruit and yoghurt, fruit and crackers, fruit and cheese.

Fruit snacks

- Fruit sticks 1–2 a day (from health food section with 100% fruit only).
- Cheese sticks 1–2 a day.
- Fruit (all the ones ending in 'berry' are very nutritious, but remember variety is the key).
- Naturally sun-dried sultanas, dates or figs (sulphur dioxide and pip free).
- Snake peel an orange and then re-wrap with the peel so it keeps fresh until eaten.

Frozen snacks, cool for kids and their lunchboxes

- Frozen grapes are a fantastic treat on hot days (slice in half if you are concerned about choking).
- The same goes for frozen melon, banana and orange quarters.
- Frozen bananas with a passionfruit yoghurt dip.
- Yoghurt can safely be frozen as a great hot day snack or for lunchboxes.
- Cold sago/tapioca mixed with natural yoghurt and sliced fruit. Freeze overnight so it can be taken in a lunchbox.

Easy wholegrain options

- Crackers (organic rice, rye, sesame and water crackers particularly those low in sugar and salt).
- A bagel with avocado and/or Philadelphia cheese.
- Healthy sugar-free biscuits.
- Wholemeal crumpet topped with a little butter.
- Cream-cheese on crackers.
- Wholemeal crumpets, bagels and muffins with a choice of toppings.
- Healthy muffins, e.g. fig (high in calcium and sultana), made from wholemeal flour and reduced or no sugar, the healthfood shop variety are often nutritious.

Fabulous recipes for fussy eaters

Other options
◎ Yoghurt is a great hot day snack.
◎ Carob and buckwheat crackers.

Home snack and lunch ideas
◎ Smoothie (with mixed berries) – you can also freeze them and give them as ice-blocks as a summer treat or at parties.
◎ Homemade ice-blocks filled with a mix of natural yoghurt and fruit pulp.
◎ Falafels and vegie sausages.
◎ Mini pizzas (using mini pocket breads) with avocado, ham, tomato, pineapple etc.

LUNCHES

So what is a healthy meal? The three basic principles of a good diet – for all of us – are variety, wholesomeness and unprocessed food. These help ensure that a diet is nutritionally sound.

Variety in a diet refers to eating a variety of food groups but it also means variety within a food group. A great, easy way to ensure variety is to check that there is a good range of colours: for example, red fruits and berries (an excellent source of vitamin C), green and yellow vegetables (high in vitamin A), wholegrain and brown bread (high in zinc), white meat (providing protein and iron), dairy (for calcium and riboflavin) and so on. Eating a little of all sorts of foods can dilute the exposure to problem food components and undesirables.

Ensure that snacks are as nutritious as meals; avoid overly fatty foods and sweetened foods or drinks (e.g. fruit juices, biscuits and cordials) that may displace more nutritious foods.

Ideas for lunchboxes

Ideally, main meals should have protein and carbohydrate/s; for example: tuna, a roll and grated vegetables. Often they can be served with a piece of fruit and always with water. Some of our ideas are portable while others are best at home.

Lastly, remember your child is likely to prefer to play than to eat, so convenience needs to be balanced with nutrition. Yes, I know that is easier said than done, but it is better to keep it in mind than be disappointed by a full lunchbox coming home each day.

Top lunchbox ideas
◎ Wholemeal salad sandwich, yoghurt, grapes (cut in half) and water.
◎ Cream-cheese, ham and avocado Lebanese bread wrap (rolled up).
◎ Bagel with avocado, sliced chicken and grated cucumber.
◎ Pumpernickel bread with cheese, hummus and red capsicum.
◎ Pocket bread with grated cheese, tomato, cucumber and yoghurt dip and canned tuna.
◎ Roast beef salad with tomato, lettuce and avocado.
◎ Prepared Nori rolls (seaweed) with a variety of fillings including tuna, avocado, cucumber, capsicum, salmon, lettuce etc. (these are extremely easy to make with or without the kids and will keep in an airtight container in the fridge overnight – no longer).

- Fish cakes with grated vegetables, fruit and yoghurt.
- Various cheeses, avocado, fruit and crackers.
- Fruit and a tub of natural yoghurt.
- Vegetarian sausages and grated/sliced vegies.
- Ham and dips wrapped in flat bread.
- Bite-size raw vegies with a separate container of dipping sauce or your favourite ranch dressing or curried tofu mayonnaise.
- Cheese cubes with tiny cherry tomatoes.

QUICK BITES AND LIGHT MEALS

Many of the following recipes can be used for lunches (freshly made or leftovers) and dinners. Once you have found a recipe, adapt it and let it expand, try using different ingredients when you make it next. Remember, the key is variety.

Nutrition tips to keep in mind:

- Sugar ideally should not be added to a child's diet. However, if a product has added sugars they should not be in the top three ingredients listed on the packet.
- Take care when using fillings such as honey, jam or other spreads as they can limit the nutrition of a meal.
- Likewise, biscuits, chips, bars, lollies, flavoured milks, cakes and pastries can severely impact on the nutrition of a meal as well as displace health foods and meals later due to the large amount of energy in such foods.
- Drinks containing caffeine should not be given to children.
- Sodium should be minimised and ideally not exceed 120mg per 100g.
- Fruit juices are not necessary. It is better to eat the fruit instead and drink water. Fruit juices may be a good source of some vitamins, but the downside is they are low in fibre, high in energy and can displace foods.
- Potato is often the most commonly eaten vegetable and variety can be lost.
- Potato chips are not the best way to eat potato. Most commercial brands are high in fat and salt, and best left for special occasions. Some healthier versions are available, and of course, homemade chips in fresh olive oil can be a tasty treat.
- Fruit bars and fruit straps are high in sugar. While these tasty morsels generally contain some fruit, they are often high in sugar (some in added sugars), low in fibre and become stuck to children's teeth (increasing the chances of decay), so are best avoided.
- Wash all fruit and vegetables. This will reduce the risk from any nasties.
- Supervise young children. To reduce the risk of choking, toddlers and young children should always be seated and supervised while eating all foods, including chopped raw fruit, vegetables and all 'hard' foods.
- Children with loose teeth or missing teeth may find softer foods, such as bread instead of a roll, easier to eat.
- Picky eaters should still be offered healthy food even if they reject it continuously.

Fabulous recipes for fussy eaters

Cheesy zucchini scrambled eggs
Ingredients
3 eggs (one for each person)
¼ of cup grated cheese
⅓ cup of milk
½ a peeled and finely grated zucchini
1 teaspoon of butter
Toast (optional)

Preparation
1. Peel then grate the zucchini using a fine grater.
2. Grate the cheese.
3. Beat the eggs, zucchini and cheese and milk until mixed.
4. Gently melt the butter in a pan, ideally non-stick.
5. Add the ingredients to the pan.
6. On a low heat gently cook the egg.
7. Stir gently with a spoon to create large pieces of scrambled egg.
8. Once ingredients are no longer moist and are cooked serve on toast soldiers.
Serves three.

Salmon croquets
Ingredients
1 medium potato
2 teaspoons of butter
1 small can of salmon, drained
1 egg beaten
2 tablespoons of finely grated and chopped carrot
2 tablespoons of finely grated and chopped zucchini
2 tablespoons of finely grated cheese
2–4 tablespoons of organic plain flour
2 tablespoons of olive oil

Preparation
1. Boil the potato and mash with the butter in a bowl, allow to cool.
2. Prepare the salmon by crushing the bones thoroughly into the salmon flesh.
3. Add the egg, salmon, vegetables and cheese to the cooled potato and blend together.
4. Make small rectangle croquettes in your palm.
5. Roll the croquettes in the flour.

6. Heat the oil in a non-stick pan and gently place croquettes in the pan.
7. Cook until golden brown on each side, remove and drain on absorbent paper.
8. Serve with yoghurt dip, pasta or rice.

Corn fritters

Ingredients
1 cup of wholemeal self-raising flour
½ cup of your choice of fluid (milk or water)
2 eggs
a medium can of creamed corn or corn kernels
Olive oil

Preparation
1. Sift the flour into a medium bowl.
2. Beat the egg lightly in a small bowl.
3. Make a well in the middle of the flour.
4. Add the fluid and egg to the mix and blend to a smooth batter.
5. Add the corn and mix.
6. Use a non-stick pan or add some oil to a flat pan and heat gently (do not burn).
7. Add a ladle-spoon of the mix to the heated pan.
8. Allow bubbles to appear before turning.
9. Cook until light brown.
10. Serve as is (cooled) or you can top with cream-cheese or your choice of topping.

Saucy balls

Ingredients
500g of quality minced lamb
1 small grated carrot
1 small peeled and grated zucchini
½ small red onion
1 teaspoon of Vegemite
1 tablespoon of Sacla bolognaise sauce (for meat mixture)
1 finely chopped clove of garlic
a sprinkle of thyme
5 medium-sized mushrooms diced finely
1 beaten egg
⅓ cup of flour
3 tablespoons of olive oil
1 jar of Sacla bolognaise sauce or equivalent tomato-based sauce (for cooking)

Fabulous recipes for fussy eaters

Preparation
1. Using a clean hand or suitable utensil combine the lamb, vegetables, herbs, Vegemite, tablespoon of bolognaise sauce and egg.
2. Heat the oil gently in a flat pan.
3. Flour your hands and make meatball-sized balls from the mix, flour the balls.
4. Place the balls into the pan and shallow-fry until brown on both sides.
5. Drain the balls on absorbent paper.
6. Gently heat the jar of bolognaise or tomato sauce and place the balls into the sauce to cook for a further 15 minutes.
7. Serve on a bed of rice or noodles or potato.

DESSERTS
Can they really be healthy? Well, of course! After all, desserts range from fresh fruit and yoghurt through to double chocolate mud pies. Like most things, it is moderation, balance and common sense that will hold you in good stead when it comes to desserts for your little ones.

In the main, desserts (if you choose to offer them) should be healthy options such as fruit and yoghurt, smoothies, cheese and crackers and other meals in this section. As a treat though, in most cases there is nothing wrong with offering something a little 'naughty' like icecream, pie or cake, but they should be offered irregularly so as not to set up an expectation of something a little tasty after the main meal.

Egg custard
Ingredients
1 cup of your choice of milk
1 beaten egg
½ teaspoon of vanilla essence
1 teaspoon of honey (not for bubs under 12 months)
¼ teaspoon of mixed spice

Preparation
1. Heat the milk in a small pot, don't allow to boil over.
2. Beat the egg in a bowl and add the honey, vanilla and spices.
3. Remove the milk from the heat and add the egg mix to the milk.
4. Place the custard back on the heat and gently simmer, stirring regularly until the custard sticks to the wooden spoon.
5. Take care not to overheat or the custard may curdle.
6. Serve when cool with sliced fruit.

Information & recipes supplied by Leanne Cooper © 2009, nutritionist & director of Sneakys www.sneakys.com.au. For more recipes visit the website & read about her book *Recipes for Fussy Foodies*.

Treating reflux in infants & children

Gastro-oesophageal reflux is a common medical issue for children of all ages. It occurs when the stomach contents (including food and stomach acid) flow upwards into the oesophagus (foodpipe). It is commonly seen in babies as they regurgitate or vomit following a feed, although not all children with this condition will vomit. Among the many other signs and symptoms these children can experience are common problems such as irritability, sleeping and settling issues, feeding difficulties and back arching.

If you suspect your child may have gastro-oesophageal reflux, or if you have any concerns, it is important to discuss this with your child's doctor or child health nurse. A thorough medical assessment is required before a diagnosis of gastro-oesophageal reflux can be made as there are many conditions that can present similarly.

Once gastro-oesophageal reflux is diagnosed, the type of treatment needed will be determined, taking into account the severity of your child's reflux, any complications, and your child's age. In some situations medical advice and reassurance may be all that is needed, while in others it may take some time to find the treatment that works best. For many, the first line of treatment includes lifestyle changes (also known as conservative treatments), however if your child's symptoms are severe or persistent, your doctor may also consider treatment with medication or referral to a paediatrician or paediatric gastroenterologist for further evaluation. A very small percentage of children with reflux may ultimately require surgery.

Nurses, allied health professionals (e.g. speech pathologists, dietitians, psychologists) and complementary medicine therapists (e.g. osteopaths, chiropractors, massage therapists, Bowen therapists) may also play a role, depending on the issues being faced and the family circumstances.

Finding the right treatment for your child may take time, and it can help if you listen to your instincts, keep looking for answers, and consult your doctor if you have any concerns.

Suggestions for infants (up to the age of two years):

- Feed your infant in an upright position, if possible, and keep them upright for at least thirty minutes after each feed. Held up to your shoulder is a good position. Avoid the upright seated position (car seat positioning) during this time as this can cause more episodes of reflux.
- Avoid slumping as this can increase intra-abdominal pressure and cause more reflux episodes.
- Avoid exposure to tobacco smoke.
- For some infants with reflux, a dummy may be useful to help settle the baby. Consider using a dummy if you are comfortable with the idea. Talk to your child health nurse if you are unsure about using a dummy or need more information about potential advantages and disadvantages of using a dummy.
- When possible, change baby's nappy before rather than after the feed. Avoid tight nappies and elastic waistbands.
- Try feeding baby smaller amounts more often.
- Avoid overfeeding; talk to your child health nurse if you are unsure about this.

❯ Try burping baby frequently during feeds.

❯ Avoid vigorous movements or bouncing baby.

❯ Consider whether food allergies or intolerances may be a factor in your child's reflux, and talk to your doctor about the possibility. Cows' milk allergy in particular is commonly associated with gastro-oesophageal reflux *(Salvatore and Vandenplas 2002)*.

❯ Always follow the SIDS and Kids safe sleeping recommendations for positioning your baby for sleep. To reduce the risk of sudden infant death and sleep baby safely, you can *(SIDS and Kids, 2007)*:

 ❯ Sleep your baby on their back from birth – never on their tummy or side. (Side positioning is unstable and not recommended as an alternative to sleeping your baby on their back. Aids and devices intended to keep baby in certain sleep positions are not recommended *(SIDS and Kids, 2007) (QLD Health, 2008)*.

 ❯ Sleep your baby with their head and face uncovered.

 ❯ Avoid exposing your baby to cigarette smoke, before and after birth.

 ❯ Sleep your baby in their own cot or bassinet in the same room as you for the first 6 to 12 months.

 ❯ Provide a safe sleeping environment, night and day: safe cot, safe mattress, safe bedding and safe sleeping place. For further information go to www.sidsandkids.org.

❯ If your baby is under twelve months of age, elevating the head of the bed is not supported by evidence from research studies *(Craig, Hanlon-Dearman, Sinclair, Taback, & Moffatt, 2004)*.

Suggestions for children (over the age of two years):

❯ Adapt strategies for younger children, e.g. avoid lying down for several hours after meals, eat smaller meals more often etcetera.

❯ Help or encourage your child to have good eating habits and make healthy decisions.

❯ Help or encourage your child to avoid large meals, especially before bedtime or exercise.

❯ Encourage your child to wear loose, comfortable clothing (and to lose weight if overweight).

❯ Minimise foods and drinks that cause irritation or increase the risk of reflux, e.g. spicy foods, citrus fruits, tomatoes and other acidic food, peppermint, carbonated drinks and fatty foods.

❯ Elevate the head of their bed as it may be helpful in reducing episodes of reflux.

❯ Encourage them to sleep on their tummy or on their left side as this may help reduce episodes of reflux.

References:

Craig, W. R., Hanlon-Dearman, A., Sinclair, C., Taback, S., & Moffatt, M. (2004). Metoclopramide, thickened feedings, and positioning for gastro-oesophageal reflux in children under two years (Review). Cochrane Database of Systematic Reviews (3), Issue 3. Art. No.: CD003502. DOI:10.1002/14651858.CD003502.pub2.

Queensland Health. (2008). Queensland Health Policy: Safe infant care to reduce the risk of sudden unexpected deaths in infancy. Brisbane: Queensland Health.

Salvatore, S., and Vandenplas, Y. "Gastroesophageal Reflux and Cow Milk Allergy: Is There a Link?" Pediatrics 110, no. 5 (November 2002): 972 - 84.

SIDS and Kids. (2007). Sudden Unexpected Death in Infancy (SUDI) Frequently Asked Questions. Melbourne: SIDS and Kids.

Written by the Reflux Infants Support Association (RISA) Inc. Content reviewed by Associate Professor (Adjunct) Jeanine Young, Nursing Director: Research, Royal Children's Hospital & Health Service District, Brisbane. www.reflux.org.au.

What is anaphylaxis?

Anaphylaxis is the most severe form of allergic reaction and is potentially life-threatening. It must be treated as a medical emergency, requiring immediate treatment and urgent medical attention. Anaphylaxis is a generalised allergic reaction, which often involves more than one body system (e.g. skin, respiratory, gastro-intestinal, cardiovascular). A severe allergic reaction usually occurs within 20 minutes of exposure to the trigger and can rapidly become life-threatening.

What causes anaphylaxis?
Common triggers of anaphylaxis include:

- **Food:** Milk, eggs, peanuts, tree nuts, sesame, fish, crustacea, wheat and soy are the most common food triggers, which cause 90% of allergic reactions, however, any food can trigger anaphylaxis. It is important to understand that even small amounts of food can cause a life-threatening reaction. Some extremely sensitive individuals can react to even the smell of a food (e.g.fish).
- **Insect venom:** Bee, wasp and jumper ant stings are the most common causes of anaphylaxis from insect stings. Ticks and fire ants also cause anaphylaxis in susceptible individuals.
- **Medication:** Medications, both over-the -counter and prescribed, can cause life-threatening allergic reactions. Individuals can also have anaphylactic reactions to herbal or 'alternative' medicines.
- **Other:** Other triggers such as latex or exercise-induced anaphylaxis are less common and occasionally the trigger cannot be identified despite extensive investigation.

Signs and symptoms
The signs and symptoms of anaphylaxis may occur almost immediately after exposure or within the first 20 minutes after exposure. Rapid onset and development of potentially life-threatening symptoms are characteristic markers of anaphylaxis. Allergic symptoms may initially appear mild or moderate but can progress rapidly. The most dangerous allergic reactions involve the respiratory system (breathing) and/or cardiovascular system (heart and blood pressure).

Mild to moderate allergic reaction:
- Tingling of the mouth
- Hives, welts or body redness
- Swelling of the face, lips, eyes
- Vomiting, abdominal pain

Severe allergic reaction – anaphylaxis:
- Difficulty and/or noisy breathing
- Swelling of the tongue
- Swelling or tightness in the throat
- Difficulty talking or hoarse voice
- Wheeze or persistent cough
- Loss of consciousness and/or collapse
- Pale and floppy (young children)

Diagnosis

A person who is suspected of having a food allergy should obtain a referral to see an allergy specialist for correct diagnosis, advice on preventative management and emergency treatment. Those diagnosed with a severe allergy must carry emergency medication as prescribed as well as an Anaphylaxis Action Plan signed by their doctor.

Food-allergic children who have a history of eczema and/or asthma are at higher risk of anaphylaxis. Administration of adrenaline is first-line treatment of anaphylaxis.

Management & treatment

Anaphylaxis is a preventable and treatable event. Knowing the triggers is the first step in prevention. Children and caregivers need to be educated on how to avoid food allergens and/or other triggers.

However, because accidental exposure is a reality, children and caregivers need to be able to recognise symptoms of anaphylaxis and be prepared to administer adrenaline according to the individual's Anaphylaxis Action Plan.

Research shows that fatalities more often occur away from home and are associated with either not using or a delay in the use of adrenaline.

In Australia, adrenaline can be purchased on the PBS in the form of an auto-injector known as the EpiPen®. More information is available from ASCIA at www.allergy.org.au.

The EpiPen® auto-injector is an intramuscular injection that contains a single, pre-measured dose of adrenaline that is given for the emergency treatment of anaphylactic reactions. It is for use by all people and is available in two doses: EpiPen® Jr or EpiPen®.

Consult your doctor for more information on allergic reactions and life-saving, emergency treatment.

Information supplied by Anaphylaxis Australia, www.allergyfacts.org.au.

Colic in babies

Many reasons are given to explain why some babies cry a lot. Colic is a popular one. However, no one is sure what colic really means in babies. Colic is usually thought to be caused by wind or gas in the bowel, but there is no proof of this. Certainly the baby looks to be in pain, but we don't really know.

What is colic?

The word colic means spasm, or painful tightening of muscle. Crying due to infant 'colic' is often thought to be due to pain coming from the baby's tummy and bowel – but the bowels of babies with colic seem healthy.

It is not known why many healthy young babies under 3 to 4 months of age cry so much in the late afternoon, evening or during the night. It may happen because it takes time for very young babies to adjust to the world. The common pattern of colic is:

- The baby cries or screams for some hours, often at the end of the day.
- The baby is hard to comfort.
- The distress comes in waves – the baby seems to calm then suddenly starts screaming again.
- The baby may arch backwards and either draw the knees up or stretch the legs out stiffly.

A baby with colic is usually calm at other times of the day, and is healthy and growing well. Colic usually gets better between 3 and 4 months of age. If a baby is very miserable at other times of the day, it may have other problems such as reflux or lactose intolerance, but many babies with these problems also have a period of evening crying which seems like 'colic'.

What you can do as a parent

Check with your doctor to be sure your baby is well. Prepare for the difficult end of the day – for example, by getting the evening meal ready early. Write out a list of things that sometimes work for your baby, and put it in a place you can see easily. Try these one by one. Get some support. Share caring for your baby with someone else if you can. It is good for the baby and good for you.

If everything has been tried and your baby still cries, try to just hold him. He will sense that you are offering comfort, even if the crying goes on. A rocking chair is great for this.

Sometimes the crying may really get to you. If this happens it is important to give the baby to someone else or put him down somewhere safe and take a break. Do something that relaxes you, have a cup of coffee or tea, play some music, read a bit. Then you will have fresh energy to go back to your baby. Sometimes going outside helps - for example, take your baby for a walk in the pram.

Medicines

It is not clear how useful medicines for colic are. Colic gets better by itself, often quite suddenly, whether you use any medicines or not. If you use them, you should follow carefully the directions on the pack about how much to give and the age of the baby to use them for. Many medicines used for colic have a warning on the packet that they should only be used for babies under 6 months if you have medical advice. See your doctor for a check of your baby's health before using them. Most colic medicines have not been shown by research to be a risk for babies, but most have also not been shown to help them either. Always check before you start these medicines.

Diet

It is common to blame the baby's feeding or the mother's diet (if breastfeeding) for colic. However this is only rarely the cause.

Occasionally babies are helped by removal of cows' milk and dairy products from their (or their mother's) diet. This should only be done with the help of a doctor.

It may be useful to reduce the amount of caffeine a mother is having through coffee, tea, cola or other drinks and foods. Breastfeeding mothers often try to avoid foods they think upset their babies. There are no particular foods to avoid. Most mothers can eat most foods in moderation.

Probiotics

In recent years there has been a lot of interest in the type of bacteria that grow in the bowel and the benefits of having a correct balance of 'good' bacteria (such as Lactobacillus acidophilus) versus 'bad' bacteria. Babies, especially if they are breastfed, are likely to have plenty of Lactobacillus acidophilus. There is no evidence that giving acidophilus powder to breastfed or bottle-fed babies helps them be more settled. We do not recommend its use, but if parents are keen to try it, it is not likely to be harmful. It is important to only give the recommended amount for young babies, mixed with cooled boiled water.

Photograph by Maple Gallery, Melbourne.

Vox Pop

We asked a number of women and men around Australia to send in their advice, tips and personal experiences on a range of topics so that you have an insight into how others cope being a new parent. We hope you find their comments interesting, informative and reassuring. Vox Pop biographies: page 652

Jessica Hatherall
Mum of two, Sydney

I've been lucky with both my kids when it came to breastfeeding as they were both relatively easy to feed. I think it helps if you can find a nice relaxing space to feed your children when you are at home in the early days. Introducing solids seemed like quite a big deal (since I am not that handy in the kitchen). But by doing lots of bulk cooking I was able to feed both kids with mostly homemade stuff. Touch wood neither of my kids is a fussy eater. I think offering lots of different things early and continuing to re-introduce things even if they don't seem to like it the first time seems to work. My son always refused to take a bottle which I found quite stressful but then by nine months I was able to wean him straight to a cup and this meant I got to skip the whole transition from bottle.

Danielle Murrihy
Mum of two, Melbourne

I managed to breastfeed my twins until they were 8 months old. (I stopped when I started to be bitten – yep, I was a sook!) So a bottle was introduced and in a way it was liberating – it meant that I could leave them with my partner and know that I could go shopping for a couple of hours instead of a quick dash there and back. Introducing solids was pretty easy. We ended up at a mother baby unit at 6 months and I had a lot of feeding advice from them. It opened up a whole new cuisine for the boys! Dropping feeds and introducing new routines was always daunting with twins; it was so easy to have a calm house one second and complete pandemonium the next if things didn't go to plan. But by changing things gradually over a week, by tweaking times of feeds by 10 minutes each day, meant that I could stretch things out or offer solids before a breastfeed or bottle which meant that the solids were eaten first.

Bianca McCulloch
Mum of two, Melbourne

I had such a hard time breastfeeding. For the first few months I was expressing and feeding my little one with a bottle. I just couldn't get him to attach properly. I tried all the nipple shields and breastfeeding consultants and it helped but I still had a hard time. I finally worked out a position that worked for me and my son. While I felt it still didn't come naturally I just persisted with it and managed to last six months until I went back to my studies. For some reason I had more trouble feeding from one breast than the other. Once I did get him to attach he refused to take a bottle so I had a hard time weaning him when I went back to school.

Ros Pittard
Mum of two, VIC

Fortunately, I found it easy to breastfeed both my babies. I had plenty of milk and they both latched on and fed beautifully from the very beginning. With my second baby, I experienced very painful nipples for the first two weeks or so. It was as though hot razor blades were slicing them every time he attached, but it settled down after the first minute or so. I felt it was definitely worth pushing through in order to breastfeed him.

My first baby absolutely refused to drink even breastmilk from a bottle until one day when he was ten months old, he suddenly wanted nothing to do with the breast anymore. I felt quite sad about it as I wasn't prepared. I'd imagined a gradual weaning process but he had other ideas!

I just had a cry and reminded myself that he wasn't rejecting me, he was just ready for something new, and he'd had months of great breastmilk. It did feel quite strange for a while that after such a long time of considering another little life, my body belonged entirely to me again … then I decided I loved that freedom!

Lee Norman
Mum of one, Melbourne

Our baby, Bliss, was in the special care nursery in an isolette then transferred to a Tertiary 3 hospital, so I didn't get to breastfeed her straight away. Initially I expressed and even though there were only a few millilitres of colostrum, we had family courier it from Cabrini where I was to the Mercy where Bliss had been transferred. When Bliss returned to Cabrini she stayed another night in the special care nursery and I still wasn't able to feed her. I kept expressing and my milk came in. The first night Bliss spent in our room at Cabrini she wouldn't take the breast which was really frustrating. I expressed then bottlefed which took a long time. We were due to go home the following day but the nurses arranged for us to have another night to help us try to get the breastfeeding happening. A nurse came in every time Bliss woke to help us both learn to feed. We used a nipple shield and finally she started to take the breast. I was really grateful to the nurses at Cabrini for getting us an extra night and helping us around the clock until she took the breast. I fed with the shield for about four weeks and slowly weaned Bliss off the shield onto the nipple. We are now 10 weeks in and feeding well. I also express a bit every day and have a great stockpile of milk in the freezer.

Anna Ngo
Mum of one, Perth

I made a personal decision to choose breastfeeding over formula. But despite what some of the literature might say it didn't happen quite as naturally as I had expected.

My husband, while a big supporter of breastfeeding, believes that mums need only bring their baby to the nipple and away she goes. A part of me agrees that logically it should be this easy.

Fortunately for learner mums like me, the staff at the maternity hospital were seasoned veterans, and with some coaching I soon had the basics figured out. I quickly learnt that there's nothing like having to feed your baby every few hours to make you feel like a real mum!

As the weeks and months went by breastfeeding became second nature and I began to feel more comfortable with it. I actually came to see it as a special bonding time between mother and baby. So much so that I still breastfeed my daughter of 7-and-a-half months. But it's not without surprises as my little one occasionally likes to test her gumming strength on me during our moment of closeness. So when I noticed a little white crown signalling the advent of her teeth, I decided that the time was right to introduce her to solids. And thus begins a new chapter …

Jess Tamblyn
Mum of one, SA

My advice to new mothers who plan to breastfeed is to learn as much as possible about it before your child is born. I chose only to learn the minimal believing it was something I couldn't really learn about until I actually had the right equipment – baby and breasts ready to go. I likened it to learning to ride a bike without actually having the bike, I didn't see the point.

But while natural (and without a doubt the best thing for babies) it is a skill that needs to be learned. Knowing very little about how to breastfeed, my initial attempts were flawed and incorrect attachment left me with sore nipples making future feeds difficult and painful. At the time I wondered how I could possibly continue. But by making the most of my time in hospital and getting as much help and advice as I could it soon became much easier.

My daughter is now 8 months old and is still breastfed. It's so easy now, neither of us need even think about what we are doing and we hope to continue for many more months to come!

Vox Pop

We asked a number of women and men around Australia to send in their advice, tips and personal experiences on a range of topics so that you have an insight into how others cope being a new parent. We hope you find their comments interesting, informative and reassuring. Vox Pop biographies: page 652

Bernadette Vella
Mum of two, Brisbane

Tiernan latched on a few minutes after being born and loved breastfeeding until he was 15 months old. I survived bouts of mastitis and my own health declined while feeding however he loved it. He could have a full bottle of formula from someone else and then see me and want a full breastfeed. He continued night feeds right through until 15 months, refusing to settle during the night unless I fed him.

I desperately wanted to be able to breastfeed Arielle. I knew if I was able to that it was only going to be for a short time. As she was born so prematurely any attempts at breastfeeding were going to be difficult. I persisted and persisted, trying every known old wives' tale and supplement to get my milk going but my body would not participate. The most I could produce in a day was about 50ml. Eventually it came time for my chemotherapy to start again and I had to give up on the idea.

Michelle Winduss
Mum of one, Sydney

Breastfeeding for my son and I did not come easy. Lack of milk was not an issue, the main problem was with him not being able to feed properly. This would make him extremely frustrated and uncomfortable.

I persevered with breastfeeding, although difficult, for 3 months. During this time I also started to gradually introduce formula so that by the end of 3 months my son was solely formula fed.

I found that that the only way that I could get my son to have a proper feed of breast milk was to express milk with a breast pump and give it to him in a bottle. This was time consuming and became very tiring.

I was glad that I persevered with the feeding, however this was a personal choice that I made. I know a lot of new mothers that could not breastfeed from day one, and I also know a mother who breastfed her baby until he was two years of age.

New mothers need to remember that all babies are different. In my experience of being a new mum I found that there is pressure to breastfeed, however mums need to remember that this is not always possible and that whatever works for you both is ok.

Nicole Hambling
Mum of one, VIC

To bottle feed or breastfeed? There was really only ever one option – breastfeeding. I would be providing the milk so it was portable, always at the right temperature – no sterilising bottles to worry about, no worrying about making sure I had enough formula when we went out.

However not everything, when children are involved, goes according to plan. Amy was jaundice and under lights for most of our hospital stay and because of this her fluid intake had to be monitored closely. I didn't want her to have a bottle just yet but it turned out it was the easiest way to feed her. I was able to express what milk I had and then top her up with formula.

This however meant that she had really only attached to the breast for one feed before we were due to go home, something I was not entirely comfortable with. I needed Plan B before we left the hospital. Plan A was that Amy would feed properly. Plan B, if needed, was to express milk and bottle feed her until I had a follow up consultation with a Lactation Consultant in five days time.

I had been using an electronic breast pump in the hospital, and if Plan B was to be put into action it was best to be prepared. So I sent my husband out to hire a pump. And boy am I glad we did. Amy wasn't too keen on attaching to my breast. Don't get me wrong she tried really hard; she just couldn't get her mouth open wide enough or something. So after trying Plan A for one day Plan B went into operation.

Less than five minutes with the Lactation

Consultation and she had our problem solved, although it would be a couple of weeks before we realised this. It was suggested I try feeding Amy using a nipple shield, and I thought they were only to be used if you had sore or cracked nipples. This little piece of plastic was to become a godsend. Almost straight away Amy mastered the art of feeding and we never looked back. I tried a couple of times to feed Amy without the plastic and she wasn't as happy, so when you find a good thing stick to it.

Christine Walsh
Mum of two, Broome

While pregnant my plan was to breastfeed for six months and I was going to give it my best shot. Our daughter attached and sucked well on my breast in hospital the first few days so I was happy. On day three she was weighed and had lost more than the initial ten percent of weight. I was given the option of topping her up with formula ... I felt so guilty giving my baby this formula nevertheless I didn't want my baby to be hungry so gave it to her.

We were discharged from hospital on day 7 and told to return in two days for Savannah to be weighed. We returned and Savannah had lost more weight; I was so upset that I wasn't producing enough milk for my daughter. My doctor saw that I was so upset and gave me the best piece of advice I have ever received: "What is best for mum is best for bubs."

Working myself up over not being able to produce enough milk was not going to help my state of mind nor my baby. Thus began the routine of feeding – breastfeed, then bottlefeed with either expressed milk or formula and then expressing. This process would take about an hour every feed. I persevered for about 8 weeks but my milk supply became less and less so I finally stopped and just bottlefed. This meant I could spend a lot less time stressing and could enjoy my baby more.

With my second baby I thought I would give breastfeeding another go and I did. Blake sucked and attached well though on weighing Blake it was found he had lost weight. I had the day 3 blues and got quite upset at the fact I could not feed my baby and felt that everyone else in the world could feed their baby except for me.

A midwife heard me sobbing and came in to console me and said that not everyone could feed and that in the maternity ward there were some who chose not to feed and others who had other feeding issues. She asked me about my daughter and if she was healthy. After that chat I felt okay with my decision to bottlefeed as I knew it would be an impossible task to do the whole feeding hour routine with a newborn and toddler.

I do still feel guilty about the fact I did not fully breastfeed my children. I know it's silly and I should not feel that guilt as both my children are healthy and happy. I think it's how society promotes breastfeeding as 'breast is best' ... full stop ... end of story. Maybe the saying should be "Breast is best if best for mum"?

Tracey Thompson
Mum of one, Brisbane

To every expectant mum out there – breastfeeding is not something that happens overnight! It takes practice and patience to learn the art of breastfeeding. It took me about two weeks to perfect the art of breastfeeding. You need to have a lot of patience and my biggest piece of advice is don't give up.

Breastfeeding is the most amazing experience once it has been perfected. Knowing that all your little bundle needs is being produced by your own body made me feel very special. Yes, it was a little painful to start with. Your breasts expand an amazing amount when the milk first comes in and your nipples are a little tender to begin with, but just keep telling yourself it's the best thing for your baby.

Plus it's so convenient – no heating bottles, no running down to the shop for formula, no going out and realising you forgot your baby's bottle. It's all ready prepared, heated and ready to go!

Vox Pop

We asked a number of women and men around Australia to send in their advice, tips and personal experiences on a range of topics so that you have an insight into how others cope being a new parent. We hope you find their comments interesting, informative and reassuring. Vox Pop biographies: page 652

Cindy Fraser
Mum of three, Melbourne

After three hard, long months of perseverance and two bouts of mastitis our first born was breastfed until he started cow's milk at around twelve months. The twins were a completely different story.

Due to a variety of reasons they were only breastfed for a brief period and that is when we learnt about bottles! We had quite a system going: 8 bottles made up ready to go would see me through the day until my husband would come home and we would sterilize and prepare the next lot.

We had a blackout one day before I had prepared any bottles which saw me sterilizing and preparing bottles for the day on the gas stove, it made me appreciate all the mod cons we rely on today!

I often hear people say that they prefer bottles to breastfeeding so they can get a break, but I honestly found it more stressful to plan and prepare bottles than I did with the convenience of being able to breastfeed any time any place without any planning.

Can you imagine having to prepare and carry 6 bottles with you just to go out for the day let alone all the other stuff you need to take!

All three are good eaters and will eat most fruits and vegetables. Our youngest is the most unpredictable even though he eats most foods; for him it is usually feast or famine and he seems to think chocolate is the main food group!

Amanda Jephtha
Mum of one, Sydney

The introduction of solids is a key milestone for you and your baby. But how will you incorporate preparing another set of meals into your already hectic life? Make your freezer your new best friend.

Cooking in bulk will save you invaluable time each day. Prepare and blend the food, and once slightly cooled, pour into ice cube trays. Slip these into large snap-lock bags to prevent freezer burn, and then pop them into the freezer.

Rather than tipping the frozen cubes back into the snap-lock bags, simply pop them into Chinese takeaway containers (purchased at your local Chinese supermarket) then write the contents on the container. They stack beautifully in the freezer, and at a glance you'll know when to replenish.

This is also a great way to measure the amount of food your babe is eating, and it is easy to increase the portions by one cube at a time.

Tip: write the contents on the side of the container facing the freezer door, and not on the lid, as once they're stacked, you won't be able to see all the lids!

Kerri Harding
Mum of one, VIC

Throughout my pregnancy, my attitude towards feeding was that I would give breastfeeding a go, but deep down I really didn't think that it would be the option for me. Once my son was born though my attitude towards feeding totally changed. I wasn't prepared for the bond that I felt with him as a result of breastfeeding and the sense of self-satisfaction that you get when you are solely responsible for the nutrition and subsequent growth and weight gain of your baby.

Needless to say that I was quite upset when, at his 4 month weigh in, his weight gain was not as it should have been. Leading up to this point I had noticed that my breasts were sometimes slow to let down and as a result, my son would be screaming and thrashing because he wasn't getting his feed straight away.

This became a vicious cycle because every time I went to feed I was tense because I didn't want the same thing to happen.

With hindsight, there are many things I would now do differently. I would demand feed to keep my supply up rather than try to stick to a four hourly feed schedule. I would consult the Australian

Breastfeeding Association for help a lot sooner than I did and I would try to rest more.

From 4 months, I found that I needed to top up my son with a bottle after a feed, and at 6 months, I knew deep down that I was persevering with breastfeeding more for my own sake, rather than for what my son was getting out of it.

Not once after I stopped feeding him at 6 months did I need to express for comfort. But I can't tell you how much I missed that bond at feeding time.

When it came to introducing solids to my son, I have to admit I felt a little bit like I was treading water. After starting him on rice cereal at 6 months of age and gradually building up the amount over quite a few days, I started trying small amounts of pureed fruit and vegetables.

Offer the same food for a few days to ensure there is no built-up reaction and to allow your baby to learn to like the new taste.

Melanie Smoothy
Mum of one, NSW

We found the topic of milk to be as heated as discussing someone's religious or political preferences. There is great emphasis placed on the importance of breastfeeding your baby. While I was lucky enough to be able to breastfeed for the first 12 months, there are a number of situations where a new mum isn't able to breastfeed. I am a firm believer in each parent having the right to decide what is best for their family without being ridiculed.

When it came to introducing solids, we experienced conflicting advice as to what age we should introduce solids. The overwhelming majority of what we had read and heard was that babies should be at least 6 months old. When Brayden began to display eagerness towards food (opening his mouth like a baby bird and eyeing us off while we were having our meals), he experienced his first taste of solids – rice cereal.

After a few weeks of happily and messily gobbling up the rice cereal, we progressed slowly to fruit, vegetables and further solids. Generally speaking, I cooked the majority of his food and I found cooking in bulk and freezing ahead of time was a great time saver. In saying that, there is absolutely nothing wrong with tin or jar food. We found it to be particularly convenient when we were out and could open a jar of custard or fruit gel to get him through until we were home.

While those initial months of blending, freezing and packing were rather time consuming, I have absolutely no regrets. Brayden has a hearty appetite and will eat just about anything put in front of him now.

Mind you, in those early days, it could be a little disheartening when you'd taken the time and care of preparation and your baby seemed to dislike the taste. We learnt not to take it personally and would simply try again, before completely ruling it out as a food he disliked.

Resources

These Resources pages list products and services relevant to "Milk & food".

To make your life easier as a parent, editorial listings have been grouped into sub categories.

Businesses then appear alphabetically under a national or a state-based subhead depending on reach.

ADVISORY SERVICES: MILK & FOOD

NATIONAL

Anaphylaxis Australia
Tel: 1300 728 000
email: coordinator@allergyfacts.org.au
website: www.allergyfacts.org.au

Anaphylaxis Australia Inc (AAI) is a charitable organisation that supports and assist those affected by potential life threatening allergies. AAI is dedicated to assisting individuals in the management of the risk of anaphylaxis. AAI's aim is to enable them to cope with every day life while minimising risk to their health and wellbeing. The organisation advocates for people living with allergies when communicating with government, health and teaching professionals, food industry and all in the community. AAI strives to raise awareness of life-threatening allergy in the Australian community and provides science-based information, resources and services to support children and adults living with the risk of anaphylaxis.

Australian Breastfeeding Association
Tel: 24-hour Breastfeeding Helpline: 1800 mum 2 mum (1800 686 2 686) or head office: (03) 9885 0855
email: info@breastfeeding.asn.au
website: www.breastfeeding.asn.au

ABA offers information and mother-to-mother support through telephone counselling and at group meetings. Group meetings provide an opportunity to meet local parents and to share information about breastfeeding and parenting. Contact the 24-hour Breastfeeding Helpline on 1800 686 2 686.

Choice
Tel: 1800 069 552
email: ausconsumer@choice.com.au
website: www.choice.com.au/baby

CHOICE has been testing products for over 45 years exposing unsafe products and providing reliable, independent buying advice. Their baby information can be accessed quickly and easily online and covers everything from strollers and cots to baby food and disposable nappies. You can view their free reports or become a member at www.choice.com.au/baby.

Natural Kitchen Strategies
Tel: (03) 9500 8003
email: jdeighan@naturalkitchenstrategies.com.au
website: www.naturalkitchenstrategies.com.au

Natural Kitchen Strategies helps parents to get their kids eating good food. By providing practical information, tips and strategies they empower parents (and kids) to eat great food and feel good about it. Natural Kitchen Strategies gives talks in schools as well as community groups and run cooking classes for everyone to learn and enjoy.

Nutrition Australia

Vic Branch: (03) 9650 5165
NSW Branch: (02) 4257 9011
QLD Branch: (07) 3257 4393
WA Branch: (08) 6304 5096
email: nsw@nutritionaustralia.org
website: www.nutritionaustralia.org

Nutrition Australia is Australia's peak nutrition education body. They sell books on nutrition (such as *Fun with Food ... for Kids* and other low cost publications relating to nutrition for children) and run nutrition workshops and in-services. Phone your state branch for assistance with nutrition enquiries or information on becoming a member.

Reflux Infants Support Association (RISA) Inc

Tel: (07) 3229 1090
email: info@reflux.org.au
website: www.reflux.org.au

RISA Inc aims to provide up-to-date information, emotional support and management strategies to families with babies or children who suffer from gastro-oesophageal reflux. RISA Inc provides this support through telephone and email contacts, newsletters and other printed literature, a library service, online support groups, online chats, a website, and more. It is run solely by families who have children with this condition on a volunteer basis. For support or further information, contact RISA Inc by phone on (07) 3229 1090, email info@reflux.org.au or go to www.reflux.org.au.

Sneakys

Tel: (02) 9400 9759
email: info@sneakys.com.au
website: www.sneakys.com.au

Looking for some guidance you can trust on how to feed children? This is a highly practical home-based course, offering a common-sense look at how to nourish your child from birth to 12 years. It is jam packed full of useful tips giving you confidence in your own knowledge. Whether it's been some time since you last studied or are akin to studying, the supported learning environment with a range of optional learning extras is ideal for parents, childcare workers, teachers or anyone with an interest in child health. No attendance is necessary, assessment is open-book, and all your study is done from the convenience of your home or office. Phone or visit their website for further information.

Epworth Freemasons Hospital

2nd Floor, 320 Victoria Parade
East Melbourne VIC 3002
Tel: (03) 9418 8333
email: info@fmh.com.au
website: www.fmh.com.au

This service is available to new mothers (who deliver at Freemasons) with breastfeeding problems with babies up to six months of age. The Centre operates on Tuesdays, Wednesdays and Fridays from 9.00am to 3.30pm by appointment only, and is run by midwives with international lactation consultancy qualifications. Out-of-pocket expenses depend on Health Fund cover. For further information or to make a booking please phone 9418 8333.

Maternal and Child Health Line

Tel: 13 22 29

The Maternal and Child Health Line is a state-wide, 24-hour telephone service. Callers can access information, advice and support regarding child health, nutrition, breastfeeding, maternal and family health. The service is available to Victorian families with children 0 to school age and complements the locally based service. Phone 13 22 29.

Karitane

PO Box 241
Villawood NSW 2163
Careline (7 days/week): 1300 227 464 or
(02) 9794 2300, Karitane@Home: (02) 9399 7147
email: karitane.online@sswahs.nsw.gov.au
website: www.karitane.com.au

Karitane provides support, guidance and information to families with children 0 to 5 years who are experiencing parenting difficulties. Assistance is available through Careline (7 day per week State-wide Service: 1300 CARING 1300 227 464), Family Care Centres, Jade House (PND support), the Toddler Clinic, Residential Unit, volunteer home visiting, Karitane@Home (private home visiting for a fee for service) and Connecting Carers NSW (for foster and kinship carer support). A specialised team of Child and Family Health professionals are available for consultation on a wide range of issues such as feeding problems, sleep and settle routines, toddler behaviour management, parent anxiety, pre and post-natal depression and other issues.

Tresillian Family Care Centres

Head Office: McKenzie Street
Belmore NSW 2192
24-hour Parents Help Line: (02) 9787 0855 or
1800 637 357
Other locations:
25 Shirley Road
Wollstonecraft NSW 2065

Resources

MILK & FOOD

Advisory services ➡ Baby & toddler food

Tel: (02) 9432 4000
2 Second Avenue
Willoughby NSW 2068
Tel: (02) 8962 8300
1b Barber Avenue
Kingswood NSW 2747
Tel: (02) 4734 2124
website: www.tresillian.net

Many women need assistance breastfeeding in the first six months after the birth of their baby. The professional staff at Tresillian help parents by offering practical advice on early feeding and all aspects relating to the care of your baby. For on the spot advice call Tresillian's 24-hour Parents Help Line on (02) 9787 5255 or 1800 637 357. Tresillian has four centres located at Canterbury, Willoughby, Wollstonecraft and Nepean. Services include 'Residential', a more intensive style of care for families experiencing difficulties with their infant or toddler. The Nepean Centre operates seven days a week while Willoughby operates Monday to Friday. 'Day Stay' operates from Tresillian's Canterbury, Nepean and Wollstonecraft Centres and offers parents with a child aged under one year the opportunity to visit for the day. Based at the Wollstonecraft and Canterbury Centres is 'Outreach', a support program where qualified child and family health professionals visit parents in their own homes within the local environs of their local Tresillian Centre. The professional staff at Tresillian Family Care Centres provide advice and care to families during the first five years of their child's life. Parents are generally referred to Tresillian after seeking help on parenting issues from their General Practitioner or Early Childhood Health Clinic.

QUEENSLAND

Bayside Breastfeeding Clinic
PO Box 9161, Wynnum Plaza
Wynnum West QLD 4178
Tel: (07) 3396 9718

Bayside Breastfeeding Clinic is Australia's original private breastfeeding clinic. Robyn Noble provides professional information and support to women who want to breastfeed their infants but encounter difficulties. There can be a range of feeding issues including lactose intolerance, allergies and medical problems in mothers and babies which may affect breastfeeding in babies of all ages. Physiological settling techniques are taught – these are especially valuable to parents when their babies are in pain. The clinic has now been running for fifteen years.

SOUTH AUSTRALIA

Women's and Children's Hospital
72 King William Road
North Adelaide SA 5006
Tel: (08) 8161 7592
website: www.wch.sa.gov.au

The Women's and Children's Hospital in South Australia is committed to supporting women wishing to breastfeed their newborn baby. The hospital offers ongoing support to mothers with babies up to 6 weeks of age through its breastfeeding unit. The unit is staffed by lactation consultants who have extensive experience working with breastfeeding women. The unit is located within the hospital's postnatal ward and is open Monday to Friday 9.00am to 4.00pm. Anyone with breastfeeding concerns may attend. Appointments are made by phoning the postnatal ward on (08) 8161 7958.

BABY & TODDLER FOOD

NATIONAL

Bellamy's Organic
Tel: 1800 010 460
email: sales@bellamysorganic.com.au
website: www.bellamysorganic.com.au

All children's food should be as pure and gentle as possible. Bellamy's Organic produces a range of organic children's food including organic cereals, organic children's first and second foods and organic snackfoods. Where possible they use only 100% Australian grown organic ingredients, free from any synthetic fertilisers, pesticides or GMOs. Bellamy's Organic product range is also gently processed without the addition of processing aids, additives or preservatives.

Healthy Kidz Online
Tel: (03) 9587 8300
email: contact@healthykidz.com.au
website: www.healthykidz.com.au

Healthy Kidz Online is an online store offering natural, organic and yummy goods for your baby, child and house. They stock natural and organic healthy snacks, allergy aware and basic pantry items, skincare and home-care products all minus the unnecessary additives and all with the environment in mind. Visit www.healthykidz.com.au for further information.

Little Tummy Tucker
Tel: (07) 3217 6649
email: info@littletummytucker.com.au
website: www.littletummytucker.com.au

Little Tummy Tucker specialises in low-allergy, delicious and nutritious food for babies, toddlers and young children. They offer a range of nutritional foods with an emphasis on low-allergy ingredients delivered directly to your door. Introduce your baby or toddler to a real food experience so that they may enjoy the wonderful tastes and textures of home-style cooking. This is the food that you would have cooked for your little one at home – if you only had the time! Available in different ranges for different ages, you're sure to find a menu suitable for your child.

Only Organic
Tel: 1800 220 003
email: onlyorganic@optusnet.com.au
website: www.onlyorganic.co.nz

Only Organic baby food is 100% certified organic. All the ingredients have been produced without the use of chemicals and the food prepared without preservatives, thickeners and other additives. Pure, natural and wholesome. Available from Woolworths/Safeway, Coles, Macro and other health food stores.

Parmalat Australia
Tel: 1800 676 961
email: customer.care@parmalat.com.au
website: www.parmalat.com.au

There is a way to make healthy eating fun for your kids. The Pauls range of dairy products featuring popular characters such as the Wiggles and Dora the Explorer are as nutritious as they are delicious. These yoghurts, dairy snacks and milks provide calcium, protein and other vitamins and minerals for growing bodies and they taste so good your kids will keep coming back for more.

Parmalat Australia
Tel: 1800 676 961
email: customer.care@parmalat.com.au
website: www.vaalia.com.au

Starting your child off with good eating habits will benefit them throughout their life. Vaalia My First Yoghurt is a great choice as it has no preservatives, colours, artificial flavours or sweeteners and less than 10% sugar. Made with full cream milk and real fruit puree, it comes in little portions ideal for little tummies. With the goodness of calcium and riboflavin for growing bodies, Omega 3 DHA for brains and eyes, as well as acidophilus, bifidus and lactobacillus GG, there are many benefits of Vaalia My First Yoghurt.

Parmalat Australia
Tel: 1800 676 961
email: customer.care@parmalat.com.au
website: www.vaalia.com.au

The benefits of Vaalia My First Yoghurt don't have to stop when your child gets older. Vaalia Yoghurt for Toddlers has Vaalia's unique blend of three active cultures including LGG, as well as Omega 3 DHA and has been created with the nutrition needs of your toddler in mind. It contains a wealth of vitamins and minerals including B group vitamins, zinc and calcium and comes in a handy six-pack of 90g pots, ideal for little appetites.

Rafferty's Garden
Tel: 64 6 877 1416
email: info@raffertysgarden.com
website: www.raffertysgarden.com

Rafferty's Garden figured the best way to get your baby to eat seriously good food was to make food that's seriously worth eating. So they have put together the very best ingredients and came up with a delicious range of nutritious and conveniently packaged baby food. Choose from 22 yummy smooth, puree and lumpy flavours plus four baby breakfast cereals. Available at your local Woolworths, Safeway, Coles, Toys R Us and IGA stores. Visit their website or phone for further information.

Yum Mum
PO Box 456
Coburg VIC 3058
Tel: 1300 YUM MUM (1300 986 686)
email: amanda@yummum.com.au
website: www.yummum.com.au

Yum Mum for toddlers are ready-made home-style meals, jammed packed with the nutrition and goodness of fresh organic ingredients. Just pure food and pure pleasure to taste with none of the baddies. Yum Mum has delicious multicultural flavours so you can rest assured even the fussiest of eaters are catered for. Perfect for the busy mum and dad on the run – just heat and serve. Suitable for children aged 9 months plus. For stockists or online sales visit their website or phone for further details.

NEW SOUTH WALES

Lettuce Deliver
Unit 8, 177 Arthur Street
Lidcombe NSW 2140
Tel: (02) 9763 7337
email: sales@lettucedeliver.com.au
website: www.lettucedeliver.com.au

Established in 1988, Lettuce Deliver is a family-owned and run business specialising in the home delivery of certified organic Australian fruit and vegetables. With over 20 years experience in fresh certified organic produce their quality, availability and service is unbeatable. Place your order by phone, fax, email or website. Try one of their seasonal boxes or jump online and go shopping. Visit their website or phone for further details.

Yummy Bubby
Tel: 0414 650 057
email: info@yummybubby.com
website: www.yummybubby.com

Yummy Bubby delivers freshly prepared, healthy food for babies and toddlers, as well as adult meals. The meals have no preservatives or additives, no artificial colours or flavours, no added salt and no added sugar. The meals are made from fresh ingredients, vacuum sealed, frozen for convenience and delivered to your door. Secure online ordering and payment.

Resources

MILK & FOOD

Baby & toddler food ➔ Breastfeeding clothing

QUEENSLAND

Rumbletums Pty Ltd
Tel: 0433 427 579
email: enquiries@rumbletums.com.au
website: www.rumbletums.com.au

Rumbletums Pty Ltd offer healthy baby food, packed with flavour and loads of fresh, nutritious ingredients. Meals are prepared by hand using simple home-style cooking methods to produce the best taste possible. Rumbletums is snap frozen to retain all their nutrients, natural colour and flavour. Free from preservatives, thickeners, fillers, gluten, added salt or sugar. Available in retails outlets and via a home delivery service. Visit their website or phone the number above for further information.

Yummies for Little Tummies Pty Ltd
Tel: (07) 3161 0585
email: y4lt@optusnet.com.au
website: www.yummiesforlittletummies.com.au

Yummies for Little Tummies' passion is to ensure children receive the best possible nutrition to help their little bodies grow and develop to reach their full potential. They specialise in the manufacture and supply of great quality, affordable, convenient, yummy and nutritious food for children – from one year of age and up. Online ordering is available. Food is delivered to your door making your life easier by saving you time and energy while at the same time ensuring your child eats well.

BOOKS, DVDs & CDs: MILK & FOOD

NATIONAL

Breastfeeders Anonymous
Tel: (08) 9831 0969
email: info@breastfeedersanonymous.com
website: www.breastfeedersanonymous.com

Breastfeeders Anonymous arms pregnant women and new mums with real-life experience and information, giving them the ammunition to succeed. The book includes factual information about all aspects of breastfeeding, loads of personal stories, gorgeous photos, 28 breastfeeding myths busted and FAQs answered by a professional lactation consultant. Order the book direct via the website www.breastfeedersanonymous.com.

Julia Sundin, Physiotherapist
Tel: (02) 9417 6467
website: www.jujusundin.com

Julia Sundin has produced a breastfeeding visualisation CD designed to assist you with preparation for breastfeeding and any post-birth anxiety and lack of confidence you may experience. It will help you develop your natural feeding instinct and build belief in yourself to be able to feed your child. $28.00 plus p&h. Available from www.jujusundin.com.

OBCT Opting for Better Cooking Techniques
website: www.bettercooking.com.au

After teaching in primary and adult education, a career change led to Ingrid training as a cook in child care centres providing her with opportunities to develop experience in creating recipes for the children centres both interstate and in Western Australia. The *Cooking Game* magazine (available October 2009) contains a culturally rich blend of delicious home-made meals, focusing on increasing the family's intake of vegetables and fruit every day. A beginner's guide to healthy cooking, following simple, tasty, low cost recipes.

Sneakys
Tel: (02) 9400 9759
email: info@sneakys.com.au
website: www.sneakys.com.au

 Starting solids is a big move and one that influences eating habits and health. *What do I Feed my Baby*, a step-by-step guide on how to introduce solids, covers when to start, what to start with, how much and how often. Written by nutritionist, mum and nutrition advisor to Huggies, Leanne Cooper, this is an absolute must for parents with infants. The closest you can get to having a nutritionist in your home but a whole lot cheaper at just $14.95.

Tweddle Child & Family Health Service
Tel: (03) 9689 1577
email: tweddle@tweddle.org.au
website: www.tweddle.org.au

 For over 80 years the expert staff at Tweddle have been assisting parents to improve their child's feeding and nutrition. *Eat Right, Don't Fight: A practical guide to feeding children from birth to the pre-school years* contains absolutely everything you need to know about feeding your baby from birth to four years. The book shows you how to master breastfeeding, when and how to introduce solids, how to encourage toddlers to broaden their diet and step-by-step advice to win over fussy eaters.

WESTERN AUSTRALIA

OBCT Opting for Better Cooking Techniques
PO Box 412
North Beach WA 6920
website: www.bettercooking.com.au

After teaching in primary and adult education, a career change led to Ingrid training as a cook in child care centres providing her with opportunities to develop experience in creating recipes for the children centres both interstate and in Western Australia. The *Cooking Game* magazine (available October 2009) contains a culturally rich blend of delicious home-made meals, focusing on increasing the family's intake of vegetables and fruit every day. A beginner's guide to healthy cooking, following simple, tasty, low cost recipes.

BREASTFEEDING CLOTHING

NATIONAL

Barefoot Maternity & Nursing Wear
Tel: (02) 4959 9050
email: sales@barefootmaternity.com.au
website: www.barefootmaternity.com.au

Barefoot Maternity are makers of stylish, comfortable and affordable maternity and nursing wear. The Barefoot range is designed and manufactured in Australia and includes garments for corporate, casual, evening and nursing. New in store for the down-to-earth girl are Barefoot Organics, soft and silky garments in organic cotton. Shop online at www.barefootmaternity.com.au.

Fertile Mind
Tel: 1800 757 777
email: sales@fertilemind.com.au
website: www.fertilemind.com.au

Glamourmom Nursing Bra Tanks and Tops have a nursing bra built in so you can feed discreetly without having to expose your midriff. They are available in a range of colours, styles and sizes. RRP $59.95. Available from maternity and baby stores or visit the website.

Fertile Mind
Tel: 1800 757 777
email: sales@fertilemind.com.au
website: www.fertilemind.com.au

Fertile Mind offers stylish fashion clothing with cleverly hidden openings for discreet breastfeeding. There is a range of styles and colours to choose from. Sleeveless and short-sleeves from $64.95, long-sleeves $69.95. They also have a Superbra and Perfect Fit Undies.

Hide'N'Drink Australia
Tel: 0402 263 241
email: sales@hidendrink.com
website: www.hidendrink.com

Breastfeeding can be tricky in public places so Hide'n'Drink have produced a stylish and comfortable accessory in order to help you feed. These breastfeeding covers promote a closeness between you and your baby. Each cover is professionally made, and the designer fabrics used are 100% cotton. They are finished off with a wide ribbon around the neckline to encourage eye contact. They are stylishly packed in an organza slip cover, making it easy for you to fit it into most bags.

KissKiss HugHug
Tel: 0414 419 345
email: jacki@kisskisshughug.com.au
website: www.kisskisshughug.com.au

The popular breastfeeding cover by KissKissHugHug features a unique neckline that provides mum with privacy and the benefit of seeing baby feed. It also has the following benefits: slips easily over any outfit; mum can breastfeed anywhere, anytime; affordable alternative to breastfeeding clothes; the assurance of having tummy covered; feels like a fashion item with the great design and original fabrics; and it's perfect for travelling on planes and in foreign countries. Visit the website for further details.

Manik Wear
Tel: (07) 3878 1671
email: tracey@manikwear.com
website: www.manikwear.com

Manik Wear is a range of three breastfeeding covers for discreet nursing on the go. Each style has been designed to blend into mum's outfit and they all fold up into a pouch or pocket for easy nappy bag storage. The different styles cater to mum's individual coverage preferences, clothing styles, occasion, baby's feeds and personal taste. Visit the website for further information.

Maternity Revolution
Tel: (07) 3205 1818
email: lisa@maternityrevolution.com.au
website: www.maternityrevolution.com.au

Maternity Revolution is an impressive online store offering bargains from $15. Subscribe to their newsletter to receive regular discounts – orders are usually processed same day and you are welcome to chat to their friendly staff if you have questions. The range includes maternity clothes, sleepwear, bras, feeding garments, support belts, nappy bags, books, premmie baby wear and much more. Visit their website for the full range. For those without a credit card Maternity Revolution accepts direct deposit and money orders.

Nursing Mums
Tel: 0412 424 269
email: nursingmums@bigpond.com

Nursing Mums breastfeeding covers are designed especially for mums when out and about. Mums can feel relaxed and feed comfortably without compromising their modesty. Covers are available in ten funky reversible patterns. Simply place your baby on your lap, place the cover over your neck and then feed discreetly. Folds compactly into your handbag when not in use. The covers also allow mum to baby eye contact when feeding. Phone or email for further information.

Nursingwear
Tel: 0410 290 849
email: info@nursingwear.com.au
website: www.nursingwear.com.au

Nursingwear has a wide online selection of breastfeeding clothes. They offer leading brands from

Resources

MILK & FOOD

Breastfeeding clothing

➔ Feeding products & accessories

around the world and Australia and have a generous returns/exchange policy. Visit www.nursingwear.com.au to shop from the comfort of your home.

Nursingwear

Tel: 0410 290 849
email: info@nursingwear.com.au
website: www.nursingwear.com.au

The Corsierre™ is a 3-in-1 bra, cami and corset. It gives full bra support and tummy coverage and has a diamond panel design that creates the illusion of slenderness. It has no hooks or clips. To access the breast simply pull up the elastic band of the bra and push down the deep v-neckline of the inner cami.

Peppermint Maternity

Tel: (07) 5455 3402
email: sales@peppermintmaternity.com.au
website: www.peppermintmaternity.com.au

Peppermint Maternity's 'peek a boo' tops consist of two layers of fabric over the breast area. This gives quick, easy, one-handed access to the breast simply by lifting the top layer of fabric to expose the nipple – no zips, clips or buttons – simple. Peppermint Maternity's 'peek-a-boo' breastfeeding tops are proudly 100% Australian made using only quality, cotton blend fabrics.

ready set mama

Tel: 0412 627 749
email: nicole@readysetmama.com.au
website: www.readysetmama.com.au

ready set mama stocks the gorgeous WOMAMA range of maternity and breastfeeding wear from New Zealand. See the full range on their website or phone for more details.

StahStuff Australia

Tel: 0414 813 255
email: info@stahstuff.com.au
website: www.stahstuff.com.au

StahStuff exclusively distributes and supplies itsi bitsi bibs and nursing shawls Australia wide. Taking pride in a strong commitment to service and style they offer a complimentary gift wrapping and card service. An itsi bitsi accessory is an ideal gift for any new mum or baby. Orders are shipped out immediately upon receipt of payment and PayPal is accepted on all purchases. Manufactured in the USA to high safety standards, each item is made of soft cotton and comes in a wide range of funky prints. All designed with an emphasis on utility and style.

Sweet Lilly Maternity

Tel: 0410 590 889
email: info@sweetlillymaternity.com.au
website: www.sweetlillymaternity.com.au

Sweet Lilly Maternity is a shop-at home-site for stylish and sexy maternity wear and practical breastfeeding clothes that have been sourced from around the world to deliver the best designs to your doorstep via a secure and stylish online store. This collection represents style, innovative designs and realistic pricing to satisfy the needs of Australian breastfeeding women. Sweet Lilly Maternity also has sexy maternity and nursing lingerie from Hotmilk New Zealand and amazing quality and comfort from Bravado Designs of Canada as well as feminine nursing sleepwear perfect for your hospital stay.

The Breastfeeding Blanket Pty Ltd

Tel: 1300 792 993
email: info@easyfeed.com.au
website: www.easyfeed.com.au

Breastfeeding in public as well as around friends and family can sometimes include uncomfortable moments. The EasyFeed® - Breastfeeding Blanket™ closes the gap between nursing rooms and breastfeeding in public by providing total privacy while feeding. The nursing cover is especially designed to allow eye contact with your baby while completely covering the breast, back and stomach area, enabling nursing mums to incorporate breastfeeding into their lifestyles by allowing them to feed in any situation. EasyFeed® - Breastfeeding Blanket™ is perfect for skin-to-skin breastfeeding. Available in a variety of colours and specialised fabrics making sure you look stylish.

Top Secret Maternity

Tel: (03) 9704 8677
email: sales@topsecretmaternity.com.au
website: www.topsecretmaternity.com.au

Top Secret Maternity is maternity fashion with a built-in nursing bra. For the discerning new mums who want to breastfeed in style, Top Secret Maternity offers a comprehensive range of fashion nursingwear for all occasions which can also be worn throughout the pregnancy. They have a range of garments which make breastfeeding as discreet as it can possibly get, thanks to the exclusive, patented "Privacy Layer" – it's supportive, discreet, versatile and stylish. View the collection and order online at or phone (03) 9704 8677 for your nearest stockist.

QUEENSLAND

Maternity Revolution

1/124 South Pine Road
Brendale QLD 4500
Tel: (07) 3205 1818
email: lisa@maternityrevolution.com.au
website: www.maternityrevolution.com.au

Maternity Revolution is one of Brisbane's largest

maternity wear stores with a huge range of feeding bras from B to I and trained staff to help you find the perfect bra. They also offer an extensive range of feeding tops, sleepwear, milk bands, milk screen, nursing pads, cream and more. Brands include Triumph, Berlei, Lovable, Anita, Hot Milk, Freshmums, Glamourmom, Blissful Babes, New Beginnings and Top Secret. Visit the superstore (open 7 days) or shop online.

FEEDING PRODUCTS & ACCESSORIES

NATIONAL

4MyEarth
email: sales@4myearth.com.au
website: www.4myearth.com.au

4MyEarth Food Wraps and Pockets are environmentally friendly and non-toxic. The wraps and pockets can be re-used again and again. Great for sandwiches, cut up fruit and snacks, and the food safe coating keeps food fresh and dry. The wrap also acts as a place mat so no matter where you are you have a clean eating surface. Visit their website or phone the number above for further information.

Advantage Health Care
Tel: 1800 227 464
email: info@advantagehealthcare.com.au
website: www.advantagehealthcare.com.au

Advantage Health Care distributes quality breastfeeding products for you and your baby. They distribute Ameda breastfeeding products, which have been serving the needs of mothers and babies for well over 60 years. Ameda breast pumps and products provide simple and effective solutions for mothers who need to express their own milk. To see the full range of breastfeeding products, visit their website or phone for further information.

Allergy Kidz Ware
Tel: (02) 4683 0445
email: info@allergykidzware.com.au
website: www.allergykidzware.com.au

Does food trigger the most horrific reactions in your child? Allergy Kidz Ware is committed to providing fun, quality products to help protect carers and children who have special dietary needs. No one wants to bring unnecessary attention to a child, but when it could be life or death a balance must be found. These trendy customised embroidered t-shirts, hats, bibs and medicine bags allow you to embroider your specific requirements. Badges and customised food bags are also available. For more information about these unique designs visit www.allergykidzware.com.au.

Annabel Trends
Tel: (07) 5593 4755
email: sales@annabeltrends.com
website: www.annabeltrends.com

Protect your baby from a big mess at mealtime with Big Baby Bibs (rrp$9.95) from Annabel Trends. These easy-to-clean plastic bibs come in six great designs. Choose from Rabbit, Frog, Cat, Pig, Duck and Elephant, all on delightfully coloured spotty backgrounds. For extra protection, the reversible pockets can be turned to the front to catch any spills. Bigger than normal bibs, Big Baby Bibs have a velcro fastening and are a gorgeous addition to mealtime.

Babeaze
Tel: (02) 4946 2807
email: enquiries@babeaze.com.au
website: www.babeaze.com.au

www.babeaze.com.au specialise in innovative parent-invented products that solve your parenting problems. They focus on practical and affordable solutions and products include the Snack & Play Travel Tray, Potty Mitts, Mac and Cool Cooling Plate and the Baby Safe Feeder. Visit their website to see their full range or phone for more details.

Belles Familles
Tel: (02) 9684 6605
email: enquiry@bellesfamilles.com.au
website: www.bellesfamilles.com.au

As your family grows your needs will change. You will start with wraps and bibs, move onto safety gear and feeding cups, then imaginative play toys and educational puzzles. Belles Familles is proud to offer you over 1,000 interesting and practical products all of which have been tested in their own family. From baby showers to christenings, first birthdays and beyond visit Belles Familles' website to see the full range and sign up for the newsletter while you are there. Phone orders are also welcome.

Born with Style
Tel: 1300 885 337
email: info@bornwithstyle.com.au
website: www.bornwithstyle.com.au

Born with Style's range includes Jeep Baby Products, United Colors of Benetton, Kolcraft, Baby Cubes, Loopa-Bowl, Kuster and more. Born with Style products are designed to be the safest, most comfortable and practical you can find, combining passion, quality and style with the latest technological advances. For more information phone the number above or visit their website.

BPM Childcare
Tel: 1300 364 474
email: equery@bpmchildcare.com
website: www.steadyco.com.au

Steadyco is an innovative range of table tools specifically designed by nutritionists for the 2 to 5 year old child to help prevent obesity by controlling portion sizes. Products range from a child's first open mouth cup to plates, bowls and cutlery. They are designed for easy grip, have a steady shape to prevent spillage and are available in a range of 4 colours. They can be used in a dishwasher, freezer or microwave. Available from Big W and baby specialist retailers nationally from $4.95rrp.

Resources

MILK & FOOD

Feeding products & accessories

BPM Childcare
Tel: 1300 364 474
email: equery@bpmchildcare.com
website: www.sillybillyz.com.au

Silly Billyz Cuddly Fleece and Snuggly Towel Bibs are high quality, nylon backed bibs that stay soft and bright wash after wash. They are quick to dry and are tumble dry safe. The double snap press closure allows you to adjust neck size so the bibs grow with your baby. The unique snuggle neck guard in the Snuggly Towel range, fits in close around baby's neck to help protect against spills. Available in a range of colours and designs from $5.95. Available at selected baby stores, pharmacies and Big W stores nationally.

Buboo
Tel: 1800 244 543
email: nurseryenquiries@funtastic.com.au
website: www.funtasticnursery.com.au

The Baby Elevator change mat is a patented product that was designed by a mother for her baby who suffered from reflux. In her frustration to find a way to help her baby, Deborah came up with the revolutionary elevated mat. The mat's elevation helps to aid your baby's digestion. Particularly suitable for reflux babies, the mat provides a much more comfortable way for every baby to have his/her nappy changed. The mat can also be used for play. Suitable for babies up to 4 months or until your baby is rolling, you can use it as a play mat by putting your baby on the mat under a hanging toy.

Caluna Loves
Tel: (03) 9974 0552 or 0402 333 291
email: info@calunaloves.com.au
website: www.calunaloves.com.au

Caluna Loves sells a large range of BPA-free and toxin-free baby feeding accessories, PVC-free bibs, organic clothing and toys and eco-friendly nappy bags. Visit www.calunaloves.com.au for further details.

Cheeky Cherubs Bibs for Kids
Tel: 0407 928 691
email: carolyn@cheekycherubs.com.au
website: www.cheekycherubs.com.au

Cheeky Cherubs Bibs for Kids provides bibs that are big, bright, beautiful and catch all the spills. They are made to last and last they do. Cheeky Cherubs Bibs are

guaranteed to keep up with the sometimes messy feeding habits of little children. They are designed for the baby/toddler who is starting to feed themselves. Funky bibs for funky kids. Proudly hand made in Australia.

Clever Babies (Kushies)
Tel: 1800 114 443
email: info@cleverbabies.com.au
website: www.cleverbabies.com.au

Kushies® Nursing Pads are a great way of dealing with leaking breasts as they draw milk into the pad keeping you and your clothing dry. Kushies® Nursing Pads have four layers of 100% cotton flannel and are contoured for a perfect fit. To view Kushies® Nursing Products call 1800 114 443 for a free mail order catalogue.

Danish by Design
Tel: (03) 9585 5944
email: info@danishbydesign.com.au
website: www.danishbydesign.com.au

The HandySitt is the ultimate in portable high chairs as it folds flat and has no weight restrictions. It attaches easily to dining chairs so your child can sit at the table for meals and play, both at home and out. Suits children from 7 months to 4.5 years.

DwellStudio
Tel: 1300 763 126
email: sales@luxurylabels.com.au
website: www.luxurylabels.com.au

Bold new colours and striking designs is the springboard for the stunning collection of Bib and Burp Sets (rrp$65) from DwellStudio. Drawing on the appealing graphics of Danish and Italian toys from the sixties and seventies, designs vary from crisp transportation icons to bold dots and floral graphics. The set includes two bibs and one burp cloth in 9 stunning patterns, including Carousel, Transportation, Chocolate Dot, Cowgirl, Cowboy and more.

Ethman Enterprises Pty Ltd
Tel: 1300 725 876
email: info@ethman.com.au
website: www.ethman.com.au

Baby Nova's range of quality German-made baby products includes eco-friendly glass feeding bottles, anti-colic bottle teats and FSC-certified wooden baby brushes. Concerned about BPA, PVC or phthalates? Baby Nova has BPA-free, PVC-free and phthalate-free feeding bottles and sippy cups, soothers, teething rings, weaning spoons and cutlery, as well as natural, low-allergen latex teats and dummies. Visit the website for further information.

Fertile Mind
Tel: 1800 757 777
email: sales@fertilemind.com.au
website: www.fertilemind.com.au

The Milkbar Feeding Pillow helps support baby's weight while feeding, reducing neck, back and arm strain. It also helps protect the delicate abdominal area after caesarean section deliveries. Fully machine washable they are available in single or twin in a range of contemporary colours. RRP $59.95 for Single, $99.95 for Twin. Visit www.fertilemind.com.au for further information.

Hello Charlie
Tel: 1300 725 876
email: info@hellocharlie.com.au
website: www.hellocharlie.com.au

Hello, Charlie! specialises in eco-friendly, natural, organic and non toxic products for babies, children and home. The site offers lots of practical and stylish products that you will use over and over, as well as everyday items like eco-friendly cloth and disposable nappies, feeding products, clothing and bedding, toiletries, pregnancy and breastfeeding products, wooden toys, baby carriers, and things to get you out and about. Visit www.hellocharlie.com.au for more details.

Icon Health
Tel: (03) 8770 5100
email: sales@iconplastics.com.au
website: www.iconplastics.com.au

The Grow baby range gives parents access to a hospital-grade, bisphenol A (BPA)-free feeding range. The Grow range includes bottles, milk storage bags, teethers, breast shield kits and the Grow Diana electric breast pump. The Grow baby range is available through leading pharmacies and Baby Buntings outlets.

Jackel Australia Pty Ltd
Tel: 1800 890 011 Customer Service
email: tommeetippee@jackel.com.au
website: www.tommeetippee.com.au

Tommee Tippee is an innovative range of baby products that are tested to Australian Safety Standards and designed for quality and functionality. The range includes the Closer to Nature range, trainer cups, bowls, utensils, feeding and comforting accessories, nursery accessories, teething and grooming aids and the Nappy Wrapper. Tommee Tippee is available from pharmacies, supermarkets and leading mass and baby specialty stores.

Kala's Little Stars Pty Ltd
Tel: (02) 4464 3232
email: sales@kalas.com.au
website: www.kalas.com.au

Kalas® Magic Cups are the first Australian-made spill-proof cups that are Bisphenol A (BPA) free. Safe for your child to use, they are light in weight, hygienic, easy to clean, will not break when dropped and have no fiddly parts. Kalas® Magic Spout is an easy flow and also fits any standard 28mm water bottle. The spouts are also available in a triple pack. See the full range online at www.kalas.com.au.

Kazoku Kids
Tel: (08) 9470 2851
email: info@kazokukids.com.au
website: www.kazokukids.com.au

The Munchee Mug range is made from toxic-free plastic and is designed to keep snacks in the cup, not all over the floor, in an easy way so kids can help themselves. The Munchee Mug has a special lid that opens when a child puts their hand inside; on the way out the lid closes leaving the rest of the snacks behind. Snacks stay inside if a child falls or tumbles and it's great for in the car or pram. The Universal Clip keeps the Munchee Mug from falling on the ground or out of arms reach. The adjustable clip attaches to a high chair, car seat, pram or shopping trolley. The airtight Munchee Mug Fresh Seal fits over the top keeping snacks fresh until ready to eat. Visit www.kazokukids.com.au or phone (08) 9470 2851 for a free brochure or to find a stockist near you.

Kiddie Food Kutter
Tel: (08) 9419 1090
email: info@kiddiefoodkutter.com
website: www.kiddiefoodkutter.com

The Kiddie Food Kutter is the knife that cuts food not fingers. This knife cuts everything a sharp knife will, but it won't cut fingers. With a moulded plastic handle and tumbled stainless steel blade it cuts by sawing rather than by being sharp, giving kids independence and parents peace of mind.

Kipiis
Tel: (02) 9300 0599
email: info@kipiis.com
website: www.kipiis.com

Kipiis (pronounced Kip-eez) Bib Clips let you make anything – a bib napkin, a cloth nappy or a kitchen towel. Just clip the two rounded fasteners onto whatever is handy, adjust the back and voila – your child is covered. The Bib Clips are designed with your flexible lifestyle in mind. They make a smart addition to your baby bag, glove box or kitchen drawer. Phone or visit the website for further information.

Label Kingdom
Tel: 1800 264 549
email: info@labelkingdom.com.au
website: www.labelkingdom.com.au

Help Identify your child's allergy with Label Kingdom's allergy labels. The label range includes: NO NUTS, NO EGGS, NO DAIRY, NO GLUTEN, NO FISH, NO SUGAR, NO WHEAT. Phone numbers can also be included on the labels in case your carer/teacher needs to contact you. Special requests are also welcome. Phone or visit Label Kingdom's website for further information: www.labelkingdom.com.au

Learning Curve Australia
Tel: (03) 9550 3600
email: service@rc2aust.com.au
website: www.rc2aust.com.au

The First Years range of products help parents keep their

Resources

MILK & FOOD
Feeding products & accessories

children healthy, happy and safe by offering products from feeding to playing and sleeping. Feeding and soothing products include the Take & Toss range of spill proof cups, bowls and spoons, booster seats and reclining feeding seats. The Play & Discovery products include unique toys and rattles including the popular 'Floating Friends teether' and 'Rolling Giggle Pals'. The Care & Safety products include hands-free safety gates, toilet training seats, bed rails, safe sleepers and monitors. The First Years also offers licensed products in Winnie the Pooh, Thomas and Friends, Cars and Princess.

Little Beetle
Tel: (03) 9579 1036
email: info@littlebeetle.com.au
website: www.littlebeetle.com.au
The Little Beetle Baby Chair is a fabric baby chair that is machine-washable, folds into a built-in pocket and is designed to fit on most dining/kitchen chairs. Visit www.littlebeetle.com.au or phone the number above for more information.

Little Kitchen
Tel: 1300 722 095
email: info@littlekitchen.com.au
website: www.littlekitchen.com.au
Little Kitchen is Australia's first and leading brand of real children's cookware. Visit their gorgeous online store and discover what all the fuss is about. Great gift ideas or a fabulous way to get your child helping in the kitchen. Visit the website or phone for more information.

Made By Mums
Tel: 0411 018 245 or (03) 9827 4770
email: info@madebymums.com.au
website: www.madebymums.com.au
Tired of that perpetual wet patch under baby's chin? Made By Mums offers a genuine solution for the dribbling wet baby with their famous Dribble Bibs – a colourful range of waterproof collar-sized bibs. The Cover-All Smock covers baby from neck to knees and greatly reduces the clean-up after meal times. All smocks and bibs are PVC-free, machine washable and cool tumble dry.

Magic in the Kitchen
Tel: 0413 914 337
email: info@magicinthekitchen.com.au
website: www.magicinthekitchen.com.au

Inspire your kids to whip up something fabulous in the kitchen by using these specially sized tools. The children's range has real tools in smaller sizes, sifters made from metal with an old fashioned crank, silicone spatulas, rolling pins, aprons and more. With a bit of help (and luck) soon they'll be taking over the cooking. Choose from one of the existing sets or make up one of your own. Available nationally (free delivery throughout Melbourne). Visit their website or phone the number above for further information.

Medela
Tel: 1800 244 543
email: nurseryenquiries@funtastic.com.au
website: www.funtasticnursery.com.au

Medela has been the market leader in breastpumps and accessories for over 30 years with their range made in Switzerland. The range includes manual and electric breast pumps, BPA free bottles and accessories and intimate apparel. They are the only product on the Australian market that is endorsed by the Australian Breastfeeding Association and is the number one choice of hospital and medical professionals throughout the world and in Australia. Visit their website or phone the number above for further information.

mumi&bubi
Tel: 0403 386 578
email: info@mumiandbubi.com.au
website: www.mumiandbubi.com.au
mumi&bubi have developed the Solids Starter Kit to help parents transition their children onto solid foods. The kit includes a simple step-by-step guide/recipe book and two pre-measured freezer trays to assist parents in transitioning their baby onto solid foods. It is an easy, do-it-yourself system, that enables you to know exactly what foods to buy and in what quantities. Shopping Lists offer a wide range of recipe choices. Each Shopping List is supported by a statement, which indicates the nutritional values in those particular foods. These recipes allow you to prepare simple, nutritious, yet economical food for your baby in your own home. Visit their website or phone the number above for further information.

Nice-Pak Products
Tel: 1800 506 750
email: info@nicepak.com.au
website: www.heinzforbaby.com.au
The Heinz Baby Basics feeding range is a bright and colourful range of accessories that includes spoons, bowls, cups, cutlery, splash mats, disposable bibs and sticky finger hand and face wipes. Heinz Baby Basics feeding accessories have been carefully designed to be attractive, practical, easy-to-use and above all safe. Available in grocery, department stores, baby stores and pharmacies. Phone 1800 506 750 or visit www.heinzforbaby.com.au for further information.

Nursing Angel

Tel: (02) 9874 8840
email: info@nursingangel.com.au
website: www.nursingangel.com.au

Nursing Angel is one of Australia's leading online stores specialising in breastfeeding products and baby carriers. Hundreds of products are available including local brands, overseas bestsellers and specialty items. Everything from breast pumps and breastfeeding accessories to nursingwear and baby carriers (largest online range in Australia). Great prices, discount shipping, free gift with purchase offers and a resident lactation consultant who writes a fantastic breastfeeding Q&A page.

Philips AVENT

Tel: 1300 364 474
email: inquiry@avent.com.au
website: www.avent.com.au

The Philips Avent range includes a complete, integrated range of baby care items including: health and monitoring, breast care, feeding equipment, non-spill cups, mother and baby skincare products and baby bags. Philips Avent feeding products are anti-colic and shaped closely to emulate the mother's natural shape. The non-spill Magic Cups have an easy sip spout, detachable handles and a snap-on lid for travel.

Philips AVENT

Tel: 1300 364 474
email: inquiry@avent.com.au
website: www.avent.com.au

Philips Avent, makers of the award-winning ISIS manual breast pump, are now adding to the range with a new generation of intelligent electronic breast pumps. New to the range is the ISIS iQ Uno a hand-held electronic pump for fast and effortless expression. Battery or mains powered, the pump is available in a Standard pack (rrp$199.95) or Out and About pack (rrp$249.95) so that you can express quickly and effortlessly anywhere. Simply begin pumping manually and when you are ready it will continue your exact rhythm. You can change the rhythm at any time at the press of a button. And of course the ISIS iQ Uno can be used with any of your existing Avent bottles and teats as a complete feeding system. Philips Avent, helping mothers to breastfeed longer. For more information or stockists details, phone the customer service line on 1300 364 474.

Piccolo Innovations

Tel: (08) 9307 1839 or 0405 797 551
email: morna@piccolo-innovations.com
website: www.piccolo-innovations.com

The Hauck highchair teaches your child to sit with the correct posture from day one, allows your child to sit with you at the table, it grows with your child, and it is easy to clean and an excellent design. The highchair means stress-free mealtimes. There is also a money back guarantee. Phone or visit the website for further details.

Piccolo Innovations

Tel: (08) 9307 1839 or 0405 797 551
email: morna@piccolo-innovations.com
website: www.piccolo-innovations.com

Petit Appetit kids cutlery is designed in Paris and handcrafted in Europe, and each piece is colourful, fun and full of character. Whether it's an animal on the farm, in the jungle or under the ocean, or even characters such as pirates, witches or princesses, these delightful accessories are sure to delight children every time they sit down to eat. Visit their website or phone for further information.

Pigeon Australia

Tel: (02) 9316 9810
email: sales@havenhall.com.au
website: www.pigeonbaby.com.au

The Pigeon range includes breastfeeding products, feeding and healthcare accessories, baby wipes and the much loved MagMag cup. Pigeon products are available from leading pharmacies and baby outlets. Visit their website or phone for further information.

Playgro Pty Ltd

Tel: (03) 8558 2000
email: sales@playgro.com
website: www.booninc.com

Boon Inc. creates innovative and stylish products that help make parents' lives easier. Often combining multiple functions, Boon products are designed with clean, modern styling, appealing to both parents and children. Available in Australia is the Boon Flair High Chair, Flo, Potty Bench, Frog Pod and an innovative new range of feeding products. Boon products are available from selected retailers and specialty baby stores nationwide. Visit their website or phone for further information.

pop maternity

Tel: 0429 693 984
email: info@popmaternity.com.au
website: www.popmaternity.com.au

Pop Maternity is the exclusive Australian distributor of the Mothers Minder Reminder Bracelets (feeding bracelets). Visit www.popmaternity.com.au for more information as well as great gift ideas. Wholesale enquiries welcome. Visit their website or phone for further information.

Possumbilities

Tel: (02) 6684 1760
email: leisagav@bigpond.net.au

The original Go Anywhere Chair transforms a regular chair into a padded, secure and safe highchair. It also fits most supermarket trolleys to safely secure baby in. Perfect for travelling, camping, restaurants, grandparents place and home. When not in use it folds neatly back into its attached bag. For frazzle-free meals anywhere, carry the Go Anywhere Chair. Visit their website or phone the number listed above for further information.

Resources

MILK & FOOD

Feeding products & accessories

➡ Lactation consultants

Probiotec Pharma
Tel: 1800 620 898 or (03) 9278 7555
email: info@miltonpharma.com
website: www.miltonpharma.com

For 93 years mums have trusted the Milton method of sterilization, clinically proven non toxic and more effective than either steaming or microwave sterilization. The Milton Method kills more than 99.9% of germs creating a safe environment for your baby. The Milton method is a safe way to disinfect teats and bottles, soothers, toys and cleaning down surfaces baby comes in contact with. Milton Antibacterial Gels are a convenient way to sanitize your hands on the run. The Antibacterial Gels disinfect 99.9% of germs and come in either natural or Aloe and Vitamin E. Available in pharmacies and supermarkets nationally.

Rose & Lily Australia Pty Ltd
Tel: 0413 977 287
website: www.roseandlily.com.au

Create fresh, fast and nutritious meals for your baby. Babymoov understands what it's like to be a busy parent. With the multifunctional Bébédelice, parents can efficiently prepare fresh, nutritious food every day. Bébédelice is the only appliance on the market that prepares baby's food right from birth. It cooks and steams, blends, warms bottles and jars, sterilises bottles and defrosts frozen food.

Sanbrook Brands Pty Ltd – Happy Baby
Tel: 1800 335 917
email: baby@sanbrook.com.au
website: www.happybaby.com.au

Happy Baby's range of innovative, practical feeding products work together as a complete feeding system. The range features the brilliant Click & Go Bowl with suction feet and heat sensing spoon; ice cube style Freezer Food Trays with protective lids; travel snack pots; 'leaning' trainer cups that make learning to drink so easy; and the Big Boy, an insulated sports cup which keeps drinks cool or warm. 'Feeding Solutions' breakthrough spout design also helps to develop baby's natural chewing action and is so gentle on teething gums. The Happy Baby Feeding Solutions range is also microwave, dishwasher and freezer safe. Designed for busy mums on the go, these practical products simply work.

Snazzy Baby
Tel: 1300 650 115
email: info@snazzybaby.com.au
website: www.snazzybaby.com.au

My Baby's Own Deluxe Travel Chair is a soft portable high chair seat for babies and toddlers that is very secure, with a unique non-slip base, four point restraint and buckle fasteners that outperform Velcro straps. Truly a portable item it rolls into its own attached storage bag and weighs only 190 grams. It fits on almost any chair, even outdoor furniture, with the added advantage it can be used in shopping trolleys to keep your baby safe while you are shopping.

SunRos Pty Ltd
Tel: (02) 9997 7625
email: info@sunros.com.au
website: www.sunros.com.au

Lanowool® breastfeeding pads are made of pure merino wool from New Zealand. Lanowool® pads are treated with medical grade lanolin. Soft, soothing and comfortable to use, Lanowool pads will not stick to sore or cracked nipples, helping to heal the nipples more effectively. Keeps breast at constant body temperature which ensures good milk flow. The pads are washable which means that they can be used time and time again.

Tee-Zed Products
Tel: (02) 9386 4000
email: sales@tee-zed.com.au
website: www.tee-zed.com

From the heat sensitive colour changing spoons to clever bibs, the Dream Baby® Feeding range provides you with all you'll need to care for and feed your baby or toddler. Their practical and affordable range is available from selected baby stores, toy stores, hardware or pharmacies or phone (02) 9386 4000 for your closest stockist.

The Product Store Pty Ltd
Tel: (07) 3857 0691
email: info@theproductstore.com.au
website: www.theproductstore.com.au

If your child pulls on your hair, pinches your skin and grabs your necklace while you're feeding him, The Breast Buddies Nursing Necklace will put a stop to all that. By giving him something else to tug on while keeping his attention focused for longer, he'll have longer, more filling feeds. Visit the website for more information.

The Wiggles
Tel: 1800 244 543
email: nurseryenquiries@funtastic.com.au
website: www.funtasticnursery.com.au

Children will have lots of wiggly fun with The Wiggles bright feeding range. You will have everything you need to feed your child including melamine plates, bottles, bibs. For more information visit the website www.funtasticnursery.com.au.

Tupperware Australia Pty Ltd

Tel: 1800 805 396

website: www.tupperware.com.au

From your toddler's first outing through to their last day of school, Tupperware will see them provided for with good looking, durable and well designed containers. Tupperware offers a myriad of bright storage containers from Tumblers with Sipper Seals for littlies learning to drink, to Sports Bottles to keep them hydrated without being too big to handle right through to environmentally friendly Sandwich Keepers that keep sandwiches fresh and lunchtime rubbish free.

Vintage Kid Designs

Tel: 0413 964 018

email: jo@vintagekid.com.au

website: www.vintagekid.com.au

Vintage Kid Designs produce unique baby bibs backed with hemp, PVC covered aprons and summer hats – all in limited edition retro prints. Visit www.vintagekid.com.au for more information.

Winnie the Pooh

Tel: 1800 244 543

email: nurseryenquiries@funtastic.com.au

website: www.funtasticnursery.com.au

Winnie the Pooh feeding range – feeding time has never been so much fun! Cute and fashionable, this cool newly designed range will have your baby licking the plate to find his/her new friends Pooh, Tigger, Piglet and Eyeore. The range includes all your standard items as well as some innovative ideas: bottle with rattle lid; sports sipper; heat sensitive spoons; embroidered bibs; melamine collection including deep plate and suction plate.

VICTORIA

Australian Breastfeeding Association

24-hour Breastfeeding Helpline: 1800 mum 2 mum (1800 686 2 686) or head office: (03) 9885 0855

email: info@breastfeeding.asn.au

website: www.breastfeeding.asn.au

The Australian Breastfeeding Association offers a breastpump hire service for short or long term. Electric breastpump hire is $15 to $25 per week for ABA members and $30 to $50 for non members depending on type of pump hired. For hire information in Victoria phone (03) 9805 5501.

NEW SOUTH WALES

Australian Breastfeeding Association

24-hour Breastfeeding Helpline: 1800 mum 2 mum (1800 686 2 686) or head office: (03) 9885 0855

email: info@breastfeeding.asn.au

website: www.breastfeeding.asn.au

The Australian Breastfeeding Association offers a breastpump hire service for short or long term. Electric breastpump hire is $15 to $25 per week for ABA members and $30 to $50 for non members depending on type of pump hired. For hire information in New South Wales phone (02) 8853 4900.

GoToddler

Tel: 1300 889 086

email: info@gotoddler.com.au

website: www.gotoddler.com.au

GoToddler provides an easy shopping experience for parents with babies or toddlers with many brands at your fingertips and the convenience of fast free delivery (Sydney metro only) to your doorstep. Apart from nappies GoToddler also features wipes, baby food and feeding products, health and safety products, as well as breastfeeding and nursing products. GoToddler loyal customers can save more by buying frequently and introducing friends.

QUEENSLAND

Australian Breastfeeding Association

24-hour Breastfeeding Helpline: 1800 mum 2 mum (1800 686 2 686) or head office: (03) 9885 0855

email: info@breastfeeding.asn.au

website: www.breastfeeding.asn.au

The Australian Breastfeeding Association offers a breastpump hire service for short or long term. Electric breastpump hire is $15 to $25 per week for ABA members and $30 to $50 for non members depending on type of pump hired.

LACTATION CONSULTANTS

NATIONAL

Australian Lactation Consultants Association (ALCA)

Tel: (02) 6260 3099

email: info@alca.asn.au

website: www.alca.asn.au

Members of ALCA are breastfeeding specialists who assist mothers with breastfeeding. Lactation Consultants (LCs) can help with breastfeeding problems including cracked bleeding nipples, painful breasts, mastitis, too much or too little milk supply, and issues with the baby/ies such as sucking problems, attachment problems, breast refusal; and support for mothers returning to work who still wish to breastfeed their baby/ies or toddlers. Members of ALCA are International Board Certified Lactation Consultants with current qualifications and practical solutions. The ALCA website has a Find a Lactation Consultant page. The website also has some information that might be useful to expectant mums and close family members who want to know more about breastfeeding and how to support the new mum while she is breastfeeding. ALCA's mission is to protect, promote and support breastfeeding by promoting the profession of IBCLC Lactation Consultants.

Resources

MILK & FOOD

Lactation consultants
➡ Women's health & wellbeing

VICTORIA

Breast Feeding Solutions
Tel: 0416 201 573
email: mary@nomlas.com

Mary Hill, private lactation consultant, provides a one-on-one consultation in your home to assist with managing any breastfeeding problems. Mary has many years of experience with all ages of babies up to 12 months. A consultation consists of taking a thorough history, observation of feeding and management of any current or recurrent problems. Close follow up during the following weeks provides a comprehensive service. Please phone Mary on 0416 201 573 for an appointment.

Pinky McKay
Tel: (03) 9801 1997
website: www.pinkymckay.com.au

Pinky McKay, author of *Sleeping Like a Baby*, *100 Ways to Calm the Crying* and an ebook *Simply Breastfeeding* is an International Board Certified Lactation Consultant and a certified Infant Massage Instructor. Pinky offers breastfeeding education and support including antenatal preparation for breastfeeding and postnatal consultations in the privacy of your own home. Packages can incorporate breastfeeding, infant massage, and gentle sleep and settling information.

The Bays Hospital
Vale Street
Mornington VIC 3931
Tel: (03) 5975 2009

The baby-friendly Maternity Unit at The Bays provides family centred care through a committed team of passionate, professional midwives ensuring excellent support and care. Many of their midwives are internationally qualified lactation consultants. Throughout your stay with their team you will gain confidence in parentcrafting and feeding your baby. They provide ongoing support and reassurance after discharge through 24-hour phone consultations, get together coffee mornings and a feeding and settling day stay program for newborns.

Tracey Gibney
Tel: 0409 130 796
email: traceygibney@yahoo.com.au

Tracey offers a home-visiting breastfeeding support service that assists mothers to identify and manage their breastfeeding challenges. In consultation a plan will be established to suit both you and your baby. On going

telephone support is also available. A lactation consultant can provide support and advice about a range of issues including attachment difficulties, nipple or breast pain, low milk production and concerns about weight gain.

NEW SOUTH WALES

Kate Hale
North Shore and the inner west of Sydney
Tel: (02) 9416 4386

Kate Hale is a midwife, lactation consultant and mother of four children. Kate does private consultations in your own home from birth to toddler covering all feeding issues along with settling, baby management and routines.

Luv-Bub Baby Massage and Successful Parenting
PO Box 392
Balmain East NSW 2041
Tel: 0438 648 465
website: www.luvbub.com.au

Moira is a qualified midwife, lactation and neo-natal specialist, and a child and family health nurse offering mobile lactation support and infant nutrition advice. Moira provides practical support, education and guidance to assist parents achieve their goals. Moira offers kind and caring support for feeding issues, newborn behaviour management, infant settling, sleep problems and routines. Other services include baby massage courses, return to work advice and baby sitting and nanny service. Sydney wide mobile service and nationally upon request.

Prenatal Plus Health & Fitness
Sydney Metro
Tel: 0419 298 586
email: monica@prenatalplushealthfitness.com.au
website: www.prenatalplus.com.au

Monica Rich is a midwife, lactation consultant and personal trainer and she offers lactation consultant sessions, prenatal and postnatal training in Neutral Bay and in your home, pilates, general training for women, rehabilitation, weight training and cardiovascular exercises. She also offers online personal training and support, programs for exercise and an exercise at home DVD/Video. One of Monica's specialities is offering advice on breastfeeding and exercise.

WESTERN AUSTRALIA

Cathy Garbin – Breastfeeding Consultancy
Tel: 0407 778 183
email: garnic@bigpond.com
website: www.cathygarbin.com

Cathy Garbin, midwife, child health nurse, lactation consultant (IBCLC), offers a personalised service for families with a new baby. She will visit your home, give you a folder of relevant information related to babies, teach you the art of breastfeeding and discuss any concerns. You will then have frequent ongoing telephone support.

Hush Postnatal Services

PO Box 479
Greenwood WA 6924
Tel: (08) 9448 5459
email: info@hushpostnatal.com.au
website: www.hushpostnatal.com.au

Hush provides a private postnatal support service in the comfort of your own home. Established by Paula Baildham and Zoe Islip, Hush is dedicated to the education and empowerment of new parents. As midwives/lactation consultants and parents, Paula and Zoe realise how daunting it can be taking your new baby home. Hush promotes knowledge, self-confidence and practical skills in all facets of newborn care. Individualised care may include breastfeeding, identification of tired signs, gentle settling techniques, bathing and baby massage and gift certificates. Private antenatal classes are also available. Visit their website for further details.

SOUTH AUSTRALIA

Roz Donnellan-Fernandez: Community Midwifery Services

Tel: (08) 8278 1429
email: elduende@chariot.net.au

Roz is a community midwife who has practised midwifery continuity of care for the past 13 years. She attends women during pregnancy, labour and birth and the postnatal period to 6 weeks following childbirth in homes, hospitals and birthing centres. She is also a qualified lactation consultant, facilitates preparation for parenthood groups with a local yoga centre and is involved in the education of midwives. Roz implemented and was Joint Co-ordinator of the inaugural Midwifery Group Practice service at (WCH) from 2004 to 2008, a public model of midwife-led care. Phone the number listed above or email for further details.

WOMEN'S HEALTH & WELLBEING

NATIONAL

Bayer Consumer Healthcare

Tel: (02) 9391 6000

Elevit* is based on the only pregnancy supplement proven in a clinical trial to reduce the risk of neural tube defects, such as spina bifida, by 92%[1]. Just one tablet of Elevit contains more folic acid, 800ug, and iron, 60mg, in combination than any other pregnancy supplement. Elevit should be taken at least one month before falling pregnant, throughout your pregnancy and while breastfeeding. Elevit is only available in pharmacy. For more information visit www.elevit.com.au.
Always read the label. Use only as directed.
*The Australian formulation of Elevit is the same as that used in the Czeizel study except that it does not contain vitamin A. [1] Czeizel A.E. Paed Drugs 2000; 2(6): 437-49.

Blackmores

Tel: 1800 803 760 tollfree Advisory Service
website: www.blackmores.com.au

Because pregnancy and breastfeeding bring specific nutritional needs, Blackmores makes a Pregnancy & Breast-Feeding Gold Formula to help both you and your baby through this special period of your life. Just two capsules a day provide 250 µg of iodine, a nutrient essential for the development of your baby's brain, hearing and eyesight, plus 16 other essential nutrients including folic acid, iron, calcium, vitamin D3, and omega-3 fatty acids. For free advice from Blackmores naturopaths phone 1800 803 760 or visit their website at www.blackmores.com.au/pregnancy.
Always read the label. Use only as directed.
CHC 36211-10/06

Key Pharmaceuticals

Tel: (02) 8113 6200
email: otc@keypharm.com.au
website: www.keypharm.com.au

Lansinoh is 100% ultra pure lanolin specially developed for breastfeeding mothers with sore nipples. It has been clinically proven to accelerate healing of sore nipples. It is natural, hypoallergenic, preservative free and does not have to be removed prior to breastfeeding. It provides soothing relief of pain and is recommended by breastfeeding specialists. Lansinoh may also be used to condition the nipples prior to breastfeeding to promote healthy, supple skin. Available from pharmacies.
Always read the label. Use only as directed.
If symptoms persist please see your doctor.

ISIS iQ UNO

Only you know what feels right for you, so it makes sense to have a breast pump that gives you complete control over your comfort. Philips AVENT IQ Electronic Breast Pumps are designed with an IQ … an electronic memory that learns and continues your personal pumping rhythm.

UNO offers everything mothers have come to expect from an AVENT breast pump – the soft let-down massage cushion and fingertip sensitive control that make the pump's action feel so gentle, natural and comfortable, almost like a baby suckling, with the addition of an iQ – an electronic brain.

For the first time you have infinitely variable fingertip control, on the breast where you need it, so there's no need to put the breast pump down to alter your rhythm. There are no predetermined factory settings and the technology behind UNO allows you to completely personalise your pumping rhythm. The 'brain' of ISIS iQ is a microprocessor. As you depress the control handle, electronic signals are sent to the microprocessor that memorises the suction, speed and – uniquely – the interval you have chosen between each depression of the handle. When you press the control button, iQ takes over until you tell it to change. ISIS IQ is available in a single (UNO) or double (DUO) pump. The DUO is the smallest and quietest double pump available and allows you to express from both breasts at once resulting in more milk in less time. Perfect for mothers who need to express milk quickly, have multiple births or have premature babies.

Philips AVENT have made milk collection easy as well. You can choose to express your milk into either one of our reusable bottles or to our innovative VIA disposable cups.

UNO can be used with either the battery pack, mains lead or as a manual pump, and is available in either Standard or Out and About version (with micro fibre carry bag) from pharmacies and baby stores nationally from $199.95rrp.

This is what using our breast pump feels like.

Our Electronic Breast Pump has patented Soft
Massage Cushions to imitate your baby's
suckling and stimulate natural milk flow. So you
can enjoy a relaxed, comfortable pumping
experience. For more information, call
customer service on 1300 364 474 or log on
to www.philips.com/AVENT

PHILIPS

AVENT

sense and simplicity

Tommee Tippee

Being a mum is the most amazing, fascinating and rewarding time of your life. Nothing matters as much as doing the very best for your baby, and that's where Tommee Tippee comes in. Tommee Tippee products have been making life better for babies and easier for mums for over 50 years. We started out with innovations for toddlers, which were so successful that we then expanded to make products for newborns, growing babies and older infants as well as expectant mums.

In many of our ranges we offer you a choice of products because every baby is different. All our products are developed in close consultation with health professionals and then tested to make sure that they not only meet but exceed industry standards.

Our aim is to look after little ones and their mums at every stage. We've worked with experts in every field and, most importantly, mums themselves to make sure every product in our range delivers top quality and real benefits for you and your little one. We involve parents at every stage of our research and development, because nobody knows better than you how to make things better at every step of the way.

We really mean it when we say "Tommee Tippee is loved by babies and recommended by mums".

So whether you are looking for sterilisers, breast pumps, bottles, cups, teats, comforters, toys, feeding utensils or the like, we are sure you will love our vast range of Tommee Tippee products.

For further product information visit our comprehensive website www.tommeetippee.com.au.

superior performance
breast pump comfort

Soft touch,
flexible cup for
perfect fit

Unique steri-box for
**sterilising
or storing**

Milk storage lid
for **storage**
and freezing
breast milk

Manual operation
means it is
discreet and **easy
to control**

The unique, 3 piece breast pump,
delivers superior performance with comfort

closer to nature™

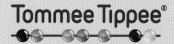

"loved by babies, recommended by mums"

Only Organic

Only Organic is a family owned company that is dedicated to providing infants and young children with deliciously wholesome quality organic food.

With today's busy lifestyles, where in many households both parents are working, it can be hard finding time to fit everything in. Only Organic baby food is made from certified organic ingredients that contain no artificial flavours or colours, no preservatives and no added sugar or salt – but does offer invaluable convenience.

At Only Organic we try to offer our customers a good variety of products which have different tastes and textures, as all babies are different and have different dietary requirements. Our range includes four stages: pureed Stage 1 from four-six months of age and up; mashed Stage 2 for six months and up and Stage 3 for nine months and up; and chunky Stage 4 for 12 months and up. Each stage has a variety of tasty, nutritious fruit and vegetable meal options. Many products are free of dairy, gluten, egg and wheat. As well as our ready meals, also look out for other offers in our range including First Cereal and First Thirst Juice.

Visit www.onlyorganic.com.au for further information.

Medela

Medela has been the market leaders in breastpumps and accessories for over 30 years with their range made in Switzerland. Renowned for quality and safety, Medela breastfeeding products are the No. 1 choice of hospitals and professionals throughout the world.

Medela believes nature has provided well for babies. However, if mother and child should still need support, Medela products are there to help them. Breast milk contains all the important nutrients and antibodies for a baby to thrive. For this reason, the World Health Organization (WHO), midwives, lactation consultants as well as pediatricians all recommend that babies should be nourished exclusively with breast milk during the first 6 months after they are born. Medela aims to give breastfeeding mothers ideal support during this important time and in the most natural way.

Australian medical researches play a large role in the development of Medela products. Medela has an ongoing working relationship with the University of Western Australia and Professor Peter Hartman. Professor Hartman provides Medela with the latest research findings on breastfeeding practices that are comfortable and efficient to the mother to help her breastfeed longer. This research is used to develop all of Medela's breastfeeding products.

Due to its strong research and quality products Medela are the only products on the Australian market that are endorsed by the Australian Breastfeeding Association. Here in Australia the Medela range includes manual and electric breast pumps, BPA free bottles, breastfeeding accessories and intimate apparel.

To find out more about Medela products visit www.funtasticnursery.com.au and for more information on breastfeeding log on to www.medela.com.au.

Works for baby, works for you!

Medela is the number one choice in Australian hospitals and the only breast pumps & accessories to be endorsed by the Australian Breastfeeding Association. Medela breastpumps; find one that suits you and your baby.

Swing

FAST AND GENTLE - The original 2-Phase Expression mimics babies initial rapid suckling to stimulate milk ejection, then the more relaxed suckling speed once milk is fowing. It makes pumping especially gentle and effective.

- Comfortable and soft thanks to the SoftFit(TM) breastshield
- Ideal for out and about
- Easy to operate and clean
- Suitable for occasional to frequent use

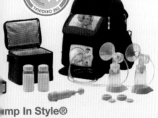

ump In Style®

vanced Breastpump - The only double ctric retail pump to feature 2-Phase ression® technology

The unique "backpack" approach to pump transportation is ideal for mums on the go

The BatteryPak offers flexibility and independence with standard or rechargeable battery options

Adjustable speed and vacuum control means mum can cutomise her pumping session

Includes manual option

Includes removable cooler carrier

Designed for daily and frequent use

Harmony Manual™

Feels more like baby than any other manual breast pump thanks to research based unique 2-Phase Expression® technology.

- Designed for faster let-down and maximum milk flow
- A soft massaging breast shield that is comfortable and effectively stimulates the breast and areola
- Swivel handle allows adjusting pumping positions for maximum comfort
- Fewer parts than other manual breast pumps
- Portable and lightweight - to pump on the go
- Ideal for occasional use

Breastfeeding Accessories

The Medela accessory range offers practical and comforting devices to help overcome any breastfeeding difficulties. These include:

- Purelan 100 – Soothes sensitive or dry nipples and is perfectly safe.
- Contact Nipple Shield – Help with breastfeeding with sore, cracked, flat or inverted nipples.
- Breast Milk Bottles – These BPA free bottles come in two handy sizes. Perfect for storage and feeding they are specially made to go with Medela breast pumps, meaning you can pump straight into the bottle.

Additional accessories also available include breast milk bags, washable & disposable bra pads, valves and membranes pack and quick clean micro bags to warm frozen breast milk. (products not featured here)

Available from Target, Kmart, David Jones, Toys R Us and leading independent Nursery stores nationwide. For stockists please call Funtastic customer service 1800 244 543 or visit www.funtasticnursery.com.au

australian breastfeeding association

Vaalia

Vaalia, leaders in better health yoghurt, helps parents give little ones the best start in life with its infant range – Vaalia My First Yoghurt. Designed specially for babies from six months old, it is the only infant yoghurt in Australia with a unique blend of three active cultures – Acidophilus, Bifidus and LGG.

LGG is unique to Vaalia yoghurt, and is the world's most studied and scientifically researched probiotic. Probiotics are bacterial cultures that have a boosting effect on the levels of good bacteria in our intestines, helping maintain healthy immune and digestive systems, and helping upset tummies recover more quickly. With 180,000,000 cfu (colony forming units) per pot, Vaalia My First Yoghurt contains enough probiotics to help your little one develop strong immunity.

Vaalia My First Yoghurt is also the only infant yoghurt with essential fatty acid Omega 3 DHA, which is vitally important for healthy brain and visual development. Vaalia My First Yoghurt has been specially formulated to meet infants' nutrition needs and contains a wealth of vitamins and minerals, including riboflavin, essential in periods of rapid growth, and calcium for healthy bones and teeth.

And the benefits of Vaalia My First Yoghurt don't have to stop when your child gets older. Vaalia Yoghurt for Toddlers has Vaalia's unique blend of three active cultures including LGG, as well as Omega 3 DHA and has been created with the nutrition needs of your toddler in mind. It contains all the goodness of dairy, including B group vitamins for energy and development of the nervous system and magnesium for healthy bones and energy production. It is also a source of riboflavin and zinc, essential in periods of rapid growth and calcium for strong bones and teeth.

Vaalia My First Yoghurt is available at all major supermarkets in 6 x 60g packs.

Vaalia Yoghurt for Toddlers is available at all major supermarkets in 6 x 90g packs.

with Omega 3 DHA
to help brain and eye development

Here doggy, doggy – think I'm gaining on him.

Time to carefully hide something of Dad's.

Ooh look, Mum's make-up drawer is unattended.

What's with those guys in the skivvies?

Think I've nailed this cute look.

Where are my toes? Well right here of course.

Incy-Wincy Spider. Gotta love the classics.

Nap? That's for babies.

We meet again doggy. But this time the advantage is mine.

Yoghurt specially formulated for your precious bundle of energy.

Vaalia My First Yoghurt is not only an excellent source of calcium, protein and riboflavin... it's also the only baby yoghurt with 3 active cultures, including acidophilus, bifidus and lactobacillus GG (LGG). Probiotic LGG is important, as it gives your baby a head start in developing healthy digestive and strong immune systems. My First Yoghurt is mild tasting and low in sugars - compare the nutrition panels with other baby yoghurts for yourself. Available in vanilla and fruit flavours, in perfect portions for happy little tummies.

DK Books – Annabel Karmel

Annabel Karmel is a respected authority on childhood nutrition and cookery. She's a firm believer that children are less likely to become fussy eaters if they are used to a good selection of fresh foods from an early age. This experience and attitude form the basis of her easy-to-use guides, which include advice, recipes and techniques designed to give your child the best possible start in life as well as practical information about things such as allergies, breastfeeding and weaning. For more information about Annabel Karmel visit www.annabelkarmel.com or www.dk.com.au/parenting.

From Annabel Karmel, respected authority on
child nutrition and cookery

Answer all your questions about feeding your baby and toddler, with tips on when to wean, advice on allergies and suggestions for introducing new foods

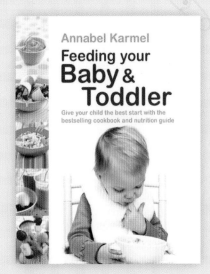

Discover how to prepare enticing meals from healthy breakfasts to tempting food for fussy eaters to give your child the best start in life

Keep a record you will treasure of that first important year with month by month advice for new parents and delicious recipes for baby's first tastes

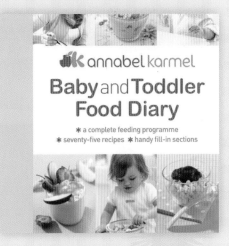

A complete weaning and feeding guide with essential nutritional information and expert tips

look inside the books at **dk.com.au/parenting**

Pauls Yoghurt

Yoghurt is a unique blend of nutritious milk and beneficial bacterial cultures that has long been recognised for the nutritional benefits it provides, such as protein, vitamins and minerals, especially calcium. Yoghurt is often used as a weaning food and is suitable for children over six months of age. Pauls Yoghurt with Real Fruit for Kids is made by blending the goodness of full cream milk with real fruit purée for a smooth, lump-free texture that young children are less likely to reject.

Yoghurt is high in nutrition because it is made from milk. During yoghurt production extra skim milk solids are added, which increases its calcium and protein content without adding any extra fat. Each 90g tub of Pauls Yoghurt with Real Fruit for Kids yoghurt provides about 140mg of calcium, which is 20% of your child's daily requirement.

Pauls Yoghurt with Real Fruit for Kids contains no preservatives, artificial colours or flavours, but does contain probiotic Acidophilus, the yoghurt culture that helps maintain the correct balance of bacteria in your child's digestive system. Each tub of this high quality yoghurt contains 90,000,000 cfu (colony forming units) of Acidophilus.

Pauls Yoghurt with Real Fruit for Kids has less than 11g of sugar per serve, most of which is lactose from the milk. A small amount of sugar is added with the fruit to make the yoghurt less tart and more palatable for little taste buds.

Pauls Yoghurt with Real Fruit for Kids comes in a range of child-friendly flavours so it is as delicious as it is nutritious and features different characters to make healthy eating more fun. Try something different by inserting a paddle pop stick through the lid and freezing for a healthy summer treat.

Pauls®

Packed with goodness

The Pauls range of children's yoghurt is perfect for kids large and small.

Goodness check list

- No preservatives, artificial colours, flavours or sweeteners
- Calcium for growing bodies. 20% RDI per serve
- Less than 11g sugar per serve
- Acidophilus for happy tummies
- Value for money multipacks
- Made from full cream milk and real fruit puree
- A fun approach to healthy food
- Ideal size for little appetites
- Gluten free

Milton Method

Since 1916 mums have trusted the Milton method of sterilization. Milton is used for a wide variety of sanitization techniques, both in hospitals and kitchens around the world.

The Milton Method is clinically proven nontoxic and international research shows that the Milton Method is more effective than other methods of sterilization such as boiling, steaming or microwave sterilization.

The Milton Method kills more than 99.9% of germs and bacteria, creating a safe environment for your baby to ensure protection against most bacterial infections. The Milton method is a safe way to disinfect teats and bottles, soothers, breast pumps, toys and to clean many other surfaces and items that your baby comes in contact with.

Milton comes conveniently packaged as tablets, solutions, antibacterial gels as well as the Milton Method Starter Kit which gives you everything you need to start sanitizing the Milton way. The Milton Antibacterial Gels are a very convenient way to sanitize your hands on the run, many mums keep Milton on the change table to clean hands after changing baby, or in their bag to clean their hands whilst out and about.

The antibacterial gels kill 99.9% of germs and come in either natural or Aloe & Vitamin E ensuring your hands stay soft and moisturised wherever you are. The gels are suitable for mum in many situations where germs need to be sanitized and is more effective at sanitizing against germs than washing your hands with soap and water.

Milton is available in supermarkets and leading pharmacies nationally.

Milton, trusted hygiene for babies since 1916.

For several generations Australian families have relied on the famous Milton Method as an effective, trusted and simple way to eliminate germs.

- ✓ **Kills 99.9% of all germs**
- ✓ Easier, simpler and quicker to use
- ✓ Uses cold water, safer for baby's items and will last longer

- ✓ Conveniently store items 'on demand' for up to 24 hours
- ✓ Clinically proven, superior to boiling or microwave steaming

TRUSTED SINCE 1916

Effective. Trusted. Simple.

For more information on Milton hygienic products visit
www.miltonpharma.com or call **1800 645 866**.

Nappies, bathtime & skincare

Photograph by Kristen Cook, Melbourne.

Nappy rash & how best to treat it

Nappy rash happens when a baby's skin is covered by a wet or dirty nappy for too long. How long is 'too long' varies a lot with different babies, and varies for any one baby depending on, for example, whether the baby is well or unwell. Nappy rash is very common and can happen no matter how careful you are. Some babies with the best care still get a lot of nappy rash, while others hardly get it at all, so a lot depends on how sensitive the child's skin is.

What does nappy rash look like?
- Nappy rash is red swollen skin that looks damp and may have some blisters or ulcers.
- The whole of the skin covered by a nappy may be damaged, or much smaller patches.
- It is usually in the area that is covered by a nappy. The skin inside the folds, such as between the buttocks, may not be so red.
- Sometimes there can be small patches of red skin on the tummy with healthy skin around them. This can be a sign of an infection on top of the nappy rash.
- A rash or sore red skin in the nappy area is not always just nappy rash. It can be caused by eczema, allergies or infections. It is important to see your doctor for any rash to be sure what it is and how it should be treated.

What triggers nappy rash?
- Many babies get nappy rash when they are unwell, particularly if they have diarrhoea. Their skin seems to become more sensitive.
- Starting a new food seems to trigger the rash for some babies.
- Having a wet or dirty nappy on for too long ('too long' is very variable).
- Chemicals in disposable nappies were a problem for some babies, but this seems to be much less of a problem now.
- An infection on the skin, such as thrush, can make the rash worse. Thrush normally lives in the gut and on skin without causing any problem, but when the skin is damaged thrush can make the damage worse.

What causes nappy rash?
- A baby's urine is sterile (there are no germs in urine), but there are germs on the baby's skin, in poo and on clothing (including nappies).
- These germs make ammonia when wet with urine or poo.
- Ammonia can burn the skin.
- The nappy can rub on the skin (especially stiff cloth nappies).
- Plastic pants over the nappy prevent air flow around the nappy, and they also hide a nappy which may be very wet or dirty, so the skin stays wet for a long time.

What to do about nappy rash:
- Change nappies often so that the skin is dry most of the time.

- Have time when there is no nappy on to help the skin to dry fully.
- Disposable nappies, with linings which absorb the urine and keep the skin dry, seem to help a lot of babies.
- Wash baby's bottom very gently so you don't rub the skin, but make sure that the skin is clean (check in all of the folds). Using a simple cleanser such as sorbolene rather than soap may be better to wash your baby's bottom.
- Only use skin wipes that are made for babies. Skin wipes for adults often have alcohol in them and this can cause pain and discomfort on damaged skin.
- Use a barrier cream to keep dampness away from the skin every time you change the nappy, e.g. zinc and castor oil, or zinc and cod liver oil. Note: these creams stain clothes and nappies. Many people use disposable nappies to avoid stains.
- If you are using cloth nappies, change them often and wash using soap powders which are labelled for sensitive skin. Drying them in a tumble dryer, if you have one, may make them softer than drying in the sun. Avoid using plastic pants whenever possible.
- Some parents find the following helpful although we know of no research to support the ideas. For washing buttocks: a solution of bicarbonate of soda – 1 teaspoon to 600ml of water. Use a cup of vinegar in the rinse water when washing nappies.

Pain relief:

- Nappy rash is painful.
- Most babies with nappy rash will be more irritable than usual, and may sleep poorly. They often need more attention, holding and comforting.
- Pain-relief using paracetamol can help. Make sure the dose is the right one for your baby.
- Covering damaged skin using a barrier cream gently and often can be soothing.

Powders:

- Powders are not necessary. There is concern that talc powder and other powders may be breathed in by a baby, and this may cause some health problems. The yeast that causes thrush feeds on cornstarch powder (corn flour), so this powder should not be used either.

What to do if nappy rash does not go away:

- Sometimes the rash does not clear up because there is an infection on the damaged skin. Thrush can make nappy rash worse as can some bacterial infections.
- A baby may have an underlying skin problem such as eczema. In this case the baby may have rashes on other parts of the body (such as the face). The rash may be inside the skin folds, while nappy rash mostly does not affect skin that is not in contact with the nappy.
- See your doctor or health care worker. Creams that treat thrush or eczema may be useful. They can be spread on the clean dry skin, left for a few minutes, then covered by the barrier cream. If it seems likely that thrush is part of the problem, oral drops which lower the amount of thrush in the gut may be useful too.

Settling techniques: newborns to 12 months

Babies need to learn how to put themselves to sleep. Like most skills, it takes time and occurs at an individual rate. In the early months of life a baby has a need to be physically connected to their mother and other significant family members. If this closeness is provided the baby learns to separate more easily from their parents as they can trust that in times of need the parent or other significant adult will come to their assistance.

Newborn babies' patterns are often unpredictable with irregular feeding and sleeping times, and generally babies do not establish a regular pattern until after 3 months of age. When assisting your baby develop a sleep pattern it is better to use levels of distress/cry as your guide to the need to comfort your child than adhering to a time schedule.

In the early weeks of life a baby will often fall asleep while being fed but then wake as soon as it is away from their parent's body.

A normal sleep cycle is approximately 40-60 minutes and some babies will stir and re-settle themselves. However, some babies may need help to resettle. When babies are overtired they may be more difficult to settle. An important starting point is to be able to recognise your baby's tired signs.

Tired signs may include: grimacing, yawning, grizzling, frowning, crying, sucking, clenched fists, staring, rigid limbs, squirming, jerky movements or becoming more active, minimal movements or activity.

When you observe baby's tired signs, prepare your baby for bed:

- Check your baby's nappy.
- Take care not to overheat.
- Position your baby in bed – on their back – according to the SIDS guidelines.

0–3 months:

- If quiet, allow to settle. If crying, introduce gentle stroking/cuddles until your baby calms.
- Swaddling your baby in a light muslin or cotton wrap may help.
- Talking/singing but without eye contact can be reassuring for both you and baby.
- Most babies will take a while to settle.
- You may need to leave your baby for a brief time to see if he or she will settle on their own.
- If your baby is crying, go in and comfort them. You may have to do this several times.
- If your baby wakes under one hour attempt to re-settle them.

3–6 months:

- Self-settling involves comforting your baby in the cot or up-in-arms for short periods while also giving your baby the opportunity to fall asleep by himself/herself.
- Your baby may initially protest and fuss when you leave the room. If you feel comfortable and your baby is not distressed, allow him/her the opportunity to settle himself/herself.
- Listen to your baby's cry and respond accordingly. If your baby continues to fuss, return and comfort until your baby calms, before leaving the room.

If you wish to safely maintain physical closeness with your child while they are asleep put their cot in your room. If your baby continues to remain unsettled – consider other management techniques. For example: offer a "top up" breastfeed within 30 minutes of completing the feed; cuddle; rhythmical movement (walk or rock); baby massage; deep relaxation bathing; play some music; offer a dummy or cooled boiled water. Choose whichever technique suits you and your baby best.

With consistency these routines may take up to two weeks to show progress. For safety, ensure the cot sides are completely raised whenever your baby is left unattended in the cot.

6–12 months:

A consistent routine is important to help your baby recognise and establish good sleep patterns.

When you start to observe your baby's 'tired signs', it is time to prepare your baby for bed:

- Check your baby's nappy.
- Put your baby in the cot – on their back – with their feet and bedding at the bottom of the cot.

In order to help your baby to fall asleep by him/herself, you may find it useful to understand normal sleep cycles and be able to identify their 'tired signs'.

Tired signs may include: grimacing, frowning, clenched fists, yawning, crying, squirming, grizzling, sucking, staring, rigid limbs, minimal movements or activity, jerky movements or becoming more active.

A normal sleep cycle is approximately 40-60 minutes and then most babies will stir and re-settle themselves. However, some babies develop sleep associations and may have difficulty re-establishing sleep unless the same conditions for re-settling are met. For example, if your baby needs the breast, bottle, dummy, to be patted or cuddled or they have a complicated ritual to assist them to sleep, you may notice after one sleep cycle that your baby wakes and cries until the same conditions that they associate with falling asleep are re-established.

It can be difficult for babies to learn to sleep by themselves and various settling techniques may help the transition from wake to sleep. When assisting your baby develop a sleep pattern it is better to use levels of distress/cry as your guide to the need to comfort your child than adhering to a time schedule.

- Give your baby an opportunity to settle. Try to leave baby, depending on their cry, for a short time. If distressed, soothe to a calm state before leaving your baby.
- Leave the room giving your baby an opportunity to self-settle.
- Remember your baby is now older and you may need to leave him for longer periods as he learns to self-settle, only if not distressed. Consistency in technique now becomes important.
- If your baby does not calm with frequent reassurances, get baby up and continue your daily routine until the next sleep period and repeat your settling technique.

If you wish to safely maintain physical closeness with your child while they are asleep put their cot in your room. If your baby continues to remain unsettled – consider other management techniques, for example offer a top up breastfeed within 30 minutes of completing the feed. Other ideas include: cuddling; rhythmical movement; walk or rocking; baby massage; deep relaxation bathing; play some music; a dummy or offer cooled boiled water. Choose whichever technique suits you and your baby best.

With consistency these routines may take up to two to four weeks to show progress. Times given are a guide only. For safety ensure cot sides are completely raised whenever a baby is left unattended in the cot.

Settling techniques: 12 months to toddlers

12 months to toddlers:

A consistent routine is important to help your child recognise and establish good sleep patterns. Developing a bedtime ritual will also help signal to your child that it is time for sleep, this may include saying goodnight to family members, cleaning their teeth, reading a bedtime story and saying goodnight to their soft toys.

When you observe your child's tired signs, prepare your baby for bed. Tired signs for this age group may include: grimacing, sucking, yawning, clenched fists, grizzling, staring, frowning, rigid limbs, crying, jerky movements or becoming restless, minimal movements or activity, increased irritability while playing.

A normal sleep cycle is approximately 40-60 minutes and some children will stir and re-settle themselves. However, some children who are dependent on their parent to help them fall asleep may have difficulty re-establishing sleep unless the same conditions for re-settling are met. For example, if your child needs the breast, bottle, dummy, cuddles or a complicated ritual to sleep, you may notice after one sleep cycle that he or she wakes and cries until the same conditions that he or she associates with falling asleep are re-established.

It can be difficult for children to learn to sleep by themselves. A consistent bedtime routine is important to help your child establish satisfactory sleep patterns. For a daytime sleep, have quiet time (story) and then bed. For a night sleep, have dinner, bath, quiet time (story), then bedtime. Other routines may include:

- Spending some quiet time with your child, either reading a story, singing a nursery rhyme or having a quiet cuddle.
- Just prior to the agreed upon bedtime, tell your child that the story will finish soon.
- Ensure your child is adequately clothed for the night, e.g. warm pyjamas, enough blankets or a sleeping bag.
- Having a favourite toy in the cot and a night light can help small children.
- Say goodnight and kiss your child. If in a cot, ensure that the sides are up and securely in place prior to leaving the room.
- Give your child an opportunity to settle. Leave the bedroom door ajar. Try to leave your child for a short time.
- If your child is not calming, return to the room and reassure them, then lay him/her down and tuck in the bedclothes.
- In a calm voice tell your child it's time for sleep.
- If his or her nappy is soiled or your child vomits, change with minimal fuss, then resume the settling technique.
- During the day, if your child still remains unsettled for the length of the sleep with frequent reassurance then cease settling. Try to avoid old habits when settling, like giving a bottle or dummy.
- Continue with the usual daily routine and settling at the next sleep. At night time, continue with settling.

With consistency these routines may take up to two weeks to show progress.

Information supplied by Tresillian, www.tresillian.net.

Building a relationship

Laughing, playing, having fun, loving and being loved. These are the things people think about when considering becoming parents. Most parents want to enjoy a close relationship with their children. For children, developing a trusting relationship between themselves and their parent, or main caregiver, is necessary for healthy development.

The most important emotional task for a child during their early years is attaching to their main caregiver, usually their parents. This means that children need to develop trust that parents are people who will meet their needs. From this basis, children are in a strong position to be able to take advantage of other learning opportunities as they grow. Promoting relationships with your own child is therefore important for the child's development as well as for the mutual enjoyment of parent and child.

Relationships with babies are formed through having eye contact while the baby's needs are being met, for instance while feeding. Through this experience, the child learns that his or her parents provide comfort and help them feel better. All it takes is using everyday opportunities to build the relationship. Smiling, laughing and talking when nappies are changed or any other activity that helps the child feel more comfortable, is helpful. Comforting the child through stroking, patting or cuddling is a useful way to promote attachment. Gazing into the eyes of a young baby and talking to them with an expressive manner, waiting for the child to respond, leads to babies mimicking the expression of their parents and this is enjoyable for both as well as relationship-building.

As babies become toddlers, they enjoy mobility and begin to develop independence. Parents need to develop a balance between how much independence to allow and what boundaries to impose. Having a predictable environment helps children develop stronger relationships with their parents. Learning that parents are reliable is helpful for children. This is a stage where again, meeting the child's gaze while the child's needs are being met is helpful in building the relationship. Having the child look at the parent when talking with the child or teaching the child something is useful. Toddlers like to laugh and play delightful games. Having fun and sharing these experiences with your toddler promotes the relationship.

With preschoolers, using routine and being predictable about expectations of the child are helpful for children in feeling secure in the relationship and safe in the environment. Playing and spending time with their parents, talking, doing chores and simply being in the presence of each other are all useful ways of promoting the relationship. There is a place for special activities, but it is the day-to-day experience of life that provides opportunities to build the foundations of the relationship.

Developing a relationship between parents and children comes naturally to many parents and occurs in the context of day-to-day experiences. Being present with your child and being in tune with the child's emotions and experiences, builds the relationship. Individual children are responded to according to their own needs and parents' own style. Parents know their children best and it is important to trust one's own sense of what is right for developing the relationship with the child.

Invest in the relationship and enjoy your children. If you do have any difficulties, consult a professional. A psychologist or social worker are well placed to provide this assistance.

Written by Bronwyn Thomas, a social worker with more than 20 years experience working with families over parenting issues. She works as a counsellor at Parentline. Parentline is a confidential telephone counselling, information and referral service for all Victorian parents and carers with children aged from birth to 18 years. Parentline is accessible from anywhere in Victoria for the cost of a local call (excluding mobiles). Phone 13 22 89.

Infant massage

Infant massage is an ancient art first practised in China and India several centuries ago. It is rapidly gaining popularity across the western world, and it's not surprising when you read the list of benefits. Not only has infant massage been shown to increase your confidence in handling your baby, it also helps your baby respond to touch and activates your maternal hormones. It helps to settle your baby, promotes good circulation, eliminates toxins, strengthens the immune system and can relieve physical discomforts such as colic and teething.

Babies learn most about their world through their sense of touch, so explain what you're doing and what part of his or her body you're working on and they'll learn far more about their own body. It will also help your baby's coordination and encourage development – and it's a wonderful practice for dads and grandparents to get involved in.

Before you begin:
Massage your baby at any time, but it's usually best after your baby's had a bath or is between feeds. Massage for as long as you and your baby are happy.

- Use almond, jojoba or virgin olive oil (any oil which is not highly perfumed). Use a few drops and put them into your palms, warming the oil before touching your baby's skin. You'll also need two towels and a warm environment. Dim the lights and play some relaxing music.
- Remove any jewellery and keep your nails short. Always keep one hand on your baby (for reassurance) and talk softly and gently.
- Massage more firmly towards your baby's heart and softly as you massage away from your baby's heart.
- Remove your baby's clothes (keep the nappy on if you prefer). Always ask your baby if he or she would like a massage – then stop and notice your baby's cues.
- Indications that your baby is happy to be massaged include: lying with open arms, eye contact, laughing, playful bouncing of arms and legs. Signs that indicate your baby is uncomfortable include: persistent crying, pushing/arching back, arms moving in and out from chest, avoiding eye contact.

A short massage routine:
Legs and feet
(You can repeat these moves for the hands and arms.)
- *Indian milking of the whole leg from thigh to ankle.*
  Support the leg at the ankle with one hand. With the other hand, make the letter 'C', wrapping your fingers around the leg and moving in long sweeping strokes towards the foot.
  When you reach the ankle swap hands and repeat the movement, so that both the outer and inner part of the leg is massaged.

⊘ *Aeroplane runway*
With the palm of your hand push and stroke up and over the sole of the foot and off.
Make a 'whoosh' noise as you do this, and your baby will think it's hilarious!

Stomach

⊘ *"I love you."*
As you stroke a big letter 'I' down the descending colon (on your baby's left side) say: 'I'.
Then draw an upside down 'L' for love, tracing a line from the right to left side across your baby's
tummy and then down the descending colon, as you say 'Love'. Lastly, draw an upside down 'U'
up the ascending colon (on your baby's right side), across the tummy and down the descending
colon, saying 'You'. Now put it all together as you tell your baby "I ... love ... you."

Chest

⊘ *Cross your heart.*
With both hands at the hip bone, slide your right hand across the chest to the opposite shoulder and
back to where it began. Then repeat this stroke with the left hand. You can give your baby's
shoulder a little squeeze when you get there.

Back

⊘ For these strokes it's best to place baby across your lap or at right angles to your body on the floor.

⊘ Stroking: place one hand on your baby's bottom and the other hand, palm facing down, on the
back of your baby's head, then stroke down your baby's back until you meet your other hand and
repeat.

⊘ Using a circular motion, massage with the pads of your thumbs along either side of your baby's
spine and your baby's bottom.

Always finish each part of the body with a touch relaxation – gently tap and vibrate the area you
have massaged and tell your baby to relax and let go.

It's always best to attend an infant massage course, but if this is not possible, then know that any
massage is beneficial, if practised with care. And always follow your baby's cues.

Written by Katie Brown, a certified massage instructor with IMA & a pre and postnatal yoga teacher, www.yogababes.com.au.

Managing your child's eczema

Eczema (atopic dermatitis) is a recurring, non-infectious, inflammatory skin condition affecting one in three Australasians at some stage throughout their lives. The condition is most common in people with a family history of an atopic disorder, including asthma or hay fever.

Atopic eczema is the most common form of the disease among Australasians. The skin becomes red, dry, itchy and scaly, and in severe cases, may weep, bleed and crust over, causing the sufferer much discomfort. Sometimes the skin may become infected. The condition can also flare and subside for no apparent reason.

Although eczema affects all ages, it usually appears in early childhood (in babies between two-to-six months of age) and disappears around six years of age. In fact, more than half of all eczema sufferers show signs within their first 12 months of life and 90 per cent of people develop eczema before the age of five. Although most children grow out of the condition, a small percentage may experience severe eczema into adulthood. The condition can not only afflict the individual sufferer, but also their family, friends and health practitioners.

What are the symptoms of eczema?
- Moderate to severely itching skin (this symptom separates eczema from other skin rashes).
- Recurring rash – dry, red, patchy or cracked skin. (In infants and toddlers, the rash usually appears on the face, elbows or knees. In older children and adults, the rash appears less often on the face, and more commonly on the hands, neck, inner elbows, backs of the knees and ankles).
- Skin weeping watery fluid.
- Rough, 'leathery', thick skin.
- Lesions which may be infected by bacteria or viruses.

What causes eczema?
Although the exact cause of eczema is unknown, it appears to be linked to the following internal and external factors:
- A family history of eczema, asthma or hayfever (the strongest predictor). If both parents have eczema, there is an 80 per cent chance that their children will too.
- Particular food and alcohol (dairy and wheat products, citrus fruits, eggs, nuts, seafood, chemical food additives, preservatives and colourings).
- Stress.
- Irritants – tobacco smoke, chemicals, weather (hot and humid or cold and dry conditions) and air conditioning or overheating.
- Allergens – house dust mites, moulds, grasses, plant pollens, foods, pets, clothing, soaps, shampoos, washing powders, cosmetics and toiletries.

How long does eczema last?
Eczema symptoms tend to become less severe over time. For many sufferers, symptoms may mostly disappear, although they will tend to suffer from dry, sensitive skin.

How do you control eczema?

Although eczema is not a life-threatening disease, it can certainly affect a sufferer's, their carer/s and family's quality of life. A child's night-time itching can cause sleepless nights for the child, his/her parents and siblings. It can place a significant strain upon family relationships. Flare-ups can often lead to absenteeism from school, work, personal activities and/or family obligations.

How do you best manage a child's eczema?

The best way to manage a child's eczema is to:

- Gain their cooperation
- Distract the child to prevent them from scratching
- Become familiar with the child's response to different environmental conditions
- Educate yourself and others about the condition and learn to be sympathetic
- Reduce stress for both yourself and the child
- See your doctor if the eczema continues to flare.

How do you avoid an eczema outbreak?

Many things can be done to avoid an eczema outbreak. Most importantly, the skin should be kept moist by using a daily moisturiser. Other ways to prevent an outbreak include:

- Wearing 100 per cent cotton or soft fabrics – avoiding rough, scratchy fibres and tight clothing
- Using rubber gloves with cotton liners
- Having lukewarm baths and showers using a non-soap cleanser or hypoallergenic bath oil and avoiding extremely hot water
- Gently patting, not rubbing, the skin dry with a soft towel
- Applying a moisturiser within three minutes after bathing to 'lock in' the moisture
- When possible, avoiding rapid changes of temperature and activities that raise a sweat
- Removing carpets and rugs from houses (if possible)
- Ventilating the house as often as possible
- Avoiding stuffed toys which harbour dust mites
- Changing bed linen regularly, vaccuuming mattresses regularly for dust mites and avoiding feather-filled pillows
- Reducing daily stress
- Learning what triggers eczema and how to avoid them.

How do you diagnose eczema?

Only a doctor or specialist can formally diagnose eczema. An accurate diagnosis requires a complete skin examination, a thorough medical history and the presence of a chronically recurring rash with intense itching that is consistent with eczema.

While there is no test to determine whether a person has eczema, tests may be conducted to rule out other possibilities.

Itching is an important clue to diagnosing eczema. If an itch is not present, chances are that the problem is not eczema.

Managing your child's eczema

Is there a cure for eczema?
Although there is no known cure for eczema and it can be a lifelong condition, treatment can offer symptom control.

What are the treatment options for eczema?
The goal of treating eczema is to heal the skin and to both prevent and minimise flare-ups. This can be done by using a moisturiser to prevent the skin from cracking or itching and to offer relief. Well-moisturised skin also helps block out germs that cause infections.

Treatment may also include:

- Topical corticoteroids that help reduce inflammation and itchiness. This is the most common form of eczema treatment. Most topical corticosteroids are available on prescription, however some milder strengths are available in pharmacies.
- Sedating antihistamines that induce sleep and reduce itchiness.
- Wet bandaging that soothes the skin, reducing itchiness and helping heal lesions.
- Antibiotics that treat secondary infections.
- Allergy testing (prick or blood tests) that may help establish trigger factors.
- Following advice from dieticians.

More severe cases of eczema may be treated by oral corticosteroids, systemic immunosuppressants and phototherapy.

It is important to seek professional medical advice before using any medication - whether over-the-counter or prescription - to determine its side-effects.

What are the complications associated with eczema?
Because eczema skin is often broken, it places the sufferer at risk of contracting skin infections. Professional medical advice should be sought at the first sign of any infection. An eczema sufferer is also at risk of developing herpes simplex type 1 (cold sores) which can spread over a large area of the skin and occasionally prove dangerous. Sufferers are also at risk of contracting a widespread skin infection known as impetigo (school sores). In order to avoid any complications associated with vaccination, the disease should be discussed with a medical professional. However, normal childhood immunisations generally pose no risk to the eczema sufferer.

Information supplied by the Eczema Association of Australasia Inc., www.eczema.org.au.

Why your baby cries

When your baby cries it is her way of communicating with you. It can be overwhelming when you do not know what she wants. Offers of advice may come from everywhere and can be conflicting, for example: "let her cry", "don't spoil the child", "don't pick her up, a good cry will do her good" and "she must be hungry".

Listed below are some things you might need to consider if you are not sure why your baby is crying. Newborn babies may cry up to two hours each day. This unsettled period is often around the same time each day, usually in the afternoon. This is common.

Some reasons for crying include:

- Having a wet or dirty nappy
- Feeling discomfort
- Being too hot or cold
- Needing to be fed, cuddled or wrapped
- Needing some quiet time
- Being tired and needing to sleep.

When you are thinking what to do next, consider what you have tried previously in your baby's routine that has worked.

A newborn will wake for approximately 1 hour and sleep for 2-3 hours. In this wake time she needs feeding and time talking to or playing with you. Finally she needs some quiet time to wind down, ready for sleep.

A breastfed baby may be hungry every 2-3 hours, bottle fed babies every 3-4 hours. Newborns may have 6-8 wet nappies and she may soil her nappy 3-4 times per day. Whether you change your baby's nappy before or after a feed is your choice – there is no evidence to suggest that either way is better.

Some babies swallow air when they feed which can cause discomfort. This is often helped by supporting them in an upright position. Sitting on your knee or leaning over your shoulder may help.

Many babies like the feeling of security by being wrapped. Babies have a reflex called the 'Moro reflex'. A sudden noise or movement can cause them to throw their arms out in fright or waken, then cry. Wrapping reduces this effect.

Your baby may like to suck between feeds. A common cause of crying is that the dummy/pacifier has fallen out of her mouth during sleep. When she returns to a light sleep she will want to suck again.

In the hotter part of the year, or if your infant is overdressed, she may easily become overheated. Using a light cotton wrap will help prevent overheating. No other bedding may by necessary. Dress your baby according to the weather – she will need to be dressed similarly to you.

In cooler weather, a cotton sheet or blanket may be needed and can be used to tuck your baby in. Once she becomes more mobile, at about 4-5 months, she may no longer like to be wrapped.

If you have tried all of the above and you still cannot settle her and feel frustrated or that you may harm her, put her safely in her cot. Phone your partner, a friend, another family member or a helpline and ask for help.

Information supplied by Karitane, www.karitane.com.au.

Toilet training a young child

Many parents feel anxious about toilet training. This can be heightened by a wish to have the child using the toilet by a specific date, such as before the start of 3-year-old kindergarten, or before another child joins the family, thinking it will lessen the workload. Unfortunately child development doesn't occur according to dates. Neither does development occur consistently. Children appear to learn skills one day and then don't seem to have retained them the next. New skills need to be learned and re-learned. Toilet training is no different. There will be steps forward and steps backward.

Most children are not ready to control their bowel and bladder until they are at least two years old, although some are older than 3 years, and boys are often later than girls. Before the child is ready to use the toilet or potty they need to be able to hold urine in their bladder for an hour or so, such as waking up from a nap dry. The child needs to be able to say when he or she is doing a wee or poo so that they can start to identify what their body feels like before they need to wee or poo. They also need to be interested in using the toilet and being independent.

Parents can feel frustrated, as though they've failed or are "bad" parents, when a child seems to be late in toilet training. In fact, a child's readiness to toilet train has little to do with parenting style and more to do with the child's physical development and their emotional readiness. It is not about the parent. It is about the child and his or her overall development. Many frustrations with toilet training can be avoided by waiting until the child is ready to use the toilet.

Once the child has learned to control bowel and bladder, the only person who can put their poos and wees in the toilet, is the child. This might seem a little obvious, but many parents get into battles with their children over where they put their poos and wees. There is not a lot of point to this. Parents do not and will never have control over this. It is a battle that no one wins, *so don't go into battle*! When it is important to the child, it will happen. The most important message for parents is *relax*. It will happen. Think about how to do it in a way that is easier for you. Some hints to try are:

- Consider staying home more for a few weeks, so your child is always near a potty or toilet
- Start toilet training at a time of little stress
- When you do go out, pack a change of undies, pants, socks, shoes and damp face washer
- Look for the positives. The words "uh-oh" and the look of dismay on your child's face can be cute; it tells you he wants to learn this skill
- Celebrate your child's achievements.

Above all, look after yourself. If you need to unload or check out what you're doing, find someone to talk with – but choose carefully. Those who say their children were trained at 14 months of age aren't particularly helpful – their children were timed to go to the toilet, not trained. Talk to people you trust, or you can discuss this issue further with your maternal and child health nurse or a counsellor at Parentline.

Written by Bronwyn Thomas, a social worker with more than 20 years experience working with families over parenting issues. She works as a counsellor at Parentline. Parentline is a confidential telephone counselling, information and referral service for all Victorian parents and carers with children aged from birth to 18 years. Parentline is accessible from anywhere in Victoria for the cost of a local call (excluding mobiles). Phone 13 22 89.

Second time around ...

When I discovered I was pregnant with my first child, I had weed on one of those pregnancy tests. It was the cheap, stick sort, and after the first hours of euphoria shared with my husband, followed by a candle-lit celebration dinner that night, I went out and bought a scrapbook and lovingly stuck that test on the first page. From then on, every milestone would be recorded – the first foetal flutterings, the drama of the birth, the first steps.

The next time I discovered I was pregnant I left the test in some urine for the requisite five minutes. My three-year-old son chose that moment to drop his porridge on the floor and then the washing machine started leaking, so we fled to a friend's house to spend the morning.

Hours later, I found the little stick in wee. I think after leaving it that long, even a man could get a positive pregnancy test but it turned out to be accurate – I was pregnant.

In my first pregnancy, my husband would sit with his hands on my belly, waiting with breath held to feel the wondrous, early movements. He would sing to the foetus, read it stories through my tummy and tell it jokes. This pregnancy, if he's not working, he's getting up at 6.00am with the three-year-old to give me a break, or he's doing dinner or bathtime. The other night in bed I grabbed his hand and said "There! It's kicking! Can you feel it?" We waited together for a few minutes, until there was a gentle snore. "That's your Dad," I told number two.

In my first pregnancy I took pictures of myself naked every month. Here's me with the first trace of a belly, here's me on the beach in a bikini with a slightly bigger belly, and here's me with a real belly at 8.5 months, trying to do a Demi Moore.

This pregnancy has so far, and will continue I suspect, gone undocumented by photos. There's too much else to do – who the hell did I lend the bassinet to, and I must get my son some dolls for his nurturing side, and today there's playgroup, and tomorrow we need to check out a kindy and there's a meal to cook and a train to push and a story to read.

In my first pregnancy I worried. When I bumped my tummy into the sharp edge of a railing, I went straight to hospital to be monitored. Was it normal to stop feeling sick? Had the movements slowed? In this pregnancy I still worry, but about things such as, is my son safe on that trike? Is he doing too much childcare? Is there any educational value in The Simpsons, or am I just kidding myself?

So, it's different the second time around. But somewhere in my desk drawers there's a yellowing pregnancy test with two pink stripes on it, rolling around under the pencils and the paper clips. And I know one day I'll get around to buying a scrapbook and sticking it in for number two. Or maybe I could just write him a note: "Dear two, try the desk drawer ..."

Written by Fran Cusworth, a mother of two & author of *The Love Child* and *Boomtown Wives*.

What to do if your child has a night terror

Night terrors are characterised by intense screaming and/or sobbing while a person is asleep. The affected person is often flailing about and seems absolutely terrified. Many sufferers truly feel as if they are seeing something in their room which is not actually there. Common sights include monsters, ghosts, snakes, spiders, intruders and fire.

Night terrors differ from nightmares in a number of ways and are less common. Where nightmares usually occur in the early hours of the morning when children have been asleep for a while, night terrors are more likely to happen in the first two to three hours of sleep. They also manifest very differently.

Children who have nightmares will wake up distressed, often crying or screaming but they will usually remember much of what the dream that woke them was about. Those who have night terrors are not actually fully awake during the experience – they are stuck between slow-wave sleep (slow-wave sleep is the deepest stage of sleep where there is a lack of eye-movement, a decreased body temperature and during which involuntary body movements occur) and wakefulness.

For this reason they often appear disoriented and unable to recognise people or their surroundings. They wake up screaming, panicked and sometimes sweating but the following morning most of them won't remember the occurrence at all. A night terror can last anywhere from five to twenty minutes.

Research shows that night terrors are not generally caused by psychiatric disorders or trauma, whereas many children experience nightmares following a particularly stressful event in their life (e.g. parents' divorce, death of a loved one). However, as with nightmares, night terrors can be very disturbing and physically exhausting for all members of the family.

How you can handle night terrors

The natural instinct is often to try to wake your child and thus alleviate the distress, but this may actually make things worse. However you do need to make sure they are not in danger of harming themselves by keeping the house as clutter free as possible, sleeping children on the ground floor, and locking doors and windows. While they are having an episode, you may gently restrain them.

Although night terrors can be unpredictable, there are a number of strategies that may help sufferers. Keeping to a strict bedtime routine and ensuring children do not get overtired or overheated may help. In extreme cases when the night terror occurs at exactly the same time each night, some parents have found waking the child up prior to this time stops the episode. Such action is generally only needed for a few nights before the terrors cease.

For the majority of children professional treatment is not necessary and most of them will grow out of the terrors in time. However, if night terrors continue over a prolonged period, it is advisable to seek medical advice to rule out other conditions that may be contributing to the episodes.

Case study: Nerelle and her daughter Alesha

"Alesha's first night terror occurred Christmas Eve last year when we were staying with my parents. She was 34 months old. During the night she woke up screaming; she proceeded to get out of bed and walk around aggressively screaming. This continued for around 2 to 3 hours in varying degrees of intensity. I offered her a drink as it was an unusually hot night and said that she could sleep with Daddy and I would sleep in her bed – however I couldn't seem to reason or communicate with her. I tried several times to re-settle her. She was thrashing around uncontrollably in her bed and would then get up and start wandering around. My mum got up and tried everything to no avail. We just followed her around getting more frustrated. Eventually, she took herself back to bed and settled. Christmas morning she awoke as though nothing had happened. None the wiser at this stage, I put it down to just a one-off bad night in a hot, different environment.

New Years Eve back at home we had a small group of friends over for a BBQ. After an hour in bed, Alesha awoke hysterically screaming; she was inconsolable. This continued for a length of time with her thrashing around in her bed – again I couldn't seem to reason, communicate with her or settle her. Our friends decided to go home. I was discussing it with one of them days later and I told her about Christmas Eve – she raised the idea of night terrors. It got me thinking and then I realised that might be why I couldn't communicate with her as she wasn't actually awake.

Sometimes she'd remain in her bed, other times she would get out. This continued for a month nearly every night. In the morning she seemed totally oblivious to it. I grew tired and frustrated. We had to get up to ensure her safety, however we were helpless and had to just let it take its course. Eventually she'd settle herself down.

I have no idea what instigated it. It just came out of the blue and I didn't even realise the first few times what was happening. It was hard to take as she had been a good sleeper, and I found myself over-tired, inpatient and frustrated. It was very disturbing to the whole family's sleep pattern. The crying and screaming was so loud and hysterical you couldn't sleep through it, and because she often got out of bed, we had to get up to ensure her safety.

We still have a few minor episodes which seem to occur if she becomes overtired. They are nowhere near as bad as before and I use them like a reminder to me that she needs to get more sleep or it could get worse again."

Written by Rachael Blair, freelance writer.

Vox Pop

We asked a number of women and men around Australia to send in their advice, tips and personal experiences on a range of topics so that you have an insight into how others cope being a new parent. We hope you find their comments interesting, informative and reassuring. Vox Pop biographies: page 652

Andrew Weldon
Dad of one, Melbourne

I entered fatherhood terrified of the poo. I found the whole thing filthy, repulsive. It seemed so odd to me – my own parents trained me carefully to think of excrement as something to scrupulously avoid, a rule that had served me well for 37 years. And yet here I was, suddenly being told by midwives, nurses, and in fact MY OWN MOTHER, to just dive into the stuff with both hands. I knew I had to conquer this repulsion, and that the only way to do this was by desensitising myself. I forced myself to change as many brown explosions as I was available to, however hard I found it. Just focus on the love, I told myself, focus on the love. Slowly I'm getting there – I gag less, I only wash my hands once afterwards. And my baby is helping by getting less explosive, god bless her. This new-found confidence feels like a significant achievement to me, one of the great milestones of parenting – I've mastered the poo. The Poo Master. It holds no fear for me now. Ha!

Amanda Jephtha
Mum of one, Sydney

Both cloth and disposable nappies vary greatly in both quality and price. While the more expensive nappies are generally better quality, every little bum is shaped differently, so the same nappy may work on one bum, but leak on another!

Trial and error is the easiest way to determine which is best for you and your baby. If you are unhappy with one brand, either buy a small packet in another brand, or swap a few nappies with another mum who uses a different brand – this way you both get to try without committing yourself to an entire packet of potential duds!

At bathtime babies thrive with body contact. The bath is the perfect opportunity to have this, and is a lovely way to unwind at the end of the day, for both you and your baby. Make sure the towel, nappy, pyjamas and cot/bassinet are ready prior to jumping in the bath, so you don't have to leave your baby unattended, and so your baby doesn't get cold waiting. Better still, have someone else prepare the paraphernalia while you enjoy the bath!

To take the edge away from your baby's cold sheets, slip a hot water bottle filled with warm water between the sheets 10 minutes before placing your baby in – remember, not too hot.

Bernadette Vella
Mum of two, Brisbane

I have been a disposable nappy fan from day one and I tend to buy them in bulk when they are on special (I have been known to buy 15 boxes at one time!). With Tiernan I was constantly being peed on when I took off his nappy. I am sure he knew what he was doing and secretly enjoyed making a mess of me. I used to change him just before leaving the house and often ended up having to get changed myself afterwards.

Ros Pittard
Mum of two, VIC

We ended up using cloth nappies for our second baby. I tried a few different sorts with number one, but didn't make a real commitment to it. Modern cloth nappies are very easy to use, just like a disposable in fact. It's an expensive outlay initially, but definitely saves you money in the long run. It is another load of washing to have to deal with, but I like not filling up the bin every week with soiled nappies. There are lots of online nappy shops to browse through and get information about modern cloth nappies and I highly recommend it. You can even buy the materials to make your own. We don't use wipes on our baby's bottom very often – a squirt of sorbelene on a tissue or two works really well to clean a little bottom, and our boys have rarely had nappy rash.

Anna Ngo
Mum of one, Perth

As a family we're a big supporter of disposable nappies. For sheer convenience alone they are worth their weight in gold.

A part of me knows that I'm just choosing the easier option but the thought of having to clean and wash every dirty nappy, which can be between 7 and 10 a day, is not a great thought.

So disposables for me are a great time saver, and I'm comforted in knowing that I don't have to carry around a great big bag of dirty nappies when I'm travelling.

Andrea Tulloch
Mum of one, NSW

We are located on a farm so the choice of nappies is really important. We do not have weekly rubbish collection and prior to the arrival of my son we would only go to the tip on an irregular basis to deliver recyclable items and other waste. All compostable items are separated out of the rubbish. So using disposable nappies and the action of disposing them became an issue.

I have been using a combination of cloth nappies during the day with a disposable nappy at night. Then disposing of the disposable happens with a weekly or fortnightly trip to the tip. This has been effective until our water tanks were getting low.

All of the additional washing as well as extra loads of cloth nappies adds up very quickly to high water usage. Thank goodness we have just had rain and while Hugh is in nappies I hope it continues to rain.

Fortunately there are new more environmental products being developed all the time but I suppose it is really important to find the right products for the right situations.

Katherine Twigg
Mum of one, VIC

When out and about, particularly in the younger months, it is a good idea to take with you a few nappies and a clean outfit for them to wear as well. Often when I was out and about with my son he dirtied his nappy and 8 out of 10 times it would escape the nappy and go all over his romper suit!

It is best to take more than just one spare nappy as well because a couple of times when we were changing my son's nappy he decided that he had more to come just as were halfway through changing him. Once we went through 4 nappies during one change!

My son loves his bath time; we give him his bath and massage just before his dinner then it's straight to bed. He then sleeps from 5.00pm till 7.30am (with a 10.00pm feed in there as well). His bath relaxes him for sleep and he associates his bath now with bedtime which makes putting him to bed a breeze!

Louise Cruz
Mum of three, NSW

As a mother of 2 children I have had some experience with the challenging world of nappies! First there is the decision between cloth and disposable or a combination of the two. My mum told me that I would need 4 dozen cloth nappies to get me through and to use disposables only when going out.

But as I was living in an apartment with no clothes line at the time it was a logistical nightmare and it would have meant that I would be constantly running my clothes dryer. So I relented to the modern way and went with the disposable option. There are many brands on the market at varying prices and through much trial and error I came to discover that some brands, although cheaper, did not provide the same absorbency or leak protection. I

Vox Pop

We asked a number of women and men around Australia to send in their advice, tips and personal experiences on a range of topics so that you have an insight into how others cope being a new parent. We hope you find their comments interesting, informative and reassuring. Vox Pop biographies: page 652

have now used one brand for all three of my kids for long periods (such as overnight sleeps or long car trips) as they provide a very good level of absorbency and I find that the leak guards are most effective.

One piece of advice I can offer is to always put a fresh nappy on your baby before sleep time as they can feel and look dry but still have some wee stored away, and it's amazing just how much a little one can do in their sleep!

Anna Brandt
Mum of one, QLD

We have given our baby nappy-free time since day one and I always find it hilarious when my husband bends down to kiss or blow raspberries on our baby and he gets piddled on. It's so funny! I'll say to my husband "you're leaving yourself wide open to get piddled on there" and within me finishing my sentence, sure enough, he's got wee on his face. As I write this my husband is holding my naked baby and has just been piddled on.

Jess Tamblyn
Mum of one, SA

I've tried most disposable nappies, seeking to find the one that is the best value for money. It does seem to be the case that you do get what you pay for with the more expensive nappies being more effective. I buy the more expensive nappies when they are on special and use them just at night as their increased absorption capacity means I don't have to change them during the night. I then use cheaper nappies during the day and find even some of the cheapest are fine as you tend to change them more regularly during the day anyway.

Always keep a look out for specials in catalogues and often buying in bulk is another great way to save money.

Danielle Murrihy
Mum of two, Melbourne

I originally wanted to try cloth nappies, but I was talked out of it by well meaning friends and family. I wish I had stuck to my guns and used cloth along with disposable nappies. I would have saved money as well as less impact on the environment. Night times we use good quality disposables as they have the best leak proofing.

Bathtimes were a big operation when they were newborns and I bathed them once or twice a week. They were winter babies so it was cold and it was awkward trying to do two babies without another set of hands. Once we moved from a baby bath to the big bath things actually got a little easier as the boys were stronger and enjoyed the water. I would fill the bath fairly deep so that they could float in the water with my hand under their neck and shoulders while the other baby was in a rocker.

When they were around 5 months of age we started running the water a lot shallower and let both boys lie on their backs at the same time in the bath. Then we got game and popped them on their tummies. They loved this! Both would face each other in the bath on their tummies and splash and laugh with each other. When they were finally sitting up I went back to one at a time as it got too dangerous with both in the bath. We started showering them at around a year– they would sit in the bottom of the shower with the water coming down onto them and they loved this as well!

Anastasia Jones
Mum of two, Melbourne

We are really lucky in Australia to have nappies designed for boys and for girls. I actually shipped about 7 boxes of disposable nappies when we moved to Hong Kong for 18 months because the nappies there are notoriously poor in comparison.

I kept my Australian brand for night and used local nappies for the day. Well, when my second baby came along I didn't have any stock of the Aussie brand left and so used the local brand like everyone else. When she was about 6 weeks old I put her in a baby sling to go to the supermarket and was at the checkout when she started squirming and crying. The supermarket has a baby change and feeding room so I went in to change her nappy – and realised that she had done a massive poo. It then went all over my top, all over her jumpsuit and up her tummy. I didn't know what to do as I didn't have a change of clothes for her (we were only going to be gone an hour). I had to strip her down and carry her home naked, except for the clean nappy.

Tracey Thompson
Mum of one, Brisbane

My little guy has very little problems with nappy rash or other skin ailments. My mother told me that to help stop nappy rash let your child have 'naked time' every day if possible. It has proved to be a great piece of advice. Every day after breakfast I go out onto my balcony with my baby and we lie on a towel (out of direct sunlight) and I give him about 15 minutes out of his nappy to air his little bottom. He loves this time and just rolls around kicking his little legs with glee while smiling at me. I hope that little piece of advice my mother passed on to me will help some of you out there too!

Christine Walsh
Mum of two, Broome

I have used fitted cloth nappies with both my children since they were about 8 weeks old. They are a fitted nappy that lasts from birth until toilet training. They require a cover that does need replacing when your child grows out of them. They come in cute designs which I find great as my son (15 months) generally just wears a shirt

with his nappy. I quite often get comments about his nappy covers. I have also recently bought another type of cloth nappy called an AIO (All in One) where you do not need a separate cover. I have managed to convince a couple of my friends to start using modern cloth nappies. It is not a difficult process and the nappies still look new even after years of use. I have to admit I still love looking at cloth nappy websites though really have no need to buy anymore! I do use a disposable at night and when travelling as it does make life easier.

A great bathtime and water saving tip: you can dust the cobwebs off your baby bath when your baby can sit up on his or her own. Just place the bathtub in the shower when you are having a shower and place your child in the bathtub. Splash splash!

Kirstin Amos
Mum of one, QLD

When we started getting ready for the birth of our son, there was debate with family and friends in relation to cloth or disposable nappies. We did both for the first three or 4 four months. When I was at home during the day I used cloth nappies and at night and when we went out we used good quality disposables. There was only one time that I ever really got caught while I was out and about with Carter. He had just finished his lunch and was smiling just before a bit of wind and then absolutely filled his nappy! The smell was out of this world and we were right in the middle of Myer trying to get to the baby change room, but I have to say his dispoable nappy held up very well!

Bathtime was always a fun and relaxing experience when Carter was younger. Now he is a little older and starting to stand on his own, it makes it a little more stressful because I don't want him to slip and hurt himself. Bathtime has become part of the bedtime routine: warm bath, gentle massage while dressing for bed and then bed. This is the best routine as it makes bedtime so much easier.

Resources

These Resources pages list products and services relevant to "Nappies, bathtime & skincare".
To make your life easier as a parent, editorial listings have been grouped into sub categories.
Businesses then appear alphabetically under a national or a state-based subhead depending on reach.

SUB-CATEGORIES

BABY & INFANT MASSAGE

NATIONAL

**Australian International Association
of Infant Massage**
Tel: 0414 825 344
email: secretary@iaim.com.au
website: www.iaim.com.au

The purpose of the International Association of Infant Massage is to promote nurturing touch and communication through training, education and research, so that parents, caregivers and their children are loved, valued and respected throughout the world community. Infant massage is easy to learn and fun. Classes foster parental confidence and competence while teaching the basics of appropriate touch, listening and responding to baby. IAIM instructors teach classes in a series of sessions usually over 4 to 5 weeks. Classes are designed for you with your pre-crawling baby. Their hands-on method ensures that you will learn the interactive massage to suit your baby's individual schedule, needs and developmental level. Private lessons and education in-services for groups are also available.

Infant Massage Australia
Tel: 0409 515 097
email: enquiries@infantmassage.org.au
website: www.infantmassage.org.au

The benefits of infant massage have been enjoyed in other cultures for centuries and now Australian parents can learn the techniques to help their babies make the most of the miracle of touch. More information on parent baby bonding and other benefits can be found on the website. Infant massage must be experienced to fully appreciate the benefits for parent and baby. To locate an instructor near you visit www.infantmassage.org.au.

Infant Massage Information Service
Tel: 1300 137 551
website: www.infantmassage-imis.com.au

The Infant Massage Information Service provides professional training for parents and professionals with the most recent information on research and effective techniques. They have a range of services and products available including a referral listing for qualified instructors, certificate training programs, and operation of the baby massage warehouse to supply infant massage products for instructors and to the general public. Gift certificates and new-parent gifts are also available from the online shop.

Pinky McKay
Tel: (03) 9801 1997
website: www.beyondhomeentertainment.com.au or
www.pinkymckay.com.au

Baby massage is proven to help your baby be smarter, happier and to sleep better. Certified Infant Massage Instructor, Internationally Certified Lactation Consultant (IBCLC), mother of five and respected baby care author, Pinky McKay will show you how to calm and connect with your baby as you follow her simple step-by-step instructions. This DVD covers the complete baby massage, mini massage, safety issues and much more. Presented by Pinky McKay, author of *Sleeping like a Baby*, *100 Ways to Calm the Crying*, and *Toddler Tactics*. For more details visit www.beyondhomeentertainment.com.au or www.pinkymckay.com.au.

VICTORIA

Baby Massage Melbourne
Tel: 0415 961 662
email: info@babymassagemelbourne.com.au
website: www.babymassagemelbourne.com.au

Baby massage courses can be run from your home, health care centre, kindergarten, gymbaroo, mother's group, or any site of your choice at a time of your choosing. Vicky holds classes on a regular basis in Prahran or she can come to you anywhere in Melbourne. Gift vouchers available.

Marcelle Oppermann
Tooronga Road
Malvern East VIC 3145
Tel: 0432 856 532
email: massagetherapy@marcelleoppermann.com
website: www.marcelleoppermann.com

Marcelle Oppermann offers infant massage classes – here you will learn a safe and effective baby massage that will provide you with a loving time of affection, enhancing bonding, improving motor co-ordination, irritability and easing colic and reflux in your baby. Suitable for premmies and special needs babies too. Member of AAMT & IMA.

Mother's Touch Baby Massage Classes
2/15 Vicki Street
Blackburn South VIC 3130
Tel: 0411 275 126
email: info@motherstouch.com.au
website: www.motherstouch.com.au

Mother's Touch baby massage classes are a great way for you to learn correct massage techniques for your baby through fun, hands-on massage classes. Baby massage helps to increase the bonding between parents and baby, improve baby's sleep, assist in pain relief, enhance the baby's development and helps with baby's body awareness. The classes are run in groups or individually in the comfort of your own home. It is a great activity to do with your mothers' group or a group of friends with babies.

Pinky McKay
Tel: (03) 9801 1997
website: www.pinkymckay.com.au

Pinky McKay teaches infant massage classes at Knox Private Hospital, offering Friday evening classes for couples as well as private sessions in your home. She will teach you how to give your baby a full body massage as well as specific strokes to help with difficulties such as colic and constipation. There is an emphasis on infant communication to help you develop confidence in your ability to interpret your baby's unique cues and discussion time at each class includes natural ways to encourage sleep and settling, how to incorporate massage in your daily routine, stress management for parents and how to continue massage as your baby becomes mobile.

Tracey Gibney
Tel: 0409 130 796
email: traceygibney@yahoo.com.au

Baby massage helps your baby to sleep better and be more sociable and settled. Infant massage also provides parents with the opportunity to interact with their baby in a unique way. Instruction is available as either a group session offered over four weeks or one-on-one sessions in your own home. As well as hands-on practice, other topics covered include infant communication and appropriate music. Easy to follow instructions provided.

Yoga Concepts
Level 1/458 Bridge Road
Richmond VIC 3121
Tel: (03) 9429 8697 or 0412 183 379
email: info@yogaconcepts.com.au
website: www.yogaconcepts.com.au

Yoga Concepts Wellness Centre in Richmond offers dynamic programs to assist with your daily life. With a family focus they have highly skilled and accredited teachers offering pre and postnatal yoga, mother and baby yoga, baby massage, prenatal massage, general relaxation massage, kids yoga, kids creative movement, pilates and parenting seminars along with general yoga, pilates and meditation classes and workshops. Phone the

NEW SOUTH WALES

Luv-Bub Baby Massage and Successful Parenting
PO Box 392
Balmain East NSW 2041
Tel: 0438 648 465
website: www.luvbub.com.au

Moira is a qualified midwife and neonatal specialist with over 20 years experience, as well as a certified infant massage instructor. A Luv-Bub baby massage course is a fantastic way to enhance bonding, loving, communication, and is relaxing for you and your baby. Baby massage is easy to learn and a great place to meet other mum's in a caring and supportive environment. Join a group or arrange a personal home visit. Baby workshops for mothers, and mothers and fathers group sessions are available Sydney wide and nationally upon request.

Resources

NAPPIES, BATHTIME & SKINCARE

Baby & infant massage ➔ Baby wipes

WESTERN AUSTRALIA

Eve Naturopathy & Massage
West Leederville
Tel: 0409 102 238
email: eve4health@yahoo.com.au

Kate Krasenstein has been a massage therapist for 11 years and a naturopath and aromatherapist for 9. She is the state representative for Infant Massage Australia and teaches the art of baby massage in individual or group class settings. Phone the number above or email for further information.

Idibidi Kids Massage
PO Box 251
Joondalup WA 6919
Tel: 0411 615 641
email: natalie@idibidikids.com.au
website: www.kidsmassage.com.au

Idibidi Kids Massage offers courses and workshops to parents and carers on how to massage their child, specialising in infant massage instruction. Infant massage has many researched benefits including assisting babies with colic, reflux, sleep problems, parents with postnatal depression and low birth weight babies. It has also shown to strengthen babies immune systems and promote relaxation. Idibidi Kids Massage covers the Perth metro area, seven days a week. View the website for further details and to enrol in a course.

BABY SKINCARE PRODUCTS

NATIONAL

Aromababy Natural Skincare
Tel: (03) 9464 0888
email: info@aromababy.com
website: www.aromababy.com

Aromababy Natural Skincare offers a specialised range of unique, organic-rich products for mum and baby including aroma-free (no essential oils) and sensitive skin products. The eczema-friendly range boasts a long history of safety and efficacy spanning 12 years including in select hospitals. Aromababy products are free from sulphates, cocoamphodiacetate, mineral oil, propylene glycol, talc, and more. Ask for it by name at your local pharmacy, baby boutique, organic store or visit online at www.aromababy.com.

Belli Skin Care Australia
Tel: 1300 884 916
email: sales@hotmama.com.au
website: www.belliskincare.com.au

Belli Baby offers the purest and mildest ingredients that nourish and protect delicate skin. Gentle oils and luxurious scents help create beautiful bonding moments during baby's bath time. Every product is allergy tested and free of artificial dyes, petroleum, mineral oil, sulfates, and parabens. Visit www.belliskincare.com.au for more information.

Caring by Nature Pty Ltd
Tel: (03) 9711 5647
email: admin@caringbynature.com
website: www.caringbynature.com

The popular Caring By Nature range consists of 5 luxurious 100% natural and organic baby skincare products. The range brings an holistic approach to baby care by taking the natural healing and soothing properties of Mother Nature and creating a specially formulated range for babies and the whole family. There are no harsh chemicals, no nut-based oils, parabens, petroleums, soaps or sulphates – instead they are sourced from the finest organic, plant derived materials. Every bottle sold comes with a 100% money-back guarantee. Contact Caring by Nature direct for a free infant massage poster and booklet and a free meditation CD for mums. Phone the number above or visit the website for further information.

GAIA Natural Baby
Tel: (03) 9703 1707
email: info@gaiaskinnaturals.com
website: www.gaiaskinnaturals.com

GAIA Natural Baby was created in 2002 by a mum for her own baby who suffered from sensitive skin and eczema. Skin-softening cleansers, moisturisers and soothing lotions make up the GAIA range and all products are free from soap, sulphates, mineral oils, petrochemicals, parabens, propylene glycol and artificial fragrance making them suitable for sensitive skin and eczema-friendly. Made from natural and certified organic ingredients, GAIA Natural Baby provides you with the purest products to gently care for your child's skin every day. Available from Woolworths/Safeway, Coles, Priceline, Big W, Target, Kmart, independent groceries, Terry White, Chemmart Chemists as well as other selected pharmacies, health food, baby stores and online (not all products available in all stores). For stockists, special offers and your chance to win prizes go to www.gaiaskinnaturals.com.

googoo
Tel: 0423 987 667
email: info@googoo.com.au
website: www.googoo.com.au

googoo sells a unique range of skin and hair care products for children. Made to order products of outstanding quality that feel great, look great and best of all smell great. With customisable organic and fusion ranges there is bound to be one of the thousands of combinations to suit your child. Visit the website for further information.

inessence Organics
Tel: 0438 252 952
email: info@inessence-organics.com
website: www.inessence-organics.com

The miessence® certified organic baby range is a new collection of nurturing products gentle enough for newborn babies. Give your baby the purest start to life. Choose from six skin and bath products for baby as well as some for mum. Order online from this secure website with free shipping on orders over $100. All orders delivered conveniently and carbon neutrally to your door.

miniOrganics
Tel: (02) 9967 0966
email: info@miniorganics.com
website: www.miniorganics.com

miniOrganics is a new skincare range for children and new mothers that has one concern at heart – creating pure, natural, and organic skincare. miniOrganic's entire range is certified under one of the most comprehensive cosmetic standards worldwide. Every product is made from a unique Australian high content organic formulation. The pack includes everything a mother will need for her infant: Superfine Jojoba, Gentle Baby Wash and Baby Washer (rrp $79.95).

Perfect Potion
Tel: 1800 988 999
email: customerservice@perfectpotion.com.au
website: www.perfectpotion.com.au

Perfect Potion provides you with certified natural and certified organic products including a large range of pure, natural and safe skincare and bodycare products for mums during pregnancy and for newborn babies. The Beautiful Baby range is made with the purest essential oils and gentle plant extracts to caress, soothe and pamper your baby's every need. Using Perfect Potion's aromatherapy products during the birthing process is a wonderful way to create a calming atmosphere that comforts and nurtures new mothers, helping to ease pain, maintain focus and sustain motivation.

Persé
Tel: (03) 9818 8700
email: info@perse.com.au
website: www.perse.com.au

Persé has evolved in response to the growing demand for everyday products derived wholly from pure natural ingredients. They create and make their own products and make it easy to find 100% natural essentials for your entire family. Persé baby products are made with Lavender and Roman Chamomile and include Baby Bath & Massage Oil, Organic Baby Wash and Organic Nappy Cream. Persé Kids products include Organic Shampoo, Organic Conditioner and Organic Body Wash and are made with Lavender and Tea Tree.

Philips AVENT
Tel: 1300 364 474
email: inquiry@avent.com.au
website: www.avent.com.au

The Philips Avent range includes a complete, integrated range of baby care items including: health and monitoring, breast care, feeding equipment, non-spill cups, mother and baby skincare products and baby bags. Philips Avent feeding products are anti-colic and shaped closely to emulate the mother's natural shape. The non-spill Magic Cups have an easy sip spout, detachable handles and a snap-on lid for travel.

Pure Spa®
Tel: (03) 9464 0888
email: info@purespa.com.au
website: www.purespa.com.au

Pure Spa® offers pure and natural, organic-rich products formulated by a leading Melbourne natural therapist. Up to 99% certified organic ingredients have been combined to provide the purest solution to all your and your baby's skincare needs. Used in select hospitals, naturally Pure Spa® is free from mineral oil, cocoamphodiacetate, parabens and sulphate. Eczema-friendly and suitable for sensitive skin, Pure Spa offers a specialist product that won't cost the earth. Go ahead and pamper yourself. Pure ingredients, pure products, pure indulgence … you'll find it all at Pure Spa®, www.purespa.com.au or from select baby boutiques, pharmacies and online stores.

BABY WIPES

NATIONAL

Church & Dwight (Australia) Pty Ltd
Tel: 1800 222 099
email: enquiries@churchdwight.com.au
website: www.curash.com.au & www.churchdwight.com.au

Curash Baby Wipes are soap free, alcohol free and pH balanced. They have been specifically designed for baby's delicate skin. They are soft, super thick and come in re-sealable clip packs. Curash Baby Care Wipes include Fragrance Free Wipes perfect for newborns with ultra sensitive skin and they come in 80s or convenient travel packs of 20. The range also includes Moisturising Wipes 80s with added Vitamin E and Sorboline to help moisturise baby's skin (and also subtly fragranced) and Regular Lightly Fragranced/Soap Free 80s, subtly fragranced to keep baby smelling fresh. Phone the number above or visit the website for further information.

Resources

NAPPIES, BATHTIME & SKINCARE

Baby wipes ➡ Baby wraps & comforters

Kazoku Kids
Tel: (08) 9470 2851
email: info@kazokukids.com.au
website: www.kazokukids.com.au

Teeny Towels are antibacterial wipes that fit on a keychain. Teeny Towels Antibacterial & Insect Repellent Wipes protect children from germs and bacteria. The all-natural 'teeny' size, portable plastic key chain holders come with refill packs that loop anywhere. Repellent are all-natural, DEET free. Teeny Pads are the only portable changing pad that comes in its own carry case. Water proof outside and soft flannel inside that's completely washable it attaches to a nappy bag with a snap ring. Visit www.kazokukids.com.au or phone (08) 9470 2851 for a free brochure or to find a store near you.

Kimberly-Clark Australia – Huggies Wipes
Tel: 1800 028 334
email: via website
website: www.huggies.com.au

Huggies® Baby Wipes are thick and especially soft and gently clean and moisturise baby's skin with a hypoallergenic formula of natural ingredients such as aloe vera and Vitamin E. All Huggies® Baby Wipes are pH balanced, dermatologically tested and free of soap and alcohol so are safe to use on baby's face, hands and bottoms. The unique texture and unbeatable thickness of Huggies® Baby Wipes means they gently get more off with each wipe, providing a quicker nappy change for baby. Huggies® Baby Wipes have a product suitable for every baby – Fragrance Free, Lightly Fragranced and Newborn and Sensitive which are clinically proven safe for newborn and sensitive skin. Huggies® Baby Wipes also come in a range of convenient pack sizes including refills, handy travel packs and Pop-Up tubs that allow for easy one hand use. Phone the number above or visit the website for further information.

Nice-Pak Products
Tel: 1800 506 750
email: info@nicepak.com.au
website: www.pudgies.com.au

Pudgies® Fragrance Free Baby Wipes are sulphate and petrol-chemical free, helping to protect your baby's delicate skin from coming into contact with irritants that may cause nappy rash and other skin complaints. Each premium quality, thick baby wipe is alcohol-free, hypoallergenic, non-chlorine bleached and contains no latex or glue in the manufacturing of the wipe. They come in a convenient soft pack of 80 with a snap-close lid to ensure they won't dry out and a handy travel 20 pack. Available in Kmart, Franklins, selected department, baby stores and pharmacies. Phone 1800 506 750 or visit www.pudgies.com.au for further information.

Nice-Pak Products
Tel: 1800 506 750
email: info@nicepak.com.au
website: www.thewiggles.com

These flushable Wiggles Toddler Wipes are soft, strong and ideal for encouraging children with toilet training and general clean-up. Sixty fruity fragranced wipes come with a resealable flip top lid making toilet training fun and easy. Dermatologically tested, biodegradable and alcohol free makes them safe enough to use on delicate skin. The Wiggles Toddler Wipes are great for on-the-go, at home, or at day care. Available in grocery, department stores and selected pharmacies. For further information contact the Consumer Information Line on 1800 506 750 or visit the website at www.thewiggles.com.

Nice-Pak Products
Tel: 1800 506 750
email: info@nicepak.com.au
website: www.thewiggles.com

The Wiggles Baby Wipes are enriched with soothing aloe vera and a mild cleansing formula to help care for your baby's soft skin. These fragrance free, hypo allergenic, and alcohol free wipes are perfect to use, from top to toe, on those wiggling bottoms at nappy change time. Available in an 80 pack or 240 value pack, the Wiggles Baby Wipes are great for on-the-go, at home or to take to day care. Available in the baby wipes aisle of your local store Big W, Kmart, Priceline, Franklins, IGA Supermarkets and selected pharmacies and baby stores. For further information contact the Consumer Information Line 1800 506 750 or visit the website www.thewiggles.com.

The Product Store Pty Ltd
Tel: (07) 3857 0691
email: info@theproductstore.com.au
website: www.theproductstore.com.au

If your child suffers from eczema, sensitive skin or nappy rash, Clearly Herbal baby wipes do not contain alcohol, lanolin or perfume that can irritate baby's skin. Each wipe is made from a superior quality spunlace cloth which is moistened with natural aloe vera, tea tree oil, green tea, and de-ionised water to cleanse and moisturise gently and naturally. With natural aromatherapy oils of Lavender and Chamomile, Clearly Herbal wipes help soothe more than just your baby's skin. For further information visit their website www.theproductstore.com.au or phone the number above for stockists.

BABY WRAPS & COMFORTERS

NATIONAL

Clever Babies (Kushies)
Tel: 1800 114 443
email: info@cleverbabies.com.au
website: www.cleverbabies.com.au

Snug As A Bug covers a range of quality, practical
Australian made products designed to make parenting a
little bit easier. The original mulit-purpose baby wrap
can be used in the car seat, pram or carry pouch and is
available in polar fleece and 100% cotton. The Comfort
Swaddle Wrap is ideal for settling unsettled babies.
Log onto www.cleverbabies.com.au or phone tollfree.

DownUnder Kids
Tel: 0407 639 113
email: sfick@downunderkids.com.au
website: www.downunderkids.com.au

DownUnder Kids brings you the AngelWrap, an easy-
to-use baby wrap that is less bulky and less restrictive on
baby's developing body without compromising security.
It provides a comfortable and uninterrupted sleep for
both baby and parent and is generously sized for
newborns through to older babies.

Fertile Mind
Tel: 1800 757 777
email: sales@fertilemind.com.au
website: www.fertilemind.com.au

Lalito's contoured shape is designed to stay wrapped.
Made from 100% breathable cotton and endorsed by the
Australian College of Midwives, it is available in white
with various trim colours. RRP $19.95.

KiwiGreen Pty Ltd
Tel: (08) 8272 9636
email: admin@kiwigreen.com.au
website: www.kiwigreen.com.au

KiwiGreen uses only high quality muslin and with two
layers in every wrap provides a soft and safe way to
wrap babies. Swaddling or wrapping is the
recommended way to settle babies as they associate
being wrapped with sleep therefore settling becomes a
lot easier. Muslin is an open weave 100% cotton cloth
which prevents your baby from over heating and makes
wrapping safe. The versatility of these cloths also means
you will use them as towels, sheets, shawls and much
more.

Miracle Blanket
Tel: 1300 886 470
email: info@miracleblanket.com.au
website: www.miracleblanket.com.au

The Miracle Blanket is an authentic 100% cotton
swaddle wrap that can solve all your swaddling
problems. Proper swaddling can increase babies' length
and quality of sleep and the Miracle Blanket is simple
and easy to use. Visit the website or phone for more
details.

Outlook Australia
Tel: (03) 9817 2311
email: outlooktm@bigpond.com
website: www.outlooktm.com

Made of 100% bamboo the Bamboo Baby® wrap fabric
has a natural stretch and generous 120cm x 120cm
proportion making it a wonderful wrap for swaddling
and settling baby. The Bamboo Baby® Wrap's benefits
include its natural antibacterial properties, ultra softness
and breathable quality. Discover the softness of Bamboo
Baby's® full range including baby towelling, wraps,
cot/bassinet blankets and sheet sets all made from 100%
bamboo.

Safe T Sleep International
Tel: +64 9 299 7589 or +64 21 73 6645
email: office@safetsleep.com
website: www.safetsleep.com

Invented by a mother, the Safe T Sleep
Sleepwrap® has become hugely popular
among parents and caregivers who want
to keep their baby in a safe, secure back
or side sleeping position. The Sleepwrap®
is a versatile, snug swaddling wrap,
allowing comfortable, natural movement for newborn
to three years plus. Comfort and security to help keep
baby's face and head uncovered and safely off the
tummy while alternate positioning also helps ensure a
nice head shape. The Sleepwraps have been widely
tested by health professionals, caregivers and have been
subject to hospital clinical trials. Safe T Sleep
Sleepwrap®'s offer convenience as well as safety, as they
fold down small enough to fit into a bag or glovebox
and can be used as an alternative to a portable cot.
Designed for everything from moses baskets, bassinets
and cradles to cots, single, king single, double, queen
and king size beds, boats and couch squabs. For those
babies who sleep extensively on their back Safe T Sleep
has also developed a little Headwedge – 100% cotton
cover over a triangle foam strip. Used best in
conjunction with a Safe T Sleep™ Sleepwrap® to assist
with positioning baby's head on alternate sides to help
prevent flat or misshapen heads. Visit
www.safetsleep.com for more information.

Sleep Sweet
Tel: 1300 786 101
email: info@cradle2kindy.com.au
website: www.cradle2kindy.com.au

Sleep Sweet baby wraps are made from top quality
100% cotton fabrics that will outlast your baby's need
for being wrapped. These infamously large wraps come
in a variety of colours and fabrics for both winter and
summer. The soft, light yet endurable cheesecloth and
stretch jersey are suitable for any season. Other fabrics
are waffle, muslin, embroidered cheesecloth, stretch silk
and flannelette. Sleep Sweet baby wraps are recommended
by Cradle 2 Kindy parenting solutions, mothercrafts
and midwives. For more information on colours and
fabrics go to the Cradle 2 Kindy website or phone the
number above.

Resources

NAPPIES, BATHTIME & SKINCARE

Baby wraps & comforters ➡ Nappies: cloth

Snugzeez
email: info@snugzeez.com.au
website: www.snugzeez.com.au

Snugzeez is an award-winning Australian company that manufactures baby comforters. Snugzeez combines the reassuring softness of baby's blanket with muslin. Babies love to touch different textures and Snugzeez provides knots to twiddle, a label to hold, satin ears and the blanket to snuggle. Snugzeez enables a gentler transition from wrapping your baby by using materials your baby already associates with sleep. Email or visit the website for further information.

BATHTIME PRODUCTS

NATIONAL

Annabel Trends
Tel: (07) 5593 4755
email: sales@annabeltrends.com
website: www.annabeltrends.com

Babies will love splashing about in the bath with gorgeous bathtime pets from Annabel Trends. The adorable wash mits add some puppet fun to bathtime as well as keeping babies squeaky clean. Choose from the yellow Duck or green Frog design (rrp$9.95) with one for small hands and one for mum or dad. Have a ribbeting and quacking time in the bath and keep baby entertained with bathtime pets. Phone the number above or visit the website for further information.

Ego Pharmaceuticals
Tel: 1800 033 706
email: ask@egopharm.com.au
website: www.egopharm.com.au

QV is a gentle, soap free cleansing and moisturising range for everybody, everyday. The QV range is free from colour, fragrance, lanolin and propylene glycol making it ideal for even the most sensitive of skin types. Highly effective and perfect for even the most precious skin, QV Bath Oil is ideal for baby's bath and for use as a massage oil to maintain the skin's natural suppleness and glow. It gently moisturises the skin as it cleanses, creating a protective film that locks in moisture to help prevent your baby's skin from becoming dry and flaky. Visit www.qvbody.com to find out more about QV Bath Oil, and the rest of the QV range. The QV range is available only in pharmacies. Visit the website for further information.
Always ready the label and use only as directed.

Humphrey's Corner
Tel: 1800 244 543
email: nurseryenquiries@funtastic.com.au
website: www.funtasticnursery.com.au

 Let your baby's imagination grow with this gorgeous range from Humphrey's Corner. Humphrey's Corner brings to life the characters from UK-author Sally Hunter's popular picture books. A complete range of baby products has been created to ensure your nursery is completely co-ordinated with the works of Humphrey's Corner. The range includes beautiful quality nursery furniture, bath and feeding plastics.

little bamboo
Tel: (03) 9016 3422
email: info@tllc.com.au
website: www.littlebamboo.com.au

Little Bamboo is a range of beautiful and soft bedroom and bathroom nursery products made using organically grown bamboo. Incorporating delicate muslin, super soft towelling, sensuous sheeting and beautiful blankets, Little Bamboo is one of the most comprehensive and innovative ranges of nursery bamboo textiles. Bringing together nearly 40 years of history in the nursery textile industry, this range has been developed to be both incredibly functional and extremely aesthetic. For more information visit www.littlebamboo.com.au.

Little Beetle
Tel: (03) 9579 1036
email: info@littlebeetle.com.au
website: www.littlebeetle.com.au

The Little Beetle Bath Towel is a baby towel that frees your hands to lift baby safely from the bath while you stay perfectly dry. Visit www.littlebeetle.com.au for more information.

Nice-Pak Products
Tel: 1800 506 750
email: info@nicepak.com.au
website: www.nicepak.com.au

The new Wiggles Wash Mitts are soft and strong. Ideal to use at bath time or shower time to make washing more fun for your child. For further information contact the Consumer Information Line on 1800 506 750 or visit the website.

Outlook Australia
Tel: (03) 9817 2311
email: outlooktm@bigpond.com
website: www.outlooktm.com

Made from 100% bamboo, Bamboo Baby® towelling is incredibly soft and the super absorbent deep pile draws water away so baby gets warm and dry quickly. The towels also stay beautifully soft wash after wash. Discover the softness of Bamboo Baby's® full range including baby towelling, wraps, cot/bassinet blankets and sheet sets all made from 100% bamboo. Phone the number above or visit the website for further information.

SunRos Pty Ltd

Tel: (02) 9997 7625
email: info@sunros.com.au
website: www.tummy-tub.com.au

TummyTub is an easy, stress-free and safe way to bath and settle your baby. The unique womb shape helps baby to relax, settle and sleep. Excellent for colicky babies, the tub uses only 5 litres of water and is lightweight. The TummyTub Multifunctional Stand makes bathtime comfortable and back friendly. Can be used for many years as it converts into a height-adjustable two-step-stool.

The Product Store Pty Ltd

Tel: (07) 3857 0691
email: info@theproductstore.com.au
website: www.theproductstore.com.au

The Coocoose® by Coochi makes bath time safer and more enjoyable for mums, dads, babies and toddlers. Made from 100% luxurious pure cotton, the Coocoose® towel fastens easily around your neck and back, leaving your hands free to bath and then cocoon and cuddle your baby dry while protecting you from splashes. Also available in the Coochi range are luxurious toddler bath and beach ponchos. Visit the website for more information.

The Wiggles

Tel: 1800 244 543
email: nurseryenquiries@funtastic.com.au
website: www.funtasticnursery.com.au

Children will enjoy bathtime even more with The Wiggles inspired bath range. The range has everything you need to bath your child including bath, step stool, toilet trainer and more. Made from quality plastic the range will inspire every little wiggle. Phone the number above or visit the website for further information.

Willy's Fun Stuff Pty Ltd

Tel: (02) 9757 3003
email: enquiry@willysfunstuff.com
website: www.willysfunstuff.com

Willy's Bath Colours are fizzing tablets that colour the bath water for bath-time fun and are suitable for ages 3–12 years. Willy's Bath Colours do not stain the bath tub or the skin and are a safe non-soap, non-fragranced product that are therefore suitable for sensitive skin. Willy's Bath Colours can even be mixed to learn to create different colours. Bath time turns into fun for everyone as the water turns into bright vivid colours for water fun.

LAUNDRY LIQUIDS

NATIONAL

Bayer Australia – Consumer Care

Tel: 1800 023 884
website: www.bayer.com.au

Your mother or grandmother may have used Amolin baby cream on your precious skin when you were a baby. In fact it has been trusted by mums for over 50 years. Today Amolin has a range of sensitive products, so you can care for your baby from top to toe. When thinking about protecting your baby's skin, one area that sometimes gets forgotten is the washing. Now there is Amolin sensitive laundry liquid. It is designed specifically for babies and people with sensitive skin, without compromising on cleaning power. This brilliant product has been tested and endorsed by the skin and cancer foundation to ensure that there is no irritation for people with sensitive skin. It is suitable for top and front loaders, in both hot and cold water. Amolin laundry liquid is available in a 1.25L bottle in the laundry section of your local supermarket. Phone the number listed above or visit the website www.bayer.com for further information.

Natures Organics

Tel: (03) 9753 5577
email: enq@naturesorganics.com.au
website: www.naturesorganics.com.au

Did you know standard laundry detergents commonly contain harsh chemicals and strong fragrances which can cause irritation to sensitive new skin? Purity's caring formulas have been dermatologically tested, they are enzyme and phosphate free, do not contain dyes or leave powder residue on clothing. Both have a light fragrance which leaves clothing feeling fresh without causing irritation to even the littlest family member. Purity contains rich plant derived ingredients, designed to lift dirt yet remain soft on frequently washed fibres. Purity Softener contains a natural softening agent, reducing wrinkles and making ironing easier. Available in Coles, Woolworths and some local independent supermarkets. Phone the number above or visit the website for further information.

NAPPIES: CLOTH

NATIONAL

Baby BeeHinds

Tel: (07) 4725 0064
email: info@babybeehinds.com.au
website: www.babybeehinds.com.au

Baby BeeHinds Modern Cloth Nappies are all about convenience, reliability and keeping our earth green. Gone are the days of folding, pinning and soaking cotton flat nappies, Baby BeeHinds are super cute, easy to use and will save you thousands of dollars over the term of your child's nappying years. They offer a range of products to suit different needs and use modern fabrics to focus on environmental sustainability, comfort and fashion. Visit the website for more information: www.babybeehinds.com.au or phone the number above.

Resources

NAPPIES, BATHTIME & SKINCARE

Nappies: cloth ➡ Nappies: disposable

Baby Soft Landings

Tel: (03) 6334 1351
email: info@babysoftlandings.com.au
website: www.babysoftlandings.com.au

 Reusable cloth nappies are an eco-friendly choice for discerning parents aiming to do their bit for the environment. Made from a range of fabrics including bamboo, hemp, wool and organic cotton, cloth nappies provide a natural alternative to disposable nappies. Baby Soft Landings can help take the confusion out of choosing a cloth nappy system to suit you, your lifestyle and your baby. Based in Launceston, Baby Soft Landings also offers local customers obligation-free demonstrations.

Bambini International

Tel: 1300 557 691
email: trade@bambiniinternational.com.au
website: www.bambiniinternational.com.au

Bambino Mio offer the complete re-useable cloth nappy solution. Multi-award winning and sold in over 70 counties around the world they are considered by so many parents as the best and most environmentally friendly alternative to disposables. Made from 100% natural materials, they are soft and comfortable against your baby's skin. Bambino Mio: a great way to save the planet, save money and so easy and convenient to use. Visit the website for more information.

Bonnibuns

Tel: 0432 733 249
email: bonnibuns@bonnibuns.com.au
website: www.bonnibuns.com.au

Bonnibuns specialise in cloth nappies including the easy-to-use Pocket Nappies as well as super trim, luxurious all-in-ones. They also have night-time nappies, a collection of reusable wipes as well as novelty nappies – fully functionable nappies customised to your footy team or favourite sport. Visit the website for further details.

Booroi Essentials

Tel: (02) 9012 0840
email: info@booroi.com.au
website: www.booroi.com.au

Booroi specialise in modern cloth nappies and organic and natural items for baby. Their cloth nappies are eco-friendly and easy to use, and include many popular brands at competitive prices. Safe, secure online shopping shipping to anywhere in Australia.

Bubblebubs

Tel: 0433 845 123
email: bubblebubs@bubblebubs.com.au
website: www.bubblebubs.com/store

Bubblebubs' nappies are an all-in-one, easy-to-use nappy made in Australia and created by Vicki Sampson. Bubblebubs also stock a fantastic collection of other products including fitted nappies and covers, night nappies, wet bags, swim nappies, cloth menstrual pads, babywear, Canningvale towels and foamy wipes wash.

Clever Babies (Kushies)

Tel: 1800 114 443
email: info@cleverbabies.com.au
website: www.cleverbabies.com.au

Established over 45 years ago and today sold in over 40 countries worldwide, Kushies® is an award-winning company leading the way in washable cloth nappy systems. Shaped to fit like a disposable, Kushies® washable nappies are made from several layers of 100% cotton flannelette. Each nappy features an exclusive patented built-in flap for extra absorbency, super soft leg elastic and adjustable hook/loop closures for optimum fit.

Easipants Cloth Nappies

Tel: 0417 318 716
email: info@easipants.com.au
website: www.easipants.com.au

Gone are the days of tricky folding, pins/clips and nappy covers. Easipants cloth nappies are simple, cuddly, fitted nappies that keep baby's skin dry and don't leak. Easipants are cloth nappies that are easy for mum, gorgeous for baby and good for the earth.

Green Bums

Tel: 0411 044 128
email: info@greenbums.com.au
website: www.greenbums.com.au

Green Bums specialises in All-In-One (AIO) nappies. No folding, no pins – just snap in and go. The AIOs come in a range of prints, denims and plain colours to suit all babies, and four sizes for a trim fit – from the tiny newborn to the late toilet trainer. Green Bums also stocks Baby Bee organic baby skin care products. For the full range visit their website.

Green Kids

Tel: 0431 431 473
email: help@greenkids.com.au
website: www.greenkids.com.au

Green Kids modern cloth nappies are cute, comfy and trim fitting, and can save you thousands of dollars. Green Kids nappies are 100% Australian made and the unique design allows them to fit most babies from birth to toilet training. Visit the website to see the fantastic range of colours and limited edition prints.

GreenBeans

Tel: (64) 7574 2984
email: sarah@greenbeans.co.nz
website: www.greenbeans.co.nz

GreenBeans is a family-owned and operated small business offering great bulk and retail prices on nappy fabrics, sewing notions and accessories. They supply bamboo, Fabrite PUL, suedecloth and microfleece, hemp, microfibre, snaps and presses and everything else you need to make modern cloth nappies. Phone the number above or visit the website for further information.

MiniLaLa

Tel: 0407 485 598
email: carli@lalababy.com.au
website: www.minilala.lalababy.com.au

The MiniLaLa range of cloth nappies includes all-in-one nappies which are super easy to use, one-size pocket nappies which will fit from newborn through to toddler, saving you lots of money, and reusable nappy accessories including wipes, liners and more. Modern cloth nappies are easy to use, save you money and are good for the planet, good for baby's skin, and best of all they're handmade in Australia. They are also extremely cute. Visit MiniLaLa today to learn more.

Nappies Covered

Tel: (08) 8558 8356
email: jodie@nappiescovered.com.au
website: www.nappiescovered.com.au

Nappies Covered is your one-stop modern cloth nappy making supply shop. They stock hemp, bamboo, printed and plain PUL fabric, Minky, Microfleece, various fasteners, elastics including FOE, labels and a great range of boosters and pre-made nappies including Chloe Toes nappies. Let your imagination run wild creating your own unique nappy designs. Whether it is pocket nappies, all-in-ones, covers, fitted or traditional nappies, they have the materials for you to design to your heart's content. Nappies Covered now proudly stock Chloe Toes nappies and covers. Phone the number above or visit the website for further information.

Nature's Child

Tel: 1300 555 632
email: orders@natureschild.com.au
website: www.natureschild.com.au

The benefits of using cloth nappies for your baby are many – no chemicals, less likely to experience skin irritation and organic cotton comfort. Nature's Child also have a good selection of fitted nappies if you want a bit more convenience, along with the health benefits of organic cotton. Compliment your routine with organic cotton nappy wipes, face wipes, breast pads and beautiful muslin baby wraps. Their certified organic bottom balm made in Australia is one of the purest in the world. Nature's Child products are available at Macro, Babies Galore and other leading and local local baby stores nationally. You can also buy online direct from Nature's Child – Australia's biggest and first online organic baby store since 2000. Phone for a free brochure.

Nip Naps

Tel: 1800 215 148
email: info@nipnaps.com.au
website: www.nipnaps.com.au

Nip Naps offer the full range of quality cloth nappy products from Mother-ease. All products are designed to provide an affordable, comfortable, durable, easy to use and leak-proof nappy system. Nip Naps also have a wealth of information about cloth nappies and offer friendly, free personalised advice on all aspects of choosing and using cloth nappies. Visit their website for more information or phone for a brochure.

Pea Pods Australia

email: info@peapods.com.au
website: www.peapods.com.au

Australian designed and owned Pea Pods Reusable Nappies save a small fortune compared to disposables and save a small planet from being filled with unnecessary waste. Simple to care for and use, Pea Pods are slim fitting and stylish. Visit their website for more information and stockists.

NAPPIES: DISPOSABLE

NATIONAL

Australian Pacific Paper Products

Tel: 1800 224 332 toll free
website: www.babyloveclub.com.au

BabyLove has a range of premium nappies for babies at every stage, from a specially designed newborn nappy through to junior size. These highly absorbent nappies are perfect for day and night use, at a great price. Babylove nappies are the only ones with The Wiggles on pack and on the nappy. BabyLove nappies are ranged in supermarkets Australia-wide. For further information phone BabyLove Consumer Enquiries on 1800 224 332 or visit www.babyloveclub.com.au for great tips, offers and information.

Australian Pacific Paper Products

Tel: 1800 224 332 toll free
website: www.babyloveclub.com.au

Cosifits is a favorite economy priced pharmacy nappy. Offering those important features, such as soft cloth-like outer cover, easy fastening grip tabs, leg leakage control guards, breathable side panels and a dry feel liner you will find Cosifits a great nappy saving you heaps. With all these useful features and high quality, Cosifits is a smart choice available nationally in pharmacies where advice is part of the service. Consumers can now get even greater value from the new Jumbo Box. For any questions or further information phone the number above.

Australian Pacific Paper Products

Tel: 1800 224 332 toll free
website: www.babyloveecobots.com.au

Resources

NAPPIES, BATHTIME & SKINCARE

Nappies: disposable ➔ Nappy & baby bags

BabyLove EcoBots are Australia's first true environmentally sensitive premium disposable nappy. Babylove has cleverly used increased biodegradable and compostable content using advanced plant based materials from renewable resources. Ecobots really are soft on baby and softer on the earth for our children's future. BabyLove EcoBots feature high absorbency and a fast acting ultra-dryness layer; a one-way liner keeps wetness away from baby's delicate skin; soft leg leakage control guards to gently hug baby's legs to prevent leakage; stretchable comfort grip tabs for secure refastening and adjustment and soft waterproof cloth-like outer cover is gentle to the touch. BabyLove EcoBots come in three sizes, crawler, walker and toddler and are available from major supermarkets and selected retail outlets. Phone 1800 224 332 for your nearest stockist or visit www.babyloveecobots.com.au for more information.

Eenee Eco Flushable Nappies
Tel: 1800 336 331 freecall
email: eenee@eenee.com.au
website: www.eenee.com

Eenee Eco Flushable Nappies are flushable disposable nappies that you can use with the new stretchy Weenees breathable, colourful, waterproof Baby Pouch Pants. Weenees care for you, your child and the environment. Weenee pants will also hold a folded cloth nappy. Also available: flushable nappy liners, breathable long lasting pilchers and Eenee undies for toilet training. Little Eenee swimmers are adjustable and designed to contain any solid 'accidents' in the pool. Phone for a free brochure or to find a store near you or visit their website for secure online ordering.

Ethman Enterprises Pty Ltd
Tel: 1300 725 876
email: info@ethman.com.au
website: www.ethman.com.au

Bambo Nature nappies are made with the environment in mind. They contain no perfumes, moisturising lotions, chlorine, latex, TBT or PVC. Thanks to their environmentally-friendly manufacturing process, Bambo Nature nappies are the only disposable nappy to hold the prestigious Nordic Swan Eco Label. They are highly absorbent and perfect for using overnight. Sizes from premature to training pants. Bambo Nature also offer sample packs. Phone the number listed above or visit the website www.ethman.com.au for further information.

Kimberly-Clark Australia – Huggies Nappies
Tel: 1800 028 334
email: via website
website: www.huggies.com.au

Huggies® Nappies are Australia's number one nappy. They are the only nappy clinically proven to help prevent nappy rash. Huggies® have a cloth-like, Breathe Dry®, all over breathable cover that allows air to circulate around a baby's bottom so baby's skin stays drier. The Unique 3-Layer Design works hard to draw wetness away from baby's skin and lock it in, which means they're second to none in terms of absorbency and a unique Fast-Absorb Layer draws moisture away from baby's skin even faster than before. Huggies® Nappies feature larger, shaped grip tabs (Crawler –Junior) for more stretch and an even better fit around the waist plus brighter and more colourful Winnie the Pooh designs across all sizes.

Kimberly-Clark Australia – Snugglers Nappies
Tel: 1800 028 334
email: via website
website: www.huggies.com.au

Snugglers® Nappies are a smart buy. They have all the great features you need at an affordable price. Snugglers® Nappies now feature extra stretchy grip tabs on sizes Crawler to Junior, a soft cloth-like cover, wide breathable sides, a dryness layer and an extra absorbent core which is now 20% more absorbent. They also have dual leakguards plus leg elastic which provides triple leakage protection. Snugglers® Nappies are available in five sizes: small, crawler, toddler, walker and junior.

Sorbies Pty Ltd
Tel: 1800 188 201
email: info@sorbies.com.au
website: www.sorbies.com.au

Sorbies is an Australian company that has developed a unique range of disposable nappies after listening to mums. Sorbies spoke to literally thousands of mums and found that mums want a great nappy that lasts all night, reducing the need for unnecessary washing and ensuring baby is kept dry through the night, while using a practical efficient nappy during the day, so as not to waste money. Sorbies is the world's first nappy pack with ultra super absorbent Night Nappies and Practical Day Nappies both in the one convenient pack.

NAPPIES: SWIM PANTS

NATIONAL

Clever Babies (Kushies)
Tel: 1800 114 443
website: www.cleverbabies.com.au

Kushies® Swim Nappies are the fantastic new bathers for babies endorsed by Swim Australia. Designed to contain any solid 'accidents' this is a quality bather that will give you peace of mind with your little one. Kushies® Swim Nappies feature wrap styling and an adjustable waist, gusseted legs for leak proof protection, lightweight nylon outer, 100% cotton inner lining system and tie at the waist for extra security. Kushies® Swim Nappies are available in a unisex style as well as a girl's style, in four different sizes and twelve different colours and prints.

Kimberly-Clark Australia – Huggies Little Swimmers

Tel: 1800 028 334
email: via website
website: www.huggies.com.au

 Babies love to play in the water, and every parent knows the importance of water safety in Australia. Huggies Little Swimmers® Disposable Swimpants allow you to start swimming with your baby from 6 months, with the complete freedom to learn and have fun. Unlike nappies, which soak up water and become heavy and uncomfortable, Huggies Little Swimmers® Swimpants don't swell up. What's more, they keep embarrassing accidents in, so you can relax. And with tear-away sides, changing with Huggies Little Swimmers® Swimpants is easy. Available in three sizes to fit children from 6-36 months. For more information visit littleswimmers.com.au.

NAPPIES: TRAINING PANTS

NATIONAL

Australian Pacific Paper Products

Tel: 1800 224 332 toll free
website: www.babyloveclub.com.au

BabyLove have a range of high quality toilet training pants to make the transition from nappies to regular underpants as easy as possible for your child. BabyLove have designed the Training Pants with The Wiggles fun and bright designs, plus easy tear open sides, soft cloth like feel cover, a stretchy and very comfortable waist. Available in Medium 8-15kgs, Large 12-18kg and Extra Large 16+kgs. Check www.babyloveclub.com.au for toilet training tips from a qualified Maternal Health Nurse. Babylove Training Pants now also feature a Feel Wet Liner allowing children to feel the wetness while protecting everything else from leaks.

Clever Babies (Kushies)

Tel: 1800 114 443
email: info@cleverbabies.com.au
website: www.cleverbabies.com.au

Kushies® training pants are a great economical alternative to disposable pull-on pants. Made from 100% soft cotton flannel that helps to prevent rashing without masking the sensation of wetness and increasing your child's motivation to be toilet trained. They offer

soft elastic waist and legs for comfort and a snug fit and are machine washable and dryable. Available in trendy bright prints and sizes from 13kg to 21kg.

Kimberly-Clark Australia – Pull-Ups

Tel: 1800 028 334
email: via website
website: www.huggies.com.au

 Pull-Ups® Training Pants are just like underpants for learners. It is the only training pant designed with a unique 'Feel Wet to Learn' Wetness Liner, so that your toddler can start to learn the difference between wet from dry to help them learn to stay dry on their own. And with colourful Disney Princess and Disney Pixar Cars designs, they look just like big kid underwear. The stretchy sides help your toddler learn to pull them on and off with ease. Remember, Pull-Ups® Training Pants are absorbent with Easy Open Sides, so little accidents are no big deal. Available in 3 sizes – Size 2 (up to 15kgs), Size 3 (15-18 kgs), Size 4 (17+ kgs). For more information or a free sample visit pull-ups.com.au.

Kimberly-Clark Australia – DryNites

Tel: 1800 028 334
email: via website
website: www.drynites.com.au

 DryNites® Pyjama Pants are a discreet way for older kids to manage the bedwetting stage while maintaining their confidence and self esteem. Kids often become dry in their own time. In the meantime, DryNites® Pyjama Pants. DryNites® Pyjama Pants come in both boy and girl designs, which make them look like regular underwear, and their trim-fit design help them disappear under pyjamas so no one can tell they're wearing them. DryNites® Pyjama Pants are available in 2 sizes: 4-7 years (17 to 30kgs) and 8-15 years (17 to 30kgs). For more information and a free sample visit drynites.com.au.

NAPPY & BABY BAGS

NATIONAL

Bespoke JaNik

Tel: 0412 538 408
email: info@bespokejanik.com
website: www.bespokejanik.com

Bespoke JaNik sells practical and fashionable baby bags with interchangeable linings, as well as pamper packs and treats for mums, fashion, footwear and gift wear. This is convenient retail therapy allowing you to update for your changing needs without sacrificing your style. Bespoke JaNik are specialists in handpicked affordable luxuries from all over the globe. They also offer a fundraising benefits program that is available for your local child care centre, kindergarten or school.

Resources

NAPPIES, BATHTIME & SKINCARE

Nappy & baby bags

Burp Baby Gear
Tel: (02) 9890 3797
email: sales@burpbabygear.com.au
website: www.burpbabygear.com.au
Burp Baby Gear is your baby boutique for hip and
sporty Burp nappy bags, organic clothing, gifts, bath
products and accessories. Their Burp nappy bags have a
unique sporty style with great features for mums and
dads. The Burp bag comes complete with a changing
mat, mobile phone, insulated bottle holders, key ring
and pacifier clasp and lots of compartments inside and
out to hold all those essential items. Visit the website for
more information.

Fat Mumma's
Tel: 0428 190 701
email: info@fatmummas.com.au
website: www.fatmummas.com.au
Fat Mumma's is all about creativity and caring. They
have created a series of fun, unique products that stand-
out in the city streets such as stylish nappy bags, groovy
kids clothing and creative, new-baby gifts. Their logo is
inspired by the cartoon styles of Japan and gives the
designs some humourous attitude. Feel like you're part
of a unique growing community of mothers with an eye
for great design and visit www.fatmummas.com.au.

gr8x®
Tel: (03) 9434 1000
email: info@gr8x.net
website: www.gr8x.net
The gr8x® baby bags and accessories are renowned for
high quality, functionality and style with the popular
and award-winning Baby Traveller®, the all-in-one baby
bag and change mat, continuing as the flagship product
and consistently receiving rave reviews from parents
around the world. With a two-year warranty on bags,
and a style and practicality that go well beyond baby, the
range continues to expand, offering innovative solutions
in stylish designs with the unique, self-inflating feeding
cushion, luxurious foot muff and popular stretch
swaddling wraps. Check out the range and the Baby
Traveller demo video online at www.gr8x.net.

Gubby
Tel: 1800 501 680
email: info@mygubby.com
website: www.mygubby.com
Contemporary designs, vibrant colour and a cheeky
character are the standout features of Gubby nappy
bags. The range includes a backpack, satchel and sling

bag and each is available in two colour schemes: red and
green. Features include a padded nappy change mat and
hide-away straps for fastening to a pram or stroller. With
each bag style, shoulder straps adjust for a comfortable
fit making Gubby an active-wear bag designed for
parents seriously on the move. Made from lightweight
and durable materials these bags offer quality at very
affordable prices. Gubby is available at leading nursery
outlets nationwide. For more information freecall 1800
501 680 or visit www.mygubby.com.

Huhana Inspired
Tel: 0406 458 619
website: www.aussienappybags.com
Huhana Inspired specialise in Nappy Pockets and Wet
Bags – simple products that make life easier. Nappy
Pockets hold baby's essentials including nappies, wipes
and creams. Stylish, durable, 100% cotton, completely
washable and a compact design, these Nappy Pockets fit
into most handbags. Wet Bags are perfect for holding
swim and sporting clothes before and after use. They
have a water-resistant lining, a zip pocket inside for
valuables and they are re-useable. Designed and made in
Sydney and 100% Australian owned.

isoki contemporary baby accessories
Tel: 1300 368 123
email: info@isoki.com.au
website: www.isoki.com.au
Isoki is about offering a fashionable alternative to baby
accessories. Their products are innovative in design and
consumer friendly. The concept of the reversible baby
bag enables the consumer choice by offering two bags in
one. The internal components of the bag are multi-
functional and can be removed and used individually.
Look for the rest of the Isoki range including the Petite
Traveller and Change Mat Clutch.

Jooki
Tel: 0404 486 573
email: info@jooki.com.au
website: www.jooki.com.au
JOOKI is a luxury mother and baby accessories brand
which epitomises the modern mums of the millennium.
JOOKI was borne from a woman's passion to deliver
quality baby bags and accessories that inspire beauty,
versatility and quality while still being functional and
practical. The bag's baby features are subtle allowing the
bags to have longevity and be used well beyond the
baby years. JOOKI is perfect as a gift for every mother
to indulge. JOOKI products are sold at selected baby
boutiques and on premium online baby stores.

Kapoochi Australia
Tel: 1800 501 680
email: info@kapoochi.net
website: www.kapoochi.net
Kapoochi sets the standard in premium baby bags by
successfully combining practicality with style. Kapoochi
have been designing and manufacturing quality,
purpose-built baby bags and baby carry pouches since
1991. Attention to detail, innovative design, product

durability and space are all hallmarks of the brand. Kapoochi pioneered features like the nappy change compartment, handy dispensers, pram fasteners and separate, secure compartments for mum's personal items. These bags are a practical tool as well as a fashion accessory. Select items are available from David Jones, Target, Big W and leading nursery outlets nationwide. For information freecall 1800 501 680 or visit www.kapoochi.net.

Little Beetle
Tel: (03) 9579 1036
email: info@littlebeetle.com.au
website: www.littlebeetle.com.au

The Little Beetle Nappy Bag holds everything you need for an expedition with baby. Pop it on your back, over your shoulder or hang it on the pram and when it comes to nappy time the bag becomes a change mat. Visit www.littlebeetle.com.au for more information.

Made By Mums
Tel: 0411 018 245 or (03) 9827 4770
email: info@madebymums.com.au
website: www.madebymums.com.au

The Nappy Wallet is a functional carry-all for all nappy changes. It has spacious compartments for nappies, moist wipes, a nappy change mat (included free of charge) and skin lotions. The Nappy Wallet is ideal for the car glove box or for short trips out. The compact design is registered and is made of supple vinyl with a waterproof lining for easy clean surfaces. Available at www.madebymums.com.au or phone (03) 9827 4770 for a free catalogue.

MYBAG
Tel: (03) 9645 7765
email: alex@mybag.com.au
website: www.mybag.com.au

Personalise your style and create your own bag using your favourite photographs with MYBAG. Select photos of family, friends, pets or holidays the choices are endless. Soft leather is carefully hand-crafted with your image which is printed on fabric in either colour, black & white or sepia tone, and is bound together to create a fully lined one-off handbag. MYBAG is available in two sizes with trim available in black, chocolate, camel, red or white leather. Purses and canvas bags are now also available.

Nic-Nac Nappywrap
Tel: 0422 912 690
email: info@nappywrap.com.au
website: www.nappywrap.com.au

Nic-Nac Nappywrap offer a range of baby bags that are streamlined, practical and durable. Best of all, they are 100% Australian made. Features include: specially designed pockets to hold all the necessities, including wipes; the Wrap features a built-in change mat – simply slide the wipes pocket aside; compatibility with slings and most baby carriers enabling parents to be hands-free. Suitable from birth to toilet training (0 to 2.5 years). Nic-Nac Nappywrap's baby bags enable parents to enjoy a simple routine when changing their baby while out and about, something greatly appreciated for the time a child is wearing nappies. Nappywraps make an ideal baby shower or blessing ceremony gift.

OiOi Pty Ltd
Tel: (03) 9500 8854
email: sales@oioi.com.au
website: www.oioi.com.au

Having a baby brings so many changes, but it doesn't mean you have to change your style. OiOi's functional and stylish bags and accessories will never date, and the OiOi range makes it easy to get organised with multiple pockets and compartments for baby things. Each OiOi bag comes with an insulated bottle holder, large padded micro fibre change mat, a PVC zip top mess purse and PVC hard wipes case. External pockets are cleverly designed for easy accessibility to phone, wallet, sunnies and keys. There are backpacks, large totes, hobos, messengers and carry all styles, all with after-baby uses.

Pebbles
Tel: 0405 027 422
email: ros@pebblespouches.com.au
website: www.pebblespouches.com.au

Pebbles is home of The PouchMISS – the handbag organiser. The PouchMISS can transform your gorgeous handbag into a nappy bag simply by packing it up and slipping it into your favourite bag of the day. The PouchMISS has pockets and compartments to hold all of your mum and baby stuff, as well as the most necessary features of a nappy bag – insulated pockets for baby's bottles and a matching change mat that folds to fit neatly inside.

Pipsqueak Designs Australia
Tel: 1800 058 000
email: info@pipsqueak.com.au
website: www.pipsqueak.com.au

The Pipsqueak Baby Swags have been produced in Australia for over 15 years. They are a practical and stylish nappy bag that carries all you need for a day out with baby and opens up to act as your portable change mat. With pockets on either side all is within easy reach while changing your baby. Made in Australia these bags make ideal gifts for expectant mothers with gift filling and wrapping that can be ordered along with the swag if desired. Order on their secure internet site for fast delivery: www.pipsqueak.com.au.

pop maternity
Tel: 0429 693 984
email: info@popmaternity.com.au
website: www.popmaternity.com.au

Pop Maternity is the exclusive Australian distributor of the designer DadGear nappy bags and vests range. Visit www.popmaternity.com.au or phone for more information.

Resources

NAPPIES, BATHTIME & SKINCARE

Nappy & baby bags ➡ Nappy disposal systems

Ramalama
Tel: 1300 729 834
email: hello@ramalama.com.au
website: www.ramalama.com.au

Ramalama's offers a range of gorgeous infant carriers and nappy bags. Made from genuine leather you will love the quality as well as the functionality of all the designs. All nappy bags come with a handy change mat and extra pockets to keep everything well organised, and are designed to be used even after baby has grown out of nappies. The infant carriers are also available in a fabric combination and are suitable from 5 months and up to 20kgs.

Shop Girl
Tel: (02) 9881 5893
email: info@shopgirl.com.au
website: www.shopgirl.com.au

Shop Girl's inspiration is creating bags for baby necessities, filling a gap between luxury handbags and mass-market brands. Their popular Grab 'n' Go Nappy Purse, roomy enough to hold wipes and nappies, comes with a matching quilted change mat. Another Shop Girl product to delight is the large beach bag with mesh bottom allowing sand to fall through. Internal zip pocket keeps phone/keys safe. Both products are machine washable in cold water. To view their range of products visit www.shopgirl.com.au.

Yojiki Australia
Tel: (08) 9524 1111
email: info@yojiki.com.au
website: www.yojiki.com.au

The Yojiki Baby Swagbag is a generously padded playmat/swag/nappy bag with cooler bag and waterproof padded change mat all rolled into one convenient and compact portable bag. Fabulous for the family on the move, this accessory for on-the-go parenting transforms as your baby grows. All premium quality elements are separate for easy care. Proudly Australian made.

NAPPY CHANGE MATS

NATIONAL

Buboo
Tel: 1800 244 543
email: nurseryenquiries@funtastic.com.au
website: www.funtasticnursery.com.au

The Baby Elevator change mat is a patented product that was designed by a mother for her baby who suffered from reflux. In her frustration to find a way to help her baby, Deborah came up with the revolutionary elevated mat. The mat's elevation helps to aid your baby's digestion. Particularly suitable for reflux babies, the mat provides a much more comfortable way for every baby to have his/her nappy changed. The mat can also be used for play. Suitable for babies up to 4 months or until your baby is rolling, you can use it as a play mat by putting your baby on the mat under a hanging toy.

Kimberly-Clark Australia
Tel: 1800 028 334
email: via website
website: www.huggies.com.au

When you're out and about, finding a clean and convenient place to change your baby's nappy can be tricky. With Huggies® Change Mats, you can change your baby's nappy anywhere. When folded, it's a compact and light mat which fits easily in your nappy bag or car glove box. When opened, it's a large mat with a soft, absorbent top and non-slip waterproof backing. Best of all, it's disposable, so with little accidents you can just throw away the germs.

StinkyBotz
Tel: 0439 556 531
email: info@stinkybotz.com.au
website: www.stinkybotz.com.au

StinkyBotz is a nappy changing accessory for every busy parent on the move. With a StinkyBotz nappy changer on hand, nappies, wipes and a clean change surface are at your fingertips, no matter where you are. StinkyBotz comes with its own wee-resistant change surface and internal pockets especially sized to house wipes, disposable nappies and nappy sacks. StinkyBotz rolls up conveniently into a small envelope shape, ready to come to the rescue of the next StinkyBotz tot.

NAPPY DELIVERY SERVICES

NATIONAL

Baby Wishes
Tel: (02) 9837 1101
email: inquiries@baby-wishes.com.au
website: www.baby-wishes.com.au

Baby Wishes is a home-delivery service that covers all areas in Australia. They deliver nappies, baby toiletries, toilet paper, toys, pull ups and party supplies. All major brands are stocked including Huggies, Baby Love nappies, My Bear nappies, Snugglers, Drynites pyjama pants, Kleenex, Wondersoft and more (over 1,200 products on the website). Phone the number above or visit the website for further information.

VICTORIA

Chris' Dial A Nappy
205A Victoria Road
Northcote VIC 3070
Tel: (03) 9489 3844
email: dialanappy@netspace.net.au
website: www.dialanappy.com.au

Chris' Dial A Nappy are the biodegradable and modern cloth nappy specialists. Conventional nappies also available and they offer free same day delivery. Chris' Dial A Nappy are committed to educating their customers in environmentally responsible nappy choices, and know that good impartial information can help parents in the confusing dilemma when choosing nappies and weighing up the environmentally friendly options. They are currently running nappy education classes (for free) in store – just phone or email to find out times – and they are also involved in environmental nappy trials in a local child care centre. All their nappies come in discounted packages. Eenees full range 100% biodegradable nappies, fitted cloth, PUL nappy covers, prefolds, Huggies, Baby love, Joeys, Factory Seconds and much more. Phone, email, or visit their website or their retail store in Northcote for more information.

The Nappy Shop
1341 Burke Road
Kew VIC 3101
Tel: (03) 9817 2661
website: www.thenappyshop.com.au

The Nappy Shop offers free home delivery – same or next day – Monday to Friday to most Melbourne metropolitan suburbs for a minimum of two boxes of nappies. To receive same day delivery (within the Nappy Shop delivery radius) make sure you place your order before 11.30am Monday to Friday.

NEW SOUTH WALES

Little Red Hen Nappy Service
PO Box 638
St Marys NSW 1790
Tel: (02) 4774 2347
website: www.nappywashservices.com.au

Little Red Hen Nappy Service offers a twice weekly delivery service to some areas from $30 a week for sixty cloth nappies (GST included). First delivery includes a nappy bucket, bin liners and nappies. All nappies are professionally laundered. Little Red Hen also delivers from the Blue Mountains to the city. Please note there is a minimum of a four-week service pre-paid. Gift vouchers are available and there are discounts for multiple births and special offers available. Introductory specials and special rates for long-term delivery are available.

AUSTRALIAN CAPITAL TERRITORY

Busy Bottoms Nappy Express
Tel: (02) 6238 1816
email: busy-bots@bigpond.com

Busy Bottoms Nappy Express nappy delivery service offer a prompt, friendly and reliable service. Their range includes My Bear, Childcare, Moltex Eco Nappies as well as bulk cleaning and paper products for both domestic and commercial. They have the Wotnot organic baby products along with the beautiful Billiegoat Soap range.

NAPPY DISPOSAL SYSTEMS

NATIONAL

CNP Brands
Tel: 1300 667 137
email: info@cnpbrands.com.au
website: www.cnpbrands.com.au

The Diaper Nanny® disposal system by Childcare Nursery Products is a quick and easy way to dispose of dirty nappies. The Diaper Nanny® has a triple seal to control odours and a foot pedal which opens the lid for hands-free use. Refills for the Diaper Nanny® disposal system are one continuous liner so you only use what you need to. Sold separately, refills come with a 'baby powder' fresh scent and last up to three months when used regularly for newborn nappies. The Diaper Nanny® is available from leading nursery retailers.

Jackel Australia Pty Ltd
Tel: 1800 890 011 Customer Service
email: tommeetippee@jackel.com.au
website: www.tommeetippee.com.au

The Tommee Tippee Nappy Wrapper Tub features an improved double blade cutter and a unique twist and seal mechanism that only requires one handle turn and seals away odours. The positive grip indicates how far in to push nappy and the bottom gripper stops the nappy chain unravelling for improved odour control. Holding 28 nappies, the Tommee Tippee Nappy Wrapper Tub comes in stylish white and lilac and has a carry handle for easy emptying. RRP $79.95. There are two types of refill cassettes to suit baby's stage of development. Stage 1 is for newborn babies and stage 2 is for when baby starts to wean and is specially formulated to stop stronger nappy smells produced by babies on solid foods. The cassettes last for about a month and use silver ion (organic) to tackle germs with a pleasant citrus floral fragrance.

Nice-Pak Products
Tel: 1800 506 750
website: www.babyu.com.au

Baby U Scented Nappy Sacks are the ideal portable nappy disposal system. Whether you're at home or on the go, these scented bags help control odour and seal in wetness and bacteria. Tie-close handles make Baby U™ Scented Nappy Sacks easy and convenient to use. Available in a 50pk or 200pk in selected Big W, Kmart, Target, Priceline, Toys R Us, baby stores and selected pharmacies.

Resources

NAPPIES, BATHTIME & SKINCARE

Nappy disposal systems ➡ Stores online

Nice-Pak Products

Tel: 1800 506 750
email: info@nicepak.com.au
website: www.babyu.com.au

The Baby U™ NappySafe™ is a smart nappy disposal system that is easy to use, environmentally friendly and economical. The smart system controls odours with its unique seal action; it's a safe, one handed operation, and there are no ongoing costs. No costly cassette refills required. Stores up to 30 nappies, and includes 10 bin liners to get you started. Available at Toys R Us and baby stores. Visit www.babyu.com.au or phone 1800 506 750 for further information.

NAPPY FASTENERS

Sanbrook Brands Pty Ltd – Happy Baby

Tel: 1800 335 917
email: baby@sanbrook.com.au
website: www.happybaby.com.au

Happy Baby's Snappi is a new age nappy fastener making nappy pins a thing of the past. Snappi allows you to fit a fresh fluffy towelling nappy in seconds – simply hook and stretch and Snappi does the rest. Snappi is easy to use and protects your baby from pins and is suitable for any nappy folding styles and supports the environment too. Happy Baby is a quality Australian brand which has been providing products for over 40 years. Happy Baby products are available from supermarkets, mass merchants and chemists Australia wide. Phone the number above or visit the website for further information.

Tee-Zed Products

Tel: (02) 9386 4000
email: sales@tee-zed.com.au
website: www.tee-zed.com

The practical and affordable range of Dream Baby® Care products includes flexible digital thermometers, nail clippers, nasal aspirators, cute comfy cold packs, nappy pins, medicine spoons, dispensers and droppers. An extensive range of safety products, toys, decor and travel accessories are also available. Look for Australian owned Dream Baby® in selected baby stores, toy stores, pharmacies or call (02) 9386 4000 for your nearest stockist.

NAPPY RASH TREATMENTS

Aspen Pharmacare Pty Ltd

Tel: (02) 8436 8300
email: sales@aspenpharmacare.com.au
website: www.aspenpharmacare.com.au

Covitol® Nappy Rash Treatment helps soothe and treat nappy rash and skin infections. Covitol® provides a thick, smooth barrier for long lasting protection. It is uniquely formulated with nutritive rich cod liver oil, high levels of zinc oxide and lanolin. Together they seal out wetness and germs to help skin irritations disappear quickly. Fragrance and colour free, it's 100% best for baby.
Always read the label. Use only as directed.
If symptoms persist see your doctor.

Bayer Australia – Consumer Care

Tel: 1800 023 884
website: www.bayer.com.au

Bepanthen Ointment has a tailored double action that both protects and promotes natural skin recovery. By providing a barrier for the skin, it helps mum to do the best she can to protect against nappy rash. In addition, it cares for the skin to help soothe and aid the natural healing of nappy rash. Clinical tests have shown that using Bepanthen Ointment as protection after every nappy change leads to a lower incidence of nappy rash. Bepanthen Ointment is also free from all colours, fragrances and preservatives so it is gentle enough to use at every nappy change, even on sensitive skin. Bepanthen Ointment is available in supermarkets and pharmacies nationally in two conveniently sized tubes: 30g and 100g. For more information, visit www.bepanthen.com.au.
Always read the label. Use only as directed.
If symptoms persist, see your doctor.

Bayer Australia – Consumer Care

Tel: 1800 023 884
website: www.bayer.com.au

For over 50 years Am-o-Lin Baby Cream has been a staple in the nursery cupboard for its oil-rich formula that helps heal and protect against nappy rash, chafing and skin irritations. Enriched with sweet almond oil, this rich cream is also ideal to soothe conditions such as minor sunburn, cracked lips and dry skin. Available in supermarkets and pharmacies nationally. For further information please phone the Consumer Helpline 1800 023 884.
Always read the label. Use only as directed.
If symptoms persist, see your doctor.

Church & Dwight (Australia) Pty Ltd

Tel: 1800 222 099
email: enquiries@churchdwight.com.au
website: www.curash.com.au & www.churchdwight.com.au

More than just nappy rash treatments, Curash has a full range of products that care for baby's delicate skin, helping to soothe, treat and prevent. Curash Anti-rash Baby Powder* and Medicated Nappy Rash Cream* are market leading products for healing and preventing nappy rash. In addition, Curash has gentle Baby Wipes which are available in Soap Free Lightly Fragranced, Fragrance Free and Moisturising variants. The Curash range also offers Moisturising Soap Free Baby Bath, and 2 in 1 Shampoo & Conditioner. Curash provides everything you need to help keep your baby's skin healthy from top to bottom. Curash is available nationally from supermarkets, pharmacies and selected stores nationally. *Always read the label. Use only as directed. Consult your health care professional if symptoms persist.*

Herron Pharmaceuticals

Tel: 1300 659 646
email: custservice@herron.com.au
website: www.herron.com.au

Herron Baby has developed a range of baby products for Australian families. Herron Baby Zinc and Castor Oil Cream is a gentle nappy rash cream, helping to soothe, heal and protect your baby's sensitive skin. Herron Baby Teething Gel is specially formulated for the temporary relief of pain caused by teething. For busy mums, keep a look out for Herron's great range of vitamins and Vita-minis for kids.
Always read the label. Use only as directed. If symptoms persist see your healthcare professional. ASMI/15681-10/08, CHC50501-10/08

Nice-Pak Products

Tel: 1800 506 750
email: info@nicepak.com.au
website: www.sudocrem.com.au

Your baby's delicate skin can easily be irritated by stools, urine, humidity, detergents, soaps, alcohol and chemicals in lotions and oils. Sudocrem® protects your baby's skin from coming into contact with irritants, which is the best prevention. Sudocrem® soothes the burning and itching sensation of nappy rash, heals the skin and provides a protective barrier to assist in the management of nappy rash. Available in pharmacies, grocery, department and baby stores. Phone 1800 506 750 or visit www.sudocrem.com.au for further information.

The Royal Children's Hospital Pharmacy

Tel: (03) 9345 5492
email: rch.pharmacy@rch.org.au
website: www.rch.org.au/nappygoo

Nappy-Goo is the nappy rash cream formulated by the Pharmacy Department at The Royal Children's Hospital in Melbourne. It is a soothing cream with mildly astringent and antiseptic properties that helps prevent, manage and treat nappy rash. Nappy-Goo is the standard nappy rash cream used throughout the hospital, and is listed on the Australian Register of Therapeutic Goods. Visit the website for further information on pharmacies that stock Nappy-Goo or phone for further details. *Active ingredients: zinc oxide, hamamelis water (witch hazel water) and melaleuca oil (tea tree oil).*

STORES ONLINE:
NAPPIES, BATHTIME & SKINCARE

NATIONAL

Australian Nappy Network

Tel: 0417 100 423
email: info@nappynetwork.org.au
website: www.nappynetwork.org.au

The Australian Nappy Network is an independent, non profit organisation working to raise the profile of reusable nappy options for modern times and modern parents. Parents considering, or already using, reusable nappies and service providers alike will find the ANN offers information, support and resources highlighting the numerous advantages of cloth nappies. The Australian Nappy Network regularly holds information sessions and informal gatherings for real-life assistance, with many during Reusable Nappy Week, held annually in October. Visit the website or phone for further information.

Baby Eco Store

Tel: (08) 7120 2275
email: babyeco@optusnet.com.au
website: www.babyecostore.com.au

Baby Eco Store has an extensive range of natural baby products including organic cotton baby clothing and accessories, gifts, natural skin care/bath time care, toys and products for mum. Their products are carefully chosen to be safe, environmentally friendly and natural – perfect for baby. Shop securely online. They deliver across Australia and are always happy to offer help and advice.

babyshop

Tel: 1800 222 437 or 1800 BABIES
email: mail@babyshop.com.au
website: www.babyshop.com.au

Experience the convenience of shopping from home with one of Australia's first online baby stores. With experience online since 1998 and hundreds of products to choose from, babyshop stocks a variety of well known brands, as well as featuring many exclusive and hard to find items. Departments include: Bathtime & Care, Bedtime & Nursery, Clothing, Feeding & Accessories, Out & About and Playtime & Development. (NSW readers can also visit their retail store at 276 Brunker Road, Adamstown.)

Darlings Downunder

Tel: (03) 9449 0290
website: www.darlingsdownunder.com.au

Darlings Downunder are specialists in the Australian

Resources

NAPPIES, BATHTIME & SKINCARE

Stores online

---

modern cloth nappy market, baby organic clothing and accessories. Darlings Downunder carry a large range of modern cloth or reusable nappies sourced locally and globally and offer retail and wholesale sales. Their range includes Haute Pockets, Baby Beehinds, Monkey Doodlez, Thirsties, Mother-ease, Tots Bots, Happy Heiny's, Kissaluvs, Bummis, Pea Pods plus many more. Reusable nappies are fitted and do not require pins or soaking. They do up easily with snap or velcro closures and are available in lovely bright colours and gorgeous prints to show off. Darlings Downunder will happily provide information and advice to suit your needs.

Down to Earth Baby

Tel: (03) 9502 3098
email: info@downtoearthbaby.com
website: www.downtoearthbaby.com

Down to Earth Baby is a one-stop organic and eco-friendly mother and baby shop. With natural products for pregnancy through to baby including fabulous skincare and aromatherapy products, organic herbal teas, as well as organic and eczema-friendly clothing. They also offer support packs and organic gifts for each stage of pregnancy, labour, postnatal recovery, breastfeeding and baby plus non-toxic toys and baby bottles. Great babycare products include cloth and disposable nappies for environmentally-conscious families.

Fluffies Knitwear Industries

Tel: (08) 8347 1343
email: fluffies@fluffies.com.au
website: www.fluffies.com.au

Fluffies Knitwear Industries is an Australian-owned company that manufactures and imports quality products such as pilchers, booties, nappies, luxury blankets, change mats, bedding, superior quality towels and much more. All available to purchase by mail order.

Healthy Kidz Online

Tel: (03) 9587 8300
email: contact@healthykidz.com.au
website: www.healthykidz.com.au

Healthy Kidz Online is an online store offering natural, organic and yummy goods for your baby, child and house. They stock natural and organic healthy snacks, allergy aware and basic pantry items, skincare and home-care products all minus the unnecessary additives and all with the environment in mind. Visit www.healthykidz.com.au or phone the number above for further information.

Hello Charlie

Tel: 1300 725 876
email: info@hellocharlie.com.au
website: www.hellocharlie.com.au

Hello, Charlie! specialises in eco-friendly, natural, organic and non toxic products for babies, children and home. The site offers lots of practical and stylish products that you will use over and over, as well as everyday items like eco-friendly cloth and disposable nappies, feeding products, clothing and bedding, toiletries, pregnancy and breastfeeding products, wooden toys, baby carriers, and things to get you out and about. Visit www.hellocharlie.com.au for more details.

La Toriana

Tel: 0408 489 268
email: info@latoriana.com.au
website: www.LaToriana.com.au

La Toriana stocks a range of baby care products including nappy creams, soaps, bath moisturisers, Gaia Skin organics, Thurlby Farm baby products and much more. This online store also stocks a great range of organic nappies. Enjoy the La Toriana experience by visiting www.latoriana.com.au.

Little Koala

Tel: 0433 296 007
email: sales@littlekoala.com.au
website: www.littlekoala.com.au

Little Koala supplies cloth nappies that are easy to use, reliable, soft on your baby's skin and cute to boot. They sell pre-folds, fitted nappies, pocket nappies, nappy covers and nappy rash balms. Little Koala sells slings and backpacks too.

Natural Form

Tel: 0414 451 250
email: info@naturalform.com.au
website: www.naturalform.com.au

Natural Form offer value for money with their top quality, organic and natural products for baby, child, mother and the home. The range includes baby skin care, bath time products, clothing, gifts, health care products and more. Visit the website for further details.

New Age Nappies

email: sales@newagenappies.com.au
website: www.newagenappies.com.au

New Age Nappies specialise in modern cloth nappies and accessories. The range includes AIOs, fitted and pre-fold nappies as well as covers, inserts, bibs, giftware, swimmers, sunglasses and more. Brands stocked include Bumkins, Imse Vimse, Kushies and Thirsties. The Imse Vimse range includes 100% certified organic nappies and covers, as well as the new fox fibre range.

Nurture Nappies

Tel: (07) 4098 7007
email: service@nurturenappies.com.au
website: www.nurturenappies.com.au

Nurture Nappies is an Australian retail and wholesale supplier of modern cloth and reusable nappies and organic baby accessories. The comprehensive range includes the multi-award winning and best-selling bumGenius range, Tots Bots bamboo nappies, Baby Beehinds, Fuzzi Bunz, Motherease, Baby Greens, itti bitti, Green Kids and Thirsties nappies. Explore, discover, learn and enjoy nappies and organic baby products that nurture your baby.

Possum Pouches
email: possumpouches@optusnet.com.au
website: www.possumpouches.com.au

Possum Pouches, incorporating KK Nappies and Possum Knits, is an online store selling a range of modern cloth nappy products. These include the KK (Keester Kovers)® Windpro AIO, a fantastic long-lasting, night-time nappy, plus Pocket and Pul AIOs, all of which require no cover. Fitted nappies and Wool AI2s are also available, and their Possum Knits Knitted Soakers, Longies, Shorts, Skirts all enjoy an excellent reputation. Possum Pouches also stock boosters and accessories. All products Australian WAHM made.

Shop for Baby
Tel: (02) 9939 3643
email: contact@shopforbaby.com.au
website: www.shopforbaby.com.au

For a huge selection of gorgeous bathtime products log on to shopforbaby.com.au. They offer a range of bath toys, bathroom accessories, organic skincare products and much more. Leave the car at home and take advantage of their fast delivery, exceptional customer service and amazing loyalty program that enables you to save every time you shop.

ShopHouse
Tel: (02) 9011 6744
email: info@shophouse.com.au
website: www.shophouse.com.au

ShopHouse is an online children's boutique offering a full range of nappies as well as bath and body products for mums and babies. ShopHouse's selection of organic products include Eco.Kid, Bod and Moltex Nappies which will have you and your child covered, from head to toe. www.shophouse.com.au is a secure website available 24/7. All purchases are delivered next day using Express Post. A hassle-free returns policy makes online shopping a breeze and gift wrapping is available. Visit www.shophouse.com.au for more information.

The Bulk Warehouse
email: support@thebulkwarehouse.com.au
website: www.thebulkwarehouse.com.au

The Bulk Warehouse is a wholesaler and distributor of baby and family-care products, toys and gifts, prams, strollers, party supplies as well as safety and cleaning products. The Bulk Warehouse delivers Australia wide and overseas.

Total Nappy Supplies
Tel: (07) 5561 0626
email: info@nappysupplies.com.au
website: www.nappysupplies.com.au

Total Nappy Supplies provides an internet based opportunity for parents to order their baby products online at any time of the day or night. The range of nappies and wipes provides parents with a variety of products to choose from. All goods ordered will be delivered to your door. They also supply to child care centres and daycare a full range of products. Check out all the products at www.nappysupplies.com.au or phone for more information.

Totally Mums and Bubs
Tel: 0431 965 113
email: natalie@totallymumsandbubs.com.au
website: www.totallymumsandbubs.com.au

Totally Mums and Bubs has everything for mums and babies delivered to your door. This is an internet store for mums and babies specialising in clothing, skincare, slings (including Peanut Shell), ISOKI nappy bags, Change Mat Clutches and Petite travellers, things for mealtime, splashtime and sleeptime, cloth nappies, training pants and accessories, gift packs and many things to make your life that little bit easier with a baby or toddler. Phone the number above or visit the website for further information.

VANCHI
Tel: 0414 346 300
email: info@vanchi.com.au
website: www.vanchi.com.au

VANCHI's range includes chic, affordable nappy bags, super-sized baby wraps, wrap & hat sets, over-sized bibs, the convenient Change 'n' Aways and the new Change Clutch. Prices start from $19.95. Visit the website for local stockists or phone 0414 346 300 for further information. VANCHI is proudly 100% Australian owned and all products are designed in Australia.

NEW SOUTH WALES

GoToddler
Tel: 1300 889 086
email: info@gotoddler.com.au
website: www.gotoddler.com.au

GoToddler is a baby and toddler online shop focused on nappies and baby necessities. GoToddler provides an easy shopping experience for parents with babies or toddlers with many brands at your fingertips and the convenience of fast free delivery (Sydney metro only) to your doorstep. Apart from nappies GoToddler also features wipes, baby food and feeding products, health and safety products, as well as breastfeeding and nursing products. GoToddler loyal customers can save more by buying frequently and introducing friends. Phone the number above or visit the website for further information.

Resources

NAPPIES, BATHTIME & SKINCARE

Stores retail ➡ Toilet training products

STORES RETAIL:
NAPPIES, BATHTIME & SKINCARE

VICTORIA

Chris' Dial A Nappy
205A Victoria Road
Northcote VIC 3070
Tel: (03) 9489 3844
email: dialanappy@netspace.net.au
website: www.dialanappy.com.au

Chris' Dial A Nappy are the biodegradable and modern cloth nappy specialists. Conventional nappies also available and they offer free same day delivery. Chris' Dial A Nappy are committed to educating their customers in environmentally responsible nappy choices, and know that good impartial information can help parents in the confusing dilemma when choosing nappies and weighing up the environmentally friendly options. They are currently running nappy education classes (for free) in store – just phone or email to find out times – and they are also involved in environmental nappy trials in a local child care centre. All their nappies come in discounted packages. Eenees full range 100% biodegradable nappies, fitted cloth, PUL nappy covers, prefolds, Huggies, Baby love, Joeys, Factory Seconds and much more. Phone, email, or visit their website or their retail store in Northcote for more information.

The Nappy Shop
1341 Burke Road
Kew VIC 3101
Tel: (03) 9817 2661
website: www.thenappyshop.com.au

The Nappy Shop provides all your nappy and accessory needs. Their friendly trained staff will give all the information needed to make the right nappy choice for your baby. Free home delivery is available – same or next day – Monday to Friday to most Melbourne metropolitan suburbs for a minimum of two boxes of nappies. To receive same day delivery (within the Nappy Shop delivery radius) make sure you place your order before 11.30am Monday to Friday.

NEW SOUTH WALES

babyshop
276 Brunker Road
Adamstown NSW 2289
Tel: 1800 222 437 or 1800 BABIES
website: www.babyshop.com.au

With experience online since 1998 and hundreds of products to choose from, babyshop stocks a variety of well known brands, as well as featuring many exclusive and hard to find items. Departments include: Bathtime & Care, Bedtime & Nursery, Clothing, Feeding & Accessories, Out & About and Playtime & Development.

QUEENSLAND

Pookey Pockets
Shop 6, 76-82 Queens Road
Kingston QLD 4114
Tel: (07) 3038 5693
email: shop@pookeypockets.com.au
website: www.pookeypockets.com.au

The Pookey Pockets shop stocks a large range of modern cloth nappies (reusable nappies) and accessories, along with the fabrics and supplies for DIY nappy-making. Previously available mainly through online stores, the shop offers customers a chance to see and touch the nappies/fabrics before purchasing. They also run regular nappy information sessions, classes and workshops for those who wish to learn to sew their own reusable nappies, catering for beginners through to more advanced sewers.

WESTERN AUSTRALIA

Hush Clothes For Kids
Shop 7 Centro Kalamunda Shopping Centre
Kalamunda WA 6076
Tel: (08) 9293 0111
website: www.kalamundaweb.com.au/hush

Hush Clothes for Kids has clothing for newborns to children aged 12 years (smart, casual and formal wear), as well as Snug as a Bug Baby Wraps and Swaddle Me wraps, Grobags, Robeez baby shoes, the breastfeeding wrap by Leah, CDs, clothing gift packs, swim nappies and chlorine-resistant bathers. Sun protective swimwear is available throughout the year. Organic clothing and nappies are also available. Mail order welcome. Phone the number above or visit the website for further information.

SOUTH AUSTRALIA

Nappies Galore Incontinence 'N' More
324 Hampstead Road
Clearview SA 5085
Tel: (08) 8359 5188
website: www.nappiesgalore.com.au

Nappies Galore, Incontinence 'N' More stock famous brand disposable nappies, pull-ups, drynites and Little Swimmers at great prices and bulk cartons of nappies from $20.95. They also sell a large range of mother and baby products, wipes, gift baskets, sanitary and incontinence products, toilet paper and cleaning products as well as Bambo environmental nappies. Delivery available to Adelaide and SA country areas or visit their store for friendly and reliable service.

TOILET TRAINING PRODUCTS

NATIONAL

BEDazzled Bed Mats

Tel: (07) 5491 1880
email: bedazzledbedmats@dodo.com.au
website: www.bedazzledbedmats.com

BEDazzled Bed Mats have all your bed wetting, toilet training and incontinence needs covered. These bed mats are washable and re-usable and come in a vast range of sizes and designs. The mattress/sheet protectors are 100% Australian owned and manufactured. This website also stocks washable and re-usable pants, pillow protectors, doona protectors and licensed manchester plus much more. Phone orders are welcome.

Bedwetting Institute of Australia

Tel: 1300 135 796
email: info@bedwettinginstitute.com.au
website: www.bedwettinginstitute.com.au

By age five one third of children still wet the bed – some occasionally, some every night. The *Bedwetting Cured* DVD, with Dr Mark Condon and Physiotherapist Margaret O'Donovan, outlines a five-step program to cure the problem. Some children will need a bedwetting alarm but very few will need medication. Waterproof absorbent mattress pads are handy for younger children. They are washable and save changing the sheets following a wet night.

Danjo Products pty Ltd

Tel: 1300 785 899
email: info@weetarget.com.au
website: www.weetarget.com.au

Wee Targets are plastic targets that you stick to the inside rim of the toilet to give little boys (and not so little) something to aim for. To make it a lot of fun, the targets have heat sensitive black ink spots on them and when the wee hits the target, the black ink 'disappears' to reveal a picture underneath. The targets go back to black once the toilet is flushed, ready for next time.

Galway Trading

Tel: 1300 721 710
email: sales@conni.com.au
website: www.conni.com.au

Conni has developed a fun range of kids' products to assist in the process of toilet training. No more total bed changes, ConniKids bed pads are absorbent on top and waterproof on bottom to keep the mattress dry and hygienic. Machine washable and tumble drier safe with no PVC, ConniKids bed pads also include a free toilet training kit. Simply remove the night nappy, place your ConniKids bed pad on the bed and let toilet training happen naturally. Phone the number above or visit the website for further information.

Nice-Pak Products

Tel: 1800 506 750
email: info@nicepak.com.au
website: www.babyu.com.au

This softly padded toilet seat offers comfort and warmth to your child during the vital toilet training period. Baby U™ Cushie Tushie™ is easily fitted onto a regular toilet seat and features glow-in-the-dark characters to guide your child at night. Using a regular toilet during the training process assists your child to become familiar with regular toilet facilities while protecting your child from the discomfort of slipping into the toilet during the early stages of toilet training. The Cushie Traveller™ Folding Padded Potty Seat provides the convenience of taking a soft, cushioned potty seat with you when you are away from home. Safety brackets hold the Cushie Traveller™ in place and enable it to fit easily on most regular toilet seats. Cushie Traveller™ is a convenient and hygienic solution to toilet training when you are on the go. Cushie Traveller™ folds easily to fit into the included washable travel bag. Phone 1800 506 750 or visit www.babyu.com.au for further information.

Nice-Pak Products

Tel: 1800 506 750
website: www.babyu.com.au

The NEW Baby U Potette is strong and ideal for encouraging children with toilet training and general use in public places. The Potette is designed to be user friendly, which in turn makes toileting convenient at any time. The Potette is a great product for people on-the-go. Set up your Potette with the super absorbent disposable liners and you are ready to go the instant your child is. It's a full-sized potty that folds flat into a carry bag. Available in Big W, Kmart, Target, Toys R Us and baby stores. Phone 1800 506 750 or visit www.babyu.com.au for further information.

Pottytraining.com.au

Tel: 1300 886 234
email: info@pottytraining.com.au
website: www.pottytraining.com.au

Pottytraining.com.au has toilet training information and products to help both parent and child. Everything is covered: from babies to toddlers, from bed-wetting to boys aiming and teaching to stand. Pottytraining is a terrific toilet training online shop. Products include toilet training kits, reward charts, Weeman, wee targets, toilet seats and inserts, folding potties and seats, bed-wetting solutions, training pants, sheet protectors, Johnny-Lights, and Wiggles wipes.

That's Great

Tel: 0407 114 180
website: www.thatsgreat.com.au

Make toilet training fun and easy with That's Great Toilet Training Packs. Each pack comes with one A4 reusable 7-day chart, two reward certificates, ten removable and reusable stickers and easy-to-use instructions. Also available: A3 non-behaviour-specific reward charts as well as chore charts. That's Great charts are bright, funky and promote positive behaviour.

Huggies® Newborn Nappies

Huggies® nappies are Australia's number one nappy, and more Huggies® Newborn nappies are sold than any other newborn nappy available on the market.

They have been specially created to keep babies drier than any other nappy. Each one has a 3-Layer Design which includes a unique Fast-Absorb Layer which draws moisture away from baby's skin even faster than before. What's more, they have a special Breathe Dry® Cover, which lets air circulate around baby's bottom, leaving it drier and healthier, making it the only nappy that's clinically proven to help prevent nappy rash.

In addition Huggies® Newborn nappies now feature Fasten-Anyway Grip tabs which ensure that you can achieve the perfect fit around the waist for your baby as well as having the softest-ever outer cover and a baby soft liner on the inside for all over softness that's gentle on your newborn's skin.

They are available in packs of 36, 54 or 108 so you can buy a smaller pack for when you're on-the-go or stock up on the larger sizes at home to ensure that you never run out. With bright and colourful Winnie the Pooh designs, Huggies® Newborn nappies are a great first-choice for you and your new baby.

It's the little things
that make them so unique

1 Only **Huggies**® nappies are clinically proven to help prevent nappy rash

2 Unique 3-Layer Design to quickly draw moisture away from baby's skin

3 **Breathe Dry**® Cover to allow air to circulate, keeping baby drier

4 Fasten-Anywhere Grip Tabs for a perfect fit

5 Softest ever Outer Cover that's gentle on newborn skin

HUGGIES
Newborn
up to 14g
36

It must be love
HUGGIES®
BRAND
huggies.com.au

Huggies® Baby Wipes

Huggies® Baby Wipes are Australia's number one baby wipe. They are thick and especially soft and gently clean and moisturise baby's skin with a hypoallergenic formula of natural ingredients such as Aloe Vera and Vitamin E.

All Huggies® Baby Wipes are pH balanced, dermatologically tested and free of soap and alcohol so are safe to use on baby's face, hands and bottoms. The unique texture and unbeatable thickness of Huggies® Baby Wipes means they gently get more off with each wipe, providing a quicker nappy change for baby. Huggies® Baby Wipes have a product suitable for every baby: Fragrance Free, Lightly Fragranced and Newborn and Sensitive which are clinically proven safe for newborn and sensitive skin.

Huggies® Baby Wipes also come in a range of convenient pack sizes including refills, handy travel packs and Pop-Up tubs that allow for easy one hand use.

The day I used a thinner baby wipe.

Huggies® Baby Wipes clean better than other wipes.
They're thickest, and won't tear even on the toughest
jobs. And with a softness that's made for baby's skin,
they're as gentle as they are strong.

It must be love
HUGGIES®
BABY WIPES
huggies.com.au

Curash Babycare

Curash Babycare is one of Australia's leading babycare brands. Curash has always been well-known for treating nappy rash however, our range extends beyond just nappy rash treatment, with products that provide complete care for baby from top to toe.

Through the years, exciting new products have been added to the Curash range helping mothers to protect their children from nappy rash as well as helping maintain healthy skin. Whether it is baby wipes, medicated nappy rash cream, soap free baby bath or a 2-in-1 shampoo & conditioner we have you and your baby's needs covered.

Curash has evolved into an Australian baby care icon with a whole range of products specifically tailored for babies and toddlers. We are constantly developing new products and conducting in-depth market research in order to meet the changing needs of today's mothers and babies.

Here at Curash we pride ourselves on our quality products, so much so that all of our products have a 100% satisfaction guarantee. To us a happy baby means happy parents.

Curash is marketed by Church & Dwight (Australia) Pty. Ltd., the makers of household names such as Discover & First Response pregnancy tests, Dencorub, Pearl Drops, Nair, Ultrafresh, Spinbrush, and Sterimar just to name a few.

For more information on the entire Curash product range please visit our website at www.curash.com.au.

For Beautiful Baby Hair

...ash 2 in 1 Shampoo and Conditioner ...enriched with chamomile extracts ...special silk proteins to leave your ...y's scalp moisturised, hair soft, shiny ...tangle free. Its dermatologically pH ...tral, no tears formula means it is ...at for sensitive skin.

For Cleaner, Healthier Skin

All Curash Baby Wipes are super soft, super thick and alcohol free to gently cleanse and freshen your baby's skin, helping protect against nappy rash. Available in Soap Free, Fragrance Free and Moisturising.

For a Happier Bath Time

Curash Soap Free Moisturising Bath, a gentle, no tears formula, enriched with vitamin E and Aloe Vera to keep your baby's skin clean, soft, smooth and moisturised whilst caring for the protective acid mantle. Ideal for sensitive skin.

Healthy skin from top to bottom.

For Teething Time

...ash Oral Pain Relieving Gel offers ...ck relief from the discomfort of infant ...thing and minor abrasions of the ...ns resulting in a calmer, happier baby. ...d a calmer, happier family.

Soothe, Heal and Prevent Nappy Rash

Curash Anti-Rash Baby Powder and Medicated Nappy Rash Cream quickly soothe and help heal nappy rash and prevent further wetness causing irritation to the skin. Use to keep baby's bottom as soft as...well...a baby's bottom.

www.curash.com.au FREE Call 1800 222 099 enquiries@churchdwight.com.au
Available from supermarkets, pharmacies and selected stores nationally.

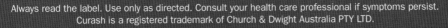

Sorbies

Sorbies disposable nappies give you a product designed by mums for mums.

Sorbies is the world's first Nappy Pack with Specialist Night Nappies and Practical Day Nappies both in the one convenient pack, all your nappy needs in the one place!

Available in sizes from Infant through to Junior, now you can use a great nappy that lasts all night, whilst using a practical efficient nappy during the day so as not to waste money.

The night nappies have extra Sorbie Beads™ for up to 12-hour protection and fun frontal designed tabs for easy identification of the night nappy. The day nappies are designed specifically for frequent daytime changes with Easygrab™ secure tabs for a stronger fit.

Sorbies disposable nappies are available in convenient, bulk and jumbo packs from supermarkets nationally. Look for the orange pack and pick one up today.

If you would like to find out more about Sorbies Disposable nappies visit our website at www.sorbies.com.au.

We are dedicated to listening to mums so if you have feedback about our products or have a great idea please drop us a line at info@sorbies.com.au or by calling 1800 188 201 and tell us how we can make your life easier.

Absolutely Unique

The only nappy pack in the world
with night nappies and day nappies

www.sorbies.com.au

Sorbies

Sorbies is an Australian company that listened to mums in order to come up with the world's first nappy pack with both night nappies and day nappies in the one convenient pack.

The Sorbies pack of nappies is convenient because all your nappy needs are in the one place. You save space because you only need the one pack of nappies for all your daytime and night time needs, you save time and money.

There are 6 key features to the Sorbies disposable nappy:

1. Absorbency – Super thirsty Sorbie Beads™ soak up to 20 times their own weight in seconds.
2. Liquid dispersion – Sorbies Quilt Lined Layer™ disperses continuously.
3. Tabs – Easygrab™ tabs for snug and secure fit.
4. Leak/Waste Guard – wide comfort guards keep liquid in protecting clothing and linen.
5. Frontal Tape – Easy-to-read labels for Night nappies and day nappies.
6. Breathable cover – Allow fresh air to circulate naturally.

The night nappy is designed to provide up to 12 hours of protection and the day nappy is practical and efficient for frequent changes. Easily identifiable the day nappy and night nappy have different designs.

The nappies are available in all sizes from Infant starting at 4kg right through to Junior 16kg+.

They are available from supermarkets nationally and if you want to find a stockist near you visit the Sorbies website at www.sorbies.com.au for more information.

NEW

SORBIES™

Night & Day
nappies   nappies

Night - 12 hour protection*
Day - Super efficient & practical

- **Night Nappies & Day Nappies all in one pack**
- **Less wastage and better value for money**

* Night Nappies will last up to 12 hours under normal conditions.

www.sorbies.com.au

Covitol

Covitol Nappy Rash Treatment Cream helps soothe and relieve nappy rash and skin infections. Covitol provides a thick, smooth barrier for long lasting protection. Primarily used as an effective nappy rash treatment cream, it also helps relieve eczema, sunburn, cuts, scrapes and skin infections.

Covitol is uniquely formulated with high levels of nutritive rich Cod Liver Oil, Zinc Oxide, Paraffin and Lanolin. Together these ingredients seal out wetness and germs to help skin irritations disappear quickly. The Cod Liver Oil is rich in vitamins A and D and omega 3. The Zinc Oxide protects and soothes wounded skin and eczema. Fragrance and colour free, it's 100% best for baby.

Always read the label. Use only as directed. If symptoms persist see your healthcare professional.

ASMI/15763-10/08

COVITOL® NAPPY RASH TREATMENT.
IT'S THICK SO IT STICKS.

Covitol® provides a thick, soothing barrier that sticks to your baby's bottom to promote healing and long lasting protection. It is specially formulated with high levels of Zinc Oxide, Cod Liver Oil and Paraffin to help seal out wetness and germs to help skin irritations disappear.

• Thick & Long Lasting • Promotes Healing • Soothes & Protects

Available in Pharmacies.

Soothing Lotion

- *Soothing on skin affected by irritations*
- *Ideal barrier at nappy change time*
- *Eczema friendly*

GAIA's Skin Soothing Lotion is a great calming lotion for any areas in need of soothing, like mozzie bites, nappy rash, itchiness and eczema. Apply in a thick layer to baby's nappy area at every nappy change to keep your baby's skin protected, soft and smooth.

Organic calendula and chamomile are calming on skin: ideal for little cheeks exposed to the elements and little noses that have been irritated by tissues.

Handy Hint: Don't rub creams into irritated areas as this can cause further friction. Instead, squeeze lotion onto the back of your hand and then using your fingertips pat the lotion onto your baby's skin. Visit www.gaiaskinnaturals.com for a free sample.

Available from selected Big W, Chemmart Chemists, Cole supermarkets, Priceline, Target, Terry White Chemists, pharmacies, health food and baby stores. Visit website for full stockist listing.

Baby Moisturiser

- *For baby soft skin*
- *NO mineral oil*
- *Ideal for sensitive skin*

Keep your little one's skin extra soft and supple with our nourishing blend of organic oils, like shea butter, evening primrose oil and wheat germ oil, to moisturise and provide softness without leaving a greasy feel. It's ideal for dry and flaky skin, to hydrate and moisturise or if you want to maintain your little one's already soft skin.

Also containing calming organic lavender and organic chamomile, making it ideal to use as part of your baby's bedtime routine – after their bath, towel dry leaving them slightly damp and give a gentle massage with GAIA Natural Baby Moisturiser. Visit www.gaiaskinnaturals.com for a free sample.

Available from All Woolworths/Safeway stores, Chemmart, Priceline, Terry White Chemists, Toys R Us, and selected Big W, Cole supermarkets, Target, pharmacies, health food and baby stores. Visit website for full stockist listing.

Baby Shampoo

• *For soft, shiny hair*
• *Ideal for cradle cap*
• *NO soap or sulphates*

GAIA Natural Baby Shampoo uses non-irritating foaming agents made from coconut and there is no soap to sting so it is kind and gentle on little scalps, skin and eyes. It's extremely mild but effectively cleanses without stripping your baby's natural protective scalp oils and has added moisturising properties to help to prevent scalp dryness, minimising cradle cap.

Organic chamomile brings out your hair's natural highlights to leave your little one with silky soft and shiny hair. Follow up with GAIA Natural Baby Conditioning Detangler to tame tangles and make combing easier on wet or dry hair.
Available from All Woolworths/Safeway, Coles supermarkets, Chemmart Chemists, Priceline, Terry White Chemists, Toys R Us, and selected Big W, Target, pharmacies, health food and baby stores. Visit website for full stockist listing.

Bath & Body Wash

• *NO soap or sulphates*
• *NO artificial fragrance*
• *Eczema friendly*

A non-drying bath and body wash containing organic sweet orange oil and extra mild foaming agents to gently cleanse and care for your baby's sensitive skin every day. Added skin-softening organic oils help to prevent dryness and will leave your baby's skin soft, fresh and moisturised at bath time.

If your baby has sensitive skin or eczema, GAIA Natural Baby Bath & Body Wash may be for you.

Handy Hint: Try to keep the bath water a fraction cooler – hot water can be drying on your baby's skin.

To get a free baby bath thermometer and bath wash sample visit www.gaiaskinnaturals.com (conditions apply).

Available from All Woolworths/Safeway, Coles supermarkets, Chemmart Chemists, Priceline, Terry White Chemists, Toys R Us, and selected Big W, Target, pharmacies, health food and baby stores. Visit website for full stockist listing.

Pea Pods

Australian designed and owned Pea Pods Reusable Nappies save a small fortune compared to disposables and save a small planet from being filled with unnecessary waste.

Simple to care for and use, Pea Pods are environmentally friendly, slim fitting and stylish.

Pea Pods make happy babies with their soft micro-fleece inner lining. The lining draws moisture away and keeps baby's skin dry. With the waterproof, breathable outer layer there is no need for a cover or pilcher. Each nappy comes complete with its own absorbent insert (no need to purchase separately) and lasts up to four hours. Need to use Pea Pods overnight? No problem, simply add a Night Booster and your reusable nappy will last up to 12 hours.

Re-usable Nappies

• Save $1,000's per child • Easy to use • Environmentally friendly

pea pods®
peapods.com.au

Available in a range of colours!

Visit our website
www.peapods.com.au
to locate your nearest stockist or order online.

Nature's Child

Nature's Child has grown from humble beginnings since July 2000. They have just opened their third and largest store in Byron Bay, Northern NSW.

Owner Jannine Barron says the passion in her team stems from the educational aspect of her business. "Some days we can really see that we change lives. Health, environment and money are the key issues. Our favourite message is showing parents how much money they save with organic products, which is the opposite of how most people logically think. When you walk past a store and see disposable nappies on special for $15 you think, wow, that's cheap but it's not! We educate parents on how to count the long-term cost of so called bargains. We can prove that you will save $5000 by using reusable, organic products instead of disposables. Parents spend $20 to $40 a week on disposable baby items that are sending them broke. Disposables create a lot of rubbish. We show parents how to replace disposables with organic cotton that cost $1.50 weekly, including electricity, water and eco-detergents. One of the many amazing facts we can share is that standard cotton accounts for around 25% of all insecticide use globally, and 11% of total pesticides. The depleted soil and water quality have further negative effects on biodiversity and human health. These facts matter when we consider our children and their future."

If you want to know more, you can phone Nature's Child for a FREE money saving info pack and colour catalogue or visit www.natureschild.com.au

PH: 1300 555 632. Nature's Child also sells nationally and the brand can be found in baby stores.

BUBOO® Baby Elevator

As with many Mumtrepeneurs it was frustration at not being able to find the right product that led Debora Kalisse to invent the BUBOO® Baby Elevator™ change mat. The idea struck in 1999 when she was a first - time mum struggling with a baby suffering reflux. Deborah had tried many different methods such as rolled-up towels and phone books under a flat change mat but none of these worked as safely or effectively as an angled changed mat. At the time there was nothing on the market like it (and it's now patent protected), hence it became the ideal opportunity to create a small business.

Different from a regular change mat, the elevation helps to aid a baby's digestion. Particularly suitable for reflux babies, the mat provides a much more comfortable way for every baby to have his/her nappy changed.

The mat can also be used for play. Suitable for babies up to 4 months or until a baby is rolling – it can be used as a play mat by putting the baby on the mat under a hanging toy.

The mat comes in an easy to clean vinyl material for $49.99*. Terry towelling covers are also available in lemon and white. The covers are made from cotton/polyester which is nice and soft and ensures your baby's comfort. They are also machine washable and can be tumble dried. Covers are sold separately for $13.99.

The Buboo Baby Elevator™ change mat is available from leading independent nursery retailers. For customer enquiries or more stockist information please contact Funtastic's free-call Customer Care Line on 1800 244 543.

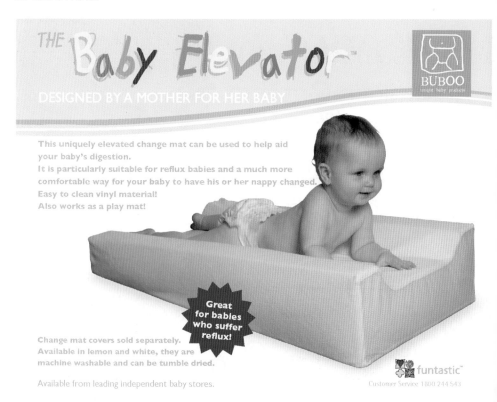

THE Baby Elevator™

BUBOO

DESIGNED BY A MOTHER FOR HER BABY

This uniquely elevated change mat can be used to help aid your baby's digestion.
It is particularly suitable for reflux babies and a much more comfortable way for your baby to have his or her nappy changed.
Easy to clean vinyl material!
Also works as a play mat!

Great for babies who suffer reflux!

Change mat covers sold separately. Available in lemon and white, they are machine washable and can be tumble dried.

Available from leading independent baby stores.

funtastic™

Customer Service 1800 244 543

Baby BeeHinds

Baby BeeHinds Modern Cloth Nappies are all about convenience, reliability and keeping our Earth green. Gone are the days of folding, pinning and soaking cotton flat nappies. Baby BeeHinds are super cute, easy to use and will save you thousands of dollars over the term of your child's nappying years. We offer a range of products to suit different needs and use modern fabrics to focus on environmental sustainability, comfort and fashion. Head on over to our website to learn about the best cloth nappies since sliced bread.

Modern cloth nappies such as Baby BeeHinds offer unbeatable value. Rather than throw your money in the bin, invest in a cloth nappy system that will save you heaps of cash, is easy to use and care for, is comfortable for baby to wear, wont impact your environment in such a negative way and, as an added bonus, will look simply adorable.

Baby BeeHinds are the leaders in modern cloth nappy innovation here in Australia, being at the forefront of new product launches consistently throughout the last 5 years. We can offer you secure online shopping, or if you value some fantastic personalised service, we also offer one-on-one product demonstrations with product consultants available in many areas throughout Australia.

Baby BeeHinds are also available through many stockists, so you can even support your local community by purchasing through a stockist near you. All this information and more can be found at www.babybeehinds.com.au.

Sit back with a cuppa and learn about our revolutionary nappies that are sure to impress. No folding. No soaking. No Pins. Just nappies that work!

Baby BeeHinds Modern Cloth Nappies

Australian designed for perfect comfort for your bub

Visit our website to learn about how easy cloth can be, and keep your baby looking super gorgeous in soft, comfy fabrics.

Best for baby, best for your hip pocket and best for your environment.

www.babybeehinds.com.au

Children's
health & safety

Photograph by Ashford Studio, Gold Coast.

Developmental milestones: 0 to 3 years

Most parents want to know if their baby or toddler is developing 'normally'. The following is a basic guide as to what you might expect for the first three years of life (often called developmental milestones). Each heading gives an idea about what a baby or child will usually do at that age. There will be individual differences, and the differences in the way you care for your child can sometimes have an effect on what your child does.

If you are worried that your child seems 'out of step' with others of the same age, talk with a child health nurse or a doctor. Another opinion will help to either reassure you or enable you to get help early.

0-3 MONTHS
Relationships and feelings (often called social and emotional development):
- Can feel, but not yet able to think – will pick up your feelings
- Watches parent's face when being talked to by 4-8 weeks
- Smiles by 5-7 weeks
- Starts to laugh aloud by 3 months.

Out of step?
- No social smile by 8 weeks
- Does not usually calm down, at least for a little while, when picked up.

Doing, seeing and hearing (often called motor skills, vision and hearing):
- When cheek is touched, turns to that side to suck from birth
- Blinks at sudden noises such as hand claps or door slamming from birth
- May open eyes to normal speech sounds just as she is dozing off from birth
- Startled by loud sounds by 1 month
- Begins to notice sudden long sounds when they start and stop (e.g. vacuum cleaner) by 1 month
- Lifts head when lying on tummy by 4-8 weeks (do not leave baby alone on tummy)
- Kicks both legs strongly by 2 months
- Arms, fingers and legs automatically move, bend, straighten and bend again
- Follows a moving light with eyes by 1 month
- Both eyes move together most of the time by 6 weeks
- Watches a moving face by 2-3 months
- Sucks well at the breast or from a bottle
- Sleep patterns vary greatly.

Out of step?
- Baby is unusually 'floppy' or stiff
- An arm and leg on one side is obviously different in muscle tone or strength to the other side

- There is unusually 'good' head control (muscles stiff).
- Fingers are always held in a tight fist
- Baby is not watching faces by 3 months
- Baby is not startled by sudden noise
- Difficulties with feeding beyond 'normal' range – discuss with child health nurse.
- Long periods of crying and continuing difficulties with settling
- Seems unusually 'good' and not demanding compared to other babies.

Learning to talk (often called speech and language development):
- Makes other sounds besides crying by 2 months
- Starts to make sounds and 'talk back' by 7-8 weeks
- Appears to listen to parent's voice and watches the face.

Out of step?
- Not watching the person's face when being spoken to by 3 months
- Not making little sounds by 3 months.

3–6 MONTHS
Relationships and feelings:
- Laughs aloud by 2-4 months
- Enjoys being played with, laughs and kicks by 4 months
- Makes eye contact with you and you will be smiling at each other.

Out of step?
- Doesn't seem interested in things around him
- Doesn't seem to show delight in being with people
- Doesn't seem to recognise his parent or other familiar people.

Doing, seeing and hearing:
- Enjoys watching others doing things
- Makes eye contact
- Likes looking at people and bright objects
- Looks at hands and plays with own fingers by 3 months
- Can grasp an object when placed in his hand by 3-4 months
- Rolls over to his side by around 5 months (range is 4-6 months)
- Lifts head and chest when lying on his tummy by 4 months – never leave baby alone on tummy
- Begins to react to familiar situations by smiling, cooing and excited movements
- Begins to turn head slowly to moderate level of sound (e.g. normal speaking voice) by 3 months
- Should quieten or smile at sound of your voice, even if he cannot see you, by 4 months
- May turn his head or eyes towards you if you speak by 4 months.

Developmental milestones: 0 to 3 years

Out of step?
- Does not open hands or straighten fingers
- Arms and legs are bent most of the time
- Is not kicking his legs
- Does not follow activities with his eyes
- Does not make eye contact with people
- Does not turn to look for you when you speak
- Is not looking to where there is a sound
- Is not startled by loud noises
- Unhappy or unsettled most of the time.

Learning to talk:
- Makes lots of little voice sounds
- Turns head towards a talking person by 5 months
- Begins babbling then listening by around 3-4 months
- Takes turn when 'talking' (making sounds) with parents.

Out of step?
- Is not making many voice sounds.

6–9 MONTHS
Relationships and feelings:
- Knows familiar people and is unsure of strangers
- At times might not go to people she knows well for a while – but wants the main carer
- May become distressed when separated from the main carer
- Delights in and plays 'peek-a-boo' games.

Out of step?
- Does not show pleasure when she sees people she knows well
- Does not make eye contact
- Cannot be comforted by parent or close carer.

Doing:
- Can swap small items from one hand to the other
- Picks objects up with thumb and one finger
- Rolls over onto tummy and back again by 7 months
- Sits without support by 8 months
- Starts to move around more and can roll and creep on her tummy by 8 months
- Can move between positions, e.g. sitting to crawling to sitting by 8 months
- Can hold a bottle to drink

- Can start to drink from a cup which is held by an adult by 8 months
- Holds a spoon, but cannot use it, by 7 months
- Shows interest in small objects and reaches out for them
- Starts to look at and feel objects before taking them to her mouth
- Looks in the right direction for things that have fallen down.

Out of step?
- Not starting to move around by any means
- Not interested in and does not reach for objects by 8 months
- Does not recognise parent or main carer
- Does not show an interest in surroundings
- Not interested in new objects.

Hearing and learning to talk:
- Should turn immediately to very quiet sounds by 7 months
- Babbles with sounds like "da da" and then starts to put these babbling sounds together by 6-7 months
- Recognises several words, e.g. looks for Daddy if "Daddy" is said
- Copies sounds made by other people.

Out of step?
- Babbling has not developed further and she does not babble in 'conversation' with others
- Not turning towards you when calling her name.

9–12 MONTHS
Relationships and feelings:
- Knows familiar people and starts to withdraw from strangers by 9 months
- Begins to turn around when his name is called
- Gives cuddles by 10 months
- Starts to become anxious if main carer is out of sight
- Stretches up arms to be picked up
- May give clues as to whether hungry or needing a cuddle
- Loves to be talked to and played with
- Copies gestures such as coughing and waving
- Cannot understand "no" or "danger".

Out of step?
- Does not show pleasure when he sees people he knows well
- Is not making eye contact
- Cannot be comforted by parent or close carer.

Developmental milestones: 0 to 3 years

Doing:
- Points with the index finger
- Drops and throws things on purpose
- Passes objects easily from one hand to the other
- Moves around by crawling or 'bottom shuffling' by 10 months
- Pulls up to standing by 11 months
- Walks with hands held and feet wide apart and facing outward by 10-12 months.

Out of step?
- Is not sitting by 9 months
- Holds his body stiff and cannot be put in a sitting position
- Is not starting to move around in any way
- Is not interested in new objects or reaching for them.

Hearing and learning to talk:
- Looks for quiet sounds made out of sight by 9 months
- Shows pleasure in babbling loudly by 9 months
- Conversation 'babble' develops further
- Knows the direction a sound comes from and turns to it immediately by 10-12 months
- Shakes his head for "no" and nods his head to signal "yes" by 10-12 months
- Knows and turns to his own name by 12 months
- Likes to look at picture books and can say some sounds at certain pictures
- May say one or two single words.

Out of step?
- Does not babble or make other sounds when someone talks to him.

1-2 YEARS
This is a time of rapid change. Your baby is on the move, full of energy and curiosity discovering the world. Parenting becomes demanding because you have to think about safety and setting limits as well as caring for your toddler. In this year your toddler is learning to be a separate person from you. The one-year-old sees everything and everyone being there for them alone. This self-centredness will continue throughout this year.

This is a year of firsts – first steps, first words, first tantrums, moving freely, running, climbing and exploring actively.

Relationships and feelings
By 18 months:
- Explores the environment around her, touching, pulling whatever she can see and reach
- Enjoys physical contact (cuddles)
- Shows different feelings and easily moves from happy to sad to angry

- Is likely to be afraid of strangers
- Shows a strong attachment to parents or main carer
- Shows distress when left by a parent – is often clingy when the parent returns.

Out of step?
- Does not show a preference for people she knows well
- Does not seem to like cuddles.

By 2 years:
- Plays near other children, but not yet with other children (unless the other children are older and able to adapt their play to fit the 2-year-old)
- Unable to share or take turns
- Gets upset by separating.

Out of step?
- Does not show awareness of different people
- Doesn't seem interested in surroundings or in people.

Doing
By 12 months can usually:
- Pull self up on a lounge chair
- Side-step around the chair whilst holding on
- Push a small trolley along in a straight line – but can't turn corners.

By 18 months can usually:
- Walk, at first with feet wide apart, but as her balance improves her feet will get closer and straighter
- Fall over if she tries to run
- Climb onto low furniture
- Push a wheeled toy such as a trolley
- Place one object such as a block deliberately onto another
- Start to scribble with a pencil
- Pick up small objects.

Out of step?
- Not yet walking
- Cannot hold a spoon and get food to her mouth
- Cannot pick up small objects.

By 2 years can usually:
- Start to explore more widely, opening doors and drawers and pushing buttons
- Run fast without falling over when turning corners or stopping
- Squat steadily to pick up objects from the floor

Developmental milestones: 0 to 3 years

- Bring a small chair to the table and sit on the chair at the table
- Walk backwards pulling a toy or trolley
- Get up without using her hands.

Out of step?
- Not walking steadily by 2 years, especially if there is a limp.

Learning to talk

By 18 months can usually:
- Babble loudly to self and others, as though having a conversation
- Listen to things said and understand some things such as "no" or "stop"
- Follow a few simple instructions such as "get your shoes"
- Identify a few familiar objects when they are named such as "show me the ball" or "where is the spoon?"
- Knows and uses 6 or more words (the words may be quite unclear, but the parent or carer can tell what is meant by the sound).

Out of step?
- Not babbling much
- Not starting to use some meaningful words
- Not listening when others speak to him.

By 2 years can usually:
- Use 20 to 50 recognisable words
- Listen to things that are said to him
- Start to put 2 words together such as "daddy's car"
- Can remember two things at a time e.g. "get the ball and bring it to daddy"
- Join in with familiar songs e.g. nursery rhymes
- Babble while playing, with a few recognisable words in the babble
- Tell you most of what he wants with words, e.g. "outside", "milk", "want more" or "go away".

Out of step?
- Is still mostly silent while playing
- Does not respond when others talk to him
- Is not able to point to objects when they are named
- Uses signs, grunts or gestures but not words when he wants something.

2–3 YEARS
This is a time of challenge – when toddlers really want to find out about themselves and what they want and don't want. Their determination, tantrums and struggle for independence are all part of normal development.

They have new skills and behaviours to learn and remember, feelings to grapple with, and these can be overwhelming. They can wait a little while … but not for long. They can hold strong feelings inside a little, but these can burst out in a rush. Losing control of such feelings can be frightening – they need lots of physical contact and reassurance that they are lovable.

Relationships and feelings
By 2.5 years can usually:
- Try hard to be independent, say "no" a lot, or "me do" (but still very dependent on parents)
- Be unable to control his feelings – tantrums are common especially when tired or frustrated
- Be unable share with others or take turns
- Start to play imaginative games, such as putting a doll to bed, driving a car around on the floor or 'feeding' toys.

Out of step?
- Is having tantrums very often
- Does not play with adults or older children.

By 3 years can usually:
- Try to copy adults, and may be able to be helpful e.g. help put toys away
- Play games using lots of imagination and start to join in with other children's play.

Out of step?
- Not playing imaginative games or using toys the way they are 'meant' to be used
- Mostly 'in his own world' rather than interacting with others.

Doing
By 2.5 years:
- Climb on and off furniture
- Run smoothly and climb on play equipment
- Kick a large ball gently but not necessarily where she wants it to go
- Throw a ball more or less where she wants it to go
- Climb up stairs
- Feed herself with a spoon and drink from an open cup
- Help to dress and undress herself
- Be very active and resist attempts to stop her doing things
- Does not understand about danger, even if she can say that something is dangerous.

Out of step?
- Cannot run smoothly, especially if there is a limp
- Cannot safely climb stairs or onto low furniture
- Is far more active or less active than other children of the same age
- Is not yet managing to feed herself most of the time.

Developmental milestones: 0 to 3 years

By 3 years can usually:
- Push or pull large toys around to where she wants them
- Walk alone up and down stairs
- Push the pedals on a pedal toy e.g. tricycle
- Stand and tiptoe
- Kick a ball forcefully
- Throw a ball and catch one with outstretched arms
- Undress and put on some simple clothes
- Eat with spoon and fork
- Manage toilet training (some children will not manage this until they are nearly 4).

Out of step?
- Not able to run as smoothly as other children of the same age
- Not climbing skilfully.

Learning to talk
By 2.5 years can usually:
- Understand a lot more than he can talk about
- Use well over 100 recognisable words, but many of the words will be unclear
- Put the words into short sentences e.g. "look mummy dog"
- Talk during play
- Let people know what he wants using words rather than signs
- Realise that language can get others to respond.

Out of step?
- Is not using words to let others know what he wants
- Is generally not talking clearly enough for parent or carer to know what he means
- Seems to be in a 'world of his own' and doesn't respond when others speak to him.

By 3 years can usually:
- Talk clearly enough so that strangers are able to understand at least some of what he is saying
- Use words such as "me" and "you" correctly
- Ask many questions starting with "what", "where" and "why"
- Listen to stories, asking repeatedly for favourite stories
- Make up long stories while playing.

Out of step?
- Is not using words to let others know what he wants.
- Is not talking clearly enough for parents or carers to know what he wants.
- Seems to be in a 'world of his own' and doesn't respond when others speak to him.

Adapted from Parenting SA Parent Easy Guide #77 with permission. Copyright Government of South Australia, www.parenting.sa.gov.au.

When do young children get their teeth?

Teething refers to the eruption of the deciduous and permanent teeth. It is a natural occurrence and can happen without any problems. However, some children may feel discomfort before their first tooth erupts (at about six months) and may continue to experience this discomfort with every one of their 20 baby teeth.

TOOTH ERUPTION

Deciduous Teeth

Although deciduous teeth begin to form in utero, they do not usually begin to erupt until six months of age. Eruption times vary from child to child just as the individual growth rate varies.

Normally no teeth are visible in the mouth at birth. Occasionally, however, some babies are born with an erupted incisor tooth (neonatal tooth), but these are not true teeth and are usually lost soon after birth. Deciduous teeth do not usually begin to erupt until six months of age.

Eruption Patterns

- Lower teeth usually erupt before the upper teeth.
- Girls usually precede boys in tooth eruption.
- The teeth in both jaws usually erupt in pairs – one on the right and one on the left.
- By the time the child reaches the age of two to three years, all the deciduous teeth should have erupted.

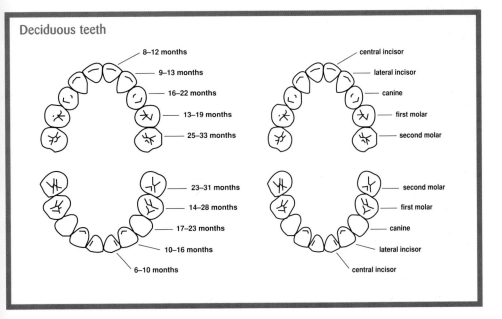

Deciduous teeth

8–12 months	central incisor
9–13 months	lateral incisor
16–22 months	canine
13–19 months	first molar
25–33 months	second molar
23–31 months	second molar
14–28 months	first molar
17–23 months	canine
10–16 months	lateral incisor
6–10 months	central incisor

Immunisation explained

Years ago, pertussis (whooping cough), diphtheria and tetanus were amongst the killer diseases of childhood. Today, we have vaccines available to protect children against these and a number of other diseases.

The word "vaccine" comes from the Latin "vacca" for cow, to show that the first vaccines (against smallpox) were derived from cowpox. Smallpox was the first killer disease to be impacted on by vaccination in the 19th century and, in 1978, became the first disease to be wiped out from the world by vaccination. However, in the first part of the 20th century, more children died from infections like pertussis and diphtheria than from all other causes of child death today. Immunisation has almost wiped out these diseases and others like measles. But if immunisation rates go down, children will again be at risk, as happened in Russia when diphtheria immunisation rates went down in the 1990s. We can now immunise against many diseases including the following:

- Pertussis (Whooping cough); Diphtheria; Tetanus; Measles; Rubella (German Measles); Mumps; Haemophilus influenzae type b (Hib); Hepatitis B; Hepatitis A; Poliomyelitis; Influenza; Varicella (Chickenpox); Pneumococcal disease (some types); Meningococcal disease (some types).

How does immunisation work?
Every time your child has an infection, the immune system in their body makes special proteins called antibodies to fight that infection. Immunisation makes the body produce antibodies. The antibodies can survive for a long time; some survive even a lifetime. So your child builds up resistance to the virus or bacteria without having to have the infection with its resulting distress and complication risk. If the vaccinated person comes into contact with the disease in the future, the body is able to make antibodies fast enough to prevent the person getting sick.

These days, children are recommended many more vaccines than in the past. Some parents may be concerned that their baby or small child might not be able to cope with so many vaccines at a time. Many vaccines can safely and effectively be given at the same time and, in fact, more and more vaccines are being made as combination vaccines. Humans are in contact with thousands of "antigens" every day and the small number of antigens in vaccines are just a "drop in the ocean" of those the body can react to at any one time, so it is very safe, and in fact recommended, that all due vaccines are given at the same visit. Giving all due vaccines at the same visit will also cause less trauma for your child and yourself than stringing them out over several visits, and some vaccines actually work better when given with others.

Where to go for immunisation
- Your local doctor.
- Your local council, hospital or community centre may have free immunisation clinics.

THE DISEASES
Pertussis (whooping cough)
Young babies with pertussis cannot stop coughing. When they gasp for air at the end of the cough, it often sounds like a "whoop". This is how the disease got its common name. When babies get pertussis, they may spend a long time in hospital and most need to be in intensive care; some of these babies die. Babies with pertussis may bleed behind the eyes and in the brain from coughing so much, or become

tired from the coughing and stop breathing. More babies are now getting pertussis in countries where immunisation rates have gone down. However, even in countries where childhood immunisation rates are high, like in Australia, babies are still at risk because teenagers and adults are getting pertussis. Unlike many diseases, protection against pertussis wears off several years after vaccination or after having the disease.

There is now a pertussis vaccine available for teenagers and adults and it is recommended that all people planning a pregnancy or who have just had a baby should be vaccinated against this very serious disease.

Diphtheria

Diphtheria affects the nose and throat and can block the windpipe. It can also affect the heart. The vaccine is very effective so we now rarely see diphtheria, with no cases in Australia since 1993. However, diphtheria still occurs overseas and people who are not adequately vaccinated can acquire it overseas or it could be brought into Australia from an overseas traveller and maybe infect young babies or those who are unimmunised.

Tetanus (lockjaw)

Tetanus (lockjaw) is caused by germs from soil entering the body through cuts and wounds. Injuries such as a scratch, a dog bite, or a prick from a thorn can also lead to tetanus. The only people who get tetanus are those who are not immunised. Unfortunately, the tetanus germ is everywhere, so anyone who is not immunised has the chance of catching tetanus. It is even possible to get tetanus twice, as the infection does not protect you long-term whereas vaccination does.

DTPa vaccine is a combination vaccine in which three vaccines (diphtheria, tetanus and pertussis) are combined in one injection to prevent these diseases.

Polio

The polio virus destroys nerves and can leave people permanently paralysed. If the disease affects the breathing muscles then the person will die unless their breathing is helped by medical equipment such as an "iron lung". Not so long ago, people with polio spent years in iron lungs. The Salk vaccine (injectable polio) was the first polio vaccine to be introduced and it effectively stopped epidemics in developed countries. Oral Sabin vaccine has been used worldwide since the 1960s because it provides protection in the gut where polio is contracted.

Polio is almost wiped out world-wide but until it is completely wiped out, all countries must continue to immunise. The last recorded polio case in Australia was in 1972. Australia, like other developed countries, is moving back to injectable polio vaccine because of the very small risk of vaccine-related polio from the oral vaccine.

Measles

Measles has become rare in Australia since the national measles control campaign in 1998 when all Australian primary school children were offered free MMR (measles, mumps, rubella) vaccine. This campaign was followed by a national campaign for young adults. The only cases now occurring in Australia are brought in from overseas or are in unimmunised contacts of those overseas cases. Children under 12 months of age, who are too young to have had the measles vaccine, and other people who are not vaccinated, are still at risk because the measles disease is very infectious. Measles is a more serious

Immunisation explained

illness than many people realise, with complications such as middle ear infections and pneumonia common and brain damage also a rare but serious complication of the disease. The very young and those with chronic illness are most at risk of these complications. Simply being older without any chronic illness is also an issue.

Rubella (German measles)
Rubella is usually a mild illness in children but can be more severe in older people. If a woman catches rubella in early pregnancy, her baby may be born deaf and/or blind and suffer from heart defects and/or intellectual disability. It is important that everyone, but particularly women prior to pregnancy, are protected against rubella by having received two MMR vaccines at least one month apart. Pregnant women generally have a blood test in early pregnancy. Rubella has become rare in Australia for much the same reason as measles. However, cases of congenital rubella can still occur when a pregnant woman is exposed to an infected person. Women born in some overseas countries who may not have received rubella vaccine are at particular risk.

Mumps
Mumps is caused by a virus. Before immunisation, mumps used to be one of the most common causes of meningitis in children. After puberty, mumps can cause inflammation of the testes in men or the ovaries in women. Mumps can affect the inner ear and cause deafness at any age.

MMR is a combination vaccine in which three vaccines (measles, mumps and rubella) are combined in one injection to prevent these diseases.

Haemophilus influenzae type b (Hib)
Haemophilus influenzae type b (Hib) is not a "flu" virus. It is a type of bacteria which can cause meningitis (inflammation of the tissues around the brain) and other life-threatening illnesses like epiglottitis which blocks the upper airway. Since the Hib vaccine was introduced in 1993, these diseases have gone from over 500 cases a year to becoming very rare. All children should have the Hib vaccine, starting at 2 months of age.

Hepatitis B vaccine
Hepatitis B is a virus that infects the liver. Individuals, and especially babies, who get this disease may have no or only mild symptoms to start. However, when the virus is caught in infancy or childhood, it is likely that it will remain in the blood (this is called being a "carrier") and is able to be passed on to other people. As many as 25% of hepatitis B carriers develop chronic liver disease, liver cancer or liver failure later in life. The hepatitis B vaccine prevents this infection – the first dose is now given at birth to maximise the protection against catching hepatitis B from a family member. For later doses, starting at 2 months, the hepatitis B vaccine is given in combination with other vaccines as a single injection.

Varicella (chickenpox)
Chickenpox is a viral illness, which is usually a mild disease of short length in otherwise healthy children, but can sometimes cause complications. Only a small percentage, the most severe cases of chickenpox, result in hospitalisation in Australia. However, as almost everyone contracts chickenpox sooner or later, this small percentage translates to 1500 Australians hospitalised each year with chickenpox. It is particularly likely to be severe in older children and adults or children with other

medical problems. Vaccines against chickenpox have been available in Australia since 2001, and are now included in the free childhood immunisation schedule (at 18 months of age). Children require one dose only, but individuals over the age of 14 years require two doses, 2 months apart.

Invasive pneumococcal disease (IPD)

The term invasive pneumococcal disease (IPD) refers to the most serious types of pneumococcal infection, where the bacteria "invade" the bloodstream. The bacterium Streptococcus pneumoniae (the pneumococcus) also causes respiratory infections like pneumonia and middle ear infection without getting into the blood, but meningitis (inflammation of the tissues around the brain) and septicaemia (or "blood poisoning") are always "invasive". Until recently, no effective vaccine was available for children under 2 years of age to prevent IPD. Between 2001 and 2005, a selective program offered free pneumococcal vaccine to infants and children most at risk of IPD, and since January 2005, all children aged less than 2 years have been eligible to receive this vaccine free of charge. The first dose is recommended at age 2 months, with the number of doses varying depending on age of first dose and medical risk. It is important for infants to start immunisation at age 2 months. Children who do not have the first dose until after 6 months require fewer doses. For more information about the vaccine ask your local doctor or clinic.

Meningococcal disease

Meningococcal disease is a bacterial infection that can cause meningitis (inflammation of the tissues surrounding the brain) and septicaemia (infection of the bloodstream). There are several strains of meningococcal bacteria in Australia, with two of these (B and C) being the most frequent causes of meningococcal disease. Meningococcal C vaccine has been available in Australia since 2002 but is protective against meningococcal C disease only. The C type of meningococcal disease accounts for around one third of meningococcal cases (and about half the deaths), so until vaccines effective against other strains, especially type B, become available, meningococcal disease will continue to be a concern. Meningococcal C vaccine is effective in all age groups including infants. A mass campaign of all pre-school and school children was carried out during 2003 and 2004, and the vaccine is now recommended at age 12 months.

Side-effects of immunisation

Immunisation is very safe and very effective. The huge benefits of immunisation far outweigh the very small risks. Like any substance, whether a medication, food or lotion, vaccines can have some side-effects in some individuals. These are usually minor, such as soreness at the injection site, mild fever or being a bit irritable. In very rare cases, a child may get a more serious reaction to a particular vaccine due to an unknown sensitivity to some component. Discuss side-effects with the doctor or nurse giving the vaccine. They will advise ways to reduce side-effects. Having a cough or cold is not a reason to delay immunisation.

Australian Baby Guide acknowledges the co-operation of The Children's Hospital at Westmead and Sydney Children's Hospital, Randwick, in making this fact sheet available. Disclaimer: This information is for education purposes only. Please consult with your doctor or health professional to make sure this information is right for your child.

What to put
in a basic first aid kit

Many people have first aid kits containing a variety of items that they believe to be suitable for their first aid needs. In addition, there are numerous first aid kits available in the marketplace.

Any first aid kit should generally be in a sturdy, dust-proof container. The container should be large enough to house its contents and to enable the first aider to readily locate required items.

The container of an occupational first aid kit should be clearly marked with the first aid symbol (i.e. white cross on a green background) and should be capable of being secured to a wall or other accessible location. It should not be locked to ensure that items are readily available in the event of an emergency. First aid kits kept or used around aquatic environments should be housed in a waterproof container.

The exact contents of a first aid kit will vary to some extent, depending on the environment, personal needs, industry requirements and regulations. In some Australian states, the contents of such kits are specified by Codes of Practice.

Following are some of the basic contents:

Telephone numbers of appropriate emergency services. These can include the local ambulance, hospital and medical centre. It can also include the Poisons Information Centre hotline and any other relevant specialist emergency hotlines. In addition to emergency numbers, the list should include the contacts for various first aid personnel, a first aid manual and/or any required leaflets.

First aid kit items:	
Triangular bandages	Adhesive tape
Cotton bandages of various sizes	Sterile eye pads
Gauze pieces	Safety pins
Alcohol swabs & wound cleaning swabs	Scissors
Adhesive dressings	Forceps & splinter probe
Sterile wound dressings of various sizes	Disposable gloves
Sterile saline for wound irrigation	Notebook and pencil
Povidone-iodine or other disinfectant	Accident report forms

Special additional modules, such as burns, eye and remote area modules, are available. First aid kits must be checked regularly to ensure that items are not missing, damaged or contaminated. Any such items should be replaced immediately.

Important note: It is important for all first aiders to ensure they are fully informed of any regulations or requirements pertaining to the administration of first aid in their locality.

Information supplied by the Royal Life Saving Society of Australia, www.royallifesaving.com.au.

What is a fever?

A fever is when the body's temperature is higher than normal. Humans usually have a body temperature within a very narrow range. Normally a child has a fever when their temperature is over 37.5°C.

A child with a fever often has a hot, flushed face and the forehead may feel hot. The child may feel hot, or sometimes even shivery. A child's hands and feet may feel cold, even when the rest of the child is hot. Children with fever are often miserable or tired.

Fever is the body's natural response to infection. Raising the body temperature helps the body to fight off the infection, so it is not always necessary to treat the fever. However, children with fever often feel uncomfortable and unwell and using measures to bring down their temperature can help.

Fevers, especially if they are rapidly increasing, may occasionally bring about convulsions (fits) in children under five-years-old. These are not dangerous but they can be frightening. Keeping a child's temperature from getting too high may prevent fits. Although paracetamol and ibuprofen is widely used for children with fever, it is often not effective in reducing fever and does not reduce the incidence of febrile convulsions.

What causes fever?

The most common cause of a fever is infection. Infections of the upper respiratory tract, such as colds and flu, are very common, especially in pre-school children. Young pre-schoolers can have five to ten infections each year. These infections are caused by a virus and get better on their own without antibiotics. Some infections, like ear infections and some throat infections, may be caused by bacteria. If your child has a bacterial infection, he or she will get better much quicker if antibiotics are prescribed by a doctor. Fever may also be caused by other factors, such as prolonged exposure to the sun on a hot day.

You need to see a doctor if your child has a fever and:
- Your child is very young (six months or younger).
- Your child seems very sick.

You also need to see a doctor if your child has an earache, has difficulty swallowing, has fast breathing, has a rash, is vomiting, has neck stiffness, has bulging of the fontanelle (the soft spot on the head in babies) and/or is very sleepy or drowsy.

Older children who have a cold, but are not very sick, generally do not need to see a doctor with every fever. Since a fever is the body's natural response to infection it is not always necessary to reduce a fever. However, if your child is very hot and uncomfortable, you can try these simple steps:
- Take off your child's clothes.
- Give medications to reduce fever, e.g. Panadol or Nurofen. This medication should be given at the correct dose, so ask your chemist or doctor for guidance.
- Give your child plenty to drink; children with a fever need more fluids.
- Consult a doctor if the fever does not settle or your child is still sick.

Australian Baby Guide acknowledges the co-operation of The Children's Hospital at Westmead and Sydney Children's Hospital, Randwick, in making this fact sheet available. Disclaimer: This information is for education purposes only. Please consult with your doctor or health professional to make sure this information is right for your child.

Babies & asthma

Asthma is a condition that affects the airways – the small tubes that carry air in and out of the lungs. People with asthma have airways that are almost always sensitive and inflamed and when someone with asthma comes into contact with an asthma trigger, the muscles around the walls of the airways tighten, narrowing the airway and making it harder to breathe. Often sticky mucus or phlegm is produced. In adults, these reactions lead to the symptoms of asthma: wheezing, tightness in the chest, shortness of breath and/or coughing. In a severe asthma attack breathing can be very difficult. In babies younger than 12 months, the airways are already small so it doesn't take much inflammation or contraction to cause symptoms. A recurring wheeze can be the first indication that a baby might have asthma.

Does wheezing always mean asthma?

Wheezing is a common symptom that is typically associated with asthma. But not everyone who wheezes has asthma. Wheezing occurs when lower airways are narrow or constricted – breathing feels difficult and there is a whistling sound in the chest on breathing out.

Wheezing is very common in the first few years of life. Infants' airways are small and if a child gets a respiratory tract infection, these already small airways become swollen and plugged with mucus – this can then lead to wheezing. For most children it is temporary and does not mean that they have asthma.

Your doctor might choose to treat your child's symptoms with asthma medications (and they are quite safe for babies) despite not diagnosing him or her with asthma, to see if the symptoms respond to treatment.

Diagnosing babies with asthma

Asthma can be a tricky disease to diagnose in babies. It is often difficult to distinguish asthma from other common respiratory conditions that also cause coughing and wheezing. Some children can seem free of asthma symptoms for long periods of time and then experience intermittent asthma 'attacks'.

It's important to remember that just one instance of wheezing isn't enough to diagnose asthma. Even if a baby is wheezing on a recurring basis, a doctor may still not be certain the cause is asthma. A doctor can't be completely sure it is asthma until he has performed a lung function test (a breathing test). Lung function tests generally involve taking a deep breath and blowing out as fast as the person can. Children under the age of seven are unable to perform this reliably.

Doctors want to avoid an incorrect diagnosis. However, uncontrolled and persistent asthma can damage the lungs over time. For these reasons, doctors might choose to treat a child's symptoms as if the child has asthma. They may prescribe asthma medications (which are quite safe for babies) to see if the symptoms respond to treatment, but may not officially diagnose a child with asthma.

The following factors will help your doctor decide whether your child has asthma. As a parent you will be asked about any family history of asthma or eczema, the pattern of your child's illness (wheezing, a dry cough, breathlessness or noisy breathing), its severity and incidence, as well as possible triggers such as allergies or colds.

You should talk to your child's doctor if your child has:

- ❯ Wheezing that happens more than once (with or without illness)
- ❯ Constant or intermittent bouts of coughing that get worse at night
- ❯ Any other breathing problem that concerns you.

Other wheezing (that is not asthma)

There are many other causes of wheezing in babies apart from asthma:

Bronchiolitis is a common condition in babies under six months old. It is caused by a virus. It starts like a cold, with a runny nose, fever and mild cough. As bronchiolitis progresses, babies can develop a wheeze and their breathing can become more rapid and shallow. Most cases of bronchiolitis are mild and get better without treatment, however in some infants, especially young babies, bronchiolitis can be severe, occasionally requiring hospitalisation. All babies should be reviewed by their doctor if they develop cold like symptoms. Symptoms to look out for include:

- ❯ Your baby developing a cold that does not settle down
- ❯ Breathing difficulties (fast or irregular)
- ❯ Wheezing.

Croup affects the voice box (larynx) and windpipe (trachea) and is caused by a viral infection. Croup is most common in children between the ages of six months and three years. Croup generally starts like a common cold. Your child may have a slight fever, sore throat and runny nose. After a few days (often beginning at night when the air is cooler) a hoarse, 'barking' cough, a hoarse voice and noisy breathing develop. This can last for a couple of hours then stop, only to return again for the next few nights.

Will my baby develop asthma?

Bronchiolitis and wheezing in babies does not mean that a baby will develop asthma later in life. In more than half of children who wheeze, the wheezing occurs when the child has an infection and stops when the child gets better. By about three years of age, the airways grow and widen, and wheezing often stops.

Asthma is more likely to develop in children who continue to wheeze beyond three years of age and have allergies, or parents with allergies. There is no proof that altering your baby's diet will reduce the risk of asthma developing, or even reduce the risk of wheezing illnesses. Colds (and other viruses) and cigarette smoke are much more common triggers.

Smoking

Mothers should not smoke during pregnancy. Maternal smoking during pregnancy has been linked to small, unwell babies, a higher rate of stillbirth, premature labour and premature birth and maternal haemorrhage. Smoking has also been linked to SIDS. Babies of smokers are more likely to suffer from asthma and respiratory infections than those of non-smokers. Other adults should not smoke near expectant mothers, children or in houses where children live. Exposing children to second-hand smoke in the home has also been shown to increase the development of asthma and other chronic respiratory illnesses. A developing lung is hugely sensitive and early damage is often permanent.

Information supplied by the Asthma Foundation of Victoria, www.asthma.org.au.

Water safety for children under 5 years

In Australia, drowning is the leading cause of death for children under the age of five. Pools are an obvious risk, but children can also drown in baths, spas, dams, rivers, creeks, garden ponds and even nappy buckets. It takes as little as 5cm of water and an unsupervised child for a drowning to occur.

Pools

- All pools must have a safety fence that completely isolates the pool and complies with the Australian Standard 1926 (AS:1926).
- The standard fence is 1.2m high with a self-closing/self-latching child resistant gate. The vertical parts must be no more than 100mm apart and the horizontal parts at least 900mm apart. The fence should not obscure the view of the pool and must be resistant to climbing.
- Gates need to be maintained to ensure they close properly. They should never be propped opened.
- Nothing should be placed near the fence that a child could use or move to climb the fence e.g. garden furniture, large pot plants and BBQs.
- Children must be supervised at all times whilst in the water and never left alone.
- Display a CPR chart by your pool.

Inflatable pools

- Be aware that children can drown in less than 5cm of water. Supervise children when they are using these products.
- Make sure the water is kept clean. Water left in inflatable pools for periods of time can become contaminated and cause illness.
- The pool should always be emptied after use and stored away from children.
- Pool fencing laws also apply to inflatable pools of 300mm or more in height.

Spas

- Outdoor spas should have the same fencing as swimming pools, including a self-closing/self-latching gate.
- Indoor spas should have a lockable door. When in use the door should be kept locked.
- All spas should be emptied when not in use.
- Display a CPR chart by your spa.

Rural properties

- Restrict your child's access to lakes, creeks, rivers, and dams by creating a 'Child Safe Area' in and around your home. You may need to fence an area around your home that separates the house from water hazards.
- Check for hidden dangers before swimming in creeks, rivers, lakes and dams.
- Supervise your children when swimming at all times.

Other potential dangers

⊙ Nappy buckets should have a secure lid and be stored in a high place such as in the laundry tub. Always empty the nappy bucket when not in use.

⊙ Fix a grill over garden ponds just beneath the water level.

⊙ Never leave children unsupervised in the bath - not even for a few minutes. Empty the bath water and take the children with you if you must leave.

⊙ After rain, check your yard and empty water that has collected in sandpits, buckets, drains and other containers.

⊙ Take extra care in heavy rain and storms as this can cause flash flooding.

⊙ Cover any open drains with a grill.

⊙ At the beach, always swim between the flags and supervise your children in the water at all times.

⊙ When swimming in rivers, lakes, dams and creeks, check the water for hidden dangers before swimming and supervise at all time.

⊙ Remember that flotation aids are not life saving devices. Children wearing flotation aids should still be supervised at all times.

⊙ Remember that children can drown in swimming pools all year around. Please be careful during the colder months as the water is often murky and dirty and children are harder to see if they have fallen into the pool.

Learn resuscitation

⊙ A child's life may be saved if the parents or carers have the proper knowledge and skills to rescue and resuscitate quickly and confidently.

⊙ Resuscitation charts are available from your local councils or The Royal Life Saving Society of Australia.

Familiarise your child with water

⊙ Water familiarisation classes help build confidence and introduce children to basic water safety. Your child can start classes as early as six months. Remember that lessons are no substitute for active supervision by adults.

Remember

⊙ It only takes 5cm of water for a child to drown.

⊙ Always supervise your children when around water.

⊙ Learn CPR.

⊙ Regularly check maintenance of pool/spa fencing.

⊙ In an emergency phone 000.

Australian Baby Guide acknowledges the co-operation of The Children's Hospital at Westmead and Sydney Children's Hospital, Randwick, in making this fact sheet available. Disclaimer: This information is for education purposes only. Please consult with your doctor or health professional to make sure this information is right for your child.

Young children & bedwetting

Wetting the bed at night (nocturnal enuresis) is very common in young children.
In fact, it is normal up to the age of five years.

Bedwetting usually happens during a type of sleep in which other things like sleep walking and sleep talking occur, particularly in younger children. The precise cause is unknown but we do know that:

- The waking response is not fully developed in all children that wet the bed.
- 60% of children who wet the bed produce more urine during sleep than other children.
- The amount of urine the bladder holds may be less than children who don't wet the bed.
- Fluid restriction in the evening doesn't prevent the episode from occurring.

Because it happens during sleep the child has no conscious control over it. Bedwetting can also be associated with constipation, urge incontinence (being unable to hold on when the child feels the urge to pass urine) or a stop and start urine stream associated with dribbling of urine after voiding.

What can you do to help?

- Do reassure your child, especially if your child is upset. You need to be patient and understanding, even though you may feel angry.
- Do try a night-light. It may be useful for children who often wake up during the night, either to go to the toilet or to change their pyjamas.
- Do encourage a good night's sleep. A restful sleep without interruptions is best for your child. Waking your child to go to the toilet during the night will not help solve the problem.
- Do try absorbent pads. The pads go under the bottom sheet to keep the bed drier and more comfortable.
- Do shower or bathe your child before you let them go to pre-school or school. The smell of urine is very strong and can hang around. This may make your child feel embarrassed and lead to other problems, such as teasing and name-calling at school.
- Do encourage your child to have plenty to drink, particularly during the day.
- Discourage your child from drinking caffeinated drinks in the evenings (e.g. chocolate or cola drinks).
- If bedwetting is becoming a problem, contact your local doctor who may refer you to an appropriate service. Your doctor will also examine your child for any other reasons for the bedwetting.

When should I get some professional help?

- If your child is still wetting the bed after the age of about six or seven, and the child is unhappy or uncomfortable about it.
- If your child has persistent daytime wetting.
- If it is causing problems in the family.
- If your child has been dry at night for over a year and suddenly starts to wet the bed again.

Australian Baby Guide acknowledges the co-operation of The Children's Hospital at Westmead and Sydney Children's Hospital, Randwick, in making this fact sheet available. Disclaimer: This information is for education purposes only. Please consult with your doctor or health professional to make sure this information is right for your child.

Teach your child to stay safe

Here are twelve very simple points that you should follow and teach to your child so that he or she can stay safe.

- Know everything you can about your children's activities and their friends. Monitor children's activities and participate with them. Don't allow children to play alone in isolated areas.

- Teach your children about strangers and to be aware of unusual behaviour in people they know. Teach them to listen to their feelings and that it is okay to say NO if any adults (including family members) ask them to do something that makes them feel uncomfortable.

- Teach your children to refuse anything from strangers including money, gifts or rides. Know where new possessions come from.

- Teach your children how to safely answer the phone if they are at home alone. One idea is to say the adult in the home is 'unavailable' to come to the phone.

- Teach your children to keep a safe distance from strangers and not give strangers directions for help. Adults need to get help from other adults.

- Teach children to use the buddy system when walking home from school, sports activities, etcetera.

- Teach your children to check first with you before going anywhere. Children need to let parents know where they are going, how they will get there, who will be going along with them and when they will return home.

- Develop a plan with your children in case they get lost. Don't have them meet you in a carpark – inside the store or shopping centre are much safer meeting places. Teach them their phone number and area code.

- Do not place your children's names on their clothing or on the outside of their possessions.

- Teach your children to say NO to anyone attempting to touch them on their private part(s).

- Teach your children about appropriate and inappropriate secrets and that some secrets have to be told if children and parents are to be kept safe.

- Establish rules to follow when your child uses the internet. Spend time on the internet with your children.

Information supplied by the Child Abuse Prevention Service Inc., www.childabuseprevention.com.au.

Resources

These Resources pages list products and services relevant to "Children's health & safety".
To make your life easier as a parent, editorial listings have been grouped into sub categories.
Businesses then appear alphabetically under a national or a state-based subhead depending on reach.

SUB-CATEGORIES

ADVISORY SERVICES: HEALTH & SAFETY

NATIONAL

Anaphylaxis Australia
Tel: 1300 728 000
website: www.allergyfacts.org.au
Anaphylaxis Australia Inc (AAI) is a charitable organisation that supports and assist those affected by potential life threatening allergies. AAI is dedicated to assisting individuals in the management of the risk of anaphylaxis. AAI's aim is to enable them to cope with every day life while minimising risk to their health and wellbeing. The organisation advocates for people living with allergies when communicating with government, health and teaching professionals, food industry and all in the community. AAI strives to raise awareness of life-threatening allergy in the Australian community and provides science-based information, resources and services to support children and adults living with the risk of anaphylaxis.

Asthma Foundations Australia
Tel: 1800 645 130
email: national@asthmaaustralia.org.au
website: www.asthmaaustralia.org.au
Asthma Foundations Australia comprises an alliance of seven state/territory Asthma Foundations. It is the national peak consumer body for people with asthma and the first choice when it comes to asthma education and resources. They aim to eliminate asthma as a major cause of ill health and disruption Australia wide through innovative programs like Asthma Friendly Schools and the Community Support Program. You can access trained Asthma Advisers via the Asthma Information Line on 1800 645 130 or visit the website for further information.

Centre for Community Child Health
Tel: (03) 9345 6150
website: www.rch.org.au/ccch
The Centre for Community Child Health has been at the forefront of early childhood development and behaviour research for over two decades. It is also involved with community projects and provides clinical services and education. The Centre aims to support parents and professionals so that children have the best possible start in life. The research the Centre conducts is about many conditions and common problems faced by children such as obesity, language and literacy delay and behavioural concerns.

Children's Medical Research Institute (Jeans for Genes® Day)
Tel: 1800 436 437
email: sryall@cmri.org.au or genie@jeansforgenes.org.au
website: www.cmri.org.au or www.jeansforgenes.org.au

The aim of the Children's Medical Research Institute (CMRI) is to conduct medical research which will advance the prevention and treatment of disease especially in children. Since 1958 CMRI has contributed significantly to paediatric health, including quality of survival of premature babies, pioneering microsurgical techniques and developing paediatric heart and lung systems. CMRI is now a world leader in the areas of cancer, congenital abnormalities, brain and nervous disorders, and gene therapy.

Choice
Tel: 1800 069 552
email: ausconsumer@choice.com.au
website: www.choice.com.au/baby

CHOICE has been testing products for over 45 years exposing unsafe products and providing reliable, independent buying advice. Their baby information can be accessed quickly and easily online and covers everything from strollers and cots to baby food and disposable nappies. You can view their free reports or become a member at www.choice.com.au/baby.

Early Childhood Australia
Tel: 1800 356 900
email: eca@earlychildhood.org.au
website: www.earlychildhoodaustralia.org.au

Early Childhood Australia is a non-profit, peak advocacy organisation acting in the best interests of children from birth to eight years. Become a member of Early Childhood Australia and support them in promoting high-quality services for young children and their families. Freecall 1800 356 900 for a free information kit and Code of Ethics brochure, or browse their free online resources online.

Eczema Association of Australasia Inc
Tel: 1300 300 182
email: itchy@eczema.org.au
website: www.eczema.org.au

The role of the Eczema Association of Australasia Inc is to support and educate eczema sufferers and carers, along with the wider community, in all aspects of eczema and its impact. The benefits of the $30 Annual Family Membership include a quarterly newsletter with tips, information and product updates, free product samples, optional social register and information sheets on a wide range of specific topics for treating and controlling eczema.

GlaxoSmithKline Consumer Healthcare
Tel: 1800 028 533
website: www.childrenspanadol.com.au

The Children's Panadol website provides essential information for parenting covering a wide range of topics including: immunisation, fever, illness, helpful hints and also a products and dosage guide. In addition you can replay the TV advertisements, print out fun games and terrific recipes, send E cards to others and also download your favourite Children's Panadol critters as wallpaper. Visit www.childrenspanadol.com.au.

Global Lead Advice & Support Service (GLASS)
Tel: 1800 626 086 freecall
email: info@lead.org.au
website: www.lead.org.au

The Global Lead Advice & Support Service (GLASS) is run by The LEAD Group, a community health promotion charity aiming to eliminate lead poisoning, and to protect the environment from lead. GLASS provides a unique service to meet all needs on lead-related issues, including written information on lead as well as an Australia-wide free call line for advice on lead poisoning prevention and counselling for cases of lead poisoning and contamination. The Global Lead Advice and Support Service (GLASS) incorporates the Lead Advisory Service Australia (LASA). Phone or visit the website for further information.

Infant & Nursery Products Association of Australia
Tel: (03) 9762 7038
website: www.babysafety.com.au or www.inpaa.asn.au

The Infant and Nursery Products Association of Australia (INPAA) is the peak industry body representing suppliers, manufacturers and retailers in the sector. The Association operates nationally, was established to improve nursery safety and is a leader in the development of industry safety standards which concentrate on suppliers identifying and managing risks associated with the use and foreseeable misuse of infant and nursery products. The Association provides members with a range of services including: an industry advocacy role to regulators, government and other agencies; development of industry product safety standards and linkages with bodies like Standards Australia; liaison with other key stakeholders in the product safety and injury prevention field; general secretariat functions; information, advice, research and guidance for members on a range of issues; regular industry events and functions. INPAA has a company accreditation and product endorsement program for items that meet the Association's safety criteria. This program is supported by an education and information element to assist consumers in the safe purchase and safe use of infant and nursery products. Phone or visit the website for further information.

Kidsafe (Child Accident Prevention Foundation of Australia)
Kidsafe ACT
Tel (02) 6290 2244
Kidsafe Hunter Valley
Tel (02) 4942 4488
Kidsafe NSW
Tel (02) 9845 0890
Kidsafe NT
Tel (08) 8985 1085

Resources

CHILDREN'S HEALTH & SAFETY

Advisory services

Kidsafe QLD
Tel (07) 3854 1829
Kidsafe SA
Tel (08) 8161 6318
Kidsafe TAS
Tel (03) 6249 1933
Kidsafe VIC
Tel (03) 9251 7725
Kidsafe WA
Tel (08) 9340 8509
website: www.kidsafe.com.au

Kidsafe is the leading non-government, charitable organisation dedicated to the prevention of child deaths from unintentional child injury and resulting disabilities through awareness campaigns, education programs, research, advocacy and environmental, legislative and behaviour change. Visit www.kidsafe.com.au or contact your local state branch.

Medibank Private

GPO Box 9999 in your capital city
Tel: 132 331
email: ask-us@medibank.com.au
website: www.medibank.com.au

No matter how many 'little additions' there are to your family, with Medibank Private you can be sure that the cost of your family's health cover premium remains the same. And with more options, tailored to help your family save money, it's no wonder Medibank Private covers more Australian families than any other health fund. For more information call 132 331.

National Prescribing Service

Tel: 1300 888 763
email: info@nps.org.au
website: www.nps.org.au

NPS Medicines Line is a national telephone service providing Australians with confidential, independent information about prescription medicines, over-the-counter medicines and herbal and natural remedies. Medicines Line pharmacists can advise how medicines work; how to take medicines; doses; side effects; interactions with other medicines; medicines during pregnancy and breastfeeding; medicines for children and storage. Medicines Line is available from 9.00am to 6.00pm EST Monday to Friday for the cost of a local call (calls from mobiles may cost more).

Nutrition Australia

Vic Branch: (03) 9650 5165
NSW Branch: (02) 4257 9011
QLD Branch: (07) 3257 4393
WA Branch: (08) 6304 5096
email: nsw@nutritionaustralia.org
website: www.nutritionaustralia.org

Nutrition Australia is Australia's peak nutrition education body. They sell books on nutrition (such as *Fun with Food ... for Kids* and other low cost publications relating to nutrition for children) and run nutrition workshops and in-services. Phone your state branch for assistance with nutrition enquiries or information on becoming a member.

Poisons Information Centre

Tel: 13 11 26
Victorian Poisons Information Centre:
www.austin.org.au/poisons
NSW Poisons Information Centre:
www.chw.edu.au/parents/factsheets/safpoisj.htm
QLD Poisons Information Centre:
www.health.qld.gov.au/PoisonsInformationCentre/
WA Poisons Information Centre:
www.scgh.health.wa.gov.au/departments/wapic/index.html

Poisons Information Centre provides telephone advice to callers needing information about first aid for poisoning, bites, stings, mistakes with medicines and poisoning prevention. The service is available 24-hours a day, seven days a week. If you or someone in your care has been poisoned, ring the Poisons Information Centre to find out what to do next. The advice is up-to-date unlike many books and charts and you may avoid an unnecessary trip to the doctor or hospital. Visit the most appropriate website for more details.

Raising Children Network

email: info@raisingchildren.net.au
website: www.raisingchildren.net.au

www.raisingchildren.net.au is Australia's first national quality-assured parenting website, covering all the basics about raising children 0 to 8 years. Features include: 50 film clips including a breastfeeding demonstration, parents tips on sleep and settling, and safety and CPR information; interactive maps showing local services and community resources; baby karaoke featuring favourite children's songs; Parenting in Pictures (visual guides for essential parenting skills); and access to the Raising Children DVD. Supported by Australian Government and quality-assured by experts.

Reflux Infants Support Association (RISA) Inc

Tel: (07) 3229 1090
email: info@reflux.org.au
website: www.reflux.org.au

RISA Inc aims to provide up-to-date information, emotional support and management strategies to families with babies or children who suffer from gastro-oesophageal reflux. RISA Inc provides this support through telephone and email contacts, newsletters and other printed literature, a library service, online support groups, online chats, a website, and more. It is run solely by families who have children with this condition on a volunteer basis. For support or further information, contact RISA Inc by phone on (07) 3229 1090, email info@reflux.org.au or go to their website www.reflux.org.au.

Royal Life Saving Society Australia
Tel: (02) 8217 3111
email: info@rlssa.org.au
website: www.royallifesaving.com.au & www.keepwatch.com.au

In Australia the number one cause of accidental death in children under the age of five is drowning. Keep watch!
There are four things to remember:
1. Supervise your child – be within arms reach.
2. Fence pools and restrict access to lakes, rivers and dams.
3. Familiarise children with water.
4. Learn resuscitation.
Courses in resuscitation and first aid are available from state branches of The Royal Life Saving Society Australia.

SIDS and Kids
Tel: National Office (03) 9819 4595 or 1300 308 307
email: national@sidsandkids.org
website: www.sidsandkids.org

To reduce the risk of SIDS and fatal sleep accidents please follow these five steps supplied by SIDS and Kids:
1. Sleep baby on the back from birth, not on the tummy or side.
2. Sleep baby with face uncovered (no doonas, pillows, lambs wool, bumpers or soft toys).
3. Avoid exposing infants to tobacco smoke before birth and after.
4. Provide a safe sleeping environment (safe cot, safe mattress, safe bedding).
5. Sleep baby in its own safe sleeping environment next to the parent's bed for the first six to twelve months of life.
If you have any questions about this Safe Sleeping Message please phone SIDS and Kids on 1300 308 307 or visit the SIDS and Kids website www.sidsandkids.org for more information.

SIDS and Kids
Tel: National Office (03) 9819 4595 or 1300 308 307
email: national@sidsandkids.org
website:www.rednoseday.com.au

Red Nose Day is on Friday 26 June 2009. Support Red Nose Day and have fun for a serious cause. SIDS and Kids is dedicated to saving the lives of babies and children during pregnancy, birth, infancy and childhood and to supporting bereaved families. They deliver on their vision through world class research; evidence-based education and bereavement support; and advocacy. Visit www.rednoseday.com.au for more information.

Sneakys
Tel: (02) 9400 9759
email: info@sneakys.com.au
website: www.sneakys.com.au

Looking for some guidance you can trust on how to feed children? This is a highly practical home-based course, offering a common-sense look at how to nourish your child from birth to 12 years. It is jam packed full of useful tips giving you confidence in your own knowledge. Whether it's been some time since you last studied or are akin to studying, the supported learning environment with a range of optional learning extras is ideal for parents, childcare workers, teachers or anyone with an interest in child health. No attendance is necessary, assessment is open-book, and all your study is done from the convenience of your home or office. Phone or visit their website for further information.

Swim Australia
Tel: (07) 3376 0933
email: info@swimaustralia.org.au
website: www.swimaustralia.org.au

Drowning is the major cause of accidental death for children under the age of five. For every drowning, many more are left with permanent brain damage. While swimming and water safety lessons are not a substitute for proper supervision and barriers, they do add another layer of protection. Additionally, they enhance the child's development and prepare them for entry into the Australian way of life. Swim Australia registers swim schools that meet industry guidelines as determined by Australian Swimming Coaches and Teachers Association.

VICTORIA

Life Saving Victoria
PO Box 353
South Melbourne DC VIC 3205
Tel: (03) 9676 6900
email: mail@lifesavingvictoria.com.au
website: www.lifesavingvictoria.com.au

Life Saving Victoria offers a range of programs for children and adults focusing on saving lives, preventing injuries and enjoying the water. They offer one of the most comprehensive Child & Infant CPR programs in the state, with over 100 years of experience in keeping families safe. They also offer Infant Aquatics, a program that helps in the development of your child while using the water to explore and practice safe water safety skills. For parents, they have a range of safety tip brochures under the Play It Safe by the Water program and also offer a range of first aid kits suitable for all homes and workplaces.

Maternal and Child Health Line
Tel: 13 22 29

The Maternal and Child Health Line is a state-wide, 24-hour telephone service. Callers can access information, advice and support regarding child health,

Resources

CHILDREN'S HEALTH & SAFETY

Advisory services ➡ Books, DVDs & CDs

nutrition, breastfeeding, maternal and family health. The service is available to Victorian families with children 0 to school age and complements the locally based service. Phone 13 22 29.

NEW SOUTH WALES

The Children's Hospital at Westmead
Cnr Hawkesbury Road & Hainsworth Street
Westmead NSW 2145
Tel: (02) 9845 3585
website: www.chw.edu.au/parents/
Kids Health is a resource centre and bookshop located in The Children's Hospital at Westmead. The centre provides parents with information on health, illness, safety and parenting issues.

QUEENSLAND

Child Health Line
Tel: (07) 3862 2333 or 1800 177 279 (24 hours)
website: www.health.qld.gov.au/cchs
The Child Health Line is a 24-hour telephone information and support service for parents, carers and service providers with infants, children and young people aged 0–18 years.

Community Child Health Service
website: www.health.qld.gov.au/cchs
On the Child Health Resource Centre website parents, prospective parents and others can access an extensive range of information on a range of issues associated with children and young people's health. This internet site makes available to the general public standardised, quality information relating to children and young people. It also enables families to locate their local child health centre and immunisation venues throughout Queensland.

Epilepsy Queensland Inc.
PO Box 1457
Coorparoo BC QLD 4151
Tel: (07) 3435 5000
email: epilepsy@epilepsyqueensland.com.au
website: www.epilepsyqueensland.com.au
Epilepsy Queensland Inc. provides support to families who have a child with febrile convulsions, infantile spasms or any other forms of childhood epilepsy. They provide support through information, referral, workshops and seminars, counselling, newsletters, advocacy and children's education programs.

Family Planning Queensland (FPQ)
100 Alfred Street
Fortitude Valley QLD 4006
Tel: (07) 3250 0240
email: enquiries@fpq.com.au
website: www.fpq.com.au
Teaching babies and young children to be sexually healthy means teaching them about their bodies, helping them to feel good about themselves and helping them to develop healthy relationships. It's never too early to start educating your child about sexuality. Use the correct names of the private body parts when you are changing and bathing them, and help them to learn that their body belongs to them. Children learn about sexuality from the time they are born. Studies show that comprehensive, age-appropriate sexuality education helps children feel good about themselves and helps them to make healthy decisions about relationships. FPQ respects parents as the primary educators of their children, and offers both education programs and resource materials to assist parents and carers to talk about sexuality with their children. FPQ is a leading provider of sexual and reproductive health services throughout Queensland with centres in Cairns, Townsville, Bundaberg, Rockhampton, Toowoomba, Sunshine Coast and Gold Coast, Brisbane and Ipswich. For more information visit www.fpq.com.au.

WESTERN AUSTRALIA

Asthma Foundation of WA
36 Ord Street
West Perth WA 6005
Tel: (08) 9289 3641
email: ask@smokefreebaby.org.au
website: www.smokefreebaby.org.au
The Newborns Asthma and Parental Smoking Project can provide you with information on the effects of smoking for you and your baby, pre and post delivery. Visit the project's website at www.smokefreebaby.org.au or contact the Asthma Foundation of WA to order your free 'Care for my air' pack. The pack is full of information on how to create a smoke-free environment for your baby.

SOUTH AUSTRALIA

Children, Youth & Women's Health Service
Tel: (08) 8303 1500
email: cywhs.webadmin@cywhs.sa.gov.au
website: www.cywhs.sa.gov.au
The Children, Youth and Women's Health Service (CYWHS) forms part of the State Government department SA Health and provides a statewide health service for children, young people and women in South Australia. The Health Service's website is a good place to start for queries about children's health and development. The site links to information and advice on many parenting and health topics, including sections written for young people across age groups.

ALLERGY & SAFETY ALERTS

NATIONAL

Allergy Kidz Ware
Tel: (02) 4683 0445
email: info@allergykidzware.com.au
website: www.allergykidzware.com.au

Does food trigger the most horrific reactions in your child? Allergy Kidz Ware is committed to providing fun, quality products to help protect carers and children who have special dietary needs. No one wants to bring unnecessary attention to a child, but when it could be life or death a balance must be found. These trendy customised embroidered t-shirts, hats, bibs and medicine bags allow you to embroider your specific requirements. Badges and customised food bags are also available. For more information about these unique designs visit www.allergykidzware.com.au.

ID Your Child
Tel: 0412 174 072
email: info@idyourchild.com.au
website: www.idyourchild.com.au

ID Your Child produces professional, high quality, PVC credit card size ID cards and name tags for special needs, illness and impairment. Make sure your loved one has medical and ID details on them at all times. They also produce ID, sport ID and medical ID wristbands for children and adults. These wristbands are an excellent way for you or your kids to carry important contact numbers (should they become lost or injured), vital medical or allergy information (stored securely and discreetly inside the band).

Label Kingdom
Tel: 1800 264 549
email: info@labelkingdom.com.au
website: www.labelkingdom.com.au

Help Identify your child's allergy with Label Kingdom's allergy labels. The label range includes: NO NUTS, NO EGGS, NO DAIRY, NO GLUTEN, NO FISH, NO SUGAR, NO WHEAT. Phone numbers can also be included on the labels in case your carer/teacher needs to contact you. Special requests are also welcome. Phone or visit Label Kingdom's website for further information: www.labelkingdom.com.au

Star Allergy Alerts
Tel: 0418 846 490
email: contact@starallergyalerts.com.au
website: www.starallergyalerts.com.au

Star Allergy Alerts are a bright fun range of allergy awareness products for children. The range includes badges, stickers, bracelets, wristbands, clothing, posters and Epipen pouches and more. Products are designed in modern colours and cute designs that kids love to wear. Perfect for child care, kindergarten/pre-school, school, camps, picnics, parties and sleep-overs.

BOOKS, DVDs & CDs: HEALTH & SAFETY

NATIONAL

Australian Competition and Consumer Commission
Tel: 1300 302 502
email: publishing.unit@accc.gov.au
website: www.accc.gov.au

Keeping baby safe: a guide to nursery furniture is a helpful booklet available free from the Australian Competition and Consumer Commission. It covers cots, prams and strollers and lists safety features and hazards. It also provides information on how to use products safely. Visit the website www.accc.gov.au or phone the number listed above for further information or to download a copy of this booklet.

Australian Competition and Consumer Commission
Tel: 1300 302 502
email: publishing.unit@accc.gov.au
website: www.accc.gov.au

Safe toys for kids is a handy guide that will help you select safe toys for your child. It also provides information on safe use of toys. The booklet is available free from the Australian Competition and Consumer Commission. Visit the website www.accc.gov.au or phone the number listed above for further information or to download a copy of this booklet.

Bedwetting Institute of Australia
Tel: 1300 135 796
email: info@bedwettinginstitute.com.au
website: www.bedwettinginstitute.com.au

By age five one third of children still wet the bed. The *Bedwetting Cured* DVD, with Dr Mark Condon and Physiotherapist Margaret O'Donovan, outlines a five-step program to cure the problem. Some children will need a bedwetting alarm but very few will need medication. Waterproof absorbent mattress pads are handy for younger children. They are washable and save changing the sheets following a wet night. Visit the website or phone the number above for further information.

Choice
Tel: 1800 069 552
email: ausconsumer@choice.com.au
website: www.choice.com.au/baby

Leave the guesswork behind with the essential buying guide for parents. Now in its twelfth edition, *The CHOICE Guide to Baby Products* is packed with independent and practical information based on CHOICE research and tests. Information covered includes test results on baby carriers, strollers, cots and highchairs. There is also general buying advice on bath time, bedtime and changing accessories, feeding, toys, walkers plus safety advice and handy "What to look for" checklists. Visit the website at www.choice.com.au/baby or phone the number listed above for further information.

Resources

CHILDREN'S HEALTH & SAFETY

Books, DVDs & CDs

➜ Health products & accessories

oKIDokie Pty Ltd
Tel: (03) 5364 2949
website: www.soundsforsilence.com.au

Developed by a paediatrician, *Sounds for Silence* is fast, easy and effective for soothing unsettled babies. *Sounds for Silence* contains soundtracks specifically designed for babies that mimic the womb. The rhythmical, familiar, reassuring sounds settle babies with 90% success. Accompanied by a 100-page book with practical advice on baby settling strategies, managing irritability and infant health issues, *Sounds for Silence* is comforting for babies and reassuring for parents.

Parenting SA
295 South Terrace
Adelaide SA 5000
Tel: (08) 8303 1660
website: www.parenting.sa.gov.au

Parent Easy Guides, produced by Parenting SA, provide information on more than 90 different parenting topics, from birth through to adolescence. Developed from research in conjunction with appropriate experts, the *Parent Easy Guides* are used widely throughout Australia. Parenting SA is an initiative of the Children, Youth and Women's Health Service (CYWHS) which forms part of the State Government department, SA Health. Parenting SA supports parents to build their knowledge, skills and confidence.

CHILDREN'S HOSPITALS

NEW SOUTH WALES

Sydney Children's Hospital
High Street
Randwick NSW 2031
Tel: (02) 9382 1111
website: www.sch.edu.au

Sydney Children's Hospital in Randwick is recognised internationally for excellence in the standards of care of children, research and clinical leadership in paediatric services and also providing ongoing preventative medicine and health promotion services, and a child protection unit. The Hospital is one of three tertiary centres for child health in NSW. It provides the most complex and comprehensive range of services in paediatric and adolescent medicine and surgery. It also looks after a local community for all matters relating to child health, including a range of community services.

The Children's Hospital at Westmead
Cnr Hawkesbury Road & Hainsworth Street
Westmead NSW 2145
Tel: (02) 9845 0000
website: www.chw.edu.au

The Children's Hospital at Westmead is a teaching hospital and is the major children's hospital in New South Wales. The Hospital cares for children from all over NSW, from other states, as well as children from other countries. The Children's Hospital at Westmead is an international leader in child health, working at the cutting edge of paediatric care for children and families. The Hospital is constantly challenging the traditional barriers of paediatric care through excellence in clinical care, research, teaching and advocacy.

QUEENSLAND

Mater Children's Hospital
Raymond Terrace
South Brisbane QLD 4101
Tel: (07) 3163 8111
website: www.mater.org.au

Operating the busiest paediatric emergency service in Queensland, the Mater Children's Hospital leads the way in specialist paediatric healthcare. A bright, airy and welcoming environment ensures that children and their families receive treatment in a way that meets the needs of the entire family. Public wards have a mix of one, two and three bedrooms, with one ensuite per room and a single bed for parents or carers to provide 24-hour support for their child if desired. Children and their siblings will enjoy the entertainment facilities offered by Radio Lollipop, the Starlight Express Room and special indoor and outdoor play areas, including teen lounges. As a tertiary level hospital, patients have access to the very best medical, nursing and allied health expertise available in Queensland.

Mater Children's Private Hospital
Raymond Terrace
South Brisbane QLD 4101
Tel: (07) 3163 2468
website: www.mater.org.au

Your entire family will feel welcome when visiting a sick child in Australia's first and only children's private hospital. New private patient rooms offer excellent views, an ensuite and parent bed facilities. Children and their siblings will enjoy the entertainment facilities offered by Radio Lollipop, the Starlight Express Room and special indoor and outdoor play areas, including teen lounges. Working in partnership with the renowned medical facilities available at the Mater Children's Hospital ensures your child will receive the very best medical, nursing and allied health expertise available in Queensland.

Mater Health & Wellness Clinic
550 Stanley Street
South Brisbane QLD 4101
Tel: (07) 3010 5744
website: www.wellnessclinic.mater.org.au

The Mater Health & Wellness Clinic provides access to a team of leading allied health specialists who work together with clients, parents, their children and the greater medical community to provide individual treatment programs to ensure optimal health and wellness. Specialised services include nutrition counselling, physiotherapy, speech pathology, occupational therapy, psychology, counselling and massage. A range of services are offered for children as well as adults, including a focus on women's health and maternity services.

FIRST AID COURSES & KITS

NATIONAL

St John Ambulance Australia
Tel: 1300 360 455
email: enquiries@stjohn.org.au
website: www.stjohn.org.au

St John is Australia's leading provider of first aid with specialised first aid training for parents of babies and young children through the Caring for Kids First Aid Course. Caring for Kids is a one-day course which covers first aid essentials for children and babies including infant/child resuscitation, control of bleeding, management of shock, wounds, burns, bites, stings, poisoning and acute illness. St John also stock a range of first aid kits to suit every situation from individual and car kits through to comprehensive family and off-road kits. Being skilled in first aid and prepared with a suitable first aid kit is sensible insurance for your and your loved ones. Locations across Australia.

VICTORIA

Babes Safety
PO Box 700
Port Melbourne VIC 3207
Tel: (03) 9646 5845 or 0409 022 237
website: www.babessafety.com.au

Would you know what to do in an emergency? Babes Safety provides mobile first aid workshops for all parents and carers. Conducted by a qualified paediatric nurse, Babes Safety covers first aid, CPR for babies and children, choking, common childhood illnesses, accident prevention and safety advice.

Little Aid
Tel: 0419 272 159
email: info@littleaid.com.au
website: www.littleaid.com.au

Little Aid provides first aid training for parents, grandparents and babysitters. All subjects are child and baby relevant. Recommended by maternal and child health health nurses, Little Aid courses are easy to understand, relaxed and professional and they can come to you. Courses start from just $25 and can even be done as a fundraiser.

NEW SOUTH WALES

All Aid Training
Tel: 1800 236 699
email: info@allaidfirstaid.com.au
website: www.allaidfirstaid.com.au

All Aid First Aid infant and child first-aid training program prepares people to act efficiently and confidently in any emergency situation involving infants and children, be it a traumatic or a medical event. These skills save lives. This is a vital area of education and training for all child care workers, new and expecting parents and grandparents and generally anyone who spends time around infants and children. Courses are flexible, interactive and practical so that skills are practical and embedded. All Aid run tailor-built courses to suit your location and schedule.

HEALTH PRODUCTS & ACCESSORIES

NATIONAL

Hug-a-bub Australia P/L
Tel: 1300 365 484
email: email@hugabub.com
website: www.hugabub.com

Occupational therapist-approved baby sling that is suitable for the tiniest premature babies through to toddlers. Excellent for digestive, colic and reflux conditions, Hug-a-bub™ has designed a baby carrier that supports your baby functionally and therapeutically. Used in special care nurseries for the many benefits it provides for premature babies and babies who need special positioning due to hip or nervous system conditions. Phone the number above for more information.

Learning Curve Australia
Tel: (03) 9550 3600
email: service@rc2aust.com.au
website: www.rc2aust.com.au

The First Years range of products help parents keep their children healthy, happy and safe by offering products from feeding to playing and sleeping. Feeding and soothing products include the Take & Toss range of spill proof cups, bowls and spoons, booster seats and reclining feeding seats. The Play & Discovery products include unique toys and rattles including the popular "Floating Friends teether" and "Rolling Giggle Pals". The Care & Safety products include hands-free safety gates, toilet training seats, bed rails, safe sleepers and monitors. The First Years also offers licensed products in Winnie the Pooh, Thomas and Friends, Cars and Princess.

MCJ Australia
Tel: 1300 558 106
email: mcjaustralia@trolleymate.com.au
website: www.trolleymate.com.au

Trolley Mate is a thickly padded shopping trolley seat cover that aims for comfort and hygiene for children.

Resources

CHILDREN'S HEALTH & SAFETY

Health products & accessories

➡ Pharmaceutical products

This product is the only one of its kind to offer various options. It can also be used as a padded high chair cover, a change mat, a capsule cover for trolleys, a pillow for the car seat and as a pram liner. Trolley Mate is compact, machine washable and suits ages 0–3 years. Prices range from $39.95 to $45 plus p&h. For more details visit the website.

Mite-Y-Fresh

Tel: (02) 9986 3432
email: sales@miteyfresh.com.au
website: www.miteyfresh.com.au

Mite-Y-Fresh is an award-winning team dedicated to bringing asthma and allergy sufferers innovative long term protective measures against some of the most commonly suffered inhaled allergens. They supply a full range of allergy protective bedding, supported and recommended by Australian GPs. Phone to talk with a consultant or place a product order by phone, email or online.

Nice-Pak Products

Tel: 1800 506 750
email: info@nicepak.com.au
website: www.thewiggles.com

The Wiggles Gel Packs are soft and strong. Ideal for soothing bumps and bruises on little legs and arms and keeping school lunches cool on hot days. They are also ideal and safe for keeping your child warm on a cold night. You have the choice of Dorothy or the Big Red Car for your gel pack. For further information contact the Consumer Information Line on 1800 506 750.

No Touch Thermometers Australia

Tel: (03) 9888 8771
email: sales@notouch.com.au
website: www.notouch.com.au

The No Touch Thermometer scans the temple without contact. It is hygienic, safe and economic, with no probe covers providing fast and accurate results. Suitable for all ages and ideal for babies and children as there is no need to stand still, wake them up or touch. No trauma, no pain, no tears and no touch. For further information visit www.notouch.com.au.

Outlook Australia

Tel: (03) 9817 2311
email: outlooktm@bigpond.com
website: www.outlooktm.com

Help protect your baby from harmful UV rays, wind, glare and insects with the original Outlook® shade-a-babe. The shade incorporates a UPF50+ sun visor and inbuilt glare guard and provides from 70-99% UVR protection. Uniquely designed to be multi-fitting, and with easy front zip access, the shade-a-babe can be adjusted to fit most models of prams and joggers. Available in twin styles and offers excellent airflow and vision for baby. Available in black and new coloured drop down visors. For further information phone or visit the website.

Outlook Australia

Tel: (03) 9817 2311
website: www.outlooktm.com

auto-shade™ is the multi-fitting sun shade for cars brought to you by Outlook, the specialists in sun protection accessories for babies. Available in two shapes that fit most vehicles, rounded or square, auto-shade™ is easily fitted to the majority of 4 door vehicles. auto-shade™ offers UV and sun glare protection, UPF 10. Car windows can be raised or lowered with the shade in place providing ventilation while still maintaining protection from the glare. For further information phone or visit the website.

Outlook Australia

Tel: (03) 9817 2311
website: www.outlooktm.com

The solar-shade™ offers up to 99% protection from harmful UV rays, considerably extending the shade cover offered to your child when you are on the move. The solar-shade™ protects eyes from sun glare, and it looks great too. Available in black, navy, cherry, sand, fuchsia and royal. For further information phone or visit the website.

Philips AVENT

Tel: 1300 364 474
email: inquiry@avent.com.au
website: www.avent.com.au

The Philips Avent range includes a complete, integrated range of baby care items including: health and monitoring, breast care, feeding equipment, non-spill cups, mother and baby skincare products and baby bags. Philips Avent feeding products are anti-colic and shaped closely to emulate the mother's natural shape. The non-spill Magic Cups have an easy sip spout, detachable handles and a snap-on lid for travel. Phone or visit the website for more details.

Probiotec Pharma

Tel: 1800 620 898 or (03) 9278 7555
email: info@miltonpharma.com
website: www.miltonpharma.com

For 93 years mums have trusted the Milton method of sterilization, clinically proven non toxic and more effective than either steaming or microwave sterilization. The Milton Method kills more than 99.9% of germs creating a safe environment for your baby. The

Milton method is a safe way to disinfect teats and bottles, soothers, toys and cleaning down surfaces baby comes in contact with. Milton Antibacterial Gels are a convenient way to sanitize your hands on the run. The Antibacterial Gels disinfect 99.9% of germs and come in either natural or Aloe and Vitamin E. Available in pharmacies and supermarkets nationally. For further information phone 1800 620 898 or visit the website www.miltonpharma.com.

Rose & Lily Australia Pty Ltd
Tel: 0413 977 287
website: www.roseandlily.com.au

The Lovenest is a paediatrician-designed head support for babies which assists in the prevention of "flat-head syndrome" (or plagiocephaly). The Lovenest's hollowed out centre and contoured shape supports baby's soft head and stops the head from touching flat surfaces for prolonged periods. Recommended for use from 0 to 4 months. For further information phone or visit the website.

Tri-Nature Pty Ltd
New South Wales
Tel: (02) 4627 2105
Victoria
Tel: 0433 TRI NAT
Queensland
Tel: (07) 3264 4885
South Australia
Tel: (08) 8346 4044
website: www.trinature.com

Tri-Nature has replaced harsh and aggressive chemicals, petroleum solvents, phosphates and other environmental pollutants found in most cleaning products with gentle, naturally-based high performance ingredients. Registered "Choose Cruelty Free". Tri-Nature also produce a safe dishwasher powder with the lowest pH of any powdered washing product and contains none of the caustic substances, alkaline or chlorinated compounds that cause so much damage when ingested. Perfect products for eczema and allergies/sensitive skin. Suitable for grey water systems. 100% guarantee. Australian owned and made. For further information phone or visit the website.

NEW SOUTH WALES

Mite-Y-Fresh
PO Box 431
Terrey Hills NSW 2084
Tel: (02) 9986 3432
website: www.miteyfresh.com.au

Mite-Y-Fresh hire out air purifiers and dehumidifiers when you need them most. Service includes delivery, instructions and pick up in the Sydney region. For an extra small fee, Mite-Y-Fresh service the Central Coast, Blue Mountains and Illawarra regions. They also provide a range of alternative, practical, easy-to-implement solutions. For further information phone or visit www.miteyfresh.com.au.

PHARMACEUTICAL PRODUCTS

NATIONAL

Aspen Pharmacare Pty Ltd
Tel: (02) 8436 8300
email: sales@aspenpharmacare.com.au
website: www.aspenpharmacare.com.au

Tixylix® is a specially formulated children's cough and cold range. Tixylix® helps ease a nagging, night-time cough and relieve a blocked, runny nose. And Tixylix® Chest Rub contains aromatic essential oils like rosemary, thyme and pine to help make breathing easier for children aged one and over. Which means the whole family can enjoy a more comfortable and restful night's sleep. Trust the Tixylix® range to take care of your children.
Always read the label.
If symptoms persist, seek medical advice.

Aspen Pharmacare Pty Ltd
Tel: (02) 8436 8300
email: sales@aspenpharmacare.com.au
website: www.aspenpharmacare.com.au

Dermeze protects, soothes and deeply moisturises very dry skin. Being an ointment it offers enhanced skin absorption and does not contain any preservatives, which can cause contact dermatitis. Dermeze provides a barrier over the skin to prevent moisture loss and to help retain the skin's natural oils. Dermeze is fragrance free and contains no artificial colours.
Always read the label. Use only as directed.
If symptoms persist please see your doctor.

Aspen Pharmacare Pty Ltd
Tel: (02) 8436 8300
email: sales@aspenpharmacare.com.au
website: www.aspenpharmacare.com.au

Orange flavoured O.R.S. helps treat and prevent dehydration in children and adults due to diarrhoea and traveller's gastroenteritis. Diarrhoea may be due to a number of conditions and can result in a loss of fluids and salts from the body. This can be particularly dangerous in babies and small children as they can become dehydrated very quickly. It is important to replace the lost fluid with a balanced mix of glucose and salts in water. O.R.S. sachets contain glucose and salts and, when mixed with fresh drinking water, aid in the prevention of dehydration.
Always read the label.
If symptoms persist, seek medical advice.

AstraZeneca Pty Ltd
Tel: 1800 805 342
website: www.emla.com.au

emla® helps erase vaccination and needles pain[2]. Research has shown that children think a needle is the

Resources

CHILDREN'S HEALTH & SAFETY

Pharmaceutical products

most frightening and painful thing about visiting the doctor. It has been shown that a child is likely to retain a fear of needles if they have been traumatised at the doctor's previously.[1] emla numbs the skin[2]. It can relieve the stress and pain of visiting the doctor for you and your child by applying it prior to the vaccination or needle.[2] It can be used in children of all ages from full-term newborn babies onwards. Emla® is available in convenient patches or cream from a pharmacist without a prescription.[2] www.emla.com.au.contains further information on emla® including application directions. To find out how emla® can help you and your child, speak to your Pharmacist or GP or call 1800 805 342.
Always read the label before using emla®.
Use only as directed.
[1] *Kleiber C et al. Pediatrics 2002;110:758-61.*
[2] *emla® Product Information May 2008.*

Bayer Australia – Consumer Care

Tel: 1800 023 884
website: www.sm33.com.au

SM33 gel gives fast, effective relief from teething pain. Most teething gels contain an analgesic to reduce pain and an antiseptic. However only SM33 contains an additional anaesthetic which quickly numbs the gums. SM33 gels is a unique formulation that works in three ways to cool, soothe and relieve teething pain. It numbs the gums to give fast relief, and it reduces inflammation and pain. SM33 gel is available from your pharmacy. Visit www.sm33.com.au for more details or phone 1800 023 884.
Always read the label. Use only as directed.
If symptoms persist see your healthcare professional.

Bayer Australia Limited

Tel: 1800 023 884
website: www.bayer.com.au

Penta-vite® multivitamins contain vitamins essential for infants and children's healthy growth and development. Some children go through times when they need a little help getting all the dietary vitamins they need, such as in instances of fussy eating or during illness. Penta-vite® can be given every day to help maintain a healthy intake of vitamins and minerals. Available in a range of chewable or liquid formulations, Pentavite® is suitable for infants and children. Visit the website www.bayer.com.au for more details or phone 1800 023 884.
Always read the label. Use only as directed.
If symptoms persist see your healthcare professional.
Vitamin supplements should not replace a balanced diet.

Care Pharmaceuticals Pty Ltd

Tel: 1800 788 870
email: info@carepharmaceuticals.com.au
website: www.littleeyes.com.au

When your little one gets eye infections, nothing can seem worse than having to wipe their eyes clean. Little Eyes' wipes provide a gentle easy way to clean your little one's eyes and lashes. Free of alcohol, fragrances and preservatives, they are pH balanced to match your child's own tears. Tested and recommended by ophthalmologists and dermatologists, Little Eyes lets you wipe away their tears (and whatever else is there) without causing more.
Always read the label. Use only as directed.
If symptoms persist please see your doctor.

Care Pharmaceuticals Pty Ltd

Tel: 1800 788 870
email: info@carepharmaceuticals.com.au
website: www.fess.com.au

A young baby's natural instinct is to breathe through their nose – even when it is blocked. It is therefore important to keep your baby's nose clear. FESS LITTLE NOSES® is a non-medicated saline solution which helps unblock your baby's nose. The saline solution will not sting baby's delicate nasal membranes and can be used as often as needed. FESS LITTLE NOSES® helps your baby breathe easier, naturally. Available from pharmacies.
Always read the label. Use only as directed.
If symptoms persist please see your doctor.

Care Pharmaceuticals Pty Ltd

Tel: 1800 788 870
email: info@carepharmaceuticals.com.au
website: www.carepharmaceuticals.com.au

Fever is a sign that your body is fighting off an infection. This may be caused by colds, ear infections, bronchitis or tonsillitis. IPROFEN FOR CHILDREN has been developed to provide temporary relief of mild to moderate pain and fever. This alcohol and sugar-free formula starts to work in 15 minutes and provides long lasting pain and fever relief for up to 8 hours. Available from pharmacies.
Always read the label. Use only as directed.
If symptoms persist please see your doctor.

Care Pharmaceuticals Pty Ltd

Tel: 1800 788 870
email: info@carepharmaceuticals.com.au
website: www.fess.com.au

FESS® NASAL GEL is specially formulated to provide soothing relief to the very delicate skin in and around the nostrils. The blending of vitamin E, olive oil and sesame seed oil in a saline base provides moisture, plus protection against further chafing and irritation. The non-medicated saline base is ideal for all ages.

Recommended for dry, sore or tender noses due to colds and flu, air conditioning, dry, cold, or windy weather, pregnancy or the harshness of tissues.
Always read the label. Use only as directed.
If symptoms persist please see your doctor.

Care Pharmaceuticals Pty Ltd

Tel: 1800 788 870
email: info@carepharmaceuticals.com.au
website: www.carepharmaceuticals.com.au

Parachoc is a non-medicated oral liquid laxative for children over 12 months of age. Parachoc works gently by lubricating and softening the faecal mass subsequently reducing pain associated with constipation and helping to restore the normal colon function. Parachoc is sugar, lactose and gluten free and available from pharmacies nationally.
Always read the label. Use only as directed.
Can be used over a long term in consultation with a doctor.

Care Pharmaceuticals Pty Ltd

Tel: 1800 788 870
email: info@carepharmaceuticals.com.au
website: www.carepharmaceuticals.com.au

Painstop Day-Time Pain Reliever for children provides fast, effective and temporary relief of moderate to strong pain in children. Painstop Day-Time can provide relief from earache, minor burns, teething and toothache, minor fractures and injuries, headaches and post-operative pain. As the only product available at pharmacies to treat moderate to strong pain in children, Painstop Day-Time works more effectively for moderate to strong pain than paracetamol or ibuprofen taken separately. Suitable for children from 12 months old. Alcohol, sugar and gluten free. Available from pharmacies.
Always read the label. Use only as directed.
If pain persists, please see your doctor.

FGB Natural Products

Tel: 1800 655 841
email: mail@fgb.com.au
website: www.fgb.com.au

There's nothing worse than a runny or blocked nose when it's time to get tucked in at night. When they're sick with a cold, children need their sleep so what can you do to make bedtime more bear-able? Luckily help is at hand with natural, gentle Euky Bearub. Australian-made Euky Bearub chest ointment helps children breathe easier and sleep better, with a blend of natural essential oils including rosemary and eucalyptus. Its gentle formula is kind to most sensitive skin, making it perfect even for little members of the family. A warm, soothing chest rub with Euky Bearub before bed helps comfort and soothe for a better night's sleep. Available at pharmacies, rrp approx. $8.95 for 50g. For stockists phone 1800 655 841 or visit www.fgb.com.au for more information.
Always read the label. Use only as directed.
If symptoms persist please see your doctor.

GlaxoSmithKline Consumer Healthcare

Tel: 1800 028 533
website: www.childrenspanadol.com.au

Children's Panadol
It's my choice

Children's Panadol is suitable for use from one month of age. Pain and fever is common in childhood and may be associated with a variety of conditions including teething, immunisation, colds and flu, sinusitis and headaches. Some analgesics are not suitable for children under 3 months of age, however paracetamol when used at the recommended dose is suitable for use from one month of age. Children's Panadol is suitable for children with asthma who are sensitive to aspirin and non steroidal anti-inflammatory drugs (NSAIDs). Children's Panadol contains paracetamol and is gentle to little stomachs. It does not contain sugar, aspirin or ibuprofen. Children's Panadol is available in a variety of formulations that have been specially prepared for children of different ages from one month right through to 12 years. The range includes infant drops, elixirs, suspensions, suppositories, chewable tablets and soluble tablets.
Always read the label. Use only as directed.
For the temporary relief of pain and fever. Incorrect use could be harmful. Consult your healthcare professional if symptoms persist. Panadol® is a registered trade mark of the GlaxoSmithKline group of companies.

Herron Pharmaceuticals

Tel: 1300 659 646
website: www.herron.com.au

Herron Baby has developed a range of baby products for Australian families. Herron Baby Zinc and Castor Oil Cream is a gentle nappy rash cream, helping to soothe, heal and protect your baby's sensitive skin. Herron Baby Teething Gel is specially formulated for the temporary relief of pain caused by teething. For busy mums, keep a look out for Herron's great range of vitamins and Vita-minis for kids.
Always read the label. Use only as directed.
If symptoms persist see your healthcare professional.
ASMI/15681-10/08, CHC50501-10/08

Hydration Pharmaceuticals

email: enquiries@hydralyte.com
website: www.hydralyte.com

Hydralyte helps prevent dehydration by replacing electrolytes lost due to vomiting, diarrhoea, fever and other dehydrating conditions. It is available as an orange or apple/blackcurrant flavoured ready-to-drink solution, ice block or sachets for travelling. Parents need to watch their children for dehydration during bouts of vomiting and diarrhoea, when the weather is hot for extended periods and if they are running a fever for extended periods. Hydralyte may be taken on the first signs of loss of fluid and is suitable for all ages. Keep some in the home ready for when you need it most. Seek further medical advice if diarrhoea persists for more than 6 hours in

Resources

CHILDREN'S HEALTH & SAFETY

Pharmaceutical products
➔ Safety products & accessories

infants under 6 months, 12 hours in children under 3 years, 24 hours in children aged between 3 to 6 years. Hydralyte is an Australian product. It is available at your local pharmacy and is used in leading children's hospitals across Australia.
Always read the label. Use only as directed.
If symptoms persist please see your doctor.

Nice-Pak Products
Tel: 1800 506 750
email: info@nicepak.com.au
website: www.infacol.com.au
Infacol Wind Drops is an effective method of treating wind in babies and infants. Babies get wind by swallowing tiny air bubbles with their milk, which become trapped causing pressure and discomfort in the stomach. Infacol relieves infant wind before painful colic can occur. Available at pharmacies, grocery, department and baby stores.
Always read the label. Use only as directed.
If symptoms persist please see your doctor.

Reckitt Benckiser – Nurofen
Tel: 1800 226 766
website: www.nurofenforchildren.com.au
Nurofen for Children targets pain and reduces the discomfort of fever to give your child fast, effective relief from symptoms associated with earache, teething, aches and pains, immunisation or a sore throat. Nurofen for Children starts to work in 15 minutes and reduces fever for up to 8 hours. Nurofen for Children Infant Drops is specially designed for infants aged 3 months to 2 years whilst regular Nurofen for Children is suitable for children aged 3 months to 12 years. Nurofen for Children is colour free and sugar free with a pleasant orange or strawberry flavour while the sugar free strawberry flavoured Nurofen for Children Infant Drops is available in a concentrated formula which means you only need to dose half the amount of liquid. An easy-to-use dosing device is provided in each pack to assist with accurate dosing. Nurofen for Children contains ibuprofen (100mg/5mL) in suspension. It is available from pharmacies in 100mL and 200mL unbreakable plastic bottles. Nurofen for Children Infant Drops contains ibuprofen (200mg/5mL). It is available from pharmacies in a 30mL unbreakable plastic bottle.
Always read the label. Use only as directed.
Incorrect use could be harmful. If symptoms persist, see your healthcare professional. Do not give to babies under 3 months. Seek medical advice for children less than 1 year.

SAFETY PRODUCTS & ACCESSORIES

NATIONAL

Babyco
Tel: 1300 130 999 Babyco Hotline
email: retail@babyco.com.au
website: www.babyco.com.au
Babyco stores have a large and diverse range of health and safety products including safety monitors, safety products for car seats and much more. Friendly staff will assist with these important choices for your baby. Contact your nearest store on the Babyco Hotline 1300 130 999. (WA, TAS and NT do not have Babyco store locations however goods are available nationally via their website www.babyco.com.au.)

Clever Babies (Kushies)
Tel: 1800 114 443
email: info@cleverbabies.com.au
website: www.cleverbabies.com.au
The Hurphy Durphy Seat Belt Buckle Guard® prevents the 'accidental' release of a seat belt that is anchoring a capsule or car seat. The devise features a black neoprene sleeve that wraps around and therefore secures the seat belt buckle with heavy duty velcro.

CNP Brands
Tel: 1300 667 137
email: info@cnpbrands.com.au
website: www.cnpbrands.com.au

BabyDan by CNP Brands creates a safe environment for your child with its range of safety gates. Uncompromising on child safety, BabyDan is uncompromising on the quality, workmanship, materials and production of their safety gate range. The range has a gate model to fit any sized opening and offers a choice of pressure-mounted gates which requires no fixing to a wall, and screw-mounted gates for larger and more unusual opening widths. The BabyDan Baby Den is a uniquely flexible gate which can be used in many ways including as a playpen, a safety gate, a hearth gate or even as a room divider. The BabyDan safety gate range is available at selected nursery specialist retailers.

Global Innovations (Aust) Pty Ltd
Tel: (07) 3805 8110
email: sales@globalinnovations.com.au
website: www.globalinnovations.com.au
The Baby Home Safety Starter Pack is a comprehensive 72-item safety pack that will assist in avoiding unnecessary accidents at home. It is an ideal pack for mothers, grandmothers or any carer who wants to prioritise safety in an effective, inexpensive manner. RRP$39.95. Kidsafe (Child Prevention Foundation of Australia) advise that each day in Australia 5,000 children seek medical attention, 170 are hospitalised and 350 children die annually, the majority from preventable accidents.

IGC DOREL Pty Ltd
Tel: 1300 809 526
email: sales@igcdorel.com.au
website: www.safety1st.com

For decades, parents all over the world have placed their trust – and their children's safety - in Safety 1st® products. Instantly recognisable for innovation, expertise and commitment to quality, the Safety 1st® product range is as extensive as it is dependable: monitors, gates, bathtubs, car seats, infant health and grooming, and childproofing products for parents' peace of mind. Safety 1st® is available in all major retailer stores and leading nursery stores. To view the latest range visit www.safety1st.com or phone IGC Dorel's Customer Service team on 1300 809 526 for your nearest stockist.

Kids Kontact
Tel: 0429 378 973
email: kidskontact@bigpond.com
website: www.kidskontact.com.au

A wandering child is every parent's worst nightmare when visiting shopping centres and events and can cause distress to both parents and children alike. Australian online business, Kids Kontact, specialises in safety and reusable ID products to ensure children remain safe and easily identifiable in an emergency. Kids Kontact carry a range of ID products to suit every child and every occasion.

Playgro Pty Ltd
Tel: (03) 8558 2000
email: sales@playgro.com
website: www.playgro.com

Playgro's safety range has been designed to help childproof your home. It's a scary fact that most childhood accidents happen in the home. Playgro's safety range is specially designed to prevent little hands from being where they shouldn't. The comprehensive range includes cupboard and cabinet drawer locks, appliance latches, window locks, stove knob covers, outlet plugs and corner cushions. Playgro's safety range will help keep your child safe within the home and put your mind at ease. Available from major retailers and specialty baby stores nationwide.

Snazzy Baby
Tel: 1300 650 115
email: info@snazzybaby.com.au
website: www.snazzybaby.com.au

The award-winning Snazzy Baby Knee Pads were designed for the ultimate protection for babies learning to crawl and walk. Endorsed by medical professionals, the uniquely developed traction beads allow babies to get the right amount of traction to get up on their knees on all types of floor surfaces hardwood, tiles, carpet and outdoor surfaces, without slipping and sliding. Developed for use over a long time frame, from 4 months to 4 years, they can be used for crawling or playground activities.

SP Products Pty Ltd
Tel: (03) 8587 4800
email: chris@specialpatterns.com.au
website: www.mickyhaha.com.au

Melbourne mother of 4, Catherine Hovenbitzer, who saw a need to prevent young children from touching "live" electrical plugs and switches while in use, originally conceived the Micky Ha Ha Power Point Safety Cover, the first of an innovative range of safety products. Its clear, durable design allows complete visibility and rounded shape prevents injury from sharp corners. Around the home, in the workshop or workplace they help retain power leads in the socket and prevent accidental unplugging. Easy and quick do-it-yourself installation. Product details and store information is available at www.mickyhaha.com.au.

SunRos Pty Ltd
Tel: (02) 9997 7625
email: info@sunros.com.au
website: www.babylook-australia.com.au

Thanks to the Babylook mirrors, you can now watch your rear-facing baby while driving your car. Just as you can see the traffic behind you in your rearview mirror, now you can also keep an eye on your baby in exactly the same way. Babylook is made in Germany.

Tee-Zed Products
Tel: (02) 9386 4000
email: sales@tee-zed.com.au
website: www.tee-zed.com

Dream Baby's® range of safety products were designed in consultation with parents, safety experts and education specialists. Recently released, the patented Magnetic Locking System (Mag Lock™) has proven a success in making homes safer. Dream Baby® has excellent child safety gates which are also suitable for use for pets. These gates are available in extra tall (one metre high), and also Hallway width gates. All gates are available in black as well as white. Extensions (9cm, 18cm and 27cm) are available for all Dream Baby® gates. Dream Baby® health and safety products are available from selected baby stores, toy stores, pharmacies and hardware stores. Phone (02) 9386 4000 for your nearest stockist.

The Product Store Pty Ltd
Tel: (07) 3857 0691
email: info@theproductstore.com.au
website: www.theproductstore.com.au

The FunPod™ is a stand-alone child safety device which elevates your toddler to kitchen bench height. Simply lift them in and let them help you with the washing up or preparation of the day's meal. It's a great way of keeping them away from electrical or hot appliances in the kitchen, not to mention stimulation or child development. The FunPod™ can be used from when your toddler stands unaided at approximately 12 months old until 5 years of age.

Children's Panadol

Children's Panadol is suitable for use from one month of age. Pain and fever is common in childhood and may be associated with a variety of conditions including teething, immunisation, colds and flu, sinusitis and headaches. Some analgesics are not suitable for children under 3 months of age, however paracetamol when used at the recommended dose is suitable for use from one month of age. Children's Panadol is suitable for children with asthma who are sensitive to aspirin and non steroidal anti-inflammatory drugs (NSAIDs). Children's Panadol contains paracetamol and is gentle to little stomachs. It does not contain sugar, aspirin or ibuprofen. Children's Panadol is available in a variety of formulations that have been specially prepared for children of different ages from one month right through to 12 years. The range includes infant drops, elixirs, suspensions, suppositories, chewable tablets and soluble tablets.

ALWAYS READ THE LABEL. Use only as directed. Children's Panadol contains paracetamol. For the temporary relief of pain and fever. Incorrect use could be harmful. Consult your healthcare professional if symptoms persist. Panadol® is a registered trade mark of the GlaxoSmithKline group of companies.

Since she was one month old.

Children's Panadol offers fast, effective relief from
pain and fever from the time a baby is one month old.

Children's
Panadol
It's my choice.

Fess Little Noses
& Little Eyes

A young baby's natural instinct is to breathe through their nose – even when it's blocked. This can make their life very frustrating, disrupting sleep, nursing and bottle feeding. That's why it's so important to keep your baby's nose clear.

The FESS Little Noses® range contains a non-medicated saline solution that provides relief of dry or blocked noses due to colds, allergies, sinusitis or dry air and being drug-free can be used as often as needed. Since it is also an alcohol free formula, FESS Little Noses solution will not sting your baby's delicate nasal membranes.

It loosens and thins nasal mucus and moisturizes dry nasal passages, helping to clear stuffy noses. The FESS Nasal Aspirator is a rubber bulb syringe with a soft tip designed to gently and effectively suction the mucus from your baby's nose so they can breathe easier, naturally. As babies insist on breathing through their nose, a clear nose is essential prior to feeding. FESS Little Noses is available as either a gentle nasal spray or nasal drops. Available from pharmacies nationally. For more information, call 1800 788 870 or visit www.fess.com.au. Little Eyes™ wipes provide a gentle easy way to clean your little one's eyes and lashes. Free of alcohol, fragrances and preservatives, Little Eyes hypoallergenic wipes are pH balanced to match your child's own tears and perfect for removing any secretions or residue from eye infections. The unique rinse-free formula contains chamomile and glycerine to gently soothe and moisturize this delicate area making it suitable for the most sensitive skins. Available in boxes of 30 handy sterilized individual sachets, from pharmacies nationally. For more information, call 1800 788 870 or visit www.littleeyes.com.au.

FESS Little Noses Spray contains saline solution equiv to 9mg/mL Sodium Chloride. Always read the label. Use only as directed. If symptoms persist, see your healthcare professional.

Care for the little things in life

When your little one has a blocked nose or sore eyes, they need a little tender loving care from more than only mum and dad. That's where **FESS Little Noses®** and **Little Eyes®** come in. Using specially formulated ingredients, they'll help provide gentle relief for babies.

FESS Little Noses® provides non-medicated relief when your baby's blocked nose disrupts their sleep, nursing or feeding. The gentle saline solution will help thin and loosen excess mucus. The soft-tip aspirator then gently removes the mucus so baby can breathe more easily. FESS Little Noses is available in both a spray and drops.

Little Eyes® hypoallergenic wipes are perfect for wiping away ocular secretions and residue without stinging. They're amazingly gentle on the delicate eye area, and ideal for cleaning between the lashes without needing to rinse afterwards.

FESS Little Noses® and **Little Eyes®** are suitable from the day baby is born.

Find out more about FESS Little Noses at www.fess.com.au, and Little Eyes at www.littleeyes.com.au. Alternatively, call 1800 788 870.

O.R.S.

To remain healthy and function well, our bodies require the correct internal balance of electrolytes and water. During certain conditions, this internal balance is impaired and dehydration develops. Dehydration can be caused by gastric illness resulting in diarrhoea and vomiting. This can be particularly worrying in babies and small children as they can become dehydrated very quickly.

Symptoms of mild dehydration may include thirst, decreased urine volume, unexplained tiredness, headache, dry mouth and dizziness.

The best treatment for minor dehydration is drinking water and stopping fluid loss. Correction of a dehydrated state can be assisted by the replenishment of necessary water and electrolytes, i.e. through oral rehydration therapy.

O.R.S. sachets contain a balanced mix of glucose and salts. When mixed with fresh drinking water, O.R.S. forms an oral rehydration solution, specially formulated to be rapidly absorbed into the body, so that water and electrolytes are restored to their optimal level.

O.R.S. is suitable for all age groups from under 6 months of age upwards.

Always read the label. Use only as directed. If symptoms persist see your healthcare professional.

ASMI/15763-10/08

Rehydrate sick kids with O.R.S.

Diarrhoea can leave us all dangerously dehydrated, especially children. Dehydration can also be caused by vomiting associated with traveller's gastroenteritis. Orange flavoured O.R.S. (Oral Rehydration Salts) not only replaces fluids, but also important electrolytes that the body needs. It's a simple and effective way to help make sure sick kids and grown-ups don't suffer from dehydration.

Don't dehydrate... rehydrate.

AVAILABLE IN PHARMACIES AND SUPERMARKETS

Dermeze

Causes of dry skin: Dry skin becomes more prevalent as we get older as our bodies don't produce enough natural oils. Babies and young children are also very susceptible to dry skin because the oil producing glands haven't developed properly.

Dry skin can be exacerbated by cold and windy weather, sun, central heating, air-conditioning, poor ventilation, chemicals, detergents, soaps, solvents, frequent showering/bathing particularly in hot water and swimming in heavily chlorinated pools.

Moisturisers: Moisturisers are used to prevent the skin from drying and they should be used frequently. They can be used alone and can also be applied under wet dressings.

Relief from dry skin conditions: Dermeze Ointment helps to relieve and soothe dry, itchy or sensitive skin. It is an intensive, low allergy, no sting moisturiser, containing no preservatives, no fragrance and with no colour added. Dermeze Ointment can be applied before and after cool compresses to help relieve redness and itching due to dry skin conditions. Wet dressings cool the skin by the water evaporating just like sweat.

Always read the label. Use only as directed. If symptoms persist see your healthcare professional.

ASMI/15763-10/08

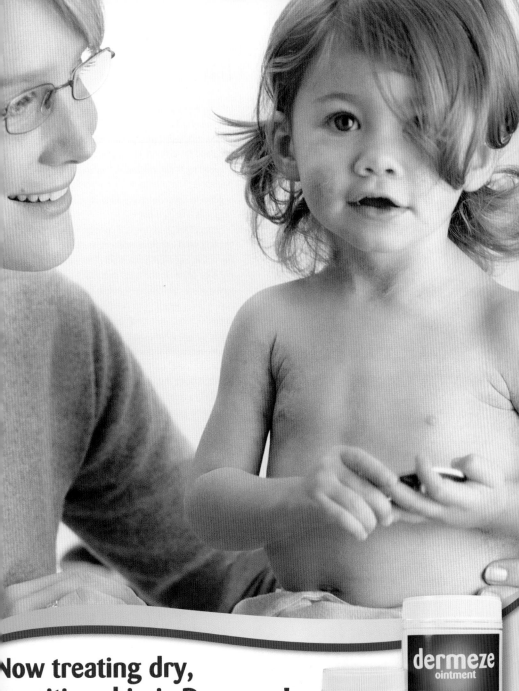

Now treating dry, sensitive skin is Dermezy!

Dermeze has been specially developed to deeply moisturise, relieve and soothe irritated skin. With no preservatives or artificial colours it's a gentle and effective choice for your child.

- **No preservatives**   • **No fragrance**   • **No artificial colours**

Infacol

Infacol Wind Drops is Australian made and has been helping reduce wind in babies for over 30 years. As a parent it is good to know that the product has been tried and tested by a few generations, and is one of the leading brands today. When your little one is in pain, and clearly suffering from a build up of wind, it is good to know there is a remedy out there that can help you and your baby.

Infacol Wind Drops is an effective method of treating wind in babies and infants. Simethicone is the active ingredient in Infacol that helps the small bubbles of gas in the baby's stomach to join together, forming a larger bubble that can be easily expelled and relieves infant wind before painful colic can occur. Given before each feed its proven formula works progressively over several days, to help reduce the frequency and severity of crying attacks associated with colic. Infacol Wind Drops is sugar free and does not contain any antacids.

Always read the label. Use only as directed. If symptoms persist see your healthcare professional.

ASMI/15791 – 11/08

Safety 1st

Stair and Hallway Safety Tips
Even though we're just passing through these areas, they should be childproofed too! Falls from stairs are especially dangerous so be sure to install gates before, or as soon as, your child starts crawling.

- Install a gate at the top and bottom of stairs to keep children off them and prevent falls.
- Teach your child how to climb the stairs but only when you are with them every step of the way.
- Cover all powerpoints in the hallway to prevent an electrical shock.
- Lock any cupboards that may contain dangerous items.
- If there is a balcony on the second floor of your home, be sure to keep the door closed and only allow access with supervision. For added safety, use a rail net to secure your balcony or stair landing.

For more helpful tips visit www.safety1st.com

Hydralyte

The main concern in children with vomiting and diarrhoea is the effect of fluid loss on the child's hydration levels. Even over a short period, consistent vomiting and or diarrhoea can quickly lead to dehydration because of a child's small size and consequent small fluid volume.

The best way to manage hydration at home is by giving small amounts of oral re-hydration fluids such as Hydralyte. This formulation, available in pharmacies and used in hospitals, contains the correct balance of electrolytes and glucose to enable rapid rehydration. Electrolytes assist in retaining fluid and glucose assists in the absorption of water and electrolytes. Plain water is not sufficient to correct this balance and soft drinks and juices contain too much sugar.

It is important that parents and carers are aware of the signs and symptoms of dehydration and when to seek medical advice.

Signs and symptoms of mild to moderate dehydration include lethargy, sunken eyes, loss of skin elasticity, reduced volume of urine and darker in colour, concentrated urine, dry mouth, sunken fontanelle (in young babies), rapid pulse and rapid weight loss of 3–7%.

Seek medical advice if diarrhoea persists for more than:
- 6 hours in infants under 6 months of age
- 12 hours in children under 3 years of age
- 24 hours in children aged 3–6 years

Ongoing management: Hydralyte should be sipped or sucked frequently while diarrhoea or vomiting persist and should continue to be consumed while symptoms of dehydration exist. Hydralyte is suitable for all age groups. Breastfed babies can be given small amounts of Hydralyte between feeds.

Choosing
furniture &
equipment

Photograph by Kristen Cook, Melbourne.

Keeping your baby safe

Providing and maintaining a safe environment for your baby can be a challenge for any parent. Children under five years old are more vulnerable to accidental death or injury than any other age group. However most accidents are preventable.

Nursery furniture and equipment has been associated with more than 20 per cent of injuries to babies in their first year of life. The most common items associated with child injuries are prams and strollers, high chairs, baby walkers, bouncinettes, change tables and cots. Child deaths have been associated with cots, prams and strollers.

This article, taken from the ACCC's *Keeping baby safe* book, identifies some of the high-risk products for babies. The 'Before you buy' sections for each product type list what to look for when buying new or second-hand products. You can also use the tips in the 'Safety at home' sections to provide a safe home environment for your baby.

While potential hazards change as your baby develops, keep these key safety rules in mind:

- Follow the advice on product warning labels
- Use products according to the manufacturer's instructions and their intended use
- Check products regularly for wear and tear.

BUYING NURSERY FURNITURE AND EQUIPMENT

Serious accidents involving baby products occur every year. To reduce the chance of this happening to your family, it is important that you select and buy safe products for your baby.

There are many products on the market for babies and it can be confusing to understand all of the safety considerations when making a selection. While this book identifies some specific risks for products, there are some general rules to consider:

- If you are buying new furniture or equipment, ask the retailer if it has been made according to Australian standards. Compliance with these standards ensures that the product meets minimum safety and design requirements.
- If you are buying or borrowing second-hand products it is important that these products comply with the checks in this guide. Wear and tear, or any modifications made to the products may make the item unsafe.
- Check furniture carefully – it should be free of rough surfaces, sharp edges, points and protrusions. It should be sturdily constructed so that it will not collapse when in use, and all locking devices should function properly.
- Before buying nursery furniture, be aware of how to create a safe sleeping environment for your child. Some items such as cot bumpers, doonas, quilts and pillows may increase the risk of sudden infant death syndrome and sleeping accidents. For information on reducing the risk of SIDS, contact the SIDS organisation in your state or territory on 1300 308 307, or visit the SIDS and Kids website www.sidsandkids.org.

Warranties

New furniture and equipment comes with an implied warranty that the product is fit for the intended use. You will usually receive a warranty card with the product. If you complete the card and return it to

he manufacturer, you can be notified of any future safety problems. You don't have to return the
varranty card to the manufacturer to be able to enforce your implied rights. If you find a safety fault
you should notify the manufacturer quickly.

HOUSEHOLD COTS

Babies and young children spend a lot of their time sleeping, so it is important that you ensure cots are
safe. Cots have been associated with fatal injuries in children under 12 months old. Young babies are
vulnerable to suffocating or choking, and toddlers are at risk of injury from falling while trying to climb
out of their cot.

Cot injuries can happen if a child's head, arms or legs are trapped between the bars and panels,
between the sides and the mattress or if their clothing is caught on the cot. When a child starts to climb,
they have outgrown their cot and it's time to move your child to a single bed.

Changes to the standard for Children's Household Cots AS/NZS 2172 in 2003 amended some of the
prescribed measurements. Many cots currently in use are made to the previous standard, and the
measurements given as a guide in this book are applicable to cots made to either standard.

Before you buy

- Select a cot that complies with the mandatory safety standard based on the Australian Standard for
  household cots AS/NZS 2172. Look for a label or sticker that says the cot complies with the
  mandatory standard. If there isn't one, ask the retailer. If the retailer cannot verify that it complies,
  do not buy it. All cots sold, even second-hand ones, must comply with this standard.
- Check that bars, panels, mattress base and drop sides are firmly attached.
- Take a tape measure with you when you go shopping so you can check the size of gaps and
  openings:
  - The mattress must fit snugly to within 25mm of sides and ends
  - With the mattress base set in the lower position, the cot sides or end need to be at least 500mm
    higher than the mattress
  - The spacing between the bars or panels in the cot sides and ends needs to be between 50mm and
    95mm – gaps wider than 95mm can trap a child's head. If the bars or panels are made from flexible
    material, the maximum spacing between the bars or panels should be less than 95mm
  - Check that there are no small holes or openings between 5mm and 12mm wide that small fingers
    can be caught in
  - Check that there are no spaces between 30mm and 50mm that could trap your child's arms or
    legs
  - Check there are no fittings (including bolts, knobs and corner posts) that might catch onto your
    child's clothing and cause distress or strangulation.

Safety at home

- Do not use U- or V-shaped pillows for children under two years old. It is safer not to use a pillow
  at all for children under two.
- Do not allow small objects that could cause your child to choke to be placed in the cot, or
  anywhere accessible to your child.

Keeping your baby safe

- Never use electric blankets or hot water bottles for babies or young children.
- Do not leave mobiles or toys with stretch/elastic cords in cots.
- Make sure the space above the cot is free of objects such as pictures or mirrors which could fall onto your child.
- Make sure the cot has no more than two legs with castors, or that at least one pair of castors has brakes.
- Keep the cot clear of heaters, stoves and power points.
- Keep the cot clear of curtain or blind cords as they are a strangulation hazard.
- Follow the manufacturer's instructions carefully (and keep them somewhere safe).
- Regularly check that nuts and bolts are tight, as per the maintenance instructions supplied with the cot.
- Set the mattress base to the lowest position before your baby can sit up.
- Remove climbing aids (such as a large toy) from the cot once your child can stand.

SECOND-HAND AND HEIRLOOM COTS
Second-hand and heirloom cots can be a hazard to children because:
- The spacing between the bars may be too wide and trap a child's head, or may be too narrow and trap a child's arms or legs
- The catches on the side of the cot may be easy for a child to undo
- Older, painted cots may be painted with lead paint that the child may chew on and swallow when they are teething
- The corners of the cot can catch on the child's clothes and create a strangulation hazard.

PORTABLE COTS
Portable cots must be assembled correctly so that they cannot collapse while a baby is in them.
Some states and territories have banned the sale and supply of some older models of portable cots with an unreliable folding mechanism. Contact your local fair trading office for further information on this product. A new mandatory safety standard for portable cots comes into effect from 1 March 2009. Portable cots supplied after that date must meet essential safety specifications.

Before you buy
- Look for a model that meets the voluntary Australian Standard AS/NZS 2195 for portable cots. Look for a label or sticker that says the portable cot complies with this voluntary standard. If there isn't one, ask the retailer. If the retailer cannot verify that it complies, ask if there is any alternative that does comply.
- Before you buy a new or second-hand portable cot, make sure that all the locking devices are secure when the cot is assembled and that your child cannot release them and collapse the cot.
- If buying a second-hand portable cot, check there are no tears in the mesh or fabric sides and no cracks in the side rails.
- Follow the assembly instructions closely when setting up the cot.

Safety at home

- Do not use a portable cot if your child weighs more than 15kg (or check instructions for your particular model).
- Check all locking devices are properly latched before putting a child in the cot. Stop using the cot before your child is able to release the locking devices and collapse it.
- Do not put pillows or an additional mattress in a portable cot. Babies can become trapped between the mattress and cot sides and may suffocate. Older children may use the extra height to help them climb out.
- Check fabric-covered rails frequently for tears – a teething child can chew off pieces and choke.
- Remove all toys from the cot when the child is sleeping.
- Repair tears in mesh or fabric sides immediately.
- Regularly check locking devices to ensure they are operating properly and have not become loose.
- Keep the portable cot clear of curtain or blind cords as they are a strangulation hazard.
- Keep the cot away from heaters, stoves and power points.

CHANGE TABLES

If you use a change table, be aware that your baby will require constant supervision when on it. Injuries from falling off a change table include serious head injuries. Most injuries occur when a baby rolls off the table onto the floor or onto another piece of furniture. A baby can roll off a change table before anyone realises it can even roll at all. *Never leave a baby unattended on a change table.*

Before you buy

- Consider whether you really want to use a change table, or if you wish to change your baby on a large doubled-over towel on the floor.
- Only buy a change table that has some form of roll-off protection such as a child safety harness, and raised sides and ends at least 100mm high.
- Make sure there are no gaps or spaces near the changing surface that could trap a child's fingers, head or limbs.
- If it's a folding table, make sure all locking devices work.

Safety at home

- Never leave a baby unattended on a change table. Ignore distractions (such as the telephone) while you change the baby. If you must attend to an emergency, put your baby in a safe place first, or take the baby with you. Even a very young baby can wriggle and fall from a change table in less time than it takes to answer the phone.
- Do not leave open pins, bottles, lotions or creams where the baby can reach them.
- Use safety harnesses at all times.
- Have everything you need to change the baby close at hand.
- Make sure no small objects that could cause choking are within your baby's reach.
- Ensure collapsible frames are locked securely in place before use.
- Repair any loose or broken parts straight away.

Keeping your baby safe

HIGH CHAIRS

Child injuries involving high chairs are mainly due to falls caused by the child standing up or trying to climb into or out of the chair. Continual supervision and the proper use of restraints will substantially reduce the risk of injury.

Before you buy

- For maximum safety, choose a high chair fitted with a five-point harness (crotch strap between the legs, straps over both shoulders and a waist belt).
- If you are buying a second-hand high chair that doesn't have a proper harness, buy a harness separately and clip or attach it securely.
- Check that the construction and framework is sturdy and robust. Put some weight on the seat and backrest to see if they squeak, sag, deform, move out of position, or collapse.
- Check that folding high chairs are stable and that the locks work. Ask for a demonstration.
- Check that moving parts cannot pinch, crush or trap a child's finger, toe, limb or head.
- Check for sharp edges and points along the edges of the chair and tray, and for any easily detachable parts which could pose a choking hazard.
- If the high chair has four castors fitted, make sure at least one pair (either front or back) has brakes.

Safety at home

- Never leave your child unattended in a high chair. If you need to leave the room, take your child with you.
- Do not allow a child to stand up in a high chair or climb into or out of it unassisted, as the chair may become unstable.
- Use the five-point harness from the very beginning and your baby will grow to accept it. Make sure it is fitted every time.
- Ensure the high chair is at least 500mm away from windows, unsecured doorways, stoves, appliance cords, curtains or blind cords.
- Fix any loose nuts and broken parts straight away.
- Repair exposed foam in the seat or back to prevent baby from choking on foam pieces.
- Make sure your child's hands are clear of moving parts when the tray is raised and lowered.
- Make sure a child cannot push against a vertical surface (such as a wall or cupboards) and push the chair over.
- Place the high chair out of reach when not in use.

PRAMS AND STROLLERS

Child deaths have occurred when a child is left to sleep in a pram or stroller with the backrest reclined. While asleep, the child may wriggle towards the end of the stroller where they are vulnerable to being strangled or smothered. The child can also slip off the backrest and be caught in the straps. *Never leave a child unattended in a pram or stroller.* Injuries involving prams and strollers are often caused by the child falling from the stroller or the stroller tipping backwards because it is overloaded. Overloading frequently occurs when bags are placed over the pram's handles. Injuries also occur when a child attempts to stand up while in the pram or stroller.

Before you buy

- Before buying a pram or stroller, decide what your requirements are. Consider whether you will need a convertible pram or stroller that will fit in your car, and whether you require a lightweight and easy-to-use model.
- Check for compliance with the mandatory safety standard for prams and strollers based on Australian Standard AS/NZS 2088. Look for a label or sticker that says the pram or stroller complies with the mandatory standard. If there isn't one, ask the retailer. If the retailer cannot verify that it complies, ask if there is any alternative that does comply.
- Check that the pram or stroller is supplied with a tether strep to help stop it rolling away.
- Make sure the pram or stroller is fitted with a restraint harness (a crotch strap between the legs, straps that go over both shoulders and a waist belt). If not, buy one separately and have it fitted.
- Look for strong components which feel rigid and not rickety. The pram or stroller should be easy to steer with solid and durable wheel components. Wheel locks must work.
- If the pram or stroller folds up for carrying, make sure frame locks are operating properly and that it won't collapse during use. Learn how to fold and use the pram or stroller before leaving the store and make sure you have been given all instructions.
- Make sure that the footrest on the pram or stroller is strong and secure, and that the pram/stroller is generally stable. A weak footrest may give way and cause the baby to be trapped.
- Check there are no gaps that could trap a head, fingers or limbs.
- Adjustable recline positions should lock securely.
- Consider a pram that has a carry basket fitted that will not tip or rock the pram when loaded with shopping (usually centrally located underneath).

Safety at home

- Do not leave a child unattended in a pram or stroller. It is not safe for a child to sleep unattended in a pram or stroller as they may get caught in its structure or unbalance the pram or stroller and tip it over. Another child may climb on and tip over or push the pram or stroller into a dangerous situation.
- Do not allow more than the intended number of child occupants in the pram or stroller. This could create tip-over hazards.
- Do not place a baby under six months old in a stroller unless the backrest can be adjusted to an angle of more than 130 degrees to the seat.
- Do not overload a pram or stroller or create a tip-over hazard by hanging shopping bags from its handles.
- Do not let a child stand on or lean out of a pram or stroller.
- Do not use a pillow or cushion in the pram or stroller because it can cause instability and possible suffocation.
- Avoid pushing loaded strollers or prams up or down stairs, or over curbs or very rough ground. Use lifts rather than stairs or escalators when transporting children in prams or strollers.
- Read and follow the manufacturer's instructions.
- Check all frame catches are locked in place and fabric fastenings are secured before use.

Keeping your baby safe

- A harness should be used from the first time a child is placed in a pram or stroller to get them used to being secured.
- Remove your child from the pram or stroller before making any adjustments as small fingers may become caught in the folding mechanism.

BABY BATH AIDS

Baby bath aids come in a range of styles, from bath rings and seats to bathing cradles. The suitability of these products changes as your baby grows. Six babies under 13 months have drowned in a bath seat or other support in Australia over 10 years. Many more babies have come close to drowning. These accidents happen when a child is left alone in a seat in the bath while their carer attends to tasks like answering the phone or preparing the child's clothes. Baby bath aids are designed to ease the strain on the carer's back while bathing a child. They are not safe without the presence and close supervision of an adult carer. It is best to always keep hold of the baby even when using a bath aid. *Bath aids are not a safety device – it is not safe to leave your child in a bath seat while you attend to other duties.*

Before you buy

- Check that the warning label about safe use is clearly displayed.
- Check that there are no sharp edges or points on the bath aid.
- Check that your child fits properly into the bath aid.
- If you are considering a second-hand baby bath aid, carefully check it for broken or worn parts that could make it unsafe.
- A second-hand baby bath aid may not comply with the current safety regulations and may not carry a safety warning.

Safety at home

- Never leave your young child alone in a bath.
- Never leave your young child in the bath in the care of an older sibling.
- Don't use a baby bath seat with suction cups in a bath with an uneven or slip-resistant base, or where the enamel is worn – the suction cups will not stick to the bath surface.
- Follow the manufacturer's instructions carefully.
- Prepare the child's clothes and towel before running a bath.
- Keep water to a minimum depth, using only enough water to wet the child using your hands.
- Ignore the telephone and the doorbell – if you need to leave the bathroom, take your child with you.
- Know how to perform resuscitation and CPR for infants.

BACKPACK AND BABY CARRIERS

Framed baby carriers should not be used before a baby is four to five months old. By this age the baby's neck should be able to withstand jolts and not sustain an injury.

Before you buy

- Buy a carrier to match your baby's size and weight, with a frame to suit your height and size. Try it on with the baby in it, and check for:

- Enough depth to support the baby's back
- Leg openings small enough to prevent the baby from slipping out
- Leg openings big enough to avoid chafing the baby's legs.
- Look for restraining straps, including over the baby's shoulders.
- Look for sturdy materials and heavy-duty fasteners.
- Look for padding on the metal frame near the baby's face to protect the baby from bumps.
- Check for sharp points, edges or rough surfaces.

Safety at home

- Use the restraining straps at all times.
- If leaning over, bend from the knees, never from the waist, to prevent the baby from falling out.
- If bending down, make sure the child is not able to reach hazards, such as hot drinks on the bench.
- Be sure the child's fingers are clear of the frame joints when folding the carrier.
- Regularly check the carrier for ripped seams, missing or loose fasteners, frayed seats or straps. Repair them promptly or discard the carrier.

BABY EXERCISE JUMPERS

A baby exercise jumper is usually a suspended sling-style seat hanging from a spring and/or rubber cable that is clamped above a door architrave. The baby bounces in the seat by pushing with their feet against the floor. Injuries have occurred while using these products when the laces (sewn into the crotch strap and threaded through the eyelets on the waiststrap) snapped under the tension of a bouncing baby, causing the baby to fall. Injuries have also occurred when babies have lurched sideways into the doorway frame, or been pushed by another young child. *Child safety experts recommend a stationary play centre as a safer alternative.*

Safety at home

- Do not leave the baby in the jumper for more than 15 minutes.
- Overuse of the jumper could lead to developmental delays when the child is learning to walk.
- Always supervise your child in the jumper.
- Always check that the equipment is securely attached above the doorway, and that the baby is securely fitted into the harness.
- Cover the spring and chain as it can entrap and pinch little fingers.
- Check the laces regularly to ensure they are in good condition and securely attached.

BABY WALKERS

Baby walkers can be dangerous as they allow infants to move more quickly around the house, and to grab things normally out of their reach. As a result, they face dangers they would not otherwise experience until a later age – such as reaching bench tops and pulling boiling kettles or irons down onto themselves, falling down stairs or reaching open fires or heaters. A baby in a walker can also tip over on uneven surfaces. For these reasons, they are not recommended. *Child safety experts recommend a stationary play centre as a safer alternative.*

Keeping your baby safe

Before you buy:

- Check for compliance with the mandatory safety standard for baby walkers based on the US ASTM F977 safety standard for baby walkers. Look for a label or sticker that says the baby walker complies with the mandatory standard. If there isn't one, ask the retailer. If the retailer cannot verify that it complies, ask if there is an alternative that does comply.
- Older second-hand baby walkers may not comply with the national safety standard introduced in November 2002 and other state and territory legislation. The safety standard requires baby walkers to have minimum levels of stability, an automatic braking system (so they cannot be easily ridden down stairs), and safety warning labels.
- Check that warning labels about safe use are clearly displayed.
- Look for an automatic braking mechanism to prevent it being ridden over a step.
- Check that any folding mechanism latches securely and will not collapse when assembled.
- Check that there are no sharp edges or points or places that can trap fingers.
- Check that your child fits properly into the baby walker.
- Look for a baby walker with an optional locking device to immobilise the baby walker when required.

Safety at home

- Never leave your child in a walker unsupervised. Your child in a walker should be within the reach of an adult at all times so they can prevent the child accessing hazardous locations.
- Do not leave the child in the walker for more than 15 minutes. Overuse of the walker can lead to developmental delays when the child is learning to walk.
- Baby walkers should only be used in a safe and flat area. Block off access to areas such as staircases, kitchens and fireplaces.
- Follow the manufacturer's instructions carefully.

CHILD CAR RESTRAINTS

Child restraints in cars are very important as they greatly reduce the risk of your child being injured or killed if you have an accident. Before you buy or rent a restraint, check that it has a label showing it complies with the Australian Standard AS/NZS 1754. Australian road laws say that you must not use a restraint if it does not comply with the Australian Standard. Each child restraint must be correctly installed and be appropriate for the weight and size of your child. The restraint must be used on every trip. *Always use a restraint for your child in the car.*

Before you buy

- Look for a label or sticker that says the child restraint complies with the mandatory safety standard, Australian Standard AS/NZS 1754. If there isn't one, ask the retailer. If the retailer cannot show you that it complies do not buy it.
- Make sure the restraint is suitable for your child's weight and size and always follow the manufacturer's guidelines.

Child's weight	Appropriate restraint (complying with AS/NZS1754)
Up to 9kg (or 70cm in length)	Infant restraint rearward facing
8kg to 18kg	Child seat forward facing
14kg to 26kg	Booster seat *Children outgrow the booster seat when they outgrow its weight range, or when their eyes are level with the top of the seat back or head rest when seated on the booster.*
14kg to 32kg	Child safety harness

- Make sure the restraint is suitable for your vehicle.
- You may need to have an extra anchorage point fitted in your car (and/or an extension strap).
- Do not buy a used child restraint if it has been in an accident or shows signs of wear, such as cracks, frayed straps or broken buckles. Make sure it complies with Australian Standard AS/NZS 1754.
- Restraints over 10 years old should not be used. They may lose their reliability and may not provide adequate protection for a child in case of an impact.
- If you wish to use a rearward facing infant restraint in a position where an airbag is fitted, you must check with the vehicle manufacturer first that it is safe to do so.
- Read and follow the manufacturer's instructions.

Safety at home

- Never carry any unrestrained passengers in your car.
- Child restraints generally must be fitted in the rear seat. Booster seats can be used in the front passenger seat under certain circumstances.
- Always follow the manufacturer's fitting instructions exactly. If you don't have fitting instructions or they are hard to understand, contact the manufacturer or an authorised safety restraint fitting station. Some specialist retailers offer an installation service.
- Make sure the restraint is properly fitted and adjusted. The baby seat restraint or harness should fit snugly (with no slack) and shouldn't be twisted.
- Always make sure your child uses the restraint properly every trip. Teach your child to always ask to use a restraint or seat belt.
- Restraints are necessary even when driving at low speeds or on short trips – you never know when a crash may happen. Many accidents occur within 10km of home.

'Cot to bed' safety

In Australia we are seeing more infants sustaining injuries from falling out of cots and beds. This is due to either not recognising the appropriate time to move a baby out of a cot, or an infant being placed prematurely in an adult's bed.

To avoid this, the following should be considered:

- Keep the fall distance to a minimum and use soft flooring materials around the cot or bed to minimise injury in the event of a fall.
- Keep the cot free of toys, pillows, bumpers, activity centres and anything else that could be 'stacked' to assist climbing.
- Keep the area into which a child could fall free of furniture, toys and other hard objects.

When to move out of a cot?

An 'Australian Standards approved' cot made up in accordance with SIDS and Kids guidelines for a safe sleeping environment is the best and safest place for a baby to sleep. However at some point, parents will consider when to move a child out of a cot and into a bed.

For safety reasons, our recommendation is that when a toddler is observed attempting to climb out of a cot (and looking like they might succeed!) it is time to move them out of the cot.

A child no longer sleeping in a cot has greater access to all living areas, so before they graduate to a bed, it is advisable to double check safety throughout the house, paying special attention to the following: drowning, falling, glass and poisoning hazards, furniture or TVs that could readily tip over and power points.

There are several reasons to consider toddler beds. These are a safe intermediate step as their height is low. They are also cost effective, as the cot mattress and bedding can be transferred to the toddler bed to provide a bed for a toddler once the cot is no longer suitable for them.

Alternatively, providing the floor is clean, the mattress from the cot could be lifted out and made up on the floor. Similarly, a mattress from a full-height single bed could be used in the same way. A child's mattress needs to be relatively firm to prevent accidents. It does not need to be soft to be comfortable.

Most furniture is now supplied with wall brackets, so in the event a child should climb drawers of furniture, it would not collapse onto them and cause serious injury.

Where children in adult-height beds are at risk of falling out of bed while sleeping, the bed can be positioned against the wall and soft materials can be placed on the floor beside the bed. Bed rails can be of assistance but must fit tightly against the side of the mattress and not allow a child's body or head to slip through.

Remember

Furniture that is not designed for sleeping, such as bean bags, sofas, large cushions, etcetera, is not safe for toddlers to sleep in. Some sleeping products such as air mattresses and water beds are not suitable for young children, and bunk beds are not recommended before the child is nine years of age.

Portacot Safety

Additional mattresses should never be used with portacots. Using an extra mattress may create a space that infants can roll into and potentially suffocate as a result of becoming trapped between the portacot side and the mattress.

Often parents and carers have the mistaken perception that soft bedding materials are needed for the comfort of their child. This often results in the introduction of an extra mattress, cushions or sheepskin rugs into a portacot. It is untrue and unnecessary to have additional bedding materials and it creates an extremely unsafe environment that may have fatal consequences. Young infants do not need soft mattresses to have a comfortable sleeping environment. Firm bedding provides a suitable and safe situation.

The mattress supplied with a portacot is the only safe mattress option when using a portable cot. When used correctly, a portable cot is a safe sleeping environment for young infants. The SIDS & Kids safe sleeping guidelines should also be followed.

From 1st March 2009 a mandatory regulation will be in place that specifically highlights warnings against using additional portacot mattresses.

For further information contact the Infant & Nursery Products Association of Australia on (03) 9762 7038 or visit www.babysafety.com.au.

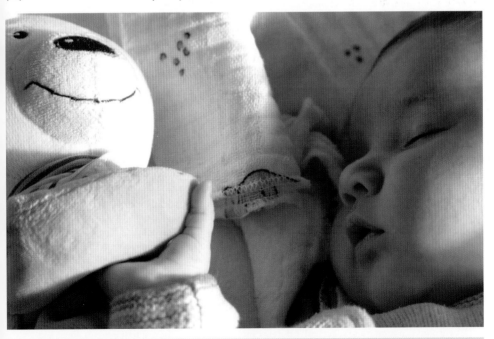

Information supplied by the Infant & Nursery Products Association of Australia, www.babysafety.com.au or www.inpaa.asn.au.

Decorating while renting

Living in a rented home can limit your options to decorate your child's bedroom, but it doesn't mean you have to forget the idea altogether. It is still your home and there are ways to decorate without upsetting the landlord.

Start with the basics

When planning your child's room there are some keys points to remember. Avoid disappointment (or eviction) by checking your rental agreement for any restrictions on decorating, before you lift a finger. When you are certain of your limits, start the process with the golden rule in mind – everything you put in that room should be able to go with you when you leave. It's a good rule for two reasons. Firstly, it will prevent you from losing your bond by permanently changing a house that doesn't belong to you. And secondly, as nice as your landlord might be, it doesn't make financial sense to increase the value of someone else's property with your hard work and money.

Other key points apply when decorating any child's room, whether you rent or own the home. Design a room with both yours and your child's decorating tastes in mind. It may be their room, but it is still part of the home and you don't want to be shuddering every time you set foot in their bedroom.

Base the room on a theme. Either an interest of your child's – trucks, fairies, the beach or animals, or a colour. Keep in mind the effect colours can have on your child's mood and behaviour. Avoid too many dark or strong colours, like black or red, as they are known to make a child feel depressed or angry. Keep these colours for highlights only. The most popular colours are paler shades of blue, green, pink, purple and yellow - and for good reason. They are known to have a calming effect and are even said to promote a sense of wellbeing and creativity.

Finally, it is important to make the room functional and safe, as well as look good. Kids need a lot of storage space for books, toys and clothes and it must be a safe environment. They will be spending a lot of time in there by themselves, away from your watchful eyes. Keep beds away from curtain cords. Make sure bookcases are stable and will not tip. Do not place heavy objects on shelves where children may be tempted to pull them down.

Decorate, don't renovate

Painting isn't usually an option and landlords aren't crazy about holes in the walls when hanging pictures, but there are clever ways to decorate the walls without renovating them permanently.

There are some great products on the market now, designed to be easily removed from walls. Wallies or wall stickers are the most obvious choice, but they are not the only option. Wall decals are similar to stickers, but are made from timber, giving them a three dimensional appearance. They are usually hand-painted and can be found in any number of designs. They can be easily applied with Blu-Tack or hung on hooks with a removable backing. 3M make these hooks in several sizes. They are easily applied and just as easily removed.

Consider creating your own little masterpiece on a canvas. Art and craft stores sell inexpensive canvases that don't require framing and are very lightweight. They can be hung using the removable hooks. Keep the artwork simple and tie it in with your chosen theme.

A bedroom can look quite spectacular if items such as lamps, toy boxes, tissue boxes, linen and curtains are co-ordinated. Decorate these items with stickers and matching iron-on transfers and motifs.

If your windows are dressed with sheer curtaining, ask your landlord if you can remove and store them, then replace them with your own. Most haberdashery stores such as Spotlight or Lincraft stock inexpensive sheer curtaining that is ready to hang. A general rule to buying curtains that will be gathered when hung, is to purchase a length two and half times the width of the window. Also remember to measure the drop (the length of curtain required, top to bottom). Decorate your new purchase with iron-on transfers. It's an inexpensive, yet effective way to bring the windows to life and tie them in with your theme. The original curtains can be hung again when you are ready to move.

If the old, tired carpet in your child's bedroom is letting down you decorating efforts, cover the stains and wear and tear with a floor rug. There are some beautiful rugs on the market specifically for children's bedrooms. It can be a feature in the room from which you co-ordinate other items.

Furniture

Furniture isn't an obvious choice when thinking about decorating walls, but it is a great way to introduce colour and interest to a blank, drab bedroom and most importantly, you can take it with you. Tall furniture such as bookshelves or wall units can cover large areas on a wall. Decorate the shelves with personal keepsakes, such as photos, birth plates, money boxes or the letters of your child's name or a special word. If you have a theme for the room, display some objects that tie in with the theme, such as toy dinosaurs, fairy statues or a selection of sports balls. I particularly like the bookshelves with the built-in toy box at the bottom. It not only provides extra storage, but adds stability to the bookcase, preventing it from tipping.

Select matching pieces of furniture such as a bed, chest of drawers and desk or bookshelf. If the budget is a little tight, choose some second-hand pieces and paint them in the same colour. There are some wonderful timber scrolls and decorative woodwork available from hardware stores that can be glued to furniture to create a special feature and tie the pieces together.

Think beyond the traditional bedroom furniture. If you have enough space, consider purchasing a raw or second-hand buffet with cupboards at the bottom and shelving above. Normally used in a kitchen or dining room, if the buffet is painted a pale colour, it can look quite spectacular in a bedroom, as well being extremely practical. The shelves can house keepsakes and books while the cupboards can store clothing, toys, towels and nappies.

Another great option is a wall unit with several square compartments for storage. Ikea has a wonderful, inexpensive unit called 'Expidit'. It comes flat-packed and ready to assemble (I hear you say "that dreaded Allen key", but fear not, this one is easy to assemble – my husband managed to put ours together without one terse word uttered!). The unit can house books, keepsakes or baskets for additional storage. Howards Storage sells woven baskets that fit in the compartments perfectly. Whatever toys and treasures my children leave lying around on the floor end up in these baskets. It saves nagging and cupboard space. Howards Storage also has a great cap organiser that hooks to the back of a door. This can be used to display special drawings from school and other important documents.

Decorating needn't be the exclusive pleasure of the homeowner. The renter has just as much scope to create a wonderful environment for their child. It might take a little more imagination, but the results will be well worth the effort.

Written by Kate Meehan, owner of Katydid Decor Company, www.katydiddecor.com.au.

Vox Pop

We asked a number of women and men around Australia to send in their advice, tips and personal experiences on a range of topics so that you have an insight into how others cope being a new parent. We hope you find their comments interesting, informative and reassuring. Vox Pop biographies: page 652

Amanda Jephtha
Mum of one, Sydney

Highchairs will be used frequently for an extended period of time and will get very dirty! It is essential that it can be cleaned easily and quickly, so look for a highchair with the least amount of nooks and crevices. Most highchairs come with a tray; not only are they handy for eating, but also for other activities such as drawing.

Some highchairs convert into proper chairs once your baby has outgrown the highchair. These are great for use at the dinner table or at a student's desk to complete homework. This type of highchair can be more expensive to purchase, but can be great value due to its longevity.

Tip: rather than plonking your crawling baby in a playpen when you shower, plonk him in the highchair in the bathroom instead. This way he'll still be supervised, and you can play games together to keep him entertained.

Bianca McCulloch
Mum of two, Melbourne

I think I changed the nursery around close to fifty times trying to make it perfect; I had every gadget and gizmo you could possibly think of with my first baby. This time around I have realised all you really need is a safe place for baby to sleep, a car seat, a pram and if you like a change table. Personally I think it was just so much easier to change nappies or clothes on the couch or you could even just lay down a towel or blanket just about anywhere and do it. I used my baby bath twice as I put him in the shower or bath with me or my partner. By the time you fill up the baby bath, bath the baby, dry and dress him then settle him, then go back and empty and clean the baby bath and pack it all away bathtime takes up half your day.

It's important to have a good pram – test it out in the shop first and make sure it's not too heavy, easy to fold and that it fits into your boot with extra room for groceries and shopping. I think that the cot and the car seat are the most important pieces of furniture you will buy. It's not a good idea to go second hand with these items in case they are no longer up to safety standards.

Jessica Hatherall
Mum of two, Sydney

I think to start with less is more when it comes to furniture and equipment. Then you can decide what works best for you. The things we have definitely had lots of use out of are:

A good cot: Both my kids have slept in it. I didn't bother with the kind that turned into a bed because I knew I was having more than one child and would just buy the older one a bed

A good pram: We have travelled and moved countries a lot since having children so we have a great stroller and have used all our prams a lot. Absolutely love our 3-wheeler but with a small gap between kids we have been unable to use it with the second child. Maclaren Quest has been great for travel and reclines a bit to help with napping.

A good high chair: We bought an expensive one but we've had years of use out of it. My toddler still sits in it and soon my new baby will get her three years of use out of it too.

Lee Norman
Mum of one, Melbourne

Having renovated our house a few years ago we had painted the entire house the same colour. When we found out about the upcoming birth of our baby we decided that we wouldn't change the colours in the nursery. We have added baby furniture of course and a huge amount of baby toys, but haven't changed the paintwork or even the artwork at this stage. We have all the usual baby furniture – a lot given to us by friends which we greatly appreciated, and have hung a couple of mobiles to provide some visual stimulation. Our favourite piece of equipment that we were given was a Tommee Tippee Nappy Wrapper Tub. In the middle of the night when you are changing a nappy just putting the dirty nappy in the bin with no mess, fuss or smell is so easy.

Ros Pittard
Mum of two, VIC

We found our rocker to be the most useful piece of equipment for our boys. Until they're sitting up well, you can pop your baby into the rocker while they watch you hang out the washing or do a bit of work in the garden or kitchen. Ours has a few different layback positions, so it's also good for sitting in the early days of feeding solids. It's easy to dismantle and put the seat part in the washing machine. It also turns into a toddler seat, so it's useful for quite a while. Don't buy equipment with too many flaps and crevices for food and mess to get stuck in. The easier to wash, the better!

Anna Ngo
Mum of one, Perth

As somewhat naive first time parents, we entered the world of baby equipment and led ourselves to believe that we would need almost every big to medium ticket item on the market. Certainly you cannot do without a good cot or a good car seat.

The most useful items are often those which don't normally spring to mind. In our household, this honour would fall on the humble activity playmat. When we first brought newborn Mikaela home, it served as a place for her to nap and we could easily keep an eye on her from nearby. It also functioned as a place to change her nappies.

The playmat of course came with various add-on toys and paraphernalia. During the early months we

made use of the special pillow designed to encourage "tummy time", and as she grew it provided ample room for her to practice rolling in all directions. In addition there was a dangling mirror which seemed to keep her amused for many a short period; and when she was able to, she often reached for the clip-on plush toys.

While I would scarcely believe that a child would be at a loss without a playmat, it certainly didn't hurt to have Mikaela flexing her motor skills on an item which we initially felt was just "nice to have". So as I reflect on our good and bad buys, I muse over the fact that a symbolic purchase bore the most fruit.

Tony Wilson
Dad of one, Melbourne

We were big fans of the baby carrier and went with the one with back support on a friend's advice. I think that was a good move. The highchair doesn't need to be very flashy – we went with a very basic white moulded plastic one. Also buy a portacot – a must for remaining mobile!

Bernadette Vella
Mum of two, Brisbane

For Tiernan I bought way too many baby things. Being my first child, I believed I had to have every baby gadget out there. Most of them last a few weeks or months and then get delegated to the back of the closet. I could have easily done without the baby bath; I used it about five times and then gave it away.

I did however use one of those little baby bath seats that you lay a newborn in in a big bath and it was fantastic. It allowed my baby freedom to kick about and enjoy the water and meant I did not have the fear of losing grip of a slippery baby in the water.

I also had a portable highchair that you attach to a normal adult seat. It was brilliant and it meant that

Vox Pop

We asked a number of women and men around Australia to send in their advice, tips and personal experiences on a range of topics so that you have an insight into how others cope being a new parent. We hope you find their comments interesting, informative and reassuring. Vox Pop biographies: page 652

I knew my child always had a good highchair to sit in when we went out and that it was clean (some highchairs in restaurants are feral). My whole mother's group had them and each week we would line our kids up in their chairs to feed them!

Cindy Fraser
Mum of three, Melbourne

We were lucky enough to have borrowed or been given much of our furniture which was a huge saving. Our main purchase would have to be our car! We needed a bigger car to fit everyone in as well as a double pram. I borrowed capsules for the first six months with the twins and these were great; I was able to strap them in inside the house and put everyone in the car at the same time, although they did start to get a bit heavy from 4 months onwards!

The other main thing we purchased was our prams – a single for our son and then a double when the twins arrived. I still prefer to walk to most places with the pram if I can, it seems to be easier than getting everyone in and out of the car and strapped in their seats (always an ongoing battle in our house).

We didn't buy two of everything for the twins, just the cots and their rockers; for everything else we found that one was plenty. The twins even shared their cot for the first month. I enjoyed setting up their rooms, although the twins room was a challenge as the furniture was loaned to us and space was minimal. I managed to buy co-ordinating linen and blankets which seemed to tie the room together nicely.

Jess Tamblyn
Mum of one, SA

Space is a real issue in our house so baby gear that takes up minimal space or that has more than one purpose is a must. As a gift my sister-in-law gave me a hook-on highchair that attaches to the kitchen table. It takes up next-to-no space, is easily

taken off and transported to family or friends for dinner. I have also seen ones that sit on a normal chair – like a highchair booster seat.

A breastfeeding pillow that can be used for breastfeeding and also to support your child as they learn to sit is also another way of saving space and money.

Katherine Twigg
Mum of one, VIC

Although we found out that we were having a boy, we decided to decorate our nursery in an antique teddy bear theme. The cot and change table were all dark wood and it was a really elegant nursery which would have suited either a boy or a girl. Everyone who sees it loves it, and if we decide to have another baby we won't have to redecorate the nursery should we have a girl next time.

Our change table is actually a chest of drawers with the change table on top. Once our son outgrows the change table we can just turn the chest of drawers upside down and it becomes a normal chest of drawers. This way we will get use out of it for years to come.

When buying a pram I would highly recommend lifting it up before you buy it. I originally bought an expensive top of the range three wheeler pram only to find that it was so heavy I could barely lift it. I ended up having to buy a normal four-wheeler pram which easily collapsed and was easy to lift.

Also, if your baby tends to have a habit of kicking off their blanket when they are in the pram you can buy these inserts which are sheepskin on the inside and therefore very comfortable, and you can actually zip them up inside it (similar to a sleeping bag). I could relax on my walk knowing my son was warm and he couldn't kick it off.

Kirstin Amos
Mum of one, QLD

When it came to decorating the nursery we could not do a lot due to the fact that we rent, so no painting but what we did was make sure that the furniture that we bought for the nursery was practical and had the ability to grow with Carter.

The best piece of furniture would have to be the cot that converts into a single bed when he is old enough and all we will have to worry about is a new mattress. The one item that we kick ourselves for buying was the portacot, it has had more use just lately but otherwise it collects dust most of the time.

Another piece of equipment that we have just bought is a play pen, but not just any play pen – this one is 3 metres from tip to tip (hexagonal shape) which means he has a huge amount of space to play in and it is big enough for either my husband or I or both of us to climb in and play and we don't have to be sitting on top of each other. The play pen is also a great area because this is where all the toys are kept and I do not have to keep moving things from room to room.

Martine Pekarsky
Mum of two, Melbourne

We bought all the major items while I was still working so financially it wasn't too much of a struggle. The change table blended in well with the décor in the lounge room and we had it set up production-style. It was definitely baby-boot camp at our house in the early days – everything was done with military precision (well it felt that way). Personally I felt that letting the house go only made things harder, so I kept everything tidy, clean and very organised. The baby bag was always packed and ready to go and I have only run out of nappies a couple of times (once when we were camping and the tab of our last nappy broke off in my hand, so we got out the duct tape and it was fixed in no time!).

Michelle Eicholtz
Mum of one, VIC

I found decorating my baby's nursery a way of welcoming our baby into the family and giving it its own little space in our house and also it made it feel real that there really was another person coming to live here with us.

I was very careful to find out what we really needed and what we would love to have but could do without. Our nursery is colourful and full of fun; we just wanted to fill it with fun stuff not have a room full of stuff just because it matched.

The most useful information we were given was to have lots of mobiles over the change table to keep baby happy while on there. We will have to move some of them out of her reach when she gets older, but she really enjoys talking to her friends during a nappy change.

Michelle Winduss
Mum of one, Sydney

The two pieces of useful equipment/furniture that we have are our son's highchair and my rocking chair.

My son received his high chair as a gift for his Baptism. It has two really useful features. Firstly, the chair has wheels that lock. When the chair is not in use and needs to be moved around, it can be wheeled to that area and not picked up (one less thing to lift!). Secondly, the highchair reclines back so sometimes he just sits there and relaxes completely.

The second useful piece of furniture is our rocking chair. At the end of our busy days I sit with our son in the rocking chair and rock him while I read him a bedtime story or sing him a lullaby. This seems to calm him down just before bed time.

Vox Pop

We asked a number of women and men around Australia to send in their advice, tips and personal experiences on a range of topics so that you have an insight into how others cope being a new parent. We hope you find their comments interesting, informative and reassuring. Vox Pop biographies: page 652

Anna Brandt
Mum of one, QLD

A girlfriend of mine lent us a rocker chair which has a vibrating motion in it. Our baby had reflux so after each feed we'd put him in this chair (without the vibrating motion on) so as to keep him upright for a while to ensure he kept his milk down. This chair was amazing too for calming our baby when he was crying and crying and crying!

If you've got a bath in your bathroom, a sink in your kitchen or a tub in your laundry, then there really is no need to buy a baby bath. Think seriously about how long you'll use it for and also keep in mind that if you've used a small baby bath for 5 or 6 months and then all of a sudden your baby's too big for it and you now need to use the 'big' bath, this is just one more thing you'll need to wean your baby into getting used to. If they've been in the 'big' bath since day one then they don't know any better.

Baby holders for the bath are another piece of equipment which you can totally do without. You will learn in hospital how to hold your baby while bathing him/her. You will do this easily for the first couple of months until your baby gets a little heavy. Once this heavy stage comes, just get an old towel, hand towel or cloth nappy and fold in a square, place this in the bottom of the bath for your baby's head to rest on. Then just lie your baby in the bottom of the bath. You will only need a tiny amount of water, up to about your baby's ears when lying in the bath. Have a cup handy to pour water over your baby. This is the easiest way to bath a baby and you save water too!

Rebecca Tragear Whiting
Mum of four, Melbourne

I love my nursery – it is simple with white walls, white furniture and dark chocolate carpet. I have used the babies' bedding (all from the linen brand Little House), cushions, accessories and artwork to personalise and add colour to the room. I joke that they have a nursery as good as a five star hotel – the best room in the house!

A good quality cot, a change table with room for all baby's bits and pieces and a great chair for breastfeeding are my nursery essentials. A bookshelf is also useful for photos, treasures, toys and books. I believe if you buy quality you will get many years of use out of the furniture and can pass them on or sell them when you have finished.

Rowena Raats
Mum of three, Kalgoorlie

One thing we can't do without is our car seat! It is a Safe-n-Sound Platinum and it has been a life saver for us all. With in-built speakers we never have to listen to another Wiggles or Dora DVD! Our car rides are now bliss! When you travel 17 hours in a car (each way) more than 3 times a year to your closest capital city you appreciate this seat and get to keep your sanity!

With the choice of baby equipment out there it can sometimes be overwhelming. I started with the basics and built on that. Good car seat, a pram that suits my lifestyle and then a cot that's practical and safe but also matches my decor. I then looked at the practical day-to-day needs such as a changing area, a bathing area, clothes storage etcetera. Once I set the basics of my nursery up I had a foundation to build on. It was also handy when family and friends wanted to know if I needed anything – because it was all set up I knew what I didn't have.

Danielle Murrihy
Mum of two, Melbourne

I suppose the biggest thing for parents of multiples (apart from a new car to fit the growing family) is buying the right pram! I bought an umbrella-style stroller and this was kept in the car for when we were out and about and the big pram was kept in the garage and used when out walking. Both prams have had a lot of use!

I definitely gave our two rockers a work out; they are essential when you have twins! My mum bought us a change table with a bath underneath it. We used the change table all the time for the first 6 months. It had wheels so we would wheel it around the house to the area where the boys were. It did save our backs! I only used the bath twice – I found it awkward to use and with a wet slippery baby trying to open and shut the cover was too dangerous in my opinion.

Anastasia Jones
Mum of two, Melbourne

Cute pink bears, farm animals, aquarium, flowers … the choices were endless. It was just too much and our baby ending up coming home to a cot, a few of my childhood toys and white walls.

The centrepiece of the room, a dark wood 3-in-1 cot, is still my favourite purchase. My youngest is currently in it and once she is too big for the bed function it will turn into a lovely seat for them both (teeth marks and all – although I think it will need a polish!).

When our second child was born I did swap the change table we had for our first child for a wooden one. What I didn't realise first time around is how heavily used an item it is. Spend the money for something that looks nice and is big enough for an 18-month-old as well as for your newborn.

Finally I have realised that I suffer from pram envy. In the past 3.5 years I have had about six prams/strollers (in my own defence, one was destroyed by an airline and the other by removalists). For my first pram I wanted to buck the three-wheel trend and so I got a four-wheeler which was good for a newborn baby but was rather large. My child sat too far back in the pram so couldn't see out when we were walking (it was also hard to manoeuvre with one hand). I then had a small fold-up one for taking my child to daycare and wanted to replace the four-wheeler for a three-wheeler. So that is three prams. The three-wheeler lasted about 8 months before it was destroyed by the airline in our move to Hong Kong. So I replaced that with a Maclaren and purchased a second for our youngest who had just been born. But the second pram was not suitable and I ended up selling that and buying a new one and … well you can see the trend here. My current, and hopefully last, pram is a three wheeler …

Tracey Thompson
Mum of one, Brisbane

The best piece of furniture we bought was a recliner chair for the nursery. It is a nice big comfortable chair that reclines right back with a footrest as well. This proved to be the best thing for me while I was breastfeeding. It made overnight feeds a lot easier and it kept my baby calm as well.

Another handy piece of equipment we received was a rocker with vibrations and music. I found that my little one was soothed by the calming vibrations and soft music and fell asleep in it many times when I couldn't console him with anything else. It was also great because it was easy to carry around so he could be with me outside when I was hanging out the washing, in the bathroom when I was showering and, well anywhere I was really!

Sophie McKellar
Mum of two, VIC

I am a huge believer in spending up on a very good pram because you use it every day and with twins even more so as they get older. I have a buggy and I love it to bits and yes it fits through most door ways. I really wanted my kids to see the world side by side not one behind the other. The twins are nearly 2 and they still often sleep in it if we are out shopping and for an hour or two. For the car it does take up a lot of room but again I love it.

Two good cots are very important as well as a change table that is a good height for you so you don't hurt your back.

Resources

These Resources pages list products and services relevant to "Choosing furniture & equipment".
To make your life easier as a parent, editorial listings have been grouped into sub categories.
Businesses then appear alphabetically under a national or a state-based subhead depending on reach.

ADVISORY SERVICES: FURNITURE & EQUIPMENT

NATIONAL

Australian Competition and Consumer Commission
Tel: 1300 302 502
website: www.accc.gov.au
Keeping baby safe: a guide to nursery furniture is a
helpful booklet available free from the Australian
Competition and Consumer Commission. It covers
cots, prams and strollers and lists safety features and
hazards. It also provides information on how to use
products safely.

Choice
Tel: 1800 069 552
website: www.choice.com.au/baby
CHOICE has been testing products for over 45 years
exposing unsafe products and providing reliable,
independent buying advice. Their baby information can
be accessed quickly and easily online and covers
everything from strollers and cots to baby food and
disposable nappies. You can view their free reports or
become a member at www.choice.com.au/baby.

Infant & Nursery Products Association of Australia
Tel: (03) 9762 7038
website: www.babysafety.com.au or www.inpaa.asn.au

The Infant and Nursery Products
Association of Australia (INPAA) is the
peak industry body representing suppliers,
manufacturers and retailers in the sector.
The Association operates nationally, was
established to improve nursery safety and
is a leader in the development of industry safety standards
which concentrate on suppliers identifying and
managing risks associated with the use and foreseeable
misuse of infant and nursery products. The Association
provides members with a range of services including: an
industry advocacy role to regulators, government and
other agencies; development of industry product safety
standards and linkages with bodies like Standards
Australia; liaison with other key stakeholders in the
product safety and injury prevention field; information,
advice, research and guidance for members on a range
of issues; regular industry events and functions. INPAA
has a company accreditation and product endorsement
program for items that meet the Association's safety
criteria. This program is supported by an education and
information element to assist consumers in the safe
purchase and safe use of infant and nursery products.

NEW SOUTH WALES

Babystyle Consultancy

PO Box 1613
Lane Cove NSW 1595
Tel: 0418 477 187
email: angela@babystyle.com.au
website: www.babystyle.com.au

Babystyle consultancy provides informative and practical advice in your home on everything you need for your baby. Babystyle consultancy covers everything from cots, car seats and prams to high chairs, feeding equipment and educational toy advice helping you make the right choice first time around. Also visit the Babystyle website to read their blog "What's hot in baby products".

nurseryknowhow

Tel: 0407 076 249
email: susan@nurseryknowhow.com.au
website: www.nurseryknowhow.com.au

First time mum? Confused about what to buy for your baby? Nurseryknowhow can help. Susan is a registered mothercraft nurse (mother of four) with 36 years experience. She will come to your home, assess your individual needs, advise you on different options, analyse different products, separate must haves from don't needs, cover clothes to cots and provide helpful literature. This is practical, reliable advice designed to save you time and money when setting up a nursery for your newborn.

Planning for Babe

PO Box 3313
St Pauls NSW 2031
Tel: 0411 126 325
email: amanda@planningforbabe.com.au
website: www.planningforbabe.com.au

Planning for Babe offers professional, time-poor, pregnant women the latest must-have – their own exclusive baby planner. Through private consultations and extensive research, Planning for Babe matches the perfect baby products to your individual lifestyle – just like a wedding planner to a wedding. From organising all the essentials, to arranging private product viewings, to having a label create a custom gown for you, this fully tailored service covers all bases for the discerning pregnant woman.

Safe Travel Solutions

32 Glennie W. Street
Gosford NSW 2250
Tel: (02) 4323 4449
email: info@safetravelsolutions.com.au
website: www.safetravelsolutions.com.au

Safe Travel Solutions is an authorised child restraint fitting station. They supply and fit child restraints and hire baby capsule and can also supply and fit extra seats in wagons, 4WDs and vans, cargo barriers and seat belts.

BABY CARRIERS & SLINGS

NATIONAL

Baba Slings

Tel: (07) 5442 9597
email: mail@babaslings.com
website: www.babaslings.com

Baba Slings allow you to carry your baby in a hands-free, no-stress hammocking position. The Baba Sling offers seven different easy-to-use positions and allows for premature babies up to toddlers to enjoy being close to you even while you fulfil daily tasks. They are comfortable for you and extremely supportive for baby. Phone the number above or visit the website for further information.

Babes In Arms

Tel: 1300 725 276
email: info@babesinarms.com.au
website: www.babesinarms.com.au

Babes in Arms is a family-run business specialising in baby carriers from around the world that are suitable for premmies to pre-schoolers. Baby carriers allow you the freedom to continue your daily routine while providing the most desirable nurturing environment for your child. Each carrier has been personally tested and chosen for the way it alleviates physical strain for parents and avoids spinal compression for your baby. Free express delivery within Australia. Phone the number above or visit the website www.babesinarms.com.au for further information.

Baby Banz

Tel: 1800 112 269
email: salesau@babybanz.com
website: www.babybanz.com

The Hipseat is a hip carrier suitable for children from six months of age. It is weight tested up to 30kg and it can be used on its own or in conjunction with shoulder sling or front pouch carriers to take the weight off the back and shoulders. Phone the number listed above or visit the website www.babybanz.com for further information.

Babybjorn

Tel: (03) 9585 8199
email: info@scanbrands.com.au
website: www.babybjorn.com.au

For over 46 years BABYBJORN's aim has been to make life easier for parents and children by creating innovative products for children up to 3 years old. Carrying your baby in a BABYBJORN baby carrier leaves both of your hands free, while your child is close to you. BABYBJORN baby carriers are developed in close collaboration with medical experts and parents. All BABYBJORN baby carriers are endorsed by the Australian College of Midwives. For more information visit www.babybjorn.com or phone the number listed above.

Resources

CHOOSING FURNITURE & EQUIPMENT

Baby carriers & slings ➡ Bedding & bed linen

Bubzilla

Tel: 1300 783 509
email: info@bubzilla.com.au
website: www.bubzilla.com.au

The continuous seaming and even width of the Bubzilla Sling eliminates the need for any buckles, rings or clips that are often unsafe, uncomfortable and tend to cause painful pressure points. As an added bonus there are handy pockets for carrying that spare nappy and some loose change. The Bubzilla Sling is perfect for breastfeeding – unlike other carriers there is no need to remove your baby to breastfeed, easy on the move. The Bubzilla Sling is sized to the wearer not the baby, so you can just throw it on and get moving every time – no hassle, no fuss. As your baby changes and grows so does the way you wear them. Suitable from 0–3 years. 100% Australian made.

Fluffies Knitwear Industries

Tel: (08) 8347 1343
email: fluffies@fluffies.com.au
website: www.fluffies.com.au

Fluffies Knitwear Industries is an Australian-owned company that supplies quality baby carriers – a convenient way to go places with your child and allowing you the freedom and mobility to set off anywhere, anytime. Designed with your and your baby's comfort in mind these carriers retail at a reasonable price. Available to purchase by mail order. Phone or visit the website for more details.

Hug-a-bub Australia P/L

Tel: 1300 365 484
email: email@hugabub.com
website: www.hugabub.com

Hug-a-Bub babywearing designs provide mothers and babies with the nurturing closeness required to build healthy bonding and attachment, while providing the ultimate in comfort, hands-free convenience and safety. Professionally acclaimed ergonomics offer unique support for both wearer and infant, gently yet securely embracing both in a loving 'hug'. Hug-a-Bub's babywearing collection includes the Original Wrap Carrier, the Pocketless Wrap Carrier, the gorgeous 100% Organic Wrap and the stylish new reversible Hug-a-Bub Side-Sling. Visit www.hugabub.com for more details.

JazSlings Baby Slings

Tel: (07) 3424 1133
email: jazsling@optusnet.com.au
website: www.jazslings.com.au

Jazslings Baby Slings are easy-to-use, practical baby carriers with their design based on the traditional native slings. Jazslings are made to properly support the developing curve of the young spine and safely contain the infant. Carrying your baby enhances the parent-child bond and can reduce crying. 'Baby wearing' has a calming effect on the infant and promotes feelings of closeness and security. Jazslings Baby Slings also allow for discreet breastfeeding in public and provide an opportunity for parents to have both hands free while keeping their baby close. Three different designs, beautiful fabrics to choose from and INPAA accredited.

Joey Sling

Tel: 1300 780 010
email: sales@joeysling.com.au
website: www.joeysling.com.au

The Joey Sling is a fashionable, fun and modern way of carrying and nurturing your baby, embracing the traditional and time honoured methods of baby wearing from birth to toddler. Designed for ultimate comfort, the Joey Sling is perfect for busy parents who need a functional and fuss-free baby carrier to suit their lifestyle without compromising on style. With its pouch-like design, the Joey Sling enables new mums to nurse their babies discreetly and comfortably. Visit the website for stockist details.

Kazoku Kids

Tel: (08) 9470 2851
email: info@kazokukids.com.au
website: www.kazokukids.com.au

The Ultimate Baby Sling gives you the ability to use your hands while holding your baby safely and comfortably, and includes instruction booklet and pillow. It is now also available in organic, made from certified organic materials. The Ultimate Baby Wrap Carrier is the perfect baby carrier that is comfortable, safe and can see you through the toddler years. Both types are versatile from birth to age 3 and can be used in various different positions, holding baby securely. Simple with no buckles, loops or straps to adjust and untangle. It comes with DVD instructions and carry bag. The Side Kick is an award-winning nappy bag with built in carrier. Converts from bag to child carrier with a simple adjustment. Visit www.kazokukids.com.au or phone for a free brochure or to find a store near you.

Snazzy Baby

Tel: 1300 650 115
email: info@snazzybaby.com.au
website: www.snazzybaby.com.au

Mom's Deluxe 3-1 Combo Carrier gives today's mums many choices as baby can face in or out and ride on either hip. The portable high chair restraint feature simply turns an ordinary chair into a temporary high chair restraint system and it can also be used in shopping trolleys for additional safety while shopping. It features a soft gel insert shoulder strap designed with mum in mind, to provide long use comfort for parents with the ergonomically designed shoulder strap that allows additional comfort to reduce back and shoulder strain and discomfort. A mesh vented panel and breathable cotton mesh lining keeps baby cool and comfortable, it can even can be used at the pool or beach. Visit www.snazzybaby.com.au to see how easy it is to use.

Tomy
Tel: 1800 244 543
email: nurseryenquiries@funtastic.com.au
website: www.funtasticnursery.com.au

 TOMY is the respected nursery brand for baby carriers and baby monitors. TOMY Baby Carriers offer a practical and stylish solution to juggling a busy life with a new baby. TOMY is the established leader for baby monitors and offers a number of monitors designed to suit the particular demands of your home and your lifestyle.

BEDDING & BED LINEN

NATIONAL

ACE Atkins Creative Embroidery
Tel: (07) 3803 2191
email: atkins.creative.embriodery@hotmail.com

ACE Atkins Creative Embroidery sell white polycotton cot sheet sets that include one flat sheet (size 112cm x 157cm), one fitted sheet (84cm x 146cm), one pillow case (65cm x 37cm) all embroidered with a heart design. Text inside can read "adorable" or "cherish". You can choose the colour thread and there's an extra cost to include your baby's name. The sheet sets come in a re-useable white muslin bag with ribbon and hearts, all with care labels. Cost $55 and postage $5.50 or an overnight satchel $12.20. Made in Australia.

Airwrap
Tel: (03) 9016 3422
website: www.airwrap.com.au

AIRWRAP supersedes traditional cot bumpers with its breathable mesh fabric allowing maximum airflow, while protecting baby from knocks and tangling in the framework of the cot. AIRWRAP's padded breathable mesh is tested to world and local standards for breathability. AIRWRAP fits most cots including larger brands like Boori. For more information about AIRWRAP visit www.airwrap.com.au.

Amby Baby Hammocks
Tel: (07) 3712 0012 or 0422 311 263
email: amby@babyhammocks.com
website: www.babyhammocks.com

Amby Baby Hammock is a patented womb-like day/night baby bed that soothes even the most restless baby to sleep. Excellent for colic, reflux and premature babies. Used extensively in hospitals, child care centres and thousands of homes worldwide. Available through www.babyhammocks.com.

Basically Baby
Tel: (02) 4577 5933
email: info@basicallybaby.com.au
website: www.basicallybaby.com.au

 Tetra Tea Tree baby bedding is a natural and safe choice when deciding on bedding for your baby. It has been Australia's leading brand of natural, organic-filled baby bedding since 1949. The range includes mattresses, pillows and the original Tetra Snuggle Bed, filled with pure organic tea tree flakes as well as chemical free, bacteria free and sterilised. Visit www.basicallybaby.com.au for more information.

BEDazzled Bed Mats
Tel: (07) 5491 1880
email: bedazzledbedmats@dodo.com.au
website: www.bedazzledbedmats.com

BEDazzled Bed Mats have all your bed wetting, toilet training and incontinence needs covered. These bed mats are washable and re-usable and come in a vast range of sizes and designs. The mattress/sheet protectors are 100% Australian owned and manufactured. This website also stocks washable and re-usable pants, pillow protectors, doona protectors and licensed manchester plus much more. Phone orders are welcome.

bespoken
Tel: 0419 593 294
email: bridget@bespoken.com.au
website: www.bespoken.com.au

This is a bedware line that will ensure your child's room stands out from the rooms of their playmates. Bespoken makes bed bandanas, door covers, baby cosies, mini bean bags, bunting and cushions for children from newborn up. The brand offers limited edition prints and hand-screened words and images. Visit their website for further information.

Blessed Earth
Tel: 1300 135 589
email: info@blessedearth.com.au
website: www.blessedearth.com.au

Blessed Earth manufactures and distributes a wide range of certified organic cotton underwear, clothing and bedding for babies, children and adults. They also manufacture a range of organic wool bedding including pillows, quilts, protectors, futons and mattresses. Australia-wide delivery available on all products. Visit their website for further information.

Branberry Pty Limited
Tel: (02) 9904 3546
email: info@branberry.com
website: www.branberry.com

Branberry combines natural fibres, classic styles and timeless colours to create a brand of knitted blankets for

Resources

CHOOSING FURNITURE & EQUIPMENT

Bedding & bed linen

babies and children like no other. They are both beautiful and functional. Although they are of the highest quality, they are meant for everyday use. Each blanket is carefully knitted and hand finished in Australia ensuring lasting quality. They are made from the finest natural fibres enabling the blankets to be soft, light and comfortable, warm in winter and cool in summer. They breathe well and are never prickly on delicate skin. And in keeping with practicality, these classics are machine washable and dryable. Made from 70% pure combed cotton and 30% extra fine merino wool, babies and children can be tucked in securely without feeling restricted as they are wonderfully elastic but don't stretch out of shape.

Brolly Sheets
Tel: 1800 809 847
email: info@brollysheets.com.au
website: www.brollysheets.com.au

Brolly Sheets take the hassle out of bedwetting. Just tuck in on top of the fitted sheet and simply whip off if your child wets the bed. No need to completely strip the bed saving you time and washing (and sanity). Brolly Sheets come in four gorgeous colours, three sizes and are easy to wash and dry.

Creswick Woollen Mills
Tel: (03) 9818 5055
email: info@creswickwool.com.au
website: www.creswickwool.com.au

Creswick Woollen Mills produce and stock a range of quality Australian-made 100% merino and 100% alpaca woollen rugs, throws, quilts and bassinet, cot and queen size blankets. They also have alpaca and wool off-cuts available for embroidery as well as wool underblankets in cot to queen sizes. Mail order available.

daboo & doshi designs
Tel: (07) 3342 2851
email: sabena@daboodoshi.com.au
website: www.daboodoshi.com.au

Specialising in quilt covers, daboo & doshi designs offer an exciting, visually stimulating and adorably bright coloured alternative that will add a vibrant look to your baby's nursery. With a gorgeous palette of colours to choose from, these fresh, fun and funky cot quilt covers (doona covers) are designed and hand made in Queensland.

DwellStudio
Tel: 1300 763 126
website: www.luxurylabels.com.au

Bold new colours and the simplicity of vintage designs is the springboard for the stunning collection of modern cot bedding from DwellStudio. DwellStudio textiles observe eco-friendly practices. They are always printed with low-impact, fibre-reactive dyes, which are the most environmentally sound and safest pigments available. Bring a new definition of style and sophistication to the modern nursery with DwellStudio Cot sets (rrp$290) in a range of stunning designs. Includes play quilt, fitted sheet, flat sheet and French pillow case.

Fluffies Knitwear Industries
Tel: (08) 8347 1343
email: fluffies@fluffies.com.au
website: www.fluffies.com.au

Fluffies Knitwear Industries is an Australian-owned company that manufactures and imports quality products such as luxury blankets, sheets, mattresses, mattress protectors, change mats, towels, pilchers, nappies and much more. Mail order available.

Galway Trading
Tel: 1300 721 710
email: sales@conni.com.au
website: www.conni.com.au

Conni has developed a fun range of kids' products to assist in the process of toilet training. No more total bed changes, ConniKids bed pads are absorbent on top and waterproof on bottom to keep the mattress dry and hygienic. Machine washable and tumble drier safe with no PVC, ConniKids bed pads also include a free toilet training kit. Simply remove the night nappy, place your ConniKids bed pad on the bed and let toilet training happen naturally.

Good-Night Sleep-Tight
Tel: (03) 9349 4927
email: goodnightsleeptight@hotmail.com

Does your child throw their covers off during sleep? Do you get up during the night to cover your infant? A mum has come up with a very simple solution – sheets that press stud together so your child stays covered. You can also easily regulate how much cover you want on your child. These sheets are available for newborns up to 10 years of age. Phone or email for more information.

IGC DOREL Pty Ltd
Tel: 1300 809 526
email: sales@igcdorel.com.au
website: www.hushamok.com/au

h⌣shamok™ The innovative design of hushamok™ enables babies to sleep soundly on their back, which is a key recommendation in the prevention of SIDS. Other health benefits include the ease of colic due to its gentle swinging motion and snug design. Available in a variety of stylish colours the hushamok™ is durable, lightweight and portable, making it ideal for around the home or packed for travel. To view the latest range visit www.hushamok.com/au or phone IGC Dorel's Customer Service team on 1300 809 526 for your nearest stockist.

Junippers

Tel: (08) 8392 2700
email: junippers@picknowl.com.au
website: www.junippers.com.au

The Sleepover® is a softly padded, fully fitted sheet which is designed to fit completely over the hard base of a portable cot, making it softer, but safe and secure as it cannot be pulled off by your sleeping child. The top of The Sleepover® is softly padded with polyester fibre creating a comfortable and safe sleeping surface for your baby. The Sleepover® is easy to fit, just fold in half, padded side in, fold the portacot base in half, padded side in and slide the base into the two pockets on the back on the sheet and then open out and pop it into the cot. No more bending! Visit the website or phone for further information.

Katie Little

Tel: (02) 9698 1899
email: infoaus@kidsline.com
website: www.kidsline.com.au

Katie Little offers a stylish range of quality linens and accessories. A refined and stylish look that's perfect for your special baby. Designed in the USA and hand finished, Katie Little offers two exciting choices: Savannah or Sofia. Both include high cotton content bed linens, nappy stackers, hampers, throw pillows along with wall borders, wall hangings and curtains. Available at all good nursery stores. Visit the website or phone for further information.

Kids Line Australia

Tel: (02) 9698 1899
email: infoaus@kidsline.com
website: www.kidsline.com.au

Kids Line will inspire you in creating a wonderful new world for your baby. Their creative, delightful hand-finished linens and matching accessories are available in a large range of luxurious nursery themes to suit and inspire your baby. With a fresh clean colour pallet, they are bound to brighten up any room. Other themes from the collection include Safari, Barn Yard and Travel. Kids Line is designed to create a special, friendly, safe and comfortable environment for your baby. Visit the website or phone for further information.

kindy kamper

Tel: 0413 408 036
email: kindykamper@iprimus.com.au
website: www.kindykamper.com.au

Kindy Kamper is a cosy, comfy and convenient all-in-one kindy bedding solution for busy mums and dads. Kindy Kamper has a comfy padded base (no more cold and uncomfortable kindy mats and beds), an attached top sheet, pillowcase (with removable insert) and a zip-on/zip-off polar fleece blanket. It also comes with adjustable Velcro corners for a snug fit and will fit most kindy mats and stretcher beds. Kindy Kamper rolls into a convenient and easy-to-carry swag with a carry handle and name label. Visit the website or phone for further information.

Kumpny Pty Ltd

Tel: 1300 586 769
email: info@kumpny.com
website: www.kumpny.com

This new patented bedding design aims to provide safer sleeping environments by reducing excess fabric. The design supports the principles of the SIDS and Kids organisation making your baby sleep at the base of the cot. Snugabub cot sheets and blankets are uniquely designed for the growth of your baby to 12-18 months of age. They re made of 100% percale cotton and complimented with 100% soft woollen or 100% quality thermal cotton blankets.

Lambykins

Tel: (03) 9306 6567
website: www.lambykins.com

Lambykins™ pure Australian merino baby blankets offer exceptional softness, quality, comfort and design. Visit www.lambykins.com for a list of nation-wide stockists or to purchase online.

Linen House

Tel: (03) 9552 6000
email: sales@linenhouse.com.au
website: www.hiccupsforkids.com.au or www.linenhouse.com.au

hiccups
linen house for kids

Hiccups is a charming kids homewares range brought to you by Linen House. Create a beautiful bedroom for your child. Printed, embroidered, yarn-dyed or flannelette bed linen designs are all designed with wonderful themes in mind. Many accessories such as cushions, coverlets, throws, canopies and bunting, bean bags, floor mats and playful novelty cushions match back with the colours of the season. Hiccups Babies provides beautiful products for the nursery, and decorating options and design elements tie the two ranges together. Visit the website for more details or phone Linen House.

little bamboo

Tel: (03) 9016 3422
email: info@tllc.com.au
website: www.littlebamboo.com.au

Little Bamboo is a range of beautiful and soft bedroom and bathroom nursery products made using organically grown bamboo. Incorporating delicate muslin, super soft towelling, sensuous sheeting and beautiful blankets, Little Bamboo is one of the most comprehensive and innovative ranges of nursery bamboo textiles. Bringing together nearly 40 years of history in the nursery textile industry, this range has been developed to be both incredibly functional and extremely aesthetic. For more information visit www.littlebamboo.com.au.

Lullaby Linen

Tel: (03) 9890 0022
email: helen@lullabylinen.com.au
website: www.lullabylinen.com.au

Resources

CHOOSING FURNITURE & EQUIPMENT

Bedding & bed linen

➔ Furniture & equipment hire

A new and exciting concept in children's bed linen and accessories has arrived. Lullaby Linen has created a full range of co-ordinating products for a complete bedroom solution. The range includes bassinet and cot comforters, single and king single doonas and co-ordinating sheets, cushions and lampshades. Lullaby Linen also has a number of gifts including aprons, smocks, bibs and Christmas gifts for your children. Hand embroidered christening gowns also compliment the range. Designed and manufactured in Australia, these products are available online and at selected stores. Visit the website or phone for further information.

Million Dollar Baby

Tel: 0413 960 673
email: m.dollarbaby@bigpond.com.au
website: www.milliondollarbaby.com.au

Million Dollar Baby sells sheets (flat and fitted) for cots, cradles, bassinets and portacots. Pillow cases and doona covers are also available separately. Bedding is available in 17 trendy colours at great prices. Child care centre orders welcome. Visit the website or phone for further information.

Mite-Y-Fresh

Tel: (02) 9986 3432
email: sales@miteyfresh.com.au
website: www.miteyfresh.com.au

Mite-Y-Fresh is an award-winning team dedicated to bringing asthma and allergy sufferers innovative long term protective measures against some of the most commonly suffered inhaled allergens. They supply a full range of allergy protective bedding, supported and recommended by Australian GPs. Phone to talk with a consultant or place a product order by phone, email or online.

Muffets Kidz Accessories Pty Ltd

Tel: 0409 906 747
email: muffetskidz@bigpond.com
website: www.muffetskidz.com.au

The Original Cot Teething Rail® is a flexible cover for the whole of the cot rail. It provides a soft biting surface for baby's top and bottom teeth while protecting the soft enamel on teeth and the aesthetics of your cot. Removable for easy cleaning – no trapped germs. Made from PVC-free, phthalate-free, halogen-free, BPA-free, eco-friendly recyclable product. Available at leading baby furniture retailers or online via their site at www.muffetskidz.com.au.

Nice-Pak Products

Tel: 1800 506 750
email: info@nicepak.com.au
website: www.babyu.com.au

Designed to lie on top of bed sheets, Baby U Waterproof Sheet Protector saves you and your child the stress and hassle of stripping beds at night when accidents occur. The waterproof backing protects sheets and mattresses and is kept in place with tuck-in bed flaps. The soft quilted poly cotton surface is comfortable to lie on, and provides assurance that little accidents will be absorbed. When wet, simply remove from the top sheet, machine wash and tumble dry. The Water Proof Sheet protector is bleachable and the vinyl backing will not crack or crinkle. Available in selected Kmart, Big W, Toys R Us, baby stores and selected pharmacies. Phone 1800 506 750 or visit www.babyu.com.au for further information.

Outlook Australia

Tel: (03) 9817 2311
email: outlooktm@bigpond.com
website: www.outlooktm.com

Developed from 100% bamboo fibres, Bamboo Baby® fabric is breathable and gentle but fully machine washable. Its natural anti-fungal, anti-bacterial qualities and gentleness on the sensitive skin of babies make Bamboo Baby® the perfect choice. Bamboo Baby® is also a great choice for eco-conscious parents as bamboo is a sustainable resource, needing no pesticides or fertilisers and requiring far less irrigation than cotton. The Bamboo Baby® blanket is beautifully silky soft and snuggly. Ideal for layering in baby's cot or bassinet.

Playgro Pty Ltd

Tel: (03) 8558 2000
email: sales@playgro.com
website: www.playgro.com

Playgro now offers parents the complete nursery solution. Playgro's co-ordinated range of infant bedding and nursery toys are available in a choice of delightful themes, designed to stimulate the imagination and create an environment full of fun, colour and adventure. With a commitment to style, quality and comfort, Playgro's co-ordinated collections have a playful charm that is sure to bring to life any room. Available nationwide.

Playgro Pty Ltd

Tel: (03) 8558 2000
website: www.playgro.com

Playgro Mattress Protection will keep your bassinet and cot mattress dry, hygienic and stain free. Playgro Mattress Protection creates an impenetrable barrier against dust mites, moisture and liquid stains. Made from a breathable Polyurethane membrane with a 100% cotton terry surface, it provides the ultimate in quality and comfort for a peaceful nights sleep.

Ramalama

Tel: 1300 729 834
email: hello@ramalama.com.au
website: www.ramalama.com.au

Have a special quilt custom made to suit your nursery or child's room, or choose from Ramalama's existing designs and colours. These quilts, pillow covers and cushion covers are handmade under fair trade practices in Vietnam, and are available in all sizes (even for mum and dad). Your support helps to fund community development, education and healthcare projects in the community.

The Kinder Kompany Pty Ltd
Tel: 1300 661 060
email: info@kinderkot.com.au
website: www.kinderkot.com.au

The dreamdome fits on a standard single bed and creates a comfy secure cubby space that's free from mozzies and other bugs. Ideal for the Australian climate, it packs up very small and can be easily transported and set up on any single bed. A range of colours are available to suit the style of your bedroom. The dreamdome is available through selected retailers and online. For your nearest retailer visit www.kinderkot.com.au/dreamdome/.

Timabare
Tel: (08) 9478 1870
email: susan@timabare.com.au
website: www.timabare.com.au

Timabare makes sheets for cradles, bassinets and cots (including Booris) that cannot be untucked once fitted. Their unique 'sack' style top sheet fits over the whole mattress and stays in place, thereby reducing the strangulation hazard in the cot. The 100% cotton interlock is free from dyes and harsh chemical finishes so it is allergy friendly for sensitive skin.

Unique Kids
Tel: (02) 9979 1125
email: info@uniquekids.com.au
website: www.uniquekids.com.au

Decorating rooms is easy with Unique Kids' gorgeous range of bed linen for both the nursery and girls' and boys' bedrooms with all the matching accessories such as rugs and cushions. Prompt delivery to your door and friendly service. Visit their website or phone for further details.

UrbanBaby.com.au
Tel: 1300 882 991
email: hello@urbanbaby.com.au
website: www.urbanbaby.com.au

UrbanBaby's padded portable cot sheets are beautifully finished and made from quality 100% cotton sheeting. The set includes one base sheet and comes in a handy drawstring bag. The padded base sheet gives your baby extra comfort and softness with the built-in insert. This eliminates the need for a separate foam mattress or folding up a towel or blanket under the sheet for extra bedding. Fits any length up to 110cm and any width up to 75cm. Fully machine washable and available in pure white. Available nationally by mail order and via their website.

FURNITURE & EQUIPMENT HIRE

NATIONAL

Bassinets & More
Tel: (02) 9871 8820
email: bassinets@bigpond.com
website: www.bassinetsandmore.com

Bassinets & More hires hospital-type bassinets for babies from birth to approximately 3 months. The bassinets can be hired in Sydney, Melbourne and Canberra. The bassinets are mobile and have braked wheels. They come complete with a mattress and two trays.

Folding Tables Direct Pty Ltd
Tel: (02) 9700 0605
email: sales@foldingtables.com.au
website: www.foldingtables.com.au

Buy or hire child-height folding tables and chairs for parties and art and craft activities. Various styles and sizes available to hire (Sydney only) or buy (delivery Australia wide). Student desks and adult height furniture also available. Visit their website for further information.

Hire for Baby
Tel: 1300 363 755
email: info@hireforbaby.com
website: www.hireforbaby.com

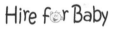

Hire for Baby can help you with all your baby equipment hire needs for a day, a week or a few months with their friendly, professional service and quality equipment at great prices. With over 50 branches all around Australia, simply visit www.hireforbaby.com and find your local branch. All equipment is purchased brand new, carefully cleaned and safety checked to ensure it is in the best possible condition for your use. Their qualified restraint fitters provide complimentary fitting of hired capsules and car seats when you collect so that you can be rest assured of your baby's safety. For holidays, reduce stress and excess baggage fees by having prams, portacots and car seats waiting for your arrival.

VICTORIA

Home & Away Baby Hire
Tel: 1300 663 672
email: babyhire@babyhire.com.au
website: www.babyhire.com.au

Home & Away Baby Hire provides quality baby equipment for hire. Perfect for newborns so you can transport them safely without the expense of purchasing a capsule. All agents are fully trained and insured for the professional installation of your carseat or capsule. Visit the website for prices, product descriptions and outlet locations. You can book online or by phone. Money-back guarantee on the safety and cleanliness of all our products.

Resources

CHOOSING FURNITURE & EQUIPMENT

Furniture & equipment hire

➜ Nursery & bedroom decor

Maxam Baby Capsule Hire

1/31 Peel Street
Eltham VIC 3095
Tel: 1300 885 645 or 0423 833 418
website: www.maxam.net.au

This is a community service managed by Maxam on behalf of many local councils throughout Melbourne and country Victoria. They provide Safe-n-Sound baby capsules for sale or hire which have been claimed by VicRoads and other state road traffic authorities as the safest option for all infants. Competitive hire fee, $80.00 (including GST), plus refundable bond. Suitable until baby is 9kg or 70cm. Short term hire available. Extensions to the standard hire period and attachments can be provided free of additional charge. Delivery and fitting available. Other baby equipment also available. For enquiries or bookings phone 1300 885 645 or 0423 833 418.

NEW SOUTH WALES

Baby Bassinet Hire

PO Box 2009
Taren Point NSW 2009
Tel: 1300 785 700
website: www.babybassinethire.com.au

Baby Bassinet Hire, located in Sydney, offers parents of newborn babies the opportunity to use the same baby bassinet at home that is used in most maternity units. These mobile bassinets are safe, hygienic, ergonomically friendly, convenient and include mattress and storage trays. There's no need to buy; just rent for a month or longer and then put your child straight into a cot at 2-4 months. Ideal for sleeping, bathing or changing. Free delivery to most suburbs in the Sydney metro area. Twin units now available. Available Sydney and outer suburbs.

Bassinets & More

Tel: (02) 9871 8820
email: bassinets@bigpond.com
website: www.bassinetsandmore.com

Bassinets & More offers a personalised hire service of Safe-n-Sound capsules to new parents. A flexible and on-time delivery service is available to most areas of Sydney, or the capsules can be picked up at Bassinets & More in West Pennant Hills. Usually just one day's notice is required for hire and in some cases same day delivery is available. Bassinets & More also hires car seats and boosters. Visit the website or phone for further information.

Mite-Y-Fresh

PO Box 431
Terrey Hills NSW 2084
Tel: (02) 9986 3432
email: sales@miteyfresh.com.au
website: www.miteyfresh.com.au

Mite-Y-Fresh hire out air purifiers and dehumidifiers when you need them most. Service includes delivery, instructions and pick up in the Sydney region. For an extra small fee, Mite-Y-Fresh service the Central Coast, Blue Mountains and Illawarra regions. They also provide a range of alternative, practical, easy-to-implement solutions. Phone to talk with a consultant or place a product order by phone, email or online.

Pearce's Child Restraints

5/6 Wilmette Place
Mona Vale NSW 2103
Tel: (02) 9997 4602
website: ww.pearceschildrestraints.com.au

Pearce's Child Restraints rent and sell baby capsules and car seats and they are also an authorised fitting station with experience in fitting all types of seats into all types of vehicles. The company visits several hospitals on a weekly basis providing rentals and fittings at various northern locations. Bookings required. Pearce's also rent the clear hospital-style mobile bassinets from which babies can move straight to a cot.

QUEENSLAND

ABC Nursery Hire

Gold Coast/Tweed Heads:
Tel: 1300 724 276
Email: info@abcnurseryhire.com
Sunshine Coast:
Tel: 1300 739 955
Email: sunshine-coast@abcnurseryhire.com
Brisbane North:
Tel: 1300 655 438
Email: brisbane-north@abcnurseryhire.com
website: www.abcnurseryhire.com

ABC Nursery Hire provides baby nursery equipment for hire to inbound tourists, local residents, local businesses and child care organisations or groups such as anti-natal classes. They provide both a delivery and pick up service (conditions apply). All baby nursery hire equipment is in excellent condition and goes through a thorough cleaning and disinfectant process prior to being hired out. Visit the website or phone for further information.

Baby Equipment Hire (Cairns & Port Douglas)

2/351 Sheridian Street
North Cairns QLD 4870
Tel: (07) 4041 1690
email: kidquip@iprimus.com.au
website: www.babyequipmenthire.com.au

Baby Equipment Hire (Cairns & Port Douglas) supplies quality baby items for hire throughout the Cairns region. Items are available by the day, week or month

...nd can be delivered. Stock includes capsules, car seats, prams, high chairs, monitors, bassinets, breast pumps and toys. They also have a great range of second-hand equipment for sale.

Bubby's Playpen

3/74 Webster Road
Stafford QLD 4053
Tel: (07) 3356 6089
website: www.bubbysplaypen.com.au

Bubby's Playpen offers baby equipment hire including hospital-grade breast pumps, hospital style bassinets, capsules and car restraints and all other needs for baby. Holiday hire, short and long term hire available. They also sell new and used baby products and factory seconds are their specialty. Bubby's Playpen is also a repair agent for brands including IGC, Mothers Choice, Bertini, Go Safe, Quinny, Babylove and Peg Perego.

Gold Coast Holiday Hire

Tel: (07) 5568 0585
email: info@burleighhire.com
website: www.burleighhire.com

Gold Coast Holiday Hire (Burleigh Hire Shop) offers a full range of baby and child hire gear. Don't have the hassle of carrying all your baby gear (and the excess luggage charges) when you go on holidays, hire it on arrival. The following goods are available (and they can deliver): portacots and wooden cots; joggers, strollers and prams; baby capsules, carseats and boosters; highchairs; baby baths; change tables; bouncers; wooden door gates; linen and folding beds; beach gear; electrical gear and more.

WESTERN AUSTRALIA

ABC Nursery Hire

Tel: 1300 787 773
Email: perth-north@abcnurseryhire.com
website: www.abcnurseryhire.com

ABC Nursery Hire provides baby nursery equipment for hire to inbound tourists, local residents, local businesses and child care organisations or groups such as anti-natal classes. They provide both a delivery and pick up service (conditions apply). All baby nursery hire equipment is in excellent condition and goes through a thorough cleaning and disinfecting process prior to being hired out.

Basics 4 Baby

Tel: 0433 293 977
email: hire@basics4baby.com.au
website: www.basics4baby.com.au

Whether you are having a new baby, going away on holidays or having guests coming to stay, Basics 4 Baby have it covered. With the A-Z of baby needs, they are sure to have what you need. Basics 4 Baby can provide the latest children's equipment and accessories in excellent condition for short or long-term hire. The range includes bassinets, highchairs, car restraints, cots, prams, play equipment, breast pumps, safety equipment and much more (even linen if required).

Go Baby Hire and Sales

Tel: 1800 300 938
email: contact@gobabyhire.com.au
website: www.gobabyhire.com.au

GoBaby Hire and Sales can provide you with everything you need for newborns through to young children when living or visiting in and around Perth, Western Australia. This will suit young families who are travelling, households with young children coming to visit for extended periods and new families with a precious bundle to get home from hospital and keep close before graduating to a cot. It's even a great way to try some of the products out before committing to a major investment in purchasing it for yourself. Centrally located in Guildford, just five minutes from the airport, for easy pick up. Delivery is available at an additional fee if required and packages are available for multiple item hire.

SOUTH AUSTRALIA

Cocoon Hire Pty Ltd

Tel: 0416 260 890
email: contact@cocoonhire.com.au
website: www.cocoonhire.com.au

Cocoon Hire specialise in the rental of mobile, clear-sided baby bassinets as used in maternity hospitals around Australia. These bassinets are an affordable, easy-to-use and safe sleeping arrangement for your newborn baby. Cocoon Hire offer convenient hire terms at great prices and free delivery and pick up of the bassinet in the Adelaide metropolitan area. Visit the website or phone for further information.

NURSERY & BEDROOM DECOR

NATIONAL

annieB's

Tel: 0410 526 145
email: annie@anniebs.com.au
website: www.anniebs.com.au

annieB's creates a world of enchantment and magic for young children with gorgeous PlayPalaces packed with extra comfy cushions, fun puppet theatres, cosy bean bags and bean bag chairs. Vibrant stripes and gingham checks will brighten up your child's room like never before. Laughter and fun guaranteed. Their new teddy bears and bunting add the finishing touch. Visit www.anniebs.com.au for more information.

Aussie Clings/Stik-ees

Tel: 1800 621 136 freecall
email: aussieclings@bigpond.com
website: www.aussieclings.com.au

Static Cling Plastic Re-usable Window Decorations and Activity Kits keep children amused for hours. They are easy to use with no mess and the range includes educational, holiday and everyday themes. Suitable for pre-schoolers to adults, they stick to most clean glossy surfaces including windows, mirrors, bathtub, tiles,

Resources

CHOOSING FURNITURE & EQUIPMENT

Nursery & bedroom decor

refrigerators and whiteboards. There are over 100 sets to choose from with prices from $7 to $30, the majority in the $10 to $13 category. Phone freecall 1800 621 136 for a free catalogue or visit their website at www.aussieclings.com.au.

Bluepaw Artwork For Children
Tel: (03) 9429 4704
email: info@bluepaw.com.au
website: www.bluepaw.com.au

Bluepaw creates modern and affordable artwork to inspire imagination in young minds. Their extensive range of images will compliment any decor or colour scheme in your child's room or baby's nursery. The artwork can be personalised to include your child's name and makes a wonderful gift. Each piece comes complete in a high quality wooden box frame, double-matt mounted with the choice of white or chocolate frame. Selected pieces include 3D elements such as flowers, buttons or tulle to bring the artwork alive. It is amazingly affordable and can be mixed and matched to suit your taste.

BoscoBear
Tel: 1300 BOSCOB
email: info@boscobear.com.au
website: www.boscobear.com.au

BoscoBear is an exciting Australian brand that has a fabulous range of products designed to celebrate children's colourful imaginations. These bright and lively products include removable room art, personalised labels, party invitations and stationery products. They have been designed to stimulate and engage a child's inquisitive nature and each theme has been carefully researched, designed and illustrated by their very experienced design team.

Bright Star Kids
Tel: 1300 668 997
email: info@brightstarkids.com.au
website: www.brightstarkids.com.au

Decorate your baby's nursery in minutes with Bright Star Kids fabulous range of removable wall decals – no painting or DIY skills needed. Choose from a great range of cute designs that will make your child's nursery feel as special and unique as they are. Visit this easy-to-use online store at www.brightstarkids.com.au where you'll find lots of fantastic offers, including up to 25% off when you purchase more than one Wall Graphic Kit in an order - great for stocking up on Christmas and birthday presents.

Cocoon Couture
Tel: (03) 9530 5199
email: info@cocooncouture.com
website: www.cocooncouture.com

Cocoon Couture offer a delightful range of boutique children's bean bag covers specially designed with everyday use in mind. Each bean bag cover features their unique quirky critters in vintage fabric appliqué on a wide selection of 100% cotton pinwale cord colours that fit in with any decor. Also available from Cocoon Couture is The Enchanted Forest range of wooden room accessories, made from environmentally friendly ply wood from plantation forests. The Enchanted Tree features the Early Bird and Sleepy Owl nesting in the branches amongst the beautiful printed leaves and acorn pegs. This beautiful collection will be a piece of childhood to treasure with love through time.

Cool Art
Tel: (02) 8005 1767
email: art@coolartvinyl.com.au
website: www.coolartvinyl.com.au

Cool Art sells custom designed wall decals that are trendy and chic. They are removable and perfect for baby nursery and kids rooms. Choose from wall quotes or from cool art designs. Made from pre-spaced ultra thin vinyl that appears hand painted when applied. Great for combining with their best-selling canvas artworks, exclusively for kids. Available online Australia-wide.

DecoArts Creations
Tel: 0419 331 884
website: www.decoart.com.au

Decoart Creations offers hand-painted original artwork for children and has recently added artworks for all ages. The types of artworks offered are personalised, ready to hang and special commissions. All artworks are individually created and rendered either in watercolour on paper or acrylic on canvas.

Duckcloth
Tel: (03) 8503 7615
website: www.duckcloth.com.au

Duckcloth is a secure online store located in Melbourne and delivering Australia-wide. They offer a fun and fresh collection of children's fabric by the metre. Use the fabric for curtains, quilts, cushions, napery, bean bags, tote bags, clothing and many other projects.

Fiona Kate
Tel: 0413 707 695
email: sales@fionakate.com.au
website: www.fionakate.com.au

If tired old boxes and storage solutions have made your life dull, then the Box Seat by Fiona Kate adds practical fun, colour and style to any room. Much more than just a storage box, the Box Seat Start-up Pack (rrp from $99.95) includes a tabletop and three boxes ready to be

illed with all matter of important treasured pieces.
Adding even more style and organising flair, apply
simple and graphic chalkboard labels and lettering for
instant identification of those all important baby's
belongings like clothes, toys and special mementoes.
Individual Box Seat priced from rrp$12.95.

Flowertot Designs
Tel: 0402 345 432
email: sales@flowertotdesigns.com.au
website: www.flowertotdesigns.com.au

Flowertot Designs is a business designed by a mum who
loves making quality decorative wall art for little ones
right through to adults. Their products range from
photo boards through to decorated shadow boxes. From
something that adds a splash of colour right through to a
product that keeps memories alive. Each product is
handmade and can be altered in design and colour. To
view the range of products visit their website
www.flowertotdesigns.com.au.

Gelati Art
Tel: (07) 3366 9304
email: online@gelatiart.com.au
website: www.gelatiart.com.au

Gelati Art specialises in designer canvas art for children's
rooms. Artwork is created on premium 100% cotton
canvas using ultrachrome pigment ink and coated
laminate for a quality finish. Gelati Art looks beautiful
in both contemporary and traditional home interiors
and comes in a range of designs, sizes and colours.
Phone for more information.

Kapow Pop Art
Tel: (02) 4784 2442
email: info@kapowpopart.com.au
website: www.kapowpopart.com.au

In the tradition of Andy Warhol and his famous Marilyn
Monroe and Campbells Tin Soup artwork, KAPOW!
Pop Art creates personalised pop art portraits on canvas.
Perfect for any art lover, it is guaranteed to become the
centrepiece of any room. Your finished Pop Art portrait
arrives stretched and ready to hang on the wall. Each
one is completely unique, created especially for you
making a Pop Art portrait the ultimate gift.

Katie Little
Tel: (02) 9698 1899
email: infoaus@kidsline.com
website: www.kidsline.com.au

Katie Little offers a stylish range of quality linens and
accessories. A refined and stylish look that's perfect for
your special baby. Designed in the USA and hand
finished, Katie Little offers two exciting choices:
Savannah or Sofia. Both include high cotton content bed
linens, nappy stackers, hampers, throw pillows along
with wall borders, wall hangings and curtains. With
everything to create that special environment for your
baby, make sure you consider the Katie Little range,
available at all good nursery stores. Phone or visit the
website for more information.

Katydid Decor Company
Tel: 1300 655 069
email: info@katydiddecor.com.au
website: www.katydiddecor.com.au

 The Katydid Décor Company
offers an innovative way to
decorate a baby's nursery or child's
bedroom and create a little
wonderland for them to enjoy. The beautifully
illustrated wallpaper borders and matching decor
stickers, transfers, motifs and hand painted wall plaques
can transform a plain room into a colourful
wonderland. Complete the room with a set of lovely
ceramic letters in your child's name, a personalised
ceramic nameplate for the door or a commemorative
plate, cup or money box as a thoughtful, personal gift to
mark a special occasion. Phone or visit the website for
more information.

Lightyear Imports
Tel: 1300 543 778
email: info@lightyearimports.com.au
website: www.lightyearimports.com.au

Lightyear Imports' extensive product range includes
their famous kids rugs – Thomas, Cinderalla, Bob the
Bulider, The Wiggles, Spiderman and lot lots more. They
also have interactive activity rugs, car mats Hopscotch
mats, educational rugs and thick designer floor rugs just
for kids. Lightyear Imports also has a growing line of
wooden toys and children's furniture. Phone or visit the
website for more information.

Linen House
Tel: (03) 9552 6000
email: sales@linenhouse.com.au
website: www.hiccupsforkids.com.au or
www.linenhouse.com.au

 Hiccups is a charming kids homewares
range brought to you by Linen House.
Create a beautiful bedroom for your child.
Printed, embroidered, yarn-dyed or
flannelette bed linen designs are all
designed with wonderful themes in mind.
Many accessories such as cushions,
coverlets, throws, canopies and bunting, bean bags,
floor mats and playful novelty cushions match back
with the colours of the season. Hiccups Babies provides
beautiful products for the nursery, and decorating
options and design elements tie the two ranges together.
Visit the website for more details or phone Linen House.

Little Pink Frog
Tel: 0412 087 382
email: info@littlepinkfrog.com.au
website: www.littlepinkfrog.com.au

Little Pink Frog specialises in signs for kids, cut-out wall
letters and plaques for all occasions. All products are
made from quality acrylic, custom designed to suit your
needs. The small plaques make a wonderful keepsake.
Visit www.littlepinkfrog.com.au or phone for further
information.

Resources

CHOOSING FURNITURE & EQUIPMENT

Nursery & bedroom decor ➜ Nursery brands

Metro-Style

Tel: 1800 683 969
email: info@metro-style.com.au
website: www.metro-style.com.au

Colourful and fun, the gorgeous range of Metro-Style wall art for babies and kids has been designed to add an element of vibrancy to a baby's nursery. Brighten up a baby girl or boy's space with cute Animal Farm, Four Elephants and Snail/Ladybird/Butterfly Wall Art. Turn a baby girl's nursery into a pretty pink paradise with wall art decorated in beautiful butterflies. Visit the website or phone the number above for further information.

Sprout Gallery

Tel: 0417 739 626
email: info@sproutgallery.com
website: www.sproutgallery.com

Sprout Gallery is an online art gallery that specialises in selling unique artworks for children's rooms. Original artworks feature fun embellishments such as fabrics, beading, buttons, ribbon and other found objects to give a wonderful three dimensional effect. Artworks do not require framing and only quality thick stretched canvases and acrylics are used. All artworks are lightweight and easy to hang.

Tee-Zed Products

Tel: (02) 9386 4000
email: sales@tee-zed.com.au
website: www.tee-zed.com

Dream Baby's® Decor range includes licensed Priss stick-ups, borders, hooks, drawer knobs, lights and character silhouettes such as Winnie the Pooh, Tweety and other Looney Tune characters. Available from selected baby stores, toy stores, hardware and pharmacies or phone (02) 9386 4000 for your nearest stockist.

Teeny Me

Tel: 0414 255 040
email: info@teenyme.com.au
website: www.teenyme.com.au

Teeny Me produce a stylish range of children's flip flop sofas, beanie bags and snooze sacs with an emphasis on fun designs and lasting quality. Tailored from washable fabrics, Teeny Me products are practical, versatile and loved by kids. Phone, email or visit the website for further information.

The Oz Material Girls

Tel: 0434 674 651
email: thematerialgirls@ozemail.com.au
website: www.theozmaterialgirls.com

The Oz Material Girls specialises in quality fabrics for quilting, patchwork, wall art and home decorating offering a huge range of licensed kids novelty prints, stunning orientals, beautiful florals, funky retro, religious themes, country cottage and rare out of print designs. Stock includes pre-cut kits, charm squares, stash builders and jelly rolls. Magazines, patterns and tools complete the extensive range.

Unique Kids

Tel: (02) 9979 1125
email: info@uniquekids.com.au
website: www.uniquekids.com.au

Unique Kids have beautiful hand-painted canvases and personalised artwork and funky wall decals to brighten any child's bedroom. Free gift wrapping, prompt delivery to your door and friendly service.

wallbuddies

Tel: 1300 655 028
email: sandy@wallbuddies.com.au
website: www.wallbuddies.com.au

wallbuddies offer instant 3-D wall murals for kid's rooms, add fantastic colour and transform your child's bedroom into a new and exciting adventure. Easy to put up and take down – no mess, no fuss. They have something for all ages and especially for a nursery. You can even add your child's name to some of the products to add that personal touch to your mural. More life like than regular stick-on decals and brighter than your regular wall art stickers.

WallCandy Arts

Tel: (02) 9300 0599
website: www.wallcandyarts.com

WallCandy is the simplest most innovative way to decorate a baby's room, create a unique atmosphere or enhance a living space. Once installed, WallCandy can be effortlessly re-arranged or removed and used again without causing damage to walls. Simply peel, stick and apply. Phone the number listed above or visit their website for further details.

VICTORIA

Books Illustrated

300 Beaconsfield Parade
Middle Park VIC 3206
Tel: (03) 9534 7751
email: info@booksillustrated.com.au
website: www.booksillustrated.com.au

Books Illustrated is a treasure trove, specialising in Australian picture book illustration and signed books. Imagine owning an original illustration from Animalia by Graeme Base, or a lively ink drawing of Old Tom by Leigh Hobbs, or a watercolour by Bob Graham or Alison Lester. Heirlooms to be treasured, but not expensive. Giclee prints of illustrations in limited ditions are also available. Gallery open by ppointment. Art can be posted by registered mail to nywhere in the world.

Bristol Eltham
Bridge Street
Eltham VIC 3095
Tel: (03) 9439 4900
email: bristoleltham@netspace.net.au
website: www.bristol.com

Bristol Eltham has a huge range of easily removable children's wall stickers and borders. They also free in-store colour consulting from colour consultant Tamara (on Thursdays) and free stain samples of your choice. Meet the team at Bristol Eltham to help with the decor of your baby's bedroom. They also have a children's play area. Open 7 days a week.

Christopher Peregrine Timms
441B Hawthorn Road
Caulfield South VIC 3162
Tel: (03) 9528 6850
email: christophertimms@bigpond.com
website: www.christophertimms.com.au

Christopher Timms makes furniture for funky kids as well as designing interiors. He says that pretty much anything can be designed or made to order. Phone the number above or check out his website.

Muralmaker
15 Orr Lane
Montmorency VIC 3094
Tel: 0402 402 024
email: russell@muralmaker.com.au
website: www.muralmaker.com.au

Muralmakers can create imaginative and original designs for your child's bedroom. A theme can be developed with an obligation-free colour illustration. The design can incorporate existing fixtures and fittings, enhancing the bedroom environment. Individual feature walls are a speciality. Phone Russell on the number above for a free quote and design.

NEW SOUTH WALES

Goldfish Gifts & Toys
Shop 2, 62 Albert Street
Berry NSW 2535
Tel: (02) 4464 3332
email: goldfish@goldfishgifts.com.au
website: www.goldfishgifts.com.au

Goldfish Gifts and Toys are designers of a great range of children's room accessories including mobiles, wall plaques, door knobs, hooks, coathangers, pencil and money boxes and more. Characters include Noah and his ark, crazy fish, gorgeous butterflies and transport. The shop is filled with colourful toys and traditional wooden toys from around the world. Ordering is possible online or via mail order. The shop is open seven days 10.00am to 5.00pm. Phone the number listed above or visit their website www.goldfishgifts.com.au for further details.

NURSERY BRANDS

NATIONAL

babydaze
Tel: 0421 946 871
email: info@babydaze.com.au
website: www.babydaze.com.au

The Marco Sky L is a unique tandem stroller that lets you transport two children in a very compact and user-friendly package. Suitable for an infant and toddler or twins from six months of age, the Marco Sky L benefits from a clearance width of 57cm and easy-to-use umbrella folding mechanism, boasting similar dimensions to that of the average single pram. No more concerns over not fitting through shop doors, down narrow aisles or in the car boot. Phone, email or visit the website for further details.

Babylove
Tel: 1300 131 477
email: info@nurseryelegance.com.au
website: www.babylove.com.au

When choosing from the extensive range of Babylove products, you can rest assured your child is in safe hands. Their design specialists are committed to proactive research and development and offer the highest available quality in child restraints, strollers, portacots, rockers, accessories and more. Babylove's philosophy is to meet and exceed customer's needs. All products go through a stringent testing process and meet all appropriate safety requirements. Products can be found in major department stores and independent specialty shops. For more information phone Nursery Elegance on the toll free number 1300 131 477.

Bambini International
Tel: 1300 557 691
email: trade@bambiniinternational.com.au
website: www.bambiniinternational.com.au

Bambini International distributes innovative and premium quality products that help make parents' lives easier and babies' lives safer. Brands include grobag, bambino mio, prince lionheart, john crane wooden toys and the new Egg bath range. In 2008 Bambini International won both major Australian "best product" awards giving parents peace of mind that it is also the experts that know what is on offer. Bambini International products can be found in major department, leading independent and specialty stores throughout Australia.

Born with Style
Tel: 1300 885 337
email: info@bornwithstyle.com.au
website: www.bornwithstyle.com.au

Born with Style's range includes Jeep Baby Products, United Colors of Benetton, Kolcraft, Baby Cubes, Loopa-Bowl, Kuster and more. Born with Style

Resources

CHOOSING FURNITURE & EQUIPMENT

Nursery brands

products are designed to be the safest, most comfortable and practical you can find, combining passion, quality and style with the latest technological advances. For more information phone the number above or visit their website.

Britax Childcare
Tel: 1300 303 330
email: custserv@britax.com.au
website: www.britax.com.au

Britax Childcare Pty Ltd is home to leading Australian juvenile brand Safe-n-Sound. In recent years Safe-n-Sound has won an Australian design award for its unique range of Safe-n-Sound AHR child car seats which feature the Active Head Restraint technology. Safe-n-Sound is a terrific choice when it comes to choosing your child's car seat.

Britax Childcare
Tel: 1300 303 330
email: custserv@britax.com.au
website: www.britax.com.au

Britax Childcare Pty Ltd is home to leading Australian juvenile brand Steelcraft. Steelcraft is at the forefront offering mums innovative products like the Strider DLX Travel System. Steelcraft is a terrific choice when it comes to choosing your child's travel system, stroller, portable cot, highchair and other nursery accessories. Visit the website or phone the number above for further information.

Buggypod
Tel: 1800 244 543
email: nurseryenquiries@funtastic.com.au
website: www.funtasticnursery.com.au

The perfect answer for parents who don't want a double stroller but whose first-born needs a safe comfortable ride from time to time. buggypod Smorph attaches easily to most A-frame strollers on the market, transforming it into a two-seater when needed, and folding up neatly when not. buggypod Smorph is sleek, black and gorgeous; with a new soft concertina fold footrest, luxury seat pad and a 5-point harness. Suitable from 6 months to 15 kilograms. Visit the website or phone the number above for further information.

CNP Brands
Tel: 1300 667 137
email: info@cnpbrands.com.au
website: www.cnpbrands.com.au

Natures Purest is a range of organic bedding, babywear and gift items made from 100% organically grown naturally coloured cotton jersey and produced without the use of dyes or chemical pesticides. The cotton buds grow in natural shades of cream, brown and green and are processed to make the most wonderful natural and pure fabrics. Another natural fibre used in the Natures Purest range is bamboo. Unrivalled as one of the most luxurious materials, bamboo handles like silk, but performs like cotton so is extremely soft yet breathable and cool. The range is packaged in attractive recycled boxes and make a perfect gift for a newborn. Natures Purest is available nationally at David Jones stores and selected nursery retailers. Visit website www.cnpbrands.com.au or contact their Customer Service on 1300 667 137 for your nearest stockist.

CNP Brands
Tel: 1300 667 137
email: info@cnpbrands.com.au
website: www.cnpbrands.com.au

The Newborn-to-Toddler Furniture Range by Fisher-Price® combines a contemporary look with practicality to accommodate a baby's changing needs. Manufactured to the highest quality, this innovative range has been specially designed with your baby in mind to create a stylish nursery that is a sensible and safe choice. Available at leading nursery specialist retailers.

CNP Brands
Tel: 1300 667 137
email: info@cnpbrands.com.au
website: www.cnpbrands.com.au

CNP Brands is a leading producer and distributor of quality nursery furniture and equipment. Passionately dedicated to safety and quality, CNP Brands enjoys an unrivalled reputation for supplying superior products and service. With a philosophy of combining safety and quality with innovative design and stylish appearance, products are easy-to-use, functional and fashionable. Its products are available at leading department stores and selected nursery specialist retailers.

CNP Brands
Tel: 1300 667 137
email: info@cnpbrands.com.au
website: www.cnpbrands.com.au

Bébé Care is a premium quality nursery brand recently launched by CNP Brands, a leading producer and distributor of quality nursery furniture and quipment. With a focus on superior materials and onstruction, the range features innovative products with exceptional styling specifically designed to appeal o discerning parents-to-be. The equipment range ncludes strollers, rockers, highchairs and travel cots, while the furniture range includes quality timber cots nd furniture pieces such as toy boxes, change tables, bookcases and chest of drawers all designed to create an ttractive and co-ordinated nursery. To view the full Bébé Care range visit www.cnpbrands.com.au or phone or more information.

CNP Brands
el: 1300 667 137
mail: info@cnpbrands.com.au
website: www.cnpbrands.com.au

Celebrated around the world as the inventor of the original buggy (stroller), Maclaren revolutionised the baby transport market with its unique compact and ghtweight umbrella-fold stroller. Since manufacturing s first buggy four decades ago, Maclaren has continued o focus on product innovation and engineering ngenuity to produce a premium line of quality baby roducts. Designed to provide convenience for families uring travel and in every day life, all Maclaren strollers eature lightweight aluminium chassis, compact mbrella-fold, lockable swivel wheels, shopping basket nd a removable seat for easy cleaning. To view the full ange available in Australia visit www.cnpbrands.com.au r phone for more information.

CNP Brands
el: 1300 667 137
mail: info@cnpbrands.com.au
website: www.cnpbrands.com.au

BabyDan by CNP Brands creates a safe environment for your child with its range of safety gates. Uncompromising n child safety, BabyDan is uncompromising on the quality, workmanship, materials and production of their afety gate range. The range has a gate model to fit any zed opening and offers a choice of pressure-mounted ates which requires no fixing to a wall, and screw-mounted gates for larger and more unusual opening idths. The BabyDan Baby Den is a uniquely flexible ate which can be used in many ways including as a aypen, a safety gate, a hearth gate or even as a room ivider. The BabyDan safety gate range is available at elected nursery specialist retailers. Visit their website at ww.cnpbrands.com.au or contact their Customer ervice on 1300 667 137 for more information.

NP Brands
el: 1300 667 137
mail: info@cnpbrands.com.au
website: www.cnpbrands.com.au

Lascal®, the manufacturer of the world's most famous stroller accessories the Buggy Board™ and Kiddy Board™, has introduced its new range into the Australian market. The new ride-on accessories offer the ultimate in comfort and convenience, and are available in a range of fun designs. Packed with ground-breaking design features, such as the advanced EASY-FIT™ connection system, designed to fit almost all travel systems and ideal for children aged two and up to 30kg, these boards are sure to impress. Lascal® – The art of moving forward™.

Danish by Design
Tel: (03) 9585 5944
website: www.danishbydesign.com.au
The Leander Cradle sways gently with baby's kicks just like in the womb and is a gorgeous stylish nest for the first 6 months. The Leander Bed is a beautiful, simple and functional cot which grows with the child. The Leander Bed follows the child's development while changing from cot to cot bed and finally to a junior bed. With one purchase you have 4 options in a single complete package.

Danish by Design
Tel: (03) 9585 5944
website: www.danishbydesign.com.au
Brand new to the Australian market, the Leander Chair offers an elegant, yet practical seating solution for your baby. The seat and foot rest are adjustable to suit the child's height and will follow the child into adulthood. The safety bar has two settings to suit baby's size. Visit www.danishbydesign.com.au for stockists.

Graco
Tel: 1800 003 178 or (03) 8787 3838
website: www.gracobaby.com
Graco is one of the world's best known and most trusted children's product companies. Graco is a Newell Rubbermaid company, with 1500 associates worldwide. Graco is dedicated and committed to designing and manufacturing top-quality products – products that inspire parents and babies alike. Today Graco continues its tradition of innovation, with products such as the patented advance comfort Air Booster Seat and the renowned Quattro Tour Duo Stroller. For information phone toll free 1800 003 178.

Humphrey's Corner
Tel: 1800 244 543
email: nurseryenquiries@funtastic.com.au
website: www.funtasticnursery.com.au

Let your baby's imagination grow with this gorgeous range from Humphrey's Corner. Humphrey's Corner brings to life the characters from UK-author Sally Hunter's popular picture books. A complete range of baby products has been created to ensure your nursery is completely co-ordinated with the works of Humphrey's Corner. The range includes beautiful quality nursery furniture, bath and feeding plastics.

Resources

CHOOSING FURNITURE & EQUIPMENT

Nursery brands

IGC DOREL Pty Ltd

Tel: 1300 809 526
email: sales@igcdorel.com.au
website: www.bertini.com.au

bertini® is recognised by parents worldwide as offering innovative designs with superior features, quality and reliability. Each piece, whether it be a chic bertini stroller, luxurious manchester set or stylish wood cot, upholds the highest standard of style, simplicity and function which bertini® is renowned. Uniquely designed to suit your lifestyle needs, the versatile and easy to use bertini range will become part of your child's growing up. To view the latest range visit www.bertini.com.au or phone IGC Dorel's Customer Service team on 1300 809 526 for your nearest stockist.

IGC DOREL Pty Ltd

Tel: 1300 809 526
email: sales@igcdorel.com.au
website: www.quinny.com

Globally known for trend-setting European style and technology, Quinny® strollers are a magical addition for mum and baby. Quinny offers three outstanding products cleverly designed with features that mums and dads love. The Quinny Buzz is available in a 3 or 4 wheeler which unfolds itself automatically with no effort at all. The Buzz can be used with the Quinny Dreami Carry Cot which is easily attached or removed from the stroller frame. The Quinny Zapp is designed for wherever life takes you. The ultra compact 3D fold and lightweight frame is perfect for travelling. The ever-versatile and sporty Quinny Speedi is extremely manoeuvrable and stable, making it perfect for use in the city or anywhere outdoors. To view the latest range visit www.quinny.com or phone IGC Dorel's Customer Service team on 1300 809 526 for your nearest stockist.

IGC DOREL Pty Ltd

Tel: 1300 809 526
email: sales@igcdorel.com.au
website: www.motherschoice.com.au

Mother's Choice® has been providing Australian families with quality nursery products for over 35 years and is driven to provide safe, comfortable and fashionable products at an affordable price. Mother's Choice® offers the largest and most comprehensive range of nursery products in Australia including strollers, portacots, bouncers, rockers, wooden cots, manchester, car and booster seats, change tables and accessories. Available at Target, Kmart and speciality stores, Mother's Choice® meets the needs of parents today and helps make the job of parenting fun, safe and a little bit easier. To view the latest range visit www.motherschoice.com.au or phone IGC Dorel's Customer Service team on 1300 809 526 for your nearest stockist.

IGC DOREL Pty Ltd

Tel: 1300 809 526
email: sales@igcdorel.com.au
website: www.gosafe.com.au

When it comes to babies, safety is everything. GoSafe® sets itself apart from other car safety brands by not only meeting Australian Standards but championing new safety standards. Offering parents an unparalleled amount of peace of mind, GoSafe® booster cushions and booster seats come in a variety of styles and fabrics suitable for any contemporary car interior. To view the latest range visit www.gosafe.com.au or phone IGC Dorel's Customer Service team on 1300 809 526 for your nearest stockist.

IGC DOREL Pty Ltd

Tel: 1300 809 526
email: sales@igcdorel.com.au
website: www.safety1st.com

For decades, parents all over the world have placed their trust – and their children's safety - in Safety 1st® products. Instantly recognisable for innovation, expertise and commitment to quality, the Safety 1st® product range is as extensive as it is dependable: monitors, gates, bathtubs, car seats, infant health and grooming, and childproofing products for parents' peace of mind. Safety 1st® is available in all major retailer stores and leading nursery stores. To view the latest range visit www.safety1st.com or phone IGC Dorel's Customer Service team on 1300 809 526 for your nearest stockist.

IGC DOREL Pty Ltd

Tel: 1300 809 526
email: sales@igcdorel.com.au
website: www.ingoodcare.com.au

Designed with practicality in mind and of course durability, ZuZu® nursery products are guaranteed to keep both parent and baby happy. Available exclusively at Big W, the ZuZu® product range includes strollers, portacots, high chairs, rockers, and modern kids manchester perfect for any decorating style and budget. To view the latest range visit www.ingoodcare.com.au or phone IGC Dorel's Customer Service team on 1300 809 526 for your nearest stockist.

IGC DOREL Pty Ltd

Tel: 1300 809 526
email: sales@igcdorel.com.au
website: www.ingoodcare.com.au

When you combine industry-leading technologies from

Australia's iconic automotive brand Aunger with IGC Dorel's 35 years experience in child nursery manufacturing, the result is child and toddler car seats offering superior design considerations and uncompromised safety features. To view the latest range visit www.ingoodcare.com.au or phone IGC Dorel's Customer Service team on 1300 809 526 for your nearest stockist.

IGC DOREL Pty Ltd
Tel: 1300 809 526
email: sales@igcdorel.com.au
website: www.bootiq.com.au

Stylish yet practical, the Bootiq range of nursery equipment and furniture ensures your child is surrounded by comfort and safety. Ideal from birth all the way through to toddler years, Bootiq offers a range of super-light strollers, portacots, rockers and interchangeable bassinettes for real family living. Also available in the Bootiq collection is styled wood furniture and fashionably designed manchester to brighten your child's nursery or bedroom. To view the latest range visit www.bootiq.com.au or phone IGC Dorel's Customer Service team on 1300 809 526 for your nearest stockist.

Learning Curve Australia
Tel: (03) 9550 3600
email: service@rc2aust.com.au
website: www.rc2aust.com.au

The First Years range of products help parents keep their children healthy, happy and safe by offering products from feeding to playing and sleeping. Feeding and soothing products include the Take & Toss range of spill proof cups, bowls and spoons, booster seats and reclining feeding seats. The Play & Discovery products include unique toys and rattles including the popular 'Floating Friends teether" and "Rolling Giggle Pals". The Care & Safety products include hands-free safety gates, toilet training seats, bed rails, safe sleepers and monitors. The First Years also offers licensed products in Winnie the Pooh, Thomas and Friends, Cars and Princess. Visit the website or phone the number above for further information.

Mako Marketing
Tel: (02) 9453 9277
website: www.babymall.com.au

The Phil & Teds new range of inline buggies offer versatility and features such as adjustable handle height, swivel or lockable front wheel and a quick-folding system. All stroller models suit from newborn to five years and are upgradable to a 'doubles' buggy later. Four positions in total: newborn, toddler, siblings and then doubles. Phone the number above for further information.

Mountain Buggy Australia
Tel: (03) 9570 2833
email: info@mountainbuggy.com.au
website: www.mountainbuggy.com

Mountain Buggy is a leading brand in Australia for three wheeled strollers. Able to carry a child from newborn to four years of age, its sturdy aluminium frame and all weather fabrics will tackle the toughest terrain. It is lightweight and easy to push with a style to suit every family whether your interests are shopping or hiking. Options include: carrycot convertibility, 'Kiddy Board' compatibility for a second child and there are also options for children with disabilities. Safe, strong and reliable buggies to last you a lifetime.

Outlook Australia
Tel: (03) 9817 2311
email: outlooktm@bigpond.com
website: www.outlooktm.com

auto-shade™ is the multi-fitting sun shade for cars brought to you by Outlook, the specialists in sun protection accessories for babies. Available in two shapes that fit most vehicles, rounded or square, auto-shade™ is easily fitted to the majority of 4 door vehicles. auto-shade™ offers UV and sun glare protection, UPF 10. Car windows can be raised or lowered with the shade in place providing ventilation while still maintaining protection from the glare.

Peg Perego
Tel: 1300 131 477
email: info@nurseryelegance.com.au
website: www.pegperego.com.au

Peg Perego is a global leader in the design and production of infant and juvenile products. Peg Perego has taken children out and about for over 50 years, in their carriages, strollers, car seats and high chairs. These unique and high quality products are designed and manufactured in Italy, using the latest technology and materials to meet all safety requirements. All products are tested to ensure they pass stringent Australian Standards requirements. Products can be found in major department stores and independent specialty shops. For more information phone Nursery Elegance on the toll free number 1300 131 477.

Philips AVENT
Tel: 1300 364 474
email: inquiry@avent.com.au
website: www.avent.com.au

Rest assured that your baby is content when you're not in the room with the Philips AVENT range of DECT baby monitors. Using digital technology you can be sure of a secure, guaranteed zero interference connection between you and your baby so that you can hear the slightest murmur if they wake. Available in three different models starting from $149.95 these monitors are easy to use and will give you peace of mind as they look after your baby's well-being with room temperature and humidity sensors. For more information or stockists details, phone the customer service line on 1300 364 474.

Resources

CHOOSING FURNITURE & EQUIPMENT

Nursery brands

➡ Pram, stroller & jogger accessories

Playgro Pty Ltd

Tel: (03) 8558 2000
email: sales@playgro.com
website: www.booninc.com

Boon Inc. creates innovative and stylish products that help make parents' lives easier. Often combining multiple functions, Boon products are designed with clean, modern styling, appealing to both parents and children. Available in Australia is the Boon Flair High Chair, Flo, Potty Bench, Frog Pod and an innovative new range of feeding products. Boon products are available from selected retailers and specialty baby stores nationwide.

Playgro Pty Ltd

Tel: (03) 8558 2000
email: sales@playgro.com
website: www.playgro.com

Playgro now makes travelling out and about with your little one easier with a range of innovative and convenient on-the-go products. The comprehensive range includes an in-car bottle warmer, car sunshades, baby rear view mirror, stroller bag, stroller rain cover and mosquito net and the Bag It – a plastic bag dispenser that hangs conveniently from the stroller. Not to mention the ingenious Kids ID Band, a simple yet effective wristband that makes finding your lost child quicker and easier. Available from major retailers and specialty baby stores nationwide.

Quicksmart

Tel: 1800 244 543
email: nurseryenquiries@funtastic.com.au
website: www.quicksmartbaby.com.au or
www.funtasticnursery.com.au

Each and every QuickSmart product is designed to be 100% portable, easy to use and lightweight so they really are a practical, convenient solution. It's the unique QuickSmart folding mechanisms that means the strollers and nursery furniture can be completely transformed and tucked away into a compact, lightweight, portable pack. The QuickSmart backpack stroller boasts a revolutionary fold away system: just six easy steps sees the QuickSmart stroller transform from a three-wheel stroller into a compact size for easy storage. With its unique patented rotating and snap lock mechanisms, the handles, seat and wheel struts swivel and fold in, reducing the overall size of the stroller to less than one third its original size. Folded up, the

QuickSmart slips into a backpack (just 56cm x 28cm x 27cm) and all up weighs in at just on 4kg. Its compact size when folded means the QuickSmart is incredibly convenient for storing or travelling. It fits easily into the boot of the smallest car and can even be stored in the overhead luggage compartment of planes, trains and buses. The QuickSmart easy fold stroller can be completely transformed in seconds to an astonishing compact size that easily fits into the boot of the smallest of cars, and neatly stored when not in use. Weighing only 6kg, the QuickSmart easy fold is easy to lift and effortless to carry. No assembly required, the easy fold stroller is ready to use straight out of the box. The QuickSmart travel cot folds and unfolds in seconds, packs away flat but is still sturdy with an alloy frame. It is the perfect lightweight addition to your transportable baby kit. Suitable from birth, the travel cot is great for quick set ups at friends houses or that last minute weekend getaway.

Sesame Beginnings

website: http://archive.sesameworkshop.org/
sesamebeginnings/new/

Sesame Beginnings is an infant brand with a range of furniture, manchester, and nursery accessories encouraging an environment of nurturing and learning between parent and baby. Baby versions of the Sesame Street characters, along with parenting tips, helps make bedtime and nursery time quality time. For more information on Sesame Beginnings product and stockists contact: Dryen (03) 8558 2222; CNP Brands (03) 9394 3000 or visit www.childcareproducts.com.au.

Silver Cross Australia

Tel: 1300 166 600
email: hello@silvercross.com.au
website: www.silvercross.com.au

Silver Cross is passionate about offering parents the highest levels of quality, baby comfort and safety with chic, contemporary design. Beginning life in 1877, Silver Cross prams became the favoured choice of the royal family. Now in the 21st century, the Silver Cross range is ever popular with celebrities – the ultimate baby accessory. Visit www.silvercross.com.au for more details.

The Kinder Kompany Pty Ltd

Tel: 1300 661 060
email: info@kinderkot.com.au
website: www.kinderkot.com.au

The KinderKot is a foldable, lightweight, 'go anywhere' travelcot. It is ideal for visiting friends, holidays, camping, airport stopovers and picnics. Designed in Europe, the KinderKot weighs only 3kgs and packs away into a shoulder bag no bigger than a daypack. The KinderKot assembles itself. Simply take it out of its bag and it will expand into its final structure. The KinderKot comes with self-inflating mattress, sleeping bag and carry bag. Made with 50% UV fabric and fully meshed, it's great for the Australian climate. For your nearest retailer visit www.kinderkot.com.au.

The Product Store Pty Ltd
Tel: (07) 3857 0691
email: info@theproductstore.com.au
website: www.theproductstore.com.au

The Baby Dream Machine™ is a pram rocker which has a cyclic and smooth continuous motion which simulates the gentle rocking motion first experienced by baby in the womb. The Baby Dream Machine™ allows either the front or rear wheels of your stroller/pram to rest upon it, before stimulating the pram to motion. Its compact design makes it ideal for safe, easy storage or taking away. Visit the website for more information.

Tomy
Tel: 1800 244 543
email: nurseryenquiries@funtastic.com.au
website: www.funtasticnursery.com.au

TOMY® TOMY is the respected nursery brand for baby carriers and baby monitors. TOMY Baby Carriers offer a practical and stylish solution to juggling a busy life with a new baby. TOMY is the established leader for baby monitors and offers a number of monitors designed to suit the particular demands of your home and your lifestyle.

PORTABLE HIGH CHAIRS

NATIONAL

Danish by Design
Tel: (03) 9585 5944
email: info@danishbydesign.com.au
website: www.danishbydesign.com.au

The HandySitt is the ultimate in portable high chairs as it folds flat and has no weight restrictions. It attaches easily to dining chairs so your child can sit at the table for meals and play, both at home and out. Suits children from 7 months to 4.5 years. Visit the website www.danishbydesign.com.au for stockists.

Ethman Enterprises Pty Ltd
Tel: 1300 725 876
email: info@ethman.com.au
website: www.ethman.com.au

Totseat is your perfect travel high chair and the only adaptable portable high chair. Simple to use and completely adjustable, it fits high-backed, low-backed, knobbly, open backed and even rounded chairs. Totseat is made of Oeko-Tex approved robust polycotton in funky colours, is fully machine washable and comes in a compact travel pouch. Perfect for keeping in your change bag. Totseat's design and safety credentials have won a host of awards and is endorsed by the Child Accident Prevention Trust. Visit the website or phone the number above for further information.

Little Beetle
Tel: (03) 9579 1036
email: info@littlebeetle.com.au
website: www.littlebeetle.com.au

The Little Beetle Baby Chair is a fabric baby chair that is machine-washable, folds into a built-in pocket and is designed to fit on most dining/kitchen chairs. Visit www.littlebeetle.com.au for more information.

Piccolo Innovations
Tel: (08) 9307 1839 or 0405 797 551
email: morna@piccolo-innovations.com
website: www.piccolo-innovations.com

The Hauck highchair teaches your child to sit with the correct posture from day one, allows your child to sit with you at the table, it grows with your child, and it is easy to clean and an excellent design. The highchair means stress-free mealtimes. There is also a money back guarantee. Phone the number above or visit the website for further details.

Possumbilities
Tel: (02) 6684 1760
email: leisagav@bigpond.net.au

The original Go Anywhere Chair transforms a regular chair into a padded, secure and safe highchair. It also fits most supermarket trolleys to safely secure baby in. Perfect for travelling, camping, restaurants, grandparents place and home. When not in use it folds neatly back into its attached bag. For frazzle-free meals anywhere, carry the Go Anywhere Chair.

Snazzy Baby
Tel: 1300 650 115
email: info@snazzybaby.com.au
website: www.snazzybaby.com.au

My Baby's Own Deluxe Travel Chair is a soft portable high chair seat for babies and toddlers that is very secure, with a unique non-slip base, four point restraint and buckle fasteners that outperform Velcro straps. Truly a portable item it rolls into its own attached storage bag and weighs only 190 grams. It fits on almost any chair, even outdoor furniture, with the added advantage it can be used in shopping trolleys to keep your baby safe while you are shopping. Visit the website or phone the number above for further information.

PRAM, STROLLER & JOGGER ACCESSORIES

NATIONAL

BuggyRug
Tel: 0411 516 241
email: info@buggyrug.com.au
website: www.buggyrug.com.au

Keep your baby snug in the buggy with an Australian made BuggyRug. A snug footmuff, pram sleeping bag and pram liner in one product. Made from quality fabrics that are both luxurious and practical. Visit www.buggyrug.com.au for more information.

Resources

CHOOSING FURNITURE & EQUIPMENT

Pram, stroller & jogger accessories

➜ Stores online

Mums on the Move
Tel: 0423 022 408
website: www.mumsonthemove.com.au

Do you like to walk when it is chilly outside? Is keeping your child warm in the pram a task? Mums on the Move have created an easy-care machine-washable PRAM POUCH™. There is a choice of various polar fleece colours surrounded by corduroy. The PRAM POUCH™ has five openings for your safety harness and front zip access.

Outlook Australia
Tel: (03) 9817 2311
email: outlooktm@bigpond.com
website: www.outlooktm.com

Outlook® pram-snug is a two piece zip-up snuggle bag for use in prams/strollers/joggers. During winter months the infant is encased in a warm cocoon of polar fleece, and during the summer months the removable pure woollen liner can be used on its own. The polar fleece outer can also be used as a playmat when you are out and about and also helps keep your pram clean. The travel-comfy is a versatile and good value 100% woollen reversible pram liner available with either a polar fleece or 100% cotton quilted backing. Both products are fully machine washable and available at all good nursery outlets or phone for your nearest stockist.

Outlook Australia
Tel: (03) 9817 2311
website: www.outlooktm.com

Help protect your baby from harmful UV rays, wind, glare and insects with the original Outlook® shade-a-babe. The shade incorporates a UPF50+ sun visor and inbuilt glare guard and provides from 70-99% UVR protection. Uniquely designed to be multi-fitting, and with easy front zip access, the shade-a-babe can be adjusted to fit most models of prams and joggers. Available in twin styles and offers excellent airflow and vision for baby. Available in black and new coloured drop down visors.

Outlook Australia
Tel: (03) 9817 2311
website: www.outlooktm.com

The solar-shade™ offers up to 99% protection from harmful UV rays, considerably extending the shade cover offered to your child when you are on the move. The solar-shade™ protects eyes from sun glare, and it looks great too. Available in black, navy, cherry, sand, fuchsia and royal.

Outlook Australia
Tel: (03) 9817 2311
email: outlooktm@bigpond.com
website: www.outlooktm.com

Give your child a comfortable pram ride with the Cotton Pram liner. With provision for a 5-point safety harness and fully reversible this liner protects your pram from spills and is universally fitting. Available in pink, sky, red, sand and black.

Pepi's Baby Products Pty Ltd
Tel: 0434 945 912
email: dee@joeyspouch.com.au
website: www.joeyspouch.com.au

Forget about shoes and blankets being dropped or dummies and rattles being lost. Keep your little one snug in their pram with the original handmade pram liner/bag, designed and made by a mum with your child's comfort and mum's practicality (and sanity) in mind.

Toi Design Limited
Tel: 1800 051 054
email: sales@toidesignz.com
website: www.toidesignz.com

Keep your new baby protected from the weather. The unique waterproof Toi Cape was designed in 1995 by new mums so that they could stay active. It goes over the car capsule, the buggy or the backpack. When baby gets older and stands up it becomes their first raincoat. The Toi cape is soft to touch and easy to wash and use. You won t wake a sleeping baby to get it on or off. For more details visit www.toidesignz.com.

REPAIR SERVICES

NEW SOUTH WALES

Sydney Luggage Centre
1147 Botany Road
Mascot NSW 2020
Tel: (02) 9669 6381
email: info@sydneyluggagecentre.com.au
website: www.sydneyluggagecentre.com.au

Sydney Luggage Centre offers a pram repair service to the general public. They service brands such as Bugaboo, Phil & Ted, Mountain Buggy, Maclaren, Steelcraft, Valco, Peg Perego, Childcare and more. The centre also has a pram upholstery shampoo service. Visit the website for further details.

SLEEPSUITS & SLEEPING BAGS

NATIONAL

Bambini International
Tel: 1300 557 691
email: trade@bambiniinternational.com.au
website: www.bambiniinternational.com.au

The multi-award winning grobag® baby sleeping bags

are designed to ensure a safe and comfortable night's sleep for your baby and peace of mind for parents. Not just a cold weather product, grobag® has developed a sleeping system that means babies will be safe and comfortable all year round. In four sizes, three different togs (warmths) and a beautiful array of fabrics there is a grobag® baby sleeping bag for every child no matter what the weather from birth to 6 years.

Bambini Warehouse

Tel: (02) 9558 2752
email: office@thedreambag.com.au
website: www.thedreambag.com.au

The Dream Bag is a UK-designed baby sleeping bag that provides babies and toddlers with a comfortable and safe sleeping environment. Distributed in Australia by Bambini Warehouse, The Dream Bag has a soft 100% cotton lining, full-length side zip for easy use and comes in three sizes and weights for all-year-round comfort. You will love the embroidered designs. A better sleep for baby means a better sleep for you. Priced from $35.99. To view the full range visit www.thedreambag.com.au.

Safe T Sleep International

Tel: +64 9 299 7589 or +64 21 73 6645
email: office@safetsleep.com
website: www.safetsleep.com

Invented by a mother, the Safe T Sleep Sleepwrap® has become hugely popular among parents and caregivers who want to keep their baby in a safe, secure back or side sleeping position. The Sleepwrap® is a versatile, snug swaddling wrap, allowing comfortable, natural movement for newborn to three years plus. Comfort and security to help keep baby's face and head uncovered and safely off the tummy while alternate positioning also helps ensure a nice head shape. The Sleepwraps have been widely tested by health professionals, caregivers and have been subject to hospital clinical trials. Safe T Sleep Sleepwrap®'s offer convenience as well as safety, as they fold down small enough to fit into a bag or glovebox and can be used as an alternative to a portable cot. For those babies who sleep extensively on their back Safe T Sleep has also developed a little Headwedge – 100% cotton cover over a triangle foam strip. Used best in conjunction with a Safe T Sleep™ Sleepwrap® to assist with positioning baby's head on alternate sides to help prevent flat or misshapen heads.

STORES ONLINE: FURNITURE & EQUIPMENT

NATIONAL

Babeaze

Tel: (02) 4946 2807
email: enquiries@babeaze.com.au
website: www.babeaze.com.au

www.babeaze.com.au specialise in innovative parent-invented products that solve your parenting problems. They focus on practical and affordable solutions and products include the Snack & Play Travel Tray, Potty Mitts, Mac and Cool Cooling Plate and the Baby Safe Feeder. Visit their website to see their full range.

Babies Galore

Tel: 1300 99 BABY (2229)
email: sales@babiesgalore.com.au
website: www.babiesgalore.com.au

Babies Galore Online has everything you need for your baby in a convenient and friendly format for those parents that are pressed for time. Shop 24 hours a day, 7 days a week. They have a wide range of products to choose from, an interactive registry, secure payment and much, much more. Log onto the website for more information (and to find store locations in NSW & QLD). Delivery not available to NT.

Baby on a Budget

Tel: (08) 9456 0700
website: www.babyonabudget.com.au

Baby on a Budget Online is an informative and specialised nursery product site with online sales. The whole range can be viewed and purchased with customer service within twelve hours. Small items can be delivered Australia wide and larger items shipped only within Western Australia. Gift vouchers available.

Baby Zone (Aust) Pty Ltd

Tel: (02) 4228 4288
website: www.babyzonedirect.com.au

www.babyzonedirect.com.au stocks all the leading brands in nursery furniture, prams, car seats, high chairs, safety products and toys. They distribute Australia wide at competitive rates.

Babycare Nursery

Tel: (02) 9724 6191
website: www.babycarenursery.com.au

Babycare Nursery pride themselves in providing customers with the best service and the lowest prices. They can take care of all of your baby needs with an extensive selection of products such as cots, car seats, prams, strollers, playpens, monitors, steam sterilisers, breastpumps and much more. All products come with a full manufacture warranty. If you can't find what you want, phone or email babycare@optusnet.com.au. Shopping is simple and easy at Babycare Nursery. (Delivery not available to WA or NT.)

Babyology

Tel: 0404 064 452
website: www.babyology.com.au

Babyology gives you daily bite-size doses of information on unique and fabulous mother and baby products from around the globe, so you can stay up-to-date with what's hip. There's also a forum where you can chat about baby gear with other parents, and all the must-have facts to help you choose and compare major products.

Resources

CHOOSING FURNITURE & EQUIPMENT

Stores online

babyshop

Tel: 1800 222 437 or 1800 BABIES
email: mail@babyshop.com.au
website: www.babyshop.com.au

Experience the convenience of shopping from home with one of Australia's first online baby stores. With experience online since 1998 and hundreds of products to choose from, babyshop stocks a variety of well known brands, as well as featuring many exclusive and hard to find items. Departments include: Bathtime & Care, Bedtime & Nursery, Clothing, Feeding & Accessories, Out & About and Playtime & Development. (NSW readers can also visit their retail store at 276 Brunker Road, Adamstown.)

Bubba Bling

Tel: 0414 455 348
email: info@bubbabling.com.au
website: www.bubbabling.com.au

Bubba Bling is a baby and toddler e-boutique specialising in funky bedding and furniture, nursery decor and artwork, accessories and gifts. All Bubba Bling products have been chosen to capture young imaginations from beautifully themed bedding sets, modern furniture, gorgeous canvas artwork and wall decals to bright and funky children's accessories and designer stationery. Visit www.bubbabling.com.au for more information.

Bubbalicious Blankies

Tel: 0427 762 774
email: mitch252@hotmail.com
website: www.bubbaliciousblankies.com.au

Bubbalicious Blankies produce top quality, personalised products for the special people in your life. They offer a huge selection of products including blankets, bunny rugs, towels, art smocks, reader bags, placemats, Santa sacks and stockings and much more. Visit their site to see the full range. Each item is embroidered individually.

Chris' Little Treasures

Tel: (03) 9404 2495
email: enquiry@chrislittletreasures.com.au
website: www.chrislittletreasures.com.au

All of Chris' Little Treasures are handcrafted and beautifully finished pieces of furniture that are functional, bright and designed to stimulate children. Perfect for either a child's bedroom or play area, Chris' have a huge choice of furniture products and accessories.

All made to last, they use only the finest finishes to ensure they are with you right through the toughest childhood. Products are all Australian made and designed. The products include table and chair settings, toy bins, toy chests, Christening boxes, keepsake boxes, lamps, height charts, bookends, mirrors and much more.

Funky Kids

Tel: (08) 9284 0051
email: info@funkykids.com.au
website: www.funkykids.com.au

Funky Kids stocks beautiful white bedroom furniture which is made in Western Australia and has a wide variety of products to decorate your child's room. They also stock fabulous brands in clothing as well as a wide variety of gifts, toys and personalised products. Visit www.funkykids.com.au.

gear4baby

email: info@gear4baby.com.au
website: www.gear4baby.com.au

Gear4baby is a family owned and operated business constantly on the lookout for new baby gear to make your life out and about less complicated. gear4baby has carefully selected baby gear and accessories that every parent needs making sure they are of the highest quality. Their range of nappy bags and wallets, slings and carriers, pram and travel accessories are stylish, practical and affordable. Visit the website for more details.

Hello Charlie

Tel: 1300 725 876
email: info@hellocharlie.com.au
website: www.hellocharlie.com.au

Hello, Charlie! specialises in eco-friendly, natural, organic and non toxic products for babies, children and home. The site offers lots of practical and stylish products that you will use over and over, as well as everyday items like eco-friendly cloth and disposable nappies, feeding products, clothing and bedding, toiletries, pregnancy and breastfeeding products, wooden toys, baby carriers, and things to get you out and about. Visit www.hellocharlie.com.au for more details.

House of Bambini

Tel: (07) 5479 6590
email: houseofbambini@yahoo.com.au
website: www.houseofbambini.com.au

House of Bambini supplies gorgeous children's bedroom furniture, children's bedlinen, bedroom decor, wallpaper and artworks as well as special gifts. Visit www.houseofbambini.com.au for more information.

Jack and Sunny Time

Tel: (07) 4154 8951
email: sales@jackandsunnytime.com.au
website: www.jackandsunnytime.com.au

Jack and Sunny Time sell locally-made quality table and chairs for children. There are two sizes available and all sets are handmade from 100% recycled timber, finished with gorgeous bright water-base colours and a high-gloss interior-exterior varnish containing no lead. All edges are rounded and the furniture is weighted for appeal and safety. Feet are padded and tables have an umbrella hole making them versatile pieces of furniture, designed to last. Australia wide delivery. Visit the website for further details.

Just for Bubs
Tel: 1300 658 490
email: jfb@justforbubs.com.au
website: www.justforbubs.com.au

Just for Bubs delivers unique and practical products for newborn babies. Through constant and thorough research they have selected popular, award-winning products overseas that are not readily available within Australia. Whether it's assistance with sleeping, feeding, speech/learning delays or simply transitioning from lying to sitting they have products to make parenting a whole lot easier. Just For Bubs also offer highly personalised products and the most gorgeous keepsakes to capture the angel that is your new baby.

Kalamazoo Kidz
Tel: 1300 887 956
email: sales@kalamazookidz.com.au
website: www.kalamazookidz.com.au

Kalamazoo Kidz offers a classic range of fun and imaginative children's products that will leave you wishing you were a child again. Specifically designed for toddlers and young children, Kalamazoo Kidz furniture, gifts and homewares feature timeless denim, delightful ginghams and stripes. Visit the website for further information.

kiddysac
Tel: 0412 077 528
email: info@kiddysac.com.au
website: www.kiddysac.com.au

Kiddysac are bright, colourful bags and storage solutions, perfectly designed for the youngest child through to 7 years. Kiddysac focuses on bright block colours, accentuated with fun designs like dinosaurs, pirates, princesses and monkeys. Made from 100% cotton drill, they are both durable and washable. Kiddysac bags are perfect to take to kindy, daycare, swimming, and the beach or just out and about. The range includes purses, pencil cases, toiletry bags, mini handbags, drawstring bags, backpacks, swim bags and wall pockets.

Kountry Kidz
Tel: (02) 6654 3006
email: kountry_kidz@bigpond.com
website: www.freewebs.com/especiallymade

Kountry Kidz makes gorgeous baby bedding and clothing, all handmade. Visit their website for further details.

Look Under the Mulberry Bush
Tel: (03) 5332 5725
email: info@underthemulberrybush.com.au
website: www.underthemulberrybush.com.au

At Look Under the Mulberry Bush you will find an array of unique, beautiful, children's clothing (0000 to 10), toys, accessories, furniture, bedding and gifts by independent designers and unique small businesses. Learn about their story, understand the creative journey and buy directly online. Shopping is secure, convenient and enjoyable with various search options available. New listings by the designer/creator always welcome. See www.underthemulberrybush.com.au for information and to join the e-newsletter.

Minimee Babies & Kids
Tel: (02) 9569 2000
email: info@minimee.com.au
website: www.minimee.com.au

Minimee can create a new baby package matching your budget and style with a bulk discount upfront. After your furniture/essentials purchase, you automatically become a VIP member and get 10% lifetime discount on all products. Offering a great range, service and prices, items include nursery furniture, prams, car seats, baby essentials, linen, fashion, toys and gifts all available online at www.minimee.com.au.

Moochie-Moo
Tel: (07) 3841 0194
email: info@moochiemoo.com
website: www.moochiemoo.com

moochiemoo.com offers a range of products not found on everyday shop shelves. Funky ID wristbands, stunning children's furniture and bedroom accessories, gorgeous night lights, Decorate My Room products and unique imported gifts and toys. Extensive research and planning has allowed them to bring you some wonderful quality products from all across the globe. The range of products is constantly updated.

My First Nursery
Tel: 0402 269 636
email: support@myfirstnursery.com
website: www.myfirstnursery.com

At My First Nursery, a web-based business, you can furnish your baby's nursery with elegant pieces of furniture and decor, stock up on essentials such as baby baths, cots, changers, cot mattresses, strollers or even travelling food bags. They offer savings to customers and ship anywhere in Australia. Visit the website for further information.

Natural Form
Tel: 0414 451 250
email: info@naturalform.com.au
website: www.naturalform.com.au

Natural Form offer value for money with their top quality, organic and natural products for baby, child, mother and the home. The range includes baby skin care, bath time products, clothing, gifts, health care products and more. Phone or visit the website for further details.

Resources

CHOOSING FURNITURE & EQUIPMENT

Stores online ➜ Stores retail

Nursing Angel

Tel: (02) 9874 8840
email: info@nursingangel.com.au
website: www.nursingangel.com.au

Nursing Angel is one of Australia's leading online stores specialising in breastfeeding products and baby carriers. Hundreds of products are available including local brands, overseas bestsellers and specialty items. Everything from breast pumps and breastfeeding accessories to nursingwear and baby carriers (largest online range in Australia). Great prices, discount shipping, free gift with purchase offers and a resident lactation consultant who writes a fantastic breastfeeding Q&A page.

Pinkietoes Pty Ltd

Tel: 0432 485 385
email: enquiry@pinkietoes.com.au
website: www.pinkietoes.com.au

Pinkietoes was started in 2007 by two mothers who appreciated the style and quality of international products that are hard to find within the Australian market place. Pinkietoes Pty Ltd sell award-winning Happy BUGU baby and toddler products ranging from bottles and skincare products to children's clothing and strollers and carriers. Most items are exclusive to Pinkietoes' online store. Wholesale enquiries are also welcome.

Shop At Home Catalogue

Tel: (02) 9453 9246
website: www.babymall.com.au

The Shop-At-Home Online catalogue enables you to experience the convenience and savings of home internet shopping from eleven product categories, covering many new and expectant parents' needs.

Totally Mums and Bubs

Tel: 0431 965 113
email: natalie@totallymumsandbubs.com.au
website: www.totallymumsandbubs.com.au

Totally Mums and Bubs has everything for mums and babies delivered to your door. This is an internet store for mums and babies specialising in clothing, skincare, slings (including Peanut Shell), ISOKI nappy bags, Change Mat Clutches and Petite travellers, things for mealtime, splashtime and sleeptime, cloth nappies, training pants and accessories, gift packs and many things to make your life that little bit easier with a baby or toddler.

UrbanBaby.com.au

Tel: 1300 882 991
email: hello@urbanbaby.com.au
website: www.urbanbaby.com.au

The UrbanBaby site is dedicated to providing the most stylish, practical and innovative products and truly useful information for pregnancy, parents and everything baby. Visit UrbanBaby for exclusive UrbanBaby products, the full Baby Einstein and Brilliant Baby ranges, fantastic wraps, the Hipseat by Hippychick, organic cotton baby clothes, gift cards and much more.

www.kids-things.com.au

Tel: (03) 9571 2596
email: kidsthings@iprimus.com.au
website: www.kids-things.com.au

www.kids-things.com.au sells a great range of Grobags, award-winning nappy bags, Merino Kids Go Go Sleeping Bags as well as quality baby wear, baby gifts and children's clothing. Visit the website for more information.

STORES PRE-LOVED & DISCOUNTED: FURNITURE & EQUIPMENT

NATIONAL

Baby & Kids Market

Tel: 1300 554 476
email: info@babykidsmarket.com.au
website: www.babykidsmarket.com.au

The Baby & Kids Market offers the biggest range of quality pre-loved baby and kids goods in Australia. Running for over five years, there are now markets in all main cities and also regional hubs. From toys to books and clothes to shoes this market has it all. The Baby & Kids Market also offers some fantastic handmade and wholesale baby and kids' goods at bargain prices. Plus free kids entertainment as well. Visit www.babykidsmarket.com.au for dates and locations.

VICTORIA

Baby Second Heaven

106–116 Walker Street
Dandenong VIC 3175
Tel: (03) 9769 2366
email: bsh@bigpond.net.au
website: www.babysecondheaven.com.au

Baby Second Heaven sells quality pre-loved and new baby goods. There are also factory seconds and samples, pram repairs and service and discounts on bulk buys. All major brands are stocked and all at extremely cheap prices.

Baby Touch Outlet

82 Grange Road
Alphington VIC 3078
Tel: (03) 9499 8436
email: outlet@babytouch.com.au

website: www.babytouch.com.au

Baby Touch Factory Outlet is staffed by experienced women who can assist you with all your enquiries and purchases. The outlet has a great range of new, discontinued and second Baby Touch manchester, accessories and toys complimented by nappy bags and strollers from Little Company. The complete Zoom Zoom Kidsline range is up to 50% off or more plus they have a great selection of quality handmade smocked dresses, knitted jumpers, beautifully embroidered blankets and soft toys galore. Open Wednesday to Saturday 9.30am to 4.30pm.

Caroline Chisholm Society
41 Park Street
Moonee Ponds VIC 3039
Tel: 1800 134 863 or (03) 9370 3933
email: info@carolinechisholmsociety.com.au
website: www.carolinechisholmsociety.com.au

The Caroline Chisholm Society Material Aid Service provides pre-loved nursery furniture, baby equipment, children's clothing, maternity clothing and nappies free of charge to families in need. The Society also provides counselling services including pregnancy and family support. If you have items to donate to help others in need please contact the Caroline Chisholm Society.

Creswick Woollen Mills
6 Roche Street
Hawthorn VIC 3122
Tel: (03) 9818 5055
email: info@creswickwool.com.au
website: www.creswickwool.com.au

Creswick Woollen Mills Factory Outlet will amaze you with its variety and quality of blankets, baby blankets, quilts, throws, craft fabric and yarn and remnant pieces all in 100% pure merino, 100% alpaca or merino wool blends. Mattress protectors, underblankets, microfibre quilts, pillows and picnic rugs are all sold direct to you at discounted prices. There is a large carpark adjacent to the shop and they are open 9.00am to 5.00pm Monday to Saturday and 10.00am to 5.00pm on Sundays.

Hand Me Downs
383 Forest Road
The Basin VIC 3154
Tel: (03) 9761 2855
website: www.handmedowns.com.au

Hand Me Downs has over 4000 square feet of all sorts of goodies, including clothes ranging from 0000 to teens, toys, shoes, linen, furniture – anything you can imagine for children. There is a kids' play area, change facilities, toilets and lots of parking.

Kids Weecycle Warehouse
3 Colin Avenue
Warrandyte VIC 3113
Tel: (03) 9844 3484
email: weecycle_warehouse@iprimus.com.au
website: www.kidsweecyclewarehouse.com.au

Kids Weecycle Warehouse specialise in good quality and affordable new and recycled baby and kids goods. Items include nursery furniture and accessories, children's clothing and shoes (including many brand name items), toys, books, puzzles, DVDs, videos, fitted cloth nappies, a large range of baby gifts and more. Hiring of goods is available (long or short term) and as well as a lay-by facility.

Pipsqueakz Recycle
Shop 8, 10 York Road
Mount Evelyn VIC 3796
Tel: (03) 9736 2211
website: www.pipsqueakz.com

Pipsqueakz Recycle has been in operation for more than seven years. This huge shop stocks an enormous and varied range of new and pre-owned items suitable for newborns through to pre-teens including nursery furniture, clothing, toys and much more. They are well known for strict standards on safety and cleanliness and all their pre-owned goods are in excellent condition and offer huge savings to buying new. They are open Monday to Friday 9.15am to 4.30pm and Saturday 10.00am to 2.00pm. They have EFTPOS facilities and great consignment rates.

NEW SOUTH WALES

Vicky's Pre-Loved Baby Shop
232 Railway Parade
Kogarah NSW 2217
Tel: (02) 9587 6016

Vicky's Pre-Loved Baby Shop specialises in pre-loved quality cots, bassinets, nursery goods, linen, clothes, toys and some maternity stock. They also have a selection of new items such as gift lines, baby knits and craft items. Phone enquiries and lay-by welcome.

WESTERN AUSTRALIA

Baby Warehouse
199 Abernethy Road
Belmont WA 6104
Tel: (08) 9477 5911

The Baby Warehouse is a unique baby store with new products at up to 50% off including furniture, clothing and everything else a baby needs. Their experienced staff are experts in child safety.

STORES RETAIL: FURNITURE & EQUIPMENT

NATIONAL

Babyco
Tel: 1300 130 999 Babyco Hotline
email: retail@babyco.com.au
website: www.babyco.com.au

Babyco stores have a diverse and large range of baby equipment, furniture and accessories from prams, strollers, cots, highchairs, car seats, door barriers, pram bags, monitors, manchester, swings, cot mattresses, change tables, wardrobes and much more. Friendly staff will assist with these important choices for your baby.

Resources

CHOOSING FURNITURE & EQUIPMENT

Stores retail

See the great range for yourself by contacting your nearest store on the Babyco Hotline 1300 130 999. (WA, TAS and NT do not have Babyco store locations however goods are available nationally via their website www.babyco.com.au.)

VICTORIA

Baby Bunting
669 Warrigal Road
East Bentleigh VIC 3165
Tel: (03) 9575 4444
1050 Burke Road
Balwyn VIC 3163
Tel: (03) 9817 1464
76 Maroondah Highway
Ringwood VIC 3134
Tel: (03) 9870 0766
6/98–108 Hampstead Road
Maribyrnong VIC 3032
Tel: (03) 9318 7444
430 Princes Highway
Narre Warren VIC 3805
Tel: (03) 9704 1444
Shop 1 Power Centre
Cranbourne-Frankston Road
Frankston VIC 3199
Tel: (03) 9769 6597
1/36 Dalton Road
Thomastown VIC 3074
Tel: (03) 9465 7770
website: www.babybunting.com.au
Baby Bunting is a one-stop baby shop. The success of the stores comes from the specialised service offered, especially to first time parents. The friendly staff are happy to demonstrate the full range of baby products, accessories and toys, all at discount prices.

Baby Mode
17 Wright Street
Sunshine VIC 3020
Tel: (03) 9311 0675
5/500 High Street
Epping VIC 3076
email: info@babymode.com.au
website: www.babymode.com.au
Baby Mode has been helping families prepare for the most precious and exciting times of their lives for over 35 years. This Australian, family-owned business continues to provide exceptional quality products and retail values with the view that there is no substitute for quality when making the right choice. They aim to provide the best quality, price and advice for you when making those choices. For a diverse range of nought to teen furniture, safety products, toys, equipment, mattresses and accessories visit the website or experience it personally at one of their stores.

Bunkers
169 Whitehorse Road
Blackburn VIC 3130
Tel: (03) 9894 4449
website: www.bunkers.com.au
Bunkers make a large range of space saving children's furniture, starting with the "convert-a-cot" which converts to a standard size single bed to bunks and beds incorporating storage or work stations underneath. Catalogue available.

Hush-A-Bye Baby Nursery Furniture
158 Cheltenham Road
Dandenong VIC 3175
Tel: (03) 9769 2016
website: www.hushabye.com.au
Hush-A-Bye Baby have a large range of cots, car safety products, nursery accessories and much more. Hush-A-Bye is a great place to shop for low prices and great savings on all popular brands.

Kiddie Country
79–85 Union Street
Armadale VIC 3143
Tel: (03) 9509 4041
Kiddie Country stocks a huge range of nursery furniture and toys. Everything you need is available under one roof, in fact four adjoining shops are devoted to nursery goods and pre-school toys. Kiddie Country sells cots, prams, car seats, change tables, high chairs, playpens, wardrobes, chests of drawers, as well as incidentals like monitors, breast pumps and manchester. They are 'Bugaboo' experts with the full range of colours in stock.

Kids Interior Designs
73 Upper Heidelberg Road
Ivanhoe VIC 3079
Tel: (03) 9499 1852
website: www.kidsinteriordesigns.com.au
Kids Interior Designs do children's furnishings including bed linen and wraps. They also carry grobags, Robeez shoes, designer PJs and dressing gowns, giftware, art smocks, toys, costumes and much more. They carry ranges to suit newborn through to early teens. Kids Interior Designs also offer an in-home decorator advice service and can help you create the perfect environment for your child.

NEW SOUTH WALES

All For Kiddiz & Bubs
163 Parramatta Road
Annandale NSW 2038
Tel: (02) 9569 2255
website: www.allforkiddizandbubs.com.au

All for Kiddiz & Bubs offers a wide range of major brands of babies and children's clothing and shoes as well as soft and educational toys, cots, bassinets, cradles, mattresses, high chairs, travel cots, prams, feeding products, monitors, car seats, safety products and accessories. The staff are helpful and prices reasonable.

Babies Galore

Shop G24, Mandarin Centre, Albert Avenue
Chatswood NSW 2067
Tel: 1300 99 BABY (2229)
Unit 1 & 2, Enterprise Park
9 Hoyle Avenue
Castle Hill NSW 2154
Tel: (02) 9894 2011
Shops 8–10/30 Karalta Road
Erina NSW 2250
Tel: (02) 4365 6860
Shop 4, 233 Mulgoa Road
Penrith NSW 2750
Tel: (02) 4722 9125
Shop 99, Level 1 Warringah Mall (cnr Old Pittwater Road & Condamine Street)
Warringah Mall NSW 2100
Tel: (02) 9939 3955
Shop 28–31 Royal Randwick Shopping Centre
Belmore Road
Randwick NSW 2031
Tel: (02) 9326 3019
Shop 9, 124 Taren Point Road
Taren Point NSW 2229
Tel: (02) 9526 6065
433 Great Western Highway
Wentworthville NSW 2145
Tel: (02) 9896 1572
Shop 1, 131–137 King Street
Warrawong NSW 2502
Tel: (02) 4272 7188
Unit 6/2 Mill Road
Campbelltown NSW 2560
Tel: (02) 4628 5606
Shop 3082, Level 3
Westfield Shopping Centre
Hornsby NSW 2077
Unit 1, 10–16 Medcalf Street
Newcastle NSW 2300
Tel: (02) 4956 7788
78–96 Pyrmont Bridge Road
Camperdown NSW 2050
Tel: (02) 9516 5622
email: sales@babiesgalore.com.au
website: www.babiesgalore.com.au

Babies Galore understand that having a baby can be both exciting, and a little daunting. That's why Babies Galore, a different kind of baby store, is with you every step of the way by offering advice, support and information to help you on your journey to parenthood. Babies Galore stock all the latest products for mum and baby, including car seats, high chairs, cots and strollers and much more. Babies Galore caters for all baby's needs from 0 to 2 years and staff at Babies Galore are up to date with the latest safety requirements for all items carried in the stores and they are happy to assist customers with advice to ensure the correct purchase to suit each individual's personal needs. There are 13 Babies Galore stores throughout NSW and a full online store.

Baby Barn Discounts

14 Industry Drive
Tweed Heads South NSW 2486
Tel: (07) 5524 5407

Established 15 years ago, Baby Barn Discounts incorporates two huge air-conditioned showrooms. The store offers friendly knowledgeable service and stocks brands such as Safe & Sound, Steelcraft, Boori, Mountain Buggy, Phil & Ted, Kidsline, Babybjorn, Childcare, Valco, Avent, Living Textiles, Oi Oi, Ergo and others as well as wooden toys and gift lines. There's off-street parking, a large playpen and lay-by is welcome. Baby Barn Discounts is also an authorised restraint fitting station and offer capsule and car seat hire services.

Baby Things

145A Anzac Parade
Kensington NSW 2033
Tel: (02) 9663 2320
email: info@babythings.com.au
website: www.babythings.com.au

Baby Things is a family-friendly store and one-stop shop where you will find everything for baby. They also hire capsules and car seats and do package deals with competitive discounts. Lay-by available.

Baby Winks

383 Goonoo Goonoo Road
Tamworth NSW 2340
Tel: (02) 6765 5811
email: amanda@babywinks.com.au
website: www.babywinks.com.au

Baby Winks Tamworth has grown to be the biggest specialty baby store in the region. Baby Winks stock only top quality products from only the best brands. Open seven days a week you are sure to find what you need for your baby. Mail and phone orders are welcome.

Baby Zone (Aust) Pty Ltd

1 Bridge Street
Wollongong NSW 2500
Tel: (02) 4228 4288
email: sales@babyzonedirect.com.au
website: www.babyzonedirect.com.au

Baby Zone is one of Australia's largest baby stores stocking all leading brands in nursery furniture, prams, car seats, high chairs, safety products and toys. Baby Zone is also one of Australia's Safety Advisory Centres offering certified child restraint fittings and qualified safety advice.

Babycare Nursery

68 John Street
Cabramatta NSW 2166
Tel: (02) 9724 6191

Resources

CHOOSING FURNITURE & EQUIPMENT

Stores retail

email: babycare@optusnet.com.au
website: www.babycarenursery.com.au

Babycare Nursery pride themselves in providing customers with the best service and the lowest prices. They can take care of all of your baby needs with an extensive selection of products such as cots, car seats, prams, strollers, playpens, monitors, steam sterilisers, breastpumps and much more. All products come with a full manufacture warranty. If you can't find what you want, phone or email babycare@optusnet.com.au. Shopping is simple and easy at Babycare Nursery.

babyshop

276 Brunker Road
Adamstown NSW 2289
Tel: 1800 222 437 or 1800 BABIES
email: mail@babyshop.com.au
website: www.babyshop.com.au

With experience online since 1998 and hundreds of products to choose from, babyshop stocks a variety of well known brands, as well as featuring many exclusive and hard to find items. Departments include: Bathtime & Care, Bedtime & Nursery, Clothing, Feeding & Accessories, Out & About and Playtime & Development. Visit babyshop at the address above or experience the convenience of shopping from home with one of Australia's first online baby stores: www.babyshop.com.au.

Bubs Baby Shops

160 Pacific Highway
Tuggerah NSW 2259
Tel: (02) 4351 5255
email: tuggerah@bubs.com.au
343 New England Highway
Rutherford NSW 2320
Tel: (02) 4932 5455
email: rutherford@bubs.com.au
92 Parramatta Road
Auburn NSW 2144
Tel: (02) 9648 3300
email: auburn@bubs.com.au
website: www.bubs.com.au

Bubs Baby Shops are some of the largest baby shops in the country with a never-before-seen range of child restraints, prams, furniture and accessories. Bubs Baby Shops have recently franchised. To find out if there is a store close to you phone 1300 79 BUBS and you will be answered by your nearest Bubs Nursery Product Expert.

Bunkers

218 Parramatta Road
Auburn NSW 2144
Tel: (02) 9648 5949
email: hanska@bunkers.com.au
website: www.bunkers.com.au

Bunkers make a large range of space saving children's furniture, starting with the "convert-a-cot" which converts to a standard size single bed to bunks and beds incorporating storage or work stations underneath. Catalogue available.

Kids Carousel

Unit 4 & 5, 390 Pacific Highway
Belmont North NSW 2280
Tel: (02) 4947 7000
email: belmontkids@optusnet.com.au

Kids Carousel was first opened in May 1996 by owners Tunia and Shane to fill a void in the market for affordable kids' fashion and nursery equipment. It now draws customers from more than 400 kilometres away on a regular basis with its friendly, down-to-earth service and advice as well as practical help and service on children's clothing, prams and car safety seats, installation and repairs. Now with over 7,000 square feet catering to baby and kids' needs. Phone or visit the website for more details.

Little Fingers

Shop 18 Centre Point Arcade
Taree NSW 2430
Tel: (02) 6550 0999
website: www.littlefingers.net.au

Little Fingers offers a wide range of baby goods such as prams, cots, linen, nappy bags, breast pumps and much more. They also have clothing for premmies up to size 14 including formal and casual wear, swimwear, beach towels, socks, bibs, hats and much more. Phone or visit the website for more details.

Minimee Babies & Kids

109 Norton Street
Leichhardt NSW 2040
Tel: (02) 9569 2000
Also located at:
123 Willoughby Road
Crows Nest NSW 2065
Tel: (02) 9436 3436
email: info@minimee.com.au
website: www.minimee.com.au

Minimee can create a new baby package matching your budget and style with a bulk discount upfront. After your furniture/essentials purchase, you automatically become a VIP member and get 10% lifetime discount on all products. Offering a great range, service and prices, items include nursery furniture, prams, car seats, baby essentials, linen, fashion, toys and gifts at Leichhardt, Crows Nest or online at www.minimee.com.au.

The Toy Loft
1 Mitchell Road
Brookvale NSW 2100
Tel: (02) 9905 4895
email: ttl@iprimus.com.au
website: www.brookvaletoylibrary.com.au
The Toy Loft sells nursery items and toys including buggies, backpacks, back carriers, trikes, go-karts, scooters, games, puzzles and baby toys. Catering for ages from 6 months to 8 years. Brands include Fitnesswise, Tri-ang, Pintoys, Baby Einstein, Kelty, Sherpa, 'Push-me-Home' Bike/Trike handles and 'Liquid Holster' drink holders.

AUSTRALIAN CAPITAL TERRITORY

Bubs Baby Shops
25 Townsville Street
Fyshwick ACT 2609
Tel: (02) 6280 6680
email: valley@bubs.com.au
website: www.bubs.com.au
email: canberra@bubs.com.au
Bubs Baby Shops are some of the largest baby shops in the country with a never-before-seen range of child restraints, prams, furniture and accessories. Bubs Baby Shops have recently franchised. To find out if there is a store close to you phone 1300 79 BUBS and you will be answered by your nearest Bubs Nursery Product Expert.

QUEENSLAND

Babies Galore
Shop 1 & 2/250 Olsen Avenue
Gold Coast QLD
Tel: (07) 5563 3437
Great Western Super Centre, Shop H2
1028 Samford Road (cnr Settlement Road)
Keperra QLD 4054
Tel: (07) 3351 1777
Shop 7 Morayfield Supa Centre
312–344 Morayfield Road
Morayfield QLD 4506
Tel: (07) 5428 6122
Shop 5 Harvey Norman Centre
3890–3892 Pacific Highway
Loganholme QLD 4129
Shop C17, Domain Central
130 Duckworth Street
Garbutt QLD 4814
Tel: (07) 47754177
363 Yaamba Road
North Rockhampton QLD 4701
Tel: (07) 49281833
email: sales@babiesgalore.com.au
website: www.babiesgalore.com.au
Babies Galore caters for all baby's needs from 0–2 years. The latest in cots and prams, car seats, high chairs, toys and accessories, manchester, mattresses and fashion are all available. Babies Galore has a large range of exclusive products that are of the highest standard and quality. Staff at Babies Galore are up to date with the latest safety requirements for all items carried in the stores and they are happy to assist customers with advice to ensure the correct purchase to suit each individual's personal needs. Babies Galore has its own Loyalty Card. To qualify just spend $2000 or more in one transaction and you will receive a 10% discount on all future full price purchases at any Babies Galore store for 12 months from the date of issue. Full terms and conditions available in store. There are six Babies Galore stores throughout QLD and a full online store. Log onto www.babiesgalore.com.au for more information.

Bubs Baby Shops
Homemaker City North, 650 Wickham Street
Fortitude Valley QLD 4006
Tel: (07) 3252 2332
email: valley@bubs.com.au
Also located at:
306 Gympie Road
Strathpine QLD 4500
Tel: (07) 3889 9111
email: strathpine@bubs.com.au
224 Nicklin Way
Warana QLD 4575
Tel: (07) 5493 1122
email: kawana@bubs.com.au
6 Venture Drive
Noosaville QLD 4566
Tel: (07) 5449 0035
email: noosa@bubs.com.au
84 Fourth Avenue
Mt. Isa QLD 4825
Tel: (07) 4743 1983
email: isa@bubs.com.au
website: www.bubs.com.au
Bubs Baby Shops are some of the largest baby shops in the country with a never-before-seen range of child restraints, prams, furniture and accessories. Bubs Baby Shops have recently franchised. To find out if there is a store close to you phone 1300 79 BUBS and you will be answered by your nearest Bubs Nursery Product Expert.

Bunkers
3405 Pacific Highway
Springwood QLD 4127
Tel: (07) 3299 2609
email: hanska@bunkers.com.au
website: www.bunkers.com.au
Bunkers make a large range of space saving children's furniture, starting with the "convert-a-cot" which converts to a standard size single bed to bunks and beds incorporating storage or work stations underneath. Catalogue available.

Kiddlee Dinks
Shop 4.03 The Zone, Deception Bay Road
Rothwell QLD 4022
Tel: (07) 3204 8688
website: www.kiddleedinks.com.au

Resources

CHOOSING FURNITURE & EQUIPMENT

Stores retail

Kiddlee Dinks is a funky children's store for babies to teens that stocks children's beds, bunks, midi sleepers, car beds, desks, hand chairs, linen, cushions, rugs, lamps and wall art. They also have a great range of unique gifts for all ages.

Pram City

4, 50 Spencer Road
Nerang QLD
Tel: (07) 5527 3318
email: prams@pramcity.com.au
website: www.pramcity.com.au

Pram City at Nerang on the Gold Coast has been established for approximately 9 years and is now under new management by a local family. They cater for all your baby needs specialising in good quality products including Safe N Sound, Peg Perego, Bertini, Valco, Steelcraft, Quinny, Mountain Buggy and Maclaren. Open 7 days a week and offering competitive prices.

WESTERN AUSTRALIA

Baby BT

Corner Railway Ave & Gillam Drive
Kelmscott WA 6111
Tel: (08) 9390 1841
email: babybt267@bigpond.com
website: www.babybt.com.au

Baby BT's friendly staff will be happy to assist and demonstrate their wide range of cots, bassinets, gliders, furniture, toddler beds, manchester and a huge range of baby equipment and accessories. Kidsline, Bright Bots and Lambs and Ivy linen and towels available. Other brands stocked include Baba slings, Snug as a Bug, Bubbaroo and Avent. The pram-friendly store has Graco, Safe-n-Sound, Childcare, Valco, INFA, Baby Hood, LovenCare, Fisher Price and Chicco. 12 week lay-by and EFTPOS facilities or shop online www.babybt.com.au.

Baby on a Budget

180 Bannister Road
Canning Vale WA 6155
Tel: (08) 9456 0770
email: canningvale@babyonabudget.com.au
Also located at:
1280 Albany Highway
Cannington WA 6107
Tel: (08) 9351 8800
email: cannington@babyonabudget.com.au
93 Joondalup Drive
Joondalup WA 6027

Tel: (08) 9301 0300
email: joondalup@babyonabudget.com.au
5 Fielden Way
Port Kennedy WA 6172
Tel: (08) 9524 6255
email: portkennedy@babyonabudget.com.au
94 Hector Street West
Osborne Park WA 6017
Tel: (08) 9242 8074
email: osbornepark@babyonabudget.com.au
9 Stanford Way
Malaga WA 6090
Tel: (08) 9249 3360
email: malaga@babyonabudget.com.au
11b 274/278 Leach Highway
Myaree WA 6154
email: myaree@babyonabudget.com.au
website: www.babyonabudget.com.au

Each of The Baby on a Budget Superstores offer personalised service with Perth's largest range of prams, cots, car seats and everything that baby requires with prices that won't be beaten. The mega stores in Osborne Park and Cannington are situated in the heart of the Perth metro area and offer everything from maternity to cots and high chairs through to goods for kids up to five years old under one roof.

Babyland

30 Frobisher Street
Osborne Park WA 6017
Also located at:
83 Stirling Highway
Nedlands WA 6009
153 High Road
Willetton WA 6155
Tel: 1300 654 959
website: www.babyland.com.au

Shopping for a baby is a very exciting time and Babyland hope to make this experience enjoyable and stress-free by delivering a huge range of nursery goods at prices you will love. Babyland delivers small items Australia wide and large items throughout WA. Their range includes car restraints, manchester, prams, cots, high chairs, change tables, monitors, back pack and slings, toys and gifts. Order online or visit one of their three store locations.

Bates Street Babies

36 Bates Street
Merredin WA 6415
Tel: (08) 9041 2200
website: www.batesstreetbabies.com.au

Bates St Babies is the only dedicated baby and maternity shop in wheatbelt WA. They stock lots of gorgeous bits and pieces for baby and little kids as well as maternity and breastfeeding clothes. They also have a lovely feeding lounge and baby change area and a great play zone for the kids to have fun while mum and dad shop. So whatever you need – cots, prams, change tables, linen, clothes, books, cards, creams, potties, bookends, motifs – visit this beautiful shop.

Bunkers

14/88 Erindale Road
Balcatta WA 6021
Tel: (08) 9344 6630
email: hanska@bunkers.com.au
website: www.bunkers.com.au

Bunkers make a large range of space saving children's furniture, starting with the "convert-a-cot" which converts to a standard size single bed to bunks and beds incorporating storage or work stations underneath. Catalogue available. Phone or visit the website for more details.

Funky Kids

Tel: (08) 9284 0051
email: info@funkykids.com.au
website: www.funkykids.com.au

Funky Kids stocks beautiful white bedroom furniture which is made in Western Australia and has a wide variety of products to decorate your child's room. They also stock fabulous brands in clothing as well as a wide variety of gifts, toys and personalised products. Two great locations: Wembley and Karrinyup Shopping Centre.

Kids Cove

Shop 9, Central Court Mall, Central Road
Kalamunda WA 6076
Tel: (08) 6293 1569
website: www.kidscove.com.au

Kids Cove offers a dream bedroom all in one shop with funky bedding for girls and boys from birth to teens. They also stock children's accessories for all ages including lamps and rugs and great brand names such as Freckles, Hiccups, Kaloo, Lilly and Lolly, Tree House, Alex and Charli Eko Peko and many more. Kids Cove personalise bedrooms with amazing hand-painted canvasses and bold bright letters for that special little one and they also stock a range of pedal cars, small retro bikes and scooters. Kids Cove also sell clothing, funky new chairs and awesome nappy bags. Phone or visit the website for more details.

SOUTH AUSTRALIA

Baby Junction

365 Magill Road
St Morris SA 5068
Tel: (08) 8361 2200
email: jody@babyjunction.com.au
website: www.babyjunction.com.au

Baby Junction understands the importance you place on making sure the products you purchase are the safest, long-wearing products available. The staff, parents themselves, have personally used many of the products they stock and only sell products that are tried and tested and safe for your baby. If you want some of the best advice in Adelaide about what products to buy and what products are suitable for your baby, then drop into their shop for a chat or phone for some free advice. Open 7 days a week.

Bug-a-lugs Baby Store

31 Light Crescent
Mt Barker SA 5251
Tel: (08) 8398 3521
email: info@bugalugsbaby.com.au
website: www.bugalugsbaby.com.au

New parents have a lot to think about and the decisions you make on purchases for your baby can make a great deal of difference to the ease with which you manage your new responsibilities. Bug-a-lugs Baby Store offers exceptional service and quality goods including nursery furniture by leading manufacturers such as Grocorp; prams and strollers by Baby Jogger, Love n Care, Valco, Steelcraft, Babylove, Maclaren and Mountain Buggy; car seats by Safe N Sound and Infa; linen by Kidsline, Living Textiles, Bubba-Blue and Sweet Dreams; and carriers by Baby Bjorn, Bubzilla, Ergo, Peanut Shell, Hugabub and Baba Slings. For more information phone the number above or visit the website.

Bunkers

1079 South Road
Melrose Park SA 5039
Tel: (08) 8277 3944
email: hanska@bunkers.com.au
website: www.bunkers.com.au

Bunkers make a large range of space saving children's furniture, starting with the "convert-a-cot" which converts to a standard size single bed to bunks and beds incorporating storage or work stations underneath. Catalogue available. Phone or visit the website for more details.

Parthenon Emporium

149 Henley Beach Road
Mile End SA 5031
Tel: (08) 8234 5733
email: enquiries@parthenon.com.au
website: www.parthenon.com.au

Parthenon Emporium provides a large range of bed linen, blankets and wraps, bedroom furniture and toys such as clocks, frames, lamps, mirrors, pin boards, coat stands and children's table and chair sets. They have exclusive toy boxes and toy crates, hand painted to match any bedroom decor and furniture may also be personalised with child's name with accessories to match. Phone or visit the website for more details.

The Infant Boutique

Shop 6/136 The Parade
Norwood SA 5067
Tel: (08) 8331 3740
email: info@theinfantboutique.com.au
website: www.theinfantboutique.com.au

The Infant Boutique is a beautiful baby and children's boutique for ages 0 to 5 years (sizes newborn to 6) stocking nursery furniture, bed linen, blankets, wraps, clothing, sleepwear, toys, games, stationery, artwork, gifts and accessories. The range includes local, national and international brands and labels. Phone or visit the website for more details.

Natures Purest

Natures purest is a gorgeous organic nursery collection made from 100% organically grown and naturally coloured cotton jersey. Designed to create an environment in which babies feel safe, secure and loved, the collection includes cot bedding, room décor, babywear, gifts and toys. The cotton used in the natures purest range is produced without the use of dyes or chemical pesticides. Grown in natural shades of cream, brown and green, the cotton buds are hand picked and processed to make the most wonderful natural and pure fabrics that gently caress baby's new skin.

The natures purest collection comprises two ranges. The Hug Me range, with an adorable bear motif, includes cot bedding, room décor, babywear and gift sets. With 28 items in the range, it is easy to create a stylish and contemporary coordinated look for your nursery.

New for 2009 is the Sleepy Safari range of toys, cot bedding and babywear. Featuring cute animal designs of a lion, elephant and giraffe, the range provides new babies with toys that not only assist development, but are safe and soft to handle.

To complement the natural cotton, natures purest has a range of baby blankets made from the natural fibre bamboo. Unrivalled as one of the most luxurious materials, bamboo handles like silk, but performs like cotton so it is extremely soft yet breathable and cool. The blanket range comes in three sizes: receiving, pram and cot.

Each natures purest product comes packaged in an attractive recycled brown box with gift tag making it the perfect gift for a new baby. Natures purest is available nationally at David Jones stores and selected nursery specialist retailers. Visit website www.naturespurest.com.au or contact Customer Service on 1300 667 137 for your nearest stockist.

Silver Cross

Congratulations! You're having a baby (or your partner, daughter, sister or friend is). Now we're guessing you're on cloud nine/over the moon/on top of the world, but you're also feeling ever-so-slightly nervous/biting your nails/pulling your hair out and waking up at 3am thinking about what on earth you've got yourself into.

Well in all honesty there's a lot of hard work to be done, but the good news is that we've been making prams and strollers for parents for over 130 years now. That means we've got a fair bit of experience in this game, experience that has helped us understand what's good for parents and what's good for babies. As a parent you'll be looking for something safe, convenient, durable and probably fashionable too, which is where we come in handy. Silver Cross have a collection of prams and strollers that act as an ideal, safe and secure second home for your child. Here's a quick overview of part of our little family that should help out with your little family:

• **Sleepover**: It's the complete package with a traditional twist. Suitable from birth to toddler, it's an overnight carrycot; it's a protective pram; it's a reversible stroller.

• **Dazzle** (shown opposite): Put simply, it's beauty with brains – a sytlish and lightweight stroller that combines with a soft carrycot to give you the perfect urban combination, suitable from birth to toddlers (25kg).

• **Pop**: A distinctive, lightweight, portable stroller that folds down quickly and easily, for use from birth to toddler.

• **Fizz**: It's an ultra-lightweight and compact stroller, suitable from six months. An ideal choice for day-to-day usage and holidays.

For more information please visit www.silvercross.com.au

Bébé Care

Bébé Care is a premium quality nursery brand developed by CNP Brands, a leading producer and distributor of nursery furniture and equipment. With a focus on superior materials and construction, the range features innovative products with exceptional styling specifically designed to appeal to the discerning parent-to-be. Exclusive to Bébé Care, a Two Year Diamond Warranty is provided across its entire range. This Diamond Warranty provides twice the standard warranty period and demonstrates the brand's commitment to superior quality. Safety is also of the utmost importance so all Bébé Care products meet the highest and most recent standards. The result is a range that is fashionable, functional, safe and easy-to-use.

The nursery equipment range includes strollers, rockers, high chairs, travel cots and accessories. New for 2009 is the Rverse stroller, a perfect example of combining stylish appeal with practical functionality. Suitable for newborn, this stroller converts easily between bassinet and stroller modes and has an easy and compact fold. Featuring a bootcover, raincover, sunshade and large shopping basket, the Rverse is manufactured in aluminum so it is ultra lightweight, strong and very fashionable.

Create a classic feel for your new nursery with the Bébé Care Classic Furniture Collection. Manufactured to the highest standards of quality, the range has been designed to accommodate a variety of lifestyle needs. Featuring quality timber cots and furniture pieces such as toy box, change table, bookcase and chest of drawers, most items are modular in design enabling a variety of assembly options. The collection comes in two colour options: the ever-popular classic white or heritage for a finish more reminiscent of a darker antique timber.

Bébé Care is available at David Jones and all good nursery stores across Australia. To view the full Bébé Care nursery range, please visit www.bebecare.com.au.

STOKKE

The Children Collection from STOKKE is an innovative and stylish range of children's furniture and stroller products. All items in the collection are designed to effectively combine function with practicality, whilst offering a truly unique and contemporary look. The collection is specifically designed to allow your child to experience its surroundings at a higher, more interactive level, and includes the popular Tripp Trapp chair/high chair which enables your child to interact with the rest of the family at the dining table by sitting at the same height and proximity.

Tripp Trapp's design includes adjustability of the seat plate and footrest in height and depth allowing the chair to grow with your child, while enabling correct ergonomic sitting, improving posture, providing legs and feet full freedom of movement for the adjusting and shifting of body weight and delivering support to your child's developing spine.

The award-winning STOKKE Xplory stroller revolutionises the entire stroller experience with its innovative, elevated seating position. Through its unique design, the Stokke Xplory provides you with an unparalleled flexibility that enables you to elevate your child to be closer to you. Being closer allows you to keep contact and interact with your child, strengthening your child's own sense of security, safety, and assurance. With its lightweight design and rotating front wheels, you will find Stokke Xplory extremely easy to handle and manoeuvre in crowded or narrow spaces, while the unique two-wheel functionality of Stokke Xplory makes getting on and of public transport and up or down stairs even easier. Available in six colours and with a wide range of optional accessories the Stokke Xplory is the only pram, pushchair, or stroller your child will ever need.

For more information on the STOKKE Children Collection products including the beautiful and innovative range of nursery furniture visit www.stokke.com and www.exquira.com.au.

TOKKE™ XPLORY®
igher is better™

TRIPP TRAPP®
The chair that grows
with your child™

bertini®

The bertini® Life Style Interaction Collection is like nothing else on the market. It is unique in that it offers mix'n'match components that allow you to create a pram, stroller, bassinette, rocker and highchair for your growing baby.

Comfort & User-friendliness: With sleek European style and 'Swiss Army Knife' practicality, the bertini Life Style Collection is far more universal than any other system available today. Suitable from birth to 20kg, the bertini Life Style Collection offers:

- Comfortable and spacious multi-position seat unit, which glides from an upright position to a lying flat position
- Forward and rear-facing seat options
- Unique five-point harness with deluxe padded fabric for safety and comfort
- Handle adjustment to accommodate different heights of parents
- Australian designed and engineered aluminium frame
- Rocker frame with stabilising feet to control movement of the Gliding seat
- Multi-function, height adjustable, stand with removable and adjustable play tray
- Bassinette with removable ventilated mattress, bootcover and soft liner for easy cleaning

Nursery Furniture & Soft Furnishings: bertini's co-ordinated nursery range of high-quality wood furniture and beautiful manchester is designed to complement your lifestyle, home, and most importantly, create a perfect atmosphere for your child. With careful attention to detail and beautiful textures, bertini's exclusive range of Australian designs offers something special for everybody.

The bertini® Life Style interaction collection is incredibly versatile and easy to use. Simply choose a frame to suit your lifestyle and transportation needs, then add a Gliding Seat or Bassinette to create a multifaceted, light weight pram.

Quick release functions allow you to mix'n'match more bertini interaction components to create a Rocker and Highchair for your growing baby.

Visit www.bertini.com.au to learn more about the bertini X series and accessories.

Gliding seat on rocker frame

Bassinette

bertini®

Maclaren

Celebrated around the world as the inventor of the original buggy (stroller), Maclaren revolutionised the baby transport market with its unique compact fold and lightweight umbrella-fold stroller. Designed to provide convenience for families during travel and everyday life, all Maclaren strollers feature lightweight aluminium chassis, lockable swivel wheels, shopping basket and a removable seat for easy cleaning. Since manufacturing its first buggy more than four decades ago, Maclaren has continued to focus on product innovation and engineering ingenuity to produce a premium line of quality baby products.

In 2009, Maclaren will introduce Grand Tour, the first true 'crossover' stroller designed to be the all-in-one solution to parents' needs. Inspired by the automotive equivalent the CUV (Crossover Utility Vehicle), the Grand Tour combines high-performance functionality and luxurious style. As the inventor of the first umbrella-fold stroller in 1965, Maclaren has now invented the first true transport system which offers parents a greater range of options including a two-way convertible forward or rearward facing seat, a bumper bar and the ability to accommodate a carrycot as well as other accessories.

Maclaren's 2009 Collection once again is designed to make life easier for parents and more comfortable for baby with high performance features and accessories. New features include a new, larger, easy-on, easy-off hood providing extra coverage, air vents and larger UV protected viewing windows; elasticised pockets to hold rain covers and mosquito nets; reflective features for safety; and newly designed ergonomically optimised handles. All Maclaren strollers are designed to be the lightest, most stylish and durable in their class. Engineered for safety and durability, they must pass a battery of 80 tests, including Maclaren's Gold Standard and testing by an independent testing house. To view the full Maclaren range in Australia visit website www.cnpbrands.com.au.

MACLAREN

maclarenbaby.com

GH PERFORMANCE
ALUMINIUM

COMPACT
UMBRELLA FOLD

5 POINT HARNESS

FOOT-OPERATED
LINKED BRAKES

SHOPPING
BASKET

WATER RESISTANT
HOOD

RAINCOVER
INCLUDED

Safe-n-Sound

Safety is far too important to be left to chance. Nobody understands that better than Safe-n-Sound.

The Safe-n-Sound MaxiRider™ and MaxiRider AHR™ is the seat that grows as your child does. It easily converts from a forward facing seat for an 8–18kg infant to a booster seat, comfortably seating children up to 26kg. This is made possible through the unique built-in harness system that stores away in a hidden compartment when not in use.

The MaxiRider AHR™ delivers additional side impact protection through AHR technology. AHR™ is a seat within a seat, featuring an adjustable head restraint that protects and contains the head in a side impact collision. The revolutionary design and construction of the headrest means greater absorption of energy during a crash and also comfortably supports the head of a sleeping child.

Other important features include the additional height provided as the AHR™ headrest extends, a tether strap that attaches to the cars anchor point, push button harness adjusters and tensioners, energy absorbing reinforced back and side wings, pivoting armrest for further comfort that can be stored away, two rotating cup holders perfect for drink bottles and fruit boxes, as well as a seat belt locator for use in booster mode included in the head rest and the unique split crotch strap and patented Anti-Submarine Clip exclusive to Safe-n-Sound.

The Anti-Submarine Clip prevents children from slipping under the seat belt ensuring the seat belt is correctly positioned on the thighs and hips, avoiding serious injury or death, so that children can survive a crash.

For further information on the full range of Safe-n-Sound products visit www.britax.com.au or ask your retailer and ensure your child arrives ... Safe-n-Sound.

QuickSmart™

At QuickSmart™ they have long recognised that busy parents are always seeking safe, reliable and innovative products that will help to make their lives easier. Their team of specialist designers have responded to the needs of today's parents by designing a clever range of products that are compact, simple to use, easy to transport and safe. The success of the original QuickSmart™ Backpack Stroller, released in Australia and internationally in 2004, started a worldwide trend in ultra compact, easy to fold strollers and marked the beginning of the QuickSmart™ project.

The QuickSmart™ mission is simply about taking products that parents use to care for their children (such as strollers, play yards, travel cots, high chairs etc) and improving them, making them more portable, more convenient, easy to store and easy to use!

The current QuickSmart™ range includes the Easy Fold Stroller, the Scuttle Bug and Scramble Bug ride ons and in 2009 the Easy Fold High Chair. The QuickSmart™ Easy Fold Stroller is unlike any other four wheeled stroller. With the revolutionary QuickSmart™ folding system, it folds and unfolds in seconds! It's easy to operate, lightweight and has all the usual comfort features like a fully retractable canopy, seat recline and utility basket. It also comes with its own travel bag and rain cover. No assembly required. In 2007 it won the prestigious Australian Design Mark for excellence in design.

The QuickSmart™ Scramble Bug and Scuttle Bug are revolutionary foot to floor ride-ons that look like cute bugs. They use castor wheels for free flowing movement in all directions, 360°. They help further develop a child's balance, pushing and steering skills and are a great way to take children from a baby walker to a ride on. Plus they fold and unfold in only 3 simple steps. In 2008 the QuickSmart™ Scramble Bug was the winner of the prestigious Australian Design Mark for excellence in design.

To find out more about QuickSmart™ products log on to www.funtasticnursery.com.au.

1
year
warranty

ages
6+
months

easy fold
stroller

New accessories available including footmuff, boot cover & organiser caddy

strollers include rain cover & carry bag

New designer colour

Latte/Black Graffiti
with bonus caddy

Packed with features the Quicksmart Easyfold Stroller is the perfect alternative to a cumbersome pram or stroller:

- Extremely compact, convenient and lightweight
- Can be caried on board most Australian domestic airlines
- Award winning contemporary design
- Practical utility basket at base
- Rear braked wheels and dual front swivel wheels
- Fully retractable canopy
- Adjustable 2 position seat recline
- Suitable for 6 months plus up to 15kgs
- comes in three designer colours
  - Latte, Red and Black

Folds and unfolds in 2 easy steps.

Step 1

Step 2

Australian DESIGN MARK

QuickSmart Easy Fold Stroller
Licence No. 0703030
Standards Australia

simply.smarter

Available from Target, Myer, David Jones
and independent Nursery stores nationwide.
For stockists please call Funtastic customer service
1800 244 543 or visit www.funtasticnursery.com.au

DECT Baby Monitors

Enjoy complete peace of mind. With the new Philips AVENT range of DECT Baby Monitors you can relax, safe in the knowledge your baby's happy even when you are out of the room.

New DECT Baby Monitors are a breakthrough in communications technology and give you guaranteed zero interference from any other device (other baby monitors, cordless phones and mobile phones). These sleekly styled baby monitors look after baby's health and well-being thanks to state-of-the-art digital technology (DECT), that creates a private, secure channel between you and your baby. They have a powerful range, so you can wander in and around the house while keeping an ear out for your baby.

Reassurance with crystal clear sound: Guarantees zero interference from any other device (other baby monitors, cordless phones and mobile phones) and provides a secure, private and continuous connection to your baby at all times.

Adjustable sound sensitivity: The adjustable sound sensitivity function will allow you to increase/decrease the microphone sensitivity to enable you to listen to your baby breathe. Plus it cleverly uses lights to indicate if the baby makes a noise, even with volume off.

Complete peace of mind: The rechargeable parent unit gives you the freedom of cordless roaming for 24 hours before recharging is required. With an extra long range of up to 330m you are assured of secure reception in and around the house.

Designed with you and your baby's needs in mind: Choosing Philips AVENT means you have the assurance of superior quality products, designed with you and your baby's needs in mind.

PHILIPS
AVENT

SCD530

Total connection with your baby

with the new range of Philips AVENT DECT Baby Monitors

As a parent, you'll know there's nothing more important than the connection with your baby, something we take to heart at Philips AVENT.

With our digitally enhanced baby monitors, we offer a fully secure means of connecting to your baby over a crystal clear & secure connection. Using the latest DECT (Digital Enhanced Cordless Telecommunication) technology, we guarantee no interference to the signal.

Your baby's peaceful relaxation can be easily affected by variations in climate, so our DECT Baby Monitors provide you with real time digital temperature & humidity readings. By remotely monitoring temperature & humidity levels, you can always check your baby's room is comfortable & healthy.

For total reassurance, the portable parent unit allows you to set the temperature monitor to instantly alert you, either by sound or vibration, to any variations which are outside the pre-set level. It also has a humidity monitor displaying the levels as a percentage, for extra reassurance.

The new range of Philips AVENT DECT Baby Monitors comprises three different models so there is one to suit everyone's needs.

For helpful tips & product information visit
www.avent.com.au

Philips AVENT
Top of the range DECT
Baby Monitor, SCD530

- Room temperature sensor
- Humidity sensor
- Extra long range of 330m and 24hr operation time
- Vibration alert
- Lullaby option
- Baby unit nightlight
- Parent talkback
- Rechargeable parent unit
- Sound level lights
- Adjustable sound sensitivity
- Volume control
- Belt clip and neck cord
- LCD screen on parent and baby units
- Travel bag

PHILIPS
sense and simplicity

Quinny®

Quinny® offers clever solutions for the self-assured woman of today, solutions that were made with you and your child's lifestyle in mind. We call this freedom of mind: not thinking in terms of limitations but in terms of opportunities. This enables you to get the most out of your life. Whether you plan to go shopping, on holiday, enjoy a drink at a café with friends or spend a day at the park, Quinny gives you the freedom to do as you please.

Visit www.quinny.com for further information.

Automatically unfolds

Dreami Carry Cot

BUZZ 3-wheeler & 4-wheeler

Unique hydraulic system designed to automatically unfold
Seat can be used in both forward and rear-facing positions
Height adjustable handle bar, foot and back rest
Seat grows with your child (additional seat for older children included)
Comes with sun canopy, Buzz box and rain cover
Dreami Carry Cot accessory available

ZAPP

- Highly compact 3D fold ideal for
  travelling [69 x 27 x 30cm]
- 360 degree lockable front wheel
- Comes with sun canopy, rain
  cover and travel bag
- Shopping basket accessory available

Available in a range of sleek and eye-catching colours.

www.quinny.com

Bootiq

Kooper, Duke and Kye – the new kids in town

Sure to make their mark for style and functionality, the Kooper, Duke and Kye are the latest strollers from the Bootiq range of nursery furniture and equipment.

With the latest styling and design and durable fabrics to keep them looking good, these Bootiq baby movers will keep you and your little one ahead in the fashion and function stakes.

Offering interchangeable bassinette and reversible stroller seats on one frame, super light aluminium frames, and large sun canopy – the Bootiq Kooper, Duke and Kye are quickly becoming a town favourite.

Visit www.bootiq.com.au for further information.

Kooper
Stroller & Bassinette

Stylish yet practical, the Bootiq Kooper transforms into three combination modes and is ideal from birth all the way through to toddler years.

Fashionably-designed, the Bootiq Kooper stroller features a high grade aluminium frame with chrome detailing, adjustable handle height, large shopping basket, lockable front swivel wheels and pneumatic rear tyres. Removable bassinette fabrics allow for flat pack storage while quick release wheels make the Bootiq Kooper a real solution for family living.

www.bootiq.com.au

An IGC DOREL Brand
www.igcdorel.com.au

⟨ BOOTIQ

hushamok

hushamok presents the newest evolution of a century's old tradition. For thousands of years, parents have relied on the secure environment of a hammock to soothe babies to sleep. Every parent wants to keep their baby safe, comfortable, and secure – and only the most trusted products will do.

hushamok is both functional and fashionable, with a trendsetting look that redefines baby furniture. The signature hammock, hushamok experience, breaks the rules about pale pinks and pastel blues, offering a wide variety of bright colours and exciting accessory options. hushamok goes beyond the merely functional: its sleek and distinctive design provides the ultimate in style and comfort for new parents and their baby.

hushamok experience includes:

- hushamok baby hammock: made with the highest-quality pre-shrunk 100% cotton, it is machine washable and available in an array of colours including pink, blue, green, orange and undyed natural.
- hushamok stand: this stylish piece will compliment any room, and its lightweight steel construction means you can use it anywhere.
- Leaf spring: the patented leaf spring guarantees a gentle, natural swaying motion.
- Mattress: soft and comfortable, this poly-filled hypoallergenic mattress fits snugly in the hammock and is machine washable for easy care.
- Two fitted sheets: the custom sheets are made of 400-count cotton, and are available in the same vivid colours as the hammock. (Additional sheets sold separately.)
- Travel bag: this convenient cotton bag makes your hushamok experience portable so your baby can enjoy a restful sleep anywhere.

h⌄shamok™ soothing babies for thousands of years

An IGC DOREL Brand
www.igcdorel.com.au

The hushamok™ experience is the ideal sleeping environment for your baby, providing you with the safety your baby requires without sacrificing style. The innovative design of the hushamok enables babies to sleep soundly on their backs, which is a key recommendation in the prevention of SIDs. Other health benefits include the ease of infant colic and acid reflux due to its gentle swinging motion and slightly elevated design.

Peg Perego

Peg Perego's world-renowned line of carriages, strollers, car seats and high chairs are known for their sophistication, style, safety and comfort.

Founded in 1949 by Giuseppe Perego, Peg Perego revolutionised the nursery product market with the introduction of rubberised fabric, a world first. Peg's unique and high quality products are designed and manufactured in Italy using the latest technology and materials which meet stringent Australian and international safety standards.

Attention to design, market changes and foresight have built a brand over time that is now internationally recognised for its original ideas in the fields of infant care. Peg Perego prides itself on unique and sophisticated design, safety and being up to speed with the expectations of the modern mum.

Products can be found in major department stores and independent specialty shops.

For more information on the iconic Peg Perego range visit www.pegperego.com or phone Nursery Elegance on toll free 1300 131 477.

Sophistication Style Safety and Comfort

Peg Perégo has taken children out and about for over 50 years, in their carriages, strollers, car seats and high chairs. Our unique and high quality products are designed and are manufactured in Italy, using the latest technology and materials to meet all safety requirements. www.pegperego.com

PRIMA PAPPA DINER
(BLACK BUBBLES)

PRIMO VIAGGIO
(BLACK BUBBLES)

SKATE
(BLACK BUBBLES)

Distributed by
nursery ELEGANCE

Peg·Pérego

For more information on products please contact us toll free on 1300 766 494

Babylove

Every parent wants the very best for their child and seeks comfort in choosing proven and trusted brands. We know that protecting your child and keeping them safe is your first priority. When choosing from our extensive range of Babylove products, you can rest assured your child is in safe hands.

Our philosophy is to meet and exceed stringent testing processes to meet all safety requirements and our customer's needs.

The Babylove design specialists are committed to proactive research and development, offering high quality products with modern and innovative designs, covering the categories in child restraints, strollers, portacots, highchairs and accessories.

With the introduction of its new Ezy range, Babylove makes the lives of new parents a whole lot more convenient. The Ezy range was developed with the needs of today's modern parent in mind, the range focuses on being easy to install, recline, fold and carry without compromising on safety. All products in the range meet Australian Standards.

With fashion options that include the tantalising Fizzy Pink, Blue Pop, Tang, Rocket Red, Charcoal and Citron Splice all intended to ignite the imagination (and taste buds!) of children and parents alike.

For more information on the full range of Babylove products or to find your nearest retailer visit www.babylove.com.au.

think smart. think ezy. babylove

ezyswitch
Convertible Car Seat

ezyUp
Expandable Booster

14kg to 26kg

Birth to 18kg

Combined with safety technology and the latest in fashion designs and accessories, the ezyswitch and the ezyUp is the revolutionary choice.

For more product information please contact Nursery Elegance toll free on 1300 131 477

nursery
ELEGANCE

Humphrey's Corner

Humphrey's Corner brings to life the characters from UK author Sally Hunter's popular picture books. They feature a charming and adorable little elephant called Humphrey. He lives in a loving home with his mummy, daddy, big sister Lottie and baby brother Jack.

Humphrey's Corner is focused around Sally's childhood memories and the experiences she has being mum to her three children on which the characters of Humphrey, Lottie and baby Jack are based. The brand was first launched in February 1998 as a range of greeting cards. Now Humphrey's Corner is enchanting mums and babies across the globe.

A complete range of nursery products has been created to ensure your nursery is beautifully coordinated with the works of Humphrey's Corner. The range includes premium quality nursery furniture, bath and feeding plastics with more to come in 2009.

Let your baby's imagination grow with this gorgeous range from Humphrey's Corner.

To find out more about Humphrey's Corner products log on to www.funtasticnursery.com.au. For more information on Humphrey's story log on to www.humphreys-corner.com.au.

Create a soft and enchanting nursery statement wtih this gorgeous range of furniture from Humphrey's Corner. Humphrey's Corner brings to life the characters from UK author Sally Hunter's popular picture books.

Designed for either boy or girl, Humphrey's Corner is the perfect decor for your new addition.

Available from David Jones and leading independent Nursery stores nationwide. For stockists please call Funtastic customer service 1800 244 543 or visit www.funtasticnursery.com.au

buggypod Smorph

buggypod Smorph is sleek, black and gorgeous with a new soft concertina fold footrest, luxury seat pad and a 5-point harness. Invented by UK mother of three Stephanie Rohl, buggypod Smorph is the perfect answer for parents who don't want a double stroller but whose first-born needs a safe comfortable ride from time to time … buggypod Smorph attaches easily to pretty much any stroller on the market, transforming it into a two-seater when needed, and folding up neatly when not.

CLIP ON: buggypod attaches simply to the side of your stroller and folds up neatly out of the way when not in use.

PULL OUT: When your toddler needs a rest, in two clicks, buggypod with its own wheel, opens and locks into place, and your child has a comfy seat to ride in.

FOLD AWAY: When your child has had a rest and is ready to walk again simply fold buggypod neatly away and off you go.

To find out more about the buggypod Smorph visit www.funtasticnursery.com.au.

the inspired choice for today's young families

**buggypod Smorph,
the perfect alternative to a double stroller**

CONNECTS IN 3 EASY STEPS

1.   2.   3.

FLEXIBILITY • COMFORT • SAFETY

 funtastic LIMITED

Safety 1st

Innovation, expertise, and commitment to quality: that's what makes our reputation first class and our products the first choice of parents all over the world.

Our product portfolio is as deep as it is dependable: car seats, monitors, gates, bath accessories, bed rails, potties, walkers, healthcare items, and more.

We invite you to experience our tradition of excellence, and to see why, year after year, we are the clear industry leader.

Visit www.safety1st.com for further information.

Family meal-times will change forever when your child sits up for feeding.

Safety 1st
Your child comes first.™
www.safety1st.com

Toys,
books & gifts

Photograph by Kristen Cook, Melbourne.

Safe toys for kids

Toys are an important part of childhood, helping children learn and develop, as well as entertaining them. Unfortunately, some toys can be dangerous. Poorly constructed toys or toys that are inappropriate for your child's age and level of development can lead to tragic results.

This article, taken from the ACCC's *Keeping baby safe* book, is a guide to help you select safe toys for your child. There are many types of toys on the market, so it isn't possible to comment on them all individually. This information covers the more common toys available and indicates some of the hazards for kids. Safety and age appropriateness are important considerations when selecting a toy for your child. When selecting toys for your child, keep these key safety rules in mind:

- Read labels and packaging. Look for and follow the age recommendations and instructions about proper assembly, use and supervision
- Toys that have small parts, or small objects such as coins, batteries and nails should not be given to children under three years of age
- Jewellery should not be given to children under three years of age
- Choose sturdy and well-made toys that can stand up to being bitten, tugged, sucked, jumped on and thrown around without falling apart
- Check for sharp edges or rough surfaces that could injure your child
- Ensure paint and fillings are non-toxic.

PLAY SAFE
Carefully selecting toys is not enough – supervising your child's play and providing them with a safe area to play in can be the best ways to protect your child from harm. It is always best to explain and demonstrate to your child the correct and safe use of a toy when first giving it to them. You can improve the safety of the play area in your home by:

- Removing and immediately discarding packaging before giving a toy to a small child
- Ensuring older children's toys are out of reach of younger children
- Checking toys for breakage or potential hazards such as a loose part that could be a choking hazard
- Never giving uninflated balloons to small children and removing burst balloons from their play area as they can cause choking
- Removing 'dead' batteries in toys, as they can leak poisons or liquid that can damage skin or eyes.

Making your own toys
Consider the appropriateness of the toy for your child's age and developmental level. Make the toy safe for use by:

- Using non-toxic paints, glue and other finishes, and always washing fabrics to remove any toxic coating
- Ensuring the materials used are not flammable – especially doll's hair, clothing and accessories. It is also important that the toy is well-made and sturdy enough to withstand playtime activity.
- Seams should be strong so that the filling can't escape

⊙ All small pieces should be securely fastened to the toy so they cannot be easily pulled off and become a choking danger

⊙ Wooden toys should be sanded smooth with no sharp edges, and preferably made from soft wood that is unlikely to splinter.

Liquid in toys

Toys that contain liquid include rolling balls, doll baby bottles, children's tumblers, necklaces, pens, paperweights, key chains and liquid timers. If the liquid is not identified on a label as safe and you suspect that it could be a harmful chemical substance, the toy could be dangerous for your child if they bite into or puncture it. *Discard the toy if the content leaks.*

Noisy toys

Be wary of toys that make loud noises as they can harm your child's hearing. Babies are more sensitive to loud noises than older children. Be particularly careful of toys that make a loud noise when held close to their ear such as toy telephones with speakers in the earpieces. Impulsive sounds like that from a cap gun or noise from a continuous siren can also be a hearing hazard for your child.

Storing toys safely

Toy boxes are useful for storing toys and helping keep bedrooms tidy, but they can be dangerous. Young children have died from being struck by heavy toy box lids as they peered inside the toy box. Some children have also been trapped inside toy boxes and been unable to lift the lid. If your toy box has a heavy lid, think about removing it for the safety of your child. If you are considering buying a toy box:

⊙ Look for one without a lid – if you choose a toy box with a lid, the lid should be lightweight and removable

⊙ If there is a lock on a toy box lid, make sure it is easy for a child to open from the inside

⊙ Make sure the toy box has ventilation holes to prevent a child suffocating should they climb inside and the lid closes

⊙ Make sure the toy box lid has rubber or other stoppers that allow a gap of 12mm or more when the lid is closed so that small fingers can't be crushed, and to help provide ventilation.

TOYS FOR KIDS UP TO THREE YEARS

Children under three years old often place toys in their mouth to explore them by sucking and chewing on them. Children in this age group are especially vulnerable to choking on small objects. *Keep small objects out of the reach of young children and always supervise their play time.*

Toys suitable for children aged up to three years must comply with the mandatory Trade Practices Act safety standard *Toys for children up to and including 36 months of age*. This means that, by law, toys suitable for ages up to 36 months (not just those marked as such) must not contain or produce during normal use any small parts that could fit inside a 35mm film canister, as they may be a choking hazard. Any object that is small enough to fit inside a 35mm film canister could choke or be swallowed or inhaled by a child under three years old. Examples of the toys suitable for children under three years of age are:

⊙ Toys to be grasped, shaken or rattled by small hands

Safe toys for kids

- Simple action toys for surprise or identifying sounds or pictures
- Toys, including books, for recognising basic letters and numbers
- Toys for sorting large shapes that do not need finger dexterity.

BABY TOYS
Before you buy
Rattles and teethers:

- Rattles and teethers must be large enough that babies can't fit them completely into their mouths as this would be a choking hazard. Small ends (such as the rattle handle) must not fit into a 50 x 35mm hole, or if round must not fit into a 43mm diameter hole.
- Never tie a teether or dummy around a baby's neck as it could strangle them.
- Rattles and other hand-held noise-producing toys should not be noisier than a loud conversation in a room.

Toys on a string or elastic cord:

- When a toy is attached to a string, the free length of the string should be shorter than 300mm so that the string is not a strangulation hazard.
- When a toy has an elastic cord to be attached across a cradle, cot or pram, the maximum stretched length of the elastic should be no more than 750mm, and the length of the elastic when relaxed should be no greater than 560mm. The elastic may be enclosed in a tube. The toy should display this warning label: *WARNING: This toy should be removed from the cradle, cot, playpen, pram, stroller etc. when the child is able to sit up unaided, because there is a possibility that the child could fall forward onto the toy in a way that would cause a restriction to breathing.*

Self retracting pull-strings:

- The last 50mm of any pull-string on toys for children younger than 18 months should stay outside the toy when the string is fully retracted so the child's fingers do not get caught.

Detachable parts:

- The detachable parts of toys intended for small children should not be small enough to be poked into the mouth, nose or ears. Smaller parts like eyes and buttons must be firmly attached to the toy.

Battery-operated toys:

- Mobiles, musical toys and night lights for children should have any batteries securely enclosed – the battery casing should only be able to be opened with a specific tool.

Mains-operated toys and appliances:

- Toys that operate on mains electricity, or appliances like night lights connected to the power supply by flexible electric cords, should be completely sealed or enclosed at the point where the power enters the toys.

STUFFED TOYS
Stuffed toys like teddy bears and cuddly dolls may seem harmless, but their eyes, nose, hair, buttons or attached jewellery are often small enough to choke small children. Check that all small parts and attachments cannot be easily removed.

Before you buy:

- The filling of stuffed toys should be clean and free of objects or substances that may be harmful.
- If possible, feel the toy for any sharp objects.
- Toys made from foam, such as bath blocks, may pose a choking danger if a child bites pieces off it. Foam toys are not recommended for children under three years.
- Only buy bean-bag style toys if you are sure the seams or material will not tear to allow the beans to escape. Polystyrene beads can be particularly hazardous as young children might inhale them.
- Seams should be securely sewn. If seams are sewn with a synthetic material like nylon thread, check the ends of the thread are secure.
- Check that all parts and small attachments like hair, jewellery and eyes cannot be easily removed from the toy.

Safety at home:

- Never let a child younger than three play with toys that have small parts that could separate and cause choking.
- Resew any split seams or dispose of the toy.
- Check toys regularly to make sure any accessories or small parts remain securely attached.

BUILDING BLOCKS

Brightly coloured toy building blocks and nesting cubes can provide young children with creative and constructive play as they stack and knock down their creations. Beware of sets containing small parts that could choke your child.

Before you buy:

- Check that paints and lacquers are non-toxic. Look for a label on a painted toy specifying that the paints are non-toxic.
- Make sure plastic pieces are durable and not brittle. When brittle plastic breaks it can form sharp, jagged edges or points that can cut.
- Select wooden items that are smoothly finished and made from soft wood that is unlikely to splinter when chewed.

Safety at home:

- Demonstrate the safe use of building sets to your child.

PUSH-PULL TOYS

Push-pull toys are ideal for young children when they start to take an active interest in exploring their surroundings and become more mobile. Toys that can be pushed or pulled along include items attached to a cord or a rigid handle such as a walking trolley with blocks or a toy stroller.

Before you buy
Pull strings:

- If your child is 18 months or younger, ensure the pull string is shorter than 22cm. Strings longer than this can tangle and form a loop or noose, and be a strangulation danger.

Safe toys for kids

- For children aged 18 months to 36 months, cords that are longer than 22cm should not have beads or other attachments that could tangle to form a loop or noose.
- Any string or cord attached to a toy should be at least 1.5mm thick to avoid being a cutting danger.

Solid handles:
- Push-along or pull-along toys with rigid handles should have protective covers firmly attached to the ends of the handle so that the exposed ends can't cut or stab an infant.
- Removal or loss of a cover should not reveal a sharp point or edge, and the cover must not be small enough to choke a child.
- Crossbars on handles should be firmly attached to the bar leading from the toy. They should not be attached by nails, as an exposed nail could form a sharp cutting edge.

Axles:
- Axles should be properly attached to the toy and the wheels firmly attached to the axles. Removal of a wheel or an axle should not produce a dangerous sharp point.

DOLLS

Children may take an interest in dolls when they begin to play make-believe games. There are many types of dolls available and you should be careful to select a safe one that suits your child's age and development.

Before you buy
Limb attachment:
- For children up to three years, ensure that the doll's limb or head, if removable, could not fit inside a 35mm film canister so it isn't a choking danger.
- If limbs or heads can be pulled from the doll's body, they should not expose sharp wires inside the body or on the end of the limb or head. Attachment with rubber bands is acceptable if the point of attachment on the limb and/or body is not a sharp screw, nail or hook that will cut fingers poked into the gap.

Construction material:
- Plastic should be soft and flexible, as brittle plastics can break and form sharp fragments and dangerous small parts.
- Wooden dolls should have smoothly finished surfaces, free of splinters. They should not contain joining nails or screws and the joins should be firmly glued.

Eyes and buttons:
- Small parts such as eyes and buttons should be securely fixed to the doll or its clothes so they cannot be easily removed by pulling, chewing or washing. Eyes and buttons should be non-toxic.

Pins:
- Nappies, liners and other clothes designed to be removed from the doll should be secured with velcro, clips or other safe fastening systems, not pins.

Handbags and purses:
- Decorations, like glitter, sequins or jewellery, on handbags, purses and other fashion accessories should be firmly attached.

Safety at home:

- Do not give small metal figures to young children. These figures are usually collectors' items and not for children – they may contain or be coated with toxic elements.
- Do not give children dolls that have exposed and dangerous sharp edges or points.
- Regularly check the dolls' clothing for bows, ribbons or other adornments that may become loose, as young children could choke on them.
- Remove any pins attached to the dolls' clothes.

TOY TRAINS, CARS AND MINIATURE VEHICLES

Vehicle toys appeal to children of all ages, but some, such as kits that require assembly and detailed models with small parts, are unsuitable for young children.

Before you buy

Construction:

- Choose toy vehicles that are strong and durable, preferably with large parts.
- Any small parts like internal fittings or mouldings, including windows, dashboards and steering wheels, should be fixed firmly so they cannot be removed by a child.

Edges should be smooth:

- Wooden vehicles should have smooth surfaces free of splinters. If vehicles are not made from a single piece of wood, the separate pieces should be firmly joined together. Glued sections fitted together with dowelling are preferable to using nails or screws that could cut or scratch if the toy breaks apart.
- Plastic vehicles should be moulded in one piece and the plastic should be strong enough to withstand rough treatment. The plastic should also be flexible enough not to form sharp or jagged sections if it breaks.
- Metal vehicles should have no sharp edges or corners. Individual parts should be firmly attached, preferably by secure rivets or welding.

Wheels and tyres:

- Wheels and tyres should be firmly attached to the vehicle. They should not, if removed, expose sharp axle rods, rough metal or splintered wheel rims. Small tyres should not be easily removed from the wheels.

Self-propelled vehicles:

- These include models with inertia motors, wound by pushing the vehicle along the floor.
- The motor should be fully enclosed with no gaps where fingers or foreign objects can get caught.
- Hand-wound mechanisms, like those on the lifting and lowering mechanisms of cranes, should be enclosed or have gears that cannot trap fingers or catch on clothing.

Dump trucks:

- Trucks and other vehicles with tilting trays should be constructed so that fingers can't be caught in the tray when it closes. Pieces that open and close should have blunt or rounded edges so fingers aren't caught or cut if the tray closes on them.

Safe toys for kids

Self-retracting strings:

◆ To ensure that the child's fingers do not get caught, check that the string does not retract too quickly and that it leaves at least 5cm length outside the toy.

Towing strings:

◆ If the string or cord is longer than 22cm, the toy should not have any slip knots or attachments that could form a loop, creating a strangulation hazard. Any string or cord on a pull-along toy for a child under three years should be at least 1.5mm thick, so it is unlikely to cut a child.

Sharp edges:

◆ There should not be any sharp points or edges on vehicles that could stab or injure a person.

WATER TOYS

When you buy toys for use in water, remember that they are not life-saving devices. Life-saving devices are covered by specific Australian standards as personal flotation devices and are not covered by this safety checklist. The Consumer Product Safety Standard for Children's Flotation Toys and Swimming Aids covers flotation toys used by children younger than 15. The standard defines a flotation toy as a device that provides buoyancy but is not attached to the body. It includes things like rings, inflatable arm bands, kick-boards and small inflatable toy boats. The standard requires that these goods must pass a series of performance tests and must be marked: *Warning: Use only under competent supervision.*

Before you buy

Inflatable arm bands and rings:

◆ Inflatable arm bands, generally worn on the child's upper arms, and inflatable rings worn around the waist, must be marked with a warning notice.

◆ The sole purpose of inflatable rings is to keep a child on the water's surface. A child who goes under the water wearing an inflatable ring may return to the surface in an unsafe position, such as feet first.

Kick-boards:

◆ Kick-boards help children develop their kicking technique and gain confidence in the water and should also be marked with the safety warning.

Floating pillows and lilos:

◆ Inflatable pillows, air mattresses or lilos provide a way to rest or play on the water, but are not intended to be life saving devices.

Face masks and goggles:

◆ Swimming goggles have a separate lens for each eye, and are not designed for underwater diving.

◆ Face masks have one large lens covering eyes and nose and are designed for underwater diving. A mask that is too small will be uncomfortable, and one that is too large may not seal and could allow water to enter.

Flippers:

◆ Flippers improve the power of a swimmer's kick, but are not flotation aids.

◆ You should also consider where the flippers will be used – flippers held in place by a strap around the heel do not usually have a base that covers the heel and the sole of the foot, and are not recommended for use on rough surfaces like rocks or coral.

RIDE-ON TOYS

Kids love wheeled toys but these can be dangerous. The most common injuries associated with wheels are falls – and over half of these are caused by irregular riding surfaces. This section includes pedal cars and sit-on toys that are propelled by the child pushing along the ground with their legs and feet.
A ride-on toy should be stable and not tip in any direction on a slope when the child is sitting on it.

Before you buy
Steering wheels:
- Column-mounted steering wheels should not be easy to remove. An exposed steering wheel shaft could spear the rider. The steering wheel should be made from a material strong enough to resist the impact of a child in an accident. If the steering wheel shatters it could expose the shaft and spear the child.

Wheels and wheel rims:
- Wheels and wheel rims, especially plastic or wooden ones, should be strong enough not to collapse or disintegrate under normal riding conditions. They should be able to withstand shocks, such as hitting kerbs, large stones or other irregular surfaces.

Seats:
- Seats should be made from a material that is not likely to split, crack or shatter on impact and place the rider at risk of being speared by the exposed seat post. All seats and surfaces, including those underneath the seat, should be smooth so they can't cut fingers.

Handlebars/grips:
- Check that the handlebar is not loose.
- If the handlebars are raised, check the supporting stem is inserted far enough down the shaft for it to be stable.
- Handlebar ends should be covered and the handgrips secure. Exposed handlebar ends can severely injure a child in a fall.
- The shaft supporting the handlebars should be strong enough to resist an impact during an accident.
- When seated, the rider's arms should be slightly bent when holding the handgrips and the child's knees should not hit the handlebar.

Support between front and back wheels:
- The support or frame between the front and back wheels should not bend or break under likely stress.

Pedal-operated toys:
- The rods connecting the pedals to the driving wheels should be firmly connected at all joints. The joints should not be sloppy or able to be disconnected, as a disconnected rod could spear upwards or dig into the ground and tip the toy.
- It should not be possible for a child's foot to become tangled in the connecting rods or the pedals. Feet should not be able to be trapped under any part of the toy when it is moving (check the pedals at their lowest position).

How to deal with temper tantrums

Temper tantrums and negativity are common behaviours during the toddler period as they learn to control their world. Nevertheless, these behaviours can be exhausting and frustrating for parents.

Reasons for temper tantrums:

- Difficulty telling parents and others what they need – not enough words to talk about their needs or emotions
- Frustration that they do not have the skill to do tasks others are doing
- Tiredness and hunger
- Difficulty controlling their emotions – quickly going from excitement to anger
- Fear – becoming scared when they lose control and not knowing how to calm down
- Not wanting to wait for things, as they can only think of their own needs
- Habit – the toddler has learnt that if they have a tantrum they will get what they want
- Testing limits – this is helping them learn about control and power
- Temperament of your toddler – some toddlers are easy going, others are shy or very active
- It is important to seek assistance if you are concerned about the number or intensity of the temper tantrums – occasionally temper tantrums can be due to more serious problems.

Things that make the situation worse:

- Being tired (both you and your toddler).
- Being hungry.
- Being too excited or overstimulated.
- Being bored or under-stimulated.
- Being unwell.
- Being told "no" or "don't" all the time.
- Being in a hurry.

Avoiding temper tantrums

Whenever possible:

- Have realistic expectations of your toddler's ability and needs
- Anticipate and avoid (if possible) difficult situations or activities for your toddler when they are tired, hungry or unwell
- Introduce new activities slowly and one at a time
- Develop routines and rituals so your toddler has a feeling of control over their world
- Limit the amount of activity and noise – have quiet times during the day
- Use a distraction when your toddler is becoming upset or agitated, e.g. "look at that car over there!"
- Provide your toddler with limited choices, e.g. "do you want milk or water?"
- Always ask your toddler to do things using one command at a time, wait for the action to be completed before giving the next task.

- Use positive language and praise – avoid saying 'no' all the time.
- Understand any stress your toddler may be experiencing, e.g. the arrival of a new baby, being left in childcare etcetera.

During a temper tantrum

There are several strategies that can be used to help your toddler gain control of their emotions:

- Holding and rocking your toddler while you provide soothing words, e.g. "daddy is here you are safe". This method can assist your toddler calm down and feel safe. It may be safer for you to hold them on your lap facing outwards if they are kicking.
- Pretend to ignore them, this can be difficult. You will need to ensure that your toddler won't hurt themselves during the tantrum, e.g. take them out of the bath, or shopping trolley, or remove furniture. It is important that you stay calm, take some deep breaths and count to ten.
- Time-out or putting your toddler in a safe place. If you are at home you can use time-out for both you and your toddler to assist you in gaining control.
- Removing them from the situation. This can be difficult as you will need to stop what you are doing and take your toddler to another area, e.g. move from one room to another.

Things that don't help:

- Getting upset and yelling at your toddler – most parents feel guilty when they have lost control.
- Giving lengthy reasons about why you wanted your toddler to do something or why you are upset – keep explanations simple.
- Bribing your toddler to behave, e.g. "if you stop yelling I will give you a chocolate".
- Physical punishments – shouting, slapping, name-calling or threats.

The good news for parents is that as your toddler develops language and physical skills, the number and severity of tantrums will reduce.

Information supplied by Tresillian, www.tresillian.net.

Choosing books for small children

It's a wonderful time to be sharing books with children. Australian publishers have responded to the baby boom and so there are more Australian books for Australian babies and toddlers than ever before.

All children learn naturally, and voraciously, through play. It's their job, and we should give them as much time for doing it as we can – especially play they structure for themselves. This is how they learn best. Play can be physical and boisterous and it can be quiet and exploratory. Books for babies and toddlers are created to mirror these needs, to allow them to engage, interpret and experience a myriad of things.

Sharing books with children is a totally satisfying experience engaging ears, eyes, hands and hearts. It's the emotional engagement between the adult and the child that is so important – often more so than the story itself.

Just as bright colours are fun and excite the senses, as do loud noises and sweet or tasty foods, subtle colours, sounds and textures can express different feelings and expressions. There is a need for variety in the books selected for children – important for their diet, an opportunity to develop broad tastes from an early age.

There are many places to find the best books for young children and many who can help with our choices: libraries and children's librarians; parents' groups; specialist children's bookshops; pre-school teachers and child carers; publications of the Children's Book Council of Australia; lists put out by state organisations; magazines: Magpies; Good Reading; Reading Time; and various institutional websites.

It is helpful to know that there are books created with very particular age ranges and development stages in mind. Babies often enjoy getting their teeth into a good board book in more ways than one. Simple shapes work best – good design, clear colours, sometimes even pure black & white. Favourites are often playful with colours, sounds or textures and focus on the familiar – sleep-time, dressing, eating, toys and tools, even facial expressions.

Toddlers are interested in the world they are exploring, recognising it through familiar activities and objects, though the characters could easily be dinosaurs or farm animals, and the settings might be outer space or deep ocean. Although children develop at different rates, many of their favourite books can span across age ranges and will be read over and over for years. Generations have shared Dr Seuss's Green eggs and Ham.

We all know how books can put you inside someone else's skin (feel their pain, learn from their mistakes, see problems from a different angle). They work for children in the same way. Although the majority of children's books are light-hearted and purely joyful, there are many books written especially to help the young child and their families deal with new, potentially tricky situations.

The best of these books have strong, well-written stories woven around a feeling: *Owl Babies* (when will mum come back); *Ginger* (a newcomer in the family); *Lucy Goosey* (fear of change).

There are books about death, sibling rivalry, new baby, twins, loneliness, selfishness, bullying, even growing sexual awareness. The important thing is that they are enjoyable stories and not didactic lessons pretending to be a story. Even for the young David Attenboroughs, there are great discovery and activity books, as well as fantasy.

Choosing books for fun and wonder will result in engagement and success. Books chosen for their worthiness or as learning exercises may, at worst, discourage the young reader. However there are many great stories, creative with concepts like numbers, colours and words (*The Very Hungry Caterpillar*; *Cat in the Hat*; *Where is the Green Sheep*), that will be read again and again.

The word count in a picture book has not much to do with suitability for age level. Books for the very young are created to be read to and with the child. Picture books often have many layers of rich visual stories which you'll discover as you read them over and over.

So choose a mix of stories that are playful and creative with both words and pictures – rhyming and rollicking, (*Hairy Maclary*), magical (*Rainbow Magic*), evocative (*Let's Escape*), exciting (*Where the Wild Things Are*), playful (*The Duck in the Truck*), painterly (*I Love Boats*), textured (*Crocodile Beat*) and naughty (*The Midnight Gang*)! The main thing is to share lots of different books with a playful enthusiasm that you'll enjoy as much as them!

List of Australian titles

BABIES +	TODDLERS +	THREE YEAR OLDS +
Go, Baby Go (4 titles) Sally Rippin, *Allen & Unwin*	**The Midnight Gang** Wild & James, *Omnibus Books*	**Doodledum Dancing** Costain & Allen, *Penguin*
Possum Magic (board book) Julie Vivas & Mem Fox *Omnibus Books*	**Ten Little Fingers, Ten Little Toes** Ormerod & Fox	**Crocodile Beat** Mullins & Jorgensen *Omnibus Books*
Crocodile Beat Mullins & Jorgensen *Omnibus Books*	**Felix** Pamela Allen, *Penguin Books*	**Possum and Wattle** Bronwyn Bancroft *Little Hare Books*
Bumping & Bouncing (4 titles) Alison Lester, *Allen & Unwin*	**Where is the Green Sheep** Judy Horacek & Mem Fox *Penguin Books*	**Mr McGee** series, Pamela Allen
Roar; Purr; Moo Alison Lester, *ABC Books*	**Puffin Babies** various titles, *Penguin Books*	**Hairy Maclary**, Lynley Dodd
Whose Feet (series) Jeannette Rowe, *ABC Books*	**Goodnight Me** Daddo & Quay	**Amy & Louis** Blackwood & Gleeson
Dear Zoo Rod Campbell	**I Went Walking**, Williams & Vivas	**Lucy Goosey** Wild & James, *Little Hare Books*
Froggy Green Anna Walker *Penguin Books*	**Baby** Cox & James	**The Way I Love You** Bedford & James
I Love to Dance (2 titles) Anna Walker, *Scholastic*	**Kisses for Daddy** Watts & Legge	**Josh** (series), Andrew & Janet McLean, *Allen & Unwin*
Tractor, Tractor (2 titles) Bedford & Watson *Little Hare Books*	**Hugo the lifesaving sailor** Lorette Broekstra	**Max**, Bob Graham, *Walker Books*
	Let's Escape Dumbleton & Gamble *Scholastic Books*	**The Firefighters** Rawlins & Whiting, *Walker Books*
	BIG and Small Bedford & Worthington *Little Hare*	**Guess the baby** Rawlins and French
	Big and Little Donna Rawlins, *Random House*	

Information supplied by Books Illustrated, www.booksillustrated.com.au.

How to handle sibling rivalry

Picture the scene: toddlers playing co-operatively, negotiating whose turn is next, giving parents time to prepare a meal without interruption. Sounds pleasant doesn't it? Is it realistic? Maybe sometimes. Probably not very often.

Many people planning children imagine an idyllic carefree family life. The reality is often far from this tranquil imagery, and sometimes parents feel disappointed when children don't seem to get along. Having more than one child in a family brings lots of opportunities for children to learn about sorting out differences, working out how to be fair and developing skills of generosity and empathy.

Many parents work hard at preparing firstborns for the birth of the next child and hope that all will go smoothly. Children between 15 months to 3.5 years enjoy cause and effect learning and babies provide a lot of opportunities for this kind of learning. Children these ages like to push buttons and turn dials to see what happens. With a baby, a toddler might think something like: "I wonder how hard I need to squeeze his hand before he reacts? Wow! That was a BIG reaction!" or "How long do I lay on her before she reacts?". Sometimes parents think of these behaviours as violence or jealousy, and understandably, wanting to protect the more vulnerable child, many parents react. When a toddler gets a reaction from both the baby and the parents, whatever led to that reaction is likely to be repeated. If we instead view this behaviour as something more akin to a scientific experiment, it can be replaced with more acceptable experiments, such as "How quickly can you get her to kick her feet by tickling her toes?". By teaching replacement behaviours to the toddler and then using words to encourage or reward these behaviours, the toddler is more likely to repeat the more acceptable behaviours.

Competition between siblings is common. It is not unusual for parents to be drawn into the conflict, wanting to protect a more vulnerable child. When parents get engaged in sorting out the problem however, young children learn that parents are needed to resolve conflict and if they want their parents to come to them, a quick way is to have a conflict together. When this happens, it is typical for conflicts between siblings to occur more frequently. It can be helpful instead to view these conflicts as opportunities to teach children about managing social relationships. With toddlers this may involve teaching them the words they need to say to assist them, teaching them to take turns, to be gentle with others, to apologise and to wait. It is more effective to teach children what you want them to do rather than what not to do. Once children are around preschool age, conflicts can be managed by asking children to sort it out together. This means giving very little attention to the problem, telling them you are not interested in who did what to whom but you do want to talk about the solution. When given the direction to work things out together, children learn to apologise and can come up with their own solutions. The challenge for parents is to put a lot of attention into rewarding the children's solution finding rather than the conflict.

So next time you see your children in conflict together, think about what you would like your children to learn and how you might teach them to resolve the issue. Each altercation between them is another opportunity to learn new skills. The learning that comes from having siblings will place the child in a good position to manage other social relationships outside the family.

Written by Bronwyn Thomas, a social worker with more than 20 years experience working with families over parenting issues. She works as a counsellor at Parentline. Parentline is a confidential telephone counselling, information and referral service for all Victorian parents and carers with children aged from birth to 18 years. Parentline is accessible from anywhere in Victoria for the cost of a local call (excluding mobiles). Phone 13 22 89.

Vox Pop

We asked a number of women and men around Australia to send in their advice, tips and personal experiences on a range of topics so that you have an insight into how others cope being a new parent. We hope you find their comments interesting, informative and reassuring. Vox Pop biographies: page 652

Melanie Smoothy
Mum of one, NSW

I'm almost certain we could one day open our own toy store with the amount of toys we've accumulated over the past two years. We cringe at the amount of toys in the 'archived toy boxes' we have in our spare room to make way for the two 'current toy boxes' in our lounge room.

Brayden seems to have acquired a love of books too, with his favourite topics being animals, farms and vehicles. We found that he seemed to recognise what he'd experienced in the books, whether via the story told or through picture books and it expanded his range of vocabulary, ie. associating the sound "baa" as belonging to a sheep and a lamb being a baby sheep, etcetera.

Our house is located on a street which has quite a heavy traffic flow, so we have always had 'background noise' CDs playing in his room – an assortment of lullabies and soft/classical music playing on repeat to dull the startling sounds of trucks early in the morning, or the school bus bringing children home. Nursery rhymes have not only become a favourite to dance to, but they are great for keeping boredom at bay when travelling. Furthermore, they are mostly quite educational, particularly songs like the alphabet song and *Five Little Ducks*.

Tanya Byrnes
Mum of one, VIC

Children will like almost any toys which is bright, colourful and noisy! Soft toys are great as pretty well everything they place in their tiny little hands goes straight in their mouths. Our son has two toys which he can't leave home without: his monkey which glows in the dark and changes colour, and his lizard. These seem to be his little security friends which he needs most of the time.

Tracey Thompson
Mum of one, Brisbane

As my child was the first grandchild on both sides he got spoilt rotten! We had so many toys and clothes, I thought I would never use them! But we sure did. When he was a newborn up to about 3 months he was happy to look at anything that was brightly coloured. He loved his playgym and it was great for me too because it kept him entertained for a while so I could do my own thing!

When he got a little older, up to about 7 months, anything that was noisy or had flashing lights was great fun. From that age onwards I am finding he likes more complex toys. Anything where he has to fit a shape into a hole and stack smaller boxes into larger boxes seems to keep his attention.

You don't need heaps of toys to keep your child entertained – just rotate them around. I put three or four different toys out at a time and swap them every week so that there are always 'new' toys out to play with.

Martine Pekarsky
Mum of two, Melbourne

Our house would turn into a 'toy tip' if we let it get out of hand. One weekend we walked through the house and found a toy on the floor of every room! I think the best strategy is to purchase very few toys but buy really good quality toys which are safe and will last for family hand-me-downs.

Only buy age-appropriate toys and be careful of those ones with little pieces as they will spread through the house.

We find that both children want the same thing so we buy two of everything, just two different colours or styles.

We purchase most of our gifts online as it seems to be cheaper and easier when you include gift wrapping, cards and all the time traipsing around the shops with two small children.

Kirstin Amos
Mum of one, QLD

Carter enjoys playing with a wide variety of toys. I try to make sure there are a wide variety of colours, textures, shapes and sizes in his playpen. We make sure that when buying toys we get age-specific toys so that Carter gets the most out of them. One of the favourites at the moment is two plastic drinking bottles: one with rice inside and the other with pasta. Carter loves these and will happily sit and shake these until he is ready to move onto the other toys sitting in his play area. The best advice I could give in relation to buying toys even before baby is born is stick to simple, bright and colourful toys that engage baby as it is amazing how much they are taking in. The only toys that I avoid at this age are hard sharp plastics and metal toys, mainly due to the fact that Carter loves sticking things in his mouth, like most children his age, and we do not want him damaging any teeth or his gums.

Anna Brandt
Mum of one, QLD

My baby's favourite thing to play with was a fluro coloured cardboard love heart which was stuck on a coloured paddle pop stick. My sister had heaps of these done for my kitchen tea party when I was getting married and I had heaps left over. I gave him one and he absolutely loved it. He would wave it around in the air and just look at it. Every time I would give him a new one he would do a little body shake with excitement. Now that everything goes in the mouth I just pull the paddle pop stick off (because the colour would come off in his mouth) and give him the cardboard love heart. He is still fascinated by it and the best part is, it didn't cost me a cent.

We've been reading books to our son since I was about 6 months pregnant. We have a huge collection so it's always a while before reading the same one

again. The little board books are great for when your baby is sucking on everything. Classics are great presents because they never date and can be passed through the generations: *Snugglepot & Cuddlepie, Peter Rabbit Collection, Little Golden Books, Dr Seuss*.

An all time favourite book of ours would have to be *Olga the Brolga*. What a great story and the pictures are just beautiful. My baby loves listening to this story and the Dr Seuss books always get a big smile too. They're so lively and the rhymes are so clever. I love listening to my husband reading these, he jumbles the rhymes so much it's hilarious.

Our favourite CD would have to be *Shoo Fly*. The songs are great and easy to learn: we do lots of singing along to this CD. It's really fun and the squealing and squirming that comes from my baby is well worth learning the words for.

Michelle Winduss
Mum of one, Sydney

My son's favourite toys are his blocks. He has wooden blocks and plastic blocks that come in different shapes and colours.

Each morning he stacks his wooden blocks on top of each other to make a tall tower. His tower must be built at the beginning of each day before he starts to play with his other toys. The blocks also have colours, pictures and the letters of the alphabet on them. As each block in the tower is built, we name the picture and say the letter of the alphabet.

The other blocks that he likes to play with are coloured and different shapes. They come with a container and lid that allows the blocks to pass through the different shapes on the lid.

Although my son is only 20 months and technically cannot yet read, he 'pretends' to read. Quite often you will find him sitting on the floor, turning the pages of a book and making little noises, which I guess is his way of reading. He has some favourite books that he likes to read – his 'sparkle' books and his musical book.

Vox Pop

We asked a number of women and men around Australia to send in their advice, tips and personal experiences on a range of topics so that you have an insight into how others cope being a new parent. We hope you find their comments interesting, informative and reassuring. Vox Pop biographies: page 652

His sparkle books have sections of pages that are highlighted by coloured aluminium foil. This is a very basic concept, but very effective in drawing a child's attention to the story. As we read the book, my son points to and touches the sparkling sections of the page. This seems to keep him very interested in listening to what we are saying. My son's other favourite book is his pop up *Thomas the Tank Engine* book that plays tunes that we can sing to. As we turn each page, we press the button that corresponds to the tune and I sing the tune to him. My son loves the way the book 'pops' up as we turn each page and his face lights up when I start singing the tunes to him. I get so much enjoyment from seeing him so happy.

Sophie McKellar
Mum of two, VIC

Our favourite book is *Where is the Green Sheep*? We all enjoy it because the pictures are fun and every page we learn something new. It is lovely and simple. Any of the lift-the-flap books have been a big hit in our house.

Music is a huge part of our day; I love to sing so this encourages the children too. In the car we always have fun kids CDs playing and lots of action ones too. When they were small we listened to lots of classical music and it calmed me as well. Be very careful as to not get too sleepy because I fell asleep at the traffic lights with very young twins on board because I was sooo tired. But music is a wonderful thing and it is so good for the whole family.

Cindy Fraser
Mum of three, Melbourne

Our most used toys are usually ones that are versatile and suitable for different ages. Blocks, puzzles, cars, tea set, crayons, train sets and dolls are all favourites in our house. Each of my children has a 'special' toy that we would be lost without (and

we have backtracked along the streets with a torch searching for a missing bear!) Our eldest had Henry the bear that went everywhere with him, until his nanny and poppy gave him Chloe the toy dog who shafted Henry as the favourite toy. Our daughter has a doll called Lilly who she enjoys bossing around and a doll called Molly who she has abbreviated and been given the unfortunate nickname Mole. And our youngest is madly in love with his bear Billy. We try very hard to not let Billy leave the house; we can't imagine how hard life would be for us all without him!

We have read to our children from day one which they have all really enjoyed. They each have their favourites which they ask for over and over again.

Bernadette Vella
Mum of two, Brisbane

My kids have way too many toys. They are the only grandchildren on one side and they are spoilt. At Christmas time I like to talk to them about the children that are not so lucky and we take some of their toys to the local Vinnies store. Tiernan gets quite excited about it and seems to understand that he is helping kids who are not so lucky.

I started reading to both my children from an early age and it is part of their bedtime routine. I like to read to each of them individually at night time. It is a little bit of special time they get with me on their own.

We tend to read two stories and then talk about what we did during the day. I used to talk about what we were planning for tomorrow however found that tends to hype them up. Whenever I read to them, they are cuddled up to me and it is a lovely time together.

When I leave the room it is always lights out but they each have a CD that they listen to. Arielle listens to classical music and Tiernan listens to stories on CD. I love watching them when they are sleeping – it is hard to believe they can be so full of life and crazy during the day and so peaceful and quiet when they are asleep.

Anastasia Jones
Mum of two, Melbourne

The day I picked my daughter up from daycare and her carer said to me "she played with a doll for about 30 minutes today," I almost ried! I am not the type of person who thinks that girls should play with dolls, and boys with cars but I have to admit that, at the same time, I did want her o at least have some interest in dolls.

Today she plays with her dolls every so often but prefers 'yellow cat', 'baby jaguar', lion or dog toys. Maybe she will be a vet when she grows up! Stuffed bears have been a total loss and take up so much room, but because they were gifts I haven't had the heart to give them up yet!

I love reading to my children. We have read to our eldest child almost every day since she was born and she still has one or two stories read to her a day. My youngest is only just now starting to like books at 18 months old – until now she would slam them in your hands every time you tried to read her one!

Jessica Hatherall
Mum of two, Sydney

Books are always a great easy gift for any age or gender. A good bookstore can help you find the right one for the right age.

Giving new mums something to help them relax and look after themselves makes a great pressie (like bath oils or massage treatments). For newborns I like to give pressies for when they are a bit older and will hopefully get more use out of them.

My toddler loves books. A lot of the books we read to him as a baby he has memorised and still enjoys reading now. He is a huge Dr Seuss fan – *Horton Hatches An Egg*, *One Fish Two Fish* etc. He also enjoys the *Spot* stories and any book about trucks. He also likes lots of different CDs – Justine Clarke's *I Like to Sing*, *Thomas the Tank Engine*, *Postman Pat* and *Bob the Builder*.

Ros Pittard
Mum of two, VIC

A great gift idea for a new mum is family and friends all contributing to pay for a cleaner for a while. One of the hardest parts of becoming a mum is learning to live with mess when there used to be none! Everyone says not to worry about the housework, but when you're trying to muddle your way through on little sleep, it's nice not to have to look at a dirty floor that you never get around to cleaning. Gift vouchers for a massage or pamper day for mum to use when things have settled down is great too. It's something indulgent to look forward to and also a great excuse to get out of the clothes with baby puke all over them and put on some lippy!

Tony Wilson
Dad of one, Melbourne

Can I plug my own books? *The Thirsty Flowers*, *Grannysaurus Rex* and *The Minister for Traffic Lights*, all by me. To be honest, Polly isn't quite up to any of those – *The Thirsty Flowers* contains the word 'prognosis' and given she struggles with 'dog', opting for her chosen pronunciation of 'gog', it's unlikely she's going to use 'prognosis' well and in a sentence. So if I was to be honest, *Hairy Maclary* and all the Lynley Dodd books. *Chatterbox* by Margaret Wild (an animal on every page), *Where the Wild Things Are* (Polly finds the magic trick hilarious, and enjoys pointing at the moon) and weirdly, the picture book version of *Clancy of the Overflow* by Banjo Patterson. She clicks her tongue for the horses' hooves, and thinks the drover's dog looks like our dog, Charley, which he does. Unfortunately, she also likes *Spot*, a disappointing glitch in her literary taste.

I love reading to her because it's a time we get to cuddle, just before bed. She'll also sometimes choose a book in the morning or during the day, because

Vox Pop

We asked a number of women and men around Australia to send in their advice, tips and personal experiences on a range of topics so that you have an insight into how others cope being a new parent. We hope you find their comments interesting, informative and reassuring. Vox Pop biographies: page 65?

she knows that book equals undivided attention on her. She definitely loves the cadence of out-loud reading, and her memory is amazing. Even without the book, if I start reciting *Clancy of the Overflow*, Polly will click her tongue, say 'gog' and bounce like a kangaroo. I hope this still happens when she's sixteen.

Lee Norman
Mum of one, Melbourne

We got so many gifts, clothes and soft toys which were all greatly appreciated. A number of items of special note are the keepsakes and unique items. We received a personalised baby blanket with Bliss' name, date and time of birth and weight at birth and we received the same information on a personalised teddy bear and wall hanging. We received a gold bracelet from one set of grandparents and a gold engraved brooch from another set. The jewellery will be great keepsakes for Bliss.

Nicole Hambling
Mum of one, VIC

Everyone wanted to know what Amy was getting for her first Christmas and I'm sure most people weren't expecting my answer – Tonka Toy Trucks. Rob and I gave Amy a Mighty Dump Truck and a Mighty Front End Loader. Sure they were almost bigger than her at Christmas but as she was just starting to walk their wide wheel base made them the perfecting "walking" toys. Amy pushed them all over the house. Then someone taught her to ride in the back of the dump truck. Amy fitted perfectly and a new game was born. Amy would climb into the back of her dump truck and cry out until we would go and push her backwards and forwards up the hallway. Hours and hours of fun for the whole family.

They were meant to end up outside in her sandpit but for some reason they are still inside and every

now and again we still hear a cry and find our little girl sitting in the back of her Dump Truck waiting for a ride up the hallway.

Amanda Jephtha
Mum of one, Sydney

Newborns are inundated with beautiful, tiny gifts. While irresistible, the reality is they are short-lived. Buying for 6 months onwards is a good idea. If clothes are on the agenda, then buy size 0 and above. A baby can never have too many singlet onesies (singlets which do up between the legs with press studs) to keep their little torsos warm. They may look absolutely enormous compared to the new baby, but the baby will grow into them shortly.

A beautiful melamine plate and cup set for the baby's first foods makes both a lovely and practical present.

Toys from birthday gifts, goodie bags and grandparents are just a small part of the toy battalion taking over your fort. So with so many toys to choose from, why does your child declare boredom?

Children become over-stimulated with too much choice, and your child may find it difficult to concentrate on the important task at hand – playing. Enter the onset of boredom, and the consequent accumulation of more toys. Bingo.

One technique to keep things fun is toy rotation. Rather than all the toys available at once, group them into age-appropriate categories, then separate each category into two (or more, depending on how many toys you have) smaller sub-groups. Simply rotate between the sub-groups so your child always has 'new' toys to play with, and you won't have a house with toys strewn underfoot!

Instead of buying more toys, why not join your local toy library? Many book libraries have this service available for a small annual fee, so your child can play with 'new' toys, while you save money buying fewer toys. This is also a great opportunity for your child to play and interact with the other children at the library.

Kerri Harding
Mum of one, VIC

We have a very extensive collection of wooden Thomas The Tank Engine toys and track at our house. My son was given a couple of the trains for his second birthday and has never looked back. Nearly three years later and it is still one of his firm favourites to play with. Lego is the other big winner.

The best thing about these toys is that they have been around for years and can always be added to. For slightly older children, I find that anything they can pull apart and rebuild into different forms seems to hold their interest a lot longer than other things.

When my son was born, one of the gifts he received was a book titled *Guess How Much I Love You*, written by Sam McBratney. It is a really lovely story and I started reading it to him every night when he was a few weeks old. My son is now nearly five and will still choose it as one of his bedtime books occasionally. He has also adapted his own version of telling us how much he loves us from the book (and with some help from Buzz Lightyear). His version is "I love you all around the world and all around the world and all around the world…. (you get the picture) up to infinity and beyond."

Some other favourite books in our household are all of Lynley Dodd's books featuring Hairy Maclary, Slinky Malinki, Schnitzel Von Krumm and the rest of the crew. Not only is the rhyming storyline so entertaining, the language she uses is great and it keeps me entertained as well. I used to be able to recite several of her books off by heart we read them so many times! Julia Donaldson also writes some great books for slightly older children.

Bedtime is synonymous with book time and snuggles at our house. We cuddle up together on my son's bed to read books and then have a 'snuggle' together before lights out. It's a really special time where we get to spend some quality bonding time together, regardless of how hectic the rest of the day has been.

Andrew Weldon
Dad of one, Melbourne

I love American cartoonist Sandra Boynton's board books for babies. She manages to be very funny at a level suitable for babies and small children, that is also genuinely funny to adults (well this adult anyway). Of all the books I've read to our baby hers are the ones that have held up the best to repeated readings – they still seem fresh and fun after dozens of repeated readings (some of the corners are a bit gnawed though). My favourite is *Hippos Go Berserk*.

Rebecca Tragear Whiting
Mum of four, Melbourne

I love reading and have read to all my children from about 3-4 months old. I find reading is a great way to establish a bedtime routine as well as a way to instill a life long love of reading. My 6 month old boy gets so excited when he sees his bedtime story he nearly falls off my knee. We started with touch and feel books and now he loves the favourite *Where is the Green Sheep?* He also knows its bedtime when we have finished our story. Bedtime stories are a great thing for dads or older siblings to do with babies too.

Rowena Raats
Mum of three, Kalgoorlie

I love reading with my baby. She is so funny mumbling away and turning the pages. I love how she memorises certain lines in familiar books and beats me to them! It can be hard to find the time to read together but making the effort is worth the reward. Just to have that cute little person enjoying a moment together and hanging on your every word makes it worthwhile.

Resources

These Resources pages list products and services relevant to "Toys, books & gifts".
To make your life easier as a parent, editorial listings have been grouped into sub categories.
Businesses then appear alphabetically under a national or a state-based subhead depending on reach.

SUB-CATEGORIES

ADVISORY SERVICES: TOYS & BOOKS

NATIONAL

Australian Competition and Consumer Commission
Tel: 1300 302 502
email: publishing.unit@accc.gov.au
website: www.accc.gov.au
Safe toys for kids is a handy guide that will help you select safe toys for your child. It also provides information on safe use of toys. The booklet is available free from the Australian Competition and Consumer Commission.

Children's Book Council of Australia
VIC Branch: 1300 360 436
email: vic@cbca.org.au or visit www.cbca.org.au/vic
NSW Branch: (02) 9818 3858
email: nsw@cbca.org.au or visit www.cbca.org.au/nsw
QLD Branch:
email: qld@cbca.org.au or visit www.cbca.org.au/qld
WA Branch:
email: wa@cbca.org.au or visit www.cbca.org.au/wa
SA Branch:
email: sa@cbca.org.au or visit www.cbca.org.au/sa
TAS Branch:
email: tas@cbca.org.au or visit www.cbca.org.au/tas
NT Branch:
email: nt@cbca.org.au or visit www.cbca.org.au/nt
ACT Branch:
email: act@cbca.org.au
website: www.cbca.org.au

The Children's Book Council is a non-profit organisation. It was established in 1945 to promote children's literature and to encourage children to read. It runs the annual Book of the Year Awards & Children's Book Week activities. The Council disseminates information related to children's literature and encourages a high standard of book reviewing. It also promotes informed discussion and debate about children's literature.

BIKES & RIDE-ON TOYS

NATIONAL

Alana Marie Educational Toys
Tel: 1300 652 808
website: www.alanamarie.com.au

A real-life miniature piano such as the Alana Marie Petit Piano offers children a head start when it comes to their musical debut. The hand-crafted, wooden piano is chromatically tuned and has 25 full-sized piano keys. It comes with a colour-coded songbook and keychart to help teach children how to play. Available in red, pink and white. Suitable for ages 6 months to 6 years (or older). Product size: 42cms x 25cms x 30cms. No assembly required and no batteries required.

LIKEaBIKE Australia
Tel: (03) 9870 4445
email: info@likeabikeaus.com
website: www.likeabikeaus.com

LIKEaBIKE is a remarkable play vehicle that provides children as young as two the opportunity to experience the joy of cycling. Riding a LIKEaBIKE is incredible fun allowing children to develop confidence and balance in a playful way. At a later stage, children can make the transition to a conventional bike without the need for training wheels. Manufactured in Germany since 1997 from sustainable timber, high-grade steel, felt, textiles and rubber, LIKEaBIKE is unequalled in design and quality.

Micro Scooters Ltd
Tel: 0420 394 348
email: info@microscooters.com.au
website: www.microscooters.com.au

Mini Micro scooters are ideal for developing children's balance, co-ordination and motor skills. Made from light-weight reinforced plastic, the Mini Micro is easy to manoeuvre and easy on little ankles and shins. The T-bar steering column and unique three-wheel scooter design provides safety and stability for the very youngest of kids, as they learn to use their body weight and balance to steer. Long walks are now whinge-free as they zoom about independently.

Modern Brands Pty Ltd
Tel: 1800 675 772
email: sales@modernbrands.com.au
website: www.modernbrands.com.au

Fropper is a brand new breed of ride-on that bounces! Perfect for children 18 to 36 months, Fropper has a unique and innovative spring system that links the two levels of the seat, for a fun, bouncy ride like no other. Featuring whisper quiet, non-abrasive wheels, Fropper is perfect for both indoor and outdoor use. Fropper folds to a fraction of its original size and with a comfortable grip handle is easy for parents to carry to and from play areas and compact to store.

Wheely Bug Toys Pty Ltd
Tel: (07) 4093 7116
email: info@wheelybug.com
website: www.wheelybug.com

The Wheelie Bug ride-on bugs are designed for years of robust fun. On castors for unlimited mobility, they help promote spatial awareness and gross motor skills. Their bodies have a layer of soft sponge covered by a durable polyurethane leather for easy cleaning. Built in Australia

from the highest quality materials and certified safety tested. Available in two sizes: Small (seat 36l x 20w x 23h for 1–3 years) and Large (46l x 26w x 28h for 3–5 years). Available from selected stockists and online.

CHILDREN'S BOOKS, DVDs & CDs

NATIONAL

BabyBlinks
Tel: (02) 9888 5052
email: info@babyblinks.com
website: www.babyblinks.com

BabyBlinks' development DVD series is a creative introduction to learning for babies and toddlers. BabyBlinks is uniquely Australian featuring native wildlife and local narration and encourages active learning by incorporating images and music that capture a young child's attention and imagination while inspiring their curiosity and development. BabyBlinks encourages positive interaction and it is recommended parents view it with their children, treating it like an interactive picture book, pointing things out and asking questions along the way.

Bright Tomato Publishing
Tel: 0421 601 759
email: info@brighttomato.com.au
website: www.brighttomato.com.au

My First Academy - Jumbo Reading Cards are A4 size cards that can be used in a variety of ways such as wall displays, during group time or even as traditional flashcards. Their large size, bright, lifelike, colourful pictures and large red word labels will really grab your child's attention and improve their concentration. If you have been looking for a simple learning aid to use with your baby Jumbo Reading Cards are the perfect choice. Use the cards to teach your baby their first words, start teaching toddlers how to read, exercise and enrich their imaginations and expand their vocabulary. The cards come in five fun and interesting categories that your little ones can really relate to: 'common items in the home', 'fruit and vegetables', 'clothes we wear', 'numbers and colours' and 'farm animals'.

Brilliant Babies
Tel: (02) 9484 9333
website: www.brilliantbabies.com.au

Inspire your child with Brilliant Baby products. Brilliant Babies *Playtime* DVD is designed to educate and entertain and there is a selection of early childhood books, baby DVDs including Baby Einstein, Music for Babies and a range of nursery art. Products designed for early childhood learning.

Hachette Children's Books
Tel: (02) 8248 0800
email: childrens.books@hachette.com.au
website: www.hachettechildrens.com.au

Hachette Children's Books has best-selling children's picture books, full of colour and imagination. They also

Resources

TOYS, BOOKS & GIFTS

Children's books, DVDs & CDs

➡ Fabulous gift ideas

have chapter books and novels for children from first readers right through to young adult. Hachette's books are available where all good books are sold.

mainly music

Tel: 1300 668 496
website: www.mainlymusic.org.au

mainly music offers children's music that is both educational and fun, DVDs that entertain and teach, books that can be read to children as well as parenting titles and more. Phone for their latest newsletter.

Pan Macmillan Australia Pty Ltd

Tel: (02) 9285 9100
email: pansyd@macmillan.com.au
website: www.panmacmillan.com.au

MACMILLAN
Pan Macmillan Australia

Pan Macmillan is one of Australia's leading publishers of young adult, children's, first concept and parenting books and has a strong focus on Australian authors. Their authors include John Marsden, Andy Griffiths, Mem Fox, Robin Barker and Tim Winton. Their range of parenting books includes Peter Mayle's classics *What's Happening To Me?* and *Where Did I Come From?*, Robin Barker's bestselling *Baby Love*, *The Mighty Toddler* and *Baby & Toddler Meals*, Mem Fox's *Reading Magic*, Tizzie Hall's *Save Our Sleep* and the *Save Our Sleep Diaries* and many more. Pan Macmillan titles are available from all good booksellers.

Sound Impressions Pty Ltd

Tel: (03) 9867 8338
email: info@soundimpressions.com.au
website: www.musicfordreaming.com

The *Music for Dreaming Collection* for Mother and Baby, a two-CD pack, consists of *Music for Dreaming for baby* and *Music for Dreaming II for mother*. It has been created to be in harmony with you and your baby's natural biological rhythm by replicating the resting heartbeat and human pulse. The pure sound of this music is created by traditional instruments rather than synthesised sounds to protect your baby's delicate ears as well as the sensitive nervous system of both mother and baby. Two hours of continuous calming music performed by an ensemble from the internationally acclaimed Melbourne Symphony Orchestra. Scientifically researched and designed to deeply relax mother and assist baby to feed effectively and be gently soothed to sleep. Trusted and used for more than a decade by leading maternity and children's hospitals, nursing mothers and childcare centres Australia wide.

NEW SOUTH WALES

Hands Can Talk

1 Delta Close
Raby NSW 2566
Tel: (02) 9824 8332
email: aileen@handscantalk.com.au
website: www.handscantalk.com.au

Hands Can Talk makes communication easy for you and your baby using sign language. Fun, interactive, Australian (Auslan based) sign language workshops are held throughout NSW. Baby/Toddler, Toddler/Preschooler, Sing & Sign, Special needs & Makaton Basic. Hands Can Talk have specialised in Australian (Auslan based) sign language workshops and resources for over ten years. Visit their website for more information on baby sign, the benefits, baby sign resources, testimonials, discount orders and online learning.

FABULOUS GIFT IDEAS

NATIONAL

Aromababy Natural Skincare

Tel: (03) 9464 0888
email: info@aromababy.com
website: www.aromababy.com

Aromababy Natural Skincare offers a divine range of gifts for mother-to-be/pregnancy, for the new baby, new mum, dad and for the entire family. Purchase through select Myer, Babies Galore, Baby Bunting, Kids Central and Bubs Baby stores or select Priceline Pharmacies, Quality Pharmacies, Terry White, Guardian, Fullife, Harrisons and other quality pharmacies, online at www.aromababy.com or via mail order. Gifts include 100% natural and organic massage oils, lotions, creams and bath products. View the entire range at www.aromababy.com.

babybuds

Tel: 1300 550 724
email: info@babybuds.com.au
website: www.babybuds.com.au

Buying one present for a mother and her newborn baby has never been easier. babybuds offer beautiful bouquets of flowers that mum will adore and baby can wear because the flower buds are actually made of quality baby clothing.

Beauford House

Tel: (03) 9458 3577
email: beaufordhouse@hotmail.com

Michelle and Judi have been producing beautiful yet practical gifts since July 1998 and continually strive to offer something different for newborns right through to those first few years at school. Why not personalise your gift with a name, a keepsake they will have forever. For more information phone Beauford House on (03) 9458 3577 or email beaufordhouse@hotmail.com.

Bubcakes
Tel: 1300 799 892
email: info@bubcakes.com.au
website: www.bubcakes.com.au

Bubcakes® offer gorgeous gifts to welcome a new baby that are a practical yet stunning alternative to flowers. Bubcakes give the new parents essential baby items, presented in a way that won't be forgotten. A great idea for when new mums go on maternity leave, when baby arrives, christenings and baby showers or even for a dad whose wife has just delivered. They offer nation-wide delivery and special requests can be catered to.

CNP Brands
Tel: 1300 667 137
email: info@cnpbrands.com.au
website: www.cnpbrands.com.au

 Natures Purest is a range of organic bedding, babywear and gift items made from 100% organically grown naturally coloured cotton jersey and produced without the use of dyes or chemical pesticides. The cotton buds grow in natural shades of cream, brown and green and are processed to make the most wonderful natural and pure fabrics. Another natural fibre used in the Natures Purest range is bamboo. Unrivalled as one of the most luxurious materials, bamboo handles like silk, but performs like cotton so is extremely soft yet breathable and cool. The range is packaged in attractive recycled boxes and makes a perfect gift for a newborn. Natures Purest is available nationally at David Jones stores and selected nursery retailers. Visit website www.cnpbrands.com.au or contact their Customer Service on 1300 667 137 for your nearest stockist.

Corporate Rewards
Tel: (08) 9364 2526
email: babygifts@corporaterewards.com.au
website: www.corporaterewards.com.au

Corporate Rewards offer gift baskets for baby arrivals, new mums, happy parents and excited siblings, delivered Australia wide. You can choose from a range of gift options including practical gifts to those that pamper. There are also helium balloons for celebrating baby's arrival and children's birthday parties (balloons delivered in Perth only).

GAIA Natural Baby
Tel: (03) 9703 1707
email: info@gaiaskinnaturals.com
website: www.gaiaskinnaturals.com

Purchase the most beautiful gift hampers for mum and babies or customise your own gorgeous gift through GAIA's totally secure online store. Delivery can be made to hospital, third party or home. You can also purchase GAIA Natural Baby and GAIA Made for Men products with special offers available to GAIA E-Club Members – joining is free and can be done online. GAIA Skin Naturals bring you the best pure, natural and organic skin care products and they are suitable for sensitive skin and those affected by eczema and dermatitis. GAIA

Natural Baby was created in 2002 by a mum for her son who had eczema, it is made entirely from natural and Australian certified organic ingredients to provide you with the purest products to gently care for your child's skin every day.

Hemer Australia
Tel: (08) 8278 3788
email: hemeraus@senet.com.au
website: www.pugglekids.com (under Gifts)

Pauline Hemer is one of Australia's leading ceramic artist/designers who has delighted children world wide with her original, hand-painted ceramics that are proudly handmade in her studio in South Australia using Australian raw materials.

IdentiKid
Tel: 1300 133 949
email: info@identikid.com.au
website: www.identikid.com.au

 IdentiKid have a range of personalised name bracelets that make the perfect and truly unique gift for kids. Bands are available in different colours and you have a lot of choice in the add-to charms available. Guaranteed to put a smile on every child's face and gifts can be sent direct to the special person. Phone 1300 133 949 or visit www.identikid.com.au for more information.

Jack & Gill Designs
Tel: 0411 232 071
website: www.jackandgilldesigns.com.au

Jack & Gill Designs offer a range of quality handmade and personalised keepsake cushions, gifts and bags for babies and children. Specialising in personalised Christening and newborn memory cushions, birthday cushions, kids cushions, scatter cushions, large floor cushions, Minky baby throws, Minky hats/beanies, art smocks, library bags, children's bags, birthday, Christmas and Easter bibs and large Christmas sacks. The fabric range features bright cotton fabrics and luxuriously soft Minky fabrics, all of which can be mixed and matched and, with the addition of your child's name, will become a unique and special gift.

Katydid Decor Company
Tel: 1300 655 069
email: info@katydiddecor.com.au
website: www.katydiddecor.com.au

 The Katydid Décor Company can create a beautiful personalised ceramic keepsake for your child or gift for someone special. The range includes commemorative plates, cups or money boxes to mark a special occasion, nameplates for a child's bedroom door and new and exclusive to Katydid, a lovely range of free-standing ceramic letters. They are a perfect gift for any child and any occasion. Select a set of letters in your child's name or special word to reflect your feelings. Your chosen gift will be enjoyed now and treasured as a keepsake in the future.

Resources

TOYS, BOOKS & GIFTS

Fabulous gift ideas ➡ Stores online

Keepsake Names

Tel: 0408 339 733

email: danielle@keepsakenames.com.au

website: www.keepsakenames.com.au

Keepsake Names manufactures bright wooden name plaques and photo frames that can be personalised with your name or someone else's special name. They make an ideal birthday, Christmas, Christening or newborn baby gift. All the timber plaques are made from pine and available in five different colours; there is also a range of different letter styles and motives and novelty plaques (made from MDF). Keepsake Names also has a range of photo frames, photo albums, personalised bracelets, children's furniture and toys which include fully furnished dolls houses and wooden toys. Products can be sent anywhere in Australia.

Little Kitchen

Tel: 1300 722 095

email: info@littlekitchen.com.au

website: www.littlekitchen.com.au

Little Kitchen is Australia's first and leading brand of real children's cookware. Visit their gorgeous online store and discover what all the fuss is about. Great gift ideas or a fabulous way to get your child helping in the kitchen. Phone the number above or visit the website for more information.

My Hamper

Tel: 0438 220 505

email: info@myhamper.com.au

website: www.myhamper.com.au

My hamper is a Melbourne-based business delivering beautiful gift hampers Australia wide. Delicious high quality products have been carefully selected to ensure maximum satisfaction. My Hamper has gifts and gift hampers for all occasions.

Oh My Giddy Aunt!

Tel: 0416 050 306

email: info@ohmygiddyaunt.com.au

website: www.ohmygiddyaunt.com.au

Oh My Giddy Aunt designs and creates beautiful personalised jewellery and keepsakes, jewellery for mothers and children, charms, lockets and arty kid's decor that will have you exclaiming "Oh My Giddy Aunt!" Visit Oh My Giddy Aunt's website or phone/email for a free catalogue.

Parents' Essentials

Tel: 1800 782 022

email: customerservice@parentsessentials.com.au

website: www.parentsessentials.com.au

Parents' Essentials makes parents' lives easier by providing innovative product solutions. They offer a collection of packs including The Maternity Hospital Pack: all your essential products for your hospital stay; the Bath Time Pack that contains the innovative Tummy Tub as the baby bath; and a Toilet Training Pack to get your toilet training journey off to a smooth start. A Parents' Essentials Pack makes a practical baby shower gift, gift for a newborn or as a solution to one of many childhood milestones.

Piktorize

Tel: 0400 883 556

email: enquiries@piktorize.com.au

website: www.piktorize.com.au

Piktorize offers beautiful high-quality photo canvases, stunning professionally bound photo books, gorgeous photo engraved pendants and fun novelty photo gift items. They also have an extensive range of personalised gift ideas and all products come with a satisfaction guarantee.

S.O.H. Sleepy Baby Bouquets

Tel: 0419 583 281

email: info@sohsleepybabybouquets.com.au

website: www.sohsleepybabybouquets.com.au

S.O.H. Sleepy Baby Bouquets offer stunning gift creations for newborn arrivals, infants and expectant/nursing mothers. They can turn an assortment of basic baby clothing into stunning bouquets made to look like fresh floral arrangements. The range presents practical and affordable alternatives to buying flowers for a newborn arrival. S.O.H. Sleepy Baby Bouquets takes all the guesswork out of buying a useful baby gift and something mum can use when she takes baby home from hospital, all elegantly presented for the cost of a bouquet of flowers.

The Fatherhood Project

Tel: (02) 6684 2309

email: info@fatherhood.com.au

website: www.fatherhood.net.au

The *Fatherhood* CD and DVD is a great gift to give to a new dad. It is a beautiful collection of songs about being a father or having a father by Australia's finest contemporary songwriters including John Butler, Xavier Rudd and Paul Kelly. It's a powerful gift for new dads or for your own father. Available from www.fatherhood.net.au or www.natureschild.com.au.

VICTORIA

Hamper Solutions

PO Box 327

Tullamarine VIC 3043

Tel: 1300 852 053

email: enquiries@hampersolutions.com.au

website: www.hampersolutions.com.au

Hamper Solutions provides unique gift hampers and gifts for all occasions. If you are looking for an alternative to flowers, hampers are the perfect choice. Hamper Solutions provides hampers and gifts for expectant arrivals, mums and babies in hospital, welcome-home and pamper hampers for mum. Hampers can be delivered to home, office or hospital. Some of the baby and children's gift ranges include: Humphrey's Corner, Pooh Bear and Peter Rabbit. Prices range from $15.00 to $500.00.

WESTERN AUSTRALIA

Corporate Rewards
Tel: (08) 9364 2526
email: babygifts@corporaterewards.com.au
website: www.corporaterewards.com.au

Corporate Rewards offer gift baskets for baby arrivals, new mums, happy parents and excited siblings, delivered Australia wide. You can choose from a range of gift options including practical gifts to those that pamper. There are also helium balloons for celebrating baby's arrival and children's birthday parties (balloons delivered in Perth only).

STORES ONLINE: TOYS, BOOKS & GIFTS

NATIONAL

Adorable Affordable
Tel: (08) 9386 3677
email: sales@adorableaffordable.com.au
website: www.adorableaffordable.com.au

Adorable Affordable has the most comprehensive range of Peter Rabbit and Humphrey's Corner licensed products currently available in Australia. Visit the website for further information.

annieB's
Tel: 0410 526 145
email: annie@anniebs.com.au
website: www.anniebs.com.au

annieB's creates a world of enchantment and magic for young children with gorgeous PlayPalaces packed with extra comfy cushions, fun puppet theatres, cosy bean bags and bean bag chairs. Vibrant stripes and gingham checks will brighten up your child's room like never before. Laughter and fun guaranteed. Their new teddy bears and bunting add the finishing touch. Visit www.anniebs.com.au for more information.

Baby Brands
Tel: (02) 9699 4315
website: www.babybrands.com.au

Baby Einstein, Taggies, Kiddopotamus are just a few of the lines brought to you by www.babybrands.com.au. Shop for gifts, essential baby accessories, toys, educational products, keepsake boxes, photo albums, sleeping and pram accessories, DVDs, furniture and lots more. Visit the website to find out about your nearest stockist or to shop online. Delivery Australia wide.

Baby BT
Tel: (08) 9390 1841
email: babybt267@bigpond.com
website: www.babybt.com.au

Baby BT has a large variety of clothing, manchester, gifts, cards, toys and teddies for babies and toddlers. There is a delightful range of prem baby clothes, clothes to 18 months and accessories. Gift vouchers, lay-by, gift registry and EFTPOS available. Shop online at www.babybt.com.au.

Baby Eco Store
Tel: (08) 7120 2275
email: babyeco@optusnet.com.au
website: www.babyecostore.com.au

Baby Eco Store has an extensive range of natural baby products including organic cotton baby clothing and accessories, gifts, natural skin care/bath time care, toys and products for mum. Their products are carefully chosen to be safe, environmentally friendly and natural – perfect for baby. Shop securely online. They deliver across Australia and are always happy to offer help and advice.

Baby Exchange
email: info@babyexchange.com.au
website: www.babyexchange.com.au

At Baby Exchange you can list your unwanted baby and children's items including clothes, toys, books, DVDs and cots and choose whatever you like in return from any category. There are bargains to be found even if you don't have anything to exchange and members receive great discounts from many online stores operated by mums.

Baby Stitch
Tel: 1300 653 880
email: info@babystitch.com.au
website: www.babystitch.com.au

Baby Stitch is a leading specialist in personalised baby gifts providing personalised soft towels, snuggly blankets, adorable bodysuits and cute bibs. Give a unique gift that is exclusively made and it will be treasured and remembered for a long time. All baby gifts are beautifully gift boxed and delivered Australia wide. Phone the number above or visit the website for more information.

Baby Zone (Aust) Pty Ltd
Tel: (02) 4228 4288
email: sales@babyzonedirect.com.au
website: www.babyzonedirect.com.au

www.babyzonedirect.com.au stocks all the leading brands in nursery furniture, prams, car seats, high chairs, safety products and toys. They distribute Australia wide at competitive rates.

Baby's Got Style
Tel: (02) 9427 2726
email: info@babysgotstyle.com.au
website: www.babysgotstyle.com.au

Resources

TOYS, BOOKS & GIFTS

Stores online

Baby's Got Style stocks beautiful, unique and funky clothing (newborn to 8 years), groovy toys, fun books, super accessories and gorgeous gifts. Brands include the best of Australian design as well as fabulous imports. Visit www.babysgotstyle.com.au for shopping that's easy, funky, fresh and stylish.

BabyExpress.com.au Pty Ltd
Tel: 1300 (PARENT) 727 368
email: babyexpress@bigpond.com
website: www.babyexpress.com.au

Babyexpress is an Australian online provider of exceptional baby and parent gift products specialising in unique gifts, personalised gift items and beautiful gift selections. For that special new arrival visit www.babyexpress.com.au or phone 1300 PARENT for more information.

Babylush
Tel: 0410 613 900
email: info@babylush.com.au
website: www.babylush.com.au

Babylush is an online boutique that offers a great range of children's clothing (newborn to size 5), fun toys, unique gifts, hair accessories, versatile baby bags, organic body products, funky shoes and socks, sleepwear, baby carriers and feeding accessories. Shop securely anytime with economical express post next day delivery. Phone the number above or visit the website for more information.

Bear Box Kids
Tel: (03) 9585 6644
email: sales@bearboxkids.com.au
website: www.bearboxkids.com.au

Bear Box Kids sells gorgeous teddies and toys as well as gifts for Christenings, cot quilts and blanket sets, porcelain dolls, tables and chairs and toy boxes of all shapes and sizes. Phone or visit the website for more information.

Bella Creations
Tel: 1300 881 981
email: sales@bellacreations.com.au
website: www.bellacreations.com.au

Bella Creations specialise in exclusive and unique gift arrangements for the celebration of women, men and new baby arrivals. Containing only quality products, visit the website for more information. Phone the number listed above or visit the website for more information.

Belles Familles
Tel: (02) 9684 6605
email: enquiry@bellesfamilles.com.au
website: www.bellesfamilles.com.au

As your family grows your needs will change. You will start with wraps and bibs, move onto safety gear and feeding cups, then imaginative play toys and educational puzzles. Belles Familles is proud to offer you over 1,000 interesting and practical products all of which have been tested in their own family. From baby showers to christenings, first birthdays and beyond visit Belles Familles' website to see the full range and sign up for the newsletter while you are there. Phone orders are also welcome.

Birth Partner
Tel: 0402 405 889
email: nicole@birthpartner.com.au
website: www.birthpartner.com.au

Birth Partner has a select range of gorgeous gifts for baby, mum and dad. You can order online, or by phone, for quick delivery Australia-wide. Visit www.birthpartner.com.au for more information.

Bucket Babies
Tel: 0419 678 039
email: info@bucketbabies.com.au
website: www.bucketbabies.com.au

Bucket Babies specialises in gifts and keepsakes for babies and young children.

Cafe Bride
Tel: (03) 9713 3572
email: carol@cafebride.com.au
website: www.cafebride.com.au

Whatever the special day or event may be, the day deserves to be unforgettable. Cafe Bride opens the door to a world of wedding and christening bomboniere, giftware, keepsakes, toys, hampers and much more. Visit www.cafebride.com.au to see their full range.

Cowtrees.com.au
Tel: (03) 9388 8997
email: sales@cowtrees.com.au
website: www.cowtrees.com.au

Cowtrees.com.au sells a range of infant, children's and family games puzzles and toys – something for the whole family. Many products are multi-award winning and all are compliant with Australian standards. Visit www.cowtrees.com.au for further information.

DigiGifts – Personalised Gifts
Tel: 0412 998 463
email: sales@digigifts.com.au
website: www.digigifts.com.au

DigiGifts sells a huge range of personalised gifts ranging from wall canvases to puzzles, photo mugs, coloured photo crystals, photo bags, personalised cartoon DVDs, apparel for all ages (babies to adults), and various other giftware. DigiGifts also provide a variety of photographic-related services including restoration and image scanning. These services all include working with digital images, printed photographs, film negatives and slides. Great gift ideas for birthdays, wedding, travel memories, anniversaries, events, yearbooks, family histories and much more.

DwellStudio

Tel: 1300 763 126
email: sales@luxurylabels.com.au
website: www.luxurylabels.com.au

Bold new colours and the simplicity of vintage toys is the springboard for the stunning collection of modern toys from DwellStudio. Drawing on the appealing graphics of Danish and Italian toys from the sixties and seventies, designs vary from animal shapes to dots and floral graphics. The range includes Soft Building Blocks (rrp$65), Soft Stacking Rings (rrp$65), Soft Mind Blocks (rrp$65), Magnetic Animals (rrp$88), Hand Puppets (rrp$165), Finger Puppets (rrp$55) and Animal Cushions (rrp$65).

E-Teddies

Tel: (07) 5428 6688
email: admin@e-teddies.com.au
website: www.e-teddies.com.au

E-Teddies is an online retail store selling a large range of quality and affordable teddy bears and soft toys, perfect for any occasion. Delivery worldwide.

Earthlink Ethnic Handcrafts

Tel: (07) 3341 2524
email: info@earthlinkhandcrafts.com
website: www.earthlinkhandcrafts.com

Earthlink has a unique range of children's products all handcrafted in developing countries. Included are hand and finger puppets and an easy-to-use puppet theatre. There is a range of authentic musical instruments from Peru and beautiful dolls from India, Africa and Peru. Earthlink also has a great selection of jute storage pockets from Bangladesh. They are proud to promote 'fair trade' ensuring all artisans receive a fair wage allowing them to improve their quality of life. All available online from www.earthlinkhandcrafts.com.

Ekidna Kidswear

Tel: 1800 606 963
email: joanne@ekidnakids.com.au
website: www.ekidnakids.com.au

Ekidna Kidswear stocks a fantastic range of giftware, accessories and baby essentials as well as gorgeous, high quality clothing in sizes for premature babies to toddlers. Phone the number above or visit the website for more information.

Entropy

Tel: (07) 4724 4555
email: info@entropy.com.au
website: www.entropy.com.au

Entropy has an amazing selection of traditional toys, sports and activity equipment for children and an extensive range of craft and craft kits. Purchase online with same day dispatch for most orders. Flat rate postage of $9.95 for orders of less than $100, FREE for all orders over $100. Phone the number above or visit the website for more information.

essentials4baby

Tel: 1300 665 229
email: enquiries@essentials4baby.com.au
website: www.essentials4baby.com.au

Essentials4baby is an online baby shop and gift registry service that specialises in a wide range of essential baby products and gifts from well known brands. Their gift registry service is free, easy to use and ensures baby gets the perfect gift every time for every occasion. Visit www.essentials4baby where you will find your shopping and gift registry experience fun, easy, inspiring and hassle-free.

Express from Heaven

website: www.expressfromheaven.com.au

Express from Heaven is a convenient, innovative way to buy all your new baby's essentials from conception to 18 months. The exclusive co-ordinated clothing, accessory and gift range has been designed specifically with your baby's needs in mind. The unique range has been made from high quality fabrics, styled for quick and easy changing and allows for total comfort for any new baby. Proudly Australian born, designed, made and owned. Available through the website via online shopping and selected outlets.

Fat Mumma's

Tel: 0428 190 701
email: info@fatmummas.com.au
website: www.fatmummas.com.au

Fat Mumma's is all about creativity and caring. They have created a series of fun, unique products that standout in the city streets such as stylish nappy bags, groovy kids clothing and creative, new-baby gifts. Their logo is inspired by the cartoon styles of Japan and gives the designs some humourous attitude. Feel like you're part of a unique growing community of mothers with an eye for great design and visit www.fatmummas.com.au.

Giftingyou

Tel: 0414 183 123
email: info@giftingyou.com.au
website: www.giftingyou.com.au

Giftingyou sells unique gifts for all occasions including products from Australian and overseas designers. They specialise in gifts for mums, babies, kids including candles, bags, homeware and exquisite jewellery. They also offer an extensive category for educational resources and special needs products used and recommended by teachers, occupational therapists, speech therapists and home-based educators. Secure online shopping, free gift wrapping and card on all orders. Visit the website for further information.

Resources

TOYS, BOOKS & GIFTS

Stores online

gorgeousgifts.com.au

Tel: 0418 218 151

email: admin@gorgeousgifts.com.au

website: www.gorgeousgifts.com.au

Gorgeousgifts.com.au supplies an amazing line up of fancy dress-ups as well hand-made themed bedroom furnishings. Browse their full range of fairy, princess, prince and pirate costumes online as well as ranges of exclusive hand-decorated pillows, wall hangings and bed linen that your little dreamers will love. Furnishings can be personalised and all orders are shipped within 7 days.

Gr8 Toys

Tel: 1300 Gr8 Toys

email: sales@gr8toys.com.au

website: www.gr8toys.com.au

Gr8 Toys sells beautiful, quality developmental and educational toys for children aged 0 to 14 years all selected by a professional. The huge range includes wooden doll houses, including Le Toy Van, dolls and accessories, wooden castles, work benches, doll sized furniture including the full range of Pintoy, plush toys including Beatrix Potter, baby toys including Boikido, toddler ride-ons, including Wheely Bugs, trikes, cubbies/tents, wooden toys, play-sets, play food, construction sets, science kits, craft sets, hammering sets, games, books, puzzles, dress-ups, Fairy Shop as well as popular character toys.

Highland Toys

Tel: 0403 804 904

website: www.highlandtoys.com.au

Highland Toys offers a great range of high quality wooden toys – solid, traditional toys that children love and that are designed to last. Their range includes rocking horses, doll's houses, trains, trucks, blocks, baby toys, musical instruments, role play, puzzles and pull-along toys. A number of the toys are handcrafted and Australian made. Highland Toys' aim is to offer toys that can sustain generations of children's love and play. You can purchase online and they deliver Australia wide.

Infancy

Tel: (02) 9565 2866

email: infancy@iinet.net.au

website: www.infancy.com.au

Infancy selects a unique range of Australian and international clothing, handcrafted toys and giftware all at highly affordable prices. Infancy also offers an online shopping service and a VIP program.

It's All About Me for Kids

Tel: 0402 108 560

email: info@itsallaboutmeforkids.com.au

website: www.itsallaboutmeforkids.com.au

It's All About Me for Kids offers original gifts for your little ones. They supply personalised books, sing-along CDs, interactive story books, growth charts, clocks and plush toys that sing your child's name when squeezed. Delivery Australia wide. Fundraising also available.

Jess & Jem

Tel: (02) 9489 4443 or 0438 822 981

email: amanda@jessandjem.com.au

website: www.jessandjem.com.au

Visit Jess & Jem's delightful website and step into a virtual toy store filled with the highest quality gifts and toys which will both delight and entertain your child. Jess & Jem stocks only premium brands and offers savings on the recommended retail price. Jess & Jem's range is divided into four shopping catalogues: traditional gifts and decor, colourful and innovative toys for boys and girls, toys for your little princess and toys for your little prince.

Juno's Blessings

Tel: 0404 353 513

website: www.junosblessings.com.au

Juno's Blessings is a family-owned internet-based business offering organic and natural products presented in gift hampers and for individual sale. Juno's Blessings specialises in Pregnancy Pamper Hampers providing options for budgets as varied as $20 to $100. Products include hand-crafted honey and goatsmilk soap, lavender hand and body lotion, handcrafted wheat packs and hand-knitted cuddlebunnies.

Just for Bubs

Tel: 1300 658 490

website: www.justforbubs.com.au

Put the wow factor into your new baby, shower or christening gift. Just for Bubs specialise in unique and beautiful baby gifts which often aren't available elsewhere in Australia. The range includes embroidered blankets, bathrobes, personalised bracelets, frames, layette sets, hand impression kits and their exclusive Just the Beginning Certificate. Hampers, gift wrapping and delivery are all part of the service.

Just Treasures

Tel: 1300 856 678

website: www.just-treasures.com.au

Just Treasures is a speciality online gift shop offering beautiful gifts for any occasion whether it's for a newborn, a Christening or for a birthday. They specialise in Disney Snowglobes with the largest Disney range in Australia, as well as jewellery boxes, costumes, figurines, blankets, plush toys, dolls and many licensed products. Delivery Australia wide and pick up on request. Eftpos and credit cards accepted.

Kazoku Kids
Tel: (08) 9470 2851
email: info@kazokukids.com.au
website: www.kazokukids.com.au

Kazoku products were invented by parents; confused by all the advice being given they decided to create what was practical, useful and value for their dollar. Visit their website at www.kazokukids.com.au and see items such as the famous Neat Nets mesh storage bags keeping toys orderly, an easy and practical way to store everything from the toy box to the bath. Now you can always find what you are looking for.

La La baby
Tel: 0407 485 598
email: carli@lalababy.com.au
website: www.lalababy.com.au

La La Baby is a funky and refreshing place for you to shop online for all things baby. With a focus on handmade items, La La Baby makes for a wonderfully unique shopping experience. From clothing, accessories and footwear, to books, toys and stationery, you'll be sure to find the perfect gift, or that special something for your own child.

LEGO Education Centre
Tel: 1800 684 068
email: anita@mooreed.com.au
website: www.mooreed.com.au

The LEGO Education Centre offers a huge and different range of LEGO items available for anyone in Australia to purchase including the hard-to-find LEGO Education items and LEGO merchandise such as watches, bags and some clothing items.

Li'l Playhouse
Tel: 0433 954 942
email: jody@lilplayhouse.com.au
website: www.lilplayhouse.com.au

www.lilplayhouse.com.au is a new online toy store that is packed with educational wooden toys, puzzles, games, dolls, castles, figurines, dress ups and much more to capture your child's heart and imagination. Easy to browse through and safe to buy from www.lilplayhouse.com.au sells fantastic quality gifts and toys that you will want to keep for generations. The site also sells gorgeous kids tableware; party gear, decor and bags; gifts to spoil mums and exclusive designer baby sleeping bags from Paris.

little brown mouse
Tel: 0414 427 798
website: www.littlebrownmouse.com.au

Little brown mouse is an online boutique dedicated to beautiful, original and lovingly made baby and toddler's clothing, bed linen, toys and gifts in an extensive range of beautiful, vintage and whimsical fabrics. Fabulous fashion where kids can still be kids with wallet-friendly prices. Proudly designed and entirely made in Australia.

Look Under the Mulberry Bush
Tel: (03) 5332 5725
email: info@underthemulberrybush.com.au
website: www.underthemulberrybush.com.au

At Look Under the Mulberry Bush you will find an array of unique, beautiful, children's clothing (0000 to 10), toys, accessories, furniture, bedding and gifts by independent designers and unique small businesses. Learn about their story, understand the creative journey and buy directly online. Shopping is secure, convenient and enjoyable with various search options available. New listings by the designer/creator always welcome. See www.underthemulberrybush.com.au for information and to join the e-newsletter.

Made By Mums
Tel: 0411 018 245 or (03) 9827 4770
email: info@madebymums.com.au
website: www.madebymums.com.au

The Luxury Baby Mat is a large creative space on which you and your child can play. With a waterproof underside it is great for indoor and outdoor activities. The mat turns into a bag and is fully machine washable and Australian made. Trust a mum to think of that.

Meemoh
Tel: 0412 140 057
email: info@meemoh.net
website: www.meemoh.net

Meemoh toys are lovingly handmade, using 100% cotton fabrics, with individual felt and stitch detail, enhancing their uniqueness. This means no one toy is the same. The chunky shape and lightweight feel of these toys are easy for those tiny hands to grab hold of and cuddle.

millie & mo
Tel: 0488 002 214
email: info@millieandmo.com.au
website: www.millieandmo.com.au

millie & mo pride themselves on making unique, funky, quality mum-made baby and toddler clothing, gifts and accessories. Products available online include bandanas, nappy covers, dresses, pants, canvas photo boards, crochet garments, gift vouchers and more. Visit www.millieandmo.com.au.

Minimee Babies & Kids
Tel: (02) 9569 2000
website: www.minimee.com.au

Minimee can provide you with all your newborn through to toddler toy needs from learning and development toys through to plush teddies/dolls and keepsakes. You will be sure to find that unique gift and you also get free gift wrapping. Offering a great range, service and prices, items include gifts/toys, nursery furniture, prams, car seats, baby essentials, linen and fashion all available online at www.minimee.com.au.

ministyle
Tel: 0419 545 366
website: www.ministyle.com.au

Resources

TOYS, BOOKS & GIFTS

Stores online

Ministyle is a chic and unique online boutique that offers an inspiring range of local and imported brands for the child in your life ranging children's fashion apparel, accessories, gifts and lifestyle products just to name a few. Gifts include bilingual talking dolls, jewellery, wall clocks, and snowglobes and a variety of children's books are also available online including Rockabye lullaby CDs imported from the United States.

Monkeytail & Wellington

Tel: 0421 993 474
email: sales@monkeytailandwellington.com.au
website: www.monkeytailandwellington.com.au

Monkeytail and Wellington is proud to present a specially selected range of independently designed and artisan crafted wares for children. This collection of locally and internationally sourced toys, clothing, books, music and children's accessories are chosen for their quality, elegance and their sprit of old fashioned fun. Visit their online store to view the entire catalogue of wonders. You can also subscribe to their VIP program and enjoy the benefits of ongoing discounts, product previews and pre-order incentives.

Moochie-Moo

Tel: (07) 3841 0194
email: info@moochiemoo.com
website: www.moochiemoo.com

moochiemoo.com offers a range of products not found on everyday shop shelves. Funky ID wristbands, stunning children's furniture and bedroom accessories, gorgeous night lights, Decorate My Room products and unique imported gifts and toys. Extensive research and planning has allowed them to bring you some wonderful quality products from all across the globe. The range of products is constantly updated. Phone the number above or visit the website for more information.

Mum & Babe

Tel: (07) 4036 4114
email: cate@mumandbabe.com.au
website: www.mumandbabe.com.au

Mum & Babe is an online boutique specialising in unique gifts for mother and child. They offer beautiful children's jewellery by Australian designers, funky clothing that won't date, go out of style and will go the distance in the sandpit, fantastic toys and exquisite children's books. Mum & Babe also sell timeless accessories for mums intended to create everlasting memories of motherhood. This is an easy to navigate site offering secure shopping and friendly service.

Nanny Pickle

Tel: (07) 3366 9006
email: nannypickle@nannypickle.com.au
website: www.nannypickle.com.au

Once upon a time, not so very long ago, there lived a sweet, savvy and slightly quirky nanny, known throughout the land as Nanny Pickle. From the wonderful world of Nanny Pickle comes her playful range of infant wear and accessories for babies and toddlers. Born out of whimsy and a daydream, Nanny Pickle creates beautiful collections of delightful infant wear, divine cards for baby and mama, sweet hand-made toys and delectable co-ordinated nursery accessories. Visit Nanny Pickle's divine website to explore the entire range.

Newborn Nursery Pty Ltd

Tel: 1300 769 269
email: info@leemiddletondolls.com.au
website: www.leemiddletondolls.com.au

Newborn Nursery is a unique concept store in Australia where children can adopt baby dolls that look and feel just like a new baby. Each baby is unique with different complexions, hair and eye colours to choose from. The dolls are displayed in a hospital maternity ward, complete with viewing windows and nurses to help the new mums with their adoption. The process includes adoption papers, a health check on the baby and a special photograph to take home.

Online Toys Australia

Tel: (03) 9394 1944
email: sales@onlinetoys.com.au
website: www.onlinetoys.com.au

Shop for toys online from the comfort, safety and privacy of your own home. Get fast, door-to-door service anywhere within Australia. Online Toys Australia offers a worry-free, 100% toy satisfaction guarantee so you can buy with confidence. They also offer a convenient gift-wrapping service, low prices and a $7.95 flat-rate shipping anywhere within Australia. Visit them online at www.onlinetoys.com.au for further information and to see their great range.

Organised Kaos 4 Kids

Tel: (03) 9432 3872
email: info@organisedkaos.com.au
website: www.ok4kids.com.au

Organised Kaos 4 Kids is a quality Australian online educational toy store featuring many unique products not found in major stores including educational games, science kits, craft kits, musical instruments, puzzles, wooden toys, traditional toys and gifts perfect for your child or someone else's. Free gift wrapping, gift tag and competitive postage rates.

Peanut Gallery Pty Ltd

Tel: (03) 9836 0302
email: info@peanutgallery.com.au
website: www.peanutgallery.com.au

Peanut Gallery is an online toy shop specialising in beautiful wooden, educational and traditional toys for children aged birth to 8 years. Their range offers many unique and hard-to-find items and features dollhouses, baby toys, art and craft, musical instruments, puzzles, soft toys, ride-ons, pull-alongs, toy kitchens, play food, cars, puppets and imaginative play toys. You can order through the website any time and they offer gift wrapping and delivery anywhere in Australia for a low cost flat fee.

Personalised Gifts

Tel: (02) 9879 7993
email: personalisedgifts@bigpond.com.au
website: www.personalisedgifts.com.au

Personalised Gifts has a unique collection of personalised products for babies and children that are not sold in retail stores. This includes a personalised baby's birth diary, personalised books, birth announcements, name meanings and personalised poems, family tree and family name origin, personalised clocks, photo mouse pads, photo jigsaw puzzles, photo mugs, photo tote bags, photo T-shirts, photo return address labels, photo jewellery, babies' fingerprint jewellery and photo crystals. You can have your photo and message on all of their products. Their range also includes personalised song CDs and personalised interactive CD-Rom stories. Visit their website for more information.

Play House Toys

Tel: (02) 9949 7984
email: sales@playhousetoys.com.au
website: www.playhousetoys.com.au

www.playhousetoys.com.au provides an extensive range of beautifully hand-crafted toys such as wooden doll's houses, knitted finger puppets, fabric hobby horses and wooden puzzles, cars and planes to name a few. They are not mass produced and are made from natural materials with non-toxic finishes. They are real toys, made by real people. Toys that are made to last, to be loved and passed on to future generations. Visit www.playhousetoys.com.au.

PlaySafe Kids

Tel: (02) 9644 6891
email: sales@playsafekids.com.au
website: www.playsafekids.com.au

PlaySafe Kids is a family-based company that imports and retails children's outdoor/indoor play equipment. Leading brands include Step 2, Little Tikes, Lerado, Eurotrike and Feber. The range include cubby houses, slides, swing sets, ride-ons and more. They also sell plastic mould injected toys through their Sydney-based store and offer shipping Australia wide. These toys will give your children hours of fun. Visit www.playsafekids.com.au for further information.

playtolearn

23 Lex Grove
Oak Park VIC 3046
Tel: 0423 644 837
email: info@playtolearn.com.au
website: www.playtolearn.com.au

playtolearn offers aesthetically pleasing and beautifully designed resources to encourage children's imagination and interaction with the world. playtolearn want to capture the essence of childhood by providing the ingredients for children's growth and development. Play is one of the most important needs a child has and playtolearn has carefully chosen resources to reflect their belief that a child plays to learn. Their resources encourage children's imagination, sense of wonder and curiosity. Browse through the website to discover the magic of their materials and equipment.

Saldon Imports

Tel: 0402 891 737
email: sames@saldonimports.com
website: www.saldonimports.com

Saldon Imports first started when two new mums began designing their own baby bibs and baseball hats. Now they also import licensed toys including Dora, Barbie, Elmo, Nemo, Bratz, Disney Cars, Care Bears and many more. Visit their website www.saldonimports.com for more information.

SAMS Handcrafts

Tel: (03) 9723 5153
email: mike@samscrafts.com.au
website: www.samscrafts.com.au

SAMS Handcrafts have been making quality handcrafted wooden toys for children for more than 25 years. The range includes vehicles (cars, trucks, trains, planes), building blocks and walker trolleys, bead frames and lacing shapes, push-along and pull-along animals, hobby horses, chunky alphabet and numerals, garages, castles, signature stools, customised jigsaw puzzles and rocking horses. Toys are bright, chunky and durable and are built to comply with Australian Standard ISO 8124-1 Safety of Toys. To order visit their website or phone the number above.

Shop for Baby

Tel: (02) 9939 3643
email: contact@shopforbaby.com.au
website: www.shopforbaby.com.au

For a huge selection of fun-filled toys and gorgeous gift ideas visit www.shopforbaby.com.au. They offer an exciting range of wooden toys, puzzles and games, beautiful gifts and much more. Leave the car at home and take advantage of their fast delivery, exceptional customer service and amazing loyalty program that enables you to save every time you shop.

Shop Online

Tel: 0424 551 699
email: admin@shop-online.net.au
website: www.shop-online.net.au

Resources

TOYS, BOOKS & GIFTS

Stores online

Shop Online is your one-stop guide to the best retailers on the net. Shop from the comfort and convenience of your home and get the best possible deals and bargains. Buy baby supplies, maternity clothing, gifts, hampers, flowers and more. You can also enter competitions and find plenty of bargains.

ShopHouse
Tel: (02) 9011 6744
email: info@shophouse.com.au
website: www.shophouse.com.au

ShopHouse is an online children's boutique offering a great range of toys and gifts for young children. The range includes craft and activity items, educational toys, rattles and squeakers as well as gorgeous soft toys. www.shophouse.com.au is a secure website available 24/7. All purchases are delivered next day using Express Post. A hassle-free returns policy makes online shopping a breeze and gift wrapping is available. Visit www.shophouse.com.au for more information.

Stylesetter International Co. Pty Ltd
Tel: (02) 9437 5588
email: custservice@optusnet.com.au
website: www.stylesetter.com.au

Stylesetter has an extensive range of plush gifts, toys, photoframes plus baby wear and accessories. Brand names include Bearington Baby and Bunnies by the Bay. Visit www.stylesetter.com.au for more details.

Sweet Creations
Tel: (08) 9304 2002
website: www.sweetcreations.com.au

Sweet Creations is a Western Australian based company who pride themselves on offering exquisite products and an exceptional boutique styled, online gift service. The online store has an incredible collection of inspirational gifts, gift baskets and boxes to suit any occasion or budget. All products are carefully selected for their finest quality, ensuring that only the best is delivered to our clients.

The Bub Club
Tel: (02) 9365 6985
website: www.thebubclub.com.au

The Bub Club is an online baby gift service that deliver gorgeous baby baskets, gift tags and albums across Australia. Visit their website for further information.

The Bulk Warehouse
email: support@thebulkwarehouse.com.au
website: www.thebulkwarehouse.com.au

The Bulk Warehouse is a wholesaler and distributor of baby and family-care products, toys and gifts, prams, strollers, party supplies as well as safety and cleaning products. The Bulk Warehouse delivers Australia wide and overseas.

The Games Shop
Tel: (03) 9650 3592
website: www.gameshop.com.au

Do you remember the first puzzle or game you played? Share the wonderful pastime of playing traditional board games with children. While it's all about having fun, there are many benefits such as developing decision-making and experiencing social interaction. Jigsaws and other puzzles challenge the mind to think in a new way. Join to receive their regular email newsletter for product releases and specials. Visit the website or email for further information.

The Kids Store
Tel: 1800 131 296
email: enquiries@thekidsstore.com.au
website: www.thekidsstore.com.au

TheKidsStore.com.au offers a huge array of fun-filled toys, amazing gift ideas, books, DVDs and CDs. Log on and check out their range of musical tunes for little ears, meaningful stories and educational DVDs. With everything for babies, toddlers and kids, leave the car at home and enjoy exceptional customer service, a generous loyalty program, beautiful packaging and fast delivery to your front door.

The Toy Bug
Tel: 040 375 351
email: thetoybug@bigpond.com
website: www.thetoybug.com.au

The Toy Bug brings educational and fun toys to you. This is an online toy store that offers a great range of toys that children will love playing and learning with at the same time. Find that something special from cute soft baby toys to traditional wooden toys. The Toy Bug offers free gift wrapping, 12 week lay-by and gift certificates. Toys to create cherished childhood memories.

Think Twins
Tel: (03) 8802 9446
email: info@thinktwins.com.au
website: www.thinktwins.com.au

Think Twins is Australia's biggest online store for families with twins, triplets and more. Whether it's finding a birthday gift or accessing a terrific range of articles and resources, Think Twins will make life as a parent of twins a little easier. Check out their range of exclusive gifts and keepsakes for all ages, a unique range of baby and toddler clothing, invitations and greeting cards for birth announcements and christenings, a huge range of twin-specific books for parents and children, safety harnesses and headrests, tandem trikes, pregnancy wear, breastfeeding products and much more.

Tonic Gifts

Tel: 0417 883 226

website: www.tonicgifts.com.au

Tonic Gifts specialises in quality and affordable gifts for all occasions including gifts for new parents and newborn babies. They also stock stunning clothing from Eternal Creation and Monstar Kids suitable for children aged from newborn up to 6 years. Vintage Kid and Alimrose Designs make great toys and bibs for baby and Tonic carries both the Bod and Bod for Bubs range of products. Renee, Glamourflage and Wild mean that mum and dad are not forgotten.

Toot Toot Toys

Tel: 1300 866 886

email: customercare@toottoottoys.com.au

website: www.toottoottoys.com.au

Toot Toot Toys offers an extensive range of Thomas and Friends, GeoTrax by Fisher-Price, BRIO, Hornby and many other train related items such as party supplies, homewares, books, games, puzzles and scrapbooking essentials so that all your needs are taken care of. Toot Toot Toys also offer free gift wrapping.

ToyBarn Australia pty Ltd

Tel: 1300 785 763

email: sales@toybarn.com.au

website: www.toybarn.com.au

ToyBarn Australia has thousands of toys at highly competitive prices. They only stock good quality toys with brands that you know and trust and provide top quality service in a high tech online shopping environment that is fun and easy to use. Personal service, speedy delivery (flat fee), rewards program and the convenience of a gift wrapping service. A super selection of toys on offer with new and exciting toys constantly being added. Visit www.toybarn.com.au to see the full range.

Toys 4 Bright Kids

Tel: (03) 9354 2763

website: www.toys4brightkids.com

Toys 4 Bright Kids specialise in educational and wooden toys for children from 3 months to 6 years of age. Their range includes high quality wooden toys, fabric books, wall hangings and role play toys and furniture.

Toys 4 Kids Ltd

Tel: +64 9 4265392

email: enquiries@toys4kids.com

website: www.toys4kids.com

Toys 4 Kids is a leading online store for baby, pre-school and educational toys for the Australasian market. They only sell brands that offer quality, creativity and imaginative learning for little hands and minds. All products meet the highest safety standard testing requirements to ensure your child's safety. Visit the website for further information.

Toys4Tikes

Tel: 1300 781 432

email: info@toys4tikes.com.au

website: www.toys4tikes.com.au

Toys4tikes toys are carefully chosen and manufactured by the world leaders in children's toys, with multi-award winning products that are durable, robust and designed with safety in mind. Toys4Tikes strives to provide exceptional customer service delivering amazing toys including Little Tikes, Eurotrike, JCB Tractors and Blue Rabbit Timber Playgrounds and more, Australia wide. Toys4Tikes is proud to be an Australian owned and managed business.

Trendy Tots Toys

Tel: 0412 366 744

email: lina@trendytotstoys.com.au

website: www.trendytotstoys.com.au

At Trendy Trendy Toys you will find a huge range of fun and funky wooden toys as well as beautiful baby gifts, role play, educational toys, puzzles and musical instruments. Brands include Plan Toys, Lark Designs, Alimrose, Djeco, Le Toy Van plus many more. $9.95 postage Australia wide.

turtlegreen

Tel: 0439 595 543

email: info@turtlegreen.com.au

website: www.turtlegreen.com.au

turtlegreen makes environmental games and stationery for children. Their range includes Go Anna!, a 3-in-1 card game set featuring beautiful watercolour illustrations of Australian bush animals. The products are Australian made and are printed on recycled or sustainably-managed forest board with minimum use of plastics. turtlegreen promotes environmental education through their website and their products are popular gifts for girls and boys of all ages. They are also perfect for postage to overseas family and friends.

Unique Kids

Tel: (02) 9979 1125

email: info@uniquekids.com.au

website: www.uniquekids.com.au

Unique Kids offers a stylish range of products for babies, boys and girls. Pamper a new baby with quality wraps, bibs, soft toys, accessories and great gift ideas. Unique Kids also has a range of baby gift boxes and a wide range of accessories, toys and bags for slightly older children. Free gift wrapping, prompt delivery to your door and friendly service. Visit their website for further details.

UrbanBaby.com.au

Tel: 1300 882 991

email: hello@urbanbaby.com.au

website: www.urbanbaby.com.au

The UrbanBaby site is dedicated to providing the most stylish, practical and innovative products and truly

Resources

TOYS, BOOKS & GIFTS

Stores online ➜ Stores retail

useful information for pregnancy, parents and everything baby. Visit UrbanBaby for exclusive UrbanBaby products, the full Baby Einstein and Brilliant Baby ranges, fantastic wraps, the Hipseat by Hippychick, organic cotton baby clothes, gift cards and much more.

Vintage Kid Designs

Tel: 0413 964 018
email: jo@vintagekid.com.au
website: www.vintagekid.com.au

Vintage Kid Designs offer a growing variety of beautifully made baby items and gifts – all sorts of things that are not only gorgeous but get us all saying 'oh I remember these'. The kinds of goodies that make us all smile and feel like we did 'way back when'. Visit www.vintagekid.com.au for more information.

Wood Puzzles

Tel: (07) 3205 1985
email: enquiries@woodpuzzles.com.au
website: www.woodpuzzles.com.au

Wood Puzzles manufacture and retail a quality range of timber toys including mobiles, nursery sets and individualised name puzzles for babies. They specialise in personalised products and their Kindy Chairs and Treasure boxes are unique gifts for birth, christening and birthdays. They have a large range of jigsaw puzzles for all ages and offer a popular service of turning your photographs into puzzles. Check out the website for the full product range. (QLD readers can visit their factory/showroom at 4/17 Kenworth Place, Brendale.)

www.sookiebaby.com.au

Tel: 0430 085 851
email: info@sookiebaby.com
website: www.sookiebaby.com

www.sookiebaby.com.au is an online boutique featuring beautiful gifts and essentials for mother and baby. Brands include Oobi, Baobab, Tea Princess Collection, Goo Goo Lotions, Diddle Dumpling, Mamas and Pappas, Kaloo and much more. Enjoy shopping from the comfort of your own home any time of the day with flat rate posting Australia wide and free gift wrapping service. Phone the number above or visit the website for more information.

Young Minds Educational Toys

Tel: (02) 9868 6521
email: sales@youngminds.com.au
website: www.youngminds.com.au

Young Minds is an Australian owned online educational toy store featuring products such as Baby Einstein, Brainy Baby, educational games and DVDs, dolls houses, science kits, craft kits, robotic kits, puzzles and wooden toys. They offer free gift wrapping and great shipping prices Australia-wide. For more information visit their website.

STORES PRE-LOVED & DISCOUNTED: TOYS, BOOKS & GIFTS

VICTORIA

Baby Touch Outlet

82 Grange Road
Alphington VIC 3078
Tel: (03) 9499 8436
email: outlet@babytouch.com.au
website: www.babytouch.com.au

Baby Touch Factory Outlet is staffed by experienced women who can assist you with all your enquiries and purchases. The outlet has a great range of new, discontinued and second Baby Touch manchester, accessories and toys complimented by nappy bags and strollers from Little Company. The complete Zoom Zoom Kidsline range is up to 50% off or more plus they have a great selection of quality handmade smocked dresses, knitted jumpers, beautifully embroidered blankets and soft toys galore. Open Wednesday to Saturday 9.30am to 4.30pm. Phone the number above or visit the website for more information.

Hand Me Downs

383 Forest Road
The Basin VIC 3154
Tel: (03) 9761 2855
website: www.handmedowns.com.au

Hand Me Downs has over 4000 square feet of all sorts of goodies, including clothes ranging from 0000 to teens, toys, shoes, linen, furniture – anything you can imagine for children. There is a kids' play area, change facilities, toilets and lots of parking. Phone the number above or visit the website for more information.

Kids Weecycle Warehouse

3 Colin Avenue
Warrandyte VIC 3113
Tel: (03) 9844 3484
email: weecycle_warehouse@iprimus.com.au
website: www.kidsweecyclewarehouse.com.au

Kids Weecycle Warehouse specialise in good quality and affordable new and recycled baby and kids goods. Items include nursery furniture and accessories, children's clothing and shoes (including many brand name items), toys, books, puzzles, DVDs, videos, fitted cloth nappies, a large range of baby gifts and more. Hiring of goods is available (long or short term) and as well as a lay-by facility. Phone the number above or visit the website for more information.

STORES RETAIL: TOYS, BOOKS & GIFTS

NATIONAL

Kids Central

Tel: 1300 850 123
email: admin@kidscentral.com.au
website: www.kidscentral.com.au

Visit Kids Central for a great range of brands in children and babies' toys, fashion, homewares and nursery products. Kids Central sells the full range of exclusive Early Learning Centre toys from the UK, and the latest in children's fashion plus much more. The stores are full of gift ideas for children aged 0 to 8 years, as well as cards and wrap to help you buy everything you need in one location. The Baby Central department caters for the needs of new or expecting parents, with newborn fashion ranges such as Bebe, Pure Baby and Rock your Baby, as well as essentials such as nappy bags, and a beautiful range of newborn gifts. Ask about the new Kids Central gift card. To find your nearest Kids Central store (in each state except NT and TAS) phone 1300 850 123 or visit www.kidscentral.com.au.

VICTORIA

1001 Things for Baby

430 Rathdowne Street
Carlton VIC 3053
Tel: (03) 9347 7007

1001 Things for Baby is a lovely baby and children's boutique situated in Rathdowne village and specialises in pieces you cannot find everywhere. The store supports local artists and designers and stocks many vintage pieces for children – anything from pull-along wagons, spinning tops and cowboy boots to beautiful linen, Moses baskets and artwork. 1001 Things for Baby specialises in baby clothing up to the age of 6 years, so you will always find something a little bit different.

Baby Bunting

669 Warrigal Road
East Bentleigh VIC 3165
Tel: (03) 9575 4444
1050 Burke Road
Balwyn VIC 3163
Tel: (03) 9817 1464
76 Maroondah Highway
Ringwood VIC 3134
Tel: (03) 9870 0766
6/98–108 Hampstead Road
Maribyrnong VIC 3032
Tel: (03) 9318 7444
430 Princes Highway
Narre Warren VIC 3805
Tel: (03) 9704 1444
Shop 1 Power Centre
Cranbourne-Frankston Road
Frankston VIC 3199
Tel: (03) 9769 6597

1/36 Dalton Road
Thomastown VIC 3074
Tel: (03) 9465 7770
website: www.babybunting.com.au

Baby Bunting is a one-stop baby shop. The success of the stores comes from the specialised service offered, especially to first time parents. The friendly staff are happy to demonstrate the full range of baby products, accessories and toys, all at discount prices.

Baby Mode

17 Wright Street
Sunshine VIC 3020
Tel: (03) 9311 0675
Also located at:
5/500 High Street
Epping VIC 3076
email: info@babymode.com.au
website: www.babymode.com.au

Baby Mode has been helping families prepare for the most precious and exciting time of their lives for over 35 years. This Australian, family-owned business continues to provide exceptional quality products and retail values with the view that there is no substitute for quality when making the right choice. They aim to provide the best quality, price and advice for you when making those choices. For a diverse range of nought to teen furniture, safety products, toys, equipment, mattresses and accessories manufactured by the world's most famous brands visit the website or experience it personally at one of their stores.

Beaumaris Books

24 South Concourse
Beaumaris VIC 3193
Tel: (03) 9589 4638
email: read@beaumarisbooks.com.au
website: www.beaumarisbooks.com.au

Beaumaris Books is a great family bookshop. With something for everyone, there is a broad range of fiction and a solid reference section. Children are delighted with the displays and parents with the welcoming toy basket (browsing is more peaceful!). Easy pram and pusher access and a congenial atmosphere. Phone for more information.

Books Illustrated

300 Beaconsfield Parade
Middle Park VIC 3206
Tel: (03) 9534 7751
email: info@booksillustrated.com.au
website: www.booksillustrated.com.au

Books Illustrated specialises in exhibitions and promotion of original Australian picture books and illustration. It is situated in a two-storey terraced house opposite the beach. Original illustrations, limited edition prints and posters are for sale. Staff at Books Illustrated also offer expert advice on the selection of picture books for children and adults.

Resources

TOYS, BOOKS & GIFTS

Stores retail

Cowtrees.com.au
152 Lygon Street
East Brunswick VIC 3057
Tel: (03) 9388 8997
email: sales@cowtrees.com.au
website: www.cowtrees.com.au

Cowtrees.com.au sells a range of infant, children's and
family games puzzles and toys – something for the
whole family. Many products are multi-award winning
and all are compliant with Australian standards. Visit
www.cowtrees.com.au for further information or their
new store at the address above.

Green Leaves
54 Mount Eliza Way
Mount Eliza VIC 3930
Tel: (03) 9787 1714

Green Leaves is Mt. Eliza's original children's fashion
boutique, and has a wonderful selection of clothing,
accessories and gifts for newborns to 14 years. Visit this
friendly, relaxed boutique with parking at the door.

Hickory Dickory Educational Toys & Books
Shop 2, 86 Mount Eliza Way
Mt Eliza VIC 3530
Tel: (03) 9787 8333

Hickory Dickory Educational Toys & Books selects
exciting and innovative toys to encourage children to
develop their learning skills in an enjoyable way. The
range includes wooden toys, puzzles, games and gifts for
children through to adults.

Honeyweather & Speight
113 Barkly Street
St. Kilda VIC 3182
Tel: (03) 9534 3380
website: www.honeyweatherandspeight.com.au

Honeyweather & Speight is a magical, old fashioned toy
shop with an art flavour. All items are non-mainstream
and either crafted by the owners themselves, or carefully
selected to encourage creative play. Priority is given to
toys that are environmentally friendly and produced by
fair trade communities. So venture into the dingy end of
St. Kilda and feel good about shopping in this
wonderland of classic and retro toys.

Hoochie Coochie
220 St Georges Road
North Fitzroy VIC 3068
Tel: (03) 9486 4200
website: www.hoochiecoochie.com.au

Owned and operated by singer Linda Bull,
Hoochie Coochie is a much loved
children's boutique nestled in the heart of
North Fitzroy village. Supporting
Australia's top children's designers, local
designers and crafty mums, you will find
clothing essentials, footwear, accessories, original
artworks, as well as manchester and homewares that are
functional , beautiful and unique. Look out for the
launch of the Hoochie Coochie Fashion Label for girls
and Mini Moochie Tees in '09. Specialising in baby wear
to size 7, Hoochie Coochie continues to inspire and
create a welcoming shopping environment for families.
Open 10.00am to 5.00pm Tuesday to Sunday, closed
Mondays.

Imagine Me
271 High Street
Northcote VIC 3070
Tel: (03) 9486 4122
email: lealie@imaginemeboutique.com.au
website: www.imaginemeboutique.com.au

As well as a beautiful range of children's clothing and
shoes, Imagine Me also stocks a great range of toys and
gifts for that special little someone. Rewarding VIP
reward program available. Imagine Me boutique offers
private baby shower functions on Sundays. Phone the
number above to make a booking.

Kiddie Country
79–85 Union Street
Armadale VIC 3143
Tel: (03) 9509 4041

Kiddie Country stocks a huge range of nursery furniture
and toys including Little Tikes, Lamaze, Fisher Price,
Chicco, Berchet and Russ. Kiddie Country has a great
range of quality wooden toys, tables and chairs, cubby
furniture and doll houses.

Kids Interior Designs
73 Upper Heidelberg Road
Ivanhoe VIC 3079
Tel: (03) 9499 1852
email: info@kidsinteriordesigns.com.au
website: www.kidsinteriordesigns.com.au

Kids Interior Designs do children's furnishings
including bed linen and wraps. They also carry grobags,
Robeez shoes, designer PJs and dressing gowns,
giftware, art smocks, toys, costumes and much more.
They carry ranges to suit newborn through to early
teens. Kids Interior Designs also offer an in-home
decorator advice service and can help you create the
perfect environment for your child.

LEGO Education Centre
37 Hall Street
Moonee Ponds VIC 3039
Tel: 1800 684 068
email: anita@mooreed.com.au
website: www.mooreed.com.au

LEGO Education Centres specialise in hands-on LEGO
workshops such as Mechanical Toy Shop and Robot

Adventures for children aged 4 and up. They offer a great range of LEGO birthday party themes too. There is a huge and different range of LEGO items available to purchase including the hard to find LEGO education items and LEGO merchandise such as watches, bags and some clothing items.

Link Educational Supplies
341 Waverley Road
Mount Waverley VIC 3149
Tel: (03) 9807 5422
website: www.linkeducational.com.au

Link Educational Supplies is an outstanding children's bookshop with experienced staff in specialised areas. Link has a large range of readers, picture books, novels and general educational materials for all levels from pre-school to Year 12. Link offers story time and activities free every Thursday during school terms between 10.30 and 11.30 am. Link welcomes children, parents, grandparents and carers. Be enchanted by stories, engaging activities and their skilled presenter.

Masquerade Costume Hire
238 High Street
Kew VIC 3101
Tel: (03) 9853 6101
email: info@masquerade.com.au
website: www.masquerade.com.au

Masquerade is a great source for costumes and quirky presents. What 2-year-old wouldn't love a pair of wings or a superhero costume? Hundreds of families have used them for the kindy and school bookweek parade. They have an amazing range of mascots to hire for birthday parties – dinosaurs, dogs and cartoon characters are among the favourites. The costumes are clean, in excellent condition and constantly updated. They pride themselves on service. In business since 1971.

The Games Shop
Shop 7, Royal Arcade (off Bourke St Mall)
Melbourne VIC 3000
Tel: (03) 9650 3592
email: contact@gameshop.com.au
website: www.gameshop.com.au

Do you remember the first puzzle or game you played? Share the wonderful pastime of playing traditional board games with children. While it's all about having fun, there are many benefits such as developing decision-making and experiencing social interaction. Jigsaws and other puzzles challenge the mind to think in a new way. Join to receive their regular email newsletter for product releases and specials.

The Little Bookroom
759 Nicholson Street
Carlton North VIC 3054
Tel: (03) 9387 9837
email: books@littlebookroom.com.au

The Little Bookroom, Australia's oldest children's bookshop, has moved to Nicholson Street, Carlton North. They continue to stock a fine and extensive range and have specialist staff on hand who are willing to help.

Packed to the rafters with fun and interesting books for newborns through to the young adult audience, The Little Bookroom has been a favourite with teachers, librarians and families since 1960. They also carry a good selection of book-related toys, hand puppets and finger puppets. All children (even naughty ones) are welcome.

Tots Stuff
5 Hamilton Walk
Mt Waverley VIC 3149
Tel: (03) 9807 8000
website: www.totsstuff.com.au

Tots Stuff specialises in educational toys suitable for children of all ages. Brands stocked include Hama Beads, Melissa and Doug, Alex, Ravensburger, Schleich and more. Join their customer email list and you will be kept up to date with new products and specials.

Toy City
2a St Georges Road
Elsternwick VIC 3185
Tel: (03) 9530 0202
website: www.toycity.com.au

Toy City sells great value and interesting different wooden toys. The vast range chosen from all over the world includes puzzles, games, dolls houses, tables and chairs, wicker prams, pedal cars and push-handle kids trikes. Free gift wrapping available and free delivery to local areas as well as national delivery by post or courier. Now open seven days a week for your convenience.

NEW SOUTH WALES

All For Kiddiz & Bubs
163 Parramatta Road
Annandale NSW 2038
Tel: (02) 9569 2255
website: www.allforkiddizandbubs.com.au

All for Kiddiz & Bubs offers a wide range of major brands of babies and children's clothing and shoes as well as soft and educational toys, cots, bassinets, cradles, mattresses, high chairs, travel cots, prams, feeding products, monitors, car seats, safety products and accessories. The staff are helpful and prices reasonable.

Baby Winks
383 Goonoo Goonoo Road
Tamworth NSW 2340
Tel: (02) 6765 5811
website: www.babywinks.com.au

Baby Winks Tamworth has grown to be the biggest specialty baby store in the region. Baby Winks stock only top quality products from only the best brands. Open seven days a week you are sure to find what you need for your baby. Mail and phone orders are welcome.

Baby Zone (Aust) Pty Ltd
1 Bridge Street
Wollongong NSW 2500
Tel: (02) 4228 4288
email: sales@babyzonedirect.com.au
website: www.babyzonedirect.com.au

Resources

TOYS, BOOKS & GIFTS

Stores retail

Baby Zone is one of Australia's largest baby stores stocking all leading brands in nursery furniture, prams, car seats, high chairs, safety products and toys. Baby Zone is also one of Australia's Safety Advisory Centres offering certified child restraint fittings and qualified safety advice.

Brays Books

268 & 335 Darling Street
Balmain NSW 2041
Tel: (02) 9810 5613 or (02) 9810 3764
email: braybook@bigpond.net.au

Brays Books now has two shops. A wonderful range of kids books is at 335 Darling Street (telephone 9810 3764) and an extended range of 'bringing up children' is at 268 Darling Street. Both shops have stroller-friendly aisle space.

Doll Repair Centre

444 Stoney Creek Road (cnr. Kingsplace)
Kingsgrove West NSW 2208
Tel: (02) 9502 2999

The Doll Repair Centre repairs dolls, doll prams and rocking horses and also sells new and old dolls as well as excellent copies of original rocking horses. Rocking horse accessories and old doll prams are for sale along with doll wigs, shoes, socks, dresses, doll stands and doll houses.

Gleebooks Children's

191 Glebe Point Road
Glebe NSW 2037
Tel: (02) 9552 2526
email: books@gleebooks.com.au
website: www.gleebooks.com.au

Gleebooks Children's Shop is a specialist children's bookseller with a comprehensive selection of children's books for all ages. Five times Australian Bookseller of the Year, Gleebooks is open seven days a week, offering a prompt and efficient mail out service and extensive website.

Goldfish Gifts & Toys

Shop 2, 62 Albert Street
Berry NSW 2535
Tel: (02) 4464 3332
email: goldfish@goldfishgifts.com.au
website: www.goldfishgifts.com.au

Goldfish Gifts and Toys are designers of a great range of children's room accessories including mobiles, wall plaques, door knobs, hooks, coathangers, pencil and money boxes and more. Characters include Noah and his ark, crazy fish, gorgeous butterflies and transport. The shop is filled with colourful toys and traditional wooden toys from around the world. Ordering is possible online or via mail order. The shop is open seven days 10.00am to 5.00pm.

Infancy

7 Wilson Street
Newtown NSW 2042
Tel: (02) 9565 2866
Also located at:
105 Booth Street
Annandale NSW 2038
584 Darling Street
Rozelle NSW 2041
email: infancy@iinet.net.au
website: www.infancy.com.au

Infancy selects a unique range of Australian and international clothing, handcrafted toys and giftware all at highly affordable prices. Infancy also offers an online shopping service, VIP program and a great children's play area.

Megalong Books

183 The Mall
Leura NSW 2780
Tel: (02) 4784 1302
email: books@megalongbooks.com
website: www.megalongbooks.com

Megalong Books has a large and varied range of children's books from first board books to chapter books for beginner readers and on to young adult titles. They also have a children's specialist to provide advice and information.

Minimee Babies & Kids

109 Norton Street
Leichhardt NSW 2040
Tel: (02) 9569 2000
Also located at:
123 Willoughby Road
Crows Nest NSW 2065
Tel: (02) 9436 3436
email: info@minimee.com.au
website: www.minimee.com.au

Minimee can provide you with all your newborn through to toddler toy needs from learning and development toys through to plush teddies/dolls and keepsakes. You will be sure to find that unique gift and you also get free gift wrapping. Offering a great range, service and prices, items include gifts/toys, nursery furniture, prams, car seats, baby essentials, linen and fashion at Leichhardt, Crows Nest or online.

Pages & Pages Children's Booksellers

878 Military Road
Mosman NSW 2088
Tel: (02) 9969 9736
email: kids@pagesandpages.com.au
website: www.pagesandpages.com.au

Pages & Pages Booksellers are one of Australia's leading specialist children's bookshops. Their Mosman bookshop features not only a well stocked general bookshop but a specialised children's bookshop and an ABC Centre and an extensive range of CDs and DVDs.

Teddy Bears Downstairs
164 Swan Street
Morpeth NSW 2321
Tel: (02) 4933 9794
email: aussiebear@kooee.com.au

Teddy Bears Downstairs stocks an extensive and extraordinary range of bears and animal friends for children and adults (who are still kids at heart). Open seven days.

The Toy Loft
1 Mitchell Road
Brookvale NSW 2100
Tel: (02) 9905 4895
email: ttl@iprimus.com.au
website: www.brookvaletoylibrary.com.au

The Toy Loft sells nursery items and toys including buggies, backpacks, back carriers, trikes, go-karts, scooters, games, puzzles and baby toys. Catering for ages from 6 months to 8 years. Brands include Fitnesswise, Tri-ang, Pintoys, Baby Einstein, Kelty, Sherpa, 'Push-me-Home' Bike/Trike handles and 'Liquid Holster' drink holders. Phone or visit the website for more information.

QUEENSLAND

Bim Bam Boom
296 Oxley Road
Graceville QLD 4075
Tel: (07) 3278 3788
email: info@bimbamboom.com.au
website: www.bimbamboom.com.au

Bim Bam Boom sells educational toys for children from birth to approx 10 to 12 years. They also run art workshops: "Toddlers Get Messy" for two to four year olds and "Boomers" for school-age children. Bim Bam Boom also runs holiday programs and hosts children's birthday parties. All you need to is bring a cake. No mess, no fuss for mum and dad, just relax and enjoy. Phone or email for more details.

Entropy
669 Flinders St West
Townsville QLD 4810
Tel: (07) 4724 4555
email: info@entropy.com.au
website: www.entropy.com.au

Entropy is an old fashioned toy store that will put a twinkle in your eye and a smile on your face. An amazing selection of traditional toys, sports and activity equipment for children and an extensive range of craft and craft kits. Purchase online with same day dispatch for most orders. Flat rate postage of $9.95 for orders of less than $100, free for all orders over $100.

Kiddlee Dinks
Shop 4.03 The Zone, Deception Bay Road
Rothwell QLD 4022
Tel: (07) 3204 8688
email: nikki@kiddleedinks.com.au
website: www.kiddleedinks.com.au

Kiddlee Dinks is a funky children's store for babies to teens that stocks children's beds, bunks, midi sleepers, car beds, desks, hand chairs, linen, cushions, rugs, lamps and wall art. They also have a great range of unique gifts for all ages.

LEGO Education Centre
2/78 Merivale Street
South Brisbane QLD 4101
Tel: 1800 684 068
email: anita@mooreed.com.au
website: www.mooreed.com.au

The LEGO Education Centre has a brand new store in South Brisbane right behind the Brisbane Convention Centre. The LEC specialises in hands-on LEGO workshops for children aged 4 and up such as Mechanical Toy Shop and Robot Adventures. They offer a great range of LEGO birthday party themes too. There is also a huge and different range of LEGO items available to purchase including the hard-to-find LEGO education items and LEGO merchandise such as watches, bags and some clothing items.

Wood Puzzles
4/17 Kenworth Place
Brendale QLD 4500
Tel: (07) 3205 1985
email: enquiries@woodpuzzles.com.au
website: www.woodpuzzles.com.au

Wood Puzzles manufacture and retail a quality range of timber toys including mobiles, nursery sets and individualised name puzzles for babies. They specialise in personalised products and their Kindy Chairs and Treasure boxes are unique gifts for birth, christening and birthdays. They have a large range of jigsaw puzzles for all ages and offer a popular service of turning your photographs into puzzles. Check out the website for the full product range or visit the store at the above address.

WESTERN AUSTRALIA

Adorable Affordable
Shop 24, Broadway Fair Shopping Centre
88 Broadway
Nedlands WA 6009
Tel: (08) 9386 3677
email: sales@adorableaffordable.com.au
website: www.adorableaffordable.com.au

Adorable Affordable has a beautiful range of baby and children's clothing, footwear, toys, gifts and accessories. The clothing range caters for premature babies through to 6 year olds with an emphasis on boys' clothing. Special occasion and Christening gowns are also available. Visit the store in Nedlands or the website for further information.

Resources

TOYS, BOOKS & GIFTS

Stores retail ➡ Toy brands

Babyland
30 Frobisher Street
Osborne Park WA 6017
Tel: 1300 654 959
Also located at:
83 Stirling Highway
Nedlands WA 6009
153 High Road
Willetton WA 6155
email: babyland1@bigpond.com
website: www.babyland.com.au

Shopping for a baby is a very exciting time and Babyland hope to make this experience enjoyable and stress-free by delivering a huge range of nursery goods at prices you will love. Babyland delivers small items Australia wide and large items throughout WA. Their range includes car restraints, manchester, prams, cots, high chairs, change tables, monitors, back pack and slings, toys and gifts. Order online or visit one of their three store locations.

Kids Cove
Shop 9, Central Court Mall, Central Road
Kalamunda WA 6076
Tel: (08) 6293 1569
website: www.kidscove.com.au

Kids Cove offers a dream bedroom all in one shop with funky bedding for girls and boys from birth to teens. They also stock children's accessories for all ages including lamps and rugs and great brand names such as Freckles, Hiccups, Kaloo, Lilly and Lolly, Tree House, Alex and Charli Eko Peko and many more. Kids Cove personalise bedrooms with amazing hand-painted canvasses and bold bright letters for that special little one and they also stock a range of pedal cars, small retro bikes and scooters. Kids Cove also sell clothing, funky new chairs and awesome nappy bags.

SOUTH AUSTRALIA

Baby Junction
365 Magill Road
St Morris SA 5068
Tel: (08) 8361 2200
website: www.babyjunction.com.au

Baby Junction understands the importance you place on making sure the products you purchase are the safest, long-wearing products available. The staff, parents themselves, have personally used many of the products they stock and only sell products that are tried and tested and safe for your baby. If you want some of the

best advice in Adelaide about what products to buy and what products are suitable for your baby, then drop into their shop for a chat or phone for some free advice. Open 7 days a week.

Parthenon Emporium
149 Henley Beach Road
Mile End SA 5031
Tel: (08) 8234 5733
website: www.parthenon.com.au

Parthenon Emporium specialises in christening wear and they also have a large range of keepsake gifts for births, christenings and birthdays. Personalised verses in frames are great ideas as well as all types of general housewares and children's gifts such as bedroom furniture, soft toys, collectors dolls, Disney lamps, jewellery, carousels, hand-painted toy boxes and hat boxes.

The Infant Boutique
Shop 6/136 The Parade
Norwood SA 5067
Tel: (08) 8331 3740
website: www.theinfantboutique.com.au

The Infant Boutique is a beautiful baby and children's boutique for ages 0 to 5 years (sizes newborn to 6) stocking nursery furniture, bed linen, blankets, wraps, clothing, sleepwear, toys, games, stationery, artwork, gifts and accessories. The range includes local, national and international brands and labels.

TASMANIA

The Growing Years
175 Elphin Road
Newstead TAS 7250
Tel: (03) 6334 7200

The Growing Years stock all your children's needs from clothing to toys. They only stock good quality items and all pre-loved clothing has been freshly washed and priced. Open Monday to Friday 9.00am to 5.00pm and Saturday by appointment.

TOY BRANDS

NATIONAL

BABY born®
Tel: 1800 244 543
email: info@funtastic.com.au
website: www.zapfcreation.com

BABY born® enables a particularly realistic role play of mother and child. Nurturing life like dolls also play a key role in the development and growth of young children. A child's language, motor skills, sense of responsibility, imagination, and emotions can all benefit from caring for a doll. No batteries are required for any of the eight lifelike features: she can drink, wet her nappy, eat and use her potty, cry and squeak, is very flexible and may also be bathed.

Bambini International

Tel: 1300 557 691
email: trade@bambiniinternational.com.au
website: www.bambiniinternational.com.au

Bambini International distributes innovative and premium quality products that help make parents' lives easier and babies' lives safer. Brands include grobag, bambino mio, prince lionheart, john crane wooden toys and the new Egg bath range. In 2008 Bambini International won both major Australian "best product" awards giving parents peace of mind that it is also the experts that love what is on offer. Bambini International products can be found in major department, leading independent and specialty stores throughout Australia.

BeesKnees 4 Kids Pty Ltd

Tel: (02) 9948 0435
email: info@beesknees4kids.com.au
website: www.beesknees4kids.com.au

Baufix is a range of high-quality wooden construction sets made in Germany using only non-toxic and environmentally friendly materials. From airplane to locomotive, crane, tractor and more, these versatile sets offer creative fun for new and more experienced little engineers aged 3 to 6 years and over. Playing with the coloured panels, bars, screws and nuts, children learn step by step how to build working models and develop their fine motor skills, logical thinking, creativity and hand-eye co-ordination. Baufix toys are available from selected toy stores and children's boutiques. Phone the or visit the website for more information.

BeesKnees 4 Kids Pty Ltd

Tel: (02) 9948 0435
email: info@beesknees4kids.com.au
website: www.beesknees4kids.com.au

Hess-Spielzeug from Germany is an exciting range of quality wooden toys for babies and toddlers. This extensive collection of rattles, pram toys, mobiles, baby-gyms and more (with its wide choice of colourful, innovative and child-friendly designs) is sure to offer something special for any little one. All toys are made in Germany using high-quality European wood and 100% non-toxic and child-safe materials. Hess-Spielzeug is distributed by BeesKnees 4 Kids and is available in selected baby boutiques and toy stores.

BeesKnees 4 Kids Pty Ltd

Tel: (02) 9948 0435
email: info@beesknees4kids.com.au
website: www.beesknees4kids.com.au

Keptin-Jr is a series of wonderfully soft and completely natural toys and comforters for babies. All Keptin-Jr toys are made from certified organic cotton and filled with pure sheep's wool. The simple designs of the toys will stimulate the child's creativity and imagination. Natural fabrics and sheep's wool easily absorb the child's smell and adjust to the body temperature, perfect attributes for babies and toddlers. Keptin-Jr soft toys and comforters are available from selected baby boutiques and toy stores.

BeesKnees 4 Kids Pty Ltd

Tel: (02) 9948 0435
website: www.beesknees4kids.com.au

Spiegelburg from Germany offers an extensive collection of unique and absolutely delightful children's toys and lifestyle products featuring Princess Lillifee, Capt'n Sharky and the new Horse Friends range. With items ranging from dolls, puzzles, games, party accessories, jewellery, beauty sets and stationery to homewares, clothing, bags and travel accessories, there is sure to be something to delight any boy or girl. Available from quality toy stores, gift shops and children's boutiques.

Born with Style

Tel: 1300 885 337
email: info@bornwithstyle.com.au
website: www.bornwithstyle.com.au

Born with Style's range includes Jeep Baby Products, United Colors of Benetton, Kolcraft, Baby Cubes, Loopa-Bowl, Kuster and more. Born with Style products are designed to be the safest, most comfortable and practical you can find, combining passion, quality and style with the latest technological advances. For more information phone the number above or visit their website.

Crayola (Australia) Pty Ltd

Tel: 1800 657 353 or (03) 9730 4400
website: www.crayola.com

Art experiences with Crayola products engage and inspire children while they create and grow, building creativity, independence and confidence through hands-on exploration. The new Beginnings range of products enables these experiences to start at a much younger age. Children aged 12 to 36 months can easily hold and manipulate each of the tiny-finger-friendly art tools to successfully scribble up a storm, while getting an early start on developing lifelong skills.

Early Learning Centre

Tel: 1300 850 123
email: admin@earlylearningcentre.com.au
website: www.elctoys.com.au

early learning centre

Early Learning Centre (ELC) is one of the world's most respected toy brands, and is passionate about helping children get off to the best possible start with their early development. These quality toys are designed to help children explore their imagination and creativity, and most importantly to make learning fun. Suitable for children from birth to 8 years of age, they meet and exceed all Australian, British and European standards for toy safety. Categories include Early Years for the under 3s, wonderful themes for boys and girls, art and craft, sport and activity, games and puzzles, and of course music and books. There are 3 easy ways to shop: online at www.elctoys.com.au; by phone 1300 850 123; or in-store. Phone or visit online for your nearest Early Learning Centre store (in all states except NT and Tasmania) and also available exclusively through all Kids Central stores.

Resources

TOYS, BOOKS & GIFTS

Toy brands

Fifi and the Flowertots

Tel: 1800 244 543
email: info@funtastic.com.au
website: www.fifiandtheflowertots.com

Fifi is a mischievous and inquisitive young Flowertot, who inhabits a colourful garden world. From growing flowers to making jam tarts, every day provides endless opportunities for fun and adventure for the energetic and forgetful young Fifi and her best friend Bumble. There is a host of Fifi and the Flowertots toys to help little people recreate the magic and adventures at home, including beanies, a playmat, musical TV and phone, talking plush and puzzles.

Graco

Tel: 1800 003 178 or (03) 8787 3838
website: www.gracobaby.com

Graco is one of the world's best known and most trusted children's product companies. Graco is a Newell Rubbermaid company, with 1500 associates worldwide. Graco is dedicated and committed to designing and manufacturing top-quality products – products that inspire parents and babies alike. For information phone toll free 1800 003 178.

Hasbro Australia Ltd

Tel: 1300 138 697

Playskool continues to bring fun and learning to young children with the newest toys and classic favourites. Playskool's extensive range of developmentally sound and entertaining toys gives youngsters the opportunity to develop through play. To help you choose the right toy at the right time for your child check out Playskool's Ages and Stages system featured on pack. Playskool brands include Gloworm, Mr Potato Head and Cool Crew amongst others. All are available at leading department and toy stores. Phone or visit the website for more information.

Hasbro Australia Ltd

Tel: 1300 138 697

Play-Doh compound, a beloved toy of children and adults, has been a part of playtime fun for many years. Play-Doh helps children create imaginary worlds and explore new colours, shapes and textures. Play-Doh is available in a wide range of colours, and offers a variety of tools and playsets providing more fun ways to play. Play-Doh compound and playsets are available at leading department and toy stores.

Jasnor

Tel: 1300 881 940
email: sales@jasnor.com.au
website: www.jasnor.com.au

Begin baby's life with new Baby Beginnings from GUNDbaby, a snugly range of plush friends for baby to cuddle. Give your baby a feel for true GUND quality with Baby Beginnings plush Lamb and Bear (rrp$24.95 each), Huggy Buddy Blankies (rrp$22.95), Lamb and Bear Chime Balls (rrp$14.95 each) and Rattles (rrp$12.95). Designed in a palette of neutral colours with delicate accent stitching, the characters are suitable for both boys and girls. Introduce your little softie to quality plush right from the start, with huggable Baby Beginnings from world-renowned GUNDbaby. Phone the number listed above or visit the website for more information.

Jasnor

Tel: 1300 881 940
email: sales@jasnor.com.au
website: www.jasnor.com.au

Peter Rabbit, every child's most loved bunny, has gotten greener with a new range made of unbleached 100% cottons, natural fibres and recycled packaging. Included in the range is the Linen Peter Rabbit (rrp$29.95), Peter Rabbit super soft comforter (rrp$26.95), Pull Along Peter (rrp$44.99) and many more. Enjoy the super soft quality of the classic Peter Rabbit with an environmentally-friendly twist. Phone the number listed above or visit the website at www.jasnor.com.au for more information.

Jasnor

Tel: 1300 881 940
email: sales@jasnor.com.au
website: www.jasnor.com.au

With bright colours, interactive accessories and gorgeous characters, the Amazing Baby range is the ultimate in developmental learning. Amazing Baby is designed to aid a child's fine and gross motor skills and developmental stages are also clearly marked on the packaging. The range includes a set of three Sound Balls (rrp$36.95), Developmental Butterfly Activity Toy (rrp$19.95) and Mirror Teether Rattles (rrp$15.95) in Cat, Bear and Puppy designs. Phone the number listed above or visit the website at www.jasnor.com.au for more information.

K's Kids

Tel: 1800 675 772
email: sales@modernbrands.com.au
website: www.modernbrands.com.au

K's Kids is a series of award-winning plush toys, featuring the wonderful K's Kids characters, specially designed for the hands and minds of babies and toddlers. The multi-award winning range is produced with the highest quality materials resulting in adorable toys that are both educational and fun to play with. Phone the number listed above or visit the website for more information.

Leapfrog

Tel: 1800 244 543
email: info@funtastic.com.au
website: www.leapfrog.com.au; www.funtastic.com.au,
www.funtasticnursery.com.au

LeapFrog products are some of the world's best selling educational toys. LeapFrog products are designed to emotionally and intellectually captivate the minds and imaginations of children. Products are designed specifically for children aged 0 to 10 years and target all the right learning milestones for each age grade. Distributed in Australia by Funtastic, LeapFrog has created fun and engaging toys that cover subjects such as phonics, reading, maths, music, geography and science. The Australian range includes infant toys, pre-school toys and exciting new learning platforms such as the Tag Reading System (2008 Australian Toy of the Year and 2008 Pre-School Toy of the Year), Leapster2 handheld Learning System which boasts the hottest software licenses on any educational gaming platform and much, much more.

Learning Curve Australia

Tel: (03) 9550 3600
email: service@rc2aust.com.au
website: www.rc2aust.com.au

The award winning Lamaze Developmental System is a unique range of infant products designed to aid babies monitor skills from birth to 24 months. Each item is colour coded to assist in choosing the right product for your child's development. All products – toys, books and play gyms – are colorful, have bright patterns and shapes, fun sounds, and different textures. Fully washable and uniquely guaranteed.

Learning Curve Australia

Tel: (03) 9550 3600
email: service@rc2aust.com.au
website: www.rc2aust.com.au

The First Years range of products help parents keep their children healthy, happy and safe by offering products from feeding to playing and sleeping. Feeding and soothing products include the Take & Toss range of spill proof cups, bowls and spoons, booster seats and reclining feeding seats. The Play & Discovery products include unique toys and rattles including the popular "Floating Friends teether" and "Rolling Giggle Pals". The Care & Safety products include hands-free safety gates, toilet training seats, bed rails, safe sleepers and monitors. The First Years also offers licensed products in Winnie the Pooh, Thomas and Friends, Cars and Princess.

Little Tikes

Tel: 1800 244 543
email: info@funtastic.com.au
website: www.littletikes.com.au

With Little Tikes products you'll be creating a world of fun that lasts. With a range that caters to babies right through to pre-schoolers and includes fun bath toys, colourful musical instruments, durable ride-ons, walkers, role-play, outdoor and activity toys, you're sure to find the perfect toy for your own little tike. Little Tikes provides the reassurance of products which are durable, colourful and educational providing long-lasting entertainment throughout the important early developmental years of their life.

Nice-Pak Products

Tel: 1800 506 750
email: info@nicepak.com.au
website: www.jollybaby.com

Jolly Baby creates fabulous infant products that are imaginative, fun, creative and innovative. Their products are designed to create positive awareness, stimulate curiosity, promote sensory progression and enhance creative imagination. Their aim is to create innovative infant development toys and the highest quality juvenile lifestyle products and infant accessories. For further information phone 1800 506 750 or visit their website www.jollybaby.com.

Playgro Pty Ltd

Tel: (03) 8558 2000
email: sales@playgro.com
website: www.playgro.com

Let your child's imagination grow with Playgro's range of infant developmental toys. Designed to stimulate an infant's sensory development, inspire their curiosity and improve their ability to explore and interact with the surrounding world, Playgro toys will help your baby reach full potential whilst being fun, entertaining and safe. With vibrant colours and patterns, different textures, and fun characters, Playgro's toy range is sure to provide hours of interactive fun and play. Available from all major retailers and selected toy and baby stores nationwide.

Roary the Racing Car

Tel: 1800 244 543
email: info@funtastic.com.au
website: www.roarytheracingcar.com

Fans of Roary The Racing Car can now create their very own Silver Hatch Race Track at home, with the arrival of the Roary cars and toys. The pre-schoolers television series, Roary The Racing Car, follows the adventures of Roary, a bright, cheeky and energetic single-seater race car, and his amazing group of loveable friends at Silver Hatch Race Track. Now race fans can create their own adventures with all their favourite characters. Choose from the Remote Control Roary, the Silver Hatch Race Track, Collectible cars, Jigsaws, Talking Plush and heaps more. Most products are suitable for kids 3 years plus.

Resources

TOYS, BOOKS & GIFTS

Toy brands ➜ Toy hire & toy libraries

Sesame Beginnings

website: http://archive.sesameworkshop.org/
sesamebeginnings/new/

Sesame Beginnings is an infant brand with a range of toy and gift ideas that teaches parents interactive techniques and fun activities that encourage early learning in a way both they and their child will enjoy. Parenting tips and baby versions of the Sesame Street characters will help make playtime quality time. The range includes DVDs, books, plush toys, block sets, chime balls, pram ties and clips, teethers and pull-down toys. For more information on the Sesame Beginnings product and stockists contact: For books: Five Mile Press (03) 8756 5500 or www.fivemile.com.au. DVDs: Madman Entertainment (03) 9419 5444 or www.madman.com.au. Toys and gift ideas: Jasnor (03) 9562 9900 or www.jasnor.com.au, Playgro (03) 8558 2000 or www.playgro.com.

Tee-Zed Products

Tel: (02) 9386 4000
email: sales@tee-zed.com.au
website: www.tee-zed.com

Dream Baby® toys and accessories provide tactile stimulation and education along with entertainment. Dream Baby® has an extensive range of fun products including plush rattles, musical toys and decor items as well as stroller and car seat toys and accessories. Their practical and affordable range is available from selected baby stores, toy stores, hardware or pharmacies or phone (02) 9386 4000 for your closest stockist.

The Wiggles

Tel: 1800 244 543
email: info@funtastic.com.au
website: www.thewiggles.com

They have been around for over 10 years and captured the hearts, minds and imaginations of kids and parents alike. Still as popular as ever, the Wiggles toys focus on enhancing physical development and encourage a love of music and dance. The new toy range has continued to adopt these values coupled with innovation and a sense of fun. Your kids can continue to grow and learn through Wiggling, dancing and singing.

Tomy

Tel: 1800 244 543
email: nurseryenquiries@funtastic.com.au
website: www.funtasticnursery.com.au

The trusted TOMY brand has launched a range of educational and interactive toys for babies 6 months plus. The range includes play gyms that evolve as baby does, toys to improve motor skills and co-ordination, and much more.

Trackmaster Thomas

Tel: 1800 244 543
email: info@funtastic.com.au
website: www.thomastrackmaster.com.au

A world of imagination is right around the bend! Whether acting out scenes from their favourite Thomas and Friends™ shows or dreaming up their own incredible adventures, it's easy for little engineers to put their favourite stories in motion with Trackmaster™ Railway systems. Every playset comes with two connectors so you can connect your new Trackmaster™ track to your blue track. Choose from the existing range of playsets, tub toys and pre-school toys as well as collectible engines.

VTech

Tel: 1800 675 772
email: sales@modernbrands.com.au
website: www.modernbrands.com.au

The VTech Baby range is designed to bring out the best in babies, infants and toddlers, encouraging them to play, learn and discover. These toys stimulate the senses and imagination to introduce age-appropriate concepts such as letters, numbers, shapes and colours. VTech Baby toys invite, inspire, engage and teach to encourage the development of a child's mental and physical abilities.

Yo Gabba Gabba

Tel: 1800 244 543
email: info@funtastic.com.au
website: www.yogabbagabba.com

Yo Gabba Gabba! is a sing-along, dance-along, magazine show for 21st century pre-schoolers and parents, with a unique blend of loveable characters, original tunes from hip hop to electronic beats, real kids, quirky animation and extraordinarily catchy songs. Meet Muno, Foofa, Toodee, and Plex as they learn concepts and simple life lessons including shapes, colours, the importance and sharing, brushing your teeth and good memories. Check out the funky range of interactive toys that reflect the shows fun life lessons, songs and dances.

TOY HIRE & TOY LIBRARIES

NATIONAL

Jumping J-Jays Castles & Slides

Australia-wide
Tel: 1300 CASTLE (1300 227 853)
website: www.partycastles.com.au

When you hire a jumping castle from Jumping J-Jays Castles & Slides you will get the world's safest inflatable games that will allow your kids to jump all day safely. Jumping J-Jays began hiring inflatable bouncy castles over 10 years ago and take pride in providing party castles that are colourful for any birthday party at home or to a much wider audience including store openings, christenings, open days, corporate events and fetes. The children are safe with inflatable front safety barriers, full inflatable side walls and sun shade. The range includes: traditional castles, combos (castle and slide), actives (combo and interactive mouth), slides and the new falling floor. Visit the website for amazing 3D virtual tours.

VICTORIA

Toy Libraries Victoria
1 Winter Street
Malvern VIC 3144
Tel: (03) 9555 4055
email: info@toylibraries.org.au
website: www.toylibraries.org.au

Toy Libraries loan play materials: generally toys, puzzles and games but some may also loan books on child development and play as well as tapes and videos. In this way parents and caregivers are encouraged to play with children. Informal, caring and friendly environments offer opportunities for networking and support. Most toy libraries charge a small annual fee and require members to fundraise and work a few hours each year. Please call the number above to find out where your local Toy Library is. There are 160 of them across Victoria.

NEW SOUTH WALES

Cubby House Toy Library Inc.
32 Howard Avenue
Dee Why NSW 2099
Tel: (02) 9971 7006
email: cubbyh@tpg.com.au

Cubby House is a community-based toy library open to children with additional needs in the Manly, Warringah, Pittwater and surrounding local areas. These needs may be physical, developmental, learning, speech, emotional or social. The range of toys available caters for babies from 6 weeks old to primary school age children. An Occupational Therapist is in attendance to help parents select suitable toys and provide ideas for play. The joining fee is $10 and an annual fee of $110 covers the loan cost of all toys.

Toy Depot
Tel: 0417 676 341
email: info@toydepot.com.au
website: www.toydepot.com.au

Toy Depot is a web-based toy hire business based in the North Shore of Sydney. They offer a great range of quality toys by Step 2 and Little Tikes along with kid-sized party tables and chairs. Toys can be delivered direct to you for a small delivery fee or can be picked up from Turramurra. Toys include ride-ons, the always-popular roller coasters, climbers, kitchens, train tables and many other items. By hiring you become a member and you are then entitled to the regular members' specials advised via newsletter.

QUEENSLAND

Little Munchkins Toy Hire
Shop 1, 6 Wongabel Street
Kenmore QLD 4069
Tel: (07) 3878 4969
email: info@littlemunchkinstoyhire.com.au
website: www.littlemunchkinstoyhire.com.au

Little Munchkins Toy Hire offers an extensive range of toys for hire. It is a fantastic way to offer your child a great variety of toys to stimulate their development at a fraction of the cost of buying them. Hire toys include: cubby houses, slides, climbing gyms, roller coasters, ride-in cars, kitchens, doll houses, farm sets, train sets, exersaucers, baby toys and lots more. Grandparents and visitors are most welcome. Great for birthday parties and playgroups too.

NORTHERN TERRITORY

Darwin Toy Library
Corner of McMillans & Marrara Roads
Moil NT 0810
Tel: (08) 8927 9077
email: dtl9077@bigpond.net.au
website: www.darwintoylibrary.org

Darwin Toy Library is a not-for-profit community based organisation. It's a toy and equipment lending service for children and families along with carers and other community groups. There is a huge variety of toys available to help develop your child's co-ordination, expression, discrimination, gross and fine motor skills. All toys are educational so the child learns through play – this is an important step in your child's development.

WESTERN AUSTRALIA

Western Australian Association of Toy Libraries
PO Box 202
Kelmscott WA 6991
Tel: 0417 887 687
website: www.waatl.org.au

For a minimal charge members of toy libraries have at their disposal a huge range of learning resources to assist in entertaining and educating young brains. From the earliest moments children love stimulation and toy libraries offer a wide variety of toys, puzzles and games that help carers fulfil the need for variety. Use toy libraries to keep your toy box changing and beat boredom with positive tools. Some of the best things about toy libraries are that they warehouse your toys saving space, and allow your child to try out toys so you will know what they actually like before you spend big and find out that once the wrapper is off they aren't interested. Visit www.waatl.org.au to find your nearest toy library in Western Australia.

LeapFrog

LeapFrog's number one aim is to help children fall in love with learning. Perfect brain food for developing kids, the LeapFrog range caters to children at every age and stage of their development from birth to 12 years.

The magic: LeapFrog always starts by looking at all the ways children love to play and learn – from books and video games through to traditional toys. From here their research identifies not just what children learn, but when and how they learn it. A six month-old just sitting up learns differently to a toddler, pre-schooler or primary school child. LeapFrog works with the best and brightest creative minds – a team of experts who form the company's Educational Advisory Board to create learning products that are relevant, engaging and highly effective.

Then there is the "ah-ha" factor. LeapFrog calls it the magic. Surprises, unexpected experiences and extra fun is built into every toy. It's what makes children pick them up and play with them, again and again and again. It comes from understanding how to intellectually captivate and emotionally engage the minds, hearts and imaginations of young learners.

Learning through play: LeapFrog's vision is to inspire in children and families a lifelong love of learning – through their collection of unique electronic interactive toys that are not only fun to play with, but also great teaching tools. LeapFrog's Baby Range includes the loveable Appy, Lulu and Ella, playful learning friends that sing, light up and introduce basic learning concepts to your baby with a single touch of their tummy. The clever LeapFrog Fridge Phonics Magnetic sets encourage letter recognition, animal recognition and basic word development while the bilingual Learn & Groove range introduces children to learning through music and play.

For the latest product news and a chance to win fabulous prizes visit www.leapfrog.com.au.

See the
learning

Share
the fun!

www.leapfrog.com.au

Lamaze

Lamaze works with child development experts to create toys that delight babies of all ages, at all stages of their learning. Suitable from birth, the Early Explorers range includes the award-winning Lamaze infant development book line of lift-the-flap and textured soft books. With teethable corners, furry bits, crinkly bits, big flaps for little fingers and a variety of interactive features, Lamaze soft books encourage imitation and discovery.

The Lamaze Play & Grow range help baby refine motor skills with different textures to grip and grab, while the bright contrasting colours and patterns will help to stimulate their vision. Other favourites in the range include the Lamaze Octotunes and Puppy Tunes that play a different note as you push each tentacle or leg. These soft, lovable characters teach baby about nurturing play and come complete with a song book and a soft vanilla scent.

Stage two toys, the Curious Explorers range for babies from 6 months, include stackers, crawl toys and the Musical Chime Garden whose sweet sounds play when baby touches a flower. Stage three, the Creative Inventors range, caters to babies over nine months with a range of bath toys for water play in the tub, the multi-sensory soft sorter with its unique green apple smell and the spin and stack rings that reward your baby with music and movement as they stack the rings.

The Spin & Explore Garden Gym is an exciting, new and innovative platform for encouraging tummy time exploration. The rotating spinner will help baby to develop upper body strength and lower leg strength through a unique shape and rotating motion, suitable from birth onwards.

For more information on the complete range of Lamaze toys and other toys in the Learning Curve range or to find your nearest retailer visit www.rc2aust.com.au.

Lamaze®

Infant Development System®

0m+   3m+   6m+   9m+   12m+

Enlightening babies through all stages

Lamaze toys encourage early development of the senses, spark creativity and introduce problem solving skills. Working with child development experts, Lamaze creates toys that delight babies at each stage:

Early explorers (0+ months), **Curious Explorers (6+months)**, Creative inventors (9+ months).

Little Tikes

With Little Tikes products you will be creating a world of fun that lasts. Little Tikes provides the reassurance of products that are durable, colourful and educational providing long-lasting entertainment throughout the important early years of their life.

The Little Tikes range caters to babies through to pre-school aged children with fun bath toys, colourful musical instruments, durable ride-ons, walkers, role-play, outdoor and activity toys covering every stage of their early development.

The colourful range of toys are made to withstand knocks, bumps and the occasional tantrum-throwing episode and are designed to help children learn about the world around them.

2009 marks the 30th anniversary of Cozy Coupe, also affectionately known as the "crazy" coupe. Over the years the Cozy Coupe has taken on a few different moulds, but it has always managed to stay true to the original basic shape and functionality and has kept the iconic red and yellow colours.

In 2009 a very special 30th anniversary edition of the Cozy Coupe will be produced, and for the first time will feature eyes!

2009 also marks an introduction to the world of Cozy Coupe for toddlers with the My First Cozy Coupe Walker Ride-on. This product grows with your child: it starts off as a walker and as your child progresses it can be expanded to include a seat effectively turning it into a ride-on.

With Little Tikes educating your little ones, play can be lots of fun and the best part is that you don't even have to tell them they're learning!

With Little Tikes you're sure to find the perfect toy for your child.

Visit www.littletikes.com.au for more information on the fabulous range of Little Tikes products and to join the official Little Tikes Club.

Children's clothing & footwear

Photograph by Iris Creations Photography, Melbourne & Geelong.

All about children's feet

The foot is a complex structure of 26 bones and 35 joints, held together and supported by scores of ligaments. A baby's foot is padded with fat and is highly flexible. Children begin to walk anywhere between eight and 18 months of age. Most toddlers are flat-footed when they first start walking, or tend to turn their feet inwards, because of poor muscle tone and weak ligaments in their feet. This will improve as the feet strengthen. Always see your podiatrist or doctor if you are concerned about your child's feet or gait.

Wearing shoes

A child learning to walk receives important sensory information from the soles of their feet. Shoes, particularly those with hard and inflexible soles, can make walking more difficult. Your toddler doesn't need shoes until they have been walking for a couple of months, and then only to protect their feet from sharp objects. It is important to allow your child to go barefoot regularly to help them develop balance, coordination and posture. Have your child's shoes professionally fitted, which should include measuring each foot for length and width. Children's feet grow very quickly and their shoe size may need updating every few months. Shoes that are too tight can hamper your child's walking and cause problems, such as ingrown toenails and bunions.

Suggestions for shoes

Shoes for your toddler should ideally have features including:

- firm, comfortable fit both lengthways and widthways
- rounded toe
- plenty of room for the toes
- flexible, flat sole
- heel support
- laces, straps or equivalent to prevent excessive movement or slipping of the foot inside the shoe.

Flat feet

The sole of a normally developed foot has an arch, called the medial arch, formed by muscles and ligaments. For the first two years, your child's feet will seem to have fallen arches. Flat feet are normal in a young child due to weak muscle tone in the foot, a generous padding of fat, and loose ankle ligaments that permit the foot to lean inwards. As your child masters walking, the ligaments and muscles will strengthen and the fat pads in the arch area won't be so noticeable. By around five years of age, your child should have normal arches in both feet.

Feet that turn inwards

Many toddlers walk 'pigeon-toed', with either one or both feet turned inwards. In most cases, this is simply a sign of developing posture and balance, and should resolve by itself (without the need for medical intervention) somewhere between the ages of three and five years. However, if the in-toeing is severe, seems to involve the leg and hip as well as the foot, or isn't improving by the time your child is around one and a half to two years of age, see your podiatrist for assessment. Excessive in-toeing may be caused by a variety of underlying difficulties, such as hip joint problems.

Feet that turn outwards

Very occasionally, toddlers walk with their feet turned outwards. This tends to be more common in children who were born prematurely. In most cases, out-toeing resolves by itself as posture and balance matures, but see your podiatrist if you are concerned.

Problems that need professional attention

You should see your doctor or podiatrist if you are worried about your child's feet or gait. Problematic symptoms may include:

- abnormally shaped toes
- ingrown toenails
- bunions or other deformities
- stiffness in the foot
- limping
- the child complaining of pain while walking
- severe in-toeing or out-toeing
- flat feet beyond the age of five years
- a sudden change in the way your child walks
- if your child isn't walking at all by two years of age.

Things to remember

- Most toddlers are flat-footed when they first start walking because the muscles and ligaments of their feet are underdeveloped.
- Toddlers should go barefoot as often as possible to encourage balance, posture and coordination.
- See your doctor or podiatrist if you are concerned about your child's feet or gait.

Photograph by Ashford Studio, Gold Coast.

Information supplied by the Australian Podiatry Association, www.podiatryvic.com.au.

Vox Pop

We asked a number of women and men around Australia to send in their advice, tips and personal experiences on a range of topics so that you have an insight into how others cope being a new parent. We hope you find their comments interesting, informative and reassuring. Vox Pop biographies: page 652

Lee Norman
Mum of one, Melbourne

My husband and I have reasonably large extended families including lots of "non related" aunties and uncles and friends so we guessed we would get a range of clothes and gifts. As a result we only purchased enough jumpsuits and singlets for the hospital. As expected our baby, Bliss, did receive a huge amount of clothes and other gifts. We found out early that when we used the two piece suits with singlets, the outfit rode up and exposed Bliss' back. We purchased a number of legless romper suits which we now use as singlets (sometimes with singlets on underneath). This provides coverage to Bliss' back when she wears a two piece outfit. Being a winter baby we often put the legless romper on under her jumpsuits as well. I suggest having a range of legless rompers and singlets when going to the hospital.

Amanda Jephtha
Mum of one, Sydney

Warning: crawling is a hazard to clothing and footwear! Pants with reinforced knees are the most durable against playground crawling, while protecting soft little knees. Flowing and frilly skirts tangle easily around learner legs, causing frustration and is an invitation for constant tripping and scraped limbs. Save these for non-playground days!

Shoes also suffer heightened wear and tear when crawling on rough surfaces. Babies don't need to wear 'proper' shoes until they're well into their walking. During the cold weather and over rough surfaces, soft shoes can be worn. Make sure they are made from soft – but durable – leather as little holes are easily worn through the toes. A good tip is to have two sets of shoes; one dedicated as 'playground' shoes so it doesn't matter how scuffed they get, and another 'nice' pair when non-abrasive crawling is on the cards, such as someone's house, or in the pram.

Little torsos are often exposed to the elements thanks to wriggling babies, no matter how deeply you tucked that singlet in. Rather than regular singlets, use singlet onesies instead. These do up between the legs with press studs so little bodies will stay toasty and warm.

Christine Walsh
Mum of two, Broome

I am quite an organised person and love to bargain hunt. So I always buy my children's clothes at the end of season sales for the following year. For example at the end of summer 2008 sales I bought my children's clothes for summer 2009. Though I have to admit this backfired on me last year when my husband got a transfer to Broome so the winter clothes I bought were hardly used at all. This is a great way to buy as I can buy brand name clothing at a fraction of the price. I quite often shop online as I am limited to clothing shops living in the country. I enjoy doing this and can spend hours just looking at different clothing and sites online. With shoes I do like to buy quality shoes for the kids as I figure they don't have as many pairs as I do at one time. I try and find them on sale when I visit Perth.

Nicole Hambling
Mum of one, VIC

Ever since my mum found out she was going to be a Nanna she has been on a continual shopping spree. But this is a different type of shopping spree. She finds the kids clothes she likes and then watches and waits, waits for the end of season sales before she buys and always in bigger sizes for the following year or even the year after if only big sizes are left. Oh, but the most important thing there is a $5 limit. No piece of clothing should cost more than $5. There are the odd items that cost a little bit more but very little is bought at full retail price. There is no loyalty to any brand either. Apparently if you watch and wait there are massive savings to be had.

The best bit? Amy's 08/09 summer wardrobe was complete in April and her winter '09 wardrobe is almost complete, all at a fraction of full retail cost. I'm now looking at this summer's clothing and dropping hints about what Amy might like for next summer!

Tanya Byrnes
Mum of one, VIC

Buying clothing for your child is an individual decision on whether you purchase label brands or alternative brands. My husband and I, after speaking to other parents, decided to purchase second-hand and some items from alternative outlets. Many second-hand clothing stores sell suitable clothing, bedding and other necessary items you may require, at reasonable prices.

Also if you start looking at seasonal shopping, such as winter clothes in summer, you can pick up clothing at reduced prices and place away in storage. When doing this, you can purchase larger sizes for your child to grow into at a later stage. Another alternative is to buy in bulk, shop around for specials, use lay-by at provided outlets and even speak to your midwife. They may have many other parents that they can place you in contact with, where you may be able to swap or buy items you require.

Alana White
Mum of one, SA

Lucky for me Jaylan is at an age where he can't tell me if he likes something or not. I think the best sort of clothes for babies is soft clothing. They get rashes easily and don't like tags etcetera rubbing on the back of their necks.

I think that Big W and Kmart have great priced baby clothing, but personally I am a Pumpkin Patch fan. They have very trendy clothing and I tend to grab a lot when it's end-of-season sale time. Everything is at least 50% off and you save heaps. My partner hates me going out shopping because I always come back with clothes for Jaylan!

Anna Ngo
Mum of one, Perth

I've never needed an excuse to go shopping, but pregnancy and motherhood did give me that extra reason if ever I needed one. Only this time I was venturing into an uncharted area of the store, and unashamedly I now spend more time in the baby clothing aisles than women's wear. There are just so many good stores and so much stuff I'd love to bring home. The only things stopping me are a limited budget, and a husband who doesn't understand that babies can never have too many clothes.

At the risk of sounding like a shopaholic, for me there is both a therapeutic side and practical side for my newfound passion of shopping for my baby. I think most women can relate with the therapeutic nature! But on a practical note, babies grow up so fast that they're in constant need of new clothing anyway.

Our household budget doesn't always allow for brand name baby clothes but thankfully there never seems to be a shortage of sales on kid's apparel.

Kerri Harding
Mum of one, VIC

Obviously personal taste and your budget are a big factor in choosing and buying your children's clothing and shoes. I have to admit that I am a bit of a label girl and that taste also largely extends to my son's wardrobe. Often I choose to buy well known and respected labels because I like the look, cut and quality of them more but that's not to say

Vox Pop

We asked a number of women and men around Australia to send in their advice, tips and personal experiences on a range of topics so that you have an insight into how others cope being a new parent. We hope you find their comments interesting, informative and reassuring. Vox Pop biographies: page 652

that I don't also purchase some of his clothes from larger discount stores as well. Regardless of where you prefer to shop, you can always pick up some great end-of-season bargains and stock up on clothing in larger sizes for the following year.

If your children are anything like my son, they will go through a stage where they will refuse to want to try on new clothes or shoes. I got to the point where I would rather have teeth pulled without an anaesthetic than take him into town clothes shopping.

My advice: always check out a store's return/refund policy and only buy from stores that allow you to take back items and that will refund your money. At least then the tantrum throwing is confined to the privacy of your own home and if it doesn't fit, you are not stuck with it.

Ebay is a great place to buy and sell children's clothing, toys and anything else you can possibly think of. I have sold some of my son's used clothing that was still in very good condition and was surprised at what people were prepared to pay for it. It is well worth a look if you are not already into it.

When it comes to shoes, I am a bit fussy. Each to their own but I only buy new shoes for my son. I also like to have them professionally fitted as he has a very narrow foot and I find that a lot of shoes are too broad for him. I also try to make the effort to get his foot measured every 3 months or so to make sure that he still has enough room inside his shoes. It is surprising how fast their feet grow!

Martine Pekarsky
Mum of two, Melbourne

Our wardrobe is a mixture of hand-me-downs, Ebay bargains and seconds shops. When buying second hand, I do buy the name brands as they tend to fit better, wash and wear well and keep their resale value on Ebay. Many of the clothes I have bought secondhand on Ebay I have sold again for the same price so we have essentially had them for free.

Bernadette Vella
Mum of two, Brisbane

I am a big fan of blue for boys and pink for girls, so my kids have been dressed accordingly. For both my children, I have always had way too many clothes. I love buying clothes for me and that love of clothes has extended to my children. Both of my kids love their clothes too. Arielle already picks what she wants to wear and loves being in skirts and dresses and almost always wants to wear pink.

For shoes I have always believed in buying the kids good quality shoes. My personal favourite are Clarks shoes. They are more expensive but I think they are worth it. I tend to just have two pairs of shoes for each season for the kids but make sure they are good quality. I don't like children running around without shoes on so I am forever arguing with my kids to put their shoes back on.

Louise Cruz
Mum of three, NSW

When buying clothes for babies and toddlers it is important to consider that spending a whole load of money on designer gear can be a wasted exercise if they are not going to wash well and still look like the expensive garments they were bought to be. I tend to be more practical when buying clothes for my active youngsters, particularly for the under 3s age group, as they are not yet fully acquainted with the idea of staying clean in their best outfit.

I find that shopping for 'play clothes' in discount stores can save you quite a bit of money and they do still have a good range of kids fashion items that will keep your little one looking "cool".

Like most mums I do like to shop and I splash out on one or two outfits per season from a more upmarket store such as Pumpkin Patch or Myer. It is nice to have that gorgeous frilly lace dress for your little princess to wear out for an occasion or a little pant and shirt suit for the handsome prince, but remember that little fingers will pick up something sticky or dirty that will invariably end up on the outfit over the course of the day. (Not to mention if your baby has reflux and will de-posit leftovers down the front of themselves!)

Cindy Fraser
Mum of three, Melbourne

I love shopping for clothes for the kids (a bit too much!) We have a mix of brands, some more expensive and plenty of bargains! The factory outlets can be a great place to hunt out a bargain; often you can get the good brands for the cheaper price, and the better quality can mean that sometimes they will survive more than one child.

We also love hand-me-downs and anything that survives my lot is well received by my girlfriends' children. Our eldest son actually didn't like wearing clothes for much of his second and third year. At home he would wear only his undies, and always complained if I tried to get him dressed. When we would come home from being out the first thing he would do was get undressed. The good thing was that his washing pile usually consisted of nothing but undies!

I take the children to get fitted for at least one pair of shoes each season, but I usually check out the shops without the kids first. That way I have a good idea of what I want before I drag all the kids in so that our trip is kept as brief as possible.

Danielle Murrihy
Mum of two, Melbourne

We were very lucky that we were given a lot of hand me down clothing so I have not bought a lot of new clothing. I love going to garage sales and buying clothes in great condition for a dollar or two! At the start of each winter and summer I do buy new clothes such as socks, skivvies and pyjamas as these are hard to find in a good second-hand condition. At 18 months I also went and had them properly fitted for shoes, so we buy a two new pairs of shoes twice a year - in summer we buy sandals and lightweight canvas runners and in winter we buy gumboots and leather runners.

I also buy jeans and jackets new when there is a end of season sale at Pumpkin Patch (I like the adjustable waist bands as both boys are different builds). The boys have always shared their clothes but there are certain outfits that look better on one, so I do always tend to dress them in the clothes that suit them.

Recently they have started wanting to wear certain clothes if they are character themed such as Thomas the Tank Engine or The Wiggles. They have not discovered action heroes yet!

Rowena Raats
Mum of three, Kalgoorlie

I think ... no, scratch that ... I know I spend more on my kid's clothes than I ever spend on mine! I love seeing my babies dressed nicely. I realise now growing up with boys that all I really wanted to do was play dress ups and have carried this into motherhood. I have enjoyed choosing outfits and making sure it all matches from top to toe. I don't mind if it is label or a discount brand as long as it looks good.

I have discovered that as they get older they don't appreciate you dressing them as much. For some reason my children don't always think that a perfectly matching outfit is cool. Thank goodness my baby is only 12 months ... plenty more dress up with her before she can really fight back. I have realised with two older children that this can also pass onto them a sense of how to match an outfit including shoes.

I am actually proud now when I realise that my eldest dresses herself really well though I have a bit more work to do with my son!

Vox Pop

We asked a number of women and men around Australia to send in their advice, tips and personal experiences on a range of topics so that you have an insight into how others cope being a new parent. We hope you find their comments interesting, informative and reassuring. Vox Pop biographies: page 652

Jess Tamblyn
Mum of one, SA

I have saved lots of money by buying secondhand clothing for my daughter. Op-shops and eBay are great for children's clothing as you can often find clothes that are as good as new but for a fraction of the price.

As they grow out of their clothes so quickly a lot of money can be wasted if you buy everything brand new.

My local opshop is brilliant; I visit it regularly and often find brand name clothing that looks as though it has hardly been worn. I find that by visiting the shop on a Monday I get the best deals as most people drop off their donations over the weekend.

eBay constantly has thousands of children's clothes listed. Clothes often sell cheap but beware of the postage costs as it often costs more than the item itself. Buying bulk lots of children's clothing is a good way to reduce postage costs.

Katherine Twigg
Mum of one, VIC

When I was pregnant, I spent up in the clothing department. I shopped at Myer and gorgeous little baby boutiques and bought the most adorable clothes.

Once my baby was born I discovered that any clothes I bought smaller than a 000 were completely useless and half of the adorable little overalls were extremely frustrating to get done up and my baby just didn't seem as comfortable. I soon learned that simple button up romper suits were much easier.

My baby grew so fast (he is now 8 months and already in a size 1), and most of his clothes barely got worn, if ever! Until he has finished his major growing spurt I will buy cheaper clothes and once he has finished I will get him some cute outfits from the more expensive places.

Sophie McKellar
Mum of two, VIC

I really love shopping in general and for kids clothes - yeah bring it on! I worked for Pumpkin Patch for a few years so I already owned loads of clothes which I now have had the chance to use.

I am also a big shopper at a couple of the large discount stores – I really like their PJs. Bonds is also on sale a lot there so keep your eyes open.

DFO is also a good spot to pick up a bargain. If you can work it out, buy ahead but you do need to be good at sizes, and with kids sometimes they grow at very strange rates!

Melanie Smoothy
Mum of one, NSW

When it comes to children's clothing, we quickly learnt two key factors: children outgrow everything far too quickly and it's almost a full time job trying to keep them clean.

When it comes to purchasing clothing and footwear, we abide by three golden rules:

We buy good quality footwear and have Brayden professionally "fitted" for his shoes. We both felt that it's important to have good fitting shoes to assist with his growth and development – in particular when they first start walking and more so when they're continuously on the go.

There is nothing wrong with your Big W, Kmart, and Target branded clothing, especially when you're having a quiet day at home, attending a playgroup or the local park, etcetera.

We buy brand name clothing on sale. I love the June/July clearance sales, factory outlets and buying online. I buy end-of-season clothing in the next size to put away for next year and the majority of people would be hard pressed to recognise what season the range is from.

Quality without the full price tag!

Michelle Winduss
Mum of one, Sydney

Before and after my son was born, he received a lot of clothing from friends and family. I did purchase some clothing, but very little.

In terms of footwear, I don't have a specific brand that I prefer my son to wear however I do try to buy footwear that is comfortable and suitable for his feet. I have purchased so many pairs of shoes for him but he still doesn't keep a pair of shoes on his feet for more than 10 minutes!

Rebecca Tragear Whiting
Mum of four, Melbourne

I confess I am a label addict when it comes to dressing my children! However I never pay full price and I buy quality not quantity.

Designer baby and children's wear is always on sale at major department stores, at specialty baby boutiques and online. I always buy the next size up at the end of season sales and put clothes away for the following year.

As children get older they need less clothes so I tend to buy a few great pieces for weekends and going out each season. For my boys I always invest in quality jeans and trainers as they wear them so much. Remember dress your kids how you like while you can because eventually they will not wear anything you like!

Lucy Mulvany
Mum of three, SA

You can never have enough socks and singlets, so they are always my first purchase of the season. I tend to really try and mix it up with items off Ebay, some 'designer' classics, some hand me downs, and some boutique items. I go for plain colours that I can mix and match all season. I am proud that my children are often complimented on their "style". I love choosing things for them and love seeing them all dressed up!

Some additional tips when buying clothes:

Gifts: friends and family will buy you lots of baby clothes as presents, so don't buy too much in advance, just a few basics to see you through the first few days.

Sizes: buy a mixture of size 0000 (newborns under 4kg from birth to 3 months) and 000 (babies under 6kg from 3 to 6 months) as you don't know how big your baby will be when they are born and they grow very quickly.

Bodysuits: easy to get on and off, and the best ones are those with press stud fasteners down the front and legs.

Singlets: singlets are handy but can often be tricky to get over your child's head.

Socks: buying lots of socks the same colour is a great idea as they have an amazing tendency to get lost!

Tags: keep tags on clothes until you are sure that your child will wear them. That way you can either take them back for a refund or sell them as 'new with tags' (NWT) on EBay.

Hand-me-downs: accept hand-me-downs from friends, as babies grow so fast that there can often be little sign of wear.

Spare clothes: toddlers get very messy, especially when you are out and about, and spare tops, pants and undies are handy to get on and off quickly, in particular when toilet training as accidents will happen!

Seasons: think about the season in which your baby is born as this will determine whether or not you buy long-sleeved or short-sleeved bodysuits.

Resources

These Resources pages list products and services relevant to "Children's clothing & footwear". To make your life easier as a parent, editorial listings have been grouped into sub categories. Businesses then appear alphabetically under a national or a state-based subhead depending on reach.

SUB-CATEGORIES

CHILDREN'S CLOTHING LABELS

NATIONAL

Annabel Trends
Tel: (07) 5593 4755
email: sales@annabeltrends.com
website: www.annabeltrends.com
The adorable Babytalk white growsuits (rrp$14.95, size 6 to 9 months) and bibs (rrp$9.95) from Annabel Trends let babies do all the talking, with witty and fun sayings that let you know exactly what your baby is thinking. Bibs include "Let's do lunch, it's on me", "Don't cry over spilt milk" and more. Growsuits include one liners such as "As seen on ultrasound", "Mine's baby fat, what's your excuse?" and many more. Made from 100% cotton.

Annabel Trends
Tel: (07) 5593 4755
email: sales@annabeltrends.com
website: www.annabeltrends.com
Keep your baby's tootsies looking their best with the divine Tippy Toes baby socks (rrp$20.95) from Annabel Trends. The fun and bright socks come in a box of 6, in a variety of loveable designs including Super Softies, Smileyworld, Super Stars, Sweet Hearts, Jolly Rogers, Baby Janes, Kickers and more. Tippy Toes Baby Socks are for babies 0-12 months and 12-18 months and are an ideal gift for tiny tots.

Aromababy Natural Skincare
Tel: (03) 9464 0888
email: info@aromababy.com
website: www.aromababy.com
At last, pure and natural certified organic cotton babywear that is as kind to baby's skin as the luxury skincare Aromababy also provides. This selection of divine mix-n-match, unisex pieces offers simplistic, practical styling for the modern day parent who demands an eco-friendly solution with a touch of class. Beautiful basics come in gorgeous waffle cotton and make the perfect gift. Pure cotton pieces in non-organic also available. Visit www.aromababy.com for further information.

Bonds
Tel: (02) 9840 1111
website: www.bonds.com.au
The BONDS Easysuit, a world first, breaks all the rules and brings you the first funky baby bodysuit and

coverall that is completely fastener free. No buttons, no studs, no ties, no zips and no Velcro. The BONDS Easysuit is a patented product and one of a kind. Nothing as simple and innovative has ever existed; you will wonder how you ever lived without the BONDS Easysuit.

Bright Bots Pty Ltd
Tel: (07) 3552 8999
email: admin@brightbots.com.au
website: www.brightbots.com.au & www.maxandtilly.com.au

Bright Bots and Max & Tilly are two very popular babywear ranges available across Australia in independent boutiques and David Jones. Bright Bots is a fun range mainly for sizes 00 through to 3, renowned for its hard wearing quality, bright colours and graphics. Max & Tilly is a newborn to size 0 range in soft pastel shades. The range has a gorgeous selection of 'better wear' pieces with practicality in mind as well. New ranges are released each season and there is also a selection of essential pieces available year round.

Cheekybubs
Tel: 1300 851 508
email: info@cheekybubs.com.au
website: www.cheekybubs.com.au

Cheekybubs can be found in stores throughout Australia. The Orginal Banbib (the abbreviated word for bandanna bib) is the most popular item; other products in the range include pram liners, blankets and covered wipe containers. Michelle continues to develop her own label stocking unique products which cannot be readily found in retail outlets. www.cheekybubs.com.au is an online store/manufacturer and supplier of innovative and stylish products with high standards of customer service and personalised service. Visit the website for more information.

cheekyteez.com.au
Tel: (08) 9408 1888
email: paul@cheekyteez.com.au
website: www.cheekyteez.com.au

Cheekyteez.com.au allows you to custom design and produce your own unique and fun clothes online. Upload your own photos, graphics, logos or select from the online gallery and you can even create your own personalised message or slogan. Put your individual designs on t-shirts, tops, singlets, bibs and other clothing items. Select different garment styles, colours or sizes and preview your design before ordering. Specialists in short-run, on-demand printed garments with fast turnaround and delivery to your door.

Chino Kids Pty Ltd
Tel: (03) 9822 9888
email: chino@designwcc.com.au
website: www.chinokids.com

Chino kids clothes are designed to inspire. Made with high quality, textured fabrics and designer fit, their seasonal ranges are available at Myer and boutiques throughout Australia. Chino designs for boys and girls 3 months to 12 years. Chino Kids' website features the complete collection and keeps you up-to-date with all the exciting Chino news. Chino Kids is proudly Australian owned and designed.

CNP Brands
Tel: 1300 667 137
email: info@cnpbrands.com.au
website: www.cnpbrands.com.au

Natures Purest is a range of organic bedding, babywear and gift items made from 100% organically grown naturally coloured cotton jersey and produced without the use of dyes or chemical pesticides. The cotton buds grow in natural shades of cream, brown and green and are processed to make the most wonderful natural and pure fabrics. Another natural fibre used in the Natures Purest range is bamboo. Unrivalled as one of the most luxurious materials, bamboo handles like silk, but performs like cotton so is extremely soft yet breathable and cool. The range is packaged in attractive recycled boxes and makes a perfect gift for a newborn. Natures Purest is available nationally at David Jones stores and selected nursery retailers. Visit website www.cnpbrands.com.au or contact their Customer Service on 1300 667 137 for your nearest stockist.

Eeni Meeni Miini Moh
Tel: (07) 3902 0088
email: info@eenimeeni.com
website: www.eenimeeni.com

eeni meeni miini moh is an innovative children's lifestyle brand committed to creating contemporary yet timeless products for children aged from newborn to 12 years. Best known for its distinct palette, naive figurative drawings and its use of natural fibres, eeni meeni miini moh creates unique products which attract attention, are fun and functional and release the free spirit and innocence of today's discerning child.

Fat Mumma's
Tel: 0428 190 701
email: info@fatmummas.com.au
website: www.fatmummas.com.au

Fat Mumma's is all about creativity and caring. They have created a series of fun, unique products that stand-out in the city streets such as stylish nappy bags, groovy kids clothing and creative, new-baby gifts. Their logo is inspired by the cartoon styles of Japan and gives the designs some humourous attitude. Feel like you're part of a unique growing community of mothers with an eye for great design and visit www.fatmummas.com.au.

Fragile
Tel: (02) 9362 0085
email: info@fragile.com.au
website: www.fragile.com.au

Fragile offers an exquisite range of maternity wear, designed in-house, for the new mum-to-be, as well as a collection of beautiful, local and imported clothing for the newborn to 6 years. Visit the website for more information.

Resources

CHILDREN'S CLOTHING & FOOTWEAR

Children's clothing labels

Itch Design

Tel: 0416 322 728
email: info@itchdesign.com.au
website: www.itchdesign.com.au

The concept behind Itch Design started in 2005 with full-time mum and graphic designer Jodi combining her two passions to bring a sense of fun and interest to children's clothing, launching a range of t-shirts that created a stir. Itch Design has now expanded to form a complete fashion statement for fabulous tots and style conscious small fry, with distinctive graphics and super cute characters children can have fun with. Itch Design has a strong focus on stimulating the creative young mind and serves up an eclectic mix of super cool tees, and pieces inspired by edgy adult fashion. Homewares have now been introduced, with bold loveable characters that will brighten any child's surroundings.

JK Kids Gear

8 stores in Australia
Tel: 1800 155 255 for your nearest store
website: www.jkonline.com.au

JK Kids offers a range of children's clothing designed for comfort, quality, affordability and style. From newborns to 12 years there is something for every child and the prices are fantastic. It is the one-stop shop for your child's clothing needs, from kindy clothes to those outfits for special occasions. Shopping is easier than ever before with JK Kids fabulous and easy-to-use online shop at www.jkonline.com.au or phone toll free on 1800 155 255 to find your nearest store.

Kinou

Tel: 0411 691 723
email: kylie@kinou.com.au
website: www.kinou.com.au

Each and every pair of Kinou's one-of-a-kind pants is hand made with love in Melbourne, Australia. Using a mix of contemporary prints and traditional classics, Kinou create pants and tees that are as unique as the babies and toddlers who wear them.

Lambykins

Tel: (03) 9306 6567
email: info@lambykins.com
website: www.lambykins.com

Lambykins™ certified organic cotton clothing offers exceptional softness, quality, comfort and design. A new premmie range will be added shortly. Visit www.lambykins.com for a list of nation-wide stockists or to purchase online.

Little Buddha Clothing

Tel: 0416 097 707
website: www.littlebuddhaclothing.com.au

Little Buddha Clothing is a small company based on the Central Coast of NSW specialising in small runs of unusual, funky and vintage kids clothing from sizes 000 up to 5. They make sweet party dresses for girls and cool boardies for boys amongst many other things and they can also custom design clothing. Most of their clothing is 100% cotton and made in Australia.

Little Grippers

Tel: (02) 9634 8119
email: littlegrippers@bigpond.com.au
website: www.littlegrippers.com.au

Little Grippers has designed a jumpsuit for active little babies. A comfortable all-in-one, cotton jumpsuit perfect for crawling, cruising, sleeping or just scuffling around the floor. 100% Australian designed and owned, Little Grippers jumpsuits include rubber grip on the knees, shins and feet for exploring with safety – no more bumps, bruises or tears. This is one of a kind play gear with safety grip. Visit the website for further information.

Little Workers

Tel: (07) 3369 4096
email: sales@littleworkers.com.au
website: www.littleworkers.com.au

Little Workers create fun and colourful fashion for kids. Quirky details, unusual fabric and original prints are some of the features of this Australian made and designed children's label. Catering for girls and boys, newborn to size12, with hats, bags and hair accessories to match. Free postage with orders over $300. Shop online (and instore of you are in Queensland – 289 Given Terrace, Paddington) or phone for a catalogue.

Lulabie

Tel: (03) 9824 8788
email: lulabie@aapt.net.au

The hallmark of Lulabie is the use of quality fabrics and exquisite embroidery on smocked gowns in Swiss Voile, satin-edged bunny rugs, change mats and embroidered wool blankets, just to name a few essential items. Lulabie sell direct to their national clientele.

Miatom

Tel: 0438 875 022
email: hello@miatom.com.au
website: www.miatom.com.au

Miatom loves to create casual, fun, kids' clothing. Best known for their unique prints, premium quality and great value for money, the simple designs are perfect for the Australian lifestyle and climate, and allow kids to run, climb and play. Miatom is proud to dress children from 1 to 12 years in age-appropriate clothing that children love to wear. Funky graphics and original prints that kids can relate to makes this label one worth wearing.

millie & mo

Tel: 0488 002 214
email: info@millieandmo.com.au
website: www.millieandmo.com.au

millie & mo pride themselves on making unique, funky, quality mum-made baby and toddler clothing, gifts and accessories. Products available online include bandanas, nappy covers, dresses, pants, canvas photo boards, crochet garments, gift vouchers and more. Visit www.millieandmo.com.au.

Minihaha & Hiawatha

Tel: (03) 9832 4832
email: info@minihaha.com.au
website: www.minihaha.com.au

Minihaha & Hiawatha manufactures and wholesales exclusive children's clothing. With a young, fresh look and European influence, Minihaha & Hiawatha has developed seven clothing labels. Bébé by Minihaha: a stunning pure cotton baby's wear range for newborns to 2 years. Bébé Jr. by Minihaha: launched in July '07 to cater for all those babies that have now outgrown the Bébé by Minihaha range. This caters for both boys and girls from age 2 years to 6 years old. Minihaha Baby: designs in baby soft fabrics exclusively for sizes 00 to 4 years. Minihaha: modern, fashionable styles using a range of their own unique fabric designs for girls aged 3 to 14 years. Woof! Baby: groovy, functional styles for boys 00 to 4 years and Woof!: cool street wear styles for 3 to 14 year olds. Hiawatha Accessories is a range of shoes to complement the clothing range. The new Tahlia range consists of a range of girls' dresses from size 3 to 14. They are a mix of funky casual to dressy and party wear using exquisite fabrics and contemporary styling. The Minihaha and Hiawatha labels are sold throughout Australia in all David Jones Department Stores, Kids Central Department Stores, leading boutiques and gift shops. Phone, email or visit the website for your nearest stockist.

minimink

Tel: 1300 887 343
email: info@minimink.com.au
website: www.minimink.com.au

The minimink range of products was introduced in 2003 and now includes several ranges: faux fur range, organic cotton and stationery. Each range is complementary to the main products in the faux fur range. The colours are natural so that they are unisex and combine with all other colours.

Monster Baby

Tel: (07) 5535 6915
email: info@monsterbaby.com.au
website: www.monsterbaby.com.au

Monster Baby is a new label that's all about edgy, graphic-driven, funky clothes for babies, infants and toddlers. They design and sell cutting-edge children's clothing including t-shirts, onesies, hoodies and jackets, hats, caps, beanies, leggings, pants, dresses, skate shorts, singlets, sleeveless ts and more. Phone or visit the website for further details.

Pash Baby

Tel: 0409 808 852
email: email@pashbaby.com
website: www.pashbaby.com

Baby Pash, luxurious baby-sized pashminas, is the ultimate in softness and warmth, made from a blend of 70 per cent pashmina (the world's finest cashmere) and 30 per cent silk. Baby Pash is an ideal baby wrap or blanket and can also be used as a scarf or pashmina once baby grows up. $185 including express delivery from www.pashbaby.com. This ultimate fashion statement for babies and toddlers is also a wonderful gift that will be treasured as a family heirloom. Visit the website or phone for further information.

Pumpkin Patch

Tel: 1800 123 430
email: info@pumpkinpatch.com.au
website: www.pumpkinpatch.com.au

Pumpkin Patch takes your little Patch stars through the new season in spectacular style. There are loads of fresh and exciting new styles to mix to the max, arriving in store and online all the time. Collections that kids just love are bursting with that legendary patch signature style. Experience the thrill of quality, affordable kids fashion styles at your nearest Patch store or check out the latest styles online at www.pumpkinpatch.com.au.

Ramalama

Tel: 1300 729 834
email: hello@ramalama.com.au
website: www.ramalama.com.au

The Ramalama range of baby basics is made from a luxuriously soft cotton/bamboo blend fabric chosen especially for its amazing properties including advanced absorbency, insulating and antibacterial properties. Bamboo is also the world's fastest growing plant requiring no harsh chemicals and little water, making it a truly organic and sustainable resource. Designed for babies up to 12 months with a palette of fresh white, warm beige, rock n roll black and earthy grey, the range consists of basic tees, leggings, rompers, wraps and bibs. Visit the website or phone the number above for further information.

Red Chalk

Tel: 0414 065 064
email: letsplay@redchalk.com.au
website: www.redchalk.com.au

Designed and made in Australia, Red Chalk is the brain child of Kate Perry. A graphic designer by trade with a background in fashion design and retail, Kate's designs are developed from cut paper, potato stamps, sticky tape, paint, illustrations and silk screens. Each season is based on a theme inspired by childhood and imagination. Visit their website at www.redchalk.com.au or phone the number above for more details.

Resources

CHILDREN'S CLOTHING & FOOTWEAR
Children's clothing labels ➔ Children's swimwear

Sesame Beginnings
website: http://archive.sesameworkshop.org/
sesamebeginnings/new/

Sesame Beginnings is an infant brand designed to teach parents interactive techniques and fun activities that encourage early learning in a way both they and their child will enjoy. With baby versions of the Sesame Street characters appearing on clothing and footwear, along with parenting tips on packaging, Sesame Beginnings helps create quality time between parents and baby. For more information on Sesame Beginnings product and stockists: For clothing available in Target contact Timeframe Clothing (03) 9499 7700 or visit www.target.com.au. For footwear available in Kmart contact Neet Feet (03) 9376 5511 or visit www.neetfeet.com.au.

Smart Stuff
Tel: (03) 5428 4822
email: info@smartstuff.com.au
website: www.smartstuff.com.au

Smart Stuff's Australian-made art smocks are bright and colourful and have no buttons, ties or elastic. Using only quality fabrics these smocks are hardwearing and offer fantastic protection against paint, glue and any messy situation. Available in sizes 2 to 14. Great for home, playgroup or school. Generous discounts for group orders too.

Wasabi Kids
Tel: 0412 399 142
email: info@wasabikids.com.au
website: www.wasabikids.com.au

Wasabi Kids has a collection of groovy kidswear for ages 6 months to 6 years – gorgeous children's clothes you won't have seen before. Wasabi Kids kids stand out from the crowd and it's not because they are standing in the naughty corner. It's because their Japanese inspired clothes are groovy, affordable and very, very cool. Give the baby shower gift that will bring smiles to everyone's faces. Visit the website for more details.

www.baobab.com.au
Tel: 0416 151 426
email: belinda@baobab.com.au
website: www.baobab.com.au

For a completely modern look that's also about comfort and ease for growing babies and mums alike, there's baobab. Check out the gorgeous range of contemporary basics for babies and toddlers 0 to 6 years. This well-priced range is made from super soft cotton knit fabrics and is available in a range of gorgeous colours with a choice of simple and graphic prints on tees, dresses, hoodies, bodysuits and babygros. Baobab is original, practical, understated, stylishly modern and fun.

Zephiregeneration.com
Tel: 0412 358 225
email: info@zephiregeneration.com
website: www.zephiregeneration.com

www.zephiregeneration.com is the home of Zephiregeneration, fashion that promotes self-expression and the importance of being unique. This is a label for girls and boys aged 3 to 14 years and babies 3 months to 2 years who dare to be different and want to make their own fashion statement. With tailor-made designs, exclusive handpicked fabrics and quality hand finishes, Zephiregeneration offers an innovative, diverse range of clothing that will create an instant impression of childhood sophistication and glamour.

CHILDREN'S CLOTHING LABELS: PREMATURE BABIES

NATIONAL

Earlybirds
Tel: 1800 666 550
email: info@earlybirds.com.au
website: www.earlybirds.com.au

Earlybirds is a beautiful collection of clothing specifically designed for those precious tiny tots who come into the world early or arrive as small bundles. You can select from two ranges: "Sunnydays" range made from 100% cotton or the new unisex "Organics" range made from 100% organic cotton. Sizes range from 800grm to newborn. Phone or visit the website for further information.

Moment by Moment
Tel: 0408 689 330
email: fiona@momentbymoment.com.au
website: www.momentbymoment.com.au

Moment by Moment is a website dedicated to premmie babies. The site offers premmie clothing, gifts, nappies and dummies all suitable for premature babies from 400grams. There is also a premmie baby support forum and Cafe Prem, a premature baby story site to provide much needed support to those experiencing premature birth. Founded by Fiona Dixon, mother of Airlie Fae born at 27 weeks due to pre-eclampsia and HELLP Syndrome in 2006. Visit the website or phone for more information.

Treasured Baby Creations
Tel: 0406 714 279
email: prembabywear@yahoo.com.au

Treasured Baby Creations specialises in beautiful, reasonably priced clothing for premmie/small birthweight babies from 1.5kg. The range includes gorgeous sets, rompers, dresses, hats, booties and more all in 100% cotton and Australian wool. Soft prints and pastels teamed with small splashes of colour ensure a classic look with character, while the designs are practical for the specific needs of little babies. Designed and made in Perth. Custom sizes can be accommodated. Email for more information or stockists.

CHILDREN'S SHOES

NATIONAL

Baby Paws Australia Pty Ltd
Tel: (03) 6245 0999
email: sales@babypaws.com
website: www.babypaws.com

 Made from soft genuine leather, Baby Paws shoes allow infants' feet to flex naturally while they learn to crawl or walk safely. Because each child and each foot is different, most Baby Paws styles have a Velcro® type fastening, or laces, to ensure that shoes fit safely and securely. The wide range of shoes are available at Myer, Shoes & Sox and other fine stockists throughout Australia. Mail order and internet sales are also available.

Beautiful Soles
Tel: 0404 845 664
email: info@beautifulsoles.com.au
website: www.beautifulsoles.com.au

 Made only for babies and toddlers from 100% leather, Beautiful Soles are designed to protect and nurture little feet. The soft suede soles gives added grip so chilly tiles or slippery floor boards are no longer a problem and they also keep socks on! View the fun range of colours and styles on their website and find the right pair for the beautiful little soul in your life. Visit the website or phone for further information.

Cheeky Little Soles
Tel: 0431 887 697
email: info@cheekylittlesoles.com.au
website: www.cheekylittlesoles.com.au

Cheeky Little Soles are the Australian designed, soft soled leather baby shoes – the perfect footwear solution for all cheeky little souls. Practical, comfortable and stylish, their padded, non slip, soft soled leather footwear has been created to naturally protect the growth and development of little feet. Visit their website for stockist information or to purchase online.

Clarks – A Pacific Brands Licence
Tel: 1800 651 185
website: www.clarks.com.au

Correct fitting shoes are vital all through a child's growing life. That's why parents look for comfort and quality when they buy their kids' shoes. Clarks is the only brand that comes in true whole and half sizes, and up to five width fittings for a perfect, professional fit. For your nearest stockist phone 1800 651 185 or visit their website.

Robeez Footwear
email: info@robeez.com
website: www.robeez.com

Robeez provides soft- and flex-soled footwear that supports the healthy development of little feet. Always functional and fashionable, Robeez footwear products carry the American Podiatric Medical Association's Seal of Approval for promoting normal foot function.

Skeanie
Tel: (02) 4822 0401
email: service@skeanie.com
website: www.skeanie.com

 Skeanie Soft Soled Shoes and Boots are made of a high quality, soft genuine leather upper to allow little feet to breathe and grow naturally. The flexible suede sole provides superior grip while crawling and walking. Infants' feet are fragile and can be easily damaged. At birth, feet are mostly cartilage and in childhood and adolescence the bones in the feet, 52 in all, will form. During this time they are very fragile and any undue pressure can cause deformities. Soft Soles are a must for pre-walkers and walkers. Skeanie Soft Soled Shoes and Boots are available in four sizes from birth to 2 years. Priced from $29.95. Available from www.skeanie.com and selected retailers.

uggys
Tel: (08) 9203 7744
email: info@uggys.com.au
website: www.uggys.com.au

Uggys sell authentic ugg boots and sheepskin products (made in Western Australia) for adults, kids and babies. Available online and at selected retail outlets. Visit www.uggys.com.au for more information.

CHILDREN'S SWIMWEAR

NATIONAL

Loose Boots
email: info@looseboots.com.au
website: www.looseboots.com.au

Loose Boots specialises in sun protective swimwear for children aged 12 months to 6 years. Loose Boots swimwear is exclusively designed and manufactured in Australia using the best quality UPF 50+ fabrics which have been tried and tested by the Australian Standards Association to protect young delicate skin from the harsh Australian climate. Designs are fresh and funky while still functional. Loose Boots also manufacture rash shirts in both long and short sleeve which is often hard to find when buying swimwear for children.

Resources

CHILDREN'S CLOTHING & FOOTWEAR

Children's swimwear ➡ Stores online

Salt Sea Tees
Tel: 0402 405 808
email: info@saltseatees.com.au
website: www.saltseatees.com.au

Designed and manufactured in Queensland, Salt Sea Tees is a boutique range of quality swimwear providing UPF 50+ protection from ultraviolet radiation. Inspired by vintage toys found in the family garage, prints are applied to the bodice of each Sea Tee as a flexible heat transfer. The finest fabric sourced from Italy, Carvico Matt Nylon Lycra provides an excellent sun protection rating of UPF50+ and also has up to 4.5 times the chlorine resistance of ordinary elastane. This product is of the highest quality, both in material, design and construction.

Zoggs Australia Pty Ltd
Tel: (02) 9453 2000
email: sales@zoggs.com.au
website: www.zoggs.com.au

Regardless of age, everyone should be able to enjoy the water. Zoggs offers a wide range of goggles to suit all face shapes that are specifically designed for kids up to 6 years, as well as an extensive range of inflatable and buoyancy aids to promote water confidence. With safety in mind, these products offer first class design and function and are made with the best materials and superb workmanship. To complete the offering, Zoggs has an extensive tots swimwear and sun protection offering. For more information visit www.zoggs.com or phone (02) 9453 2000.

VICTORIA

Swimwear Galore
430 Brunswick Street
Fitzroy VIC 3065
Tel: (03) 9417 2222
310 St. Kilda Road
St. Kilda VIC 3182
Tel: (03) 9534 6222
1297 Nepean Highway
Cheltenham VIC 3192
Tel: (03) 9585 5622
131 Ocean Beach Road
Sorrento VIC 3943
Tel: (03) 5984 0322
138 Malop Street
Geelong VIC 3220
Tel: (03) 9529 9100
website: www.swimweargalore.com.au

Swimwear Galore is the largest retail swimwear shop in Australia. They cater for the whole family: girls' two piece, singlets and one piece sizes 1–14; boys' swimwear and shorts, sizes 1–14; men's swimwear, trunks and shorts, sizes 14-28 and ladies' two piece, singlet sets and one piece, sizes 8–32. They also have a large range of sun protection t-shirts and all-in-ones for children. Maternity swimwear also available. Open Monday to Friday 9.30am to 5.30pm, Saturday 9.00am to 5.00pm, extended hours during summer.

HATS, JEWELLERY & ACCESSORIES

NATIONAL

Flirty Bird Hair Accessories
Tel: 0411 332 490
email: hello@flirtybird.com.au
website: www.flirtybird.com.au

Flirty Bird offers a great range of handmade hair accessories including clips, headbands, ponytail holders and barrette clips. With a low flat rate of only $4.00 postage you can afford to give your child's hair some flair. Custom orders or requests are always welcome.

VICTORIA

missmouse
Tel: 0408 811 352
email: missmousetrading@bigpond.com
website: www.missmouse.com.au

missmouse specialises in gorgeous hand-knitted hats in bamboo yarns, reversible cotton hats, non-slip bow hairclips, brooches and library bags. The focus is on creating unique and contemporary accessories in 100% natural fibre. All items are extremely gentle and luxurious to wear which is also perfect for sensitive or allergy-prone skin. Designed and made in Melbourne and thoroughly tested by kids in all types of play conditions.

LABELS: IRON-ON, STICK-ON AND SEW

NATIONAL

ABC Labels
Tel: 1300 136 515
email: info@abclabels.com.au
website: www.abclabels.com.au

ABC Labels offer vinyl stick-on name labels, iron-on labels, mini name labels, shoe name labels, bag tags and packs including budget and speciality packs. They specialise in fundraising. Express delivery available and a 100% money back guarantee. Available nationally. Visit their website at www.abclabels.com.au and check out their new range of products.

Apparel Labels/R. Draper & Co
Tel: (08) 8332 9344
email: apparel@internode.on.net
website: www.apparellabels.com.au

Apparel Labels has been supplying woven name tags for over 15 years. The name tags are ideal for child care, kindergarten and school children and are available in both sew-on or iron-on. Stickers suitable for lunch boxes, books, pencils are also available saving the cost of lost items.

IdentiKid
Tel: 1300 133 949
email: info@identikid.com.au
website: www.identikid.com.au

 IdentiKid labels offers cute designs, gorgeous colours and great quality and price. They have dishwasher-safe vinyl stickers, wristbands, iron-on
www.identikid.com.au clothing labels and bag tags. Check out their innovative kids ID products too. 100% guaranteed and 100% Australian. Fundraising enquiries welcome. Phone 1300 133 949 for a free brochure or visit www.identikid.com.au.

Label Kingdom
Tel: 1800 264 549
email: info@labelkingdom.com.au
website: www.labelkingdom.com.au

Label Kingdom has a fantastic range of personalised identification labels, bag tags and invitations. Stick-on labels include shoe labels, allergy labels, glitter labels, pantry labels, shape labels plus their new stick on dot labels. They also have iron-on labels that really bond to the fabric, durable full colour bag tags which come in 19 designs and gorgeous invitations which include birthday invitations, baby shower and bridal shower invitations, BBQ invitations, 'Just Moved' notes plus much more. These labels are a must for childcare, kindy or school. Label Kingdom is a proud Australian family business. Free postage within Australia and New Zealand.

Stuck on You
Tel: 1800 645 849
website: www.stuckonyou.biz

Stuck on You is a fun, innovative company that strives to help parents organise their hectic households. Designed and manufactured in Australia, their vinyl labels are waterproof, microwave safe, dishwasher safe and UV resistant and clothing labels are made to stay put, and survive all your washer and dryer wear-and-tear. Visit the website for further information.

You Name It - Labels!
Tel: 1300 360 677
email: info@younameitlabels.com
website: www.younameitlabels.com

No more lost property! You Name It - Labels! offers a range of easy to apply iron-on clothing labels. Durable, washing machine and dryer resistant, these are great for naming your clothing, bunny rugs, bibs, sheet bags and other items. You Name It - Labels! also offers brightly coloured dishwasher and microwave safe vinyl labels perfect for lunch boxes, toys, toiletries and even shoes. There is a huge range available. Phone for a catalogue or visit their website.

STORES ONLINE: CHILDREN'S CLOTHING & FOOTWEAR

NATIONAL

Adorable Affordable
Tel: (08) 9386 3677
email: sales@adorableaffordable.com.au
website: www.adorableaffordable.com.au

Adorable Affordable has a beautiful range of baby and children's clothing, footwear and accessories. Their website and online shopping cart make choosing the perfect baby gift easy and fun. The clothing range is for premature babies to 6 year olds with an emphasis on boys' clothing. Special occasion and Christening gowns are also available. Phone the number listed above or visit the website www.adorableaffordable.com.au for further information.

All You Need
Tel: 0402 400 846
email: info@allyouneed.com.au
website: www.allyouneed.com.au

All You Need is an online boutique and children's emporium where you can find all you need for babies, children and mother. Find TikiBoo Kids boutique children's clothing, designer baby clothes, hair accessories, hats and aprons, children's decor, handmade toys and Cardamums handmade cards. They also offer a custom boutique service where they can custom design the perfect outfit. Find that perfect gift, unique kids clothing designs, party dresses, sock monkeys and so much more. Phone the number listed above or visit the website www.allyouneed.com.au for further information.

Baby BT
Tel: (08) 9390 1841
email: babybt267@bigpond.com
website: www.babybt.com.au

Baby BT has a large variety of clothing, manchester, gifts, cards, toys and teddies for babies and toddlers. There is a delightful range of prem baby clothes, clothes to 18 months and accessories. Gift vouchers, lay-by, gift registry and EFTPOS available. Shop online at www.babybt.com.au. Email or phone for further information.

Baby Eco Store
Tel: (08) 7120 2275
email: babyeco@optusnet.com.au
website: www.babyecostore.com.au

Baby Eco Store has an extensive range of natural baby products including organic cotton baby clothing and accessories, gifts, natural skin care/bath time care, toys and products for mum. Their products are carefully chosen to be safe, environmentally friendly and natural – perfect for baby. Shop securely online. They deliver across Australia and are always happy to offer help and advice. Phone the number listed above or visit the website for further information.

Resources

CHILDREN'S CLOTHING & FOOTWEAR

Stores online

Baby Exchange
email: info@babyexchange.com.au
website: www.babyexchange.com.au
At Baby Exchange you can list your unwanted baby and children's items including clothes, toys, books, DVDs and cots and choose whatever you like in return from any category. There are bargains to be found even if you don't have anything to exchange and members receive great discounts from many online stores operated by mums. Visit the website or phone for further information.

Baby Goes Retro
Tel: 0448 123 230
email: info@babygoesretro.com.au
website: www.babygoesretro.com.au
Baby goes Retro is the place to shop for funky and unique designer labels with a retro flavour. Create an individual look for your baby and toddler with stylish clothing directly from Europe. They also stock a great range of cool gift ideas, accessories, nursery items and organic cotton wear. Labels include Katvig, Plastisock, nanoou, Ej sikke lej, Snoffs, Elodie Details, Ida T and more. Order securely online and pay only $5 for shipping Australia wide. Visit the website or phone for further information.

Baby's Got Style
Tel: (02) 9427 2726
email: info@babysgotstyle.com.au
website: www.babysgotstyle.com.au
Baby's Got Style stocks beautiful, unique and funky clothing (newborn to 8 years), groovy toys, fun books, super accessories and gorgeous gifts. Brands include the best of Australian design as well as fabulous imports. Visit www.babysgotstyle.com.au for shopping that's easy, funky, fresh and stylish or phone the number above for more information.

Babylush
Tel: 0410 613 900
email: info@babylush.com.au
website: www.babylush.com.au
Babylush is an online boutique that offers a great range of children's clothing (newborn to size 5), fun toys, unique gifts, hair accessories, versatile baby bags, organic body products, funky shoes and socks, sleepwear, baby carriers and feeding accessories. Shop securely anytime with economical express post next day delivery. Visit the website or phone for further information.

babyshop
Tel: 1800 222 437 or 1800 BABIES
email: mail@babyshop.com.au
website: www.babyshop.com.au

Experience the convenience of shopping from home with one of Australia's first online baby stores: www.babyshop.com.au. With experience online since 1998 and hundreds of products to choose from, babyshop stocks a variety of well known brands, as well as featuring many exclusive and hard to find items. Departments include: Bathtime & Care, Bedtime & Nursery, Clothing, Feeding & Accessories, Out & About and Playtime & Development. (NSW readers can also visit their retail store at 276 Brunker Road, Adamstown.)

Bibs and Rattles
Tel: (07) 3324 9403
email: info@bibsandrattles.com
website: www.bibsandrattles.com
Bibs and Rattles is an online baby boutique that prides itself on variety, quality and affordability from newborn to 2 years old. Bibs and Rattles aim to provide exceptional service and each order is gorgeously gift wrapped with care.

Blossom Tots
Tel: (03) 9749 3702
email: info@blossomtots.com.au
website: www.blossomtots.com.au
Blossom Tots is an online boutique of Australian brands of baby and children's clothing including Papoose, Max and Tilly, Bright Bots and Ka-Boosh. They offer a range of baby clothes including outfits, singlets, hats, pants, bodysuits, coveralls, rompers, dresses, bootees, blankets and other accessories. Sizes range from 00000 for your precious premature newborns to 8 years. Blossom Tots aim to offer you the best in Australian designed products at affordable prices with prompt delivery and secure payment options.

Brite Babes
Tel: 0408 460 910
email: info@britebabes.com.au
website: www.britebabes.com.au
Brite Babes is an online store featuring unique baby and kids accessories. Brands include Little Packrats & Ribbies Clippies and a range of baby blankets, bibs, burp cloths, soft soled shoes, swim nappies, swaddling blankets, backpacks, hair accessories, hats, melamine sets and much more.

Caluna Loves
Tel: (03) 9974 0552 or 0402 333 291
email: info@calunaloves.com.au
website: www.calunaloves.com.au
Caluna Loves sells a range of organic clothing, PVC-free bibs, organic toys and eco-friendly nappy bags. This online store also has a range of infant swimwear that has built-in reusable swim nappies.

ClothingStoreOnline.com.au

Tel: 0404 366 999
email: admin@clothingstoreonline.com.au
website: www.clothingstoreonline.com.au

Shopping on www.clothingstoreonline.com.au is fun
and easy. Each designer has their own dedicated home
and product pages and also has a selection of their range
displayed in the various multi category pages. Simply
find what you're looking for and then drop as many
things into the one shopping basket, from as many
different designers as you wish. Then you can pay in
one, easy checkout. Once that's done, it's simply a
matter of sitting back and waiting for your purchase to
arrive. While there's nothing new about shopping online what makes ClothingStoreOnline.com.au special is
the designers it brings together on a single pain-free site.

Duckcloth

Tel: (03) 8503 7615
email: info@duckcloth.com.au
website: www.duckcloth.com.au

Duckcloth is a secure online store located in Melbourne
and delivering Australia-wide. They offer a fun and
fresh collection of children's fabric by the metre. Use the
fabric for curtains, quilts, cushions, napery, bean bags,
tote bags, clothing and many other projects.

Eclectic Baby

Tel: 0407 663 115
email: emma@eclecticbaby.com.au
website: www.eclecticbaby.com.au

Eclectic Baby is a baby boutique offering an amazing
collection of stylish handmade items. Many of the
brands are exclusive to Eclectic Baby and behind each
brand is a talented Australian crafter, creating and
designing unique pieces for modern mums and kids.

Ekidna Kidswear

Tel: 1800 606 963
email: joanne@ekidnakids.com.au
website: www.ekidnakids.com.au

Ekidna Kidswear stocks gorgeous, high quality clothing
in sizes for premature babies to toddlers. In addition to
clothing, Ekidna Kidswear also stocks a fantastic range
of giftware, accessories and baby essentials. Visit the
website or phone for further information.

Express from Heaven

website: www.expressfromheaven.com.au

Express from Heaven is a convenient,
innovative way to buy all your new
baby's essentials from conception to 18
months. The exclusive co-ordinated
clothing, accessory and gift range has
been designed specifically with your
baby's needs in mind. The unique range has been made
from high quality fabrics, styled for quick and easy
changing and allows for total comfort for any new baby.
Proudly Australian born, designed, made and owned.
Available through the website via online shopping and
selected outlets.

FrockYou.com.au

Tel: 0439 353 645
email: info@frockyou.com.au
website: www.frockyou.com.au

FrockYou.com.au is a hip eboutique stocking a massive
range of Australian and international clothing labels for
mums, kids and babies. From Monster Baby, Moppit,
Gabrial Saynte, Smirk, Ej Sikke Lej, Baby Legs, Cuski,
Itch Deisgns, Yunginz shoes and up and coming new
designers, to a covetable range of the latest in clothing,
shoes, bags and jewellery for mums. Shop for yourself
and the cool little people in your lives, all on the one
site, 24/7. Visit the website or phone for further
information.

Funky Kids

Tel: (08) 9284 0051
email: info@funkykids.com.au
website: www.funkykids.com.au

Funky Kids stock fabulous brands in clothing and
accessories including Guess, Fred Bare, Big By Fiona,
eeni meeni and much more as well as a wide variety of
gifts, toys and personalised products. Visit
www.funkykids.com.au.

Hello Charlie

Tel: 1300 725 876
email: info@hellocharlie.com.au
website: www.hellocharlie.com.au

Hello, Charlie! specialises in eco-friendly, natural,
organic and non toxic products for babies, children and
home. The site offers lots of practical and stylish
products that you will use over and over, as well as
everyday items like eco-friendly cloth and disposable
nappies, feeding products, clothing and bedding,
toiletries, pregnancy and breastfeeding products,
wooden toys, baby carriers, and things to get you out
and about. Visit www.hellocharlie.com.au for more
details.

Infancy

Tel: (02) 9565 2866
email: infancy@iinet.net.au
website: www.infancy.com.au

Infancy selects a unique range of Australian and
international clothing, handcrafted toys and giftware all
at highly affordable prices. Infancy also offers an online
shopping service and a VIP program. Visit the website
or phone for further information.

Infant Tiny Steps

email: info@tinysteps.com.au
website: www.tinysteps.com.au

Infant Tiny Steps offers a fantastic range of shoes and
accessories for the fashionable infant and toddler. Their
collection of stylish products has been sourced from
around the globe. Brands include 2feettall, shooshoos,
Pediped, Bibi, Pedoodles, Blabla, Sweet Shoes, Diddle
dumpling, Kinder Clobber and more. Free gift wrapping
is available and delivery available Australia wide. Visit
www.tinysteps.com.au to view the full range.

Resources

CHILDREN'S CLOTHING & FOOTWEAR

Stores online

Junior World Discounts Pty Ltd
Tel: (03) 9898 3816
website: www.juniorworld.com.au

Junior World Discounts are a wholesaler of quality, budget-priced kids' clothes. Sizes range from newborn through to teens. Their range is available to retail shops and party planners Australia wide. Contact them for information regarding products and pricing.

Kids Exclusive
Tel: 0405 152 549
email: sales@kidsexclusive.com.au
website: www.kidsexclusive.com.au

Kids Exclusive offers high quality European kids' shoes and clothing. Their catalogue includes brands sourced from all over Europe such as Primigi, Petit Shoes, Compagnucci, Jack & Lily, Girandola, Laranjinha, Confetti & Absorba. Phone or visit the website for further information.

Kidz Brandz
Tel: (03) 9016 0543
email: info@kidzbrandz.com.au
website: www.kidzbrandz.com.au

Kidz Brandz is an Australian company that specialises in selling high quality, well-known US children's designer brands such as OshKosh B'Gosh, Gap, Baby Gap, Levis, Carters, Nike, Quiksilver, Roxy, Calvin Klein, Polo Ralph Lauren and Tommy Hilfiger. From time to time they may also carry a limited amount of stock in other popular brands like Adidas, Billabong, Timberland and others. Kidz Brandz is also now starting to source some non-US brands such as Zara, Next UK, Pumpkin Patch and Esprit.

Kidzwear Online
Tel: 1300 731 140
email: headoffice@wikidz.com.au
website: www.kidzwearonline.com.au

Kidzwear Online is a comprehensive online factory outlet for quality children's wear for ages newborn to 8 years. They offer massive genuine discounts of 50 to 80% off everyday with new lines added weekly. Sign up as a Kidzwear Online VIP member and receive updates and further store discounts. Low price, fast delivery Australia wide.

Kountry Kidz
Tel: (02) 6654 3006
email: kountry_kidz@bigpond.com
website: www.freewebs.com/especiallymade

Kountry Kidz makes gorgeous baby bedding and clothing, all handmade. Visit their website for further details.

La La baby
Tel: 0407 485 598
email: carli@lalababy.com.au
website: www.lalababy.com.au

La La Baby is a funky and refreshing place for you to shop online for all things baby. With a focus on handmade items, La La Baby makes for a wonderfully unique shopping experience. From clothing, accessories and footwear, to books, toys and stationery, you'll be sure to find the perfect gift, or that special something for your own child.

La Toriana
Tel: 0408 489 268
email: info@latoriana.com.au
website: www.LaToriana.com.au

La Toriana stocks designer labels for babies and children from premmies to 7 years old. Quality is paramount so their quality, designer products and exceptional service will surpass your expectations in retail online shopping. Enjoy the La Toriana experience by visiting www.latoriana.com.au.

Lil Miss Tutu
Tel: 0405 462 579
email: lil_miss_tutu_@hotmail.com
website: www.lilmisstutu.com.au

Lil Miss Tutu sells gorgeous and unique tutus, skirts and tees, wonderful as everyday wear or for fancy/dress-up. These clothes make great birthday and Christmas presents and there are many theme items on offer fro throughout the year.

little brown mouse
Tel: 0414 427 798
email: mail@littlebrownmouse.com.au
website: www.littlebrownmouse.com.au

Little brown mouse is an online boutique dedicated to beautiful, original and lovingly made baby and toddler's clothing, bed linen, toys and gifts in an extensive range of beautiful, vintage and whimsical fabrics. Fabulous fashion where kids can still be kids with wallet-friendly prices. Proudly designed and entirely made in Australia. Visit the website or phone for further information.

Little Smarties
Tel: (03) 9857 0102
email: kate@fewster.biz
website: www.littlesmarties.com.au

Little Smarties stocks fun and funky children's wear, accessories and gifts catering for newborn to size 10. Labels include Eeni Meeni, Minihaha, Woof, Munster and Ouch as well as European brands and niche labels with a special interest in boyswear. Online ordering and worldwide shipping available. Visit the website or phone for further information.

Look Under the Mulberry Bush

Tel: (03) 5332 5725
email: info@underthemulberrybush.com.au
website: www.underthemulberrybush.com.au

At Look Under the Mulberry Bush you will find an array of unique, beautiful, children's clothing (0000 to 10), toys, accessories, furniture, bedding and gifts by independent designers and unique small businesses. Learn about their story, understand the creative journey and buy directly online. Shopping is secure, convenient and enjoyable with various search options available. New listings by the designer/creator always welcome. See www.underthemulberrybush.com.au for information and to join the e-newsletter.

Madison Lane

Tel: 1800 804 994
email: info@madisonlane.com.au
website: www.madisonlane.com.au

Madison Lane offers designer children's clothes, shoes and accessories and goes to lengths to ensure your shopping experience is five star from log in to check out. You will not only find all the best labels in one easy location, there is free shipping for all orders over $150. Visit the website for further details.

MikyB:-) Fun Kids Clothes

Tel: (07) 5607 1708
email: sales@mikyb.com.au
website: www.mikyb.com.au

MikyB:-) Fun Kids Clothes is a new Australian label designing fun, affordable kid's and baby's everyday wear. With a focus on using only quality 100% cotton, this range is perfect for the Australian climate and sensitive skin. Designed by a mum for mums, these clothes are not only heaps of fun but practical. Items are printed as they are ordered which allows them to offer a huge selection of fun garments with unique, age-appropriate prints. The entire range is available all year online at www.mikyb.com.au.

mini eco

Tel: 0411 558 940
email: enquiries@minieco.com.au
website: www.minieco.com.au

mini eco specialise in gorgeous organic baby and children's wear. Organic and eco-friendly kids wear can be fun, fashionable, colourful and stylish – plus it's better for your family and the planet. With over 20 brands from overseas never seen in Australia before, mini eco also stock accessories, bedding, toys, toiletries, party supplies and gifts as well as products for adults.

Minimee Babies & Kids

Tel: (02) 9569 2000
email: info@minimee.com.au
website: www.minimee.com.au

Minimee can provide you with all your newborn through to toddler fashion needs. With brands like Bebe, Marquise, Oobi, Pure Baby Organic, Fresh Baked and Ouch you will find fashion and quality at the best prices. Offering a great range, service and prices, items include nursery furniture, prams, car seats, baby essentials, linen, fashion, toys and gifts all available online at www.minimee.com.au.

ministyle

Tel: 0419 545 366
email: info@ministyle.com.au
website: www.ministyle.com.au

Ministyle is a chic and unique online boutique that offers an inspiring range of local and imported brands for the child in your life ranging children's fashion apparel, accessories, gifts and lifestyle products just to name a few. Fashion brands include Kenzo, Ed Hardy, Willow & Finn, Sudo, Moppit and more. MiniStyle is a one stop shop for the latest and greatest in children's fun and fashion.

Monkey Caboose

Tel: 1300 551 343
email: info@monkeycaboose.com.au
website: www.monkeycaboose.com.au

Monkey Caboose aims to provide contemporary and design conscious fashion, toys and accessories from Australia and overseas that celebrate your child's individuality and personality. Their labels are fun, unique and will provide inspiration for a truly memorable childhood. Enjoy the convenience of 24 hour a day, 7 day a week shopping, speedy delivery and beautiful free gift wrapping. From newborn to size 4, Monkey Caboose has something for every budget and style.

Monkeytail & Wellington

Tel: 0421 993 474
email: sales@monkeytailandwellington.com.au
website: www.monkeytailandwellington.com.au

Monkeytail and Wellington is proud to present a specially selected range of independently designed and artisan crafted wares for children. This collection of locally and internationally sourced toys, clothing, books, music and children's accessories are chosen for their quality, elegance and their sprit of old fashioned fun. Visit their online store to view the entire catalogue of wonders. You can also subscribe to their VIP program and enjoy the benefits of ongoing discounts, product previews and pre-order incentives.

Mum & Babe

Tel: (07) 4036 4114
email: cate@mumandbabe.com.au
website: www.mumandbabe.com.au

Mum & Babe is an online boutique specialising in funky clothing that won't date, go out of style and will go the distance in the sandpit, as well as fantastic toys and exquisite children's books. This is an easy to navigate site offering secure shopping and friendly service.

Mums 'n Bubs Maternity Wear

Tel: (08) 8945 6867
email: info@mumsnbubsmaternity.com
website: www.mumsnbubsmaternity.com

Resources

CHILDREN'S CLOTHING & FOOTWEAR

Stores online

Mums 'n Bubs Maternity Wear stock maternity wear, baby nappy bags, baby gifts, premature baby wear, children's wear, breastfeeding tops as well as baby and toddler hats. Visit the online store or phone for further details.

Nanny Pickle

Tel: (07) 3366 9006
email: nannypickle@nannypickle.com.au
website: www.nannypickle.com.au

Once upon a time, not so very long ago, there lived a sweet, savvy and slightly quirky nanny, known throughout the land as Nanny Pickle. From the wonderful world of Nanny Pickle comes her playful range of infant wear and accessories for babies and toddlers. Visit Nanny Pickle's divine website to explore the entire range.

Posh Totty

Tel: 0400 128 114
email: info@poshtotty.com.au
website: www.poshtotty.com.au

Posh Totty specialises in the latest and trendiest new products from all over the world carrying a range of children's clothing, shoes, gift sets, organic items and toys. At Posh Totty you will always be able to shop easily and securely from the comfort of your own home. Visit the website or phone for further information.

Pumpkin Patch

Tel: 1800 123 430
email: info@pumpkinpatch.com.au
website: www.pumpkinpatch.com.au

Pumpkin Patch takes your little Patch stars through the new season in spectacular style. There are loads of fresh and exciting new styles to mix to the max, arriving in store and online all the time. Collections that kids just love are bursting with that legendary patch signature style. Experience the thrill of quality, affordable kids fashion styles at your nearest Patch store or check out the latest styles online at www.pumpkinpatch.com.au.

Quinn Macool

Tel: (02) 8850 5159
email: info@quinnmacool.com.au
website: www.quinnmacool.com.au

Quinn Macool streetwear for babies and boys in sizes 000 to 8 has over 150 original designs that are fun, colourful and a little bit cheeky. All clothing is 100% cotton and is tagless at the neck so no more tag rage and the neck size is generous to allow clothing to go on easily and off easily, so no more tantrums. Made from 100% cotton Quinn Macool clothes are affordably priced so your boys can always look cool without breaking the family budget. All clothing comes beautifully packaged in the Quinn Macool signature drawer boxes so they make great gifts.

Redhill Footwear & Childrenswear

Tel: (03) 5728 1771
email: info@redhillchildrenswear.com.au
website: www.redhillchildrenswear.com.au

Red Hill Footwear & Childrenswear offers an extensive range of children's clothing, footwear and accessories online and as well as a mix of ladies' footwear and handbags. Red Hill's main focus is to provide quality products from Australian designers and where possible Australian made and endeavour to provide you with products that are unique, fun and different.

Rosie Pose

Tel: (02) 4647 6533 or 0438 543 683
email: nicole@rosiepose.com.au
website: www.rosiepose.com.au

Rosie Pose is an online boutique specialising in gorgeous clothing pieces for newborns to age 6 years. Dress and accessorise your youngsters with simplicity, character or flare. Rosie Pose stock a huge range of clothing, shoes, gifts and accessories including the labels Bebe by Minihaha, Alex & Charli, Sooki Baby, ID Tee, Albetta and many more including exclusive labels, And Me Too, Ivy Designs and the famous Koo-di Pop Up cot.

Ruby Lime Design

Tel: (07) 4973 7065
email: carolynethornton@yahoo.com.au
website: www.rubylimedesign.blogspot.com

Ruby Lime Design sells hand-made children's t-shirts embellished with designer and vintage print fabrics as well as original jewellery from recycled scrabble tiles for both children and adults, and beautiful purses and bags for both children and adults.

Saldon Imports

Tel: 0402 891 737
email: sames@saldonimports.com
website: www.saldonimports.com

Saldon Imports first started when two new mums began designing their own baby bibs. There are now four in the range: Missy Moo, Cheeky Monkey, Pumpkin Pie and Sweet Pea. They have also designed baseball caps (for summer protection) for babies in pink, grey, orange and red. Saldon Imports now imports licensed kids clothing as well including Bratz, Miss Kitty, My little Pony, Hi 5, Spiderman and more.

Shop and Swap 4 Baby

Tel: (03) 9636 0700
email: info@shopandswap4baby.com.au
website: www.shopandswap4baby.com.au

Shop and Swap 4 Baby is a funky and innovative website

stocking your favourite brands at affordable prices. You can buy designer maternity, baby and toddler items (up to size 6) as well as exchange your own items for credits or cash. Designer brands include Fred Bare, Baby Gap, Country Road, Oilily, Seed, Petit Bateau and Pumpkin Patch. Only items that are new, near-new or in excellent condition are stocked, all up to 50% off the retail price.

ShopHouse
Tel: (02) 9011 6744
email: info@shophouse.com.au
website: www.shophouse.com.au

ShopHouse is an online children's boutique offering designer children's clothing, accessories and unique gifts for children. ShopHouse's collection includes delectable pieces from Oobi Baby, Mill & Mia, Pure Baby, Penny Scallan, Cocoon Couture and introducing And The Little Dog Laughed, exclusively online at ShopHouse. www.shophouse.com.au is a secure website available 24/7. All purchases are delivered next day using Express Post. A hassle-free returns policy makes online shopping a breeze and gift wrapping is available.

Sweet Lilly Maternity
Tel: 0410 590 889
email: info@sweetlillymaternity.com.au
website: www.sweetlillymaternity.com.au

Sweet Lilly Maternity is home to a great collection of fun, fabulous, edgy newborn baby wear. Practical, sweet and gorgeous, this range of newborn baby clothes and exquisite designer baby gifts are something all new mums would welcome as they bring their gorgeous little babies into the world. Sweet Lilly Maternity also has a stunning range of practical and easy-to-use baby carriers in exquisite fabric designs by Peanut Shell from the USA.

The Kids Store
Tel: 1800 131 296
email: enquiries@thekidsstore.com.au
website: www.thekidsstore.com.au

TheKidsStore.com.au offers a gorgeous selection of funky clothing and fancy footwear. Log on and check out stylish brands including Oobi, Annabel Trends, Skeanie and many more. With everything for babies, toddlers and kids, leave the car at home and enjoy exceptional customer service, a generous loyalty program, beautiful packaging and fast delivery to your front door.

Tonic Gifts
Tel: 0417 883 226
email: louisa@tonicgifts.com.au
website: www.tonicgifts.com.au

Tonic Gifts stocks stunning clothing from Eternal Creation and Monstar Kids suitable for children aged from newborn up to 6 years. Vintage Kid and Alimrose Designs make great toys and bibs for baby and Tonic carries both the Bod and Bod for Bubs range of products. Renee, Glamourflage and Wild mean that mum and dad are not forgotten.

Totally Mums and Bubs
Tel: 0431 965 113
website: www.totallymumsandbubs.com.au

Totally Mums and Bubs has everything for mums and babies delivered to your door. This is an internet store for mums and babies specialising in clothing, skincare, slings (including Peanut Shell), ISOKI nappy bags, Change Mat Clutches and Petite travellers, things for mealtime, splashtime and sleeptime, cloth nappies, training pants and accessories, gift packs and many things to make your life that little bit easier with a baby or toddler.

Twenty Three Skidoo
Tel: (08) 8357 3377
email: kylie@twentythreeskidoo.com.au
website: www.twentythreeskidoo.com.au

Twenty Three Skidoo specialises in medium to high-end fashion labels such as Nolita Pocket, Confetti, DKNY, Fred Bare and Eeni Meeni just to name a few. Sizes range from 0 to 10 years. They also stock a large range of designer play toys, gifts and accessories with products sourced from around the globe. Visit www.twentythreeskidoo.com.au for more details.

UrbanBaby.com.au
Tel: 1300 882 991
email: hello@urbanbaby.com.au
website: www.urbanbaby.com.au

The UrbanBaby site is dedicated to providing the most stylish, practical and innovative products and truly useful information for pregnancy, parents and everything baby. Visit UrbanBaby for exclusive UrbanBaby products, the full Baby Einstein and Brilliant Baby ranges, fantastic wraps, the Hipseat by Hippychick, organic cotton baby clothes, gift cards and much more.

Wikidz Kids Wear
Tel: 1300 731 140
email: party@wikidz.com.au
website: www.wikidz.com.au

Wikidz is a leading distributor of quality, affordable, fashionable infant and children's wear. They carry a great selection of boys and girls garments ranging from newborn to 8 years and bring them to you via party plan. The Wikidz collections are designed in Australia and made overseas. Visit the website for further information.

www.sookiebaby.com.au
Tel: 0430 085 851
website: www.sookiebaby.com

www.sookiebaby.com.au is an online boutique featuring beautiful gifts and essentials for mother and baby. Brands include Oobi, Baobab, Tea Princess Collection, Goo Goo Lotions, Diddle Dumpling, Mamas and Pappas, Kaloo and much more. Enjoy shopping from the comfort of your own home any time of the day with flat rate posting Australia wide and free gift wrapping service.

Resources

CHILDREN'S CLOTHING & FOOTWEAR

Stores pre-loved & discounted ➡ Stores retail

STORES PRE-LOVED & DISCOUNTED: CHILDREN'S CLOTHING & FOOTWEAR

NATIONAL

Baby & Kids Market
Tel: 1300 554 476
email: info@babykidsmarket.com.au
website: www.babykidsmarket.com.au

The Baby & Kids Market offers the biggest range of quality pre-loved baby and kids goods in Australia. Running for over five years, there are now markets in all main cities and also regional hubs. From toys to books and clothes to shoes this market has it all. The Baby & Kids Market also offers some fantastic handmade and wholesale baby and kids' goods at bargain prices. Plus free kids entertainment as well. Visit the website www.babykidsmarket.com.au for dates and locations or phone the number above.

VICTORIA

Caroline Chisholm Society
41 Park Street
Moonee Ponds VIC 3039
Tel: 1800 134 863 or (03) 9370 3933
email: info@carolinechisholmsociety.com.au
website: www.carolinechisholmsociety.com.au

The Caroline Chisholm Society Material Aid Service provides pre-loved nursery furniture, baby equipment, children's clothing, maternity clothing and nappies free of charge to families in need. The Society also provides counselling services including pregnancy and family support. If you have items to donate to help others in need please contact the Caroline Chisholm Society. Visit the website or phone the number above for further information.

Hand Me Downs
383 Forest Road
The Basin VIC 3154
Tel: (03) 9761 2855
website: www.handmedowns.com.au

Hand Me Downs has over 4000 square feet of all sorts of goodies, including clothes ranging from 0000 to teens, toys, shoes, linen, furniture – anything you can imagine for children. There is a kids' play area, change facilities, toilets and lots of parking.

Kids Weecycle Warehouse
3 Colin Avenue
Warrandyte VIC 3113
Tel: (03) 9844 3484
email: weecycle_warehouse@iprimus.com.au
website: www.kidsweecyclewarehouse.com.au

Kids Weecycle Warehouse specialise in good quality and affordable new and recycled baby and kids goods. Items include nursery furniture and accessories, children's clothing and shoes (including many brand name items), toys, books, puzzles, DVDs, videos, fitted cloth nappies, a large range of baby gifts and more. Hiring of goods is available (long or short term) and as well as a lay-by facility.

Little Wonders Baby Shop
1–36 Station Street
Cranbourne VIC 3977
Tel: (03) 5995 3464
email: sales@littlewonders.com.au
website: www.littlewonders.com.au

Little Wonders Baby Shop offers a range of pre-loved items such as children's clothes for newborns through to size 10, maternity clothes and a range of items and accessories to make your pregnancy more comfortable. Located in Cranbourne with an outlet in Baranduda, this shop is run by mothers with young children. Open 10.30am to 3.00pm Tuesday to Friday or by appointment. Visit the website or phone for further information.

Pipsqueakz Recycle
Shop 8, 10 York Road
Mount Evelyn VIC 3796
Tel: (03) 9736 2211
email: info@pipsqueakz.com
website: www.pipsqueakz.com

Pipsqueakz Recycle has been in operation for more than seven years. This huge shop stocks an enormous and varied range of new and pre-owned items suitable for newborns through to pre-teens including nursery furniture, clothing, toys and much more. They are well known for strict standards on safety and cleanliness and all their pre-owned goods are in excellent condition and offer huge savings to buying new. They are open Monday to Friday 9.15am to 4.30pm and Saturday 10.00am to 2.00pm. They have EFTPOS facilities and great consignment rates. Visit the website or phone for further information.

WESTERN AUSTRALIA

Baby Warehouse
199 Abernethy Road
Belmont WA 6104
Tel: (08) 9477 5911

The Baby Warehouse is a unique baby store with new products at up to 50% off including furniture, clothing and everything else a baby needs. Their experienced staff are experts in child safety.

STORES RETAIL:
CHILDREN'S CLOTHING & FOOTWEAR

NATIONAL

Kids Central
Tel: 1300 850 123
email: admin@kidscentral.com.au
website: www.kidscentral.com.au

Visit Kids Central for a great range of brands in children and babies' toys, fashion, homewares and nursery products. Kids Central sells the full range of exclusive Early Learning Centre toys from the UK, and the latest in children's fashion plus much more. The stores are full of gift ideas for children aged 0 to 8 years, as well as cards and wrap to help you buy everything you need in one location. The Baby Central department caters for the needs of new or expecting parents, with newborn fashion ranges such as Bebe, Pure Baby and Rock your Baby, as well as essentials such as nappy bags, and a beautiful range of newborn gifts. Ask about the new Kids Central gift card. To find your nearest Kids Central store (in each state except NT and Tasmania) phone 1300 850 123 or visit www.kidscentral.com.au.

Pumpkin Patch
Tel: 1800 123 430
email: info@pumpkinpatch.com.au
website: www.pumpkinpatch.com.au

Pumpkin Patch takes your little Patch stars through the new season in spectacular style. There are loads of fresh and exciting new styles to mix to the max, arriving in store and online all the time. Collections that kids just love are bursting with that legendary patch signature style. Experience the thrill of quality, affordable kids fashion styles at your nearest Patch store or check out the latest styles online at www.pumpkinpatch.com.au.

Shoes & Sox Pty Ltd
Tel: (02) 9420 8755
email: support@shoesandsox.com.au
website: www.shoesandsox.com.au

At Shoes & Sox they believe that your child's footwear is part of your child's overall healthcare. Independent research as well as their own experience indicates that children who wear correctly fitted and appropriate footwear are healthier for it. The comfort, support and cushioning features of correctly fitted, quality footwear translate into healthier and better performing children with fewer foot, joint, back, posture and walking problems in adult life. Shoes & Sox's goal is to provide you with reasonably priced and fashionable footwear that is appropriate for your child and that fits correctly. Stores in Sydney, Melbourne and Canberra. Visit the website for store locations or phone the number listed above.

VICTORIA

1001 Things for Baby
430 Rathdowne Street
Carlton VIC 3053
Tel: (03) 9347 7007
email: debravoight@yahoo.com.au

1001 Things for Baby is a lovely baby and children's boutique situated in Rathdowne village and specialises in pieces you cannot find everywhere. The store supports local artists and designers and stocks many vintage pieces for children – anything from pull-along wagons, spinning tops and cowboy boots to beautiful linen, Moses baskets and artwork. 1001 Things for Baby specialises in baby clothing up to the age of 6 years, so you will always find something a little bit different.

Ann Lewis Shoes Hawthorn
684 Glenferrie Road
Hawthorn VIC 3122
Tel: (03) 9818 6151
website: www.annlewis.com.au

Ann Lewis Children's Shoes in Hawthorn is a Clarks Platinum store. Specialising in a full range of children's shoes from the very first pair through to the last pair of school shoes. A continuous care program is now available looking after mums and dads pockets.

Belly Babes
85 Cunninghame Street
Sale VIC 3850
Tel: (03) 5144 4600
Shop 2, 108 Franklin Street
Traralgon VIC 3844
Tel: (03) 5176 0610
email: info@bellybabesmaternity.com.au
website: www.bellybabesmaternity.com.au

Belly Babes has become one of Gippsland's favourite maternity, baby and children's fashion stores. They stock a large range of baby and children's wear (premmie to size 8) including labels such as Freshbaked, Purebaby, Tiny Tribe, Sooki Baby, Ouch, Soda Kids, Oobi, Robeez, Scooter and Krickets just to name a few. New stock arrives daily so if you're looking for funky or fashionable you're sure to find it at Belly Babes.

Fragile
285-287 Coventry Street
South Melbourne VIC 3202
Tel: (03) 9686 4111
email: info@fragile.com.au
website: www.fragile.com.au

Fragile offers an exquisite range of maternity wear, designed in-house, for the new mum-to-be, as well as a collection of beautiful, local and imported clothing for the newborn to 6 years.

Glow Maternity & Newborn
197 Main Street
Mornington VIC 3931
Tel: (03) 5973 5655
website: www.glowmaternitywear.com.au

Resources

CHILDREN'S CLOTHING & FOOTWEAR

Stores retail

Glow Maternity & Newborn has a great range of baby clothes and gifts from premmie to size 4. Visit the website or phone the number above for further information.

Golly Gosh Children's Wear
165 Liebig Street
Warrnambool VIC 3280
Tel: (03) 5562 7230
email: gollygosh@westvic.com.au

Golly Gosh Children's Wear is a specialist children's wear store offering an extensive range of baby and children's clothing from prem to size 14. Customers can choose from leading brands Fred Bare, Osh Kosh, Esprit, Soda Kids, FreshBaked Kids, Minihaha, Woof and Osh Kosh shoes, as well as exquisite baby brands Bébé, Pure Baby, Max & Tilly and Le Bon. Let the friendly team at Golly Gosh help you dress your children with style. Phone orders available.

Green Leaves
54 Mount Eliza Way
Mount Eliza VIC 3930
Tel: (03) 9787 1714

Green Leaves is Mt. Eliza's original children's fashion boutique, and has a wonderful selection of clothing, accessories and gifts for newborns to 14 years. Visit this friendly, relaxed boutique with parking at the door or phone for more details.

Hoochie Coochie
220 St Georges Road
North Fitzroy VIC 3068
Tel: (03) 9486 4200
website: www.hoochiecoochie.com.au

Owned and operated by singer Linda Bull, Hoochie Coochie is a much loved children's boutique nestled in the heart of North Fitzroy village. Supporting Australia's top children's designers, local designers and crafty mums, you will find clothing essentials, footwear, accessories, original artworks, as well as manchester and homewares that are functional , beautiful and unique. Look out for the launch of the Hoochie Coochie Fashion Label for girls and Mini Moochie Tees in '09. Specialising in baby wear to size 7, Hoochie Coochie continues to inspire and create a welcoming shopping environment for families. Open 10.00am to 5.00pm Tuesday to Sunday, closed Mondays. Visit the website or phone the number above for further information.

Imagine Me
271 High Street
Northcote VIC 3070
Tel: (03) 9486 4122
email: lealie@imaginemeboutique.com.au
website: www.imaginemeboutique.com.au

Imagine Me has an exciting range of top clothing and shoe brands for kids. Sizes range from newborn to 14 and brands include Minihaha, Woof, Sooki Baby, Tiny Tribe, Fresh Baked, Oobi Baby, Noise, Bebe, PureBaby, Minymo, Rock your baby, Cheeky Little Soles, Ohme Ohmy, Tea Princess and many more wonderful local and international brands. Rewarding VIP reward program available. Imagine Me boutique offers private baby showers on Sundays. Phone to make a booking.

Jack & Jill Children's Wear
80 South Parade
Blackburn VIC 3130
Tel: (03) 9877 9667

Jack & Jill Children's Wear offers great personal service and designer label clothing including Guess. They also design their own baptism and communion gowns, keepsake boxes and bomboniere. Sizes range from newborn to size 8.

Jungle Junior
39 Malop Street
Geelong VIC 3220
Tel: (03) 5224 2362
website: www.junglejunior.com.au

One, Two Buckle My Shoe (located within Jungle Junior) is Geelong's only fully-imported, European footwear supplier for children. Quality italian, spanish, french and other international shoes range in sizes from 18 to 40, from first walkers through to school shoes and gumboots. Give your child's feet the attention they deserve with professionally fitted, gorgeous European shoes from Landos, Ciao Bimbi, Andanines, Gulliver, Panda and most recently Lelli Kelly.

Little Smarties
657 High Street
Kew East VIC 3102
Tel: (03) 9857 0102
email: kate@fewster.biz
website: www.littlesmarties.com.au

Little Smarties stocks fun and funky children's wear, accessories and gifts catering for newborn to size 10. Labels include Eeni Meeni, Minihaha, Woof, Munster and Ouch as well as European brands and niche labels with a special interest in boyswear. Online ordering and worldwide shipping available.

Mumma Mia Maternity Lifestyle
365 Glenhuntly Road
Elsternwick VIC 3185
Tel: (03) 9528 1375
website: www.mummamia.com.au

Mumma Mia Maternity Lifestyle offers a great shopping experience for parents-to-be. They stock everything you need from maternity wear through to clothing for children size 3. They specialise in funky maternity wear in sizes small to extra large and kids' wear in sizes 0000 to 3. There is also a playroom, a feeding and change area and the shop is pram-friendly. Open Monday to friday 9.30am to 5.30pm and Saturday 9.30am to 4.00pm.

Pelican's Belly
Shop 1099 Westfield Doncaster
Doncaster VIC 3108
Tel: (03) 9840 1268
email: pelicansbellychadstone@gmail.com

Pelicans Belly offer delicious kids' clothes and accessories from some of the world's best designer labels. They also stock fantastic Australian labels such as Blu Bikki and Sudo and prices start at around $20. They do mail order around Australia, send text messages and email pictures to you to help you find the best outfit for your child. They also stock Kenzo, Confetti, Collette Dinnigan, Diesel, Guess, Blu Bikki, Tommy Rocket, Paul Frank, Lelli Kelly and Jean Bourget. Join their VIP list to receive pre-sale notifications and special offers.

Redhill Footwear & Childrenswear
49 Ford Street
Beechworth VIC 3747
Tel: (03) 5728 1771
website: www.redhillchildrenswear.com.au

Red Hill Footwear & Childrenswear offers an extensive range of children's clothing, footwear and accessories and as well as a mix of ladies' footwear and handbags. Red Hill's main focus is to provide quality products from Australian designers and where possible Australian made and endeavour to provide you with products that are unique, fun and different. You can also shop online at www.redhillchidrenswear.com.au.

Second Childhood
44 Glenferrie Road
Malvern VIC 3144
Tel: (03) 9509 6898
website: www.secondchildhood.com.au

Second Childhood specialises in clothing and items for children aged newborn to 14 years. Second Childhood was established over 18 years ago and is renowned as carrying leading local and international designer-labelled clothing and items. The quality and condition of all items is outstanding and prices are a fraction of their original retail price. Many items are often brand-new. Toys, games and costumes are generally brand-new also. New items arrive daily.

The Red Balloon Children's Wear
281 High Street
Ashburton VIC 3147
Tel: (03) 9885 8946

The Red Balloon carries the following babywear labels: Bébé, Le Bon, Marquise, Papoose, Minihaha, Gumboots and Fred Bare, as well as budget priced babywear. The Red Balloon's specialty is all-cotton babywear.

NEW SOUTH WALES

All For Kiddiz & Bubs
163 Parramatta Road
Annandale NSW 2038
Tel: (02) 9569 2255
website: www.allforkiddizandbubs.com.au

All for Kiddiz & Bubs offers a wide range of major brands of babies and children's clothing and shoes as well as soft and educational toys, cots, bassinets, cradles, mattresses, high chairs, travel cots, prams, feeding products, monitors, car seats, safety products and accessories. The staff are helpful and prices reasonable.

babyshop
276 Brunker Road
Adamstown NSW 2289
Tel: 1800 222 437 or 1800 BABIES
email: mail@babyshop.com.au
website: www.babyshop.com.au

 With experience online since 1998 and hundreds of products to choose from, babyshop stocks a variety of well known brands, as well as featuring many exclusive and hard to find items. Departments include: Bathtime & Care, Bedtime & Nursery, Clothing, Feeding & Accessories, Out & About and Playtime & Development. Visit babyshop at the address above or experience the convenience of shopping from home with one of Australia's first online baby stores: www.babyshop.com.au.

Fragile
76a Paddington Street
Paddington NSW 2021
Tel: (02) 9362 0085
Also located at:
Shop 5003, Level 5
Westfield Shopping Centre
Bondi Junction NSW 2022
Tel: (02) 9389 3522
email: info@fragile.com.au
website: www.fragile.com.au

Established in 1995, Fragile has over the years become somewhat of an Australian icon — the place to visit when shopping for all things beautiful. Fragile offers an exquisite range of maternity wear, designed in-house, for the new mum-to-be, as well as a collection of beautiful, local and imported clothing for the newborn to 6 years.

Girotondo
Shop 4, 10 Dover Road
Rose Bay NSW 2029
Tel: (02) 9388 1383
email: girotondo@aapt.net.au
website: www.girotondo.com.au

Girotondo is a specialised baby shop with a great selection of clothing, manchester and toys. Children's clothing ranges from size 0000 to 8 years of age and includes many of Australia's leading designers as well as imports from France and Italy.

Resources

CHILDREN'S CLOTHING & FOOTWEAR

Stores retail

Infancy
7 Wilson Street
Newtown NSW 2042
Tel: (02) 9565 2866
Also located at:
105 Booth Street
Annandale NSW 2038
584 Darling Street
Rozelle NSW 2041
email: infancy@iinet.net.au
website: www.infancy.com.au

Infancy selects a unique range of Australian and international clothing, handcrafted toys and giftware all at highly affordable prices. Infancy also offers an online shopping service, VIP program and a great children's play area.

Kids Carousel
Unit 4 & 5, 390 Pacific Highway
Belmont North NSW 2280
Tel: (02) 4947 7000
email: belmontkids@optusnet.com.au

Kids Carousel was first opened in May 1996 by owners Tunia and Shane to fill a void in the market for affordable kids' fashion and nursery equipment. It now draws customers from more than 400 kilometres away on a regular basis with its friendly, down-to-earth service and advice as well as practical help and service on children's clothing, prams and car safety seats, installation and repairs. Now with over 7,000 square feet catering to baby and kids' needs. Phone or email for more details.

Little Dream
Shop 6, 427A Parramatta Road
Leichhardt NSW 2040
Tel: (02) 9560 2311
email: info@littledream.com.au
website: www.littledream.com.au

Little Dream is an exclusive children's boutique catering for newborn babies, girls and boys of all ages. Little Dream specialises in exclusive handmade christening gowns, Holy Communion, flower girls, page boys and for that special occasion. They are a stockist for Eternal Creation, Safer Baby, Shemiz, Koby and many more. Little Dream also specialises in smocking, honeycomb and all hand embroidery using the finest materials. A broad range of gifts is available too. Phone the number listed above, email or visit their website for more information.

Little Fingers
Shop 18 Centre Point Arcade
Taree NSW 2430
Tel: (02) 6550 0999
website: www.littlefingers.net.au

Little Fingers offers a wide range of baby goods such as prams, cots, linen, nappy bags, breast pumps and much more. They also have clothing for premmies up to size 14 including formal and casual wear, swimwear, beach towels, socks, bibs, hats and much more.

Minimee Babies & Kids
109 Norton Street
Leichhardt NSW 2040
Tel: (02) 9569 2000
Also located at:
123 Willoughby Road
Crows Nest NSW 2065
Tel: (02) 9436 3436
email: info@minimee.com.au
website: www.minimee.com.au

Minimee can provide you with all your newborn through to toddler fashion needs. With brands like Bebe, Marquise, Oobi, Pure Baby Organic, Fresh Baked and Ouch you will find fashion and quality at the best prices. Offering a great range, service and prices, items include nursery furniture, prams, car seats, baby essentials, linen, fashion, toys and gifts at Leichhardt, Crows Nest or online at www.minimee.com.au.

Redhill Footwear & Childrenswear
477 Dean Street
Albury NSW 2640
Tel: (02) 6021 7747
email: info@redhillchildrenswear.com.au
website: www.redhillchildrenswear.com.au

Red Hill Footwear & Childrenswear offers an extensive range of children's clothing, footwear and accessories and as well as a mix of ladies' footwear and handbags. Red Hill's main focus is to provide quality products from Australian designers and where possible Australian made and endeavour to provide you with products that are unique, fun and different. You can also shop online at www.redhillchildrenswear.com.au.

Tots Encore
2/306 Bronte Road
Waverley NSW 2024
Tel: (02) 9387 5286
email: tots@totsencore.com
website: www.totsencore.com

Tots Encore offer a wide range of new and recycled premium-brand children's wear from newborn to age 12. There are exciting new collections from up and coming designers, artists and new consignments are presented in the store each week. So whether you are looking for a one-off piece or have premium-brand clothing that you would like to consign, drop in to see us. Open 10.00 am to 4.00pm Monday to Saturday. Phone or email for more details.

NORTHERN TERRITORY

Mums 'n Bubs Maternity Wear
Shop 16B Hibiscus Shopping Town
Leanyer Darwin NT 0812
Tel: (08) 8945 6867
email: info@mumsnbubsmaternity.com
website: www.mumsnbubsmaternity.com
Mums 'n Bubs Maternity Wear stock maternity wear, baby nappy bags, baby gifts, premature baby wear, children's wear, breastfeeding tops as well as baby and toddler hats. Visit the store at the address above or online at www.mumsnbubsmaternity.com.

WESTERN AUSTRALIA

Adorable Affordable
Shop 24, Broadway Fair Shopping Centre, 88 Broadway
Nedlands WA 6009
Tel: (08) 9386 3677
email: sales@adorableaffordable.com.au
website: www.adorableaffordable.com.au
Adorable Affordable has a beautiful range of baby and children's clothing, footwear, toys, gifts and accessories. The clothing range caters for premature babies through to 6 year olds with an emphasis on boys' clothing. Special occasion and Christening gowns are also available. Visit the store in Nedlands or the website for further information.

Funky Kids
Tel: (08) 9284 0051
email: info@funkykids.com.au
website: www.funkykids.com.au
Funky Kids stock fabulous brands in clothing and accessories including Guess, Fred Bare, Big By Fiona, eeni meeni and much more as well as a wide variety of gifts, toys and personalised products. Two great locations: Wembley and Karrinyup Shopping Centre.

Hush Clothes For Kids
Shop 7 Centro Kalamunda Shopping Centre
Kalamunda WA 6076
Tel: (08) 9293 0111
website: www.kalamundaweb.com.au/hush
Hush Clothes for Kids has clothing for newborns to children aged 12 years (smart, casual and formal wear), as well as Snug as a Bug Baby Wraps and Swaddle Me wraps, Grobags, Robeez baby shoes, the breastfeeding wrap by Leah, CDs, clothing gift packs, swim nappies and chlorine-resistant bathers. Sun protective swimwear is available throughout the year. Organic clothing and nappies are also available. Mail order welcome.

SOUTH AUSTRALIA

Bug-a-lugs Baby Store
31 Light Crescent
Mt Barker SA 5251
Tel: (08) 8398 3521
email: info@bugalugsbaby.com.au
website: www.bugalugsbaby.com.au

Bug-a-lugs Baby Store stocks a gorgeous range of children's wear from premature to 7 years including brands such as Baby Kids, Bright Bots, Ouch and Marquis. Bug-a-lugs Baby Store also offers a range of maternity wear as well as huge range of nursery furniture and equipment.

Parthenon Emporium
149 Henley Beach Road
Mile End SA 5031
Tel: (08) 8234 5733
email: enquiries@parthenon.com.au
website: www.parthenon.com.au
Parthenon Emporium specialises in all types of christening wear and matching accessories in a variety of colours and fabrics, such as silk, Swiss voile and satin as well as formal and casual wear from sizes 000–4 including many European styles. They also stock christening and confirmation bomboniere, as well as gifts and accessories such as candles, bibs and towel sets, stylish European pre-walkers, leather shoes and christening booties.

The Infant Boutique
Shop 6/136 The Parade
Norwood SA 5067
Tel: (08) 8331 3740
email: info@theinfantboutique.com.au
website: www.theinfantboutique.com.au
The Infant Boutique is a beautiful baby and children's boutique for ages 0 to 5 years (sizes newborn to 6) stocking nursery furniture, bed linen, blankets, wraps, clothing, sleepwear, toys, games, stationery, artwork, gifts and accessories. The range includes local, national and international brands and labels.

Twenty Three Skidoo
298-300 Unley Road
Hyde Park SA 4812
Tel: (08) 8357 3377
email: kylie@twentythreeskidoo.com.au
website: www.twentythreeskidoo.com.au
Located in Hyde Park, Twenty Three Skidoo specialises in medium to high-end fashion labels such as Nolita Pocket, Confetti, DKNY, Fred Bare and Eeni Meeni just to name a few. Sizes range from 0 to 10 years. The spacious heritage-listed store also houses a large range of designer play toys, gifts and accessories with products sourced from around the globe. Pram friendly with eay parking at the rear of the store.

TASMANIA

The Growing Years
175 Elphin Road
Newstead TAS 7250
Tel: (03) 6334 7200
The Growing Years stock all your children's needs from clothing to toys. They only stock good quality items and all pre-loved clothing has been freshly washed and priced. Open Monday to Friday 9.00am to 5.00pm and Saturday by appointment.

Pumpkin Patch

No one can really explain the emotional rollercoaster ride of a first time parent – the array of 'butterflies' that seem to be constantly bombarding. It's a unique, totally personal experience to go through.

At the Patch, we know your bundle of joy must only have the very best – so we've designed a gorgeous cotton-rich collection packed with fashion styles, guaranteed comfort, and all at family-friendly prices.

It's never too early for fashion – dressing your stars in playful prints, delightful details and appliques – all bursting with that legendary Patch style.

Best of all you can be the first to know about:

- trend alerts & new collections in store & online
- exclusive offers
- early notice of promotions and sales.

Just become a Patch eClub VIP. You'll also go into the monthly eClub draw to win a $250 Patch wardrobe. Register your email today online at www.pumpkinpatch.com.au or in store.

Pumpkin Patch for all your fashion first looks.

Fun things to do

Photograph by Lifeworks Photography, Melbourne.

Learning through play

Playgroup-aged children are going through a stage of rapid brain and skill development, and play is vital to healthy growth. Playgroup Australia recognises parents as a child's first educator, and values all families with small children aged birth to five years learning and developing together through play. The following activities have been designed to give parents ideas of how to help their children learn through age-appropriate activities – and to have fun!

Under 3 months
Music fun
Put on a CD and help your baby clap hands, clap feet, and bicycle his legs. Show your baby how you clap hands, wriggle fingers, twirl, and bob up and down.

Foot tapping
Lie your baby safely on their back. Tap the bottom of your baby's feet gently in time to a song that you are singing, for example Twinkle, Twinkle Little Star.

Looking in the mirror
Hold your baby in front of a mirror so they can explore what they look like.

Mobile
Hang colourful and black and white things, things that move, and things that make noise over your baby's cot. Tie securely and don't use anything smaller than what would fit in a film canister.

Looking fun
Babies learn by watching. Take your baby outside and hold them where they can see things moving – streamers, trees or washing on the line.

Aeroplanes
Let your baby follow things with their eyes – move your face, a rattle, or a coloured toy in front of them. Play aeroplanes with your hands – fly through the air and land on your baby's tummy!

3–6 months
Singing
Sing and help your baby do action songs: Twinkle Twinkle Little Star, Incy Wincy Spider, Put a Spot Over Here, Round and Round the Garden etc.

Exploring and touching
Give your baby safe objects from around the house to explore their shapes and textures – plastic things from the kitchen, pots and pans, sponges, paper, empty tins with lids, velvet, fur, lace, towelling, cardboard, fine sandpaper etc.

Make a book
Make a 'feely book' by gluing textured objects onto squares of cardboard. Punch two holes in the side of each square and make them into a book by securing with string or shower curtain rings – easy to take out with you!

Listening fun
Use rice, pasta or a bell to fill a plastic container – make sure the container is well sealed. Shake to your baby's side or behind baby and see if they can find it.

Looking and movement
Lay your baby down on a rug. Hold a toy to your baby's side and fly it over their head and land on the other side so your baby can follow the toy with their eyes.

6–9 months

Shakers for baby to hold
Fill and tightly seal small (no smaller than a film canister), light-weight containers with rice for your baby to hold and shake.

Milk carton blocks
Use milk cartons to make blocks for your baby. Draw or stick pictures of objects such as animals on the sides. Talk to your baby about the pictures as they play with the blocks.

Where's teddy?
Hide a toy in one room of the house and carry your baby from room to room saying 'Where's teddy?' and telling them what rooms you are looking in.

Roll the ball
Roll a soft, brightly coloured ball to your baby and teach them how to stop it and push it back to you.

Using feet
Hang rattles or similar noise-making toys where your baby can kick them, or put socks with securely attached bells on your baby's feet so they make noise when they move their feet.

Noise and movement
Fill empty plastic bottles that will roll with small/colourful/noisy things, e.g. bells, scrunched coloured paper, or small stones. Secure lids tightly.

9–12 months

Music from the kitchen
Make fun instruments from up-turned pots and pans with wooden spoons, or two saucepan lids for cymbals. Use your instruments to explore different concepts such as loud and soft, fast and slow.

Water fun
A great summer activity! Fill a low, wide container with a few centimetres of water and place it on the ground. Float small objects such as flowers or corks in the water and let your baby reach and splash. Always supervise children when playing with water.

Toys overboard!
Using elastic, tie small soft toys to the top of your baby's high-chair. Show them how you drop the toys and pull them back up again.

Reading fun
Sit your baby on your lap and read stories with simple action words and pictures. Stories with repetitive phrases are fun, like 'Run, run, as fast as you can, you can't catch me I'm the Gingerbread Man!'.

Learning through play

Hide and Seek

Show your baby a toy, then hide it under a towel or small blanket and help them find it.

Outside fun

Take your baby into the backyard or to the park. Let your baby feel different surfaces, let them sit and crawl on the grass and feel stones and leaves with supervision – some objects can look like a tasty treat!

12–18 months

Action songs

Repeat action songs with your baby often so they can learn words and actions. Make up songs about the things you or your baby are doing throughout your day – 'I am walking, you are bouncing'.

Sand play

If you don't have a sand-pit at home, create one out of an old tyre filled with sand. Your baby can explore the feeling of sand between their fingers and toes, and experience the different temperatures and textures of wet and dry sand.

Give your baby small containers such as butter containers with holes pierced in the bottom to make a sieve, or cut open milk bottles to dig the sand with.

What's that smell?

Put some cotton wool in small containers the size of film canisters, and drop a small amount of different smelly substances into each container. You could use: perfume, mint leaves, vanilla essence, spices such as cloves, cinnamon or ginger, or vinegar. Attach the lids securely and poke a small hole in the lid so they can be smelled. Sit your child on your lap and let them smell each one, while talking about how they use their nose to smell, and suggesting simple terms to describe the smell.

Stacking and nesting

Use plastic cups from the kitchen or different sized boxes to make towers, or nest them inside each other.

Scribbling

Provide your child with paper and crayons for some scribbling fun. You may have some masterpieces that can be framed for your walls!

18–24 months

Body parts

It is fun to learn body parts through songs. Sing about, point to and use different body parts in Heads and Shoulders and If You're Happy and You Know It.

Scrapbook

Make a scrapbook of objects, and pictures of objects and people that your child knows. You can stick these into a book or slip them into a photo album.

Dress-ups

Encourage your child to play dress-ups by providing a full-length mirror and an assortment of old clothes such as hats, scarves, and shoes.

Playdough

A simple recipe for playdough:

>   2 cups plain flour
>   ½ cup oil
>   Food colouring
>   Water

Add the oil to the flour and mix; mix food colouring or Edicol dye with water and add to mixture until it forms a soft dough. This recipe is safe if eaten by little mouths!

Give your child things to stick in the dough (paddle-pop sticks, straws etcetera), things to pound with (like a toy mallet), and things to make impressions with (jar lids, cookie cutters, or bottle caps).

Hiding places

Big places to hide are often popular with toddlers. If you or someone you know has a large cardboard box after having something delivered, turn it into a cubby house for your toddler to play and hide in. You can even make some slits in the cardboard to allow for opening windows and doors.

Simon Says

Action games keep toddlers busy while they are learning to move and follow directions. Simon says is a simple game where you use commands such as 'Simon says, clap your hands' and give time for your toddler to follow. Encourage your child when they follow correctly.

2–3 years

Walk and Stop

A great game for practising listening skills! This can be played inside or outside and encourages children to try different ways of moving their bodies:

>   "You walk and you walk and you walk and you stop.
>   You walk and you walk and you walk and you stop.
>   You walk and you walk and you walk and you stop.
>   You walk and you walk and you walk and you stop."

>   When the children hear 'stop!' they should freeze until the song starts again. Other movements can be sung in the song too, such as skip, hop, run, dance, jump or wriggle.

Making instruments

Hooters: cover the end of a cardboard cylinder with paper with a hole poked through – children can blow or sing through the other end.

Rhythm sticks: cut two 20cm lengths of dowel for hitting together

Sandpaper blocks: cover two small timber off-cuts with sandpaper and rub together.

Play your instruments along with your child's favourite CD.

Simple puzzle

Glue a picture from a magazine onto a sheet of cardboard, and cut the picture into a few pieces. Help your child to learn how to put the pieces back together again to make the picture.

Information supplied by Playgroup Australia, www.playgroupaustralia.com.au.

What is a playgroup?

Playgroup is an informal session where mums, dads, grandparents, caregivers, children and babies meet together in a relaxed environment.

Playgroups are set up and run by parents and caregivers, with children choosing from a range of activities set up to meet their varying needs. Activities at playgroup are either free or low cost, and may include:

- music and singing
- imaginative play
- outdoor and free play
- art and craft activities
- outings.

In a playgroup, parents and caregivers stay to interact with the other adults and to play with the children.

Playgroup can be held anywhere that is safe for children and where groups of people can meet - community and neighbourhood centres, health clinics, women's centres, preschools and kindergartens, church halls and even in someone's house

No child is too young for playgroup. All children from 0-5 years, including babies, love new experiences and benefit from developing sensory, social and communication skills through activities at playgroup. Children like playgroup because they can:

- participate in new experiences
- develop and increase their social skills
- learn sharing, co-operation and simple routines
- interact with other adults and children in a safe environment
- enjoy learning more about their world.

Adults also benefit from playgroup – a time to talk, make friends and share experiences, while children learn through their play experiences. Adults like playgroup because they can:

- meet other local families and develop new friendships
- relax and talk in a friendly environment
- share experiences and ideas
- play with children and nurture a spirit of co-operation
- take up opportunities for personal development.

There is a Playgroup Association in every state and territory to help you find a local playgroup which suits your needs and/or set up a new playgroup.

If you would like to start a new playgroup in your area or join an existing playgroup, phone your Playgroup Association on 1800 171 882 (free call).

Information supplied by Playgroup Australia, www.playgroupaustralia.com.au.

Swimming lessons with Starfish & Salmon

We have two fish in our family, and they couldn't be more different. My Starfish, aged 3, approaches swimming lessons with protests, negotiations, and finally when the inevitable moment approaches, a headlock grip on me, his mother.

It's a shame to admit, but he's not clinging to my neck for love. It's fear. If that Canadian backpacker teacher with her sing-song voice lunges at him and sweeps him under the water, he's taking me down with him. And if he's learned anything with clarity in swimming lessons, it's that his mum doesn't want to get her hair wet.

Meanwhile, over in lane two, my swimming-crazy Salmon, aged 6, is doing his thing. He has invented a new stroke: a version of the Australian crawl in which, instead of turning the head neatly to one side to draw breath, you turn and then take your whole body around in a full-body roll before resuming normal freestyle. One, two, three and roll again. The teenage instructor is apparently guffawing too much to intervene.

In our family, we generally hold back from swimming lessons until about age two. Until that time, get your youngsters entering the water safely. Keep them familiar with the feeling of their body in the water, teach them how to exhale or blow bubbles when their face is under water, get them to mimic basic stroke actions and teach them to float.

Up until age four, parents need to be in the pool doing lessons with their children. Swim coach Laurie Lawrence has taken aim at parents (read mothers) who won't get into the water with kids because they want to keep their lipstick on and their hair dry. (OK, OK, I really am getting in now.)

Saturday is Dads' Day at our local pool. It's uncomfortably steamy and overcrowded and a stretch of the foot is liable to meet with someone's submerged buttocks. The water is suspiciously warm and fathers are breaking rules everywhere; leaping over lane barriers with glee, tossing babies into the air and generally getting their own hair wet with abandon.

We have a new appreciation for indoor swimming pools, having just returned from 18 months living in a small mining town – with no pool – in remote coastal Western Australia.

There, my Salmon did only two weeks of swimming lessons a year; all that was available. (My little one was more like caviar at that stage, and there were no lessons for toddlers.) The kids wore wetsuits in the freezing waters of the Indian Ocean and they had to push on through salty waters often choppy and clogged with seaweed. The mothers kept an anxious watch for sharks and stingrays.

Maybe one day out of ten, the waters would fall flat and turn ultramarine blue, the skies would be perfect and the air would be toasty warm. The sea would be clear right to the bottom, all seaweed gone – unforgettable.

These days, back in the steamy comfort of a Melbourne YMCA, while our Starfish might hate it, he is already learning the skills of entering safely, breathing underwater, and paddling back to a pool edge. Tiny victories that may yet save his life.

And one day as he locks eyes with me from under the water, reaching his fingers out and kicking and paddling his way back up to the surface, his face is suddenly triumphant as he realises he's starting to do the same thing as his big brother – swimming.

Written by Fran Cusworth, a mother of two & author of *The Love Child* and *Boomtown Wives*.

Family fun in the garden

In a busy modern world obsessed with consumerism and a mentality that pre-packaged anything is the best and easiest option, isn't it time that we literally stop and smell the roses? It's a sad reality that the kids of the millennium and beyond are destined to miss out on some of life's simple pleasures unless we take our children by the hand and guide them down the garden path to explore our own backyards. Recent research suggests that gardening actually reduces stress levels. I am yet to meet a mother who has not been stressed at one time or another, and of course a less stressed mother makes for better parenting.

There are multiple benefits to this simple but pleasurable activity, including but not limited to, getting out in the fresh air, letting children learn about nature, the textures of all things outdoors (dirt, mud, sand, water, grass, bugs and worms) and the enormous pleasure derived from watching something grow (a bit like mothering, isn't it!). And if your mothering role is making it hard for you to make the time for exercise, think about what gardening is doing for you – walking, bending, stretching, digging, and lifting!

Gardening doesn't have to be an expensive pastime, in fact it can be dirt cheap. A simple project to get the kids started is to collect seeds from some food you have bought and eaten. Pumpkin and zucchini are large enough for small hands to manage and they germinate easily. They can take up a bit of space in the garden though, so if space is limited, give peas, beans or radishes a try.

Not only will growing your own vegetables nurture your child's interest in nature, your food will be healthier and free of pesticides and chemicals. I have known even the fussiest of eaters to devour an entire plate of vegies after growing, nurturing and harvesting their own spoils. One fussy eater who visited our garden was shocked to learn that peas actually originated from a plant!

To really stimulate your child's interest in growing their own food, involve your child in every part of the process. You can even make your own organic fertilisers by making a worm farm or compost teas. If you do resort to using commercial fertilisers, be sure to buy organic products to give your plants and children the safest and most environmentally friendly growth.

Bean seeds are practically fail-safe and child proof. Try our experiment below to allow your children to watch the whole process.

The possibilities of allowing your children into the garden are endless. Herb and flower gardens are easy projects for children to undertake. Send the children on a nature treasure hunt in your backyard. You'll be surprised at the great number of unusual shaped leaves or patterned bark they find. Plant a sensory garden where each plant stimulates one of the senses. Some simple suggestions include paper daisy, lavender, spearmint, herbs, and strawberries.

The simple joy a child derives from watching the first buds burst open is priceless, and I guarantee you'll be presented with countless hand-picked posies. In the long term, your children will develop an appreciation for the earth and adopt their own environmentally sound practices to eventually pass on to their own children.

Bean observatory

- Cut a 1.25 litre soft drink bottle horizontally just above the lower bulbous shaped part to form a bowl and half fill with water.
- Remove and discard the lid. Cover the bottle opening with a sheet of paper towel and invert into the water filled cavity. The paper towel will act as a filter to stop potting mix falling into the water.
- Fill the upturned part of the bottle with potting mix and push a bean seed into the soil.
- Give the soil a sprinkle of water so that the soil is moist. Keep your pot in a light place such as a kitchen window sill and watch your bean grow.

The beauty of this self-watering pot is that if you forget to water your bean it will still thrive as it will draw water from its reserve. In other words the kids can't kill it! Just make sure that the upside down bottle top is in the water well. Soon your children will see the roots reaching down into the water and the green shoots reaching for the sun in the opposite direction.

Once you can see the roots extend to the water, transplant into your garden and await harvest time! Be sure to leave some of the beans on the vine until they wither and dry. Let your children collect the seeds to demonstrate the complete cycle.

Photograph by Appleseed Photography, Adelaide.

Written by Rose Alexander, freelance writer.

Music experiences for young children

Most young children enjoy music and they respond positively and naturally to it. They like to dance and bob around to CDs and tapes, make sounds with instruments and toys, laugh and giggle at finger plays and knee bounces and join in with songs they know well. Besides being enjoyable, music activities are also good for children: they can stimulate their learning and development in language, memory and listening, as well as physical and social skills. Music can be a regular part of young children's daily family routines, play and group activities.

Music as part of a daily routine

There are many ways in which music can become part of daily family routines, such as dressing, bathtime or bedtime. Songs and rhymes need not add extra time to these regular tasks but they can significantly enhance the quality of the interactions.

You can sing lullabies to settle a baby at sleep time, or gentle songs to soothe an upset toddler, or ritualised songs for greeting, goodbye and pack-away times. Songs and rhymes can be created or adapted to match specific routines. For example: *Here we go round the mulberry bush* can be adapted to fit most situations by changing the words. The lyrics can become 'this is the way we ... wash our hands', or 'put on our hats' or 'pack up our toys'. Singing about the task you are doing helps build children's language by giving them a model of appropriate language for what the child is actually doing at the time. *This is the way we wash our hands* can easily be extended to include other parts of the routine: 'this is the way we roll up our sleeves'; '... use the soap'; '... turn on the tap'; and '... dry our hands'. Songs often involve the repetition of words and phrases and this helps with language development. For older children music can be combined with movement. The song *Let's go walking*, for example, can be adapted to include alternative ways of moving, such as jumping, galloping, tiptoeing or sidestepping.

Music also offers endless possibilities to help young children learn. Advertisers know that tunes help messages stay in people's minds. In the same way, songs can be used to reinforce fundamental learning like basic literacy (alphabet songs) and numeracy (counting songs).

Music as play

Young children learn about their world through play, and therefore benefit from having opportunities to play with music. Children can explore sounds and create them using simple instruments, sound-producing toys and sound-makers (everyday objects like pots and pans that can be used to make sounds).

Music in groups

Music activities are also great with groups of children. When adults lead children in group music activities, they can model musical behaviours for the children to copy, such as singing, playing instruments, listening and creating sounds. Adult participation and enthusiasm also encourages the children to join in music making while also helping develop positive attitudes towards music.

Information provided by the Centre for Community Child Health, www.rch.org.au/ccch.

Nursery rhymes

Here are a few nursery rhymes to get you back up to speed on the words (so that when the repetitive rhyme recitals begin in your house you don't look blank!)

Humpty Dumpty

Humpty Dumpty sat on a wall.
Humpty Dumpty had a great fall.
All the King's horses,
And all the King's men,
Couldn't put Humpty together again!

Teddy Bear, Teddy Bear

Teddy bear, teddy bear, turn around.
Teddy bear, teddy bear, touch the ground.
Teddy bear, teddy bear, stand on your head.
Teddy bear, teddy bear, go to bed.
Teddy bear, teddy bear, wake up now.
Teddy bear, teddy bear, take your bow.

Eensy Weensy Spider

Eensy Weensy Spider climbed up the water spout.
Down came the rain and washed poor Eensy out.
Out came the sunshine and dried up all the rain.
So Eensy weensy spider climbed up the spout again.

Miss Polly Had a Dolly

Miss Polly had a dolly who was sick, sick, sick.
So she called for the doctor to come quick, quick, quick.
The doctor came with his bag and his hat,
And he knocked on the door with a rat-a-tat-tat.
He looked at the dolly and he shook his head.
He said "Miss Polly put her straight to bed".
He wrote on the paper for a pill, pill, pill,
"I'll be back in the morning, yes I will will will".

Once I Caught a Fish

One, two, three, four, five,
Once I caught a fish alive,
Six, seven, eight, nine, ten,
Then I let it go again.
Why did you let it go?
Because it bit my finger so.
Which finger did it bite?
This little finger on the right.

Twinkle Twinkle

Twinkle twinkle little star,
How I wonder what you are.
Up above the world so high,
Like a diamond in the sky.
Twinkle twinkle little star,
How I wonder what you are.

Mary Had a Little Lamb

Mary had a little lamb,
Its fleece was white as snow.
And everywhere that Mary went,
The lamb was sure to go.

Vox Pop

We asked a number of women and men around Australia to send in their advice, tips and personal experiences on a range of topics so that you have an insight into how others cope being a new parent. We hope you find their comments interesting, informative and reassuring. Vox Pop biographies: page 652

Cindy Fraser
Mum of three, Melbourne

On a nice day we enjoy getting outside and playing with water. A small amount in a bucket and a paint brush keeps the kids entertained for ages. Swap the brushes for some sponges and the kids will spend hours washing the windows or get the bikes out and add some soap suds and give them a good wash. On wet weather days we love playing with homemade playdough, blowing bubbles and more importantly popping them, dancing to music and cooking. The empty boxes the nappies arrive in always seem to be a big hit too; they climb in and out of them, drag each other around in them and recreate them into robots, cars, houses … As a special treat we rug up and head out for a walk early in the evening after we have had dinner. The kids each take a torch and we go in search of frogs, possums and anything else exciting! The kids think it is very exciting to be out walking at night and it has the added bonus of wearing them out ready for bed!

Andrew Weldon
Dad of one, Melbourne

I wish I could get as much pleasure out of anything, anything at all, as my 10 month daughter gets from lying on her belly in the nude. Man, she likes that. Her little legs kick wildly, and she screeches with uncontainable delight. And looking in the mirror – she's crazy for that. Is it her she's seeing, or some other baby? Dunno. But whoever it is, she sure is pleased to see them. And sucking things – wow! Is that some fun! Her granny calls it 'docking'. She can put the entire speaking end of a telephone in her mouth. I've tried putting the entire end of the phone in my mouth, and I enjoy it, sure, but my legs don't flap uncontrollably. What's wrong with me? I can't help thinking that somewhere along the way, I've lost touch with the simple pleasures of life.

Jessica Hatherall
Mum of two, Sydney

On rainy days I often take my little ones on an outing. We either go to a friend's house or head to the aquarium or a museum. Other great outings are going to the zoo, heading to almost any playground/park and every once in a while we will go have lunch with daddy.

Katherine Twigg
Mum of one, VIC

My son absolutely loves swimming! I first took him to swimming lessons when he was six months old and he took to it straight away, kicking his legs like he had done it a million times before. He didn't like going under at first but now he's getting much more used to it. He gets really excited now when I tell him he's going swimming and it has so many benefits. It's good exercise for him (and me), it's fun for him and he gets to swim with other babies, and it's much safer if he knows how to swim. It's something he can do with me or daddy or altogether as a family and it's something you can do if it's too hot or if it's cold and rainy.

Tanya Byrnes
Mum of one, VIC

After looking at the GymbaRoo website recently I gave them a call to investigate the program further. The program is tailored for various age groups and caters towards each child's development and skill levels. Each week you can use the lessons and continue on at home with your child to further enhance their development. Both your child and you will enjoy what you have learned each week, and it's a great interactive time for each involved.

Bernadette Vella
Mum of two, Brisbane

Both my kids love cooking. I cooked at home from a young age as did my parents and grandparents, so I suppose it is hereditary. I tend to be more focussed on the fun of cooking than the end result so we often have the kitchen in a complete mess and the end product is not always what we expected. I let them take on a fair bit of responsibility with cooking. Tiernan for instance has been breaking eggs since he was 2 and at 4 can easily separate the white from the yolk of an egg. I let them taste as we go along and basically try to just supervise and let them do the bulk of the cooking. They are so proud of the end result and the more responsibility I give them the more they seem to do.

The other thing we love doing together is gardening. We try to plant herbs and vegetables and I sometimes buy seeds, other times seedlings. We carefully tend the plants and take great pleasure in watching them grow. Whenever we are cooking we try to use something from the garden that we have grown. The kids just love it.

Cooking pancakes or cupcakes on a rainy day (or really on any day) is great too – they can help with the mixing and decorating and they are quick to cook and yummy to eat.

Playgroups are also a lot of fun watching your child's face when they see all the other kids. We found playgroups the were part of the Playgroup Association a lot more beneficial to our kids as they were structured with guidelines and had insurance in case anything ever happened (not that it ever did).

Danielle Murrihy
Mum of two, Melbourne

I am actually going to admit this … I don't like doing craft with my kids! We will do playdough and drawing with crayons but that is as far as it goes! We go to playgroups a couple of times a week, plus still have our weekly mothers' group meet ups and the boys go to occasional care one day a week, so they get to do craft at other places!

At home on rainy days we do puzzles and blocks, reading books plus we also put on a DVD sometimes. Warm weather is outside time and the TV is very limited.

We have a yearly pass to a local council run farm, and so we go to the farm every couple of weeks and it is a great morning out. We last about 2 hours there, have some lunch and of course go and feed all the animals.

The staff now recognise the boys and will tell me in which direction one has disappeared. It is one of the few places that I let them run around. Everywhere else they have to be holding my hand, in a shopping trolley or in a pram.

Kerri Harding
Mum of one, VIC

Rainy days don't necessarily mean having to put up with whinging, whining, bored children. Let your imagination run wild and you will discover heaps of things around your home that you can do to keep confined children entertained.

Make your own playdough and then have fun making things with it.

Do some baking. Making gingerbread men and then decorating them can be lots of fun.

Go on an excursion to Spotlight or a craft store and buy things like patterned felt, glitter, stick on eyes, feathers, non-toxic glue etcetera. Children will have a ball choosing things to put in their own little basket.

Keep your odd or holey socks and decorate them to make a puppet. You can then put on a puppet show afterwards.

Write and illustrate your own book together.

Make things out of some of the items that go into the recycling bin.

Paint. Have some butchers' paper on hand. Draw an outline of your child's body and have them paint

Vox Pop

We asked a number of women and men around Australia to send in their advice, tips and personal experiences on a range of topics so that you have an insight into how others cope being a new parent. We hope you find their comments interesting, informative and reassuring. Vox Pop biographies: page 652

it so that it looks the same as what they are wearing that day.

Have a movie afternoon with popcorn and snuggle up with blankets.

Balloons can provide endless entertainment. Play indoor soccer or see how many times you can take it in turns to hit the balloon before it hits the floor.

Put on some music and have your own private disco.

Invite a play mate over.

Go to an indoor play centre, swimming pool, ten pin bowling or attend story time at your local library – perfect options if you just want to get out of the house.

If you don't mind the idea of your child getting wet, it is good fun to look for snails, worms and frogs on a rainy day and what child doesn't love to jump around in puddles? My son has his own umbrella and loves to go outside with it at the slightest hint of rain.

On nice days when you want to get out and do something for the day, going to the zoo is always lots of fun for everybody involved.

Simple things like going to a playground and having a picnic, feeding ducks somewhere, going to the beach, playing in the autumn leaves or visiting friends on a farm can also be great activities that don't cost you money.

Martine Pekarsky
Mum of two, Melbourne

On weekends that we can't get away camping, we end up going to the museum, or a new park or play centre just for a change of scenery and to try something new. During the week, in the first year we did GymbaRoo and now we are doing swimming.

We've spent a lot of time catching up with friends from mothers' club, those we met in hospital, and the local twins club has actually been great for all of us. The Botanical Gardens and the Heidi Modern Art Museum in Heidelberg are our favourite places to go for a stroll.

Leanne Cummins
Mum of two, NSW

Children are ego-centric and love stories and pictures relating to them. A great way to keep them busy and have fun while learning is to make a book about them. All you need is a camera, paper and a pen. Take photos of your child doing various different things, and then print them out and make them into a book. You can stick the pictures onto a page, write your story on the page, and put them into plastic sleeves to make the book. Or you could get the pages laminated and bound together at a local stationary store.

You don't have to make it a bestseller, your kids will love them because it's about you and your family. I like educational books, such as *Days of the week*, eg. "On Monday, Meg went to visit Nan" with a picture of Meg and Nan.

I also like to get new mums to make a book when they're expecting a new baby. The story could be something like " I like to listen to the new baby in mummy's tummy" with a picture of the child listening to a pregnant belly.

These books will soon become their favourite stories. They last forever and are a wonderful reminder of your time together while your child is little. My kids still read theirs!

Sophie McKellar
Mum of two, VIC

Free play down at the beach or a walk in the park is so good for you and your baby – find a new park to visit every week, you'll be amazed at just how many there are. Take your picnic rug and some soft toys and off you go … cheap, fun and easy.

Anna Brandt
Mum of one, QLD

Lying out in the backyard or park watching the trees blowing in the breeze is great fun for a baby and very relaxing too (mums, take care you don't nod off). We made a cardboard and crepe paper wind spinner for my baby who absolutely loves it. Watching the colourful crepe paper spinning around is very entertaining for a baby.

If it's raining you can take your baby to the local pool. The babies' pools are usually always under cover and heated so a good thing to do to get out of the house.

Most cinemas do 'Bubs in Arms' viewing sessions for parents with babies. It doesn't matter if your baby cries or is loud during the movie because there are heaps of other parents in the same situation.

Cubby houses made from sheets and dress ups is a great way for kids to be entertained during rainy days.

Catherine Manuell
Mum of two, Melbourne

If you are going away with a young baby on a family holiday pack as little as possible! At least one pair of quick dry pants and lots of t-shirts for kids. These take up so little room and let them layer up if needed as well as change their look/cleanliness easily without overloading the luggage!

If you are travelling on a plane carry onboard: wipes, two disposable plastic bags or three for rubbish (or worse!), two to three light changes of tops and bottoms for each child and one to two for each parent.

Use a safety pin to attach a clear window key tag to 'can't live without' teddies etcetera. Put the teddy's name (not the child's) and any phone numbers you can be reached at, saying which country the phone number is for. This really can save much stress and distress. We have experienced many tears and had airport security looking for our lost teddy as we have run for our next connection. Luckily because he was tagged he turned up just before the plane took off!

Travel at all times with a small notebook and pen, it is amazing how much entertainment can come from these two light and simple things.

Travel with a small shopping trolley, sized to take on board. When you arrive it is big enough to pile in all of the coats, drinks, food, umbrellas and other extras that parents always get left to worry about and end up carting around day to day.

Fun activities with playdough

Make a pizza.

Talk about what you'd like on your pizza, then make vegetables and toppings.

Make a zoo or farm.

Use icy-pole sticks or cut straws to make a fence around plastic animals.

Make a volcano or garden.

An ice-cream lid covered in dough makes a good base, then decorate with twigs, leaves, flowers and pebbles.

Use a garlic crusher or play dough machine to make noodles, worms or hair.

Make imprints, pressing hands, fingers, leaves and (large) coins into the dough.

Roll a long sausage and then cut the sausage with scissors, or make bracelets and rings.

Make a face. Roll dough into balls for eyes, nose and mouth.

Shape numbers, letters or their name. Older children may enjoy trying this or they can try 'writing' on playdough 'paper' with a toothpick.

Resources

These Resources pages list products and services relevant to "Fun things to do".
To make your life easier as a parent, editorial listings have been grouped into sub categories.
Businesses then appear alphabetically under a national or a state-based subhead depending on reach.

SUB-CATEGORIES

ACTIVITY, CREATIVE PLAY & SPORTS PROGRAMS

NATIONAL

Toddler Kindy GymbaROO Pty Ltd
Tel: 1800 559 426
email: office@gymbaroo.com.au
website: www.gymbaroo.com.au

Enjoy quality time with your baby or toddler and learn how to enhance your child's development. At GymbaROO classes, qualified instructors guide programs of movement, music, massage, baby games and activities on specially designed equipment to enhance co-ordination and critical skills for early learning. GymbaROO programs begin with BabyROO classes for infants from six weeks old, to classes for toddlers and preschoolers. Phone the number above for information on your nearest class. (In Brisbane and the Gold Coast these classes are run by KindyROO – see separate listing in the Queensland section.)

VICTORIA

Gymnastics Victoria
144 High Street
Prahran VIC 3181
Tel: (03) 9214 6020
email: info@gymnasticsvictoria.org.au
website: www.gymnasticsvictoria.org.au

Kindergym assists children's co-ordination, body and spatial awareness through fun and stimulating activities. Kindergym is a movement based program for children under 5 and their care giver. The program encourages children to learn through play by structuring the environment rather than the child. It is a wonderful way to spend quality time with your child. Classes are offered throughout Victoria. Gymnastics Victoria can refer you to a Kindergym program in your area if you phone (03) 9214 6020.

KiddyGym
St George's Hall, 296 Glenferrie Road
Malvern VIC 3144
Tel: (03) 9822 3301
email: office@stgeorgesmalvern.org
website: www.stgeorgesmalvern.org

KiddyGym is a fun, safe, social environment for parent/carer and child to play and learn together. The program encourages body awareness, improves confidence, strength, co-ordination, gross and fine motor skills and musicality. KiddyGym have classes for babies, toddlers and kinder kids. Make a booking for your hour of fitness and fun on Wednesdays, Thursdays and Fridays.

LEGO Education Centre
37 Hall Street
Moonee Ponds VIC 3039
Tel: 1800 684 068
email: anita@mooreed.com.au
website: www.mooreed.com.au

LEGO Education Centres specialise in hands-on LEGO workshops such as Mechanical Toy Shop and Robot Adventures for children aged 4 and up. They offer a great range of LEGO birthday party themes too. There is a huge and different range of LEGO items available to purchase including the hard to find LEGO education items and LEGO merchandise such as watches, bags and some clothing items.

Playful Parenting
12 Surrey Road
South Yarra VIC 3141
Tel: 0408 321 011
email: paula@playfulparenting.com.au

Playful Parenting offers creative 'play and learn' classes for children from 10 months to under 4 years with their parent, grandparent or carer. Physical activities, music and movement, art and sensory play are presented in a supportive and playful environment where the child gets to discover, learn, share and grow in confidence in age-appropriate groups. Mothers' groups welcome. Bookings are essential.

Wiz Kids Kindergym
Level 1, 574A North Road
Ormond VIC 3204
Tel: (03) 9578 2332
email: info@wizkids.org.au
website: www.wizkids.org.au

Wiz Kids Kindergym offers weekly classes including singing, dancing, gymnastics and play for children 10 months to 5 years old to explore and develop their physical, cognitive and social skills in a fun and safe environment. The weekly programs are creative, stimulating and lots of fun. Try a class for free. They have state-of-the-art Kindergym equipment, innovative programs, lively dances, caring leaders trained and registered with Gymnastics Victoria and different themes every two weeks such as Circus and Under the Sea. Email or visit the website for more information.

NEW SOUTH WALES

Jumping Jacks Playtime
PO Box 200
Crows Nest NSW 2065
Tel: 1800 811 764
email: info@jumpingjacksplaytime.com.au
website: www.jumpingjacksplaytime.com.au

Jumping Jacks Playtime is a physio-designed and physio-operated kinda gym for children in the Sydney area. They help same-aged kids (with their parents/carers) to interact and exercise for one hour of fun and fitness with colourful and challenging equipment designs that change weekly plus music group and parachute time. The program is designed for kids aged approx. 6 months to 5 years in age-related classes. Short and long term options available; classes are small and allow for one-on-one attention. Phone or visit the website for your closest gym location. Birthday parties catered for.

QUEENSLAND

KindyROO
Shop 3, 17 Billabong Street
Stafford QLD 4053
Tel: (07) 3352 5022
email: kindyroo@bigpond.com
website: www.kindyroo.com.au

KindyRoo is a parent/child-education program run by qualified educators. Its aim is to promote learning in children by encouraging completion of the early childhood developmental stages through the use of specialised equipment, movement and dance activities. It caters for babies from 6 weeks up to children of pre-school age. The classes and activities are age appropriate and children are grouped according to development stage. Through fun and movement they help children become capable and confident for future learning.

LEGO Education Centre
2/78 Merivale Street
South Brisbane QLD 4101
Tel: 1800 684 068
email: anita@mooreed.com.au
website: www.mooreed.com.au

The LEGO Education Centre has a brand new store in South Brisbane right behind the Brisbane Convention Centre. The LEC specialises in hands-on LEGO workshops for children aged 4 and up such as Mechanical Toy Shop and Robot Adventures. They offer a great range of LEGO birthday party themes too. There is also a huge and different range of LEGO items available to purchase including the hard-to-find LEGO education items and LEGO merchandise such as watches, bags and some clothing items.

WESTERN AUSTRALIA

Monkey Bars Play & Learn Centre
Unit 1/2 Batman Road
Canning Vale WA 6155
Tel: (08) 6254 2555
email: info@monkeybars.com.au
website: www.monkeybars.com.au

Monkey Bars Play & Learn Centre provides children up to 5 years with the opportunity to learn through play as they engage in a learning journey full of fun and exciting adventures. With the focus on mind and body, each session is different and designed to stretch your child's imagination. The program is based on various

Resources

FUN THINGS TO DO

Activity, creative play & sports prgrams

➡ Aquariums, museums & zoos

developmental objectives and guaranteed to provide your child with loads of fun. The centre also hosts sessions for new mums including Mums & Bubs Yoga, for expectant mums including antenatal yoga, and their after-school program offers a variety of fitness and yoga classes for school-aged children. The cafe area provides a relaxed atmosphere for mums and dads to enjoy.

SOUTH AUSTRALIA

Colonel Light Kindergym Inc.

Westbourne Park Memorial Hall
388 Goodwood Road
Cumberland Park SA 5041
Tel: (08) 8271 8912

Colonel Light Kindergym offers movement-based activities including balance, sliding, climbing, jumping and dance, allowing children to develop co-ordination, confidence, creativity and self-esteem. An opportunity for you and your child to participate in free play, and individual, partner and group activities in a safe environment, with enthusiastic, friendly accredited leaders. Their one-hour programs are for children aged 6 months to 5 years, operating Monday to Thursday mornings during school terms. Established 25 years. Phone or email for more information.

Gymnastics SA Inc

PO Box 183
Park Holme SA 5043
Tel: (08) 8294 8288
email: admin@gymsa.com.au
website: www.gymsa.com.au

Kindergym is a fun program where children learn to move and to develop balance and co-ordination skills through play, providing the foundations for a lifetime of positive attitudes towards physical activity. Specially designed Kindergym equipment provides positive learning experiences for every child aged between 6 months and five years of age. Discover the fun of jumping, climbing, rolling and dancing in a fun, safe and exciting environment where child and parent learn play together. Qualified Kindergym Leaders guide the children and parents through each phase of the program. Centres are located throughout metropolitan and country areas of South Australia.

Sportybots

Tel: (08) 8370 6378
email: sportybots@optusnet.com.au
website: www.sportybots.com.au

Basic skills from eight sports are taught in a fun non-

contact and non-competitive environment. The programs also focus on the development of gross motor skills that are important for sports based play. Whether you have an active child, a child needing to develop some gross motor skills, or you want to introduce them to a variety of sports or simply want to have some fun and meet new friends, then Sportybots is the place to be.

AQUARIUMS, MUSEUMS & ZOOS

VICTORIA

Healesville Sanctuary

Badger Creek Road
Healesville VIC 3777
Tel: (03) 5957 2800
email: hs@zoo.org.au
website: www.zoo.org.au

Located just one hour from Melbourne in the stunning Yarra Valley, Healesville Sanctuary gives visitors a chance to view the sights, sounds and scents of the beautiful Aussie bush, while experiencing some close encounters with our native wildlife. Highlights include the breathtaking Birds of Prey show, colourful Parrots in Flight presentation and the Sanctuary's new interactive wildlife hospital.

Melbourne Aquarium

Corner King & Flinders Streets
Melbourne VIC 3000
Tel: (03) 9923 5999
email: melb_aquarium@melbourneaquarium.com.au
website: www.melbourneaquarium.com.au

Melbourne Aquarium is packed with adventure and excitement for people of all ages. It's an awesome journey over four thrilling and interactive levels, where you will meet thousands of aquatic animals. Experience life underwater in the 2.2 million litre Oceanarium, where daily feeds and presentations will capture your imagination, while surrounded by sharks, giant stingrays and turtles. Do not miss the amazing new Antarctica exhibit, featuring King and Gentoo penguins. Watch them splash in the penguin pool and slip and slide across the snow covered ice. Even the youngest of children will be enchanted by the colour, movement and hands-on learning experiences at Melbourne Aquarium.

Melbourne Museum

Carlton Gardens
Carlton VIC 3001
Tel: 13 11 02
website: www.museum.vic.gov.au

A special feature of the Melbourne Museum is the Children's Museum, designed for families with children aged 3 to 8 years. The Museum includes the Children's Gallery which houses children's artwork, and the Children's Garden which provides a venue for many different activity programs. Big Box, a giant, coloured cube structure, features a wonderful exhibition about physical growth using some of the Museum's fascinating natural history specimens.

Melbourne Zoo

Elliott Avenue
Parkville VIC 3052
Tel: (03) 9285 9300
email: mz@zoo.org.au
website: www.zoo.org.au

The Zoo is one of the most family-friendly venues in Melbourne. Children under four are admitted free and there are discounted family tickets available. There are baby changing rooms, a playground in Carousel Park and plenty of picnic lawns. During every school holiday period there is a special program designed to interest children. Keeper talks and animal feeding times are also educational and entertaining events. Special events are held throughout the year. During summer the Zoo stays open until 9.30pm for Zoo Twilights on Saturdays and Sundays. Admission charges apply.

National Wool Museum

26 Moorabool Street
Geelong VIC 3220
Tel: (03) 5272 4701
email: nwminfo@geelongcity.vic.gov.au
website: www.nwm.vic.gov.au

Located in a century-old refurbished bluestone wool store, the National Wool Museum uses unique objects and innovative displays to tell the story of the Australian wool industry from early settlement to the present day. The National Wool Museum provides a unique learning setting for groups of all ages and programs for all levels, from pre-school through to adult learning, are catered for. There is a constantly changing program of temporary exhibitions, many of which feature special children's activities and the Museum frequently runs programs especially designed for playgroups. Visit their website for further information.

Werribee's Open Range Zoo

K Road
Werribee VIC 3030
Tel: (03) 9731 9600 Information Hotline
email: worz@zoo.org.au
website: www.zoo.org.au

Experience a taste of African adventure at Werribee Open Range Zoo. Go on safari and see rhino, giraffe and zebra grazing on the grassy plains. Then come face to face with a pride of lions, see playful monkeys and discover a family of hippos in their new wild wetland home. Facilities include 45-minute guided safari tour, African and Australian walking trails, Meerkat bistro and safari shop. Open every day from 9.00am to 5.00pm. Safari tours depart from 10.30am. Last tour departs 3.40pm.

NEW SOUTH WALES

Australian Museum

6 College Street (opposite Hyde Park)
Sydney NSW 2010
Tel: (02) 9320 6000 General Enquiries
website: www.australianmuseum.net.au

Kidspace is a mini museum that stimulates under-5s to investigate the natural world. Kidspace features five 'pods' bug pod, marine pod, volcano pod, observation pod and imagination pod. Each pod will intrigue children they can feel animal textures, enjoy wall puzzles, make crazy mixed-up animals and peek out of the observation pod to see what animals they can spot. The Museum is open 9.30am to 5.00pm every day except Christmas Day. Admission is free for under 5s, Australian Government 'Blue' Pension Concession Card Holders and The Australian Museum Members. Family (1 adult & 2 children) $18, Family (2 adult & 2 children) $30, Adults $12, Children $6 and Concession/Senior $8 (price does not include special exhibitions).

Oceanworld Manly

West Esplanade
Manly NSW 2095
Tel: (02) 8251 7877
email: info@oceanworld.com.au
website: www.oceanworld.com.au

Dive in to Oceanworld Manly, home of Shark Dive Extreme. See the sharks being fed, get up close and personal with snakes, spiders, baby crocs and more in their Dangerous Australians show, interact with the creatures in the touch pool and enjoy the beauty of the coral fish displays. Oceanworld is just 200m from Manly Ferry Wharf and is open daily, except Christmas Day, from 10.00am to 5.30pm. Visit www.oceanworld.com.au or call (02) 8251 7877 for feed times, shows and special events and for information on unique sleepover adventures, fantastic birthday parties, kids club for mini marine biologists and a great special entry offer – under 3s are free.

Powerhouse Museum

500 Harris Street
Ultimo NSW 2007
Tel: (02) 9217 0444
email: info@phm.gov.au
website: www.powerhousemuseum.com

Australia's largest and most popular museum explores almost every aspect of human creativity from science and technology to social history, space exploration, decorative arts and design. See over 400,000 objects which promote the past, present and future of Australia. Interact with fascinating exhibits and be entertained by extraordinary performances and activities guaranteed to delight children and adults alike. A dedicated program of children's activities are staged in school holidays throughout the year. Open 10.00am to 5.00pm daily (except Christmas Day). Adults $10, Children $5 (4-15 years), Concession $6, Family $25. Members and children under 4 are free. (Additional fees apply to some temporary exhibitions.)

Sydney Aquarium

Aquarium Pier, Darling Harbour
Sydney NSW 2000
Tel: (02) 8251 7800
website: www.myfun.com.au

Nowhere else will you find a larger collection of

Resources

FUN THINGS TO DO

Aquariums, museums & zoos ➡ Arts & crafts

Australian aquatic life with over 12,000 marine animals. Take a journey through one of the most spectacular aquariums in the world, exploring Australia's rich and diverse waterways, marine ecosystems and unique aquatic environments. Walk underwater and come face to face with dozens of sharks of many different species – some over 3.5 metres long and weighing 300kg. Marvel at the majestic giant rays as they pass overhead, confront Nancy the ferocious 3 metre saltwater crocodile and be entertained and amazed by the secretive platypus and adorable penguins. Sydney Aquarium is also home to the largest Great Barrier Reef exhibit in the world. Visit the home of Nemo and see clown fish dart amongst the wavering tentacles of an anemone, as well as stunningly beautiful hard and soft corals. And the interactive touch pools let you get truly up close, just like being at Sydney's sea-side rock pools. Featuring 60 tanks and three oceanariums holding over five million litres of water, as well as 160 metres of underwater tunnels, Sydney Aquarium is an ideal all-weather venue conveniently located at Sydney's Darling Harbour. Open every day from 9.00am to 10.00pm. Phone or visit the website for more information.

Sydney Tramway Museum
Corner Princes Highway & Pitt Street
Loftus NSW 2232
Tel: (02) 9542 3646
website: www.sydneytramwaymuseum.com.au
The Sydney Tramway Museum (near The Royal National Park) offers a 'hands-on' experience with tram rides as well as a variety of trams on display, photographs, souvenir shop, kiosk and family picnic and BBQ area. Open Sundays and public holidays (except Christmas day) 10.00am to 5.00pm and Wednesdays 10.00am to 3.00pm. Adults $15.00, seniors/pensioners $10.00, school-aged children $8.00 (includes tram rides for the day; note: prices may change in 2009). Pre-booked group visits available any day. Wholly operated by volunteers. Additional opening days during school holidays; phone for details or visit their website. Easy access by train (every half-hour) - alongside Loftus Railway Station on Waterfall Line, or by car through Sutherland Shopping Village. Phone or visit the website for more information.

Sydney Wildlife World
Aquarium Pier, Darling Harbour
Sydney NSW 2000
Tel: (02) 9333 9288
website: www.myfun.com.au
Discover an authentic Australian wildlife experience in the heart of Sydney's Darling Harbour. Explore 3 levels, 9 habitats and over 65 exhibits, featuring the largest variety of Australian animals under one roof. Meet the most dangerous bird in the world, the cassowary, plus get up close to iconic kangaroos, cuddly koalas, colourful butterflies and vivid birds in remarkable walk-through habitats. Guided by experienced keepers, limited-capacity tours give you an exclusive and unique interactive experience with the animals of Sydney Wildlife World. Gain valuable insights about amazing wildlife as you go behind the scenes of exhibits and animal facilities. And you'll take home priceless memories of your animal encounters as you collect and release, feed, pat and touch Australian wildlife. Or you can try Breakfast with the Koalas. Gain early entry to Sydney Wildlife World at 7.30am to escape the morning crowds and see the animals at their most active time. Enjoy a hot buffet breakfast in a bush garden setting with gum trees and banksias overlooking the red sands of the semi-arid habitat surrounded by koalas. Experienced animal keepers will entertain you with informative talks, followed by your chance to cuddle up next to the iconic Australian koalas for a magic photographic moment. Open every day from 9.00am to 6.00pm. Phone or visit the website for more information.

Taronga Western Plains Zoo
Obley Road
Dubbo NSW 2830
Tel: (02) 6881 1400
website: www.taronga.org.au
Taronga Western Plains Zoo is like a wild and wonderful slice of Africa located in Dubbo, right in the heart of New South Wales. With over 300 hectares of bushland, Taronga Western Plains Zoo is more than just a zoo experience, it's an African safari. Like Africa you will see big game roaming across wide open spaces, however, unlike Africa, Dubbo is only hours away. So when planning your safari, just remember that all tickets to Taronga Western Plains Zoo are valid for two consecutive days, giving you ample time to access all that the Zoo has to offer. Home to over 800 animals, the Zoo is widely recognised as Australia's greatest open range Zoo. Your safari adventure takes you on a 6km journey, navigable by car, bike, electric carts or, for the really keen, on foot. As you travel the Zoo's circuit you will encounter animals hailing from each corner of the globe, however you will also find yourself immersed in the great Australian bush, teaming with free-range wildlife – this Zoo adventure will really bring you back to nature. A full daily schedule of keeper activities and special tours, such as Animal Encounters and Early Morning Walks, deliver magical up close animal experiences you will never forget. Hungry humans are also catered for by the Zoo's café and takeaway outlets, however, for those wishing to bring their own, free picnic and barbecue areas are dotted throughout the circuit. The Zoo is open from 9.00am to 4.00pm (exit gates close at 5.00pm). For further information visit www.taronga.org.au or phone (02) 6881 1400.

Taronga Zoo
Bradleys Head Road
Mosman NSW 2088
Tel: (02) 9969 2777
website: www.zoo.nsw.gov.au

Situated on Sydney Harbour at Mosman, Taronga Zoo is open every day of the year from 9.00am to 5.00pm. One of Sydney's most famous attractions, Taronga is home to almost 4,000 animals including rare and endangered creatures as well as Australian native wildlife. The Zoo has many popular exhibits including Koala Encounters, Australian Walkabout, Gorilla Forest, Backyard to Bush, Wild Asia and its newest exhibit Great Southern Oceans. At the new 1.2 hectare exhibit visitors can come face-to-face with a swimming seal or watch little penguins 'fly' through the water from a simulated Submarine Research Station. This amazing wildlife experience is just 12 minutes from the city by ferry and all shows are included in entry.

QUEENSLAND

Australia Zoo
Steve Irwin Way
Beerwah QLD 4519
Tel: (07) 5436 2000
email: info@australiazoo.com.au
website: www.australiazoo.com.au

Australia Zoo is your ultimate wildlife adventure. At 70 acres in size with over one thousand native and exotic animals; a line up of interactive animal encounters there is never a dull moment at Australia Zoo. If you've ever wanted to hand-feed an Asian Elephant (for free), cuddle a koala, walk alongside a cheeky cheetah, get up close to a gorgeous lemur, wrap a Burmese python around your shoulders or waddle with a wombat, then Australia Zoo is your ultimate destination.

WESTERN AUSTRALIA

AQWA – The Aquarium of Western Australia
Hillarys Boat Harbour, 91 Southside Drive
Hillarys WA 6025
Tel: (08) 9447 7500
website: www.aqwa.com.au

Explore 12,000 kilometres of Western Australia's coastline in just one day. AQWA takes you on an underwater journey to discover the incredible and unique marine life of Western Australia.

ARTS & CRAFTS

NATIONAL

Aussie Clings/Stik-ees
Tel: 1800 621 136 freecall
email: aussieclings@bigpond.com
website: www.aussieclings.com.au

Static Cling Plastic Re-usable Window Decorations and Activity Kits keep children amused for hours. They are easy to use with no mess and the range includes educational, holiday and everyday themes. Suitable for pre-schoolers to adults, they stick to most clean glossy surfaces including windows, mirrors, bathtub, tiles, refrigerators and whiteboards. There are over 100 sets to choose from with prices from $7 to $30, the majority in the $10 to $13 category. Phone freecall 1800 621 136 for a free catalogue or visit their website at www.aussieclings.com.au.

Crafty Critters (Australia) Pty Ltd
Tel: (03) 6344 4939
email: theteam@craftycritters.com.au
website: www.craftycritters.com.au

Crafty Critters is your one-stop craft and gift shop. Buy online for a great range of craft supplies: scrapbooking, beading, kids craft, needlework, paints, stamping, giftware and so much more.

VICTORIA

Artmania
Tel: 0412 434 508
email: bray1@bigpond.net.au
website: www.artmania.com.au

Artmania is run by Elena Sacks who is a qualified art/craft teacher with more than 10 years experience teaching in primary schools, as well as conducting private art classes and children's birthday parties. The art programs aim to inspire, enrich and build up children's confidence and self esteem. In 2009 Artmania will be introducing toddler art groups where you and your child can explore and experience a range of age appropriate art activities and mediums.

Books Illustrated
300 Beaconsfield Parade
Middle Park VIC 3206
Tel: (03) 9534 7751
email: info@booksillustrated.com.au
website: www.booksillustrated.com.au

Books Illustrated

Through its workshop program Books Illustrated aims to provide children and adults with a range of quality creative experiences with practising children's book illustrators. Books Illustrated runs workshops at Gasworks Arts Park and other venues. Register online for the Books Illustrated ENews to receive information about their workshop program.

The Art Factory
28 Glenferrie Road
Malvern VIC 3144
Tel: (03) 9576 0135
307 Buckley Street
Essendon VIC 3040
249a Belmore Road
North Balwyn VIC 3104
177 Ferguson Street
Williamstown VIC 3016
email: info@theartfactory.com.au
website: www.theartfactory.com.au

Resources

FUN THINGS TO DO

Arts & crafts ➔ Books & websites: family activities

The Art Factory conducts kids art programs for all ages and adult mosaic workshops. The Art Factory is also a great party venue where every guest gets the chance to create a masterpiece and take home their fabulous creation. They can make treasure boxes, photo frames, CD houses and more. Birthday parties are for kids aged from 4 to teens. Phone the number above for more information.

Wiz Kids Kindergym

Level 1, 574A North Road
Ormond VIC 3204
Tel: (03) 9578 2332
website: www.wizkids.org.au

Wiz Kids Kindergym offers weekly craft workshops for children 2.5 to 5 years old. Each week children create masterpieces using different materials and techniques. Phone, email or visit the website for further information.

Wonder Play

Tel: (03) 9502 7749
email: sacha@wonderplay.com.au
website: www.wonderplay.com.au

Wonder Play is a fun weekly class filled with painting, pasting, colouring and creating for kids aged 18 months to 5 years. Children can explore up to 8 different creative activities in each session and there are new activities every week. Your child will have lots of fun exploring new materials and making wonderful keepsakes such as fridge magnets, mobiles, magic wands and of course lots of paintings for the fridge door. Classes are offered at various locations across Melbourne – visit the website to find your nearest location.

NEW SOUTH WALES

Art 'N' Move

46 Hardy Street
Dover Heights NSW 2030
Tel: (02) 9371 6773
website: www.artnmove.com.au

Art 'N' Move is a fun, interactive program for toddlers to pre-schoolers aged 15 months to 4 years. Each week a teacher and an assistant guide the children through a themed lesson which incorporates: story time, 4 to 5 songs using different percussion instruments, an art activity, age-appropriate developmental toys and the parachute. Children develop many skills including fine and gross motor skills, language skills, socialising and music appreciation in a warm and intimate environment. Small classes cater for four age groups.

Plaster Painting Studios

The Entertainment Quarter, Lang Road
Moore Park NSW 2031
Tel: 0415 944 498
email: michelle@plasterpainting.com
website: www.plasterpainting.com

At Plaster Painting Studios you can plaster 3D figurines, plaques, canvas, picture frames, candle holders and money boxes. They can be sprayed shiny, glittered and ready in 15 minutes. Drop in and paint anytime no need to book. Priced from $1 to $20 there's a piece for every budget. Vacation care outings are only $15 per child. Wholesale pricing is available for 50 plus pieces – a great idea for fetes and fundraising.

QUEENSLAND

Bim Bam Boom

296 Oxley Road
Graceville QLD 4075
Tel: (07) 3278 3788
email: info@bimbamboom.com.au
website: www.bimbamboom.com.au

Bim Bam Boom sells educational toys for children from birth to approx 10 to 12 years. They also run art workshops: "Toddlers Get Messy" for two to four year olds and "Boomers" for school-age children. Bim Bam Boom also runs holiday programs and hosts children's birthday parties. All you need to to is bring a cake. No mess, no fuss for mum and dad, just relax and enjoy. Phone or email for more details.

Entropy

669 Flinders St West
Townsville QLD 4810
Tel: (07) 4724 4555
email: info@entropy.com.au
website: www.entropy.com.au

Entropy is an old fashioned toy store that will put a twinkle in your eye and a smile on your face. An amazing selection of traditional toys, sports and activity equipment for children and an extensive range of craft and craft kits. Purchase online with same day dispatch for most orders. Flat rate postage of $9.95 for orders of less than $100, free for all orders over $100.

The Patch Place

Shop 2, 326 Gympie Road
Strathpine QLD 4500
Tel: (07) 3881 0965
email: info@thepatchplace.com.au
website: www.thepatchplace.com.au

The Patch Place provides opportunities for children of all ages to explore their creative side, increase their academic skills and create new friendships, all while having fun. They run regular workshops ranging from jewellery making to abstract art, provide tuition services and run birthday parties that are not to be missed. The Patch Place also has a fantastic range of craft and fun educational products available for purchase, as well as a selection of designed kids clothes.

TASMANIA

Crafty Critters (Australia) Pty Ltd
16–18 Reuben Court
Kings Meadows (next to Meadow Mews) TAS 7249
Tel: (03) 6344 4939
email: theteam@craftycritters.com.au
website: www.craftycritters.com.au

Crafty Critters is your one-stop craft and gift shop. Buy online or visit the store for a great range of craft supplies: scrapbooking, beading, kids craft, needlework, paints, stamping, giftware and so much more.

BOOKS & WEBSITES: FAMILY ACTIVITIES

NATIONAL

887 Ideas for Busy Families
Tel: (08) 9368 4135
email: slossie@optusnet.com.au

887 Ideas for Busy Families is a compendium of tips and suggestions that includes ideas for kids of all ages. There are problem-solving ideas for first time parents, quick ideas for frazzled parents, enjoyable activities for the weekend and fun things that grandparents can be involved in too. The tried and tested ideas come from parents from around the world and are inexpensive or cost nothing at all. Available from all good bookstores.

Fun in the Sack
Tel: 1300 731 727
email: info@funinthesack.com.au
website: www.funinthesack.com.au

Fun in the Sack provides fun outdoor activities and games that will keep everyone entertained while playing outside together during a birthday party or a family outing. Many activities are old favourites that you will remember from when you were little such as the three-legged races or the jumping sack, jumping with all your might as you head for the finish line. They can make it easy for you to organise a child's birthday party or structured activities for a group by providing you with clear instructions to get everyone joining in – even the grown-ups.

Little Explorers
Tel: 0405 419 123
email: talktous@littleexplorers.com.au
website: www.littleexplorers.com.au

Part online store and part information site, Little Explorers is a resource for parents and children who love to be outdoors. The online store features a huge range of fabulous products for being out and about, including kids swimwear, floatsuits, child carriers – anything to do with the outdoors and travel. The directory listings are a searchable library of child-friendly facilities and attractions including parks and playgrounds, beaches, eating out, and places to stay all across Australia. Phone or visit the website for more information.

Moving To Learn
Tel: 1300 881 202
email: begintomove@bigpond.com
website: www.movingtolearn.com

Finally the manual your child didn't come with. *Moving To Learn* is for all parents, carers and educators of children aged birth to 3 years. It contains vital information about developmental stages and the impact movement, music and play has on learning. Fully illustrated activities showing the fun you can have in your own home for little or no cost. An accompanying 67 track CD of original songs and chants is great value at $44.95. Available at www.movingtolearn.com or www.robyncrowe.com.

Natural Parenting Tips
Tel: (08) 9206 1275
email: kiera@naturalparentingtips.com
website: www.naturalparentingtips.com

Natural Parenting Tips is your resource for gentle discipline ideas, recipes, resources, and creative play ideas for infants and toddlers. Updated daily with new articles and resources. Phone or visit the website for more information.

Our Little Treasure
Tel: (02) 9899 2191
email: admin@ourlittletreasure.com.au
website: www.ourlittletreasure.com.au

Our Little Treasure is a free website overflowing with teacher-designed activities, recipes, articles, competitions, shopping and much more to provide you and your child with hours of learning and fun. Our Little Treasure's activities are created with your child's education in mind and simplicity as the key. Your child benefits from quality educational content and you save time and money, so everyone wins. With so many things to choose from, your little one will never be bored again. For more information about who they are and what they do, visit their free website or phone the number above.

playtolearn
23 Lex Grove
Oak Park VIC 3046
Tel: 0423 644 837
email: info@playtolearn.com.au
website: www.playtolearn.com.au

playtolearn offers aesthetically pleasing and beautifully designed resources to encourage children's imagination and interaction with the world. playtolearn want to capture the essence of childhood by providing the ingredients for children's growth and development. Play is one of the most important needs a child has and playtolearn has carefully chosen resources to reflect their belief that a child plays to learn. Their resources encourage children's imagination, sense of wonder and curiosity. Browse through the website to discover the magic of their materials and equipment. Phone the number listed above or visit the website for more information.

Resources

FUN THINGS TO DO

Books & websites: family activities ➔ Day outings

QuickCraft
Tel: 0422 038 355
email: info@quickcraftonline.com
website: www.quickcraftonline.com

QuickCraft has hundreds of printable activities for children to make and do, plus craft and cooking recipes, carer/parent resources, and children's poems by an award-winning Australian poet. All printable to A4, quick and easy to use and easily stored. Their new innovative CDs are also quick and easy to use – each CD has over 150 printable pages for children to make and do. Choose from masks, puzzles, writing sheets, alphabets, finger puppets, craft and cooking recipes, poems and so much more. Each CD offers endless activities relating to its theme.

COOKING CLASSES

VICTORIA

Little Kitchen
371 St Georges Road
North Fitzroy VIC 3068
Tel: 1300 722 095
email: info@littlekitchen.com.au
website: www.littlekitchen.com.au

Little Kitchen is Australia's first organic cookery school designed and custom-built especially for children. The centre features children's cooking lessons, cooking birthday parties, a children's cooking concept store, organic herb garden and children's dining room. Lessons and parties book out fast.

CRY-BABY SESSIONS

VICTORIA

Cinema Nova
380 Lygon Street
Carlton VIC 3053
Tel: (03) 9347 5331
email: info@cinemanova.com.au
website: www.cinemanova.com.au

The CRY-BABY Sessions allow parents to come back to the movies again. Sessions are open only to parents and their babies (and of course toddlers and young children) where anything is allowed – crying, kicking, screaming, and yes breastfeeding too. They will even leave the lights half on so you can see what you're doing. Check out their website for the next scheduled session. Ticket

prices are $15.50 adult; $11.00 unemployed, students and seniors; $9.00 for pensioners and $13.50 for industry concessions; $11 Privilege Card Members. Phone the number listed above or visit the website for more information.

NEW SOUTH WALES

Roseville Cinemas
112 Pacific Highway
Roseville NSW 2069
Tel: (02) 9416 8555
email: lisa@rosevillecinemas.com.au
website: www.rosevillecinemas.com.au

Roseville Cinemas has sound-proof rooms built into both cinemas. Each has built-in volume controls, seating for 6 in cinema 2 and 8 in cinema 1. There is also a bouncinette, change table and a subtle light you can turn on when needed. They do not allow prams into the rooms so suggest a capsule, nor are there discounts for mothers groups (discounts apply only to 10+ people in the group and the crying rooms don't fit that many). You can watch any film you choose at any time you wish. Phone the number listed above or visit the website for more information.

DANCE CLASSES

NEW SOUTH WALES

Big Steps Little Feet
Francis Street & Wairoa Avenue
Bondi NSW 2026
Tel: (02) 9388 0118
email: enquiries@bigstepslittlefeet.com.au
website: www.bigstepslittlefeet.com.au

Big Steps Little Feet specialises in creative dance and ballet tuition for children from 2 to 8 years, allowing them to have fun and focus on the process of learning rather than the results. Their Rainbow Ballet program is a unique, inspiring and magical program, revealing each child's unique talents in fun and engaging ways. Each educational class is designed around a term theme. Classical ballet and contemporary dance form the curriculum and each different lesson is brought to life with all-things-beautiful and incorporates drama, creative play, story-time, music, free movement and gross motor development.

Oz Tots
193 Avoca Street
Randwick NSW 2031
Tel: 0407 453 418
email: marcia@oztots.com
website: www.oztots.com

Oz Tots is a program that guides and encourages a child's ability to think creatively through movement. This helps bring out the best of a child's imagination especially in the early 'magical years' of a child's development. Classes are held for the 3–5 year old age group.

Parramatta Ballet Theatre Academy at Merrylands
Scout Hall, Windsor Road
Merrylands NSW 2160
Tel: (02) 9953 1848
email: ballettheatreacademy@gmail.com

The Parramatta Ballet Theatre Academy at Merrylands offers pre-ballet for three and four-year-olds to foster the enjoyment and love of dance, to encourage co-ordination, concentration, confidence, and to develop listening and learning skills.

DAY OUTINGS

VICTORIA

Bundoora Park – Coopers Settlement
1069 Plenty Road
Bundoora VIC 3083
Tel: (03) 8470 8170
email: bundpark@darebin.vic.gov.au
website: www.bundoorapark.com.au

Coopers Settlement is located in the largest park in the northern suburbs – Bundoora Park just 15 kilometres from the centre of Melbourne. The urban farm presents an authentic farm experience with a variety of animals to touch and hold. While at the farm you can ride a pony, take a tractor ride or the more adventurous can brave the flying fox.

CERES Community Environment Park
Corner of Roberts & Stewart Streets
Brunswick East VIC 3057
Tel: (03) 9387 2609
email: ceres@ceres.org.au
website: www.ceres.org.au

CERES is an urban oasis of native bush gardens including a biodynamic farm only five minutes from the centre of Melbourne. CERES is relaxing destination for young families, where children can safely roam and play in a natural environment and where you can learn more about living sustainably. With a cafe, market (Wednesdays and Saturdays 9.00am to 1.00pm), nursery and numerous trails, there is plenty to see and do at CERES. Add to that a busy calendar of weekend workshops and large outdoor festivals including the Harvest Festival in March and Return of the Sacred Kingfisher Festival in November CERES is a vibrant and community focused centre. CERES is a great venue for your next party, wedding and all kinds of events. Phone 9387 2609 for more information.

Collingwood Children's Farm
St Heliers Street
Abbotsford VIC 3067
Tel: (03) 9417 5806
website: www.farm.org.au

The Collingwood Children's Farm is open every day of the year from 9.00am–5.00pm. Learn about life on a farm, milk the cows, see the orchards and feed the animals. Entry fees: $8 adult, $4 child, $16 family. Group bookings Monday–Friday $6 per person. Family Day is the first Sunday of each month. The Farmer's Market is the second Saturday of each month 8.00am to 1.00pm. $2 donation entry fee.

Craft Markets Australia
PO Box 337
Mount Martha VIC 3934
Tel: (03) 5974 4710
email: marketinfo@craftmarkets.com.au
website: www.craftmarkets.com.au

Few things are more enjoyable than browsing around the very best of Australia's craft markets taking in the colour, friendliness and quality and having a fabulous shopping experience. The philosophy is simple – everything sold at these markets has to be fresh, home grown, good value and above all great quality.

Dromkeen Collection Art Gallery
1012 Kilmore Road
Riddells Creek VIC 3431
Tel: (03) 5428 6799
email: dromkeen@scholastic.com.au
website: www.scholastic.com.au

Dromkeen is the home of Australian children's literature. Open Tuesday to Friday 9.00am to 5.00pm and Sundays 12.00 to 4.00pm (closed all public holidays) with authors and illustrators visiting on the last Sunday of the month. Free entry. Enjoy the gallery rooms featuring exhibitions of original illustrations from children's picture books. Take a picnic lunch and wander through the gardens of the historical homestead. Enquire about the Dromkeen Dragons, a club for children.

Fairy Park
Geelong-Ballan Road
Anakie VIC 3221
Tel: (03) 5284 1262
website: www.fairypark.com

Fairy Park is one of Victoria's best kept secrets. Visit a fairyland to see, listen and learn about fairy tales. There is excitement around every corner as you pass through fairy castles, cottages and caves. Wonderfully detailed displays come to life at the push of a button. There is medieval fun at Camelot's playground complete with castle towers, a dungeon, secret slides and passages. Pram and pusher friendly paths. Kiosk and full picnic facilities. Open daily. Melways page 11, A10.

Myuna Farm
182 Kidds Road
Doveton VIC 3177
Tel: (03) 9706 9944
email: shill@casey.vic.gov.au
website: www.casey.vic.gov.au/myunafarm

Myuna Farm is located approximately 35 kilometres south east of Melbourne. It is a working community farm which enables people of all ages, abilities and backgrounds to experience hands-on contact with a variety of animals and learn about farming life.

Resources

Parks Victoria
10/535 Bourke Street
Melbourne VIC 3000
Tel: 13 1963
email: info@parks.vic.gov.au
website: www.parkweb.vic.gov.au

Parks Victoria manages an outstanding system of parks, reserves, heritage sites, bays and waterways across Victoria. As well as protecting natural and cultural values, the parks are there to be appreciated and enjoyed by people. Many of the parks have walking tracks which cater for parents with prams and many other fabulous features that can be enjoyed by the whole family. Go for a relaxing stroll along the lake, have a picnic with the family, or just sit back and watch the kids on the playground. Here is a list of some of the many parks within the Melbourne metropolitan area which would make a special day out with the kids. These parks provide facilities such as toilets, playgrounds, BBQ/fireplaces, picnic shelters, walking tracks and many more.

Albert ParkAlbert Park   2K D6
Banksia Park Bulleen   32 D4
Braeside Park Braeside   88 D8
Brimbank Park Keilor   14 H9
Cardinia Reservoir Park Narre Warren East   210 D2
Dandenong Ranges National Park Olinda   22 C1
Greenvale Reservoir Park Greenvale   179 B5
Hawstowe Park South Morang   183 H5
Horseshoe Bend Farm Keilor East   15 A9
Jells Park Wheelers Hill   71 K7
Karkarook Park Heatherton   78 D7
Mornington Peninsula NP
 Frankston North   252, 254, 258
Point Cook Coastal Park Point Cook   208 J12
Silvan Reservoir Park Olinda   120 H11
Wattle Park Burwood   60 J2
Werribee Park Werribee   201 D1
Westerfolds Park Templestowe   33 EI
Yarra Bend Park Fairfield   22 J10

Parks Victoria hosts a variety of activities and events for children and their families during school holidays and some public holidays. For more information contact the Parks Victoria Information Centre on 13 1963.

Phillip Island Nature Park
Ventnor Road, Summerlands Peninsula
Phillip Island VIC 3922
Tel: (03) 5951 2800
website: www.penguins.org.au

Breathtaking coastlines, unique wildlife and spectacular attractions all located a mere 90 minutes from Melbourne. Phillip Island Nature Parks is home to the world famous Penguin Parade®, Koala Conservation Centre and Churchill Island Heritage Farm. A 3 Parks Pass allows you to experience all Phillip Island has to offer. Phone the number above or visit the website for more information.

Puffing Billy
Old Monbulk Road
Belgrave VIC 3160
Tel: (03) 9757 0700
email: info@pbr.org.au
website: www.puffingbilly.com.au

Puffing Billy, Australia's oldest steam railway and one of the finest preserved steam railways in the world, travels for 24 kilometres through the beautiful forests and fern gullies of the Dandenong Ranges to Emerald Park Lake and Gembrook. Puffing Billy operates every day of the year except Christmas Day. Located in Belgrave only 40 kilometres or one hour east of Melbourne, Puffing Billy is easily accessed by electric trains. Phone the number above or visit the website for more information.

Rain Hayne and Shine Farmyard
490 Stumpy Gully Road
Balnarring VIC 3926
Tel: (03) 5983 1691
email: info@rhsfarm.com.au
website: www.rhsfarm.com.au

The Rain Hayne and Shine Farmyard is a family-friendly venue located in the picturesque Mornington Peninsula. The farm features a large variety of friendly farm animals to pat, feed and cuddle and offers pony and goat cart rides (for a small extra charge) and has an emphasis on 'hands on' activities. Indoor and outdoor picnic areas are available with free gas BBQs, microwave and tea and coffee facilities. Open daily (except Christmas Day) from 10.00am to 4.00pm (extended hours at peak times). Special school holiday activities. (Melway map 163 E5.) Phone the number above or visit the website for more information.

Royal Botanic Gardens Cranbourne
Cnr Ballarto Road and Botanic Drive
Cranbourne VIC 3977
Tel: (03) 5990 2200
email: rbg@rbg.vic.gov.au
website: www.rbg.vic.gov.au

There is something for everyone in the Australian Garden where all the family can enjoy exploring the Exhibition Gardens and the Rockpool Waterway. Once you have visited the Australian Garden head into the rest of RBG Cranbourne where you can enjoy the extensive walking tracks through native bushland. The Boonerwurring Cafe offers coffee and light meals and botanically themed gifts are available at the Gardens Shop. Entry to the Australian garden is $9.50 for adults and children under-16 can enter for free. Phone the number above or visit the website for more information.

Royal Botanic Gardens Melbourne
Birdwood Avenue
South Yarra VIC 3141
Tel: (03) 9252 2300
email: rbg@rbg.vic.gov.au
website: www.rbg.vic.gov.au

A great place to take your children for a day out, a picnic or a party! There are lawns and open spaces, interesting pathways through weird and wonderful plants, and swans on the lake. Eating facilities include a lakeside restaurant and Observatory Café. There are also summer children's theatre productions and year round guided walks of the gardens and observatory. The Garden's Shop at Observatory Gate and Lakeside stock a diverse range of botanically themed items for children and adults alike. The Ian Potter Foundation Children's Garden is open Wednesday to Sunday from 10.00am to 4.00pm and entry is free. Phone or visit the website for more information.

Scienceworks
2 Booker Street
Spotswood VIC 3015
Tel: (03) 9392 4800
email: scienceworks@museum.vic.gov.au
website: www.museumvictoria.com.au/scienceworks

Scienceworks is Melbourne's award-winning, hands-on science and technology museum. It makes finding out about science fun for everyone. Spend the day at Scienceworks and see the exhibitions, particularly Nitty Gritty Super City. Designed specifically for 3 to 8 year olds, this exhibition allows children to explore science in the city. They can create in the construction zone, visit the exhibition cafe, record their own weather report, steer a ship, explore a recycling factory, pedal the pianola and much more.

NEW SOUTH WALES

Australia Walkabout Wildlife Park
Corner Peats Ridge & Darkinjung Roads
Calga NSW 2250
Tel: (02) 4375 1100
email: info@walkaboutpark.com.au
website: www.walkaboutpark.com.au

Australia Walkabout Wildlife Park provides great fun for the kids with some of the friendliest wild animals in New South Wales. Enjoy a cup of coffee on the veranda while the kids play in the sandpit, or take part in up to ten tours, talks and demonstrations daily. Experience wildlife, bush tucker and bush medicine, nature walks and ancient Aboriginal sites and ask about birthday parties, kindergarten excursions and school holiday programs. Phone or visit the website for more information.

Australian Reptile Park
Pacific Highway
Somersby NSW 2250
Tel: (02) 4340 1022
email: reception@reptilepark.com.au
website: www.reptilepark.com.au

Located less than one hours drive north of Sydney's Harbour Bridge and south of Newcastle, the Australian Reptile Park is home to unique families of reptiles and mammals. Experience loads of exciting daily wildlife shows, unique exhibits, Lost World of Reptiles and Spider World – the only place in the world where you will see the deadly funnel web spider milked of venom. Walk with dingoes and giant Galapagos tortoises, hand-feed friendly kangaroos, pat cuddly koalas and 'smile' when you snuggle up for a photo with a huge python. Come and say hi to Elvis, the largest crocodile in NSW, see Tasmanian devils and learn how the Park is helping to save this endangered Australian icon from extinction. Take a leisurely stroll through the wildflowers, sizzle a sausage on the free gas barbecues and relax under the gum trees, or enjoy the Hard Croc Café. There's a children's adventure playground, the Reptile Park's gift shop and so much more. Open 9.00am to 5.00pm every day except Christmas Day. Visit the website or phone (02) 4340 1022 for more information.

Fairfield City farm
31 Darling Street
Abbotsbury NSW 2176
Tel: (02) 9823 3222
email: cityfarm@fairfieldcity.nsw.gov.au
website: www.cityfarm.com.au

Fairfield City Farm is a beautiful 600-acre working and educational farm less than an hour away from Sydney. Enjoy a variety of native and farmyard animal exhibits and shows including cow milking, sheep shearing and koala talk. Free parking, electric BBQs and picnic areas available. Takeaway available from the café. Family passes and group discounts available.

Featherdale Wildlife Park
217–229 Kildare Road
Doonside (near Blacktown) NSW 2767
Tel: (02) 9622 1644
email: info@featherdale.com.au
website: www.featherdale.com.au

Featherdale Wildlife Park is a multi-award winning tourist attraction. The park is home to the largest collection of Australian animals in the world. You can cuddle up to a koala, hand feed kangaroos, wallabies and emus and watch Nghukur the saltwater crocodile munch his way through breakfast each day at 10.15am (except during winter). The park has pram and wheelchair access, café facilities, leafy picnic areas and coin-operated BBQs and a baby change table is available.

Thomas the Tank Engine Rides
The Train Shed at Vicary's Winery, The Northern Road
Luddenham NSW 2745
Tel: (02) 4739 0199
website: www.thetrainshed.com.au

Kids love the train rides on Thomas, Toby, James and Percy which run every Saturday, Sunday and Public Holiday 10.00am to 4.00pm. There's no admission charge and train rides are just $4.00 for one child and one adult together. You can stay for lots of rides with an Unlimited Rides Pass for $25 per child (and they can still

Resources

FUN THINGS TO DO

Day outings ➡ Indoor playcentres

take an adult with them on the pass if they like). There's hot and cold food, drinks, ice creams and Devonshire teas available from the kiosk or you can bring a picnic. Drive the "U-Drive" model trains and see the great selection of Thomas gifts in the shop.

QUEENSLAND

Daisy Hill Koala Centre
Daisy Hill Conservation Park, Daisy Hill Road
Daisy Hill QLD 4127
Tel: (07) 3299 1032
website: www.epa.qld.gov.au

Run by the Environmental Protection Agency, Go Bush is a school holiday-based program, offering a wide range of fun and educational activities. Join a ranger and experience what nature has to offer through night-time family spotlights, wildlife shows and guided bushwalking. Children's activities are offered for 6 to 12 year olds, while family activities are open to all ages. For all enquiries phone Daisy Hill Koala Centre on the number above.

Paradise Country
Entertainment Road
Oxenford QLD 4210
Tel: 133 FUN
website: www.myfun.com.au

Paradise Country offers an authentic half day Aussie Farm Tour that reflects the traditional Australian bush culture. From the moment you enter through the traditional Aussie Homestead you will be fascinated by the authentic charm and hospitality of the traditional way of life that is only found in Australia. Paradise Country's half-day farm tours include a barbeque lunch with live entertainment and bush dancing – a fun-filled interactive day the whole family will enjoy.

Sea World
Sea World Drive
Main Beach QLD 4217
Tel: 133 FUN
website: www.myfun.com.au

Get below the surface to discover a world of fun and adventure at Sea World where you will be enchanted by the amazing dolphins in their new show "Imagine", laugh along with the crowd at the hilarious new sea lion show Fish Detectives and be in awe of the beautiful polar bears at Polar Bear Shores and awesome sharks and marine life at Shark Bay. Meet your favourite Sesame Street characters at Sesame Street Beach and enjoy all the rides, shows and attractions.

The Valley Rattler
Tozer Street
Gympie QLD 4570
Tel: (07) 5482 2750
email: rattler@mvhr.org.au
website: www.thevalleyrattler.com

Experience the Cooloola Region's Mary Valley aboard the 'Valley Rattler' – easily one of Queensland's most scenic railway lines. The Valley Rattler operates steam train tours on Wednesday, Saturday and Sunday and a rail motor tour on Tuesday. Tours depart from the Old Gympie Railway Station and travel through the country towns of Dagun, Amamoor, Kandanga and Imbil. The Valley Rattler is a great, affordable day out for the whole family where you can enjoy good old-fashioned country hospitality.

Warner Bros. Movie World
Pacific Motorway
Oxenford QLD 4210
Tel: 133 FUN
website: www.myfun.com.au

Experience the magic and excitement of a world where everyone's a star. Warner Bros. Movie World is the only place where you can become lost in a world of fantasy and fun, meet your favourite stars and super-heroes, and experience the exhilaration of world-class adventure rides, movie attractions and an array of stunning shows where an exciting encounter or adventure takes place at every turn. Proud to be the only movie-related theme park in the Southern Hemisphere, Warner Bros. Movie World provides a fun-filled, exciting and memorable day.

Wet'n'Wild Water World
Pacific Motorway
Oxenford QLD 4210
Tel: 133 FUN
website: www.myfun.com.au

Wet n Wild Water World offers a splashtacular day out with pools and slides for the young and young at heart. From the kids aquatic playground Buccaneer Bay to the ultimate adrenaline rush at the Extreme H2O Zone, there's something for the whole family at Wet n Wild. Dive n Movies screen over summer and all pools and slides are heated during the cooler months for year round fun.

NORTHERN TERRITORY

Territory Wildlife Park
Cox Peninsula Road
Berry Springs NT 0838
Tel: (08) 8988 7200
email: twp@nt.gov.au
website: www.territorywildlifepark.com.au

The Territory Wildlife Park is the territory's wildest wildlife experience. Discover the native wildlife of the Top End up close or take part in one of the many interactive displays, feeding Barramundi and freshwater Whip-ray in the Billabong or enjoy a hands on encounter with wildlife during Creature Feature. Entry or adults $20.00, children (5 to 16 years) $10.00, under 5 years free. Family Passes available. Phone or visit the website for more information.

INDOOR PLAYCENTRES

VICTORIA

Billy Lids Pty Ltd
86 Lynch Street
Hawthorn VIC 3122
Tel: (03) 9818 2225
email: b_lids@bigpond.net.au
website: www.billylids.com

Billy Lids Indoor Playcentre is a colourful, clean, safe place for your children to play while you relax and enjoy true cafe food. Billy Lids specialises in children's parties and cater for all occasions from the smaller gathering of a few friends to larger birthday parties and corporate functions. Billy Lids is a great place not only for the kids but for all the family.

Bonkers Playcentre
497 Nepean Highway
Brighton East VIC 3187
Tel: (03) 9530 6601
email: kids@bonkersplaycentre.com.au
website: www.bonkersplaycentre.com.au

Bonkers Playcentre is based on a jungle theme and with a fun jungle maze, special tree house, selection of educational toys and variety of computer games, everyone will have a great time at this unique playcentre. Bonkers Playcentre provides exciting and safe play equipment for babies and toddlers, specialises in kids entertainment, children's and adults birthday parties, educational programs, music programs, music kindergarten, family celebrations, Christmas parties, corporate events, catering, family breakfasts, lunches and dinners, holiday programs, kids shows and live music. Phone or visit the website for more information.

Jungle Junior
39 Malop Street
Geelong VIC 3220
Tel: (03) 5224 2362
email: jujunior@bigpond.net.au
website: www.junglejunior.com.au

Located in the centre of Geelong, Jungle Junior is an indoor playcentre catering specifically for children under seven years of age. Ideal for parents on the run for a quick coffee break, or for mothers' groups who love to chat and relax. There is an area for non-walking babies, a toddler area and large playgym, all of which are fully padded and vinyl covered and sanitised daily. The gourmet café will fill any hungry tummy offering a yummy selection of salad sandwiches, fruit platters, focaccias, slices, muffins and even fully cooked breakfasts. Jungle Junior is fully heated and air-conditioned and also provides baby change areas and highchairs.

Kidz Zone Indoor Playcentre & Café
219 Sydney Road
Coburg VIC 3058
Tel: (03) 9383 1977
email: parties@kidzzone.com.au
website: www.kidzzone.com.au

Kidz Zone Indoor Playcentre & Cafe has a big inflatable jumping castle, toddler area with soft play equipment, four birthday party rooms and table reservations can be made at the cafe for mothers' groups or playgroups. They now also have special kids activities like craft and storytelling.

Kidzmania
Central West Shopping Centre, 67 Ashley Street
West Footscray VIC 3012
Tel: (03) 9689 9800
email: info@kidzmania.com.au
website: www.kidzmania.com.au

Kidzmania is a cool play centre for kids. Fully heated and air conditioned, it offers a large cafe area with a great range of food and drink. The large enclosed 0 to 3 years toddler area has its own jumping castle, ball pool and play structure. The 4 to 12 year olds have a nautical themed playground with a large 3 level play structure, twin astro slides, super slide and large multi-functional ball room and pirate jumping castle. Kidzmania also offer birthday parties in their new themed party rooms. Open 7 days a week 9.00am to 6.00pm.

Rare Bears
1134 Toorak Road
Camberwell VIC 3124
Tel: (03) 9889 9444
10 Bridge Street
Eltham VIC 3095
Tel: (03) 9439 6619
email: camprarebears@optusnet.com.au
website: www.rarebears.com.au

Rare Bears is a great place to take the kids for fun and entertainment while you relax in the café, having a coffee and eating fantastic food. Rare Bears is open seven days a week and caters for children of all ages, with toddlers in separate defined areas and exciting play possibilities for the older ones. On Friday and Saturday nights Rare Bears converts to a family restaurant open to 9.00pm (the Camberwell location has a BYO license). Children's parties are a specialty.

Wriggle It
Shop 1, 197 Star Zone, Karingal Drive
Karingal (Melway 103 C4) VIC 3199
Tel: (03) 9789 8434
email: wriggleitplaycentre@yahoo.com.au

Wriggle It is an indoor party and play centre providing activities for children parties and casual play. They have a giant padded play structure, jump castle and under 3's area, cubby houses and a cafe with a wide selection of food and drink. They are open Monday to Sunday and offer group discounts and fundraising options for schools and other organisations.

Resources

FUN THINGS TO DO

Indoor playcentres ➡ Music programs

NEW SOUTH WALES

Lollipop's Playland & Café in Castle Hill

10 Hudson Avenue
Castle Hill NSW 2154
Tel: (02) 9680 8868
website: www.lollipopsplayland.com.au/castlehill

Lollipop's Playland & Café in Castle Hill has a wide range of play equipment including a new bouncy barrel, speed slide, teacups ride, huge playframe, bouncy super slide, separate fenced toddler area with playframe, bouncy and best ball pool, ride on cars area, creative areas plus heaps more. Children's parties are a speciality. Great for group visits and they also offer an action-packed school holiday program. Unlimited play. Fully air conditioned with full wristband security. Ample free parking and a quality café. Open 7 days. Flooded with natural light.

Wiggly Play Centre

1A Stanton Road
Seven Hills NSW 2147
Tel: (02) 9838 9564
email: kim@thewiggles.com.au
website: www.wigglyplaycentre.com.au

One of Sydney's premier indoor play centres, Wiggle Play Centre caters exclusively for the fun, entertainment and development of children up to the age of 10 years. The Wiggle Play Centre is packed with fun things to do including a large maze, ball pits, jumping castles and great birthday parties. Wiggles merchandise and activities are also available. Visit or phone the number above for further details.

Wizzy World

9, 372 Eastern Valley Way
Chatswood NSW 2067
Tel: (02) 9882 1444
email: info@wizzyworld.com.au
website: www.wizzyworld.com.au

Wizzy World is one of Sydney's newest and brightest indoor play centres. It makes you wish you were a kid again – a huge play frame with six slippery dips, flying fox, rope bridge and more – playing has never been so safe or so much fun. Play mini soccer, netball or book one of the themed party rooms for a birthday party. And while the kids are playing, you can relax with great food and coffee in the cafe. Phone the number above or visit the website for more information.

AUSTRALIAN CAPITAL TERRITORY

KidCity

25 Kemble Court
Mitchell ACT 2911
Tel: (02) 6241 3144
email: info@kidcity.com.au
website: www.kidcity.com.au

KidCity is Canberra's biggest and most exciting indoor cafe, play and party centre. KidCity provides an enjoyable, safe and fun play environment for 0 to 11 year olds, and is as relaxing for parents and carers as it is fun for the kids. A great meeting place for friends to catch up over a scrumptious morning tea, lunch or afternoon tea, while children play. Birthday parties are also available. Open Monday to Friday 9.30am to 4.30pm, Saturday and Sunday 9.30am to 5.30pm. Phone the number listed above or visit the website for more information.

QUEENSLAND

Mulligrubs Play Centre & Cafe

25–31 Shore Street
Cleveland QLD 4163
Tel: (07) 3286 9766
email: mulligrubs2@aapt.net.au
website: www.mulligrubs.net.au

Mulligrubs Play Centre & Cafe caters for children from 0 to 11 years of age. Children can play on the climbing structure, ride bikes, jump on the jumping castle and slide down the air slide. They also cater for the older children with air hockey table, play stations, soccer table, and during school holidays there is free art and craft. Also have a look at their Playgroup information, it's a great way to meet other families. Adults are free, children under 12 months are free and for kids 1 to 11 years an entry fee is required. Socks must be worn. Phone or the number listed above or visit the website for more information.

Smileez Playhouse & Cafe

3B/250 Olsen Avenue
Parkwood QLD 4214
Tel: (07) 5574 4491
email: smileezfun@yahoo.com.au
website: www.smileez.com.au

Smileez Playhouse and Cafe caters for children aged 0 to 11 years. There's a separate under-3s area with lots of fun toys, slides and ball pits, a huge 3-level maze with flying fox, ball pits, two slides and jumping castles. Birthday parties are also a speciality – there are three party rooms with your own host who dress up in theme. Other features include a brand new arcade games area, basket ball, air hockey and Sega rally cars. A great cafe lets you relax while the kids play. Phone or the number listed above or visit the website www.smileez.com.au for more information.

LANGUAGE CLASSES

VICTORIA

Language Champs
50 Station Street
Moorabbin VIC 3189
Tel: (03) 9555 5355 for locations around Melbourne
email: info@languagechamps.com.au
website: www.languagechamps.com.au

Language Champs delivers premium educational language programs. They teach languages such as French, Spanish, German, Mandarin, Japanese, Italian and English. Classes and kinder programs are fun, play-based and for children aged 2 years plus, teens and adults. Language Champs children's programs are taught using a mix of games, songs, puppets, arts and crafts and many other activities taught by native speaking teachers. A free preview session is available. Language Champs can teach in your home, in child care centres or schools or in their own centres in Moorabbin, Prahran, Surrey Hills or at another location of your choice.

NEW SOUTH WALES

Fun French
Beecroft NSW 2119
Tel: (02) 9875 5097
email: info@funfrench.com.au
website: www.funfrench.com.au

Fun French conducts small group classes for 3 to 12 year olds. French is taught in a fun way with songs, games, mime and activities. Children learn in the same way that they learn their first language. For pre-schoolers, mum stays with the child, getting a free lesson and making new friends too.

MUSIC PROGRAMS

NATIONAL

Creative Capers
Tel: 1300 881 202
email: info@creativecapers.com.au
website: www.creativecapers.com.au

Creative Capers is a unique, original, high quality early childhood movement and music program, specifically designed for children aged 6 weeks to 7 years. The focus is on movement and co-ordination, enhanced by a variety of musical experiences. Creative Capers is suitable for all parent, childcare, health, community and educational environments. Phone or visit the website for more information.

do-re-mi
Tel: (07) 3801 1154
email: gc.godfrey@hotmail.com
website: www.do-re-mi.com.au

do-re-mi music for children classes (est. 1980) are offered to parents/carers with babies and young children in private music groups or in child care centres. The

heartbeat of the mother is the first regular beat familiar to the child and babies hear clearly in the womb from 28 weeks. Nerve areas – neurons in the brain function – are at their peak when a child is approximately age one; a time when song and rhymes are absorbed quickly. By the age of two or three children will begin to say or sing back songs and rhymes which were absorbed from infancy. Children learn to sing in the same way they learn to speak, through repetition, good role modelling, fun and a nurturing environment. Do-re-mi also offer professional workshops and courses especially designed for child care staff while providing appropriate books, CDs and others resources. Visit the website for more information.

hey dee ho music
Tel: 1300 139 631
email: info@heydeehomusic.com.au
website: www.heydeehomusic.com.au

hey dee ho music is an exciting, interactive music program designed to stimulate early childhood development. Musical concepts of beat, rhythm, tempo, pitch and dynamics are introduced along with your favourite nursery rhymes and popular children's songs. hey dee ho music provides babies, toddlers, pre-schoolers and their parents or carers an opportunity to have fun together sharing the pleasure of music. Auslan signing, spatial awareness, multicultural languages and the solfa are included in classes that operate throughout Victoria, New South Wales, South Australia and Queensland as well as creches, kindergartens, preschools, playgroups, birthday parties and wherever else you find children under 5.

International School of Music
Tel: (02) 9489 8388
email: ros@ismaustralia.com
website: www.ismaustralia.com

Little Jitterbugs Music (2 year olds) and Little Beebopper Music (3 year olds) are structured stimulating programs of music and action. They aim to develop early music fundamentals such as rhythm, aural, pitch, co-ordination, fine and gross motor skill and the developmental procedures of creative ability. Lots of fun in a class maximum of ten children with fully qualified music educators. The programs provide a strong foundation for further study. Group music courses for students aged from 4 years to adult are also available.

Kinderjazz
Tel: (02) 9742 5717
email: info@kinderjazz.com
website: www.kinderjazz.com

Kinderjazz offers a selection of children's music CDs that have been recorded live by the world's only "Big JAZZ Band" for kids and recommended by Sesame Street Whether you're looking for ways to stimulate a developing young mind or you'd like to introduce children to the pleasures of music or you just want your kids to have fun, you will find this collection of blues,

Resources

FUN THINGS TO DO

Music programs

latin, ragtime, jazz and swing music perfect for children under the age of 12. Kinderjazz's recorded music is specifically written to engage young children while simultaneously appealing to adults of all ages. Visit the website for further information.

Kindermusik

Tel: 1300 721 722
email: info@kindermusik.com.au
website: www.kindermusik.com.au

Research proves that early integration of music into your child's daily routine means improving their ability to think, reason, create and express. Music makes children smarter. With more than 25 years experience in early childhood development, Kindermusik is a well-respected name in musical learning. Their trained and licensed educators provide carefully researched, developmentally appropriate music and movement programs for children (newborn to age seven) both in class and at home. This music program offers fun, learning and laughter. Phone 1300 721 722 for a free class preview coupon.

mainly music

Tel: 1300 668 496
email: johood@mainlymusic.org.au
website: www.mainlymusic.org.au

Started in 1990, mainly music is a fun music session suitable for parent and child. From birth to school age, children will love participating with their parent or caregiver in action songs, rhymes and other music-based activities. Everyone gets to enjoy morning tea afterwards in a relaxed setting. Your local mainly music can be located on www.mainlymusic.org.au.

Toptots Early Development Centre

Tel: 0412 481 708
email: mail@toptots.net.au
website: www.toptots.net.au

Toptots® offers DIY books and music programs for children aged 3 to 10 years. They also have English and LOTE readers. Phone 0412 481 708 or visit www.toptots.net.au for further information.

VICTORIA

Baby Love Music Fun

Clifton Hall 314 Church Street
Richmond VIC 3121
Tel: (03) 9429 9738
email: babylovemusicfun@climatechangesin.com.au
website: www.babylovemusicfun.blogspot.com

This unique and quality music, singing and movement program has been especially developed for babies and the adults who love them. The age and developmentally-specific classes for babies 3 months to 3 years feature Music for Milestones and Opera for Babies with professional opera singer Melanie Maslin.

Kidz Can HQ

1 Sinclair Street
Elsternwick VIC 3185
Tel: (03) 9523 8373
email: marcelle@kidzcanhq.com.au
website: www.kidzcanhq.com.au

Kidz Can HQ is a comprehensive children's development program catering for children aged 6 months to 4 years. Join in for 1.5 hours (age dependent) of fun-filled, interactive time with your child. Programs include time in the toy room, music time developing rhythm and a love of music, physical playtime on gross motor skill equipment, snack and story time ending with an art and craft session. Visit the website or phone for more information.

Little Feet Music

Tel: (03) 9515 3993
email: info@littlefeetmusic.com.au
website: www.littlefeetmusic.com.au

Little Feet Music classes are suitable for all young children. Babies, toddlers and pre-school children are introduced to singing, games, dance, rhythm and playing percussion instruments in fun, creative and imaginative ways. Children attend the sessions with an adult and participate in all aspects of music development, learning skills that are not only used in class, but also to be enjoyed at home. Contact Little Feet Music and unlock that door to your child's creativity.

Moving Into Music

1/89a Mont Albert Road
Canterbury VIC 3126
Tel: (03) 9836 2686
email: laurishing@movingintomusic.com.au
website: www.movingintomusic.com.au

Moving Into Music offers creative music learning for babies through to pre-school children. Parents share classes with their children learning to build and strengthen the musical bond which lays the foundations for guiding and providing for future music learning. Classes are held in Camberwell, Toorak, Ivanhoe, Kew and East Melbourne. At school age, children can learn piano, keyboard, acoustic or electric guitar at their music studios situated in AllansMusic in Kew.

Music Works Magic

Main Studio: 263 Glenhuntly Road
Elsternwick VIC 3185
Tel: (03) 9029 6879
email: anna@musicworksmagic.com
website: www.musicworksmagic.com

Music Works Magic! offers interactive group music classes for babies through to 12 years, including birthday parties and private tuition all around

Melbourne. All instruments tuition available at Elsternwick. They have a wonderful educational Resource Centre with books, CDs, puppets, toys and instruments. There are Professional Development sessions for adults working with children. Staff are highly qualified, experienced and Kodaly accredited. Visit their website at www.musicworksmagic.com. Venues all over Melbourne. They also provide visits or ongoing services to child care centres. Phone or visit the website for more information.

Victorian Orff Schulwerk Association
300 Huntingdale Road
Huntingdale VIC 3166
Tel: (03) 9535 7020
email: glenys@stockdaleacs.com.au
website: www.vosa.org

Victorian Orff Schulwerk Association (VOSA) is an holistic approach to music education. VOSA promotes this through participation in music using the integration of speech, singing, instrument playing, movement, listening and dance. VOSA runs Family Marimba Days, an annual Marimba camp for families, an Early Childhood Conference of Performing Arts and it has also developed an online Early Childhood Music Resource Library.

NEW SOUTH WALES

Australian Music Schools
PO Box 810
Randwick NSW 2031
Tel: (02) 9314 7282
email: info@australianmusicschools.com.au
website: www.australianmusicschools.com.au

Australian Music Schools (AMS) offer beginner classes for babies to adults. AMS courses incorporate a wide range of musical activities presented in an engaging way. They are designed for each individual age group. All courses include: keyboard/piano playing, singing, note and rhythm reading, music appreciation, percussion, theory, ensemble playing, creative and composition work, aural development and musical games. There are always lots of extra activities throughout the year such as concerts, camps and workshops. AMS also provides entertainment for children's birthday parties. Phone or visit the website for more information.

Einsteinz Music
Tel: (02) 9343 0333
email: info@einsteinzmusic.com.au
website: www.einsteinzmusic.com.au

Einsteinz Music is where fun and learning go hand-in-hand for children aged 6 months to 4 years and their parents/carers. Join the Einsteinz Music Program and learn music alongside your child while encouraging their development. All Einsteinz programs are carefully developed and run by professional musicians. Venues are located in Bondi, Camperdown, Concord, Coogee, Crows Nest, Leichhardt, Lilyfield, Neutral Bay, Newtown, Randwick and Rozelle.

Go Seek
Tel: (02) 9388 2361
email: info@goseek.com.au
website: www.goseek.com.au

Go Seek is a funky and vibrant children's entertainment group well known for their unique and exciting entertainment packages including: interactive, musical stage shows; kids birthday parties; fun games workshops; face painting; roving characters and powerful and catchy award-winning songs (and music CDs). A fantastic explosion of colour, movement and funky music, Go Seek take children on a musical journey of discovery and adventure, educating and entertaining through exciting themes, catchy tunes, bright funky costumes, clever props, imaginative story lines and high-energy routines. Go Seek perform their interactive, adventure-filled shows and workshops at festivals, clubs, schools, child care centres, corporate functions, Christmas parties, family fun days, shopping centres, birthday parties and special events in NSW, Victoria, Queensland and ACT.

Sydney Youth Orchestras
Level 1, 10 Hickson Road
The Rocks NSW 2000
Tel: (02) 9251 2422
email: info@syo.com.au
website: www.syo.com.au

Packed with enormous fun and entertainment, SYO Toddlers' Proms introduce music to pre-school and primary children (and their parents) through a hands-on and high-octane concert experience. Dance, sing, march along to the music, beat the bass drums, whack the timpani or conduct the whole orchestra. For dates and bookings phone (02) 8256 2222 or visit www.syo.com.au.

QUEENSLAND

The Beats Bus
Tel: (07) 3366 8010
email: info@thebeatsbus.com.au
website: www.thebeatsbus.com.au

The Beats Bus is a fun, energy-packed, hands-on musical experience offering music edutainment to young people and their caregivers in a unique and creative environment. Once onboard Betty the Bus, a custom-designed marquee, children are immersed in an imaginary world as they take off to exciting destinations. With the help of characters like Brendan the Bus Driver and Sonic Shea, children will discover musical concepts through songs, sounds, games, stories and the use of percussion instruments.

WESTERN AUSTRALIA

Rhymes 'n' Chimes
Various music locations
Tel: 0410 236 846
email: colette@rhymesnchimes.com.au
website: www.rhymesnchimes.com.au

Rhymes 'n' Chimes run fun music groups for mums and

Resources

FUN THINGS TO DO

Music programs ➡ Playgroups

children aged 6 months to 5 years. Take part in their cheerful sing-along using musical instruments. Participate in action and movement songs and discover sounds and rhythm while having fun.

SOUTH AUSTRALIA

Musical Child
32 Military Road
Semaphore South SA 5019
Tel: (08) 8449 8451
website: www.musicalchild.com.au

Provide your child with opportunities for early learning through music with Musical Child classes, shows and products. Children aged from 12 months enjoy playing percussion instruments, singing, moving to music, circle dancing, mimicry, puppetry nursery rhymes and songs with illustrations. The children's traditional repertoire is presented by their endearing qualified music educators. Your child will love the singers and the songs. Locations across Adelaide and in the Riverland.

Tritones Music Classes
Prospect/Ovingham, Aberfoyle Park & Blackwood
Tel: (08) 8270 3847
website: www.tritones.com.au

Tritones Music Classes presents Kindermusik and other exciting, fun, educational music and movement programs for children aged 6 weeks to 7 years across Adelaide, South Australia. Early integration of music into your child's daily routine improves his/her ability to think, reason, create and express. Children learn best through music and movement, especially in a fun environment.

PLAYGROUPS

NATIONAL

Playgroup Australia
Tel: (07) 3394 8448
email: info@playgroupaustralia.com.au
website: www.playgroupaustralia.com.au

Playgroup Australia is the national peak and administrative body for playgroups in Australia. It is a federation of the eight peak state and territory Playgroup Associations across Australia who collectively represent more than 110,000 families and 145,000 children at 8,300 playgroup sessions every week. Playgroup Australia is a not-for-profit organisation reliant on community and member organisation support to develop and promote playgroup activities across

Australia. For information on how to start a new playgroup or to join an existing one, phone your local Playgroup Association on 1800 171 882 (tollfree).

VICTORIA

Playgroup Victoria
346 Albert Street
Brunswick VIC 3056
Tel: (03) 9388 1599 or 1800 171 882 (tollfree)
email: pgvic@playgroup.com.au
website: www.playgroupaustralia.com.au

Playgroup is an informal session where mums, dads, grand parents, caregivers, children and babies meet together in a relaxed environment. They are community based, parent run, and usually held weekly. Playgroups are held in almost every region of Victoria. Playgroup Victoria is a non-profit Association which administers and supports playgroups across Victoria. They connect families with playgroups in their area, and provide assistance for those wanting to start their own playgroup. For a low annual fee Playgroup Association members benefit from regular magazines and publications; comprehensive insurance cover for all playgroup activities; access to a member's hotline and website gateway; member discounts for Playgroup Shop, concerts, courses, speaker's tours, resources and more.

NEW SOUTH WALES

Playgroup NSW Inc
PO Box 6665
Wetherill Park DC NSW 1851
Tel: (02) 9604 5513 or 1800 171 882 (tollfree)
email: admin@playgroupnsw.com.au
website: www.playgroupaustralia.com.au

Playgroup is an informal session where mums, dads, grand parents, caregivers, children and babies meet together in a relaxed environment. They are community based, parent run, and usually held weekly. Playgroups are held in almost every region of NSW. Playgroup NSW is a non-profit Association which administers and supports playgroups across NSW. They connect families with playgroups in their area, and provide assistance for those wanting to start their own playgroup. For a low annual fee Playgroup Association members benefit from regular magazines and publications; comprehensive insurance cover for all playgroup activities; access to a member's hotline and website gateway; member discounts for Playgroup Shop, concerts, courses, speaker's tours, resources and more.

AUSTRALIAN CAPITAL TERRITORY

ACT Playgroups Association Inc.
PO Box 513
Jamison Centre ACT 2614
Tel: (02) 6251 0261 or 1800 171 882 (tollfree)
email: playgroupsact@ixa.net.au
website: www.playgroupaustralia.com.au

Playgroup is an informal session where mums, dads,

grandparents, care givers, children and babies meet together in a relaxed environment. They are community based, parent run, and usually held weekly. ACT Playgroups Association is a non-profit Association which administers and supports playgroups across ACT and some surrounding NSW areas. They connect families with playgroups in their area, and provide assistance for those wanting to start their own playgroup. For a low annual fee Playgroup Association members benefit from regular magazines and publications; comprehensive insurance cover for all playgroup activities; free Australian Baby Card; access to the Association's development and support staff; toy library and other resources (for a small fee); as well as events for playgroup members.

QUEENSLAND

Playgroup Queensland Inc
PO Box 339
Alderley QLD 4051
Tel: (07) 3855 9600 or 1800 171 882 (tollfree)
email: info@playgroupqld.com.au
website: www.playgroupaustralia.com.au

Playgroup is an informal session where mums, dads, grand parents, caregivers, children and babies meet together in a relaxed environment. They are community based, parent run, and usually held weekly. Playgroups are held in almost every region of Queensland. Playgroup Queensland is a non-profit Association which administers and supports playgroups across Queensland. They connect families with playgroups in their area, and provide assistance for those wanting to start their own playgroup. For a low annual fee Playgroup Association members benefit from regular magazines and publications; comprehensive insurance cover for all playgroup activities; access to a member's hotline and website gateway; member discounts for Playgroup Shop, concerts, courses, speaker's tours, resources and more.

NORTHERN TERRITORY

Playgroup Association of NT Inc.
PO Box 13
Nightcliff NT 0814
Tel: (08) 8945 7775 or 1800 171 882 (tollfree)
email: admin@playgroupnt.com.au
website: www.playgroupaustralia.com.au

Playgroup is an informal session where mums, dads, grand parents, caregivers, children and babies meet together in a relaxed environment. They are community based, parent run, and usually held weekly. Playgroups are held in almost every suburb of Darwin and rural and remote towns across the Northern Territory. The Playgroup Association of NT is a non-profit community organisation providing support for playgroups in the Northern Territory. They connect families with playgroups in their area, and provide assistance for those wanting to start their own playgroup. For a low annual fee Playgroup Association members benefit from regular magazines and

publications; comprehensive insurance cover for all playgroup activities; use of Playgroup House facilities; low cost craft resources; fun days and more.

WESTERN AUSTRALIA

Playgroup WA
PO Box 61
North Perth WA 6906
Tel: (08) 9228 8088 or 1800 171 882 (tollfree)
email: admin@playgroupwa.com.au
website: www.playgroupaustralia.com.au

Playgroup is an informal session where mums, dads, grand parents, caregivers, children and babies meet together in a relaxed environment. They are community based, parent run, and usually held weekly. Playgroups are held in almost every region of Western Australia. Playgroup WA is a non-profit Association which administers and supports playgroups across Western Australia. They connect families with playgroups in their area, and provide assistance for those wanting to start their own playgroup. For a low annual fee Playgroup Association members benefit from regular publications and e-newsletters; extensive range of Playgroup WA resource material; comprehensive insurance cover for all playgroup activities; access to a member's hotline and website gateway; member discounts and more.

SOUTH AUSTRALIA

Playgroup SA
91 Prospect Road
Prospect SA 5082
Tel: (08) 8344 2722 or 1800 171 882 (tollfree)
email: info@playgroupsa.com.au
website: www.playgroupaustralia.com.au

Playgroup is an informal session where mums, dads, grand parents, caregivers, children and babies meet together in a relaxed environment. They are community based, parent run, and usually held weekly. Playgroups are held in almost every region of South Australia. Playgroup SA is a non-profit Association which administers and supports playgroups across SA. They connect families with playgroups in their area, and provide assistance for those wanting to start their own playgroup. For a low annual fee Playgroup Association members benefit from regular magazines and publications; comprehensive insurance cover for all playgroup activities; access to a member's hotline and website gateway; member discounts for Playgroup Shop, concerts, courses, speaker's tours, resources and more.

TASMANIA

Playgroup Tasmania
PO Box 799
Launceston TAS 7250
Tel: (03) 6228 0362 or 1800 171 882 (tollfree)
email: playgroup@playgrouptas.org.au
website: www.playgroupaustralia.com.au

Resources

FUN THINGS TO DO

Story times ➜ Travel advisory services

Playgroup is an informal session where mums, dads, grand parents, caregivers, children and babies meet together in a relaxed environment. They are community based, parent run, and usually held weekly. Playgroups are held in almost every region of Tasmania. Playgroup Tasmania is a non-profit Association which administers and supports playgroups across Tasmania. They connect families with playgroups in their area, and provide assistance for those wanting to start their own playgroup. For a low annual fee Playgroup Association members benefit from regular magazines and publications; comprehensive insurance cover for all playgroup activities; access to resource centres in Hobart, Launceston and Burnie offering toys and books for hire; member discounts for Playgroup Shop, concerts, courses, speaker's tours, resources and more.

STORY TIMES

VICTORIA

Link Educational Supplies
341 Waverley Road
Mount Waverley VIC 3149
Tel: (03) 9807 5422
website: www.linkeducational.com.au

Link Educational Supplies is an outstanding children's bookshop with experienced staff in specialised areas. Link has a large range of readers, picture books, novels and general educational materials for all levels from pre-school to Year 12. Link offers story time and activities free every Thursday during school terms between 10.30 and 11.30 am. Link welcomes children, parents, grandparents and carers. Be enchanted by stories, engaging activities and their skilled presenter. Phone or visit the website for more information.

SWIM CLASSES

VICTORIA

Learn to Swim Victoria
116 Cape Street
Heidelberg VIC 3084
Tel: (03) 9455 1330
email: learntoswimvic@optusnet.com.au
website: www.learntoswimvic.com.au

Learn to Swim Victoria turns water babies into world champions by providing a streamlined pathway from infants to competitive squads. Class sizes are small and

staff professionally qualified to ensure that your child gets the best possible tuition. They offer an 8-lane, 25m crystal-clear indoor salt water pool and ensure that both air and water temperatures are correctly maintained. Many friendships are formed at LTSV that extend beyond the swimming pool. Visit www.learntoswimvic.com.au for more details.

Life Saving Victoria
PO Box 353
South Melbourne DC VIC 3205
Tel: (03) 9676 6900
email: mail@lifesavingvictoria.com.au
website: www.lifesavingvictoria.com.au

Life Saving Victoria offers a range of programs for children and adults focusing on saving lives, preventing injuries and enjoying the water. They offer one of the most comprehensive Child & Infant CPR programs in the state, with over 100 years of experience in keeping families safe. They also offer Infant Aquatics, a program that helps in the development of your child while using the water to explore and practice safe water safety skills. For parents, they have a range of safety tip brochures under the Play It Safe by the Water program and also offer a range of first aid kits suitable for all homes and workplaces.

St. Kilda Sea Baths
10–18 Jacka Boulevard
St. Kilda VIC 3182
Tel: (03) 9525 4888
email: enquiries@southpacifichc.com.au
website: www.southpacifichc.com.au

South Pacific Swim Club offers a comprehensive learn-to-swim club catering for all levels of swimming ability and ages. The program also includes a water-safety component that provides participants with the opportunity to develop water safety and survival skills. Classes take place in the beautiful St Kilda Sea Baths, a warm sea water, 25m pool and hydrotherapy spa.

Sunshine Leisure Centre
5 Kennedy Street
Sunshine VIC 3020
Tel: (03) 9249 4615
email: sslc@brimbank.vic.gov.au
website: www.brimbank.vic.gov.au

Sunshine Leisure Centre has indoor heated swimming pools with ramp access to the program pool, beach entry and toddler play area, swimming lessons for age 6 months to adult, steam room, spa, gym, group fitness classes, crèche, café and family change rooms. For more information regarding their programs phone the centre on the number above.

QUEENSLAND

Aquatic Achievers
Cnr Old Cleveland & Tilley Roads
Chandler QLD 4155
Tel: (07) 3823 3877
Also located at:

Aspley Hypermarket
59 Albany Creek Road
Aspley QLD 4034
Tel: (07) 3863 3446
948 New Cleveland Road
Gumdale QLD 4154
Tel: (07) 3823 1091
Level 1, Sunnybank Hills Shoppingtown
Sunnybank Hills QLD 4109
Tel: (07) 3711 5252
email: chan-rec@aquaticachievers.com.au
website: www.aquaticachievers.com.au

Aquatic Achievers Solo 1 teaching program instils pride
and confidence in you and your child. Solo 1 is a unique
14-level teaching program catering for babies from 3
months to 12-year-old children. The level structure
ensures your child will progress on ability through the
14 levels and receive certificates to reward their progress
on the way. Discover the easy gentle way to water
confidence at Aquatic Achievers.

Giggles Swim School

558 Kingston Road
Kingston QLD 4114
Tel: (07) 3290 2725
email: giggleslogan@gmail.com
website: www.gouldadamspark.com.au

Giggles Swim Schools offer
water safety and swimming
skills in a fun, safe
environment using fun
accelerated lessons with new
innovative teaching techniques for babies through to
primary school children. Excellent indoor facilities,
astute professional Playmates (instructors) and an
internationally renown program using elements of NLP
and new teaching techniques ensure successes for every
child. Giggles Swim Schools also offers pool parties,
themed functions, a huge range of aquatic merchandise
and sun protection products and mobile swimming
services are available on request. Phone or email for
further information.

THEATRE SHOWS & WORKSHOPS

NEW SOUTH WALES

Puppeteria

48A Carrington Road
Randwick NSW 2031
Tel: (02) 9371 7328
Also located:
12 Denawen Avenue
Castle Cove NSW 2069
website: www.puppeteria.com

'Puppeteria' puppet theatre stages public performances
during school holidays and during term time on
weekends and on selected mornings during the week at
their two theatre locations in Sydney. Phone for further
details.

QUEENSLAND

Brisbane Arts Theatre

210 Petrie Terrace
Brisbane QLD 4000
Tel: (07) 3369 2344
email: info@artstheatre.com.au
website: www.artstheatre.com.au

Capture your child's imagination by taking them to a
live theatre experience at Brisbane Arts Theatre. The
company has earned a reputation for producing quality
theatrical productions for young children. Shows often
feature lots of singing and dancing. For a list of 2009
children's theatre shows and times please phone the
Theatre on (07) 3369 2344. Admission prices are very
reasonable. Phone or visit the website for more
information.

Livewire Theatre

Tel: 0414 536 414
email: livewiretheatre@hotmail.com

Livewire Theatre offers workshops for 3 to 17 year olds
in drama, acting, art, improvisation, clowning, circus
skills and creative writing. All sessions allow participants
to have maximum input, encouraging creativity,
independent thought, collaboration skills and, most
importantly, fun while learning. They travel everywhere.
Phone the number listed above or email for more
information.

TRAVEL ADVISORY SERVICES

NATIONAL

BYOkids

Tel: 1300 BYOkids (1300 296 543)
email: admin@byokids.com.au
website: www.byokids.com.au

www.byokids.com.au is a 700+ page online resource for
families planning a holiday. With information on family-
friendly accommodation, destinations, kids club resorts,
attractions, holiday parks, exclusive family deals and
packages within Australia or worldwide. Book online or
have a BYOkids travel consultant arrange your perfect
holiday via phone or email. Book your next family
escape from the comfort of your own home. Phone the
number above or visit their website for more
information.

Kids Holidays Online

Tel: 0408 966 101
email: peter@kidsholidaysonline.com.au
website: www.kidsholidaysonline.com.au

Kids Holidays Online is a family travel website with
accommodation, videos, guides, family travel reviews,
travel tips and travel packages. The site has information
on holidays in Fiji, Vanuatu, Cook Islands, Samoa,
Hawaii, Queensland and NSW family destinations. Visit
their website www.kidsholidaysonline.com.au for more
information.

Resources

FUN THINGS TO DO

Travel advisory services ➡ Travel destinations

Travel with Kidz

Tel: (02) 9932 4019

email: wendy@travelwithkidz.com.au

website: www.travelwithkidz.com.au

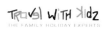

Launched in 1995 in Sydney, Travel With Kidz specialises in family holidays worldwide. Based on experience, knowledge and building relationships, Travel With Kidz has grown to be the family holiday experts. Consultants have travelled the world and offer years of family travelling experiences. They believe an informed decision eliminates the unknown factors, ensuring a successful family holiday. The series collection caters for children from 0 through to 18 years, eco tourism and multi-generational travel.

VICTORIA

Family Affair Travel

Level 9, 310 King Street

Melbourne VIC 3000

Tel: (03) 9602 2042

email: familytravel@iprimus.com.au

Family Affair Travel is a team of dedicated "travelling mothers" who have combined their parenting skills with family travel experiences. They specialise in all aspects of both domestic and international travel and with their careful pre-planning they can take the stress out of organising your holiday making it a wonderful family experience.

TRAVEL DESTINATIONS

VICTORIA

Campbell Homestead B&B

295 Toomeys Road Mardan

Mirboo North VIC 3871

Tel: (03) 5664 1282

email: inq@campbellhomestead.com.au

website: www.campbellhomestead.com.au

Set in a cottage garden, this charming country homestead, circa 1890s, is lovingly decorated creating an elegant 'old worlde charm' yet with modern amenities. Perfect romantic getaway, excellent for families and small groups. Relax by open fires, play tennis, walk and talk to farm animals. Milk a cow, pat a pig, cuddle a lamb and ride a billycart. Completely self-contained with full breakfast provisions and a moderate tariff. Two hours drive from Melbourne.

Countrywide Cottages

1205 Deans Marsh Road

Bambra VIC 3241

Tel: (03) 5288 7399

email: stay@countrywidecottages.com.au

website: www.countrywidecottages.com.au

Award winning cottages. Just 25 minutes inland from Lorne, Countrywide Cottages offers 4-star self-contained themed cottages, sleeping 5 to 8 per cottage, 27 in total. Help feed the alpacas, bunnies, and chickens. There are delightful bush walks from your door, private bonfires (outside fire season), a yabby dam and recreation area. High chair, portacot and baby bath available free of charge. Reconnect family to earth with their 'Back to Nature' platypus tour packages. Indulge yourselves with a Pamper Package. Off peak 4 midweek nights special rate. Your dogs are also very welcome, with home made doggie treats on arrival. Purpose built disabled access.

Hazelwood Cottage

105 Hazelwood Road

Warburton East VIC 3779

Tel: (03) 9882 1760 or (03) 5966 9517

website: www.visitvictoria.com.au

Hazelwood Cottage is a self-contained house on 30 acres catering for all, but in particular people with disabilities. Aids are provided including hospital beds, a hoist and a wheelchair. There are seven bedrooms, a playroom, toys, table tennis, pianola, books and games. Yarra Valley views, large garden, huge English trees, bushwalks, wonderful bird life and fern gullies. Excellent day trips, walks and bike trails. Reasonable rates. For more information visit the website listed above.

Sanctuary Park Cottages

85 Badger Avenue

Healesville VIC 3777

Tel: (03) 5962 6240

email: info@sanctuarypark.com.au

website: www.sanctuarypark.com.au

Sanctuary Park Cottages offers self-contained cottages with double spas, wood fires, undercover pool and spa, BBQ area, children's playground and beautiful gardens all set on 20 acres with picturesque views. Situated right behind Healesville Sanctuary and close to all the Yarra Valley attractions. Phone or visit the website for more information.

Seahaven Village

1–7 Geelong Road

Barwon Heads VIC 3227

Tel: (03) 5254 1066

email: info@seahavenvillage.com.au

website: www.seahavenvillage.com.au

Why not escape for the weekend to Barwon Heads. Chosen for the hit ABC series Seachange this small town has that laid back coastal lifestyle feel to it. Seahaven Village cottages have reverse cycle air-conditioning, they are cosy and well-fitted and offer family-friendly accommodation with breakfast baskets, chocolates, log fires, spas, cots, fenced garden for kids, videos, fireguards, dishwasher, BBQ, washer and dryer. Phone the number above for reservations and further information.

South Mokanger Farm Cottages
728 Mokanger Road
Cavendish VIC 3314
Tel: (03) 5574 2398
email: info@smfarmcottages.com.au
website: www.smfarmcottages.com.au

Enjoy peace and quiet on this historic farm near the Grampians. Stay in one of the self-contained cottages – cot and highchair provided. The farm is also dog friendly. Phone or visit the website for more information.

The Oaks Bed & Breakfast
20 Victoria Parade
Frankston VIC 3199
Tel: (03) 9783 2355
email: oaks@bigpond.net.au

The Oaks is a great place for a relaxing break either with the kids or without them. The Conservatory Unit has a QS bed with ensuite including corner spa, a TV and kitchen with microwave. The Courtyard Unit has two single beds and private bathroom. Gourmet continental breakfast supplies are included. The Oaks is a short walk to the Botanic Gardens, Bunarong Aquarium, the beach and pier as well as Mornington Peninsula's attractions and wineries. Special weekly rates are available. Phone for a free holiday planner to be posted to you.

NEW SOUTH WALES

Belford Cabins
659 Hermitage Road
Pokolbin NSW 2320
Tel: (02) 6574 7100
email: nappybag@belfordcabins.com.au
website: www.belfordcabins.com.au

Comfortable self-contained country cabins offering peace and privacy in a natural bushland setting. Perfect for a weekend or extended getaway for couples, or the whole family, this retreat is close to many wineries, attractions and activities and lets you enjoy the great Australian outdoors. Phone or visit the website for more information.

QUEENSLAND

Hamilton Island
PO Box 162
Hamilton Island QLD 4803
Tel: 13REEF (137333)
email: vacation@hamiltonisland.com.au
website: www.hamiltonisland.com.au

Hamilton Island is the perfect holiday destination where children can stay and eat for free when they share a room with their parents (the self-contained holiday apartments can sleep five people). Children eat for free, from an innovative menu, in some of the island's ten restaurants. The Clownfish Club offers low-cost childcare facilities for children aged from 6 weeks. Younger children stay in the safety of the colourful centre while older children embark on adventures around the island. Hamilton Island has a choice of hotels as well as privately-owned accommodation, ten restaurants, an endless array of activities and is serviced by daily flights by the major airlines. Phone the number above or visit the website for more information.

Lilyponds Holiday Park
26 Warruga Street
Mapleton QLD 4560
Tel: (07) 5445 7238
email: frogmaster@lilyponds.com.au
website: www.lilyponds.com.au

Lilyponds Holiday Park on the Blackall Range, overlooking Queensland's Sunshine Coast, is set among beautiful gardens and magnificent trees. Either enjoy one of their fully-equipped ensuite cabins (one with disabled facilities) or bring your own van and camp among the trees in their avocado orchard. Lilyponds offers the best of both worlds: rural calm and cool nights. Phone the number above or visit the website for more information.

Novotel Rockford Palm Cove Resort
Coral Coast Drive
Palm Cove QLD 4879
Tel: (07) 4059 1234
email: daycare-palmcove@rockfordhotels.com.au
website: www.novotel-pcr.com.au

The Novotel Rockford Palm Cove is a popular family resort in tropical north Queensland, 25 minutes north of Cairns. 5 to 12 year olds can enjoy a range of fun activities at Novotel Kids Club where individual abilities and interests are catered for. Typical activities include crafts, construction, sand play, water play, play dough and puzzles. Novotel Day Care hosts children between the ages of 6 weeks up to 5 years including those with special needs. The centre is fully accredited. Bookings essential. Phone or visit the website for more information.

Paradise Resort Gold Coast
122 Ferny Avenue
Surfers Paradise QLD 4217
Tel: 1800 074 111
email: book@paradiseresort.com.au
website: www.paradiseresort.com.au

Paradise Resort Gold Coast is a low-rise, tropical family resort and home to Australia's largest kids' club, a themed fantasy fun park (for 0 to 12 year-olds). Parents can relax and enjoy all the resort facilities knowing that their children are having a ball under the care of qualified minders. Phone or visit the website for more information.

Playgroup Australia

Playgroup Australia is the national peak body for playgroups. Our members are the State and Territory Playgroup Associations who administer the delivery of community and facilitated playgroup programs to around 108,000 families. It's an exciting time for playgroups in Australia. Community, parent-managed playgroups continue to thrive over 40 years since they first began in Australia. This makes the playgroup movement one of Australia's largest not-for-profit, volunteer-run organisations, with something like 1.6 million voluntary hours contributed per annum.

Through the national Supported Playgroup Program over 200 playgroups have been established, targeted at socially-isolated and disadvantaged families. Our latest national program, PlayConnect Playgroups, are for families with children with Autism Spectrum Disorders. Both of these programs receive funding from the Australian Government.

Our coordination of National Playgroup Week during March, in partnership with our member associations, results in many new families discovering the joy of playgroup. A playgroup is a group of mums, dads, grandparents and caregivers who meet together each week with their babies, toddlers and preschoolers for interaction and fun.

Recent research indicates that your baby's first three years are really important for brain development and future health and well being. Playgroups offer babies a stimulating environment to play and learn. Babies love playgroup and best of all, playgroups are fun!

Playgroup gives parents and caregivers a chance to meet to discuss ideas, problems and the joys of parenting. Many long-term friendships begin at playgroup.

Join or start a playgroup today! Call your state or territory Playgroup Association on 1800 171 882 (tollfree) or visit www.playgroupaustralia.com.au.

Birthday parties

Photograph by Lifeworks Photography, Melbourne.

Dear Polly ...

Dear Polly,

Okay, you've turned one, and here is the joke of the night. I've cooked pasta, and deposited it in one of your Bunnykins bowls on the off chance that you might eat something that is fed to you, rather than insisting on feeding yourself. I've cut up the penne and doused it in bolognaise. For a while, you let me spoon you bits, particularly if I favour the meat over the pasta, and then, again showing an independence that is well in advance of any actual ability to be independent, you scoop up the penne in your fists.

No laughs from you yet. This is all par for the course, every night of the week, fist-feeding at dinner time. But then, sensing that I might be a little hungry, you shove your fists in my mouth and drop the pasta in there. Wanting to be a sport (and frankly, because it was a pretty reasonable bolognaise made by your Granny Margaret) I eat your food. And that's when you started giggling. You dip back into the bowl for more and feed me more. By now you're in hysterics. The big guy who's slightly less appealing than Mum is eating my penne! And I'm feeding it to him! You seem to have an innate sense of the law of comedy trios, and decide to go back one more time. Again, I'm force-fed by you. Hawwwwwwww!! You can barely go on. Together we have struck comedy gold. It's surely destined to become a running gag.

I actually can't believe you are one. It's been so much fun having you around this year. That makes it sound like we've had you around for a barbecue or something, when really I'm trying to say that in an existential sense, you have changed everything — as though the world was in black and white before, and now is in colour.

When you came home from the hospital you were so adorably defenceless and tiny that Mum and I hugged you most of the day and half of the night, and it only got a bit annoying when you wanted to make it the whole of the night. Mum did most of the waking. She, after all, was pushing the drinks trolley and I had a breakfast radio alarm to contend with. I also failed to hear you on many occasions. I think that for a while there, you had a cry that was exactly the same timbre as my dreams.

Back then you loved being cuddled against a shoulder or a breast. I also adored having you lie over the crook of my elbow, and you enjoyed that position too, especially when I patted your bottom. We watched ten episodes of Band of Brothers like that, and as limbs flew from bodies and bloody battle unfolded after bloody battle, Mum did ask whether I really thought it was suitable. And I said, yep, because it was just loud bangs which you didn't yet know were scary, nor could you tell that the brave man on screen had just lost his face. It was pretty full on, come to think of it. I highly recommend seeing it once I let you, which will now be some time. You were so small and delicate, and apart from a sort of yellow flakiness on your scalp, utterly flawless.

You used to make an 'o' shape with your mouth, sort of like a prim and proper lady expressing surprise, with a touch of disapproval. It was so cute. Mum and I would stand over your change table with the camera, trying to get you to make an 'o' shape with your mouth. We might have a photo of it, but I fear that we might also have missed it.

You had an enormous head, right from the start. It was in the 99th percentile, straight off, which was bad news for your mother, because she had to birth you, and bad news for you, because of the likelihood you too will have to birth similarly big bonces when your turn comes. The good news might be however, that packed in that enormous melon of yours, is a GARGANTUAN BRAIN. Mum and I have promised ourselves that we will never become boastful parents, in Mum's case because she believes it's kind of pathetic, and in my case because my first priority has to be boasting about me. Nevertheless, in your short one year on Earth, you have already impressed me with your intellectual prowess.

Here, recorded for posterity, are some of things you already have in the 'can do' basket:

Pointing: Boy can you point. Generally you say 'ook' as you point, which we have rather ambitiously interpreted as a meaningful attempt to say 'look'. For the last three months, 'ook' has been pretty much your only repeated word, although 'gog' has emerged recently as a challenger (see below). I have tried to capitalise on your knowledge of the word 'ook' by asking you leading questions such as "what is the predominant sound in the word 'chook'?" and, "how would a cockney Englishman say the word 'hook'?". Your pointing is generally very enthusiastic, especially if you have spotted a 'gog' which we are assuming is a 'dog' although it's worth pointing out that spiders, cats, ants, flies and of course your beloved Charley Dog all get called 'gogs'.

Smiling: You knocked this over at about 5 or 6 weeks. One of the things that made you smile was me moving my mouth like a fish. Not my worst material, if I do say so myself. Now your smile is full of teeth, and half teeth, and an impending gap that you (if you could drive) could drive a truck through.

Laughing: I think the first time I ever heard you laugh was when Granny Margaret was changing you on the change table. It's an absolutely life affirming sound. Now you are one, the best ways to get you laughing include peekaboo, popping up out of the pool like a sea monster, sneezing (and saying 'sneezy', as we do after every sneeze), tummy raspberries and tickling. You also might laugh if you see something for the first time. The other day, you laughed up a riot when I held you in my arms and we chased pigeons in Johnson Park. "Gog," you said, when you finally got a grip.

Crawling: You showed signs of crawling when you were about 10 months old, which was a little slower than some of your contemporaries. When you did start, you developed a tentative one knee forward movement, and then followed it by bringing your back foot right up level with the front of your knee. Then you'd topple back into a sit, because even with your impressive flexibility, nobody can actually function like that. Your friend Dash Daalder is an even funnier crawler, doing a sort of commando thing that reminds everyone of Bruce Willis in the last scenes from Die Hard. You are now an absolute crawling whiz, and I love hearing you patter up and down the halls. Today, we played your favourite game of the moment, which is called 'Chasing'. This involves me saying the word 'chasing!' to you in an excited voice, which sets you on a frantic trip across the floorboards. Once you get to the corridor rugs, you are really moving, but I'm right there with you, because I'm 35 years older and am a fair bit better at 'chasing' than you. Then, with Charley trying to mount me (he gets excited when I get on hands and knees) and you exhausted by the sheer thrill of it all, I gobble you up in my arms. Then I turn around, and you chase me back, and just let it be said right now that I LET YOU WIN. At the moment, I think you believe you are actually catching me, but like I said before, I've got 35 years on you, and I'm a much better 'chasing' player than I'm letting on. I get a little sad playing 'chasing'

Dear Polly ...

because I know that one day soon you'll walk, and then run, and given the state of my knee and ankle cartilage, I'll never have the fun that I'm having right now.

Eating: You were a pretty good eater right from birth. You preferred one of Mum's breasts over the other, I think it was the left. Your favourite foods this year have been pumpkin, apple, sweet potato, grapes, broccoli and yes, party pies. You have worked out that meat is more fun, and annoyingly, as I mentioned above, nobody is allowed to feed you. Last night we had a tug-of-war over your rubber spoon. Me pulling as hard as I could. You pulling as hard as you could. I won, for the same reasons that I win 'chasing'. You spat it, and Mum came into the room to see what all the fuss was. Perhaps the worst extreme of your independent streak is your desire to change your own nappies. I mean to be honest, I'd be pretty goddamn happy for you to take over, but our worry is that despite your screaming and wriggling and flipping and complaining, you are not actually up to the task.

Dancing: You love to dance, particularly to Barry White and the theme from The Muppet Show. Your main move is to bop up and down in a sitting position with your arms above your head, flapping your hands. To mix things up, you sometimes throw in a variation, a sort of fists clenched in front, elbows bent, twisting at the hips manoeuvre that is popular with all who see it. If I could give you any advice, it would be to use the variation move a little more, although maybe it's the shock value that makes it such a winner.

Peekaboo: You peekabooed early, perhaps as early as 8 months. For a while, you enjoyed us doing all the hiding, but once you worked out that you could do it too, WHACKO! Who needs Hollywood when you've got peekaboo. Mum loved it when you took peekaboo to the nappy table, pulling nappies and linen and clothes up over your face, and then popping out again, grinning. Of course you are also a horrible cheat at peekaboo. Every time your hands go up to your face, we can see you split your fingers, so you can monitor just how absolutely great it's going to be when the people see you reveal yourself.

Swimming: You can't actually swim, but that doesn't stop you from crawling as fast as you can down the slope of the toddler pool at Fitzroy Pool, until I catch you, just before you disappear under the water. These are strange little suicide missions you go on, because you have yet to work out what not being able to swim means. You do let me dip your head under, however. We count to three — one, two, three, and then I blow on your face, which makes you close your eyes, and then I put you under.

Kissing: At around 6-8 months, whenever Mum and I said 'kissing' you would lean into us and make this lovely cooing little singing noise while you planted a wide open mouth on our faces. We loved this, and I sometimes try to get you to do it now, but the phase seems to have passed. Although you did kiss Mum last night. Which was beautiful.

In a year of so many highlights, it's perhaps easiest to remember the crashing lowlights — two trips to the Children's Hospital. The first occurred in November, when you were sick with gastro. You were so floppy and listless that your Aunty Sam recommended a trip to the hospital. For a while, because you didn't have diarrhoea, the doctors thought it might be a urinary tract infection, and to test for that, we had to either catch some of your urine or have it drawn out of your bladder with a big needle. Naturally the first option was the one we were hoping for, so we milled around for an hour, comforting you when you cried from the stomach pains. Eventually I saw some action down there, and dived for the catch with my pristine, glass sample catcher. "I got it, I think!" I exclaimed to your Mum, holding up the captured liquid. "I'm not sure you did," she replied, looking at the mess on the bed and the colour of the sample. Still, we had confirmation for gastro, and you were allowed to go home.

The second trip to the hospital was even more stressful. I came home from my writing office and Mum and your Aunty Char were worried about some grunting noises you were making, as if suffering from cramps again. I drove you around to Aunty Sam's house, and she immediately thought it was respiratory — that you might have swallowed something. So we were off again.

My main memory of the drive there was how distressed you were, struggling for breath, and that I got TWO CONSECUTIVE TRAINS going through the level crossing. You cried all the way until Flemington Road when suddenly you stopped crying, and started to go all floppy and listless. I panicked, reaching into the back seat to wake you up, to stop your eyelids drooping shut. Two minutes later, I'd parked in Flemington Road, had you in arms, and was dashing for emergency. (I did actually put money in the meter on the way out of the car. I'm not sure what this says about my personality, but I know it's something profound.)

The hospital staff were amazing. You were taken into a little resuss room, not because you were unconscious (you were awake again by now) but because all airways cases are treated there first. Then six doctors surrounded you, pushing and prodding while you flirted – smiling and pointing and showing off, working the crowd even in your weakened state. Then they bundled you off to X-ray, and I had to hold your little arms above your head, and keep you still while they took the pics of your tiny chest. The X-rays revealed nothing, but your breathing was still laboured, your pulse 200 and your temperature running at 40, so the respiratory specialist concluded that you did have a partially blocked airway. I tried to think what you might have swallowed — a pistachio shell was my best guess — but really, with the amount of crap from the house renovation, it could have been anything. I felt like the worst parent in the world.

The bad news kept on coming when the doctors told us that it was too late to have a bronchioscope that evening and that you'd have to stay overnight. By now Mum was with me too, and she kept asking, "what if she gets suddenly worse?" and the doctor said, "well you'll be there to let us know, and she'll be monitored, and if that happens, then she'll be operated on immediately". Needless to say, Mum didn't get a whole lot of sleep that night.

You were pretty brave getting your drip inserted, when they splinted your arm. For a while you found it amazing that it was suddenly so big and heavy. "Ook" you said to the nurses, waving your gigantic white foam arm. It was very cute, and you quickly wowed the hospital staff as well as the two little girls in the ward with you, who were struggling with the much more permanent problem of cystic fibrosis. Not surprisingly you barely slept that night, and your temperature and pulse continued to soar. When I arrived back at the hospital in the morning, it was time for surgery. Just before you went down, you gave a tired and somewhat pained sneeze. The sneeze might have done the trick, however, because the news from the bronchioscope was perplexing. There was no blockage, and no evidence of there having been a blockage. Mum had found a brown paper samosa bag on the floor at home which was missing a corner, so the final conclusion was that you ate the paper, stored it in your lung for the night (yuck, samosa breath) and then coughed it up and ate it the following morning, just before surgery. We waited in the recovery room for you to wake up, and it was so lovely getting that first cuddle.

Dear Polly ...

I'm finishing this letter a month or so after I started it. Since your birthday, your Mum and I have got married, meaning your parents are no longer living in sin. If you look at the succession rules of the British aristocracy, you'll note that kids born out of wedlock can't inherit anything from their parents. Your mother and I have decided to stick rigorously to that rule, as well as the ones about elbows on table and ripping foxes apart with hounds. This means, all our stuff will go to the other kids, if there are any. Hopefully you are reading this at an age where you can tell that I'm joking. If not, don't come crying to me. Go crying to your Mum.

The wedding was beautiful, your Mum looked amazing, and you sat in the front row and heckled. The highlight for many people was when the celebrant talked about the serious nature of the commitment, and you laughed. It was so lovely having you there.

Bubs ... have I mentioned that we sometimes call you 'Bubs'? Really, it's your Mum's name for you, and she also calls you 'Bubbsy'. I've tried to coin the nickname 'babbit' which is used for the word 'baby' in the middle section of David Mitchell's Cloud Atlas (you really should read that, I can PROMISE it's still in print and it's so great) but I'm not very good at keeping up usage on 'babbit'. It's usually just 'Polly' for me. Anyway Bubs, I really should sign off and go and write my novel which is the story of an English tabloid editor who sets up a former Premier League footballer to be part of a sex scandal. If you're an adult and it's published (likely) and still in print (unlikely), your Dad is a happy man. Even if it's not in print, which is the more likely scenario, I'm still a happy man — and that's mostly to do with being Mum's husband and your Dad.

I'll write you another letter next year. I know you are going to be so different by then. Already, you're showing signs that you want to walk. You can stand up in the middle of a room (look, no furniture!), and just two days ago you took five assisted steps with Mum holding your hand. Whenever you stand up you give yourself a clap, which normally destabilises your effort. I'm guessing that by next year, your favourite book won't be *That's Not My Kitten*. Your favourite food won't be broccoli and your favourite game won't be 'chasing'. I'll miss you, my one-year-old babbit.

All my love.

Dad

Written by Tony Wilson, author & broadcaster, www.tonywilson.com.au.

Building family traditions

Blowing candles out on a birthday cake, toasting marshmallows over a camp fire, swishing sparklers through the air on New Year's Eve, Sunday lunch with the extended family, fish and chips on Friday night …

If any of these phrases bring a smile to your face or give you a warm feeling inside, it is likely that your thoughts were turned back in time to a tradition you experienced with your family, when you were a child. Having special memories of shared experiences with a group of others, gives people a strong sense of belonging to that group. Repeated shared experiences in a family are known as family traditions.

As parents, building memories of rituals and shared experiences within the family is an important exercise to undertake. Family traditions are an opportunity to build bonds within the family. These experiences require the family's members to give something of themselves and connect with other members of the family and to foster a sense of belonging to the family as a whole. Children who grow up with a rich source of memories of shared experiences in their family of origin are more resilient to the challenges that life brings. As they grow and have challenging life experiences, the knowledge that they belonged to their family of origin and that they share enjoyable memories with these people, can place them in good stead to avoid being overwhelmed by more unhelpful life events.

Rituals and shared memories can be built around celebrations or regular events that happen at similar times each week, month, season or year. They occur many times over and the shared memory of these experiences is just as important as the experience. Building memories for your children do not have to cost money, but they will always take your time. Family traditions can be built around many experiences, but don't limit your imagination. Some ideas for family traditions are:

- Doing something regularly at the same time each week such as Sunday morning bike rides, dinner on your laps every Sunday evening, playing board games every Saturday afternoon.
- Planning a routine around family celebrations such as what you do on birthdays – singing Happy Birthday, blowing out candles on a cake, having a birthday cake.
- A regular meal with the extended family such as Sunday roast at grandma's.
- Regular holidays at the same place with the same group of people.
- Sitting together around an open fire when the weather is cold.

For families that have had a change in structure, such as where a two-parent family has become a one parent family or vice versa, it may be helpful to keep the traditions of the family so all members have a sense of continuity. Over time it can be useful to re-examine the traditions of the original family and develop new rituals that give a sense of identity to the new family. It is easy to assume the family will continue to do things as before, but at times this will not be possible or desirable. Formulating traditions help develop the family's identity and bond the new members together through their shared experience.

Take note of the things your children enjoy doing with the family. Those that they repeat in conversation with each other and other adults may well be the events that you can repeat regularly and develop into traditions which strengthen their sense of belonging to you.

Written by Bronwyn Thomas, a social worker with more than 20 years experience working with families over parenting issues. She works as a counsellor at Parentline. Parentline is a confidential telephone counselling, information and referral service for all Victorian parents and carers with children aged from birth to 18 years. Parentline is accessible from anywhere in Victoria for the cost of a local call (excluding mobiles). Phone 13 22 89.

Fabulous kids' parties

Anyone can host a kids' party, but it doesn't take too much effort to make your child's party a fabulous event which will be the talk of the playground for the year to come.

'Fabulous' doesn't mean an over-the-top extravaganza costing hundreds running into thousands of dollars. The key is to find a theme, stick to it and make a plan. Write down everything you need to do, make or bake. Do whatever you can before the big day so you'll be organised and relaxed.

Let your child's interests inspire you when choosing your theme. This could be as simple as a favourite animal, place, activity, or even a colour. Be creative with your invitations, table decorations, lolly bags and props.

Decorated tiny noodle boxes make wonderful treasure boxes instead of lolly bags for a pirate themed party. Instead of a regular table cloth, lay down brown craft paper and draw a treasure map across the length of the table, incorporating the guests' names in the map's landmarks. Make a pirate patch for each guest, or even newspaper pirate hats …

If going to a café is your child's favourite treat, recreate one at home. Line little tables with white paper and have a jar of crayons instead of sugar sticks laid out on the table. You could draw an outline of a placemat at each place and let the kids decorate their own spot. Make party menus on the computer for each table. Have aprons for any parent helpers to wait on the tables. Use take-away containers or bags for the take-home party bags.

If you are raising a budding artist, you might like to use a long roll of paper, either hung or laid on the ground, supply pots of paint and brushes and let the guests make a Happy Birthday mural for your child. If you're going to do a messy activity like this, ask your guests not to wear their best party outfits and to bring an art smock if you are not supplying them! You might also have other craft activities set up at tables, such as making a small cardboard photo frame, and you could supply each guest with a photo of them with the party host as a keepsake of your fabulous event.

If you are hosting a small group, you might like to consider a cooking party, and let the guests cook their own party food before they devour it. Mini pizzas, cupcakes, fruit salad and sausage rolls are simple enough fare. Instead of lolly bags, wrap the goodies in a tea towel tied with ribbon, and include a miniature kitchen utensil, such as a cookie cutter or whisk. Invitations could be written on the back of a wooden spoon.

Incorporate the theme into all aspects of the party, from the invitations and decorations, to food and games, and of course, the cake. Decorate tables with plain paper overlaid with inexpensive coloured tissue paper to match your theme. Hats or masks add another dimension to the fun, and can be made quite easily or bought from party suppliers.

Brainstorm all of your ideas onto paper. Start with a general list of your child's interests and expand from there. Some themes to get you started might be magic, farm, zoo, dancing, glamour, football, beach, fairies, pink, gardening, cats and so on.

Try to be different, the possibilities are endless. Let your imagination run wild, and sit back and watch as your little one hosts the unique event of the season!

Written by Rose Alexander, freelance writer.

Vox Pop

We asked a number of women and men around Australia to send in their advice, tips and personal experiences on a range of topics so that you have an insight into how others cope being a new parent. We hope you find their comments interesting, informative and reassuring. Vox Pop biographies: page 652

Kerri Harding
Mum of one, VIC

My son's birthday last year was the first 'official' birthday party we have thrown; we sent out invitations and invited quite a few of his friends. Before this, it had always been family and just a couple of friends. We found that once he started kindergarten and was regularly invited to other children's birthday parties throughout the year, he too wanted to have a party and invite his friends.

At a young age, regardless of how much or how little money you choose to spend on your child's party, they will have a ball whatever you organise. Children make fun out of nothing when there are a few of them together. We have been to quite a few backyard parties at people's homes and they are no less enjoyable than those that are held at a play centre or any other venue. The important thing is to do something that you are comfortable with and not end up in debt over it. Sometimes I think it is too easy for parents to get caught up in the competitiveness of who can throw the best party for their child.

Jumping castles and all the old favourites such as pin the tail on the donkey, pass the parcel, musical chairs, treasure hunts and piñatas are always popular party games if you choose to have something at home. Indoor play centres are a very popular option among my son's friends and have the added bonus of minimal organisation and being able to walk out and leave all the mess behind you. We have also been to quite a few parties held at local playgrounds and one at a local animal farm. Adding a dress-up theme to any of these also seems to be very popular!

I have seen some fantastic home-made birthday cakes – personally I don't have the patience to tackle my own masterpiece but if you are that way inclined, the possibilities are endless as to what you can create. As for party food, the usual party pies and sausage rolls, fairy bread, cocktail frankfurts and potato chips still seem to be as popular as ever. Healthier alternatives such as sandwiches and fruit kebabs also seem to go down well.

Martine Pekarsky
Mum of two, Melbourne

Okay, so I am a self-confessed party junkie and have been buying party books for years. So our first birthday was a Pirate party, and the second birthday was a Jungle party. Everyone got dressed up and the themes are just so much fun. We are thinking about doing something special at the Botanical Gardens for the twins' third birthday, or maybe Cowboys and Indians at home again. That's a downside of having twins … only being able to have one party a year!

Anastasia Jones
Mum of two, Melbourne

For us the 'silly season' – the months of December and January – are full of birthdays and specials events. In addition to Christmas and New Year we have two children's birthdays, two grandparent birthdays, and a wedding anniversary.

If I am going to organise a party for any of our silly season occasions I notify people in October so that they can put it in their diary and I don't get the usual response "I am so partied out – I have had a Christmas Party every day this week, I just don't think I can do another!" My girls are still young so I haven't organised too many. Last year we hired a playroom for a couple of hours and let the kids play with the toys in the room.

Regarding food, I went to a party where spaghetti was served first before the lollies and cake came out. The kids didn't care – they wanted to play and enjoy the balloons and confetti all over the place and no big deal was made of it. They ate as much as they wanted and then they went and played.

I also read that someone organised a party for their child and linked up with a charity, explaining on the invite that the baby had many toys and donations to the charity would be appreciated instead of a gift. What a great idea for a baby party!

Christine Walsh
Mum of two, Broome

For both my children's first birthday party we held a party and invited our closest friends and relatives. For my daughter's party we just had chicken and an assortment of salads. At this stage we didn't have too many friends with children. A friend decorated the backyard with fairies and butterflies and it looked absolutely gorgeous. I made a butterfly cake from the *Women's Weekly Birthday Cake* book and I made a small round cake 'smash' cake for my daughter.

By the time it was my son's first birthday party we had quite a few friends with toddlers so we hired a bouncy castle. This was great as it kept the kids entertained for most of the party. We played two games, the first being an animal hunt where the kids found scattered plastic animals around the yard. I also bought a string piñata and put lollies and balloons inside. All the kids held one string and on the count of 1, 2, 3 they all pulled the string and the contents fell out. We had a sausage sizzle and salads for food. The cake was a 'construction' cake keeping with the bouncy castle theme of Bob the Builder. Instead of lolly bags I purchased bubbles that were on a string necklace and the lid had a whistle. The kids loved it but the parents were cursing me on the ride home.

For my daughter's second birthday I was heavily pregnant so we took the easy option and had a party at an indoor playgym centre. This time we only invited our friends that had children. The climbing structures and ball pit kept the kids busy the whole time. Food was catered by the centre including tea and coffee for the mums and dads. So the only thing I had to worry about was the cake and lolly bags. At $10 a head it was a bargain!

My daughter's third birthday party was a Teddy Bear's picnic. We had teddy bears (painted by my daughter) hung around the decking area. There were paw prints leading from the driveway to the party and lots of balloons. The kids sat on a picnic rug on the ground. There was an assortment of food such as teddy bear fairy bread (using a cookie cutter cut out teddy shaped bread and put chocolate sprinkles on), teddy bear paw print cupcakes, teacups, tiny teddies and some hot food. The kids had all brought a teddy with them and did a bear hunt around the yard looking for animal stickers. We also played pass the bear – when the music stopped the child holding the bear got a small prize. The children had a lovely time and enjoyed the teddy bear cake. I really enjoyed planning this party and found a lot of ideas on the internet. I am starting to think about a joint party for my children next year … now I just have to decide on a theme!

Melanie Smoothy
Mum of one, NSW

For Brayden's first birthday I set out to plan the perfect party. I envisaged cooking skills to leave Gordon Ramsay envious and our house being presented as though it were for a *Better Homes & Gardens* photo shoot.

What actually happened were last minute cancellations, a range and quantity of food that exceeded the number of guests attending, and atrocious weather that was far from the clear and sunny day I'd envisaged!

The weather quickly turned cold and windy and I was doing my best to remain dignified while chasing decorations, balloons, and party utensils across our backyard. After admitting defeat, my perfectly planned sun-filled outdoor party was moved inside.

Sure, his party was different to what I had planned, but I soon realised it was perfect just the way it was – we were surrounded by family and friends who we love and mean the most to us and who had come to celebrate his birthday (not to inspect my presentation or party planning skills). Realistically, cancellations and unpredictable weather are factors which are bound to happen, some things are simply beyond your control.

Vox Pop

We asked a number of women and men around Australia to send in their advice, tips and personal experiences on a range of topics so that you have an insight into how others cope being a new parent. We hope you find their comments interesting, informative and reassuring. Vox Pop biographies: page 652

For Brayden's second birthday we were much the wiser! We chose to have dinner in a restaurant on the day of his birthday and we visited an animal nursery the following day, and guests had the opportunity to attend either or both celebration, according to their time commitments.

Cindy Fraser
Mum of three, Melbourne

We have kept birthdays in our house fairly low key celebrating them mainly with family at home. Our son had his first big party for his fifth birthday earlier this year. The idea of having a crowd of noisy 5-year-olds tear through my house did not appeal, so we opted to have it at a play centre and limit his guests to 10 friends (including his siblings). I highly recommend doing this and believe it was money well spent. A basic party provided us with a private party room, food and drink, and games and activities. We opted to supply our own cake as our son had thoughtfully requested a 'Hot wheels car cake' (and making that was another story!). We worked out that we would have spent at least half of what we did if we had done it ourselves, only this way we were able to enjoy the party because everything was organised for us and at the end we got to walk away from the mess.

Danielle Murrihy
Mum of two, Melbourne

For the twins' first birthday we made a big deal and invited a lot of people, but for their second and third birthday we kept it low key; we actually were away for both birthdays so we spent it with family interstate. The boys have been to a few birthdays and they now realise about parties, birthday cakes, presents and singing Happy Birthday and blowing out the candles. At three they didn't really understand the party games, but I am sure their fourth birthday will be a lot more exciting!

Leanne Cummins
Mum of two, NSW

I have volunteered as a Joey Scout leader over the past two years, and it has given me great insight into how kids want to be entertained! It gives you great satisfaction when you hear from one of the kids at 'your' birthday party say "this is the best birthday party I've been to" and I've heard it from the last four parties in a row (okay, my head is swelling!)

My secrets:

Put a theme on the party, and vary the theme of the games to go with the party.

Use the same old games that kids love and play at school.

Include a craft and let them do something they're not allowed to do at home.

Favourite games:

Pin the tail on the donkey: we have turned this into 'pin the tiara on the princess' (Princess party), 'pin the sword on Mallory' (spiderwick party), 'pin the mummy on the sarcophagus' (ancient Egyptian party), and 'pin the bat in the tree' (scary party).

Duck, duck, goose: variations have included 'frog, frog, prince' (princess), 'sprite, sprite, goblin' (spiderwick), 'pyramid, pyramid, tomb' (Egypt), and 'ogre, ogre, witch' (scary)

Obstacle courses are always great. Get the kids to go over, under, around, and they are not allowed to fall off the tightrope (on the ground), and then they get to find some kind of sword on the way through and attack the baddy at the other end (that's what they aren't usually allowed to do at home!). The baddy is a cardboard cutout from a box – the kids can draw their own character. The prince might kill a dragon or a witch, the kids can kill a goblin at the spiderwick party, the pharaoh might kill a crocodile at the river Nile, or the tunnel could have anything dark and scary at the end in a scary party.

Cake and food – the best part! Themed cakes are so easy... bake an ordinary everyday cake, ice it, and add a toy and candles (the kids don't care!). Our cakes have included: the princess party had a castle and we used upturned icecream cones for the turrets with paper flags on toothpicks; spiderwick had a big blob of red 'wax' to seal it (like the book in the movie) and sour red lollies for the tape around the cake (kids fought over it); and the Egyptian party was the best – no cake, just pile lamingtons into a step pyramid!

Your kids will love to help you plan the theme and the games. They have great imaginations and if you have an older child, they can invite a friend and run the whole party for you!

Great party ideas sourced from www.partykids.com.au

Wake up surprise: Start the birthday off right with a wonderful wake up surprise. When your child falls asleep decorate their room with a bunch of balloons and a Happy Birthday banner. You could also decorate the breakfast table with balloons on the back of chairs and streamers or confetti on the table.

Keep the party simple: Keep the number of guests down and more than likely your party will run a lot smoother. Inviting every child in the class is only inviting a couple of hours of chaos for you. This is especially true for sleepovers. The tried and true method of the number of guests is the age of the child. So a five-year-old would have five guests – you can always add a couple of extra guests but if you stick close to this number things will be easier.

Lootbag twist: Instead of the usual take home lollybag try using party hats turned upside down and lined with a napkin. They can be filled with lollies ready to take home and when all the lollies are gone the guests have a fun hat to use! Also a nice idea is to attach a thank you note from the birthday child on each lollybag, thanking each child for their gift and for attending.

First birthdays: A great idea to make a first birthday special is to have a time capsule party. All guests have to bring something to put in the capsule. You can video everyone explaining what they are putting in and why. Then put the tape in the time capsule as well. Recover the capsule for their 18th birthday and relive some wonderful memories.

Ice-cream birthday cake: To save on mess and the expense of plates if you are having an ice-cream cake, simply scoop some cake into an ice-cream cone for each party guest. Place a marshmallow in the bottom of each cone to stop ice-cream dripping out the bottom.

Icebreaker party game: Fill a jar with jellybeans and when each guest arrives they have to guess how many there are. The closest wins the whole jar to take home. Don't announce the winner until the end of the party. This is a great party game for keeping kids busy while waiting for everyone to arrive.

Squeak squeak: All children sit in a circle with one child blindfolded and standing in the middle. Spin the one in the middle around 3 times, they then go round the circle, sit on one of the others laps and say "squeak squeak", the other player must "squeak squeak" like a piggy. If they guess whose lap they are sitting on the one sitting goes into the middle. Make sure that each time someone new goes into the middle everyone moves places.

Bubble walk: Take a length of bubble wrap packaging material (available from most post offices). The length should be around 2 metres long. The players take turns walking the length of the bubble wrap. The first one to walk the entire length without popping any bubbles is the winner. This game is a lot of fun.

Catch me if you can: The party guests form a large circle facing inwards. Each player is given a number. One player stands in the centre keeping the broom upright by resting the palm of his hand on the top. The player in the centre calls out a number and removes his hand. The player whose number is called tries to catch the broom before it hits the ground. If that player manages to catch it they take their place in the centre, otherwise the original player stays in the centre.

Number hunt: Give each person a sheet of newspaper from the classified section and a pen. On the word go each person has two minutes to find and circle as many numbers that match the age of the birthday child. Most numbers wins.

Resources

These Resources pages list products and services relevant to "Birthday parties".
To make your life easier as a parent, editorial listings have been grouped into sub categories.
Businesses then appear alphabetically under a national or a state-based subhead depending on reach.

SUB-CATEGORIES

BIRTHDAY PARTY ENTERTAINMENT

NATIONAL

Jumping J-Jays Castles & Slides
Australia-wide
Tel: 1300 CASTLE (1300 227 853)
email: enquiries@partycastles.com
website: www.partycastles.com.au

When you hire a jumping castle from Jumping J-Jays Castles & Slides you will get the world's safest inflatable games that will allow your kids to jump all day safely. Jumping J-Jays began hiring inflatable bouncy castles over 10 years ago and take pride in providing party castles that are colourful for any birthday party at home or to a much wider audience including store openings, christenings, open days, corporate events and fetes. The children are safe with inflatable front safety barriers, full inflatable side walls and sun shade. The range includes: traditional castles, combos (castle and slide), actives (combo and interactive mouth), slides and the new falling floor. Visit the website for amazing 3D virtual tours.

VICTORIA

Dinosaur Diggers
Tel: (03) 9571 6626
email: sandra@dinosaurdiggers.com.au
website: www.dinosaurdiggers.com.au

If you have ever wanted to have something special for your child's birthday party then why not get Dinosaur Diggers to bring museum quality exhibits to your home or venue and run an amazing show. They start with an interactive presentation on fossils and dinosaurs where the children get to touch everything they bring with them. A fossil dig follows the presentation – the children get to find, identify and keep real fossils. They also get a "budding paleontologist" certificate at the end of the party. Dinosaur Diggers also performs an educational series as a pre-school or school incursion.

Fire Engine Rides
PO Box 1111
Waverley Gardens VIC 3170
Tel: (03) 9795 0714
website: www.fireengines.com.au

Birthday parties have to be interesting and in 158 suburbs in Melbourne that's where Firefighter Rob arrives in his bright shiny red 1940s vintage Fire Engine and stays for 45 minutes minimum. The children (2 plus years) can be shown over the engine, go for a ride or two and, for the adventurous, squirt the hoses! Children will be told stories about the engine and will receive colouring-in pages by Weg. They also now have an online Firefighters Party Shop. Visit www.fireengines.com.au for further information.

Myuna Farm Mobile Ark
82 Magpie Road
Clematis VIC 3782
Tel: (03) 5968 4713
Myuna Farm Mobile Ark can be hired to bring 25 to 30 farm animals out to events across Melbourne. Let your children cuddle and feed farm animals with friendly staff supervision at your next children's birthday party.

Pinnacle Puppet Theatre
Tel: (03) 9727 2347
email: mariam1955@bigpond.com
The Pinnacle Puppet Theatre presents entertainment for children from 3 years of age and upwards at your venue, home or hall or anywhere else. Their 20 years of experience covers everything from birthday and Christmas parties to music festivals. There is always a lot of interaction between puppets and children and their stories always have an unexpected 'twist' in the plot.

Wild Action
PO Box 253
Macedon VIC 3440
Tel: 0419 385 245
email: waction@netspace.net.au
website: www.wildaction.com.au
Wild Action is the zoo that comes directly to you. Learn about the fascinating world of Australian wildlife. Smile at a live salt water crocodile, cuddle a python snake, hold a turtle or green tree frog, laugh at a goanna lizard, tickle a joey kangaroo, chat with a rainbow lorikeet and much more at your child's next birthday party.

NEW SOUTH WALES

Fancy Faces
Tel: 0414 505 982 or (02) 9634 8119
email: littlegrippers@live.com.au
website: www.natsfancyfaces.spaces.live.com/photos
Create a world of fantasy for your child's next birthday party with beautiful butterflies, flower fairies, pretty princesses and many more. Natalee will light up your party with beautiful face art, temporary tattoos, cheek art and glitter the works and a photo of each of your guests emailed to the host. Only quality professional face and body paint used, safe and hygienic. To book phone Natalee on 0414 505 982 or email littlegrippers@live.com.au.

Go Seek
Tel: (02) 9388 2361
email: info@goseek.com.au
website: www.goseek.com.au

Go Seek is a funky and vibrant children's entertainment group well known for their unique and exciting entertainment packages including: interactive, musical stage shows; kids birthday parties; fun games workshops; face painting; roving characters and powerful and catchy award-winning songs (and music CDs). A fantastic explosion of colour, movement and funky music, Go Seek take children on a musical journey of discovery and adventure, educating and entertaining through exciting themes, catchy tunes, bright funky costumes, clever props, imaginative story lines and high-energy routines. Go Seek perform their interactive, adventure-filled shows and workshops at festivals, clubs, schools, child care centres, corporate functions, Christmas parties, family fun days, shopping centres, birthday parties and special events in NSW, Victoria, Queensland and ACT.

Kindifarm
PO Box 11
Terrey Hills NSW 2084
Tel: (02) 9970 8708
website: www.kindifarm.com
Kindifarm offers a country encounter that lasts forever where children of all ages are encouraged to interact with animals. This team of farmyard friends includes lambs, kids and a calf for the children to bottle feed, a piglet, sheep and goats for hand feeding as well as baby chicks, a duck and bunny rabbits the children are able to pat and cuddle. With over 16 years experience Kindifarm loves visiting parties, kindergartens, playgroups, schools and fetes all year round.

AUSTRALIAN CAPITAL TERRITORY

Jelly Bean Amusements
12/43 Bayldon Road
Queanbeyan NSW 2620
Tel: 1300 136 825
website: www.jba.net.au
Jelly Bean Amusements takes the hassle out of having a party. Since their establishment in 1999 they have participated in over 1,800 parties, corporate functions and other events. Jelly Bean Amusements will entertain the children at the venue of your choice at any time of the day or night. All rides are fully supervised from the time they arrive to the time they pack up. There are packages suitable for any party or event and free entertainment for fundraising events.

QUEENSLAND

Livewire Theatre
Tel: 0414 536 414
email: livewiretheatre@hotmail.com
Give your child a special day to remember with over 60 male and female characters to choose from with Livewire Theatre. Suitable for all ages with fully themed games, interactive storytelling, balloon sculpting, facepainting, stilts and circus acts, jumping castles, amusements and more. Servicing all of Brisbane, Sunshine Coast, hinterland and surrounds.

Resources

BIRTHDAY PARTIES

Birthday party entertainment
➔ Birthday party invitations & cards

WESTERN AUSTRALIA

Face Painting Fun & Games
PO Box 450
Fremantle PLB WA 6959
Tel: 0402 933 161
website: www.facepainting.net.au

Face Painting is all about having fun. At Face Painting Fun & Games they provide a fun way of opening up children's creativity and encourage their freedom of expression. With imagination a few strokes of paint transforms a child's world and creates a 'theatre of the face'. Face Painting Fun and Games are available for theme birthdays, festivals, shopping centres, schools and your special event. Phone or visit the website for further information.

Fire Engine Fun
PO Box 261
Inglewood WA 6932
Tel: 0413 569 698
website: www.fireenginefun.com.au

With Fire Engine Fun you can have a genuine 1960 retired fire engine visit your child's next birthday party. Fireman Kevin has a one-hour program that includes an interactive story, squirt the fire hose game, rides for the family and a fire fighter certificate with a photo for the birthday child. Kevin has a 'Working with Children' clearance and their vehicles are transport-approved with annual licence checks. Visit their website at www.fireenginefun.com.au for pictures and further information.

SOUTH AUSTRALIA

Animal Capers
Metro & country areas
Tel: (08) 8557 4240 or 0423 106 580
email: animalcapers@aapt.net.au
website: www.animalcapers.com.au

Animal Capers come to you, inside or out, day and night. You can invite 8 animals of your choice including an owl, bandicoot, possum, lizard, frog and rabbit and experience the tame and friendly native and farm animals. Children will get to touch, hold and sometimes feed these amazing animals. Animal Capers caters for all age groups and provides lots of fun and education. Available for birthday parties, playgroups, child care centres or kindergartens. Phone, email or visit the website www.animalcapers.com.au for further information.

Animals Anonymous
Mobile Service
Tel: (08) 8388 5104
email: info@animalsanonymous.com.au
website: www.animalsanonymous.com.au

Animals Anonymous' native bush friends come to you in a fun and fascinating hands-on wildlife show featuring gliders, goannas, potoroos, pythons and much more. They bring 10-15 friendly, hand-reared native Australian animals and one fun-loving, passionate presenter. All ages and all areas catered to suit your needs. Email or visit the website for further information.

BIRTHDAY PARTY FOOD

NATIONAL

Caluna Loves
Tel: (03) 9974 0552 or 0402 333 291
email: info@calunaloves.com.au
website: www.calunaloves.com.au

If you are planning a birthday party or celebration, Caluna Loves can create wonderful decorative icing pictures to top your cake or your favourite photo can be transferred onto a sheet of icing. Visit www.calunaloves.com.au for further details.

VICTORIA

Borg's Cakes
20 Harrington Square
Altona VIC 3018
Tel: (03) 9398 3783
email: borgs.cakes@optusnet.com.au

Borg's Cakes has cakes for birthday parties as well as helium-filled balloons, party food, party goods and handmade pastizzi and ravioli. A delivery service is available 7 days to all suburbs. Email for further information.

NEW SOUTH WALES

Crumbs Cake Art
10 Blue Gum Road
Annangrove NSW 2156
Tel: (02) 9679 1808
email: sales@crumbscakeart.com.au
website: www.crumbscakeart.com.au

Specialising in delicious, customised cakes to complement the theme of your special event, the team of talented cake designers creates cakes to suit your tastes and requirements. You may also decide to have a sculpture made out of cake in the theme of your event. Indulge in a delectable mudcake (24 varieties), or a classic fruitcake, decorated with elegance and flair. For a contemporary edge, Crumbs Cake Art can create stunning cupcake towers or little individual cakes. Delivery available in the Sydney area. Phone and arrange an appointment at their studio or visit the website for further information.

BIRTHDAY PARTY INVITATIONS & CARDS

NATIONAL

Announcements & Invitations by Little Dance

Tel: (03) 9752 6602
email: enquiries@littledanceinvitations.com
website: www.littledanceinvitations.com

Announcements & Invitations by Little Dance specialise in beautiful photo invitations for birthdays, Christmas and other special and fun occasions. They offer an original range of invitations from funny to stylish, classic designs as well as RSVP cards, place cards and bomboniere tags, also fantasy art and photo montages. Announcements & Invitations by Little Dance create gorgeous photo memory gifts.

BoscoBear

Tel: 1300 BOSCOB
email: info@boscobear.com.au
website: www.boscobear.com.au

BoscoBear is an exciting Australian brand that has a fabulous range of products designed to celebrate children's colourful imaginations. These bright and lively products include removable room art, personalised labels, party invitations and stationery products. They have been designed to stimulate and engage a child's inquisitive nature and each theme has been carefully researched, designed and illustrated by their very experienced design team.

cardamon seed

Tel: (03) 9383 3247
email: info@cardamonseed.com.au
website: www.cardamonseed.com.au

cardamon seed makes it easy for you to have birth announcement cards for your new baby using your own photos. Their designs are original and can be changed to suit your taste. Their website displays a range of card designs to choose from for birth announcements, thank you cards, christening invitations, Christmas cards, birthday and wedding invitations. All you need to do is send them a photo by email and then choose the design you like, the message and quantity. Within 24 hours they will email you a proof for your approval, before sending your cards to print. The cardamon seed service takes between 5 to 10 working days from the time you order through to receipt of your cards. The cards are available nationally and internationally. Visit their website or phone for further information.

Creative Cards

Tel: (03) 9873 4081
email: info@creativecards.com.au
website: www.creativecards.com.au

Creative Cards specialise in creating personalised, beautiful and unique photo cards using your photo and words. Their high quality yet affordable range includes, birth announcements, thank you cards, birthday invitations, Christmas cards and much more. Simply choose from the wide range of gorgeous designs, email a photo from your collection, write your own words or choose theirs and let them do the rest. Your personalised cards and free envelopes will be returned to you within 10 days. Available nationally.

Designed with Love

email: designedwithlove@bigpond.com
website: www.designedwithlove.com.au

Designed with Love offers beautiful, affordable stationery for all of your child's events – birth announcements, christening invitations, birthday invitations and much more. Each is personalised with your photos and many different colour combinations. Starting at only $1 each.

Designer Photo Cards

Tel: 0412 579 599
email: enquiry@designerphotocards.com.au
website: www.designerphotocards.com.au

Designer Photo Cards design customised cards for special occasions and they also offer standard designs as well. Designer Photo Cards can be created for just about anything – announcements, invitations, greetings and thank you cards. Once you've purchased a customised design it is yours to do what you like with. Some people like to use their design to make matching mugs, calendars, mouse-mats – the possibilities are endless.

InkPink Design

Tel: 0407 545 925
email: cards@inkpinkdesign.com.au
website: www.inkpinkdesign.com.au

Kick off your party plans or announce your new baby in style with a personalised photo greeting card that will grab the attention of your guests when they receive it and can be added to the family photo album after the event is over. InkPink Design can create invitation and announcement designs for all occasions: baby showers, baby birth announcements, christenings and naming days, birthdays and thank-you cards. Cards come with optional magnets on the back, envelopes and folding cards. Enlargement prints of photo collages and family keepsake designs are also available.

Inviting Invitations

Tel: (02) 9999 6597
email: enquiries@invitinginvitations.com.au
website: www.invitinginvitations.com.au

Inviting Invitations sells unique, personalised baby invitations and cards. The range includes baby shower invitations, birth announcement cards, christening invites, birthday party invitations and cards. You can also customise your own unique and personalised invitations and cards with your child's photo. Prices range from $2.95 including envelopes and delivery Australia wide within 7 days.

Label Kingdom

Tel: 1800 264 549
email: info@labelkingdom.com.au
website: www.labelkingdom.com.au

Add a little sparkle to your birthday with a new range of

Resources

BIRTHDAY PARTIES

Birthday party invitations & cards
➡ Birthday party suppliers: online

invitations from Label Kingdom. With a wide range
now available which include birthday invitations, baby
shower and bridal shower invitations, BBQ invitations,
they even supply 'Just Moved' notes plus much more.
Label Kingdom's invitations are bright and colourful,
and they also come with magnets which can be stuck
onto the back of your invite so once your guests receive
their special invitation they can display it on the fridge.
Invitations are also supplied with envelopes as well.
Label Kingdom is a proud Australian family business.
Free postage within Australia and New Zealand. Email
or visit the website for further information.

Mini Ink
Tel: 0408 936 031
email: design@miniink.com.au
website: www.miniink.com.au

Mini Ink creates individually designed birthday cards.
These cards aim to make parents, family and friends
smile, as well as convey a message of joy or an invitation
to celebrate, using your own personal photos of your
special little one. Each contemporary and stylish baby
card is custom created and printed onto archive quality
photo paper, then delivered to your door ready to make
a big impression. Visit www.miniink.com.au for more
information.

Photocards
email: lexandscott@unwired.com.au
website: www.photocards.ueuo.com

Photocards custom design the perfect photo
announcement, invitation or greeting card for birthday
parties, farewells, thank-you cards, baby showers, birth
announcements, christenings and baptisms,
congratulations, anniversaries, graduations, change of
address, Christmas cards, engagements, weddings,
kitchen teas, hens nights and much more. Visit the
website for further information.

Stationery Online
Tel: 1800 501 075
email: sales@stationeryonline.com
website: www.stationeryonline.com.au

Stationery Online offers a great range of invitations and
accessories in fun colours and designs that kids will love.
Make your next party special with themes that will
excite little ones (and parents). Choose from designs
such as fairies, pirates, trains, butterflies, rockets and
more. Available in traditional or magnetic formats. View
and order online or phone for further information. They
deliver anywhere in Australia.

BIRTHDAY PARTY PLANNERS

NATIONAL

Children's Parties
email: email@childrensparties.com.au
website: www.childrensparties.com.au

Planning a child's party? Looking for ideas to entertain
them? Then check out the Children's Parties' website.
With specialised pages on themes, food and games they
can find a solution for all your questions when planning
your child's next birthday party.

BIRTHDAY PARTY SUPPLIERS: ONLINE

NATIONAL

Belles Familles
Tel: (02) 9684 6605
email: enquiry@bellesfamilles.com.au
website: www.bellesfamilles.com.au

Belles Familles is proud to offer you
over 1,000 interesting and practical
products all of which have been
tested in their own family. From
baby showers to christenings, first
birthdays and beyond visit Belles Familles' website to
see the full range and sign up for the newsletter while
you are there. Phone orders are also welcome.

Complete Party Boxes
Tel: 1300 668 619
email: customerservice@completepartyboxes.com.au
website: www.completepartyboxes.com.au

Complete Party Boxes has the
ultimate in children's party supplies.
Visit their website and see their divine
meal boxes and party favor boxes –
they have plates, cups, napkins, invitations, party favors,
sweets and much more. Their complete party packs will
take the hassle out of shopping around for all the
different items – Complete Party Boxes has put all your
party needs together and will deliver them to your door.
Quality products and excellent service.

Folding Tables Direct Pty Ltd
Tel: (02) 9700 0605
email: sales@foldingtables.com.au
website: www.foldingtables.com.au

Buy or hire child-height folding tables and chairs for
parties and art and craft activities. Various styles and
sizes available to hire (Sydney only) or buy (delivery
Australia wide). Student desks and adult height furniture
also available. Visit their website for further information.

Fun in the Sack
Tel: 1300 731 727
email: info@funinthesack.com.au
website: www.funinthesack.com.au

Fun in the Sack provides fun outdoor activities and
games that will keep everyone entertained while playing

outside together during a birthday party or a family outing. Many activities are old favourites that you will remember from when you were little such as the three-legged races or the jumping sack, jumping with all your might as you head for the finish line. They can make it easy for you to organise a child's birthday party or structured activities for a group by providing you with clear instructions to get everyone joining in – even the grown-ups.

Gorgeous Little Parties Pty Ltd
Tel: (03) 9499 7944
email: shop@gorgeouslittleparties.com.au
website: www.gorgeouslittleparties.com.au

Create that perfect little princess or super hero party with an array of gorgeous party products and accessories. Gorgeous Little Parties offer the coolest themed party products including invitations, plates, cups, balloons, treat bags, pinatas, games, tattoos, stickers, masks and much more. Simply visit the online store and browse the huge range of fully co-ordinated party themes: www.gorgeouslittleparties.com.au.

gorgeousgifts.com.au
Tel: 0418 218 151
email: admin@gorgeousgifts.com.au
website: www.gorgeousgifts.com.au

Gorgeousgifts.com.au supplies an amazing line up of fancy dress-ups as well hand-made themed bedroom furnishings. Browse their full range of fairy, princess, prince and pirate costumes online as well as ranges of exclusive hand-decorated pillows, wall hangings and bed linen that your little dreamers will love. Furnishings can be personalised and all orders are shipped within 7 days.

Groovy Kids Parties
Tel: (08) 9315 1004
email: admin@groovy-kids-parties.com
website: www.groovy-kids-parties.com

Groovy Kids Parties is a free resource site for kids birthday party ideas, novelty birthday cakes recipes (with photos and instructions), kids birthday party games, party themes, birthday party planning, free birthday party invitations, free printable drawings and much more.

Kids Theme Parties
email: kidsthemeparties@bigpond.com
website: www.kidsthemeparties.com.au

Kids Theme Parties have party supplies for all types of parties and can deliver to your door anywhere in Australia. Some of the themes include Dora, Elmo, Princess, Transformers, Ben 10, Sesame Street and many more. Email or visit the website for more information.

Magic in the Kitchen
Tel: 0413 914 337
email: info@magicinthekitchen.com.au
website: www.magicinthekitchen.com.au

Be inspired to host your kids cooking party using Magic in the Kitchen's special Party Packs. They will provide you with the tools to make your own magic. The children's range has real tools in smaller sizes, sifters made from metal with an old fashioned crank, silicone spatulas, rolling pins, aprons and more. With a bit of help (and luck) soon they'll be taking over the cooking. Choose from one of the existing party sets or make up one of your own. Bulk discounts apply. Available nationally (free delivery throughout Melbourne).

Party Squad
Tel: 0414 326 396
email: info@partysquad.com.au
website: www.partysquad.com.au

Planning a children's event? Let Party Squad bring the party to you. They offer child-sized chair and table hire, helium balloons, lolly bags, games packs, entertainers and entertainment, novelties, party essentials, catering and cakes. Party Squad specialise in affordable children's events in Victoria and now have an online shop servicing all of Australia. Phone 0414 326 396 or visit their website.

Partykids
Tel: 0412 103 444
email: info@partykids.com.au
website: www.partykids.com.au

Partykids is Australia's original online party shop and the perfect place to find all your children's birthday party supplies. Partykids offer a huge range of party products that make organising your child's birthday party a piece of cake. Choose from over 50 fully co-ordinated themes plus free ideas for party food, kids party games and other party tips. Shop at your leisure and have all your party essentials delivered to your door, anywhere in Australia within 4 working days.

Shop for Baby
Tel: (02) 9939 3643
email: contact@shopforbaby.com.au
website: www.shopforbaby.com.au

ShopForBaby.com.au can supply all your party needs. They offer a gorgeous range of birthday invitations, thank-you cards, party bags and much more. Leave the car at home and take advantage of their fast delivery, exceptional customer service and amazing loyalty program that enables you to save every time you shop. Email or visit the website for further information.

The Party Parlour
Tel: (02) 9869 1001
email: info@thepartyparlour.com.au
website: www.thepartyparlour.com.au

Beautifully co-ordinated party products delivered to your door. The Party Parlour aims to provide you with a great range of co-ordinated party products and imaginative party ideas that inspire you. You can design your own party by mixing and matching products from their extensive range, or use some of their party ideas if you are short on time and creativity. Shop online and save yourself time and money.

Resources

BIRTHDAY PARTIES

Birthday party suppliers: online
➡ Birthday party venues

Theme In A Box
Tel: (02) 9327 7888
email: info@themeinabox.com.au
website: www.themeinabox.com.au

Theme In A Box have over 70 complete themed party packages containing all the party supplies you need to host a fantastic party from the invitations to the loot bags. Choose from baby's first birthday, Thomas, Shrek, The Wiggles, fairies, pirates, dinosaurs, your child's favourite colour and lots more. Themed extras include balloons, piñatas, banners, cards, scatters, cake decorating kits, candles and streamers. Order online and it can be delivered to your door.

Toot Toot Toys
Tel: 1300 866 886
email: customercare@toottoottoys.com.au
website: www.toottoottoys.com.au

Buy all your Thomas the Tank party supplies without running around. Pinatas, plates, candles, blowers, hats, invitations, loot bags all at the one shop. Toot Toot Toys also have small items that can be added to party loot bags like bath gels and stickers etcetera, or costumes to really enhance the theme. Toot Toot Toys is your one-stop party shop.

BIRTHDAY PARTY SUPPLIERS: RETAIL

VICTORIA

Cheaper Party Supplies Pty Ltd
3 The Strand
Preston Market VIC 3072
Tel: (03) 9478 2453

Cheaper Party Supplies has a large range of discounted, disposable catering supplies including the popular "First Birthday" range now available in pink and blue. They also stock balloons and hire balloon gas.

Gorgeous Little Parties Pty Ltd
41 Lower Heidelberg Road
Ivanhoe VIC 3079
Tel: (03) 9499 7944
email: shop@gorgeouslittleparties.com.au
website: www.gorgeouslittleparties.com.au

Gorgeous Little Parties offer the coolest themed party products including invitations, plates, cups, balloons, treat bags, pinatas, games, tattoos, stickers, masks and much more. Browse the huge range of fully co-ordinated party themes at their Ivanhoe store.

Masquerade Costume Hire
238 High Street
Kew VIC 3101
Tel: (03) 9853 6101
email: info@masquerade.com.au
website: www.masquerade.com.au

Masquerade is a great source for costumes and quirky presents. What 2-year-old wouldn't love a pair of wings or a superhero costume? Hundreds of families have used them for the kindy and school bookweek parade. They have an amazing range of mascots to hire for birthday parties – dinosaurs, dogs and cartoon characters are among the favourites. The costumes are clean, in excellent condition and constantly updated. They pride themselves on service. In business since 1971.

NEW SOUTH WALES

Tracky Beans
Hornsby Heights NSW 2077
Tel: (02) 9940 4482
email: party@trackybeans.com.au
website: www.trackybeans.com.au

Tracky Beans is a comprehensive decorating service supplying helium balloons, decorations, balloon bouquets, party hire, fairy lights, table centrepieces, balloon topiary trees, piñatas, party hire and disposable tableware including plates, cups and table covers. Parties for children, adults, christenings, weddings, engagements, end-of-year functions at home or at your chosen venue. They offer a delivery service and can help with private parties, school and social club functions.

SOUTH AUSTRALIA

Wheelie Kids
Tel: (08) 8263 2025
email: wheeliekids@optusnet.com.au
website: www.wheeliekids.com.au

Wheelie Kids provide a variety of ride-on electric vehicles for kids parties, fetes and social functions. Great package deals include hall hire, lolly bags, balloons and invitations. Wheelie Kids can come to you or you can go to them. The range of vehicles is also available to purchase. Visit the website for more information.

BIRTHDAY PARTY VENUES

NATIONAL

Creative Memories
Tel: (03) 9561 6089 or 0414 299 923
email: davis_kelly@optusnet.com.au

If your daughter is too old for fairy parties, Creative Memories run fun, relaxed children's parties where participants create their own scrapbook photo album page by learning cropping, mounting, journalling and decorating techniques. Excellent value for money, no mess and tailored to suit your child and her friends. Consultants available Australia wide.

Bonkers Playcentre
497 Nepean Highway
Brighton East VIC 3187
Tel: (03) 9530 6601
email: kids@bonkersplaycentre.com.au
website: www.bonkersplaycentre.com.au

Bonkers Playcentre offers babies and toddlers play areas, specialises in children's birthday parties including first and second birthday parties, karaoke and music birthday parties and adults' birthday parties. Loved by all kids and adults, Free Bonkers & Magic Show runs every Saturday and Sunday at 12.00pm (except some holidays & subject to magician's availability) and is offered as family entertainment for the public and for birthdays. Birthday packages include a free gift from Bonkers the Monkey (valued at $15.95), party box, helium balloon and a party hat for the birthday child, Jungle treats (lolly bags) for all kids, two free coffees, a free return entry pass, party music and lights, invitations, loads of food and drinks. As added extras Bonkers Playcentre can also organise games, provide a piñata, face painting or favourite Bonkers the Monkey Music Show.

Fairies of South Yarra
528 Malvern Road
Prahran VIC 3181
Tel: (03) 9510 9188
email: info@partyforkids.com.au
website: www.partyforkids.com.au

Fairies of South Yarra have created a unique world and called it "Children's Fairy World" to host boys and girls parties. To ensure that you see the party rooms and know what occurs in each room, they have put the room online for your convenience. Experience the most memorable birthday party with a wide selection of themes performed by their professional entertainers and with a broad range of costumes, gifts and accessories available in their retail shop. Receive a free birthday present for your birthday child when you book and celebrate a party at Fairies of South Yarra. For a free Party Planner Consultation phone (03) 9510 9188 or visit the website for more details.

Fairy Park
Geelong-Ballan Road
Anakie VIC 3221
Tel: (03) 5284 1262
email: info@fairypark.com
website: www.fairypark.com

Fairy Park is one of Victoria's best kept secrets. There is excitement around every corner as you pass through fairy castles, cottages, caves and wonderfully detailed displays come to life at the push of a button. Enjoy hours of medieval fun at Camelot's playground. Children's parties are welcome – BYO decorations, fairy wings, gnome hats and a picnic. There is shelter for over 400 guests, a kiosk and full picnic facilities. Pram and pusher-friendly paths. Open daily. Melways page 11, A10. Visit the website for more details.

Jungle Junior
39 Malop Street
Geelong VIC 3220
Tel: (03) 5224 2362
email: jujunior@bigpond.net.au
website: www.junglejunior.com.au

Jungle Juniors birthday parties take all the mess and hassle out of parties so you can sit back and enjoy your child's special day. Catering for 5 to 30 children per party, no request is too large and they can even take care of the cake. Special dietary requirements and allergies are also taken care of with tailor-made menus including slices, fruit and cheese platters, hot and cold food and gourmet sandwiches to suit yourself and your guests. Even table settings and decorations can be done for you in bright party colours.

Kidz Can HQ
1 Sinclair Street
Elsternwick VIC 3185
Tel: (03) 9523 8373
email: marcelle@kidzcanhq.com.au
website: www.kidzcanhq.com.au

Kidz Can HQ offers a great venue to celebrate your child's birthday. This is a bright and colourful wonderland and includes an obstacle course, train, trampoline, ball pool, castle, swings and much more. Kidz Can HQ can cater for the party if you wish and you can enjoy the premises exclusively as it will not be open to the public for the duration of the party. Phone for more information or have a look at www.kidzcanhq.com.au.

Kidz Zone Indoor Playcentre & Café
219 Sydney Road
Coburg VIC 3058
Tel: (03) 9383 1977
email: parties@kidzzone.com.au
website: www.kidzzone.com.au

Kidz Zone Indoor Playcentre & Cafe specialises in children's parties so you can just sit back and relax and watch the kids enjoy. Organised parties include free invitations, a hostess, admission fee, private theme party rooms for 1.5 hours, food and drink from selected menus and lolly bags for each child. The birthday child will also receive a photo of the birthday party. They now also have special kids activities like craft and storytelling.

Little Kitchen
371 St Georges Road
North Fitzroy VIC 3068
Tel: 1300 722 095
email: info@littlekitchen.com.au
website: www.littlekitchen.com.au

Little Kitchen is Australia's first organic cookery school designed and custom-built especially for children. The centre features children's cooking lessons, cooking birthday parties, a children's cooking concept store, organic herb garden and children's dining room. Lessons and parties book out fast so phone the number above or visit the website for further information.

Resources

BIRTHDAY PARTIES

Birthday party venues

Music Works Magic
Main Studio: 263 Glenhuntly Road
Elsternwick VIC 3185
Tel: (03) 9029 6879
email: anna@musicworksmagic.com
website: www.musicworksmagic.com
Music Works Magic offers interactive group music
classes for babies through to 12 years, including
birthday parties and private tuition. All instruments are
available. Venues all over Melbourne.

Playful Parenting
12 Surrey Road
South Yarra VIC 3141
Tel: 0408 321 011
email: paula@playfulparenting.com.au
Playful Parenting is a delightful 'play and learn' centre
offering classes and parties for pre-school aged children.
Birthday parties (1 to 5 years) can be designed to suit
your child's individual needs with play equipment, toys,
musical entertainment and games to amuse each age
group. Their party space is exclusive to only your group
with a separate room for party food (catering available)
and off-street parking. They can also provide
entertainment to your home party to keep all young
guests happy. Enquiries welcome.

Rare Bears
1134 Toorak Road
Camberwell VIC 3124
Tel: (03) 9889 9444
Also located at:
10 Bridge Street
Eltham VIC 3095
Tel: (03) 9439 6619
email: camprarebears@optusnet.com.au
website: www.rarebears.com.au
Rare Bears is a great place to take the kids for fun and
entertainment while you relax in the café, having a coffee
and eating fantastic food. Rare Bears is open seven days
a week and caters for children of all ages, with toddlers
in separate defined areas and exciting play possibilities
for the older ones. On Friday and Saturday nights Rare
Bears converts to a family restaurant open to 9.00pm
(the Camberwell location has a BYO license). Children's
parties are a specialty.

The Art Factory
28 Glenferrie Road
Malvern VIC 3144
Tel: (03) 9576 0135

307 Buckley Street
Essendon VIC 3040
249a Belmore Road
North Balwyn VIC 3104
177 Ferguson Street
Williamstown VIC 3016
email: info@theartfactory.com.au
website: www.theartfactory.com.au
The Art Factory is a great party venue where every guest
gets the chance to create a masterpiece and take home
their fabulous creation. They can make treasure boxes,
photo frames, CD houses and more. Birthday parties are
for kids aged from 4 to teens. The Art Factory also
conducts kids art programs for all ages and adult mosaic
workshops. Phone the number above for more
information.

Wiz Kids Kindergym
Level 1, 574A North Road
Ormond VIC 3204
Tel: (03) 9578 2332
email: info@wizkids.org.au
website: www.wizkids.org.au
Wiz Kids runs active parties for children aged 1 to 7
years that are a pleasure for both parents and kids.
Parties include moving to music, games and play on
gymnastics equipment. They have state-of-the-art
Kindergym equipment, innovative programs, lively
dances, caring leaders trained and registered with
Gymnastics Victoria. Bring your own food or Wiz Kids
can cater for you.

Wriggle It
Shop 1, 197 Star Zone, Karingal Drive
Karingal (Melway 103 C4) VIC 3199
Tel: (03) 9789 8434
email: wriggleitplaycentre@yahoo.com.au
Wriggle It is an indoor party and play centre providing
activities for children parties and casual play. They have
a giant padded play structure, jump castle and under 3's
area, cubby houses and a cafe with a wide selection of
food and drink. They are open Monday to Sunday and
offer group discounts and fundraising options for
schools and other organisations.

NEW SOUTH WALES

Australia Walkabout Wildlife Park
Corner Peats Ridge & Darkinjung Roads
Calga NSW 2250
Tel: (02) 4375 1100
website: www.walkaboutpark.com.au
Birthday parties at Australia Walkabout Wildlife Park
are packed full of fun with your own ranger to entertain
the children and grown-ups too. Get painted up with
ochre face paint, ready for the adventure, then you can:
track real wild kangaroos and emus through the bush;
eat bush tucker; see how to get water from the trees; feed
the pademelons; learn about Aboriginal medicine; wash
up with bush soap, and finish up with a sausage sizzle
and lolly bag.

Fairyland
733 Military Road
Mosman NSW 2088
Tel: (02) 9960 7222
email: customerservice@magicinfairyland.com.au
website: www.magicinfairyland.com

Treat your child to the latest dress-up outfits and accessories, book a fantasy party of their dreams, choose from a vast array of unique gift ideas or fly in for Fairyland's popular school holiday workshops and weekly storytime tales. Open 7 days a week. Email or visit the website for further information.

Jumping Jacks Playtime
PO Box 200
Crows Nest NSW 2065
Tel: 1800 811 764
email: info@jumpingjacksplaytime.com.au
website: www.jumpingjacksplaytime.com.au

Jumping Jacks Playtime is a physio-designed and physio-operated kinda gym for children in the Sydney area. They help same-aged kids (with their parents/carers) to interact and exercise for one hour of fun and fitness with colourful and challenging equipment designs that change weekly plus music group and parachute time. The program is designed for kids aged approx. 6 months to 5 years in age-related classes. Short and long term options available; classes are small and allow for one-on-one attention. Phone or visit the website for your closest gym location. Birthday parties catered for.

Plaster Painting Studios
The Entertainment Quarter, Lang Road
Moore Park NSW 2031
Tel: 0415 944 498
email: michelle@plasterpainting.com
website: www.plasterpainting.com

At Plaster Painting Studios you can plaster 3D figurines, plaques, canvas, picture frames, candle holders and money boxes. They can be sprayed shiny, glittered and ready in 15 minutes. Birthday parties are $20 per child or they can do a 'Party in a Box' which can be couriered to you if you can t get to them in Moore Park. Phone for more details.

Puppeteria
48A Carrington Road
Randwick NSW 2031
Tel: (02) 9371 7328
Also located:
12 Denawen Avenue
Castle Cove NSW 2069
website: www.puppeteria.com

'Puppeteria' puppet theatre offers a range of creative and exciting individually themed parties, including professional puppet shows featuring 'jeral puppets', craft, interactive puppetry and party food. Phone the number above or visit the website www.puppeteria.com for further details.

Wiggly Play Centre
1A Stanton Road
Seven Hills NSW 2147
Tel: (02) 9838 9564
email: kim@thewiggles.com.au
website: www.wigglyplaycentre.com.au

 One of Sydney's premier indoor play centres, Wiggle Play Centre caters exclusively for the fun, entertainment and development of children up to the age of 10 years. The Wiggle Play Centre is packed with fun things to do including a large maze, ball pits, jumping castles and great birthday parties. Wiggles merchandise and activities are also available. Visit or phone the number above for further details.

QUEENSLAND

Bim Bam Boom
296 Oxley Road
Graceville QLD 4075
Tel: (07) 3278 3788
email: info@bimbamboom.com.au
website: www.bimbamboom.com.au

Bim Bam Boom sells educational toys for children from birth to approx 10 to 12 years. They also run art workshops: "Toddlers Get Messy" for two to four year olds and "Boomers" for school-age children. Bim Bam Boom also runs holiday programs and hosts children's birthday parties. All you need to to is bring a cake. No mess, no fuss for mum and dad, just relax and enjoy.

Brisbane Arts Theatre
210 Petrie Terrace
Brisbane QLD 4000
Tel: (07) 3369 2344
website: www.artstheatre.com.au

The Brisbane Arts Theatre provides a venue for great children's parties with a difference. Take your children to see a live theatre performance, celebrate at interval with party food and cut your cake (families provide party food) and then after the show meet all the cast members and get their autographs. Your child's birthday celebration will be a memorable experience for years to come. For 2009 shows and bookings phone (07) 3369 2344.

The Patch Place
Shop 2, 326 Gympie Road
Strathpine QLD 4500
Tel: (07) 3881 0965
website: www.thepatchplace.com.au

The Patch Place provides opportunities for children of all ages to explore their creative side, increase their academic skills and create new friendships, all while having fun. They run regular workshops ranging from jewellery making to abstract art, provide tuition services and run birthday parties that are not to be missed. The Patch Place also has a fantastic range of craft and fun educational products available for purchase, as well as a selection of designed kids clothes.

Child care
& early education

Preparing for child care

Placing your child in child care is an exciting, though sometimes overwhelming, experience for many families. Before you begin using child care, you will need to consider issues such as when you want to start using care, what child care options are available, how to access child care, and what you might expect when your child starts care. This article by the National Childcare Accreditation Council Inc. provides you with information to guide you through these issues, and to assist you to make informed decisions about the type of child care your family wants to use.

When should my child start care?

There is no 'best time' to start child care - it depends on what suits your family and child. Current research in child development indicates that the quality of the child care they receive is more important to good outcomes for children than the age at which they start care, or the amount of time they spend in care.

Many families are seeking quality child care, so it is important to consider your child care options as early as possible and to begin the process of finding suitable services well before you need to start using care.

Most services have a waiting list, and it is a good idea to place your child's name on the lists of several services to increase the chances of a place being available when you require it. It is also important that you remove your name from any waiting lists that you are on once you find a child care place so that services can keep their waiting lists up-to-date for other families.

Even though you may not know the exact details of the days and hours that you will want for child care, it is helpful to think in advance about what may be most likely to suit your family situation. However, child care services understand that a family's anticipated needs may change by the time a child care place is offered.

What child care options are available?

There is a variety of child care options available, including family day care, long day care and outside school hours care. You will need to consider the characteristics of each type of care, as well as the individual service to decide whether the care being offered will suit your child and family. Many families find that their child care needs change over time, and they may use two or more different service types either at the same time, or one after another. For example, a family may choose to place their baby in a family day care service, but move them to a long day care service in the year before they start school so that they can engage with a larger group of children.

The child care services types that currently participate in the Child Care Quality Assurance (CCQA) systems administered by NCAC are:

- Family Day Care – provides care for small groups of children from birth to 12 years of age in the family home of a registered carer.
- Long Day Care – provides care for children from birth to 5 years of age in a centre-based environment.
- Outside School Hours Care – provides care for school age children before and/or after school and/or during school holidays (vacation care).

Other child care types include occasional child care, preschool services or care provided by family or friends, babysitters and nannies. When considering your child care options, you may wish to visit different child care services to assist you to decide whether to place your child's name on the waiting list. Please note that many child care services charge a non-refundable waiting list administration fee.

How can I find a child care service?

NCAC provides the names, contact details and accreditation history of registered child care services on the NCAC website (www.ncac.gov. au) through a search facility that enables you to search for services by postcode or suburb. If you are unable to access NCAC's website you can telephone NCAC on 1300 136 554 and speak with a child care adviser. Friends and family members can often provide you with a good source of information about the child care they use, and it can be useful to find out what others think about the child care they use. You may also be able to find out about child care services through:

- your local business or telephone directory
- local council listings
- classified advertisements
- public noticeboards in schools and shopping centres
- work/study colleagues
- your employer or educational institution
- the Child Care Access Hotline: 1800 670 305.

How will I know if the child care is good quality?

There are some useful questions that you can ask when visiting child care services to decide whether the care they offer will meet your needs. NCAC produces a free *Family Information Kit* that outlines what to look for in quality child care. To receive this kit, please visit the 'Families and Children' page on NCAC's website. NCAC has also developed a range of other resources for families that will assist you to determine whether a service is offering quality care. These include:

- A *Choosing Quality Child Care* brochure that includes information about NCAC, how to find quality child care, questions to assist families to choose quality care and the Child Care Quality Assurance (CCQA) system standards.
- *Quality Assurance* brochures, including CCQA information for each specific service type.
- NCAC *Factsheets for Families* about aspects of quality care in child care services.

NCAC requires child care services to provide families with information about the service's participation in the CCQA systems. If a service is accredited, they need to display a current Certificate of Accreditation and a Quality Profile Certificate that shows the ratings they received for each area of practice when they were accredited.

Not accredited services are also required to display the most recent Quality Profile Certificate. It is important to note that not accredited services should be working to improve the quality of care they provide, and you may find that a not accredited service has improved their practices to a satisfactory or higher level since they were not accredited.

Services that are newly registered with NCAC, and have not yet had an accreditation decision should display a NCAC Certificate of Registration.

Preparing for child care

What happens when my child begins care?

Enrolment

Once a child care place has been offered, the service should guide you through an enrolment process. Effective enrolment processes are very important as this time is used for families and child care professionals to share important information about your child, family and the child care service. An enrolment form may request information including:

- Family contact details and information.
- Authorised contact details and access information for your child. This helps services to know who is authorised to collect them from care, as well as authorised contacts that may be used in an emergency, when you cannot be contacted.
- Specific information about your child, including their eating and sleeping routines, interests and likes/dislikes, illnesses, allergies, medical conditions, health insurance information and health care professional contact details.
- Your child's immunisation history. This may be provided by taking a photocopy of the child's child health record, or by obtaining an immunisation history statement from the Australian Childhood Immunisation Register on the Medicare Australia website (www. medicareaustralia.gov.au).
- Your child's birth certificate.

Orientation

Starting child care can often be an emotional experience for both you and your child. An orientation visit usually takes place before your child starts care, and is an important step as it provides time for you, your child and the child care professionals to get to know each other.

By spending time in the service you can begin to understand what you can expect from the service. An orientation visit also provides valuable time for you to discuss the enrolment form, your child's needs, interests, routines and rituals with the child care professionals who will work with your child.

It is also a good opportunity to ask questions and to become more familiar with the service.

During an orientation visit, you should be able to spend time with your child in the service. This enables them to explore their new environment, establish the beginnings of a relationship with child care professionals, and to meet potential 'new friends', with the security of having you close by. It can also make you feel reassured when you see how your child responds to the child care environment.

Services often provide a handbook to families at orientation time which outlines information about the service, the staff, opening hours, and policies on issues such as holidays, managing illness, fees and other issues which may affect care arrangements.

What will help my child to settle into care?

Children can often experience some difficulty settling into a child care environment, particularly if they find it hard to separate from family or familiar caregivers. Each child's response to care and the length of time they take to settle depends on the individual child and their past experiences. However, there are strategies that families and services can use to support children to settle successfully. Families may find the following suggestions helpful when they are supporting their child to settle into care:

- If possible, start child care before work or study commitments commence and try to allow your child to have shorter days initially, then gradually increase the time spent in care.

❯ Seek out a preferred child care professional or peer that your child can stay with when you leave the service.

❯ Spend some time settling your child at a favoured activity before you leave.

❯ Inform the service about what comforts your child, and discuss how you manage activities or times of the day they find unsettling. For example, does your child have a comfort item such as a toy or blanket that can help them to settle when they become upset?

❯ Show your child that you feel secure about leaving them at the service and that you trust the child care professionals. Say 'goodbye' confidently, and reassure them that you will be back later. While it may be tempting to leave while they are engaged happily in play, it can be very distressing for your child to realise you have left without saying goodbye.

❯ You should feel that you can contact the service at any time to check how your child is settling, and the child care professionals should provide you with sensitive, honest feedback about this.

Child care often plays a major role in your family's life. It is important to build a good relationship with your child care service, to exchange important information about your child and to share your values and expectations for your child with child care professionals. Using quality child care offers many positive outcomes for children, including opportunities to develop meaningful relationships and to engage in experiences that will benefit them both now and in their future life course.

Some practical things to consider when choosing child care:

❯ What hours of care does the service offer? Will you be able to drop off and collect your child within these hours?

❯ Will it be more practical to seek child care closer to home or closer to your place of work or study?

❯ Does the service have closure periods during the year, how long are these, and when do they occur?

❯ Does the service have an 'open door' policy that allows you to visit or telephone the service at any time?

❯ Does the service charge fees for public holidays, or when your child is absent?

❯ Does the service provide things such as nappies and meals, or will these need to be provided from home?

❯ What ages does the service cater for? For example, a service may provide care for children aged 0-3, so your family may also need to consider future child care options.

A guide to early education

School is compulsory in Australia for children aged 6 (5 in TAS) to 15 (ACT, NSW, NT), 16 (QLD, VIC) or 17 (Tasmania, WA, SA), although each state has different cut-off dates for entry/exit. Regardless of the type of school – public (government/state), home schooling, private or otherwise – a curriculum is in place setting the framework of education across the country.

Prior to year 1, early education (preschool, kindergarten, pre-prep and the like) is relatively unregulated and not compulsory in most states. Early education is play-based and varies, depending on the age and program. Below is an introduction to early education across Australia, by state.

Please note that the Council of Australian Governments (COAG), in partnership between the Commonwealth and state and territory governments, is developing a new national framework for early childhood education and care. Following national endorsement, the final framework is expected to be introduced as of July 2009.

Victoria
Three-year-olds
At present the public school system does not generally offer programs for 3-year-olds. Many child care centres offer 3-year-old programs with registered early childhood education teachers on staff. Some non-government schools and kindergartens also have 3-year-old programs.

Four-year-olds
Children who are 4, or turn 4 by 30 April may attend kindergarten. Kindergarten is generally 10 hours a week and offered in a range of settings, including purpose-built kindergartens (public and private run), children's centres, community-based and private child care centres, community halls and some schools. Public school enrolments go through the local council with which the school resides.

Five-year-olds
This is called prep (the first year of formal schooling) and a child may enrol in a school at the preparatory level if he/she is 5 years of age by 30 April of that year.

By law, a child must start school in the year they turn 6. Note that entry into prep or year 1 will be determined by the school if the child has not started school prior to turning 6.

New South Wales
Three-year-olds
At present the government school system does not generally offer programs for 3-year-olds. Some non-government schools offer 3-year-old programs, as do Montessori and Steiner.

Four-year-olds
Children who are 4 or turn 4 by 31 July may attend preschool which can be part of the public school system or private/community-based or as part of long day care.

Five-year-olds

Children enter kindergarten (the first year of formal schooling) if they are five or turn 5 before 31 July in that year. By law, a child must start school by their 6th birthday (note that entry into kindergarten or year 1 will be determined by the school if the child has not started school prior to turning 6).

Australian Capital Territory

Three-year-olds

The public school system does offer limited programs for 3-year-olds (Charnwood and Narrabundah). In 2009 four Early Childhood Schools (birth to 8) will open offering early learning programs. Some non-government schools offer 3-year-old programs. Children attend 2, 3 or 5 days a week. Some day care centres are also beginning to offer a more formalised program for 3-year-olds. The Playschool Parent Association also offers programs on preschool premises.

Four-year-olds

Children who are 4 or turn 4 by 30 April are entitled to 12 hours per week of preschool (free of charge if in the public system) in that year; which is usually either 2 long days (9.00am to 3.00pm) or 3 short days (9.00am to 1.00pm) depending on what the preschool offers. Each preschool is amalgamated with a nearby primary school.

Five-year-olds

Children who are 5 or turn 5 by 30 April may attend kindergarten, which is the first formal year of school. By law, a child must start school by their 6th birthday (note that entry into kindergarten or year 1 will be determined by the school if the child has not started school prior to turning 6).

Queensland

Three-year-olds

At present the public school system does not generally offer programs for 3-year-olds. Many long day care centres offer 3-year-old programs with registered kindergarten teachers on staff. Some non-government schools also have 3-year-old programs.

Four-year-olds

Children who are 4, or turn 4 by 30 June may access programs and services provided in kindergartens or other early education and care facilities. Kindergarten may be part-time, to school terms and hours, or on a half-day basis; and is offered in a range of settings, including the Crèche and Kindergarten Association of Queensland (C&K), community groups, non-government schools, or other non-government organisations.

Five-year-olds

This is called prep and although not compulsory, a child can enrol in a school at the preparatory level if he/she is five years of age by 30 June of that year. Generally, enrolments are direct with the school of choice. A child reaches compulsory school age when they are aged at least 6 years and 6 months, and parents have a legal obligation to enroll their child in school. This may be as part of their prep year or year 1.

A guide to early education

Northern Territory

Three-year-olds

At present the public school system does not generally offer programs for 3-year-olds. Many child care centres offer 3-year-old programs with registered child care workers on staff. Some non-government schools and kindergartens also have 3-year-old programs.

Four-year-olds

Children who are 4, or turn 4 by 30 June may attend preschool (not compulsory). Preschool may run as part of the public school system or privately; there are also mobile preschool services in remote areas. A preschool program is generally 12 hours per week (such as four half days, two full days or a combination).

Five-year-olds

This is called transition and although not compulsory, a child must be five years of age by 30 June of the year they enter transition. By law, if a child turns 6 before 30 June they must be enrolled in school (year 1). Children do not need to have taken transition to enter year 1.

Western Australia

Three-year-olds

At present the public school system does not generally offer programs for 3-year-olds. Many child care centres offer 3-year-old programs with registered early childhood education teachers on staff. Some non-government schools and kindergartens also have 3-year-old programs.

Four-year-olds

Children who are 4, or turn 4 by 30 June, may attend kindergarten (not compulsory). Kindergarten may run as part of the public school system or privately. A kindergarten program is generally 11 hours per week (such as four half days, two full days or a combination).

Five-year-olds

This is called pre-primary and, although not compulsory, a child must be five years of age by 30 June of the year they enter pre-primary. By law, a child must start school in the year they turn 6 (year 1).

South Australia

Three-year-olds

The public school system does not generally offer programs for 3-year-olds. Many child care centres and some non-government schools and kindergartens offer 3-year-old programs. Children start a 3-year-old program not before their 3rd birthday.

Four-year-olds

Children who are 4+ may attend preschool (also called kindergarten). Preschool is generally 12 hours per week and offered in kindergartens, children's centres, child parent centres and early childhood development centres as well as non-government schools. Public school enrolments go through the local council with which the school resides.

Five-year-olds

Five-year-old children who attend public school can start at the beginning of each of the four terms. This is a child's first formal year of education and is called reception.

By law, a child must start school (year 1 or reception) by their 6th birthday (note that entry into reception or year 1 will be determined by the school if the child has not started school prior to turning 6).

Tasmania

Three-year-olds

The public school system does offer limited programs for 3-year-olds (called pre-kindergarten) and many schools offer "Launching into Learning" programs (birth to 4 years old). Most child care centres and some non-government schools offer 3-year-old programs.

Four-year-olds

To start kindergarten (which is not compulsory), your child must be four years of age by 1 January in the year in which they start. Kindergartens may run as part of the government or non-government school system or as a registered school in a child care centre. A kindergarten program is generally 10 hours per week (either half day or full day sessions).

Five-year-olds

By law, a child who is 5 by 1 January must start school. This year is called prep and is the first formal year of education.

Written by Anastasia Jones, freelance writer.

Survival tips for working parents

Being a working parent is a challenging role. It involves a balancing act between meeting your child's needs for care and attention, sharing a satisfying relationship with your partner and friends and being a reliable and competent employee while trying to enjoy life and parenthood.

As a parent you can make life easier by:

- setting realistic and achievable goals for you and your family
- asking for help
- changing your expectations and priorities around the house
- involving other supportive adults in the planning and sharing of parenting and household responsibilities
- being realistic about what can be achieved each day.

Routine is important. Having an unpredictable lifestyle is time-consuming and unsettling for everyone. Young children become frustrated, overwhelmed, and rushed when routines are frequently changing (understandably, sometimes it cannot be helped).

Talk to your partner about household responsibilities and expectations as a parent and an adult household member.

Start and finish the day on a happy note

- Give yourself extra time in the morning.
- Re-think what is essential to be completed before leaving the house each morning.
- Pack your work and child care bags the night before.
- Use time in the car as a valuable opportunity to connect with your child both on the way to child care and on the way home. Sing songs, and listen to your child when they speak to you.
- Most importantly, leave work stresses at work.
- Organise the next day's clothing the night before, for you and your child.
- Avoid conflicts and fights in the morning – it is always a no-win situation for everyone.
- Make sure your child goes to bed early enough as this ensures they have adequate sleep for development and growth and gives you and your partner time to interact as adults and friends.
- Feeding the family does not need to be stressful! Prepare double amounts of food and freeze for later.
- Invest in a slow cooker and put dinner on before you leave for work.
- Also remember your evening meal does not always have to be a hot meal.
- Depending on the age of your child, try and enjoy dinner around the table with the television off and all family members present. This is a good habit to get into and provides a great opportunity to meaningfully interact with your family.
- Consider a no TV rule in the morning as this can distract everyone from getting ready.

Shopping

- Add an extra hour to child care for shopping later in the day.
- Avoid taking tired and hungry children shopping.
- Consider shopping online, or in the evening ask your partner to do the shopping.
- Another suggestion is to do a big weekly shop to avoid the need to shop every day.

Washing

- Wash and hang the clothes the night before.
- Fold washing properly and save ironing.

Children do get sick when you least expect it

- Ensure your employer knows you are also a parent, so if your child does become sick you can take leave.
- Otherwise, have an alternative plan – either arrange for your partner to care for your child or have a back-up such as a grandparent or good friend on standby.
- Babysitting clubs are a great idea if you want to go out at night time with no extra child care costs, but remember you do need to 'repay' the hours and babysit other people's children.

Maintain family harmony and think of yourself

- Take time out for yourself and your partner to reconnect and maintain a healthy relationship.
- Go for a walk, taking time to talk and listen to each other even if it is only for a short time.
- Plan regular enjoyable family activities that are simple. It's these activities that provide your children with family memories later in life!
- Continue or start to do a regular exercise program. This is an essential part of caring for yourself.

Information supplied by Tresillian, www.tresillian.net.

The importance of kindergarten programs

Kindergarten is an educational program for children in the year prior to starting primary school. Kindergarten programs can be offered in a sessional kindergarten setting as well as in long day care, often called children's services or child care centres.

Kindergarten can be seen as preparing your child for school, however it should not be seen as a school program. Kindergarten programs should be based on the developmental needs of the children at the time, not on what they may be doing at school the following year. Therefore most kindergarten programs are based on the play-based approach. This approach is seen by many early childhood educators as the best way for kindergarten children to learn.

Play-based programs

All children learn best through play. Research has shown early childhood professionals that children who are engaged in the program, whose interests are met through stimulating and challenging experiences, are the children who 'love to learn'. This in turn supports their learning later in life. Most kindergartens base the program on what is known as a 'play-based curriculum'. This means that children are in a program that is based on their developmental needs and is met through play experiences and environments. Play-based programs ensure that children's interests and needs are met through a stimulating, challenging and engaging program. Adults need to remember that play is the children's work. Through play children begin to learn how the world works and how they fit into that world. They can begin to make sense of the world through play, they can feel safe in their play world, and they can be whoever they want in their play world. They can be in charge!

What should a play-based program provide?

The program should allow the children time to explore, experiment and investigate. Programs also:

- Encourage and stimulate children's development socially, emotionally, intellectually and physically.
- Allow children to explore the world in ways that are interesting and fun, whilst developing their independence, confidence and self-esteem.
- Include educational experiences including early literacy, numeracy, music, drama, art and science.
- Empower children to develop self-esteem and confidence.
- Provide opportunities for children to express themselves through language, art and imaginative play.
- Encourage children to become more independent, ensuring strong foundations for learning.
- Include family and community into the curriculum.
- Assist children in developing a positive self-image to enable effective learning and development of positive social attitudes.
- Children who are engaged in what adults might see as 'just playing' are actually learning life skills such as co-operation, problem solving and negotiation.

Your child's experience at kindergarten will support them at school. School readiness is about your child's self-confidence, self-esteem and being socially mature. The program that is offered through play experiences and environments is going to provide that. Enjoy your child's kindergarten year.

Written by Cathy Tighe, Early Childhood Management Services (ECMS), www.ecms.org.au.

Vox Pop

We asked a number of women and men around Australia to send in their advice, tips and personal experiences on a range of topics so that you have an insight into how others cope being a new parent. We hope you find their comments interesting, informative and reassuring. Vox Pop biographies: page 652

Cindy Fraser
Mum of three, Melbourne

As a qualified early childhood professional with over 10 years' experience working with young children, the first thing I can say is it is so much harder when they are your own children and you don't give them back at the end of the day! My eldest attended child care on the days that I was teaching, and while it was expensive it was still very worthwhile, especially as he was in the same building as me and I had known his carers for many years. When the twins arrived we really struggled. Child care was not an affordable option with three children to consider, and our family live in the country so were unable to help us out. This is when I found out about In Home Care. Although I had been in the child care industry for so long I had never heard of this wonderful service. Within a week of filling out the paperwork I had a fantastic nanny commence work in my home that I was comfortable with. This was affordable for us as In Home Care is approved care, which gave us access to the child care benefit, and the 50% tax rebate. Our nanny is paid $20 per hour yet it is only costing us $6 per hour … and that is to care for all three children! She is also really flexible and has been able to accommodate our family's ever changing needs. I cannot recommend this service enough; I think it is one of child care's best kept secrets!

Jessica Hatherall
Mum of two, Sydney

I wanted to wait until my eldest child was three before I sent him to child care. But once my daughter came along and with no extended family nearby I knew it would be quite challenging not to have any help. I have found a fantastic nanny who comes to us two days a week. Lucky for us, they all get along brilliantly and enjoy the one-on-one attention.

Bianca McCulloch
Mum of two, Melbourne

In the past I have had a hard time dropping my son off at child care because he would cry and I felt really bad leaving him there. Now when I drop him off he waves and says goodbye and can't get in there fast enough, so it feels great dropping him off now because he actually enjoys being there.

I think the small child care centres are great and while they may not be new and fancy they usually have staff that really enjoy spending time with your kids and giving them the attention they need.

I will be going on maternity leave from work soon and I'm really looking forward to taking my little boy to playgroups and libraries for toddler readings and things. I think it's important for young children to experience active play and also the library is a good way to teach kids that there are times we have to be quiet.

Nicole Hambling
Mum of one, VIC

Be a working mum or a stay-at-home mum? It was a big decision. Occasional adult conversation versus talking to a 6-month-old and a 17-month-old Labrador puppy all week? That decision was a little easier. Go back to work full-time or part-time? Easier decision. I like being home with Amy, I just occasionally need some real conversation. Part-time it was. But the biggest decision of all was what to do with Amy while I was back at work. Family day care, full-time day care, occasional care, the creche at work, friends, grandparents? After a lot of research, meetings, interviews, we finally decided to put Amy into family day care (FDC).

One of the things we like about FDC was that Amy would be looked after in the carer's home. She would be one of only a few and she wouldn't get lost in the system. It wasn't an easy decision and I remember wondering on that first day when I dropped Amy off, if we had done the right thing. Almost 12 months later I know we did the right thing. Amy goes to Maria's three days a week and loves it. I have trouble trying to get her to come home with me when I go to pick her up! Amy has fitted in really well and is just like another member of the family.

Bernadette Vella
Mum of two, Brisbane

Both my children attend child care three days per week. Tiernan started when he was a year old and Arielle started when she was 5 months old. I am lucky to have them in a wonderful, small, family-owned centre. The staff there are incredibly caring and supportive. They have been very understanding of my health issues and take extra special care of the kids. The kids love going to child care. They love their teachers and have made some really good friendships there. At the start and the end of each day they are in the same room and it is great seeing them interact with each other with their friends. They learn so many social skills being there and have learnt to be a little bit more independent from me which is great.

Danielle Murrihy
Mum of two, Melbourne

At 12 months of age I started putting the boys into occasional care for 5 hours once a week (oh bliss!) and when they turned 3 they went into the bigger room, so now they go for 7 hours. They really enjoy it, and I do too!

We also attend an early intervention kinder program one morning a week as one of my boys is autistic. Next year he will be going to two day sessions a week at a centre that will go from 9.00am to 3.00pm. It will be great for him and it means I will have some one-on-one time with his brother which I'm looking forward to.

Jess Tamblyn
Mum of one, SA

I'm a big fan of family day care. My daughter started attending family day care at 7 months for 3 days a week when I returned to part-time work. The low numbers of children and the consistency of the same carer meant my daughter experienced minimal distress when she first started.

Set within a family home with a maximum of four children under school age, family day care offers more flexibility than normal child care centres. My daughter also gets to go out and about every day as her carer goes on school runs, trips to the library and playground which help break up her day and offers her more variety and stimulation.

As a secondary school teacher my workload is spread across the week so on some days I only need care for a few hours. Family day care is much more cost effective than most child care centres that often charge for a full day even if you only need care for a couple of hours.

Kirstin Amos
Mum of one, QLD

Since I was going back to work full time after 12 months maternity leave my husband and I made the decision to put Carter in day care two days a week and for grandma to have Carter three days. Carter was a bit apprehensive at first as you would expect. I started him at day care a couple of weeks before going back to work and that meant if he was not happy and settled I could go and pick him up early and this did happen for the first couple of days. Then all of sudden Carter started enjoying himself and when I left him he made no fuss and just played happily. It definitely reduced my stress level when returning to work, knowing that Carter was happy and settled in the day care environment. I do believe that Carter spending time at a day care centre is a good thing because he is

Vox Pop

We asked a number of women and men around Australia to send in their advice, tips and personal experiences on a range of topics so that you have an insight into how others cope being a new parent. We hope you find their comments interesting, informative and reassuring. Vox Pop biographies: page 652

learning important social interaction tools – as he grows up he will be able to interact and play with others and not withdraw into himself because he is not use to being around other children.

Leanne Cummins
Mum of two, NSW

Many children are excited when they go off to school or child care with their special backpacks and drink bottles bought for this special occasion. We have spent a lot of time getting them used to the place, it feels good and we're happy leaving our most precious possessions in the hands of fully qualified people.

The day finally arrives. We walk them in, sign the book, carefully unpack their lunches and set them up at the playdough table to leave them with a special friend so that we can make a quick exit to our long list of places to be or things to do.

But after 2-3 days, they know the drill! Quick as a flash they attach themselves like a leech to your leg and start screaming to not leave them there! You feel like a failure, it wasn't supposed to be like this … what have you done wrong? You look around for someone to help.

The carer detaches your child and you run out feeling like your heart is in your throat. You are leaving your baby behind, the tears are flowing down your cheeks as you drive out, wondering whether to look back at that little face, still screaming for you to stay for 'just one more hug'.

Sometimes all you need is a sympathetic mum to give you a hug and say that she understands (no, you're not alone). My suggestion is to give your child a special hanky to keep tucked in their pocket – something very special, filled with hugs from mummy that they can carry with them all day and hug whenever they need you.

I often hear that children who need a little more love settle much faster when mums try this. I'm not sure how often it really helps, but I'm sure that leaving them with plenty of hugs certainly helps the mums!

Lucy Mulvany
Mum of three, SA

My three children all attend a local child care centre for two days a week while I work part time. I drop them at around 8.30am and pick them up at around 4.30pm. I went with my gut feeling on the carers when I chose the centre, and that seems to worked. The children love it, and I love to be able to work and be relaxed knowing that all three of my children are being so well cared for.

Rowena Raats
Mum of three, Kalgoorlie

My first went to part-time day care at 18 months to full-time at 2 years old. My second went at 12 weeks full-time. My third will start at 13 months for 2 days a week. I had always used long day care because in a small town your choices are limited and waiting lists are long. With my third child I put my name on the waiting list when I was 8 weeks pregnant and got a call when she was 8 months old!

Tracey Thompson
Mum of one, Brisbane

I put my son in child care when he was 9 months old. I have the luxury of not having to work but so many of my friends and even my GP said that child care is a great way for my son to learn from just interacting with the other children. I decided to put him in one day a week and it's the best thing I did. He loves it! He has learnt so much since he has been there and it's also somewhere that's different to being at home every day, which makes it interesting for him! Even though I didn't need to work I now work on the day he is there just to keep me up to date in the work force. (I am a nurse so things are always changing on a day-to-day basis.)

Anastasia Jones
Mum of two, Melbourne

I went back to work three days a week when my first child was three months old. Thankfully I didn't have to have her on a waiting list to get her into the day care centre that I felt was best. I visited about three centres near work and, in the end, went with my gut feeling. We are not lucky enough to have any family living near us so formal day care was our only option.

With our second child, we were living overseas and had a helper (maid/nanny) who looked after her (and the older one, then aged two). She has just started at day care back here in Australia and is settling in beautifully. I had originally thought she would have trouble settling into an environment with so many other children instead of the one-on-one care she was used to (when we were overseas).

While we were overseas, our eldest daughter attended a 'playgroup' which is the norm for children where we lived. For 2.5 hours a day they join a group of about 10 other children and paint, play and read books to the theme of the month (some groups have mothers attend also). Now that we are back in Australia, things are at the other end of the spectrum. No pre-school programs really exist that are similar to what our daughter had been doing overseas. Pre-school education is heavily reliant on education through informal play only and all the extra activities are considered too much for one child to be doing. Our daughter will start 4-year-old kindy next year and I am keen to see what this will involve.

Anna Brandt
Mum of one, QLD

If you want your baby/child to attend child care you will need to have yourself listed with the child care centre well in advance. Arrange a day and go around to several centres and check out how the different centres operate. Put your name down at a few centres to which you would be happy to send your baby/child and then you will just need to wait for that spot to become available. We were hoping for our baby to commence child care at approximately 6 months of age and so when I was 3 months pregnant we went around to the centres and put our name on the waiting lists. My baby has recently just started child care at 5.5 months old but we have been preparing for a little while in advance.

William started off by going to grandma's each week for a day and this has helped him become more independent and has given me the courage to leave him in somebody else's care and know that he'll be okay.

When we knew which centre he would be attending we went there two or three times for short visits so he would know the place before I actually dropped him off for the first time. This helped him and the carers meet so it wasn't all new the first day. During these short visits it gave me the opportunity to see how the children interacted with the carers and each other and also to see how the children are disciplined, put to bed, fed etcetera.

The centre we chose for William to attend suggested William start at the centre a couple of weeks prior to my returning to work. This helps make the transition easier and you can prepare for your return to work and actually be useful on your first day.

On our first day I don't think William even noticed I was gone. He was so excited to see the other babies and children that I had become 'old news' to him. To start out we only did half days and gradually increased the time William was at day care so he was staying there for full days prior to my returning back work.

If your baby/child has a routine type it out and give a copy to your baby/child's carer at the centre. I have found that having a routine but being flexible with the routine also is the easiest way to be. I have also found that day to day generally I am happier and I can plan my day so the day runs smoothly. If your routine has flexibility this helps also with the carers in the centre being able to follow it.

Resources

These Resources pages list products and services relevant to "Child care & early education".
To make your life easier as a parent, editorial listings have been grouped into sub categories.
Businesses then appear alphabetically under a national or a state-based subhead depending on reach.

SUB-CATEGORIES

ADVISORY SERVICES: CHILD CARE & EDUCATION

NATIONAL

Australian Scholarships Group
Tel: 1800 648 945
website: www.asg.com.au
In 1974 a small group of parents established the Australian Scholarships Group (ASG) as an independent not-for-profit Friendly Society helping families to provide for the future costs of their children's education. Today ASG is Australia's specialist provider of education scholarship benefits that enable families to provide an all-important start in life for their children. ASG's members believe education provides a means for their children to pursue their dreams and fulfil their potential. For more information on the Australian Scholarships Group phone 1800 648 945 or visit www.asg.com.au.

CareforKids.com.au
Tel: (02) 9235 2807
email: enquiries@careforkids.com.au
website: www.careforkids.com.au
Finding child care can be a daunting and time consuming process. How do you select the best child care services near you? That's exactly where CareforKids.com.au can help. It brings together all the pieces of the child care puzzle to make it faster and simpler for families to match children with the right care. Thousands of parents across Australia regularly turn to CareforKids.com.au in search of child care services which includes child care centres, babysitters, nannies, au pairs and more.

Family Day Care Australia
Tel: (02) 4320 1100 or freecall 1800 621 218
email: enquiries@fdca.com.au
website: www.familydaycare.com.au
Family day care is a child care experience like no other. Your child will learn through play in small groups of 4-5 pre-school aged children in the home of a trained child care professional. Activities such as story telling, singing, art and craft, playing games, visiting the park or the library are planned to suit your child's individual needs. They cater for the flexible needs of modern families through long day care programs, before/after school care, vacation care, overnight and weekend care by negotiation. Family day care is licensed and accredited to ensure the quality of care is of the highest standard. Carers are supported by a central co-ordination unit

which monitors care, places children and administers child care fee subsidies. To find a family day care place for your child near your home or work freecall 1800 621 218 or visit their website www.familydaycare.com.au.

Loretta Pace
Tel: (03) 9332 2611

Play Matters Handbook is an effective tool for guiding you through the early childhood basics. It is a simple and informative 50 page handbook that demonstrates how over 80 stimulating and exciting experiences can be offered to children. The handbook makes parents aware of teaching the right skill or using the right tool at the right time. Each age group from 0 to 5 is colour coded and it is simple, clear and easy to read.

National Childcare Accreditation Council Inc. (NCAC)
Tel: (02) 8260 1900
email: qualitycare@ncac.gov.au
website: www.ncac.gov.au

 NCAC administers Child Care Quality Assurance systems and can assist families looking for child care. Visit the NCAC website or phone NCAC for information on quality child care, advice on what to look for in a child care service and to find the names of registered and accredited child care services in any local area.

Seriously!! Kids!! Pty Ltd
Tel: 0449 639 195
email: info@seriouslykids.com.au
website: www.seriouslykids.com.au

Seriously!! Kids!! is an online, personable, hands-on, complete care connection providing parents with all the information you may need when caring for kids. It is a free resource with thousands of articles and videos packed with practical information, help, support and advice.

SIDS and Kids
Tel: National Office (03) 9819 4595 or 1300 308 307
email: national@sidsandkids.org
website: www.sidsandkids.org

 SIDS and Kids have created a Child Care Kit to spread the safe sleeping message. The kit contains vital training resources and information on infant health, specifically designed for child care centres.

VICTORIA

Child Care Centres Association of Victoria Inc.
Suite 6, 539 Highett Road
Highett VIC 3190
Tel: (03) 9532 2017
email: info@cccav.org.au
website: www.cccav.org.au

As the recognised peak body in Victoria, the Association constantly strives to be a leader in the future directions of children's services. Through their members they deliver high-quality childcare in caring and nurturing environments.

NEW SOUTH WALES

NSW Association for Gifted and Talented Children
C/- Hilltop Road Public School, Hilltop Road
Merrylands NSW 2160
Tel: (02) 9633 5399
website: www.nswagtc.org.au

The NSW Association for Gifted and Talented Children provides support for gifted young people, their parents and teachers. Services include a resource centre, website, counselling, playgroup and other activities.

NSW Family Day Care Association
PO Box N107
Petersham North NSW 2049
Tel: (02) 9572 9440
website: www.nswfdc.com.au

Family Day Care (FDC) is a government-approved child care service that provides quality care for children 0–12 years in a registered home environment. Family Day Care Carers offer individual attention to children in small group settings and ensure each child's health, safety and wellbeing while working with families to provide excellent care and education experiences. FDC is supported by the Children's Services Regulation 2004 and operates under the Australian Government's national accreditation system through the NCAC.

QUEENSLAND

Association for the Pre-School Education of Deaf Children
PO Box 177
Moorooka QLD 4105
Tel: (07) 3848 0080
email: preschool.assoc.deafchildren@uqconnect.net

The Association for the Pre-School Education of Deaf Children plays a vital role in promoting total communication of hearing impaired children aged 0–6 years. The Association provides specialised therapy teams including speech, occupational and physiotherapy.

BABYSITTER, NANNY & AU-PAIR AGENCIES

NATIONAL

Au-Pair Australia
Tel: (02) 9571 6121
email: info@aupairaustralia.com.au
website: www.aupairaustralia.com.au

 Au-Pair Australia places international live-in au pairs and live-in nannies in Victoria, new South Wales and Queensland. Overseas au-pairs can help the family with childcare and some light domestic duties. Placement starts from $180 for 30 hours work or $210 for 35 hours plus room and board. The common placement period is between 6 to 9 months. Most au-pairs have a driver's licence for school drop-off and pick-up and all au-pairs are referenced, health checked and have police clearance.

Resources

CHILD CARE & EARLY EDUCATION

Babysitter, nanny & au-pair agencies

Charlton Brown Nanny Agency and College

Tel: (07) 3221 3855 or 1300 nannies

email: info@charltonbrown.com.au

website: www.charltonbrown.com.au

Whether you need a couple of hours care or a couple of years, Charlton Brown can place a nanny to suit your specific requirements. (Charlton Brown is also an approved In Home Care provider). In addition to their nanny placement services, Charlton Brown provides hands-on, flexible and accredited training of nannies, child care professionals, aged care workers and disability support workers. For more information phone the number above or visit their website.

Dial-an-Angel Pty Limited

Vic: Melbourne (03) 9593 9888

NSW: Lindfield: (02) 9416 7511

NSW: Penrith: (02) 4722 3355

NSW: Gosford: (02) 4323 6688

NSW: Newcastle: (02) 4929 3065

Qld: Gold & Sunshine Coasts (07) 5591 8891

Qld: Brisbane (07) 3878 1077

WA: East Perth (08) 9364 5488

SA: North Adelaide (08) 8267 3700

ACT: Phillip (02) 6282 7733

(Not available in Tasmania or Northern Territory.)

email: administration@dialanangel.com

website: www.dialanangel.com

DIAL-AN-ANGEL, one of Australia's leading agencies in home and family care since 1967, provides families with mothercraft nurses, evening babysitters, after-school carers and nannies for daytime childcare. Phone DIAL-AN-ANGEL on one of the state numbers above for prompt professional service. All angels are personally interviewed and fully screened.

Expect a Star Education Services

Tel: 1300 669 653

email: services@expectastar.com.au

website: www.expectastar.com.au

Expect A Star Education Services offer a range of services to parents with children aged 0 to 3 years, including a nanny and babysitting service where you can conveniently place bookings online. Expect A Star also have an online store with a range of products sorted by age and/or development area. Other services include a national child care centre search to locate your nearest child care centre and family fun ideas for you and your family. Visit the website www.expectastar for more information.

Find a Babysitter.com.au

Tel: 1300 789 073

email: info@findababysitter.com.au

website: www.findababysitter.com.au

Find A Babysitter.com.au is Australia's leading introduction site helping parents find great nannies, after-school carers and babysitters. Parents pay a one-off joining fee to access the detailed carer profiles and place a Job Posting online. Parents interview, select and pay their own carers. There are no further overheads or costs. Find A Babysitter.com.au pride themselves on being a quality site, offering the most affordable and effective way of finding great carers. See the range of carers available in your area by doing a free trial search. Visit www.findababysitter.com.au and simply enter your postcode.

JCR Aupairs and Nannies

Tel: (03) 9557 0300

email: sorrel@jcraus.com.au

website: www.jcraus.com.au

JCR Aupair & Nannies can help you find your perfect live-in international aupair. From only $150 per week, it is flexible, economical and an affordable alternative. Aupairs stay for a minumum of 6 months, maximum 12 months. Fully referenced with at least 200 hours childcare experience. JCR Aupair & Nannies is a professional service that has been in business of matching families and aupairs for over 9 years working only with overseas associates.

VICTORIA

Abracadabra Brighton Domestic Agencies Pty Ltd

Suite 9, 214 Bay Street

Brighton VIC 3186

Tel: 0448-4-nanny

website: www.abrabrighton.com

The Abracadabra agency was established in 1984 and still operates under the original management headed by Sandy Faure. Abracadabra Brighton Domestic Agencies Pty Ltd is open seven days and can provide nannies and babysitters around the clock on a permanent or casual basis. Staff hold current police checks/WWC and first aid certificates and are all referenced checked. Approved provider for Workcover, TAC and In-Home Care (child care) with Government Child Care Benefit with 50% tax rebate for out-of-pocket expenses when passing the work/training/study test. The Child Care Tax Rebate is not income tested.

Asharon Agency

1381a Malvern Road

Malvern VIC 3144

Tel: (03) 9822 6964

email: asharon.agency@bigpond.com

Asharon Agency has been providing assistance to families for 40 years in the area of nannies, child care and domestic home help. Carers are selected for their reliability, punctuality and relevant experience. Carers may be engaged on a casual or permanent basis. All carers have police checks and first aid training. Asharon

Agency also offers assistance with domestic help, by way of cleaning and ironing. An after-hours service is available by phoning (03) 9822 6964.

Bambini Child Care Services
PO Box 234
Hawthorn VIC 3122
Tel: (03) 9813 5680
email: enquiries@bambini.com.au
website: www.bambini.com.au

Having trouble finding good quality affordable child care? Looking for an alternative to busy child care centres? Bambini is a privately owned family day care and in-home care service. Run by early childhood professionals and mothers who understand the difficulties in finding reliable child care that is affordable and flexible. As a provider of 'approved care' our In Home Care and Family Day Care offer you access to the Child Care Benefit and the 50% child care tax rebate.

Forest Hill Babysitting Service
33 Dorset Street
Glen Waverley VIC 3150
Tel: (03) 9562 0110

The Forest Hill Babysitting Service has been established for 46 years. They offer casual babysitting, day and evening, in the eastern suburbs. Their policy has been to only employ mothers as sitters and their office hours are 9.00am to 5.00pm Monday to Friday.

Help-On-The-Way
Level 1, 139 Glen Eira Road
St Kilda East VIC 3183
Tel: (03) 9528 6688
email: wehelp@helpontheway.com.au
website: www.helpontheway.com.au

Help-On-The-Way was established in 1990 to provide their clients with the ultimate in personal service, care and attention. Their home help services cover all aspects of childcare (nannies, babysitters, mothercraft nurses) and cleaning, elderly care and party help. All staff are insured and have either police clearances or wwcc and all child carers must have a current First Aid Certificate. Open Monday to Saturday. All areas. Gift vouchers available.

Mothers Dream Team t/a Placement Solutions
Tel: 1300 854 624
email: info@mothersdreamteam.com.au
website: www.mothersdreamteam.com.au

Placement Solutions, established in 1988, have the solutions for your family and home. They offer government-approved and rebated in-home child care including premier nannies for day, evening or night nannying services. Other services include placement services across Melbourne, cleaning and de-cluttering as well as seminars and training on all aspects of in-home care and home help.

Susan Rogan Family Care
504C-198 Harbour Esplanade
Docklands VIC 3008
Tel: (03) 9670 7686
email: office@susanrogan.com.au
website: www.susanrogan.com.au

Susan Rogan Family Care has provided trained and experienced nannies since 1991 for private and corporate clients. Services include recruitment of permanent nannies, providing nannies for short term and casual care and child care staff for functions. Susan Rogan Agency Nannies are not only carefully screened, they are employed and insured by the agency, giving you complete peace of mind. The agency is approved as a provider of In Home Care and these families can claim Child Care Benefit to reduce the cost of using a nanny. Phone for further details.

The Elite Nanny Service
Tel: (03) 9824 2484
email: elitenannyservice@bigpond.com
website: www.elitenannyservice.com.au

Elite Nanny Service offers advice and suitable options when providing assistance to cater for your childcare needs from casual day or evening care, a planned weekend away, a permanent full or part time nanny or just one morning per week. Mothercraft Nurses are available to assist new parents with all aspects of care for your newborn child including casual days, evenings and overnight care. All Elite nannies are professional, reliable and carefully screened. All nannies are qualified and experienced with Paediatric First Aid and all are reference and Australia-wide police checked. The Elite Nanny Service provides expertise when determining your childcare needs with the utmost professionalism.

Victorian Babysitting Service
117A Esplanade
Altona VIC 3018
Tel: (03) 9315 9880
email: rose@vicbab.com
website: www.vicbab.com

Victorian Babysitting Service provides experienced babysitters who care for your children in your own home up to a 30 kmilometre radius of Melbourne. Servicing many hotels in Melbourne suburbs and Geelong, all babysitters are reference and police checked, have first aid training and public liability insurance. Victorian Babysitting Service is registered with the Family Assistance Office and offers casual and ongoing care, day, evening and weekends. Phone for further details.

Virtual Personal Management
10 Apsley Court
Point Cook VIC 3030
Tel: (03) 9459 6857 or 0412 853 261
email: ntoleman@vpmanagement.com.au
website: www.vpmanagement.com.au

Resources

CHILD CARE & EARLY EDUCATION

Babysitter, nanny & au-pair agencies
➡ Early education programs

VPM specialises in the recruitment of nannies and lifestyle managers and are providers of the government-funded In Home Care Programme – 50% childcare tax rebate. VPM builds long-term relationships with clients and has a reputation for integrity, customer satisfaction and efficiency. Their people are driven by clear and consistent principles. Email or phone for more information.

NEW SOUTH WALES

Blue Ribbon Nannies & Carers
13 Third Street
Ashbury NSW 2193
Tel: (02) 9799 1077
email: blueribbonnanny@optusnet.com.au
website: www.blueribbonnannies.com.au
Blue Ribbon Nannies and Carers (established in 1995) caters for busy Sydney parents and their need for reliable home help. They provide nannies, babysitters, mother's helpers and before and after-school carers. Phone or visit www.blueribbonnannies.com.au for further details.

Modern Family Focus
PO Box 440
Waverley NSW 2024
Tel: (02) 9326 4111
email: info@modernfamilyfocus.com.au
website: www.modernfamilyfocus.com.au
Modern Family Focus provides a reliable, easy-to-use service. They deliver personalised, professional in-home childcare and domestic workers to support you and your family. They can cater to your individual needs with competitive prices and a unique service. Ask about their loyalty discounts, gift certificates or the unique Focus Care Kits.

Snow White Babysitting Agency
41 Berringar Road
Valentine NSW 2280
Tel: (02) 4946 8125
email: bemartin@tpg.com.au
Snow White Babysitting Agency has been arranging child care/babysitting since 1970. Competent carers, all screened by the NSW Commission for Children and Young People via their Working with Children Check come to the child's/children's home or to a hospitality establishment by appointment. 'At short notice' is their specialty. Phone for a comprehensive information package.

StarSitters Nanny & Babysitting Agency
Tel: 0406 404 285
email: info@starsitters.com.au
website: www.starsitters.com.au

StarSitters Nanny and Babysitting Agency is a friendly and reliable company dedicated to providing you with a wide range of child care services for all your family's needs. All carers are personally interviewed and thoroughly screened including reference checks and "working with children" background checks. Nannies and babysitters are available for full-time, part-time and casual work, before and after-school care, as mothers' helpers, for nanny-share positions as well as overnight, weekday/nights and weekends. For the St. George and Sutherland Shire phone Sarah Borg on 0406 404 341 and all other areas phone Jess Moyes on 0406 404 285.

QUEENSLAND

Gold Coast Nannies
Tel: 0431 301 916
email: justine@goldcoastnannies.com.au
website: www.goldcoastnannies.com.au
Gold Coast Nannies' qualified child care professionals and nannies will provide a safe and exciting experience for your children. Parents will have peace of mind, knowing their most precious assets are in the hands of an experienced and professional team. Available 24 hours a day, 7 days a week for all your babysitting needs. Gold Coast Nannies has full-time and part-time nannies that can care for your children in your home. All staff have blue cards, first aid experience and/or qualifications.

Indigo Services
PO Box 2165
Toowong QLD 4066
Tel: 1300 669 460
email: info@indigoservices.com.au
website: www.indigoservices.com.au
Indigo take the hard work out of sourcing, interviewing and recruiting domestic staff and offer an efficient and professional service. Formerly known as Musden Emergency Mums, they have been successfully operating since 1979 and take pride in matching the right people to the right clients and giving premium customer service. Their workers will live-in or live-out on a casual, temporary or permanent basis.

WESTERN AUSTRALIA

mrs doubtfire
PO Box 843
Claremont WA 6910
Tel: 1300 882 493
email: info@mrsd.com.au
website: www.mrsd.com.au
Established in 1999 mrs doubtfire offers a personal service, tailored to your needs, in your home. They offer

qualified professional nannies, night time babysitters, mothers helpers and au pairs. Gift vouchers are available.

Results Nannies – Au-Pairs International
PO Box 3266
Success WA 6964
Tel: (08) 9499 4685
email: robert@theresultsgroup.com.au
website: www.theresultsgroup.com.au

Results Nannies & Au-Pairs International offer local and international nanny placement with affordable and reliable nannies, au-pairs, mother's helpers with prompt, courteous and efficient service at all times. Phone for further details.

Toptots Early Development Centre
Tel: 0412 481 708
email: mail@toptots.net.au
website: www.toptots.net.au

Toptots® Edu-Centre WA is an early development education centre focusing on parent and child classes. In house and at home tutoring is available from birth to age 10 years – baby school, pre-kindy, kindergarten, pre-school to Grade 7 and beyond. Phone 0412 481 708 or visit www.toptots.net.au for further information.

EARLY EDUCATION PROGRAMS

NATIONAL

Baby Hands Insitute Pty Ltd
Tel: (02) 8230 1513
email: info@australianbabyhands.com
website: www.australianbabyhands.com

Baby Hands Institute provide fun educational classes on communicating with your baby using Australian Sign Language. Baby Hands Institute classes are unique as they incorporate Auslan and they also offer parents and babies the opportunity to increase their baby signing vocabulary in a fun environment. Baby signing is a communication tool which has been successfully implemented in homes around the world. For more information on teachers and classes available visit their website.

VICTORIA

Early Childhood Management Services
Tel: (03) 8481 1100
email: ecms@ecms.org.au
website: www.ecms.org.au

ECMS is a not-for-profit organisation which manages community kindergarten, childcare and family day care services throughout Victoria. They believe that all young children should have access to high quality care and educational programs which provide a stimulating, safe and caring environment. Their programs aim to promote the physical, social, emotional and intellectual development of children.

ECMS Family Day Care
Tel: (03) 9731 7948
email: fdc@ecms.org.au
website: www.ecms.org.au/familydaycare.html

ECMS Family Day Care is a unique home-based childcare service providing quality childcare in the homes of caring and professional care providers. With its warm home like environments, family day care provides flexible childcare and caters to the individual needs of children and their families. They acknowledge that all children have the right to grow and develop in a warm, safe and secure environment.

Edworks Active Learning
PO Box 1008
Camberwell VIC 3124
Tel: (03) 9882 8777
email: edworks@edworksglobal.com
website: www.edworks.com.au

Edworks Active Learning teaches children to work smart. Edworks develops the highest skill level in its students to maximise their achievement for the year at hand and, importantly, for the challenging years ahead. In a positive and stimulating atmosphere, students acquire the confidence to develop independent learning skills that lay the vital foundations for your child's future. Contact them to organise a free assessment.

The Tutor Place
147 Miller Street
Thornbury VIC 3071
Tel: (03) 9416 7849
email: annette@thetutorplace.com.au

Give your child the educational edge in a challenging learning environment. The Tutor Place tailors programs according to your child's needs and offers: Pre-Prep Programs; Beginners Prep Programs; Literacy Recovery Programs (Prep to Grade 3) and Literacy Enhancement Programs (Grade 4 to Grade 6). All programs include reading strategies, writing and comprehension skills, spelling and phonological awareness. Guaranteed successful positive quality outcomes with fully qualified experienced teachers.

NEW SOUTH WALES

Hands Can Talk
1 Delta Close
Raby NSW 2566
Tel: (02) 9824 8332
website: www.handscantalk.com.au

Hands Can Talk makes communication easy for you and your baby using sign language. Fun, interactive, Australian (Auslan based) sign language workshops are held throughout NSW. Baby/Toddler, Toddler/Preschooler, Sing & Sign, Special needs & Makaton Basic. Hands Can Talk have specialised in Australian (Auslan based) sign language workshops and resources for over ten years. Visit their website for more information on baby sign, the benefits, baby sign resources, testimonials, discount orders and online learning.

Resources

CHILD CARE & EARLY EDUCATION

Fundraising
→ Kindy bags, lunchboxes & paraphernalia

QUEENSLAND

C&K (Creche & Kindergarten Association)
14 Edmondstone Street
Newmarket QLD 4051
Tel: 1800 177 092
website: www.candk.asn.au

C&K, which has more than 400 services throughout Queensland, offers kindergarten (pre-prep programs), child care, family day care and in-home care. C&K is the only state-wide early childhood organisation that is recognised and funded by the Department of Education, Training and the Arts. They employ university-qualified early childhood teachers, have high staff/children ratios, big play areas and welcome parent involvement.

FUNDRAISING

NATIONAL

Creative Memories
Tel: (03) 9561 6089 or 0414 299 923
email: davis_kelly@optusnet.com.au

Want a fun, relaxed fundraiser where participants receive excellent value for money? Creative Memories helps you create safe and meaningful scrapbook photo albums through beginner classes and workshops. Classes are tailored to suit your organisation's needs and consultants are available Australia wide.

Direct Publications
Tel: 1300 653 305
email: admin@directdigital.com.au
website: www.fundraisingdirectory.com.au

The Fundraising Directory is a book and website that offers a comprehensive search and browse facility for fundraising products and suppliers in Australia. Both are available at no cost to the community sector in Australia, including schools, kindergartens sporting clubs and special interest groups. On the Fundraising Directory website, each supplier has a full page of information on their fundraising program so that all your fundraising research can done from the one resource.

Expressions Australia Pty Ltd
Tel: 1300 855 509
website: www.expressions.com.au

Expressions Australia offers tea towels and aprons screen printed with drawings or handprints done by everyone in your school, club or kinder. Their group projects are a fun and easy way to raise funds, with no upfront costs. They pride themselves on providing high standards of customer service and quality products that make wonderful mementoes and fabulous gifts. Phone them on 1300 855 509 for a free sample tea towel.

Fundraising Adventures
Tel: 1300 554 282
email: info@fundraisingadventures.com.au
website: www.fundraisingadventures.com.au

Fundraising Adventures has individual /personalised fundraising programs to help schools, preschools, clubs and charities raise funds. These fundraising programs are easy to implement as they do 90% of the work yet your organisation gets to keep up to 70% of all the monies raised. For a free information pack phone 1300 554 282 or visit the website for more information.

Highland Toys
Tel: 0403 804 904
email: enquiries@highlandtoys.com.au
website: www.highlandtoys.com.au

Highland Toys offer fundraising opportunities for child care centres, preschools and playgroups with their great range of high quality wooden toys – solid, traditional toys that children love and that are designed to last. Their range includes rocking horses, doll's houses, trains, trucks, blocks, baby toys, musical instruments, role play, puzzles and pull-along toys. A number of the toys are handcrafted and Australian made.

Jelly Bean Amusements
12/43 Bayldon Road
Queanbeyan NSW 2620
Tel: 1300 136 825
email: enquiries@jba.net.au
website: www.jba.net.au

Jelly Bean Amusements can supply pre-packaged fairy floss suitable for resale to the general public. Their pre-packaged fairy floss and popcorn is made to order which ensures that it is fresh on the day it is delivered. Pre-packaged fairy floss and popcorn keeps well and has a shelf life of three months. Each fairy floss order is supplied with a minimum of three different coloured bags in order to increase the visual impact when you are selling it. Specific colours are also available on request. Product is priced at $2.00 per 65g bag with a recommended resale price of $3 to $3.50 per bag. Free delivery is available for orders within the ACT.

Mr. Showbags
Tel: 1300 MR SHOWBAGS (1300 677 469)
email: sales@mrshowbags.com.au
website: www.mrshowbags.com.au

Mr. Showbags is a national supplier providing pre-packed, value for money, exciting showbags for all your fundraising needs. If you're having a fete or would like to raise money for a community group then give the staff at Mr Showbags a call and they will be happy to answer your questions.

Prospect Wines

Tel: (03) 9877 1099
email: sales@prospectwines.com.au
website: www.prospectwines.com.au

Your group can make between 30 to 50% profit selling wine with Prospect Wines. They source wines from premium regions around Australia and provide them direct to fundraisers. All wine is labelled with your exclusive design and logo and they offer an Australia-wide service (excluding WA and NT) with no minimum quantity. Contact Prospect Wines to arrange for an information kit to be emailed or posted.

KINDY BAGS, LUNCHBOXES & PARAPHERNALIA

NATIONAL

4MyEarth

email: sales@4myearth.com.au
website: www.4myearth.com.au

4MyEarth Food Wraps and Pockets are environmentally friendly and non-toxic. The wraps and pockets can be re-used again and again. Great for sandwiches, cut up fruit and snacks, and the food safe coating keeps food fresh and dry. The wrap also acts as a place mat so no matter where you are you have a clean eating surface. Email for more information.

Allergy Kidz Ware

Tel: (02) 4683 0445
email: info@allergykidzware.com.au
website: www.allergykidzware.com.au

Does food trigger the most horrific reactions in your child? Allergy Kidz Ware is committed to providing fun, quality products to help protect carers and children who have special dietary needs. No one wants to bring unnecessary attention to a child, but when it could be life or death a balance must be found. These trendy customised embroidered t-shirts, hats, bibs and medicine bags allow you to embroider your specific requirements. Badges and customised food bags are also available. For more information about these unique designs visit www.allergykidzware.com.au.

Bubbalicious Blankies

Tel: 0427 762 774
email: mitch252@hotmail.com
website: www.bubbaliciousblankies.com.au

Bubbalicious Blankies produce top quality, personalised products for the special people in your life. They offer a huge selection of products including blankets, bunny rugs, towels, art smocks, reader bags, placemats, Santa sacks and stockings and much more. Visit their site to see the full range. Each item is embroidered individually.

kiddysac

Tel: 0412 077 528
email: info@kiddysac.com.au
website: www.kiddysac.com.au

Kiddysac are bright, colourful bags and storage solutions, perfectly designed for the youngest child through to 7 years. Kiddysac focuses on bright block colours, accentuated with fun designs like dinosaurs, pirates, princesses and monkeys. Made from 100% cotton drill, they are both durable and washable. Kiddysac bags are perfect to take to kindy, daycare, swimming, and the beach or just out and about. The range includes purses, pencil cases, toiletry bags, mini handbags, drawstring bags, backpacks, swim bags and wall pockets.

kindy kamper

Tel: 0413 408 036
email: kindykamper@iprimus.com.au
website: www.kindykamper.com.au

Kindy Kamper is a cosy, comfy and convenient all-in-one kindy bedding solution for busy mums and dads. Kindy Kamper has a comfy padded base (no more cold and uncomfortable kindy mats and beds), an attached top sheet, pillowcase (with removable insert) and a zip-on/zip-off polar fleece blanket. It also comes with adjustable Velcro corners for a snug fit and will fit most kindy mats and stretcher beds. Kindy Kamper rolls into a convenient and easy-to-carry swag with a carry handle and name label.

Little Beetle

Tel: (03) 9579 1036
email: info@littlebeetle.com.au
website: www.littlebeetle.com.au

Little Beetle has a gorgeous new range of kiddie bags offering a choice of 4 great designs. Excellent quality and value with plenty of room and a drink bottle is included. These make a fantastic gift and are perfect for crèche or kinder.

Smart Stuff

Tel: (03) 5428 4822
email: info@smartstuff.com.au
website: www.smartstuff.com.au

Smart Stuff's Australian-made art smocks are bright and colourful and have no buttons, ties or elastic. Using only quality fabrics these smocks are hardwearing and offer fantastic protection against paint, glue and any messy situation. Available in sizes 2 to 14. Great for home, playgroup or school. Generous discounts for group orders too.

Tupperware Australia Pty Ltd

Tel: 1800 805 396
website: www.tupperware.com.au

Tupperware® From your toddler's first outing through to their last day of school, Tupperware will see them provided for with good looking, durable and well designed containers. Tupperware offers a myriad of bright storage containers from Tumblers with Sipper Seals for littlies learning to drink, to Sports Bottles to keep them hydrated without being too big to handle right through to environmentally friendly Sandwich Keepers that keep sandwiches fresh and lunchtime rubbish free.

NCAC

In recent years, the changing and diverse needs of families in Australia has increased the demand for quality child care services. The quality of care children receive and their learning experiences, particularly in their first few years of life, are critical in shaping their future.

Quality child care services provide more than just child care. They promote the development of positive relationships between children, families and child care professionals and provide experiences which foster the way children think, imagine, create, problem solve, interact with others and understand their place in the world.

The National Child Care Accreditation Council (NCAC) aims to assist families understand the value of quality care and help them make informed decisions when selecting a child care service. NCAC assists families by setting quality standards for child care services receiving Child Care Benefit funding. These standards aim to ensure children's health and safety and to promote play, learning and development through positive experiences and interactions.

Placing your child in child care is an exciting though sometimes overwhelming experience for many families. Before you can begin using child care, you will need to consider issues such as when you want to start using care, what child care options are available, how to access child care, and what you might expect when you child starts care. Families seeking quality child care are encouraged to consider what the best questions to ask are and what to look for in a child care service.

For further information about finding and choosing a quality child care service telephone NCAC on 1300 136 554, e-mail qualitycare@ncac.gov.au or visit the NCAC website www.ncac.gov.au. Family Factsheets, which are available from the Families and Children section on the website have advice and tips to assist families to prepare for child care.

You want the best care for your child...
We can help you find it

The National Childcare Accreditation Council (NCAC) supports families looking for quality child care.

NCAC can give you advice on what to look for in a quality child care environment and can also provide you with the names and contact details of registered and accredited child care services in your area through an easy search facility on our website, or by contacting us.

For more information about quality child care services, or the Child Care Quality Assurance systems administered by NCAC, please visit our website (www.ncac.gov.au) or telephone NCAC on 1300 136 554 for a free Family Information Pack.

Level 3, 418a Elizabeth Street, Surry Hills NSW 2010
Telephone: (02) 8260 1900 or 1300 136 554 (toll free)
Facsimile: (02) 8260 1901
E-mail: qualitycare@ncac.gov.au

www.ncac.gov.au

NCAC
National Childcare
Accreditation Council Inc.

Help,
advice
& referrals

Photograph by Maple Gallery, Melbourne.

Postnatal depression

Adjusting to life as a mother can be difficult. In fact, for many women, having a baby is the most significant life-changing event they will ever experience. Adjusting to this major life change, as well as coping with the day-to-day demands of a new baby, can make some women more likely to experience depression at this time, particularly if they've experienced depression in the past.

How common is postnatal depression?

Postnatal depression (PND) affects 14 per cent of new mothers in Australia. As with depression, PND is common. On average, one in five people will experience depression at some point in their lives – one in four females and one in six males. Around one million Australian adults and 100,000 young people live with depression each year.

What causes postnatal depression?

Like depression which occurs at any other time, postnatal depression doesn't have one definite cause – but it's likely to result from a combination of factors including:

- a past history of depression and/or anxiety
- a stressful pregnancy
- depression during the current pregnancy
- a family history of mental disorders
- experiencing severe 'baby blues'
- a prolonged labour and/or delivery complications
- problems with the baby's health
- difficulty breastfeeding
- a lack of practical, financial and/or emotional support
- past history of abuse
- difficulties in close relationships
- being a single parent
- having an unsettled baby (e.g. difficulties with feeding and sleeping)
- having unrealistic expectations about motherhood
- moving house
- making work adjustments (e.g. stopping or re-starting work).

How do you know if you have postnatal depression?

Postnatal depression has the same signs and symptoms as depression. Women with PND can experience a prolonged period of low mood, reduced interest in activities, tiredness and disturbance of sleep and appetite and negative thoughts and feelings.

To find out about the general symptoms of depression, go to the series of depression checklists at www.beyondblue.org.au.

How is postnatal depression treated?

There is a range of effective treatments for managing PND.

Psychological treatment

Psychological treatment, which is often referred to as 'talking therapy' has generally been found to be the most effective way of treating postnatal depression. Psychological treatment can help by:

- changing negative thoughts and feelings
- encouraging involvement in activities
- speeding recovery
- preventing depression from getting serious again.

Medication

Medication can play an important role in helping people with depression manage from day to day. Some people may worry about how anti-depressants will affect a baby who is breastfed. However, remaining on medication can be important in order to avoid significant depression which can have a negative impact for both mother and baby. If the mother is breastfeeding, specific types of medications are preferred. While a number of factors will influence the choice of antidepressant, SSRIs – sertraline, citalopram and fluvoxamine – have been found to be least likely to cause any harm to infants.

The decision to take medication is up to the individual and should be made in consultation with a doctor, after considering the risks and benefits to both the mother and infant. For more details visit www.beyondblue.org.au or call the beyondblue info line on 1300 22 4636 (local call).

How to help yourself if you have postnatal depression

- Seek help and treatment from a doctor or other qualified health professional.
- Seek friendships with other women, including other mums who have postnatal depression.
- Organise child care or ask friends or family to look after the child/ren occasionally to allow you to have time to yourself.
- Make sure you take time to do the things you enjoy like reading a book, listening to music or having a bath.
- Spend some time with your partner to help nurture the relationship.
- Develop a support system of friends, family and professionals and accept help.
- Restrict visitors when feeling unwell, overwhelmed or tired.
- Take things one step at a time.
- Don't bottle up feelings – discuss them with friends, family and your partner.
- Eat a balanced diet.
- Practise deep breathing and muscle relaxation techniques.
- Try to establish good sleeping patterns.
- Learn about postnatal depression.
- Call a postnatal depression support service or mental health crisis line if things are getting tough and other help is not available.

Information supplied by beyondblue, www.beyondblue.org.au.

Managing strong emotions

When people think about becoming parents, they often imagine the delight of gazing into their child's loving face. Many people are surprised and concerned by some of their responses to their children.

There are some healthy and typical behaviours in young children that can be challenging to loving parents. Toddlers tantrum when frustrated or angry, and although these behaviours are to be expected at this developmental stage, they can be unpleasant to witness and difficult when the behaviour disrupts a family's plans. For some parents, these experiences raise strong feelings.

Some parents feel worried about their children's behaviour. They can feel frustrated and angry and often these feelings have not been anticipated. This can lead to parents doubting their abilities to contain their own behaviour. Parent helplines often receive calls from parents who are alarmed about their responses and behaviour towards their children. Anger is a healthy emotion with the purpose of giving us great energy to address an issue. Anger in itself is not the issue, it is what you do with it. When parents lose their cool, children's behaviour can escalate. Children need assistance with managing their strong feelings and learn acceptable behaviours by watching their parents. It is important for parents to learn to manage strong feelings and they are more likely to enjoy their parenting experience. Many parents have found it useful to have some tips for managing their own strong feelings:

- View the child's behaviour as being within the scope of 'normal' behaviour. When this occurs, many parents find they feel more comfortable and relaxed. The child's behaviour is not about you, the parent; it is about the child and his or her feelings of emotions, such as frustration.
- Predict high-risk times. If you are aware that you are more vulnerable when you are tired or busy, then plan around these times and avoid situations that will challenge your child.
- Identify what happens before you become distressed. Many people find that their breathing changes, they clench their teeth or a 'knot' appears in their stomach. With these signs your body is telling you that you are at risk of behaving in a manner you might regret.
- Plan to do something specific when your body gives you these signs, walk out of the room, breathe slowly, picture yourself somewhere pleasant, count to 10 or 100, whatever it takes for you to be in a calm place again. Planning ahead for managing these high-risk times can be very helpful.
- Ensure you spend time with the people who help you feel good about yourself.
- Take care of yourself by doing some things for you.
- Be fair on yourself. Parents don't have to get it right all the time for children to be okay.
- Talk to a professional. If you feel that you are angrier than you can manage or you are behaving aggressively towards your children, it is time to seek professional help. Psychologists, social workers and family counsellors are all people well trained to assist you in your parenting role. Telephone services such as Parentline talk to many parents who feel guilty about their levels of anger and are distressed about their own behaviours in trying to manage the situation.

Learning ways of managing strong emotions is important so that parenting is enjoyable.

Written by Bronwyn Thomas, a social worker with more than 20 years experience working with families over parenting issues. She works as a counsellor at Parentline. Parentline is a confidential telephone counselling, information and referral service for all Victorian parents and carers with children aged from birth to 18 years. Parentline is accessible from anywhere in Victoria for the cost of a local call (excluding mobiles). Phone 13 22 89.

Is it my fault?

A woman who is living with a violent partner is often told that the violence is her fault. You know that if you are told something often enough you begin to believe it. A violent partner will constantly put you down in front of friends and family. You begin to lose your self-esteem and confidence in your own abilities and you start to think "if only I was a better wife, lover and mother this would not be happening". Unfortunately, it does not matter what you do or say.

The violence will continue to happen. *The violence is not your fault.* Domestic violence occurs because a male partner chooses to use power to control and frighten his intimate partner. The perpetrators of domestic violence are mainly men and the vast majority of victims are women.

Violence against women is a major issue in Australia and it is prevalent and widespread in all of our communities. The Commonwealth's Office for Women in Canberra states that "domestic violence occurs when a family member, partner or ex-partner attempts to physically dominate or harm the other. Domestic violence can be exhibited in many forms, including physical violence, sexual abuse, emotional abuse, intimidation, economic deprivation or threats of violence".

Throughout Australia there is now a growing awareness of the significance of animal abuse in domestic violence. Pet animals are often threatened or harmed to coerce women into staying within an abusive relationship.

In the past women have delayed leaving because of concern for their pets. Shelter programs for pets are being established so that women can now leave knowing that their animals will be safe too.

If you are in an abusive relationship you should tell a trusted friend or relative what is happening. Remember that the perpetrator is violent, usually behind closed doors, and is relying on your silence to keep the abuse secret.

Do not feel ashamed to talk about the abuse because *the violence is not your fault.* Ring a local domestic violence service and talk about what is happening and discuss with them what you want to do and how it can be achieved.

Many women say that they "just want the violence to stop" but unfortunately it will not stop until the perpetrator takes responsibility for his violence. This will only happen when the abusive behaviour is exposed and appropriate services can then be involved.

| If you are experiencing domestic violence then call the Crisis Line in your state for information and support. | State Domestic Violence Crisis Lines: | **VIC:** (03) 9322 3555 or 1800 015 188 **ACT:** (02) 6280 0900 **NT:** 1800 019 116 **QLD:** 1800 811 811 | **WA:** 1800 199 008 **SA:** 1300 782 200 **NSW:** 1800 656 463 **TAS:** 1800 633 937 |

Written by Judy Johnson, OAM.

Australian Childhood Foundation

Child abuse is one of Australia's most critical social problems. There were more than 309,517 reported cases of child abuse in Australia in 2007 – that is one report every two minutes. The number of reports has doubled in the past decade.

More infants under the age of 12 months were found to have been abused or neglected than children in any other age group. In 2007 there were more children living away from their family for their own protection than ever before. The number of children in care has more than doubled in the past decade. There are five main types of child abuse. Many children experience more than one form of abuse.

Physical abuse occurs when a parent or carer physically injures a child or young person intentionally. The physical abuse of children is illegal and includes hitting, shaking, throwing, burning and biting children and young people. Certain types of punishment, whilst not causing injury can also be considered physical abuse if they place a child at risk of being hurt, for example, locking a child outside in cold weather.

Emotional and psychological abuse occurs when children or young people do not receive the love, affection or attention they need to feel good about themselves or develop properly. Constant criticism, teasing, ignoring, yelling and rejection are all examples of emotional and psychological abuse.

Child sexual abuse occurs when an adult or someone bigger or older involves a child or young person in any sexual activity. Perpetrators of sexual abuse take advantage of their power, authority or position over the child or young person to gratify themselves. Child sexual abuse is a crime.

Neglect is when a child or young person's basic needs for food, housing, health care and warm clothing are not met. Children who are made to live in unhygienic conditions are said to experience neglect. Leaving children without adequate supervision for their age is also a form of neglect.

Exposure to family violence between adults in a child's home is harmful to children. It can include witnessing violence or being aware of it happening between adults in the home.

Why does child abuse happen?

Eliza (17 years) was sexually abused by her father from a very early age. She cannot remember how old she might have been when it began. For her, the abuse was as much a part of her life as 'washing the dishes or taking the dog for a walk'. She thought it was normal and had no idea that there were words for what her father was doing to her. Eliza believed that her family was ordinary and normal.

Child abuse and neglect are complex problems. There is no one single cause. Different forms of child abuse are caused by different factors or different combinations of factors. Some of the factors which can lead to child abuse are described below. At the core of all forms of child abuse is a lack of basic respect for children.

Community tolerance of violence against children. There is still some acceptance in the community for the use of physical force for the purposes of discipline and punishment of children. When held strongly by individual parents, these attitudes can support the physical and emotional abuse of children. This behaviour would not be tolerated between adults.

Lack of community understanding about the consequences of child abuse and neglect on children. Research has shown that the general public have a poor understanding of the true extent of the problem of child abuse in Australia. As a result, child abuse does not readily register as an issue of community concern. This leaves all of us without the knowledge and the confidence to know what to do to prevent child abuse in the first place or take action if we are worried about the safety of a child.

Adults who are sexually and physically violent. Some adults engage in physical and sexual violence towards other adults and children. This violence may often stem from individual psychological problems, low self-esteem and a history of abuse and violence in their own childhood. Sex offenders hurt children because of a range of complex psychological and emotional problems.

Parents under stress. Child abuse can occur when parents experience stress and find it difficult to ask for or use support. Stress can be caused by unemployment, financial problems, divorce and separation. Parents under stress can sometimes transfer their feelings of frustration onto their children. The stress can also affect their judgement and decision making as a parent.

Parents with health or mental health problems. Child abuse and neglect can sometimes occur when parents have a personal problem or illness which affects their ability to parent their children. Many parents with a mental illness that is being treated and who receive adequate support can parent their children well. Parents who have a mental illness that is unrecognised or untreated or who lack important supports may neglect or abuse their children. Their illness may make it difficult for them to identify or meet their child's growing needs for security or stimulation. Parents who are addicted to illicit drugs or alcohol can leave their children in unsafe environments or without adequate supervision. When substance or alcohol affected, some parents may be more prone to using violence against their partners and/or their children. Without adequate support, parents with an intellectual disability may sometimes not be able to care for their children.

Parents who lack parenting skills. Sometimes child abuse and neglect can be caused by parents who have poor parenting skills. This may be because they did not have positive role models in their own parents. Sometimes, a lack of confidence and low self-esteem prevent parents from knowing how to change harmful or negative parenting styles.

Families who are isolated. Families who are socially isolated are sometimes not able to find people to support them if they start having problems parenting their children. Often families who are isolated have no extended family network and often feel left out of their community. Sometimes, families experience isolation because of the loss of a parent through death or separation. Some families experience isolation because they become homeless and have to live in temporary accommodation.

Child abuse does not happen to other children who live in families and neighbourhoods that are somehow different from yours. It can happen to children just like your own children, grandchildren, nieces and nephews. It can happen to children who attend the local school or play in the local football team. It can happen in your neighbourhood.

Children do not have the power to stop their abuse. Adults do.

Every action counts, no matter how small.

Play your part.

Visit www.stopchildabusenow.com.au.

Vox Pop

We asked a number of women and men around Australia to send in their advice, tips and personal experiences on a range of topics so that you have an insight into how others cope being a new parent. We hope you find their comments interesting, informative and reassuring. Vox Pop biographies: page 652

Bernadette Vella
Mum of two, Brisbane

My mum has been the most wonderful source of support throughout. She gives her advice when I ask but never forces her ideas upon me. She always seems to be there just when I need her. The past few years have been difficult for her, being faced with potentially losing her daughter to cancer, but she has been a tower of strength for me. The rest of my family, dad, brothers, sister and partners, have also been wonderful support. They are always there when I need them and have shared all of the ups and downs of my journey.

I suppose I did not realise how important family really was until I had kids and especially since getting sick.

I am also lucky enough to belong to a wonderful mothers' group and in addition to me having cancer, one of the little boys in our group drowned last year. We have supported each other through these two awful events and grown incredibly close. We have had other various challenges to face and we are lucky enough to be able to share both our stresses and our happiness. We met five years ago in ante-natal classes and we are still going strong today.

I also tend to find online forums wonderful. I use online forums for all areas of life, be it work, technology, my cancer or my kids. There is lots of good advice floating around and they are also a great place to be able to have a vent anonymously!

My most difficult time was obviously having cancer with two young children. Seeing the lack of support available was what prompted me to start Mummy's Wish – a charity supporting mums with cancer. Our aim is to help mothers diagnosed with cancer while they have under school-aged children.

We provide information about other support available, make the cancer wards in hospitals more child friendly, provide treat bags to brighten their day and provide emotional and financial support.

Just knowing that someone else has been there and survived can help you get through.

Alana White
Mum of one, SA

Once Jaylan was born I wanted answers to everything, but soon found out that babies don't come with a manual! I have a Child and Youth Health Services nurse come out to me once a fortnight to weigh and check Jaylan and myself. Because I have suffered from postnatal depression I have needed the extra attention and support.

The nurse brings out information on topics such as babies' milestones, when to feed solids, etcetera. The Children, Youth & Women's Health Service website is also very helpful for parent's questions and baby information – www.cywhs.sa.gov.au.

I think the best advice you can get is from other mothers. Asking your mum or grandma can be annoying and their answers are likely to be quite ancient! Attending Playgroups and mothers groups can also be very beneficial for you and your bubs.

Cindy Fraser
Mum of three, Melbourne

I wanted a speech assessment for our eldest son. I was lucky to know of a few through my work as a kindergarten teacher and within no time I had organised an assessment for him. Our therapist was wonderful – she would give us games and activities to take home as 'homework' which our son loved doing. Overall we had 10 sessions, spaced out over 6 months and the results are wonderful; we couldn't believe how quickly his speech developed in such a short space of time. I was also keen for one of the twins to have an assessment, and for me to also gain some ideas on how to promote his language development. Our speech therapist was no longer practicing so referred us to a colleague of hers. The best thing about our new therapist is that she comes to us. This means that the children are comfortable in their own environment which usually means they open up and respond to her faster. The other bonus is that I do not need to organise child care for my other children as I can just provide them with activities in other rooms of the house.

Danielle Murrihy
Mum of two, Melbourne

When my boys were 6 months old and I was at the end of my tether we ended up at a mother baby unit (sleep school) for a 5-day stay. I learnt so much and it really helped with their sleeping and my sanity. I am also an active member of my local Multiple Birth Association. This club has been a great deal of comfort, friendship and acceptance for me as a mum and as a person. It is great to go somewhere that's safe for the kids and where you can blend in with the crowd. Here I get no second looks, no silly advice from people who do not have a clue, no silly personal questions and no disapproving looks when two toddler twins go into a simultaneous meltdown. If you have multiples do yourself a favour and join your local club!

Kaz Cooke
Mum of one, Melbourne

I think it's perfectly logical to feel depressed or sad sometimes about the life and independence you left behind. But if you feel like that all the time, or a lot, then you need to get help (maybe even just so you can get more sleep). Sleep deprivation makes everything seem so much harder. Don't go into yourself – reach out for help. I did, I used to ring the advice lines, and went to a sleep clinic: it made me feel reassured, more normal and less alone. If you put on a lot of weight, put away full-length mirrors and don't buy magazines with stories about people like Angelina Jolie losing 67 kilos in 3 days after the birth: just concentrate on getting to know your baby in the early days. This is no time to be wondering what Angelina has done with her arse.

Ros Pittard
Mum of two, VIC

We found many of the behaviours of our first baby to be very challenging, and called the Maternal and Child Health Help Line countless times for help. We also had to see health professionals at the Royal Children's Hospital and I was usually very tired and teary. Without exception, the services and professionals we accessed were non-judgmental, caring and patient. Whatever you do, don't be afraid to ask for help. There is a lot available and it is likely to make a big difference to how you manage challenging times. While you wouldn't wish your hard times on any parent, it is very comforting to know there are many others having similar experiences. Not talking or seeking help can feel very isolating, which is of course not good for you, and not good for your baby.

Leanne Cummins
Mum of two, NSW

From the minute a new mum finds out she is pregnant, she becomes susceptible to stories and advice from just about everyone she meets …
how big (or small) the baby is, whether it's a boy or a girl, 'horror labour' stories, and then everything you need to know about your baby.

Pregnancy is a great time to practice sorting the information that you get from well-meaning family, friends and acquaintances. Practice nodding your head and allowing the information to flow straight through!

Many of my new mums will talk about the amount of confusing information they receive from health professionals, and well-meaning people in their lives. Remember that many different strategies have worked for different parents and babies over the years, and their advice is meant to help. It is ok to keep some of their suggestions in mind to try, and if they don't work, try a different one next time.

Vox Pop

We asked a number of women and men around Australia to send in their advice, tips and personal experiences on a range of topics so that you have an insight into how others cope being a new parent. We hope you find their comments interesting, informative and reassuring. Vox Pop biographies: page 652

You are new at this, and your baby has not read the same parenting books as you! It can be a very frustrating time with the bombardment of new information – and you just want one thing that will make it right!

It is important that you find one or two friends and health professionals that you admire and/or trust and seek your opinions from them. The more people you ask, the more varied the responses may be. Eventually you will find a happy medium that suits you and your baby.

Support can come from your GP, midwife, paediatrician, child health nurse, and telephone support lines such as the Australian Breastfeeding Association. Your main carer in hospital will be able to put you in touch with your local child health facilities and their telephone support as well. It is also becoming popular for some health insurers to offer a pregnancy program to their members where you can speak to an experienced midwife, lactation consultant or child health nurse on the phone.

Louise Cruz
Mum of three, NSW

When my daughter was around 12 months old I sought a referral to the Tresillian Centre at Nepean Hospital in Penrith for help with her sleeping arrangements. I had allowed her to share my bed after having great difficulty in settling her for her sleeps and after a while of putting up with many poor night's sleep from having her kick me through the night, I decided it was time to address the problem.

I stayed at the residential unit for 5 nights where the trained staff gave me the strategies for how to settle her and the assistance to implement them. It was very hard to use the controlled crying technique, but with their support and advice I was able to get my daughter into a new sleep routine and at the end of our stay we were feeling confident that we could continue with the plan at home.

If I was to give any advice to other mums going through a similar situation it would be to seek advice and help if you find you cannot manage the situation at home on your own. If you choose to go to a facility like Tresillian you need to be prepared to follow through with the strategies they give you once you go home and you will find they are successful.

Martine Pekarsky
Mum of two, Melbourne

We have used the Victorian Nurse-On-Call hotline a couple of times when there has been a fall or gastro or something a little bit borderline as to whether they need to go to the doctor or not. The service has been excellent and I'd highly recommend it (it is also free).

We went to sleep school at South Eastern Private when they were 9 months old and the nurses there taught me some amazing things – not only about sleeping but routines, discipline, eating and parenting in general.

If you are having problems with sleeping then persevere and try to get into a good sleep school. They are hard to get into but they are well worth it if you follow their professional advice – they have seen it all before.

Melanie Smoothy
Mum of one, NSW

We quickly learned that babies don't come with an instruction manual or how-to guide! Even the most maternal or paternal parent can still find themselves in a state of confusion or bewilderment.

We've referred to a number of sources for help and advice. In the early months we regularly met with the local Childhood Nurse for feeding advice, growth measurements, sleep advice and general information. We've also contacted the Tresillian helpline for advice, even as recently as this year to obtain advice on transferring Brayden from his cot to his very own 'big boy bed'.

We also learned quite quickly that:

Children will do things at their own pace and should not be compared.

You, as the parents, are the experts when it comes to your child.

You will receive endless amounts of advice from everyone – family, friends, work colleagues, even the lady in the supermarket seems to want to give you advice!

Don't get me wrong, people can be a wealth of information. But from our experience, we often found that when people give you their advice and/or information, there is often the expectation for you to follow it.

At the end of the day, we've learned to treat any advice we're given as 'general' advice. It may not necessarily pertain to our situation, or it may fit like a glove. No two babies are the same and your instincts as parents are the best thing for your baby.

But if you find yourself feeling unsure, seeking reassurance or just wanting to know more, refer to any of the countless sources of information available.

Michelle Eicholtz
Mum of one, VIC

I have had to call a 24-hour helpline twice and I found it a great source of comfort. The first time was when I was having trouble feeding my baby and she was choking and spitting her milk out. I didn't know whether to call an ambulance or take her to the hospital or just wait and see. The advice from the person on the helpline was great and calmed me right down and pointed me in the right direction.

It was nice to know that there were experienced people on the end of the line and they were there to help and guide me.

The best advice I think is to find a really good doctor that you can tell anything to; someone who won't dismiss your worries and one that you can

trust to listen to you and who knows the system and can refer you to the right people. Also get to know your Maternal Health Nurse. Every healthcare professional has their own way of dealing with things and keep looking for one that you feel comfortable with. I got frustrated to start with because people weren't listening to me probably because I was a first time mum. Just don't give up if something doesn't feel right – keep pushing for answers.

Rowena Raats
Mum of three, Kalgoorlie

Living in a remote town can be tough when it comes to babies and in my case families. There is limited support and services. I have regularly used the Princess Margaret Hospital (Children's Hospital in Perth) for advice and support.

We live in a mining town and my family are all hours away and so it has meant that I need to rely on myself a lot more. For example when my baby is not well and the doctor doesn't have an available appointment for that week, it is my call whether we spend three hours at the Emergency Department. This can be tough especially as teething can make a baby miserable and can be mistaken for something more serious.

My advice is to know what is available in your town and what you can access outside of this. Ask you GP, Child Health Nurse, your friends and wider community. Keep a list of numbers and services handy. It is also a great way to see what playgroups and other supportive, interactive opportunities are around.

Resources

These Resources pages list products and services relevant to "Help, advice & referrals".
To make your life easier as a parent, editorial listings have been grouped into sub categories.
Businesses then appear alphabetically under a national or a state-based subhead depending on reach.

SUB-CATEGORIES

ADVISORY SERVICES: CHILD ABUSE PREVENTION

NATIONAL

Australian Childhood Foundation
Tel: (03) 9874 3922
email: info@childhood.org.au
website: www.stopchildabusenow.com.au

Australian
Childhood Foundation
Protecting Children

If you have serious concerns about the safety of a child contact the Child Protection Service in your state. Anyone can ring the child protection service at any time if they are concerned about the welfare of a child or young person. You do not have to prove that abuse or neglect is happening. Your name remains confidential if you give it when you make a report and cannot be released. You can make a report anonymously. The phone numbers are:

Victoria	13 22 89
New South Wales	13 20 55
ACT	6205 8800
Queensland	1300 301 300
Northern Territory	1800 019 116
Western Australia	1800 654 432
South Australia	1300 364 100
Tasmania	1800 808 178

Barnardos Australia
Tel: 1800 061 000
email: barnmktg@zip.com.au
website: www.barnardos.org.au

Every two minutes an Australian child is reported as neglected or abused. If no-one is providing these children with the basic protection they need how can they grow and build a life of their own? Barnardos helps break the cycle of neglect and abuse, giving these children back their childhood. You can help give a child a brighter future by supporting this work or by becoming a carer or mentor. Phone or email for more information.

Child Abuse Prevention Service
Tel: 1800 688 009 or (02) 9716 8000
email: mail@childabuseprevention.com.au
website: www.childabuseprevention.com.au

For the past 30 years CAPS has offered support to parents and carers when the stress and pressures have become too great. CAPS offer 24-hour, 7 days a week confidential telephone support and referrals. For help please phone 1800 688 009 or (02) 9716 8000.

The National Association for Prevention of Child Abuse & Neglect (NAPCAN)

Tel: (02) 9211 0224
email: contact@napcan.org.au
website: www.napcan.org.au

NAPCAN is a leading advocate for the prevention of child abuse and neglect, and works to achieve this goal through advocacy, promoting social change, building resilience in parents, children and young people, developing professional and parental skills and knowledge, and strengthening community capacity.

ADVISORY SERVICES: DEAF CHILDREN

NATIONAL

Deaf Australia Incorporated

Tel: (07) 3357 8266
email: info@deafau.org.au
website: www.deafau.org.au

Deaf Australia provides information about deaf people, issues that affect them, and options for communication and education. It can also put parents of deaf children in touch with deaf adults who can offer positive support and encouragement.

QUEENSLAND

Association for the Pre-School Education of Deaf Children

PO Box 177
Moorooka QLD 4105
Tel: (07) 3848 0080
email: preschool.assoc.deafchildren@uqconnect.net

The Association for the Pre-School Education of Deaf Children plays a vital role in promoting total communication of hearing impaired children aged 0–6 years. The Association provides specialised therapy teams including speech, occupational and physiotherapy.

ADVISORY SERVICES: DEVELOPMENTAL DELAY OR DISABILITY

VICTORIA

Stride Early Intervention Centre

44 Balmoral Avenue
Lower Templestowe VIC 3107
Tel: (03) 9850 8080

Stride Forward Early Intervention Program provides teaching and therapy services such as speech pathology and physiotherapy to families who have a child, aged between birth and six years/school entry, experiencing a developmental delay and/or disability.

Uncle Bobs Child Development Centre

56 Chapman Street
North Melbourne VIC 3051
Tel: (03) 9345 5092
email: unclebobs.cdc@rch.org.au

The Uncle Bobs Child Development Centre, auspiced by the Royal Children's Hospital, is an early childhood intervention program providing therapy and educational programs to children 0–6 years with developmental delay and/or disability. The program also offers a range of family support and community education.

NEW SOUTH WALES

Northcott Disability Services

1 Fennell Street
North Parramatta NSW 2151
Tel: (02) 9890 0100
email: nc@northcott.com.au
website: www.northcott.com.au

Northcott Disability Services provides support to people with disabilities throughout New South Wales in over 70 programs. The Early Childhood Support Service in Sydney assists children with physical disabilities from 0 to 6 years of age, working together with the family to develop a program that meets the needs of their child. The Early Childhood Support Service aims to support the child within the family, promote the child's strengths and abilities and assist integration into a range of children's services including pre-school and school. Phone for more information.

QUEENSLAND

Down Syndrome Association Of Queensland

PO Box 3223
Stafford QLD 4053
Tel: (07) 3356 6655
email: dsa.qld@uq.net.au
website: www.dsaq.org.au

DSAQ is a parent organisation that provides support and information to intending and new parents on Down syndrome throughout Queensland. Services offered include: an education consultant, prenatal information kits, new parent kits, seminars and workshop referrals, new baby playgroup, e-group and coffee mornings.

NORTHERN TERRITORY

Down Syndrome Association of the Northern Territory

PO Box 41545
Casuarina NT 0811
Tel: (08) 8985 6222
email: dsant@octa4.net.au

Down Syndrome Association of the Northern Territory (DSA NT) is a support service for individuals with Down syndrome; families who have a member with Down Syndrome; health, education and recreational workers dealing with people with Down Syndrome. DSA NT offers information to new parents including hospital visits; an extensive resource library; quarterly newsletter; parent support meetings; community awareness; a Computer Aided Learning Program for children aged 2 to 16 years and an educational software library service.

Resources

HELP, ADVICE & REFERRALS

Advisory services: domestic violence
➜ Advisory services: general counselling

ADVISORY SERVICES: DOMESTIC VIOLENCE

VICTORIA

Domestic Violence Outreach Services

Domestic Violence Outreach Services provide individual support, information, advocacy and referral for women and children who are experiencing domestic violence. Services are free and confidential. To contact an Outreach Service near you call:

EASTERN METROPOLITAN

Ringwood   (03) 9870 5939

NORTHERN METROPOLITAN

Heidelberg   (03) 9458 5788

SOUTHERN METROPOLITAN

Mornington Peninsula (03) 5971 9454

INNER SOUTH   (03) 9536 7777

OUTER SOUTH

Dandenong   (03) 9791 6111

Narre Warren   (03) 9703 0044

Frankston   (03) 9781 4658

WESTERN METROPOLITAN

Footscray   (03) 9689 9588

If you live in the country call the Women's Domestic Violence Crisis Service of Victoria on 1800 015 188 for the telephone number of the nearest rural Outreach Service.

Women's Domestic Violence Crisis Service of Victoria

GPO Box 4396
Melbourne VIC 3000
Tel: (03) 9373 0123 or 1800 015 188 (Crisis Line)
email: wdvcs@wdvcs.org.au
website: www.wdvcs.org.au

The Women's Domestic Violence Crisis Service is a 24-hour, 7 days-a-week crisis telephone service. Any woman in Victoria who is experiencing or in fear of violence within her family or home from her husband, partner or other family member is welcome and encouraged to phone this service for support, information or access to safe emergency housing for herself and her children. Open 24 hours every day. Visit the website for more information.

NEW SOUTH WALES

Domestic Violence Line

Tel: 1800 656 463

Domestic violence is any abusive behaviour used by one partner in a relationship to gain and maintain control over another's life. Domestic violence is the use of violence and control by men to stop women and children living in safety and free of fear in their own home. Wherever you live in New South Wales, the Domestic Violence Line can assist you with support and assistance at a local level or, if you would prefer, can help you further away from home. Domestic violence: You can live without it.

ADVISORY SERVICES: FOR MEN

NATIONAL

Dadstheword Pty Ltd

Tel: 1300 306 802
email: rosvroom@bigpond.net.au
website: www.dadstheword.com

Discover the secrets to your baby and quickly become a great dad – this DVD shows you all you need to know. It will save you hours of distress and quickly skyrocket you to enjoying those first days home with your baby. Endorsed by Australian College of Midwives and Steve Biddulph. Information on the DVD is suitable for all new mums and dads.

Mensline Australia

Tel: 1300 789 978
email: talkitover@menslineaus.org.au
website: www.menslineaus.org.au

Mensline Australia is a professional and anonymous telephone support and information service for men, specialising in relationship and family concerns. Concerned partners and children are also encouraged to call. Mensline Australia is available nationally, 24 hours a day, 7 days a week for the cost of a local call.

The Fatherhood Project

Tel: (02) 6684 2309
email: info@fatherhood.com.au
website: www.fatherhood.net.au

The Fatherhood Project offers programs for expectant and new fathers. They also organise the Fatherhood Festival on Fathers' Day weekend where fathers and families meet to speak about the role of fathers and celebrate. Visit www.fatherhood.net.au for more information.

NEW SOUTH WALES

Beer + Bubs

Tel: (02) 9440 9099
email: cheers@beerandbubs.com.au
website: www.beerandbubs.com.au

Beer + Bubs is all about learning how to be the best childbirth support person you can be at this two-and-a-half-hour workshop at the pub. Learn what to say and what not to say, great ideas for pain relief, how to be an advocate for the birthing mother, practical tips on what to do at each stage of labour and much more. Cost is $50 per person which includes dinner.

ADVISORY SERVICES: GENERAL COUNSELLING

NATIONAL

Centre for Community Child Health
Tel: (03) 9345 6150
email: enquiries.ccch@rch.org.au
website: www.rch.org.au/ccch

The Centre for Community Child Health has been at the forefront of early childhood development and behaviour research for over two decades. It is also involved with community projects and provides clinical services and education. The Centre aims to support parents and professionals so that children have the best possible start in life. The research the Centre conducts is about many conditions and common problems faced by children such as obesity, language and literacy delay and behavioural concerns. For further information about how they can help you, visit the website or contact them directly.

Early Childhood Australia
Tel: 1800 356 900
email: eca@earlychildhood.org.au
website: www.earlychildhoodaustralia.org.au

Early Childhood Australia is a non-profit, peak advocacy organisation acting in the best interests of children from birth to eight years. Become a member of Early Childhood Australia and support them in promoting high-quality services for young children and their families. Freecall 1800 356 900 for a free information kit and Code of Ethics brochure, or browse their free online resources on their website www.earlychildhoodaustralia.org.au.

Positive Parenting Network of Australia
email: lois.haultain@parent.net.au
website: www.parent.net.au

The Positive Parenting Network is an alliance of professional educators who support and encourage parents in their challenging and important job. They help parents understand how to deal with misbehaving children in loving, positive ways and how they can bring peace to their families. Visit the website www.parent.net.au to find classes, workshops, resources and private consultations ('supernanny' visit or by phone) with experienced and certified educators. Sign up for a free email newsletter with helpful hints at www.parent.net.au. Educators are available in NSW, Victoria and Queensland.

Tresillian Family Care Centres
24-hour Parents Help Line: (02) 9787 0855 or 1800 637 357
website: www.tresillian.net

Messenger Mums is an exciting initiative between Tresillian Family Care Centres and ninemsn for parents having difficulties in the early years of their child's life. Tresillian's registered nurses are available online from Monday to Friday between 9.00am to 3.30pm to offer parenting advice and support via 'instant-messaging'. This is a free service. Visit http://health.ninemsn.com.au/messengermums/default.aspx.

Triple P International
email: contact@triplep.net
website: www.triplep.net

As we all know, kids don't come with an instruction manual. No matter what your parenting needs, Triple P – Positive Parenting Program® has practical parenting information, advice and support to help you. As an internationally awarded evidence-based parenting program with over 30 years of proven clinical research to back it up, you can be sure Triple P will provide you with the tips and advice to get through these early years.

VICTORIA

Being a Mother
Tel: (03) 9882 7958 or 0407 819 519
email: betty@beingamother.com
website: www.beingamother.com

Feel like you're the only one who struggles with being a mum? Tired of yelling or being frustrated? Want to know how to feel happier and less stressed? Being a Mother is a tailored workshop addressing these issues with techniques that are practical, easy to use and work immediately. East Hawthorn venue. Rebates and concession available. For more information phone Betty Chetcuti, Psychologist (BBSc (Hons.), MEdPysch, MAPS), wife and mother of three. Private appointments also available.

Caroline Chisholm Society
41 Park Street
Moonee Ponds VIC 3039
Tel: 1800 134 863 or (03) 9370 3933
email: info@carolinechisholmsociety.com.au
website: www.carolinechisholmsociety.com.au

The Caroline Chisholm Society provides counselling (pregnancy, grief – pregnancy loss and post abortion – individual and family counselling, parent/child relationships counselling and financial counselling), a 7-day-a-week counselling line, free pregnancy testing, support groups (postnatal depression support groups and constructive parenting programs), in-home family support program, material aid and accommodation service.

Centre for Child & Family Development
721A Riversdale Road
Camberwell VIC 3124
Tel: (03) 9830 0422
email: ccfdau@ozemail.com.au
website: www.childandfamily.com.au

The Under Fives Counselling Service provides skilled psychotherapy help for problems which may arise for

Resources

HELP, ADVICE & REFERRALS

Advisory services: general counselling
➜ Advisory services: grief counselling

new babies and new parents and for toddlers and young children with eating, sleeping, toilet training difficulties and general behavioural problems.

Mercy Health O'Connell Family Centre
6 Mont Albert Road
Canterbury VIC 3126
Tel: (03) 8416 7600
website: www.mercy.com.au
Mercy Health O'Connell Family Centre, a facility of Mercy Health, is a government-funded service providing family focused education and support to families experiencing parenting difficulties with children up to four years of age. Services include day-stay programs and a residential program and most costs are covered by Medicare. The Centre also conducts parent education workshops around various early parenting topics and issues in response to community request and need.

Parent Infant Research Institute
Austin Health 330 Waterdale Road
Heidelberg Heights VIC 3081
Tel: (03) 9496 4496
website: www.piri.org.au
The Infant Clinic is a not-for-profit clinic staffed by specialist psychologists who provide a comprehensive service to families in the ante and postnatal period. Cutting edge research, teaching and treatment programs are available to address the needs of parents facing the challenges of parenthood, especially prematurity, relationship changes, anxiety, depression and understanding and managing babies and toddlers. The Infant Clinic also has antenatal programs to assist in the transition to parenthood.

Satir Centre of Australia for the Family
Suite 2, 1051 A/B High Street
Armadale VIC 3143
Tel: (03) 9824 7755
website: www.satiraustralia.com
Satir Centre of Australia for the Family offers psychotherapy and psychological support for mothers, fathers, grandparents and families of pregnant women, new parents, toddlers, young children and adolescents. All consultations are offered in a private psychological and medical setting.

WIRE – Women's Information
210 Lonsdale Street
Melbourne VIC 3000
Tel: 1300 134 130
website: www.wire.org.au

WIRE - Women's Information has been providing free information, support and referrals to Victorian women since 1984. Need to talk something over? Talk things through with a sensitive, supportive woman on 1300 134 130. Women phone WIRE for all sorts of reasons – from problems at home, to finding work. You don't need to be in crisis. No problem is too big or too small. You can also drop into their Women's Information Centre for free public access computers, information resources and seminars on a wide rage of topics.

NEW SOUTH WALES

Dial-A-Mum Inc
PO Box 241
Wahroonga NSW 2076
Tel: (02) 9477 6777
email: dial_a_mum@hotmail.com
website: www.dial-a-mum.org.au
Dial-A-Mum is a telephone support service that has been in operation since 1979 and is operated and funded by a group of trained, volunteer mothers. Callers come from all age groups, from all areas of Sydney and New South Wales and from all walks of life. Their issues are varied: conflict in relationships (spouse/partner, family, friends, neighbours and the workplace), domestic abuse, parenting, mental health, grief and isolation. Callers are adults and children who just want to talk to a mum.

Karitane
PO Box 241
Villawood NSW 2163
Careline (7 days/week): 1300 227 464 or
(02) 9794 2300, Karitane@Home: (02) 9399 7147
email: karitane.online@sswahs.nsw.gov.au
website: www.karitane.com.au

Karitane leaders in parenting services since 1923

Karitane provides support, guidance and information to families with children 0 to 5 years who are experiencing parenting difficulties. Assistance is available through Careline (7 day per week State-wide Service: 1300 CARING 1300 227 464), Family Care Centres, Jade House (PND support), the Toddler Clinic, Residential Unit, volunteer home visiting, Karitane@Home (private home visiting for a fee for service) and Connecting Carers NSW (for foster and kinship carer support). A specialised team of Child and Family Health professionals are available for consultation on a wide range of issues such as feeding problems, sleep and settle routines, toddler behaviour management, parent anxiety, pre and post-natal depression and other issues.

Tresillian Family Care Centres
Head Office: McKenzie Street
Belmore NSW 2192
24-hour Parents Help Line: (02) 9787 0855 or
1800 637 357
Other locations:
25 Shirley Road
Wollstonecraft NSW 2065
Tel: (02) 9432 4000

2 Second Avenue
Willoughby NSW 2068
Tel: (02) 8962 8300
1b Barber Avenue
Kingswood NSW 2747
Tel: (02) 4734 2124
website: www.tresillian.net

Arriving home with a new baby can be daunting and often it's hard to know who to turn to for help. If you need assistance with any issue relating to the care of your baby contact the Tresillian 24-hour Parents Help Line on (02) 9787 0855 in Sydney or 1800 637 357(outside Sydney). Parents needing help from Tresillian are usually experiencing difficulties ranging from breastfeeding, settling the newborn, a baby who continues to wake several times a night, toddler behaviour, nightwaking and postnatal depression. Tresillian employs professional staff including Child and Family Health Nurses, Paediatricians, Psychologists, Psychiatrists and Social Workers who offer families practical advice. They also hold a range of Parent Education Seminars across Sydney.

QUEENSLAND

Epilepsy Queensland Inc.
PO Box 1457
Coorparoo BC QLD 4151
Tel: (07) 3435 5000
website: www.epilepsyqueensland.com.au

Epilepsy Queensland Inc. provides support to families who have a child with febrile convulsions, infantile spasms or any other forms of childhood epilepsy. They provide support through information, referral, workshops and seminars, counselling, newsletters, advocacy and children's education programs.

WESTERN AUSTRALIA

Ngala Inc.
9 George Street
Kensington WA 6151
Tel: (08) 9368 9368
website: www.ngala.com.au

Ngala is an early parenting centre with a passion for supporting and guiding families through the journey of early parenting via a range of opportunities to increase and enhance knowledge of parenting skills. They offer education courses, coffee mornings, consults, day stay and overnight stay and the Ngala Helpline. Helpline staff provide guidelines and reassurance for parents, and seek to encourage confidence. Parents can contact the Ngala Helpline between the hours of 8.00am and 8.00pm on (08) 9368 9368 (metro callers) or 1800 111 546 (country) 7 days a week.

Parenting With Ease
Tel: (08) 9408 1372
email: chantelle@parentingwithease.com.au
website: www.parentingwithease.com.au

Parenting With Ease offers real solutions to real problems including sleep issues, the daily battle of wills with your toddler and feeling a greater sense of calm and ease in your role as a parent. Parenting With Ease helps parents to enter the world of a child and understand how to integrate with it through the manuals The 12 Ingredients to Miracle Parenting and The Baby Ease Sleep Solution and the CD Harmonious Mother Harmonious Baby. Parenting With Ease also offers workshops on Baby Ease and Toddler Ease and consultations on sleep and behaviour.

ADVISORY SERVICES: GRIEF COUNSELLING

NATIONAL

Bonnie Babes Foundation Inc
Tel: (03) 9803 1800
email: enquiry@bbf.org.au
website: www.bbf.org.au

The Bonnie Babes Foundation is a non-profit volunteer based charity which is established for the health and wellbeing of families. Sadly one in every four pregnancies ends in a loss from miscarriage and stillbirth. Over 17,000 babies are born prematurely, many of them often struggling for life. The Bonnie Babes Foundation helps to save babies' lives and counsel families through this extreme hardship. All proceeds the Foundation raises are for vital medical research projects, and for the 24-hour, 7-day-per-week family counselling services. They also support families with seriously ill babies and infants with childhood diseases.

SIDS and Kids
National Office (03) 9819 4595 or 1300 308 307
email: national@sidsandkids.org
website: www.sidsandkids.org

 SIDS and Kids offers a range of support and counselling services to Australian families following the death of a baby or child during pregnancy, birth, infancy and childhood, regardless of the cause. Bereavement support is offered 24 hours a day, 7 days a week and is completely free of charge.

VICTORIA

SANDS (Vic)
Suite 208, 901 Whitehorse Road
Box Hill VIC 3128
Tel: (03) 9899 0217 (admin) or (03) 9899 0218 (support)
email: info@sandsvic.org.au
website: www.sandsvic.org.au

SANDS (Vic) is a state-wide self-help support organisation for parents who have experienced the death of a baby through miscarriage, stillbirth or shortly after birth. SANDS offers 24-hour phone support for bereaved parents, families and friends. It holds monthly support meetings and has a bi-monthly newsletter. SANDS has also produced the book *Your Baby has Died* and many other pamphlets and educates parents, professionals and the general community through seminars, workshops, media releases and literature.

Resources

HELP, ADVICE & REFERRALS

Advisory services: helplines

ADVISORY SERVICES: HELPLINES

NATIONAL

Child Abuse Prevention Service

Tel: 1800 688 009 or (02) 9716 8000
email: mail@childabuseprevention.com.au
website: www.childabuseprevention.com.au

For the past 30 years CAPS has offered support to parents and carers when the stress and pressures have become too great. CAPS offer 24-hour, 7 days a week confidential telephone support and referrals. For help please phone 1800 688 009 or (02) 9716 8000.

Child Safety After Hours Service Centre

Tel: (07) 3235 9999 or 1800 177 135 in Queensland
email: info@childsafety.qld.gov.au
website: www.childsafety.qld.gov.au

The Child Safety After Hours Service Centre (formerly Crisis Care) is the 24-hour service of the Department of Child Safety and provides after-business-hours responses to clients of the department, the community, other government departments and community agencies in response to child protection matters.

Mensline Australia

Tel: 1300 789 978
website: www.menslineaus.org.au

Mensline Australia is a professional and anonymous telephone support and information service for men, specialising in relationship and family concerns. Concerned partners and children are also encouraged to call. Mensline Australia is available nationally, 24 hours a day, 7 days a week for the cost of a local call.

Poisons Information Centre

Tel: 13 11 26
Victorian Poisons Information Centre:
www.austin.org.au/poisons
NSW Poisons Information Centre:
www.chw.edu.au/parents/factsheets/safpoisj.htm
QLD Poisons Information Centre:
www.health.qld.gov.au/PoisonsInformationCentre/
WA Poisons Information Centre:
www.scgh.health.wa.gov.au/departments/wapic/index.html

Poisons Information Centre provides telephone advice to callers needing information about first aid for poisoning, bites, stings, mistakes with medicines and poisoning prevention. The service is available 24-hours a day, seven days a week. If you or someone in your care has been poisoned, ring the Poisons Information Centre

to find out what to do next. The advice is up-to-date unlike many books and charts and you may avoid an unnecessary trip to the doctor or hospital.

Suicide Call Back Service

Tel: 1300 657 467
website: www.suicideline.org.au or www.crisissupport.org.au

The Suicide Call Back Service is a national, free, appointment-based telephone support service, specifically designed to support people at risk of suicide, their carers and those bereaved by suicide. The service offers people in need six professional telephone counselling sessions, available 7 days a week and after traditional hours. Speak to one of the counsellors or leave your contact details so they may call you back.

VICTORIA

Maternal and Child Health Line

Tel: 13 22 29

The Maternal and Child Health Line is a state-wide, 24-hour telephone service. Callers can access information, advice and support regarding child health, nutrition, breastfeeding, maternal and family health. The service is available to Victorian families with children 0 to school age and complements the locally based service. Phone 13 22 29.

Parentline

Tel: 13 22 89
website: www.parentline.vic.gov.au

Don't cope alone

Parentline is a confidential telephone counselling, information and referral service for all Victorian parents and carers with children aged from birth to 18 years. The service is available from 8.00am to 12 midnight during the week, and 10.00am to 10.00pm on weekends. Professional counsellors are available to discuss a wide range of parenting issues including child behaviour, family relationships, transition to school, and parent/adolescent conflict. Parentline's aim is to work with families to support and strengthen them, and to link families with community resources. Parentline is accessible from anywhere in Victoria for the cost of a local call (excluding mobiles). Phone 13 22 89.

SuicideLine (VIC)

Tel: 1300 651 251
website: www.suicideline.org.au

Help when you need it most. The specialist counsellors of SuicideLine (VIC) provide professional telephone counselling and information to people at risk of suicide and self harm as well as support to family, friends and the bereaved. Free and anonymous 24/7 support.

WIRE – Women's Information

210 Lonsdale Street
Melbourne VIC 3000
Tel: 1300 134 130
email: inforequests@wire.org.au
website: www.wire.org.au

WIRE - Women's Information has been providing free information, support and referrals to Victorian women since 1984. Need to talk something over? Talk things through with a sensitive, supportive woman on 1300 134 130. Women phone WIRE for all sorts of reasons – from problems at home, to finding work. You don't need to be in crisis. No problem is too big or too small. You can also drop into their Women's Information Centre for free public access computers, information resources and seminars on a wide rage of topics. Visit the website for further details.

Women's Domestic Violence Crisis Service of Victoria

GPO Box 4396
Melbourne VIC 3000
Tel: (03) 9373 0123 or 1800 015 188 (Crisis Line)
email: wdvcs@wdvcs.org.au
website: www.wdvcs.org.au

The Women's Domestic Violence Crisis Service is a 24-hour, 7 days-a-week crisis telephone service. Any woman in Victoria who is experiencing or in fear of violence within her family or home from her husband, partner or other family member is welcome and encouraged to phone this service for support, information or access to safe emergency housing for herself and her children. Open 24 hours every day.

NEW SOUTH WALES

Domestic Violence Line

Tel: 1800 656 463

Domestic violence is any abusive behaviour used by one partner in a relationship to gain and maintain control over another's life. Domestic violence is the use of violence and control by men to stop women and children living in safety and free of fear in their own home. Wherever you live in New South Wales, the Domestic Violence Line can assist you with support and assistance at a local level or, if you would prefer, can help you further away from home. Domestic violence: You can live without it.

AUSTRALIAN CAPITAL TERRITORY

ParentLine

Tel: (02) 6287 3833
website: www.parentlineact.org.au

ParentLine is open from 9.00am to 9.00pm, Monday to Friday for parents and other people concerned with issues of parenting. The service aims to enhance the development, health and emotional wellbeing of children by supporting parents and carers and connecting them with the network of services available to families in the ACT and surrounding areas. The assistance provided is confidential, immediate and anonymous. Professionally trained staff provide callers with counselling, guidance, information about parenting issues and programs offered by other agencies, and referral to other organisations. ParentLine also provides face-to-face counselling and ongoing telephone support through trained volunteers.

QUEENSLAND

Child Health Line

Tel: (07) 3862 2333 or 1800 177 279 (24 hours)
website: www.health.qld.gov.au/cchs

The Child Health Line is a 24-hour telephone information and support service for parents, carers and service providers with infants, children and young people aged 0–18 years.

Parentline Counselling Service

PO Box 2000
Milton QLD 4064
Tel: 1300 301 300
website: www.parentline.com.au

Parentline is a confidential telephone counselling service that provides education, guidance and support to parents and carers of children. Parenting is the most important task in our community, however sometimes it can be puzzling, frustrating, worrying or stressful. At times you just need to talk things over with someone. Parentline's professional counsellors are available for the cost of a local call between 8.00am and 10.00pm, seven days a week.

WESTERN AUSTRALIA

Ngala Inc.

9 George Street
Kensington WA 6151
Tel: (08) 9368 9368
email: ngala@ngala.com.au
website: www.ngala.com.au

Ngala is an early parenting centre with a passion for supporting and guiding families through the journey of early parenting via a range of opportunities to increase and enhance knowledge of parenting skills. They offer education courses, coffee mornings, consults, day stay and overnight stay and the Ngala Helpline. Helpline staff provide guidelines and reassurance for parents, and seek to encourage confidence. Parents can contact the Ngala Helpline between the hours of 8.00am and 8.00pm on (08) 9368 9368 (metro callers) or 1800 111 546 (country) 7 days a week.

SOUTH AUSTRALIA

24/7 Parent Helpline

Tel: 1300 364 100

The Parent Helpline is a 24/7 service providing information, support and referral to parents and young people from birth to 25 years. Parents can access information on a large range of topics including behaviour, feeding or sleeping difficulties, diet and toilet training, risk taking and managing the transition to adulthood. The information is provided by a multi-disciplinary team of registered nurses, community health workers, social workers and specially trained volunteers. The Helpline has a local call cost. The Parent Helpline is an initiative of the Children Youth and Women's Health Service, which forms part of the State Government Department SA Health.

Resources

HELP, ADVICE & REFERRALS

Advisory services: legal advice & referral
➔ Advisory services: premature babies

24/7 Youth Healthline
Tel: 1300 131 719
website: www.cyh.com

The Youth Healthline provides information, support and referral for young people from 12 to 25 years from anywhere in SA on any topic including anxiety, depression, school or family issues. Staff link callers to services within their local community to enable networks and supports to be developed. The Youth Heathline is an initiative of the Children, Youth and Women's Health Service, which forms part of the State Government department, SA Health.

ADVISORY SERVICES: LEGAL ADVICE & REFERRAL

VICTORIA

Women's Legal Service Victoria
3rd Floor, 43 Hardware Lane
Melbourne VIC 3000
Tel: (03) 9642 0877
email: Justice@vicnet.net.au

Women's Legal Service Victoria offers free legal advice for all women in Victoria covering the following areas of law: family law, intervention orders and victims of crime assistance matters. Where they are unable to give advice they will attempt to give appropriate referral. Phone or email for more information.

ADVISORY SERVICES: MULTIPLE BIRTHS

NATIONAL

Australian Multiple Birth Association (AMBA)
Tel: 1300 886 499
email: secretary@amba.org.au
website: www.amba.org.au

AMBA is a voluntary community organisation of families with twins, triplets, quadruplets and more. A national network of associated groups provides activities and services that encourage the exchange of information, education and mutual support. AMBA is committed to increasing awareness of the special needs of multiple birth families, and to improve the resources available to them. AMBA is a non-profit, non-political and non-sectarian organisation co-operating with organisations having related interests. Phone or visit the website for more information.

Think Twins
Tel: (03) 8802 9446
email: info@thinktwins.com.au
website: www.thinktwins.com.au

Think Twins is Australia's biggest online store for families with twins, triplets and more. Whether it's finding a birthday gift or accessing a terrific range of articles and resources including a huge range of twin-specific books for parents and children, Think Twins will make life as a parent of twins a little easier.

ADVISORY SERVICES: MUMS IN BUSINESS

NATIONAL

Business Mums Network
Tel: (03) 9018 8947
email: admin@businessmums.com
website: www.businessmums.com.au

Are you a mum starting or running a business? Or wanting to start one? Then the Business Mums Network can support you. Founded in 2002 and run by a mum, they understand the unique needs of mums running a business. They can provide online and offline networking opportunities, information written especially with business mums in mind, an offline bi-monthly magazine and an annual conference.

Creative Mums
Tel: (02) 9907 6627
email: creativemums@optusnet.com.au
website: www.creativemums.com.au

Creative Mums is an Australian wide network of mums. Creative Mums supports mums and mums-to-be in starting up or running their 'creative' businesses or practising their artistic profession with raising children in a balanced way. Creative Mums supports other mums by promoting their products and services and as such creates a new economy based on local produce and artistic quality. Creative Mums organises seminars, workshops, exhibitions, network events and creative entertainment for your children. Membership is free. Phone or email for more information.

How to Start a Business With Less Than $100
website: www.biznessbasics.com

Ever dreamed of going into business but thought you couldn't afford it? Then you need to read *How to Start a Business With Less Than $100*. It is the essential survival guide for anyone who wants to learn how to do it cheaper and better.

Single Parents in Business
website: www.singleparentsinbusiness.com

Single Parents in Business is a network for all working single parents. They offer support, networking opportunities and much more. Learn how to start a business with less than $100 and be mentored by some of the most successful single parents in Australia.

WAHM Network Australia
Tel: (08) 9206 1275
website: www.wahmnetwork.com.au

WAHM Network Australia is a free support community for work-at-home mums. The site offers a networking forum, member blogs and a network of wonderful women to help you grow your at-home business.

ADVISORY SERVICES: PREMATURE BABIES

NATIONAL

Earlybirds
Tel: 1800 666 550
email: info@earlybirds.com.au
website: www.earlybirds.com.au

Earlybirds' website is a useful source for parents and carers of premature babies. Earlybirds Network page provides access to information and links to national and local premature support groups together with latest copies of newsletters from Austprem and Premmie Press. Earlybirds proudly supports Austprem and the National Premmie Foundation.

L'il Aussie Prems
Tel: 0412 248 583
website: www.lilaussieprems.com.au

L'il Aussie Prems is an Australian online support site for parents and families of premature babies. You will find links to Australian support groups, clothing stores, read amazing birth stories, blogs, premmie articles and view premature baby galleries. They have a great community forum featuring live chats, personal diaries, premmie buddies and more.

Miracle Babies
Tel: 1300 PREMMIE (1300 773 664)
email: info@miraclebabies.com.au
website: www.miraclebabies.com.au

Miracle Babies supports families of babies who enter the world challenged by prematurity or sickness. Their mission is to help families during their journey through a Neonatal Intensive Care Unit (NICU), the transition to home and onwards. They provide support through hospital visits, newsletters, an online forum, playgroups and a 1300 phone number. Founding members have all experienced the birth of a premature or sick newborn. By sharing their strength and knowledge, they can help families celebrate their own miracle babies.

Moment by Moment
Tel: 0408 689 330
email: fiona@momentbymoment.com.au
website: www.momentbymoment.com.au

Moment by Moment is a website dedicated to premmie babies. The site offers premmie clothing, gifts, nappies and dummies all suitable for premature babies from 400grams. There is also a premmie baby support forum

and Cafe Prem, a premature baby story site to provide much needed support to those experiencing premature birth. Founded by Fiona Dixon, mother of Airlie Fae born at 27 weeks due to pre-eclampsia and HELLP Syndrome in 2006.

Parent Infant Research Institute
Heidelberg Repat Hospital, PO Box 5444
Heidelberg West VIC 3081
Tel: (03) 9496 4496
email: carol.newnham@austin.org.au

The birth of a premature baby affects both the baby and his/her parents in unexpected ways. *Premiepress* explains these differences along with the normal emotional, physical and social needs of babies. By understanding these needs as well as the baby's difficulties, parents are encouraged to help their baby's development.

VICTORIA

Life's Little Treasures
Tel: 0437 254 360
website: www.lifeslittletreasures.org.au

Lifes Little Treasures is a charity run by volunteer parents who themselves have had a premature baby. They provide support and assistance to other families of premature babies throughout Victoria, either in hospital, neonatal intensive care units, special care nurseries or in the community when families get home. They provide this support and information to parents via a supportive parent network to match like parents together for support; morning teas/playgroups at various venues including hospitals and community settings; a quarterly newsletter and website to provide parents with updated and relevant information on premature baby issues; a Parent Information guide and parent packs providing relevant tips and information specific to these families. Social occasions are also organised throughout the year.

Parent Infant Research Institute
Heidelberg Repat Hospital, PO Box 5444
Heidelberg West VIC 3081
Tel: (03) 9496 4496
email: carol.newnham@austin.org.au

The Prematurity Clinic runs the following groups to help parents with premature babies: Playgroups: therapeutic/educational/early intervention play program designed to promote infant brain/motor/social/ cognitive/language development; Workshops: educational sessions for parents; Counselling: the clinic provides targeted counselling by senior psychologists for parents who have difficulties adjusting to the premature birth and baby experience. All services are provided by psychologists or a neuropsychologist.

The Featherweight Club
C/- Mercy Hospital for Women, 163 Studley Road
Heidelberg VIC 3084
Tel: 0412 976 224
email: fwc@featherweightclub.com
website: www.featherweightclub.com

Resources

HELP, ADVICE & REFERRALS

Advisory services: relationships
➜ Advisory services: women's health

The Featherweight Club is a voluntary organisation established to support families who have had an infant admitted to a Special Care Nursery, including the Neonatal Intensive Care Unit, due to prematurity or other complications. It seeks to raise awareness of these families' needs within the hospital environment and the broader community. Members have all had personal experiences of babies in a Special Care Nursery and they support families using the practical experiences of, and funds raised by, their volunteer members.

ADVISORY SERVICES: RELATIONSHIPS

NATIONAL

Relationships Australia

Tel: 1300 364 277
email: enquiries@ransw.org.au
website: www.relationships.com.au

Relationships Australia provides individual, couple and family counselling, mediation, relationship and parenting education, counselling and mediation for adolescents in crisis and their families, professional training and consultation and corporate/business consultancy.

ADVISORY SERVICES: SINGLE PARENTS

NATIONAL

National Council of Single Mothers & their Children

Tel: (08) 8226 2505 or tollfree 1300 725 470
email: ncsmc@ncsmc.org.au
website: www.ncsmc.org.au

The National Council of Single Mothers and their Children fights for the rights of single mothers and their children to the benefit of all single parent families. NCSMC offers practical help and support for single mothers and their children in every state and territory including lobby and advocacy work for Centrelink, family law, child support and domestic violence issues. NCSMC is a peak body representing the rights and voice of single mothers and their children across Australia.

prisms.com.au

Tel: 0438 007 059
email: info@prisms.com.au
website: www.prisms.com.au

prisms provides newly separated and single mothers with a comprehensive range of information, online resources and support. The website includes an online forum, resource centre, expert panel (with advice about child psychology, career, early childhood education, finance, real estate, health and fitness) and inspirational case studies of single mothers who have survived separation and divorce. prisms holds regular meetings for single mothers around Australia. The prisms website is updated daily.

SingleParentdom – Single Parent Support Groups

website: www.singleparentdom.com

SingleParentdom is the home of single parents in Australia. They have single parent support and social groups across the country. Register your interest and be put in touch with a group in your area. It is free to join and if there isn't a group in your district then they will start one.

The Single Parent Bible

website: www.singleparentbible.com.au

The Single Parent Bible is a free online magazine including everything the single parent needs to know, delivered in a brightly wrapped fun package. *The Single Parent Bible* is produced by single parents for single parents and promises to be as essential to the single parent as chocolate and child care. Visit the website for more information.

NEW SOUTH WALES

Lone Parent Family Support Service NSW

15–17 Young Street
Circular Quay NSW 2001
Tel: (02) 9251 5622
email: admin@lpfsscityeast.ngo.org.au

Lone Parent Family Support Service offers free telephone and face-to-face counselling, support groups, social outings and a free newsletter. They aim to assist lone parents (women and men) and their families create a support network in order to achieve a high degree of self sufficiency. Email or phone the number above for further information.

ADVISORY SERVICES: SLEEP PROBLEMS

NATIONAL

It's Time to Sleep Pty Ltd

Tel: 1300 137 110
email: info@itstimetosleep.com
website: www.itstimetosleep.com

It's Time to Sleep is an educational DVD and book that teaches parents how to get babies and toddlers to sleep independently. It was produced with Rhonda Abrahams who created and runs the Baby Sleep and Settling Centre in the Sunshine Hospital. The DVD covers all aspects of baby sleep and settling that Rhonda uses in the centre, educating parents on why babies have trouble sleeping and demonstrating techniques used to teach babies and toddlers to sleep independently. Phone 1300 137 110.

Parenting With Ease

Tel: (08) 9408 1372
email: chantelle@parentingwithease.com.au
website: www.parentingwithease.com.au

Parenting With Ease offers real solutions to real problems including sleep issues, the daily battle of wills with your toddler and feeling a greater sense of calm and ease in your role as a parent. Parenting With Ease helps parents to enter the world of a child and understand how to integrate with it through the manuals *The 12 Ingredients to Miracle Parenting* and *The Baby Ease Sleep Solution* and the CD *Harmonious Mother Harmonious Baby*. Email or visit the website for more information.

Sleep Rescue & Home Support Services

Tel: (03) 9439 1367 or 0428 439 136
email: admin@sleeprescue.com
website: www.sleeprescue.com

If your baby is not sleeping there is help. The Sleep Rescue and Home Support Service provides practical support, education and advice to help parents develop skills to confidently manage the challenges of early parenthood. Staff provide guidance and continuity of support to assist families achieve their goals in their home environment. Families receive care and support for infant settling, feeding issues, sleep problems and routines. They offer day/night overstays, 24 hours and no waiting list. Email or visit the website for more information.

VICTORIA

Melbourne Children's Sleep Unit

Dept. of Respiratory & Sleep Medicine/
Monash Medical Centre
Clayton VIC 3168
Tel: (03) 9594 5656
website: www.mscu.org.au

Melbourne Children's Sleep Unit offers assessment and management of all sleep problems in children from babies through to 18 years of age. If needed, overnight sleep studies are performed. The Unit is staffed by paediatricians and sleep scientists. Visit the website for more information.

Positive Parenting Services

Tel: 0408 102 552
email: katieshafar@yahoo.com.au
website: www.positiveparenting.com.au

Never underestimate the impact on a family of sleeplessness due to a wakeful baby or child/infant. Katie Shafar provides infant/toddler sleep/behaviour management in your own home. Her work is to keep families together by decreasing family stresses, to encourage quiet times and talking, and to empower people to solve their own problems by giving them the knowledge and confidence to trust their own intuition and follow through. Phone Katie on the number above or visit her website www.postiveparenting.com.au for more information.

Tweddle Child & Family Health Service

53 Adelaide Street
Footscray VIC 3011
Tel: (03) 9689 1577
email: tweddle@tweddle.org.au
website: www.tweddle.org.au

Tweddle is an early parenting centre which provides support and education for families with children up to four years of age. Tweddle has day-stay and residential programs for parents who are experiencing sleeping, feeding and behaviour problems with their baby or young child. Tweddle's range of services and programs are tailored to suit an individual family's needs. Tweddle also has two new services: Tweddle@Home is a fee-based, home-visiting service with expert advice tailored to your individual needs in the privacy of your own home; Tweddle Psychology Service has recently commenced where clients can be referred by a health professional or contact them direct. Rebates may be available through Medicare and private insurance agencies.

NEW SOUTH WALES

The Hills Parenting Centre

105 Showground Road
Castle Hill NSW 2154
Tel: (02) 9659 7760
email: michele@hillsparentingcentre.com.au
website: www.hillsparentingcentre.com.au

The Hills Parenting Centre provides for families from birth to five years of age with a speciality in infant sleep programs. Services include pregnancy groups, help with the management of a newborn infants, setting up routines, avoiding problems. Their other area of expertise is in providing help throughout the toddler years with a focus on building healthy relationships and teaching parents how to understand and manage difficult toddler behaviour. This is the first private service of its kind in Australia.

ADVISORY SERVICES: WOMEN'S HEALTH & WELLBEING

NATIONAL

beyondblue: the national depression initiative

email: Info line: 1300 22 4636
website: www.beyondblue.org.au

One of the key roles of beyondblue is to produce, and refer people to, accurate, up-to-date, easy-to-read information on depression, anxiety and related disorders. This includes information relating to: depression, anxiety disorders, postnatal depression, bipolar disorder, diagnosis, treatment, recovery, young people, men, family and friends and chronic physical illness. Phone their Information Line 1300 22 4636 or visit www.beyondblue.org.au for more information.

Resources

HELP, ADVICE & REFERRALS

Advisory services: women's health

➡ Home support services

Cancer Council Australia

Tel: (02) 8063 4100
email: info@cancer.org.au
website: www.cancer.org.au

Cancer Council Australia is Australia's national cancer control organisation. It comprises Australia's peak state and territory cancer councils. Cancer Council members fund vital research and provide information, education, support and services for cancer patients, their families and carers. For information, resources or support, contact your local cancer council or call the Cancer Helpline on 13 11 20 (the cost of a local call from anywhere in Australia).

Mummy's Wish Inc

Tel: 0419 682 860
email: bernadette@mummyswish.org.au
website: www.mummyswish.org.au

Mummy's Wish helps mums diagnosed with cancer while they have children. Visit the website www.mummyswish.org.au for lots of useful information and tips. For mums in Brisbane with a child under school age, they can also offer a treat bag full of goodies as well as other support.

VICTORIA

PANDA

810 Nicholson Street
North Fitzroy VIC 3068
Tel: Phone support: 1300 726 306; Admin (03) 9481 3377
email: info@panda.org.au
website: www.panda.org.au

PANDA is a statewide, not-for-profit organisation for women and families affected by postnatal and antenatal depression in Victoria. PANDA acknowledges that social, biological and psychological factors play a role in postnatal and antenatal depression. PANDA works to: support and inform women and their families who are affected by postnatal and antenatal mood disorders; and educate health care professionals and the wider community about postnatal and antenatal mood disorders. PANDA runs a support, information and referral helpline which is staffed by specially trained volunteers and staff, many of whom have experienced postnatal or antenatal depression.

Women's Health Information Centre (WHIC)

Corner Flemngton Road & Grattan Street
Carlton VIC 3053
Tel: (03) 8345 3045, 1800 442 007 country callers
website: www.thewomens.org.au

The Women's Health Information Centre is a free confidential statewide health service offering information, individualised support and referral options on a wide range of women's health issues. The experienced women's health nurses and midwives are available by telephone, email or visit the centre for one-on-one support.

QUEENSLAND

Healthecare Belmont Private Hospital

1220 Creek Road
Carina QLD 4152
Tel: (07) 3398 0238

The Brisbane Centre for Post Natal Disorders is an in-patient and day patient specialised unit for women experiencing emotional disturbances during the childbearing period. Mothers and their babies are supported by a multi-disciplinary team, a comprehensive therapy program and supportive environment with an opportunity to gain insight, develop more satisfactory ways of relating to others, build a sense of confidence and enhance enjoyment of parenting. For further information contact the unit on (07) 3398 0238.

Women's Health Queensland Wide

165 Gregory Terrace
Spring Hill QLD 4000
Tel: (07) 3839 9962
Health Information Line (07) 3839 9988
Toll Free outside Brisbane 1800 017 676
TTY (07) 3831 5508
email: admin@womhealth.org.au
website: www.womhealth.org.au

Women's Health Queensland Wide is a non-profit health promotion service providing information and education services to women and health workers throughout the state. Services include a Health Information Line staffed by registered nurses and midwives, library services, fact sheets and quarterly publication, as well as a website and health education programs. Women can contact the service for information on a wide range of topics including pregnancy, childbirth, breastfeeding, early childhood and postnatal depression.

ADVISORY SERVICES: YOUNG PARENTS

NATIONAL

Young Mums Online

Tel: 0431 173 053
email: admin@youngmumsonline.com
website: www.youngmumsonline.com

Young Mums Online is an online community dedicated to young parents around Australia. YMO is designed to be a non-judgemental environment where new or young mothers won't feel silly asking questions and/or giving advice. Visit the website for further details or phone the number above.

VICTORIA

The Royal Women's Hospital
132 Grattan Street
Carlton VIC 3053
Tel: (03) 8345 2127
email: angela.steele@thewomens.org.au
website: www.ypp.org.au

The Young Women's Health Program offers antenatal and postnatal support and outreach services for women aged 19 years and under who are pregnant and parenting. Service hours are 9.00am to 5.00pm Monday to Friday.

QUEENSLAND

YHES House
11 Hicks Street
Southport QLD 4215
Tel: (07) 5531 1577
email: yypcoord@yhes.org.au
website: www.yhes.org.au

The Youth Health and Education Service (YHES House) Young Parents Support Program aims to improve the health and wellbeing of young parents aged 12 to 25 years, and their children, during the prenatal and early childhood periods. By offering a Childbirth Education Support Group and a New Parents Group, YHES House provides information, socialisation and ongoing support to empower young people to make informed decisions about their own and their child's health and wellbeing.

HOME SUPPORT SERVICES

NATIONAL

Cradle 2 Kindy Parenting Solutions
Tel: 1300 786 101
email: info@cradle2kindy.com.au
website: www.cradle2kindy.com.au

Cradle 2 Kindy Parenting Solutions provides an optimum start for any parent. This includes ongoing help, bi-monthly newsletters and age-appropriate e-letters. This service includes advice on setting up the nursery, newborn care, breast and bottle feeding, weaning, age-appropriate routines, sleep and settling, night waking, colic/reflux, behavioural and twin management all in the comfort of your home. Cradle 2 Kindy also provide phone and email consultation to those in rural areas. Their motto is "bringing confidence to parenting". Read more about their services on their website www.cradle2kindy.com.au or email/phone for more details.

Sleep Rescue & Home Support Services
Tel: (03) 9439 1367 or 0428 439 136
email: admin@sleeprescue.com
website: www.sleeprescue.com

If your baby is not sleeping there is help. The Sleep Rescue and Home Support Service provides practical support, education and advice to help parents develop skills to confidently manage the challenges of early parenthood. Staff provide guidance and continuity of support to assist families achieve their goals in their home environment. Families receive care and support for infant settling, feeding issues, sleep problems and routines. They offer day/night overstays, 24 hours and no waiting list.

VICTORIA

Help-On-The-Way
Level 1, 139 Glen Eira Road
St Kilda East VIC 3183
Tel: (03) 9528 6688
email: wehelp@helpontheway.com.au
website: www.helpontheway.com.au

Help-On-The-Way was established in 1990 to provide their clients with the ultimate in personal service, care and attention. Their home help services cover all aspects of childcare (nannies, babysitters, mothercraft nurses) and cleaning, elderly care and party help. All staff are insured and have either police clearances or wwcc and all child carers must have a current First Aid Certificate. Open Monday to Saturday. All areas. Gift vouchers available.

Hospital to Home
Tel: (03) 9818 8807 or 0427 818 848
email: hospitaltohome@bigpond.com
website: www.hospitaltohome.com.au

Hospital to Home is a quality home nursing support service caring for mothers and families. Services include: home nursing (home visit by an experienced midwife providing breastfeeding support, settling techniques and parentcraft assistance); lactation consultants; maternal massage, aromatherapy facial, feet treat; infant massage tuition; luscious meals, gourmet biscuits and champagne; home assistance, house cleaning or home and family support; nappy service (Huggies and cloth); classic flowers and gift vouchers. All in the comfort of your home either as an Early Discharge Package or purchased singularly.

Positive Parenting Services
Tel: 0408 102 552
email: katieshafar@yahoo.com.au
website: www.positiveparenting.com.au

Never underestimate the impact on a family of sleeplessness due to a wakeful baby or child/infant. Katie Shafar provides infant/toddler sleep/behaviour management in your own home. Her work is to keep families together by decreasing family stresses, to encourage quiet times and talking, and to empower people to solve their own problems by giving them the knowledge and confidence to trust their own intuition and follow through. Phone Katie on the number above or visit her website www.postiveparenting.com.au for more information.

Resources

HELP, ADVICE & REFERRALS

Home support services
➜ Organising & staying on top of family life

Tweddle Child & Family Health Service

53 Adelaide Street
Footscray VIC 3011
Tel: (03) 9689 1577
email: tweddle@tweddle.org.au
website: www.tweddle.org.au

tweddle
child + family health service

Tweddle is an early parenting centre which provides support and education for families with children up to four years of age. Tweddle has day-stay and residential programs for parents who are experiencing sleeping, feeding and behaviour problems with their baby or young child. Tweddle's range of services and programs are tailored to suit an individual family's needs. Tweddle also has two new services: Tweddle@Home is a fee-based, home-visiting service with expert advice tailored to your individual needs in the privacy of your own home; Tweddle Psychology Service has recently commenced where clients can be referred by a health professional or contact them direct. Rebates may be available through Medicare and private insurance agencies.

NEW SOUTH WALES

babybliss

Tel: 0417 487 439
email: jo@babybliss.com.au
website: www.babybliss.com.au

Babybliss is a home visiting service, established by Jo Ryan, for parents of babies and toddlers. Jo's calm and relaxed approach to tackling early childhood issues like sleeping, feeding and establishing routines makes her a welcome inclusion for young families and empowers parents to feel confident in dealing with their children. Jo works with families in their own home or remotely, to their own standards and in a way that is suitable to each family's unique beliefs and practice. Her support and advice will ultimately assist in reducing the stress that is felt by all parents, creating a better experience of early parenthood and young family life.

Blissful Babies

PO Box 7263
Penrith South LPO NSW 2750
Tel: 0400 673 881
website: www.blissfulbabies.com.au

Blissful Babies has over 20 years experience and can assist families with setting up a nursery, providing support for newborns, establishing a flexible daily routine, assisting and coaching parents in Mothercraft skills, teaching feeding techniques, breastfeeding care and advice, reflux management, teaching settling techniques, relaxation bathing and baby massage, night waking and looking after pre-term and special needs infants. Blissful Babies has also worked extensively with neonates, postnatal depression and other medical conditions. Effective techniques for managing multiple births. A follow-up phone service is also offered.

QUEENSLAND

My Helping Hand

Tel: 0405 222 153
email: lynne@myhelpinghand.com.au
website: www.myhelpinghand.com.au

My Helping Hand provides a personalised, in-home service to help you in the first few weeks at home with your baby. The service is tailored to suit your individual requirements and needs. My Helping Hand is beneficial to all mums and especially those who do not have any family close by. They are passionate about helping others and providing a professional and friendly service so let them take care of your housework while you have time with your baby.

ORGANISING & STAYING ON TOP OF FAMILY LIFE

NATIONAL

Busy Mothers

Tel: (02) 4731 1199
email: info@busymothers.com.au
website: www.busymothers.com.au

busy mothers.com.au

The *Busy Mothers Companion* – the resource for all busy households. It is full of practical resources and a wealth of tips and ideas that you can use to help you manage and organise your family life. You will get: menu planners, shopping lists, medical information, household charts, budget planners, direct debit schedules, reward charts and much, much more. Everything at your fingertips to help you get organised.

Milestone Press

Tel: 0401 671 707
email: sales@milestonepress.com.au
website: www.milestonepress.com.au

Milestone Press publishes *The Master Plan Diary* which will help take the stress out of organising family life. Every parent knows that it's possible to do five things on a Saturday morning and here at last is a diary that gives you the room to organise the schedules of your family. With plenty space for mum or dad, plus space for individual family members, you can see at a glance what needs to be done. Week to an opening. Starts October 2008 and finishes January 2010. it also comes with a separate address book with birthday/anniversary planner that you can transfer from year to year and space to plan/record dinner plans.

Mother's Helper

Tel: 0429 950 227
email: samantha@mothershelpers.com.au
website: www.mothershelpers.com.au

Mother's Helper Diary Second Edition is now complete with a pregnancy journal – everything you will need from pregnancy to birth and parenting. There are sections for: recording your pregnancy, birth plan, hospital bag and labour and birth; baby's birth details, emergency contacts and notes; a practical guide for baby's first eight months; medication, Illness and allergy. The activity and feeding companion is the best way to make sense of those early, sleep deprived days with your baby. The simple layout prompts you to jot down baby's feeds, sleeps, nappies and routines – all those things that will fly out of your mind in the first few weeks after birth. *Mother's Helper*: everything you will need to know about you and your baby in one convenient place.

Organize Your Life!

Tel: (03) 5289 1657 or 0400 057 912
email: claire@organizeyourlife.com.au
website: www.organizeyourlife.com.au

The *Organize Your Life Interactive Organizer* has over 300 ready-made lists covering every aspect of your life. It is within a convenient computer filing system giving you more time and energy. Visit the website for further details.

OTi organiser

Tel: (02) 9905 1082
email: sales@oti.net.au
website: www.oti.net.au

OTi organiser is an innovative handbag size organiser to provide busy women with a stylish and practical combined diary/organiser to help streamline and better manage busy lives. The tools, information and content will make it easier to develop a lifestyle plan, better manage time, meals, budgets and achieve a richer, healthier and more fulfilled life. Other sections include: Contacts – medical, household, kids, friends and family; Event planning – for holidays and entertaining; Info – passwords and budgeting; Shopping list pad. Phone/email or visit the website www.oti.net.au for further information.

Schoolwise

Tel: 1300 786 484
email: info@schoolwise.com.au
website: www.schoolwise.com.au

The *Schoolwise* family organiser is a comprehensive folder that puts an end to lost phone numbers, forgotten birthday parties, notices covering the fridge and clutter piling up on the kitchen bench. From child care through to secondary school, the paperwork never stops. The stylish and handy folder with a wipe clean surface also includes a 12-month calendar, address book, ready-made forms and clear pocket pouches that help guide and motivate you to stay organised. Purchase online at www.schoolwise.com.au or phone 1300 786 484.

Simple Savings International Pty Ltd

email: info@simplesavings.com.au
website: www.simplesavings.com.au

Save thousands of dollars every year with simplesavings.com.au. This online service is devoted to helping you save money – from slashing your weekly food bill and ditching expensive habits to cutting the cost of raising a family. Join today for loads of free money-saving information: great tip sheets, a bill payment system, yearly planner and newsletters or become a fully paid member for $47 to access an extra 13,000 tips, a busy forum, hilarious blog and member-only downloads. Phone the number above or visit the website for more information.

Smart-Mums

Tel: 0417 892 155
email: shelley@smart-mums.com.au
website: www.smart-mums.com.au

www.smart-mums.com.au is a quick, easy-to-use website for busy Australian mums, grandparents and carers. It provides parenting and lifestyle articles, quick links to informative and relevant websites, a fantastic shopping directory, healthy recipes as well as great competitions. Everything is in the one location – whether you need to help the children with their homework, send a gift, organise the family holiday or cook a quick nutritious meal – save time and do it online. Phone the number above or visit the website for more information.

That's Great

Tel: 0407 114 180
email: sales@thatsgreat.com.au
website: www.thatsgreat.com.au

Are you at your wit's end? Does your child have an annoying habit you would like to stop? Is nothing working? Then try a That's Great reward product – the range includes bright and funky A3 reusable reward carts, toilet training packs and chore charts. You will be amazed how quickly and enthusiastically your child wants to complete the reward chart. No more nagging required. Phone the number above or visit the website for more information.

NEW SOUTH WALES

LessMess

Tel: (02) 9712 4159 or 0407 772 663
email: mail@lessmess.com.au
website: www.lessmess.com.au

A professional organiser is someone who creates customised solutions to help others get organised. LessMess can come to a client's home to identify the problems and provide ideas, information, structure, solutions, tools and systems, which increase productivity, reduce stress and lead to more control. To teach customers they de-clutter with them to show that no project is too big because often the hardest thing is to get started. They believe that organising is a skill everybody can learn. Phone the number above or visit the website for more information.

beyondblue

beyondblue is a national, independent, not-for-profit organisation working to address issues associated with depression, anxiety and related substance misuse disorders in Australia.

beyondblue is a bipartisan initiative of the Australian, state and territory governments with a key goal of raising community awareness about depression and reducing stigma associated with the illness.

beyondblue works in partnership with health services, schools, workplaces, universities, media and community organisations, as well as people living with depression, to bring together their expertise around depression.

'Postnatal depression is like living in a fog. You wonder how you're going to keep going.'

ing pregnant or having a baby can increase your risk of experiencing
pression and anxiety. Postnatal depression affects one in six women
ving birth in Australia, so it's important to be aware of the signs and
eck it out. The sooner you seek help, the sooner you can recover.

find out more visit our website or call the infoline.

300 22 4636

beyondblue
the national depression initiative

www.beyondblue.org.au

Tizzie Hall

Tizzie Hall has gained an international reputation as a baby interpreter, baby whisperer and miracle worker. Her book *Save our Sleep* has sold over 40,000 copies and is a must-have for all new parents and *SOS: My Very First Diary* works as an essential companion or a stand-alone purchase. They are the perfect gift for a new mother.

Save Our Sleep is the essential baby book with fool-proof routines for getting your baby to sleep through the night, every night. It is the book that parents have asked Tizzie to write. It provides specific routines for sleeping and feeding for all stages from newborns to two years, as well as addressing issues that can affect a baby's sleep pattern such as colic, through to travelling and moving house.

SOS: My Very First Diary has been created in response to many mothers asking Tizzie to provide a diary where they can chart their baby's sleep and feed routines, as well as record their first precious milestones. The diary also provides Tizzie's indispensable advice about getting your baby into good sleeping patterns.

Together, *Save Our Sleep* and *SOS: My Very First Diary* show how both parents and baby can achieve the ultimate goal of a full night's sleep.

Stop child abuse

How much do you know about the problem of child abuse? Why not take a few minutes to complete a questionnaire at stopchildabusenow.com.au. Just click through to Know More and then Myths and Realities.

The Stop Child Abuse Now campaign is about motivating the Australian community to stop being bystanders and to act and do something about child abuse. And while facing the issue of child abuse is not easy, doing nothing is no longer an option.

10 things you can do to help:
1. Be a support for a stressed parent
2. Listen to and believe children
3. Strengthen relationships in your local neighbourhood
4. Improve your knowledge about child abuse
5. Raise awareness about child abuse
6. Consider becoming a foster parent
7. Become a volunteer for children and families in need
8. Share information about positive parenting
9. Become an advocate for children
10. Wear a Childhood Hero badge

Relationships Australia

Relationships Australia is one of the largest Australian community based, not for profit organisations providing relationship support to individuals, couples, families and communities.

We deliver a wide range of services including counselling, family dispute resolution, relationship education and parenting skills education, special programs for men, early intervention services and specialised family violence programs. There are also programs which are focused on the needs of children, and others which specifically engage Indigenous and Culturally Diverse (CALD) families, groups, and communities.

We are committed to enhancing the lives of communities, families and individuals and supporting positive and respectful relationships.

Index &
vox biographies

Index

Index

Index

Index

ⓜ

Index

Index

U

V

W

Y

Z

Vox Pop biographies

Here are short biographies for each of the women and men that contributed to the Vox Pop sections throughout the *Australian Baby Guide*. We hope you have found their comments insightful.

ALANA White

I have a baby boy, Jaylan, and I am a stay-at-home mum. I am currently involved in a mothers' group with five other mothers. I am also attending a nine-week PND group while Jaylan attends child care for two hours once a week. I also have a Child and Youth Services Health Nurse come out once a fortnight to catch up with me and Jaylan to see how we are doing.

AMANDA Jephtha

I am an eastern Sydneysider, and mum of Lex and wife to Alan. I am also the owner of Planning for Babe, exclusive baby planners. Like a wedding planner to a wedding, I help professional, time-poor pregnant women match the perfect products to their individual needs and lifestyle.

ANASTASIA Jones

I am the mother of two girls living in suburban Victoria after recently returning from 18 months living in Hong Kong. After ten-plus years in the corporate world I am taking a break from the 12-hour a day grind, working as a freelancer and blogger and studying for my 'PhD' in Dora the Explorer, The Wiggles and Hi-5.

ANDREA Tulloch

I used to work in film and television production but then fell in love with Andrew when we met in Sydney through mutual friends. We now live on a mixed grazing farm in the South West Slopes of NSW. We hope that Hugh will grow up to be a healthy multicultural boy that can cross between rural life and life in the big smoke!

ANDREW Weldon

I am a freelance cartoonist. My work has appeared in *The Sunday Age*, *The Big Issue*, *The Chaser* books, and various other publications.

ANNA Brandt

I live in Queensland with my son William, husband Anthony and handsome roman nose bull terrier Dachs. We were a little worried that on the arrival of our first baby Dachs would feel left out. However Dachs and William just love each other. Wherever William is, Dachs is … Guaranteed.

ANNA Ngo

I live in Perth with my husband Tuan and daughter Mikaela. Sometimes it feels like I'm living with two babies given my husband's obsession with a cartoon called *Transformers*. I am mostly a stay-at-home mum, but not long ago I returned to part-time work in my usual field of beauty therapy. I am also a member of a local mothers' group, love watching movies, and I'm addicted to shopping.

BERNADETTE Vella

I live in Brisbane and I am a single mum to two children, Tiernan and Arielle. I work part-time in software consulting and also operate a charity, Mummy's Wish, supporting mums with cancer.

BIANCA McCulloch

I live in Melbourne (I moved here from New Zealand when I was 5 years old). I have a beautiful little boy named Jhan and a little girl on the way. I enjoy most outdoor activities such as camping, fishing and basically anything that gets me out in the sun. I work as a support worker for the Young Women's Health Program at The Women's hospital in Melbourne and I love my job.

CATHERINE Manuell

Originally training and working as a teacher and then travelling overseas, I returned to Australia and started designing hats 19 years ago. After another overseas trip, I returned to work as a freelance designer for labels such as Metalicus, Stussy Sista and Kookai before launching my own Catherine Manuell Design brand ten years ago. I never really thought it would grow into something quite so large. I always thought as long as I was enjoying it and it was working then I'd stick with it. There have been a few turning points in the business – getting my first order was pretty big! But I think I made the decision to pursue it seriously about seven years ago. I'd just given birth to my daughter and I knew that if I was going to keep the business going, I'd have to employ someone to help me. I'd need to make enough money to pay that person, so it was no longer just about me. When I realised that the business was able to do that, that was pretty satisfying.

CHRISTINE Walsh

I am a mother of two children Savannah and Blake. My husband got a transfer about a year ago to Broome, WA, so that is where we call home for now. I miss not having family support around but I'm finding that this town really caters for families with young children. The first thing I did when I moved to town was join Playgroup. I am a primary school teacher and have worked in a part-time and full-time capacity between having the kids. Though without family support up here I haven't yet returned to the classroom since having Blake. I love being a mum and all that it entails. Just seeing your child light up when they see you for a cuddle really makes it all worthwhile. I have come to a stage where I find two kids relatively easy to look after so am thinking "do I want to have another child?" I don't think you really understand unconditional love until you hold your own child in your arms that very first time.

CINDY Fraser

I live in Melbourne with my husband and three children – Luke and twins Taya and Brad. I am a qualified kindergarten teacher with 10 years' teaching experience, and I have worked in various child care settings and been a nanny. When my firstborn arrived, I was fortunate to be teaching a kindergarten class within a child care centre, so he was able to 'come to work' with me. His room was near mine so I was able to continue breastfeeding and spend some time with him on my breaks. Six months after my twins were born I started working for a privately owned family day care and in-home care company. This has allowed me the flexibility to work the days and hours that suit me. I now have a really good balance between work and home, as well as the flexibility of being able to work from home which seems to keep us all happy.

DANIELLE Murrihy

I am a mum to twin boys and life is busy, busy, busy with playgroups, twin groups and mothers' groups each week. I am a stay-at-home mum during the week, but I do freelance work on the weekends as a hair and make-up artist for weddings. Dad has to look after the boys every weekend and he does a terrific job! I am involved in a couple of multiple birth forums: AMBA and Multiplicity World Wide and I am the club president for my local multiple birth association. Being a mum to twins is an awesome experience and it has been so far (most of the time) a really easy journey. Okay, the first 6 months I survived on four broken hours of sleep a night and a lot of

sugar, but hey I survived it and everything is going well now. One of my boys has just been diagnosed with high functioning autism Asperger's syndrome, so we are going down a slightly different path than what I had dreamed. But at the end of the day I have two happy, healthy boys who absolutely adore each other and they don't give me too much grief. (I just wish they would stop picking all my flowers so I have something left to admire in my garden!)

JESS Tamblyn

I became a mother when my gorgeous daughter Madison was born. Recently I returned to part-time work as a P.E. and recreation teacher at our local high school. I enjoy playing netball, spending time outdoors and catching up with my friends. I live with my partner Robbie in the Adelaide Hills and we hope to add to our family in the near future.

JESSICA Hatherall

I am from Sydney and a mother of two beautiful children – Felix and Ivy. I am a former lawyer and film producer who, since the birth of my son, has tried my hand at being a stay-at-home mum.

KATHERINE Twigg

My name is Katherine Twigg and I live in Victoria. I am 27 years old and I have a baby boy named Jacob. I am a stay-at-home mum although I work one day a week while my mum looks after Jacob. I absolutely love being at home with Jacob, watching the way he changes every day. It's definitely hard some days, like not having any time to yourself, and having to keep going even if you're unwell, but I do feel I'm very lucky. I have a wonderful husband and a wonderful mum and dad who support and help me as much as they can. I am never alone and I have nothing but admiration for anyone who has to raise a child on their own. It is most definitely a full-time job that lasts 24 hours a day, 7 days a week, with no sick leave or annual leave and no wage. But it's the only job in which you get to feel every single emotion on any given day.

KAZ Cooke

Kaz Cooke is an Australian author and cartoonist widely known for her bestselling books *Up the Duff*, *Kidwrangling* and *Girl Stuff: Your Full-On Guide to the Teen Years*, which are funny, friendly, thoroughly researched and full of common sense. She has also written two picture books for kids, *The Terrible Underpants* and *Wanda-Linda Goes Berserk*.

Vox Pop biographies

KERRI Harding

I live in Victoria and I'm currently a stay-at-home mum to my son. I love the whole new social network that having a child has exposed me to, and I'm looking forward to (but at the same time feeling a little bit sad about) the prospect of my son starting school next year. I readily admit that parenthood is often challenging but nothing compares to that overwhelming feeling of love that you have for your child as you watch them sleep.

KIRSTIN Amos

I am married and the mother of one cute and adorable boy, Carter. I currently reside in Queensland, half way between Brisbane and the Gold Coast. I work full time and enjoy evening walks with Carter after a hard day … It is the best way to relax and enjoy mummy and baby time. When I get some spare time I enjoy scrapbooking, card making, puzzles and cross stitch panels. When I can get away from work I also enjoy taking Carter to swimming classes, another way of relaxing for me as well.

LEANNE Cummins

I am a midwife, lactation consultant (IBCLC), childbirth educator and busy mother – a joey scout leader and mum of two girls in the Illawarra, NSW. I moved into midwifery from ICU nursing twelve years ago and had a passion for childbirth education in both public and private hospitals, as well as teaching independantly. Over the past six years I have worked on a telephone helpline, speaking to parents all over Australia about pregnancy, birth and beyond. I have also produced the Birthing Sense Birth Education DVDs.

LEE Norman

I am married and my first child Bliss was born June 2008. I am a human resources professional and my hobbies include horse riding, travelling, softball and going to the footy in Melbourne.

LINDA Bull

After a long and much loved career as a singer I branched out into the world of retail and opened my first children's boutique, Hoochie Coochie, in Melbourne in 2005. I am now enjoying juggling a retail store and two beautiful children.

LOUISE Cruz

I am a mother of two gorgeous kids with our third due shortly. We have a beautiful daughter, Mikayla, and an energetic son, Kendrick. My daughter is in year 2 at school and enjoys playing many sports which keeps my afternoons full taking her to various activities. Our son is full of energy and loves to be outdoors running around and playing with his Thomas trains. Our family is a regular fixture at all The Wiggles concerts and also the Disney On Ice spectaculars. I love being a full-time, stay-at-home mum and wouldn't trade it for anything in the world, even on the bad days!

LUCY Mulvany

I have three gorgeous children aged 4, 3 and 2 years. I work part-time in sales as well as care for my family, and I am finally taking time to take care of myself by getting fit! My support network enables me to be the best mum I can be – I have an amazing family, a wonderful mothers' group, and a fantastic online parenting community.

MARTINE Pekarsky

I am a mum to twins Astrid and Olsen. My husband and I tried for six years to start a family and were just thrilled when we finally found out that not only were we pregnant, but pregnant with twins. We love our new life; it's pretty full on but we have never been happier. Running our own business means there's great flexibility to spend time with our two gorgeous toddlers during the day and work in the evenings. Camping has been a huge part of our lifestyle since the children could walk and when the weather is good we go away by ourselves or with friends to some of the scenic places around Victoria.

MELANIE Smoothy

I was once told that having a child is a privilege, not a right, and I truly believe that. Having suffered a miscarriage in our first pregnancy, every day that our pregnancy with Brayden progressed was another day to be thankful for another day closer to his arrival. Our experience as parents thus far has been the most rewarding, frustrating, exciting, challenging, tiring and exhilarating time of our lives and yet, if we had the chance to do it all again, we wouldn't change a single thing. While we've made mistakes along the way, we've learnt from each and every experience. As parents you quickly become your own worst critic – give yourself a break. The most important thing is that you're doing the best you can and that your child feels safe, secure and loved. Happy parenting from our household to yours.

MICHELLE Eicholtz

I have one child and I am a stay-at-home mum. I never thought I would be driving along singing nursery rhymes, and I still resent the fact that every time I go shopping I have to fight with all the other mums for that magic car spot!

MICHELLE Winduss

I live in NSW, I am married, have a son and I work as an accountant in Sydney. I found that working and being a first-time mum is very challenging and keeps me busy. Hobbies include cooking and baking and spending time with my family and friends.

NICOLE Hambling

I am mum to Amy and work 15 hours per week in the accounts department for the State Sports Centres Trust. In what little spare time I have left I help co-ordinate the Victorian Banner Crew and Supporters Group for the Fremantle Football Club.

REBECCA Tragear Whiting

I live in Melbourne and have four children – Rhiannon, Declan, Angus and D'Arcy. I am a fashion and beauty publicist and I work from home, although since baby D'Arcy arrived I have done very little work as I never seem to have a minute spare. I am going out of my mind with a teenager and a toddler in the same house; I have found the two are quite similar except locking the big one in the laundry when she is 'naughty' doesn't work! I end each day physically and mentally exhausted but wouldn't have it any other way. I have a fabulously supportive husband, Stefan, and without him I could not do what I do every day.

ROS Pittard

I am a teacher, student counsellor, wife and, most importantly, mother of two gorgeous boys, Riley and Joshua. I live in regional Victoria, and dream of one day being able to once again drink a cup of tea before it goes cold.

ROWENA Raats

I was raised in a large foster family (I am adopted). I grew up in a small Aboriginal community and then moved to Kalgoorlie, WA. I met the love of

my life during a short work trip to Port Hedland. Thirteen years and three children later and I am still here and still in love and am now running my own business.

SARAH Murdoch

Sarah lives in Sydney, Australia, with her husband Lachlan and their children Kalan and Aidan. In 1997 Sarah began working with the National Breast Cancer Foundation of Australia. Since then she has committed herself to charity work and is now patron of the National Breast Cancer Foundation, an ambassador for the Murdoch Children's Research Institute and a director of The Australian Ballet. Sarah's book *Birth Skills*, co-authored with Juju Sundin, was released in March 2007.

SOPHIE McKellar

I am a first-time mum and had twins, so wow, what a big shock! I live in Victoria and love to sing and have a good time every day. I hope for more babies but I'm not sure my husband totally agrees, but hey we'll see. I hope my comments help all those new parents out there.

TANYA Byrnes

My husband Allan and I received our little gift after a 13.5 hour labour. I have a background in business management, and my husband and I now run our own company within the transport industry.

TONY Wilson

Tony Wilson is a writer and broadcaster and has made short films around the world, written novels, and penned children's books, but it was always his ambition to become a cautionary tale. His website is www.tonywilson.com.au.

TRACEY Thompson

I have one child, Joshua, and we live in sunny Brisbane, QLD. I am a nurse and have recently started working again two days a week to keep my skills up. I absolutely love being a mum and can't wait until 2009 when we will start trying for baby number two!